Visit Our Web Site:
http://www.prenhall.com/heizer

- **What's New:** This features gives a quick overview of the new articles and resources that we just posted or updated.
- **Study Hall:** A student resource guide including Ask the Tutor, Career Center, Writing Center, and Study Skills Center.
- **Faculty Lounge:** This Faculty page is password protected and provides a wealth of resources which include downloadable supplements and current events articles, plus offers help with computers, teaching archives, Internet skills, and a conference and chat system.
- **Research Area:** Links to domestic and international news organizations, Web browsers, and Web tutorials.

What's New	Study Hall	Faculty Lounge	Help!?!
Home Page	Global Info	Research Area	Feedback

Every Chapter features the following additional interactive materials:

- **Interactive Study Guide:** On a chapter-by-chapter basis, we provide a graded quiz as a self-review of each chapter.
- **Internet Exercises/Projects:** Exercises for each chapter to encourage you to use the Internet for learning and research.
- **Internet Resources:** Specific Internet resources linked to the chapter and topic you are studying.
- **Current Events:** A summary and analysis of current OM news events, with links to this text, discussion questions, group activities, a glossary, and a bibliography.
- **Case Studies:** Thirty-three additional case studies to supplement those already in your text.
- **Virtual Company Tours:** Exciting walk-through tours of 17 companies, including Dole, Red Hook Ale, Honda, and others.
- **The New York Times:** A special operations management issue of the *New York Times*, edited by Professor Render, is available free from the textbook publisher. Included here are discussion questions that tie each article to a chapter in your text.
- **PowerPoint Slides:** Over 1,000 PowerPoint slides to help you review text material and organize your studies.

TWO VERSIONS AVAILABLE

We recognize that everyone teaches Operations Management a little differently. Some instructors want to cover more quantitative tools and some don't. We have a version for either approach! *Operations Management*, **Fifth edition**, is available in hardcover and *Principles of Operations Management*, **Third edition**, is available in paperback. The versions are virtually identical except the paperback, *Principles of Operations Management,* **Third edition, doesn't** include **6 quantitative modules**. The following modules are not included in the paperback version:

- Decision-Making Tools
- Linear Programming
- Transportation Models
- Waiting Line Models
- Learning Curves
- Simulation

To determine which book will work for you, please see the head-to-head comparisons of the table of contents listed below.

OPERATIONS MANAGEMENT FIFTH EDITION	PRINCIPLES OF OPERATIONS MANAGEMENT THIRD EDITION
I. Introduction to Operations Management	**I. Introduction to Operations Management**
1. Operations and Productivity	1. Operations and Productivity
2. Operations Strategy for Competitive Advantage	2. Operations Strategy for Competitive Advantage
3. Operations in a Global Environment*	3. Operations in a Global Environment*
II. Designing Operations	**II. Designing Operations**
4. Managing Quality	4. Managing Quality
4S. Statistical Process Control	4S. Statistical Process Control
5. Forecasting	5. Forecasting
6. Design of Goods and Services	6. Design of Goods and Services
7. Process Strategy and Capacity Planning	7. Process Strategy and Capacity Planning
7S. State-of-the-Art Technology in Operations	7S. State-of-the-Art Technology in Operations
8. Location Strategies	8. Location Strategies
9. Layout Strategy	9. Layout Strategy
10. Human Resources and Job Design	10. Human Resources and Job Design
10S. Work Measurement	10S. Work Measurement
III. Managing Operations	**III. Managing Operations**
11. Supply-Chain Management*	11. Supply-Chain Management*
12. Inventory Management	12. Inventory Management
12S. Just-in-Time Systems	12S. Just-in-Time Systems
13. Aggregate Scheduling	13. Aggregate Scheduling
14. Material Requirements Planning (MRP)	14. Material Requirements Planning (MRP)
15. Short-Term Scheduling	15. Short-Term Scheduling
16. Project Management	16. Project Management
17. Maintenance and Reliability	17. Maintenance and Reliability
IV. Quantitative Modules	
A. Decision-Making Tools	
B. Linear Programming	
C. Transportation Models	
D. Waiting-Line Models	
E. Learning Curves	
F. Simulation	* Chapters 3 and 11 are new to this edition.

Would you like to customize this book?

Utilizing our **Just-In-Time Program**, you have the option of creating your own version of this text, or mixing and matching chapters of this text and those texts listed on the following page. You can choose chapters from any of these titles to create a custom textbook that will fulfill your course needs exactly. In addition, you have the option of including your own material, or material from other publishers. Plus, your custom book can be packaged with any Prentice Hall Decision Science or Business Statistics software or shrink-wrapped with any Prentice Hall textbook. The Harvard Business Cases are also available as part of the JIT Program.

THE JIT PROGRAM OFFERS:

FLEXIBILITY:
You can revise and update your book every semester.

INSTRUCTIONAL SUPPORT:
You have access to all instructor's materials that accompany the traditional textbook and desk copies of your JIT book.

COST SAVINGS:
Because you use only the material you select, JIT books are often less expensive than traditional textbooks.

QUICK TURNAROUND:
You can have your custom book delivered in four weeks.

ADDITIONAL RESOURCES:
You can package your JIT book with Prentice Hall Decision Science/Business Statistics software and shrink-wrap your book with other Prentice Hall books.

ADDITIONAL ACCESS:
All Harvard Business Cases are available to include in your custom text.

The Highest Quality Production Available Includes:

- Custom cover and title page: including your name, school, department, course title, and section number
- Paperback, perfect bound, black-and-white laser printed text
- Customized table of contents and index
- Sequential pagination throughout the text
- Chapters, text figures, and problems renumbered to correspond with custom organization
- Solutions to selected problems included at the end of each chapter

Please see the next page for our current list of available titles!

TEXTS AVAILABLE ON THE JIT DATABASE

OPERATIONS MANAGEMENT

Handfield/Nichols, Jr., *Introduction to Supply Chain Management*
Heineke/Meile, *Games and Exercises in Operations Management*
Heizer/Render, *Operations Management,* Fifth Edition
Heizer/Render, *Principles of Operations Management,* Third Edition
Latona/Nathan, *Cases and Readings in POM*
Russell/Taylor, *Operations Management,* Second Edition
Schmenner, *Plant and Service Tours in Operations Management,* Fifth Edition

MANAGEMENT SCIENCE/OPERATIONS RESEARCH

Eppen/Gould, *Introductory Management Science,* Fifth Edition
Render/Stair, *Quantitative Analysis for Management,* Sixth Edition
Render/Stair, *Introduction to Management Science*
Render/et al., *Cases and Readings in Management Science*
Taylor, *Introduction to Management Science,* Sixth Edition
Wright/et al., *Strategic Management: Texts and Cases*

BUSINESS STATISTICS

Berenson/Levine, *Basic Business Statistics,* Seventh Edition
Klimberg/et al., *Cases in Business Statistics*
Levin/Rubin, *Statistics for Management,* Seventh Edition
Levine/et al., *Statistics for Managers Using Microsoft Excel,* Updated and Second Edition
McClave/Benson, *Statistics for Business and Economics,* Seventh Edition
Neter, *Applied Statistics,* Fourth Edition
Watson/et al., *Statistics for Management and Economics,* Fifth Edition

SOFTWARE

Weiss, POM for Windows
Weiss, QM for Windows
Weiss, DS for Windows

If you are interested in creating your own JIT book, please give us a call at **1-800-777-6872** or email us at **JIT_DecScience@prenhall.com**. For further information on this program, you can visit our website at **www.sscp.com/just_in_time.html** !

OPERATIONS MANAGEMENT

Fifth Edition

Jay Heizer
Jesse H. Jones Professor of Business Administration
Texas Lutheran University

Barry Render
Charles Harwood Professor of Operations Management
Crummer Graduate School of Business
Rollins College

Prentice Hall
Upper Saddle River, New Jersey 07458

Acquisitions Editor: Tom Tucker
Developmental Editor: Ron Librach
Editorial Assistant: Melissa Back
Editor-in-Chief: Natalie E. Anderson
Marketing Manager: Debbie Clare
Senior Production Editor: Cynthia Regan
Permissions Editor: Monica Stipanov
Managing Editor: Dee Josephson
Manufacturing Buyer: Arnold Vila
Manufacturing Manager: Vincent Scelta
Senior Designer/Cover Design: Cheryl Asherman
Design Manager: Patricia Smythe
Interior Design: Meryl Levavi/Digitext
Photo Research Supervisor: Melinda Lee Reo
Image Permission Supervisor: Kay Dellosa
Photo Researcher: Teri Stratford
Cover Illustration/Photo: Hisao Matsui/SIS
Composition/Illustrator (Interior): UG

Microsoft Excel, Solver, and Windows are registered trademarks of the Microsoft Corporation in the U.S.A. and other countries. Screen shots and icons reprinted with permission from the Microsoft Corporation. This book is not sponsored or endorsed by or affiliated with the Microsoft Corporation.

 Copyright 1999, 1996 by Prentice-Hall, Inc.
A Simon & Schuster Company
Upper Saddle River, New Jersey 07458

All rights reserved. No part of this book may be reproduced, in any form or by any means, without permission from the publisher.

Library of Congress Cataloging-in-Publication Data
Heizer, Jay H.
    Operations management / Jay Heizer, Barry Render. — 5th ed.
       p.   cm.
    Prev. eds. published under title: Production and operations management.
    Includes bibliographical references and index.
    ISBN 0-13-905068-X
    1. Production management.   I. Render, Barry.   II. Heizer, Jay H.
Production and operations management.   III. Title.
TS155.H3725   1999
658.5—dc21   98-20778
                                                     CIP

Prentice-Hall International (UK) Limited, London
Prentice-Hall of Australia Pty. Limited, Sydney
Prentice-Hall Canada, Inc., Toronto
Prentice-Hall Hispanoamericana, S.A., Mexico
Prentice-Hall of India Private Limited, New Delhi
Prentice-Hall of Japan, Inc., Tokyo
Simon & Schuster Asia Pte. Ltd., Singapore
Editora Prentice-Hall do Brasil, Ltda., Rio de Janeiro

Printed in the United States of America

10 9 8 7 6 5 4 3 2 1

To:
Tristan and Sebastian

Michael, Beth, Zachary,
Charlie and Joey

ABOUT THE AUTHORS

Jay Heizer holds the Jesse H. Jones Chair of Business Administration at Texas Lutheran University in Seguin, Texas. He received his B.B.A. and M.B.A. from the University of North Texas and his Ph.D. in Management and Statistics from Arizona State University (1969). He was previously a member of the faculty at Memphis State University, the University of Oklahoma, Virginia Commonwealth University, and the University of Richmond. He has also held visiting positions at Boston University, George Mason University, and the Czech Management Center.

Dr. Heizer's industrial experience is extensive. He learned the practical side of operations management as a machinist apprentice at Foringer and Company, production planner for Westinghouse Airbrake, and at General Dynamics, where he worked in engineering administration. Additionally, he has been actively involved in consulting in the OM and MIS areas for a variety of organizations including Philip Morris, Firestone, Dixie Container Corporation, Columbia Industries, and Tenneco. He holds the CPIM certification from the American Production and Inventory Control Society.

Professor Heizer has co-authored five books and has published over thirty articles on a variety of management topics. His papers have appeared in the *Academy of Management Journal, Journal of Purchasing, Personnel Psychology, Production & Inventory Control Management, APICS-The Performance Advantage, Journal of Management History,* and *Engineering Management,* among others. He has taught operations management courses in undergraduate, graduate, and executive programs.

Barry Render is the Charles Harwood Distinguished Professor of Operations Management at the Crummer Graduate School of Business at Rollins College, in Winter Park, Florida. He received his M.S. in Operations Research and his Ph.D. in Quantitative Analysis at the University of Cincinnati (1975). He previously taught at George Washington University, University of New Orleans, Boston University, and George Mason University, where he held the GM Foundation Professorship in Decision Sciences and was Chair of the Decision Science Department. Dr. Render has also worked in the aerospace industry for General Electric, McDonnell Douglas, and NASA.

Professor Render has co-authored nine textbooks with Prentice-Hall, including *Quantitative Analysis for Management, Service Operations Management, Introduction to Management Science,* and *Cases and Readings in Management Science.* His more than one hundred articles on a variety of management topics have appeared in *Decision Sciences, Production and Operations Management, Interfaces, Information and Management, Journal of Management Information Systems, Socio-Economic Planning Sciences,* and *Operations Management Review,* among others.

Dr. Render has also been honored as an AACSB Fellow and named as a Senior Fulbright Scholar in 1982 and again in 1993. He was twice vice-president of the Decision Science Institute Southeast Region and served as Software Review Editor for *Decision Line* from 1989 to 1995. He has also served as Editor of the *New York Times* Operations Management special issues since 1996. Finally, Professor Render has been actively involved in consulting for government agencies and for many corporations, including NASA, FBI, U.S. Navy, Fairfax County, Virginia, and C&P Telephone.

He teaches operations management courses in Rollins College's MBA and Executive MBA programs. In 1995 he was named as that school's Professor of the Year, and in 1996 was selected by Roosevelt University to receive the St. Claire Drake Award for Outstanding Scholarship.

Photo Credits

CHAPTER 1: p. 2 L: Courtesy of Whirlpool Corporation, p. 2 R: Kevin Horan, p. 3: Michael L. Abramson Photography, p. 22: Courtesy of Siemens Corporation.

CHAPTER 2: p. 32: Courtesy of Komatsu Ltd., p. 33 Top&Bottom: Courtesy of Komatsu Ltd., p. 38: Andy Sacks/Tony Stone Images.

CHAPTER 3: p. 54: Courtesy of Boeing Commercial Airplane Group, p. 55 Top & Bottom: Courtesy of Boeing Commercial Airplane Group, p. 60: Copyright Disney/NPC, p. 62: Paulo Fridman/ Gamma-Liaison, Inc., p. 67: John Chiasson/Gamma-Liaison, Inc.

CHAPTER 4: p. 76 L&R: Michael L. Abramson, p. 77: Courtesy of Motorola, Inc., p. 81: Claus Meyer/Black Star, p. 84 L: Courtesy of Barry Render, p. 84 C: Courtesy of M. J. Juran Institute, p. 84 R: Courtesy of Philip B. Crosby and Associates, p. 94: Ted Kawalerski Photography Inc., p. 95: Courtesy of TRW Incorporated, p. 98: Barry Bomzer/Tony Stone Images.

SUPPLEMENT 4: p. 108: P. L. Vidor/BetzDearborn, Inc., p. 117: Courtesy of New United Motor Manufacturing, Inc. (NUMMI), p. 118: Courtesy of Harley-Davidson, Inc., p. 120: Ted Horowitz/ The Stock Market.

CHAPTER 5: p. 140 L&R: Courtesy of Tupperware USA, Inc., p. 149: Jeff Greenberg/Picture Cube, Inc., p. 152: B. Daemmrich/ The Image Works, p. 165: Courtesy of The Glidden Company.

CHAPTER 6: p. 192 Top&Bottom: Courtesy of Regal Marine Industries, Inc., p. 193: Courtesy of Regal Marine Industries, Inc., p. 195: Courtesy of Shouldice Hospital, p. 197 L: Rick Etkin/Tony Stone Images, p. 197 CL: Al Messerschmidt/Folio, Inc., p. 197 C: Courtesy of Polaris, p. 197 CR: Courtesy of Sony Electronics, Inc., p. 197 R: Don Spiro/Medichrome/The Stock Shop, Inc., p. 200 Top: Courtesy of BMW of North America, Inc., p. 200 Bottom: Courtesy of National Cash Register, p. 203: Courtesy of Maytag, p. 206 L&R: Courtesy of Structural Dynamics Research Corporation (SDRC), p. 209: Courtesy of J. R. Simplot Company, p. 214: Tom Lyle/ Medichrome/The Stock Shop, Inc.

CHAPTER 7: p. 226 Top & Bottom: Courtesy of Nucor Steel Corporation, p. 227: Courtesy of Nucor Steel Corporation, p. 235 L&R: Louis Psihoyos/Matrix International, p. 238: Courtesy of Sterling Software, Inc., p. 241 L&R: Courtesy of Red Lobster/Darden, p. 245 L&R: Steve Woit, p. 249: James Schnepf Photography, Inc., p. 254: John Madere/International Paper.

SUPPLEMENT 7: p. 272: R. A. Flynn, Inc./Textile Clothing Technology Corp. (TC)[2], p. 274: Courtesy of Ford Motor Company, Detroit, p. 276: Courtesy of Iconics, p. 277: Andrew Sacks/Tony Stone Images, p. 281: David Walberg, p. 282: Tim Rue/True Photo, p. 284: William Taufic Photography, Inc.

CHAPTER 8: p. 290 Top & Bottom: Courtesy of Federal Express Corporation, p. 291 Top & Bottom: Courtesy of Federal Express Corporation, p. 295: A. Tannenbaum/Sygma, p. 298: Jay Heizer, p. 305: Jay Heizer, p. 307: Courtesy of National Decision Systems.

CHAPTER 9: p. 320: John A. Wee/Pittsburgh International Airport, p. 321 Top & Bottom: Courtesy of Pittsburgh International Airport, p. 324: Michael Grecco/Stock Boston, p. 335: Jay Daniel/Autodesk, Inc., p. 338: Chris Usher/Chris Usher Photography, p. 345: Courtesy of Tyson Corporation.

CHAPTER 10: p. 364 L&R: Property of AT&T Archives. Reprinted with permission of AT&T., p. 365: Property of AT&T Archives. Reprinted with permission of AT&T., p. 376: Andy Freeberg Photography, p. 377 Top L: Courtesy of Apple Computer, Inc., p. 377 Top C: Courtesy of Kinesis Corporation, p. 377 Top R: Courtesy of Industrial Innovations, Inc., p. 377 Bottom: Courtesy of 3M Corporation, p. 379: Collins/Monkmeyer Press.

SUPPLEMENT 10: p. 392: Joseph Nettis/Stock Boston, p. 396: Courtesy of Choice Hotels International, p. 403: David A. Zickl.

CHAPTER 11: p. 415 Top: H. John Maier, Jr./New York Times Permissions, p. 415 Bottom: New York Times Permissions, p. 423: Michael L. Abramson Photography, p. 424: Mike Wilkinson/FSP/ Gamma-Liaison, Inc., p. 426: Gary Grimes.

CHAPTER 12: p. 438: Courtesy of Harley-Davidson, Inc., p. 439 L&R: Courtesy of Harley Davidson, Inc., p. 445: Courtesy of Warner-Lambert Company, p. 451: Courtesy of Levi Strauss & Co., p. 456: Lonal V. Harding/UNOVA, Inc.

SUPPLEMENT 12: p. 480: Copyright 1998 G.M. Corp. used with permission GM Media Archives, p. 484: Malcolm S. Kirk/Peter Arnold, Inc., p. 491: W.B. Spunbarg/Picture Cube, Inc., p. 494: Courtesy of McDonald's Corporation.

CHAPTER 13: p. 502 L&R: Courtesy of Anheuser-Busch Companies, Inc. p. 503: Courtesy of Anheuser-Busch Companies, Inc., p. 507: Charles Thatcher/Tony Stone Images, p. 509: Courtesy of Deere & Company.

CHAPTER 14: p. 536: Courtesy of Collins Industries, p. 537 L&R: Courtesy of Collins Industries, p. 543: Courtesy of Harley-Davidson Inc., p. 552: William Strode/Woodfin Camp & Associates.

CHAPTER 15: p. 578: Courtesy of Delta Airlines, p. 579: Etienne de Malglaive/Gamma-Liaison, Inc., p. 580: Courtesy of Northrop-Grumman, p. 590: Duomo Photography, p. 593: Charles Gupton/The Stock Market, p. 598: John Maher/The Stock Market, p. 603: The Arizona Daily Star.

CHAPTER 16: p. 622 Top & Bottom: Courtesy of Bechtel Group, Inc., p. 623: Courtesy of Bechtel Group, Inc., p. 635: Reprinted with permission of SAS Institute, Inc.

CHAPTER 17: p. 664 L&R: Courtesy of NASA Kennedy Space Center, p. 665: Courtesy of NASA Kennedy Space Center, p. 671: Courtesy of Orlando Utilities Commission.

MODULE A: p.684: Robert R. Mercer/Gamma-Liaison, Inc., p. 689: Courtesy of Applied Decision Analysis.

MODULE B: p. 704: Harry M. Walker/Monkmeyer Press.

MODULE C: p. 740: Michael Quan/Tony Stone Images, p. 749: Reuters/Corbis-Bettmann.

MODULE D: p. 764: Paul Damien/Tony Stone Images, p. 773: George Hunter/Tony Stone Images, p. 776: Vlastinir Shone/Gamma-Liaison, Inc.

MODULE E: p. 796: Courtesy of Samsung Electronics America, Inc.

MODULE F: p. 812: Courtesy of Micro Analysis & Design Simulation Software, Inc., p. 814: Lester Sloan/Woodfin Camp & Associates, p. 824: Courtesy of Imagine That, Inc.

Foreword

FOREWORD TO THE FIFTH EDITION OF OPERATIONS MANAGEMENT

When I first entered a production operation in 1952 the world of business was divided into two parts, like the Red Sea had been. One part made big things out of little things; the other part purchased the little things, found the customers, took care of the money, sold stuff, and complained about the activities of the first part. The two portions of the company had nothing in common and little interest in each other.

Over the years it was discovered that there are no separate parts of an organization. It is a body that requires all components to function together as a unit if a successful life is to be obtained.

However everyone knew that the world was made up of separate parts. Markets were described as domestic and international. The latter was not part of the organization and often had a great deal of difficulty obtaining information about plans, products, and people. Now we have learned that the world of business has no boundaries and there are only domestic markets. We have also learned that we have suppliers and customers who do not speak our language or observe our holidays.

Functional operations used to be responsible for whatever noun was in their title. Manufacturing manufactured, purchasing purchased, personnel personneled, and quality was done by the quality department. When I was a quality manager top management held me personally responsible if a customer received something that was not proper. Everyone else were "bad guys" trying to get stuff by quality, and we were the "good guys." When enough things went wrong the practice was to find a tougher, smarter cop. There was no thought of getting things done right.

When I began preaching the prevention of problems, called quality management, it took a while for people to catch on. The breakthrough came with the determination of the "price of nonconformace." How much did it cost to do things wrong, and then fix them. Most companies came to the realization that it took 25% and more of their revenues to live that way. That was the beginning of the quality revolution.

When I talk to Professor Render's classes each year I am always impressed that the students are learning to look at the world from a platform that did not exist in my early career. The broad scope of this book assures that this will happen. It provides a place to begin the future by reviewing the past. The students always want to know about the "reality" of quality management, which is the general subject of my chat. I tell them that basic concepts are the important part of business management, that there are no "systems" to do the executive's work. Concepts come from understanding, understanding begins with learning, and learning comes from examining credible resources with an open mind.

I know you will enjoy yourself in this course.

PHILIP CROSBY
Winter Park, Fl.

Brief Contents

PART ONE
INTRODUCTION

1. Operations and Productivity 1
2. Operations Strategy for Competitive Advantage 31
3. Operations in a Global Environment 53

PART TWO
DESIGNING OPERATIONS

4. Managing Quality 75
   Supplement 4: Statistical Process Control 107
5. Forecasting 139
6. Design of Goods and Services 191
7. Process Strategy and Capacity Planning 225
   Supplement 7: State-of-the-Art Technology in Operations 271
8. Location Strategies 289
9. Layout Strategy 319
10. Human Resources and Job Design 363
    Supplement 10: Work Measurement 391

PART THREE
MANAGING OPERATIONS

11. Supply-Chain Management 413
12. Inventory Management 437
    Supplement 12: Just-in-Time Systems 479
13. Aggregate Scheduling 501
14. Material Requirements Planning (MRP) 535
15. Short-Term Scheduling 577
16. Project Management 621
17. Maintenance and Reliability 663

PART FOUR
QUANTITATIVE MODULES

A. Decision-Making Tools 683
B. Linear Programming 703
C. Transportation Models 739
D. Waiting-Line Models 763
E. Learning Curves 795
F. Simulation 811
   Appendices A1
   Indices I1

Contents

ABOUT THE AUTHORS vi
FOREWORD BY PHILIP E. CROSBY ix
PREFACE xxi

PART ONE INTRODUCTION

1. Operations and Productivity 1

Global Company Profile: Whirlpool 2
What Is Operations Management? 4
The Heritage of Operations Management 4
Why Study OM? 6
What Operations Managers Do 7
  How This Book Is Organized 8
Organizing to Produce Goods and Services 8
Where Are the OM Jobs? 10
Exciting New Trends in Operations Management 11
Operations in the Service Sector 12
  Differences between Goods and Services 12
  Growth of Services 14
  Service Pay 16
The Productivity Challenge 16
  Productivity Measurement 17
  Productivity Variables 19
  Productivity and the Service Sector 22
The Challenge of Social Responsibility 23

  Summary 24 • Key Terms 24 • Solved Problems 24 • Discussion Questions 25 • Critical Thinking Exercise 26 • Problems 26 • Case Study: National Air Express 28 • Bibliography 29 • Internet Resources 29

2. Operations Strategy for Competitive Advantage 31

Global Company Profile: Komatsu 32
Identifying Missions and Strategies 34
  Mission 34
  Strategy 36
Achieving Competitive Advantage Through Operations 36
  Competing on Differentiation 36
  Competing on Cost 37
  Competing on Response 37
Ten Decisions of OM 39
Issues in Operations Strategy 42
  Research 42
  Preconditions 43
  Dynamics 43
Strategy Development and Implementation 44
  Identify Critical Success Factors 45
  Build and Staff the Organization 47

  Summary 47 • Key Terms 47 • Solved Problem 48 • Discussion Questions 48 • Critical Thinking Exercise 48 • Problems 49 • Case Study: Minit-Lube, Inc. 49 • Case Study: Global Strategy at Motorola 50 • Video Case 1: Strategy at Regal Marine 51 • Internet Case Study 51 • Bibliography 51 • Internet Resources 52

3. Operations in a Global Environment 53

Global Company Profile: Boeing 54
Defining Global Operations 57
  Globalization of Production 59
Why Global Operations Are Important 59

xii CONTENTS

Achieving Global Operations 62
    Global Product Design 62
    Global Process Design and Technology 63
    Global Facility Location Analysis 63
    Impact of Culture and Ethics 66
Global Issues in Service Operations 67
    Managing Global Service Operations 68
    Summary 68 • Key Terms 69 • Using POM for Windows for Location Analysis 69 • Using Excel OM to Solve Location Problems 69 • Discussion Questions 70 • Critical Thinking Exercise 71 • Problems 71 • Case Study: Ford and Mazda Share the Driver's Seat 73 • Bibliography 74 • Internet Resources 74

PART TWO
DESIGNING OPERATIONS

4. Managing Quality 75

Global Company Profile: Motorola 76
Quality and Strategy 78
Defining Quality 79
    Other Implications of Quality 80
International Quality Standards 80
    Japan's Industrial Standard 80
    Europe's ISO 9000 Standard 81
    Environmental Management Standard 82
    U.S. Standards 82
Total Quality Management 82
    Continuous Improvement 83
    Employee Empowerment 83
    Benchmarking 84
    Just-in-Time (JIT) 85
    Knowledge of TQM Tools 86
Tools of TQM 86
    Quality Function Deployment (QFD) 86
    Taguchi Technique 89
    Pareto Charts 90
    Process Charts 91
    Cause-and-Effect Diagram 92
    Statistical Process Control (SPC) 92
The Role of Inspection 93
    When and Where to Inspect 95

    Source Inspection 96
    Service Industry Inspection 96
    Inspection of Attributes vs. Variables 96
Total Quality Management in Services 97
    Summary 99 • Key Terms 99 • Discussion Questions 100 • Critical Thinking Exercise 100 • Problems 100 • Case Study: Westover Electrical, Inc. 102 • Case Study: Quality Cleaners 104 • Video Case 2: Quality at the Ritz-Carlton Hotel Company 105 • Internet Case Study 106 • Bibliography 106 • Internet Resources 106

Supplement 4: Statistical Process Control 107

Statistical Process Control (SPC) 108
    Control Charts for Variables 110
    The Central Limit Theorem 111
    Setting Mean Chart Limits ($\bar{x}$-Charts) 113
    Setting Range Chart Limits (R-Charts) 115
    Using Mean and Range Charts 115
    Control Charts for Attributes 117
    Process Capability 121
Acceptance Sampling 123
    Operating Characteristic Curve 123
    Average Outgoing Quality 125
    Summary 126 • Key Terms 126 • Using POM for Windows 126 • Using Excel OM for SPC 127 • Solved Problems 128 • Discussion Questions 130 • Problems 130 • Data Base Application 133 • Case Study: Bayfield Mud Company 135 • Case Study: SPC at the Gazette 136 • Internet Case Study 137 • Bibliography 137 • Internet Resources 138

5. Forecasting 139

Global Company Profile: Tupperware Corporation 140
What Is Forecasting? 142
    Forecasting Time Horizons 142
    The Influence of Product Life Cycle 143
Types of Forecasts 143
The Strategic Importance of Forecasting 143
    Human Resources 144
    Capacity 144
    Supply-Chain Management 144

Seven Steps in the Forecasting System 144
Forecasting Approaches 145
   Overview of Qualitative Methods 145
   Overview of Quantitative Methods 146
Time-Series Forecasting 147
   Decomposition of a Time Series 147
   Naive Approach 148
   Moving Averages 148
   Exponential Smoothing 151
   Exponential Smoothing with Trend Adjustment 155
   Trend Projections 158
   Seasonal Variations in Data 161
Causal Forecasting Methods: Regression and Correlation Analysis 163
   Using Regression Analysis to Forecast 163
   Standard Error of the Estimate 165
   Correlation Coefficients for Regression Lines 167
   Multiple-Regression Analysis 168
Monitoring and Controlling Forecasts 170
   Adaptive Smoothing 172
   Focus Forecasting 172
   The Computer's Role in Forecasting 172
Forecasting in the Service Sector 172

Summary 173 • Key Terms 174 • Using POM for Windows in Forecasting 174 • Using Excel Spreadsheets in Forecasting 174 • Solved Problems 177 • Discussion Questions 179 • Critical Thinking Exercise 179 • Problems 179 • Data Base Application 187 • Case Study: North-South Airline 188 • Case Study: Akron Zoological Park 189 • Internet Case Study 189 • Bibliography 190 • Internet Resources 190

6. Design of Goods and Services 191

Global Company Profile: Regal Marine 192
Goods and Services Selection 194
   Product Strategy Options 194
   Generation of New Product Opportunities 195
   Product Life Cycles 196
   Life Cycle and Strategy 198
   Environmentally Friendly Products 199
Product Development 200
   Product Development System 200
   Organizing for Product Development 201
   Manufacturability and Value Engineering 202
Issues for Product Development 203
   Robust Design 204
   Time-Based Competition 204
   Modular Design 204
   Computer-Aided Design (CAD) 205
   Value Analysis 206
   Product-by-Value Analysis 206
Defining the Product 207
   Make-or-Buy Decisions 209
   Group Technology 209
Documents for Production 210
Service Design 211
   Documents for Services 213
Application of Decision Trees to Product Design 215
Transition to Production 217

Summary 217 • Key Terms 217 • Solved Problems 218 • Discussion Questions 218 • Critical Thinking Exercise 218 • Problems 218 • Case Study: De Mar's Product Strategy 221 • Case Study: GE's Rotary Compressor 222 • Video Case 3: Product Design at Regal Marine 223 • Bibliography 224 • Internet Resources 224

7. Process Strategy and Capacity Planning 225

Global Company Profile: Nucor 226
Three Process Strategies 228
   Process Focus 229
   Repetitive Focus 230
   Product Focus 232
   Comparison of Process Choices 233
Process Analysis and Design 235
   Flow Diagrams 236
   Process Charts 236
   Time-Function Mapping 237
   Work-Flow Analysis 237
Process Reengineering 239
   Moving Toward Lean Production 239
Service Process Strategy 241
   Service-Sector Considerations 241
   Customer Interaction and Process Strategy 242

More Opportunities to Improve Service Processes 243
Selection of Equipment and Technology 244
Environmental Issues 245
Capacity 246
   Defining Capacity 246
   Forecasting Capacity Requirements 247
   Applying Decision Trees to Capacity Decisions 249
   Managing Demand 250
Break-Even Analysis 251
   Single-Product Case 254
   Multiproduct Case 255
Strategy-Driven Investments 257
   Investment, Variable Cost, and Cash Flow 257
   Net Present Value 258

Summary 261 • Key Terms 261 • Using Excel OM for Break-Even Analysis 262 • Solved Problems 263 • Discussion Questions 263 • Critical Thinking Exercise 264 • Problems 264 • Case Study: Matthew Yachts, Inc. 268 • Video Case 4: Process Strategy at Wheeled Coach 269 • Bibliography 270 • Internet Resources 270

Supplement 7: State-of-the-Art Technology in Operations 271

Design Technology 272
   Computer-Aided Design (CAD) 273
   Standard for the Exchange of Product Data (STEP) 273
   Computer-Aided Manufacturing (CAM) 274
   Virtual Reality Technology 274
Production Technology 275
   Numerical Control 275
   Process Control 275
   Vision Systems 276
   Robots 276
   Automated Storage and Retrieval System (ASRS) 277
   Automated Guided Vehicle (AGV) 278
   Flexible Manufacturing System (FMS) 278
   Computer-Integrated Manufacturing (CIM) 279
Technology in Services 280
Information Sciences in Operations 281

   Transaction Processing 281
   Management Information System (MIS) 282
   The Internet 282
   Artificial Intelligence 283
Managing Technology in a Global Environment 284

Summary 286 • Key Terms 286 • Discussion Questions 286 • Problems 287 • Case Study: Rochester Manufacturing Corporation 287 • Bibliography 288 • Internet Resources 288

8. Location Strategies 289

Global Company Profile: Federal Express 290
The Strategic Importance of Location 292
Factors That Affect Location Decisions 293
   Labor Productivity 294
   Exchange Rates 296
   Costs 296
   Attitudes 296
   Proximity to Markets 297
   Proximity to Suppliers 297
Methods of Evaluating Location Alternatives 298
   The Factor-Rating Method 298
   Locational Break-Even Analysis 300
   Center-of-Gravity Method 301
   Transportation Model 303
Service Location Strategy 304
   How Hotel Chains Select Sites 305
   The Telemarketing and Internet Industries 306
   Geographic Information Systems 306

Summary 307 • Key Terms 308 • Using POM for Windows 308 • Using Excel OM to Solve Location Problems 308 • Solved Problems 309 • Discussion Questions 311 • Critical Thinking Exercise 311 • Problems 312 • Data Base Application 315 • Case Study: Southern Recreational Vehicle Company 317 • Internet Case Study 318 • Bibliography 318 • Internet Resources 318

9. Layout Strategy 319

Global Company Profile: Pittsburgh International Airport 320
The Strategic Importance of Layout Decisions 322

Types of Layout 322
Fixed-Position Layout 323
Process-Oriented Layout 325
   Expert Systems in Layout 331
   Work Cells 331
   The Focused Work Center and the Focused Factory 333
Office Layout 334
Retail Layout 336
Warehousing and Storage Layouts 337
   Cross-Docking 338
   Random Stocking 338
   Customizing 339
Repetitive and Product-Oriented Layout 339
   Assembly-Line Balancing 341

Summary 345 • Key Terms 345 • Using POM for Windows for Layout Design 346 • Solved Problems 348 • Discussion Questions 351 • Critical Thinking Exercise 352 • Problems 352 • Data Base Application 358 • Case Study: Des Moines National Bank 358 • Case Study: State Automobile License Renewals 360 • Video Case 5: Facility Layout at Wheeled Coach 361 • Internet Case Studies 362 • Bibliography 362 • Internet Resources 362

10. Human Resources and Job Design 363

Global Company Profile: Lucent Technologies 364
Human Resource Strategy for Competitive Advantage 366
   Constraints on Human Resource Strategy 366
Labor Planning 367
   Employment-Stability Policies 367
   Work Schedules 368
   Job Classifications and Work Rules 369
Job Design 369
   Labor Specialization 369
   Job Expansion 370
   Psychological Components of Job Design 371
   Self-Directed Teams 372
   Motivation and Incentive Systems 374
   Ergonomics and Work Methods 375
The Visual Workplace 381
Labor Standards 383

Summary 383 • Key Terms 383 • Solved Problems 384 • Discussion Questions 386 • Critical Thinking Exercise 386 • Problems 386 • Case Study: The Fleet That Wanders 387 • Case Study: Lincoln Electric's Incentive Pay System 388 • Bibliography 389 • Internet Resources 389

Supplement 10: Work Measurement 391

Labor Standards and Work Measurement 392
Historical Experience 393
Time Studies 393
Predetermined Time Standards 398
Work Sampling 400

Summary 403 • Key Terms 403 • Solved Problems 403 • Discussion Questions 406 • Problems 406 • Case Study: Telephone Operator Standards at AT&T 411 • Bibliography 412 • Internet Resources 412

PART THREE
MANAGING OPERATIONS

11. Supply-Chain Management 413

Global Company Profile: Volkswagen 414
The Strategic Importance of the Supply Chain 416
   Global Supply-Chain Issues 417
Purchasing 418
   Manufacturing Environments 419
   Service Environments 419
   Make-or-Buy Decisions 419
Supply-Chain Strategies 420
   Many Suppliers 420
   Few Suppliers 421
   Vertical Integration 422
   Keiretsu Networks 423
   Virtual Companies 423
Vendor Selection 425
   Vendor Evaluation 425
   Vendor Development 426
   Negotiations 426

Managing the Supply Chain 427
Materials Management 429
   Distribution Systems 430
Benchmarking Supply-Chain Management 431
   Summary 431 • Key Terms 432 • Discussion Questions 432 • Critical Thinking Exercise 432 • Problems 432 • Case Study: Factory Enterprises, Inc. 433 • Case Study: Thomas Manufacturing Company 434 • Video Case 6: Supply Chain Management at Regal Marine 435 • Internet Case Studies 436 • Bibliography 436 • Internet Resources 436

12. Inventory Management 437

Global Company Profile: Harley-Davidson 438
Functions of Inventory 440
   Types of Inventory 440
Inventory Management 441
   ABC Analysis 441
   Record Accuracy 443
   Cycle Counting 444
   Control of Service Inventories 444
Inventory Models 446
   Independent versus Dependent Demand 446
   Holding, Ordering, and Setup Costs 446
Inventory Models
for Independent Demand 447
   The Basic Economic Order Quantity (EOQ) Model 447
   Minimizing Costs 447
   Reorder Points 453
   Production Order Quantity Model 454
   Quantity Discount Models 457
Probabilistic Models with Constant Lead Time 460
Fixed-Period Systems 464

   Summary 465 • Key Terms 466 • Using POM for Windows to Solve Inventory Problems 466 • Using Excel OM for Inventory 466 • Solved Problems 469 • Discussion Questions 471 • Critical Thinking Exercise 471 • Problems 471 • Case Study: Sturdivant Sound Systems 476 • Case Study: LaPlace Power and Light 476 • Video Case 7: Inventory Control at Wheeled Coach 477 • Internet Case Studies 477 • Bibliography 478 • Internet Resources 478

Supplement 12: Just-in-Time Systems 479

Just-in-Time Philosophy 480
Suppliers 481
   Goals of JIT Partnerships 483
   Concerns of Suppliers 484
JIT Layout 485
   Distance Reduction 485
   Increased Flexibility 486
   Impact on Employees 486
   Reduced Space and Inventory 486
Inventory 486
   Reduce Variability 487
   Reduce Inventory 487
   Reduce Lot Sizes 488
   Reduce Setup Costs 489
Scheduling 490
   Level Material-Use Schedules 490
   Kanban 490
Quality 493
Employee Empowerment 493
JIT in Services 494

   Summary 495 • Key Terms 495 • Solved Problems 495 • Discussion Questions 496 • Problems 496 • Case Study: Electronic Systems, Inc. 498 • Bibliography 499 • Internet Resources 499

13. Aggregate Scheduling 501

Global Company Profile: Anheuser-Busch 502
The Planning Process 504
The Nature of Aggregate Scheduling 505
Aggregate Planning Strategies 507
   Capacity Options 508
   Demand Options 509
   Mixing Options to Develop a Plan 510
Methods for Aggregate Scheduling 511
   Graphical and Charting Methods 511
   Mathematical Approaches to Planning 516
   Comparison of Aggregate Planning Methods 518
Aggregate Scheduling in Services 518
   Restaurants 519
   Miscellaneous Services 520

CONTENTS   xvii

National Chains of Small Service Firms 520
Airline Industry 520
Hospitals 521

Summary 522 • Key Terms 522 • Using POM for Windows for Aggregate Planning 522 • Using Excel OM for Aggregate Planning 523 • Solved Problems 525 • Discussion Questions 527 • Critical Thinking Exercise 527 • Problems 527 • Data Base Application 532 • Case Study: Southwestern State College 532 • Internet Case Study 533 • Bibliography 534 • Internet Resources 534

14. Material Requirements Planning (MRP) 535

Global Company Profile: Collins Industries 536
Dependent Inventory Model Requirements 538
   Master Production Schedule 539
   Bills of Material 541
   Accurate Inventory Records 544
   Purchase Orders Outstanding 545
   Lead Times for Each Component 545
MRP Structure 545
MRP Management 550
   MRP Dynamics 550
   MRP and JIT 550
Lot-Sizing Techniques 551
Extensions of MRP 555
   Closed-Loop MRP 555
   Capacity Planning 556
   Material Requirements Planning II (MRP II) 557
   Enterprise Resource Planning (ERP) 558
MRP in Services 560
Distribution Resource Planning (DRP) 561
   DRP Structure 562
   Allocation 562

Summary 562 • Key Terms 563 • Using POM for Windows to Solve MRP Problems 563 • Solved Problems 565 • Discussion Questions 568 • Critical Thinking Exercise 568 • Problems 568 • Data Base Application 573 • Case Study: Service, Inc. 574 • Case Study: Ruch Manufacturing 574 • Video Case 8: MRP at Wheeled Coach 575 • Bibliography 576 • Internet Resources 576

15. Short-Term Scheduling 577

Global Company Profile: Delta Airlines 578
The Strategic Importance
of Short Term Scheduling 580
Scheduling Issues 580
   Forward and Backward Scheduling 582
   Scheduling Criteria 582
Scheduling Process-Focused Work Centers 583
Loading Jobs in Work Centers 584
   Input-Output Control 584
   Gantt Charts 585
   Assignment Method 587
Sequencing Jobs in Work Centers 590
   Priority Rules for Dispatching Jobs 590
   Critical Ratio 594
   Sequencing N Jobs on Two Machines: Johnson's Rule 594
Limitations of Rule-Based Dispatching Systems 596
Finite Scheduling 596
Theory of Constraints 597
   Bottleneck Work Centers 598
Repetitive Manufacturing 599
Scheduling for Services 601
   Scheduling Nurses with Cyclical Scheduling 602

Summary 603 • Key Terms 604 • Using POM for Windows to Solve Scheduling Problems 604 • Using Excel OM for Short-Term Scheduling 605 • Solved Problems 607 • Discussion Questions 611 • Critical Thinking Exercise 611 • Problems 611 • Data Base Application 616 • Case Study: Old Oregon Wood Store 617 • Bibliography 619 • Internet Resources 619

16. Project Management 621

Global Company Profile: Bechtel 622
The Strategic Importance
of Project Management 624
Project Planning 625
   The Project Manager 625
   Work Breakdown Structure 626
Project Scheduling 627
Project Controlling 629

Project Management Techniques: PERT and CPM 629
  The Framework of PERT and CPM 629
  Activities, Events, and Networks 630
  Dummy Activities and Events 632
  PERT and Activity Time Estimates 633
  Critical Path Analysis 634
  The Probability of Project Completion 638
  Case Study of PERT: Schware Foundry 639
Cost-Time Trade-Offs and Project Crashing 643
Applying Project Scheduling to Service Firms 645
A Critique of PERT and CPM 646

  Summary 647 • Key Terms 648 • Using POM for Windows for Project Scheduling 648 • Solved Problems 648 • Discussion Questions 652 • Critical Thinking Exercise 653 • Problems 653 • Data Base Application 659 • Case Study: Shale Oil Company 660 • Internet Case Studies 661 • Bibliography 661 • Internet Resources 662

17. Maintenance and Reliability 663

Global Company Profile: NASA 664
The Strategic Importance of Maintenance and Reliability 666
Reliability 667
  Improving Individual Components 667
  Providing Redundancy 670
Maintenance 671
  Implementing Preventive Maintenance 671
Increasing Repair Capabilities 675
  Total Productive Maintenance 675
Techniques for Establishing Maintenance Policies 676

  Summary 676 • Key Terms 677 • Using POM for Windows to Solve Reliability Problems 677 • Solved Problems 677 • Discussion Questions 678 • Critical Thinking Exercise 678 • Problems 679 • Case Study: Worldwide Chemical Company 681 • Internet Case Studies 682 • Bibliography 682 • Internet Resources 682

PART FOUR QUANTITATIVE MODULES

A. Decision-Making Tools 683

The Decision Process in Operations 684
Fundamentals of Decision Making 685
Decision Tables 686
  Decision Making under Risk 686
  Expected Value of Perfect Information (EVPI) 688
Decision Trees 689
  A More Complex Decision Tree 690

  Summary 692 • Key Terms 693 • Using POM for Windows to Solve Decision Table and Tree Problems 693 • Using Excel OM for Decision Models 694 • Solved Problems 695 • Discussion Questions 696 • Problems 696 • Case Study: Nigel Smythe's Heart Bypass Operation 700 • Internet Case Studies 701 • Bibliography 701

B. Linear Programming 703

Requirements of a Linear Programming Problem 705
Formulating Linear Programming Problems 706
  Shader Electronics Example 706
Graphical Solution to a Linear Programming Problem 707
  Graphical Representation of Constraints 707
  Iso-Profit Line Solution Method 708
  Corner-Point Solution Method 711
Sensitivity Analysis 713
Solving Minimization Problems 714
Linear Programming Applications 716
  Production-Mix Example 717
  Diet Problem Example 718
  Production Scheduling Example 718
  Labor Scheduling Example 720
The Simplex Method of LP 722

  Summary 722 • Key Terms 723 • Using POM for Windows to Solve LP Problems 723 • Using Excel Spreadsheets to Solve LP

Problems 724 • Solved Problems 725 • Discussion Questions 728 • Problems 729 • Data Base Application 735 • Case Study: Golding Landscaping and Plants, Inc. 736 • Internet Case Studies 737 • Bibliography 737

C. Transportation Models 739

Transportation Modeling 740
Developing an Initial Solution:
The Northwest-Corner Rule 742
The Stepping-Stone Method 743
Special Issues in Modeling 748
   Demand Not Equal to Supply 748
   Degeneracy 748

Summary 750 • Key Terms 750 • Using POM for Windows to Solve Transportation Problems 750 • Using Excel OM to Solve Transportation Problems 751 • Solved Problems 752 • Discussion Questions 755 • Problems 755 • Data Base Application 760 • Case Study: Andrew-Carter, Inc. 761 • Internet Case Studies 762 • Bibliography 762

D. Waiting-Line Models 763

Queuing Costs 765
Characteristics of a Waiting-Line System 765
   Arrival Characteristics 766
   Waiting-Line Characteristics 767
   Service Facility Characteristics 767
   Measuring the Queue's Performance 770
The Variety of Queuing Models 770
   Model A: Single-Channel Queuing Model with Poisson Arrivals and Exponential Service Times 771
   Model B: Multiple-Channel Queuing Model 774
   Model C: Constant Service Time Model 776
   Model D: Limited Population Model 777
Other Queuing Approaches 780

Summary 781 • Key Terms 781 • Using POM for Windows for Queuing 782 • Using Excel OM for Queuing 782 • Solved Problems 783 • Discussion Questions 786 • Problems 786 • Case Study: New England Castings 790 • Case Study: The Winter Park Hotel 792 • Internet Case Study 793 • Bibliography 793

E. Learning Curves 795

Learning Curves in Services and Manufacturing 797
Applying the Learning Curve 798
   Arithmetic Approach 799
   Logarithmic Approach 799
   Learning-Curve Coefficient Approach 800
Strategic Implications of Learning Curves 802

Summary 803 • Key Term 803 • Using POM for Windows for Learning Curves 803 • Using Excel OM for Learning Curves 804 • Solved Problems 805 • Discussion Questions 806 • Problems 806 • Case Study: SMT's Negotiation with IBM 809 • Bibliography 810

F. Simulation 811

What Is Simulation? 813
Advantages and Disadvantages of Simulation 813
Monte Carlo Simulation 815
Simulation of a Queuing Problem 818
Simulation and Inventory Analysis 820
The Role of Computers in Simulation 823

Summary 824 • Key Terms 824 • Using POM for Windows for Simulation 825 • Simulation with Excel Spreadsheets 825 • Solved Problems 827 • Discussion Questions 828 • Problems 829 • Case Study: Alabama Airlines 836 • Internet Case Studies 837 • Bibliography 837

APPENDIX I Normal Curve Areas and How to Use the Normal Distribution A2
APPENDIX II Poisson Distribution Values A5
APPENDIX III Values of $e^{-\lambda}$ for Use in the Poisson Distribution A7
APPENDIX IV Table of Random Numbers A8
APPENDIX V Using POM for Windows and Excel OM A9
APPENDIX VI Solutions to Even-Numbered Problems A10

Name Index I1
General Index I7

Preface

Welcome to *Operations Management,* Fifth Edition, written as a broad introduction to the field of operations management. This book presents a state-of-the-art view of the activities of the operations function. Operations is an exciting area of management that has a profound effect on production and productivity. Indeed, few other activities have as much impact on the quality of our lives. The goal of this text is to present the field of operations as realistic, practical activities that improve the quality of our lives.

Operations management includes a blend of topics from accounting, industrial engineering, management, management science, and statistics. Operations management jobs can be challenging, important, and rewarding, and can lead to successful careers. Even if you are not employed in the operations area, the concepts can often be applied to other disciplines, and can help you understand how the discipline functions and impacts your life.

The authors are well aware that the majority of readers are not OM majors. However, students of marketing, finance, management, economics, accounting, quantitative methods, and information systems will find the material both interesting and useful. Over 200,000 readers of earlier editions of *Operations Management* seem to have endorsed this premise.

ORGANIZATION OF THE TEXT

This text is organized around the 10 decisions that are critical to effective operations management. These 10 decisions are divided into strategic (or longer term) and tactical (or shorter term) decisions and correspond to *designing* operations and then *managing* them. This approach, presented in a realistic, global, and exciting environment will help managers understand the critical role of operations and the decisions it entails.

Part One provides an introduction to OM; productivity, strategy, and global issues that drive operations decisions. Part Two describes *designing* operations by addressing issues related to quality, product and service design, process/technology selection, facility location, human resources and job design, and facility layout. Part Three describes *managing* operations in terms of performances such as scheduling (aggregate, short-term, and project), supply-chain management/purchasing, inventory control, just-in time systems, and maintenance. Part Four contains six quantitative modules which outline analytical techniques that are used in making a series of operations decisions. The techniques are decision trees and tables, linear programming, the transportation model, waiting-line models, learning curves, and simulation. The four parts of the book are illustrated in the diagram on the next page.

Two Versions of the Text This text is available to professors and students in two versions: *Operations Management,* Fifth Edition, which is casebound and *Principles of Operations Management,* Third Edition, a paperback. Parts One, Two and Three of both books are identical. However, Part Four is available only in *Operations Management,* Fifth Edition.

xxi

xxii   PREFACE

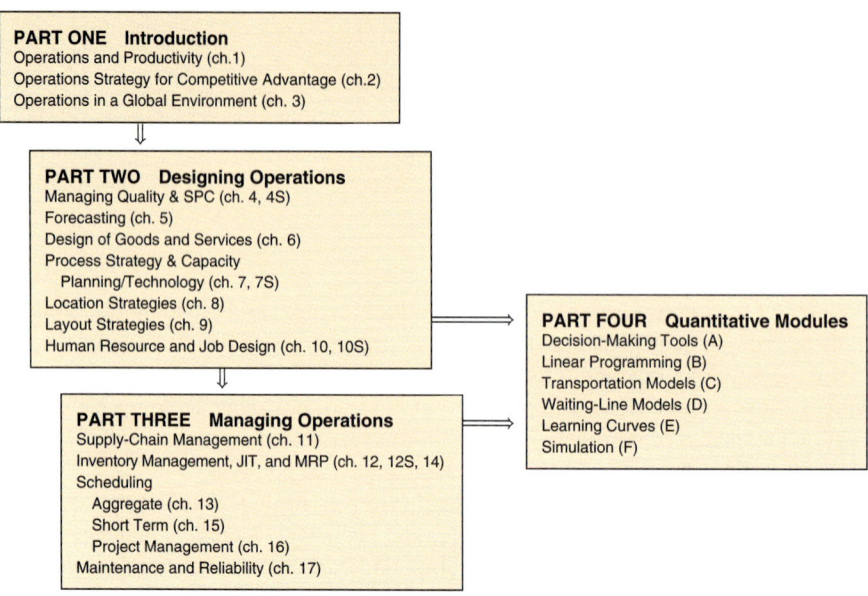

TEN DECISIONS OF OM
Managing Quality
Design of Goods & Services
Process Strategy
Location Strategies
Layout Strategies
Human Resources
Supply-Chain Management
Inventory Management
Scheduling
Maintenance

FOCUS OF THE NEW EDITION

This fifth edition of *Operations Management* represents a major revision in our treatment of this dynamic topic. Our new thrust is to take a much more strategic and managerial approach to OM and to use strategy as a unifying link in every chapter. We have also chosen the ten decisions that operations managers make as an organizing theme. These decisions are introduced in chapters 1 and 2 and repeated with the icon (on the left) in the margin of successive chapters.

We also continue to place much greater emphasis on the role of service operations and on global issues. We have even dropped the word *Production* from our previous edition's title. In addition, without neglecting the importance of analytical tools, we have moved six of these topics into Part Four.

Here are some details about our changes in content.

Strategic Focus Our revision of chapter 2, "Operations Strategy for Competitive Advantage," sets the stage for the importance of strategy as a competitive weapon in every organization. We have expanded our coverage to focus on how managers achieve strategies of *differentiation, low cost,* and *response*. We then continue the differentiation, cost leadership, and response strategies in our chapters dealing with the 10 decisions of OM to illustrate how strategy can impact on the functions of an operations manager. Chapter 2 also provides sample missions for Circle K and Merck, research from the Strategic Planning Institute, and a strategic link to the process analysis choices developed by Hayes and Wheelwright.

Global Focus We are proud to be the first OM test to develop a full chapter (chapter 3) on the importance of operations in a global environment. The chapter defines global operations, justifies their importance, and describes how to achieve global product design, process designs, make location decisions, and deal with foreign cultures and ethics. The subject of managing global service operations like Air France, Arthur Anderson, Dai-Ichi Kangyo Bank, IBM, McDonald's, Euro Disney, and Motel 6 are addressed. Input from our colleague Marc Schniederjans, at the University of Nebraska, who is author of *Opera-*

tions Management: A Global Context, has made this chapter a wonderful topic that will enrich any OM course.

Each chapter, 17 in all, also opens with a *Global Company Profile*—a two page photo essay describing such world-class global players as Komatsu, Motorola, Volkswagen, Boeing, Whirlpool, Nucor, Anheuser-Busch, Delta Air Lines, and others. These profiles introduce each chapter by providing an example of how a well-known firm addresses the subject of that chapter. The global focus is a major theme of this new edition.

Service Operations Focus OM has a strong service as well as a traditional manufacturing aspect. This edition stresses the service aspects of operations, and regularly notes the distinction between service and manufacturing in OM. With the integration of service coverage throughout the text, the tone is set in chapter 1, in a section entitled "Operations in the Service Sector." Each chapter then follows up with further discussion. For example, in chapter 6, "Design of Goods and Services," we now deal with service selection, service design, and documents for services as major topics. Numerous new service cases have been added to those carried over from the previous edition.

A Focus on Keeping Current The exciting part of teaching and studying in the OM field is the constant change. Globalization, for example, is having a big impact on location strategies, supply-chain management, human resource issues, quality, and process strategies. Some of the current topics that we introduce in this edition are:

1. *Positioning strategies,* such as *process* versus *product* focus, determine how operations are organized (chapters 2 and 7).
2. A new chapter in *Supply-Chain Management.* This chapter opens with a profile of VW's new plant in Brazil and includes such state-of-the-art developments as *channel assembly, global supply chains, keiretsu networks, virtual (hollow) companies, drop shipping,* and *advanced shipping notice* (ASN) (chapter 11).
3. Changes in the field of quality, including the *ISO 14000* environmental standards, *"best practices," global benchmarking,* new material on *quality function deployment* (QFD), and *process capability* (chapter 4).
4. Environmental issues facing OM. The green movement, designing environmentally friendly products (such as a recyclable BMW), and environmental process design are topics seriously treated in this edition (chapters 6, 7, and others).
5. *Geographical information systems* and the use of the *Internet* are new topics covered as a part of location analysis (chapter 8).
6. New layout issues (chapter 9) include *cross-docking, random stocking, customizing,* and *automatic identification systems* (AIS).
7. The *visual workplace,* and the many forms it can take (including andons), are now addressed along with changing issues of *flexible workweeks, job empowerment,* and *learning organizations* (chapter 10).
8. New coverage of *buckets, backflushing* and Enterprise Resource Planning (ERP) are provided as part of MRP systems (chapter 14).
9. *Work breakdown structure* (WBS) is introduced as a step in project management, (chapter 16).

Focus on the Real World of Operations To maximize interest and excitement in OM we made maximum use of real companies and their stories. In addition to noting these companies in text discussion, we *feature* leading organizations in 17 *Global Company Profiles* and 44 *OM in Action* boxes. These features bring OM to life and help drive home the points made in the chapters. Actual OM issues in the business world spark students' interest and enliven class discussion.

xxiv   PREFACE

Focus on OM Software Two of the best OM student software packages are available with our texts: **POM for Windows** and **Excel OM.** POM for Windows can be packaged as an option with this text, at a reasonable price. The Excel OM package is distributed free with this textbook on the CD-ROM in the back of the book.

POM for Windows is the most popular microcomputer-based decision support software in college OM courses. The newest version, by developer Howard Weiss (Temple University), is a major upgrade containing 20 modules (see Appendix V). POM for Windows continues to improve in both breadth of functions and user friendliness. Instructors can structure their course with or without the use of the software. At the end of each problem-oriented chapter, students will also find an explanation of how to use the software for that particular application. For most effective learning, the software has been structured to closely match the approach, notation, and terms found in this text. Problems that can be solved with POM for Windows are noted with the symbol ■. A sample screen capture for an inventory/quantity discount problem appears below. To order this package, please use ISBN: 0-13-989815-8.

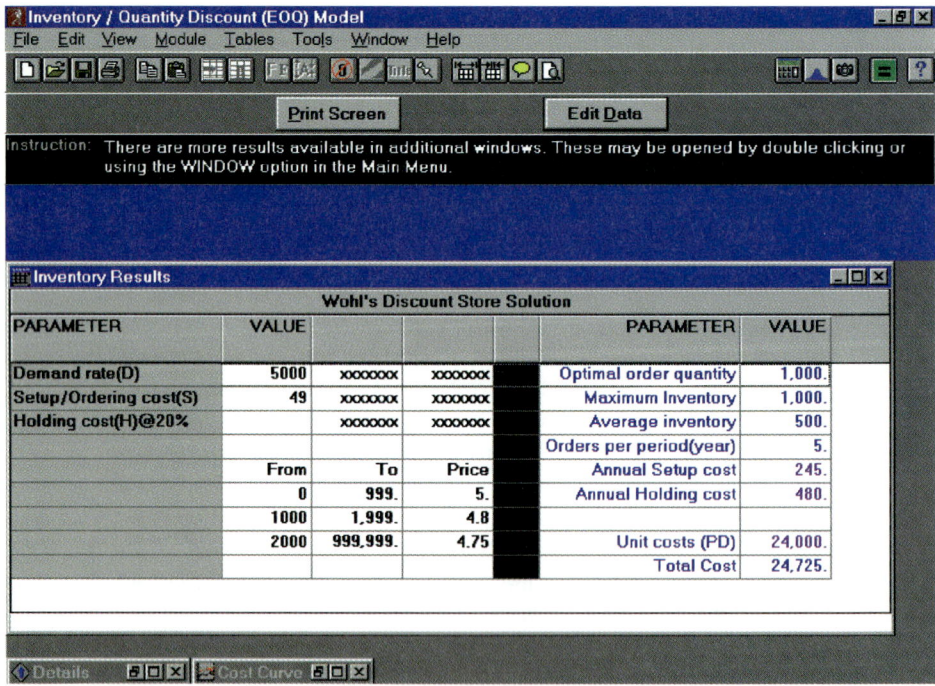

Excel OM is a new Excel spreadsheet approach to OM problem solving. These easy-to-use Excel add-ins are free to those who purchase this textbook and contain 14 modules:

1. aggregate planning
2. assignment models
3. break-even/cost-volume
4. center-of-gravity
5. decision analysis
6. factor weighting
7. forecasting
8. inventory modules (6 of them)
9. job shop scheduling
10. learning curves
11. lot sizing
12. quality control
13. transportation modeling
14. waiting lines

Developed by Professor Howard Weiss, this program illustrates the actual formulas used to make calculations, and is thus an "open" or "symbolic" approach in which students can observe and even modify formulas. Standard Excel can also be used to tackle such applications as linear programming and simulation, and these uses are illustrated in appropriate chapters. Problems that can be solved using Excel or Excel OM are identified by ✗. Sample Excel OM input and output screens are illustrated with a breakeven example below.

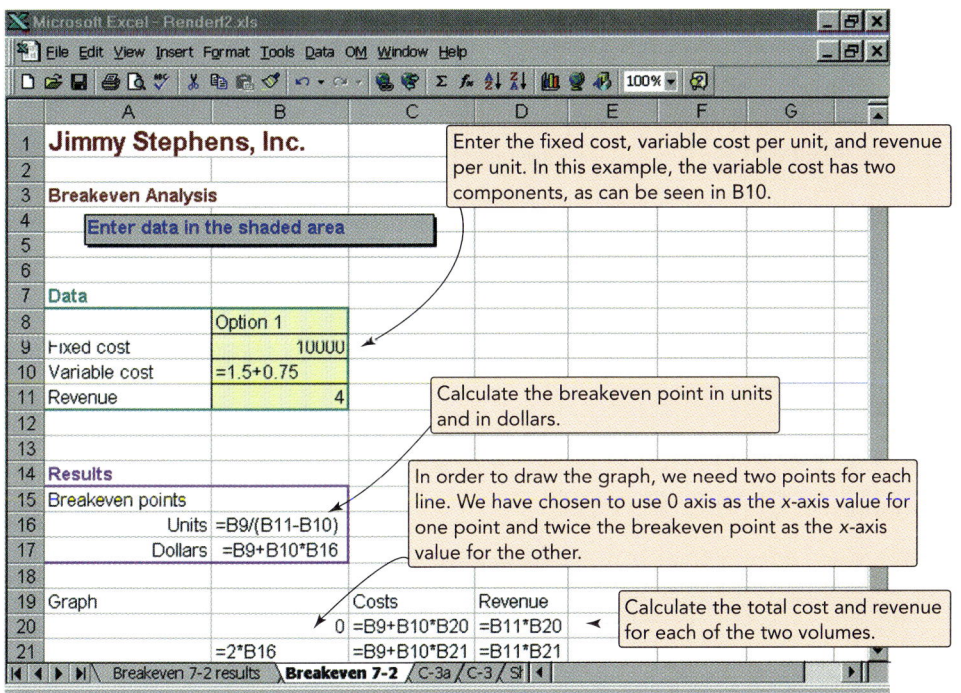

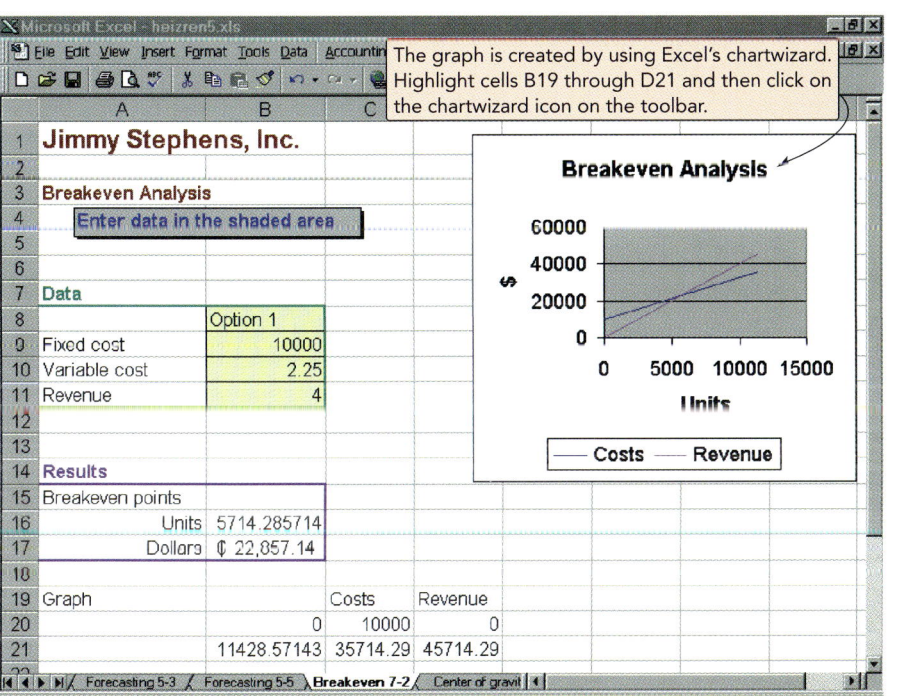

Extend, a Simulation Software Package The fifth edition of *Operations Management* by Heizer/Render includes a limited version of Extend+Manufacturing 4.0, the simulation software developed by Imagine That, Inc. Extend is provided on the CD-ROM in the back of this book.

Extend is a powerful simulation package suitable for modeling or reengineering almost any process. Although the textbook contains a limited version of Extend, it is a very rich package complete with a tutorial, on-line manuals, a variety of libraries (model components), and save and print capabilities. It includes several pre-built models, in both manufacturing and service systems, along with examples of cases discussed in the simulation module. This limited version of Extend is useful for modeling small but meaningful problems and can be used for classroom demonstration, homework, and class projects. It is an excellent package for demonstrating and teaching simulation.

Two Focuses: Managerial and Quantitative Topics in OM As the operations course evolves into a more managerially-oriented subject, many professors have chosen to provide more coverage of strategy, services, quality, JIT and other non-quantitative topics. Our new edition has placed the topics of decision trees and tables, linear programming, the transportation method, learning curves, queuing theory, and simulation in Part Four of the book.

OUR INTERNET CONNECTION AND HOME PAGE

This text has its own home page on the Internet, with challenging new exercises and assignments. The **www.prenhall.com/heizer** link to the Internet uses the benefits of this worldwide network to provide you with additional up-to-the-minute illustrations from actual companies. It also includes numerous additional case studies and homework exercises. The Internet is available for research and operations problem-solving, and we encourage professors to integrate the Internet into the operations management course. You can link to this home page inside Prentice Hall's World Wide Web site via either a university or home Internet service.

The home page for this text is organized both chapter-by-chapter and by topic. For example, almost every chapter includes additional cases, Internet homework projects, a student study guide, self tests, and assignments for touring and investigating an operations topic at companies that are linked to our home page. There is also a *New York Times* "OM Theme of the Times" section on the home page. This relates *New York Times* articles, which are available free to your class, to a series of discussion and homework questions that appear only on the home page. And with our virtual tours section, you can visit 17 exciting companies, ranging from an automobile manufacturer to a hospital, directly through the home page. These tours also contain discussion questions that can be used as a class assignment.

To summarize, here are the features available at **www.prenhall.com/heizer**:

1. Internet exercises and projects for each chapter.
2. Dozens of extra case studies, in addition to the 46 already in the text. These cases are named at the end of each text chapter.
3. Virtual company tours, with questions that can be answered and e-mailed to the instructor.
4. Discussion questions for the current issue of *New York Times* "OM Theme of the Times."
5. A complete study guide, including PowerPoint slides.
6. Self tests for each topic.

CHAPTER-BY-CHAPTER CHANGES

To highlight the extent of the revisions compared to our previous edition, here are a few of the changes on a chapter-by-chapter basis.

Chapter 1: Operations and Productivity This revision sets the tone for goods and services throughout the book. It also introduces six exciting new trends in operations (globalization, just-in-time performance, supply-chain partnering, rapid product development, mass customization, and empowering employees), brings in the new subject of multi-factor productivity, and sets the tone for OM social responsibility for the rest of the book.

Chapter 2: Operations Strategy for Competitive Advantage This chapter features a major expansion of our coverage of strategy, with a focus on differentiation, cost, and response. There is also a new discussion of the Hayes and Wheelwright process choice decisions. A new video case (Regal Marine) has been added.

Chapter 3: Operations in a Global Environment This new chapter stresses how our world economies tie together and the impact of globalization on the OM function. A case study on how Ford and Mazda partnered for success concludes the chapter. Homework problems focus on location decision analysis.

Chapter 4: Managing Quality This chapter includes new material dealing with ISO standards (including ISO 14000) and the house of quality. It also stresses the strategic impact of quality on the firm. A new video case features Ritz Carlton Hotels.

Supplement to Chapter 4: Statistical Process Control We have expanded our discussion of $\bar{x}$ charts, R charts, and sampling distributions and included process capability (C_{pk}) as a new topic. Our treatment of sampling plans has been shortened.

Chapter 5: Forecasting This chapter contains new material on strategy and on the service sector. It now delineates the seven steps of forecasting and provides a revised treatment of exponential smoothing with trend.

Chapter 6: Design of Goods and Services This chapter takes on a more strategic focus and includes more material on service design. It also introduces modular design and environmental product design issues. There are two new case studies, including a video case on Regal Marine.

Chapter 7: Process Strategy and Capacity Planning This chapter is also a major revision, with an expanded treatment of the work of Hayes and Wheelwright on process strategies and their continuum. Flow diagrams for Nucor Steel, Standard Register, and Harley Davidson illustrate these strategies. New treatment of process reengineering (with time function mapping and work flow analysis), a new section on environmental process issues, and additional material on capacity planning appear. A new video case on Wheeled Coach is included.

Supplement to Chapter 7: State-of-the-Art Technology in Operations This supplement introduces the subject of managing technology for global operations and such topics as STEP, 3-D object modeling, virtual reality, and the use of the Internet as an OM tool.

Chapter 8: Location Strategies This chapter places further emphasis on the strategic implication of location decisions. It now includes a ranking of the business environments in 20 countries, introduces the subject of geographical information systems, and discusses the Internet as a new location concept.

Chapter 9: Layout Strategies Strategic implications of layout are emphasized in this chapter, along with the topics of cross docking, customizing and random stocking. There is more detail on assembly-line balancing heuristics and a new video case featuring layout issues at Wheeled Coach.

Chapter 10: Human Resources and Job Design Our reorganization of this chapter includes new material on empowerment, learning organizations, and the visual workplace. Lincoln Electric provides a new case study on incentive pay systems.

Supplement to Chapter 10: Work Measurement Our revisions include a new service-oriented case on AT&T's time standards.

Chapter 11: Supply-Chain Management This mostly new chapter expands on our earlier treatment of purchasing management with emphasis on strategic implications of supply-chain management. The opening *Global Company Profile,* describing VW's new plant in Brazil (the brainchild of former G.M. executive José Lopez), sets the stage for global issues in supply chains. New material includes coverage of drop shipping, postponement, channel assembly, ASN, virtual companies, and Keiretsu. There is also a video case on Regal Marine.

Chapter 12: Inventory Management We deleted the topic of marginal analysis, enhanced our treatment of probabilistic models, and added two new cases, including a video case on Wheeled Coach.

Supplement to Chapter 12: Just-in-Time Systems This new supplement emphasizes suppliers and relationships. It contains sections on JIT layout, inventory, scheduling, quality, empowerment, and JIT in services. There is also a new section and problems on how to compute the appropriate number of kanbans.

Chapter 13: Aggregate Scheduling This chapter now precedes MRP and contains new material on yield management and on aggregate scheduling in the service sector.

Chapter 14: Material Requirements Planning (MRP) Our revision includes material linking MRP and JIT, including "buckets" and "backflushing," and a new section on Enterprise Resource Planning (ERP). There are two new case studies, including a video case on Wheeled Coach.

Chapter 15: Short-Term Scheduling Our opening *Global Company Profile* highlights scheduling at Delta Air Lines' new operations control center. There is also new material on the Theory of Constraints and on services. We have deleted material on scheduling of N jobs on 3 machines and on m machines.

Chapter 16: Project Management This revised chapter has a greater emphasis on strategy. It also includes detailed examination of work breakdown structure and introduces activity-on-node (AON) networks.

Chapter 17: Maintenance and Reliability This chapter has been shortened, but more emphasis has been placed on strategic issues. NASA's space shuttle provides a *Global Company Profile* to open the chapter.

Quantitative Module A: Decision-Making Tools The focus on this module is on decision trees and decision tables, with less material on mathematical models. We have also deleted coverage of decision making under uncertainty, but added numerous new problems.

Quantitative Module B: Linear Programming In this major revision, we have deleted material on the simplex method in order to focus on the graphical approach and sensitivity analysis. A major new section on LP applications has been added, with realistic examples in product mix, diet problems, production scheduling, and labor scheduling.

Quantitative Module C: Transportation Models This module has also been shortened with a deletion of material on the MODI method.

Quantitative Module D: Waiting-Line Models This module is unchanged, but contains several new homework problems.

Quantitative Module E: Learning Curves This major revision now includes an arithmetic approach, a logarithmic approach, and a coefficient approach (tables). There is additional learning material on learning curves in services and numerous new problems.

Quantitative Module F: Simulation This topic is basically unchanged, but Extend, a commercial simulation software package, is now available to illustrate the wide use of simulation to adopters.

PEDAGOGICAL FOCUS AND FEATURES

Our goal in this revision is to provide the finest pedagogical package available to students and instructors in the operations discipline. We think we have succeeded. Here are some of the features to help enhance learning and teaching.

Global Company Profiles Each of our 17 chapters now opens with a two-page analysis of a leading global organization such as: NASA, Delta Air Lines, Komatsu, Boeing, Motorola, Whirlpool, Lucent Technologies, and many more. Chosen for its leadership in the area of OM covered in each chapter, the company profiled provides a motivational introduction to each topic.

OM In Action Boxes Forty-four half-page examples of recent OM practices are drawn from a wide variety of sources, including *The Wall Street Journal, New York Times, Fortune, Forbes,* and *Harvard Business Review*. These boxes bring OM to life.

Case Studies We introduce 46 case studies in this edition, 16 of them new, and 18 focused on the service sector. Most of these have been developed by leading academics and represent real-world companies. The cases are generally 1–2 pages in length, making them short enough to cover in weekly assignments, but detailed enough to add depth to each topic they represent.

Video Cases New to this edition are eight video cases, short videos (5–8 minutes), plus case studies at the end of appropriate chapters. Three firms that are highlighted include: Ritz Carlton (hotel), Regal Marine (boat manufacturer), and Wheeled Coach (ambulance maker).

Critical Thinking Exercises To challenge students to face cultural, ethical, or critical issues of business today, these paragraph-long thinking exercises are ideal for class break-out or discussion. They involve thought-provoking topics that can spice up a class or allow for small group discussion analysis.

Solved Problems Once again, solved problems are included in this edition. They are provided as models for students as they work unsolved problems on their own. In addition to in-chapter examples, there are 61 solved problems in this new edition.

Data Base Applications A feature called "Data Base Applications" appears in chapters on quality control, forecasting, location strategy, layout, aggregate planning, material requirements planning, short-term scheduling, and project management, and in the quantitative modules on linear programming and transportation models These very large problems are intended for analysis by computer. They permit students to spend more time interpreting outputs of realistic problems to supplement problem-solving skills developed with a regular program.

Three Levels of Problems The number of end-of-chapter problems has been increased by 15%, for a total of 435, and each is identified as one of three levels; introductory (one dot), moderate (two dots), and challenging (three dots). In addition, these problems focus on problem formulation and interpretation as well as calculation. There are also over 300 discussion questions.

Marginal Notes and Definitions Notes in the margins provide interesting and motivational sidebars to students. There are more than six per chapter, including quotes from famous people, tips for learning, and highlights of major points. New to this edition are margin definitions that emphasize each term that is boldfaced in the text.

Solutions to Even-Numbered Problems Brief answers to all the even-numbered problems in the book appear in Appendix VI.

ACKNOWLEDGMENTS

We thank the many individuals who were kind enough to assist us in this endeavor. The following professors provided insights that guided us in this revision. Rick Carlson, Metropolitan State University; Warren W. Fisher, Stephen F. Austin State University; Sue Helm, University of Wisconsin–River Falls; Johnny Ho, Columbus State University; John Nicolay, University of Minnesota; Zinovy Radovilsky, California State University–Hayward; Narendra K. Rustagi, Howard University; Girish Shambu, Canisius College; and L. W. Shell, Nicholls State University.

We also wish to acknowledge the help of the reviewers of the earlier editions of this text. Without the help of these fellow professors, we would never have received the feedback needed to put together a teachable text. The reviewers are listed in alphabetical order:

Preface

Sema Alptekin
University of Missouri–Rolla

Jean-Pierre Amor
University of San Diego

Moshen Attaran
California State University–Bakersfield

John H. Blackstone
University of Georgia

Theodore Boreki
Hofstra University

Mark Coffin
Eastern Carolina University

Henry Crouch
Pittsburg State University

Larry A. Flick
Norwalk Community Technical College

Barbara Flynn
Iowa State University

Damodar Golhar
Western Michigan University

Jim Goodwin
University of Richmond

James R. Gross
University of Wisconsin–Oshkosh

Donald Hammond
University of South Florida

Marilyn K. Hart
University of Wisconsin–Oshkosh

James S. Hawkes
University of Charleston

George Heinrich
Wichita State University

Zialu Huq
University of Nebraska–Omaha

Paul Jordan
University of Alaska

Larry LaForge
Clemson University

Hugh Leach
Washburn University

B. P. Lingeraj
Indiana University

Andy Litteral
University of Richmond

Laurie E. MacDonald
Bryant College

Mike Maggard
Northeastern University

Arthur C. Meiners, Jr.
Marymount University

Joao Neves
Trenton State College

Niranjan Pati
University of Wisconsin–LaCrosse

Michael Pesch
St. Cloud State University

David W. Pentico
Duquesne University

Leonard Presby
William Patterson State
 College of New Jersey

Ranga V. Ramasesh
Texas Christian University

M. J. Riley
Kansas State University

Narendrea K. Rustagi
Howard University

Teresita S. Salinas
Washburn University

Ronald K. Satterfield
University of South Florida

Robert J. Schlesinger
San Diego State University

Shane J. Schvaneveldt
Webber State College

Avanti P. Sethi
Wichita State University

Girish Shambu
Canisius College

Susan Sherer
Lehigh University

Vicki L. Smith-Daniels
Arizona State University

Stan Stockton
Indiana University

John Swearingen
Bryant College

Kambiz Tabibzadeh
Eastern Kentucky University

Bruce M. Woodworth
University of Texas–El Paso

Rao J. Taikonda
University of Wisconsin–Oshkosh

In addition, we appreciate the fine people at Prentice Hall who provided both help and encouragement: Tom Tucker, our decision sciences editor; Ron Librach, our development editor, Cindy Harford, our Internet editor; Cynthia Regan, our production editor; and Kristen Imperatore, our supplements editor. Reva Shader developed the subject indexes for this text. Donna Render, Jessie Render, Sue Crabill, Kay Heizer, Christy Van Geldren, and Kathy Webb provided the accurate typing and proofing so critical in a rigorous textbook.

We also appreciate the efforts of colleagues who have helped to shape the entire learning package that accompanies this text: Professor Howard Weiss (Temple University) developed Excel OM and POM for Windows microcomputer software; Professor John McGill (Trenton State University) developed a portion of the excellent PowerPoint graphics; Professor John Swearingen (Bryant College) created The Instructor's Resource Manual, numerous PowerPoint slides, and CD-ROM materials; Dr. Vijay Gupta helped proof our Solutions Manual; Beverly Amer (Northern Arizona University) produced and directed our video series; and Professor Phillip Angelillo (Polytechnic University of Brooklyn) who so carefully checked the accuracy of our manuscript. We have been fortunate to have been able to work with all of these people.

We wish you a pleasant and productive introduction to operations management.

Barry Render
Roy E. Crummer Graduate
School of Business
Rollins College
Winter Park, FL 32789
Phone: (407) 646-2657
Fax: (407) 646-1550
Email:brender@rollins.edu

Jay Heizer
Texas Lutheran University
1000 W. Court Street
Seguin, TX 78155
Phone: (830) 372-6056
Fax: (830) 372-8096
Email: heizer_j@txlutheran.edu

NEW CONTENT

The exciting part of teaching and studying in the OM field is the constant change! We've thoroughly updated this state of the art text to reflect the trends taking place in Operations Management. Here is a quick overview of some of the changes.

- ## STRATEGIC FOCUS

  We have expanded our coverage to focus on how managers achieve strategies of *differentiation*, *low cost*, and *response*. We then continue the differentiation, cost leadership, and quick response strategies in our subsequent chapters to illustrate how strategy can impact everything an operations manager does. Chapter 2 also provides sample missions for Circle K and Merck, research from the Strategic Planning Institute, and a strategic link to the process analysis choices developed by Hayes and Wheelwright.

- ## SERVICE OPERATIONS FOCUS

  This edition increases the coverage of service operations. With an integration of service coverage throughout the text, the tone is set in chapter 1, with a major section entitled "Operations in the Service Sector." Each chapter then follows up with further discussion. We now deal with service selection, service design, and documents for services as major topics. Numerous new service cases have been added.

- ## GLOBAL FOCUS

  We are proud to be the first OM text to develop a full chapter on the importance of Operations in a Global Environment. The chapter defines global operations, justifies their importance, and describes how to achieve global product design, process designs, make location decisions, and deal with foreign cultures and ethics. In addition, each chapter opens with a ***Global Company Profile***, a two-page photo essay describing such world-class global players.

- ## OPERATIONS PROCESSES

  Processes and process analysis get increased coverage in this edition. For example, chapter 7 (Process Strategy and Capacity Planning) is a major revision, with an expanded treatment of the work of Hayes and Wheelwright (first mentioned in chapter 2) on process strategies and their continuum. Flow diagrams for Nucor Steel, Standard Register, and Harley Davidson illustrate these strategies. New treatment of process reengineering (with time function mapping and work flow analysis), a new section on environmental process issues, and additional material on capacity planning appear.

Part I • Introduction to Operations Management

Operations and Productivity 1

CHAPTER OUTLINE

GLOBAL COMPANY PROFILE: WHIRLPOOL
WHAT IS OPERATIONS MANAGEMENT?
THE HERITAGE OF OPERATIONS MANAGEMENT
WHY STUDY OM?
WHAT OPERATIONS MANAGERS DO
   How This Book Is Organized
ORGANIZING TO PRODUCE GOODS AND SERVICES
WHERE ARE THE OM JOBS?
EXCITING NEW TRENDS IN OPERATIONS MANAGEMENT
OPERATIONS IN THE SERVICE SECTOR
   Differences between Goods and Services
   Growth of Services
   Service Pay

THE PRODUCTIVITY CHALLENGE
   Productivity Measurement
   Productivity Variables
   Productivity and the Service Sector
THE CHALLENGE OF SOCIAL RESPONSIBILITY
SUMMARY
KEY TERMS
SOLVED PROBLEMS
DISCUSSION QUESTIONS
CRITICAL THINKING EXERCISE
PROBLEMS
CASE STUDY: NATIONAL AIR EXPRESS
BIBLIOGRAPHY
INTERNET RESOURCES

LEARNING OBJECTIVES

When you complete this chapter you should be able to:

Identify or Define:

Production and productivity

Operations management (OM)

What operations managers do

Services

Describe or Explain:

A brief history of operations management

Career opportunities in operations management

The future of the discipline

Measuring productivity

GLOBAL COMPANY PROFILE:

Productivity Increases Make a Difference at Whirlpool

Visual inspection takes place as parts are packed for shipment. A focus on total quality and reduction in scrap has been a major ingredient in productivity improvement at Whirlpool's plant in Benton Harbor, Michigan.

The U.S. home-appliance market is growing annually at 2% or less, about half of that projected for Europe. Therefore, Whirlpool chairman David Whitwam's strategy has been to take Whirlpool global. Whirlpool acquired major interest in Ingils Limited of Canada, Vitromatic of Mexico, and a 53% stake in Philips Electronics NV in the Netherlands. It has now set its sights on Asia, with the purchase of four competitors in China and two in India. Appliance giants Maytag, Electrolux, and GE have similarly developed and implemented global strategies to enable them to compete internationally.

As traditional economic barriers collapse, Whirlpool is establishing a global network of plants, from Canada to Brazil and from Mexico to China. In each of these facilities, Whirlpool fights for increases in productivity. Productivity makes a difference to employees, to customers, and to stockholders.

For employees, enhanced productivity at Whirlpool's washing machine factory in Benton Harbor, Michigan, means that, in recent years, each employee has received more than $2,000 in extra pay.

For customers, Whirlpool continues to defy inflation by holding the line on consumer prices. Even in the face of a consumer price index that is up about 16% in the last four years, some Whirlpool washers have dropped in price.

Productivity increases have benefited stockholders, too. Whirlpool has

WHIRLPOOL

At Whirlpool's Clyde, Ohio, plant, washing machines are assembled with perfect parts received on time from Benton Harbor

gained market share while outpacing its rivals in profitability. Consequently, Whirlpool's stock price is also up.

None of this happens without increases in productivity. Parts manufactured per labor hour is up and scrap is down. How did Whirlpool do it? First, there was a change in attitude by management and employees who now "live" quality as well as talk about it. Second, companywide training now stresses that employees use their heads as well as their hands. Third, flexible work rules allow employees to work where needed. Fourth, a gain-sharing agreement keeps everyone focused on productivity improvements. And fifth, Whirlpool has moved toward global procurement of 35 strategic materials and components.

The global business system is changing not only the way Whirlpool enhances productivity and procures material but also the way firms throughout the world organize and communicate. New global information links connect suppliers, customers, and manufacturers with the stroke of a key, the click of a mouse button, or even the touch of a screen. Ideas, designs, money transfers, and orders now move in seconds instead of days or weeks.

Moreover, the new information age has all but collapsed traditional barriers. Companies now make worldwide products. Ford makes a world car. Gillette makes a world razor. Microsoft makes Internet programs used around the world. McDonald's hamburgers taste the same in Moscow, Tel Aviv, Bangkok, and Chicago. These firms are just a few examples of the integrated international production system. Not only is movement of information by electrons cheap and fast, but huge ships and airplanes make the movement of goods less expensive and increasingly rapid.

These changes have a tremendous impact on the operations of firms. Companies that were once local became national, then regional, and now global. The technology that manifests itself in computers, communication, and lower transportation costs are terrific drivers toward the globalization of economic growth and world trade. This globalization explosion means we are living in an exciting and challenging time, with new jobs, new opportunities, and wonderful new options for operations managers.

As we progress through this text, we will discover how to manage operations in this global economy. An array of informative examples, charts, text discussions, and pictures illustrate concepts and provide information. Examples of operations management range from Minit-Lube and McDonald's to Whirlpool and Disney World. We will see how operations managers create the goods and services that enrich our lives.

In this chapter, we first define *operations management,* explaining its heritage and the exciting role operations managers play in a huge variety of businesses. Then we discuss production and productivity in both goods- and service-producing firms. This is followed by a discussion of operations in the service sector and the challenge of managing an effective production system.

WHAT IS OPERATIONS MANAGEMENT?

Production The creation of goods and services.

Operations management (OM) Activities that relate to the creation of goods and services through the transformation of inputs to outputs.

Production is the creation of goods and services. **Operations management (OM)** is the set of activities that creates goods and services through the transformation of inputs into outputs. Activities creating goods and services take place in all organizations. In manufacturing firms, the production activities that create goods are usually quite obvious. In them, we can see the creation of a tangible product such as a Sony TV or a Ford Taurus.

In organizations that do not create physical products, the production function may be less obvious. It may be "hidden" from the public and even from the customer. An example is the transformation that takes place at a bank, hospital, airline office, or college.

Often when services are performed, no tangible goods are produced. Instead, the product may take such forms as the transfer of funds from a savings account to a checking account, the transplant of a liver, the filling of an empty seat on an airline, or the education of a student. Regardless of whether the end product is a good or service, the production activities that go on in the organization are often referred to as operations or *operations management*.

THE HERITAGE OF OPERATIONS MANAGEMENT

The field of OM is relatively young, but its history is rich and interesting. Our lives and the OM discipline have been enhanced by the innovations and contributions of numerous

The Heritage of Operations Management

individuals. We introduce a few of these people in this section; and a summary of significant events in operations management is shown in Figure 1.1.

Eli Whitney (1800) is credited for the early popularization of interchangeable parts, which was achieved through standardization and quality control in manufacturing. Through a contract he signed with the U.S. government for 10,000 muskets, he was able to command a premium price because of their interchangeable parts.

Frederick W. Taylor (1881), known as the father of scientific management, contributed to personnel selection, planning and scheduling, motion study, and the now popular field of ergonomics. One of his major contributions was his belief that management should be much more resourceful and aggressive in the improvement of work methods. Taylor and his colleagues, Henry L. Gantt and Frank and Lillian Gilbreth, were among the first to seek systematically the best way to produce.

Another of Taylor's contributions was the belief that management should assume more responsibility for:

1. Matching employees to the right job.
2. Providing the proper training.
3. Providing proper work methods and tools.
4. Establishing legitimate incentives for work to be accomplished.

By 1913, Henry Ford and Charles Sorensen combined what they knew about standardized parts with the quasi-assembly lines of the meatpacking and mail-order industries and added the revolutionary concept of the assembly line where men stood still and material moved.

Quality control is another historically significant contribution to the field of OM. Walter Shewhart (1924) combined his knowledge of statistics with the need for quality

> Frederick W. Taylor's *Principles of Scientific Management* revolutionized manufacturing. A scientific approach to the analysis of daily work and the tools of industry frequently increased productivity 400%.

> One of the Gilbreth's techniques was to use cameras to record movement by attaching lights to an individual's arms and legs. In that way they could track the movement of individuals while performing various jobs.

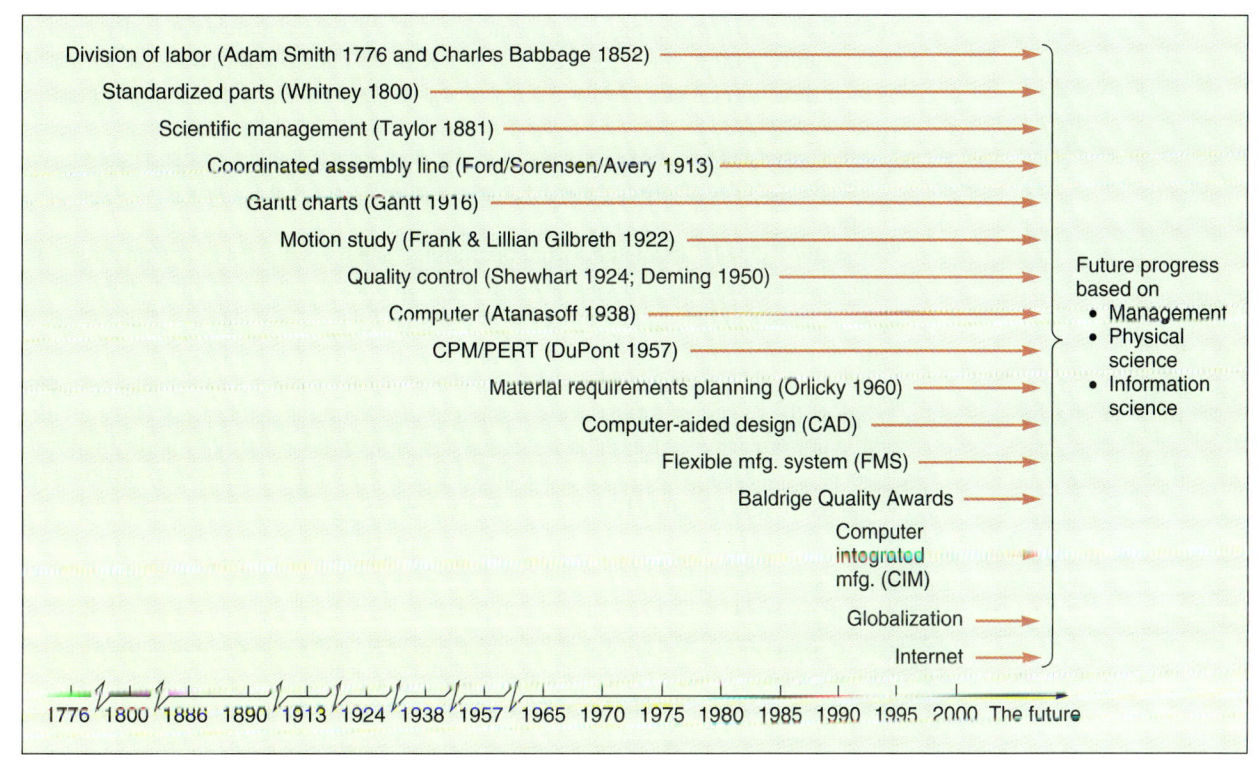

FIGURE 1.1 ■ **Significant Events in Operations Management**

- Division of labor (Adam Smith 1776 and Charles Babbage 1852)
- Standardized parts (Whitney 1800)
- Scientific management (Taylor 1881)
- Coordinated assembly line (Ford/Sorensen/Avery 1913)
- Gantt charts (Gantt 1916)
- Motion study (Frank & Lillian Gilbreth 1922)
- Quality control (Shewhart 1924; Deming 1950)
- Computer (Atanasoff 1938)
- CPM/PERT (DuPont 1957)
- Material requirements planning (Orlicky 1960)
- Computer-aided design (CAD)
- Flexible mfg. system (FMS)
- Baldrige Quality Awards
- Computer integrated mfg. (CIM)
- Globalization
- Internet

Future progress based on
- Management
- Physical science
- Information science

Timeline: 1776, 1800, 1886, 1890, 1913, 1924, 1938, 1957, 1965, 1970, 1975, 1980, 1985, 1990, 1995, 2000, The future

6 CHAPTER 1 OPERATIONS AND PRODUCTIVITY

Charles Sorensen was the man who towed an automobile chassis on a rope over his shoulders through the Ford plant while others added parts.

control and provided the foundations for statistical sampling in quality control. W. Edwards Deming (1950) believed, as did Frederick Taylor, that management must do more to improve the work environment and processes so that quality can be improved.

Operations management will continue to progress with contributions from other disciplines, including *industrial engineering* and *management science*. These disciplines, along with statistics, management, and economics, have contributed substantially to greater productivity.

Innovations from the *physical sciences* (biology, anatomy, chemistry, physics) have also contributed to advances in OM. These advances include new adhesives, chemical processes for printed circuit boards, gamma rays to sanitize food products, and molten tin tables on which to float higher-quality molten glass as it cools. The design of products and processes often depend on the biological and physical sciences.

An especially important contribution to OM has come from the *information sciences,* which we define as the systematic processing of data to yield information. The information sciences are contributing in a major way toward improved productivity while providing society with a greater diversity of goods and services.

Decisions in operations management require individuals who are well versed in management science, in information science, and often in one of the biological or physical sciences. In this chapter, we take a look at the diverse ways a student can prepare for careers in operations management.

WHY STUDY OM?

We study OM for four reasons:

1. OM is one of the three major functions of any organization, and it is integrally related to all the other business functions. All organizations market (sell), finance (account), and produce (operate), and it is important to know how the OM segment functions. Therefore, we study *how people organize themselves for productive enterprise*.
2. We study OM because we want to know *how goods and services are produced*. The production function is the segment of our society that creates the products we use.
3. We study OM to understand what operations managers do. By understanding what these managers do, you can develop the skills necessary to become such a manager. This will help you explore the numerous and lucrative career opportunities in OM.
4. We study OM *because it is such a costly part of an organization*. A large percentage of the revenue of most firms is spent in the OM function. Indeed, OM provides a major opportunity for an organization to improve its profitability and enhance its service to society. Example 1 considers how a firm might increase its profitability via the production function.

EXAMPLE 1

Fisher Technologies is a small firm that must double its dollar contribution to fixed cost and profit in order to be profitable enough to purchase the next generation of production equipment. Management has determined that, if the firm fails to increase contribution, its bank will not make the loan and the equipment cannot be purchased. If the firm cannot purchase the equipment, the limitations of the old equipment will force Fisher to go out of business and, in doing so, put its employees out of work and discontinue producing goods and services for its customers.

Table 1.1 shows a simple profit-and-loss statement and three strategic options for the firm. The first option is a *marketing option* where good management may increase sales by 50%. By increasing sales by 50%, contribution will in turn increase 71%, but increasing sales 50% may be more than difficult; it may even be impossible.

The second option is a *finance/accounting option* where finance costs are cut in half through good financial management. But even a reduction of 50% is still inadequate for generating the necessary increase in contribution. Contribution is increased by only 21%.

The third option is an *OM option* where management reduces production costs by 20% and increases contribution by 114%. Given the conditions of our brief example, Fischer Technologies has increased contribution from $10,500 to $22,500 and will now have a bank willing to lend it additional funds.

TABLE 1.1 ■ Options for Increasing Contribution

	CURRENT	Marketing Option[a] INCREASE SALES REVENUE 50%	Finance/ Accounting Option[b] REDUCE FINANCE COSTS 50%	OM Option[c] REDUCE PRODUCTION COSTS 20%
Sales	$100,000	$150,000	$100,000	$100,000
Costs of goods	−80,000	−120,000	−80,000	−64,000
Gross margin	20,000	30,000	20,000	36,000
Finance costs	− 6,000	− 6,000	− 3,000	− 6,000
	14,000	24,000	17,000	30,000
Taxes at 25%	− 3,500	− 6,000	− 4,250	− 7,500
Contribution[d]	$ 10,500	$ 18,000	$ 12,750	$ 22,500

[a] Increasing sales 50% increases contribution by $7,500 or 71.0% (7,500/10,500).
[b] Reducing finance costs 50% increases contribution by $2,250 or 21.0% (2,250/10,500).
[c] Reducing production costs 20% increases contribution by $12,000 or 114.0% (12,000/10,500).
[d] Contribution to fixed cost (excluding finance costs) and profit.

Example 1 underscores the important role of developing an effective strategy for the operations activity of a firm. It is also the approach taken by many companies as they face growing global competition.

WHAT OPERATIONS MANAGERS DO

All good managers perform the basic functions of the management process. The **management process** consists of *planning, organizing, staffing, leading,* and *controlling.* Operations managers apply this management process to the decisions they make in the OM function. Managers contribute to production and operations through the decisions shown in Table 1.2. Successfully addressing each of these decisions requires planning, organizing, staffing, leading, and controlling. Typical issues relevant to these decisions and the chapter where each is discussed are also shown.

Management process
The application of planning, organizing, staffing, leading, and controlling to the achievement of objectives.

Table 1.2 ■ **Ten Critical Decisions of Operations Management**

Ten Decision Areas	Issues	Chapter(s)
Quality management	Who is responsible for quality? How do we define the quality we want in our service or product?	4, 4 Supplement
Service and product design	What product or service should we offer? How should we design these products and services?	6
Process and capacity design	What process will these products require and in what order? What equipment and technology is necessary for these processes?	7, 7 Supplement
Location	Where should we put the facility? On what criteria should we base the location decision?	8
Layout design	How should we arrange the facility? How large must the facility be to meet our plan?	9
Human resources and job design	How do we provide a reasonable work environment? How much can we expect our employees to produce?	10, 10 Supplement
Supply-chain management	Should we make or buy this component? Who are our good suppliers and how many should we have?	11
Inventory, material requirements planning, and JIT ("just-in-time")	How much inventory of each item should we have? When do we reorder?	12, 12 Supplement, 14
Intermediate, short-term, and project scheduling	Is subcontracting production a good idea? Are we better off keeping people on the payroll during slowdowns?	13, 15, 16
Maintenance	Who is responsible for maintenance?	17

TEN DECISIONS OF OM

Managing Quality
Design of Goods & Services
Process Strategy
Location Strategies
Layout Strategies
Human Resources
Supply-Chain Management
Inventory Management
Scheduling
Maintenance

How This Book Is Organized

The 10 decisions shown in Table 1.2 are activities required of operations managers. The ability to make good decisions in these areas and allocate resources to ensure their effective execution goes a long way toward an efficient operations function. The text is structured around these 10 decisions. Throughout the book, we will discuss the issues and tools that help managers make these 10 decisions. We will also consider the impact that these decisions can have on the firm's strategy and productivity.

ORGANIZING TO PRODUCE GOODS AND SERVICES

To create goods and services, all organizations perform three functions (see Figure 1.2). These functions are the necessary ingredients not only for production but also for an organization's survival. They are:

Organizing to Produce Goods and Services

(A)
Commercial Bank

Operations
- Teller scheduling
- Check clearing
- Collection
- Transactions processing
- Facilities design/layout
- Vault operations
- Maintenance
- Security

Finance
- Investments
  - Securities
  - Real estate
- Accounting
- Auditing

Marketing
- Loans
  - Commercial
  - Industrial
  - Financial
  - Personal
  - Mortgage
- Trust department

(B)
Airline

Operations
- Ground support equipment
- Maintenance
- Ground operations
  - Facility maintenance
  - Catering
- Flight operations
  - Crew scheduling
  - Flying
  - Communications
  - Dispatching
- Management science

Finance/accounting
- Accounting
  - Accounts payable
  - Accounts receivable
  - General ledger
- Finance
  - Cash control
  - International exchange

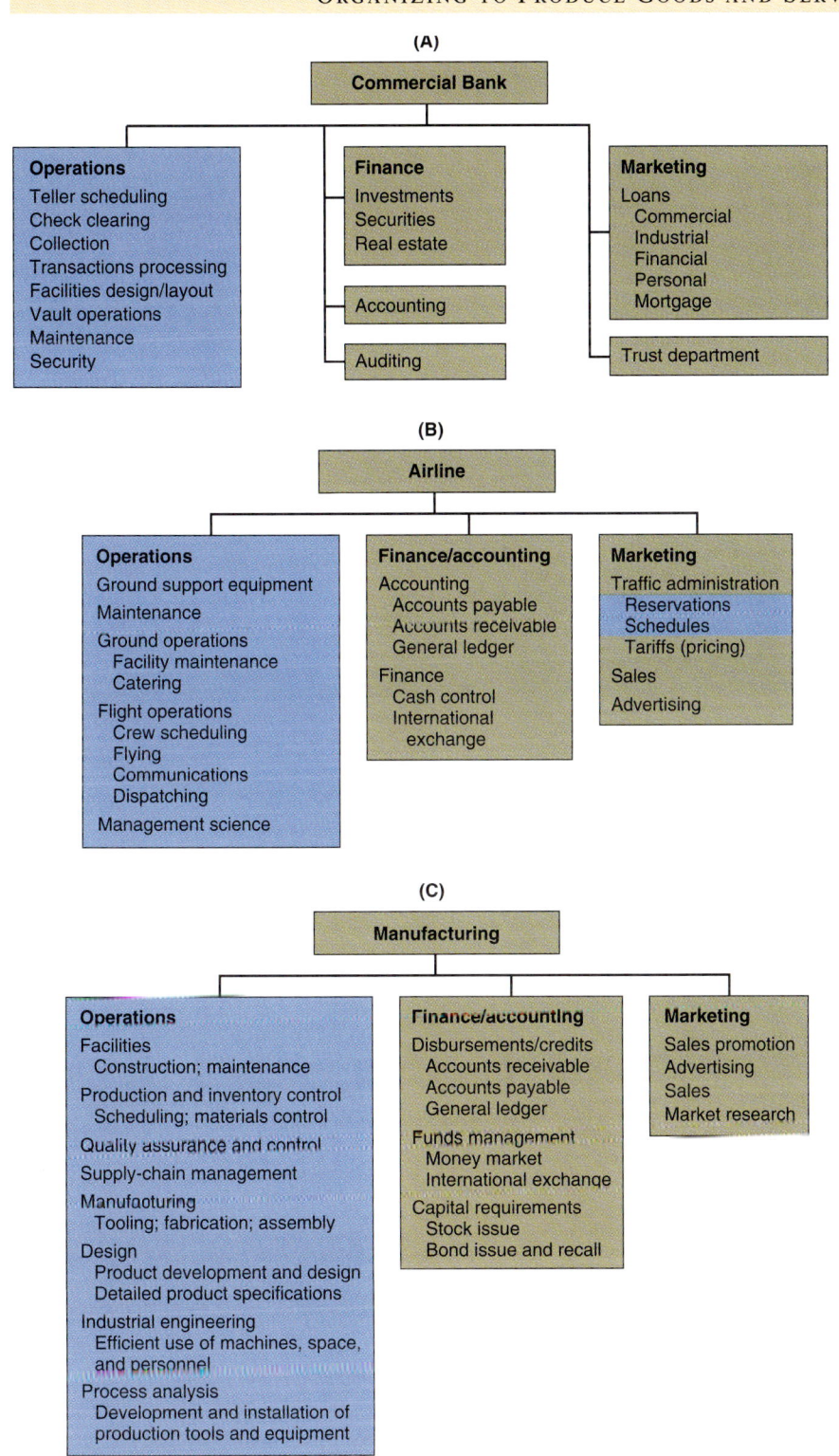

Marketing
- Traffic administration
  - Reservations
  - Schedules
  - Tariffs (pricing)
- Sales
- Advertising

(C)
Manufacturing

Operations
- Facilities
  - Construction; maintenance
- Production and inventory control
  - Scheduling; materials control
- Quality assurance and control
- Supply-chain management
- Manufacturing
  - Tooling; fabrication; assembly
- Design
  - Product development and design
  - Detailed product specifications
- Industrial engineering
  - Efficient use of machines, space, and personnel
- Process analysis
  - Development and installation of production tools and equipment

Finance/accounting
- Disbursements/credits
  - Accounts receivable
  - Accounts payable
  - General ledger
- Funds management
  - Money market
  - International exchange
- Capital requirements
  - Stock issue
  - Bond issue and recall

Marketing
- Sales promotion
- Advertising
- Sales
- Market research

FIGURE 1.2 ■ Organization Charts for Two Services and One Manufacturing Organization *(A) A Bank, (B) an Airline, and (C) a Manufacturing Organization. The blue areas are OM activities.*

1. *Marketing,* which generates the demand, or at least takes the order for, a product or service (nothing happens until there is a sale).
2. *Production/operations,* which creates the product.
3. *Finance/accounting,* which tracks how well the organization is doing, pays the bills, and collects the money.

Universities, churches or synagogues, and businesses all perform these functions.

Any institution, even a volunteer group such as the Boy Scouts of America, is organized to perform these three basic functions. Figure 1.2 shows how a bank, an airline, and a manufacturing firm organize themselves to perform these functions. The blue-shaded areas of Figure 1.2 show the operations functions in these firms.

WHERE ARE THE OM JOBS?

How does one get started on a career in operations? The 10 OM decisions identified in Table 1.2 are made by individuals who work in the disciplines shown in the blue areas of Figure 1.2. Competent business students who know their accounting, statistics, finance, and OM have an opportunity to enter the entry-level positions in all of these areas. As you read this text, look at the disciplines that can assist you in making these decisions. Then take courses in those areas. The more background an OM student has in accounting, statistics, information systems, and mathematics, the more job opportunities will be available. About 40% of *all* jobs are in OM. The following are just a few of the areas where opportunities exist for OM graduates in the year 2000:[1]

1. *Technology/methods:* The greatest opportunities today are in the fields that make use of technology and the techniques of continuous improvement. These include computer applications, maintenance, process improvement, and ergonomics.
2. *Facilities/space utilization:* The development of work cells, facility consolidation, layout improvements for storage of raw materials, warehousing, work-in-progress, and finished goods all provide tremendous opportunities.
3. *Strategic issues:* Identifying new opportunities, providing vision, organizational development, measurement and reporting systems, benchmarking, and creating and sustaining peak performance are ranked as major opportunities.
4. *Response time:* Speed and reaction time by an organization and its suppliers, reduction of setup times, and product design times are viewed as critical in today's fast-paced environment.
5. *People/team development:* Throughout the production and distribution system, the topics of employee involvement and empowerment, leadership, communication, and team development are all crucial for maximizing productivity opportunities.
6. *Customer service:* As customers demand more customized products, as services become more important, and as technology becomes a larger ingredient in many products, order fulfillment, after-sale service, and equipment uptime all are key for operational success.
7. *Quality:* Product quality and information quality remain crucial to operations success.
8. *Cost reduction:* As always, operations managers must focus on doing more with less through simplification, streamlining, and focusing on resources to get the job done at minimal costs.

---

[1] *Sources:* Tompkins Associates, Inc., Raleigh, NC, as reported in *OR/MS Today*; and *New York Times*, November 6, 1996, p. C4.

9. *Inventory reduction and supply-chain management:* Reduction and faster movement of inventory throughout the supply chain, cutting damage and shrinkage, and just-in-time arrival of inventory all help release assets for more productive purposes.
10. *Productivity improvement:* Productivity enhancements are the only way we can improve our standard of living. It is the operations manager's continuing task to see that this is done.

EXCITING NEW TRENDS IN OPERATIONS MANAGEMENT

One of the reasons OM is such an exciting discipline is that the operations manager is confronted with an ever-changing world. Consequently, both the approach to and the results of the 10 OM decisions in Table 1.2 are subject to change. These dynamics are the result of a variety of forces, from globalization of world trade to the transfer of ideas, products, and money at electronic speeds. The direction now being taken by OM—where it has been and where it is going—is shown in Figure 1.3. We now introduce some of the challenges shown in Figure 1.3.

- *Global focus:* The rapid decline in communication and transportation costs has, of course, made markets global. But at the same time, resources in the form of materials, talent, and labor have also become global. Contributing to this rapid globalization are countries throughout the world that are vying for economic growth and industrializa-

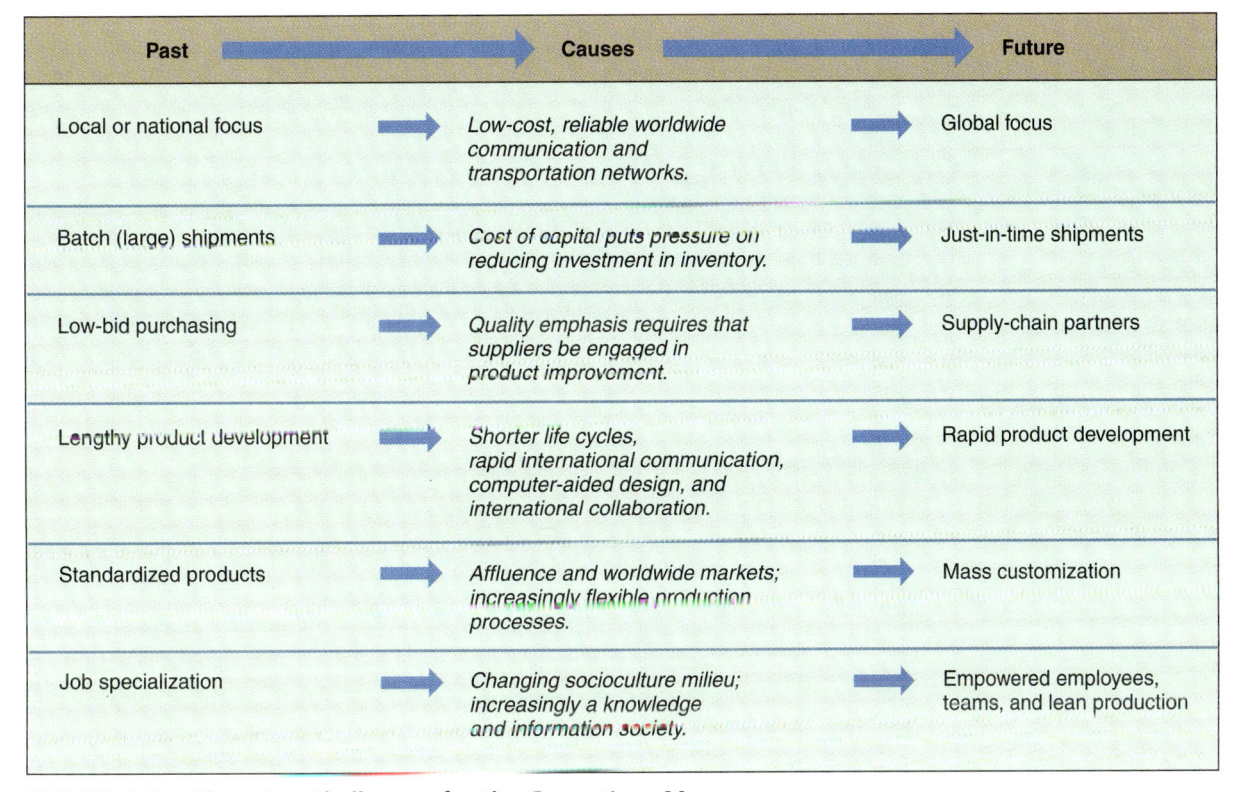

Past	Causes	Future
Local or national focus	Low-cost, reliable worldwide communication and transportation networks.	Global focus
Batch (large) shipments	Cost of capital puts pressure on reducing investment in inventory.	Just-in-time shipments
Low-bid purchasing	Quality emphasis requires that suppliers be engaged in product improvement.	Supply-chain partners
Lengthy product development	Shorter life cycles, rapid international communication, computer-aided design, and international collaboration.	Rapid product development
Standardized products	Affluence and worldwide markets; increasingly flexible production processes.	Mass customization
Job specialization	Changing socioculture milieu; increasingly a knowledge and information society.	Empowered employees, teams, and lean production

FIGURE 1.3 ■ Changing Challenges for the Operations Manager

tion. Operations managers are responding with innovations that generate and move ideas, parts, and finished goods rapidly, wherever and whenever needed.
- *Just-in-time performance:* Vast financial resources are committed to inventory. And inventory impedes response to the dynamic changes in the marketplace. Operations managers are viciously cutting inventories at every level, from raw materials to finished goods.
- *Supply-chain partnering:* Shorter product life cycles, as well as rapid changes in material and process technology, require more participation by suppliers. Suppliers usually supply over half of the value of products. Consequently, operations managers are building long-term partnerships with critical players in the supply chain.
- *Rapid product development:* Rapid international communication of news, entertainment, and lifestyles is dramatically chopping away at the life of products. Operations managers are responding with design technology that is faster and design management that is more effective.
- *Mass customization:* Once we begin to consider the world as the marketplace, then the individual differences become quite obvious. Cultural differences, compounded by individual differences, in a world where consumers are increasingly aware of options, places substantial pressure on firms to respond. Operations managers are responding with production processes that are flexible enough to cater to individual whims of consumers. The goal is to produce individual products, whenever and wherever needed.
- *Empowered employees:* More sophisticated employees and a more technical workplace have combined to require more competence at the workplace. Operations managers are responding by moving more decision making to the individual worker.

These and many more topics that are part of the exciting challenges to operations managers are discussed in this text.

OPERATIONS IN THE SERVICE SECTOR

The service sector is defined differently by different people. Even the U.S. government has trouble generating a consistent definition. Because definitions vary, much of the data and statistics generated about the service sector are inconsistent. However, we will define **services** as including repair and maintenance, government, food and lodging, transportation, insurance, trade, financial, real estate, education, legal, medical, entertainment, and other professional occupations.[2]

Services Those economic activities that typically produce an intangible product (such as education, entertainment, lodging, government, financial and health services).

Differences between Goods and Services

Let's examine some of the differences between goods and services:

- Services are *usually intangible* (for example, your purchase of a ride in an empty airline seat between two cities) as opposed to a tangible good.
- Services are often *produced and consumed simultaneously;* there is no stored inventory. For instance, the beauty salon produces a haircut that is "consumed" simultaneously, or the doctor produces an operation that is "consumed" as it is produced. We have not yet figured out how to inventory haircuts or appendectomies.

[2] This definition is similar to the categories used by the U.S. Bureau of Labor Statistics.

- *Services are often unique.* Your mix of financial coverage, such as investments and insurance policies, may not be the same as anyone else's, just as the medical procedure or a haircut produced for you is not exactly like anyone else's.
- Services have *high customer interaction.* Services are often difficult to standardize, automate, and make as efficient as we would like because customer interaction demands uniqueness. In fact, in many cases this uniqueness is what the customer is paying for; therefore, the operations manager must ensure that the product is designed so that it can be delivered in the required unique manner.
- Services have *inconsistent product definition.* Product definition may be rigorous, as in the case of an auto insurance policy, but inconsistent because policyholders change cars and mature.
- Services are often *knowledge-based,* as in the case of educational, medical, and legal services, and therefore hard to automate.
- Services are frequently *dispersed.* Dispersion occurs because services are frequently brought to the client/customer via a local office, a retail outlet, or even a house call.

Table 1.3 indicates some additional differences between goods and services that impact OM decisions. Although service products are different from goods, the operations function continues to transform resources into products. Indeed, the activities of the operations function are often very similar for both goods and services: The 10 OM decisions in Table 1.2 must be performed for each. For instance, both goods and services must have quality standards established, and both must be designed and processed on a schedule, in a facility where human resources are employed.

TABLE 1.3 ■ Differences between Goods and Services

Attributes of Goods (Tangible product)	Attributes of Services (Intangible product)
Product can be resold.	Reselling a service is unusual.
Product can be inventoried.	Many services cannot be inventoried.
Some aspects of quality are measurable.	Many aspects of quality are difficult to measure.
Selling is distinct from production.	Selling is often a part of the service.
Product is transportable.	Provider, not product, is often transportable.
Site of facility is important for cost.	Site of facility is important for customer contact.
Often easy to automate.	Service is often difficult to automate.
Revenue is generated primarily from the tangible product.	Revenue is generated primarily from the intangible services.

Having made the distinction between goods and services, we should point out that in many cases, the distinction is not clear-cut. In reality, almost all services are a mixture of a service and a tangible product; similarly, the sale of many goods includes or requires a service. For instance, many products have the service components of financing and transportation (e.g., automobile sales). Many also require after-sale training and maintenance (e.g., office copiers). When a tangible product is *not* included in the service, we may call it a **pure service**. Although there are not very many pure services, one example is counseling.

Figure 1.4 shows the range of *services* in a product. The range is extensive and shows the pervasiveness of service activities.

Pure service A service that does not include a tangible product.

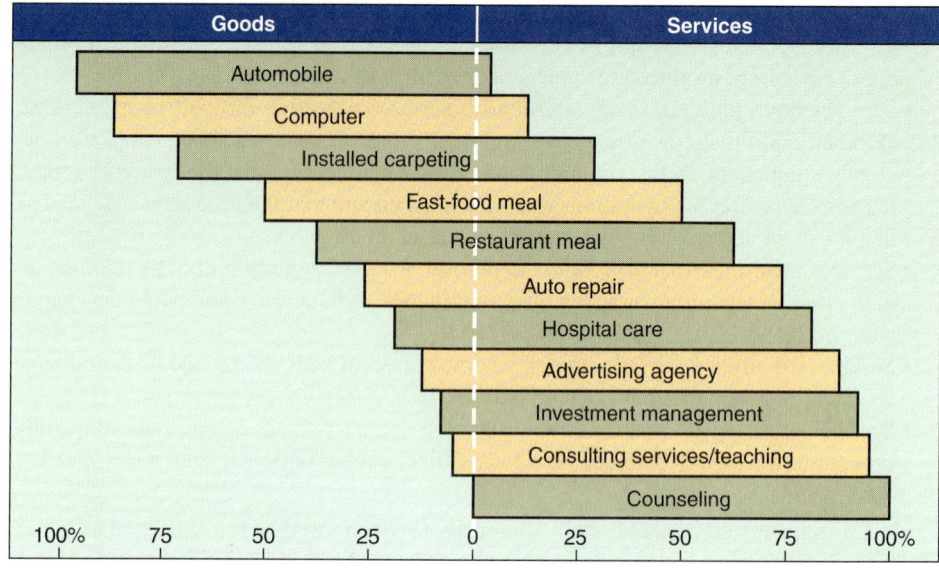

FIGURE 1.4 ■ **Most Goods Contain a Service and Most Services Contain a Good**
Sources: For similar presentations, see Earl W. Sasser, R. P. Olsen, and D. Daryl Wyckoff, *Management of Service Operations* (Boston: Allyn & Bacon), p. 11; and G. Lynn Shostack, "Breaking Free from Product Marketing," *Journal of Marketing,* April 1987.

Growth of Services

Services now constitute the largest economic sector in advanced societies. For example, service-sector employment in the United States is shown in Figure 1.5(a). Until about 1900, most Americans were employed in agriculture. Increased agricultural productivity allowed people to leave the farm and seek employment in the city. The manufacturing and

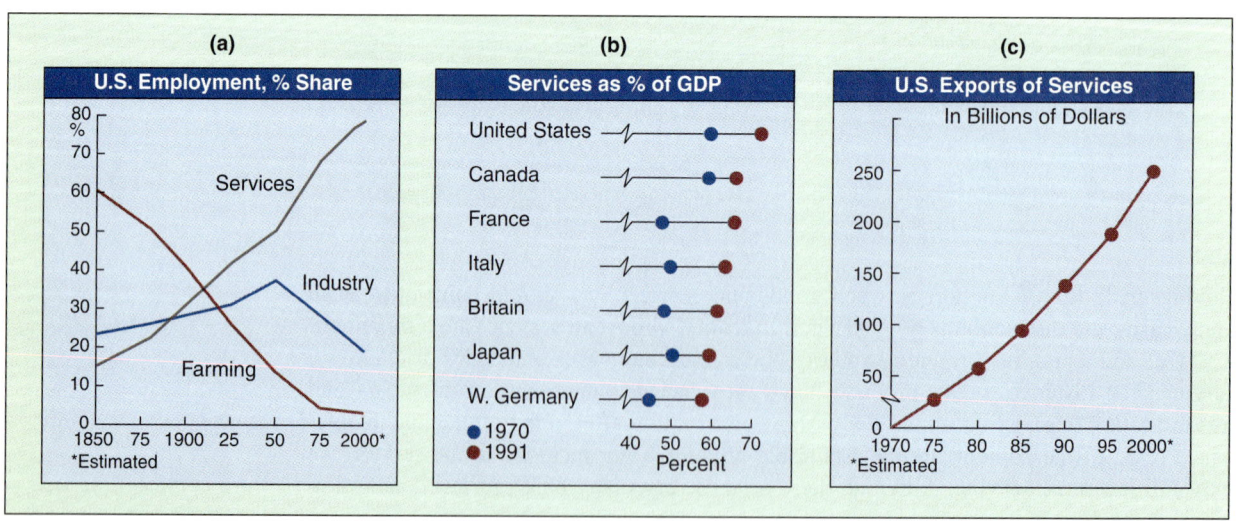

FIGURE 1.5 ■ **Development of the Service Economy**
Sources: Adapted from U.S. Labor Statistics Bureau; OECD; National statistics; U.S. Commerce Department U.S. Foreign Trade Highlights 1995; "The Final Frontier," *The Economist,* February 20, 1993, p. 63; *Statistical Abstract of the United States,* 1995.

service sectors began to grow, with services becoming the dominant employer in the early 1920s and manufacturing employment peaking at about 32% in 1950. Similarly, as Figures 1.5(a) and (b) show, productivity increases in manufacturing have allowed more of our economic resources to be devoted to services. Consequently, much of the world can now enjoy the pleasure of education, health services, entertainment, and the myriad of other things that we call services. Figure 1.5(c) indicates the explosive growth of U.S. export of services. Examples of firms and percentage of employment in the **service sector** are shown in Table 1.4. Table 1.4 also provides employment percentages for the nonservice sectors of manufacturing, construction, mining, and agriculture on the bottom four lines.

Service sector That segment of the economy that includes trade, financial, education, legal, medical, and other professional occupations.

TABLE 1.4 ■ Examples of Organizations in Each Sector

Sector	Example	Percentage of All Jobs
Service Sector		
Government	U.S., State of Alabama, Cook County	12.5%
Education	New York City P.S. 108, Notre Dame University	7.5
Food, Lodging	McDonald's, Luby's Cafeteria, Motel 6, Hilton Hotels	1.8
Entertainment	Walt Disney, Paramount Pictures	1.7
Trade (retail, wholesale)	Walgreen's, Wal-Mart, Nordstrom's	20.8
Utilities, Transportation	Pacific Gas & Electric, American Airlines, Santa Fe R.R., Roadway Express	7.1
Finance, Insurance, Real Estate	Citicorp, American Express, Prudential, Aetna, Trammell Crow	6.5
Legal	Hunton & Williams, local law offices	1.0
Medical	Mayo Clinic, Humana Hospitals	8.5
Social Services and Other	San Diego Zoo, Smithsonian Museum	2.4
Repair and Maintenance	IBM maintenance, Xerox maintenance, Pitney-Bowes	3.0
Business Services	Snelling and Snelling, Waste Management, Inc.	1.5
Manufacturing Sector	General Electric, Ford, U.S. Steel, Intel	16.4
Construction Sector	Bechtel, McDermott	6.1
Mining Sector	Homestake Mining	0.5
Agriculture	King Ranch	2.7

Source: Statistical Abstract of the United States, 1996, Table 641.

Service Pay

Although there is a common perception that service industries are low-paying, in fact, many service jobs pay very well. Operations managers in the maintenance facility of an airline are very well paid, as are the operations managers who supervise computer services to the financial community. About 42% of all service workers receive wages above the national average. However, the service-sector average is driven down because 14 of the Commerce Department categories of the 33 service industries do indeed pay below the all-private industry average. Of these, retail trade, which pays only 61% of the national private industry average, is large. But even considering the retail sector, the average wage of all service workers is about 96% of the average of all private industries.[3]

THE PRODUCTIVITY CHALLENGE

The creation of goods and service requires changing resources into goods and services. The more efficiently we make this change the more productive we are. **Productivity** is the ratio of outputs (goods and services) divided by the inputs (resources, such as labor and capital) (see Figure 1.6). The operations manager's job is to enhance (improve) this ratio of outputs to inputs. Improving productivity means improving efficiency.[4]

Productivity The ratio of outputs (goods and services) divided by one or more inputs (such as labor, capital, or management).

This improvement can be achieved in two ways: a reduction in inputs while output remains constant, or an increase in output while inputs remain constant. Both represent an improvement in productivity. In an economic sense, inputs are land, labor, capital, and management, which are combined into a production system. Management creates this production system, which provides the conversion of inputs to outputs. Outputs are goods and services, including such diverse items as guns, butter, education, improved judicial

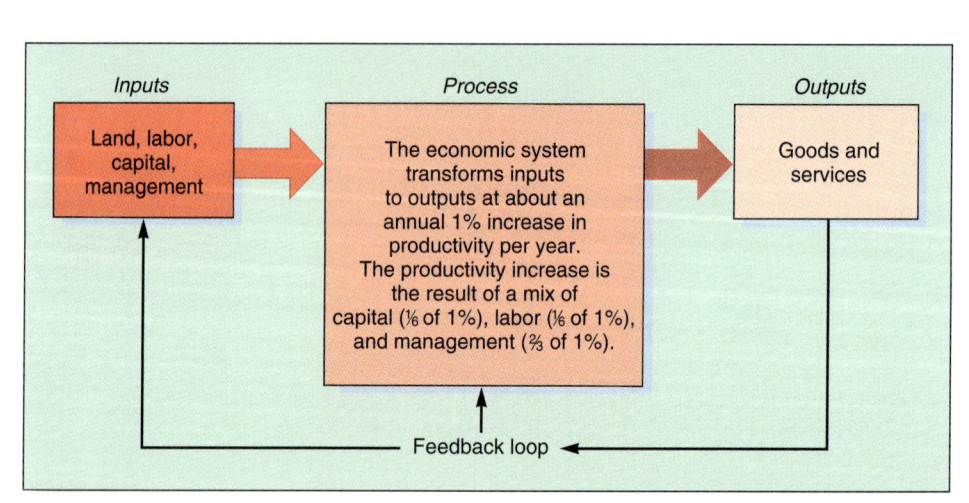

FIGURE 1.6 ■ **The Economic System Transforms Inputs to Outputs** *An effective feedback loop evaluates process performance against a plan. In this case, it also evaluates customer satisfaction and sends signals to those controlling the inputs and process.*

---

[3] Herbert Stein and Murray Foss, *The New Illustrated Guide to the American Economy* (Washington, D.C.: The AIE Press, 1995), p. 30.

[4] *Efficiency* means doing the job well—with a minimum of resources and waste. Note the distinction between being *efficient*, which implies doing the job well, and *effective*, which means doing the right thing. A job well done—say, by applying the 10 decisions of operations management—helps us be *efficient*; developing and using the correct strategy helps us be *effective*.

OM IN ACTION

WHAT HAPPENS WHEN PRODUCTIVITY IMPROVES?

When productivity improved (a) at Whirlpool's Benton Harbor, Michigan, plant cost went down (b) and wages increased (c). Productivity improvements allowed increased returns to both labor and capital *and* provided a dividend in the form of lower prices to consumers.

Source: Whirlpool Corp.; American Productivity and Quality Centers, as reported in *The Wall Street Journal*, May 4, 1992, pp. A1–A4. Reprinted by permission of *The Wall Street Journal*, © 1992 Dow Jones & Company, Inc. All Rights Reserved.

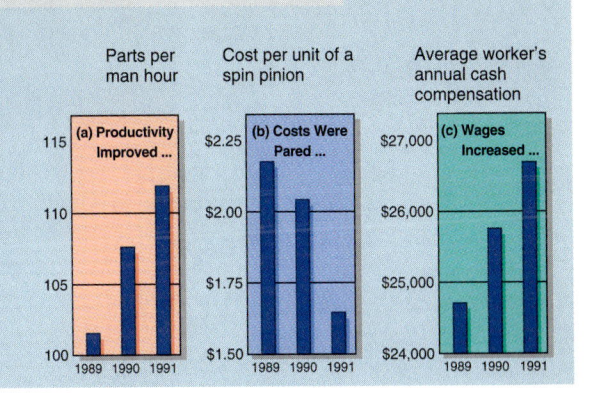

---

systems, and ski resorts. *Production* is the total goods and services produced. High production may imply only that more people are working and that employment levels are high (low unemployment), but it does not imply high *productivity*.

Measurement of productivity is an excellent way to evaluate a country's ability to provide an improving standard of living for its people. *Only through increases in productivity can the standard of living improve.* Moreover, only through increases in productivity can labor, capital, and management receive additional payments. If returns to labor, capital, or management are increased without increased productivity, prices rise. On the other hand, downward pressure is placed on prices when productivity increases, because more is being produced with the same resources.

The benefits of increased productivity are illustrated in the *OM in Action* box, "What Happens When Productivity Improves?"

For almost 100 years, the United States was able to increase productivity at an average rate of 2.5% per year. Such growth doubled our wealth every 30 years. Since the early 1970s, however, the United States has been unable to sustain that level of productivity increase, and productivity has averaged less than 1.0% per year.[5] From an economic-growth perspective, this is disastrous and explains much of the national concern with "stagnation of wages" and two-income families. However, there are bright spots in the U.S. productivity picture. The manufacturing sector, although a decreasing portion of the U.S. economy, has recently had productivity increases exceeding 3% per year. For example, the mid-1990s marked the return of the U.S. steelmaking industry after it was given up for dead a decade ago. With costs down and quality up, U.S. steel plants are now exporting to Europe and Japan.

In this text, we examine how to improve productivity through the operations function. Productivity is a significant issue for our society and one that the operations manager is uniquely qualified to address.

Productivity Measurement

The measurement of productivity can be quite direct. Such is the case when productivity can be measured as labor-hours per ton of a specific type of steel or as the energy necessary to generate a kilowatt of electricity.[6] An example of this can be summarized in the following equation:

---

[5] Bureau of Labor Statistics, U.S. Department of Labor, 1997

[6] The quality and time period are assumed to remain constant.

$$\text{Productivity} = \frac{\text{Units produced}}{\text{Input used}} \tag{1.1}$$

For example, if units produced = 1000 and labor hours used is 250, then:

$$\text{Productivity} = \frac{\text{Units produced}}{\text{Labor-hours used}} = \frac{1000}{250} = 4 \text{ units per labor-hour}$$

Single-factor productivity Indicates the ratio of one resource (input) to the goods and services produced (outputs).

The use of just one resource input to measure productivity, as shown above, is known as **single-factor productivity.** However, a broader view of productivity is **multifactor productivity,** which includes all inputs (e.g., labor, material, energy, capital). Multifactor productivity is also known as *total factor productivity*. Multifactor productivity is calculated by combining the input units, as shown below:

$$\text{Productivity} = \frac{\text{Output}}{\text{Labor} + \text{Material} + \text{Energy} + \text{Capital} + \text{Miscellaneous}} \tag{1.2}$$

Multifactor productivity Indicates the ratio of many or all resources (inputs) to the goods and services produced (outputs).

To aid in the computation of multifactor productivity, the individual inputs (the denominator) can be expressed in dollars and summed as shown in Example 2.

EXAMPLE 2

Collins Title Company has a staff of 4 each working 8 hours per day (for a payroll cost of $640/day) and overhead expenses of $400 per day. Collins processes and closes on 8 titles each day. The company recently purchased a computerized title-search system that will allow the processing of 14 titles per day. Although the staff, their work hours, and pay will be the same, the overhead expenses are now $800 per day.

$$\text{Labor productivity with the old system: } \frac{8 \text{ titles per day}}{32 \text{ labor-hours}} = .25 \text{ titles per labor-hour}$$

$$\text{Labor productivity with the new system: } \frac{14 \text{ titles per day}}{32 \text{ labor-hours}} = .4375 \text{ titles per labor-hour}$$

$$\text{Multifactor productivity with the old system: } \frac{8 \text{ titles per day}}{640 + 400} = .0077 \text{ titles per dollar}$$

$$\text{Multifactor productivity with the new system: } \frac{14 \text{ titles per day}}{640 + 800} = .0097 \text{ titles per dollar}$$

Labor productivity has increased from .25 to .4375. The change is .4375/.25 = 1.75, or a 75% increase in labor productivity. Multifactor productivity has increased from .0077 to .0097. This change is .0097/.0077 = 1.259, or a 25.9% increase in multifactor productivity.

Use of productivity measures aids managers in determining how well they are doing. The multifactor-productivity measures provide better information about the trade-offs among factors, but substantial measurement problems remain. Some of these measurement problems are:

1. *Quality* may change while the quantity of inputs and outputs remains constant. Compare a radio of this decade with one of the 1940s. Both are radios, but few people would deny that the quality has improved. The unit of measure—a radio—is the same, but the quality has changed.

2. *External elements*[7] may cause an increase or decrease in productivity for which the system under study may not be directly responsible. A more reliable electric power service may greatly improve production, thereby improving the firm's productivity because of this support system rather than because of managerial decisions made within the firm.
3. *Precise units of measures* may be lacking. Not all automobiles require the same inputs: Some cars are subcompacts, others 911 Turbo Porsches.

Productivity measurement is particularly difficult in the service sector, where the end product can be hard to define. For example, the quality of your haircut, the outcome of a court case, or service at a retail store are all ignored in the economic data. In some cases, adjustments are made for the quality of the product sold, but *not* the quality of the sales performance or a broader product selection, each of which allows for a more intelligent purchase by the consumer. Note the quality-measurement problems in a law office, where each case is different, altering the accuracy of the measure "cases per labor-hour" or "cases per employee."

Productivity Variables

As we saw in Figure 1.6, productivity increases are dependent upon three **productivity variables:**

1. *Labor*, which contributes about $\frac{1}{6}$ of the annual increase.
2. *Capital*, which also contributes about $\frac{1}{6}$ of the annual increase.
3. *Management*, which contributes about $\frac{2}{3}$ of the annual increase.

These three factors are critical to improved productivity. They represent the broad areas in which managers can take action to improve productivity.

Labor Improvement in the contribution of labor to productivity is the result of a healthier, better-educated, and better-nourished labor force. Some increase may also be attributed to a shorter workweek. Historically, about 17% of the annual improvement in productivity is attributed to improvement in the quality of labor. Three key variables for improved labor productivity are:

1. Basic education appropriate for an effective labor force.
2. Diet of the labor force.
3. Social overhead that makes labor available, such as transportation and sanitation.

In developed nations, a fourth challenge to management is *maintaining and enhancing the skills of labor* in the midst of rapidly expanding technology and knowledge. Recent data suggest that the average American 17-year-old knows significantly less mathematics than the average Japanese at the same age, and about half cannot answer the questions in Figure 1.7.

Overcoming shortcomings in the quality of labor while other countries have a better labor force is a major challenge. (See the *OM in Action* box, "Getting a Job at Carrier Is Like Applying for College.") Perhaps improvements can be found not only through increasing competence of labor but also via a fifth item, *better utilized labor with a stronger commitment*. Training, motivation, flextime, team building, and the human resource strategies discussed in Chapter 10, as well as improved education, may be among the many techniques that will contribute to increased labor productivity. Improvements in labor productivity are possible; however, they can be expected to be increasingly difficult and expensive.

Productivity variables
The three factors critical to productivity improvement—labor, capital, and the arts and science of management.

Many American high schools have nearly a 50% dropout rate in spite of offering a wide variety of programs.

---

[7] These are exogenous variables—that is, variables outside of the system under study that influence it.

20 CHAPTER 1 OPERATIONS AND PRODUCTIVITY

OM IN ACTION

GETTING A JOB AT CARRIER IS LIKE APPLYING FOR COLLEGE

On a pothole-filled road across from a chicken processor in the remote town of Arkadelphia, Arkansas, sits a Carrier Corp. plant that could be a blueprint for the future of U.S. manufacturing.

The sleek, spotless plant looks more like an insurance office than a factory. Full of automation, with a lean workforce of only 150, quiet enough to hear a whisper, it is "probably cleaner than most of our houses," says Fred Cobb, a Carrier worker.

This plant, however, is distinguished by its workers, who are a breed apart from most factory workers. Instead of knuckling under to foreign competition, Carrier, a world-class supplier of air conditioners, is opening small plants that require small, educated workforces. Job applicants at Carrier must complete a grueling course. The selection process, which results in a job for only 1 of every 16 applicants yields a top-quality workforce.

The application process starts with a standard state test for applicants who already hold high school diplomas. Only those scoring in the top third advance to having their references checked. Then applicants are interviewed by managers *and* assembly-line workers to see how well they would fit in. Those who survive these interviews enter a six-week course. For five nights a week plus Saturdays, applicants learn blueprint reading, math, computer skills, and quality control. They still receive no assurance of a job at Carrier—and they do not get paid!

But if hired, they have a say in how the plant is run and have unusual authority. They can shut down production if they spot a problem and can order their own supplies. Carrier and the workers at this plant have found that selective recruiting and aggressive training yield an effective workforce, improving productivity.

Sources: Memphis Business Journal (December 16, 1996): 32; *The Wall Street Journal,* March 13, 1993, p. A-1; and *Quality Digest,* May 1994, p. 40.

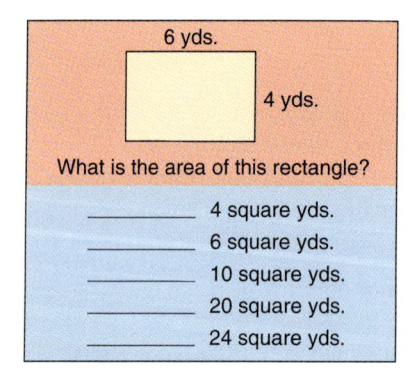

---

6 yds.

4 yds.

What is the area of this rectangle?

_____ 4 square yds.
_____ 6 square yds.
_____ 10 square yds.
_____ 20 square yds.
_____ 24 square yds.

If $9y + 3 = 6y + 15$ then $y =$

_____ 1   _____ 4
_____ 2   _____ 6

Which of the following is true about 84% of 100?

_____ It is greater than 100
_____ It is less than 100
_____ It is equal to 100

FIGURE 1.7 ■ **About Half of the 17-Year-Olds in the United States Cannot Correctly Answer Questions of This Type**

Between 20% and 30% of U.S. workers lack the basic skills they need for their current jobs.
(*Source:* Nan Stone, *Harvard Business Review*)

Capital Human beings are tool-using animals. Capital investment provides those tools. Capital investment has increased in the U.S. every year except during a few very severe recession periods. Annual capital investment in the United States has increased until recent years at the rate of 1.5% of the base investment. This means that the amount of capital invested after allowances for depreciation has grown by 1.5% per year.

Inflation and taxes increase the cost of capital, making capital investment increasingly expensive. When the capital invested per employee drops, as it has in recent years, we can expect a drop in productivity. Using labor rather than capital may reduce unemployment in the short run, but it also makes economies less productive and therefore lowers wages in the long run. The trade-off between capital and labor is continually in flux. Additionally, the higher the interest rate, the more projects requiring capital are "squeezed

THE PRODUCTIVITY CHALLENGE

out": They are not pursued because the potential return on investment for a given risk has been reduced. Managers adjust their investment plans to changes in capital cost.

Management Management is a factor of production and an economic resource. Management is responsible for ensuring that labor and capital are effectively used to increase productivity. Management accounts for about two thirds of the annual one-percent increase in productivity. It includes improvements made through the application of technology and the utilization of knowledge.

This application of technology and utilization of new knowledge requires training and education. Education will remain an important high-cost item in postindustrial societies. Postindustrial societies are technological societies requiring training, education, and knowledge. Consequently, they are also known as knowledge societies. **Knowledge societies** are those in which much of the labor force has migrated from manual work to technical and information-processing tasks requiring education and knowledge. Effective operations managers build workforces and organizations that recognize the continuing need for education and knowledge. They ensure that technology, education, and knowledge are used effectively.

More effective utilization of capital, as opposed to the investment of additional capital, is also important. The manager, as a productivity catalyst, is charged with the task of making improvements in capital productivity within existing constraints. Productivity gains in knowledge societies require managers who are comfortable with technology and management science.

The productivity challenge is difficult. A country cannot be a world-class competitor with second-class inputs. Poorly educated labor, inadequate capital, and dated technology are second-class inputs. High productivity and high-quality outputs require high-quality inputs.

Although current U.S. productivity growth is lower than those of most other industrialized countries, the United States still leads in gross domestic product (GDP) per capita. The American worker remains the most productive in the world, producing on average $49,600 in goods and services—$5,000 to $10,000 more per worker than their Japanese and German counterparts. However as Figure 1.8 (b) shows, the U.S. lead in productivity is narrowing.

> A panel of academics and business executives called for lightening the taxation of corporate profits and broadening tax breaks for capital gains in order to reduce the cost of capital, spur corporate investment, and improve U.S. living standards.
>
> **Knowledge society**
> A society in which much of the labor force has migrated from manual work to work based on knowledge.

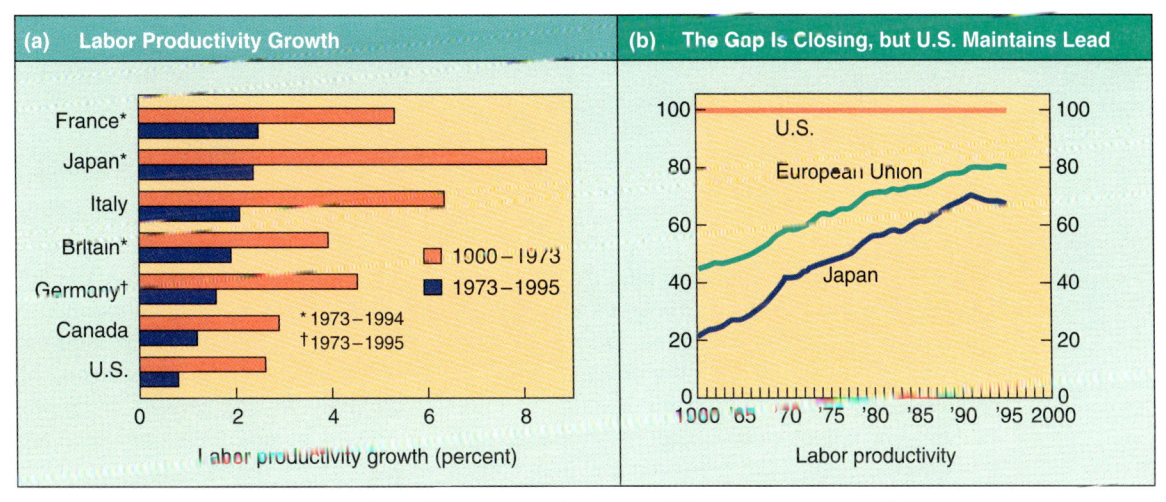

FIGURE 1.8 ■ A Comparison of Productivity in the United States, Japan, and Germany

Sources: Adapted from *The Economist,* November 23, 1996, p. B55; U.S. Labor Department statistics; European Commission; and *Scientific American,* July 1997, p. 84.

Siemens, the multi-billion-dollar German conglomerate, has long been known for its apprentice programs in its home country. Because education is often the key to efficient operations in a technological society, Siemens has spread its apprentice-training programs to its U.S. plants. These programs are laying the foundation for the highly skilled workforce that is essential for global competitiveness.

Productivity and the Service Sector

The service sector provides a special challenge to the accurate measurement of productivity and productivity improvement. The traditional analytical framework of economic theory is based primarily on goods-producing activities. Consequently, most published economic data relate to goods production. But the data do indicate that in recent years, as our contemporary service economy has increased in size, we have had slower growth in productivity. As Figure 1.8(a) shows, the recent overall U.S. productivity growth rate is well below the historical 2.5% and below current productivity increases in Japan, Germany, and other western countries. When U.S. manufacturing productivity is computed separately, productivity growth is over 3%, but with services included, total productivity drops to less than 1%.[8]

Productivity of the service sector has proven difficult to improve because service-sector work is:

1. Typically labor-intensive (for example, counseling, teaching).
2. Frequently individually processed (for example, investment counseling).
3. Often an intellectual task performed by professionals (for example, medical diagnosis).
4. Often difficult to mechanize and automate (for example, a haircut).
5. Often difficult to evaluate for quality (for example, performance of a law firm).

The more intellectual and personal the task, the more difficult it is to achieve increases in productivity. Low-productivity improvement in the service sector is also attributable to the growth of low-productivity activities in the service sector. These include activities not previously a part of the measured economy, such as child care, food preparation, house cleaning, and laundry service. These activities have moved out of the home and into the measured economy as more and more women have joined the workforce. Inclusion of these activities has probably resulted in lower productivity for the service sector, although, in fact, actual productivity has probably increased because these activities are now more efficiently produced than previously.[9]

Playing a Mozart string quartet still takes four musicians the same length of time.

---

[8] According to the U.S. Labor Department, U.S. productivity for 1995 was 0.3% and for 1996 0.7%.

[9] Allen Sinai and Zaharo Sofianou, "The Service Economy–Productivity Growth Issues" (CSI Washington, DC), *The Service Economy*, January 1992, pp. 11–16.

> ### OM IN ACTION
>
> **TACO BELL USES PRODUCTIVITY TO LOWER COSTS**
>
> Founded in 1962 by Glenn Bell, Taco Bell became a part of PepsiCo in 1978. Since then, PepsiCo has been working to improve Taco Bell's productivity. Like many services, Taco Bell increasingly relies on its operations function to improve productivity and reduce cost.
>
> First, it revised the menu and designed meals that were easy to prepare. Taco Bell then shifted a substantial portion of food preparation to suppliers who could perform food processing more efficiently than a stand-alone restaurant. Ground beef was precooked prior to arrival and then reheated, as were many dishes that arrived in plastic boil bags for easy sanitary reheating. Similarly, tortillas arrived already fried and onions prediced. Efficient layout and automation cut to 8 seconds the time needed to prepare tacos and burritos. These advances have been combined with training and empowerment to increase the span of management from one supervisor for 5 restaurants to one supervisor for 30 or more.
>
> Operations managers at Taco Bell believe they have cut in-store labor by 15 hours per day and reduced floor space by more than 50%. The result is a store that can handle twice the volume with half the labor. Effective operations management has resulted in productivity increases that support Taco Bell's low-cost strategy. Taco Bell is now the fast-food low-cost leader.
>
> *Sources: Fortune,* August 4, 1997, p. 27.; OR/MS Today, October 1997, pp. 20–21; and Leonard L. Berry, *On Great Service* (New York: The Free Press, 1995).

However, in spite of the foregoing discussion about the difficulty of improving productivity in the service sector, improvements can be made. This text presents a multitude of ways to do it. Indeed, a recent article in the *Harvard Business Review* reinforces the concept that managers can improve service productivity. The authors argue that "the primary reason why the productivity growth rate has stagnated in the service sector is management,"[10] and they find astonishing what can be done when management pays attention to how work actually gets done.

Although the evidence indicates that all industrialized countries have the same problem with service productivity, the United States remains the world leader in overall productivity *and* service productivity. Retailing is twice as productive in the United States as in Japan, where laws protect shopkeepers from discount chains. The U.S. telephone industry is at least twice as productive as Germany's government monopoly. The U.S. banking system is also 33% more efficient than Germany's banking oligopolies. However, because productivity is central to the operations manager's job and because the service sector is so large, we take special note in this text of how to improve productivity in the service sector. (See, for instance, the *OM in Action* box, "Taco Bell Uses Productivity to Lower Costs.")

THE CHALLENGE OF SOCIAL RESPONSIBILITY

Operations managers function in a system where they are subjected to constant changes and challenges: These come from stakeholders such as customers, suppliers, owners, lenders, and employees. These stakeholders and government agencies require that managers respond in a socially responsible way in maintaining a clean environment, a safe

---

[10] Michael van Biema and Bruce Greenwald, "Managing Our Way to Higher Service-Sector Productivity," *Harvard Business Review* 75, no. 4 (July–August 1997): 89. Their conclusions are not unique. Management *does* make a difference: See for instance: Frederick Harbison and Charles A. Myers, *Management in the Industrial World* (New York: McGraw-Hill, 1959); and Robert H. Hayes and William J. Abernathy, "Managing Our Way to Economic Decline," *Harvard Business Review* 59, no. 4 (July–August 1980): 67–77.

SUMMARY

Operations, marketing, and finance/accounting are the three functions basic to all organizations. The operations function creates goods and services. Much of the progress of operations management has been made in the twentieth century, but since the beginning of time, humankind has been attempting to improve its material well-being. Operations managers are key players in the battle for improved productivity.

However, as societies have become increasingly affluent, more of their resources are devoted to services. In the United States, three quarters of the workforce is employed in the service sector. Although productivity improvements are difficult to achieve in the service sector, operations management is the primary vehicle for making that improvement.

KEY TERMS

Production *(p. 4)*
Operations management (OM) *(p. 4)*
Management process *(p. 7)*
Services *(p. 12)*
Pure service *(p. 13)*
Service sector *(p. 15)*
Productivity *(p. 16)*
Single-factor productivity *(p. 18)*
Multifactor productivity *(p. 18)*
Productivity variables *(p. 19)*
Knowledge society *(p. 21)*

SOLVED PROBLEMS

Solved Problem 1.1

Productivity can be measured in a variety of ways, such as by labor, capital, energy, material usage, and so on. At Modern Lumber, Inc., Art Binley, president and producer of apple crates sold to growers, has been able, with his current equipment, to produce 240 crates per 100 logs. He currently purchases 100 logs per day, and each log requires 3 labor-hours to process. He believes that he can hire a professional buyer who can buy a better-quality log at the same cost. If this is the case, he can increase his production to 260 crates per 100 logs. His labor-hours will increase by 8 hours per day.

What will be the impact on productivity (measured in crates per labor-hour) if the buyer is hired?

Solution

(a) Current labor productivity $= \dfrac{240 \text{ crates}}{100 \text{ logs} \times 3 \text{ hours}}$

$= \dfrac{240}{300}$

$= .8$ crates per labor-hour

(b) Labor productivity with buyer $= \dfrac{260 \text{ crates}}{(100 \text{ logs} \times 3 \text{ hours}) + 8 \text{ hours}}$

$= \dfrac{260}{308}$

$= .844$ crates per labor-hour

Using current productivity (.80 from [a]) as a base, the increase will be 5.5%. (.844/.8 = 1.055, or a 5.5% increase).

Solved Problem 1.2

Art Binley has decided to look at his productivity from a multifactor (total factor productivity) perspective (refer to Solved Problem 1.1). To do so, he has determined his labor, capital, energy, and material usage and decided to use dollars as the common denominator. His total labor-hours are now 300 per day and will increase to 308 per day. His capital and energy costs will remain constant at $350 and $150 per day, respectively. Material costs for the 100 logs per day are $1,000 and will remain the same. Because he pays an average of $10 per hour (with fringes), Binley determines his productivity increase as follows:

Current System		System with Professional Buyer	
Labor:	300 hrs @ $10 = $3,000	308 hrs. @ $10 =	$3,080
Material:	100 logs/day 1,000		1,000
Capital:	350		350
Energy:	150		150
Total Cost:	$4,500		$4,580

Productivity of current system:
= 240 crates/4,500 = .0542

Productivity of proposed system:
= 260 crates/4,580 = .0567

Using current productivity (.0542) as a base, the increase will be .047. That is, .0567/.0542 = 1.047, or a 4.7% increase.

DISCUSSION QUESTIONS

1. Define operations management in your own words. Will your definition accommodate both manufacturing and service operations?
2. Consider the potential contribution of information sciences to OM. Why is the management of information of such great importance in the management of "production"?
3. Figure 1.2 outlines the operations, finance/accounting, and marketing functions of three organizations. Prepare a chart similar to Figure 1.2 outlining the same functions for:
   a. a large metropolitan newspaper
   b. a local drugstore
   c. a college library
   d. a local service organization (such as Boy Scouts, Girl Scouts, Rotary International, Lions, Grange)
   e. a doctor's or dentist's office
   f. a jewelry factory
4. Do the preceding assignment for some other enterprise of your choosing, perhaps an organization where you have worked.
5. What is the difference between production and operations?
6. Identify three disciplines that will contribute in a major way to the future development of OM.

7. Can you identify the operation function(s) of a past or current employer? Draw an organization chart for the operations function of that firm.
8. What are the three classic functions of a firm?
9. What departments might you find in the OM function of a home appliance manufacturer?
10. Describe the registration system at your university. What are its inputs, transformations, and outputs?
11. What are the similarities and differences in the transformation process between a fast-food restaurant and a computer manufacturer?
12. Identify the transformation that takes place in your automobile repair garage.
13. As the administrative manager in a law office, you have been asked to develop a system for evaluating the productivity of the 15 lawyers in the office. What difficulties are you going to have in doing this, and how are you going to overcome them?

CRITICAL THINKING EXERCISE

As Figure 1.7 and the discussion in this chapter suggest, the U.S. educational system is far from the best in the world. Other nations, such as Japan and Israel, excel in academic education, and Germany is the leader in technical training through apprenticeship programs. What are the strengths and weaknesses of the U.S. educational system? What features would we want to emulate from Japan, Germany, or other nations? What is the role of business and the operations manager when the education system fails to provide world-class inputs while consumers expect world-class outputs?

PROBLEMS

- 1.1 Art and Sandy Binley make apple crates for resale to local growers. They and their three employees invest 50 hours per day making 150 crates.
  a) What is their productivity?
  b) They have discussed reassigning work so the flow through the shop is smoother. If they are correct and can do the necessary training, they think they can increase crate production to 155 per day. What would be their new productivity?
  c) What would be their *increase* in productivity?

- 1.2 Joanna produces Christmas tree ornaments for resale at local craft fairs and Christmas bazaars. She is currently working a total of 15 hours per day to produce 300 ornaments.
  a) What is Joanna's productivity?
  b) Joanna thinks that by redesigning the ornaments and switching from contact cement to a hot-glue gun she can increase her total production to 400 ornaments per day. What would be her new productivity?
  c) What would be the increase in productivity?

- 1.3 Carl Sawyer makes billiard balls in his Dallas plant. With a recent increase in taxes, his costs have gone up and he has a newfound interest in efficiency. Carl is interested in determining the productivity of his organization. He has data for a month last year and good current data. He would like to know if his organization is maintaining the manufacturing average of 3.0% increase in productivity. He has the following monthly data:

	Last Year	Now
Production	1,000	1,000
Labor (hours)	300	275
Resin	50	45
Capital invested ($)	10,000	11,000
Energy (BTU)	3,000	2,850

Show the productivity change for each category and then determine the annual improvement for labor-hours, the typical standard for comparison.

- **1.4** Mr. Sawyer, (Using data from Problem 1.3) determines his costs to be as follows:
  - labor $10 per hour;
  - resin $5 per lb;
  - capital cost per month $1,000;
  - energy $.50 per BTU.

  Show the productivity change on a multifactor basis with dollars as the common denominator.

- **1.5** The approximate figures for service jobs in certain countries are shown in the following table. Overall productivity increases are highest in Japan, followed by Germany and then the United States. What conclusions might you draw about productivity and the percentage of services in each economy?

  Percentage of Jobs That Are Service Jobs

United States	75%
Germany	62
Japan	57

- **1.6** Lackey's, a local bakery, is worried about increased costs—particularly energy. Last year's records can provide a fairly good estimate of the parameters for this year. Charles Lackey, the owner, does not believe things have changed much, but he did invest an additional $3,000 for modifications to the bakery's ovens to make them more energy-efficient. The modifications were supposed to make the ovens at least 15% more efficient, but extra labor-hours were required for workers to become familiar with the process changes. Lackey has asked you to check the energy savings of the new ovens and also to look over other measures of the bakery's productivity to see if the modifications were beneficial. You have the following data to work with:

	Last Year	Now
Production (dozen)	1,500	1,500
Labor (hours)	350	325
Capital investment ($)	15,000	18,000
Energy (BTU)	3,000	2,750

- **1.7** As part of a study for the Department of Labor Statistics, you are assigned the task of evaluating the improvement in productivity of small businesses. One of the small businesses you are to evaluate is Lackey's (see Problem 1.6). Determine the multifactor productivity using the following costs:
  - labor $10 per hour;
  - capital 1% per month of investment;
  - energy $.50 per BTU.

  You are to provide your boss with a multifactor indication of the productivity increase or decrease between last year and this year.

- **1.8** As a library or Internet assignment, find the U.S. productivity rate for the (a) latest quarter and (b) latest year.

- **1.9** As a library or Internet assignment, find the U.S. productivity rate (increase) last year for the (a) national economy, (b) manufacturing sector, and (c) service sector.

Case Study

National Air Express

National Air is a competitive air-express firm with offices around the country. Frank Smith, the Chattanooga, Tennessee, station manager, is preparing his quarterly budget report, which will be presented at the Southeast regional meeting next week. He is very concerned about adding capital expense to the operation when business has not increased appreciably. This has been the worst first quarter he can remember: snowstorms, earthquakes, and bitter cold. He has asked Martha Lewis, field services supervisor, to help him review the available data and offer possible solutions.

Service Methods

National Air offers door-to-door overnight air-express delivery within the United States. Smith and Lewis manage a fleet of 24 trucks to handle freight in the Chattanooga area. Routes are assigned by area, usually delineated by zip code boundaries, major streets, or key geographical features, such as the Tennessee River. Pickups are generally handled between 3:00 P.M. and 6:00 P.M., Monday through Friday. Driver routes are a combination of regularly scheduled daily stops and pickups that the customer calls in as needed. These call-in pickups are dispatched by radio to the driver. Commitments are made in advance, with regular pickup stops concerning the time the package will be ready. However, most call-in customers want as late a pickup as possible, just before closing (usually at 5:00 P.M.).

When the driver arrives at each pickup location, he or she provides supplies as necessary (an envelope or box if requested) and must receive a completed air waybill for each package. Because the industry is extremely competitive, a professional, courteous driver is essential to retaining customers. Therefore, Smith has always been concerned about drivers not rushing a customer to complete his or her package and paperwork.

Budget Considerations

Smith and Lewis have found that they have been unable to meet their customers' requests for a scheduled pickup on many occasions in the past quarter. While on average, drivers are not handling any more business, they are unable on some days to arrive at each location on time. Smith does not think he can justify increasing costs by $1,200 per week for additional trucks and drivers while productivity (measured in shipments per truck/day) has remained flat. The company has established itself as the low-cost operator in the industry but has at the same time committed itself to offering quality service and value for its customers.

Discussion Questions

1. Is the productivity measure of shipments per day per truck still useful? Are there alternatives that might be effective?
2. What, if anything, can be done to reduce the daily variability in pickup call-ins? Can the driver be expected to be at several locations at once at 5:00 P.M.?
3. How should we measure package pickup performance? Are standards useful in an environment that is affected by the weather, traffic, and other random variables? Are other companies having similar problems?

Source: Adapted from a case by Phil Pugliese under the supervision of Professor Marilyn M. Helms, University of Tennessee at Chattanooga. Reprinted by permission.

BIBLIOGRAPHY

Babbage, C. *On the Economy of Machinery and Manufacturers,* 4th ed. London: Charles Knight, 1835.

Drucker, P. F. *The Concept of the Corporation.* New York: Mentor, 1946.

———"The New Productivity Challenge." *Harvard Business Review* 69, no. 6 (November–December 1991): 69.

Fabricant, S. A. *Primer on Productivity.* New York: Random House, 1969.

Gale, B. T. "Can More Capital Buy Higher Productivity?," *Harvard Business Review* 58, no. 4 (July–August 1980): 78–86.

Harbison, F., and C. A. Myers. *Management in the Industrial World.* New York: McGraw-Hill, 1959.

Hounshell, D. A. *From the American System to Mass Production 1800–1932: The Development of Manufacturing.* Baltimore: Johns Hopkins University Press, 1985.

Smith, A. *An Inquiry into the Nature and Causes of the Wealth of Nations.* London: Strahan and Cadell, 1776.

Taylor, F. W. *The Principles of Scientific Management.* New York: Harper & Brothers, 1911.

van Biema, Michael, and Bruce Greenwald "Managing Our Way to Higher Service-Sector Productivity," *Harvard Business Review* 75, no. 4 (July–August 1997): 87–95.

Wrege, C. D. *Frederick W. Taylor, the Father of Scientific Management: Myth and Reality.* Homewood, IL: Business One Irwin, 1991.

Wren, D. A. *The Evolution of Management Thought.* New York: Ronald Press, 1994.

INTERNET RESOURCES

American Productivity and Quality Center:
http://www.apqc.org/

Center for Productivity Enhancement at the University of Massachusetts:
http://dragon.cpe.uml.edu/index.html

U.S. Government Bureau of Labor Statistics:
http://stats.bls.gov/

Operations Strategy for Competitive Advantage

2

CHAPTER OUTLINE

GLOBAL COMPANY PROFILE: KOMATSU

IDENTIFYING MISSIONS AND STRATEGIES
- Mission
- Strategy

ACHIEVING COMPETITIVE ADVANTAGE THROUGH OPERATIONS
- Competing on Differentiation
- Competing on Cost
- Competing on Response

TEN DECISIONS OF OM

ISSUES IN OPERATIONS STRATEGY
- Research
- Preconditions
- Dynamics

STRATEGY DEVELOPMENT AND IMPLEMENTATION
- Identify Critical Success Factors
- Build and Staff the Organization

SUMMARY

KEY TERMS

SOLVED PROBLEM

DISCUSSION QUESTIONS

CRITICAL THINKING EXERCISE

PROBLEMS

CASE STUDIES: MINIT-LUBE, INC.; GLOBAL STRATEGY AT MOTOROLA

VIDEO CASE 1: STRATEGY AT REGAL MARINE

INTERNET CASE STUDY

BIBLIOGRAPHY

INTERNET RESOURCES

LEARNING OBJECTIVES

When you complete this chapter you should be able to:

Identify or Define:
- Mission
- Strategy
- Ten decisions of OM

Describe or Explain:
- Specific approaches used by OM to achieve strategic concepts
- Differentiation
- Low Cost
- Response

31

GLOBAL COMPANY PROFILE:

Komatsu Dresser's Global Strategy

In direct competition with Caterpillar, Komatsu Dresser sells products (crawler tractors, loaders, hydraulic excavators, and wheel loaders) to construction and mining markets in North America.

Komatsu, a long-time Japanese manufacturer of construction and mining equipment, competes worldwide in some very competitive markets. Like other organizations, Komatsu must constantly review how to organize its resources for maximum benefit. This review of resource allocation often means modifications in Komatsu's strategy. Over the years, these modifications have taken many forms.

In the 1960s, Komatsu augmented its product line and reduced development costs by licensing designs and technology from others, such as Cummins Engine and International Harvester. This period also saw a strategic move toward improved quality.

In the 1970s, Komatsu's strategy was to become a global enterprise and build export markets, while reducing costs because of the increasing value of the yen. It expanded into Eastern bloc countries and established subsidiaries in Europe and America, as well as service departments in newly industrializing countries.

In the 1980s, Komatsu responded to an even stronger yen through joint ventures with Dresser Industries (to form the Komatsu Dresser Company) and manufacturing outside of Japan. As of the 1990s, the strategy includes the latest in manufacturing technology to improve quality and drive down costs, as well as added focus on electronic engine controls for environmentally friendly engines.

The global battle for construction equipment is fierce. World-class competitors such as Caterpillar, John Deere, Champion, and Ingersoll-Rand fight Komatsu for these markets.

KOMATSU

Strategic changes at Komatsu mean more emphasis on environmental issues. Here research is being conducted on diesel engine exhaust-gas emission control to make Komatsu equipment more environmentally friendly.

In its continuing fierce worldwide battle with Caterpillar for the global heavy equipment customer, Komatsu is building equipment throughout the world as cost and logistics dictate. This worldwide strategy allows Komatsu to move production as markets and exchange rates change.

33

In its continuing worldwide battle for the global heavy equipment customer, Komatsu is now able to build equipment throughout the world and move production as markets, cost, politics, and exchange rates dictate. The firm's constant strategic adjustments to its environment have allowed it to be number one or two in a variety of world markets.

Each of Komatsu's strategies was established in light of (1) the threats and opportunities in the environment and (2) the strengths and weaknesses of the organization. Ultimately, every strategy is an attempt to answer the question, "How do we satisfy a customer?" within these constraints.

IDENTIFYING MISSIONS AND STRATEGIES

An effective operations management effort must have a *mission* so it knows where it is going and a *strategy* so it knows how to get there.

Mission

Mission The purpose or rationale for an organization's existence.

Economic success, indeed survival, is the result of identifying missions to satisfy a customer's needs and wants. We define the organization's **mission** as its purpose—what it will contribute to society. Mission statements provide boundaries and focus for organizations and the concept around which the firm can rally. The mission states the rationale for the organization's existence. Developing a good strategy is difficult, but it is much easier if the mission has been well defined. The mission can also be thought of as the *inten*t of the strategy—what the strategy is designed to achieve. Figure 2.1 provides two examples of mission statements.

Once an organization's mission has been decided, each functional area within the firm determines its supporting mission. By "functional area" we mean the major disciplines required by the firm, such as marketing, finance/accounting, and production/opera-

---

Circle K

We believe our primary business is not so much retail as it is service oriented.

Certainly, our customers buy merchandise in our stores. But they can buy similar items elsewhere, and perhaps pay lower prices.

But they're willing to buy from Circle K because we give them added value for their money.

That added value is service and convenience.

As a service company, our mission is to:
 Satisfy our customers' immediate needs and wants by providing them with a wide variety of goods and services at multiple locations.

Merck

The mission of Merck is to provide society with superior products and services–innovations and solutions that improve the quality of life and satisfy customer needs–to provide employees with meaningful work and advancement opportunities and investors with a superior rate of return.

FIGURE 2.1 ■ **Mission Statements for Two Organizations** *Source:* Annual reports. Reprinted with permission from Tosco Marketing Company.

tions. Missions for each function are developed to support the firm's overall mission. Then within that function lower-level supporting missions are established for the OM functions. Figure 2.2 provides such a hierarchy of sample missions.

Sample Company Mission

To manufacture and service a growing and profitable worldwide microwave communications business that exceeds our customers' expectations.

Sample Operations Management Mission

To produce products consistent with the company's mission as the worldwide low-cost manufacturer.

Sample OM Department Missions

Department	Mission
Quality management	To attain the exceptional value that is consistent with our company mission and marketing objectives by close attention to design, procurement, production, and field service opportunities.
Product design	To lead in research and engineering competencies in all areas of our primary business, designing and producing products and services with outstanding quality and inherent customer value.
Process design	To determine and design or produce the production process and equipment that will be compatible with low-cost product, high quality, and a good quality-of-work life at economical cost.
Location selection	To locate, design, and build efficient and economical facilities that will yield high value to the company, its employees, and the community.
Layout design	To achieve, through skill, imagination, and resourcefulness in layout and work methods, production effectiveness and efficiency while supporting a high quality-of-work life.
Human resources	To provide a good quality-of-work life, with well-designed, safe, rewarding jobs, stable employment, and equitable pay, in exchange for outstanding individual contribution from employees at all levels.
Supply-chain management	To cooperate with suppliers and subcontractors to develop innovative products and stable, effective, and efficient sources of supply.
Inventory	To achieve low investment in inventory consistent with high customer service levels and high facility utilization.
Scheduling	To achieve high levels of throughput and timely customer delivery through effective scheduling.
Maintenance	To achieve high utilization of facilities and equipment by effective preventive maintenance and prompt repair of facilities and equipment.

FIGURE 2.2 ■ Sample Missions for a Company, the Operations Function, and Major Departments in an Operations Function

Strategy

Strategy How an organization expects to achieve its missions and goals.

With the mission established, strategy and its implementation can begin. **Strategy** is an organization's action plan to achieve the mission. Each functional area has a strategy for achieving its mission and for helping the organization reach the overall mission. These strategies exploit opportunities and strengths, neutralize threats, and avoid weaknesses. In the following sections we will describe how strategies are developed and implemented.

We suggest that firms achieve missions in three conceptual ways: (1) differentiation, (2) cost leadership, and (3) quick response.[1] This means operations managers are called on to deliver goods and services that are (1) *better,* or at least different, (2) *cheaper,* and (3) more *responsive.* Operations managers translate these *strategic concepts* into tangible tasks to be accomplished. Any one or combination of these three strategic concepts can generate a system that has a unique advantage over competitors. For example, Hunter Fan has differentiated itself as a premier maker of quality ceiling fans that lower heating and cooling costs for its customers. Nucor Steel, on the other hand, satisfies customers by being the lowest-cost steel producer in the world. And Dell achieves rapid response by building personal computers with each customer's requested software in a matter of hours.

Clearly strategies differ. And each strategy puts different demands on operations management. Hunter Fans strategy is one of *differentiating* itself via quality from others in the industry. Nucor focuses on value at *low cost,* while Dell's dominant strategy is quick, reliable *response.*

ACHIEVING COMPETITIVE ADVANTAGE THROUGH OPERATIONS

Competitive advantage The creation of a unique advantage over competitors.

Each of the three strategies provides an opportunity for operations managers to obtain competitive advantage. **Competitive advantage** implies the creation of a system that has a unique advantage over competitors. The idea is to create customer value in an efficient and sustainable way. Pure forms of these strategies may exist, but operations managers will more likely be called on to implement some combination of them. Let us briefly look at how managers achieve competitive advantage via *differentiation, low cost, and response.*

Competing on Differentiation

Differentiation To distinguish the offerings of the organization in any way that the customer perceives as adding value.

Safeskin Corporation is number one in latex exam gloves because it has differentiated itself and its products. It did so by producing gloves that were designed to prevent allergic reactions about which doctors were complaining. When other glove makers caught up, Safeskin developed hypoallergenic gloves. Then it added texture to its gloves. Then it developed a synthetic disposable glove for those allergic to latex—always staying ahead of the competition. Safeskin's strategy is to develop a reputation for designing and producing reliable state-of-the-art gloves, thereby differentiating itself.

Differentiation is concerned with providing *uniqueness.* A firm's opportunities for creating uniqueness are not located within a particular function or activity, but can arise in virtually everything that the firm does. Moreover, because most products include some service and most services include some product, the opportunities for creating this uniqueness are limited only by imagination. Indeed, **differentiation** should be thought of

---

[1] See related discussion in Michael E. Porter, *Competitive Strategy: Techniques for Analyzing Industries and Competitors* (New York: The Free Press, 1980).

as going beyond both physical characteristics and service attributes to encompass everything about the product or service that influences the value that the customers derive from it. Therefore, effective operations managers assist in defining everything about a product or service that will influence the potential value to the customer. This may be the convenience of a broad product line, product features, or product service. Product service can manifest itself through convenience (location of distribution centers or stores), training, product delivery and installation, or repair and maintenance services.

Competing on Cost

Southwest Airlines has been a consistent moneymaker while other U.S. airlines have lost billions. Southwest has done this by fulfilling a need for low-cost and short-hop flights. Its operations strategy has included use of secondary airports and terminals, first-come, first-served seating, few fare options, smaller crews flying more hours, snacks-only or no-meal flights, and no downtown ticket offices.

Additionally, and less obviously, Southwest has very effectively matched capacity to demand and effectively utilized this capacity. It has done this by designing a route structure that matches the capacity of its Boeing 737, the only plane in its fleet. Second, it obtains more air miles than other airlines by faster turnarounds—its planes are on the ground less.

One driver of a low-cost strategy is an optimal facility that is effectively utilized. Southwest and others with low-cost strategies understand this and utilize resources effectively. Identifying the optimum size can allow firms to spread overhead costs over enough units to drive down costs and to provide a cost advantage. For instance, Wal-Mart continues to pursue its low-cost strategy with superstores, open 24 hours per day. For 20 years, it has successfully grabbed market share. Wal-Mart has driven down store overhead costs, shrinkage, and distribution costs. Its rapid transportation of goods, reduced warehousing costs, and direct shipment from manufacturers have resulted in high inventory turnover and made it a low-cost leader.

Low-cost leadership entails achieving maximum *value* as defined by your customer. It requires examining each of the 10 OM decisions in a relentless effort to drive down costs while meeting customer expectations of value. A low-cost strategy does *not* imply low value or low quality.

Competing on Response

The third strategy option is response. Response is often thought of as *flexible* response, but it also refers to *reliable* and *quick* response. Indeed, we define **response** as including the entire range of values related to timely product development and delivery, as well as reliable scheduling and flexible performance.

Flexible response may be thought of as the ability to match changes in a marketplace in which design innovations and volumes fluctuate substantially.

Compaq is an exceptional example of a firm that has demonstrated flexibility in both design and volume changes in the volatile world of personal computers. Compaq's products often have a life cycle of months, and volume and cost changes during that brief life cycle are dramatic. However, Compaq has been successful at institutionalizing the ability to change products and volume to respond to dramatic changes in product design and costs—thus building a *sustainable competitive advantage*.

The second aspect of response is the *reliability* of scheduling. One way the German machine industry has maintained its competitiveness despite having the world's highest labor costs is through reliable response. This response manifests itself in reliable scheduling. German machine firms have meaningful schedules—and they perform to these sched-

---

"By breaking the rules of the game and thinking of new ways to compete, a company can strategically redefine its business and catch its bigger competitors off guard. The trick is not to play the game better than the competition but to develop and play an altogether different game."

Prof. C. Markides,
Sloan Management Review

Low-cost leadership Achieving maximum value as perceived by the customer.

Response That set of values related to rapid, flexible, and reliable performance.

OM IN ACTION

GLOBAL STRATEGY AT HONG KONG'S JOHNSON ELECTRIC

Patrick Wang, managing director of Johnson Electric Holdings, Ltd., walks through his Hong Kong headquarters with a micromotor in his hand. This tiny motor, about twice the size of his thumb, powers a Dodge Viper power door lock. Although most people have never heard of Johnson Electric, we all have several of its micromotors nearby. This is because Johnson is the world's leading producer of micromotors for cordless tools, household appliances (such as coffee grinders and food processors), personal care items (such as hair dryers and electric shavers), and cars. A luxury Mercedes, with its headlight wipers, power windows, power seat adjustments, and power side mirrors, may use 50 Johnson micromotors per vehicle.

Like all truly global businesses, Johnson spends liberally on communications to tie together its global network of factories, R&D facilities and design centers. For example, Johnson Electric installed a $20 million videoconferencing system that allows engineers in Cleveland, Ohio, and Stuttgart, Germany, to monitor trial production of their micromotors in China.

Johnson's first strength is speed in product development, speed in production, and speed in delivering—13 million motors a month, mostly assembled in China but delivered throughout the world. Its second strength is the ability to stay close to its customers. Johnson has design and technical centers scattered across the United States, Europe, and Japan. "The physical limitations of the past are gone" when it comes to deciding where to locate a new center, says Patrick Wang. "Customers talk to us where they feel most comfortable, but products are made where they are most competitive."

Sources: The Economist, June 22, 1996, p. 65; and Forbes, November 8, 1993, pp. 292–293.

---

ules. Moreover, the results of these schedules are communicated to the customer and the customer can, in turn, rely upon them. Consequently, the competitive advantage generated through reliable response has value to the end customer.

The third aspect of response is *quickness.* Johnson Electric, discussed in the *OM in Action* box, competes on speed—speed in design, production, and delivery. Whether it is a production system at Johnson Electric, a lunch delivered in 15 minutes at Bennegin's, or customized pagers delivered in 3 days from Motorola, the operations manager who develops systems that respond quickly can have a competitive advantage.

Compaq Computer Corp. has demonstrated that it knows how to respond to the market in an industry in which life cycles are measured in months. With a constant stream of new products ranging from desktop PCs to servers, as well as new facilities such as this, operations personnel have responded so well that Compaq's sales have skyrocketed from $4.1 billion in 1991 to $25 billion in 1997.

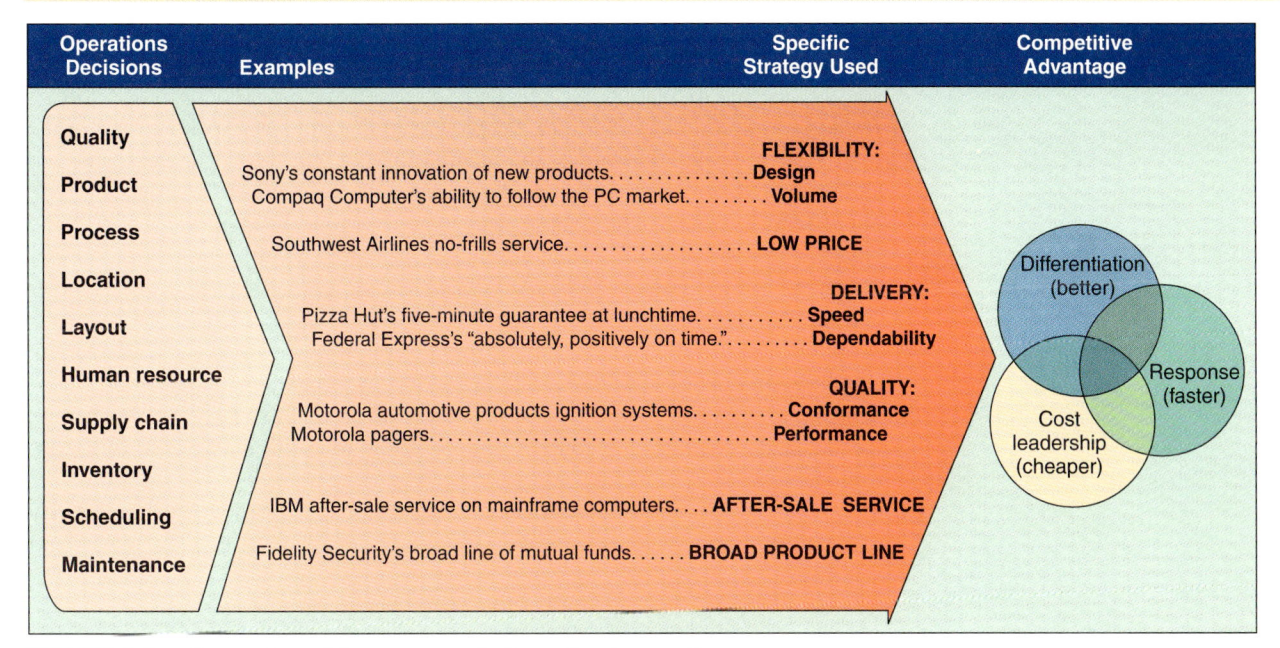

FIGURE 2.3 ■ Operations Management's Contribution to Strategy

Operations Decisions	Examples	Specific Strategy Used	Competitive Advantage
Quality		**FLEXIBILITY:**	
Product	Sony's constant innovation of new products............. **Design**		
Process	Compaq Computer's ability to follow the PC market......... **Volume**		Differentiation (better)
Location	Southwest Airlines no-frills service................... **LOW PRICE**		
Layout		**DELIVERY:**	Response (faster)
Human resource	Pizza Hut's five-minute guarantee at lunchtime........... **Speed**		
Supply chain	Federal Express's "absolutely, positively on time."........ **Dependability**		Cost leadership (cheaper)
Inventory		**QUALITY:**	
Scheduling	Motorola automotive products ignition systems........ **Conformance**		
Maintenance	Motorola pagers................................... **Performance**		
	IBM after-sale service on mainframe computers.... **AFTER-SALE SERVICE**		
	Fidelity Security's broad line of mutual funds...... **BROAD PRODUCT LINE**		

Source: For related presentation, see Jeffrey G. Miller and Aleda Roth, "A Taxonomy of Manufacturing Strategies," *Management Science* 40, no. 3 (March 1994): 285–304.

In practice, these three *concepts*—differentiation, low cost, and response—are often translated into the six *specific strategies* shown in Figure 2.3: (1) flexibility in design and volume, (2) low price, (3) delivery, (4) quality, (5) after-sale service, and (6) a broad product line. Through these six specific strategies, OM can increase productivity and generate a sustainable competitive advantage. Proper implementation of the following decisions by operations managers will allow these strategies to be achieved.

TEN DECISIONS OF OM

Differentiation, low cost, and response can be achieved when managers make effective decisions in 10 areas of OM. These are collectively known as **operations decisions**. The 10 decisions of OM that support missions and implement strategies follow:

1. *Quality.* The customer's quality expectations must be determined and policies and procedures established to identify and achieve that quality.
2. *Goods and service design.* Designing goods and services defines much of the transformation process. Costs, quality, and human resource decisions interact strongly with design decisions. Designs usually determine the lower limits of cost and the upper limits of quality.
3. *Process and capacity design.* Process options are available for products and services. Process decisions commit management to specific technology, quality, human resource use, and maintenance. These expenses and capital commitments will determine much of the firm's basic cost structure.
4. *Location selection.* Facility-location decisions for both manufacturing and service organizations may determine the firm's ultimate success. Errors made at this juncture may overwhelm other efficiencies.

"In the future, there will be just two kinds of firms: those who disrupt their markets and those who don't survive the assault."

Professor Richard D'Aveni, author of *Hypercompetition*

Operations decisions
The critical decisions of OM. They are quality, product design, process design, location selection, layout design, human resources and job design, supply-chain management, inventory, scheduling, and maintenance.

5. *Layout design.* Capacity needs, personnel levels, purchasing decisions, and inventory requirements influence layout. Additionally, processes and materials must be sensibly located in relation to each other.
6. *Human resources and job design.* People are an integral and expensive part of the total system design. Therefore, the quality-of-work life provided, the talent and skills required, and their costs must be determined.
7. *Supply-chain management.* These decisions determine what is to be made and what is to be purchased. Consideration is also given to quality, delivery, and innovation, all at a satisfactory price. An atmosphere of mutual respect between buyer and supplier is necessary for effective purchasing.
8. *Inventory.* Inventory decisions can be optimized only when customer satisfaction, suppliers, production schedules, and human resource planning are considered.
9. *Scheduling.* Feasible and efficient schedules of production must be developed; the demands on human resources and facilities must be determined and controlled.
10. *Maintenance.* Decisions must be made regarding desired levels of reliability and stability, and systems must be established to maintain that reliability and stability.

TABLE 2.1 ■ Differences in the Demands of Goods and Services Influence How the 10 Operations Management Decisions Are Used

Operations Decisions	Goods	Services
Quality	Many objective quality standards.	Many subjective quality standards.
Goods and service design	Product is usually tangible.	Product is not tangible. A new range of product attributes—a smile.
Process and capacity design	Customer is not involved in most of the process.	Customer may be directly involved in the process—a haircut. Capacity must match demand to avoid lost sales—customers often avoid waiting.
Location selection	May need to be near raw materials or labor force.	May need to be near customer—car rental.
Layout design	Layout can enhance production efficiency.	Can enhance product as well as production—layout of a fine-dining restaurant.
Human resources and job design	Workforce focused on technical skills. Labor standards can be consistent. Output-based wage system possible.	Direct workforce usually needs to be able to interact well with customer—bank teller. Labor standards vary depending on customer requirements—legal cases.
Supply-chain management	Supply-chain relationships critical to final product.	Supply-chain relationships important but may not be critical.
Inventory	Raw materials, work-in-process, and finished goods may be inventoried.	Most services cannot be stored so other ways must be found to accommodate changes in demand.
Scheduling	Ability to inventory may allow leveling of production rates.	Primarily concerned with meeting the customer's immediate schedule.
Maintenance	Maintenance is often preventive and takes place at the production site.	Maintenance is often "repair" and takes place at the customer's site.

Operations managers implement these 10 decisions by identifying key tasks and the staffing needed to achieve them. However, the implementation of decisions is influenced by a variety of issues, including a product's proportion of goods and services (see Table 2.1). Few products are either all goods or all services. While the 10 decisions remain the same for both goods and services, their relative importance and method of implementation depend upon this ratio of goods and services. Throughout this text, we discuss how strategy is selected and implemented for both goods and services through these 10 operations management decisions.

Let's look at an example of strategy development through one of the ten decisions.

EXAMPLE 1

Pierre Alexander has just completed chef school and is ready to open his own restaurant. After examining both the external environment and his prospective strengths and weaknesses, he makes a decision on the mission for his restaurant, which he defines as "To provide outstanding French fine dining for the people of Chicago." His supporting operations strategy is to ignore the options of *cost leadership* and *quick response* and focus on *differentiation*. Consequently, his operations strategy requires him to evaluate product designs (menus and meals) and selection of process, layout, and location. He must also evaluate the tactics for dealing with human resources, suppliers, inventory, scheduling, and maintenance that will support his mission and a differentiation strategy.

Examining just one of these ten decisions, *process design*, requires that Pierre consider the issues presented in the following figure.

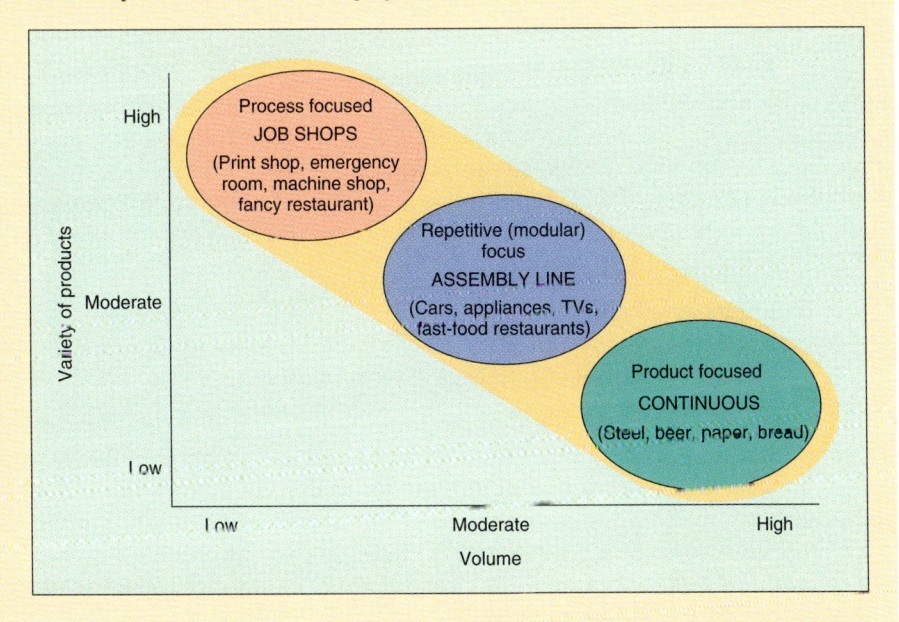

The first option is to operate in the lower-right corner of the preceding figure, where he could produce high volumes of food with a limited variety, much as in an institutional kitchen. Such a process could produce large volumes of standard items such as baked goods and mashed potatoes prepared with state-of-the-art automated equipment. Alexander concludes that this is not an acceptable process option.

Alternately, he can move to the middle of the figure, where he could produce more variety and lower volumes. Here he would have less automation and use prepared modular components for meals, much as a fast-food restaurant does. Again, he deems such a process design inappropriate for his mission.

> Finally, Alexander can design a process that operates in the upper-left corner of the figure, which requires little automation but lends itself to high variety. This process option suggests that he build an extremely flexible kitchen suitable for a wide variety of custom meals catering to the whims of each customer. With little automation, such a process would be suitable for a huge variety. This process strategy will support his mission and desired product differentiation. Only with a process such as this can he provide fine French-style gourmet dining that he has in mind.

As we go through this text, we will discuss and demonstrate similar ways that each of the ten decisions of operations management is evaluated in order to provide competitive advantage, not just for fine dining restaurants, but for all the goods and services that enrich our lives.

ISSUES IN OPERATIONS STRATEGY

Once a firm has formed a mission, developing and implementing a specific strategy requires that the operations manager consider a number of issues. We will examine these issues in three ways. First, we look at what *research* tells us about effective operations management strategies. Second, we identify some of the *preconditions* to developing effective OM strategy. Third, we look at the *dynamics* of OM strategy development.

Research

PIMS A program established in cooperation with GE to identify characteristics of high return-on-investment firms.

Strategic insight has been provided by the findings of the Strategic Planning Institute.[2] Its **PIMS** program (profit impact of market strategy) was established in cooperation with the General Electric Corporation. PIMS has collected nearly 100 data items from about 3,000 cooperating organizations. Using the data collected and high *return on investment* (ROI)[3] as a measure of success, PIMS has been able to identify some characteristics of high ROI firms. Among those characteristics that impact strategic OM decisions are:

1. High product quality (relative to the competition).
2. High capacity utilization.
3. High operating effectiveness (the ratio of expected to actual employee productivity).
4. Low investment intensity (the amount of capital required to produce a dollar of sales).
5. Low direct cost per unit (relative to the competition).

These five findings support a high return on investment and should therefore be considered as an organization develops a strategy. In the analysis of a firm's relative strengths and weaknesses, these characteristics can be measured and evaluated. The specific strategic approaches suggested earlier in Figure 2.3 indicate where an operations manager may want to go, but without achieving the five characteristics of firms with a high return on investment, that journey may not be successful.

Another research study, summarized in Table 2.2, indicates the significant role that OM can play in competitive strategy. When a wide mix of 248 businesses were asked to evaluate the importance of 32 categories in obtaining a sustainable competitive advantage, 28% of the categories selected fell under operations management. When quality/ser-

---

[2] R. D. Buzzel and B. T. Gale, *The PIMS Principles* (New York: The Free Press, 1987).

[3] Like other performance measures, *return on investment* (ROI) has limitations, including sensitivity to the business cycle, depreciation policies and schedules, book value (goodwill), and transfer pricing.

vice is added, the total goes to 44%. The study supports the major role OM strategy plays in developing a competitive advantage.[4]

Table 2.2 ■ Categories of Strategic Options Where Managers Seek a Sustainable Competitive Advantage

Percentages	Categories
28%	**Operations Management**
	Low-cost product
	Product-line breadth
	Technical superiority
	Product characteristics/differentiation
	Continuing production innovation
	Low-price/high-value offering
	Efficient, flexible operations adaptable to customers
	Engineering research development
	Location
	Scheduling
18%	**Marketing/distribution**
17%	**Momentum/name recognition**
16%	**Quality/service**
14%	**Good management**
4%	**Financial resources**
3%	**Other**

Preconditions

Before establishing and attempting to implement a strategy, the operations manager needs to understand that the firm is operating in an open system in which a multitude of factors exists. These factors influence strategy development and execution. The more thorough the analysis and understanding of both the external and internal factors, the more the likelihood of success. Although the list of factors to be considered is extensive, at a minimum it entails an understanding of the:

1. Strengths and weaknesses of competitors, as well as possible new entrants into the market, substitute products, and commitment of suppliers and distributors.
2. Current and prospective environmental, technological, legal, and economic issues.
3. Product life cycle, which may dictate the limitations of operations strategy.
4. Resources available within the firm and within the OM function.
5. Integration of the OM strategy with the company's strategy and other functional areas.

> "To the Japanese, strategy is so dynamic as to be thought of as 'accommodation' or 'adaptive persistence.'"
> Richard Pascale,
> Sloan Management Review

Dynamics

Strategies change for two reasons. First, strategy is dynamic because of *changes within the organization*. All areas of the firm are subject to change. Changes may be in a variety of areas, including purchasing, finance, technology, and product life. All may make a difference in an organization's strengths and weaknesses and therefore its strategy. Figure 2.4 shows possible change in both overall strategy and OM strategy during the product's life. For instance, as a product moves from introduction to growth, product and process design typically move from development to stability. As the product moves to the growth stage, forecasting and capacity planning become issues

---

[4] See David A. Aaker, "Creating a Sustainable Competitive Advantage," *California Management Review*, winter 1989, pp. 91–106.

44 CHAPTER 2 OPERATIONS STRATEGY FOR COMPETITIVE ADVANTAGE

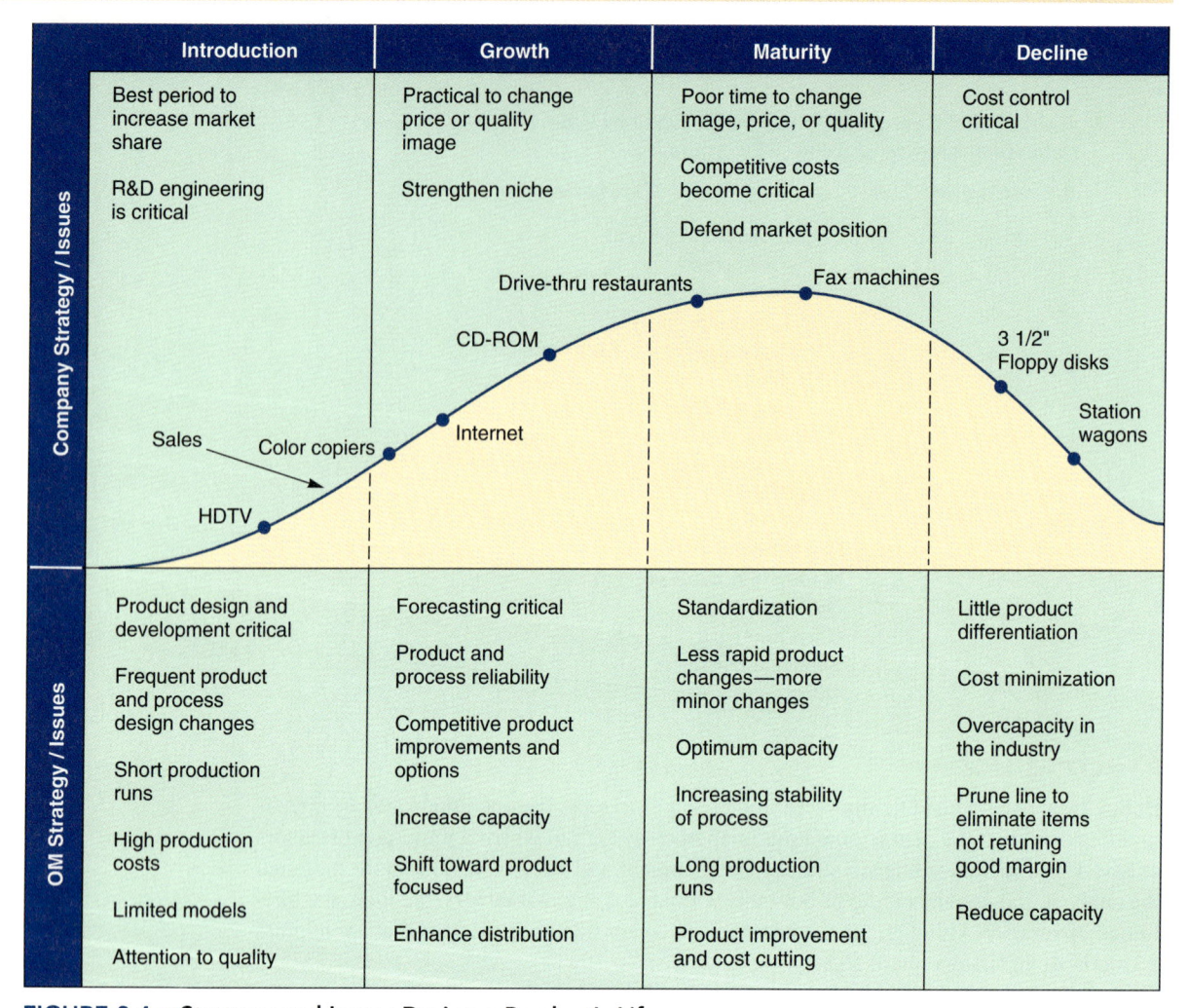

	Introduction	Growth	Maturity	Decline
Company Strategy / Issues	Best period to increase market share R&D engineering is critical	Practical to change price or quality image Strengthen niche	Poor time to change image, price, or quality Competitive costs become critical Defend market position	Cost control critical
	HDTV, Sales, Color copiers	CD-ROM, Internet	Drive-thru restaurants, Fax machines	3 1/2" Floppy disks, Station wagons
OM Strategy / Issues	Product design and development critical Frequent product and process design changes Short production runs High production costs Limited models Attention to quality	Forecasting critical Product and process reliability Competitive product improvements and options Increase capacity Shift toward product focused Enhance distribution	Standardization Less rapid product changes—more minor changes Optimum capacity Increasing stability of process Long production runs Product improvement and cost cutting	Little product differentiation Cost minimization Overcapacity in the industry Prune line to eliminate items not retuning good margin Reduce capacity

FIGURE 2.4 ■ Strategy and Issues During a Product's Life
Sources: Various; see, for instance, Michael E. Porter, *Techniques for Analyzing Industries and Competitors* (New York: The Free Press, 1980).

Strategy is also dynamic because of *changes in the environment.* Komatsu, an international manufacturer of large earth-moving equipment, provides an example in the opening Global Company Profile of this chapter of how strategy must change as the environment changes. Its strategies, like many OM strategies, are increasingly global. Microsoft also had to adapt quickly to a changing environment. Microsoft's shift in strategy was caused by the Internet. Microsoft moved to distributing some software products over the Internet to provide both fast and economic delivery.

STRATEGY DEVELOPMENT AND IMPLEMENTATION

SWOT analysis
Determining internal strengths and weaknesses and external opportunities and threats.

Once firms understand the issues involved in developing an effective strategy, they evaluate their internal strengths and weaknesses as well as the opportunities and threats of the environment. This is known as **SWOT analysis** (for *S*trength, *W*eakness, *O*pportunities, and *T*hreats). Beginning with SWOT analyses, firms position themselves, through their strategy, to have a competitive advantage. The firm may have excellent design skills or great talent at identifying outstanding locations. However, the firm may recognize limitations of its manufacturing process or in finding good suppliers. The idea is to maximize opportunities and minimize threats in the environment while maximizing the advantages of the organization's strengths and minimizing the weaknesses. Any preconceived ideas about mission are then reevaluated to ensure they are consistent with the SWOT analysis. Subsequently, a strategy for achieving the mission is developed. This strategy is continually evaluated against the value provided customers and competitive realities. The process is shown in Figure 2.5. From this process critical success factors are identified.

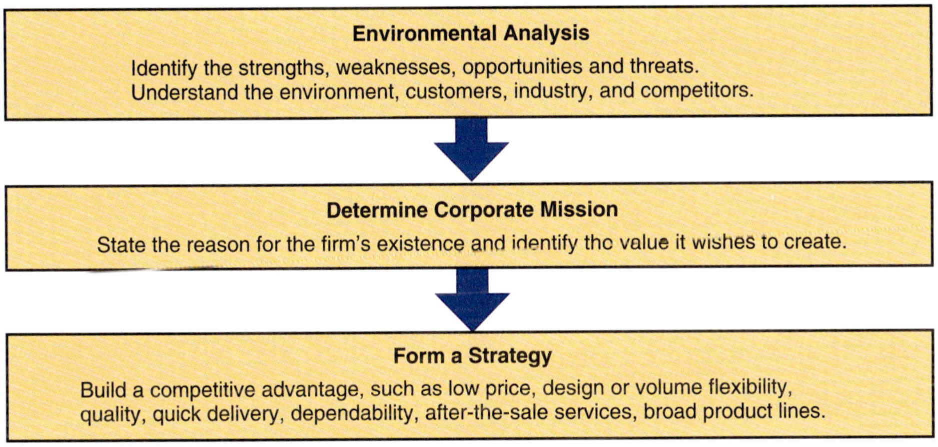

Environmental Analysis
Identify the strengths, weaknesses, opportunities and threats.
Understand the environment, customers, industry, and competitors.

↓

Determine Corporate Mission
State the reason for the firm's existence and identify the value it wishes to create.

↓

Form a Strategy
Build a competitive advantage, such as low price, design or volume flexibility, quality, quick delivery, dependability, after-the-sale services, broad product lines.

FIGURE 2.5 ■ Strategy Development Process

Identify Critical Success Factors

Because no firm does everything particularly well, a successful strategy implementation requires identifying those tasks that are critical to success. The operations manager asks, "What tasks must be done particularly well for a given operations strategy to succeed? Which elements contain the highest likelihood of failure, and which will require additional commitment of managerial, monetary, technological, and human resources? Which activities will help the OM function provide a competitive advantage?"

Critical success factors are selected in light of achieving the mission, as well as the organization's internal strengths. **Critical success factors** (CSFs) are those relatively few activities that make a difference between having and not having a competitive advantage. Ultimately the CSFs make a difference between an organization's success and failure. Successful organizations identify and use critical success factors to develop a unique and distinct competence that allows them to achieve a competitive advantage.[5] CSFs for Compaq and Microsoft are discussed in the *OM in Action* box.

The critical success factors can overlap functional areas of the firm such as marketing or finance, or they may be within one functional area. In this text, we are, of course, going to focus primarily on the 10 decisions within the operations management function that often are critical success factors. Potential CSFs for marketing, finance, and operations are shown in Figure 2.6.

Critical success factors
Those activities or factors that are key to achieving competitive advantage.

---

[5] For a discussion of distinct competence, see Michael E. Porter, *Competitive Advantage* (New York: The Free Press, 1985).

OM IN ACTION

CRITICAL SUCCESS FACTORS AT COMPAQ AND MICROSOFT

Two world-class companies, Compaq and Microsoft, lead in bringing new products to market with quality and marketability. They share these five traits in doing so:

- *They focus on one business.* For example, Compaq makes only one product, personal computers. Microsoft focuses on software for personal computers, resisting the tempting desire to get into the chip, router, or PC market.
- *They are global.* Both Microsoft and Compaq are so strong that they are able to compete globally. And they pursue international markets that have stiff competition, which forces them to remain world-class. Compaq is the leading supplier of PCs in the U.S., Canadian, and European markets and has 45% of its sales abroad.
- *Their senior management is actively involved in defining and improving the product development process.* Microsoft's Bill Gates, for example, keeps in contact with his engineers by electronic mail memos, sometimes 30 in a day.
- *They recruit and retain the top people in their fields.* Microsoft is always known for hiring the best and brightest possible. Thousands have become millionaires by staying on and helping the company grow.
- *They understand that speed to market reinforces product quality.* Microsoft's Windows NT, with a staggering 4.3 million lines of code, almost killed the 200 programmers on the project in rushing it to market in 1993. But it redefined the concept of network software and windows software by marrying them. It also reflects Gates's aggressive goals of continuous improvement.

Sources: New York Times, May 5, 1997, pp. C1, C6; and *The Wall Street Journal,* May 26, 1993, pp. A1, A12.

The 10 operations management decisions developed in this text provide an excellent checklist for determining the critical success factors within the operations function. For instance, the 10 decisions and related CSFs can manifest themselves in a firm's ability to differentiate. That differentiation may be via innovation and new products, where the

Implement Strategy by Identifying and Executing the Critical Success Factors in the Functional Areas

Marketing	Finance/Accounting	Production/Operations
Service Distribution Promotion Price Channels of distribution Product positioning (image, functions)	Leverage Cost of capital Working capital Receivables Payables Financial control Lines of credit	

Decisions	Sample Options	Chapter
Quality	Define customer expectations and how to achieve them	4, S4
Product	Customized or standardized	6
Process	Facility size, technology	7, S7
Location	Near supplier or near customer	8
Layout	Work cells or assembly line	9
Human resource	Specialized or enriched jobs	10, S10
Supply chain	Single or multiple source suppliers	11, S12
Inventory	When to reorder; how much to keep on hand	12, 14
Schedule	Stable or fluctuating production rate	13, 15, 16
Maintenance	Repair as required or preventive maintenance	17

FIGURE 2.6 ■ Implement the Strategy by Identifying the Critical Success Factors

CSF is product design, as is the case for 3M and Rubbermaid. Similarly, differentiation may be via quality, where the CSF is institutionalizing that quality, as at McDonald's. And differentiation may be via maintenance, where the critical success factors are providing reliability and after-sale service, as is the case at IBM.

Build and Staff the Organization

The operations manager's job is a three-step process. Once a strategy and critical success factors have been identified, the second step is to group the necessary activities into an organizational structure. The third step is to staff it with personnel who will get the job done. The manager works with subordinate managers to build plans, budgets, and programs that will successfully implement strategies that achieve missions. Firms tackle this organization of the operations function in a variety of ways. The organization charts shown in chapter 1 (Figure 1.2) indicate the way some firms have organized to perform the required activities.

The organization of the operations function and its relationship to other parts of the organization vary with the OM mission. Moreover, the operations function is most likely to be successful when the operations strategy is integrated with other functional areas of the firm and supports overall company objectives. For example, short-term scheduling in the airline industry is dominated by volatile customer travel patterns. Day-of-week preference, holidays, seasonality, college schedules, and so on, all play a role in changing flight schedules. Consequently, airline scheduling, although an OM activity, can be a part of marketing. Effective scheduling in the trucking industry is reflected in the amount of time trucks travel loaded. However, scheduling of trucks requires information from delivery and pickup points, drivers, and other parts of the organization. When the organization of the OM function results in effective scheduling in the air passenger and commercial trucking industries, a competitive advantage can exist.

The operations manager provides a means of transforming inputs into outputs. The transformations may be in terms of storage, transportation, manufacturing, dissemination of information, and utility of the product or service. *The operations manager's job is to implement an OM strategy, increase productivity, and provide competitive advantage.*

> Ford has identified four core processes of its automobile business
> — product development
> — manufacturing
> — vehicle ordering and distribution
> — after-sale service

> "The manufacturing business of tomorrow will not be run by financial executives, marketers, or lawyers inexperienced in manufacturing, as so many U.S. companies are today."
> — Peter Drucker

SUMMARY

Although it is a challenging task, operations managers can improve productivity in a competitive, dynamic global economy. They can build and manage OM functions that contribute in a significant way to the competitiveness of an organization. Organizations identify their strengths and weaknesses. They then develop effective missions and strategies that account for these strengths and weaknesses and complement the opportunities and threats in the environment. If this procedure is performed well, the organization can have competitive advantage, through some combination of product differentiation, low cost, and response. Such performance is the responsibility of the professional manager, and professional managers are among the few in our society who *can* achieve this performance. The challenge is great, and the rewards to the manager and to society substantial.

KEY TERMS

Mission *(p. 34)*
Strategy *(p. 36)*
Competitive advantage *(p. 36)*
Differentiation *(p. 36)*
Low-cost leadership *(p. 37)*
Response *(p. 37)*
Operations decisions *(p. 39)*
PIMS *(p. 42)*
SWOT analysis *(p. 44)*
Critical success factors *(p. 45)*

SOLVED PROBLEM

Strategy at Pirelli SpA

The global tire industry continues to consolidate. Michelin buys Goodrich and Uniroyal and builds plants throughout the world. Bridgestone buys Firestone, expands its research budget, and focuses on world markets. Goodyear spends almost 4% of its sales revenue on research. These three aggressive firms have come to dominate the world tire market with a 15% to 20% market share each. Against this formidable array the old-line Italian tire company, Pirelli SpA, responded, but with two mistakes: the purchase of Armstrong Tire and a disastrous bid to take over the German tire maker Continental AG. Pirelli still had only 5% of the market and by 1991 was losing $500 million a year while the competition was getting stronger. Tires are a tough, competitive business that rewards companies with strong market shares and long production runs.

Use a SWOT analysis to establish a feasible strategy for Pirelli.

Solution

1. Find an opportunity in the world market that avoids the mass market onslaught by the big three.
2. Maximize the internal strength represented by Pirelli tires winning World Rally Championships in 1995 and 1996 and having of one of the world's strongest brand names.

Pirelli established exclusive deals with Jaguar's new XJ-8 and Lotus Elise and takes a large share of tire sales on Porsches, S-Class Mercedes, BMWs, and Saabs. People are willing to pay a premium for Pirellis. Pirelli also switched out of low-margin standard tires and into higher-margin performance tires. The operations function responded by focusing its design efforts on performance tires and developing a system of modular tire manufacture that allows much faster switching between models. This modular system, combined with investments in new manufacturing flexibility, has driven batch sizes down to as small as 150 to 200, making small lot performance tires economically feasible. A threat from the big three going after the performance market remains, but Pirelli has bypassed its weakness of having a small market share. And the firm has returned to profitability.

Sources: Forbes, May 19, 1997, pp. 106–113; and *The Wall Street Journal,* August 1, 1997, p. B3.

DISCUSSION QUESTIONS

1. Identify the 10 decisions of operations management.
2. Identify the mission and strategy of your automobile repair garage. What are the manifestations of the 10 OM decisions at the garage? That is, how is each of the 10 decisions accomplished?
3. Answer question 2 for some other enterprise of your choosing.
4. Based on what you know about the automobile industry, how has the OM strategy of General Motors or Ford changed in the last 10 years?
5. As a library or Internet assignment, identify the mission of a firm and the strategy that supports that mission.
6. How does an OM strategy change during a product's life cycle?
7. What unique *OM strengths* has Wal-Mart exhibited as it has pursued its low-cost strategy?

CRITICAL THINKING EXERCISE

IBM at one time had a 70% market share in the computer business. Most of that business was in large computers, known as mainframes. Throughout the 1980s and 1990s, technology and markets favored computer networks, then personal computers (PCs), and now client-server networks. IBM has had a difficult time adjusting. Sales, employment, and percentage of installed computers have all dropped. From an OM perspective, how might IBM have better matched its strengths and weaknesses with the opportunities and threats of the environment?

PROBLEMS

- **2.1** Find an article in the business literature (such as *Business Week, The Wall Street Journal, Forbes,* or *Fortune*) that (1) documents an organization's current OM strategy and (2) documents a *change* in an organization's OM strategy.
- **2.2** Identify how changes in the external environment affect the OM strategy for a company. For instance, discuss what impact the following external factors might have on OM strategy:
    a) Major increases in oil prices.
    b) Water- and air-quality legislation.
    c) Fewer young prospective employees entering the labor market in 1985 through 1995.
    d) Inflation versus stable prices.
    e) Legislation moving health insurance from a benefit to taxable income.
- **2.3** Identify how changes in the internal environment affect the OM strategy for a company. For instance, discuss what impact the following internal factors might have on OM strategy:
    a) Maturing of a product.
    b) Technology innovation in the manufacturing process.
    c) Changes in product design that move Compaq's disk drives from 3-inch floppy drives to CD-ROM drives.
- **2.4** Determine from library or Internet research the mission of the following—AT&T, United Way, Microsoft, Southwest Airlines, and another organization of your choosing.
- **2.5** For the organization chosen in Problem 2.4, determine the strategy of the operations function.

Case Study

Minit-Lube, Inc.

In recent years, a substantial market has developed for automobile tune-up and lubrication shops. This demand came about because of the change in consumer buying patterns as self-service gas stations proliferated. Consumers started pumping their own gas, which made a second stop necessary for oil and lubrication. Consequently, Minit-Lube, Mobil-Lube, Jiffy-Lube, and others developed a strategy to accommodate this opportunity.

Minit-Lube stations perform oil changes, lubrication, and interior cleaning in a spotless environment. The buildings are clean, painted white, and often surrounded by neatly trimmed landscaping. To facilitate fast service, cars can be driven through three abreast. At Minit-Lube, the customer is greeted by service representatives who are graduates of the Minit-Lube school in Salt Lake City. The Minit-Lube school is not unlike McDonald's Hamburger University near Chicago or Holiday Inn's training school in Memphis. The greeter takes the order, which typically includes fluid checks (oil, water, brake fluid, transmission fluid, differential grease) and the necessary lubrication, as well as filter changes for air and oil. Service personnel in neat uniforms then move into action. The standard three-person team has one person checking fluid levels under the hood, another assigned interior vacuuming and window cleaning, and the third in the garage pit, removing the oil filter, draining the oil, checking the differential and transmission, and lubricating as necessary. Precise task assignments and good training are designed to put the car in and out of the bay in 10 minutes. The idea is to charge no more, and hopefully less, than gas stations, automotive repair chains, and auto dealers, while providing better service.

Discussion Questions

1. What constitutes the mission of Minit-Lube?
2. How does the Minit-Lube operations strategy provide competitive advantage? (*Hint:* Evaluate how Minit-Lube's traditional competitors perform the 10 decisions of operations management vs. how Minit-Lube performs them.)
3. Is it likely that Minit-Lube has increased productivity over its more traditional competitors? Why? How would we measure productivity in this industry?

Case Study

Global Strategy at Motorola

For years Motorola and other U.S. firms such as RCA, Magnavox, Philco, and Zenith were among the world's most successful consumer electronics firms. In the face of withering competition from the Japanese, however, these firms began to fall by the wayside. Motorola has remained the exception: Today it is a world leader in mobile communication technology, ranking as the leading maker of cellular telephones, paging devices, automotive semiconductors, and microchips used to operate devices other than computers. By first attaining and then maintaining this lofty position, Motorola has taken on the Japanese head-to-head. Although it may have lost a few battles here and there, the firm has won many more.

Motorola heard the call to battle in the early 1980s. The firm then controlled the emerging U.S. market for cellular telephones and pagers but, like many other firms at the time, was a bit complacent and not aggressively focused on competing with the Japanese. Meanwhile, Japanese firms began to flood the U.S. market with low-priced, high-quality telephones and pagers. Motorola was shoved into the background.

At first, managers at Motorola were unsure how they should respond. They abandoned some business areas and even considered merging the firm's semiconductor operations with those of Toshiba. Finally, however, after considerable soul searching, they decided to fight back and regain the firm's lost market position. This fight involved a two-part strategy: First learn from the Japanese and then compete with them.

To carry out these strategies, executives set a number of broad-based goals that essentially committed the firm to lowering costs, improving quality, and regaining lost market share. Managers were sent on missions worldwide, but especially to Japan, to learn how to compete better. Some managers studied Motorola's own Japanese operation to learn more fully how it functioned; others focused on learning about other successful Japanese firms. At the same time, the firm dramatically boosted its budgets for R&D and employee training worldwide.

One manager who visited Japan learned an especially important lesson. While touring a Hitachi plant north of Tokyo, he noticed a flag flying in front of the factory emblazoned with the characters *P200*. When he asked what it meant, he was told by the plant manager that the factory had hoped to increase its productivity by 200% that year. The manager went on to note somewhat dejectedly that it looked as if only a 160% increase would be achieved. Because Motorola had just adopted a goal of increasing its own productivity by 20%, the firm's managers soberly realized that they had to forget altogether their old ways of doing business and reinvent the firm from top to bottom.

Old plants were shuttered as new ones were built. Workers received new training in a wide range of quality-enhancement techniques. The firm placed its new commitment to quality at the forefront of everything it did. It even went so far as to announce publicly what seemed at the time to be an impossible goal: to achieve *Six Sigma* quality, a perfection rate of 99.9997%. When Motorola actually achieved this level of quality, it received the prestigious Malcolm Baldrige National Quality Award.

Even more amazing have been Motorola's successes abroad, especially in Japan. The firm has 20 offices and more than 3,000 employees there. It is currently number three in market share there in both pagers and cellular telephones but is closing fast on number two. Worldwide, Motorola controls 45% of the total market for these products, has regained its number-two position in semiconductor sales, and is furiously launching so many new products that its rivals seem baffled.

Today, Motorola generates over 56% of its revenues abroad. Major new initiatives are underway in Asia, Latin America, and Eastern Europe. The firm has also made headway in Western Europe against entrenched rivals Philips and Thomson. But not content to rest on its laurels, Motorola has set new—and staggering—goals for itself. It wants to take quality to the point where defects will be counted in relation to billions rather than millions. It wants to cut its cycle times (the time required to produce a new product, the time to fill an order, and/or the time necessary to change a production system from one product to another) tenfold every five years. It also wants over 75% of its revenues to come from foreign markets by 2000.

Discussion Questions

1. What are the components of Motorola's international strategy?
2. Describe how Motorola might have arrived at its current strategy as a result of a SWOT analysis.
3. Discuss Motorola's primary business strategy.

Source: Adapted from R. W. Griffin and M. W. Pustay *International Business* (Reading MA: Addison-Wesley 1996), pp. 373–374.

Video Case 1

Strategy at Regal Marine

Regal Marine, one of the U.S.'s 10 largest power-boat manufacturers, achieves its mission—providing luxury performance boats to customers worldwide—using the strategy of differentiation. It differentiates its products through constant innovation, unique features, and high quality. Increasing sales at the Orlando, Florida, family-owned firm suggest that the strategy is working.

As a quality boat manufacturer, Regal Marine starts with continuous innovation, as reflected in computer aided design (CAD), high-quality molds, and close tolerances that are controlled through both defect charts and rigorous visual inspection. In-house quality is not enough, however. Because a product is only as good as the parts put into it, Regal has established close ties with a large number of its suppliers to ensure both flexibility and perfect parts. With the help of these suppliers, Regal can profitably produce a product line of 22 boats, ranging from the $11,000 3-passenger Rush to the $250,000 40-foot Commodore Yacht.

"We build boats," says VP Tim Kuck, "but we're really in the 'fun' business. Our competition includes not only 300 other boat, canoe, and yacht manufacturers in our $17 billion industry, but home theatres, the Internet, and all kinds of alternative family entertainment." Fortunately for Regal, with the strong economy and the repeal of the boat luxury tax on its side, it has been paying down debt and increasing market share.

Regal has also joined with scores of other independent boat makers in the American Boat Builders Association. Through economics of sale in procurement, Regal is able to navigate against billion-dollar competitor Brunswick (makers of the Sea Ray and Bayliner brands). The *Global Company Profile* featuring Regal Marine (which opens Chapter 6) provides further background on Regal and its strategy.

Discussion Questions

1. State Regal Marine's mission in your own words.
2. Identify the strengths, weaknesses, opportunities, and threats that are relevant to the strategy of Regal Marine?
3. How would you define Regal's strategy?
4. How would each of the 10 operations management decision apply to operations decision making at Regal Marine?

Internet Case Study

See our Internet home page at http://www.prenhall.com/heizer for an additional case study: Johannsen Steel Company.

BIBLIOGRAPHY

Barney, Jay B. "Looking Inside for Competitive Advantage." *Academy of Management Executive* IX, no. 4 (November 1995): 49–61.

Drucker, P. F. "The Emerging Theory of Manufacturing." *Harvard Business Review* (May-June 1990): 94.

Edmondson, H. E., and S. C. Wheelwright. "Outstanding Manufacturing in the Coming Decade." *California Management Review* 31 (summer 1989): 70–90.

Gerwin, Donald. "Manufacturing Flexibility: A Strategic Perspective," *Management Science* 39 (April 1993).

Kaplan, Robert S., and David P. Norton. "Using the Balanced Scorecard as a Strategic Management System." *Harvard Business Review* (January-February 1996): 75–85.

Kim, Yearnmin, and Jinjoo Lee. "Manufacturing Strategy and Production Systems: An Integrated Framework." *Journal of Operations Management* 11 (1993): 3–15.

MacMillan, Ian C., and Rita Gunther McGrath. "Discovering New Points of Differentiation." *Harvard Business Review* 75 (July-August 1997): 135–145.

Malhotra, M. K., D. C. Steele, and V. Grover. "Important Strategic and Tactical Manufacturing Issues in the 1990s." *Decision Sciences* 25, no. 2 (March-April 1994): 189–214.

Markides, Constantinos. "Strategic Innovation." *Sloan Management Review* 38 (spring 1997): 9–24.

Ohmae, K. "The Borderless World." *Sloan Management Review* 32 (winter 1991): 117.

Ohmae, K. "Getting Back to Strategy." *Harvard Business Review* 66 (November-December 1988): 149–156.

Porter, M. E. *The Competitive Advantage of Nations.* New York: The Free Press, 1990.

Skinner, W. *Manufacturing: The Formidable Competitive Weapon.* New York: John Wiley, 1985.

Stalk, George, Jr. "Time—The Next Source of Competitive Advantage." *Harvard Business Review* 66 (July-August 1988): 41–51.

Womack, J. P., D. T. Jones, and D. Roos. *The Machine That Changed the World.* New York: Rawson Associates, 1990.

INTERNET RESOURCES

Business Policy and Strategy, Division of the Academy of Management:
http://comsp.com.latrobe.edu.au/bps.html

Global Industry Profiles of Strategies:
http://www.agilityforum.org/

Manufacturing Strategies, maintained at Cranfield University:
http://www.cranfield.ac.uk/public/mn/

Operations in a Global Environment

3

CHAPTER OUTLINE

GLOBAL COMPANY PROFILE: BOEING
DEFINING GLOBAL OPERATIONS
　Globalization of Production
WHY GLOBAL OPERATIONS ARE IMPORTANT
ACHIEVING GLOBAL OPERATIONS
　Global Product Design
　Global Process Design and Technology
　Global Facility Location Analysis
　Impact of Culture and Ethics
GLOBAL ISSUES IN SERVICE OPERATIONS
　Managing Global Service Operations

SUMMARY
KEY TERMS
USING POM FOR WINDOWS FOR LOCATION ANALYSIS
USING EXCEL OM TO SOLVE LOCATION PROBLEMS
DISCUSSION QUESTIONS
CRITICAL THINKING EXERCISE
PROBLEMS
CASE STUDY: FORD AND MAZDA SHARE THE DRIVER'S SEAT
BIBLIOGRAPHY
INTERNET RESOURCES

LEARNING OBJECTIVES

When you complete this chapter you should be able to:

Identify or Define:

　International business
　Multinational corporation
　Transnational company
　Global company
　Maquiladora
　Critical success factors in location analysis

Describe or Explain:

　Global facility location analysis
　Cultural and ethical issues in operations
　Why global issues are important
　Four global operations considerations

GLOBAL COMPANY PROFILE:

Building a Global Plane Yields Competitive Advantage

In building its newest product, the 777, Boeing took a huge financial risk of $4 billion. Global competition meant finding not only exceptional suppliers, wherever they may be, but also suppliers willing to step up to the risk associated with new products. Boeing found its 777 partners in over a dozen countries, a few of which are shown in the table below. These "partners," investing $1.5 billion, not only spread the risk but also added the advantage to all parties of including local content in the plane. Countries that have a manufacturing stake in the 777, says Boeing, are more likely to buy from Boeing than from European competitor Airbus Industries. One such nation is Japan, whose consortium of Fuji, Kawasaki, and Mitsubishi complete one fifth of the plane's body, including most of the

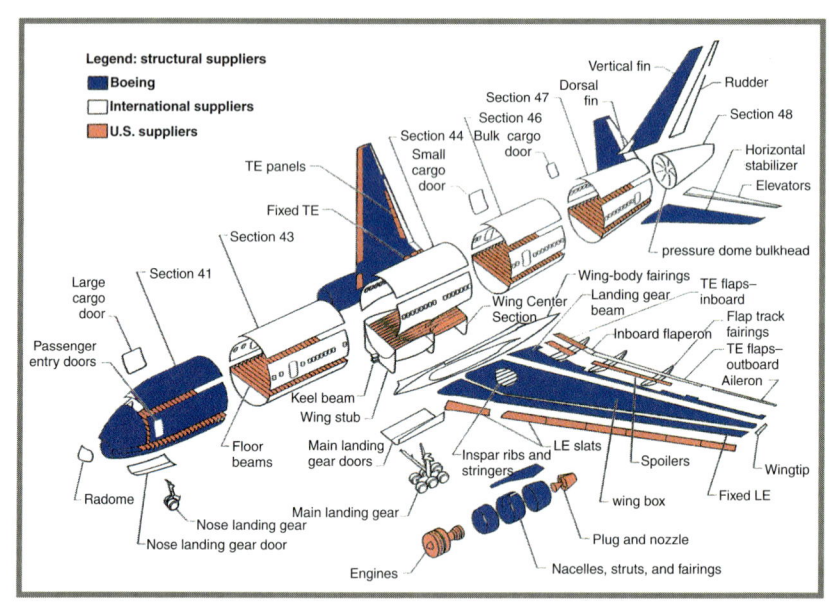

This figure shows the worldwide purchasing effort for Boeing's new 777, with 20% of the plane's structure contracted to a Japanese consortium of Fuji, Kawasaki, and Mitsubishi Heavy Industries.

Some International Suppliers of Boeing 777 Components		
Firm	**Country**	**Parts**
Alenia	Italy	Wing flaps
AeroSpace Technologies	Australia	Rudder
CASA	Spain	Ailerons
Fuji	Japan	Landing gear doors, wing section
GEC Avionics	United Kingdom	Flight computers
Hawker de Havilland	Australia	Elevators
Kawasaki	Japan	Fuselage sections 43, 44, cargo doors
Korean Air	Korea	Flap supports
Menasco Aerospace	Canada	Landing gears
Messier-Bugatti	France	Landing gears
Mitsubishi	Japan	Fuselage sections 46, 47, 48, passenger doors
Short Brothers	Ireland	Landing gear doors
Singapore Aerospace	Singapore	Landing gear doors
Smiths Industries	United Kingdom	Electronic systems

BOEING

The aircraft fuselage section, or belly of the aircraft, is manufactured in Japan. This 14,000-pound section houses the aft lower cargo hold and the economy section for the interior passenger cabin.

fuselage, parts of the wing, and landing gear doors.

Starting in 1996, Boeing has contracted more than half its work outside the U.S., a savings of $600 million per year. To Boeing machinists, who earn an average of $22 per hour, this practice means pickets with signs such as "Export Planes—Not Our Jobs." But Boeing claims it is impossible to export planes without sending a significant number of jobs overseas. When a foreign nation now agrees to buy planes from Boeing, it typically does so on condition that some work will be done in that country. Union workers disagree. Our biggest competitor is not Airbus, they say; it is workers in Mexico, Korea, and Poland.

Tight supplier contracts ensure that quality components are delivered on time and within cost to Boeing's final assembly line. It all comes together in Everett. For details of this assembly line, see chapter 9, "Layout Strategies."

55

Boeing's merger with McDonnell Douglas strengthens its position as the world's largest aerospace company, with over 200,000 employees and 1997 revenues of $48 billion.

SONY's TV plant in Bridgend, Wales, has such close cooperation with its 140 suppliers that the factory has had "no incoming inspection" since 1989.

Global competition is here to stay. Rapid growth in emerging world markets like China and Eastern Europe means that even medium-size companies must extend their operations globally. Making a product only in the United States and then exporting it no longer guarantees success or even survival. There are new standards of global competitiveness that include quality, variety, customization, convenience, timeliness, and cost. This globalization of production contributes efficiency and adds value to the products and services offered the world, but it also complicates the operations manager's job.

Companies today respond to global competition with strategies and speeds unheard of in the past. For instance:

- Boeing is flourishing because both its sales and production are worldwide.
- Italy's Benetton moves inventory to stores around the world faster than its competition by building flexibility into design, production, and distribution.
- Sony purchases components from suppliers in Thailand, Malaysia, and around the world for assembly in its electronic products.
- Coleco, the U.S. toy company, meets surges in demand for Cabbage Patch dolls by contracting with firms in China and Hong Kong—and then whisking the dolls to the U.S. Christmas market in jumbo jets supplied by global carriers such as Singapore and Korean Airlines.

International operations management refers to the process by which global firms transform inputs into goods and services. Figure 3.1 shows how such firms' strategy (be it differentiation, cost leadership, or response—all discussed in chapter 2) relates to their operations function. This strategy hinges on the three complex and important decisions illustrated in Figure 3.1.

Global Strategic Context
- Differentiation
- Cost leadership
- Response

Supply-Chain Management
- Sourcing
- Vertical integration
- Make-or-buy decisions
- Partnering

Location Decisions
- Country-related issues
- Product-related issues
- Government policies/political risk
- Organizational issues

Materials Management
- Flow of materials
- Transportation options and speed
- Inventory levels
- Packaging
- Storage

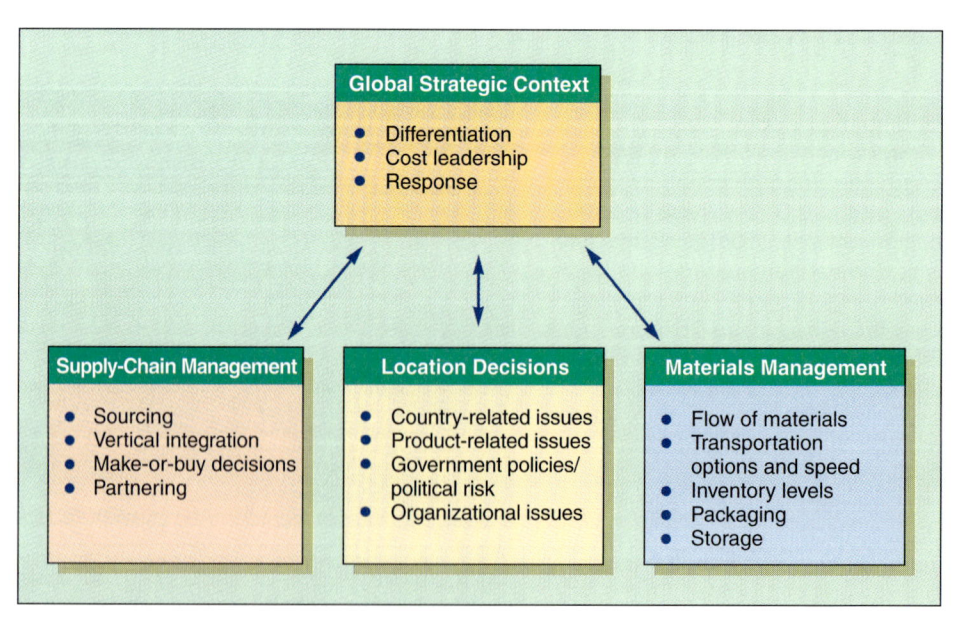

FIGURE 3.1 ■ Management Issues in Global Operations
Source: Adapted from R. W. Griffin and M. W. Pustay, *International Business* (Reading, MA: Addison-Wesley, 1996), p. 584.

The authors wish to thank Professor Marc J. Schniederjans, University of Nebraska, for his extensive input and assistance in developing this chapter. Professor Schniederjans is author of *Operations Management: A Global Context* and *International Facility Location and Acquisition Analysis,* both published by Quorum Books, 1998.

1. How to design products and where to build plants and offices.
2. Where and how to obtain the resources needed to create a good or service.
3. What modes of transportation to use and how to manage inventory.[1]

Every firm, whether domestic or global, faces these decisions. However, in the global game, competition is intensified. Competitors such as film makers Kodak and Fuji confront each other in over 100 nations. The globalization of world markets, the introduction of "global products" (like Ford Tempo, Coke, Levi jeans), and the advent of the "global factory" and the "global village" are all having a profound effect on operations management.

DEFINING GLOBAL OPERATIONS

To help understand international business activity, experts have categorized firms according to the extent of their global activities. An **international business** is any firm that engages in international trade or investment. This is a very broad category and is the opposite of a domestic, or local, firm.

A **multinational corporation (MNC)** is a firm with *extensive* international business involvement. MNCs buy resources, create goods or services, and sell goods or services in a variety of countries. The term *multinational corporation* applies to most of the world's large, well-known businesses. Certainly IBM is a good example of an MNC. It imports electronics components to the U.S. from over 50 countries, exports computers to over 130 countries, has facilities in 45 countries, and earns more than half of its sales and profits abroad. Other well-known MNCs and their sales, assets, and percentage workforce outside their home country are shown in Table 3.1.

Two more widely used terms differentiate MNCs a bit more precisely. A **global company** views the world as a single marketplace, with standardized goods and services to meet the needs of customers worldwide. Global firms, such as Microsoft, may be able to capture a competitive advantage, such as lower costs through economies of scale, by con-

International business
A firm that engages in cross-border transactions.

Multinational corporation (MNC) A firm that has extensive involvement in international business, owning or controlling facilities in more than one country.

Global company A firm that integrates operations from different countries and views the world as a single marketplace.

TABLE 3.1 ■ Some Multinational Corporations (MNCs)

Company	Home Country	% Sales Outside Home Country	% Assets Outside Home Country	% Foreign Workforce
Citicorp	United States	66	51	NA
Colgate-Palmolive	United States	65	47	NA
Daimler-Benz	Germany	61	NA	25
Dow Chemical	United States	54	45	NA
Gillette	United States	68	66	NA
Honda	Japan	63	36	NA
IBM	United States	59	55	51
ICI	Britain	78	50	NA
Nestlé	Switzerland	98	95	97
Philips Electronics	Netherlands	94	85	82
Siemens	Germany	51	NA	38
Unilever	Britain/Netherlands	95	70	64

NA = Not Available
Sources: *The Wall Street Journal*, September 26, 1996, p. R6; *Forbes*, July 18, 1994; and *Fortune*, July 25, 1994, p. 143.

---

[1] R. W. Griffin and M. W. Pustay, *International Business* (Reading, MA: Addison-Wesley, 1996), pp. 584–586.

Transnational company
A firm that seeks to combine the benefits of global-scale efficiencies with the benefits of local responsiveness.

centrating production in a handful of highly efficient factories. However, authority and responsibility may still be identified as residing at headquarters in the home country.

A **transnational company**, sometimes called a "world company," is a truly internationalized firm whose country identity is not as important as its interdependent network of worldwide operations. Key activities in a transnational company are neither centralized in the parent company nor decentralized so that each subsidiary can carry out its own tasks on a local basis. Instead, the resources and activities are dispersed, but specialized, so as to be both efficient and flexible in an interdependent network.[2] Nestlé is a good example of such a company. Although it is legally Swiss, 95% of its assets are held and 98% of its sales are made outside of Switzerland (see Table 3.1). Less than 10% of its workers are Swiss. Similarly, service firms such as Asea Brown Boveri (an engineering firm that is Swedish but headquartered in Switzerland), Reuters (a news agency), Bertelsmann (a publisher), and Citicorp (a banking corporation) can be viewed as transnationals.

So it is no wonder that writers such as Alvin Toffler think that international firms will ultimately become *stateless*.[3] National identities increasingly fade as decisions are made on economic, not national, merits.

As a test of *your* knowledge about international companies, try to answer the questions in our quiz in Table 3.2. You may be surprised to discover the parents of the eleven famous product lines listed in the first column.

Table 3.2 ■ Global Quiz: Can You Match the Product with the Proper Parent Company and Country?

Product	Parent Company	Country of Parent
Arrow Shirts		
Braun Household Appliances		
Burger King		
Firestone Tires		
Godiva Chocolate		
Haagen-Dazs Ice Cream		
Jaguar Autos		
MGM Movies		
Lamborghini Autos		
Goodrich Tires		
Alpo Petfoods		

Choose from these parent companies:
a. Automobili Lamborghini
b. Bidermann International
c. Bridgestone
d. Campbell Soup
e. Credit Lyonnais
f. Ford Motor Company
g. Gillette
h. Grand Metropolitan
i. Michelin
j. Nestlé

Choose from these countries:
1. France
2. Great Britain
3. Indonesia
4. Japan
5. United States
6. Switzerland

Answers: Arrow: b, 1; Braun: g, 5; Burger King: h, 2; Firestone: c, 4; Godiva: d, 5; Haagen-Dazs: h, 2; Jaguar: f, 5; MGM: e, 1; Lamborghini: a, 3; Goodrich: i, 1; Alpo: j, 6.

---

[2] Christopher Bartlett and Sumantra Ghoshal, *Transnational Management* (Homewood, IL.: Richard B. Irwin, 1992), p. 14.

[3] Alvin Toffler quoted in "Recipe for Intelligence," *Information Today*, March 1994, pp. 61–63.

Globalization of Production

More and more firms are clearly dispersing parts of their production processes to locations around the world to take advantage of national differences in the cost and quality of labor, talent, energy, facilities, and capital. Thus, it is not always meaningful to talk about "Japanese products," "British products," or "American products." Consider General Motor's Pontiac Le Mans, which is perceived to be "made in the USA." With the globalization of production, GM has spread many of its Le Mans production activities abroad.[4] As a result, of the $20,000 paid by each buyer to GM for the purchase of a Le Mans,

- About $6,000 heads to South Korea for the auto's assembly.
- $3,500 goes to Japan for engines, axles, and electronics.
- $1,500 goes to Germany for design.
- $800 goes to Taiwan, Singapore, and Japan for smaller parts.
- $500 heads to England for marketing.
- $100 goes to Ireland for information technology.
- The rest, $7,600, goes to GM and its U.S. bankers, insurance agents, and attorneys.

The Le Mans is not alone. Ford's Mercury Capri is designed in Italy; its engine and drivetrain are made in Japan; and the car itself is assembled in Australia. Because the Capri's only U.S. part may be its Ford nameplate, it has become, in fact, a *global product*.[5]

We have mentioned several reasons why companies globalize their operations. Let's now consider this issue in further detail.

> Ford treats western Europe as a single market, with parts and final auto assembly at 12 plants in 6 countries: Ireland, Britain, France, Germany, Spain, and Holland.

WHY GLOBAL OPERATIONS ARE IMPORTANT

There are many reasons why a domestic business operation will decide to change to some form of international operation. These can be viewed as a continuum ranging from tangible reasons to intangible reasons (see Figure 3.2). Let us examine, in turn, each of the seven reasons listed in Figure 3.2.

> German apparel maker Hugo Boss AG is being forced by German labor costs to shift over half its production to central Europe and North America.

Tangible → Intangible

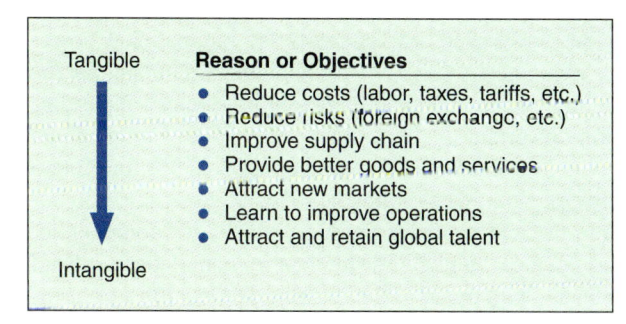

Reason or Objectives
- Reduce costs (labor, taxes, tariffs, etc.)
- Reduce risks (foreign exchange, etc.)
- Improve supply chain
- Provide better goods and services
- Attract new markets
- Learn to improve operations
- Attract and retain global talent

FIGURE 3.2 ■ Reasons to Globalize Operations
Sources: Adapted from M. J. Schniederjans, *Operations Management: A Global Context* (New York: Quorum Books, 1998); and K. Ferdows "Making the Most of Foreign Factories," *Harvard Business Review* (March–April 1997): 73–88.

Reduce Costs Virtually all international operations seek to take advantage of the tangible opportunities in reducing their costs. Lower wage scales in foreign countries can help to lower direct and indirect labor costs. (See the *OM in Action* box, "U.S. Cartoon Production at Home in Manila.") Less stringent government regulations on a wide variety of operation practices (i.e., environmental control, health and safety, etc.) can directly reduce

---

[4] R. B. Reich, *The Work of Nations* (New York: Alfred A. Knopf, 1991).

[5] Charles W. L. Hill, *International Business* (Homewood, IL.: Richard B. Irwin, 1994), pp. 6–7.

OM IN ACTION

U.S. CARTOON PRODUCTION AT HOME IN MANILA

Fred Flintstone is not from Bedrock. He is actually from Manila, capital of the former American colony of the Philippines. So are Tom and Jerry, Aladdin, and Donald Duck. About 90% of American television cartoons are produced in Asia, with the Philippines leading the way. With their natural advantage of English as an official language and a strong familiarity with U.S. culture, animation companies in Manila now employ more than 1,700 people. Filipinos think Western, and "you need to have a group of artists that can understand the humor that goes with it," says Bill Dennis, a Hanna-Barbera executive.

Major studios like Disney, Marvel, Warner Brothers, and Hanna-Barbera send *storyboards*—cartoon action outlines—and voice tracks to the Philippines. Artists there draw, paint, and film about 20,000 sketches for a 30-minute episode. The cost of $130,000 to produce an episode in the Philippines compares to $160,000 in Korea and $500,000 in the U.S.

Source: Orlando Sentinel, September 5, 1995, p. B8.

Maquiladoras Mexican factories located along the U.S.-Mexico border that receive preferential tariff treatment.

GATT An international treaty that helps promote world trade by lowering barriers to the free flow of goods across borders.

NAFTA A free trade agreement between Canada, Mexico, and the United States.

the cost of operations in a foreign country. Opportunities to cut the cost of taxes and tariffs are also a reason to establish operations in foreign countries. In Mexico, the creation of **maquiladoras** (free trade zones) allows manufacturers to cut their costs of taxation by paying only on the value added by Mexican workers.[6] If a U.S. manufacturer, such as IBM, brings a $500 computer to a maquiladora operation for assembly work costing $25, tariff duties will be charged only on the $25 of work performed in Mexico.

Trade agreements have also helped reduce tariffs and thereby reduced the cost of operating facilities in foreign countries. The **General Agreement on Tariffs and Trade (GATT)** has helped to reduce tariffs from 40% in 1940 to 7% in 1990.[7] Another important trade agreement in the American continent is the **North American Free Trade Agreement (NAFTA)**. Passed in 1993 by the U.S. Congress, NAFTA seeks to phase out all trade and tariff barriers during the next 15 years among Canada, Mexico, and the United States.[8]

Reduce Risks Going global has become easier and less risky for international operations because of international trade agreements. NAFTA, in addition to reducing tariffs, also seeks to promote conditions of fair competition and increased investment opportunities as well as provide for protection on certain intellectual property rights. For example, if we wanted to move a U.S. factory to Mexico, we could apply under NAFTA for protection for our investment capital. This protection would obligate the U.S. government to underwrite the risk of financial loss for our factory and help reduce our cost of capital by obtaining a lower interest rate on the loan to build it. Currently the maquiladoras afford foreign operations a means of dispensing with much of the complicated legalities of opening a factory in Mexico.

Improve the Supply Chain The supply chain can often be improved by locating facilities in countries where unique resources are available. These resources may be expertise, labor, or raw material. For example, auto-styling studios are migrating to the auto mecca

---

[6] L. E. Koslow, *Business Abroad* (Houston: Gulf Publishing, 1996), pp. 55–56.

[7] K. Ferdows, "Making the Most of Foreign Factories," *Harvard Business Review* (March/April 1997): p. 74.

[8] *North American Free Trade Agreement*, Volumes I and II (Washington, DC: Superintendent of Documents, U.S. Government Printing Office, 1993).

of the world, southern California, to ensure the necessary expertise in contemporary auto design. Similarly, world athletic shoe production has migrated from South Korea to Guangzhou, China: This location takes advantage of the low-cost labor and production competence in a city where 40,000 people work making athletic shoes for the world. And a perfume essence manufacturer wants a presence in Grasse, France, where much of the world's perfume essences are prepared from the flowers of the Mediterranean.

Provide Better Goods and Services While the characteristics of goods and services can be objective and measurable in nature (e.g., number of on-time deliveries), they can also be subjective and less measurable (e.g., sensitivity to culture). As we move from tangible to intangible reasons for internationalizing operations, we need an ever better understanding of differences in culture and of the way business is handled in different countries. Improved understanding as the result of a local presence permits firms to customize products and services to meet unique cultural needs in foreign markets.

Another reason for international operations includes nearness to foreign customers, which improves response time to meet customers' changing product and service requirements. Customers who purchase goods and services from U.S. firms are increasingly located in foreign countries. Providing them with quick and adequate service is often improved by locating facilities in their home countries.

Attract New Markets Because international operations require local interaction with foreign customers, suppliers, and other competitive businesses, international firms inevitably learn about unique opportunities for new products and services. Knowledge of these markets may not only help to increase sales but also may permit organizations to diversify their customer bases and smooth the business cycle. Global operations also add production flexibility so products and services can be switched between economies that are booming and those that are not.

Another reason to go into foreign markets is the opportunity to expand the *life cycle* (i.e., stages a product goes through; see chapter 6) of an existing product. While some products in the United States are in a "mature" stage of their product life cycle, they may represent state-of-the-art products in less developed countries. For example, the U.S. market for personal computers in the late 1990s could be characterized as "mature." In the same time period, PCs are in the "introductory" stage in many developing countries such as Albania, China, and Burma (Myanmar).

Learn to Improve Operations Learning does not take place in isolation. Because the world is full of ideas, firms serve themselves and their customers well when they remain open to the free flow of ideas. For example, General Motors found that it could improve operations by jointly building and running, with the Japanese, an auto assembly plant in San Jose, California. This strategy allows GM to contribute its capital and knowledge of U.S. labor and environmental laws while the Japanese contribute production and inventory ideas. GM also used its employees and experts from Japan to help design its U.S. Saturn plant around production ideas from Japan. Similarly, operations managers have improved equipment and layout by learning from the ergonomic competence of the Scandinavians.

Attract and Retain Global Talent Global organizations can attract and retain better employees by offering more employment opportunities. They need people in all functional areas and areas of expertise worldwide. For example, Sweden's leading pharmaceutical companies are building research and production facilities near American universities and pharmaceutical institutes so that they can better recruit and retain skilled researchers

Free trade may take us into the era of the floating factory: A six-person crew will take a factory from port to port in order to obtain the best market, material, labor, and tax advantages.

Some international businesses provide the same levels of technology, compensation, safety, and environmental awareness in every country. This IBM plant in Brazil, for example, uses the same protective "bunnysuits" and "cleanrooms" as IBM plants in the U.S. and Japan.

and technicians important to the development of new drugs.[9] Global firms can recruit and retain good employees because they provide both greater growth opportunities and insulation against unemployment during times of economic downturn. During economic downturns in one country or continent, a global firm has the means to relocate unneeded personnel to more prosperous locations. Global organizations also provide incentives for people who like to travel or take vacations in foreign countries.

So, to recap Figure 3.2, successfully achieving a competitive advantage in our shrinking world means maximizing all of the possible opportunities, from tangible to intangible, that the international operations can offer.

ACHIEVING GLOBAL OPERATIONS

How an operation makes the transition from domestic to global to achieve its strategy requires careful analysis. This section introduces four global considerations: (1) product design, (2) process design and technology, (3) facility location, and (4) culture and ethics.

Global Product Design

Because products are designed for the user, social and cultural differences must be taken into consideration in any global product design. While packaging and marketing can help make foreign products seem domestic in origin, very small differences in product orientation can spell disaster for manufacturers. For example, a European manufacturer overesti-

---

[9] H. K. Robinson and M. Nicolin, "Winning Strategies in the Competitive Markets of the United States: A Swedish Perspective," in *Collaborating to Compete*, J. Bleeke and D. Ernst, eds. (New York: John Wiley, 1993), pp. 187–210.

mated the willingness of U.S. consumers to accept liter packaging of liquid products (which is the norm in Europe). Instead of packaging in U.S. quart or gallon measures, this European manufacturer used liter package sizes and the product was shunned by U.S. buyers.[10] Conversely, Coca Cola has been very successful in the global marketplace by making subtle product design changes, specifically by varying the sugar content and taste of its beverages to better suit customer expectations in different countries.

Global Process Design and Technology

The real costs of information processing and communication have fallen so fast in the past decade that it is now possible for a firm to manage effectively a highly integrated, globally dispersed operation. Global communication networks, based on either ground or satellite systems, are now available virtually everywhere. Texas Instruments (TI), for example, communicates between 50 plants in 19 countries. Its communication system allows it to coordinate globally its supply chain, production scheduling, and people, as well as financial planning and customer service. Over 140 mainframe computers instantly drive the vast amounts of information between TI's plants to effect tight coordination.

Similarly, Hewlett-Packard (H-P) uses satellite-based information processing to coordinate new product development teams located in the U.S., Japan, Great Britain, and Germany. Team members "meet" by teleconferencing on a weekly basis, as well as communicating daily by phone, fax, e-mail, and the Internet. All of this technology has enabled H-P to reduce the time needed to develop new products and to increase the integration of its globally dispersed operations.

In 1989, Hewlett-Packard let its Singapore operation handle the design, production, distribution, and marketing of its Desk Jet printer, marking the first time for H-P that an Asian operation would have full responsibility for a business.

Global Facility Location Analysis

One of the first steps in going international is to determine the country in which to locate a new factory or service facility. One approach to this decision requires parent organizations to identify what they believe are **critical success factors (CSFs)**. CSFs, as discussed in chapter 2, are those activities or factors necessary to achieve competitive advantage. They can be any or all of the reasons for internationalization presented in Figure 3.2. Other criteria, such as availability of technology, a nation's level of education, political and legal risks, social and cultural differences, and economic factors, may also be CSFs. (An example of a negative factor, crime, is seen in the *OM in Action* box.) CSFs are identified by their ability to support specific strategic objectives that the parent organization may be pursuing. For example, GE's entry into Hungarian lightbulb production met that firm's goal of market growth and a CSF of a potentially low-cost production facility in eastern Europe. The goal is to try to find the best fit between the parent country's CSFs and the foreign location that will support it.

One procedure for applying CSFs to country selection is to use a rating scale with the following four steps:

1. Select CSFs based on the parent organization's strategic or operations objectives.
2. Obtain country-specific information on the CSFs.
3. Evaluate each country's CSFs using a 1 to 5 (or similar) rating scale, where 1 is an undesirable rating and a 5 is a most desirable rating, for determining how a facility will support an operations strategy.
4. Sum the ratings. The country with the largest summed ratings is the best in which to locate the facility.

Critical success factors (CSFs) Activities or factors critical to an organization's success.

NCR's factory in Dundee, Scotland, is a world-class manufacturer of ATMs, helping NCR hold the number one position in the worldwide ATM market.

---

[10] Robinson and Nicolin, "Winning Strategies," p. 197.

OM IN ACTION

THE CRIME FACTOR IN SELECTING A FOREIGN SITE

It's a risky business doing business in Mexico City. U.S. officials and multinationals have warned the Mexican government that foreign investment will suffer if petty crime, corrupt cops, armed robberies, murder, rape, and carjacking continue unabated in this smoggy capital of 16 million people.

In 1996 and 1997, top executives from Goodyear Tire, Eastman Kodak, and the U.S. Embassy have faced armed assaults. Embassy staffers have even been warned not to take taxis without companions. According to Kroll Associates, security consultants, Mexico City is in danger of being raised in its risk ranking to a 7, the level of drug-run Bogota, Colombia.

The accompanying table rates the overall risk, including political stability and personal security, for a multinational. A ranking of 1 is the safest ranking and a 10, the most dangerous.

Safest ←   → Most Dangerous

1	2	3	4	5	6	7	8	9	10
None	Tokyo	Hong Kong	Buenos Aires	Belize City	Caracas	Bogota	Rio de	Kabul	None
		La Paz	Quito	New York	Lima (Peru)	(Colombia)	Janeiro	(Afghanistan)	
		(Bolivia)	(Equador)	Los Angeles	Manila	Sao Paulo			
		London	Santiago	San Juan	Mexico City	(Brazil)			
		Montevideo	(Chile)		Moscow				
		(Uruguay)	San Jose		Panama City				
			(Costa Rica)						

Note: No country or city has ever received a 1 or a 10.
Sources: *The Wall Street Journal*, October 29, 1996, p. A18; and *Orlando Sentinel*, December 20, 1997, p. A-3.

Example 1 illustrates this procedure.

EXAMPLE 1

Matsuhito of Japan has decided to add a new factory to its international manufacturing system. It wants to select one from among four possible countries in which to locate the new factory. Matsuhito management identified 13 CSFs it felt to be important in helping it achieve a strategic organizational goal of worldwide efficiency. These 13 CSFs were important in the success of the firm's Japanese plants, and company officials wanted to make sure that the new international plant would work well in conjunction with current operating systems. Matsuhito managers used a 1 to 5 rating system to evaluate each possible country as a candidate for the new factory. For example, it was determined that country 2 had the best "rate of technological change" and country 4 had the least.

	Candidate Country Ratings			
Critical Success Factors	Country 1	Country 2	Country 3	Country 4
Technology				
1. rate of technology change	3	5	2	1
2. innovations in process design	5	3	1	5
Level of education				
3. number of skilled workers	5	4	3	4
4. national literacy rate	4	1	1	2

	Candidate Country Ratings			
Critical Success Factors	Country 1	Country 2	Country 3	Country 4
Political and legal aspects				
5. stability of government	5	5	2	5
6. product liability laws	4	3	3	5
7. export restrictions	4	3	3	1
Social and cultural aspects				
8. similarity in language	5	1	5	4
9. work ethic	4	2	3	1
Economic factors				
10. tax rates	3	3	2	5
11. inflation	3	5	5	5
12. availability of raw materials	2	4	3	5
13. interest rates	3	4	2	5
Total Rating Points	50	43	35	48

On the assumption that each of the 13 CSFs are equally important, the best choice for locating the new factory is country 1, which has the largest CSF rating of 50.

The procedure in Example 1 assumes each of the individual CSFs is equally important in the decision process. A weighting factor can also be added to the procedure if the importance of one or more of the CSFs is greater than another. The weighting factor can be expressed as a mathematical weight ranging from 0 to 1, summing to 1 for all CSFs. This weighting factor is similar to probabilities used in expected monetary value (EMV). In this case, the mathematical weight is multiplied times the rating to generate an expected rating point value. Example 2 shows how the mathematical weighting can be included in Example 1 calculations.

EXAMPLE 2

Matsuhito's management has now made the subjective decision to weight the importance of economic factors at 70% (i.e., seven tenths of the weight is to be allocated to economic factors alone) and to weight the total of noneconomic factors at 30%. We can now see what such a weighting does to the original country-selection decision.

	Total Candidate Country Ratings			
Critical Success Factors	Country 1	Country 2	Country 3	Country 4
Technology	8	8	3	6
Level of education	9	5	4	6
Political and legal aspects	13	11	8	11
Social and cultural aspects	9	3	8	5
Total Noneconomic	39	27	23	28
Economic factors	11	16	12	20
Total Economic	11	16	12	20
Total Rating Points	50	43	35	48

1. Expected value of rating points for country 1: 39(0.3) + 11(0.7) = 19.4
2. Expected value of rating points for country 2: 27(0.3) + 16(0.7) = 19.3
3. Expected value of rating points for country 3: 23(0.3) + 12(0.7) = 15.3
4. Expected value of rating points for country 4: 28(0.3) + 20(0.7) = 22.4

Based on the largest expected rating points value of 22.4, the best selection is now country 4.

OM IN ACTION

GOING GLOBAL AT MAYTAG—WITH CAUTION

In a bid to become a major global player, in 1984 appliance giant Maytag Corp. spent almost $1 billion to buy the company that makes the world-famous Hoover vacuum cleaner. This acquisition, plus an earlier $800-million binge on three other well-known global brand names, turned into an earnings disaster.

In a tough, painful decision, Maytag bit the bullet in 1994 and began its pullback into the U.S. It is keeping Hoover but sold its Australian business that year and got rid of its European operation the next year. Today, Maytag draws just 6% of its sales from overseas—versus 21% in 1990. The message from the CEO Leonard Hadley: "The word *global* is a little like the word *cancer*. One word is used to cover a wide range of issues."

Maytag's advice to others is this: "Go overseas, but pick your spots carefully." In the next few years, Maytag will be pumping $70 million into a joint venture with the Chinese appliance maker Hefei Rengshida. This selective caution contrasts with rival Whirlpool's decision to slug it out on a broad scale in Europe and Asia, resulting in a 26% drop in 1997 earnings per share. Maytag's results since 1989: It has gone from a $3-billion company with 26,000 employees to a $3-billion company with 17,000 employees and 9 fewer factories. In cutting losses and admitting defeat in the broad global market, Maytag may have made a tough, but sound decision.

Sources: Forbes, March 10, 1997, pp. 64, 66; and *New York Times*, November 25, 1997, pp. C1, C4.

Impact of Culture and Ethics

> "The ethics of the world market are very clear. Manufacturers will move wherever it is cheapest or most convenient to their interests." Carlos Arias Macelli, owner of a Guatemala plant that supplies J.C. Penney

One of the greatest challenges to global operations is reconciling differences in social and cultural behavior. Managers sometimes do not know how to behave when operating a business with people of different social or cultural backgrounds. Significant differences in what one country's culture deems acceptable may be considered unacceptable in another country's culture. For instance, cultural variations in punctuality by employees and suppliers makes a marked difference in preparation of production and delivery schedules. Similarly, the traditional long lunch hour that prevails in many countries can play havoc with a three-shift operation.

Ethics vary, too. When Philip Morris took over a former state-owned cigarette manufacturer in the Czech Republic, it had to contend with an ethical standard that accepted thievery: Stealing from the state had been acceptable under communism. Such differences provide interesting problems for operations managers as privatization spreads throughout eastern Europe.

Bribery likewise creates substantial ethical problems in the global arena. In the U.S., strict laws define bribery as not only unethical but also unlawful. Cultural variations in some Arab, Latin American, and Southeast Asian countries present a significant challenge to operations managers when building effective supply chains that include foreign firms.

In the last decade, changes in international laws, agreements, and codes of conduct have been applied to define ethical behavior among managers around the world.[11] GATT, for example, helps to make uniform the protection of both governments and industries from foreign firms that engage in unethical conduct. Even on issues where significant differences between cultures exist, as in the area of bribery or the protection of intellectual property, global uniformity is slowly being accepted by most nations.[12]

---

[11] S. J. Carroll and M. J. Gannon, *Ethical Dimensions of International Management* (Thousand Oaks, CA: Sage Publications, 1997).

[12] C. Hotchkiss, *International Law for Business* (New York: McGraw-Hill, 1994).

Companies often move production to countries that offer lower labor costs. However, international firms must pay close attention to how their workers are treated in countries like China, Pakistan, and Vietnam. When child labor is used (as shown here in Bangladesh), companies that buy from manufacturers reinforce the practice. They may also incur negative publicity, as has been the case recently.

GLOBAL ISSUES IN SERVICE OPERATIONS

Globalization affects services just as it does manufacturing. An **international service provider** is a firm that creates utility for global customers by transforming resources into services. Examples of international service firms are Air France (transporting passengers and cargo), Arthur Andersen (auditing global corporations), Dai-Ichi Kangyo Bank (processing international business accounts), and IBM (using programmers in India to test accounting software).

Global service operations are on the rise all over the world. One quarter of all international trade is estimated to derive from the sale of services. Experts generally agree that providing services to foreign markets offers greater growth potential than either manufacturing or agriculture. Typically, procedures for establishing global service operations involve four steps.[13]

> **Step 1:** Determine if sufficient *people* or *facilities* exist to support the service. Service firms such as Sumitomo Bank and Saatchi & Saatchi (the giant ad agency) are heavily dependent on fax, Internet, and voice-link technology, as well as on the foreign-language personnel needed to support it.

> **Step 2:** Identify foreign markets that are open—that is, not protected by foreign countries. Agreements like NAFTA, for example, identify 61 specific professional-service categories as being eligible for U.S., Mexican, or Canadian employ-

International service provider A firm that transforms resources into a service-creating utility for its global customers.

---
[13] *Sources:* Adapted from L. E. Koslow *Business Abroad* (Houston: Gulf Publishing, 1996); and G. Berle and P. Kirschner, *The International Instant Business Plan* (Santa Maria, CA: Puma Publishing, 1996).

ment. These include such service jobs as accounting, economics, engineering, dentistry, management consulting, registered nursing, and teaching.

Step 3: Determine what services are of most interest to foreign customers. Start with services that the domestic operation does well. Then see if similar services are offered and what resources would be needed to enter the foreign market.

Step 4: Determine how to reach global customers. Approaches include exploring the Internet, buying clientele lists, using existing business suppliers for initial referrals, and getting information from local colleges and government agencies in the foreign country.

Managing Global Service Operations

Managing global service operations involves several interesting issues, including the following:[14]

- Capacity planning
- Location planning
- Facilities design and layout
- Operations scheduling

With a decade of neglect, Russia's chip factories are like a semiconductor caboose. Today they produce chips equivalent to IBM PCs of the early 1980s.

Capacity planning is deciding how many customers the firm will be able to serve at one time. To accommodate a high anticipated sales demand for its "Big Mek," the first McDonald's restaurant in Russia was built seven times larger than any of its other outlets.

Location planning is also important. Auto, subway, railways, bike, or other transportation facilities must be available to facilitate the flow of clients and employees. Most international services involve setting up branch facilities in foreign markets and then staffing with locals.

Disney narrowed its choices for locating Euro-Disney to two: a site in France (near Paris) and one in Spain (near Barcelona). Spain had a more favorable climate, similar to Florida's, but the French site was closer to Europe's major population centers. It was selected.

To establish the appropriate look and layout, global facilities must also have careful designs. U.S. companies typically try to create a look that blends their national culture with the local culture. At EuroDisney, for example, signs are in both French and English. Some foreign firms, however, try to blend into the local environment so as to appear local. Most Motel 6 guests in the U.S. are unaware that the chain is foreign-owned.

Finally, global firms must schedule operations to meet customers' needs. For example, British Air, Air France, Swiss Air, KLM, Delta Airlines, and others generally depart from the U.S. to Europe between 6 P.M. and 9 P.M. This schedule gives passengers at least part of the day for working, before arriving in Europe between 6 A.M. and 8 A.M. the next morning. Westbound flights generally depart Europe in mid-morning and arrive in the U.S. later that same afternoon. This scheduling takes into account time zones, customer preferences, and aircraft-maintenance needs.

SUMMARY

Production and service operations have life cycles. Moving from a domestic operation to an international operation has become a part of the life cycle of many companies. Consistent with this life cycle, opportunities for adding value change just as markets do. Consequently, operations managers take action to meet these challenges and opportunities. Many domestic organizations have chosen to develop international operations for chiefly tangible strategic reasons such as improving the supply chain or reducing costs. As firms learn more about tangible and intangible opportunities throughout the world, they often choose to become more global. The topics in this chapter constitute only a brief introduction to some of the ways organizations can move toward successful global operations.

[14] Adapted from R. W. Griffin and M. W. Pustay *International Business* (Reading, MA: Addison-Wesley, 1996), pp. 601–602.

International business *(p. 57)*
Multinational corporation (MNC) *(p. 57)*
Global company *(p. 57)*
Transnational company *(p. 58)*
Maquiladoras *(p. 60)*

General Agreement on Tariffs and Trade (GATT) *(p. 60)*
North American Free Trade Agreement (NAFTA) *(p. 60)*
Critical success factors (CSFs) *(p. 63)*
International service provider *(p. 67)*

KEY TERMS

USING POM FOR WINDOWS FOR LOCATION ANALYSIS

POM for Windows, a PC-based software package available with this text, includes a facility location module that can be used to solve Examples 1 and 2, as well as other problems in this chapter. (Refer to Appendix V). To illustrate, consider the case of Globalco Oil Company, which wishes to expand its corporate presence in the Middle East. After extensive preliminary analysis, Globalco has refined its site choices to either Egypt or Morocco. Program 3.1 provides the data inputs for five important factors, including their importance weights, and ratings on a 1–10 scale for each country. As we see, Egypt is more highly rated, with a 6.2 score versus 4.8 for Morocco.

Location / Factor rating

Globalco Oil Solution

	Weights	Egypt	Morocco
Technology	0.3	6.	5.
Education	0.2	5.	3.
Political	0.1	6.	7.
Cultural	0.1	4.	5.
Economic	0.3	8.	5.
Total	1.		
Weighted Total		6.2	4.8
Weighted Average		6.2	4.8

PROGRAM 3.1 ■ Using POM for Windows Facility Location Module to Solve Globalco Oil's Problem.

If you wish to solve Example 1 with POM for Windows, note that the weights are all equal, so a "1" may be entered for each factor. Solving Example 2 involves setting a weight of .3 for each of the "non-economic" factors and a weight of .7 for each of the four "economic" factors.

USING EXCEL OM TO SOLVE LOCATION PROBLEMS

Our Excel spreadsheet add-in software, Excel OM, may also be used to solve location problems. (Appendix V lists all of the modules available in Excel OM). Program 3.2 illustrates input data and the formulas used to compute factor weightings with Excel OM. Data in the above discussion of POM for Windows, from Globalco Oil Company, are used again here. Program 3.3 provides the output screen that corresponds to Program 3.2.

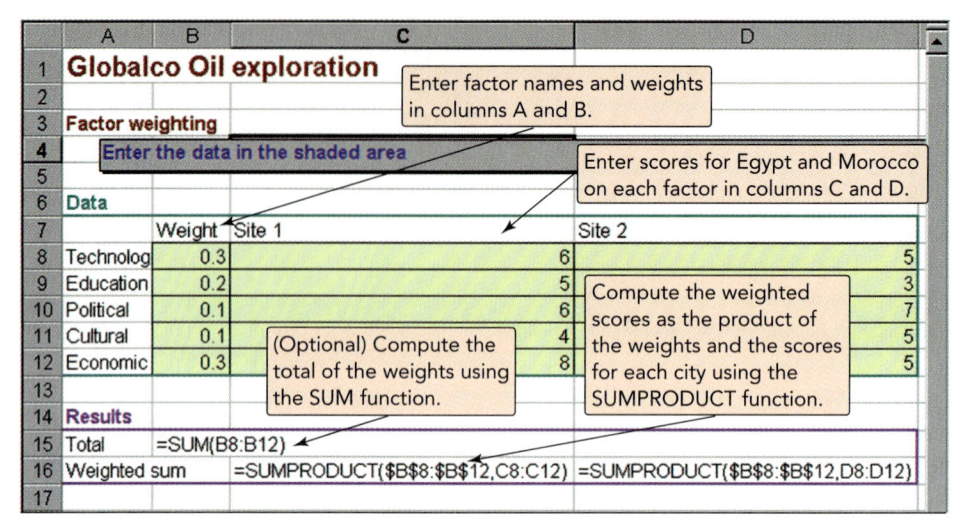

PROGRAM 3.2 ■ Excel OM's Factor Rating Module Input Screen and Formulas, Using Globalco Oil Data.

	A	B	C	D
1	Globalco Oil exploration			
2				
3	Factor weighting			
4	Enter the data in the shaded area			
5				
6	Data			
7		Weight	Site 1	Site 2
8	Technolog	0.3	6	5
9	Education	0.2	5	3
10	Political	0.1	6	7
11	Cultural	0.1	4	5
12	Economic	0.3	8	5
13				
14	Results			
15	Total	=SUM(B8:B12)		
16	Weighted sum		=SUMPRODUCT($B$8:$B$12,C8:C12)	=SUMPRODUCT($B$8:$B$12,D8:D12)

- Enter factor names and weights in columns A and B.
- Enter scores for Egypt and Morocco on each factor in columns C and D.
- (Optional) Compute the total of the weights using the SUM function.
- Compute the weighted scores as the product of the weights and the scores for each city using the SUMPRODUCT function.

PROGRAM 3.3 ■ Output from Program 3.2, using Excel OM to Solve Globalco Oil's Problem.

	A	B	C	D
1	Globalco Oil exploration			
2				
3	Factor weighting			
4	Enter data in the shaded area			
5				
6	Data			
7		Weight	Egypt	Morocco
8	Technology	0.3	6	5
9	Education	0.2	5	3
10	Political	0.1	6	7
11	Cultural	0.1	4	5
12	Economic	0.3	8	5
13				
14	Results			
15	Total		1	
16	Weighted sum		6.2	4.8

Although not a requirement of the procedure, choosing weights that sum to 1 makes it easier to communicate the decision process to others involved.

DISCUSSION QUESTIONS

1. What are the differences between an international firm, a multinational corporation, a global company, and a transnational company?
2. In what ways may a global operation be better suited to take advantage of the benefits of the international area?
3. For what reasons do domestic operations typically become international operations?
4. Explain how the critical success factor model can be used to select a country for international expansion.
5. What considerations should be involved in establishing a global service operation?
6. Explain and give an example of how product design should be considered when offering a product in a global market.
7. How do various cultural differences affect ethics?

CRITICAL THINKING EXERCISE

As a manufacturer of athletic shoes whose image, indeed performance, is widely regarded as socially responsible, you find your costs increasing. Traditionally, your athletic shoes have been made in Indonesia and South Korea. Although the ease of doing business in those countries has been improving, wage rates have also been increasing. The labor-cost differential between your present suppliers and a contractor who will get the shoes made in China now exceeds $1 per pair.

Your sales next year are projected to be 10 million pairs, and your analysis suggests that this cost differential is not offset by any other tangible costs; you face only the political risk and potential damage to your commitment to social responsibility. Thus, this $1 per pair savings should improve your bottom line. There is no doubt that the Chinese government remains repressive and is a long way from a democracy. What do you do and on what basis do you make your decision?

PROBLEMS

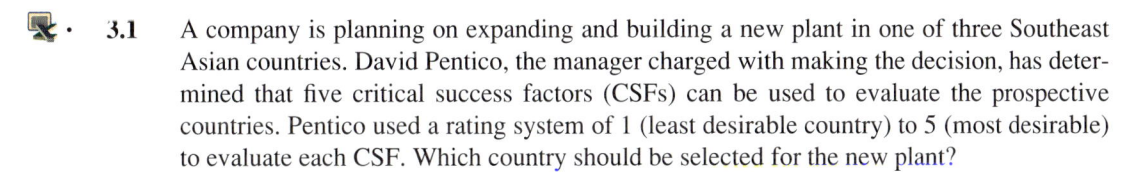

3.1 A company is planning on expanding and building a new plant in one of three Southeast Asian countries. David Pentico, the manager charged with making the decision, has determined that five critical success factors (CSFs) can be used to evaluate the prospective countries. Pentico used a rating system of 1 (least desirable country) to 5 (most desirable) to evaluate each CSF. Which country should be selected for the new plant?

	Candidate Country Ratings		
Critical Success Factors	Taiwan	Thailand	Singapore
Technology	4	5	1
Level of education	4	1	5
Political and legal aspects	1	3	3
Social and cultural aspects	4	2	3
Economic factors	3	3	2

3.2 The country-selection decision in Problem 3.1 now requires a consideration of a mathematical weighting, where the weights are 0.2 for technology, 0.1 for level of education, 0.4 for political and legal aspects, 0.1 for social and cultural aspects, and 0.2 for economic factors. Based on this mathematical weighting, which country should now be selected?

3.3 An international legal firm is planning to expand globally by opening a law office in one of four countries: Italy, Portugal, Turkey, or France. The chief partner entrusted with the decision, Norean Sharpe, has identified eight critical success factors (CSFs) that she views as essential for the success of any law office. She used a rating system of 1 (least desirable country) to 5 (most desirable) to evaluate each CSF. Which country should be selected for the new law office?

	Candidate Country Ratings			
Critical Success Factors	Italy	Portugal	Turkey	France
Level of education				
1. number of lawyers	5	5	2	4
2. national literacy rate	2	1	1	4

CHAPTER 3 OPERATIONS IN A GLOBAL ENVIRONMENT

| | Candidate Country Ratings ||||
Critical Success Factors	Italy	Portugal	Turkey	France
Political and legal aspects				
3. stability of government	5	5	2	5
4. product liability laws	2	3	5	5
5. number of suits per year	4	1	3	1
Social and cultural aspects				
6. similarity in language	2	1	1	4
7. acceptability of lawyers	4	4	3	1
Economic factors				
8. number of courts	3	1	5	2

3.4 The country-selection decision in Problem 3.3 now requires a consideration of a mathematical weighting, where the weights are 0.1 for level of education, 0.6 for political and legal aspects, 0.2 for social and cultural aspects, and 0.1 for economic factors. Based on this mathematical weighting, which country should now be selected?

3.5 Prentice Hall Publishing is going to add two additional distribution centers to its European theater of operations. One center will be located in each of two countries selected from the set of four candidates. The 4 potential countries and 15 CSF ratings are given below. The CSFs were evaluated on the basis of 1 to 5 rating system, where 1 means least desirable country and 5, the most desirable.

| | Candidate Country Ratings ||||
Critical Success Factors	Spain	England	Italy	Poland
1. rate of technology change	1	3	5	2
2. innovations in process design	3	5	5	4
3. number of skilled workers	1	5	3	5
4. national literacy rate	2	5	2	3
5. stability of government	5	1	1	1
6. product liability laws	1	2	1	2
7. export restrictions	4	2	1	5
8. similarity in language	1	3	1	2
9. work ethic	4	2	5	2
10. tax rates	1	3	5	2
11. inflation	5	3	5	2
12. availability of raw materials	5	5	5	5
13. interest rates	4	5	2	4
14. population	1	3	4	1
15. number of miles of highway	1	5	5	1

On the assumption that each of the 15 CSFs is equally important, which two countries would be the best choices for locating the two new distribution centers?

3.6 In Problem 3.5, if the first five CSF ratings are each given a mathematical weight of 0.1 and the remaining ten CSFs should be equally weighted at 0.05, what are the best two countries for the new distribution centers?

Case Study

Ford and Mazda Share the Driver's Seat

Ford Motor Company and Mazda Motor Corporation have one of the more unusual working relationships in the automobile industry. Ford is a major U.S. firm; Mazda is based in Japan. The two have collaborated on several different projects, and each agrees that the partnership has paid off handsomely.

It all started in 1979. Mazda, a relatively small player in the world automobile market at the time, wanted a strong international partner in order to make the transformation from a small niche player to a major global automaker. At the same time, Ford was looking for a foreign partner to help it design and produce smaller automobiles. The two firms agreed that they were logical partners. Mazda sold approximately 25% of its stock to Ford, and the two firms have collaborated on various projects since.

One significant success story involves the Ford Probe and the Mazda MX-6. Mazda engineers designed the basic platform, engine, and drivetrain for the cars. Mazda then designed the outside for the MX-6, and Ford did the same for the Probe. Finally, both cars are assembled at a factory in Flat Rock, Michigan, which is owned by the two firms. Thus consumers who buy a Ford Probe or a Mazda MX-6 are getting essentially the same car but with a different appearance.

Another successful collaboration between Ford and Mazda has been the Ford Escort. Again, Mazda engineers design the car, and Ford makes it. With the Escort, however, Mazda's involvement started at the very beginning of the process, and the Japanese firm played the dominant role in establishing a detailed schedule for getting the car into production. Engineers in U.S. firms like Ford have a reputation for continually raising problems and issues during design that result in delays and extensions. Mazda, however, refused to bow to scheduling delays and kept everyone focused on moving ahead and staying on schedule. As a result, the first new Escorts rolled off a Ford assembly line almost to the day of the production target—a target that had been set seven years earlier! Further, the Escort came in under budget and with higher EPA gas mileage estimates than had been projected at the start of the project. Managers at Ford estimated Mazda's contributions saved the firm over $1 billion on design and production.

There have been some rough spots in the alliance, however. The popular Mazda Navaho recreational vehicle, launched in 1990, was actually made by Ford, based on the also popular Ford Explorer. Unfortunately for Mazda, however, Ford announced in 1994 that demand for its Explorer was so great that it would soon cease providing Navahos for its Japanese partner. More importantly, Mazda fell into severe financial difficulties in the mid-1990s due to overexpansion of capacity, costly proliferation of its vehicle models, and a recession in its home market. To restore Mazda's financial health, its chief creditor, Sumitomo Bank Ltd., has given effective management control of Mazda to Ford. Ford now manages that Flat Rock plant—after sending 320 Mazda executives back home to Japan—and has changed the name of Mazda's chain of Japanese dealerships from Autorama to Ford. To conserve cash, Ford executives also canceled Mazda's plans to start manufacturing in Europe. Instead, Mazda's European dealers will focus on marketing imports from Mazda's Japanese plants and Ford-made products sold under the Mazda nameplate.

Discussion Questions

1. Is the arrangement between Ford and Mazda a joint venture rather than a more general strategic alliance? Why or why not?
2. What fundamental questions might managers at Ford and Mazda have asked themselves before becoming strategic allies?
3. What are the apparent benefits that each firm derives from this relationship?
4. What might eventually cause Ford and Mazda to dissolve their alliance?
5. Why don't more automakers follow the lead of Ford and Mazda and enter partnerships for design and manufacturing?
6. Will Mazda's recent financial problems—and Ford's reaction to them—cause their 15-year-old alliance to break up?

Source: Adapted from R. W. Griffin and M. W. Pustay, *International Business* (Reading, MA: Addison-Wesley, 1996), pp. 437–438.

BIBLIOGRAPHY

Berle, G., and P. Kirschner. *The International Instant Business Plan*. Santa Maria, CA: Puma Publishing, 1996.

Bleeke J., and D. Ernst. *Collaborating to Compete*. New York: John Wiley, 1993.

Carroll, S. J., and M. J. Gannon. *Ethical Dimensions of International Management*. Thousand Oaks, CA: Sage Publications, 1997.

Chilton, K., M. Weidenbaum, and R. Batterson. *The Dynamic American Firm*. Boston: Kluwer, 1996.

Ferdows, K. "Making the Most of Foreign Factories." *Harvard Business Review* (March–April 1997): 73–88.

Hoffman, J. J., and M. J. Schniederjans. "A Two-Stage Model for Structuring Global Facility Site Selection Decisions: The Case of the Brewing Industry." *Facilities,* December 14, 1996, pp. 23–34.

Hotchkiss, C. *International Law for Business*. New York: McGraw-Hill, 1994.

Koslow, L. E. *Business Abroad*. Houston: Gulf Publishing, 1996.

Marquardt, M., and A. Reynolds. *The Global Learning Organization*. Burr Ridge, IL: Richard B. Irwin, 1994.

Porter, M. E. *Competition in Global Industries*. Boston: Harvard Business School Press, 1986.

Rodrigues, C. *International Management*. Minneapolis/St. Paul: West Publishing, 1996.

Schniederjans, M. J. *International Facility Location and Acquisition Analysis*. New York: Quorum Books, 1998.

Schniederjans, M. J. *Operations Management: A Global Context*. New York: Quorum Books, 1998.

INTERNET RESOURCES

Global Inventory Project (GIP) of the G7 countries. These are country efforts to inventory projects and studies relevant to the information society. Many countries are joining this effort. Three sites are:
http://nii.nist.gov/g7/g7-gip.html (United States)
http://www.ispo.ece.be/g7/projects/theme1.html (European Community)
http://strategis.ic.gc.ca/ (Canada)

International Trade Net:
http://www.intl-tradenet.com/

Yahoo International Economy:
http://www.yahoo.com/Business_and_Economy/International_Economy/

Part II · Designing Operations

MANAGING QUALITY 4

CHAPTER OUTLINE

GLOBAL COMPANY PROFILE: MOTOROLA
QUALITY AND STRATEGY
DEFINING QUALITY
   Other Implications of Quality
INTERNATIONAL QUALITY STANDARDS
   Japan's Industrial Standard
   Europe's ISO 9000 Standard
   Environmental Management Standard
   U.S. Standards
TOTAL QUALITY MANAGEMENT
   Continuous Improvement
   Employee Empowerment
   Benchmarking
   Just-in-Time (JIT)
   Knowledge of TQM Tools
TOOLS OF TQM
   Quality Function Deployment (QFD)
   Taguchi Technique
   Pareto Charts
   Process Charts

Cause-and-Effect Diagram
Statistical Process Control (SPC)
THE ROLE OF INSPECTION
   When and Where to Inspect
   Source Inspection
   Service Industry Inspection
   Inspection of Attributes vs. Variables
TOTAL QUALITY MANAGEMENT IN SERVICES
SUMMARY
KEY TERMS
DISCUSSION QUESTIONS
CRITICAL THINKING EXERCISE
PROBLEMS
CASE STUDIES: WESTOVER ELECTRICAL, INC.; QUALITY CLEANERS
VIDEO CASE 2: QUALITY AT THE RITZ-CARLTON HOTEL COMPANY
INTERNET CASE STUDY
BIBLIOGRAPHY
INTERNET RESOURCES

LEARNING OBJECTIVES

When you complete this chapter you should be able to:

Identify or Define:

   Quality

   Malcolm Baldrige National Quality Award

   Deming, Juran, and Crosby

   Taguchi technique

Describe or Explain:

   Why quality is important

   Total quality management (TQM)

   House of quality

   Pareto charts

   Process charts

   Quality robust products

   Inspection

75

GLOBAL COMPANY PROFILE:

Managing Quality Provides a Competitive Advantage at Motorola

Motorola's Accelerated Life Testing (ALT) facility also tests extreme conditions of temperature shock, dust, water, and vibrations. Here cellular phones are undergoing a water test.

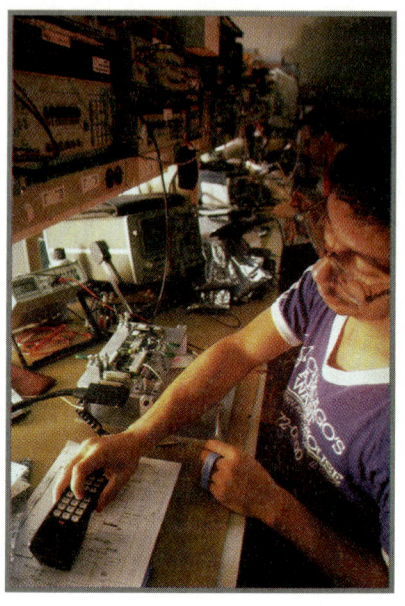

When automated inspection devices work, Motorola uses them. However, when manual intervention in the testing process is appropriate, as is shown here, it is used.

Motorola decided some years ago to be a world leader in quality. Indeed, Motorola is so good that it became the first winner of the Malcolm Baldrige National Quality Award. Motorola believes in total quality management and practices it from the top, specifically from Honorary Chairman Robert Galvin. It achieves outstanding quality through a demonstrated top-management commitment that permeates this entire global organization.

To make the quality focus work, Motorola did a number of things:

76

MOTOROLA

Motorola's strong emphasis on employee participation and total quality management often puts employees in teams that are responsible for evaluating and improving their own processes. This team is from Penang, Malaysia.

- Aggressively began a worldwide education program to be sure that employees understood quality and statistical process control.
- Established goals—namely, its Six Sigma program. Motorola's Six Sigma program means that it can expect to have a defect rate of no more than a few parts per million.
- Established extensive employee participation and employee teams. More than 4,000 Total Customer Satisfaction teams from throughout the world vie for awards based on team performance.

Motorola's divisions can expect a quality service review every two years. Five-member teams are selected from various parts of the company to perform the review. After the review, the general manager and staff have a session with the teams and go over the review. The strengths and weaknesses are discussed, and recommendations are given to the local management about improvements that must be made.

The system is working; it gives Motorola uniformity and consistency. Corporate goals receive commitment throughout the organization, and that is a powerful quality tool. The quality effort has allowed Motorola to move from 6,000 rejects per million just 5 years ago to only 40 defects per million now. Motorola believes it has saved $700 million in manufacturing costs over those five years.

TEN DECISIONS OF OM

Managing Quality
Design of Goods & Services
Process Strategy
Location Strategies
Layout Strategies
Human Resources
Supply-Chain Management
Inventory Management
Scheduling
Maintenance

QUALITY AND STRATEGY

As Motorola and many other firms have found, quality is a wonderful tonic for improving operations. Managing quality helps build successful strategies of *differentiation, low cost,* and *response.* For instance, defining customer quality expectations has helped Bose Corp. successfully *differentiate* its stereo speakers as among the best in the world. Nucor has learned to produce quality steel at *low cost* by developing efficient processes that produce consistent quality. And Dell Computers rapidly *responds* to customer orders because quality systems, with little rework, have allowed it to achieve rapid throughput in its plants. Indeed, quality may be the critical success factor for these firms just as it is at Motorola.

As Figure 4.1 suggests, improvements in quality help firms increase market share and reduce costs, both of which can increase profitability. Increases in market share often occur as firms speed response, lower selling prices as a result of economies of scale, and improve their reputation for quality products. Similarly, improved quality allows costs to drop as firms increase productivity and lower rework, scrap, and warranty costs.

One analysis of air conditioner manufacturers has documented that quality and productivity are positively related. In that study, companies with the highest quality were five times as productive (as measured by units produced per labor-hour) as companies with the poorest quality.[1] Indeed, when the implications of an organization's long-term costs and the potential for increased market share are considered, total costs may well be at a minimum when 100% of the goods or services are perfect and defect-free.

Quality, or the lack of quality, impacts the entire organization from supplier to customer and from product design to maintenance. However, perhaps more importantly, *building* an organization that can achieve quality also affects the entire organization—and it is a demanding task. Figure 4.2 lays out the flow of activities for an organization to use to achieve total quality management (TQM). A successful set of activities begins with an organizational environment that fosters quality, followed by an understanding of the principles of quality, and then an effort to engage employees in the necessary activities to implement quality. When these things are done well, the organization typically satisfies its customers and obtains a competitive advantage. The ultimate goal is to win customers. Because quality causes so many other good things to happen, it is a great place to start.

Two Ways Quality Can Improve Profitability

Improved Quality →

Sales Gains
- Improved response
- Higher prices
- Improved reputation

Reduced Costs
- Increased productivity
- Lower rework and scrap costs
- Lower warranty costs

→ Increased Profits

FIGURE 4.1 ■ **Ways Quality Improves Profitability**

---

[1] David A. Garvin, "What Does 'Product Quality' Really Mean?" *Sloan Management Review* 26, no.1 (fall 1984): 36.

Organizational practices
- Leadership
- Mission statement
- Effective operating procedures
- Staff support
- Training

Yields: What is important and what is to be accomplished.

Quality principles
- Customer focus
- Continuous improvement
- Employee empowerment
- Benchmarking
- Just-in-time
- Tools of TQM

Yields: How to do what is important and to be accomplished.

Employee fulfillment
- Empowerment
- Organizational commitment

Yields: Employees attitudes that can accomplish what is important and to be accomplished.

Customer satisfaction
- Meeting customer needs
- Repeat customers

Yields: An effective organization with a competitive advantage.

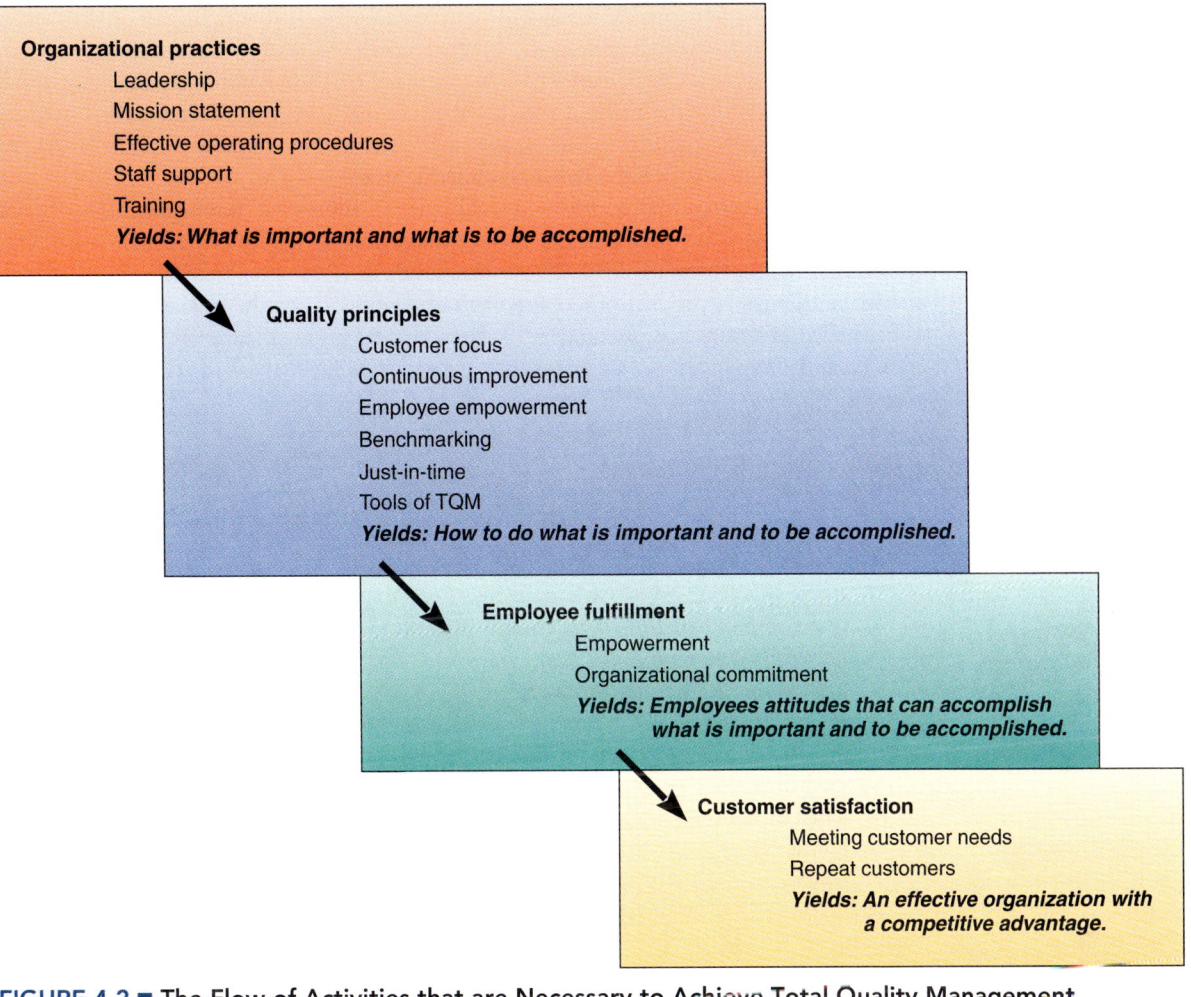

FIGURE 4.2 ■ The Flow of Activities that are Necessary to Achieve Total Quality Management

In this chapter we define quality and discuss international quality standards. We then present the concept of total quality management and its tools. In the supplement to this chapter, we explore the subject of statistical quality control.

DEFINING QUALITY

Total quality management systems are driven by identifying and satisfying customer needs. Total quality management takes care of the customer. Consequently, we accept the definition of **quality** as adopted by the American Society for Quality: "The totality of features and characteristics of a product or service that bears on its ability to satisfy stated or implied needs."[2]

However, others believe that definitions of *quality* fall into several categories.[3] Some definitions are *user-based*. They propose that quality "lies in the eyes of the beholder."

Quality The ability of a product or service to meet customer needs.

---

[2] Ross Johnson and William O. Winchell, *Production and Quality* (Milwaukee, WI: American Society for Quality, 1989), p. 2.

[3] Garvin, "What Does 'Product Quality' Really Mean?": 25–43.

Quality may be in the eyes of the beholder, but to build a product, operations managers must define what the beholder (the consumer) expects.

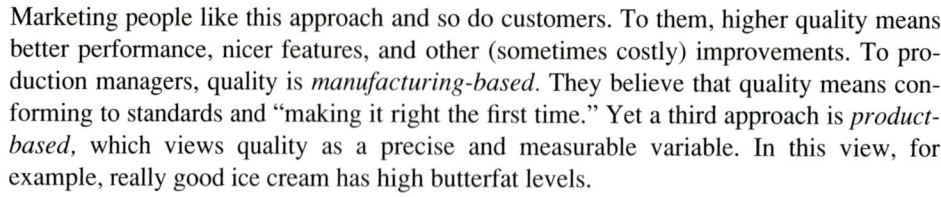

Marketing people like this approach and so do customers. To them, higher quality means better performance, nicer features, and other (sometimes costly) improvements. To production managers, quality is *manufacturing-based*. They believe that quality means conforming to standards and "making it right the first time." Yet a third approach is *product-based*, which views quality as a precise and measurable variable. In this view, for example, really good ice cream has high butterfat levels.

This text develops approaches and techniques to address all three categories of quality. The characteristics that connote quality must first be identified through research (a user-based approach to quality). These characteristics are then translated into specific product attributes (a product-based approach to quality). Then the manufacturing process is organized to ensure that products are made precisely to specifications (a manufacturing-based approach to quality). A process that ignores any one of these steps will not result in a quality product.[4]

Other Implications of Quality

In addition to being a critical element in operations, quality has other implications. Here are three other reasons why quality is important:

1. *Company reputation.* An organization can expect its reputation for quality—be it good or bad—to follow it. Quality will show up in perceptions about the firm's new products, employment practices, and supplier relations. Self-promotion is not a substitute for quality products.
2. *Product liability.* The courts increasingly hold organizations that design, produce, or distribute faulty products or services liable for damages or injuries resulting from their use. The Consumer Product Safety Act of 1972 sets and enforces product standards by banning products that do not reach those standards. Impure foods that cause illness, nightgowns that burn, or auto fuel tanks that explode upon impact can all lead to huge legal expenses, large settlements or losses, and terrible publicity.
3. *Global implications.* In this technological age, quality is an international, as well as OM, concern. For both a company and a country to compete effectively in the global economy, products must meet global quality, design, and price expectations. As the Korean Yugo demonstrated, inferior products harm a firm's profitability and a nation's balance of payments.

"Well, as a last ditch measure, we could improve the corporate image by improving the product."
Source: The Wall Street Journal, with permission of Cartoon Features Syndicate.

INTERNATIONAL QUALITY STANDARDS

Quality is so important globally that a number of quality standards have been developed. Japan, the European Community, and the United States have each developed their own quality standards.

Japan's Industrial Standard

The Japanese specification for quality management is published as Industrial Standard Z8101-1981. It emphasizes continuous improvement and stresses the role of organization-wide coordination and commitment. The standard states:

> Implementing quality control effectively necessitates the cooperation of all people in the company, involving top management, managers, supervisors, and workers in all areas of corporate activities such as market research, research and development, product planning

[4]Ibid., p. 29.

design, preparations for production, purchasing, vendor management, manufacturing, inspection, sales, and afterservices, as well as financial control, personnel administration, and training and education.

Europe's ISO 9000 Standard

The European Community (EC) has developed quality standards called **ISO 9000, 9001, 9002, 9003,** and **9004.** The focus of the EC standards are to force the establishment of quality management procedures, through detailed documentation, on firms doing business in the EC. A firm becomes certified by a qualified external examiner upon complying with all quality documentation standards. After the firm is certified, it gains listing in the ISO directory, which many organizations consult when selecting a new vendor. This listing, we should note, says nothing about the product's *actual* quality—it deals entirely with standards that are followed.

Several factors make the ISO 9000 series a subject of interest: (1) The standards are achieving worldwide acceptance, (2) the standards are now being applied to some products made or imported by the EC, and (3) adherence to the standards may be necessary for product certification.

Even small U.S. firms, such as New York's Rice Aircraft, are recognizing the value of ISO 9000 certification. This family-owned parts distributor saw the strategic implications of undergoing the rigorous ISO 9000 rules. For instance, Rice won a $3-million contract with American Airlines, which confirms that the airline was impressed that a firm as small as Rice was meeting international quality standards.

ISO 9000 focuses on the manuals, procedures, work instructions, records, and related standards for activities in the firm. Because it is not oriented toward leadership or the product, ISO 9000 is not without critics. Quality expert Philip Crosby, for example, states: "It is a delusion that sound management can be replaced by an information format. It is like putting a Bible in every hotel room with the thought that occupants will act according to its content."[5]

ISO 9000 A set of quality standards developed by the European Community.

"ISO" is Greek for *uniform*, as *uniform* throughout the European Community.

"If quality isn't ingrained in the organization, it will never happen."
— Philip Crosby

An emphasis on quality has helped many businesses improve profitability. Mobil Oil's lubricant-blending plant in Bogota, Colombia, attained ISO certification and, through a number of quality initiatives, reached record production. Here an employee monitors a filling machine.

[5]*Quality Digest,* April, 1997, p. 24.

Environmental Management Standard

ISO 14000 An environmental management standard established by the European Community.

The continuing internationalization of quality is evident with the EC's development of **ISO 14000**. ISO 14000 is a new EC environmental management standard that contains five core elements: (1) environmental management, (2) auditing, (3) performance evaluation, (4) labeling, and (5) life-cycle assessment. The new standard could have several advantages:

- Positive public image and reduced exposure to liability.
- Good systematic approach to pollution prevention through the minimization of ecological impact of products and activities.
- Compliance with regulatory requirements and opportunities for competitive advantage.
- Reduction in need for multiple audits.

This standard, or some variation of it, will probably soon be accepted worldwide.

U.S. Standards

The United States has long had military specifications for defense contracts, and in recent years, the American Society for Quality has developed specifications equivalent to those of the EC. They are Q90, Q91, Q92, Q93, and Q94. Q90 provides an overview and introduction to the other standards, definitions, and concepts related to quality.

- Q91 is the general standard for design, development, manufacturing, installation, and servicing of products or services.
- Q92 provides more detail than Q91 for organizations involved in production, installation, and servicing of products or services.
- Q93 provides more detail than Q91 for organizations specifically involved in inspection and tests and for distributors and value-added contractors.
- Q94 provides guidelines for managing and auditing a quality control system.

The global implications of quality are so important that, in 1988, the United States established the *Malcolm Baldrige National Quality Award* for quality achievement. The award is named for former Secretary of Commerce Malcolm Baldrige. Winners include such firms as Motorola, Milliken, Xerox, Federal Express, Ritz-Carlton Hotels, AT&T, Cadillac, and Texas Instruments.

TOTAL QUALITY MANAGEMENT

Total quality management (TQM) Management of an entire organization so that it excels in all aspects of products and services that are important to the customer.

Total quality management (TQM) refers to a quality emphasis that encompasses the entire organization, from supplier to customer. TQM stresses a commitment by management to have a continuing companywide drive toward excellence in all aspects of products and services that are important to the customer.

TQM is important because quality decisions influence each of the 10 decisions made by operations managers. Every chapter that follows deals with some aspect of identifying and meeting customer expectations. Meeting those expectations requires an emphasis on TQM if a firm is to compete as a leader in world markets.

Quality expert W. Edwards Deming used 14 points (see Table 4.1) to indicate how he implemented TQM.[6] We develop these into five concepts for an effective TQM program: (1) continuous improvement, (2) employee empowerment, (3) benchmarking, (4) just-in-time (JIT), and (5) knowledge of TQM tools.

---

[6] John C. Anderson, Manus Rungtusanatham, and Roger G. Schroeder, "A Theory of Quality Management Underlying the Deming Management Method," *Academy of Management Review* 19, no. 3 (1994): 472–509.

TABLE 4.1 ■ Deming's 14 Points for Implementing Quality Improvement

1. Create consistency of purpose.
2. Lead to promote change.
3. Build quality into the product; stop depending on inspections to catch problems.
4. Build long-term relationships based on performance instead of awarding business on the basis of price.
5. Continuously improve product, quality, and service.
6. Start training.
7. Emphasize leadership.
8. Drive out fear.
9. Break down barriers between departments.
10. Stop haranguing workers.
11. Support, help, and improve.
12. Remove barriers to pride in work.
13. Institute a vigorous program of education and self-improvement.
14. Put everybody in the company to work on the transformation.

Source: Deming revised his 14 points a number of times over the years. See W. Edwards Deming," Philosophy Continues to Flourish," *APICS—The Performance Advantage* 1, no. 4 (October 1991): 20.

The critical element for improving quality is management leadership.

Continuous Improvement

Total quality management (TQM) requires a never-ending process of continuous improvement that covers people, equipment, suppliers, materials, and procedures. The basis of the philosophy is that every aspect of an operation can be improved. The end goal is perfection, which is never achieved but always sought.

The Japanese use the word *kaizen* to describe this ongoing process of unending improvement—the setting and achieving ever-higher goals. In the United States, *TQM, zero defects,* and *six sigma* are used to describe such efforts. Whatever word or phrase is used, operations managers are key players in building a work culture that endorses continuous improvement.

Kaizen The Japanese word for the ongoing process of incremental improvement.

Employee Empowerment

Employee empowerment means involving employees in every step of the production process. Consistently, business literature suggests that some 85% of quality problems have to do with materials and processes, not with employee performance. Therefore, the task is to design equipment and processes that produce the desired quality. This is best done with a high degree of involvement by those who understand the shortcomings of the system. Those dealing with the system on a daily basis understand it better than anyone else. When nonconformance occurs, the worker is seldom wrong. Either the product was designed wrong, the system that makes the product was designed wrong, or the employee was improperly trained.[7] Although the employee may be able to help solve the problem, the employee rarely causes it.

Techniques for building employee empowerment include (1) building communication networks that include employees; (2) developing open, supportive supervisors; (3) moving responsibility from both managers and staff to production employees; (4) building high-morale organizations; (5) and creating such formal organization structures as teams and quality circles.

Employee empowerment Enlarging employee jobs so that the added responsibility and authority is moved to the lowest level possible in the organization.

---

[7] See a related discussion in Asher Israeli and Bradley Fisher, "The Worker Is Never Wrong," *Quality Progress,* October 1989, p. 95.

Leaders in the Fight for Quality

W. Edwards Deming. *(left) The awarding of the Deming Prize for quality control on Japanese TV is a national event. After World War II, Deming went to Japan to teach quality, and the Japanese learned. In his quality crusade, Deming insisted that management accept responsibility for building good systems. The employee, he believed, cannot produce products that on the average exceed the quality of what the process is capable of producing. Dr. Deming died in 1993.*

J. M. Juran. *(middle) A pioneer in teaching the Japanese how to improve quality, Juran believes strongly in top-management commitment, support, and involvement in the quality effort. He is also a believer in teams that continually seek to raise quality standards. Juran varies from Deming somewhat in focusing on the customer and defining quality as fitness for use, not necessarily the written specifications.*

Philip B. Crosby. *(right)* Quality Is Free *was Crosby's attention-getting book published in 1979. Crosby's traditional view has been "with management and employee commitment great strides can be made in improving quality." He also believes that in the traditional trade-off between the cost of improving quality and the cost of poor quality, the cost of poor quality is understated. The cost of poor quality should include all of the things that are involved in not doing the job right the first time.*

Quality circle A group of employees meeting regularly with a facilitator to solve work-related problems in their work area.

Teams can be built to address a variety of issues. One popular focus of teams is quality. Such teams are often known as quality circles. A **quality circle** is a group of employees who meet regularly to solve work-related problems. The members receive training in group planning, problem solving, and statistical quality control. They generally meet once a week (usually after work, but sometimes on company time). Although the members are not rewarded financially, they do receive recognition from the firm. A specially trained team member, called the facilitator, usually helps train the members and keeps the meetings running smoothly. Teams with a quality focus have proven to be a cost-effective way to increase productivity as well as quality.

Benchmarking

Benchmarking Selecting a demonstrated standard of performance that represents the very best performance for a process or activity.

Benchmarking is another ingredient in an organization's TQM program. **Benchmarking** involves selecting a demonstrated standard of products, services, costs, or practices that represent the very best performance for processes or activities very similar to your own. The idea is to develop a target at which to shoot and then to develop a standard or benchmark against which to compare your performance. The steps for developing benchmarks are:[8]

---

[8] Adapted from Michael J. Spendolini, *The Benchmarking Book* (New York: AMACOM, 1992).

- Determine what to benchmark.
- Form a benchmark team.
- Identify benchmarking partners.
- Collect and analyze benchmarking information.
- Take action to match or exceed the benchmark.

In the ideal situation, you find one or more similar organizations that are leaders in the particular areas you want to study. Then you compare yourself (benchmark yourself) against them. The company need not be in your industry. Indeed, to establish world-class standards, it may be best to look outside of your industry. If one industry has learned how to compete via rapid product development while yours has not, it does no good to study your industry. As discussed in the *OM in Action* box, "L. L. Bean's Reputation Makes It a Benchmark Favorite," this is exactly what Xerox and Chrysler did when they went to L. L. Bean for order-filling and warehousing benchmarks. Benchmarks often take the form of "best practices" found in other firms. Table 4.2 illustrates best practices for resolving customer complaints.

> "There is absolutely no reason for having errors or defects in any product or service."
> Philip Crosby

TABLE 4.2 ■ Best Practices for Resolving Customer Complaints

- *Make it easy for clients to complain:* It is free market research.
- *Respond quickly to complaints:* It adds customers and loyalty.
- *Resolve complaints on the first contact:* It reduces cost.
- *Use computers to manage complaints:* Discover trends, share them, and align your services.
- *Recruit the best for customer service jobs:* It should be part of formal training and career advancement.

Source: Canadian Government Guide on Complaint Mechanism.

Benchmarks can and should be established in a variety of areas. Total quality management requires no less.

Just-in-Time (JIT)

The philosophy behind just-in-time (JIT) is one of continuing improvement and enforced problem solving. JIT systems are designed to produce or deliver goods just as they are needed. When implemented, JIT reduces the amount of inventory that a firm has on hand by establishing quality and purchasing controls that bring inventory to the firm just-in-time for use. JIT is related to quality in three ways.

- *JIT cuts the cost of quality.* This occurs because scrap, rework, inventory investment, and damage costs are directly related to inventory on hand. Because there is less inventory on hand with JIT, costs are lower. Additionally, inventory hides bad quality whereas JIT immediately *exposes* bad quality.
- *JIT improves quality.* As JIT shrinks lead time, it keeps evidence of errors fresh and limits the number of potential sources of error. JIT creates, in effect, an early warning system for quality problems, both within the firm and with vendors.
- *Better quality means less inventory and a better, easier-to-employ JIT system.* Often the purpose of keeping inventory is to protect against poor production performance resulting from unreliable quality. If consistent quality exists, JIT allows firms to reduce all the costs associated with inventory.

OM IN ACTION

L. L. BEAN'S REPUTATION MAKES IT A BENCHMARK FAVORITE

Managers in the United States smiled knowingly in the 1950s when Japanese engineers made the rounds at trade shows, endlessly snapping photos. The smiles faded in the 1970s and 1980s as those photos led to world-class products. Now, the United States is embracing an effective response: benchmarking. "Too many companies suffer because they refuse to believe others can do things better," says Robert Camp, Xerox's benchmarking manager.

The spread of benchmarking has created many role models at home. When Xerox set out to improve its order filling, for example, it went to L. L. Bean. What did copier parts have in common with Bean's outdoor paraphernalia? Nothing. But Xerox managers felt that their order-filling processes were similar: They both involve handling products so varied in size and shape that the work must be done by hand. Bean, it turns out, was able to "pick" orders three times as fast as Xerox. The lesson learned, Xerox pared its warehouse costs by 10%.

Then Chrysler came to study Bean's warehousing methods. Bean employees use flowcharts to spot wasted motions. This practice resulted in an employee suggestion to stock high-volume items close to packing stations. So impressed was Chrysler that it decided to follow suit and rely more on problem solving at the worker level.

L. L. Bean now receives up to five requests a week for benchmark visits—too many to handle. The company schedules only those with a "genuine interest in quality, not the merely curious," says Bean plant manager Robert Olive.

Sources: Business Week, September 18, 1995, pp. 122–132; and *Journal of Services Marketing* (1995): 11–14.

Knowledge of TQM Tools

To empower employees and implement TQM as a continuing effort, everyone in the organization must be trained in the techniques of TQM. In the following section, we focus on some of the diverse and expanding tools that are used in the TQM crusade.

TOOLS OF TQM

> "Quality is never an accident; it is always the result of intelligent effort."
>
> John Ruskin

Six tools/techniques that aid the TQM effort are:

1. quality function deployment (house of quality)
2. Taguchi technique
3. Pareto charts
4. process charts
5. cause-and-effect diagrams (fish-bone charts)
6. statistical process control.

We will now introduce these tools.

Quality Function Deployment (QFD)

We earlier defined *quality* as "the totality of features and characteristics of a product or service that bears on its ability to satisfy stated or implied needs." Consequently, an effective TQM program translates the customer's stated or implied needs into specific features and services. One very effective technique for doing so is quality function deployment.

TOOLS OF TQM

Quality function deployment (QFD) refers to both (1) determining what will satisfy the customer and (2) translating those customer desires into the target design.[9] We use QFD early in the production process to help us determine *what* will satisfy the customer and also *where* to deploy quality efforts.

One of the tools of QFD is the house of quality. The **house of quality** is a graphic technique for defining the relationship between customer desires and product (or service). Only by defining this relationship in a rigorous way can operations managers build products and processes with features desired by customers. Defining this relationship is the first step in building a world-class production system. To build the house of quality, we perform six basic steps:

1. Identify customer *wants*. (What do prospective customers want in this product?)
2. Identify *how* the good/service will satisfy customer wants. (Identify specific product characteristics, features, or attributes and show how they will satisfy customer *wants*.)
3. Relate customer *wants* to product *hows*. (Build a matrix, as in Example 1, that shows this relationship.)
4. Identify relationships between the firm's *hows*. (How do our *hows* tie together? For instance, in the following example, there is a high relationship between low electricity requirements and auto focus, auto exposure, and auto film advance because they all require electricity. This relationship is shown in the "roof" of the house in Example 1.)
5. Develop importance ratings. (Using the *customer's* importance ratings and weights for the relationships shown in the matrix, compute *our* importance ratings, as in Example 1.)
6. Evaluate competing products. (How well do competing products meet customer wants? Such an evaluation, as shown in the two columns on the right of the figure in Example 1, would be based on market research.)

Example 1 shows how to construct a house of quality.

Quality function deployment (QFD) A process for determining customer requirements (customer "wants") and translating them into the attributes (the "hows") that each functional area can understand and act upon.

House of quality A part of the quality function deployment process that utilizes a planning matrix to relate customer "wants" to "how" the firm is going to meet those "wants."

EXAMPLE 1

First, through extensive market research, Great Cameras, Inc. determined what the customer *wants*. Those *wants* are shown on the left of the house of quality on page 88 and are: lightweight, easy to use, reliable, easy to hold steady, and no double exposures. Second, the product development team determined *how* the organization is going to translate those customer *wants* into product design and process attribute targets. These *hows* are entered across the top portion of the house of quality. These characteristics are low electricity requirements, aluminum components, auto focus, auto exposure, auto film advance, and ergonomic design.

Third, the product team evaluated each of the customer *wants* against the *hows*. In the relationship matrix of the house, the team evaluated how well its design will meet customer needs. Fourth, in the "roof" of the house, the product development team developed the relationship between the attributes.

Fifth, the team developed importance ratings for its design attributes on the bottom row of the table. This was done by assigning values (5 for high, 3 for medium, and 1 for low) to each entry in the relationship matrix, and then multiplying each of these values by the customer's importance rating. These values in "Our importance ratings" row provide a ranking of how to proceed with product and process design, with the highest values being the most critical to a successful product.

---

[9] See Yoji Akao, ed., *Quality Function Deployment: Integrating Customer Requirements into Product Design* (Cambridge, MA: Productivity Press, 1990).

88 CHAPTER 4 MANAGING QUALITY

Sixth, the house of quality is also used for the evaluation of competitors. How well do *competitors* meet customer demand? The two columns on the right indicate how market research thinks competitors satisfy customer wants (**G**ood, **F**air, or **P**oor). So company A does a good job on "lightweight," "easy to use," and "easy to hold steady," a fair job on "reliability," and a poor job "no double exposures." Company B does a good job with "reliability" but poor on other attributes. Products from other firms and even the proposed product can be added next to company B.

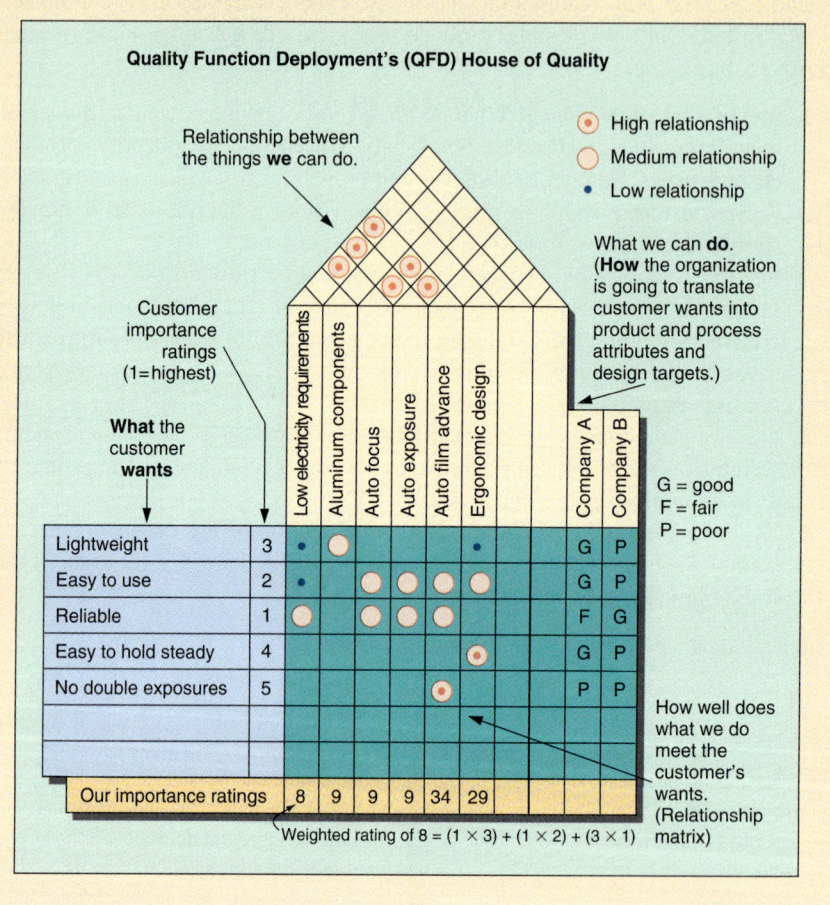

Quality Function Deployment's (QFD) House of Quality

- ⦿ High relationship
- ○ Medium relationship
- • Low relationship

Relationship between the things **we** can do.

What we can do. (**How** the organization is going to translate customer wants into product and process attributes and design targets.)

Customer importance ratings (1=highest)

What the customer **wants**

		Low electricity requirements	Aluminum components	Auto focus	Auto exposure	Auto film advance	Ergonomic design			Company A	Company B
Lightweight	3	•	○				•			G	P
Easy to use	2	•		○	○	○	○			G	P
Reliable	1	○		○	○	○				F	G
Easy to hold steady	4						⦿			G	P
No double exposures	5					⦿				P	P
Our importance ratings		8	9	9	9	34	29				

G = good
F = fair
P = poor

How well does what we do meet the customer's wants. (Relationship matrix)

Weighted rating of 8 = (1 × 3) + (1 × 2) + (3 × 1)

The earlier a potential loss can be identified, the better the potential loss can be addressed by design or process change.

Another use of quality function deployment (QFD) is to show how the quality effort will be *deployed*. As Figure 4.3 shows, *design characteristics* of House 1 become the inputs to House 2, which are satisfied by *specific components* of the product. Similarly, the concept is carried to House 3, where the specific components are to be satisfied through particular *production processes*. Once those production processes are defined, they become requirements of House 4 to be satisfied by a *quality plan* that will ensure conformance of those processes. The quality plan is a set of specific tolerances, procedures, methods, and sampling techniques that will ensure that the production process meets the customer requirements.

Much of the QFD literature and effort is devoted to meeting customer requirements with design characteristics (House 1 in Figure 4.3), and its importance is not to be underestimated. However, *the sequence* of houses is a very effective way of identifying, communicating, and allocating resources throughout the system. The series of houses helps operations managers determine where to *deploy* quality resources. In this way we meet customer requirements, produce quality products, and win orders.

TOOLS OF TQM 89

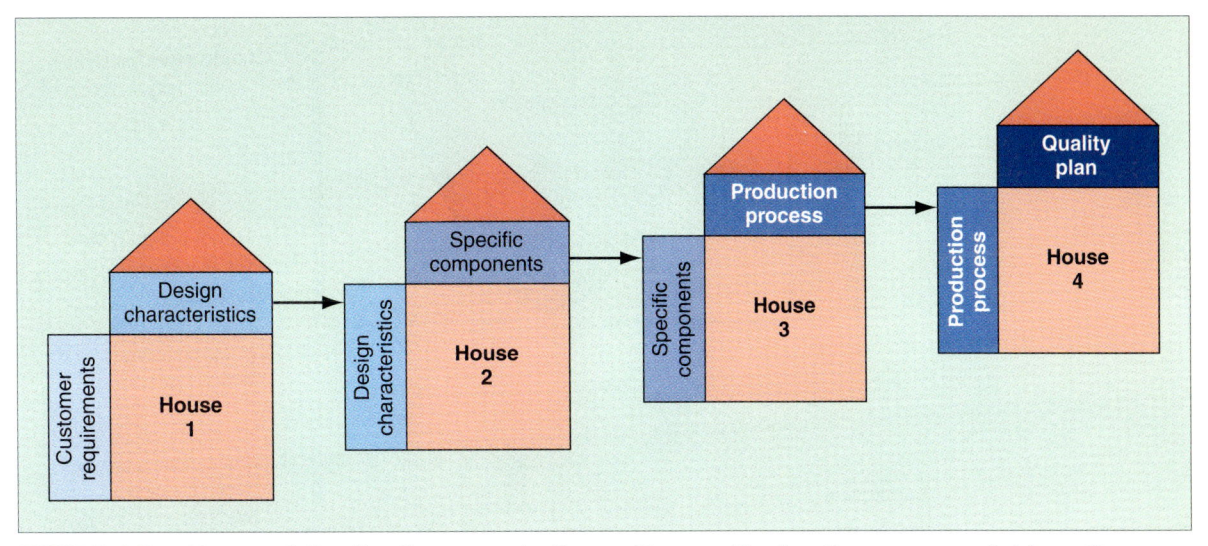

FIGURE 4.3 ■ House of Quality Sequence Indicates How to Deploy Resources to Achieve Customer Requirements

Taguchi Technique

Most quality problems are the result of product and process design. Therefore, tools are needed to address these areas. One of those tools is the **Taguchi technique,** a quality improvement technique aimed at both product and process design.[10]

Taguchi Concepts Three concepts are important to understanding Taguchi's approach and method: *quality robustness, quality loss function,* and *target-oriented quality.*

Quality robust products are products that can be produced uniformly and consistently in adverse manufacturing and environmental conditions. Taguchi's idea is to remove the *effects* of adverse conditions instead of removing the causes. Taguchi suggests that removing the effects is often cheaper than removing the causes and more effective in producing a robust product. In this way, small variations in materials and process do not destroy product quality.

A **quality loss function (QLF)** identifies all costs connected with poor quality and shows how these costs increase as the product moves away from being exactly what the customer wants. These costs include not only customer dissatisfaction but also warranty and service costs; internal inspection, repair, and scrap costs; and costs that can best be described as costs to society. Notice that Figure 4.4(a) shows the quality loss function as a curve that increases at an increasing rate. It takes the general form of a simple quadratic formula:

$$L = D^2 C$$

where L = loss
D^2 = square of the deviation from the target value
C = cost of avoiding the deviation

All the losses to society due to poor performance are included in the loss function. The smaller the loss, the more desirable the product. The farther the product is from the target value, the more severe the loss.

Taguchi technique A quality control technique that focuses on improving the product at the design stage.

Quality robust Products that are consistently built to meet customer needs in spite of adverse conditions in the production process.

Quality loss function (QLF) A mathematical function that identifies all costs connected with poor quality and shows how these costs increase as product quality moves from what the customer wants.

[10] Lance Ealey, "Taguchi Basics," *Quality,* November 1988, pp. 30–32; and Glen Stuart Peace, *Taguchi Methods: A Hands-On Approach* (Reading, MA: Addison-Wesley, 1993).

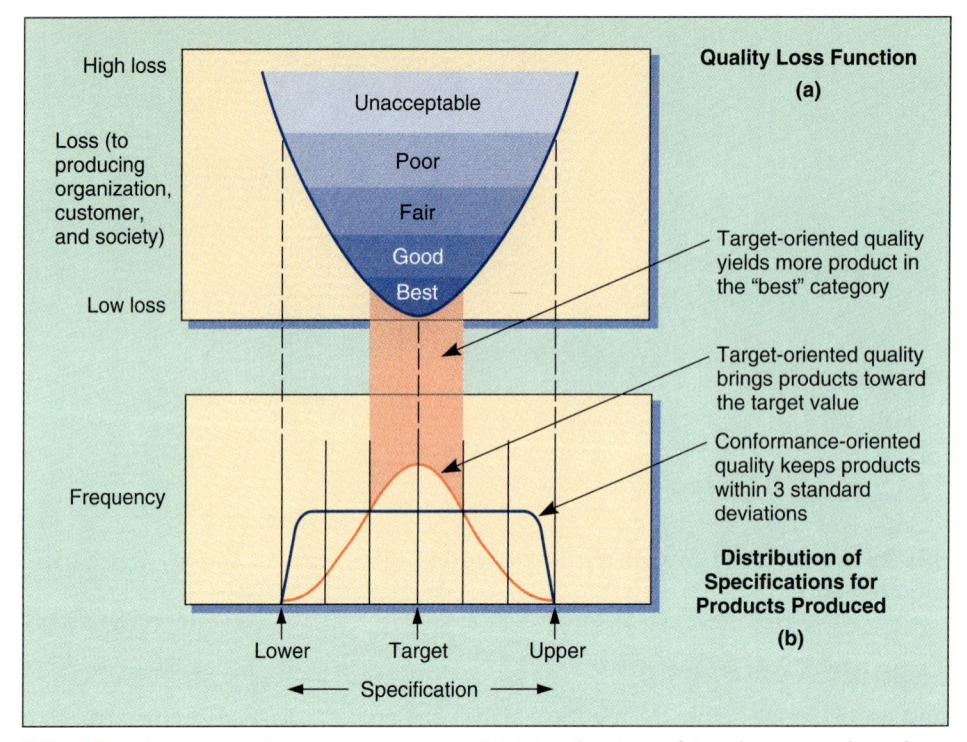

FIGURE 4.4 ■ **(a) Quality Loss Function; (b) Distribution of Products Produced**
Taguchi aims for the target, because products produced near the upper and lower acceptable specifications result in higher quality loss function.

Taguchi observed that traditional conformance-oriented specifications (that is, the product is good as long as it falls within the tolerance limits) are too simplistic. As shown in Figure 4.4(b), conformance-oriented quality accepts all products that fall within the tolerance limits, producing more units farther from the target. Therefore, the loss (cost) is higher in terms of customer satisfaction and benefits to society. Target-oriented quality, on the other hand, strives to keep the product at the desired specification, producing more (and better) units near the target.

Target-oriented quality is a philosophy of continuous improvement to bring the product exactly on target.

Target-oriented quality A philosophy of continuous improvement to bring the product exactly on target.

Pareto Charts

Pareto charts are a method of organizing errors, problems, or defects to help focus on problem-solving efforts. They are based on the work of Vilfredo Pareto, a nineteenth-century economist. Joseph M. Juran popularized Pareto's work when he suggested that 80% of a firm's problems are a result of only 20% of the causes.

Example 2 indicates that of the five types of defects identified, the vast majority were of one type, scratches.

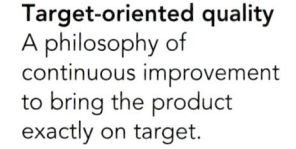

Pareto charts A graphic way of identifying the few critical items as opposed to many less important ones.

EXAMPLE 2

Custom Wine Glasses of Leadville, Colorado, has just collected the data from 75 defects from the day's production. The boss decides to prepare a Pareto analysis of the defects. The data provided are scratches, 54; porosity, 12; nicks, 4; contamination, 3; and miscellaneous, 2.

TOOLS OF TQM

The Pareto chart shown indicates that 72% of the defects were the result of one cause, scratches. The majority of defects will be eliminated when this one cause is corrected.

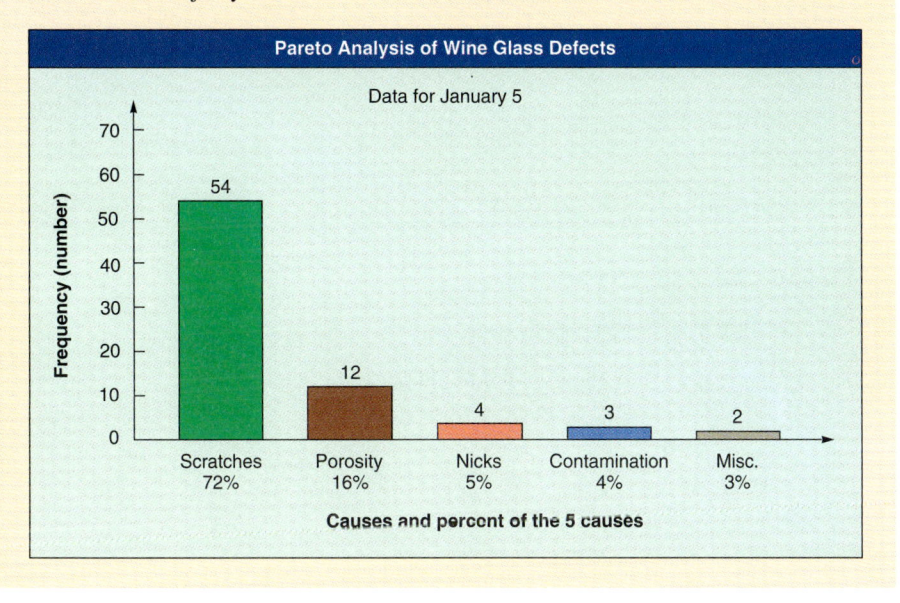

Pareto Analysis of Wine Glass Defects
Data for January 5

Cause	Frequency	Percent
Scratches	54	72%
Porosity	12	16%
Nicks	4	5%
Contamination	3	4%
Misc.	2	3%

Pareto analysis indicates which problems may yield the greatest payoff. Pacific Bell discovered this when it tried to find a way to reduce damage to buried phone cable, the number-one cause of phone outages. Pareto analysis showed that 41% of cable damage was caused by construction work. Armed with this information, Pacific Bell was able to devise a plan to reduce cable cuts by 24% in one year, saving $6 million.[11]

Process Charts

Process charts are designed to help us understand a sequence of events (that is, the process) through which a product travels. The process chart graphs the steps of the process and their relationship. This type of analysis can:

1. Help identify the best inspection and data-collection points.
2. Isolate and track the origin of problems.
3. Identify nonvalue-added activities such as delay and storage.
4. Identify opportunities for travel-distance reduction.

As shown in Example 3, a process chart organizes information about a process in a graphical matter, using five standard symbols and distance.

Process chart Chart using symbols to analyze the movement of people or material.

EXAMPLE 3

The WJC Chicken Processing Plant in Little Rock, Arkansas, would like to understand more about its packing and shipping process. After observation of the packing and shipping line and discussion with operators, you prepare the following process chart. This type of analysis should help you determine (1) where inspection and data collection could take place (perhaps prior to sealing, weighing, and labeling to check for bacteria counts, and after quick freeze to check once again); (2) the opportunities for reducing distance

---

[11] *The Wall Street Journal*, February 24, 1994, p. A1.

92   CHAPTER 4   MANAGING QUALITY

traveled; (3) where to remove delays; and (4) where to look should certain types of problems arise.

Present Method [X]	PROCESS CHART	Proposed Method [ ]

SUBJECT CHARTED _Packing and Shipping Process_   DATE _1/1/98_
to Determine Inspection Points   CHART BY _HRC_
                                                  CHART NO. _1_
DEPARTMENT _Packing and Shipping_   SHEET NO. _1_ OF _1_

DIST. IN FEET	TIME IN MINS.	CHART SYMBOLS	PROCESS DESCRIPTION
10'	.05	○⇨□D▽	To Packing Station
—	.1	○⇨□D▽	Pack
2'	.03	○⇨□D▽	To Airtight Sealing, Weighing, and Labeling
—	.2	○⇨□D▽	Airtight Sealing, Weighing, and Labeling
50'	.25	○⇨□D▽	To Quick Freeze Storage
—	35	○⇨□D▽	Quick Freeze Storage
	60	○⇨□D▽	Wait
25'	.15	○⇨□D▽	To Bulk Packing
—	.7	○⇨□D▽	Bulk Packing
	240	○⇨□D▽	Storage
40'	2.0	○⇨□D▽	To Shipping Dock
	2.5	○⇨□D▽	Load on Shipping Truck
		○⇨□D▽	
127'	340.98	5 5 0 1 1	TOTALS

The standard American Society of Mechanical Engineers (ASME) process symbols are
○ = operation; ⇨ = transportation; □ = inspection; D = delay; ▽ = storage

As you will see in our discussion of human resources and job design in chapter 10, process charts can be useful analytical tools in a wide variety of other applications.

Cause-and-Effect Diagram

Cause-and-effect diagram A schematic technique used to discover possible locations of quality problems.

Another tool for identifying possible locations of quality problems and inspection points is the **cause-and-effect diagram,** also known as an **Ishikawa diagram** or a **fish-bone chart.** Figure 4.5 illustrates a chart (note the shape resembling the bones of a fish) for an everyday quality control problem—a dissatisfied airline customer. Each "bone" represents a possible source of error.

The operations manager starts with four categories: material, machinery/equipment, manpower, and methods. These four M's are the "causes." They provide a good checklist for initial analysis. Individual causes associated with each category are tied in as separate bones along that branch, often through a brainstorming process. For example, the machinery branch in Figure 4.5 has problems caused by deicing equipment, mechanical delays, and broken carousels. When a fish-bone chart is systematically developed, possible quality problems and inspection points are highlighted.

Statistical Process Control (SPC)

Statistical process control (SPC) A process used to monitor standards, making measurements and taking corrective action as a product or service is being produced.

Statistical process control monitors standards, makes measurements, and takes corrective action as a product or service is being produced. Samples of process outputs are examined; if they are within acceptable limits, the process is permitted to continue. If they

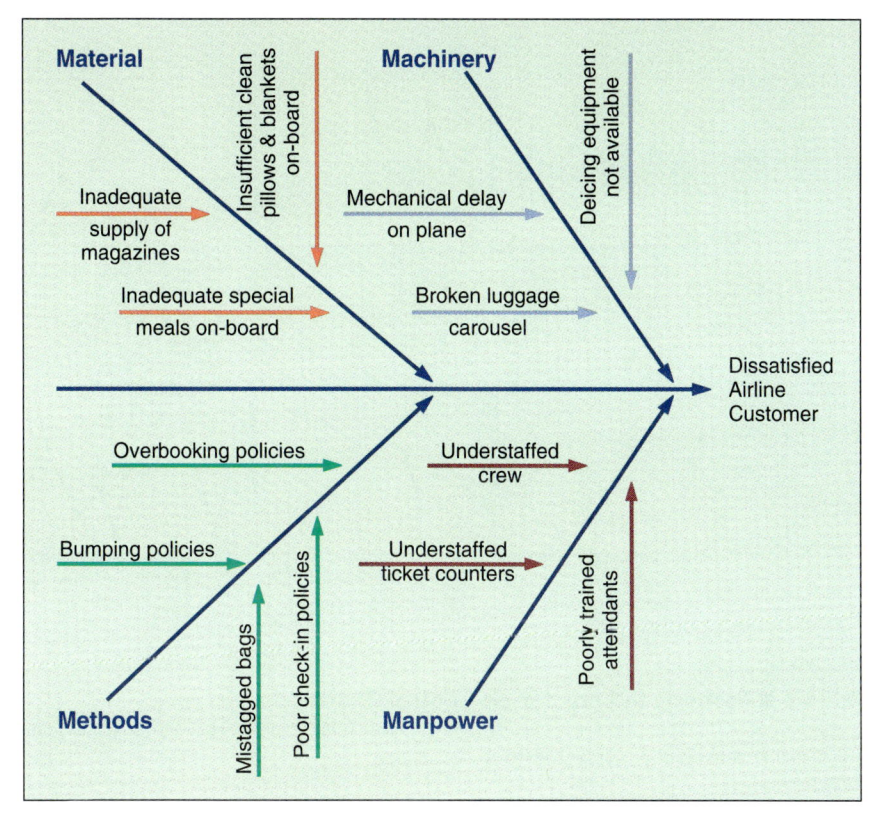

FIGURE 4.5 ■ Fish-Bone Chart (or Cause-and-Effect Diagram) for Problems with Airline Customer Service

fall outside certain specific ranges, the process is stopped and, typically, the assignable cause located and removed.

Control charts are graphic presentations of data over time that show upper and lower limits for the process we want to control. Control charts are constructed in such a way that new data can be quickly compared to past performance data. We take samples of the process output and plot the average of these samples on a chart that has the limits on it. The upper and lower limits in a control chart can be in units of temperature, pressure, weight, length, and so on.

Figure 4.6 shows the useful information that can be portrayed in control charts. When the average of the samples falls within the upper and lower control limits and no discernible pattern is present, the process is said to be in control with only natural variation present. Otherwise, the process is out of control or out of adjustment.

The supplement to this chapter details how control charts of different types are developed. It also deals with the statistical foundation underlying the use of this important tool.

Control charts Graphic presentations of process data over time.

THE ROLE OF INSPECTION

To make sure a system is producing at the expected quality level, control of the process is needed. The best processes have little variation from the standard expected. The operations manager's task is to build such systems and to verify, often by inspection, that they

94　CHAPTER 4　MANAGING QUALITY

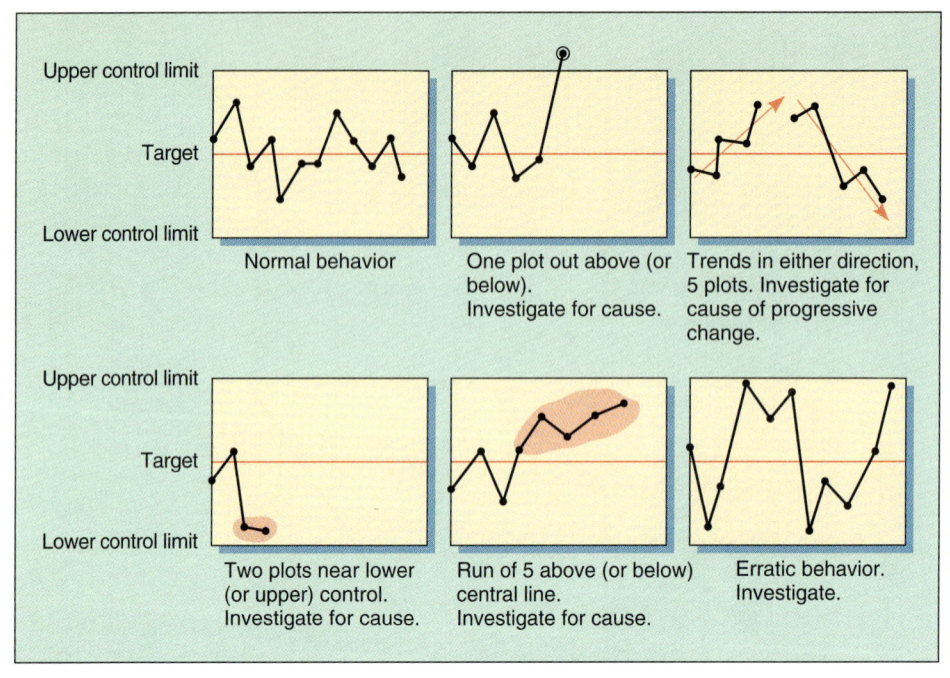

FIGURE 4.6 ■ Patterns to Look for on Control Charts
Source: Adapted from Bertrand L. Hansen, *Quality Control: Theory and Applications,* 1991, p. 65. Reprinted by permission of Prentice-Hall, Upper Saddle River, New Jersey.

Inspection A means of ensuring that an operation is producing at the quality level expected.

are performing to standard. This **inspection** can involve measurement, tasting, touching, weighing, or testing of the product (sometimes even destroying it when doing so). Its goal is to detect a bad process immediately. Inspection does not correct deficiencies in the system or defects in the products; nor does it change a product or increase its value. Inspection only finds deficiencies and defects, and it is expensive.

Inspection should be thought of as an audit. Audits do not add value to the product. However, operations managers, like financial managers, need audits, and they need to

Although we increasingly rely upon automated inspection techniques, much inspection is still done manually. Here an employee of Bausch & Lomb in Indonesia inspects contact lenses.

At TRW's new plant in Dijon, France, a technician inspects power-steering system pinions. TRW's internal quality audit program includes such aspects as measuring quality costs, procedures to make sure new products are designed and delivered with quality, inspection at all points in the process, quality circles, close relations with suppliers, and a business plan stressing quality.

know when and where to audit. So there are two basic issues relating to inspection: (1) *when to inspect* and (2) *where to inspect*.

When and Where to Inspect

Deciding when and where to inspect depends on the type of process and the value added at each stage. Inspections (audits) can take place at any of the following points.

1. At your supplier's plant while the supplier is producing.
2. At your plant upon receipt of goods from your supplier.
3. Before costly or irreversible processes.
4. During the step-by-step production process.
5. When production is complete.
6. Before shipment from your plant.
7. At the point of customer contact.

Pareto charts, process charts, and cause-and-effect diagrams, as discussed in the previous section, are TQM tools to aid in this "when and where" to inspect decision. However, inspection is not a substitute for a robust product produced by well-trained employees in a good process. In one well-known experiment conducted by an independent research firm, 100 defective pieces were added to a "perfect" lot of items and then subjected to 100% inspection.[12] The inspectors found only 68 of the defective pieces in their first inspection. It took another three passes by the inspectors to find the next 30 defects. The last two defects were never found. So the bottom line is that there is variability in the inspection process. Additionally, inspectors are only human: They become bored, they become tired, and the inspection equipment itself has variability. Even with 100% inspection, inspectors cannot guarantee perfection. Therefore, employee empowerment is usually a better solution than trying to find defects by inspection.

One of the themes of our treatment of quality is that "quality cannot be inspected into a product."

---

[12] *Statistical Quality Control* (Springfield, MA: Monsanto Chemical Company, n.d.), p. 19.

For example, at Velcro Industries, as in many organizations, quality was viewed by machine operators as the job of "those quality people." Inspections were based on random sampling, and if a part showed up bad, it was thrown out. The company decided to pay more attention to operators, machine repair and design, measurement methods, communications, and responsibilities, and to invest more money in training. Over time as defects declined, Velcro was able to pull half its quality control people out of the process.

Source Inspection

The best inspection can be thought of as no inspection at all; this "inspection" is always done at the source—it is just doing the job properly with the operator ensuring that this is so. This may be called **source inspection** (or source control) and is consistent with the concept of employee empowerment, where individual employees self-check their own work. The idea is that each supplier, process, and employee *treats the next step in the process as the customer,* ensuring perfect product to the next "customer." This inspection may be assisted by the use of checklists and controls such as a fail-safe device called a *poka-yoke*, a name borrowed from the Japanese.

A **poka-yoke** is a foolproof device or technique that ensures production of good units every time.[13] These special devices avoid errors and provide quick feedback of problems. A simple example of a poka-yoke device is the diesel or leaded gas pump nozzle that will not fit into the "unleaded" gas tank opening on your car. In McDonald's, the French-fry scoop and standard-size bag used to measure the correct quantity are poka-yokes. Similarly, in a hospital, the prepackaged surgical coverings that contain exactly the items needed for a medical procedure are poka-yokes. Checklists are another type of poka-yoke. The idea of source inspection and poka-yokes is to ensure that 100% good product or service is provided at each step in the process.

Service Industry Inspection

In *service*-oriented organizations, inspection points can be assigned at a wide range of locations, as illustrated in Table 4.3. Again, the operations manager must decide where inspections are justified. Pareto charts and process charts may prove useful when making these judgments.

Inspection of Attributes vs. Variables

When inspections take place, quality characteristics may be measured as either *attributes* or *variables*. **Attribute inspection** classifies items as being either good or defective. It does not address the *degree* of failure. For example, the lightbulb burns or it does not. **Variable inspection** measures such dimensions as weight, speed, height, or strength to see if an item falls within an acceptable range. If a piece of electrical wire is supposed to be 0.01 inch in diameter, a micrometer can be used to see if the product is close enough to pass inspection.

Knowing whether attributes or variables are being inspected helps us decide which statistical quality control approach to take, as we will see in the supplement to this chapter.

---

[13] For further discussion, see Alan Robinson, *Modern Approaches to Management Improvement: The Shingo System* (Cambridge, MA: Productivity Press, 1990).

Source inspection Controlling or monitoring at the point of production or purchase—at the "source" rather than "flow."

Poka-yoke Literally translated, "foolproof"; it has come to mean a device or technique that ensures the production of a good unit every time.

Attribute inspection An inspection that classifies items as being either good or defective.

Variable inspection Classifications of inspected items as falling on a continuum scale such as dimension, size, or strength.

TABLE 4.3 ■ Inspection Points in Three Service Organizations

Organization	Some points of Inspection	Issues to consider
Bank America	Teller stations	Shortages, courtesy, speed, accuracy
	Loan accounts	Collateral, proper credit checks, rates, terms of loans, default rates, loan ratios
	Checking accounts	Accuracy, speed of entry, rate of overdraws
Nordstrom's Department Store	Stockrooms	Clean, uncluttered, organized, level of stockouts, ample supply, rotation of goods
	Display areas	Attractive, well-organized, stocked, visible goods, good lighting
	Sales counters	Neat, courteous, knowledgeable personnel; waiting time; accuracy in credit checking and sales entry
Chili's Restaurant	Kitchen	Clean, proper storage, unadulterated food, health regulations observed, well-organized
	Cashier station	Speed, accuracy, appearance
	Dining areas	Clean, comfortable, regular monitoring by personnel

TOTAL QUALITY MANAGEMENT IN SERVICES

Quality of services is more difficult to measure than quality of manufactured goods. Generally, however, a user of a service has a few features in mind as a basis for comparison among alternatives. Lack of one feature may eliminate a service firm from consideration. Quality also may be perceived as a bundle of attributes in which many lesser characteristics are superior to those of competitors.

Extensive, in-depth interviews with consumer focus groups identified 10 general attributes or determinants of service quality (see Table 4.4).[14] The same study also drew the following conclusions:

1. *Consumers' perceptions of service quality result from a comparison of their before-service expectations with their actual service experience.* In other words, service quality is judged on the basis of whether it meets expectations.
2. *Quality perceptions are derived from the service process as well as from the service outcome.* From the consumer's point of view, the way the service is performed can be as important as the actual service.
3. *Service quality is of two types, normal and exceptional.* First, there is the quality level at which the regular service is delivered, such as the bank teller's handling of a transaction. Second, there is the quality level at which "exceptions" or "problems" are handled. This implies that a quality control system must recognize and have prepared a set of alternate plans for less-than-optimal operating conditions.

---

[14] L. Berry, V. Zeithaml, and A. Parasuraman, "Quality Counts in Services, Too," *Business Horizons*, May–June 1985, pp. 45–46.

> **TABLE 4.4 ■ Determinants of Service Quality**
>
> **Reliability** involves consistency of performance and dependability. It means that the firm performs the service right the first time and also means that the firm honors its promises.
>
> **Responsiveness** concerns the willingness or readiness of employees to provide service. It involves timeliness of service.
>
> **Competence** means possession of the required skills and knowledge to perform the service.
>
> **Access** involves approachability and ease of contact.
>
> **Courtesy** involves politeness, respect, consideration, and friendliness of contact personnel (including receptionists, telephone operators, etc.).
>
> **Communication** means keeping customers informed in language they can understand and listening to them. It may mean that the company has to adjust its language for different consumers—increasing the level of sophistication with a well-educated customer and speaking simply and plainly with a novice.
>
> **Credibility** involves trustworthiness, believability, and honesty. It involves having the customer's best interests at heart.
>
> **Security** is the freedom from danger, risk, or doubt.
>
> **Understanding/knowing the customer** involves making the effort to understand the customer's needs.
>
> **Tangibles** include the physical evidence of the service.
>
> *Source:* Excerpted from A. Parasuraman, Valerie A. Zeithaml, and Leonard L. Berry, "A Conceptual Model of Service Quality and Its Implications for Future Research," *Journal of Marketing*, Fall 1985, p. 44.

Follow-up interviews with service managers suggest that service quality can be measured by how effectively a service can close the gaps between expectations and the service provided. The *OM in Action* box, "TQM at Work in the Service Sector," provides another glimpse of how OM managers improve quality in services.

Designing a high-quality process that fills these pharmaceutical bottles in sterile conditions is much more fruitful than having an inspector evaluate the bacteria count on bottles filled in a poor system. Good quality systems focus on quality processes, not after-the-fact inspections.

OM IN ACTION

TQM AT WORK IN THE SERVICE SECTOR

The U.S. service industry in the 1990s distinctly resembles U.S. manufacturing in the 1970s. Quality is inconsistent, costs are high, profit margins are narrow, and competition increases each year.

Moreover, in some industries, such as copiers, technology in copier design has evened out product distinctions. Savin, a copier manufacturer owned by Japan's Ricoh Corp., believes that competitive advantage is to be found in service and is stressing customer service rather than product specifications. Says Savin VP, Robert Williams: "A company's fortunes ride on the quality of its service."

Here are just two ways in which Savin cut service expenses while improving service quality:

- Using statistical analysis, Savin found that significant time on service calls was being wasted when engineers had to go back to their trucks for spare parts. The firm assembled a "call kit," which allows engineers to carry onto customer premises all parts with highest probability for use. Now service calls are faster and cost less, and more can be made per day.
- The Pareto principle, that 20% of your staff causes 80% of your errors, was used to tackle the "callback" problem. Callbacks meant the job was not done right the first time and that a second visit, at Savin's expense, was needed. Retraining only the 11% of customer engineers with the most callbacks resulted in a 19% drop in return visits.

"Total quality management," according to Williams, "is an approach to doing business that should permeate every job in the service industry."

Sources: Business Marketing, July–August 1996, p. 1, The Wall Street Journal, November 4, 1991, p. A18; and Office, October 1993, pp. 26, 69.

Measuring Quality in Hospitals Because quality is so difficult to measure in many services, a number of imprecise measures have been developed. For instance, the main hospital accrediting group (JCAHO) uses a number of financial measures and counts of credentials to evaluate performance. However, many experts question whether the quality of care is really measured by number of licensed nurses—a criterion that JCAHO uses. Perhaps, they should look instead at the ratio of nurses to patients or the appropriateness of treatments administered. "We spend a lot of time doing paper trails," says one doctor at Columbia Hospital, near Jacksonville, Florida, but "there is very little time spent anymore on actual quality."[15]

SUMMARY

Quality is a term that means different things to different people. It is defined in this chapter as "the totality of features and characteristics of a product or service that bears on its ability to satisfy stated or implied needs." Defining quality expectations is critical to effective and efficient operations.

Quality requires building a total quality management (TQM) environment because quality cannot be inspected into a product. The chapter also addresses five TQM concepts: continuous improvement, employee empowerment, benchmarking, just-in-time, and knowledge of TQM tools. The six TQM tools introduced in this chapter are quality function deployment, Taguchi technique, Pareto charts, process charts, cause-and-effect diagrams, and statistical process control (SPC).

KEY TERMS

Quality *(p. 79)*
ISO 9000 *(p. 81)*
ISO 14000 *(p. 82)*
Total quality management (TQM) *(p. 82)*
Kaizen *(p. 83)*
Employee empowerment *(p. 83)*
Quality circle *(p. 84)*
Benchmarking *(p. 84)*

---

[15] *New York Times*, May 11, 1997, p. F11.

Quality function deployment (QFD) *(p. 87)*
House of quality *(p. 87)*
Taguchi technique *(p. 89)*
Quality robust *(p. 89)*
Quality loss function *(p. 89)*
Target-oriented quality *(p. 90)*
Pareto charts *(p. 90)*
Process chart *(p. 91)*

Cause-and-effect diagram, Ishikawa diagram, or fish-bone chart *(p. 92)*
Statistical process control (SPC) *(p. 92)*
Control charts *(p. 93)*
Inspection *(p. 94)*
Source inspection *(p. 96)*
Poka-yoke *(p. 96)*
Attribute inspection *(p. 96)*
Variable inspection *(p. 96)*

DISCUSSION QUESTIONS

1. Provide your own definition of *product quality*.
2. Name several products that do not require high quality.
3. Do you think the establishment of the Malcolm Baldrige National Quality Award has had much effect on the quality of products actually produced in the United States?
4. How can a university control the quality of its output (that is, its graduates)?
5. What are the major concepts of TQM?
6. Find a recent article on QFD and summarize its major points. Do you think QFD will be commonplace in U.S. firms? Why?
7. How can a firm build a climate of continuous improvement?
8. What are the three basic concepts of the Taguchi technique?
9. What are six tools of TQM?
10. What is the "house of quality"?
11. Why is target-oriented performance better than conformance-oriented performance?
12. What are 10 determinants of service quality?
13. What is the quality loss function (QLF)?
14. What does the formula $L = D^2C$ mean?
15. As a library or Internet exercise, determine the Baldrige Award criteria.
16. What are the four *M*'s of a cause-and-effect diagram?

CRITICAL THINKING EXERCISE

The Oklahoma City plant of Tursine Electronics assembles printed circuit boards with a quality rating that is both deplorable and dropping. Indeed, it is worse than any of the company's other plants. To complicate matters, labor relations are difficult and morale low, resulting in high turnover and absenteeism. The new plant manager, who has been sent in to straighten things out, believes that the facility will be closed unless dramatic productivity and quality improvements are made. Quality has become too important a factor in the industry.

How can the manager turn this plant around, build a quality product, and instill quality into the workforce?

PROBLEMS

4.1 Use the quality function deployment's house of quality technique to construct a relationship matrix between customer *wants* and *how* you as an operations manager would address them. Consider the *wants* and *hows* of the following:
a) ice cream
b) a soft drink
c) a quick lunch

4.2 Using the house of quality, pick a real product (perhaps the ice cream, soft drink, or lunch in Problem 4.1) and identify how an existing organization satisfies customer requirements.

4.3 Using a sequence of "houses of quality," as described in Figure 4.3, determine how you might deploy resources to achieve the desired quality. (*Hint:* Choose a product/service that you understand.)

4.4 Conduct an interview with a prospective purchaser of a new bicycle and translate the customer's *wants* into the specific *hows* of the firm.

4.5 Use Pareto analysis to investigate the following data collected on a printed-circuit-board assembly line.
  a) Prepare a graph of the data.
  b) What conclusions do you reach?

Defect	Number of Defect Occurrences
Wrong component	217
Components not adhering	146
Excess adhesive	64
Misplaced transistors	600
Defective board dimension	143
Mounting holes improperly positioned	14
Circuitry problems on final test	92

4.6 Develop a process chart for one of the following:
  a) changing an automobile tire
  b) paying a bill in a restaurant
  c) making a deposit at your bank

4.7 Prepare a process chart for one of the following:
  a) a fast-food drive-thru window (single window)
  b) a two-station drive-thru window (pay at one, pick up at second)
  c) the registration process at your college

4.8 Draw a fish-bone chart detailing reasons why a bolt might not be correctly matched to a nut on an assembly line.

4.9 Draw a fish-bone chart showing why a typist you paid to prepare a term paper produced a document with numerous errors.

4.10 Draw a fish-bone chart describing problems that your college or university has with its registration system.

4.11 Develop a Pareto analysis of the following causes of delay in a production process.

Reason for delay	frequency
Test equipment down	22
Delay in inspection	15
Inadequate parts	40
Lack of personnel available	3
Awaiting engineering decision	10
No schematic available	11

Case Study

Westover Electrical, Inc.

Westover Electrical, Inc., is a medium-sized Houston manufacturer of wire windings used in making electric motors. Joe Wilson, V-P Operations, has experienced an increasing problem with rejected product found during the manufacturing operation. "I'm not sure where to begin," admitted Joe at the weekly meeting with his boss. "Rejects in the Winding Department have been killing us the past 2 months. Nobody in operations has any idea why. I have just brought in a consultant, Roger Gagnon, to take a look at the situation and make recommendations about how we can find out what is going on. I don't expect Roger to make technical recommendations—just see if he can point us in the right direction."

Gagnon's first stop later that day was the production floor. His discussions with the production supervisors in the Winding Department indicated that they had no real grasp of what the problem was or what to do to correct it. A tour of the winding operation indicated that there were three machines that wound wire onto plastic cores to produce the primary and secondary electric motor windings. After inspection by quality control (QC), these windings then went to the Packaging Department. Packaging personnel, Gagnon found, inspect their own work and make corrections on the spot. The problem is that too many windings are found to be defective and require reworking before they can be packaged.

Gagnon's next stop was the Quality Control Department, where he obtained the records for the past month's Winding Department rejects (Table 4.5).

Discussion Questions

1. Prepare an outline for Roger Gagnon's report.
2. What charts, graphs, computer printouts, and so forth might be included in the report?
3. Prepare Gagnon's recommendation, with justification, on one page.
4. Prepare the detail necessary to supplement Gagnon's recommendation and justification so that Joe Wilson will understand how Gagnon arrived at his recommendations.

Source: Professor Victor E. Sower, Ph.D., C.Q.E., Sam Houston State University.

TABLE 4.5 ■ January Transformer Reject Log: Winding Process

No. of Reject Units by Cause

Date	No. Inspected	Winder	Bad Wind	Twisted Wire	Broken Leads	Abraded Wire	Wrong Core	Wrong Wire	Failed Electrical Test
1	100	1	1	0	4	1	0	0	1
	100	2	2	1	0	0	1	5	0
	100	3	0	0	0	5	0	0	3
2	100	1	0	1	3	0	0	0	0
	100	2	3	1	0	0	2	3	0
	100	3	0	0	1	6	0	0	0
3	100	1	1	0	0	2	0	0	0
	100	2	0	0	0	0	0	3	0
	100	3	0	0	1	4	0	0	3
4	100	1	0	0	3	0	0	0	0
	100	2	0	0	0	0	0	2	0
	100	3	0	0	0	3	1	0	3
5	100	1	0	1	5	0	0	0	0
	100	2	0	0	0	0	0	2	1
	100	3	0	0	0	3	0	0	2
8	100	1	0	0	2	0	0	0	0
	100	2	0	0	0	0	0	1	0
	100	3	0	0	0	3	0	0	3
9	100	1	0	1	2	0	0	0	0
	100	2	0	0	0	0	0	1	0
	100	3	0	0	0	3	0	0	4

TABLE 4.5 ■ January Transformer Reject Log: Winding Process (Continued)

Date	No. Inspected	Winder	Bad Wind	Twisted Wire	Broken Leads	Abraded Wire	Wrong Core	Wrong Wire	Failed Electrical Test
10	100	1	0	0	5	0	0	0	0
	100	2	1	0	0	0	1	0	0
	100	3	0	0	0	5	0	0	4
11	100	1	0	0	4	0	0	0	0
	100	2	0	0	0	0	0	0	0
	100	3	0	0	0	4	0	0	4
12	100	1	0	0	3	0	1	0	0
	100	2	1	0	1	0	0	0	0
	100	3	0	0	0	5	0	0	4
15	100	1	0	0	2	0	0	1	0
	100	2	0	0	0	0	0	1	0
	100	3	0	0	0	3	0	0	3
16	100	1	0	0	6	0	0	0	0
	100	2	0	0	0	0	0	0	0
	100	3	0	0	0	3	0	0	3
17	100	1	0	1	1	0	0	0	0
	100	2	0	0	0	0	0	0	1
	100	3	0	0	0	3	0	0	3
18	100	1	1	0	2	0	0	0	0
	100	2	0	0	0	0	0	1	0
	100	3	0	0	0	4	0	0	1
19	100	1	0	0	2	0	0	0	0
	100	2	0	0	0	0	0	0	0
	100	3	0	0	0	3	0	0	1
22	100	1	0	1	4	0	0	0	0
	100	2	0	0	0	0	0	0	0
	100	3	0	0	0	3	0	1	2
23	100	1	0	0	4	0	0	0	0
	100	2	0	0	0	0	0	0	1
	100	3	0	0	0	4	0	0	3
24	100	1	0	0	2	0	0	1	0
	100	2	0	1	0	0	0	0	0
	100	3	0	0	0	4	0	0	3
25	100	1	0	0	3	0	0	0	0
	100	2	0	0	0	1	0	0	0
	100	3	0	0	0	2	0	0	4
26	100	1	0	0	1	0	0	0	0
	100	2	0	1	0	1	0	0	0
	100	3	0	0	0	2	0	0	3
29	100	1	0	0	2	0	0	0	0
	100	2	0	0	1	0	0	0	0
	100	3	0	0	0	2	0	0	3
30	100	1	0	0	2	0	0	0	0
	100	2	0	0	0	0	1	0	0
	100	3	0	0	0	2	0	0	3

Note: Assume that each defective unit was rejected because of one single defect.

Case Study

Quality Cleaners

The owner of Quality Cleaners has decided that a quality improvement program must be implemented in his dry cleaning service. Customers bring clothes to one of five stores or pickup stations. Orders are then delivered to the cleaning plant twice each day (morning and afternoon), with deliveries of orders being made to the stores at the same time, allowing for same-day service by customer request.

The stores are opened at 7:00 A.M. by a full-time employee. This person is relieved at 3:00 P.M. by a part-time employee, who closes the store at 6:00 P.M.

When the clothes are received from the customer, a five-ply ticket showing the customer name, phone number, due date, and special requests is prepared. One ply is given to the customer as a claim check and the store keeps one ply (to show what it has in process). The clothes and the remaining plies of the ticket are put in a nylon laundry bag for delivery to the plant.

At the cleaning plant, the departments are:

Mark-in Each order is removed from the bag; items are tagged for identification later and sorted into large buggies according to due date, type of garment, and cleaning requirements. Buggies are moved to the cleaning department as they become full. Also at mark-in, garments are checked for spots, stains, tears, or other special handling. The problem is written on a strip-tag (a ½-in. wide paper tape) and attached to the garment with the identification tag.

Cleaning The buggies are emptied into the cleaning machine one item at a time to allow for inspection. The primary items checked are spots and stains requiring special attention and foreign objects. For example, an ink pen left in a pocket could ruin the whole load. As items are removed from the cleaning machine, they are placed on hangers and moved by conveyor to the pressing department.

Pressing There are four presses: one for silks, one for pants, and two general-purpose. On an ordinary day, three of the presses will be operating, but which three of the four are operating will depend upon the total demand and product mix that particular day. As items are pressed, they are placed on a conveyor that delivers them to the assembly department.

Assembly Cleaned items are grouped into customer orders, bagged, and put in the appropriate queue for delivery to the respective store. At this time, two plies (of the remaining three) of the ticket are attached to the order, and one ply stays at the plant to show that the order was completed. When the customer picks up the order, one ply will stay on the order.

The store will retain the last ply and pull the corresponding ply from its work-in-process file to show that the order is complete.

Note: Although Quality Cleaners is a larger-than-average cleaning operation, total annual revenues are approximately $600,000. Therefore, any suggestions must be relatively inexpensive.

At present, a majority of the employees are cross-trained to allow for flexibility. The table below indicates the production employees and the positions for which they are trained. *P* indicates this is the primary duty, or the one they perform most often. A check indicates they are also trained in that function.

		Presses		
Employee	Cleaning	General Purpose	Silks	Pants
David	P	✓		✓
Tasha	✓	✓		P
Len	✓	P	✓	
Mary		✓	P	✓
Betty (part-time)	✓	✓		✓
Mike (part-time)	✓	✓		✓

For example, one day David may only clean; the next day he cleans a while and then presses pants. This presents a problem in determining who put a double crease in Mrs. Jones's slacks, but the owner believes this flexibility in scheduling is valuable and must be maintained.

Discussion Questions

1. Design the quality program. Consider the following issues:
   a) Where should inspection(s) occur?
   b) How will accountability be achieved?
   c) What factors (variables, attributes, other considerations) should be checked?
   d) Is statistical process control (SPC) appropriate?
      i. Variable or attribute?
      ii. At what point?
2. What are the cost items for implementing your plan? Give a budget, including equipment, supplies, and labor-hours (divided into types of labor).
3. What records should be kept to measure the success of the program in terms of cost, quality performance, and service to the customer?

Source: Professor Marilyn S. Jones, Winthrop University.

Video Case 2

Quality at the Ritz-Carlton Hotel Company*

Ritz-Carlton. The name alone evokes images of luxury and quality. As the first hotel company to win the Malcolm Baldrige National Quality Award, the Ritz treats quality as if it is the heartbeat of the company. This means a daily commitment to meeting customer expectations and making sure that each hotel is free of any deficiency.

In the hotel industry, quality can be hard to quantify. Guests do not purchase a product when they stay at the Ritz: They buy an experience. Thus, creating the right combination of elements to make the experience stand out is the challenge and goal of every employee, from maintenance to management.

Before applying for the Baldrige Award, company management undertook a rigorous self-examination of its operations in an attempt to measure and quantify quality. Nineteen processes were studied, including room-service delivery, guest reservation and registration, message delivery, and breakfast service. This period of self-study included statistical measurement of process work flows and cycle times for areas ranging from room service delivery times and reservations to valet parking and housekeeping efficiency. The results were used to develop performance benchmarks against which future activity could be measured.

With specific, quantifiable targets in place, Ritz-Carlton managers and employees now focus on continuous improvement. The goal is 100% customer satisfaction: If a guest's experience does not meet expectations, the Ritz-Carlton risks losing that guest to competition.

One way the company has put more meaning behind its quality efforts is to organize its employees into "self-directed" work teams. Employee teams determine work scheduling, what work needs to be done, and what to do about quality problems in their own areas. In order that they can see the relationship of their specific area to the overall goals, employees are also given the opportunity to take additional training in hotel operations. Ritz-Carlton believes that a more educated and informed employee is in a better position to make decisions in the best interest of the organization.

Discussion Questions

1. In what ways could the Ritz-Carlton monitor its success in achieving quality?
2. Many companies say that their goal is to provide quality products or services. What actions might you expect from a company that intends quality to be more than a slogan or buzzword?
3. Why might it cost the Ritz-Carlton less to "do things right" the first time?
4. How could control charts, pareto diagrams, and cause-and-effect diagrams be used to identify quality problems at a hotel?
5. What are some nonfinancial measures of customer satisfaction that might be used by the Ritz-Carlton?

*Source: Adapted from C.T. Horngren, G. Foster, and S.M. Dator, *Cost Accounting*, 9th ed. (Upper Saddle River, NJ: Prentice Hall, 1997): 334.

■ Internet Case Study ■

See our Internet home page at http://www.prenhall.com/heizer for this additional case study: Falls Church General Hospital.

BIBLIOGRAPHY

Akao, Y., ed. *Quality Function Deployment: Integrating Customer Requirements into Product Design.* Cambridge, MA: Productivity Press, 1990.

Berry, L. L., A. Parasuraman, and V. A. Zeithaml. "Improving Service Quality in America: Lessons Learned." *The Academy of Management Executive* 8, no. 2 (May 1994): 32–52.

Black, Simon A., and Leslie J. Porter. "Identification of the Critical Factors of TQM." *Decision Sciences* 27, no. 1 (winter 1996): 1–17.

Carr, L. P. "Applying Cost of Quality to a Service Business." *Sloan Management Review* 33, no. 4 (summer 1992): 72.

Costin, H. *Readings in Total Quality Management.* New York: Dryden Press, 1994.

Crosby, P. B. *Let's Talk Quality.* New York: McGraw-Hill, 1989.

———. *Quality Is Free.* New York: McGraw-Hill, 1979.

Deming, W. E. *Out of the Crisis.* Cambridge, MA: Center for Advanced Engineering Study, 1986.

Denton, D. K. "Lessons on Competitiveness: Motorola's Approach." *Production and Inventory Management Journal* 32, no. 3 (third quarter 1991): 22.

Evans, J. R., and W. M. Lindsay. *The Management and Control of Quality,* 2nd ed. New York: West, 1993.

Feigenbaum, A. V. *Total Quality Control,* 3rd ed. New York: McGraw-Hill, 1991.

Foster, S. T., Jr. "Designing and Initiating a Taguchi Experiment in a Services Setting." *Operations Management Review* 9, no. 3 (September 1990): 37–50.

Hart, M. K. "Quality Tools for Decreasing Variation and Defining Process Capability." *Production and Inventory Management Journal* 33, no. 2 (second quarter 1992): 6.

Hauser, J. R. "How Puritan-Bennett Used the House of Quality." *Sloan Management Review* 34, no. 3 (spring 1993): 61–70.

Juran, J. M. "Made in the U.S.A.: A Renaissance in Quality." *Harvard Business Review* 14, no. 4 (July–August 1993): 35–38.

Miller, J. G. *Benchmarking.* Homewood, IL: Business One Irwin, 1992.

Paton, S. M. "Service Quality: Disney Style." *Quality Digest,* January 1997, pp. 24–29.

Peace, G. S. *Taguchi Methods: A Hands-On Approach.* Reading, MA: Addison-Wesley, 1993.

Price, F. *Right Every Time: Using the Deming Approach.* New York: Marcel Dekker, 1990.

Schonberger, R. J. "Is Strategy Strategic? Impact of Total Quality Management on Strategy." *The Executive* 6, no. 3 (August 1992): 80.

INTERNET RESOURCES

American Society for Quality:
    http://www.asq.org/
ISO Central Secretariat:
    http://www.iso.ch/welcome.html
Juran Institute:
    http://www.juran.com/
National Institute of Standards and Technology:
    http://www.quality.nist.gov/

Quality Digest:
    http://www. qualitydigest.com/
Quality Progress:
    http://www.qualityprogress.asqc.org/
Vilfredo Pareto and other economists:
    http://www.diogenes.Baylor.edu/

SUPPLEMENT 4

STATISTICAL PROCESS CONTROL

SUPPLEMENT OUTLINE

STATISTICAL PROCESS CONTROL (SPC)
  Control Charts for Variables
  The Central Limit Theorem
  Setting Mean Chart Limits ($\bar{x}$-Charts)
  Setting Range Chart Limits (*R*-Charts)
  Using Mean and Range Charts
  Control Charts for Attributes
  Process Capability
ACCEPTANCE SAMPLING
  Operating Characteristic Curve
  Average Outgoing Quality
SUMMARY
KEY TERMS
USING POM FOR WINDOWS
USING EXCEL OM FOR SPC
SOLVED PROBLEMS
DISCUSSION QUESTIONS
PROBLEMS
DATA BASE APPLICATION
CASE STUDIES: BAYFIELD MUD COMPANY; SPC AT THE *GAZETTE*
INTERNET CASE STUDY
BIBLIOGRAPHY
INTERNET RESOURCES

LEARNING OBJECTIVES

When you complete this supplement you should be able to:

Identify or Define:

  Natural causes of variations
  Assignable causes of variations
  Central limit theorem
  Attribute inspection
  Variable inspection
  Process control
  $\bar{x}$-charts
  R-charts
  LCL and UCL
  P-charts
  C charts
  C_{pk}
  Acceptance sampling
  OC curve
  AQL and LTPD
  AOQ
  Producer's risk
  Consumer's risk

Describe or Explain:

  The role of statistical quality control

107

BetzDearborn, Inc., headquartered in Trevose, Pennsylvania, is one of the world's largest water-testing laboratories, with operations in over 90 countries. The company uses statistical process control to monitor the quality of water, wastewater, and other chemicals for the petroleum, paper, auto, electric utility, food processing, and steel industries. In addition to process monitoring, BetzDearborn's quality assurance laboratory (shown here) uses statistical sampling techniques to conduct further product quality tests. Using this combination of constant monitoring and lab testing, BetzDearborn ensures consistent quality of discharge water and chemicals on aquatic life.

Statistical process control (SPC) A process used to monitor standards, making measurements and taking corrective action as a product or service is being produced.

In this supplement, we address statistical process control—the same techniques used at BetzDearborn, at IBM, at GE, and at Motorola to achieve quality standards. We also introduce acceptance sampling. **Statistical process control** is the application of statistical techniques to the control of processes. *Acceptance sampling* is used to determine acceptance or rejection of material evaluated by a sample.

STATISTICAL PROCESS CONTROL (SPC)

Statistical process control (SPC) is a statistical technique that is widely used to ensure that processes meet standards. All processes are subject to a certain degree of variability. While studying process data in the 1920s, Walter Shewhart of Bell Laboratories made the distinction between the common and special causes of variation. Many people now refer to these variations as *natural* and *assignable* causes. He developed a simple but powerful tool to separate the two—**the control chart.**

Control chart A graphic presentation of process data over time.

We use statistical process control to measure performance of a process. A process is said to be operating *in statistical control* when the only source of variation is common (natural) causes. The process must first be brought into statistical control by detecting and eliminating special (assignable) causes of variation.[1] Then its performance is predictable, and its ability to meet customer expectations can be assessed. The *objective* of a process control system is to *provide a statistical signal when assignable causes of variation are present*. Such a signal can quicken appropriate action to eliminate assignable causes.

Natural Variations Natural variations affect almost every production process and are to be expected. **Natural variations** are the many sources of variation that occur within a process that is in statistical control. Natural variations behave like a constant system of chance causes. Although individual values are all different, as a group they form a pattern that can be described as a *distribution*. When these distributions are *normal*, they are characterized by two parameters. These parameters are

- mean, μ (the measure of central tendency—in this case, the average value)
- standard deviation, σ (the measure of dispersion)

As long as the distribution (output measurements) remains within specified limits, the process is said to be "in control," and natural variations are tolerated.

Natural variations
Variabilities that affect almost every production process to some degree and are to be expected; also known as common causes.

Assignable Variations **Assignable variation** in a process can be traced to a specific reason. Factors such as machine wear, misadjusted equipment, fatigued or untrained workers, or new batches of raw material are all potential sources of assignable variations.

Natural and assignable variations distinguish two tasks for the operations manager. The first is to ensure that the process is capable of operating under control with only natural variation. The second is, of course, to identify and eliminate assignable variations so that the processes will remain under control.

Assignable variation
Variation in a production process that can be traced to specific causes.

Samples Because of natural and assignable variation, statistical process control uses averages of small samples (often of five items) as opposed to data on individual parts. Individual pieces tend to be too erratic to make trends quickly visible.

Figure S4.1 provides a detailed look at the important steps in determining process variation. The horizontal scale can be weight (as in the number of ounces in boxes of cereal) or length (as in fence posts) or any physical measure. The vertical scale is frequency. The samples of five boxes of cereal in Figure S4.1 (a) are weighed; (b) they form a distribution, (c) that can vary. The distributions formed in (b) and (c) will fall in a predictable pattern, (d) if only natural variation is present. If assignable causes of variation are present, then we can expect either the mean to vary or the dispersion to vary, as is the case in (e).

Control Charts The process of building control charts is based on the concepts presented in Figure S4.2. This figure shows three distributions that are the result of outputs from three types of processes. We plot small samples and then examine characteristics of the resulting data to see if the process is within "control limits." The purpose of control charts is to help distinguish between natural variations and variations due to assignable causes. As seen in Figure S4.2, a process is (a) in control *and the process is capable of producing within established control limits*, (b) in control *but the process is not capable*

---

[1] Removing assignable causes is work. As quality guru W. Edwards Deming observed, "A state of statistical control is not a natural state for a manufacturing process. It is instead an achievement, arrived at by elimination, one by one, by determined effort, of special causes of excessive variation." See W. Edwards Deming, "On Some Statistical Aids Toward Economic Production," *Interfaces* 5, no. 4 (1975): 5.

(a) Samples of the product, say five boxes of cereal taken off the filling machine line, vary from each other in weight.

each of these represents one sample of five boxes of cereal

(b) After enough samples are taken from a stable process, they form a pattern called a distribution.

the solid line represents the distribution

(c) There are many types of distributions, including the normal (bell-shaped) distribution, but distributions do differ in terms of central tendency (mean), standard deviation or variance, and shape.

Measure of central tendency (mean)   Variation (Std. deviation)   Shape

(d) If only natural causes of variation are present, the output of a process forms a distribution that is stable over time and is predictable.

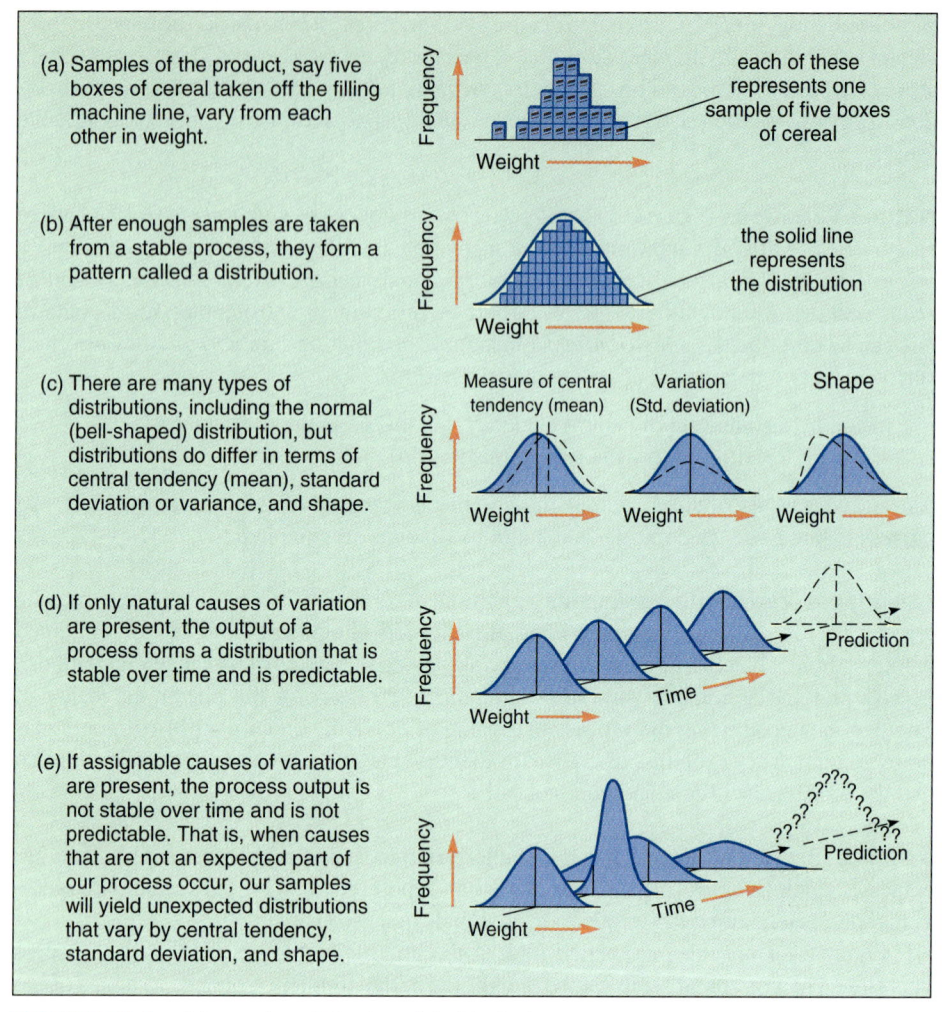

Prediction

(e) If assignable causes of variation are present, the process output is not stable over time and is not predictable. That is, when causes that are not an expected part of our process occur, our samples will yield unexpected distributions that vary by central tendency, standard deviation, and shape.

??? Prediction

FIGURE S4.1 ■ **Natural and Assignable Variation**

of producing within established limits, or (c) out of control. We now look at ways to build control charts that help the operations manager keep a process under control.

$\bar{x}$-chart A quality control chart for variables that indicates when changes occur in the central tendency of a production process.

R-chart A control chart that tracks the "range" within a sample; indicates that a gain or loss in uniformity has occurred in a production process.

Control Charts for Variables

Variables are characteristics that have continuous dimensions. They have an infinite number of possibilities. Examples are weight, speed, length, or strength. Control charts for the mean, $\bar{x}$, and the range, R, are used to monitor processes that have continuous dimensions. The $\bar{x}$- (x-bar) **chart** tells us whether changes have occurred in the central tendency (the mean, in this case) of a process. These changes might be due to such factors as tool wear, a gradual increase in temperature, a different method used on the second shift, or new and stronger materials. The **R-chart** values indicate that a gain or loss in dispersion has occurred. Such a change might be due to worn bearings, a loose tool, an erratic flow of lubricants to a machine, or to sloppiness on the part of a machine operator. The two types of charts go hand in hand when monitoring variables, because they measure the two critical parameters, central tendency and dispersion.

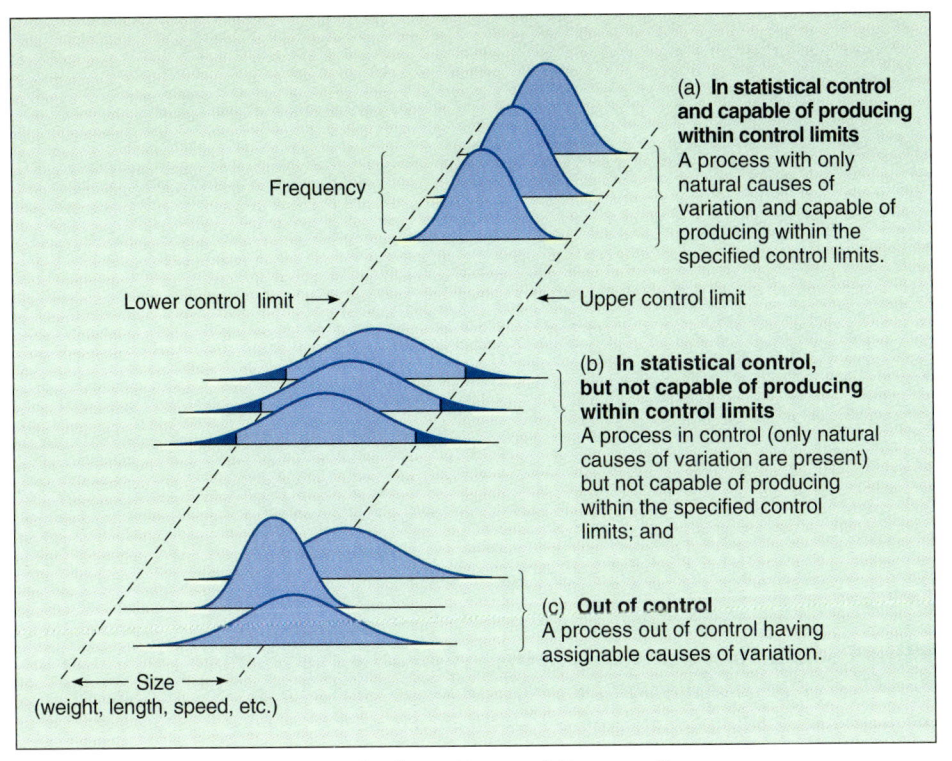

FIGURE S4.2 ■ Process Control: Three Types of Process Outputs

(a) **In statistical control and capable of producing within control limits**
A process with only natural causes of variation and capable of producing within the specified control limits.

(b) **In statistical control, but not capable of producing within control limits**
A process in control (only natural causes of variation are present) but not capable of producing within the specified control limits; and

(c) **Out of control**
A process out of control having assignable causes of variation.

The Central Limit Theorem

The theoretical foundation for $\bar{x}$-charts is the **central limit theorem**. In general terms, this theorem states that regardless of the distribution of the population of all parts or services, the distribution of $\bar{x}$'s (each of which is a mean of a sample drawn from the population) will tend to follow a normal curve as the sample size grows larger. Fortunately, even if the sample (n) is fairly small (say, 4 or 5), the distributions of the averages will still roughly follow a normal curve. The theorem also states that: (1) the mean of the distribution of the $\bar{x}$'s (called $\bar{\bar{x}}$) will equal the mean of the overall population (called μ); and (2) the standard deviation of the *sampling distribution*, $\sigma_{\bar{x}}$, will be the *population standard deviation*, σ, divided by the square root of the sample size, n.[2] In other words,

$$\bar{\bar{x}} = \mu \tag{S4.1}$$

and

$$\sigma_{\bar{x}} = \frac{\sigma}{\sqrt{n}} \tag{S4.2}$$

Figure S4.3 shows three possible population distributions, each with its own mean, μ, and standard deviation σ. If a series of random samples ($\bar{x}_1, \bar{x}_2, \bar{x}_3, \bar{x}_4$, and so on), each of size n, is drawn from any population distribution (which could be normal, beta, uniform, and so on), the resulting distribution of $\bar{x}_i$'s will appear as they do in the graph.

Central limit theorem
The theoretical foundation for $\bar{x}$-charts that states that regardless of the distribution of the population of all parts or services, the distribution of $\bar{x}$'s will tend to follow a normal curve as the sample size grows large.

The two parameters are:
Mean → measure of central tendency.
Range → measure of dispersion.

[2] *Note:* The standard deviation is easily calculated as: $\sigma = \sqrt{\dfrac{\sum_{i=1}^{n}(x_i - \bar{x})^2}{n-1}}$

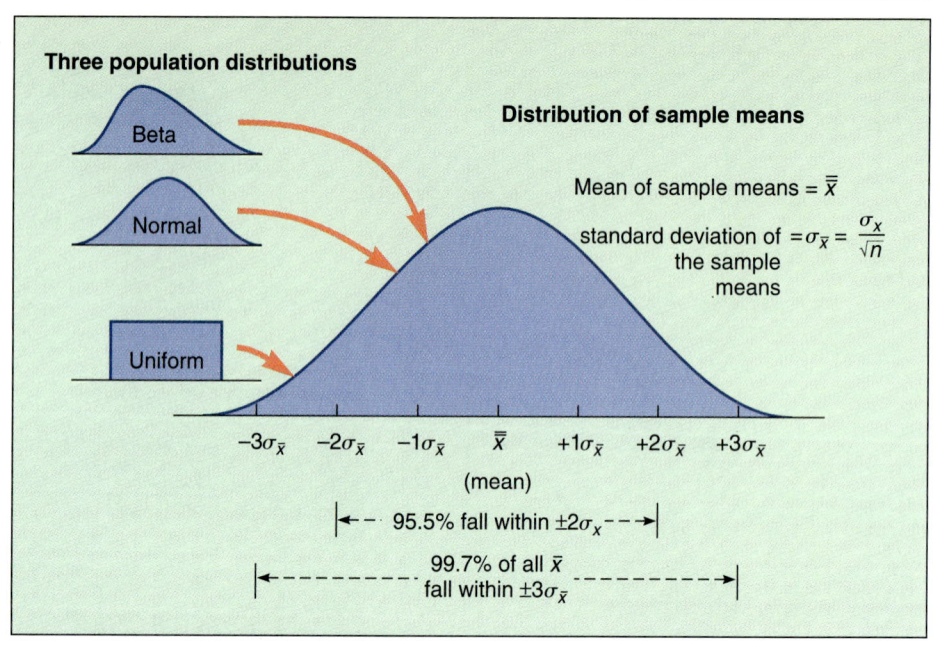

FIGURE S4.3 ■ **The Relationship between Population and Sampling Distributions.**
Regardless of the population distribution (e.g., normal, beta, uniform), each with its own mean (μ) and standard deviation (σ), the distribution of sample means is normal.

Moreover, the sampling distribution, as is shown in Figure S4.4, will have less variability than the process distribution. Because the sampling distribution is normal, we can state that:

- 95.5% of the time, the sample averages will fall within $\pm 2\sigma_{\bar{x}}$ if the process has only natural variations.
- 99.7% of the time, the sample averages will fall within $\pm 3\sigma_{\bar{x}}$ if the process has only natural variations.

If a point on the control chart falls outside of the $\pm 3\sigma_{\bar{x}}$ control limits, then we are 99.7% sure the process has changed. This is the theory behind control charts.

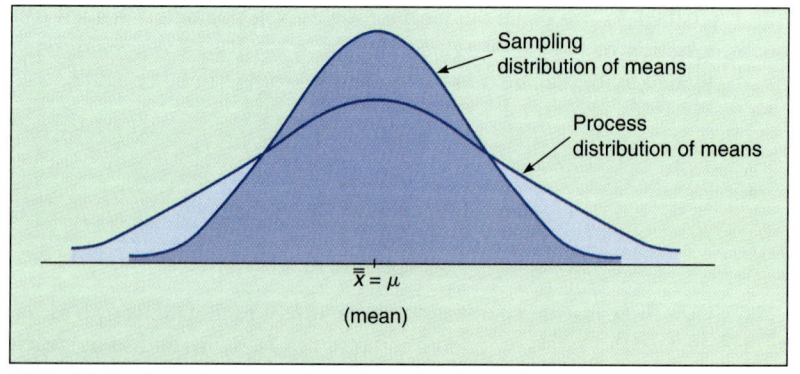

FIGURE S4.4 ■ **The Sampling Distribution of Means Is Normal and Has Less Variability Than the Process Distribution.**
In this figure, the process distribution from which the sample was drawn was also normal, but it could have been any distribution.

Setting Mean Chart Limits ($\bar{x}$-Charts)

If we know, through past data, the standard deviation of the process population, σ, we can set upper and lower control limits by these formulas:

$$\text{Upper control limit (UCL)} = \bar{\bar{x}} + z\sigma_{\bar{x}} \quad \text{(S4.3)}$$

$$\text{Lower control limit (LCL)} = \bar{\bar{x}} - z\sigma_{\bar{x}} \quad \text{(S4.4)}$$

where $\bar{\bar{x}}$ = mean of the sample means or a target value set for the process
z = number of normal standard deviations (2 for 95.5% confidence, 3 for 99.7%)
$\sigma_{\bar{x}}$ = standard deviation of the sample means = $\sigma/\sqrt{n}$
σ = population (process) standard deviation
n = sample size

"All quality control does is find our mistakes. I want to start avoiding them."

Example S1 shows how to set control limits for sample means using standard deviations.

EXAMPLE S1

The weights of boxes of Oat Flakes within a large production lot are sampled each hour. To set control limits that include 99.7% of the sample means, samples of nine boxes are randomly selected and weighed. The *population* standard deviation (σ) is known to be 1 ounce. Here are the results for the past 12 hours:

Hour	Weight of Sample (Avg. of 9 Boxes)	Hour	Weight of Sample (Avg. of 9 Boxes)	Hour	Weight of Sample (Avg. of 9 Boxes)
1	16.1	5	16.5	9	16.3
2	16.8	6	16.4	10	14.8
3	15.5	7	15.2	11	14.2
4	16.5	8	16.4	12	17.3

The average mean of the 12 samples is calculated to be exactly 16 ounces. We therefore have $\bar{\bar{x}} = 16$ ounces, $\sigma = 1$ ounce, $n = 9$, and $z = 3$. The control limits are:

$$\text{UCL}_{\bar{x}} = \bar{\bar{x}} + z\sigma_{\bar{x}} = 16 + 3\left(\frac{1}{\sqrt{9}}\right) = 16 + 3\left(\frac{1}{3}\right) = 17 \text{ ounces}$$

$$\text{LCL}_{\bar{x}} = \bar{\bar{x}} - z\sigma_{\bar{x}} = 16 - 3\left(\frac{1}{\sqrt{9}}\right) = 16 - 3\left(\frac{1}{3}\right) = 15 \text{ ounces}$$

The 12 samples are then plotted on the control chart shown below. Because the means of several recent sample averages fall outside the upper and lower control limits of 17 and 15, we can conclude that the process is becoming erratic and *not* in control.

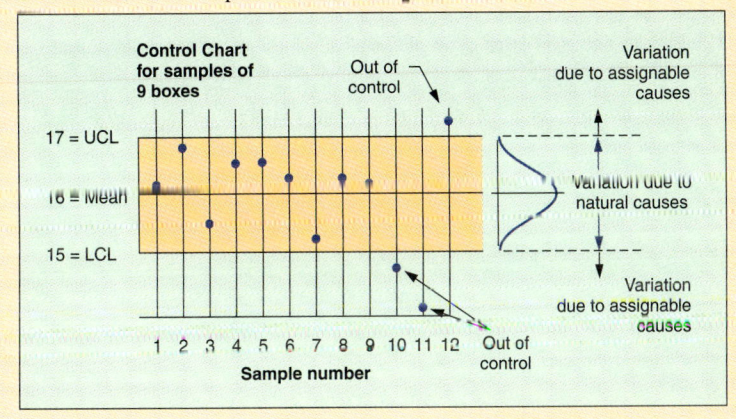

Because process standard deviations are either not available or difficult to compute, we usually calculate control limits based on the average *range* values rather than on standard deviations. Table S4.1 provides the necessary conversion for us to do so. The *range* is defined as the difference between the largest and smallest items in one sample. For example, if the heaviest box of Oat Flakes in hour 1 of Example S1 was 19 ounces and the lightest was 14 ounces, the range for that hour would be 5 ounces. We use Table S4.1 and the equations

$$\text{UCL}_{\bar{x}} = \bar{\bar{x}} + A_2 \bar{R} \tag{S4.5}$$

and

$$\text{LCL}_{\bar{x}} = \bar{\bar{x}} - A_2 \bar{R} \tag{S4.6}$$

where $\bar{R}$ = average range of the samples
A_2 = value found in Table S4.1
$\bar{\bar{x}}$ = mean of the sample means

Table S4.1 ■ Factors for Computing Control Chart Limits

Sample Size, n	Mean Factor, A_2	Upper Range, D_4	Lower Range, D_3
2	1.880	3.268	0
3	1.023	2.574	0
4	.729	2.282	0
5	.577	2.115	0
6	.483	2.004	0
7	.419	1.924	0.076
8	.373	1.864	0.136
9	.337	1.816	0.184
10	.308	1.777	0.223

Source: Reprinted by permission of American Society for Testing Materials. Copyright 1951. Taken from Special Technical Publication 15-C, "Quality Control of Materials," pp. 63 and 72.

Example S2 shows how to set control limits for sample means using Table S4.1 and the average range.

EXAMPLE S2

Super Cola bottles soft drinks labeled "net weight 16 ounces." An overall process average of 16.01 ounces has been found by taking several batches of samples, in which each sample contained 5 bottles. The average range of the process is .25 ounce. Determine the upper and lower control limits for averages in this process.

Looking in Table S4.1 for a sample size of 5 in the mean factor A_2 column, we find the number .577. Thus, the upper and lower control chart limits are

$$\text{UCL}_{\bar{x}} = \bar{\bar{x}} + A_2 \bar{R}$$
$$= 16.01 + (.577)(.25)$$
$$= 16.01 + .144$$
$$= 16.154 \text{ ounces}$$

$$\text{LCL}_{\bar{x}} = \bar{\bar{x}} - A_2 \bar{R}$$
$$= 16.01 - .144$$
$$= 15.866 \text{ ounces}$$

Setting Range Chart Limits (*R*-Charts)

In Examples S1 and S2, we determined the upper and lower control limits for the process *average*. In addition to being concerned with the process average, operations managers are interested in the process *dispersion,* or *range*. Even though the process average is under control, the dispersion of the process may not be. For example, something may have worked itself loose in a piece of equipment that fills boxes of Oat Flakes. As a result, the average of the samples may remain the same, but the variation within the samples could be entirely too large. For this reason, operations managers use control charts for ranges in order to monitor the process variability, as well as control charts for the process average, which monitor the process average. The theory behind the control charts for ranges is the same as that for process average control charts. Limits are established that contain ±3 standard deviations of the distribution for the average range $\bar{R}$. We can use the following equation to set the upper and lower control limits for ranges:

$$\text{UCL}_R = D_4 \bar{R} \qquad (S4.7)$$

$$\text{LCL}_R = D_3 \bar{R} \qquad (S4.8)$$

where UCL_R = upper control chart limit for the range
LCL_R = lower control chart limit for the range
D_4 and D_3 = values from Table S4.1

Example S3 shows how to set control limits for sample ranges using Table S4.1 and the average range.

EXAMPLE S3

The average *range* of a process for loading trucks is 5.3 pounds. If the sample size is 5, determine the upper and lower control chart limits.

Looking in Table S4.1 for a sample size of 5, we find that $D_4 = 2.115$ and $D_3 = 0$. The range control limits are

$$\text{UCL}_R = D_4 \bar{R}$$

$$= (2.115)(5.3 \text{ pounds})$$

$$= 11.2 \text{ pounds}$$

$$\text{LCL}_R = D_3 \bar{R}$$

$$= (0)(5.3 \text{ pounds})$$

$$= 0$$

Using Mean and Range Charts

We can define the normal distribution with two parameters, the *mean* and *standard deviation*. The $\bar{x}$ (mean)-chart and the *R*-chart mimic these two parameters. The $\bar{x}$ chart is sensitive to shifts in the process mean, whereas the *R*-chart is sensitive to shifts in the process standard deviation. Consequently, by using both charts we can track changes in the process distribution.

For instance, the samples and the resulting $\bar{x}$-chart in Figure S4.5(a) show the shift in the process mean, but because the dispersion is constant, no change is detected by the R-chart. Conversely, the samples and the $\bar{x}$-chart in Figure S4.5(b) detect no shift (because none is present), but the R-chart does detect the shift in the dispersion. Both charts are required to track the process accurately.

Steps to Follow When Using Control Charts There are five steps that are generally followed in using $\bar{x}$- and R-charts:

1. Collect 20 to 25 samples of $n = 4$ or $n = 5$ each from a stable process and compute the mean and range of each.
2. Compute the overall means ($\bar{\bar{x}}$ and $\bar{R}$), set appropriate control limits, usually at the 99.7% level, and calculate the preliminary upper and lower control limits. *If the process is not currently stable,* use the desired mean, μ, instead of $\bar{\bar{x}}$ to calculate limits.

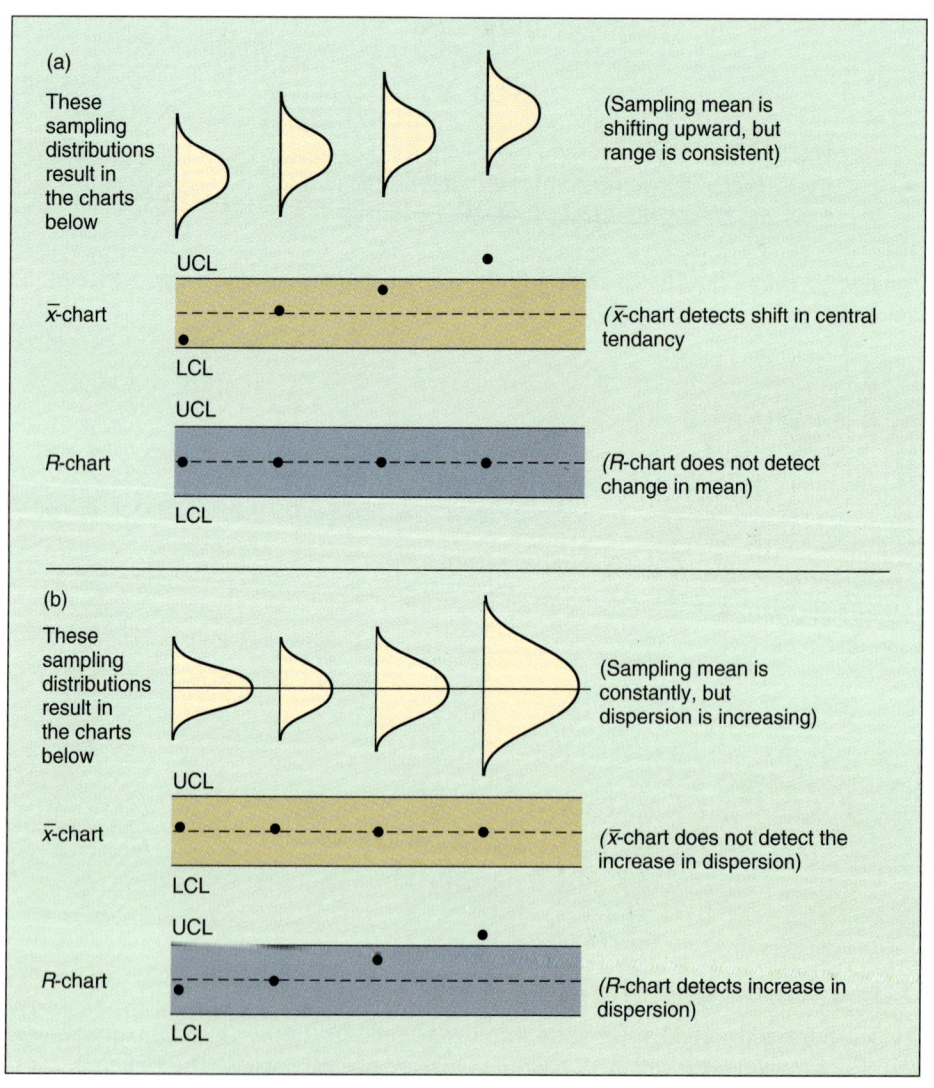

FIGURE S4.5 ■ **Mean and Range Charts Complement Each Other by Showing the Mean and Dispersion of the Normal Distribution**

OM IN ACTION

GREEN IS THE COLOR OF MONEY FOR DUPONT AND THE ENVIRONMENT

DuPont has found that statistical process control (SPC) is an excellent approach to solving environmental problems. With a goal of slashing manufacturing waste and hazardous waste disposals by 35%, DuPont brought together information from its quality control systems and its material management data bases.

Cause-and-effect diagrams and Pareto charts revealed where major problems occurred. Then the company began reducing waste materials through improved SPC standards for production. Tying together shop-floor information-based monitoring systems with air-quality standards, DuPont identified ways to reduce emissions. Using a vendor evaluation system linked to JIT purchasing requirements, the company initiated controls over incoming hazardous materials.

DuPont now saves more than 15 million pounds of plastics annually by recycling them into products rather than dumping them into landfills. Through electronic purchasing, the firm has reduced wastepaper to a trickle, and by using new packaging designs, it has cut in-process material wastes by nearly 40%.

By integrating SPC with environmental-compliance activities, DuPont has made major quality improvements that far exceed regulatory guidelines. DuPont's innovations in solving environmental problems have, at the same time, realized huge cost savings.

Sources: Automotive Industries, June 1996, p. 93; Business Week/Quality, October 25, 1991, pp. 44–46, 49; and E. E. Dwinells and J. P. Sheffer, APICS—The Performance Advantage, March 1992, pp. 30–31.

---

3. Graph the sample means and ranges on their respective control charts and determine whether they fall outside the acceptable limits.
4. Investigate points or patterns that indicate the process is out of control. Try to assign causes for the variation and then resume the process.
5. Collect additional samples and, if necessary, revalidate the control limits using the new data.

Applications of control charts appear in examples in this supplement, as well as in the *OM in Action* box, "Green Is the Color of Money for DuPont and the Environment."

Control Charts for Attributes

Control charts for $\bar{x}$ and R do not apply when we are sampling *attributes*, which are typically classified as *defective* or *nondefective*. Measuring defectives involves counting them (for example, number of bad lightbulbs in a given lot or number of letters or data entry

Acceptable tolerance levels on auto body parts at this New United Motor Manufacturing (NUMMI) plant in Fremont, California, are so small that the company uses computers to see whether the process is in or out of control. Workers at NUMMI (which makes the Toyota Corolla and GM Prizm) are empowered to stop the entire production line by pulling the overhead cord if any quality problems are spotted.

Harley-Davidson, like other world-class firms, makes extensive use of statistical process control (SPC). At the work cell shown here, an employee measures the dimensions of a part and posts the data on the control chart.

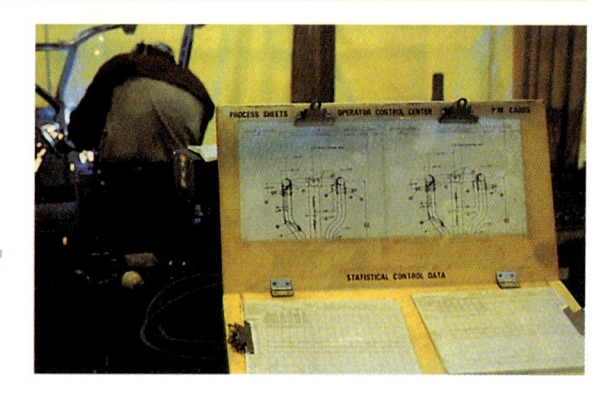

records typed with errors), whereas *variables* are usually measured for length or weight. There are two kinds of attribute control charts: (1) those that measure the *percent* defective in a sample—called *p*-charts—and (2) those that count the *number* of defects—called *c*-charts.

P-charts A quality control chart that is used to control attributes.

P-Charts Using **P-charts** is the chief way to control attributes. Although attributes that are either good or bad follow the binomial distribution, the normal distribution can be used to calculate *p*-chart limits when sample sizes are large. The procedure resembles the $\bar{x}$-chart approach, which was also based on the central limit theorem.

The formulas for *p*-chart upper and lower control limits follow:

$$\text{UCL}_p = \bar{p} + z\sigma_{\hat{p}} \tag{S4.9}$$

$$\text{LCL}_p = \bar{p} - z\sigma_{\hat{p}} \tag{S4.10}$$

where $\bar{p}$ = mean fraction defective in the sample
z = number of standard deviations ($z = 2$ for 95.5% limits; $z = 3$ for 99.7% limits)
$\sigma_{\hat{p}}$ = standard deviation of the sampling distribution

$\sigma_{\hat{p}}$ is estimated by the formula:

$$\sigma_{\hat{p}} = \sqrt{\frac{\bar{p}(1-\bar{p})}{n}} \tag{S4.11}$$

where n = size of each sample.

Example S4 shows how to set control limits for *p*-charts for these standard deviations.

EXAMPLE S4

Data-entry clerks at ARCO key in thousands of insurance records each day. Samples of the work of 20 clerks are shown in the table. One hundred records entered by each clerk were carefully examined and the number of errors counted. The fraction defective in each sample was then computed.

Set the control limits to include 99.7% of the random variation in the entry process when it is in control.

Statistical Process Control (SPC)

Sample Number	Number of Errors	Fraction Defective	Sample Number	Number of Errors	Fraction Defective
1	6	.06	11	6	.06
2	5	.05	12	1	.01
3	0	.00	13	8	.08
4	1	.01	14	7	.07
5	4	.04	15	5	.05
6	2	.02	16	4	.04
7	5	.05	17	11	.11
8	3	.03	18	3	.03
9	3	.03	19	0	.00
10	2	.02	20	4	.04
				80	

$$\bar{p} = \frac{\text{total number of errors}}{\text{total number of records examined}} = \frac{80}{(100)(20)} = .04$$

$$\sigma_{\hat{p}} = \sqrt{\frac{(.04)(1-.04)}{100}} = .02$$

(*Note:* 100 is the size of each sample = n)

$$\text{UCL}_p = \bar{p} + z\sigma_{\hat{p}} = .04 + 3(.02) = .10$$

$$\text{LCL}_p = \bar{p} - z\sigma_{\hat{p}} = .04 - 3(.02) = 0$$

(because we cannot have a negative percent defective)

When we plot the control limits and the sample fraction defectives below, we find that only one data-entry clerk (number 17) is out of control. The firm may wish to examine that individual's work a bit more closely to see if a serious problem exists (see Figure S4.6).

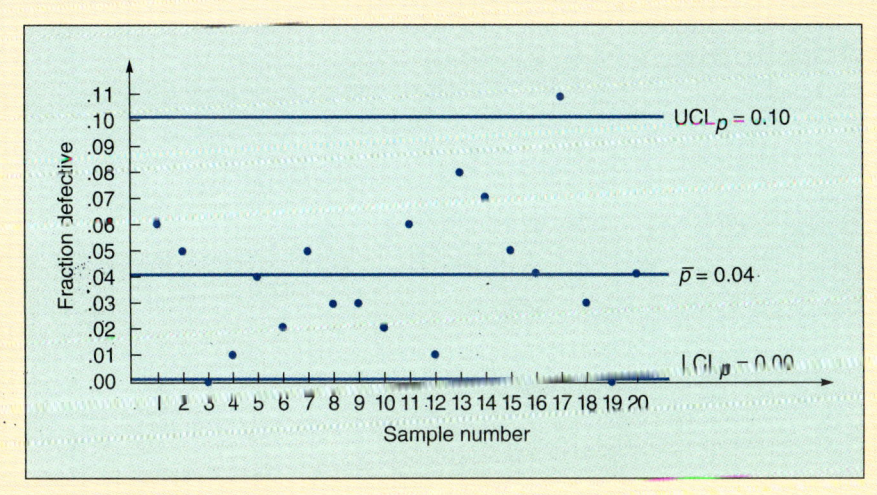

FIGURE S4.6 ■ *p*-Chart for Data Entry for Example S4

Space-age robotics and computerized analytical equipment are used by Waste Management Corp. to protect groundwater. Waste Management processing and disposal centers analyze up to 60,000 samples annually in the company's attempt to assure the highest standards of environmental quality.

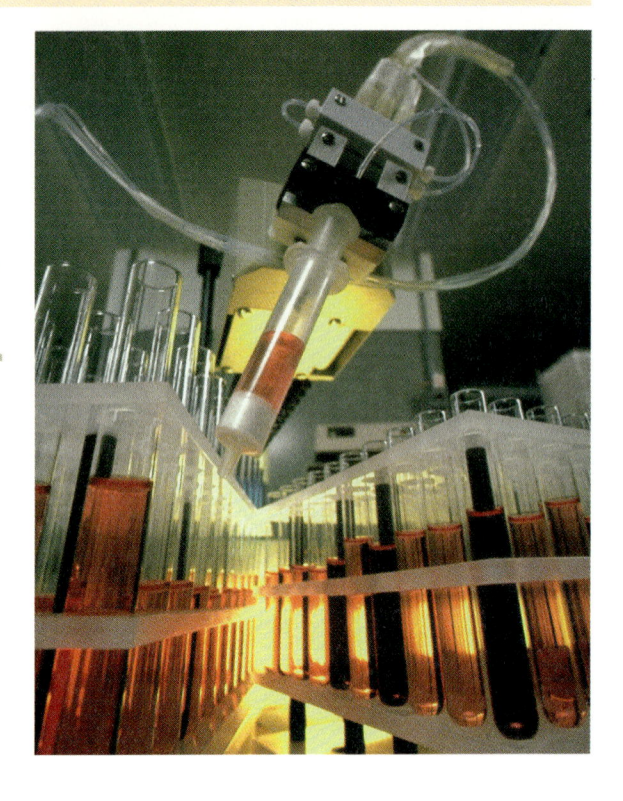

C-Charts In Example S4, we counted the number of defective records entered. A defective record was one that was not exactly correct because it contained at least one defect. However, a bad record may contain more than one defect. We use **c-charts** to control the *number* of defects per unit of output (or per insurance record in the preceding case).

Control charts for defects are helpful for monitoring processes in which a large number of potential errors can occur but the actual number that do occur is relatively small. Defects may be errors in newspaper words, bad circuits in a microchip, blemishes on a table, or missing pickles on a fast-food hamburger.

The Poisson probability distribution,[3] which has a variance equal to its mean, is the basis for *c*-charts. Because *c* is the mean number of defects per unit, the standard deviation is equal to $\sqrt{c}$. To compute 99.7% control limits for $\bar{c}$, we use the formula

$$\bar{c} \pm 3\sqrt{\bar{c}} \qquad \text{(S4.12)}$$

C-charts *A quality control chart used to control the number of defects per unit of output.*

Example S5 shows how to set control limits for a $\bar{c}$-chart.

EXAMPLE S5

Red Top Cab Company receives several complaints per day about the behavior of its drivers. Over a 9 day period (where days are the units of measure), the owner received the following numbers of calls from irate passengers: 3, 0, 8, 9, 6, 7, 4, 9, 8, for a total of 54 complaints.

---

[3] A Poisson probability distribution is a discrete distribution commonly used when the items of interest (in this case, defects) are infrequent and/or occur in time and space.

To compute 99.7% control limits, we take

$$\bar{c} = \frac{54}{9} = 6 \text{ complaints per day}$$

Thus,

$$UCL_c = \bar{c} + 3\sqrt{\bar{c}} = 6 + 3\sqrt{6} = 6 + 3(2.45) = 13.35$$

$$LCL_c = \bar{c} - 3\sqrt{\bar{c}} = 6 - 3\sqrt{6} = 6 - 3(2.45) = 0$$

After the owner plotted a control chart summarizing these data and posted it prominently in the drivers' locker room, the number of calls received dropped to an average of three per day. Can you explain why this occurred?

Note that although we have discussed process charts and control limits, focusing on the target value, not the limits, is best. An example of the advantage of such a focus is provided in the *OM in Action* box, "Robust Quality at Mazda."

Process Capability

Statistical process control means we want to keep the process in control. This means that the natural variation of the process must be small (narrow) enough to produce products that meet the standards (quality) required. The most popular way of expressing this process capability is a C_{pk} index. C_{pk} measures the difference between desired and actual dimensions of products made on the process.

Two assumptions are appropriate for measures of C_{pk}. The process should be (1) under control (the only variation is the process's natural variation) and (2) normally distributed.

C_{pk} A proportion of natural variation (3σ) between the center of the process and the nearest specification limit.

OM IN ACTION

ROBUST QUALITY AT MAZDA

Ford Motor Company, which now controls the Japanese-based Mazda Company, asked Mazda to build transmissions for one of Ford's models sold in the United States. Although the transmissions built by Mazda were identical in specification to those built by Ford, the Ford transmissions produced higher rates of malfunction and customer complaints. Consequently, Ford incurred increased levels of warranty costs.

Wanting to correct the situation, Ford investigated by comparing samples of transmissions from both companies. Ford found that although its own transmissions fell within a preset range of acceptability on a zero-defect standard, the Mazda samples were more exact, with little, if any, variation from the engineering specification. In some Ford transmissions, many components fell near the *outer limits* of tolerance from the target. When randomly assembled together, a series of deviations tended to "stack up." Otherwise trivial variations in one part compounded variations in others. Because of deviations, parts interacted with greater friction than they could withstand individually or with greater vibration than customers were prepared to endure.

Further investigation also indicated that creative management played a part in Mazda's more reliable transmissions. Instead of focusing on a range of acceptability, Mazda management aimed at manufacturing products that consistently met target values. Mazda became the first Japanese automaker to receive ISO 9002 certification.

Sources: Automotive Industries, June, 1996, p. 25; and *Harvard Business Review* (January–February 1990): 65–75.

FIGURE S4.7 ■ Meanings of C_pk Measures

A C_{pk} index of 1.0 indicates that the process variation is centered within the upper and lower control limits. As the C_{pk} index goes above 1, the process becomes more and more target-oriented with fewer defects. If the C_{pk} is less than 1.0, the process will not produce within the specified tolerance.

Source: Adapted from Jim Pearson, "NYPRO People Deliver Effective Process Control with Seasoned C_{pk} Measures," *Target,* spring 1991, p. 51.

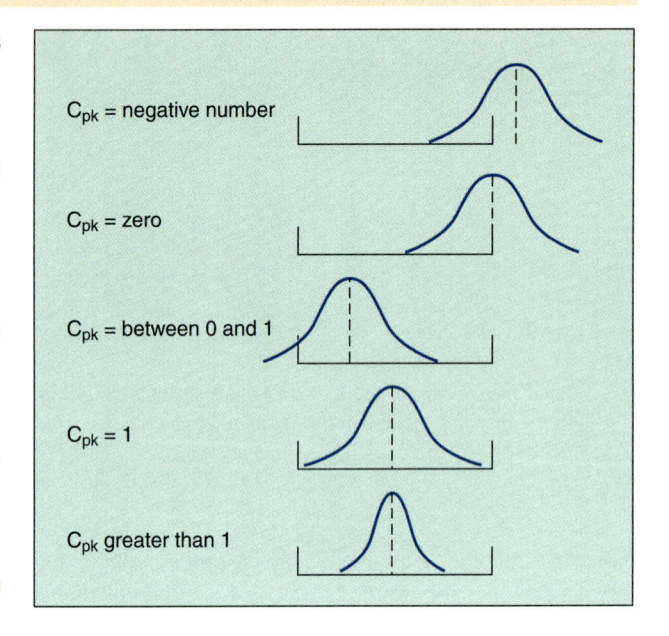

C_{pk} = negative number

C_{pk} = zero

C_{pk} = between 0 and 1

C_{pk} = 1

C_{pk} greater than 1

The formula for C_{pk} is:

$$C_{pk} = \text{minimum of} \left[\frac{\text{Upper Specification Limit} - \bar{X}}{3\sigma}, \frac{\bar{X} - \text{Lower Specification Limit}}{3\sigma} \right] \quad (S4.13)$$

where $\bar{X}$ = process mean
σ = standard deviation of the process population

When the C_{pk} index equals 1.0, the process variation is centered within the upper and lower specification limits and the process is capable of producing within ±3 standard deviations (fewer than 2,700 defects per million). A C_{pk} of 2.0 means the process is capable of producing fewer than 3.4 defects per million. Figure S4.7 shows the meaning of various measures of C_{pk}, and Example S6 shows an application of C_{pk}.

EXAMPLE S6

You are the process improvement manager and have developed a new machine to cut insoles for the company's top-of-the-line running shoes. You are excited because the company's goal is no more than 3.4 defects per million and this machine may be the innovation you need. The insoles cannot be more than ±.001 of an inch from the required thickness of .250″. You want to know if you should replace the existing machine, which has a C_{pk} of 1.0. You decide to determine the C_{pk} for the new machine and make a decision on that basis.

Upper Specification Limit = .251″

Lower Specification Limit = .249″

Mean of the new process = $\bar{X}$ = .250″
Estimated standard deviation of the new process = σ = .0005″

> $$C_{pk} = \text{minimum of } \left[\frac{\text{Upper Specification Limit} - \bar{X}}{3\sigma}, \frac{\bar{X} - \text{Lower Specification Limit}}{3\sigma} \right]$$
>
> $$C_{pk} = \text{minimum of } \left[\frac{(.251) - .250}{(3).0005}, \frac{.250 - (.249)}{(3).0005} \right]$$
>
> Both calculations result in: $\frac{.001}{.0015} = 0.67$
>
> Because the new machine has a C_{pk} of only 0.67, the new machine should *not* replace the existing machine.

If the mean of the process is not centered on the desired (specified) mean, then the smaller numerator in Equation (S4.13) is used (the minimum of the difference between the Upper Specification Limit and the mean or the Lower Specification Limit and the mean). This application of C_{pk} is shown in Solved Problem S4.4.

ACCEPTANCE SAMPLING

Acceptance sampling is a form of testing that involves taking random samples of "lots" or batches of finished products and measuring them against predetermined standards. Sampling is more economical than 100% inspection. The quality of the sample is used to judge the quality of all items in the lot. Although both attributes and variables can be inspected by acceptance sampling, attribute inspection is more commonly used, as illustrated in this section.

Acceptance sampling can be applied either when materials arrive at a plant or at final inspection, but it is usually used to control incoming lots of purchased products. A lot of items rejected, based on an unacceptable level of defects found in the sample, can (1) be returned to the supplier or (2) be 100% inspected to cull out all defects, with the cost of this screening usually billed to the supplier. However, acceptance sampling is not a substitute for adequate process controls. In fact, the current approach is to build statistical quality controls at the supplier level so that acceptance sampling can be eliminated.

Operating Characteristic Curve

The **operating characteristic (OC) curve** describes how well an acceptance plan discriminates between good and bad lots. A curve pertains to a specific plan—that is, to a combination of *n* (sample size) and *c* (acceptance level). It is intended to show the probability that the plan will accept lots of various quality levels.

In acceptance sampling, two parties are usually involved: the producer of the product and the consumer of the product. In specifying a sampling plan, each party wants to avoid costly mistakes in accepting or rejecting a lot. The producer usually has the responsibility of replacing all defects in the rejected lot or of paying for a new lot to be shipped to the customer. The producer, therefore, wants to avoid the mistake of having a good lot rejected (**producer's risk**). On the other hand, the customer or consumer wants to avoid the mistake of accepting a bad lot because defects found in a lot that has already been accepted are usually the responsibility of the customer (**consumer's risk**). The OC curve

Acceptance sampling A method of measuring random samples of lots or batches of products against predetermined standards.

Operating characteristic (OC) curve A graph that describes how well an acceptance plan discriminates between good and bad lots.

Producer's risk The mistake of having a producer's good lot rejected through sampling.

Consumer's risk The mistake of a customer's acceptance of a bad lot overlooked through sampling.

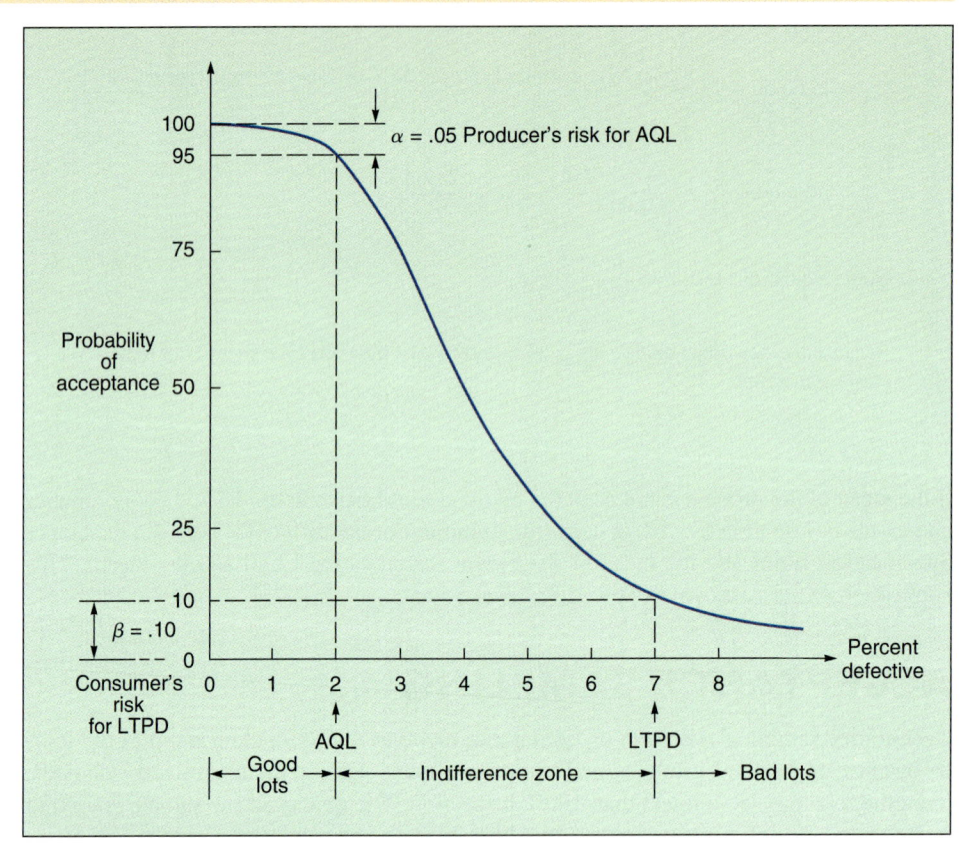

FIGURE S4.8 ■ **An Operating Characteristic (OC) Curve Showing Producer's and Consumer's Risks**

A good lot for this particular acceptance plan has less than or equal to 2% defectives. A bad lot has 7% or more defectives.

shows the features of a particular sampling plan, including the risks of making a wrong decision.[4]

Figure S4.8 can be used to illustrate one sampling plan in more detail. Four concepts are illustrated in this figure.

The **acceptable quality level (AQL)** is the poorest level of quality that we are willing to accept. In other words, we wish to accept lots that have this or better level of quality, but no lower. If an acceptable quality level is 20 defects in a lot of 1,000 items or parts, then AQL is 20/1,000 = 2% defectives.

The **lot tolerance percent defective (LTPD)** is the quality level of a lot that we consider bad. We wish to reject lots that have this or poorer level of quality. If it is agreed that an unacceptable quality level is 70 defects in a lot of 1,000, then the LTPD is 70/1,000 = 7% defective.

Acceptable quality level (AQL) The quality level of a lot considered good.

Lot tolerance percent defective (LTPD) The quality level of a lot considered bad.

---

[4] Note that sampling always runs the danger of leading to an erroneous conclusion. Let us say in this example that the total population under scrutiny is a load of 1,000 computer chips, of which in reality only 30 (or 3%) are defective. This means that we would want to accept the shipment of chips, because 4% is the allowable defect rate. However, if a random sample of $n = 50$ chips were drawn, we could conceivably end up with 0 defects and accept that shipment (that is, it is OK), or we could find all 30 defects in the sample. If the latter happened, we could wrongly conclude that the whole population was 60% defective and reject them all.

To derive a sampling plan, producer and consumer must define not only "good lots" and "bad lots" through the AQL and LTPD, but they must also specify risk levels.

Producer's risk (α) is the probability that a "good" lot will be rejected. This is the risk that a random sample might result in a much higher proportion of defects than the population of all items. A lot with an acceptable quality level of AQL still has an α chance of being rejected. Sampling plans are often designed to have the producer's risk set at $\alpha = .05$, or 5%.

Consumer's risk (β) is the probability that a "bad" lot will be accepted. This is the risk that a random sample might result in a lower proportion of defects than the overall population of items. A common value for consumer's risk in sampling plans is $\beta = .10$, or 10%.

The probability of rejecting a good lot is called a **type I error**. The probability of a bad lot being accepted is a **type II error**.

Sampling plans and OC curves may be developed by computer (as seen in the software available with this text), by published tables such as the U.S. Military Standard MIL-STD-105 or Dodge-Romig table, or by calculation, using binomial or Poisson distributions.[5]

Type I error Statistically, the probability of rejecting a good lot.

Type II error Statistically, the probability of a bad lot being accepted.

Average Outgoing Quality

In most sampling plans, when a lot is rejected, the entire lot is inspected and all defective items replaced. Use of this replacement technique improves the average outgoing quality in terms of percent defective. In fact, given (1) any sampling plan that replaces all defective items encountered and (2) the true incoming percent defective for the lot, it is possible to determine the **average outgoing quality (AOQ)** in percent defective. The equation for AOQ is:

$$\text{AOQ} = \frac{(P_d)(P_a)(N - n)}{N} \quad \text{(S4.14)}$$

where P_d = true percent defective of the lot
P_a = probability of accepting the lot
N = number of items in the lot
n = number of items in the sample

Average outgoing quality (AOQ) The percent defective in an average lot of goods inspected through acceptance sampling.

The maximum value on the AOQ curve corresponds to the highest average percent defective or the lowest average quality for the sampling plan. It is called the *average outgoing quality limit (AOQL)*.

Acceptance sampling is useful for screening incoming lots. When the defective parts are replaced with good parts, acceptance sampling helps to increase the quality of the lots by reducing the outgoing percent defective.

Figure S4.9 compares acceptance sampling, SPC, and C_{pk}. As Figure S4.9 shows, (a) acceptance sampling by definition accepts some bad units, (b) control charts try to keep the process in control, but (c) the C_{pk} index places the focus on improving the process. As operations managers, that is what we want to do—improve the process.

---

[5] The two most frequently used tables for acceptance plans are *Military Standard Sampling Procedures and Tables for Inspection by Attributes* (MIL-STD-105D)(Washington, DC: U.S. Government Printing Office, 1963); and H. F. Dodge and H. G. Romig, *Sampling Inspection Tables—Single and Double Sampling*, 2nd ed. (New York: John Wiley, 1959).

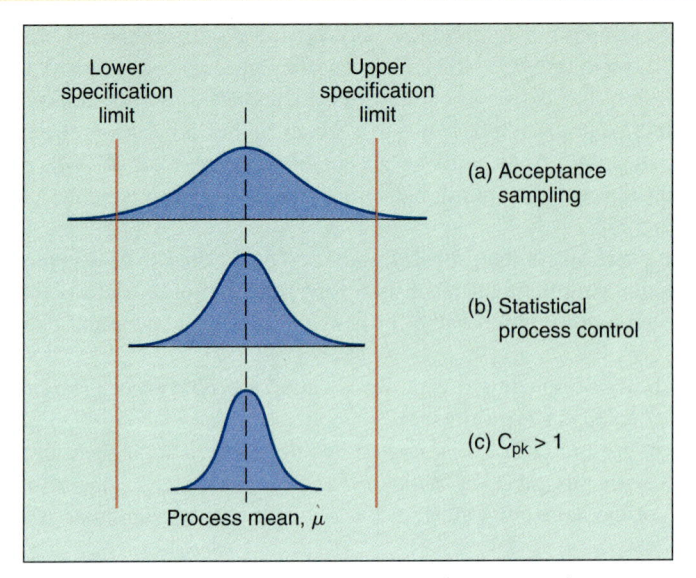

FIGURE S4.9 ■ The Application of Statistical Process Techniques Contributes to the Identification and Systematic Reduction of Process Variability

SUMMARY

Statistical process control is a major statistical tool of quality control. Control charts for SPC help operations managers distinguish between natural and assignable variations. The $\bar{x}$-chart and the R-chart are used for variable sampling, and the p-chart and the c-chart for attribute sampling. The C_{pk} index is a way to express process capability. Operating characteristic (OC) curves facilitate acceptance sampling and provide the manager with tools to evaluate the quality of a production run or shipment.

KEY TERMS

Statistical process control (SPC) *(p. 108)*
Control chart *(p. 108)*
Natural variations *(p. 109)*
Assignable variation *(p. 109)*
$\bar{x}$-chart *(p. 110)*
R-chart *(p. 110)*
Central limit theorem *(p. 111)*
p-charts *(p. 118)*
c-charts *(p. 120)*
C_{pk} *(p. 121)*

Acceptance sampling *(p. 123)*
Operating characteristic (OC) curve *(p. 123)*
Producer's risk *(p. 123)*
Consumer's risk *(p. 123)*
Acceptable quality level (AQL) *(p. 124)*
Lot tolerance percent defective (LTPD) *(p. 124)*
Type I error *(p. 125)*
Type II error *(p. 125)*
Average outgoing quality (AOQ) *(p. 125)*

USING POM FOR WINDOWS

POM for Windows' Quality Control module has the ability to compute all of the SPC control charts we introduced in this supplement. To illustrate, Program S4.1 uses the *p*-chart data for ARCO found in Example S4. It computes *p*-bar, the standard deviation, and the upper and lower control limits. Students need only enter the number of defects for each of the 20 samples.

Acceptance Sampling

USING EXCEL OM FOR SPC

PROGRAM S4.1 ■ POM for Windows' Analysis of ARCO's Data to Compute P-Chart Control Limits

USING EXCEL OM FOR SPC

Excel and other spreadsheets are extensively used in industry to maintain control charts. Excel OM's Quality Control module has the ability to develop $\bar{x}$-charts, p-charts, and c-charts. Programs S4.2 and S4.3 illustrate Excel OM's spreadsheet approach to computing the $\bar{x}$ control limits for the Oat Flakes company in Example S1. Program S4.2 provides both the data input and formulas screen. Program S4.3 provides output. Excel also contains a built-in graphing ability with Chart Wizard.

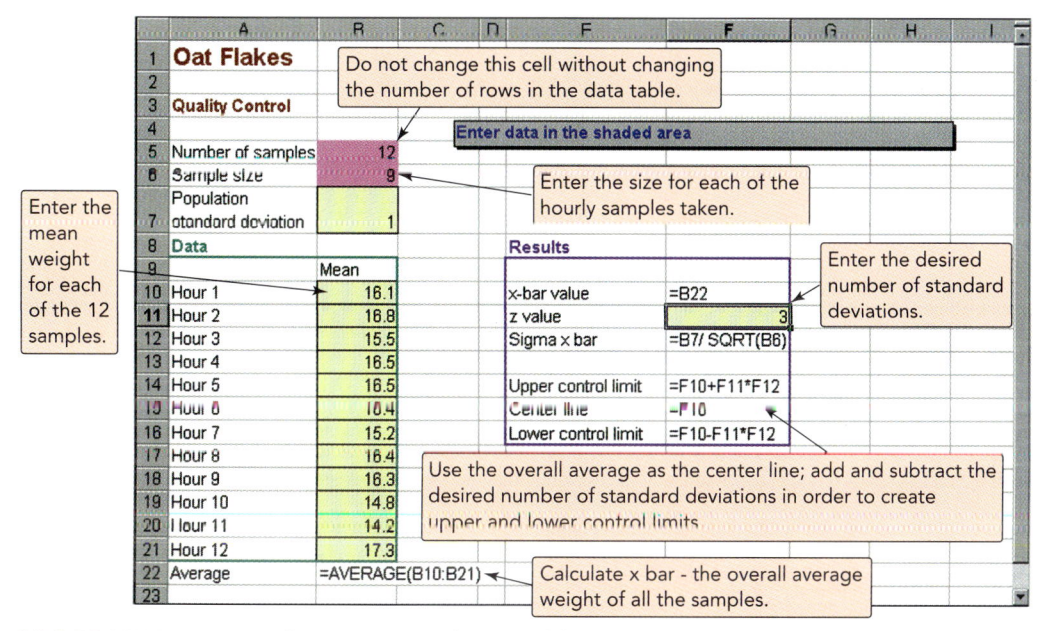

PROGRAM S4.2 ■ Excel OM Input and Spreadsheet Formulas for Oat Flakes Example S1

SUPPLEMENT 4 STATISTICAL PROCESS CONTROL

	A	B	C	D	E	F	G	H	I
1	Oat Flakes								
2									
3	Quality Control								
4					Enter data in the shaded area				
5	Number of samples	12							
6	Sample size	9							
7	Population standard deviation	1							
8	Data				Results				
9		Mean							
10	Hour 1	16.1			x-bar value	16			
11	Hour 2	16.8			z value	3			
12	Hour 3	15.5			Sigma x bar	0.333333			
13	Hour 4	16.5							
14	Hour 5	16.5			Upper control limit	17			
15	Hour 6	16.4			Center line	16			
16	Hour 7	15.2			Lower control limit	15			
17	Hour 8	16.4							
18	Hour 9	16.3							
19	Hour 10	14.8							
20	Hour 11	14.2							
21	Hour 12	17.3							
22	Average	16							
23									

PROGRAM S4.3 ■ Output Using Excel OM to Solve Oat Flakes Example S1 Using Program S4.2 as Input

SOLVED PROBLEMS

Solved Problem S4.1

A manufacturer of precision machine parts produces round shafts for use in the construction of drill presses. The average diameter of a shaft is .56 inch. Inspection samples contain 6 shafts each. The average range of these samples is .006 inch. Determine the upper and lower control chart limits.

Solution

The mean factor A_2 from Table S4.1 where the sample size is 6, is seen to be .483. With this factor, you can obtain the upper and lower control limits:

$$\text{UCL}_{\bar{x}} = .56 + (.483)(.006)$$
$$= .56 + .0029$$
$$= .5629''$$
$$\text{LCL}_{\bar{x}} = .56 - .0029$$
$$= .5571''$$

Solved Problem S4.2

Nocaf Drinks, Inc., a producer of decaffeinated coffee, bottles Nocaf. Each bottle should have a net weight of 4 ounces. The machine that fills the bottles with coffee is new, and the operations manager wants to make sure that it is properly adjusted. Bonnie Crutcher, the operations manager, takes a sample of $n = 8$ bottles and records the average and range in ounces for each sample. The data for several samples is given in the following table. Note that every sample consists of 8 bottles.

Sample	Sample Range	Sample Average	Sample	Sample Range	Sample Average
A	.41	4.00	E	.56	4.17
B	.55	4.16	F	.62	3.93
C	.44	3.99	G	.54	3.98
D	.48	4.00	H	.44	4.01

Is the machine properly adjusted and in control?

Solution

We first find that $\bar{\bar{x}} = 4.03$ and $\bar{R} = .51$. Then, using Table S4.1, we find:

$$\text{UCL}_{\bar{x}} = \bar{\bar{x}} + A_2\bar{R} = 4.03 + (.373)(.51) = 4.22$$

$$\text{LCL}_{\bar{x}} = \bar{\bar{x}} - A_2\bar{R} = 4.03 - (.373)(.51) = 3.84$$

$$\text{UCL}_R = D_4\bar{R} = (1.864)(.51) = .95$$

$$\text{LCL}_R = D_3\bar{R} = (.136)(.51) = .07$$

It appears that the process average and range are both in control.

Solved Problem S4.3

Altman Distributors, Inc. fills catalog orders. Among the last 100 orders shipped, the percent of errors was .05. Determine the upper and lower limits for this process for 99.7% confidence.

Solution

$$\text{UCL}_p = \bar{p} + 3\sqrt{\frac{\bar{p}(1-\bar{p})}{n}} = .05 + 3\sqrt{\frac{(.05)(1-.05)}{100}}$$

$$= .05 + 3(0.0218) = .1154$$

$$\text{LCL}_p = \bar{p} - 33\sqrt{\frac{\bar{p}(1-\bar{p})}{n}} = .05 - 3(.0218)$$

$$= .05 - .0654 = 0 \text{ (because percent defective cannot be negative)}$$

Solved Problem S4.4

Ettlie Engineering has a new catalyst injection system for your countertop production line. Your process engineering department has conducted experiments and determined that the mean is 8.01 grams with a standard deviation of .03. Your specifications are

$\mu = 8.0$ and $\sigma = .04$, which means an Upper Specification Limit of 8.12 ($= 8.0 + 3(.04)$)

and a Lower Specification Limit of 7.88 ($= 8.0 - 3(.04)$).

What is the C_{pk} performance of the injection system? Using our formula:

$$C_{pk} = \text{minimum of} \left[\frac{\text{Upper Specification Limit} - \bar{X}}{3\sigma}, \frac{\bar{X} - \text{Lower Specification Limit}}{3\sigma} \right]$$

where $\bar{X}$ = process mean
σ = standard deviation of the process population

$$C_{pk} = \text{minimum of} \left[\frac{8.12 - 8.01}{(3).03}, \frac{8.01 - 7.88}{(3).03} \right]$$

$$\left[\frac{.11}{.09} = 1.22, \frac{.13}{.09} = 1.44 \right]$$

The minimum is 1.22, so the C_{pk} is 1.22 with an implied error rate of less than 2,700 defects per million.

DISCUSSION QUESTIONS

1. Why is the central limit theorem so important in statistical quality control?
2. Why are $\bar{x}$- and R-charts usually used hand in hand?
3. Explain the differences among the four types of control charts.
4. What might cause a process to be out of control?
5. What was the contribution of Walter Shewhart?
6. What is the difference between natural and assignable causes of variation?
7. Explain why a process can be out of control even though all samples fall within the upper and lower control limits.
8. What do the terms *producer's risk* and *consumer's risk* mean?
9. Define *type I* and *type II errors*.
10. Define C_{pk} and explain what a C_{pk} of 1.0 means.

PROBLEMS

S4.1 The overall average on a process you are attempting to monitor is 75 units. The average range is 6 units. What are the upper and lower control limits if you choose to use a sample size of 10?

S4.2 The overall average on a process you are attempting to monitor is 50 units. The average range is 4 units. What are the upper and lower control limits if you choose to use a sample size of 5?

S4.3 Your supervisor, Lisa Lehmann, has asked that you report on the output of a machine on the factory floor. This machine is supposed to be producing optical lenses with a mean weight of 50 grams and a range of 3.5 grams. The following table contains the data for a sample size of $n = 10$ taken during the past 3 hours:

Sample Number	Sample Average	Sample Range
1	55	3
2	47	1
3	49	5
4	50	3
5	52	2
6	57	6
7	55	3
8	48	2
9	51	2
10	56	3

Prepare your report.

S4.4 Food Storage Technologies produces refrigeration units for food producers and retail food establishments. The overall average temperature that these units maintain is 46°Fahrenheit. The average range is 2°Fahrenheit. Samples of 6 are taken to monitor the production process. Determine the upper and lower control chart limits for averages and ranges for these refrigeration units.

S4.5 Autopitch devices are made for both major- and minor-league teams to help them improve their batting averages. When set at the standard position, Autopitch can throw hard balls toward a batter at an average speed of 60 mph. To monitor these devices and to maintain the highest quality, Autopitch executives take samples of 10 Autopitch devices at a time. The average range is 3 mph. Using control chart techniques, determine control chart limits for averages and ranges for Autopitch.

- **S4.6** Major Products, Inc., produces granola cereal, granola bars, and other natural food products. Its natural granola cereal is sampled to ensure proper weight. Each sample contains 8 boxes of cereal. The overall average for samples is 17 ounces. The range is only 0.5 ounces. Determine the upper and lower control chart limits for averages for the boxes of cereal.

- **S4.7** Small boxes of NutraFlakes cereal are labeled "net weight 10 ounces." Each hour, random samples of size $n = 4$ boxes are weighed to check process control. Five hours of observations yielded the following data:

		Weights		
Time	Box 1	Box 2	Box 3	Box 4
9 A.M.	9.8	10.4	9.9	10.3
10 A.M.	10.1	10.2	9.9	9.8
11 A.M.	9.9	10.5	10.3	10.1
Noon	9.7	9.8	10.3	10.2
1 P.M.	9.7	10.1	9.9	9.9

Using these data, construct limits for $\bar{x}$- and R-charts. Is the process in control? What other steps should the quality control department follow at this point?

- **S4.8** Sampling 4 pieces of precision-cut wire (to be used in computer assembly) every hour for the past 24 hours has produced the following results:

Hour	$\bar{x}$	R	Hour	$\bar{x}$	R
1	3.25"	.71"	13	3.11"	.85"
2	3.10	1.18	14	2.83	1.31
3	3.22	1.43	15	3.12	1.06
4	3.39	1.26	16	2.84	.50
5	3.07	1.17	17	2.86	1.43
6	2.86	.32	18	2.74	1.29
7	3.05	.53	19	3.41	1.61
8	2.65	1.13	20	2.89	1.09
9	3.02	.71	21	2.65	1.08
10	2.85	1.33	22	3.28	.46
11	2.83	1.17	23	2.94	1.58
12	2.97	.40	24	2.64	.97

Develop appropriate control charts and determine whether there is any cause for concern in the cutting process.

- **S4.9** In the past, the defect rate for your product has been 1.5%. What are the upper and lower control chart limits if you wish to use a sample size of 500 and $z = 3$?

- **S4.10** In the past, the defect rate for your product has been 3.5%. What are the upper and lower control chart limits if you wish to use a sample size of 500 and $z = 3$?

- **S4.11** You are attempting to develop a quality monitoring system for some parts purchased from Warton & Kotha Manufacturing Co. These parts are either good or defective. You have decided to take a sample of 100 units. Develop a table of the appropriate upper and lower control chart limits for various values of the fraction defective in the sample taken. The values for p in this table should range from 0.02 to 0.10 in increments of 0.02. Develop the upper and lower control limits for a 99.7% confidence level.

- **S4.12** Due to the poor quality of various semiconductor products used in their manufacturing process, Microlaboratories has decided to develop a quality control program. Because the semiconductor parts that it gets from suppliers are either good or defective, quality control manager George Haverty has decided to develop control charts for attributes. The total number of semiconductors in every sample is 200. Furthermore, Haverty would like to determine the upper control chart limit and the lower control chart limit for various values of the fraction defective (p) in the sample taken. To allow more flexibility, he has decided to develop a table that lists values for p, UCL, and LCL. The values for p should range from .01 to 0.10, incrementing by .01 each time. What are the UCLs and the LCLs for 99.7% confidence?

S4.13 For the last two months, Mary Hart has been concerned about the number 5 machine at the West Factory. In order to make sure that the machine is operating correctly, samples are taken, and the average and range for each sample is computed. Each sample consists of 12 items produced from the machine. Recently 12 samples were taken and the sample range and sample average computed for each. The sample range and sample average were 1.1 and 46 for the first sample, 1.31 and 45 for the second, .91 and 46 for the third, and 1.1 and 47 for the fourth. After the fourth sample, the sample averages increased. For the fifth sample, the range was 1.21 and the average was 48; for number 6, it was .82 and 47; for number 7, it was .86 and 50; and for the eighth sample, it was 1.11 and 49. After the eighth sample, the sample average continued to increase, never getting below 50. For sample number 9, the range and average were 1.12 and 51; for number 10, they were .99 and 52; for number 11, they were .86 and 50; and for number 12, they were 1.2 and 52.

During installation, the supplier set an average of 47 for the process with an average range of 1.0. It was Hart's feeling that something was definitely wrong with machine number 5. Do you agree?

S4.14 Pet Products, Inc. caters to the growing market for cat supplies, with a full line of products ranging from litter to toys to flea powder. One of its newer products, a tube of fluid that prevents hairballs in long-haired cats, is produced by an automated machine set to fill each tube with 63.5 grams of paste.

To keep this filling process under control, four tubes are pulled randomly from the assembly line every four hours. After several days, the data shown in the table below resulted. Set control limits for this process and graph the sample data for both the $\bar{x}$- and R-charts.

SAMPLE NUMBER

	1	2	3	4	5	6	7	8	9	10	11	12	13
$\bar{x}$	63.5	63.6	63.7	63.9	63.4	63.0	63.2	63.3	63.7	63.5	63.3	63.2	63.6
R	2.0	1.0	1.7	0.9	1.2	1.6	1.8	1.3	1.6	1.3	1.8	1.0	1.8

SAMPLE NUMBER

	14	15	16	17	18	19	20	21	22	23	24	25
$\bar{x}$	63.3	63.4	63.4	63.5	63.6	63.8	63.5	63.9	63.2	63.3	64.0	63.4
R	1.5	1.7	1.4	1.1	1.8	1.3	1.6	1.0	1.8	1.7	2.0	1.5

S4.15 The smallest defect in a computer chip will render the entire chip worthless. Therefore, tight quality control measures must be established to monitor these chips. In the past, the percentage defective at a California-based company has been 1.1%. The sample size is 1,000. Determine upper and lower control chart limits for these computer chips. Use $z = 3$.

S4.16 Chicago Supply Company manufactures paper clips and other office products. Although inexpensive, paper clips have provided the firm with a high margin of profitability. The percentage defective for paper clips produced by Chicago Supply Company has been averaging 2.5%. Samples of 200 paper clips are taken. Establish upper and lower control chart limits for this process at 99.7% confidence.

- : S4.17 Daily samples of 100 power drills are removed from Drill Master's assembly line and inspected for defects. Over the past 21 days, the following information has been gathered. Develop a 3 standard deviation (99.7% confidence) *p*-chart and graph the samples. Is the process in control?

Day	Number of Defective Drills	Day	Number of Defective Drills
1	6	12	5
2	5	13	4
3	6	14	3
4	4	15	4
5	3	16	5
6	4	17	6
7	5	18	5
8	3	19	4
9	6	20	3
10	3	21	7
11	7		

- : S4.18 A random sample of 100 Modern Art dining room tables that came off the firm's assembly line is examined. Careful inspection reveals a total of 2,000 blemishes. What are the 99.7% upper and lower control limits for the number of blemishes? If one table had 42 blemishes, should any special action be taken?

- : S4.19 A new process has just been established on your assembly line. The process is suppose to add 4 grams of a deep red coloring to each bottle of nail polish with an Upper Specification Limit of 4.1 grams and a Lower Specification Limit of 3.9 grams. Although the mean is 4 grams, the standard deviation is 0.1 gram. What is the C_{pk} of the new process?

- : S4.20 The manager of the Oat Flakes plant (see Example S1) desires a quality specification with a mean of 16 ounces, an Upper Specification Limit of 16.5, and a Lower Specification Limit of 15.5. What is the actual performance of the system using the 12 samples in Example S1?

- : S4.21 The NutraFlakes cereal in Problem S4.7 is to be packaged with a mean of 10 ounces plus or minus 0.1 ounces. Using the data in Problem S4.7, determine the standard deviation of the 20 weights and then determine the C_{pk} of the process. (*Hint:* For a review of how to compute a standard deviation, see footnote 2 on page 111.)

- : S4.22 Blackburn, Inc., an equipment manufacturer in Nashville, has submitted a sample cutoff valve to improve your manufacturing process. Your process engineering department has conducted experiments and found that the valve has a mean (μ) of 8.01 and a standard deviation (σ) of .04. Your desired performance is $\mu = 8.0$ and $\sigma = .045$. What is the C_{pk} of the Blackburn valve?

DATA BASE APPLICATION

- : S4.23 West Battery Corp. has recently been receiving complaints from retailers that its 9-volt batteries are not lasting as long as other name brands. James West, head of the TQM program at West's Austin plant, believes there is no problem because his batteries have had an average life of 50 hours, about 10% longer than competitors' models. To raise the lifetime above this level would require a new level of technology not available to West. Nevertheless, he is concerned enough to set up hourly assembly line checks. He decides to take size-5 samples of 9-volt batteries for each of the next 25 hours to create the standards for control chart limits (see the following table):

West Battery Data—Battery Lifetimes (in hours)

Hour	1	2	3	4	5	$\bar{X}$	R
1	51	50	49	50	50	50.0	2
2	45	47	70	46	36	48.8	34
3	50	35	48	39	47	43.8	15
4	55	70	50	30	51	51.2	40
5	49	38	64	36	47	46.8	28
6	59	62	40	54	64	55.8	24
7	36	33	49	48	56	44.4	23
8	50	67	53	43	40	50.6	27
9	44	52	46	47	44	46.6	8
10	70	45	50	47	41	50.6	29
11	57	54	62	45	36	50.8	26
12	56	54	47	42	62	52.2	20
13	40	70	58	45	44	51.4	30
14	52	58	40	52	46	49.6	18
15	57	42	52	58	59	53.6	17
16	62	49	42	33	55	48.2	29
17	40	39	49	59	48	47.0	20
18	64	50	42	57	50	52.6	22
19	58	53	52	48	50	52.2	10
20	60	50	41	41	50	48.4	19
21	52	47	48	58	40	49.0	18
22	55	40	56	49	45	49.0	16
23	47	48	50	50	48	48.6	3
24	50	50	49	51	51	50.2	2
25	51	50	51	51	62	53.0	12

With these limits in place, West now takes 5 more hours of data, which are shown in the following table:

Hour	1	2	3	4	5
26	48	52	39	57	61
27	45	53	48	46	66
28	63	49	50	45	53
29	57	70	45	52	61
30	45	38	46	54	52

a) Is the manufacturing process in control?
b) Comment on the lifetimes observed.

Case Study

Bayfield Mud Company

In November 1997, John Wells, a customer service representative of Bayfield Mud Company, was summoned to the Houston warehouse of Wet-Land Drilling, Inc., to inspect three boxcars of mud-treating agents that Bayfield had shipped to the Houston firm. (Bayfield's corporate offices and its largest plant are located in Orange, Texas, which is just west of the Louisiana–Texas border.) Wet-Land had filed a complaint that the 50-pound bags of treating agents just received from Bayfield were short-weight by approximately 5%.

The light-weight bags were initially detected by one of Wet-Land's receiving clerks, who noticed that the railroad scale tickets indicated that net weights were significantly less on all three boxcars than those of identical shipments received on October 25, 1997. Bayfield's traffic department was called to determine if lighter-weight pallets were used on the shipments. (This might explain the lighter net weights.) Bayfield indicated, however, that no changes had been made in loading or palletizing procedures. Thus, Wet-Land engineers randomly checked 50 bags and discovered that the average net weight was 47.51 pounds. They noted from past shipments that bag net weights averaged exactly 50.0 pounds, with an acceptable standard deviation of 1.2 pounds. Consequently, they concluded that the sample indicated a significant short-weight. (The reader may wish to verify this conclusion.) Bayfield was then contacted, and Wells was sent to investigate the complaint. Upon arrival, Wells verified the complaint and issued a 5% credit to Wet-Land.

Wet-Land management, however, was not completely satisfied with the issuance of credit. The charts followed by their mud engineers on the drilling platforms were based on 50-pound bags of treating agents. Lighter-weight bags might result in poor chemical control during the drilling operation and thus adversely affect drilling efficiency. (Mud-treating agents are used to control the pH and other chemical properties of the cone during drilling operation.) This defect could cause severe economic consequences because of the extremely high cost of oil and natural gas well-drilling operations. Consequently, special-use instructions had to accompany the delivery of these shipments to the drilling platforms. Moreover, the light-weight shipments had to be isolated in Wet-Land's warehouse, causing extra handling and poor space utilization. Thus, Wells was informed that Wet-Land might seek a new supplier of mud-treating agents if, in the future, it received bags that deviated significantly from 50 pounds.

The quality control department at Bayfield suspected that the light-weight bags may have resulted from "growing pains" at the Orange plant. Because of the earlier energy crisis, oil and natural gas exploration activity had greatly increased. In turn, this increased activity created increased demand for products produced by related industries, including drilling muds. Consequently, Bayfield had to expand from a one-shift (6:00 A.M. to 2:00 P.M.) to a two-shift (2:00 P.M. to 10:00 P.M.) operation in mid-1995, and finally to a three-shift operation (24 hours per day) in the fall of 1997.

The additional night-shift bagging crew was staffed entirely by new employees. The most experienced foremen were temporarily assigned to supervise the night-shift employees. Most emphasis was placed on increasing the output of bags to meet ever-increasing demand. It was suspected that only occasional reminders were made to double-check the bag weight-feeder. (A double-check is performed by systematically weighing a bag on a scale to determine if the proper weight is being loaded by the weight-feeder. If there is significant deviation from 50 pounds, corrective adjustments are made to the weight-release mechanism.)

To verify this expectation, the quality control staff randomly sampled the bag output and prepared the chart on the following page. Six bags were sampled and weighed each hour.

Discussion Questions

1. What is your analysis of the bag-weight problem?
2. What procedures would you recommend to maintain proper quality control?

Source: Professor Jerry Kinard, Western Carolina University.

136 Supplement 4 Statistical Process Control

Time	Average Weight (Pounds)	Range Smallest	Range Largest	Time	Average Weight (Pounds)	Range Smallest	Range Largest
6:00 A.M.	49.6	48.7	50.7	6:00	46.8	41.0	51.2
7:00	50.2	49.1	51.2	7:00	50.0	46.2	51.7
8:00	50.6	49.6	51.4	8:00	47.4	44.0	48.7
9:00	50.8	50.2	51.8	9:00	47.0	44.2	48.9
10:00	49.9	49.2	52.3	10:00	47.2	46.6	50.2
11:00	50.3	48.6	51.7	11:00	48.6	47.0	50.0
12 Noon	48.6	46.2	50.4	12 Midnight	49.8	48.2	50.4
1:00 P.M.	49.0	46.4	50.0	1:00 A.M.	49.6	48.4	51.7
2:00	49.0	46.0	50.6	2:00	50.0	49.0	52.2
3:00	49.8	48.2	50.8	3:00	50.0	49.2	50.0
4:00	50.3	49.2	52.7	4:00	47.2	46.3	50.5
5:00	51.4	50.0	55.3	5:00	47.0	44.1	49.7
6:00	51.6	49.2	54.7	6:00	48.4	45.0	49.0
7:00	51.8	50.0	55.6	7:00	48.8	44.8	49.7
8:00	51.0	48.6	53.2	8:00	49.6	48.0	51.8
9:00	50.5	49.4	52.4	9:00	50.0	48.1	52.7
10:00	49.2	46.1	50.7	10:00	51.0	48.1	55.2
11:00	49.0	46.3	50.8	11:00	50.4	49.5	54.1
12 Midnight	48.4	45.4	50.2	12 Noon	50.0	48.7	50.9
1:00 A.M.	47.6	44.3	49.7	1:00 P.M.	48.9	47.6	51.2
2:00	47.4	44.1	49.6	2:00	49.8	48.4	51.0
3:00	48.2	45.2	49.0	3:00	49.8	48.8	50.8
4:00	48.0	45.5	49.1	4:00	50.0	49.1	50.6
5:00	48.4	47.1	49.6	5:00	47.8	45.2	51.2
6:00	48.6	47.4	52.0	6:00	46.4	44.0	49.7
7:00	50.0	49.2	52.2	7:00	46.4	44.4	50.0
8:00	49.8	49.0	52.4	8:00	47.2	46.6	48.9
9:00	50.3	49.4	51.7	9:00	48.4	47.2	49.5
10:00	50.2	49.6	51.8	10:00	49.2	48.1	50.7
11:00	50.0	49.0	52.3	11:00	48.4	47.0	50.8
12 Noon	50.0	48.8	52.4	12 Midnight	47.2	46.4	49.2
1:00 P.M.	50.1	49.4	53.6	1:00 A.M.	47.4	46.8	49.0
2:00	49.7	48.6	51.0	2:00	48.8	47.2	51.4
3:00	48.4	47.2	51.7	3:00	49.6	49.0	50.6
4:00	47.2	45.3	50.9	4:00	51.0	50.5	51.5
5:00	46.8	44.1	49.0	5:00	50.5	50.0	51.9

■ *Case Study* ■

SPC at the *Gazette*

Of critical importance to a newspaper is accurate typesetting. To assure typesetting quality, a quality improvement team was established in the printing department at the *Gazette* in Geronimo, Texas. The team developed a procedure for monitoring the performance of typesetters over a period of time. Such a procedure involves sampling output, establishing control limits, comparing the *Gazette's* accuracy with that of the industry, and occasionally updating the resulting information.

The team randomly selected 30 editions of the *Gazette* published during the preceding 12 months.

From each paper, 100 paragraphs were randomly chosen and read for accuracy. The number of paragraphs with errors in each paper was recorded and the fraction of paragraphs with errors in each sample determined. The following table shows the results of the sampling:

Sample	Paragraphs with Errors in the Sample	Fraction of Paragraphs with Errors (per 100)	Sample	Paragraphs with Errors in the Sample	Fraction of Paragraphs with Errors (per 100)
1	2	.02	16	2	.02
2	4	.04	17	3	.03
3	10	.10	18	7	.07
4	4	.04	19	3	.03
5	1	.01	20	2	.02
6	1	.01	21	3	.03
7	13	.13	22	7	.07
8	9	.09	23	4	.04
9	11	.11	24	3	.03
10	0	.00	25	2	.02
11	3	.03	26	2	.02
12	4	.04	27	0	.00
13	2	.02	28	1	.01
14	2	.02	29	3	.03
15	8	.08	30	4	.04

Discussion Questions

1. Using a 95.45% confidence level, plot the overall fraction of errors (p) and the upper and lower control limits on a control chart.
2. Assume that the industry upper and lower control limits are .1000 and .0400, respectively. Plot them on the control chart.
3. Plot the fraction of errors in each sample. Do all samples fall within the firm's control limits? When one falls outside the control limits, what should be done?

Source: Professor Jerry Kinard, Western Carolina University.

Internet Case Study

See our Internet home page at http://www.prenhall.com/heizer for this additional case study: Green River Chemical Company.

BIBLIOGRAPHY

Besterfield, D. H. *Quality Control,* 2nd ed. Englewood Cliffs, NJ: Prentice Hall, 1986.

Evans, J. R., and W. M. Lindsay. *The Management and Control of Quality,* 3rd ed. Minneapolis/St. Paul: West Publishing, 1993.

Kumar, S., and Y. P. Gupta. "Statistical Process Control at Motorola's Austin Assembly Plant." *Interfaces* 23, no. 2 (March–April 1993): 84–92.

Montgomery, D. C. *Introduction to Statistical Quality Control,* 2nd ed. New York: John Wiley, 1991.

Runger, G. C., and D. C. Montgomery. "Adaptive Sampling Enhancements for Shewhart Control Charts." *IIE Transactions* 25, no. 3 (May 1993): 41–51.

Wheeler, Donald J. "Why Three Sigma Limits?" *Quality Digest,* August 1996, pp. 63–64.

INTERNET RESOURCES

American Society of Quality:
  http://www.asq.org
American Statistical Association:
  http://www.amstat.org/
Associated Quality Consultants:
  http://www.quality.org/
Carnegie Mellon University: Maintained by the Statistics Department with excellent links to American Statistical Association abstracts and a number of statistical algorithms:
  http://lib.stat.cmu.edu/
Poka-yoke examples, tutorials and links page:
  http://www.cox.smu.edu/jgrout/pokayoke.html
Princeton University: Extensive links to a number of interesting sites:
  http://www.princeton.edu/~cap/contrib.html
Statistical Engineering Division of the Department of Commerce:
  http://www.itl.nist.gov/div898/
Statistical Service at Duke University:
  http://www.isds.duke.edu/
Total quality engineering:
  http://www.tqe.com/
University of Florida: Extensive links to a variety of statistical sites maintained by the Department of Statistics:
  http://www.stat.edu/ulib/statistics/html

FORECASTING 5

CHAPTER OUTLINE

GLOBAL COMPANY PROFILE: TUPPERWARE
WHAT IS FORECASTING?
   Forecasting Time Horizons
   The Influence of Product Life Cycle
TYPES OF FORECASTS
THE STRATEGIC IMPORTANCE OF FORECASTING
   Human Resources
   Capacity
   Supply-Chain Management
SEVEN STEPS IN THE FORECASTING SYSTEM
FORECASTING APPROACHES
   Overview of Qualitative Methods
   Overview of Quantitative Methods
TIME-SERIES FORECASTING
   Decomposition of a Time Series
   Naive Approach
   Moving Averages
   Exponential Smoothing
   Exponential Smoothing with Trend Adjustment
   Trend Projections
   Seasonal Variations in Data
CAUSAL FORECASTING METHODS: REGRESSION AND CORRELATION ANALYSIS
   Using Regression Analysis to Forecast

   Standard Error of the Estimate
   Correlation Coefficients for Regression Lines
   Multiple-Regression Analysis
MONITORING AND CONTROLLING FORECASTS
   Adaptive Smoothing
   Focus Forecasting
   The Computer's Role in Forecasting
FORECASTING IN THE SERVICE SECTOR
SUMMARY
KEY TERMS
USING POM FOR WINDOWS IN FORECASTING
USING EXCEL SPREADSHEETS IN FORECASTING
SOLVED PROBLEMS
DISCUSSION QUESTIONS
CRITICAL THINKING EXERCISE
PROBLEMS
DATA BASE APPLICATION
CASE STUDIES: NORTH-SOUTH AIRLINE; AKRON ZOOLOGICAL PARK
INTERNET CASE STUDY
BIBLIOGRAPHY
INTERNET RESOURCES

LEARNING OBJECTIVES

When you complete this chapter you should be able to:

Identify or Define:
   Forecasting
   Types of forecasts
   Time horizons
   Approaches to forecasts

Describe or Explain:
   Moving averages
   Exponential smoothing
   Trend projections
   Regression and correlation analysis
   Measures of forecast accuracy

GLOBAL COMPANY PROFILE:

Forecasting Provides Tupperware's Competitive Advantage

Stainless steel alloy molds, each requiring over 1,000 hours of skilled handcrafting, are the heart of the manufacturing process. Each mold creates the exact shape of a new product: Molds cost an average of $100,000 and can weigh up to 5 tons. When a specific product is scheduled for a production run, its mold is carefully placed, as we see in the photo, into an injection molding machine.

When most people think of Tupperware, they envision plastic food-storage containers sold through home parties. However, Tupperware happens to be a successful global manufacturer, with more than 85% of its $1.2 billion in sales outside the United States. A household name in nearly 100 countries, the firm has 15 plants located around the world: one in South Carolina, four in Latin America, one in Africa, five in Europe, and four in Asia. Throughout the world, Tupperware stands for quality, providing a lifetime warranty that each of its 400 plastic products will not chip, crack, break, or peel.

Forecasting demand at Tupperware is a critical, never-ending process. Each of its 50 profit centers around the world is responsible for computerized monthly, quarterly, and 12-month sales projections. These are aggregated by region and then globally at Tupperware's World Headquarters in Orlando, Florida. These forecasts drive production at each plant.

The variety of statistical forecasting models used at Tupperware includes every technique discussed in this chapter, including moving averages, exponential smoothing, and regression analysis. At world headquarters, huge databases are maintained to map the sales of each product, the test-market results of each *new* product (20% of the firm's sales come from products less than two years old), and the stage of each product in its own life cycle.

Three factors are key in Tupperware's sales forecasts: (1) the number of registered "consultants" or sales representatives, (2) the percentage of currently "active" dealers (this number changes each week and month), and (3) sales per active

The plastic pellets that are melted at 500 degrees into Tupperware products are dropped through pipes from second-floor bins into the machine holding a mold. After being injected into water-cooled molds at a pressure up to 20,000 pounds per square inch, the product cools and is removed and inspected.

140

TUPPERWARE CORPORATION

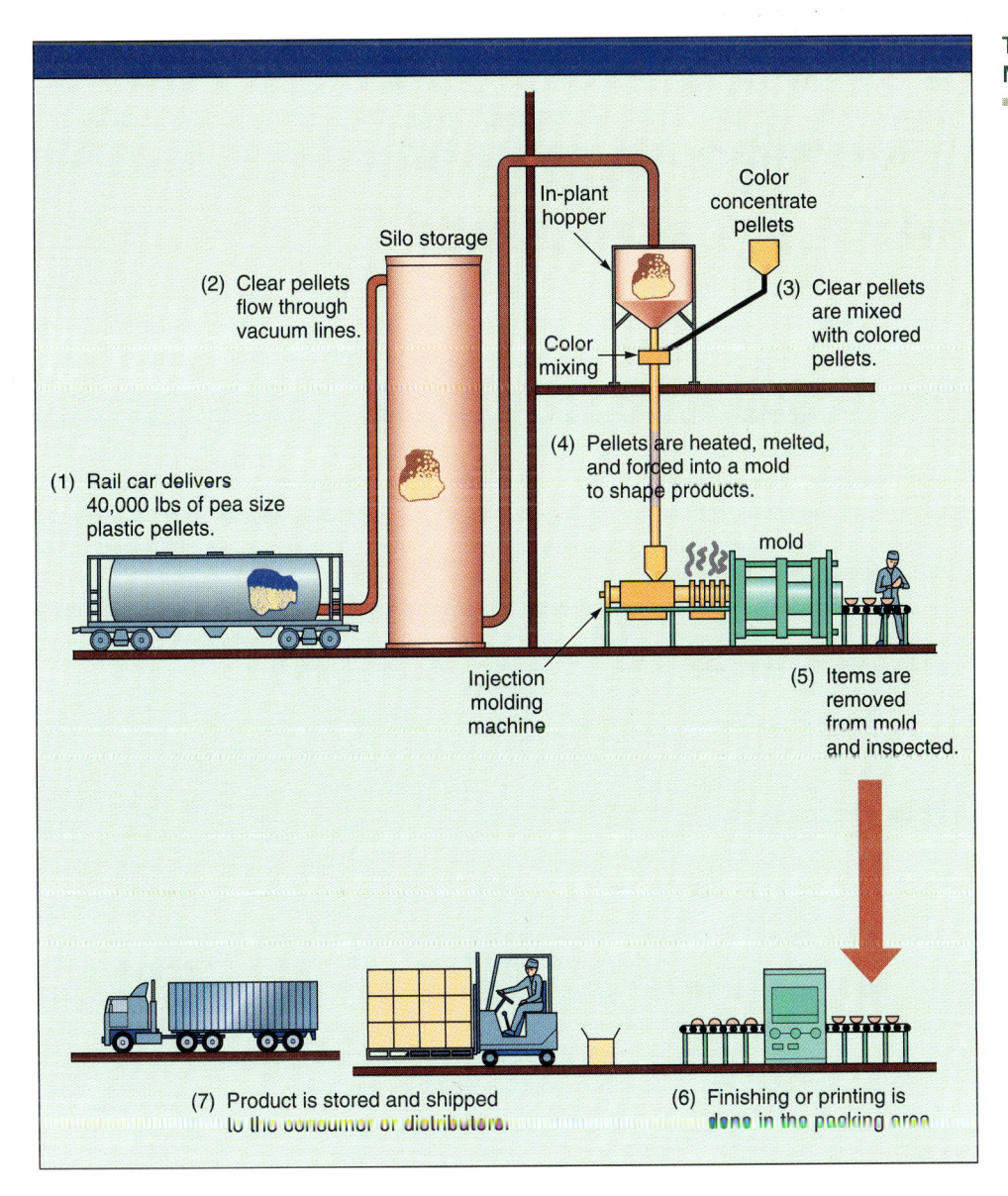

Tupperware's Manufacturing Process

(1) Rail car delivers 40,000 lbs of pea size plastic pellets.
(2) Clear pellets flow through vacuum lines.
(3) Clear pellets are mixed with colored pellets.
(4) Pellets are heated, melted, and forced into a mold to shape products.
(5) Items are removed from mold and inspected.
(6) Finishing or printing is done in the packing area.
(7) Product is stored and shipped to the consumer or distributors.

dealer, on a weekly basis. Forecasts incorporate historical data, recent events, and promotional events.

Tupperware maintains its edge over strong competitors like Rubbermaid by using a *group process* to refine its statistical forecasts: Although inputs come from sales, marketing, finance, and production, final forecasts are the consensus of all participating managers. This final step is Tupperware's version of the "jury of executive opinion" described in this chapter.

141

Every day managers like those at Tupperware make decisions without knowing what will happen in the future. They order inventory without knowing what sales will be, purchase new equipment despite uncertainty about demand for products, and make investments without knowing what profits will be. Managers are always trying to make better estimates of what will happen in the future in the face of uncertainty. Making good estimates is the main purpose of forecasting.

In this chapter, we examine different types of forecasts and present a variety of forecasting models. Our purpose is to show that there are many ways for managers to forecast the future. We also provide an overview of business sales forecasting and describe how to prepare, monitor, and judge the accuracy of a forecast. Good forecasts are an *essential* part of efficient service and manufacturing operations. They are also an important modeling tool in both strategic and tactical decision making.

WHAT IS FORECASTING?

Forecasting The art and science of predicting future events.

Forecasting is the art and science of predicting future events. It may involve taking historical data and projecting them into the future with some sort of mathematical model. It may be a subjective or intuitive prediction. Or it may involve a combination of these—that is, a mathematical model adjusted by a manager's good judgment.

As we introduce different forecasting techniques in this chapter, you will see that there is seldom one single superior method. What works best in one firm under one set of conditions may be a complete disaster in another organization, or even in a different department of the same firm. In addition, you will see that there are limits as to what can be expected from forecasts. They are seldom, if ever, perfect. They are also costly and time-consuming to prepare and monitor.

Few businesses, however, can afford to avoid the process of forecasting by just waiting to see what happens and then taking their chances. Effective planning in both the short and long run depends on a forecast of demand for the company's products.

Forecasting Time Horizons

A forecast is usually classified by the *future time horizon* that it covers.[1] Time horizons fall into three categories:

1. *Short-range forecast.* This forecast has a time span of up to one year but is generally less than three months. It is used for planning purchasing, job scheduling, workforce levels, job assignments, and production levels.
2. *Medium-range forecast.* A medium-range, or intermediate, forecast generally spans from 3 months to 3 years. It is useful in sales planning, production planning and budgeting, cash budgeting, and analyzing various operating plans.
3. *Long-range forecast.* Generally 3 years or more in time span, long-range forecasts are used in planning for new products, capital expenditures, facility location or expansion, and research and development.

Medium-range and long-range forecasts are distinguished from short-range forecasts by three features:

1. First, intermediate and long-run forecasts *deal with more comprehensive issues* and support management decisions regarding planning and products, plants, and processes. Implementing some facility decisions, such as GM's decision to open a

---

[1] For details, see Peter W. Stonebraker and G. Keong Leong, *Operations Strategy* (Boston: Allyn & Bacon, 1994).

new Saturn manufacturing plant, can take 5 to 8 years from inception to completion.
2. Second, short-term forecasting usually *employs different methodologies* than longer-term forecasting. Mathematical techniques, such as moving averages, exponential smoothing, and trend extrapolation (all of which we shall examine shortly), are common to short-run projections. Broader, *less* quantitative methods are useful in predicting such issues as whether a new product, like the optical disk recorder, should be introduced into a company's product line.
3. Finally, as you would expect, short-range forecasts *tend to be more accurate* than longer-range forecasts. Factors that influence demand change every day. Thus, as the time horizon lengthens, it is likely that one's forecast accuracy will diminish. It almost goes without saying, then, that sales forecasts must be updated regularly in order to maintain their value and integrity. After each sales period, forecasts should be reviewed and revised.

> Our forecasting ability has improved, but it has been outpaced by an increasingly complex world economy.

The Influence of Product Life Cycle

Another factor to consider when developing sales forecasts, especially longer ones, is product life cycle. Products, and even services, do not sell at a constant level throughout their lives. Most successful products pass through four stages: (1) introduction, (2) growth, (3) maturity, and (4) decline.

Products in the first two stages of the life cycle (such as virtual reality and high definition TVs) need longer forecasts than those (such as 3½″ floppy disks and station wagons) in the maturity and decline stages. Forecasts that reflect life cycle are useful in projecting different staffing levels, inventory levels, and factory capacity as the product passes from the first to the last stage. The challenge of introducing new products is treated in more detail in chapter 6.

TYPES OF FORECASTS

Organizations use three major types of forecasts in planning future operations.

1. **Economic forecasts** address the business cycle by predicting inflation rates, money supplies, housing starts, and other planning indicators.
2. **Technological forecasts** are concerned with rates of technological progress, which can result in the birth of exciting new products, requiring new plants and equipment.
3. **Demand forecasts** are projections of demand for a company's products or services. These forecasts, also called *sales forecasts,* drive a company's production, capacity, and scheduling systems and serve as inputs to financial, marketing, and personnel planning.

Economic and technological forecasting are specialized techniques that may fall outside the role of the operations manager. The emphasis in this book will therefore be on demand forecasting.

Economic forecasts
Planning indicators valuable in helping organizations prepare medium- to long-range forecasts.

Technological forecasts
Long-term forecasts concerned with the rates of technological progress.

Demand forecasts
Projections of a company's sales for each time period in the planning horizon.

THE STRATEGIC IMPORTANCE OF FORECASTING

Good forecasts are of critical importance in all aspects of a business: *The forecast is the only estimate of demand until actual demand becomes known.* Forecasts of demand therefore drive decisions in many areas. Let's look at the impact of product forecast on three activities: (1) human resources, (2) capacity, and (3) supply-chain management.

Human Resources

Hiring, training, and laying off workers all depend on anticipated demand. If the human resources department must hire additional workers without warning, the amount of training declines and the quality of the workforce suffers. A large Louisiana chemical firm almost lost its biggest customer when a quick expansion to round-the-clock shifts led to a total breakdown in quality control on the second and third shifts.

Capacity

When capacity is inadequate, the resulting shortages can mean undependable delivery, loss of customers, and loss of market share. This is exactly what happened to Nabisco in 1993, when it underestimated the huge demand for its new low-fat Snackwell Devil's Food Cookies. Even with production lines working overtime, Nabisco could not keep up with demand, and it lost customers.[2] When excess capacity is built, on the other hand, costs can skyrocket.

Supply-Chain Management

Good supplier relations and the ensuing price advantages for materials and parts depend on accurate forecasts. For example, auto manufacturers who want TRW Corp. to guarantee sufficient airbag capacity must provide accurate forecasts to justify TRW plant expansions. In the global marketplace, where components for Boeing 777 jets are manufactured in dozens of countries, coordination driven by forecasts is critical. Scheduling transportation to Seattle for final assembly at the lowest possible cost means no last-minute surprises that can harm already low profit margins.

SEVEN STEPS IN THE FORECASTING SYSTEM

> An interesting quote: "Those who can predict the future have never been appreciated in their own times."
> —Philip Crosby

Forecasting follows these seven basic steps:

1. *Determine the use of the forecast.* What objectives are we trying to obtain? Let's use Tupperware Corporation, the focus of this chapter's Global Company Profile, as an example. Tupperware needs accurate demand forecasts to drive production at each of its 15 plants, so the use is to forecast production requirements.
2. *Select the items to be forecasted.* For Tupperware, there are over 400 products, each with its own SKU (stock-keeping unit). Tupperware, like other firms of this type, does demand forecasts by families (or groups) of SKUs.
3. *Determine the time horizon of the forecast.* Is it short-, medium-, or long-term? Tupperware develops forecasts monthly, quarterly, and for 12-month sales projections.
4. *Select the forecasting model(s).* Tupperware uses a variety of statistical models that we shall discuss, including moving averages, exponential smoothing, and regression analysis. It also employs judgmental, or nonquantitative, models.

---

[2] "Man Walked on the Moon, but Man Can't Make Enough Devil's Food Cookie Cakes," *The Wall Street Journal,* September 28, 1993, pp. 1–2.

5. *Gather the data needed to make the forecast.* Tupperware's world headquarters maintains huge databases to monitor the sale of each product.
6. *Make the forecast.*
7. *Validate and implement the results.* At Tupperware, forecasts are reviewed in sales, marketing, finance, and production departments to make sure that the model, assumptions, and data are valid. Forecasts are then used to schedule material, equipment, and personnel at each plant.

These seven steps present a systematic way of initiating, designing, and implementing a forecasting system. When the system is to be used to generate forecasts regularly over time, data must be routinely collected. Then actual computations are usually made by computer.

Regardless of the system that firms like Tupperware use, each company faces several realities:

1. Forecasts are seldom perfect. This means that there are often outside factors that we cannot predict or control that impact the forecast. Companies need to allow for this reality.
2. Most forecasting techniques assume that there is some underlying stability in the system. Consequently, some firms automate their predictions using computerized forecasting software, then closely monitor only the product items whose demand is erratic.
3. Both product family and aggregated forecasts are more accurate than individual product forecasts. Tupperware, for example, aggregates product forecasts by both family (e.g., mixing bowls versus cups versus storage containers) and region. This approach helps balance the over- and under-predictions of each product and country.

FORECASTING APPROACHES

There are two general approaches to forecasting, just as there are two ways to tackle all decision modeling. One is quantitative analysis; the other is a qualitative approach. **Quantitative forecasts** use a variety of mathematical models that rely on historical data and/or causal variables to forecast demand. Subjective or **qualitative forecasts** incorporate such factors as the decision maker's intuition, emotions, personal experiences, and value system in reaching a forecast. Some firms use one approach and some use the other. In practice, a combination of the two is usually most effective, as we see in the *OM in Action* box, "Forecasting the Demand for HDTV Sales."

Overview of Qualitative Methods

In this section, we consider four different *qualitative* forecasting techniques.

1. **Jury of executive opinion.** Under this method, the opinions of a group of high-level experts or managers, often in combination with statistical models, are pooled to arrive at a group estimate of demand. Bristol-Meyers Squibb Company, for example, uses 220 well-known research scientists as its jury of executive opinion to get a grasp on future trends in the world of medical research.
2. **Sales force composite.** In this approach, each salesperson estimates what sales will be in his or her region. These forecasts are then reviewed to ensure that they are realistic. Then they are combined at the district and national levels to reach an overall forecast.

Quantitative forecasts Forecasts that employ one or more mathematical models that rely on historical data and/or causal variables to forecast demand.

Qualitative forecasts Forecasts that incorporate such factors as the decision maker's intuition, emotions, personal experiences, and value system.

Jury of executive opinion A forecasting technique that takes the opinion of a small group of high-level managers and results in a group estimate of demand.

Sales force composite A forecasting technique based upon salesperson's estimates of expected sales.

OM IN ACTION

FORECASTING THE DEMAND FOR HDTV SALES

Developing sales forecasts is an important component of any business plan, even for products still in their infancy. Three especially challenging markets are personal digital assistants, multimedia and interactive television, and high-definition TV (called HDTV and considered the next generation of television). In all three cases, accurately estimating demand is extremely challenging because the products and services are so new—and hence, sales data are not yet available. Still, demand estimates are important for critical decisions involving billions of dollars.

Qualitative forecasting methods, based on managerial judgment, are common under such conditions. Interestingly, however, we find that based on studies of previous products, this approach usually overestimates the future. To deal with the U.S. market for HDTV, historical data from three other products in the high-priced consumer segment were examined closely. Forecasters at the American Electronics Association looked to their experience with sales-demand curves for color TV sets, refrigerators, and VCRs, using early estimates of price and costs to match these products' experiences.

Assumptions about government policy for funding the new HDTV industry complicate the forecasting process and accuracy. The head of the Congressional Budget Office "finds the forecast very optimistic about market size and certainly about timing." Yet by blending quantitative and qualitative modeling of potential demand, analysts can have a major impact on corporate decisions.

Sources: Barry L. Bayus, *OR/MS Today* 22, no. 4 (August 1995): 36–38; *The Wall Street Journal* (September 12, 1997): A1, A8; and *Barrons*, October 3, 1994, p. 14.

Delphi method A forecasting technique using a group process that allows experts to make forecasts.

3. **Delphi method.** There are three different types of participants in the Delphi method: decision makers, staff personnel, and respondents. Decision makers usually consist of a group of 5 to 10 experts who will be making the actual forecast. Staff personnel assist decision makers by preparing, distributing, collecting, and summarizing a series of questionnaires and survey results. The respondents are a group of people, often located in different places, whose judgments are valued. This group provides inputs to the decision makers before the forecast is made.

The state of Alaska, for example, has used the Delphi method to develop its long-range economic forecast. An amazing 90% of the state's budget is derived from 1.5 million barrels of oil pumped daily through a pipeline at Prudhoe Bay. The large Delphi panel of experts had to represent all groups and opinions in the state and all geographic areas. But Delphi was the perfect forecasting tool because panelist travel could be avoided. It also meant that leading Alaskans could participate because their schedules were not impacted by meetings and distances.

Consumer market survey A forecasting method that solicits input from customers or potential customers regarding future purchasing plans.

4. **Consumer market survey.** This method solicits input from customers or potential customers regarding future purchasing plans. It can help not only in preparing a forecast but also in improving product design and planning for new products.

Overview of Quantitative Methods

Five quantitative forecasting methods, all of which use historical data, are described in this chapter. They fall into two categories:

1. Naive approach
2. Moving averages   ⎫
3. Exponential smoothing   ⎬ time-series models
4. Trend projection   ⎭
5. Linear regression   } causal model

Time-Series Models *Time-series* models predict on the assumption that the future is a function of the past. In other words, they look at what has happened over a period of time and use a series of past data to make a forecast. If we are predicting weekly sales of lawn mowers, we use the past weekly sales for lawn mowers in making the forecast.

Time series
A forecasting technique that uses a series of past data points to make a forecast.

Causal Models Causal (or associative) models, such as linear regression, incorporate the variables or factors that might influence the quantity being forecast. For example, a causal model for lawn mower sales might include such factors as new housing starts, advertising budget, and competitors' prices.

TIME-SERIES FORECASTING

A time series is based on a sequence of evenly spaced (weekly, monthly, quarterly, and so on) data points. Examples include weekly sales of Nike Air Jordans, quarterly earnings reports of Microsoft stock, daily shipments of Coors beer, and annual consumer price indices. Forecasting time-series data implies that future values are predicted *only* from past values and that other variables, no matter how potentially valuable, may be ignored.

Here are two famous quotes: "You can never plan the future from the past." Sir Edmund Burke; "I know of no way of judging the future but by the past." Patrick Henry

Decomposition of a Time Series

Analyzing time series means breaking down past data into components and then projecting them forward. A time series typically has four components: trend, seasonality, cycles, and random variation.

1. *Trend* is the gradual upward or downward movement of the data over time. Changes in income, population, age distribution, or cultural views may account for movement in trend.
2. *Seasonality* is a data pattern that repeats itself after a period of days, weeks, months, or quarters. There are six common seasonality patterns:

Period of Pattern	"Season" Length	Number of "Seasons" in Pattern
Week	Day	7
Month	Week	4–4½
Month	Day	28–31
Year	Quarter	4
Year	Month	12
Year	Week	52

Restaurants and barber shops, for example, experience weekly seasons, with Saturday being the peak of business. Beer distributors forecast yearly patterns, with monthly seasons. Three "seasons"—May, July, and September—each contain a big beer-drinking holiday.

3. *Cycles* are patterns in the data that occur every several years. They are usually tied into the business cycle and are of major importance in short-term business analysis and planning. Predicting business cycles is difficult because they may be affected by political events, by international turmoil.
4. *Random variations* are "blips" in the data caused by chance and unusual situations. They follow no discernible pattern, so they cannot be predicted.

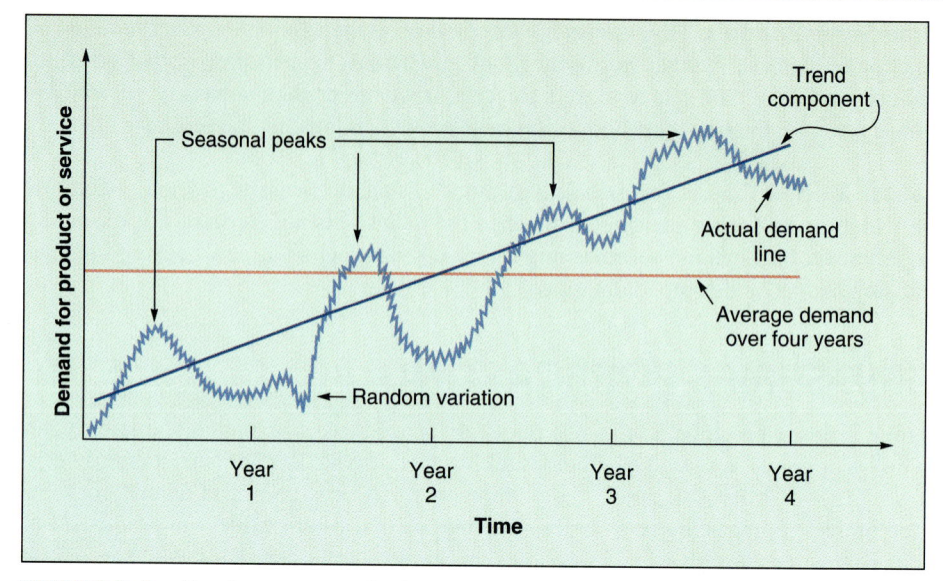

FIGURE 5.1 ■ **Product Demand Charted over 4 Years with a Growth Trend and Seasonality Indicated**

Figure 5.1 illustrates a demand over a 4-year period. It shows the average, trend, seasonal components, and random variations around the demand curve. The average demand is the sum of the demand for each period divided by the number of data periods.

Naive Approach

The simplest way to forecast is to assume that demand in the next period will be equal to demand in the most recent period. In other words, if sales of a product—say, Motorola cellular phones—were 68 units in January, we can forecast that February's sales will also be 68 phones. Does this make any sense? It turns out that for some product lines, this **naive approach** is the most cost-effective and efficient objective forecasting model. At least it provides a starting point against which more sophisticated models that follow can be compared.

Moving Averages

A **moving-average** forecast uses a number of historical actual data values to generate a forecast. Moving averages are useful *if we can assume that market demands will stay fairly steady over time*. A 4-month moving average is found by simply summing the demand during the past 4 months and dividing by 4. With each passing month, the most recent month's data are added to the sum of the previous 3 months' data, and the earliest month is dropped. This practice tends to smooth out short-term irregularities in the data series.

Mathematically, the simple moving average (which serves as an estimate of the next period's demand) is expressed as

$$\text{Moving average} = \frac{\Sigma \text{ demand in previous } n \text{ periods}}{n} \quad (5.1)$$

where *n* is the number of periods in the moving average—for example, 4, 5, or 6 months, respectively, for a 4-, 5-, or 6-period moving average.

During stable times, forecasting is easy; it is just this year's performance plus or minus a few percentage points.

Naive approach
A forecasting technique that assumes demand in the next period is equal to demand in the most recent period.

Moving averages
A forecasting method that uses an average of the n most recent periods of data to forecast the next period.

TIME-SERIES FORECASTING 149

L. L. Bean, Inc., uses two time-series models to forecast incoming calls at its Freeport, Maine, order center. Modeling call volumes allows for efficient scheduling of staff and saves $300,000 annually that might have been lost to unanswered calls or overscheduling of operators.

Example 1 shows how moving averages are calculated.

EXAMPLE 1

Storage shed sales at Donna's Garden Supply are shown in the middle column of the table below. A 3-month moving average appears on the right.

Month	Actual Shed Sales	3-Month Moving Average
January	10	
February	12	
March	13	
April	16	(10 + 12 + 13)/3 = 11⅔
May	19	(12 + 13 + 16)/3 = 13⅔
June	23	(13 + 16 + 19)/3 = 16
July	26	(16 + 19 + 23)/3 = 19⅓
August	30	(19 + 23 + 26)/3 = 22⅔
September	28	(23 + 26 + 30)/3 = 26⅓
October	18	(26 + 30 + 28)/3 = 28
November	16	(30 + 28 + 18)/3 = 25⅓
December	14	(28 + 18 + 16)/3 = 20⅔

Thus we see that the forecast for December is 20⅔. To project the demand for sheds in the coming January, we sum the October, November, and December sales and divide by 3: January forecast = (18 + 16 + 14)/3 = 16.

When a detectable trend or pattern is present, *weights* can be used to place more emphasis on recent values. This practice makes forecasting techniques more responsive to changes because more recent periods may be more heavily weighted. Choice of weights is somewhat arbitrary because there is no set formula to determine them. Therefore, deciding

Using data that are 20 years old (e.g., from housing prices or tuition rates) may not be so useful that all the past data are needed to forecast next year's values. It is not always necessary to use *all* data.

which weights to use requires some experience. For example, if the latest month or period is weighted too heavily, the forecast might reflect a large unusual change in the demand or sales pattern too quickly.

A weighted moving average may be expressed mathematically as

$$\text{Weighted moving average} = \frac{\Sigma\,(\text{weight for period } n)\,(\text{demand in period } n)}{\Sigma\,\text{weights}} \quad (5.2)$$

Example 2 shows how to calculate a weighted moving average.

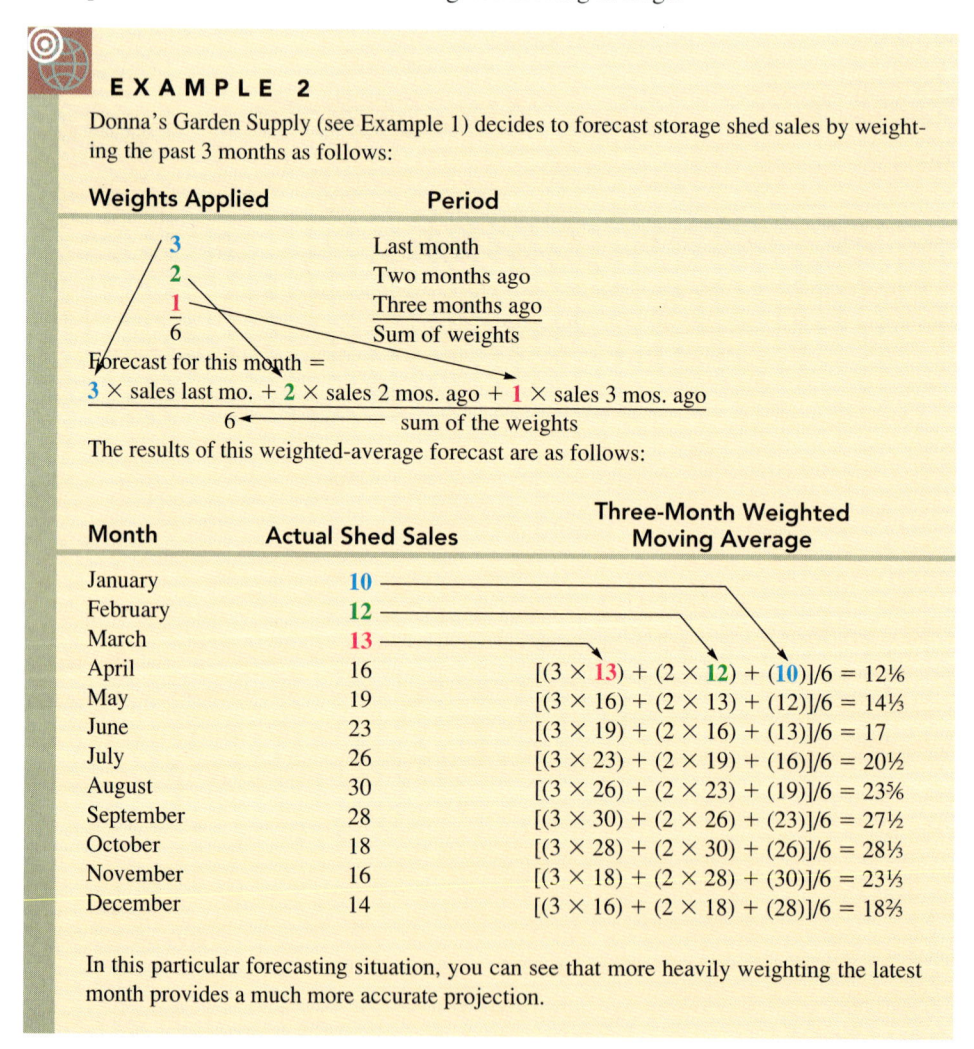

EXAMPLE 2

Donna's Garden Supply (see Example 1) decides to forecast storage shed sales by weighting the past 3 months as follows:

Weights Applied	Period
3	Last month
2	Two months ago
1	Three months ago
6	Sum of weights

Forecast for this month =

$$\frac{3 \times \text{sales last mo.} + 2 \times \text{sales 2 mos. ago} + 1 \times \text{sales 3 mos. ago}}{6 \leftarrow \text{sum of the weights}}$$

The results of this weighted-average forecast are as follows:

Month	Actual Shed Sales	Three-Month Weighted Moving Average
January	10	
February	12	
March	13	
April	16	[(3 × 13) + (2 × 12) + (10)]/6 = 12⅙
May	19	[(3 × 16) + (2 × 13) + (12)]/6 = 14⅓
June	23	[(3 × 19) + (2 × 16) + (13)]/6 = 17
July	26	[(3 × 23) + (2 × 19) + (16)]/6 = 20½
August	30	[(3 × 26) + (2 × 23) + (19)]/6 = 23⅚
September	28	[(3 × 30) + (2 × 26) + (23)]/6 = 27½
October	18	[(3 × 28) + (2 × 30) + (26)]/6 = 28⅓
November	16	[(3 × 18) + (2 × 28) + (30)]/6 = 23⅓
December	14	[(3 × 16) + (2 × 18) + (28)]/6 = 18⅔

In this particular forecasting situation, you can see that more heavily weighting the latest month provides a much more accurate projection.

Both simple and weighted moving averages are effective in smoothing out sudden fluctuations in the demand pattern in order to provide stable estimates. Moving averages do, however, present three problems.

1. Increasing the size of *n* (the number of periods averaged) does smooth out fluctuations better, but it makes the method less sensitive to *real* changes in the data.
2. Moving averages cannot pick up trends very well. Because they are averages, they will always stay within past levels and will not predict changes to either higher or lower levels. That is, they *lag* the actual values.
3. Moving averages require extensive records of past data.

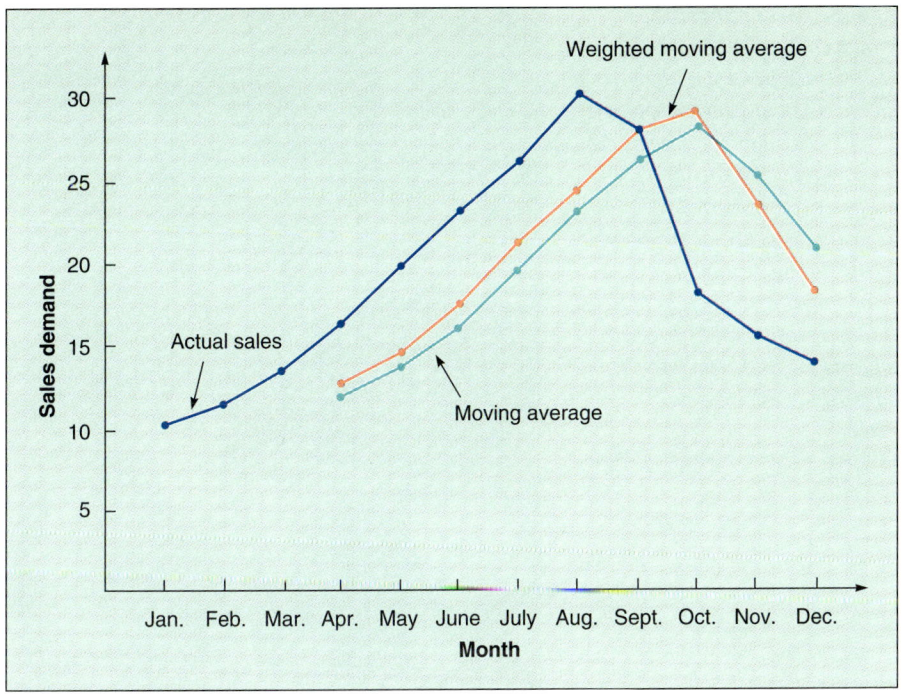

FIGURE 5.2 ■ Actual Demand vs. Moving-Average and Weighted Moving-Average Methods for Donna's Garden Supply

Figure 5.2, a plot of the data in Examples 1 and 2, illustrates the lag effect of the moving-average models. Note that both the moving average and weighted moving-average lines lag the actual demand from April on. The weighted moving average, however, usually reacts more quickly to demand changes. Even in periods of downturn (see November and December), it more closely tracks the demand.

Exponential Smoothing

Exponential smoothing is a sophisticated weighted moving-average forecasting method that is still fairly easy to use. It involves very *little* record keeping of past data. The basic exponential smoothing formula can be shown as follows.

New forecast = last period's forecast
 + α (last period's actual demand − last period's forecast)   (5.3)

where α is a weight, or **smoothing constant,** chosen by the forecaster, that has a value between 0 and 1. Equation (5.3) can also be written mathematically as

$$F_t = F_{t-1} + \alpha(A_{t-1} - F_{t-1}) \quad (5.4)$$

where F_t = new forecast
 F_{t-1} = previous forecast
 α = smoothing (or weighting) constant ($0 \leq \alpha \leq 1$)
 A_{t-1} = previous period's actual demand

Exponential smoothing
A weighted moving-average forecasting technique in which data points are weighted by an exponential function.

Smoothing constant
The weighting factor used in an exponential smoothing forecast, a number between 0 and 1.

Just three weeks after IBM announced its new home computer line in September 1994, the firm sold out its supply through year's end and was unable to fill holiday orders. Why? IBM attributes the shortage to conservative forecasting—a chronic problem in miscalculating demand for PCs. The potential revenue loss of $100 million repeats similar forecasting problems for IBM's popular Think Pad portable PC two years earlier.

Exponential smoothing may have an obscure-sounding name, but it is actually widely used in business and an important part of many computerized inventory control systems.

The concept is not complex. The latest estimate of demand is equal to our old estimate adjusted by a fraction of the difference between the last period's actual demand and the old estimate. Example 3 shows how to use exponential smoothing to derive a forecast.

EXAMPLE 3

In January, a car dealer predicted February demand for 142 Ford Mustangs. Actual February demand was 153 autos. Using a smoothing constant chosen by management of $\alpha = .20$, we can forecast March demand using the exponential smoothing model. Substituting our sample data into the formula, we obtain

New forecast (for March demand) = 142 + .2(153 − 142)
= 144.2

Thus, the March demand forecast for Ford Mustangs is rounded to 144.

The *smoothing constant*, α, is generally in the range from .05 to .50 for business applications. It can be changed to give more weight to recent data (when α is high) or more weight to past data (when α is low). To demonstrate this weighting concept, we can rewrite equation (5.4) algebraically in the form

$$F_t = \alpha A_{t-1} + \alpha(1-\alpha)A_{t-2} + \alpha(1-\alpha)^2 A_{t-3} \\ + \alpha(1-\alpha)^3 A_{t-4} + \cdots + \alpha(1-\alpha)^{n-1} A_{t-n} \quad (5.5)$$

where the weights add to 1. Even though this time series goes back *n* periods (where n can be a very long time), the importance of older past periods declines quickly as α is increased.

TIME-SERIES FORECASTING

When α reaches the extreme of 1.0, then in equation (5.5), $F_t = 1.0A_{t-1}$. All the older values drop out, and the forecast becomes identical to the naive model mentioned earlier in this chapter. That is, the forecast for the next period is just the same as this period's demand.

The following table helps illustrate this concept. For example, when $\alpha = .5$, we can see that the new forecast is based almost entirely on demand in the last 3 or 4 periods. When $\alpha = .1$, the forecast places little weight on recent demand and takes many periods (about 19) of historic values into account.

			Weight Assigned to		
SMOOTHING CONSTANT	MOST RECENT PERIOD (α)	2ND MOST RECENT PERIOD $\alpha(1-\alpha)$	3RD MOST RECENT PERIOD $\alpha(1-\alpha)^2$	4TH MOST RECENT PERIOD $\alpha(1-\alpha)^3$	5TH MOST RECENT PERIOD $\alpha(1-\alpha)^4$
$\alpha = .1$	.1	.09	.081	.073	.066
$\alpha = .5$	.5	.25	.125	.063	.031

Selecting the Smoothing Constant The exponential smoothing approach is easy to use, and it has been successfully applied in virtually every type of business. However, the appropriate value of the smoothing constant, α, can make the difference between an accurate forecast and an inaccurate forecast. In picking a value for the smoothing constant, the objective is to obtain the most accurate forecast. The overall accuracy of a forecasting model can be determined by comparing the forecasted values for past known periods with the actual or observed demand for those periods.

The forecast error is defined as

$$\text{Forecast error} = \text{demand} - \text{forecast}$$

Mean Absolute Deviation One measure of the overall forecast error for a model is the **mean absolute deviation (MAD)**. This value is computed by taking the sum of the absolute values of the individual forecast errors and dividing by the number of periods of data (n):

$$\text{MAD} = \frac{\Sigma |\text{forecast errors}|}{n} \quad (5.6)$$

Mean absolute deviation (MAD)
A measure of the overall forecast error for a model.

Example 4 applies this concept with a trial-and-error testing of two values of α.

EXAMPLE 4

During the past eight quarters, the Port of Baltimore has unloaded large quantities of grain from ships. The port's operations manager wants to test the use of exponential smoothing to see how well the technique works in predicting tonnage unloaded. He guesses that the forecast of grain unloaded in the first quarter was 175 tons. Two values of α are examined: $\alpha = .10$ and $\alpha = .50$. The following table shows the *detailed* calculations for $\alpha = .10$ only:

Quarter	Actual Tonnage Unloaded	Rounded Forecast with $\alpha = .10$*	Rounded Forecast with $\alpha = .50$*
1	180	175	175
2	168	176 = 175.00 + .10(180 − 175)	178
3	159	175 = 175.50 + .10(168 − 175.50)	173
4	175	173 = 174.75 + .10(159 − 174.75)	166

Quarter	Actual Tonnage Unloaded	Rounded Forecast with $\alpha = .10$*	Rounded Forecast with $\alpha = .50$*
5	190	173 = 173.18 + .10(175 − 173.18)	170
6	205	175 = 173.36 + .10(190 − 173.36)	180
7	180	178 = 175.02 + .10(205 − 175.02)	193
8	182	178 = 178.02 + .10(180 − 178.02)	186
9	?	179 = 178.22 + .10(182 − 178.22)	184

*Forecasts rounded to the nearest ton.

To evaluate the accuracy of each smoothing constant, we can compute forecast errors in terms of absolute deviations and MADs.

Quarter	Actual Tonnage Unloaded	Rounded Forecast with $\alpha = .10$	Absolute Deviation for $\alpha = .10$	Rounded Forecast with $\alpha = .50$	Absolute Deviation for $\alpha = .50$
1	180	175	5	175	5
2	168	176	8	178	10
3	159	175	16	173	14
4	175	173	2	166	9
5	190	173	17	170	20
6	205	175	30	180	25
7	180	178	2	193	13
8	182	178	4	186	4
		Sum of absolute deviations	84		100
		$\text{MAD} = \frac{\Sigma |\text{deviations}|}{n}$	10.50		12.50

On the basis of this analysis, a smoothing constant of $\alpha = .10$ is preferred to $\alpha = .50$ because its MAD is smaller.

Most computerized forecasting software includes a feature that automatically finds the smoothing constant with the lowest forecast error. Some software modifies the α value if errors become larger than acceptable.

Mean squared error (MSE) The average of the squared differences between the forecasted and observed values.

Mean Squared Error The **mean squared error (MSE)** is another way of measuring overall forecast error. MSE is the average of the squared differences between the forecasted and observed values. Its formula is

$$\text{MSE} = \frac{\Sigma \, (\text{forecast errors})^2}{n} \quad (5.7)$$

Example 5 finds the MSE for the Port of Baltimore introduced in Example 4.

EXAMPLE 5

Quarter	Actual Tonnage Unloaded	Forecast for $\alpha = .10$	(Error)²
1	180	175	$5^2 = 25$
2	168	176	$(-8)^2 = 64$
3	159	175	$(-16)^2 = 256$
4	175	173	$2^2 = 4$

TIME-SERIES FORECASTING

Quarter	Actual Tonnage Unloaded	Forecast for $\alpha = .10$	(Error)²
5	190	173	17² = 289
6	205	175	30² = 900
7	180	178	2² = 4
8	182	178	4² = 16
			Sum of errors squared = 1,558

$$\text{MSE} = \frac{\Sigma \text{ forecast errors}^2}{n} = 1{,}558/8 = 194.75$$

Is this MSE good or bad? It all depends on the MSEs for other values of a. As a practice exercise, find the MSE for $\alpha = .50$. (You should get MSE = 201.5.) The result indicates that $\alpha = .10$ is a better choice because we want to minimize MSE. Coincidentally, this confirms the conclusion we reached using MAD in Example 4.

Exponential Smoothing with Trend Adjustment

As with *any* moving-average technique, simple exponential smoothing fails to respond to trends. Other forecasting techniques that can deal with trends are certainly available. However, because exponential smoothing is such a popular modeling approach in business, let us look at it in more detail.

Here is why exponential smoothing must be modified when a trend is present. Assume that demand for our product or service has been increasing by 100 units per month and that we have been forecasting with $\alpha = 0.4$ in our exponential smoothing model. The following table shows a severe lag in the 2nd, 3rd, 4th, and 5th months, even when our initial estimate for month 1 is perfect.

Month	Actual Demand	Forecast for Month t (F_t)
1	100	$F_1 = 100$ (given)
2	200	$F_2 = F_1 + \alpha (A_1 - F_1) = 100 + .4\,(100 - 100) = 100$
3	300	$F_3 = F_2 + \alpha (A_2 - F_2) = 100 + .4\,(200 - 100) = 140$
4	400	$F_4 = F_3 + \alpha (A_3 - F_3) = 140 + .4\,(300 - 140) = 204$
5	500	$F_5 = F_4 + \alpha (A_4 - F_4) = 204 + .4\,(400 - 204) = 282$

To improve our forecast, let us illustrate a more complex exponential smoothing model, one that adjusts for trend. The idea is to compute an exponentially smoothed average of the data and then adjust for positive or negative lag in trend. The new formula is:

$$\text{Forecast including trend } (FIT_t) = \text{exponentially smoothed forecast } (F_t)$$
$$+ \text{ exponentially smoothed trend } (T_t) \quad (5.8)$$

With trend-adjusted exponential smoothing, estimates for both the average and the trend are smoothed. This procedure requires two smoothing constants, α for the average and β for the trend. We then compute the average and trend each period:

$$F_t = \alpha \,(\text{Actual demand this period}) + (1 - \alpha)\,(\text{Forecast last period}$$
$$+ \text{ Trend estimate last period})$$

or

$$F_t = \alpha\,(A_t) + (1 - \alpha)\,(F_{t-1} + T_{t-1}) \quad (5.9)$$

$$T_t = \beta \text{ (Forecast this period} - \text{Forecast last period)}$$
$$+ (1 - \beta) \text{ (Trend estimate last period)}$$

or

$$T_t = \beta (F_t - F_{t-1}) + (1 - \beta) T_{t-1} \tag{5.10}$$

where F_t = exponentially smoothed forecast of the data series in period t
T_t = exponentially smoothed trend in period t
A_t = actual demand in period t
α = smoothing constant for the average ($0 \leq \alpha \leq 1$)
β = smoothing constant for the trend ($0 \leq \beta \leq 1$)

So the three steps to compute a trend-adjusted forecast are:

Step 1: Compute F_t, the exponentially smoothed forecast for period t, using equation (5.9).

Step 2: Compute the smoothed trend, T_t, using equation (5.10).

Step 3: Calculate the forecast including trend, FIT_t, by the formula $FIT_t = F_t + T_t$.

Example 6 shows how to use trend-adjusted exponential smoothing.

EXAMPLE 6

A large Portland manufacturer uses exponential smoothing to forecast demand for a piece of pollution-control equipment. It appears that an increasing trend is present.

Month (t)	Actual Demand (A_t)	Month (t)	Actual Demand (A_t)
1	12	6	21
2	17	7	31
3	20	8	28
4	19	9	36
5	24		

Smoothing constants are assigned the values of $\alpha = .2$ and $\beta = .4$. Assume the initial forecast for month 1 (F_1) was 11 units and the trend over that period (T_1) was 2 units.

Step 1: Forecast for month 2 (F_2) = $\alpha A_2 + (1 - \alpha)(F_1 + T_1)$
$F_2 = (.2)(17) + (1 - .2)(11 + 2)$
$= 3.4 + (.8)(13) = 3.4 + 10.4 = 13.8$ units

Step 2: Compute the trend in period 2.
$T_2 = \beta(F_2 - F_1) + (1 - \beta) T_1$
$= .4(13.8 - 11) + (1 - .4)(2)$
$= (.4)(2.8) + (.6)(2) = 1.12 + 1.2 = 2.32$

Step 3: Compute the forecast including trend (FIT_t):
$FIT_2 = F_2 + T_2$
$= 13.8 + 2.32$
$= 16.12$ units

TIME-SERIES FORECASTING

We will also do the same calculations for the third month.

Step 1: $F_3 = \alpha A_3 + (1 - \alpha)(F_2 + T_2) = (.2)(20) + (1 - .2)(13.8 + 2.32)$
$= 4 + (.8)(16.12) = 4 + 12.9 = 16.9$

Step 2: $T_3 = \beta(F_3 - F_2) + (1 - \beta)T_2 = (.4)(16.9 - 13.8) + (1 - .4)(2.32)$
$= (.4)(3.1) + (.6)(2.32) = 1.24 + 1.39 = 2.63$

Step 3: $FIT_3 = F_3 + T_3$
$= 16.90 + 2.63 = 19.53$

Table 5.1 completes the forecasts for the 9-month period. Figure 5.3 compares actual demand to forecast including trend (FIT_t).

TABLE 5.1

Month	Actual Demand	Smoothed Forecast, F_t	Smoothed Trend, T_t	Forecast Including Trend FIT_t
1	12	11.00	2.00	—
2	17	13.80	2.32	16.12
3	20	16.90	2.63	19.53
4	19	19.40	2.58	21.98
5	24	22.38	2.74	25.12
6	21	24.30	2.41	26.71
7	31	27.57	2.75	30.32
8	28	29.86	2.57	32.43
9	36	33.14	2.85	35.99

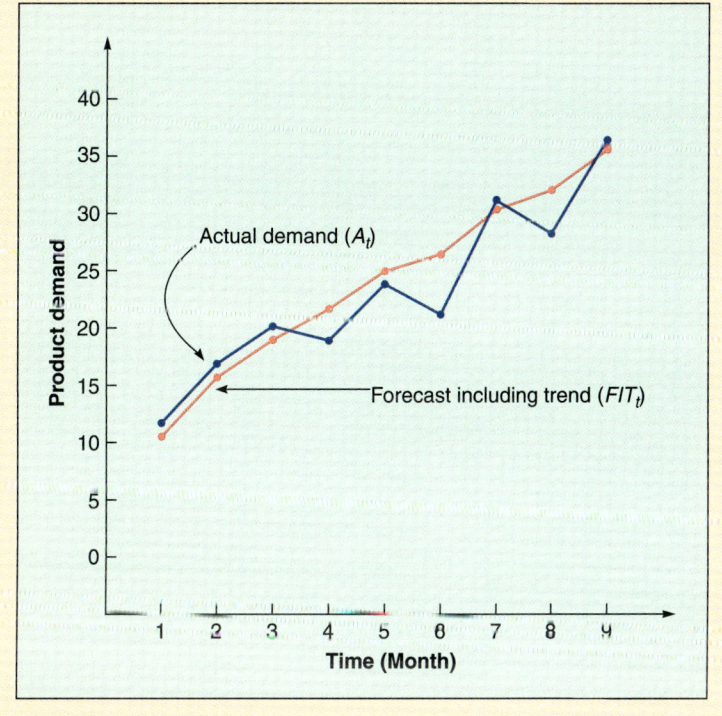

FIGURE 5.3 ■ Exponential Smoothing with Trend-Adjustment Forecasts Compared to Actual Demand Data

The value of the trend-smoothing constant, β, resembles the α constant because a high β is more responsive to recent changes in trend. A low β gives less weight to the most recent trends and tends to smooth out the present trend. Values of β can be found by the trial-and-error approach or by using sophisticated commercial forecasting software, with the MAD used as a measure of comparison.

Simple exponential smoothing is often referred to as *first-order smoothing,* and trend-adjusted smoothing is called *second-order,* or *double, smoothing.* Other advanced exponential-smoothing models are also used, including seasonal-adjusted and triple smoothing, but these are beyond the scope of this book.[3]

Trend Projections

Trend projection A time-series forecasting method that fits a trend line to a series of historical data points and then projects the line into the future for forecasts.

The last time-series forecasting method we will discuss is **trend projection.** This technique fits a trend line to a series of historical data points and then projects the line into the future for medium-to-long-range forecasts. Several mathematical trend equations can be developed (for example, exponential and quadratic), but in this section, we will look at *linear* (straight-line) trends only.

If we decide to develop a linear trend line by a precise statistical method, we can apply the *least squares method.* This approach results in a straight line that minimizes the sum of the squares of the vertical differences or deviations from the line to each of the actual observations. Figure 5.4 illustrates the least squares approach.

A least squares line is described in terms of its *y*-intercept (the height at which it intercepts the *y*-axis) and its slope (the angle of the line). If we can compute the *y*-intercept and slope, we can express the line with the following equation:

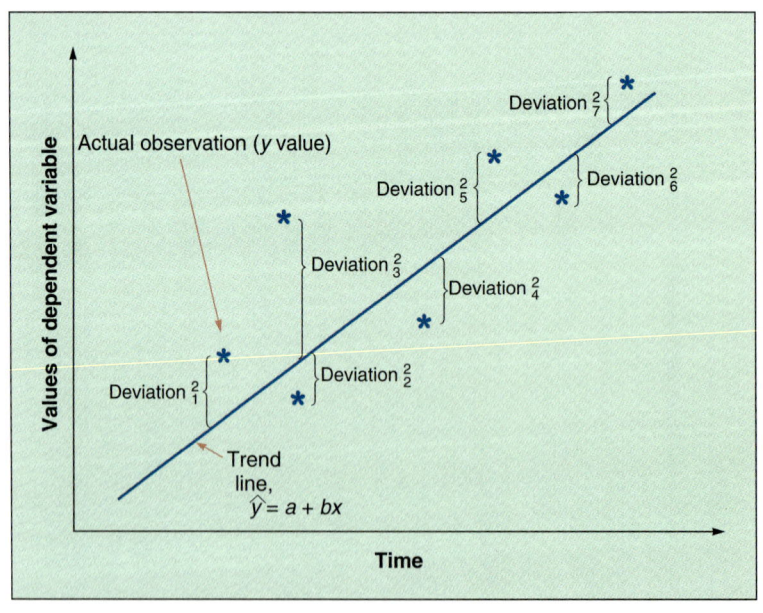

FIGURE 5.4 ■ The Least Squares Method for Finding the Best-Fitting Straight Line, Where the Asterisks Are the Locations of the Seven Actual Observations or Data Points

---

[3] For more details, see E. S. Gardner, "Exponential Smoothing: The State of the Art," *Journal of Forecasting* 4, no. 1 (March 1985); or G.E.P. Box et al., *Time Series Analysis, Forecasting, and Control,* 3rd ed. (Englewood Cliffs, NJ: Prentice Hall, 1994).

TIME-SERIES FORECASTING   159

$$\hat{y} = a + bx \quad (5.11)$$

where $\hat{y}$ (called "y hat") = computed value of the variable to be predicted
                            (called the dependent variable)
         a = y-axis intercept
         b = slope of the regression line (or the rate of change in
             y for given changes in x)
         x = the independent variable (which in this case is *time*)

Statisticians have developed equations that we can use to find the values of a and b for any regression line. The slope b is found by

$$b = \frac{\Sigma xy - n\bar{x}\bar{y}}{\Sigma x^2 - n\bar{x}^2} \quad (5.12)$$

where b = slope of the regression line
        Σ = summation sign
        x = values of the independent variable
        y = values of the dependent variable
        $\bar{x}$ = average of the value of the x's
        $\bar{y}$ = average of the value of the y's
        n = number of data points or observations

We can compute the y-intercept a as follows:

$$a = \bar{y} - b\bar{x} \quad (5.13)$$

Example 7 shows how to apply these concepts.

EXAMPLE 7

The demand for electrical power at N.Y. Edison over the period 1992–1998 is shown below, in megawatts. Let's forecast 1999 demand by fitting a straight-line trend to these data.

Year	Electrical Power Demand	Year	Electrical Power Demand
1992	74	1996	105
1993	79	1997	142
1994	80	1998	122
1995	90		

With a series of data over time, we can minimize the computations by transforming the values of x (time) to simpler numbers. Thus, in this case, we can designate 1992 as year 1, 1993 as year 2, and so on.

Year	Time Period	Electric Power Demand	x^2	xy
1992	1	74	1	74
1993	2	79	4	158
1994	3	80	9	240
1995	4	90	16	360
1996	5	105	25	525
1997	6	142	36	852
1998	7	122	49	854
	$\Sigma x = 28$	$\Sigma y = 692$	$\Sigma x^2 = 140$	$\Sigma xy = 3,063$

$$\bar{x} = \frac{\Sigma x}{n} = \frac{28}{7} = 4 \qquad \bar{y} = \frac{\Sigma y}{n} = \frac{692}{7} = 98.86$$

$$b = \frac{\Sigma xy - n\bar{x}\bar{y}}{\Sigma x^2 - n\bar{x}^2} = \frac{3{,}063 - (7)(4)(98.86)}{140 - (7)(4^2)} = \frac{295}{28} = 10.54$$

$$a = \bar{y} - b\bar{x} = 98.86 - 10.54(4) = 56.70$$

Thus, the least squares trend equation is $\hat{y} = 56.70 + 10.54x$. To project demand in 1999, we first denote the year 1999 in our new coding system as $x = 8$:

$$\text{Demand in 1999} = 56.70 + 10.54(8)$$

$$= 141.02, \text{ or } 141 \text{ megawatts}$$

We can estimate demand for 2000 by inserting $x = 9$ in the same equation:

$$\text{Demand in 2000} = 56.70 + 10.54(9)$$

$$= 151.56, \text{ or } 152 \text{ megawatts}$$

To check the validity of the model, we plot historical demand and the trend line in Figure 5.5. In this case, we may wish to be cautious and try to understand the 1997–1998 swing in demand.

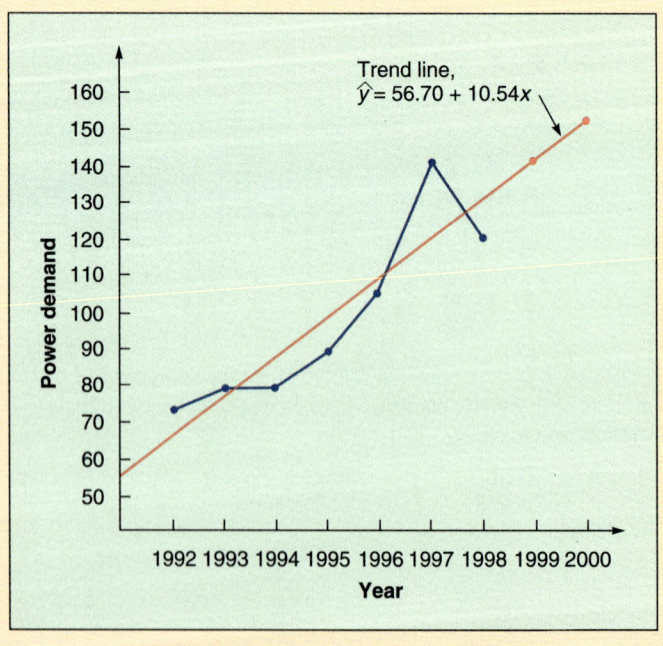

FIGURE 5.5 ■ Electrical Power and the Computed Trend Line

Time-Series Forecasting

Notes on the use of the least squares method Using the least squares method implies that we have met three requirements:

1. We always plot the data first, because least squares data assume a linear relationship. If a curve appears to be present, curvilinear analysis is probably needed.
2. We do not predict time periods far beyond our given data base. For example, if we have 20 months' worth of average prices of Microsoft stock, we could forecast only 3 or 4 months into the future. Forecasts beyond that have little statistical validity. Thus, you cannot take 5 years' worth of sales data and project 10 years into the future. The world is too uncertain.
3. Deviations around the least squares line (see Figure 5.4) are assumed to be random. They are normally distributed with most observations close to the line and only a smaller number farther out.

Seasonal Variations in Data

Time-series forecasting like that in Example 7 involves looking at the *trend* of data over a series of time. As we stated before, however, seasonality sometimes makes adjustment in the trend-line forecast necessary. Demand for coal and fuel oil, for example, peaks during cold winter months. Demand for golf clubs or suntan lotion may be highest in summer. Analyzing data in monthly or quarterly terms usually makes it easy for a statistician to spot seasonal patterns. Seasonal indices can then be developed by several common methods.

In what is called a *multiplicative seasonal model,* seasonal factors are multiplied by an estimate of average demand to produce a seasonal forecast. Our assumption in this section is that trend has been removed from the data. Otherwise, the magnitude of the seasonal data will be distorted by the trend.

Here are the steps we will follow for a company that has "seasons" of one month.

1. Find the *average historical demand each season* (or month in this case) by summing the demand for that month in each year and dividing by the number of years of data available. For example, if, in January, we have seen sales of 8, 6, and 10 over the past 3 years, average January demand equals (8 + 6 + 10)/3 = 8 units.
2. Compute the *average demand over all months* by dividing the total average annual demand by the number of seasons. For example, if the total average demand for a year is 120 units and there are 12 seasons (each month), the average monthly demand is 120/12 = 10 units.
3. Compute a *seasonal index* for each season by dividing that month's actual historical demand (from step 1) by the average demand over all months (from step 2). For example, if the average historical January demand over the past 3 years is 8 units and the average demand over all months is 10 units, the seasonal index for January is 8/10 = .80. Likewise, a seasonal index of 1.20 for February would mean that February's demand is 20 percent larger than the average demand over all months.
4. Estimate next year's total annual demand.
5. Divide this estimate of total annual demand by the number of seasons, then multiply it by the seasonal index for that month. This provides the *seasonal forecast.*

Because John Deere understands seasonal variations, it has been able to obtain 70% of its orders in advance of seasonal use (through price reductions and incentives such as free interest) so it can smooth production.

Example 8 illustrates this procedure as it computes seasonal factors from historical data.

EXAMPLE 8

Monthly sales of Compaq Company laptop computers at Reva Computerland for 1996–1997 are shown in the following table.

Month	Sales Demand 1996	Sales Demand 1997	Average 1996–1997 Demand	Average Monthly Demand*	Seasonal Index†
Jan.	80	100	90	94	.957
Feb.	75	85	80	94	.851
Mar.	80	90	85	94	.904
Apr.	90	110	100	94	1.064
May	115	131	123	94	1.309
June	110	120	115	94	1.223
July	100	110	105	94	1.117
Aug.	90	110	100	94	1.064
Sept.	85	95	90	94	.957
Oct.	75	85	80	94	.851
Nov.	75	85	80	94	.851
Dec.	80	80	80	94	.851

Total average annual demand = 1,128

*Average monthly demand = $\dfrac{1{,}128}{12 \text{ months}} = 94$

†Seasonal index = $\dfrac{\text{average 1996–1997 monthly demand}}{\text{average monthly demand}}$

If we expected the 1998 annual demand for computers to be 1,200 units, we would use these seasonal indices to forecast the monthly demand as follows:

Month	Demand	Month	Demand
Jan.	$\dfrac{1{,}200}{12} \times .957 = 96$	July	$\dfrac{1{,}200}{12} \times 1.117 = 112$
Feb.	$\dfrac{1{,}200}{12} \times .851 = 85$	Aug.	$\dfrac{1{,}200}{12} \times 1.064 = 106$
March	$\dfrac{1{,}200}{12} \times .904 = 90$	Sept.	$\dfrac{1{,}200}{12} \times .957 = 96$
April	$\dfrac{1{,}200}{12} \times 1.064 = 106$	Oct.	$\dfrac{1{,}200}{12} \times .851 = 85$
May	$\dfrac{1{,}200}{12} \times 1.309 = 131$	Nov.	$\dfrac{1{,}200}{12} \times .851 = 85$
June	$\dfrac{1{,}200}{12} \times 1.223 = 122$	Dec.	$\dfrac{1{,}200}{12} \times .851 = 85$

For simplicity, trend calculations are ignored and only two periods used for each monthly index in the above example. Example 9 illustrates how indices that have already been prepared can be applied to adjust trend-line forecasts.

EXAMPLE 9

Management at Davis's Department Store has used time-series regression to forecast retail sales for the next 4 quarters. Sales estimates are $100,000, $120,000, $140,000, and $160,000 for the respective quarters. Seasonal indices for the 4 quarters have been found to be 1.30, .90, .70, and 1.15, respectively.

To compute a seasonalized or adjusted sales forecast, we just multiply each seasonal index by the appropriate trend forecast:

$$\hat{y}_{seasonal} = \text{Index} \times \hat{y}_{trend\ forecast}$$

Thus for

Quarter I: $\hat{y}_I = (1.30)(\$100,000) = \$130,000$
Quarter II: $\hat{y}_{II} = (.90)(\$120,000) = \$108,000$
Quarter III: $\hat{y}_{III} = (.70)(\$140,000) = \$98,000$
Quarter IV: $\hat{y}_{IV} = (1.15)(\$160,000) = \$184,000$

CAUSAL FORECASTING METHODS: REGRESSION AND CORRELATION ANALYSIS

Unlike time-series forecasting, *causal forecasting* models usually consider *several* variables that are related to the quantity being predicted. Once these related variables have been found, a statistical model is built and used to forecast the item of interest. This approach is more powerful than the time-series methods that use only the historic values for the forecasted variable.

Many factors can be considered in a causal analysis. For example, the sales of IBM PCs might be related to IBM's advertising budget, the company's prices, competitors' prices and promotional strategies, and even the nation's economy and unemployment rates. In this case, PC sales would be called the *dependent variable* and the other variables would be called *independent variables*. The manager's job is to develop *the best statistical relationship between PC sales and the independent variables*. The most common quantitative causal forecasting model is **linear-regression analysis**.

Linear-regression analysis A straight-line mathematical model to describe the functional relationships between independent and dependent variables.

Using Regression Analysis to Forecast

We can use the same mathematical model that we employed in the least squares method of trend projection to perform a linear-regression analysis. The dependent variables that we want to forecast will still be $\hat{y}$. But now the independent variable, x, need no longer be time. We use the equation

$$\hat{y} = a + bx$$

where $\hat{y}$ = value of the dependent variable (in our example, sales)
a = y-axis intercept
b = slope of the regression line
x = independent variable

Chapter 5 Forecasting

Example 10 shows how to use linear regression.

EXAMPLE 10

Nodel Construction Company renovates old homes in Orono, Maine. Over time, the company has found that its dollar volume of renovation work is dependent on the Orono area payroll. The following table lists Nodel's revenues and the amount of money earned by wage earners in Orono during the years 1993 to 1998.

Nodel's Sales ($000,000), y	Local Payroll ($000,000,000), x	Nodel's Sales ($000,000), y	Local Payroll ($000,000,000), x
2.0	1	2.0	2
3.0	3	2.0	1
2.5	4	3.5	7

Nodel management wants to establish a mathematical relationship to help predict sales. First, it needs to determine whether there is a straight-line (linear) relationship between area payroll and sales, so it plots the known data on a scatter diagram.

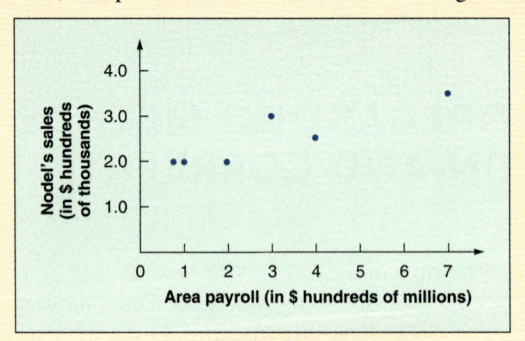

It appears from the six data points that there is a slight positive relationship between the independent variable (payroll) and the dependent variable (sales): As payroll increases, Nodel's sales tend to be higher.

We can find a mathematical equation by using the least squares regression approach.

Sales, y	Payroll, x	x^2	xy
2.0	1	1	2.0
3.0	3	9	9.0
2.5	4	16	10.0
2.0	2	4	4.0
2.0	1	1	2.0
3.5	7	49	24.5
$\Sigma y = 15.0$	$\Sigma x = 18$	$\Sigma x^2 = 80$	$\Sigma xy = 51.5$

$$\bar{x} = \frac{\Sigma x}{6} = \frac{18}{6} = 3$$

$$\bar{y} = \frac{\Sigma y}{6} = \frac{15}{6} = 2.5$$

$$b = \frac{\Sigma xy - n\bar{x}\bar{y}}{\Sigma x^2 - n\bar{x}^2} = \frac{51.5 - (6)(3)(2.5)}{80 - (6)(3^2)} = .25$$

$$a = \bar{y} - b\bar{x} = 2.5 - (.25)(3) = 1.75$$

The estimated regression equation, therefore, is

$$\hat{y} = 1.75 + .25x$$

or

$$\text{Sales} = 1.75 + .25 \text{ (payroll)}$$

If the local chamber of commerce predicts that the Orono area payroll will be $600 million next year, we can estimate sales for Nodel with the regression equation:

$$\text{Sales (in hundred thousands)} = 1.75 + .25(6)$$
$$= 1.75 + 1.50 = 3.25$$

or

$$\text{Sales} = \$325{,}000$$

The final part of Example 10 shows a central weakness of causal forecasting methods like regression. Even when we have computed a regression equation, we must provide a forecast of the independent variable x—in this case, payroll—before estimating the dependent variable y for the next time period. Although this is not a problem for all forecasts, you can imagine the difficulty of determining future values of *some* common independent variables (such as unemployment rates, gross national product, price indices, and so on).

Standard Error of the Estimate

The forecast of $325,000 for Nodel's sales in Example 10 is called a *point estimate* of y. The point estimate is really the *mean,* or *expected value,* of a distribution of possible values of sales. Figure 5.6 illustrates this concept.

Glidden Paints assembly lines fill thousands of cans per hour. To predict demand, the firm uses causal forecasting methods such as linear regression, with independent variables such as disposable personal income and GNP. Although housing starts would be a natural variable, Glidden found that it correlated poorly with past sales. It turns out that most Glidden paint is sold through retailers to customers who already own homes or businesses.

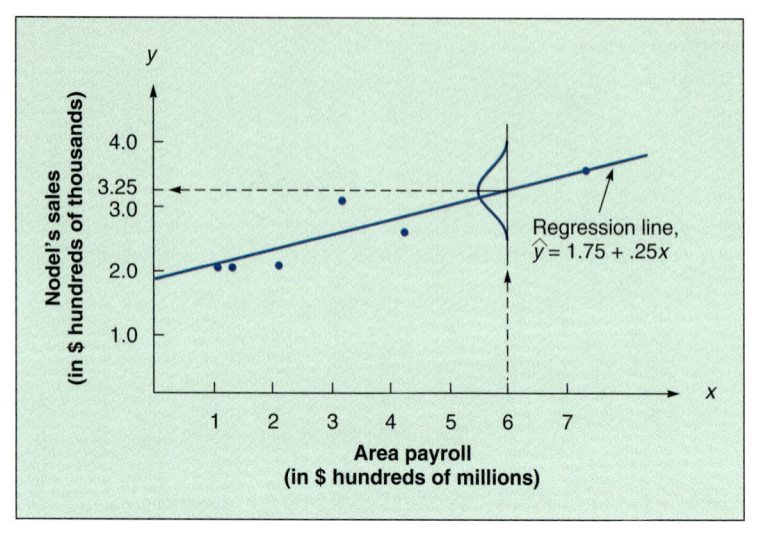

FIGURE 5.6 ■ Distribution about the Point Estimate of $600 Million Payroll

Standard error of the estimate A measure of variability around the regression line—its standard deviation.

To measure the accuracy of the regression estimates, we must compute the **standard error of the estimate,** $S_{y,x}$. This computation is called the *standard deviation of the regression:* It measures the error from the dependent variable, *y*, to the regression line, rather than to the mean. Equation (5.14) is a similar expression to that found in most statistics books for computing the standard deviation of an arithmetic mean:

$$S_{y,x} = \sqrt{\frac{\Sigma(y - y_c)^2}{n - 2}} \tag{5.14}$$

where y = *y*-value of each data point
  y_c = computed value of the dependent variable, from the regression equation
  n = number of data points

Equation (5.15) may look more complex, but it is actually an easier-to-use version of equation (5.14). Both formulas provide the same answer and can be used in setting up prediction intervals around the point estimate.[4]

$$S_{y,x} = \sqrt{\frac{\Sigma y^2 - a\Sigma y - b\Sigma xy}{n - 2}} \tag{5.15}$$

Example 11 shows how we would calculate the standard error of the estimate in Example 10.

---

[4] When the sample size is large ($n > 30$), the prediction interval value of *y* can be computed using normal tables. When the number of observations is small, the *t*-distribution is appropriate. See J. Neter, W. Wasserman, and S. Whitmore, *Applied Statistics,* 3rd ed. (Newton, MA: Allyn & Bacon, 1991).

EXAMPLE 11

To compute the standard error of the estimate for Nodel's data in Example 10, the only number we need that is not available to solve for $S_{y,x}$ is Σy^2. Some quick addition reveals $\Sigma y^2 = 39.5$. Therefore,

$$S_{y,x} = \sqrt{\frac{\Sigma y^2 - a\Sigma y - b\Sigma xy}{n - 2}}$$

$$= \sqrt{\frac{39.5 - 1.75(15.0) - .25(51.5)}{6 - 2}}$$

$$= \sqrt{.09375} = .306 \text{ (in \$ hundred thousands)}$$

The standard error of the estimate is then $30,600 in sales.

Correlation Coefficients for Regression Lines

The regression equation is one way of expressing the nature of the relationship between two variables. Regression lines are not "cause-and-effect" relationships. They merely describe the relationships among variables. The regression equation shows how one variable relates to the value and changes in another variable.

Another way to evaluate the relationship between two variables is to compute the **coefficient of correlation.** This measure expresses the degree or strength of the linear relationship. Usually identified as r, the coefficient of correlation can be any number between $+1$ and -1. Figure 5.7 illustrates what different values of r might look like.

Coefficient of correlation A measure of the strength of the relationship between two variables.

(a) Perfect positive correlation: $r = +1$

(b) Positive correlation: $0 < r < 1$

(c) No correlation: $r = 0$

(d) Perfect negative correlation: $r = -1$

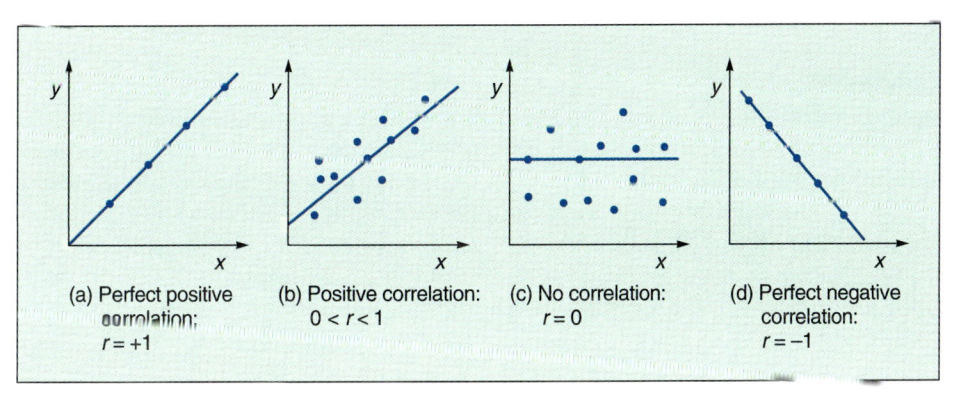

FIGURE 5.7 ■ Four Values of the Correlation Coefficient

To compute r, we use much of the same data needed earlier to calculate a and b for the regression line. The rather lengthy equation for r is

$$r = \frac{n\Sigma xy - \Sigma x\Sigma y}{\sqrt{[n\Sigma x^2 - (\Sigma x)^2][n\Sigma y^2 - (\Sigma y)^2]}} \quad (5.16)$$

Example 12 shows how to calculate the coefficient of correlation for the data given in Examples 10 and 11.

EXAMPLE 12

In Example 10, we looked at the relationship between Nodel Construction Company's renovation sales and payroll in its hometown of Orono. To compute the coefficient of correlation for the data shown, we need add only one more column of calculations (for y^2) and then apply the equation for r:

y	x	x^2	xy	y^2
2.0	1	1	2.0	4.0
3.0	3	9	9.0	9.0
2.5	4	16	10.0	6.25
2.0	2	4	4.0	4.0
2.0	1	1	2.0	4.0
3.5	7	49	24.5	12.25
$\Sigma y = 15.0$	$\Sigma x = 18$	$\Sigma x^2 = 80$	$\Sigma xy = 51.5$	$\Sigma y^2 = 39.5$

$$r = \frac{(6)(51.5) - (18)(15.0)}{\sqrt{[(6)(80) - (18)^2][(6)(39.5) - (15.0)^2]}}$$

$$= \frac{309 - 270}{\sqrt{(156)(12)}} = \frac{39}{\sqrt{1,872}}$$

$$= \frac{39}{43.3} = .901$$

This r of .901 appears to be a significant correlation and helps to confirm the closeness of the relationship between the two variables.

Coefficient of determination
A measure of the amount of variation in the dependent variable about its mean that is explained by the regression equation.

A high r^2 doesn't always mean one variable will be a good predictor of the other. Skirt lengths and stock market prices may be correlated, but raising one doesn't mean the other will go up or down.

Although the coefficient of correlation is the measure most commonly used to describe the relationship between two variables, another measure does exist. It is called the **coefficient of determination** and is simply the square of the coefficient of correlation—namely, r^2. The value of r^2 will always be a positive number in the range of $0 \le r^2 \le 1$. The coefficient of determination is the percent of variation in the dependent variable (y) that is explained by the regression equation. In Nodel's case, the value of r^2 is .81, indicating that 81% of the total variation is explained by the regression equation.

Multiple-Regression Analysis

Multiple regression
A causal forecasting method with more than one independent variable.

Multiple regression is a practical extension of the simple regression model we just explored. It allows us to build a model with several independent variables instead of just one variable. For example, if Nodel Construction wants to include average annual interest rates in its model for forecasting renovation sales, the proper equation would be

$$\hat{y} = a + b_1 x_1 + b_2 x_2 \qquad (5.17)$$

OM IN ACTION

FORECASTING SPARE PARTS AT AMERICAN AIRLINES

To support the operation of its fleet of over 400 aircraft, American Airlines maintains a vast inventory of spare repairable (rotatable) aircraft parts. Its PC-based forecasting system, the Rotables Allocation and Planning System (RAPS), provides demand forecasts for spare parts, helps allocate these parts to airports, and computes the availability of each spare part. With 5,000 different kinds of parts, ranging from landing gear to wing flaps to coffeemakers to altimeters, meeting demand for each part at each station can be extremely difficult—and expensive. The average price of a rotatable part is about $5,000, with some parts (such as avionics computers) costing well over $500,000 each.

Before developing RAPS, American used only time-series methods to forecast the demand for spare parts. The time-series approach however, was slow to respond to even moderate changes in aircraft usage, let alone major fleet expansions. Instead, RAPS uses linear regression to establish a relationship between monthly part removals and various functions of monthly flying hours. Correlation coefficients and statistical significance tests are used to find the best regressions, which now take only one hour instead of the days that the old system needed.

The results? Using RAPS, American says that it had a one-time savings of $7 million and recurring annual savings of nearly $1 million.

Sources: Mark I. Tedone, "Repairable Part Management," *Interfaces* 19, no. 4 (July–August 1989): 61–68; and *New York Times*, March 21, 1997, p. D2.

where $\hat{y}$ = dependent variable, sales
a = a constant
x_1 and x_2 = values of the two independent variables, area payroll and interest rates, respectively
b_1 and b_2 = coefficients for the two independent variables

The mathematics of multiple regression becomes quite complex (and is usually tackled by computer), so we leave the formulas for a, b_1, and b_2 to statistics textbooks. However, Example 13 shows how to interpret equation (5.17) in forecasting Nodel's sales.

EXAMPLE 13

The new multiple-regression line for Nodel Construction, calculated by computer software, is

$$\hat{y} = 1.80 + .30x_1 - 5.0x_2$$

We also find that the new coefficient of correlation is .96; implying the inclusion of the variable x_2, interest rates, adds even more strength to the linear relationship.

We can now estimate Nodel's sales if we substitute values for next year's payroll and interest rate. If Orono's payroll will be $600 million and the interest rate will be .12 (12%), sales will be forecast as

$$\text{Sales (\$ hundred thousands)} = 1.80 + .30(6) - 5.0(.12)$$
$$= 1.8 + 1.8 - .6$$
$$= 3.00$$

or

$$\text{Sales} = \$300,000$$

MONITORING AND CONTROLLING FORECASTS

Once a forecast has been completed, it should not be forgotten. No manager wants to be reminded that his or her forecast is horribly inaccurate, but a firm needs to determine why actual demand (or whatever variable is being examined) differed significantly from that projected. If the forecaster is accurate, that individual usually makes sure that everyone is aware of his or her talents. Very seldom does one read articles in *Fortune, Forbes,* or *The Wall Street Journal,* however, about money managers who are consistently off by 25% in their stock market forecasts.

One way to monitor forecasts to ensure that they are performing well is to use a tracking signal. A **tracking signal** is a measurement of how well the forecast is predicting actual values. As forecasts are updated every week, month, or quarter, the newly available demand data are compared to the forecast values.

The tracking signal is computed as the *running sum of the forecast errors (RSFE)* divided by the *mean absolute deviation (MAD)*:

$$\begin{pmatrix} \text{Tracking} \\ \text{signal} \end{pmatrix} = \frac{\text{RSFE}}{\text{MAD}}$$

$$= \frac{\Sigma(\text{actual demand in period } i - \text{forecast demand in period } i)}{\text{MAD}} \qquad (5.18)$$

where

$$\text{MAD} = \frac{\Sigma|\text{forecast errors}|}{n}$$

as seen earlier in equation (5.6).

Positive tracking signals indicate that demand is *greater* than forecast. *Negative* signals mean that demand is *less* than forecast. A good tracking signal—that is, one with a low RSFE—has about as much positive error as it has negative error. In other words, small deviations are okay, but positive and negative errors should balance one another so that the tracking signal centers closely around zero.

Once tracking signals are calculated, they are compared to predetermined control limits. When a tracking signal exceeds an upper or lower limit, there is a problem with the forecasting method, and management may want to reevaluate the way it forecasts demand. Figure 5.8 shows the graph of a tracking signal that is exceeding the range of acceptable variation. If the model being used is exponential smoothing, perhaps the smoothing constant needs to be readjusted.

How do firms decide what the upper and lower tracking limits should be? There is no single answer, but they try to find reasonable values—in other words, limits not so low as to be triggered with every small forecast error, and not so high as to allow bad forecasts to be regularly overlooked. George Plossl and Oliver Wight, two inventory control experts, have suggested using maximums of ±4 MADs for high-volume stock items and ±8 MADs for lower-volume items.[5] Other forecasters suggest slightly lower

---

Tracking signal
A measurement of how well the forecast is predicting actual values.

A few famous forecasts somewhat lacking in accuracy: "I think there is a world market for maybe five computers." Thomas Watson, chairman of IBM, 1943; "I have traveled the length and breadth of this country and talked with the best people, and I can assure you that data processing is a fad that won't last out the year." The editor in charge of business books for Prentice Hall, 1957; "There is no reason anyone would want a computer in their home." Ken Olson, president, chairman, and founder of Digital Equipment Corp., 1977

---

[5] See G. W. Plossl and O. W. Wight, *Production and Inventory Control* (Englewood Cliffs, NJ: Prentice Hall, 1967).

MONITORING AND CONTROLLING FORECASTS

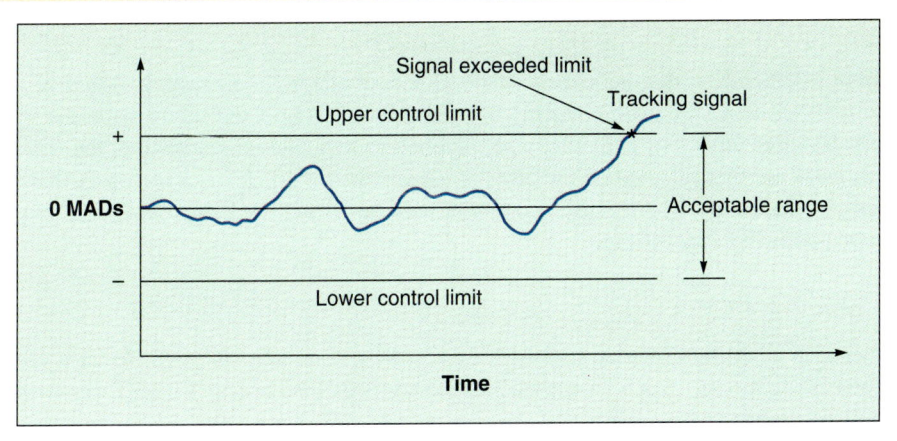

FIGURE 5.8 ■ A Plot of Tracking Signals

ranges. Because one MAD is equivalent to approximately .8 standard deviations, ±2 MADs = ±1.6 standard deviations, ±3 MADs = ±2.4 standard deviation, and ±4 MADs = ±3.2 standard deviations. This fact suggests that for a forecast to be "in control," 89% of the errors are expected to fall within ±2 MADs, 98% within ±3 MADs, or 99.9% within ±4 MADs.[6]

Example 14 shows how the tracking signal and RSFE can be computed.

EXAMPLE 14

Kevin Stone Bakery's quarterly sales of croissants (in thousands), as well as forecast demand and error computations, are shown below. The objective is to compute the tracking signal and determine whether forecasts are performing adequately.

Quarter	Forecast Demand	Actual Demand	Error	RSFE	|Forecast Error|	Cumulative Forecast Error	Cumulative MAD	Tracking Signal
1	100	90	−10	−10	10	10	10.0	−1
2	100	95	− 5	−15	5	15	7.5	−2
3	100	115	+15	0	15	30	10.0	0
4	110	100	−10	−10	10	40	10.0	−1
5	110	125	+15	+ 5	15	55	11.0	+ .5
6	110	140	+30	+35	30	85	14.2	+2.5

At the end of quarter 6, $\text{MAD} = \dfrac{\Sigma |\text{forecast errors}|}{n} = \dfrac{85}{6} = 14.2$

and $\text{Tracking signal} = \dfrac{\text{RSFE}}{\text{MAD}} = \dfrac{35}{14.2} = 2.5 \text{ MADs}$

This tracking signal is within acceptable limits. We see that it drifted from −2.0 MADs to +2.5 MADs.

---

[6] To prove these three percentages to yourself, just set up a normal curve for ±1.6 standard deviations (z values). Using the normal table in Appendix I, you find that the area under the curve is .89. This represents ±2 MADs. Likewise, ±3 MADs = ±2.4 standard deviations encompass 98% of the area, and so on for ±4 MADs.

Adaptive smoothing An approach to exponential smoothing forecasting in which the smoothing constant is automatically changed to keep errors to a minimum.

Adaptive Smoothing

A lot of research has been published on the subject of adaptive forecasting. *Adaptive forecasting* refers to computer monitoring of tracking signals and self-adjustment if a signal passes a preset limit. For example, when applied to exponential smoothing, the α and β coefficients are first selected on the basis of values that minimize error forecasts, and then adjusted accordingly whenever the computer notes an errant tracking signal. This process is called **adaptive smoothing.**

Focus Forecasting

Focus forecasting Forecasting that tries a variety of computer models and selects the best one for a particular application.

Rather than adapt by choosing a smoothing constant, computers allow us to try a variety of forecasting models. Such an approach is called focus forecasting. **Focus forecasting** is based on two principles:

1. Sophisticated forecasting models are not always better than simple ones.
2. There is no single technique that should be used for all products or services.

Bernard Smith, inventory manager for American Hardware Supply, is the man who coined the term *focus forecasting*. Smith's job was to forecast quantities for 100,000 hardware products purchased by American's 21 buyers.[7] He found that buyers neither trusted nor understood the exponential-smoothing model then in use. Instead, they used very simple approaches of their own. So Smith developed his new computerized system for selecting forecasting methods.

Smith chose seven forecasting methods to test. They ranged from the simple ones that buyers used (such as the naive approach) to some of the more statistical models. Every month, Smith applied the forecasts of all seven models to each item in stock. In these simulated trials, the forecast values were subtracted from the most recent actual demands, giving a simulated forecast error. The forecast method yielding the least error is selected by the computer, which then uses it to make next month's forecast. Although buyers still have an override capability, American Hardware finds that focus forecasting provides excellent results.

The Computer's Role in Forecasting

As we can see from American Hardware Supply, forecast calculations are seldom performed by hand in the age of computers. Many academic and commercial programs are readily available to handle time-series and causal projections.

Popular commercial packages include General Electric's *Time Series Forecasting* and IBM's IMPACT (Inventory Management Program and Control Technique). Popular packages for PCs are SAS, SPSS, BIOMED, SYSTAB, Minitab, Excel OM, and POM for Windows. POM for Windows and Excel OM are both illustrated shortly.

FORECASTING IN THE SERVICE SECTOR

Forecasting in the service sector presents some unusual challenges. A major technique in the retail sector is tracking demand by maintaining good short-term records. For instance, a barbershop catering to men expects peak flows on Fridays and Saturdays. Indeed, most barbershops will be closed on Sunday and Monday, and many call in extra help on Friday

---

[7] Bernard T. Smith, *Focus Forecasting: Computer Techniques for Inventory Control* (Boston: CBI Publishing, 1978).

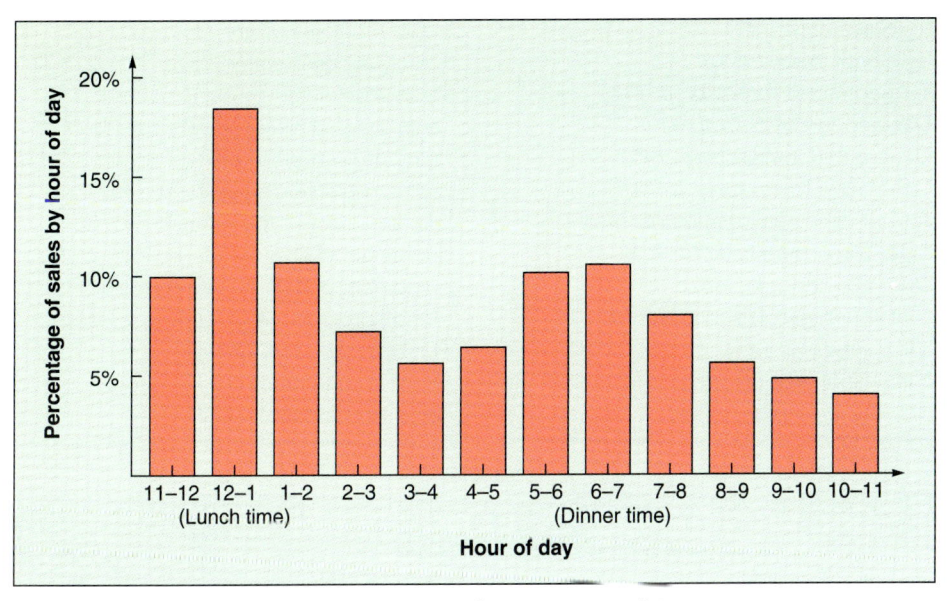

FIGURE 5.9 ■ Forecast of Sales by Hour for a Fast-Food Restaurant

and Saturday. A downtown restaurant, on the other hand, may need to track conventions and holidays for effective short-term forecasting.

Specialty retail facilities, such as flower shops, may have other unusual demand patterns, and those patterns will differ depending on the holiday. When Valentine's Day falls on a weekend, for example, flowers can't be delivered to offices and those romantically inclined are likely to celebrate with outings rather than flowers. If a holiday falls on a Monday, some of the celebration may also take place on the weekend, reducing flower sales. However, when Valentine's Day falls in midweek, busy midweek schedules often make flowers the optimal way to celebrate. Because flowers for Mother's Day are to be delivered on Saturday or Sunday, this holiday forecast varies less. Due to special demand patterns, many service firms maintain records of sales, noting not only the day of the week but also unusual events, including the weather, so that patterns and correlations that influence demand can be developed.

Fast-food restaurants are well aware not only of weekly and daily but even hourly demands that influence sales. Therefore, detailed forecasts of demand are needed. Rather than maintain a manual log, many firms now use point-of-sale computers that track sales by time period, perhaps every 15 minutes. Figure 5.9 shows the hourly forecast for a typical fast-food restaurant. Note the lunch-time and dinner-time peaks.

SUMMARY

Forecasts are a critical part of the operations manager's function. Demand forecasts drive a firm's production, capacity, and scheduling systems and affect the financial, marketing, and personnel planning functions.

There are a variety of qualitative and quantitative forecasting techniques. Qualitative approaches employ judgment, experience, intuition, and a host of other factors that are difficult to quantify. Quantitative forecasting uses historical data and causal relations to project future demands. No forecasting method is perfect under all conditions. And even once management has found a satisfactory approach, it must still monitor and control forecasts to make sure errors do not get out of hand. Forecasting can often be a very challenging, but rewarding, part of managing.

KEY TERMS

Forecasting *(p. 142)*
Economic forecasts *(p. 143)*
Technological forecasts *(p. 143)*
Demand forecasts *(p. 143)*
Quantitative forecasts *(p. 145)*
Qualitative forecasts *(p. 145)*
Jury of executive opinion *(p. 145)*
Sales force composite *(p. 145)*
Delphi method *(p. 146)*
Consumer market survey *(p. 146)*
Time series *(p. 147)*
Naive approach *(p. 148)*
Moving averages *(p. 148)*

Exponential smoothing *(p. 151)*
Smoothing constant *(p. 151)*
Mean absolute deviation (MAD) *(p. 153)*
Mean squared error (MSE) *(p. 154)*
Trend projection *(p. 158)*
Linear-regression analysis *(p. 163)*
Standard error of the estimate *(p. 166)*
Coefficient of correlation *(p. 167)*
Coefficient of determination *(p. 168)*
Multiple regression *(p. 168)*
Tracking signal *(p. 170)*
Adaptive smoothing *(p. 172)*
Focus forecasting *(p. 172)*

USING POM FOR WINDOWS IN FORECASTING

In this section, we look at our forecasting software package, POM for Windows. POM for Windows can project moving averages (both simple and weighted), handle exponential smoothing (both simple and trend-adjusted), forecast with least squares trend projection, and solve linear-regression (causal) models.

Program 5.1 uses Example 4's Port of New Orleans data to illustrate an exponential-smoothing forecast. A summary screen of error analysis and a graph of the data can also be generated. As a special example of adaptive forecasting, when using an alpha of 0, POM for Windows will find the alpha value that yields the minimum MAD.

Forecasting / Time series analysis - [Details and Error Analysis]

Method: Exponential Smoothing
Alpha for smoothing: .1
Note: Error analysis begins at first period with forecast.

Port of New Orleans Solution

	Demand(y)	Forecast	Error	|Error|	Error^2
Quarter 1	180.	175.	5.	5.	25.
Quarter 2	168.	175.5	-7.5	7.5	56.25
Quarter 3	159.	174.75	-15.75	15.75	248.0625
Quarter 4	175.	173.175	1.825	1.825	3.3306
Quarter 5	190.	173.3575	16.6425	16.6425	276.9729
Quarter 6	205.	175.0217	29.9783	29.9783	898.6959
Quarter 7	180.	178.0196	1.9804	1.9804	3.9221
Quarter 8	182.	178.2176	3.7824	3.7824	14.3064
TOTALS	1,439.		35.9586	82.4586	1,526.54
AVERAGE	179.875		4.4948	10.3073	190.8175
Next period forecast		178.5959	(Bias)	(MAD)	(MSE)
				Std err	15.9507

PROGRAM 5.1 ■ POM for Windows Exponential-Smoothing Example, Using Example 4 Data

USING EXCEL SPREADSHEETS IN FORECASTING

Excel and spreadsheets in general are frequently used in forecasting. Both exponential smoothing and regression analysis (simple and multiple) are supported by built-in Excel functions. You may also use Excel OM's forecasting module, which has five components:

Using Excel Spreadsheets in Forecasting

(1) moving averages, (2) weighted moving averages, (3) exponential smoothing, (4) regression (with one variable only), and (5) decomposition. Excel OM's error analysis is much more complete than that available with the Excel add-in.

Programs 5.2 and 5.3 illustrate Excel OM's formulas and output, respectively, using Example 2's weighted moving average data.

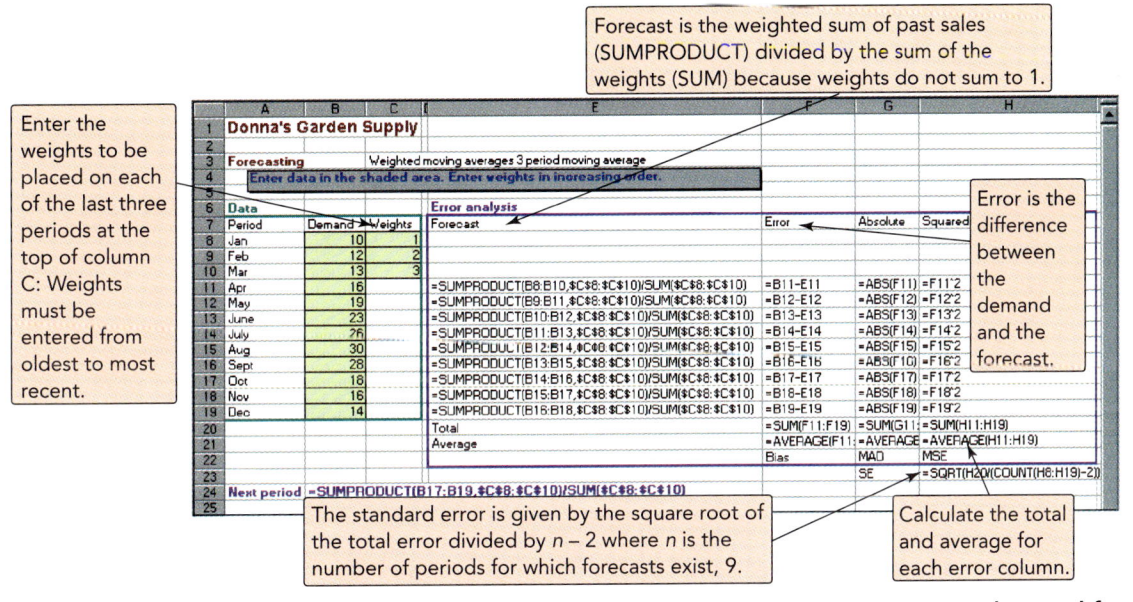

Forecast is the weighted sum of past sales (SUMPRODUCT) divided by the sum of the weights (SUM) because weights do not sum to 1.

Enter the weights to be placed on each of the last three periods at the top of column C: Weights must be entered from oldest to most recent.

Error is the difference between the demand and the forecast.

	A	B	C	D	E	F	G	H
1	Donna's Garden Supply							
2								
3	Forecasting			Weighted moving averages 3 period moving average				
4	Enter data in the shaded area. Enter weights in increasing order.							
5								
6	Data			Error analysis				
7	Period	Demand	Weights	Forecast		Error	Absolute	Squared
8	Jan	10	1					
9	Feb	12	2					
10	Mar	13	3					
11	Apr	16		=SUMPRODUCT(B8:B10,$C$8:$C$10)/SUM($C$8:$C$10)		=B11-E11	=ABS(F11)	=F11^2
12	May	19		=SUMPRODUCT(B9:B11,$C$8:$C$10)/SUM($C$8:$C$10)		=B12-E12	=ABS(F12)	=F12^2
13	June	23		=SUMPRODUCT(B10:B12,$C$8:$C$10)/SUM($C$8:$C$10)		=B13-E13	=ABS(F13)	=F13^2
14	July	26		=SUMPRODUCT(B11:B13,$C$8:$C$10)/SUM($C$8:$C$10)		=B14-E14	=ABS(F14)	=F14^2
15	Aug	30		=SUMPRODUCT(B12:B14,$C$8:$C$10)/SUM($C$8:$C$10)		=B15-E15	=ABS(F15)	=F15^2
16	Sept	28		=SUMPRODUCT(B13:B15,$C$8:$C$10)/SUM($C$8:$C$10)		=B16-E16	=ABS(F16)	=F16^2
17	Oct	18		=SUMPRODUCT(B14:B16,$C$8:$C$10)/SUM($C$8:$C$10)		=B17-E17	=ABS(F17)	=F17^2
18	Nov	16		=SUMPRODUCT(B15:B17,$C$8:$C$10)/SUM($C$8:$C$10)		=B18-E18	=ABS(F18)	=F18^2
19	Dec	14		=SUMPRODUCT(B16:B18,$C$8:$C$10)/SUM($C$8:$C$10)		=B19-E19	=ABS(F19)	=F19^2
20				Total		=SUM(F11:F19)	=SUM(G11:G19)	=SUM(H11:H19)
21				Average		=AVERAGE(F11:F19)	=AVERAGE(G11:G19)	=AVERAGE(H11:H19)
22						Bias	MAD	MSE
23							SE	=SQRT(H20/(COUNT(H6:H19)-2))
24	Next period	=SUMPRODUCT(B17:B19,$C$8:$C$10)/SUM($C$8:$C$10)						

The standard error is given by the square root of the total error divided by n – 2 where n is the number of periods for which forecasts exist, 9.

Calculate the total and average for each error column.

PROGRAM 5.2 ■ Using Excel OM for Weighted Moving-Average Forecasting. Input data and formulas from Example 2 are shown.

	A	B	C	D	E	F	G	H	I
1	Donna's Garden Supply								
2									
3	Forecasting			Weighted moving averages 3 period moving average					
4	Enter data in the shaded area. Enter weights in increasing order.								
5									
6	Data				Error analysis				
7	Period	Demand	Weights		Forecast	Error	Absolute	Squared	
8	Jan	10	1						
9	Feb	12	2						
10	Mar	13	3						
11	Apr	16			12.16667	3.833333	3.833333	14.69444	
12	May	19			14.33333	4.666667	4.666667	21.77778	
13	June	23			17	6	6	36	
14	July	26			20.5	5.5	5.5	30.25	
15	Aug	30			23.83333	6.166667	6.166667	38.02778	
16	Sept	28			27.5	0.5	0.5	0.25	
17	Oct	18			28.33333	-10.3333	10.33333	106.7778	
18	Nov	16			23.33333	-7.33333	7.333333	53.77778	
19	Dec	14			18.66667	-4.66667	4.666667	21.77778	
20					Total	4.333333	49	323.3333	
21					Average	0.481481	5.444444	35.92593	
22						Bias	MAD	MSE	
23							SE	6.796358	
24	Next period	15.333333							

PROGRAM 5.3 ■ Output of Excel OM's Weighted Moving-Average Program Using Data from Example 2 as Input

176 CHAPTER 5 FORECASTING

Programs 5.4 and 5.5 provide an Excel OM regression analysis, using the electrical power data from Example 7. As an alternative, you may want to experiment with Excel's built-in regression analysis. To do so, under the *Tools* menu bar selection choose *Analysis,* then *Regression*. Enter your *Y* and *X* data into two columns (say C and D). When the regression window appears, enter the *Y* and *X* ranges, then select *OK*. Excel offers several plots and tables to those interested in more rigorous analysis of regression problems.

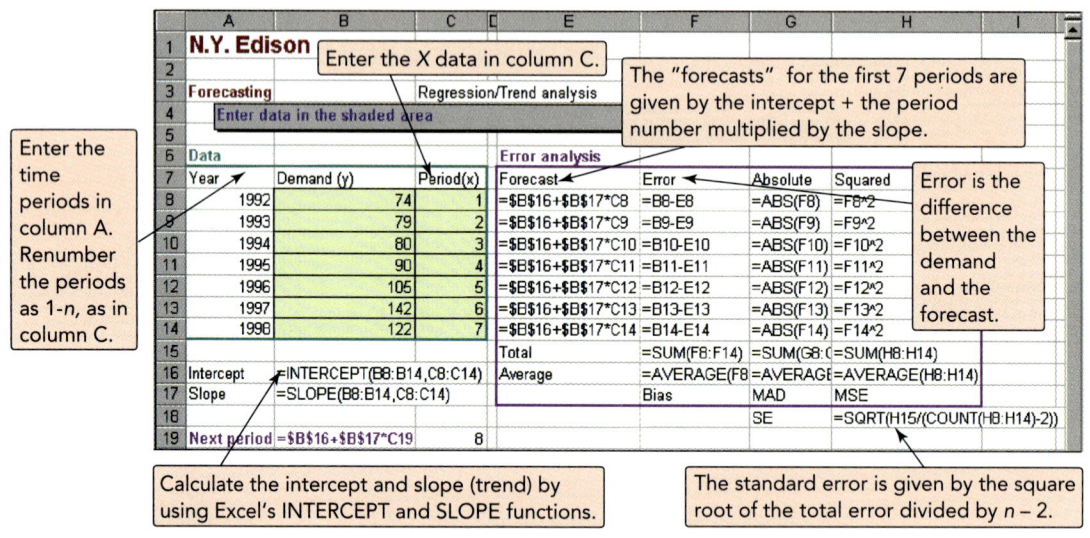

PROGRAM 5.4 ■ Excel OM's Regression Analysis Using Example 7 Data as Input

PROGRAM 5.5 ■ Output from Excel OM's Regression Analysis, with Data from Example 7

SOLVED PROBLEMS

Solved Problem 5.1

Sales of Green Line Jet Skis have grown steadily during the past 5 years (see table to the right). The sales manager had predicted in 1993 that 1994 sales would be 410 air conditioners. Using exponential smoothing with a weight of $\alpha = .30$, develop forecasts for 1995 through 1999.

Year	Sales	Forecast
1994	450	410
1995	495	
1996	518	
1997	563	
1998	584	
1999	?	

Solution

Year	Forecast
1994	410.0
1995	$422.0 = 410 + .3 (450 - 410)$
1996	$443.9 = 422 + .3 (495 - 422)$
1997	$466.1 = 443.9 + .3 (518 - 443.9)$
1998	$495.2 = 466.1 + .3 (563 - 466.1)$
1999	$521.8 = 495.2 + .3 (584 - 495.2)$

Solved Problem 5.2

In Example 6, we applied trend-adjusted exponential smoothing to forecast demand for a piece of pollution-control equipment for months 2 and 3 (out of 9 months of data provided). Let us now continue this process for month 4. We want to confirm the forecast for month 4 shown in Table 5.1 (p. 157) and Figure 5.3 (p. 157).

For month 4, $A_4 = 19$, with $\alpha = .2$, and $\beta = .4$

Solution

$$F_4 = \alpha A_4 + (1 - \alpha)(F_3 + T_3)$$
$$= (.2)(19) + (1 - .2)(16.9 + 2.63)$$
$$= 3.8 + (.8)(19.53)$$
$$= 3.8 + 15.62$$
$$= 19.4$$
$$T_4 = \beta (F_4 - F_3) + (1 - \beta) T_3$$
$$= (.4)(19.4 - 16.9) + (1 - .4)(2.63)$$
$$= (.4)(2.5) + (.6)(2.63)$$
$$= 1.0 + 1.58$$
$$= 2.58$$
$$FIT_4 = 19.4 + 2.58$$
$$= 21.98$$

Solved Problem 5.3

Room registrations in the Toronto Towers Plaza Hotel have been recorded for the past 9 years. In order to project future occupancy, management would like to determine the mathematical trend of guest registration. This estimate would help the hotel determine whether future expansion will be needed. Given the following time-series data, develop a regression equation relating registrations to time. Then forecast 1999 registrations. Room registrations are in the thousands:

1990: 17   1991: 16   1992: 16   1993: 21   1994: 20
1995: 20   1996: 23   1997: 25   1998: 24

Solution

Year	Transformed Year, x	Registrants, y (in thousands)	x^2	xy
1990	1	17	1	17
1991	2	16	4	32
1992	3	16	9	48
1993	4	21	16	84
1994	5	20	25	100
1995	6	20	36	120
1996	7	23	49	161
1997	8	25	64	200
1998	9	24	81	216
	$\Sigma x = 45$	$\Sigma y = 182$	$\Sigma x^2 = 285$	$\Sigma xy = 978$

$$\bar{x} = \frac{45}{9} = 5, \quad \bar{y} = \frac{182}{9} = 20.22$$

$$b = \frac{\Sigma xy - n\bar{x}\bar{y}}{\Sigma x^2 - n\bar{x}^2} = \frac{978 - (9)(5)(20.22)}{285 - (9)(25)} = \frac{978 - 909.9}{285 - 225} = \frac{68.1}{60} = 1.135$$

$$a = \bar{y} - b\bar{x} = 20.22 - (1.135)(5) = 20.22 - 5.675 = 14.545$$

$$\hat{y} \text{ (registrations)} = 14.545 + 1.135x$$

The projection of registrations in the year 2000 (which is $x = 11$ in the coding system used) is

$$\hat{y} = 14.545 + (1.135)(11) = 27.03$$

or 27,030 guests in 2000

Solved Problem 5.4

Quarterly demand for Jaguar XJ6's at a New York auto dealer is forecast with the equation

$$\hat{y} = 10 + 3x$$

where x = quarters, and

Quarter I of 1997 = 0
Quarter II of 1997 = 1
Quarter III of 1997 = 2
Quarter IV of 1997 = 3
Quarter I of 1998 = 4
and so on

and

$\hat{y}$ = quarterly demand

The demand for sports sedans is seasonal, and the indices for Quarters I, II, III, and IV are 0.80, 1.00, 1.30, and 0.90, respectively. Forecast demand for each quarter of 1999. Then seasonalize each forecast to adjust for quarterly variations.

Solution

Quarter II of 1998 is coded $x = 5$; Quarter III of 1998, $x = 6$; and Quarter IV of 1998, $x = 7$. Hence, Quarter I of 1999 is coded $x = 8$; Quarter II, $x = 9$; and so on.

$\hat{y}$(1999 Quarter I) = 10 + 3(8) = 34
$\hat{y}$(1999 Quarter II) = 10 + 3(9) = 37
$\hat{y}$(1999 Quarter III) = 10 + 3(10) = 40
$\hat{y}$(1999 Quarter IV) = 10 + 3(11) = 43

Adjusted forecast = (.80)(34) = 27.2
Adjusted forecast = (1.00)(37) = 37
Adjusted forecast = (1.30)(40) = 52
Adjusted forecast = (.90)(43) = 38.7

DISCUSSION QUESTIONS

1. Briefly describe the steps that are used to develop a forecasting system.
2. What is a time-series forecasting model?
3. What is the difference between a causal model and a time-series model?
4. What is a qualitative forecasting model, and when is it appropriate?
5. What is the meaning of *least squares* in a regression model?
6. What are some of the drawbacks of the moving-average forecasting model?
7. What effect does the value of the smoothing constant have on the weight given to the past forecast and the past observed value?
8. Briefly describe the Delphi technique. How would it be used by an employer you have worked for?
9. What is MAD, and why is it important in the selection and use of forecasting models?
10. Describe the three forecasting time horizons and their use.
11. Name and discuss three *qualitative* forecasting methods.
12. Which forecasting technique can place the most emphasis on recent values? How does it do this?
13. What does it mean to "decompose" a time series?
14. What is the basic difference between a weighted moving average and exponential smoothing?
15. Describe two popular measures of forecast accuracy.
16. What is the difference between a dependent and an independent variable?
17. Define the meaning of the *coefficient of determination* in your own words. Provide an example.
18. What is the purpose of a tracking signal?

CRITICAL THINKING EXERCISE

In 1997, the Board of Regents, which is responsible for all public higher education funding in a large midwestern state, hired a consultant to develop a series of enrollment forecasting models, one for each college. These models used historical data and exponential smoothing to forecast the following year's enrollments. Based on the model, which included a smoothing constant (α) for each school, each college's budget was set by the Board. The head of the Board personally selected each smoothing constant, based on what she called her "gut reactions and political acumen."

What do you think the advantages and disadvantages of this system are? Answer from the perspective of (a) the Board of Regents and (b) the president of each college. How can this model be abused and what could be done to remove any biases? How can a *regression model* be used to produce results that favor one forecast over another?

PROBLEMS

- **5.1** Registration numbers for an accounting seminar over the past 10 weeks are shown below:

Week	1	2	3	4	5	6	7	8	9	10
Registrations	22	21	25	27	35	29	33	37	41	37

  a) Use a 3-week moving average to forecast weeks 4 through 11.
  b) Plot the actual data (weekly registrations) and your 3-week moving-average forecast on a graph.

- **5.2** Compute the MAD for your forecast in Problem 5.1.
- **5.3** Using the data in Problem 5.1, compute the 2-week moving average for weeks 3 through 11.

5.4 Compute the MAD for your forecast in Problem 5.3. Which moving average forecast has had fewer errors in the past—the 3-week or the 2-week forecast? Use the data in Problem 5.2 to make the comparison.

5.5 Apply exponential smoothing to the data in Problem 5.1, with a given forecast for week 1 of 25 and $\alpha = .5$.
  a) Forecast weeks 2 through 11.
  b) Compute the MAD.

5.6 The following data relate the sales figures of the bar in a small "bed and breakfast" inn to the number of guests registered that week.

Week	Guests	Bar Sales
1	16	$330
2	12	270
3	18	380
4	14	300

(Bar Sales ← dependent variable (y))

  a) Perform a linear regression that relates bar sales to guests (not to time).
  b) If the forecast is for 20 guests next week, what are the sales expected to be? 410

5.7 Refer back to the trend-adjusted exponential-smoothing illustration in Example 6. Using $\alpha = .2$ and $\beta = .4$, we forecast sales for 9 months, showing the detailed calculations for months 2 and 3. In Solved Problem 5.2, we continued the process for month 4.

In this problem, show your calculations for months 5 and 6 for F_t, T_t, and FIT_t.

5.8 Refer to Problem 5.7. Complete the trend-adjusted exponential-smoothing forecast computations for periods 7, 8, and 9. Confirm that your numbers for F_t, T_t, and FIT_t match those in Table 5.1 (p. 157).

5.9 Daily high temperatures in the city of Houston for the last week have been as follows: 93, 94, 93, 95, 96, 88, 90 (yesterday).
  a) Forecast the high temperature today, using a 3-day moving average.
  b) Forecast the high temperature today, using a 2-day moving average.
  c) Calculate the mean absolute deviation based on a 2-day moving average.

5.10 For the data below, develop a 3-month moving-average forecast.

Month	Automobile Battery Sales	Month	Automobile Battery Sales
January	20	July	17
February	21	August	18
March	15	September	20
April	14	October	20
May	13	November	21
June	16	December	23

5.11 Given the following data, develop a 3-year moving-average forecast of demand.

Year	1	2	3	4	5	6	7	8	9	10	11
Demand	7	9	5	9	13	8	12	13	9	11	7

5.12 Jon Ahlbrand has developed the following forecasting model:

$$\hat{y} = 36 + 4.3x$$

where $\hat{y}$ = demand for Aztec air conditioners and
  x = the outside temperature (°F).

a) Forecast demand for the Aztec when the temperature is 70°F.
b) What is demand when the temperature is 80°F?
c) What is demand when the temperature is 90°F?

5.13 Data collected on the yearly demand for 50-lb. bags of grass seed at Bob's Hardware Store are shown in the following table. Develop a 3-year moving average to forecast sales. Then estimate demand again with a weighted moving average in which sales in the most recent year is given a weight of 2 and sales in the other two years are each given a weight of 1. Which method do you think is better?

Year	1	2	3	4	5	6	7	8	9	10	11
Demand for Grass Seed (thousands of bags)	4	6	4	5	10	8	7	9	12	14	15

5.14 Develop a 2- and a 4-year moving average for the demand for bags of grass seed in Problem 5.13.

5.15 In Problems 5.13 and 5.14, four different forecasts were developed for the demand for grass seed. These four forecasts are a 2-year moving average, a 3-year moving average, a weighted moving average, and a 4-year moving average. Which one would you use? Explain your answer.

5.16 Use exponential smoothing with a smoothing constant of .3 to forecast the demand for grass seed given in Problem 5.13. To begin the procedure, assume that last period's forecast for year 1 is 5,000 bags. Would you prefer to use the exponential smoothing model or the weighted-average model developed in Problem 5.13? Explain your answer.

5.17 Refer to Solved Problem 5.1. Using smoothing constants of .6 and .9, develop a forecast for the sales of Green Line Jet Skis.

5.18 Refer to Solved Problem 5.1 and Problem 5.17. What effect did the smoothing constant have on the forecast for Green Line Jet Skis? Which smoothing constant gives the most accurate forecast?

5.19 Refer to Solved Problem 5.1. Use a 3-year moving-average forecasting model to forecast the sales of Green Line Jet Skis.

5.20 Refer to Solved Problem 5.1. Using the trend-projection method, develop a forecasting model for the sales of Green Line Jet Skis.

5.21 Refer to Solved Problem 5.1 and Problems 5.19 and 5.20. Would you use exponential smoothing with a smoothing constant of .3, a 3-year moving average, or trend to predict the sales of Green Line Jet Skis?

5.22 As you can see in the following table, demand for heart transplant surgery at Washington General Hospital has increased steadily in the past few years:

Year	1	2	3	4	5	6
Heart Transplant Surgeries Performed	45	50	52	56	58	?

The director of medical services predicted 6 years ago that demand in year 1 would be 41 surgeries.
a) Use exponential smoothing, first with a smoothing constant of .6 and then with one of .9, to develop forecasts for years 2 through 6.
b) Use a 3-year moving average to forecast demand in years 4, 5, and 6.
c) Use the trend-projection method to forecast demand in years 1 through 6.
d) With MAD as the criterion, which of the above four forecasts is best?

5.23 A careful analysis of the cost of operating an automobile was conducted by a firm. The following model was developed:

$$Y = 4,000 + 0.20X$$

where Y is the annual cost and X is the miles driven.
a) If a car is driven 15,000 miles this year, what is the forecasted cost of operating this automobile?
b) If a car is driven 25,000 miles this year, what is the forecasted cost of operating this automobile?
c) Suppose that one car is driven 15,000 miles at an actual operating cost of $6,000; suppose that a second car is driven 25,000 miles at an actual operating cost of $10,000. Calculate the mean absolute deviation.

5.24 Given the following data, use exponential smoothing ($\alpha = 0.2$) to develop a demand forecast. Assume the forecast for the initial period is 5.

Period	1	2	3	4	5	6
Demand	7	9	5	9	13	8

5.25 Consulting income at Dr. Thomas W. Jones Associates for the period February to July has been as follows:

Month	February	March	April	May	June	July
Income (in $ thousands)	70.0	68.5	64.8	71.7	71.3	72.8

Use trend-adjusted exponential smoothing to forecast August's income. Assume that the initial forecast for February is $65,000 and the initial trend adjustment is 0. The smoothing constants selected are $\alpha = .1$ and $\beta = .2$.

5.26 Resolve Problem 5.25 with $\alpha = .1$ and $\beta = .8$. Using MAD, which smoothing constants provide a better forecast?

5.27 Calculate (a) MAD and (b) MSE for the following forecast versus actual sales figures.

Forecast	100	110	120	130
Actual	95	108	123	130

5.28 Given the following data, use least squares regression to derive a forecasting equation. What is your estimate of the demand in period 7?

Period	1	2	3	4	5	6
Demand	7	9	5	11	10	13

5.29 Given the following data, use least squares regression to develop a relation between the number of rainy summer days and the number of games lost by the Boca Raton Cardinal baseball team.

Year	1989	1990	1991	1992	1993	1994	1995	1996	1997	1998
Rainy Days	15	25	10	10	30	20	20	15	10	25
Games Lost	25	20	10	15	20	15	20	10	5	20

5.30 Sales of industrial vacuum cleaners at Larry Armstrong Supply Co. over the past 13 months are shown below:

Month	Jan.	Feb.	March	April	May	June	July
Sales (in thousands)	11	14	16	10	15	17	11

Month	Aug.	Sept.	Oct.	Nov.	Dec.	Jan.
Sales (in thousands)	14	17	12	14	16	11

a) Using a moving average with 3 periods, determine the demand for vacuum cleaners for next February.
b) Using a weighted moving average with 3 periods, determine the demand for vacuum cleaners for February. Use 3, 2, and 1 for the weights of the most recent, second most recent, and third most recent periods, respectively. For example, if you were forecast-

PROBLEMS

ing the demand for February, November would have a weight of 1, December would have a weight of 2, and January would have a weight of 3.

c) Evaluate the accuracy of each of these methods.
d) What other factors might Armstrong consider in forecasting sales?

: 5.31 The operations manager of a musical instrument distributor feels that demand for bass drums may be related to the number of television appearances by the popular rock group Green Shades during the previous month. The manager has collected the data shown in the following table:

Demand for Bass Drums	3	6	7	5	10	8
Green Shades TV Appearances	3	4	7	6	8	5

a) Graph these data to see whether a linear equation might describe the relationship between the group's television shows and bass drum sales.
b) Use the least squares regression method to derive a forecasting equation.
c) What is your estimate for bass drum sales if the Green Shades performed on TV nine times last month?

· 5.32 A study to determine the correlation between bank deposits and consumer price indices in Birmingham, Alabama, revealed the following (which was based on $n = 5$ years of data):

$$\Sigma x = 15$$
$$\Sigma x^2 = 55$$
$$\Sigma xy = 70$$
$$\Sigma y = 20$$
$$\Sigma y^2 = 130$$

a) Find the coefficient of correlation. What does it imply to you?
b) What is the standard error of the estimate?

: 5.33 The accountant at Carl Baker Coal Distributors, Inc., notes that the demand for coal seems to be tied to an index of weather severity developed by the U.S. Weather Bureau: When weather was extremely cold in the United States over the past 5 years (and the index was thus high), coal sales were high. The accountant proposes that one good forecast of next year's coal demand could be made by developing a regression equation and then consulting the *Farmer's Almanac* to see how severe next year's winter will be. For the data in the following table, derive a least squares regression and compute the coefficient of correlation of the data. Also compute the standard error of the estimate.

Coal Sales, y (in millions of tons)	4	1	4	6	5
Weather Index, x	2	1	4	5	3

: 5.34 Thirteen students entered the OM program at Rollins College 2 years ago. The following table indicates what each student scored on the high school SAT exam and their grade point averages (GPAs) after students were in the Rollins program for 2 years. Is there a meaningful relationship between SAT scores and grades? If a student scores a 350 on the SAT, what do you think his or her GPA will be? What about a student who scores 800?

Student	A	B	C	D	E	F	G	H	I	J	K	L	M
SAT Score	421	377	585	690	608	390	415	481	729	501	613	709	366
GPA	2.90	2.93	3.00	3.45	3.66	2.88	2.15	2.53	3.22	1.99	2.75	3.90	1.60

· 5.35 Dr. Jerilyn Ross, a New York City psychologist, specializes in treating patients who are agoraphobic (afraid to leave their homes). The following table indicates how many patients Dr. Ross has seen each year for the past 10 years. It also indicates what the robbery rate was in New York City during the same year.

Year	1	2	3	4	5	6	7	8	9	10
Number of Patients	36	33	40	41	40	55	60	54	58	61
Crime Rate (Robberies) per 1,000 Population	58.3	61.1	73.4	75.7	81.1	89.0	101.1	94.8	103.3	116.2

Using trend analysis, predict the number of patients Dr. Ross will see in years 11, 12, and 13. How well does the model fit the data?

- **5.36** Using the data in Problem 5.35, apply linear regression to study the relationship between the crime rate and Dr. Ross's patient load. If the robbery rate increases to 131.2 in year 11, how many phobic patients will Dr. Ross treat? If the crime rate drops to 90.6, what is the patient projection?

- **5.37** Accountants at the firm Doke and Reed believed that several traveling executives submit unusually high travel vouchers when they return from business trips. First, they took a sample of 200 vouchers submitted from the past year. Then they developed the following multiple-regression equation relating expected travel cost ($\hat{y}$) to number of days on the road (x_1) and distance traveled (x_2) in miles:

$$\hat{y} = \$90.00 + \$48.50x_1 + \$.40x_2$$

The coefficient of correlation computed was .68.

a) If Bill Tomlinson returns from a 300-mile trip that took him out of town for 5 days, what is the expected amount he should claim as expenses?

b) Tomlinson submitted a reimbursement request for $685. What should the accountant do?

c) Should any other variables be included? Which ones? Why?

- **5.38** In the past, Melissa Bryant's tire dealership sold an average of 1,000 radials each year. In the past 2 years, 200 and 250, respectively, were sold in fall, 350 and 300 in winter, 150 and 165 in spring, and 300 and 285 in summer. With a major expansion planned, Bryant projects sales next year to increase to 1,200 radials. What will be the demand during each season?

- **5.39** Suppose the number of auto accidents in a certain region is related to the regional number of registered automobiles in thousands (X_1), alcoholic beverage sales in $10,000s ($X_2$), and rainfall in inches (X_3). Furthermore, imagine that the regression formula has been calculated as

$$Y = a + b_1X_1 + b_2X_2 + b_3X_3$$

where Y = number of automobile accidents,

$$a = 7.5, b_1 = 3.5, b_2 = 4.5, \text{ and } b_3 = 2.5$$

Calculate the expected number of automobile accidents under the following conditions:

	X_1	X_2	X_3
a)	2	3	0
b)	3	5	1
c)	4	7	2

- **5.40** The following multiple-regression model was developed to predict job performance as measured by a company job performance evaluation index based on a preemployment test score and college grade point average (GPA):

$$Y = 35 + 20X_1 + 50X_2$$

where Y = job performance evaluation index
X_1 = preemployment test score
X_2 = college GPA

a) Forecast the job performance index for an applicant who had a 3.0 GPA and scored 80 on the preemployment score.
b) Forecast the job performance index for an applicant who had a 2.5 GPA and scored 70 on the preemployment score.

5.41 City government has collected the following data on annual sales tax collections and new car registrations:

Annual Sales Tax Collections (in millions)	1.0	1.4	1.9	2.0	1.8	2.1	2.3
New Car Registrations (in thousands)	10	12	15	16	14	17	20

Determine the following:
a) The least squares regression equation.
b) Using the results of part (a), find the estimated sales tax collections if new car registrations total 22 thousand.
c) The coefficients of correlation and determination.

5.42 Passenger miles flown on Northeast Airlines, a commuter firm serving the Boston hub, are shown for the past 12 weeks:

Week	1	2	3	4	5	6
Actual Passenger Miles (in thousands)	17	21	19	23	18	16

Week	7	8	9	10	11	12
Actual Passenger Miles (in thousands)	20	18	22	20	15	22

a) Assuming an initial forecast for week 1 of 17,000 miles, use exponential smoothing to compute miles for weeks 2 through 12. Use $\alpha = .2$.
b) What is the MAD for this model?
c) Compute the RSFE and tracking signals. Are they within acceptable limits?

5.43 Summer-month bus and subway ridership in Washington, DC, is believed to be tied heavily to the number of tourists visiting the city. During the past 12 years, the following data have been obtained:

Year	Number of Tourists (in millions)	Ridership (in millions)	Year	Number of Tourists (in millions)	Ridership (in millions)
1	7	1.5	7	16	2.4
2	2	1.0	8	12	2.0
3	6	1.3	9	14	2.7
4	4	1.5	10	20	4.4
5	14	2.5	11	15	3.4
6	15	2.7	12	7	1.7

a) Plot these data and decide if a linear model is reasonable.
b) Develop a regression relationship.
c) What is expected ridership if 10 million tourists visit the city in a year?

Chapter 5 Forecasting

d) Explain the predicted ridership if there are no tourists at all.
e) What is the standard error of the estimate?
f) What is the model's correlation coefficient and coefficient of determination?

5.44 Emergency calls to the 911 system of Gainesville, Florida, for the past 24 weeks are shown in the following table:

Week	1	2	3	4	5	6	7	8	9	10	11	12
Calls	50	35	25	40	45	35	20	30	35	20	15	40
Week	13	14	15	16	17	18	19	20	21	22	23	24
Calls	55	35	25	55	55	40	35	60	75	50	40	65

a) Compute the exponentially smoothed forecast of calls for each week. Assume an initial forecast of 50 calls in the first week, and use $\alpha = .1$. What is the forecast for week 25?
b) Reforecast each period using $\alpha = .6$
c) Actual calls during week 25 were 85. Which smoothing constant provides a superior forecast? Explain and justify the measure of error that you used.

5.45 Using the 911 call data in Problem 5.44, forecast calls for weeks 2 through 25 with a trend-adjusted exponential smoothing model. Assume an initial forecast for 50 calls for week 1 and an initial trend of zero. Use smoothing constants of $\alpha = .3$ and $\beta = .1$. Is this model better than that of Problem 5.44? What adjustment might be useful for further improvement? (Again, assume actual calls in week 25 were 85.)

5.46 Des Moines Power and Light has been collecting data on demand for electric power in its western subregion for only the past 2 years. Those data are shown in the following table:

Month	Demand in Megawatts Last Year	Demand in Megawatts This Year	Month	Demand in Megawatts Last Year	Demand in Megawatts This Year
Jan.	5	17	July	23	44
Feb.	6	14	Aug.	26	41
Mar.	10	20	Sept.	21	33
Apr.	13	23	Oct.	15	23
May	18	30	Nov.	12	26
June	15	38	Dec.	14	17

In order to plan for expansion and to arrange to borrow power from neighboring utilities during peak periods, the utility needs to be able to forecast demand for each month next year. However, the standard forecasting models discussed in this chapter will not fit the data observed for the 2 years.

a) What are the weaknesses of the standard forecasting techniques as applied to this set of data?
b) Because known models are not really appropriate here, propose your own approach to forecasting. Although there is no perfect solution to tackling data such as these (in other words, there are no 100% right or wrong answers), justify your model.
c) Forecast demand for each month next year using the model you propose.

5.47 Attendance at Orlando's newest Disneylike attraction, Vacation World, has been as follows:

Quarter	Guests (in thousands)	Quarter	Guests (in thousands)
Winter '96	73	Summer '97	124
Spring '96	104	Fall '97	52
Summer '96	168	Winter '98	89
Fall '96	74	Spring '98	146
Winter '97	65	Summer '98	205
Spring '97	82	Fall '98	98

Compute seasonal indices using all of the data.

- **5.48** Joe Barrow, owner of Barrow's Department Store, has used time-series extrapolation to forecast retail sales for the next 4 quarters. The sales estimates are $120,000, $140,000, $160,000, and $180,000 for the respective quarters. Seasonal indices for the 4 quarters have been found to be 1.25, .90, .75, and 1.15, respectively. Compute a seasonalized or adjusted sales forecast.

DATA BASE APPLICATION

5.49 Thornton Savings and Loan is proud of its long tradition in Tampa, Florida. Begun by Angela Thornton 6 years after World War II, the S&L has bucked the trend of financial and liquidity problems that has plagued the industry since 1985. Deposits have increased slowly but surely over the years, despite recessions in 1960, 1983, 1988, and 1991. Ms. Thornton believes it necessary to have a long-range strategic plan for her firm, including a 1-year forecast and preferably even a 5-year forecast of deposits. She examines the past deposit data and also peruses Florida's Gross State Product (GSP), over the same 44 years. (GSP is analogous to Gross National Product, GNP, but on the state level.) The resulting data are in the following table:

Year	Deposits*	GSP†	Year	Deposits*	GSP†	Year	Deposits*	GSP†
1955	.25	.4	1970	2.3	1.6	1985	24.1	3.9
1956	.24	.4	1971	2.8	1.5	1986	25.6	3.8
1957	.24	.5	1972	2.8	1.6	1987	30.3	3.8
1958	.26	.7	1973	2.7	1.7	1988	36.0	3.7
1959	.25	.9	1974	3.9	1.9	1989	31.1	4.1
1960	.30	1.0	1975	4.9	1.9	1990	31.7	4.1
1961	.31	1.4	1976	5.3	2.3	1991	38.5	4.0
1962	.32	1.7	1977	6.2	2.5	1992	47.9	4.5
1963	.24	1.3	1978	4.1	2.8	1993	49.1	4.6
1964	.26	1.2	1979	4.5	2.9	1994	55.8	4.5
1965	.25	1.1	1980	6.1	3.4	1995	70.1	4.6
1966	.33	.9	1981	7.7	3.8	1996	70.9	4.6
1967	.50	1.2	1982	10.1	4.1	1997	79.1	4.7
1968	.95	1.2	1983	15.2	4.0	1998	94.0	5.0
1969	1.7	1.2	1984	18.1	4.0			

*In $ millions.
†In $ billions.

a) Using exponential smoothing, with $\alpha = .6$, then trend analysis, and finally linear regression, discuss which forecasting model fits best for Thornton's strategic plan. Justify the selection of one model over another.

b) Carefully examine the data. Can you make a case for excluding a portion of the information? Why? Would that change your choice of model?

Case Study

North-South Airline

In 1997, Northern Airlines[*] merged with Southeast Airlines to create the fourth largest U.S. carrier. The new North-South Airline inherited both an aging fleet of Boeing 737-200 aircraft and Stephen Ruth. Ruth was a tough former secretary of the Navy who stepped in as new president and chairman of the board.

Ruth's first concern in creating a financially solid company was maintenance costs. It was commonly believed in the airline industry that maintenance costs rose with the age of the aircraft. Ruth quickly noticed that, historically, there has been a significant difference in reported B737-200 maintenance costs (from ATA Form 41s) both in the airframe and engine areas between Northern Airlines and Southeast Airlines, with Southeast having the newer fleet.

On November 12, 1997, Ruth assigned Peg Young, vice president for operations and maintenance, to study the issue. Specifically, Ruth wanted to know (1) whether the average fleet age was correlated to direct airframe maintenance costs and (2) whether there was a relationship between average fleet age and direct engine maintenance costs. Young was to report back with the answer, along with quantitative and graphical descriptions of the relationship, by November 26.

First, Young had her staff construct the average age of Northern and Southeast B737-200 fleets, by quarter, since the introduction of the aircraft to service by each airline in late 1988 and early 1989. The average age of each fleet was calculated by first multiplying the total number of calendar days that each aircraft had been in service at the pertinent point in time by the average daily utilization of the respective fleet to total fleet hours flown. The total fleet hours flown was then divided by the number of aircraft in service at that time, giving the age of the "average" aircraft in the fleet.

The average utilization was found by taking the actual total fleet hours flown at September 30, 1996, from Northern and Southeast data, and dividing by total days in service for all aircraft at that time. The average utilization for Southeast was 8.3 hours per day, and the average utilization for Northern was 8.7 hours per day. Because the available cost data were calculated for each yearly period ending at the end of the first quarter, average fleet age was calculated at the same points in time.

The fleet data are shown in the following table. Airframe cost data and engine cost data are both shown paired with fleet average age.

Discussion Question

Prepare Peg Young's response to Stephen Ruth.

North-South Airline Data for Boeing 737-200 Jets

	Northern Airline Data			Southeast Airline Data		
Year	Airframe Cost per Aircraft	Engine Cost per Aircraft	Average Age (hours)	Airframe Cost per Aircraft	Engine Cost per Aircraft	Average Age (hours)
1990	$51.80	$43.49	6,512	$13.29	$18.86	5,107
1991	54.92	38.58	8,404	25.15	31.55	8,145
1992	69.70	51.48	11,077	32.18	40.43	7,360
1993	68.90	58.72	11,717	31.78	22.10	5,773
1994	63.72	45.47	13,275	25.34	19.69	7,150
1995	84.73	50.26	15,215	32.78	32.58	9,364
1996	78.74	79.60	18,390	35.56	38.07	8,259

[*]Dates and names of airlines and individuals have been changed in this case to maintain confidentiality. The data and issues described here are actual.

Case Study

Akron Zoological Park

During the late 1980s, global changes in consumer preferences for radial tires, inflation, and changes in governmental priorities, almost resulted in the permanent closing of the Akron Children's Zoo. Lagging attendance and a low membership level did not help matters. Faced with uncertain prospects, the city of Akron opted out of the zoo business. In response, the Akron Zoological Park was organized as a corporation to operate the zoo under contract with the city.

To be successful, the zoo must maintain its image as a quality place for its visitors to spend their time. Its animal exhibits are clean and neat. The animals, birds, and reptiles look well cared for. As resources become available for construction and continuing operations, the zoo also keeps adding new exhibits and activities. The independent organization's efforts seem to be working, because attendance increased from 53,353 in 1989 to an all-time record of 133,762 in 1994.

Due to its northern climate, the zoo's open season lasts from mid-April until mid-October. It reopens for 1 week at Halloween and for the month of December. Zoo attendance depends largely on the weather. For example, attendance was down during the month of December 1995, which established many local records for the coldest temperature and the most snow. Variations in weather also affect crop yields and prices of fresh animal foods, thereby influencing the costs of animal maintenance.

In normal circumstances, the zoo may be able to achieve its target goal and attract an annual attendance equal to 40% of its community. Akron has not grown appreciably during the past decade. But the zoo became known as an innovative community resource, and as indicated in the table, annual paid attendance has doubled. Approximately 35% of all visitors are adults. Children account for one half of the paid attendance. Group admissions remain a constant 15% of attendance.

The zoo does not have an advertising budget. To gain exposure in its market, it depends on public service announcements, the zoo's public television series, and local press coverage of its activities. Many of these activities are only a few years old and are a strong reason why attendance has increased.

Although the zoo is a nonprofit organization, it must ensure that its income sources equal or exceed operating and physical plant costs. Its continued existence remains totally dependent on its ability to generate revenues while reducing its expenses.

Annual Attendance at the Akron Zoological Park

Year	Total Persons	Admission Fee ($) Adult	Child	Group
1998	117,874	4.00	2.50	1.50
1997	125,363	3.00	2.00	1.00
1996	126,853	3.00	2.00	1.50
1995	108,363	2.50	1.50	1.00
1994	133,762	2.50	1.50	1.00
1993	95,504	2.00	1.00	.50
1992	63,034	1.50	.75	.50
1991	63,853	1.50	.75	.50
1990	61,417	1.50	.75	.50
1989	53,353	1.50	.75	.50

Discussion Questions

1. The president of the Akron Zoo has asked you to calculate the expected gate admittance figures and revenues for both 1999 and 2000. Would simple linear-regression analysis be the appropriate forecasting technique?
2. Besides admission price, what other factors that influence annual attendance should be considered in the forecast?

Source: Professor F. Bruce Simmons, III, The University of Akron.

Internet Case Study

See our Internet home page at http://www.prenhall.com/heizer for this additional case study Human Resources, Inc.

BIBLIOGRAPHY

Box, G. E. P., and G. Jenkins. *Time Series Analysis: Forecasting and Control.* San Francisco: Holden Day, 1970.

Brown, R. G. *Statistical Forecasting for Inventory Control.* New York: McGraw-Hill, 1959.

Chambers, J. C., C. Satinder, S. K. Mullick, and D. D. Smith. "How to Choose the Right Forecasting Techniques." *Harvard Business Review* 49 (July-August 1971): 45-74.

Collopy, F., and J. S. Armstrong. "Rule-Based Forecasting: Development and Validation of an Expert Systems Approach to Combining Time Series Extrapolations." *Management Science* 38, no. 10 (October 1992): 1094.

Gardner, E. S. "Exponential Smoothing: The State of the Art." *Journal of Forecasting* 4, no. 1 (March 1985).

Georgoff, D. M., and R. G. Murdick. "Manager's Guide to Forecasting." *Harvard Business Review* 64 (January-February 1986): 110-120.

Gips, J., and B. Sullivan. "Sales Forecasting-Replacing Magic with Logic." *Production and Inventory Management Review* 2 (February 1982).

Murdick, R., and D. M. Georgoff. "Forecasting: A Systems Approach." *Technological Forecasting and Social Change* 44 (1993): 1-16.

Murdick, R., B. Render, and R. Russell. *Service Operations Management.* Boston: Allyn and Bacon, 1990.

Render, B., and R. M. Stair. *Quantitative Analysis for Management,* 6th ed. Upper Saddle River, NJ: Prentice Hall, 1997.

INTERNET RESOURCES

Guide to the web for Statisticians-Statistical Methodology:
    http://www.maths.uq.oz.au/~qis.webguide/methods.html

Journal of Time Series Analysis:
    http://www.blackwellpublishers.co.uk/scripts/webjrn1.idc?issn=01439782

Nonlinear Analysis of Retail Performance:
    http://attila.stevens-tech.edu/~dvaccari/ieee.html

Design of Goods and Services

CHAPTER OUTLINE

GLOBAL COMPANY PROFILE: REGAL MARINE

GOODS AND SERVICES SELECTION
- Product Strategy Options
- Generation of New Product Opportunities
- Product Life Cycles
- Life Cycle and Strategy
- Environmentally Friendly Products

PRODUCT DEVELOPMENT
- Product Development System
- Organizing for Product Development
- Manufacturability and Value Engineering

ISSUES FOR PRODUCT DEVELOPMENT
- Robust Design
- Time-Based Competition
- Modular Design
- Computer-Aided Design (CAD)
- Value Analysis
- Product-by-Value Analysis

DEFINING THE PRODUCT
- Make-or-Buy Decisions
- Group Technology

DOCUMENTS FOR PRODUCTION

SERVICE DESIGN
- Documents for Services

APPLICATION OF DECISION TREES TO PRODUCT DESIGN

TRANSITION TO PRODUCTION

SUMMARY

KEY TERMS

SOLVED PROBLEM

DISCUSSION QUESTIONS

CRITICAL THINKING EXERCISE

PROBLEMS

CASE STUDIES: DE MAR'S PRODUCT STRATEGY; GE'S ROTARY COMPRESSOR

VIDEO CASE 3: PRODUCT DESIGN AT REGAL MARINE

BIBLIOGRAPHY

INTERNET RESOURCES

LEARNING OBJECTIVES

When you complete this chapter you should be able to:

Identify or Define:

- Product life cycle
- Product development team
- Manufacturability and value engineering
- Robust design
- Time-based competition
- Modular design
- Computer-aided design
- Value analysis
- Group technology
- Configuration management

Explain:

- Japanese approach to product development
- Concurrent engineering
- Product-by-value analysis
- Product documentation

GLOBAL COMPANY PROFILE:

Product Strategy Provides Competitive Advantage at Regal Marine

Twenty-five years after its founding by potato farmer Paul Kuck, Regal Marine has become a powerful force on the waters of the world. The world's third-largest boat manufacturer (by global sales), Regal exports to 30 countries, including Russia and China. Almost one third of its sales are overseas.

Product design is critical in the highly competitive pleasure boat business: "We keep in touch with our customers and we respond to the marketplace," says Kuck. "We're introducing six new models this year alone. I'd say we're definitely on the aggressive end of the spectrum." With changing consumer tastes, compounded by material changes and ever-improving marine engineering, the design function is under constant pressure. Added to these pressures is the constant issue of cost competitiveness combined with the need to provide good value for customers.

CAD/CAM is used to design the hull of a new product. This process results in faster and more efficient design and production.

Once a hull has been pulled from the mold, it travels down a monorail assembly path. JIT inventory delivers engines, wiring, seats, flooring, and interiors when needed.

Consequently, Regal Marine is a frequent user of computer-aided design (CAD). New designs come to life via Regal's three-dimensional CAD system, borrowed from automotive technology. Regal's naval architects' goal is to continue to reduce the time from concept to prototype to production. The sophisticated CAD system not only has reduced product development time but also has reduced problems with tooling and production, resulting in a superior product.

All of Regal's products, from the $11,000 14-foot Rush to the $225,000 40-foot Commodore yacht, follow a similar production process. Hulls and bows are separately hand-produced by spraying preformed molds with 3 to 5 layers of a fiberglass laminate. The hulls and bows harden and are

REGAL MARINE

removed to become the lower and upper structure of the boat. As they move to the assembly line, they are joined and components added at each workstation.

Wooden decks, precut in-house by computer-driven routers, are delivered on a just-in-time basis for installation at one station. Engines—one of the few purchased components—are installed at another. Racks of electrical wiring harnesses, engineered and rigged in-house, are then installed. An in-house upholstery department delivers customized seats, beds, dashboards, or other cushioned components. Finally, chrome fixtures are put in place, and the boat is sent to Regal's test tank for watertight, gauge, and system inspection.

At the final stage, boats are placed in this test tank, where a rain machine ensures watertight fits.

193

> **TEN DECISIONS OF OM**
>
> Managing Quality
>
> **Design of Goods & Services**
>
> Process Strategy
> Location Strategies
> Layout Strategies
> Human Resources
> Supply-Chain Management
> Inventory Management
> Scheduling
> Maintenance

Product decision The selection, definition, and design of products.

Global firms like Regal Marine know that the basis for an organization's existence is the good or service it provides society. Great products are the keys to success. Anything less than an excellent product strategy can be devastating to a firm. To maximize the potential for success, top companies focus on only a few products and then concentrate on those products. For instance, Honda's focus is engines. Virtually all of Honda's sales (autos, motorcycles, generators, lawn mowers) are based on its outstanding engine technology. Likewise, Intel's focus is on computer chips, and Microsoft's is PC software. However, because most products have a limited and even predictable life cycle, companies must constantly be looking for new products to design, develop, and take to market. Good operations managers insist upon strong communication between customer, product, processes, and suppliers that results in a high success rate for their new products. Benchmarks, of course, vary by industry, but Regal introduces six new boats a year, and Rubbermaid introduces a new product each day!

One product strategy is to build particular competence in customizing an established family of goods or services. This approach allows the customer to choose product variations while reinforcing the organization's strength. Dell Computers, for example, has built a huge market by delivering computers with the exact hardware and software desired by end users. And Dell does it fast—it understands that speed to market is imperative to gain a competitive edge. Motorola also understands the importance of quick response and has built its pager business based on speed to market. In fact, it has reduced the time from order to delivery from over a month to less than 3 hours!

Note that many service firms also refer to their offerings as products. For instance, when Allstate Insurance offers a new homeowner's policy, it is referred to as a new "product." Similarly, when Citicorp opens a mortgage department, it offers a number of new mortgage "products." Although the term *products* may often refer to tangible goods, it also refers to offerings by service organizations.

An effective product strategy links product decisions with investment, market share, product life cycle, and defines the breadth of the product line. The objective of the **product decision** is to develop and implement a product strategy that meets the demands of the marketplace with a competitive advantage. One of the 10 decisions of OM, product strategy may focus on developing a competitive advantage via differentiation, low cost, rapid response, or a combination of these.

GOODS AND SERVICES SELECTION

Product Strategy Options

A world of options exists in the selection, definition, and design of products. Product selection is choosing the good or service to provide customers or clients. For instance, hospitals specialize in various types of patients and various types of medical procedures. A hospital's management may decide to operate a general-purpose hospital or a maternity hospital or, as in the case of the Canadian hospital Shouldice, specialize in hernias. Hospitals select their products when they decide what kind of hospital to be. Numerous other options exist for hospitals, just as they exist for McDonald's or General Motors.

Organizations like Shouldice Hospital *differentiate* themselves through their product. Shouldice differentiates itself by offering a distinctly unique and high-quality product. Its hernia-repair service is so fast that it discharges patients 3 days earlier than other hospitals—and with very few complications. Shouldice customers come from throughout the world, and the hospital is so popular that it can't handle all those desiring service.

Taco Bell has developed and executed a *low-cost* strategy through product design. By designing a product (its menu) that can be produced with a minimum of labor in small

Product selection occurs in services as well as manufacturing. Shown here is Shouldice Hospital, renowned for its world-class specialization in hernia repair—no emergency room, no maternity ward, no open heart surgery, just hernias. Shouldice's cost is about one third of general-purpose hospitals. Local anesthetics are used; patients enter and leave the operating room on their own; rooms are spartan, discouraging patients from remaining in bed; and all meals are served in a common dining room. As Shouldice has demonstrated, product selection affects the entire production system.

kitchens, Taco Bell has developed a product line that is both low-cost and high-value. Successful product design has allowed Taco Bell to increase the food content of its products from 27¢ to 45¢ of each sales dollar.

Toyota's strategy is *rapid response* to changing consumer demand. By executing the fastest automobile design in the industry, Toyota has driven the speed of product development down to well under 2 years in an industry whose standard is still close to 3 years. Although competitors often operate in a 3 year guess, shorter design time allows Toyota to get a car to market before consumer tastes change.

Product decisions are fundamental to an organization's strategy and have major implications throughout the operations function. For instance, GM's Pontiac Grand Am steering columns are a good example of the strong role product design plays in both quality and efficiency. The new steering column has a simpler design, with about 30% fewer parts than its predecessor. The result: assembly time is one third of the older column, and the new column's quality is about seven times higher. As an added bonus the new line's machinery costs a third less than that in the old line.

Generation of New Product Opportunities

Product selection, definition, and design take place on a continuing basis because so many new product opportunities exist. Five factors influencing market opportunities are:

1. *Economic change,* which brings increasing levels of affluence in the long run but economic cycles and price changes in the short run. In the long run, for instance, more and more people can afford automobiles, but in the short run, a recession may weaken the demand for automobiles.

OM IN ACTION

STRYKER'S PRODUCT IDEAS COME FROM ITS CUSTOMERS

Homer Stryker's hospital products firm has made *Forbes'* list of the Best Small Companies in America for 10 years straight. From its humble start 50 years ago by its clever orthopedist founder, Stryker Corporation now offers an array of niche products, including bone drills and saws, hospital beds, hip implants, and video cameras for internal surgery.

Churning out new products has been Stryker's strength. By operating with autonomous divisions, each with its own highly trained, specialized sales staff, Stryker knows how to listen to its customers. Stryker's salespeople act as a de facto research-and-development team. Most of the company's new product ideas come from salespeople standing in the operating room next to the physician. There they can observe the doctor in action, write down their comments, and come up with ways to improve a saw, a hip implant, or a bed.

As a case in point, eye surgeons kept complaining about a bed's lack of flexibility at the head level. It was hard, they said, to position a patient's head. Stryker people took note and the firm rolled out a profitable bed with a moveable headrest.

Another hot new product is a tiny $18,000 video camera used inside a long tube inserted through the abdomen for gallbladder surgery. Aided by the camera, the surgeon can swiftly remove the gallbladder with only a minute incision. Instead of a 1-week hospital stay, the patient is out the next day. This product and similar Stryker products reflect the continuing focus on holding down health-care costs while producing brisk sales. Effective product development remains a key ingredient of Stryker's profitability.

Sources: The Wall Street Journal (July 7, 1997): B10; and *Sales and Marketing Management* (November, 1994): 64.

---

2. *Sociological and demographic change*, which may appear in such factors as decreasing family size. This trend alters the size preference for homes, apartments, and automobiles.
3. *Technological change*, which makes possible everything from home computers to cellular phones to artificial hearts.
4. *Political/legal change*, which brings about new trade agreements, tariffs, and government contract requirements.
5. Other changes, which may be brought about through *market practice, professional standards, suppliers*, and *distributors*.

Operations managers must be aware of these factors and be able to anticipate changes in product opportunities, the products themselves, product volume, and product mix. The *OM in Action* box, "Stryker's Product Ideas Come from Its Customers," discusses how Stryker maintains its flow of new ideas.

Product Life Cycles

Products are born. They live and they die. They are cast aside by a changing society. It may be helpful to think of a product's life as divided into four phases. Those phases—introduction, growth, maturity, and decline—are illustrated for several products in Figure 6.1. That figure also reveals the relative positions of five products.

Product life cycles may be a matter of a few hours (a newspaper), months (seasonal fashions and personal computers), years (Betamax video recorders), or decades Volkswagen Beetle). Regardless of the length of the cycle, the task for the operations manager is the same: to design a system that helps introduce new products successfully. If the operations function cannot perform effectively at this stage, the firm may be saddled with losers—products that cannot be produced efficiently and perhaps not at all.

Figure 6.2 shows the four life cycle stages and the relationship of product sales, costs,

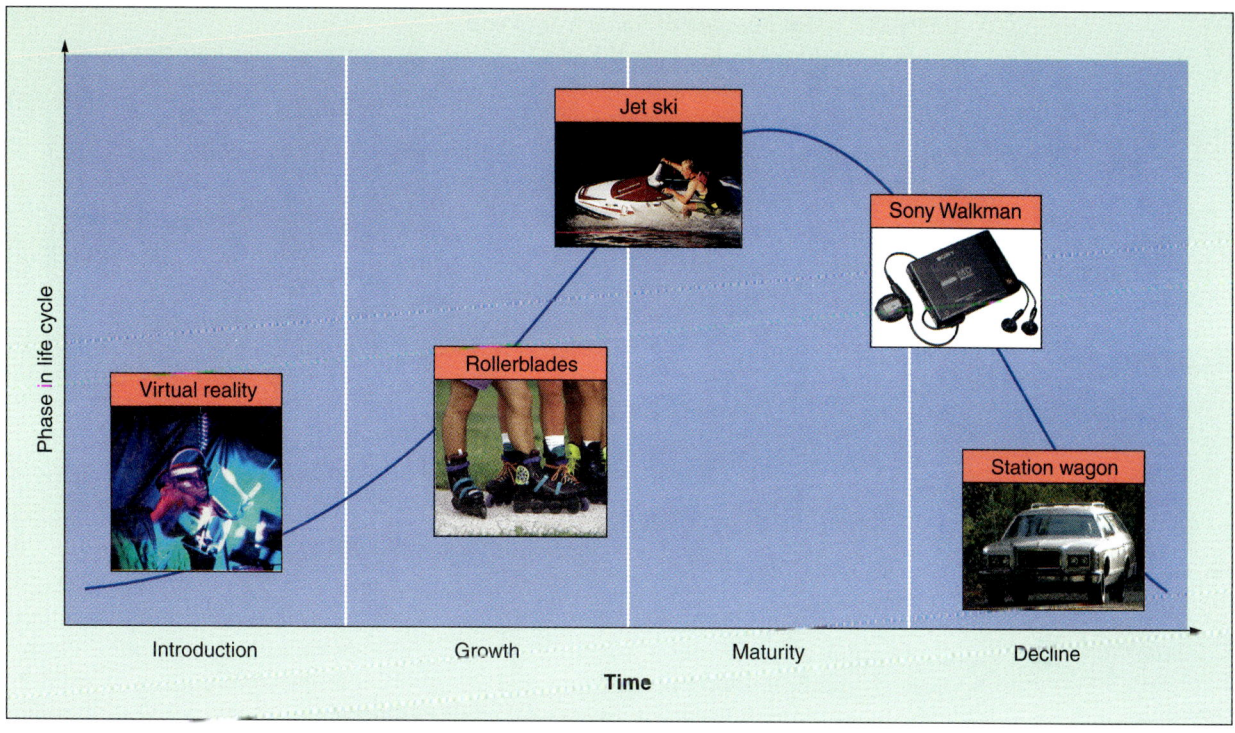

FIGURE 6.1 ■ **Products in Various Stages of Life Cycle**

and profit over the life cycle of a product. Note that typically a firm has a negative cash flow while it develops a product. When the product is successful, those losses may be recovered. Eventually, the successful product may yield a profit prior to its decline. However, the profit is fleeting. As Figure 6.3 on page 198 shows, leading companies generate a substantial portion of their sales from products less than 5 years old.

Despite constant efforts to introduce viable new products, many new products do not succeed. Indeed, for General Mills to come up with a winner in the breakfast cereal market—defined as a cereal that gets a scant one half of 1% of the market—isn't easy. Among the top 10 brands of cereal, the youngest, Honey Nut Cheerios, was created in

More than 30% of Rubbermaid sales each year come from products less than 5 years old.

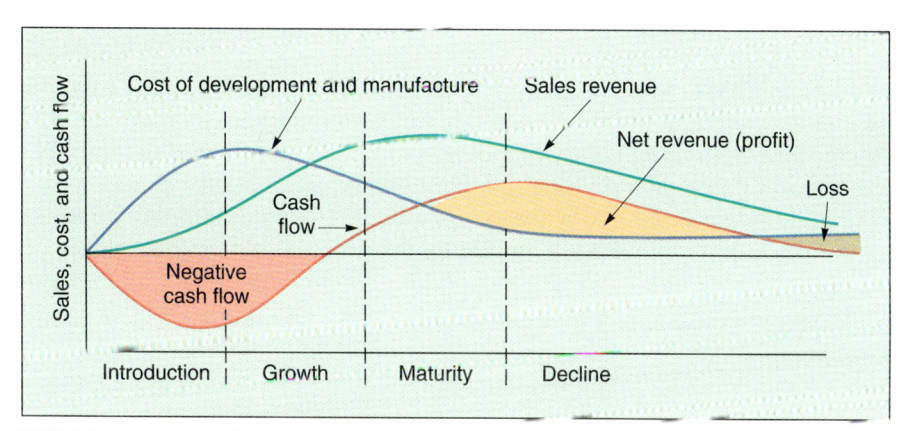

FIGURE 6.2 ■ **Product Life Cycle, Sales, Cost, and Profit**

FIGURE 6.3 ■ Percent of Sales from Products Introduced in the Last 5 Years

The higher the percent of sales from products introduced in the last 5 years, the more likely the firm is to be a leader.

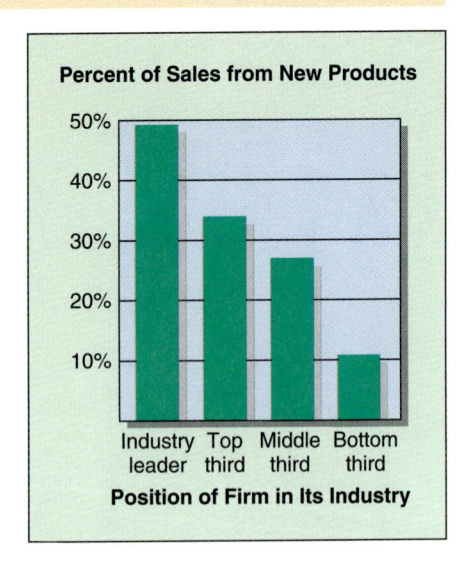

Motorola went through 3,000 working models to develop its first pocket-size cellular telephone.

1979.[1] DuPont estimates that it takes 250 ideas to yield one *marketable* product.[2] In fact, it is estimated that only 1 out of 25 products *introduced* actually succeeds! Consequently, product selection, definition, and design occur frequently—perhaps as many as 500 times for each financially successful product. Operations managers and their organizations must be able to accept risk and tolerate failure. They must accommodate a high volume of new product ideas while maintaining the activities to which they are already committed.[3]

Life Cycle and Strategy

Just as operations managers must be prepared to develop new products, they must also be prepared to develop *strategies* for new and existing products. Periodic examination of products is appropriate to determine their positions in the life cycle because *strategies change as products move through their life cycle.* Successful product strategies require determining the best strategy for each product based on its position in its life cycle. A firm, therefore, identifies products or families of products and their position in the life cycle. Let us review some strategy options as products move through their life cycles.

Introductory Phase Because products in the introductory phase are still being "fine-tuned" for the market, as are their production techniques, they may warrant unusual expenditures for (1) research, (2) product development, (3) process modification and enhancement, and (4) supplier development. For example, when cellular phones were first introduced, the features desired by the public were still being determined. At the same time, production managers were still groping for the best manufacturing techniques.

---

[1] Richard Gibson, "A Cereal Maker's Quest for the Next Grape-Nuts," *The Wall Street Journal,* January 23, 1997, p. B1.

[2] Rosabeth Kanter, John Kao and Fred Wiersema, *Innovation Breakthrough Thinking at 3M, DuPont, GE, Pfizer, and Rubbermaid* (New York: Harper-Business, 1997).

[3] See a discussion of this issue in Rosabeth Moss Kanter, "Swimming in New Streams: Mastering Innovation Dilemmas," *California Management Review* 31, no. 4 (summer 1989): 45–69.

Growth Phase In the growth phase, product design has begun to stabilize, and effective forecasting of capacity requirements is necessary. Adding capacity or enhancing existing capacity to accommodate the increase in product demand may be necessary.

Maturity Phase By the time a product is mature, competitors are established. So high-volume, innovative production may be appropriate. Improved cost control, reduction in options, and a paring down of the product line may be effective or necessary for profitability and market share.

Decline Phase Management may need to be ruthless with those products whose life cycle is at an end. Dying products are typically poor products in which to invest resources and managerial talent. Unless dying products make some unique contribution to the firm's reputation or its product line or can be sold with an unusually high contribution, their production should be terminated.[4]

Environmentally Friendly Products

Another way to achieve a differentiation strategy—and even a low-cost strategy—is for the operations manager to systematically identify opportunities for products to be environmentally friendly throughout the products' life cycle.[5] These opportunities range from activities that society perceives as socially responsible to actions that are legally required, such as pollution prevention. The British cosmetic firm Body Shop, for example, has successfully differentiated its products by stressing product design. Body Shop pursues a product design, development, and testing strategy that it believes to be socially responsible. This includes environmentally friendly ingredients and elimination of animal testing.

Bristol-Meyers Squibb has responded to environmental issues with a pollution-prevention program called Environment 2000.[6] This program addresses environmental, health, and safety issues at all stages of the product life cycle. Ban Roll-On was one of the first products studied. Repackaging Ban in smaller cartons resulted in a reduction of 600 tons of recycled paperboard. The product then required 55% less shelf space for display. As a result, not only was pollution prevented but store operating costs were also reduced.

One way to accomplish programs like these is to get employees from different functional areas to work together to reduce the environmental impact of a product throughout its life.

The benefits of such a strategy include:

1. Developing safe and more environmentally sound products.
2. Minimizing waste of raw materials and energy.
3. Differentiating products from the competition.
4. Reducing environmental liabilities.
5. Increasing cost-effectiveness of complying with environmental regulations.
6. Being recognized as a good corporate citizen.

General Electric is currently developing a refrigerator that will require substantially less electricity during its life.

---

[4] *Contribution* is defined as the difference between direct cost and selling price. Direct costs are labor and material that go into the product.

[5] Marc J. Epstein, *Measuring Corporate Environmental Performance—Best Practices for Costing and Managing an Effective Environment Strategy* (The IMA Foundation for Applied Research, 1996), p. 39.

[6] A. A. Atkinson, R. D. Banker, R. S. Kaplan, and S. M. Young, *Management Accounting* (Upper Saddle River, NJ: Prentice Hall 1997), p. 613.

200　CHAPTER 6　DESIGN OF GOODS AND SERVICES

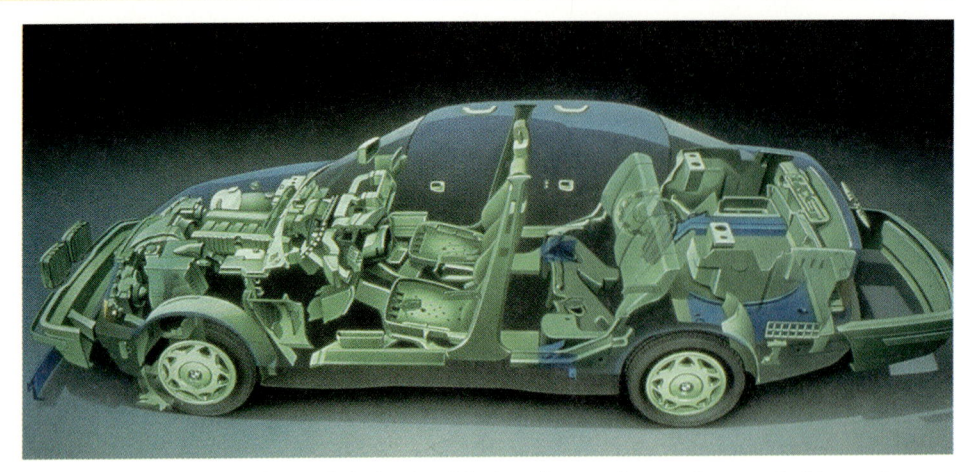

BMW uses parts made of recycled plastics (blue) and parts that can be recycled (green). "Green manufacturing" means companies can reuse, refurbish, or dispose of a product's components safely and reduce total life cycle product costs.

The German auto firm, BMW, has successfully addressed the decline stage of the life cycle by being environmentally friendly at the design stage; its designs now include recyclable plastic components, as shown in the photo.

PRODUCT DEVELOPMENT

Product Development System

An effective product strategy links product decisions with cash flow, market dynamics, product life cycle, and the organization's capabilities. A firm must have the cash for product development, understand the changes constantly taking place in the marketplace, and

NCR Corporation has demonstrated the success of the team approach with an electronic cash register. The cash register goes together with no screws or bolts. The entire terminal consists of just 15 vendor-produced components. Assembly is so easy that this engineer can put the terminal together blindfolded. NCR has reduced the number of parts by 85%, the number of suppliers by 65, and the time to assemble by 25%.

PRODUCT DEVELOPMENT

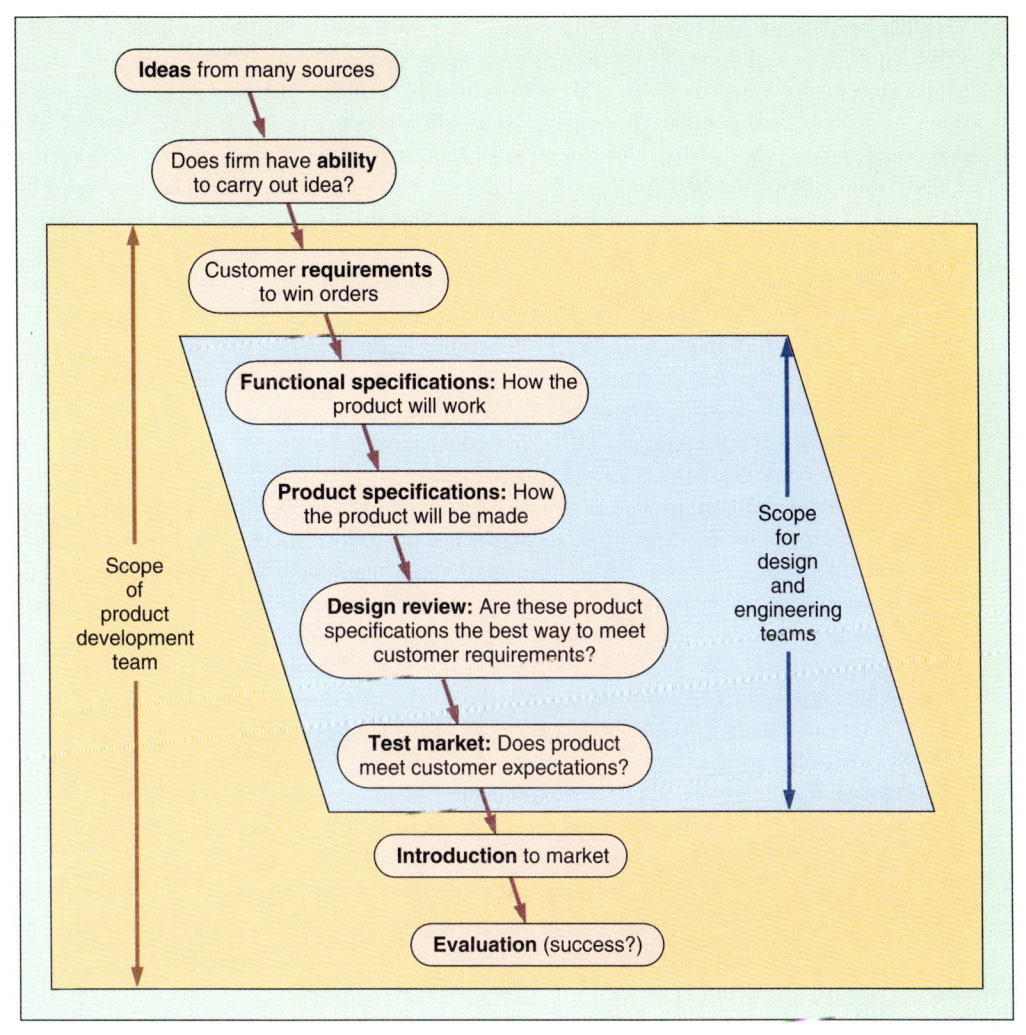

FIGURE 6.4 ■ Product Development Stages

Product concepts are developed from a variety of sources, both external and internal to the firm. Concepts that survive the product-idea stage progress through various stages, with nearly constant review in a highly participative environment to minimize failure.

have the necessary talents and resources available. The product development system may well determine not only product success but also the firm's future. Figure 6.4 shows a product development system. In this system, product options go through a series of steps, starting with ideas that may come from either internal or external sources and ending with the evaluation of new products.

Organizing for Product Development

The traditional U.S. approach to product development is an organization with distinct departments. These departments are: first, a research and development department to do the necessary research; then an engineering department to design the product; then a manufacturing engineering department to design a product that can be produced; and finally, a production department that produces the product. The distinct advantage of this approach

Product excellence means determining what the customer wants and providing it.

is that fixed duties and responsibilities exist. The distinct disadvantage is lack of forward thinking: How will downstream departments in the process deal with the concepts, ideas, and designs presented to them, and ultimately what will the customer think of the product? A second and popular approach is to assign a product manager to "champion" the product through the product development system and related organizations. However, a third, and perhaps the best, product development approach used in the U.S. seems to be the use of teams. Such teams are known variously as *product development teams, design for manufacturability teams,* and *value engineering teams.*

The Japanese bypass the team issue by not subdividing organizations into research and development, engineering, production, and so forth. Consistent with the Japanese style of group effort and teamwork, these activities are all in one organization. Japanese culture and management style are more collegial and the organization less structured than in most Western countries. Therefore, the Japanese find it unnecessary to have "teams" provide the necessary communication and coordination. However, the typical Western style and the conventional wisdom is to use teams.

Product development teams Teams charged with moving from market requirements for a product to achieving product success.

Product development teams are charged with the responsibility of moving from market requirements for a product to achieving a product success (Figure 6.4). Such teams often include representatives from marketing, manufacturing, purchasing, quality assurance, and field service personnel. Many teams also include representatives from vendors. Regardless of the formal nature of the product development effort, research suggests that success is more likely in an open, highly participative environment where those with potential contributions are allowed to make them. The objective of a product development team is to make the good or service a success. This includes marketability, manufacturability, and serviceability.

Concurrent engineering Use of participating teams in design and engineering activities.

Use of such teams is also called **concurrent engineering** and implies a team representing all affected areas (known as a *cross-functional* team). Concurrent engineering also implies speedier product development through simultaneous performance of various aspects of product development. A recent study suggests that the team approach is the dominant structure for product development by leading organizations in the U.S.[7]

Manufacturability and Value Engineering

Manufacturability and value engineering activities to help improve a product's design, production, maintainability and use.

Manufacturability and value engineering activities are concerned with improvement of design and specifications at the research, development, design, and production stages of product development. In addition to immediate, obvious cost reduction, design for manufacturability and value engineering may produce other benefits. These include:

1. Reduced complexity of the product;
2. Additional standardization of components;
3. Improvement of functional aspects of the product;
4. Improved job design and job safety;
5. Improved maintainability (serviceability) of the product;
6. Robust design.

Manufacturability and value engineering activities may be the best cost-avoidance technique available to operations management. They yield value improvement by focusing on achieving the functional specifications necessary to meet customer requirements in an optimal way. Value engineering programs, when effectively managed, typically reduce costs between 15% and 70% without reducing quality. Some studies have indicated that for every dollar spent on value engineering, $10 to $25 in savings can be realized.

---

[7] "Best Practices Survey 1994: Product Definition," *Target* 11, no. 3 (May–June 1995): 22–24.

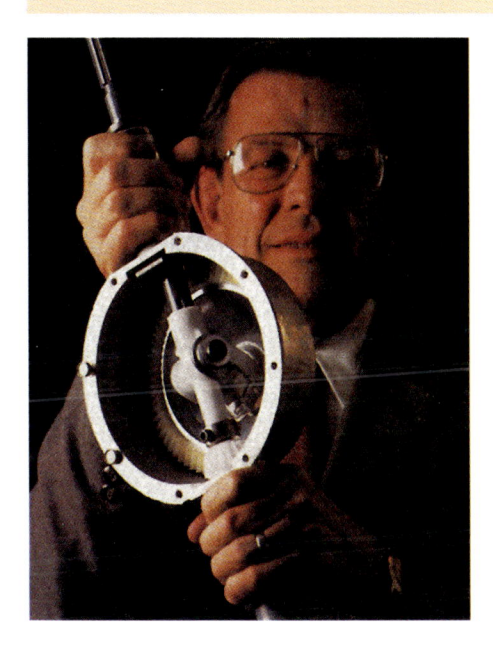

The new washer transmission designed by Maytag can switch from slow reciprocal motion of the agitator shaft during the wash cycle to fast rotary motion of the washtub during the wring cycle. The new design using only 40 pieces is more reliable. The reduction in number of parts means a substantial reduction in cost, with fewer designs and purchases as well as less inventory and manufacturing expense.

Product design affects virtually all aspects of operating expense. Consequently, the development process needs to ensure a thorough evaluation of design prior to a commitment to produce. The cost reduction achieved for a specific bracket via value engineering is shown in Figure 6.5.

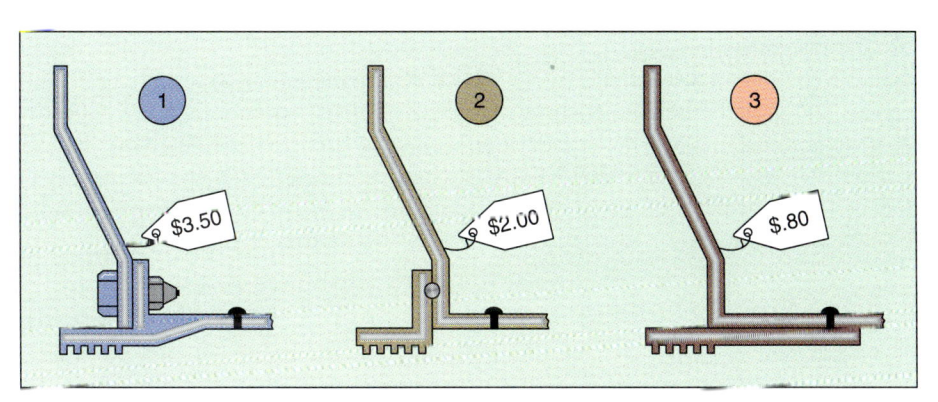

FIGURE 6.5 ■ Cost Reduction of a Bracket via Value Engineering
Each time the bracket is redesigned and simplified, we are able to produce it for less.
Source: Adapted from Robert Goodell Brown, *Management Decisions for Production Operations* (Hinsdale, IL: Dryden Press, Inc., 1971), p. 353.

ISSUES FOR PRODUCT DEVELOPMENT

In addition to developing an effective system and organization structure for product development, several techniques are important to product development. We will now review six of these: (1) robust design, (2) time-based competition, (3) modular design, (4) computer-aided design, (5) value analysis, and (6) product-by-value analysis.

Robust design a design that can be produced to requirements even with unfavorable conditions in the production process.

Robust Design

Robust design means that the product is designed so that small variations in production or assembly do not adversely affect the product. For instance, AT&T developed an integrated circuit that could be used in many products to amplify voice signals. As originally designed, the circuit had to be manufactured very precisely to avoid variations in the strength of the signal. Such a circuit would have been costly to make because of stringent quality controls needed during the manufacturing process. However, after testing and analyzing the design, AT&T engineers realized that if the resistance of the circuit were reduced—a minor change with no associated costs—the circuit would be far less sensitive to manufacturing variations. The result was a 40% improvement in quality.

Time-Based Competition

Time-based competition Competition based on time; may take form of rapidly developing products and moving them to market or rapid product or service delivery.

Product life cycles are becoming shorter. This trend increases the importance of product development. Therefore, faster developers of new products continually gain on slower developers and obtain a competitive advantage. This concept is called **time-based competition**.[8]

With many products, the first company into production may have its product adopted for use in a variety of applications that will generate sales for years. It may become the "standard." Consequently, there is often more concern with getting the product to market than with optimum product design or process efficiency. Even so, rapid introduction to the market may be good management because until competition begins to introduce copies or improved versions, the product can sometimes be priced high enough to earn a profit even using somewhat inefficient production design and methods. For example, when Kodak first introduced its Ektar film, it sold for 10% to 15% more than conventional film. Motorola's innovative pocket-sized cellular telephone was 50% smaller than any Japanese competitor's and sold for twice the price.[9]

Much of the current competitive battlefield is focused around the speed of product to market. If an organization loses here, catching up in other areas is very difficult.

Rather than developing entirely new products, some firms look at new product development as a continuum that extends from enhancement to migrations to inventions. Cellular phones and global wireless networks may be inventions, but more modest enhancements or migrations may use the organization's existing strengths and, therefore, be less risky and faster. Enhancements may be modest changes in color, size, and features, such as Boeing's enhancements of the 737 described in the *OM in Action* box. However, Boeing also practices a migration strategy as it moves to new models of aircraft.[10]

Modular Design

Modular design Parts or components of a product are subdivided into modules that are easily interchanged or replaced.

Products designed in easily segmented components are known as **modular designs**.[11] Modular designs offer flexibility to both production and marketing. The production department typically finds modularity helpful because it makes product development, production, and subsequent changes easier. Moreover, marketing may like modularity because it adds flexibility to the ways customers can be satisfied. For instance, virtually all

---

[8] Joseph Blackburn, *Time-Based Competition: The Next Battleground in American Manufacturing* (Homewood, IL: Irwin/Business One, 1990); see also Kim Clark, as reported in James P. Womack, Daniel T. Jones, and Daniel Roos, *The Machine That Changed the World* (New York: Rawson Associates, 1990), p. 111.

[9] J. Dean and J. Evans, *Total Quality* (Minneapolis/St. Paul: West Publishing, 1994), p. 251.

[10] For a related discussion see Thomas S. Robertson, "How to Reduce Market Penetration Cycle Times," *Sloan Management Review,* fall 1993, pp. 87–89.

[11] See related discussion in C. Y. Baldwin and Kim B. Clark, "Managing in an Age of Modularity," *Harvard Business Review,* 75, no. 5 (September–October 1997): 84–93.

OM IN ACTION

ENHANCING THE BOEING 737 LIFE CYCLE

Many firms have found that they can extend the life cycles of their products by enhancing them. In this way, they prolong earnings streams and generate additional profits. One multinational successfully doing this is Boeing. Its key products include the 737, the 747, the 757, the 767, and the 777.

Boeing delivered its first 737 in 1967. The plane sold well for several years; many carriers initially bought 20 or 30 at a time. However, in the mid-1970s, it began to lose ground. Boeing decided that the 737's life cycle was ending and was preparing to end its production. It decided to try one last measure, however, by marketing the plane to fledgling airlines in developing countries. Instead of trying to sell 20 planes at a time to KLM or United, Boeing intended to sell 1 or 2 at a time to small airlines in countries in Africa, South America, and other developing regions.

Boeing first realized that it had to make a few modifications to the basic 737 so that it would better fit local conditions. For example, pilots in developing countries were not as skilled as their Western counterparts and tended to "bounce" more during landing. So Boeing redesigned the landing system to be better able to handle extreme landing conditions.

The plan was a big success. Boeing sold enough 737s, even in small quantities, to justify keeping the plane in production. And as those small airlines began to grow, they continued to buy 737s as well as upgrading to newer, larger Boeing aircraft. Surprisingly, domestic orders also continued to come in on a regular basis from airlines such as Southwest, which uses 737s exclusively. As a result, Boeing continues to make the 737, which recently became the largest-selling commercial aircraft in aviation history.

Sources: Fortune (March 8, 1993): 66–73; and R. W. Griffin and M. W. Pustay *International Business* (Addison-Wesley: Reading, MA, 1996), p. 91.

---

premium high-fidelity stereos are produced and sold this way. The customization provided by modularity allows customers to mix and match to their own taste. This is also the approach taken by Harley-Davidson, where relatively few different engines, chassis, gas tanks, and suspension systems are mixed to produce a huge variety of motorcycles. It has been estimated that many automobile manufacturers can, by mixing the available modules, never make two cars alike. This same concept of modularity is carried over to many industries, from airframe manufacturers to fast-food restaurants. Airbus uses the same wing modules on several planes, just as McDonald's and Burger King use relatively few modules (cheese, lettuce, buns, sauces, pickles, meat patties, french fries, etc.) to make a variety of meals.

Computer-Aided Design

Computer-aided design (CAD) is the use of computers to interactively design and document products. Increasingly, manufactured products are being developed through CAD, which greatly enhances the speed and integrity of product design.

When CAD is used, a design engineer starts by developing a rough sketch or, conceivably, just an idea. The designer then uses a graphic display as a drafting board to construct the geometry of a design. As a geometric definition is completed, a sophisticated CAD system allows the designer to determine various kinds of engineering data, such as strength or heat transfer. CAD also allows the designer to ensure that parts fit together so there will be no interferences when parts are subsequently assembled. Thus, if the designer is sketching the fender for an automobile, the brackets and related panels are changed as the fender is changed. Analysis of both existing and new designs can be done expediently and economically. (Note the photo of Regal Marine's CAD designers in the Global Company Profile that opens this chapter.)

> **Computer-aided design (CAD)** Use of a computer to interactively develop, design, and document products.

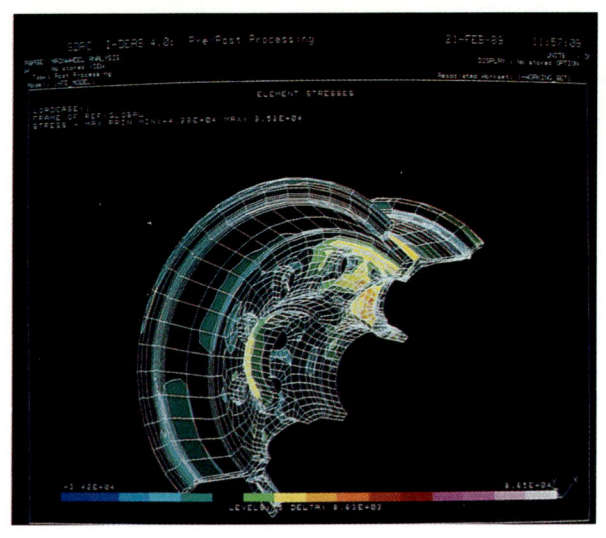

Computer-aided design: B. F. Goodrich engineers and managers use software from Structural Dynamics Research Corporation (SDRC) to model wheel and brake assemblies. By analyzing stress and heat, they can often avoid costly design and production mistakes. Whereas errors that are found at the design stage on a CRT screen can often be fixed for a nominal cost, the cost is substantial once production has begun.

Proctor & Gamble used CAD when designing its Crest toothpaste pump dispenser.

Once the designer is satisfied with the design, it becomes part of a drawing database on electronic media. Through a library of symbols, the CAD system also helps to ensure adherence to drafting standards. Additionally, because CAD data are available for subsequent use by others, tool-design personnel and programmers of numerically controlled machines find CAD technology helpful. They can now proceed to design tooling and programs with confidence that they have the latest accurate engineering data and drawings.

Value Analysis

Value analysis A review of successful products that takes place during the production process.

Although value engineering focuses on *preproduction* design improvement, value analysis, a related technique, takes place *during* the production process, when it is clear that a new product is a success. **Value analysis** seeks improvements that lead to either a better product or a product made more economically. The techniques and advantages for value analysis are the same as for value engineering, although minor changes in implementation may be necessary because value analysis is taking place while the product is being produced.

Product-by-Value Analysis

Product-by-value analysis A listing of products in descending order of their individual dollar contribution to the firm, as well as the *total annual* dollar contribution of the product.

The effective operations manager directs efforts toward those items that show the greatest promise. This is the Pareto principle (i.e., focus on the critical few, not the trivial many) applied to product mix: Resources are to be invested in the critical few and not the trivial many. **Product-by-value analysis** lists products in descending order of their *individual dollar contribution* to the firm. It also lists the *total annual dollar contribution* of the product. Low contribution on a per-unit basis by a particular product may look substantially different if it represents a large portion of the company's sales.

A product-by-value report allows management to evaluate possible strategies for each product. These might include increasing cash flow (for example, increasing contribution by raising selling price or lowering cost), increasing market penetration (improving quality and/or reducing cost or price), or reducing costs (improving the production process). The report may also tell management which product offerings should be eliminated and which fail to justify further investment in research and development or capital equipment. The report focuses management's attention on the strategic direction for each product.

DEFINING THE PRODUCT

Once new goods or services are selected for introduction, they must be defined. First, a good or service is defined in terms of its *functions*—that is, what it is to *do*. The product is then designed: That is, it is determined how the functions are to be achieved. Management typically has a variety of options as to how a product should achieve its functional purpose. For instance, when an alarm clock is produced, aspects of design such as the color, size, or location of buttons may make substantial differences in ease of manufacture, quality, and market acceptance.

Rigorous specifications of a product are necessary to assure efficient production. Equipment, layout, and human resources cannot be determined until the product is defined, designed, and documented. Therefore, every organization needs documents to define its products. This is true of everything from meat patties, to cheese, to computers, to a medical procedure. In the case of cheese, a written specification is typical. Indeed, written specifications or standard grades exist and provide the definition for many products. For instance, Monterey Jack cheese has a written description that specifies the characteristics necessary for each Department of Agriculture grade. A portion of the Department of Agriculture grade for Monterey Jack Grade AA is shown in Figure 6.6. Similarly, McDonald's Corp. has 60 specifications for potatoes that are to be made into french fries.

---

§ 58.2469 Specifications for U.S. grades of Monterey (Monterey Jack) cheese

(a) *U.S. grade AA*. Monterey Cheese shall conform to the following requirements:
(1) *Flavor*. Is fine and highly pleasing, free from undesirable flavors and odors. May possess a very slight acid or feed flavor.
(2) *Body and texture*. A plug drawn from the cheese shall be reasonably firm. It shall have numerous small mechanical openings evenly distributed throughout the plug. It shall not possess sweet holes, yeast holes, or other gas holes.

(3) *Color*. Shall have a natural, uniform, bright attractive appearance.
(4) *Finish and appearance—bandaged and paraffin-dipped*. The rind shall be sound, firm, and smooth providing a good protection to the cheese.

Code of Federal Regulation, Parts 53 to 109, Revised as of Jan. 1, 1985, General Service Administration.

FIGURE 6.6 ■ Monterey Jack
A portion of the general requirements for the U.S. grades of Monterey cheese is shown here.

Most manufactured items as well as their components are defined by a drawing, usually referred to as an engineering drawing. An **engineering drawing** shows the dimensions, tolerances, materials, and finishes of a component. The engineering drawing will be an item on a bill of material. An engineering drawing is shown in Figure 6.7.

Engineering drawing
A drawing that shows the dimensions, tolerances, materials, and finishes of a component.

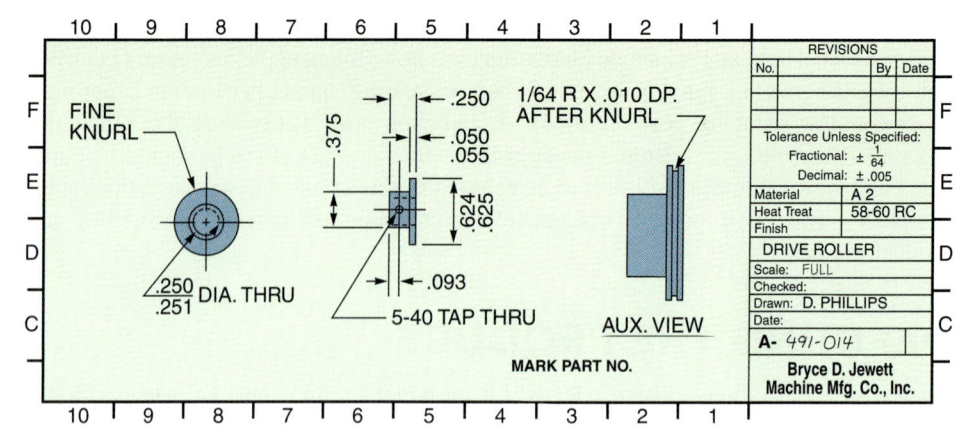

FIGURE 6.7 ■ Engineering Drawings Such as This One Show Dimensions, Tolerances, Materials, and Finishes

Bill of material (BOM)
A listing of the components, their description, and the quantity of each required to make one unit of a product.

The **bill of material (BOM)** lists the components, their description, and the quantity of each required to make one unit of a product. A bill of material for a manufactured item is shown in Figure 6.8(a). An engineering drawing shows how to make one item on the bill of material.

(a) **Bill of Material for a Panel Weldment**

NUMBER	DESCRIPTION	QTY
A 60-71	PANEL WELDM'T	1
A 60-7	LOWER ROLLER ASSM.	1
R 60-17	ROLLER	1
R 60-428	PIN	1
P 60-2	LOCKNUT	1
A 60-72	GUIDE ASSM. REAR	1
R 60-57-1	SUPPORT ANGLE	1
A 60-4	ROLLER ASSEM.	1
02-50-1150	BOLT	1
A 60-73	GUIDE ASSM. FRONT	1
A 60-74	SUPPORT WELDM'T	1
R 60-99	WEAR PLATE	1
02-50-1150	BOLT	1

(b) **Portion-Control Standard for a Hamburger**

PRODUCT: Juicy Burger

DESCRIPTION	QTY
Buns	1
Cheese	1 slice
Meat patties	2
Pickle slice	2
Dehydrated onions	1/250 pkg.
Sauce	1/137.5
Lettuce	1/26 head

FIGURE 6.8 ■ Bills of Material Take Different Forms in a Manufacturing Plant (a) and a Fast-Food Restaurant (b), but in Both Cases, the Product Must Be Defined

In the food-service industry, bills of material manifest themselves in *portion-control standards*. The portion-control standard for a "Juicy Burger" is shown in Figure 6.8(b). In a more complex product, a bill of material is referenced on other bills of material of which they are a part. In this manner, subunits (subassemblies) are part of the next higher unit (their parent bill of material) that ultimately make a final product. In addition to being defined by written specifications, portion-control documents, or bills of material, products

The J. R. Simplot potato-processing facility in Caldwell, Idaho, is responsible for making many of the billions of french fries that McDonald's serves each year. Sixty specifications define how these strips of potatoes become french fries at McDonald's. These specifications define this product by first specifying a russet Burbank potato. The russet Burbank potato has a distinctive taste and high ratio of solid to water. It specifies a special blend of frying oil and a unique steaming process. The fries are then prefried and dried; the exact time and heat is covered by a patent. Mac fries are sprayed (instead of dipped in sugar like many other fries) to brown them evenly. The product is further defined by requiring that 40% of all fries be between 2 and 3 inches long and another 40% must be over 3 inches long. A few stubby ones constitute the final 20%.

can be defined in other ways. For example, products such as chemicals, paints, and petroleums may be defined by formulas or proportions that describe how they are to be made. Movies are defined by scripts, and insurance coverage by legal documents known as policies.

Make-or-Buy Decisions

For many components of products, firms have the option of producing the components themselves or purchasing them from outside sources. Choosing between these options is known as the make-or-buy decision. The **make-or-buy decision** distinguishes between what the firm wants to *produce* and what it wants to *purchase*. Because of variations in quality, cost, and delivery schedules, the make-or-buy decision is critical to product definition. Many items can be purchased as a "standard item" produced by someone else. Such a standard item does not require its own bill of material or engineering drawing because its specification as a standard item is adequate. Examples are the standard bolts listed on the bill of material shown in Figure 6.8(a), for which there will be SAE (Society of Automotive Engineers) specifications. Therefore, there typically is no need for the firm to duplicate this specification in another document. We discuss what is known as the make-or-buy decision in more detail in chapter 11.

Make-or-buy decision
The choosing between producing a component or a service and purchasing it from an outside source.

Group Technology

Engineering drawings may also include codes to facilitate group technology. **Group technology** requires that components be identified by a coding scheme that specifies the type of processing (such as drilling) and the parameters of the processing (such as size). This facilitates standardization of materials, components, and processes as well as the identification of families of parts. As families of parts are identified, activities and machines can

Group technology
A product and component coding system that specifies the type of processing and the parameters of the processing; it allows similar products to be grouped.

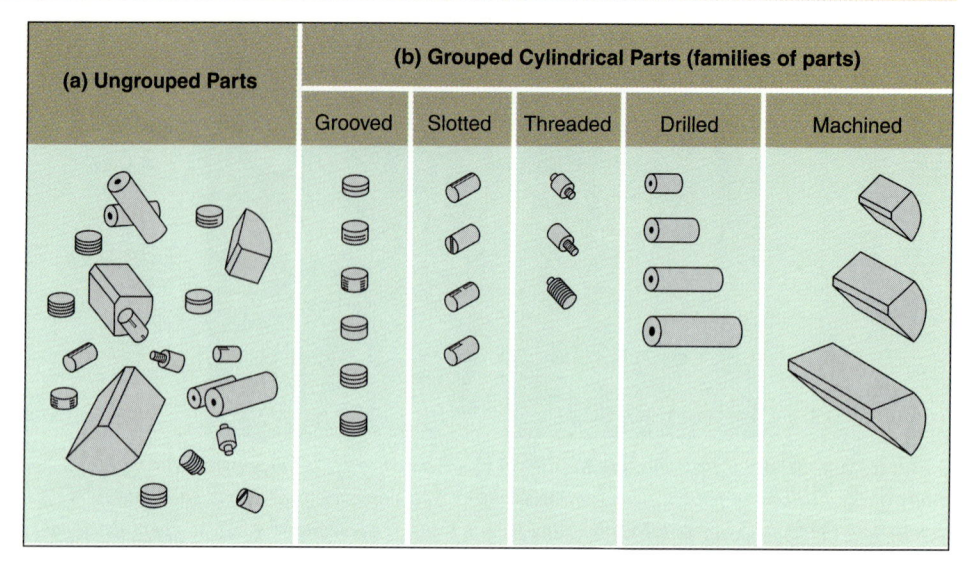

FIGURE 6.9 ■ A Variety of Group Technology Coding Schemes Move Manufactured Components from (a) Ungrouped to (b) Grouped (families of parts)

be grouped to minimize setups, routings, and material handling. An example of how families of parts may be grouped is shown in Figure 6.9. Group technology provides a systematic way to review a family of components to see if an existing component might suffice on a new project. Using existing or standard components eliminates all the costs connected with the design and development of the new part, which is a major cost reduction. For these reasons, successful implementation of group technology leads to the following advantages:

1. Improved design (because more design time can be devoted to fewer components),
2. Reduced raw material and purchases,
3. Simplified production planning and control,
4. Improved layout, routing, and machine loading,
5. Reduced tooling setup time, and work-in-process and production time.

The application of group technology helps the entire organization, as many costs are reduced.

Assembly drawing
An exploded view of the product, usually via a three-dimensional or isometric drawing.

Assembly chart
A graphic means of identifying how components flow into subassemblies and ultimately into a final product.

DOCUMENTS FOR PRODUCTION

Once a product is selected and designed, its production is assisted by a variety of documents. We will briefly review some of these.

An **assembly drawing** simply shows an exploded view of the product. An assembly drawing is usually a three-dimensional drawing, known as an *isometric drawing;* the relative locations of components are drawn in relation to each other to show how to assemble the unit (see Figure 6.10[a]).

The **assembly chart** shows in schematic form how a product is assembled. Manufactured components, purchased components, or a combination of both may be shown on an assembly chart. The assembly chart identifies the point of production where components flow into subassemblies and ultimately into a final product. An example of an assembly chart is shown in Figure 6.10(b).

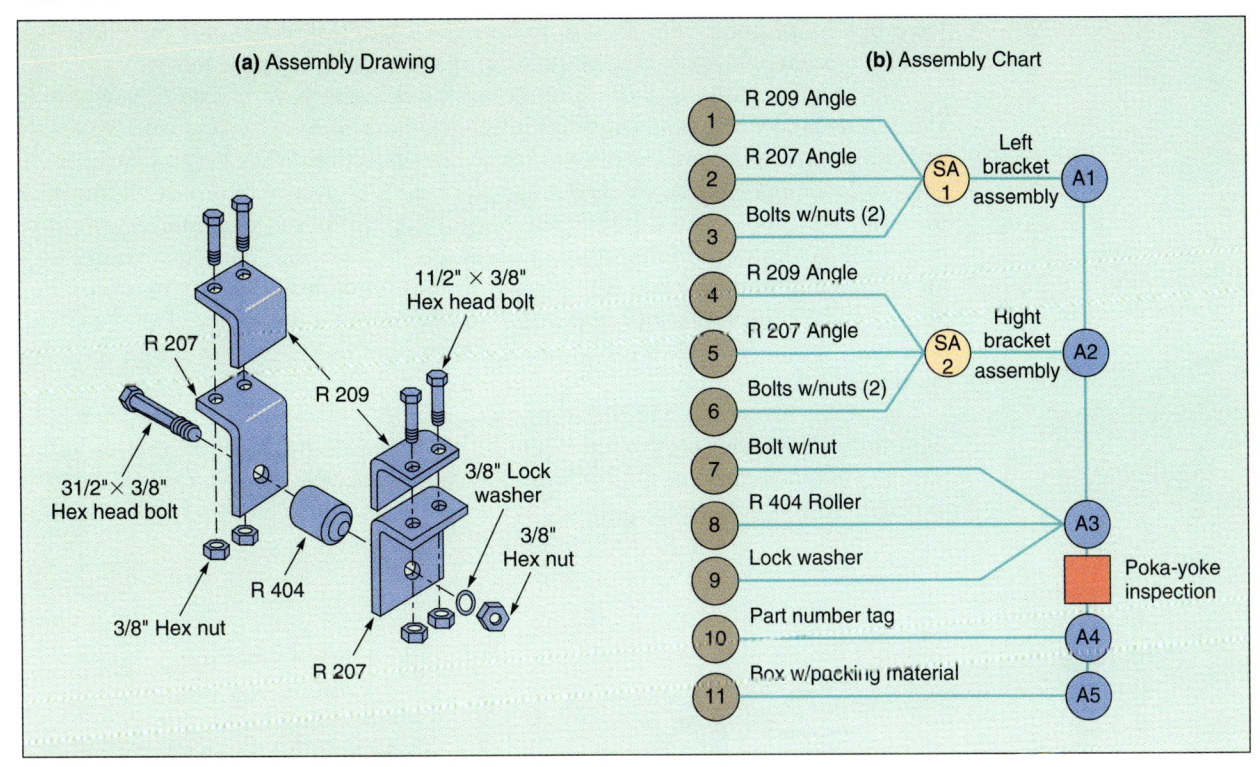

FIGURE 6.10 ■ Assembly Drawing and Assembly Chart

The **route sheet** lists the operations (including assembly and inspection) necessary to produce the component with the material specified in the bill of material. The route sheet for an item will have one entry for each operation to be performed on the item. When route sheets include specific methods of operation and labor standards, they are often known as *process sheets*.

The **work order** is an instruction to make a given quantity of a particular item, usually to a given schedule. The ticket that a waiter writes in your favorite restaurant is a work order. In a hospital or factory, the work order is a more formal document that provides authorization to draw various pharmaceuticals or items from inventory, to perform various functions, and to assign personnel to perform those functions.

Engineering change notices (ECNs) change some aspect of the product's definition or documentation, such as an engineering drawing or a bill of material. For a complex product that has a long manufacturing cycle, such as a Boeing 757, the changes may be so numerous that no two 757s are built exactly alike—which is indeed the case. Such dynamic design change has fostered the development of a discipline known as configuration management, which is concerned with product identification, control, and documentation. **Configuration management** is the system by which a product's planned and changing configurations are accurately identified and for which control and accountability of change are maintained.

SERVICE DESIGN

Much of our discussion so far has focused on what we can call tangible products, that is, goods. On the other side of the product coin are, of course, services. Service industries include banking, finance, insurance, transportation, and communications. The products of-

Route sheet A listing of the operations necessary to produce the component with the material specified in the bill of material.

Work order An instruction to make a given quantity of a particular item, usually to a given schedule.

Engineering change notice (ECN) A correction or modification of an engineering drawing or bill of material.

Configuration management A system by which a product's planned and changing components are accurately identified and for which control and accountability of change are maintained.

fered by service firms range from a medical procedure that leaves only the tiniest scar after an appendectomy, to a shampoo and cut at a hair salon, to a great movie.

Designing services is challenging because they often have unique characteristics. One reason productivity improvements in services are so low is because both the design and delivery of service products include customer interaction. When the customer participates in the design process, the service supplier may have a menu of services from which the customer selects options (see Figure 6.11[a]). At this point, the customer may even participate in the *design* of the service. Design specifications may take the form of a contract or a narrative description with photos (such as for cosmetic surgery or a hairstyle). Similarly, the customer may be involved in the *delivery* of a service (see Figure 6.11[b]) or in both design and delivery, a situation that maximizes the product-design challenge (see Figure 6.11[c]).

However, like goods, a large part of cost and quality of a service is defined at the design stage. Conveniently, there are a number of techniques available for services just as there are for goods that can both reduce costs and enhance the product. One technique is to design the product so that *customization* occurs as late in the process as possible. This

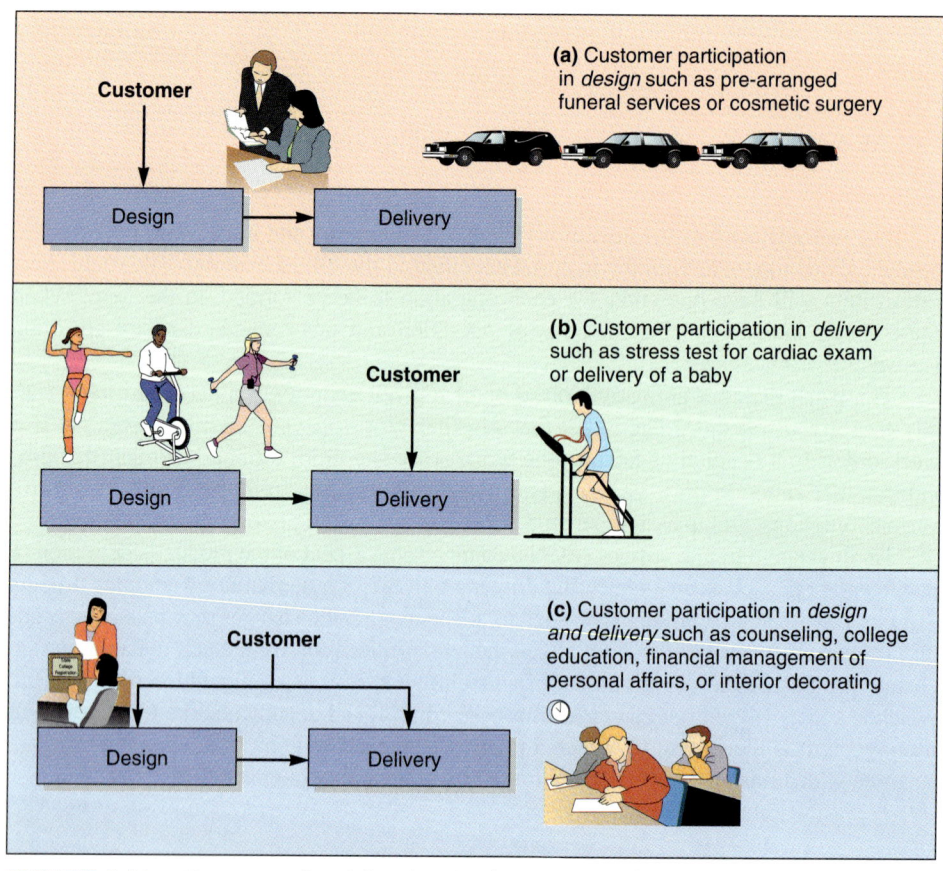

FIGURE 6.11 ■ Customer Participation in the Design of Services
Source: Robert Murdick, Barry Render, and Roberta Russell, *Service Operations Management* (Boston: Allyn & Bacon, 1990).

is the way a hair salon operates: Although shampoo and rinse are done in a standard way with lower-cost labor, the tint and styling (customizing) are done last. It is also the way most restaurants operate: "How would you like that cooked?" "Which dressing would you prefer with your salad?"

The second approach is to *modularize* the product so that customization takes the form of changing modules. This strategy allows modules to be designed as "fixed," standard entities. The modular approach to product design has applications in both manufacturing and service. Just as modular design allows you to buy a Harley-Davidson motorcycle or a high-fidelity stereo with just the features you want, modular flexibility also lets you buy meals, clothes, and insurance on a mix-and-match (modular) basis. Similarly, investment portfolios are put together on a modular basis. Certainly college curricula are another example of how the modular approach can be used to customize a service (in this case, education).

A third approach to the design of services is to divide the service into small parts and identify those parts that lend themselves to *automation* or *reduced customer interaction*. For instance, by isolating check-cashing activity via ATM machines, banks have been very effective at designing a product that both increases customer service and reduces costs. Similarly, Southwest Airlines has ticketless service. Because airlines spend $15 to $30 to produce a single ticket (including labor, printing, and travel agents' commission), ticketless systems save the industry a billion dollars a year. Reducing both costs and lines at airports—and thereby increasing customer satisfaction—provides a win-win "product" design.

Because of the high customer interaction in many service industries, a fourth technique is to focus design on the so-called *moment-of-truth*. Jan Carlzon, former president of Scandinavian Airways, believes that in the service industry there is a moment-of-truth when the relationship between the provider and the customer is crucial.[12] At that moment, the customer's satisfaction with the service is defined. The **moment-of-truth** is the moment that exemplifies, enhances, or detracts from the customer's expectations. That moment may be as simple as a smile or having the checkout clerk focus on you rather than talking over his shoulder to the clerk at the next counter. Moments-of-truth can occur when you order at McDonald's, get a haircut, or register for college courses. Figure 6.12 on page 214 shows a moment-of-truth analysis for a computer company's customer service hotline. The operations manager's task is to identify moments-of-truth and design a service that meets or exceeds the customer's expectations.

Moment-of-truth In the service industry that crucial moment between the service provider and the customer that exemplifies, enhances, or detracts from the customer's expectation.

Documents for Services

Because of the high customer interaction of most services, the documents for moving the product to production are different from those used in goods producing operations. The documentation for a service will often take the form of explicit job instructions that specify what is to happen at the moment-of-truth. For instance, regardless of how good a bank's products may be in terms of checking, savings, trusts, loans, mortgages, and so forth, if the moment-of-truth is not done well, the product may be poorly received. Example 1 shows the kind of documentation a bank may use to move a product (drive-up window banking) to "production." In a telemarketing service, the product design and its related transmittal to production may take the form of telephone script, and a "storyboard" is frequently used for a motion picture.

---

[12]Jan Carlzon, *Moments of Truth* (Cambridge: Ballinger Publishing, 1987).

214   CHAPTER 6   DESIGN OF GOODS AND SERVICES

Experience Detractors
- I had to call more than once to get through.
- A recording spoke to me rather than a person.
- While on hold, I get silence, and I wonder if I am disconnected.
- The operator sounded like he was reading a form of routine questions.
- The operator sounded uninterested.
- The operator rushed me.

Standard Expectations
- Only one local number needs to be dialed.
- I never get a busy signal.
- I get a human being to answer my call quickly and he or she is pleasant and responsive to my problem.
- A timely resolution to my problem is offered.
- The operator is able to explain to me what I can expect to take place next.

Experience Enhancers
- The operator was sincerely concerned and apologetic about my problem.
- He asked intelligent questions that allowed me to feel confident in his abilities.
- The operator offered various times to have work done, to suit my schedule.
- Ways to avoid future problems were suggested.

FIGURE 6.12 ■ **MOMENT-OF-TRUTH: The Customer Contacts the Service Hotline at a Computer Company**

Like all storyboards, this exhibit lays out the product clearly so that each activity is identified and its contribution to the process known.

EXAMPLE 1

Documentation for Moving a Service Product to Production

Customers who use drive-up teller stations rather than walk-in lobbies may require different customer-relations techniques. The distance and machinery between you and the customer raises communication barriers. Communication tips to improve customer relations at a drive-up window are:

- Be especially discreet when talking to the customer through the microphone.
- Provide written instructions for customers who must fill out forms you provide.
- Mark lines to be completed or attach a note with instructions.
- Always say "please" and "thank you" when speaking through the microphone.
- Establish eye contact with the customer if the distance allows it.
- If a transaction requires that the customer park the car and come into the lobby, apologize for the inconvenience.

Source: Adapted from *Teller Operations* (Chicago, IL: The Institute of Financial Education, 1987), p. 29.

APPLICATION OF DECISION TREES TO PRODUCT DESIGN

Decision trees can be used for new product decisions as well as for a wide variety of other management problems. They are particularly helpful when there are a series of decisions and various outcomes that lead to *subsequent* decisions followed by other outcomes. To form a decision tree, we use the following procedure:

1. Be sure that all possible alternatives and states of nature are included in the tree. This includes an alternative of "doing nothing."
2. Payoffs are entered at the end of the appropriate branch. This is the place to develop the payoff of achieving this branch.
3. The objective is to determine the expected value of each course of action. We accomplish this by starting at the end of the tree (the right-hand side) and working toward the beginning of the tree (the left), calculating values at each step and "pruning" alternatives that are not as good as others from the same node.

Example 2 shows the use of a decision tree applied to product design.

EXAMPLE 2

Silicon, Inc., a semiconductor manufacturer, is investigating the possibility of producing and marketing a microprocessor. Undertaking this project will require either purchasing a sophisticated CAD system or hiring and training several additional engineers. The market for the product could be either favorable or unfavorable. Silicon, Inc., of course, has the option of not developing the new product at all.

With favorable acceptance by the market, sales would be 25,000 processors selling for $100 each. With unfavorable acceptance, sales would be only 8,000 processors selling for $100 each. The cost of CAD equipment is $500,000, but that of hiring and training three new engineers is only $375,000. However, manufacturing costs should drop from $50 each when manufacturing without CAD to $40 each when manufacturing with CAD.

The probability of favorable acceptance of the new microprocessor is .40; the probability of unfavorable acceptance is .60. See Figure 6.13 on page 216.

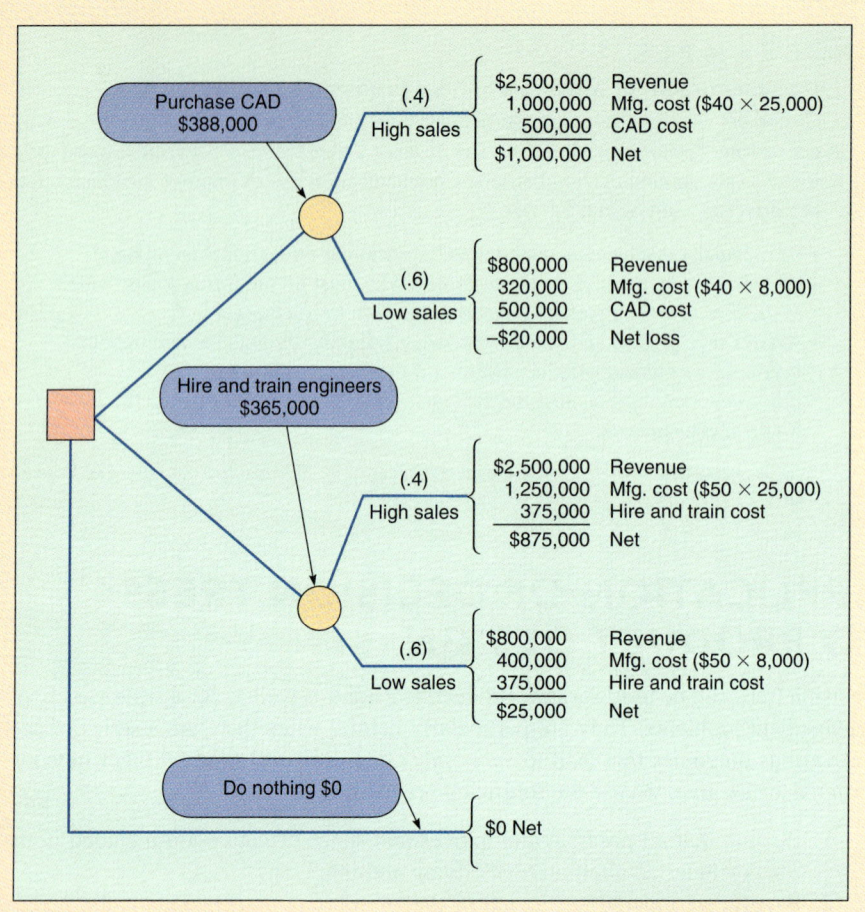

FIGURE 6.13 ■ Decision Tree for Development of a New Product

Purchase CAD $388,000
- High sales (.4):
  - $2,500,000 Revenue
  - 1,000,000 Mfg. cost ($40 × 25,000)
  - 500,000 CAD cost
  - $1,000,000 Net
- Low sales (.6):
  - $800,000 Revenue
  - 320,000 Mfg. cost ($40 × 8,000)
  - 500,000 CAD cost
  - −$20,000 Net loss

Hire and train engineers $365,000
- High sales (.4):
  - $2,500,000 Revenue
  - 1,250,000 Mfg. cost ($50 × 25,000)
  - 375,000 Hire and train cost
  - $875,000 Net
- Low sales (.6):
  - $800,000 Revenue
  - 400,000 Mfg. cost ($50 × 8,000)
  - 375,000 Hire and train cost
  - $25,000 Net

Do nothing $0
- $0 Net

The expected monetary values (EMVs) have been circled at each step of the decision tree. For the top branch:

$$\text{EMV (purchase CAD system)} = (.4)(\$1,000,000) + (.6)(-\$20,000)$$

$$= \$388,000$$

This figure represents the results that will occur if Silicon, Inc., purchases CAD.

The expected value of hiring and training engineers is the second series of branches:

$$\text{EMV (hire/train engineers)} = (.4)(\$875,000) + (.6)(\$25,000)$$

$$= \$365,000$$

The EMV of doing nothing is $0.

Because the top branch has the highest expected monetary value (an EMV of $388,000 vs. $365,000 vs. $0), it represents the best decision. Management should purchase the CAD system.

TRANSITION TO PRODUCTION

Eventually, our product, whether a good or service, has been selected, designed, and defined. It has progressed from an idea, to a functional definition, and then perhaps to a design. Now, management must make a decision as to further development and production or termination of the product idea. One of the arts of modern management is knowing when to move a product from development to production; this move is known as *transition to production*. The product development staff is always interested in making improvements in a product. Because this staff tends to see product development as evolutionary, they may never have a completed product, but as we noted earlier, the cost of late product introduction is high. Although these conflicting pressures exist, management must make a decision—more development or production.

Once this decision is made, there is usually a period of trial production to ensure that the design is indeed producible. This is the manufacturability test. This trial also gives the operations staff the opportunity to develop proper tooling, quality-control procedures, and training of personnel to ensure that production can be initiated successfully. Finally, when the product is deemed both marketable and producible, line management will assume responsibility.

Some companies appoint a project manager, while others use product development teams to ensure that the transition from development to production is successful. Both approaches allow a wide range of resources and talents to be brought to bear to ensure satisfactory production of a product that is still in flux. A third approach is integration of the product development and manufacturing organizations. This approach allows for easy shifting of resources between the two organizations as needs change. The operations manager's job is to make the transition from R&D to production—seamless—as smooth as possible.

SUMMARY

Effective product strategy requires selecting, designing, and defining a product and then transitioning that product to production. Only when this strategy is carried out effectively can the production function contribute its maximum to the organization. The operations manager must build a product development system that has the ability to conceive, design, and produce products that will yield a competitive advantage for the firm. As products move through their life cycle (introduction, growth, maturity, and decline), the options that the operations manager should pursue change. Both manufactured and service products have a variety of techniques available to aid in performing this activity efficiently.

Written specifications, bills-of-material, and engineering drawings aid in defining products. Similarly, assembly drawings, assembly charts, route sheets, and work orders are often used to assist in the actual production of the product. Once a product is in production, value analysis is appropriate to ensure maximum product value. Engineering change notices and configuration management provide product documentation.

KEY TERMS

Product decision *(p. 194)*
Product development teams *(p. 202)*
Concurrent engineering *(p. 202)*
Manufacturability and value engineering *(p. 202)*
Robust design *(p. 204)*
Time-based competition *(p. 204)*
Modular design *(p. 204)*
Computer-aided design (CAD) *(p. 205)*
Value analysis *(p. 206)*
Product-by-value analysis *(p. 206)*
Engineering drawing *(p. 207)*

Bill of material (BOM) *(p. 208)*
Make-or-buy decision *(p. 209)*
Group technology *(p. 209)*
Assembly drawing *(p. 210)*
Assembly chart *(p. 210)*

Route sheet *(p. 211)*
Work order *(p. 211)*
Engineering change notice (ECN) *(p. 211)*
Configuration management *(p. 211)*
Moment-of-truth *(p. 213)*

SOLVED PROBLEM

Solved Problem 6.1

Sarah King, president of King Electronics, Inc., has two design options for her new line of high-resolution cathode-ray tubes (CRTs) for computer-aided design workstations. The life cycle sales forecast for the CRT is 100,000 units.

Design option A has a .90 probability of yielding 59 good CRTs per 100 and a .10 probability of yielding 64 good CRTs per 100. This design will cost $1,000,000.

Design option B has a .80 probability of yielding 64 good units per 100 and a .20 probability of yielding 59 good units per 100. This design will cost $1,350,000.

Good or bad, each CRT will cost $75. Each good CRT will sell for $150. Bad CRTs are destroyed and have no salvage value. Because units break up when thrown in the trash, there is little disposal cost. Therefore, we ignore any disposal costs in this problem.

Solution

We draw the decision tree to reflect the two decisions and the probabilities associated with each decision. We then determine the payoff associated with each branch. The resulting tree is shown in Figure 6.14.

FIGURE 6.14 ■ Decision Tree for Solved Problem 6.1

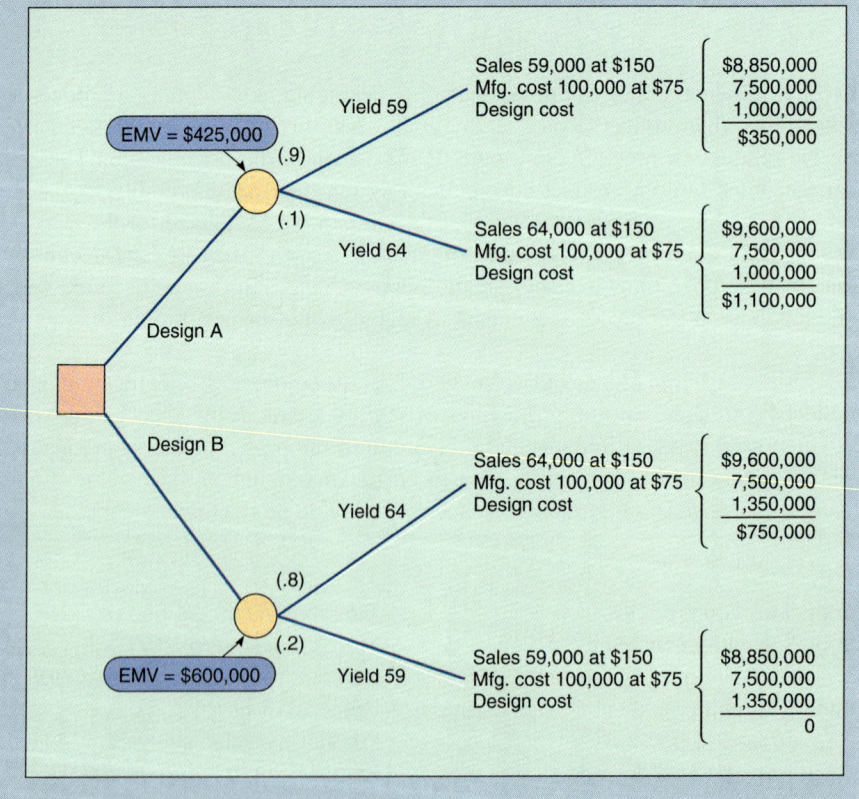

Design A:
- EMV = $425,000
- Yield 59 (.9): Sales 59,000 at $150 = $8,850,000; Mfg. cost 100,000 at $75 = 7,500,000; Design cost = 1,000,000; Net = $350,000
- Yield 64 (.1): Sales 64,000 at $150 = $9,600,000; Mfg. cost 100,000 at $75 = 7,500,000; Design cost = 1,000,000; Net = $1,100,000

Design B:
- EMV = $600,000
- Yield 64 (.8): Sales 64,000 at $150 = $9,600,000; Mfg. cost 100,000 at $75 = 7,500,000; Design cost = 1,350,000; Net = $750,000
- Yield 59 (.2): Sales 59,000 at $150 = $8,850,000; Mfg. cost 100,000 at $75 = 7,500,000; Design cost = 1,350,000; Net = 0

For design A,

$$\text{EMV (design A)} = (.9)(\$350{,}000) + (.1)(\$1{,}100{,}000)$$

$$= \$425{,}000$$

For design B,

$$\text{EMV (design B)} = (.8)(\$750{,}000) + (.2)(\$0)$$

$$= \$600{,}000$$

The highest payoff is design option B at $600,000.

DISCUSSION QUESTIONS

1. What management techniques may prove helpful in making the transition from design to production?
2. Why is it necessary to document a product explicitly?
3. What techniques do we use to document a product?
4. Configuration management has proved particularly useful in which industries? Why?
5. What are the advantages of computer-aided design?
6. What is group technology, and why is it proving helpful in our quest for productivity improvement?
7. What savings can be expected by computer-aided design?
8. What strategic advantages does computer-aided design provide?
9. What are the four phases of the product life cycle?
10. How do product selection and design affect quality?
11. Once a product is defined, what documents are used to assist production personnel in its manufacture?
12. How does configuration management manifest itself when you ask for service on your automobile?
13. What are the similarities and dissimilarities between a manufactured product and a new type of life insurance policy referred to by the salespeople as their new "product"?
14. What is time-based competition?
15. Describe three product strategy options
16. Why should a firm try to prevent pollution?

CRITICAL THINKING EXERCISE

Rubbermaid's record of new product innovation is remarkable. With almost 5,000 products, the firm continues to crank out a new one almost every day—and with great success. Rubbermaid has divided its product line into four dozen categories. Then it creates entrepreneurial teams of five to seven members in each category. Each team includes a product manager, research and manufacturing engineers, and financial, sales, and marketing executives. Teams conceive their own products, shepherding them from design stage to marketplace.

Compare Rubbermaid's product approach to the American and Japanese approaches discussed in this chapter.

PROBLEMS

- **6.1** Prepare a bill of material for a ballpoint pen.
- **6.2** Draw an assembly chart for a ballpoint pen.
- **6.3** Prepare a bill of material for a simple table lamp. Identify those items that you, as

manufacturer of the body and related components, are likely to make and those that you are likely to purchase. Justify your decision for each item.

6.4 Prepare an assembly chart for the table lamp in Problem 6.3.

6.5 As a library or Internet project, find a series of group technology codes.

6.6 Given the contribution made on each of the three products in the following table and their position in the life cycle, identify a reasonable operations strategy for each.

Product	Product Contribution (Percent of Selling Price)	Company Contribution (Percent of Total Annual Contribution Divided by Total Annual Sales)	Position in Life Cycle
Notebook computer	30	40	Growth
Palm-held computer	30	50	Introduction
Hand calculator	50	10	Decline

6.7 The product planning group of Hawkes Electric Supplies, Inc., has determined that it needs to design a new series of switches. It must decide upon one of three design strategies. The market forecast is for 200,000 units. The better and more sophisticated the design strategy and the more time spent on value engineering, the less will be the variable cost. The chief of engineering design, Dr. Gerry Johnson, has decided that the following costs are a good estimate of the initial and variable costs connected with each approach. These are:

a) Low-tech: a low-technology, low-cost process consisting of hiring several new junior engineers. This option has a cost of $45,000 and variable cost probabilities of .2 for $.55 each, .5 for $.50, and .3 for $.45.

b) Subcontract: a medium-cost approach using a good outside design staff. This approach would have an initial cost of $65,000 and variable cost probabilities of .7 of $.45, .2 of $.40, and .1 of $.35.

c) High-tech: a high-technology approach using the very best of the inside staff and the latest computer-aided design technology. This approach has a fixed cost of $75,000 and variable cost probabilities of .9 of $.40 and .1 of $.35.

What is the best decision based on an expected monetary value (EMV) criterion? (*Note:* We want the lowest EMV as we are dealing with costs in this problem.)

6.8 Faber Manufacturing, Inc., of St. Paul, Minnesota, has the option of (a) proceeding immediately with production of a new top-of-the-line stereo TV that has just completed prototype testing or (b) having the value analysis team complete a study. If Melissa Steffens, VP for Operations, proceeds with the existing prototype (option a), the firm can expect sales to be 100,000 units at $550 each, with a probability of .6 and a .4 probability of 75,000 at $550. If, however, she uses the value analysis team (option b), the firm expects sales of 75,000 units at $750, with a probability of .7 and a .3 probability of 70,000 units at $750. Cost of the value analysis is $100,000. Which option has the highest expected monetary value (EMV)?

6.9 Ritz Products' materials manager, Wayne Parkins, must determine whether to make or buy a new semiconductor for the wrist TV that the firm is about to produce. One million units are expected to be produced over the life cycle. If the product is made, start-up and production costs of the *make* decision total $1 million with a probability of .4 that the product will be satisfactory and .6 probability that it will not. If the product is not satisfactory, the firm will have to reevaluate the decision. If the decision is reevaluated, the choice will be whether or not to spend another $1 million to redesign the semiconductor or to purchase. Likelihood of success the second time that the make decision is made is .9. If the second make decision also fails, the firm must purchase. Regardless of when the purchase takes place, Parkins's best judgment of cost is that Ritz will pay $.50 for each purchased semiconductor plus $1 million in vendor development cost.

a) Assuming that Ritz must have the semiconductor (stopping or doing without is not a viable option), what is the best decision?
b) What criteria did you use to make this decision?
c) What is the worst that can happen to Ritz as a result of this particular decision? What is the best that can happen?

6.10 Use the data in Solved Problem 6.1 to examine what happens to the decision if King can increase the yield when the yield is 59 out of each 100. If the yield is 59 per 100, a special expensive phosphorus can be applied to the screen at an added cost of $50 per CRT. This procedure will be good for only 5 units per 100 (that is, it can bring the yield up to only 64 per 100). Prepare the modified decision tree. What are the payoffs, and which branch has the greatest EMV?

Case Study

De Mar's Product Strategy

De Mar, a plumbing, heating and air-conditioning company located in Clovis-Fresno, California, has a simple but powerful product strategy: *Solve the customer's problem no matter what, solve the problem when the customer needs it solved, and make sure the customer feels good when you leave.* De Mar offers guaranteed, same-day service for customers requiring it. The company provides 24-hour-a-day, 7-day-a-week service at no extra charge for customers whose air conditioning dies on a hot summer Sunday or whose toilet overflows at 2:30 in the morning. As assistant service coordinator Janie Walter puts it: "We will be there to fix your A/C on the fourth of July, and it's not a penny extra. When our competitors won't get out of bed, we'll be there!"

De Mar guarantees the price of a job to the penny before the work begins. Whereas most competitors guarantee their work for 30 days, De Mar guarantees all parts and labor for one year. The company assesses no travel charge because "it's not fair to charge customers for driving out." Owner Larry Harmon says: "We are in an industry that doesn't have the best reputation. If we start making money our main goal, we are in trouble. So I stress customer satisfaction; money is the by-product."

De Mar uses selective hiring, ongoing training and education, performance measures and compensation that incorporate customer satisfaction, strong teamwork, peer pressure, empowerment, and aggressive promotion to implement its strategy. Says credit manager Anne Semrick: "The person who wants a nine-to-five job needs to go somewhere else."

De Mar is a premium pricer. Yet customers respond because De Mar delivers value—that is, benefits for costs. In 8 years, annual sales increased from about $200,000 to more than $3.3 million.

Discussion Questions

1. What is De Mar's product? Identify the tangible parts of this product and its service components.
2. How should other areas of De Mar (marketing, finance, personnel) support its product strategy?
3. Even though De Mar's product is primarily a service product, how should each of the 10 OM decisions in the text be managed to ensure that the product is successful?

Source: Adapted from: Leonard L. Berry, *On Great Service* (New York: The Free Press, 1995), p. 64.

Case Study

GE's Rotary Compressor

In 1981, market share and profits in General Electric's appliance division were falling. The company's technology was antiquated compared to that of foreign competitors. For example, making refrigerator compressors required 65 minutes of labor in comparison to 25 minutes for competitors in Japan and Italy. Moreover, GE's labor costs were higher. The alternatives were obvious: Either purchase compressors from Japan or Italy or design and build a better model.

By 1983, the decision to build a new rotary compressor in-house was made, along with a commitment for a new $120-million factory. GE was not a novice in rotary compressor technology; in fact, it had invented the technology and been using it in air conditioners for many years. A rotary compressor weighs less, has one-third fewer parts, and is more energy-efficient than the current reciprocating compressors. The rotary compressor also takes up less space, thus providing more room inside the refrigerator and better meeting customer requirements.

Some engineers argued against rotary compressors, citing the fact that they run hotter. This is not a problem in most air conditioners because the coolant cools the compressor. In a refrigerator, however, the coolant flows only one-tenth as fast, and the unit runs about four times longer in 1 year than an air conditioner. GE had problems with the early rotary compressors in air conditioners. Although the bugs had been eliminated in smaller units, GE quit using rotaries in larger units due to frequent breakdowns in hot climates.

GE managers and design engineers were concerned about other issues. Rotary compressors make a high-pitched whine, and managers were afraid that this feature would adversely affect consumer acceptance. Managers and consumer test panels spent many hours addressing this issue. The new design also required key parts to work together with a tolerance of only 50-millionths of an inch. Nothing had been mass-produced with such precision before, but manufacturing engineers felt sure they could do it.

The compressor they finally designed was nearly identical to that used in air conditioners, with one change. Two small parts inside the compressor were made out of powdered metal rather than the hardened steel and cast iron used in air conditioners. This material was chosen because it could be machined to much closer tolerances and reduced machining costs. Powdered metal had been tried a decade earlier on air conditioners but did not work. The design engineers who were new to designing compressors did not consider the earlier failure important.

A consultant suggested that GE consider a joint venture with a Japanese company that had a rotary refrigerator compressor already on the market. The idea was rejected by management. The original designer of the air conditioner rotary compressor, who had left GE, offered his services as a consultant. GE declined his offer, writing him that it had sufficient technical expertise.

About 600 compressors were tested in 1983 without a single failure. They were run continuously for 2 months under elevated temperatures and pressures supposed to simulate 5 years' operation. GE normally conducts extensive field-testing of new products; its original plan to test models in the field for 2 years was reduced to 9 months due to time pressure to complete the project.

The technician who disassembled and inspected the parts thought they did not look right. Parts of the motor were discolored, a sign of excessive heat. Bearings were worn, and it appeared that high heat was breaking down the lubricating oil. The technician's supervisors discounted these findings and did not relay them to upper levels of management. Another consultant who evaluated the test results believed that something was wrong because only one failure was found in 2 years and recommended that test conditions be intensified. This suggestion was also rejected by management.

By 1986, only 2½ years after board approval, the new factory was producing compressors at a rate of 10 per minute. By the end of the year, more than 1 million had been produced. Market share rose, and the new refrigerator appeared to be a success. But in July 1987, the first compressor failed. Soon after, reports of other failures in Puerto Rico arrived. By September, the appliance division knew it had a major problem. In December, the plant stopped making the compressor. Not until 1988 was the problem diagnosed as excessive wear in the two powdered-metal parts that burned up the oil. The cost in 1989 alone was $450 million. By mid-1990, GE had voluntarily replaced nearly 1.1 million compressors with replacements purchased from six suppliers, five of them foreign.

Discussion Questions

1. What factors in the product development process caused this disaster? Which individuals were responsible?
2. How might this disaster have been prevented? What lessons do you think GE learned for the future?
3. On what basis was GE attempting to achieve a competitive advantage? How did it fail?

Source: James Dean and James Evans, *Total Quality* (Minneapolis/St. Paul: West Publishing, 1994), pp. 256–257.

Video Case 3

Product Design at Regal Marine

With hundreds of competitors in the boat business, Regal Marine must work to differentiate itself from the flock. As we saw in the *Global Company Profile* that opened this chapter, Regal continuously introduces innovative, high-quality new boats. Its differentiation strategy is currently reflected in a product line consisting of 22 models.

To maintain this stream of innovation, and with so many boats at varying stages of their life cycles, Regal constantly seeks design input from customers, dealers, and consultants. Design ideas rapidly find themselves in the styling studio, where they are placed onto CAD machines in order to speed the development process. Existing boat designs are always evolving as the company tries to stay stylish and competitive. Moreover, with life cycles as short as 3-years, a steady stream of new products is required. A few years ago, the new product was the 3-passenger $11,000 Rush, a small, but powerful boat capable of pulling a water-skier. Last year, it was a 20-foot inboard-outboard performance boat with so many innovations that it won prize after prize in the industry. And this year, the new boat is a redesigned 40-foot Commodore that sleeps six in luxury staterooms. With all these models and innovations, Regal designers and production personnel are under pressure to respond quickly.

By getting key suppliers on board early and urging them to participate at the design stage, Regal improves both innovations and quality while speeding product development. Regal finds that the sooner it brings suppliers on board, the faster it can bring new boats to the market. After a development stage that constitutes concept and styling, CAD designs yield product specification. The first stage in actual production is the creation of the "plug," a foam-based carving used to make the molds for fiberglass hulls and decks. Specifications from the CAD system drive the carving process. Once the plug is carved, the permanent molds for each new hull and deck design are formed. Molds take about 4–8 weeks to make and are all handmade. Similar molds are made for many of the other features in Regal boats—from galley and stateroom components to lavatories and steps. Finished molds can be joined and used to make thousands of boats.

Discussion Questions

1. How does the concept of product life cycle apply to Regal Marine products?
2. What strategy does Regal use to stay competitive?
3. What kind of engineering savings is Regal achieving by using CAD technology rather than traditional drafting techniques?
4. What are the likely benefits of the CAD design technology?

BIBLIOGRAPHY

Akao, Y., ed. *Quality Function Deployment: Integrating Customer Requirements into Product Design.* Cambridge, MA: Productivity Press, 1990.

Ali, A., M. U. Kalwani, and D. Kovenock. "Selecting Product Development Projects: Pioneering versus Incremental Innovation Strategies." *Management Science* 39, no. 3 (March 1993): 255–274.

Bower, J. L., and T. M. Hout. "Fast Cycle Capacity for Competitive Power." *Harvard Business Review,* November–December 1988, pp. 110–118.

Burbidge, J. L. "Production Flow Analysis for Planning Group Technology." *Journal of Operations Management* 10, no. 1 (January 1991): 5–27.

Capon, N., J. U. Farley, D. R. Lehmann, and J. M. Hulbert. "Profiles of Product Innovators Among Large U.S. Manufacturers." *Management Science* 38, no. 2 (February 1992): 157.

Choi, M., and W. E. Riggs. "GT Coding and Classification Systems for Manufacturing Cell Design." *Production and Inventory Management Journal* 32 (first quarter 1991): 28.

Cooper, Robin, and W. Bruce Chew. "Control Tomorrow's Costs Through Today's Designs." *Harvard Business Review* 74 (January–February 1996): 88–97.

Fitzsimmons, J. A., P. Kouvelis, and D. N. Mallick. "Design Strategy and Its Interface with Manufacturing and Marketing: A Conceptual Framework." *Journal of Operations Management* 10, no. 3 (August 1991): 398.

Garza, O., and T. L. Smunt. "Countering the Negative Impact of Intercell Flow in Cellular Manufacturing." *Journal of Operations Management* 10, no. 1 (January 1991): 92–118.

Hastings, N. A., and C. Yeh. "Bill of Manufacture." *Production and Inventory Management Journal* 33, no. 4 (fourth quarter 1992): 27–31.

Iansiti, M. "Real-World R&D: Jumping the Product Generation Gap." *Harvard Business Review* 71, no. 3 (May–June 1993): 131–147.

Khurana, A., and S. R. Rosenthal. "Integrating the Fuzzy Front End of New Product Development." *Sloan Management Review,* winter 1997, pp. 103–119.

Mosier, C. T., and R. E. Janaro. "Toward a Universal Classification and Coding System for Assemblies." *Journal of Operations Management* 9, no.1 (January 1990): 44.

Neibel, B. W., and A. B. Draper. *Product Design and Process Engineering.* New York: McGraw-Hill, 1974.

Samoras, T. T., and F. L. Czerwinski. *Fundamentals of Configuration Management.* New York: John Wiley, 1971.

Smith, P. G., and D. G. Reinertsen. *Developing Products in Half the Time.* New York: Van Nostrand Reinhold, 1991.

Stalk, G., Jr., and T. M. Hout. *Competing Against Time.* New York: The Free Press 1990.

Wheelwright, S. C., and W. E. Sasser, Jr. "The New Product Development Map." *Harvard Business Review* 67 (May–June 1989): 112–125.

INTERNET RESOURCES

Examples of bad design:
  http://www.baddesigns.com
Center for Design at the Royal Melbourne Institute of Technology:
  http://daedalus.edc.rmit.edu.au/
Concurrent Engineering Virtual Environment Demo: University of Hertfordshire:
  http://www.mansys.herts.ac.uk/ider/design.html
Consortium on Green Design and Manufacturing:
  http://greenmfg.me.brkeley.edu/

Green Design Initiative: Carnegie Mellon University:
  http://www.cc.cmu.edu/GreenDesign/research.html
ISO 14000 Information Center sponsored by the Environmental Industry Web Site:
  http://www.iso14000.com/
Rapid Design Exploration and Optimization Program, Defense Advance Research Projects Program:
  http://elib.cme.nist.gov/radeo/
Saturn Case Study in Engineering Design:
  http://bishop.berkeley.edu/develop/saturn/banner.html

Process Strategy and Capacity Planning

7

CHAPTER OUTLINE

GLOBAL COMPANY PROFILE: NUCOR
THREE PROCESS STRATEGIES
   Process Focus
   Repetitive Focus
   Product Focus
   Comparison of Process Choices
PROCESS ANALYSIS AND DESIGN
   Flow Diagrams
   Process Charts
   Time-Function Mapping
   Work-Flow Analysis
PROCESS REENGINEERING
   Moving toward Lean Production
SERVICE PROCESS STRATEGY
   Service-Sector Considerations
   Customer Interaction and Process Strategy
   More Opportunities to Improve Service Processes
SELECTION OF EQUIPMENT AND TECHNOLOGY
ENVIRONMENTAL ISSUES
CAPACITY
   Defining Capacity
   Forecasting Capacity Requirements
   Applying Decision Trees to Capacity Decisions
   Managing Demand
BREAK-EVEN ANALYSIS
   Single-Product Case
   Multiproduct Case
STRATEGY-DRIVEN INVESTMENTS
   Investment, Variable Cost, and Cash Flow
   Net Present Value
SUMMARY
KEY TERMS
USING EXCEL OM FOR BREAK-EVEN ANALYSIS
SOLVED PROBLEMS
DISCUSSION QUESTIONS
CRITICAL THINKING EXERCISE
PROBLEMS
CASE STUDY: MATTHEW YACHTS, INC.
VIDEO CASE 4: PROCESS STRATEGY AT WHEELED COACH
BIBLIOGRAPHY
INTERNET RESOURCES

LEARNING OBJECTIVES

When you complete this chapter you should be able to:

Identify or Define:
   Process focus
   Repetitive focus
   Product focus
   Process reengineering
   Service process issues
   Environmental issues

Describe or Explain:
   Process analysis
   Lean production
   Green manufacturing
   The capacity issue
   Break-even analysis
   Financial considerations
   Strategy-driven investments

GLOBAL COMPANY PROFILE:

Process Selection Yields a Competitive Advantage at Nucor

This ladle, equipped with magnetic stirring and vacuum degassing features, pours steel via a ceramic nozzle into a metering vessel called a tundish and then into a special mold that can adjust the slab's dimensions.

Nucor Steel's very successful process strategy has been to build and operate a type of steel mill known as the "mini mill." This means having a "product-oriented" facility that is smaller, cheaper, less complex, and more efficient than a larger integrated mill. It is a classic low-cost strategy. Nucor's Crawfordsville, Indiana, plant makes steel in an innovative process that was designed and built to produce one product, sheet steel. However, by modest changes in the steel mix, the supplemental alloys, and changes in the size and finish of the steel, Nucor meets the needs of a wide variety of markets for high-quality sheet steel.

Steel is produced in two phases at Nucor. First, scrap steel is loaded into two 125-ton electric-arc furnaces. A massive electric charge with a thunderous roar melts the scrap. Then an

Here the shaped steel exits the caster mold as a 2-inch-thick-by-52-inch-wide slab and enters the hot tunnel furnace, where its temperature is uniformly raised to the level needed for rolling. A higher-quality sheet can be produced if slab temperature is uniform.

226

NUCOR

analysis is made of the alloy, and a variety of additional ingredients are added, depending upon the nature of the scrap and the product desired. The melted steel, at about 3,000°F, is called a *heat*. It is poured into a ladle and carried by an overhead crane to a casting machine. There steel solidifies as a red-hot 2-inch-thick ribbon of steel and is cut into lengths as it cools. The lengths are called *slabs*, each weighing about 25 tons.

In the second phase, the characteristics of the steel can be modified modestly, primarily determining shape and finish. This is accomplished in a rolling mill and related operations. The rolling mill, with steel flying by at 30 miles per hour, progressively presses the red-hot slabs into the desired shapes.

At Nucor, process strategy provides a competitive advantage in several ways. First, Nucor casts steel close to the final shape of the product, eliminating unnecessary capital equipment and personnel. Second, the continuous process eliminates a substantial amount of reheating prior to rolling, yielding a major savings in energy cost. Third, an efficient process, combined with an effective employee incentive system, yields the highest productivity of any steel mill in the world. Nucor's labor-hours per ton of steel may be half that of some competitors. Fourth, the process technology used at Crawfordsville results in high productivity *and* high quality. The process results not only in excellent control of steel characteristics, but in reduced labor, energy, and work-in-process, as well as a net savings in capital investment.

The coiling of rolled sheet steel results in rolls of about 25 tons.

Process strategy An organization's approach to transform resources into goods and services.

TEN DECISIONS OF OM
Managing Quality
Design of Goods & Services
Process Strategy
Location Strategies
Layout Strategies
Human Resources
Supply-Chain Management
Inventory Management
Scheduling
Maintenance

In chapter 6, we examined the need for the selection, definition, and design of goods and services. We now turn to their production. A major decision for the operations manager is finding the best way to produce. Let's look at ways to help managers design a process for achieving this goal.

A **process** (or transformation) **strategy** is an organization's approach to transform resources into goods and services. We use both terms, *process* and *transformation*, to describe this strategy. The *objective of a process strategy* is to find a way to produce goods and services that meet customer requirements and product specifications within cost and other managerial constraints. The process selected will have a long-term effect on efficiency and production, as well as the flexibility, cost, and quality of the goods produced. Therefore, much of a firm's strategy is determined at the time of this process decision.

THREE PROCESS STRATEGIES

Virtually every good or service is made by using some variation of one of three process strategies: (1) process focus, (2) repetitive focus, and (3) product focus. Notice the relationship of these three strategies to volume and variety shown in Figure 7.1. Although the figure shows only three strategies, an innovative operations manager can build processes anywhere on a continuum between these three to meet the necessary volume and variety requirements.

Let's look at each of these strategies with an example and a flow diagram. We examine *Standard Register* as a process-focused firm, *Harley-Davidson* as a repetitive producer, and *Nucor Steel* as a product-focused operation.

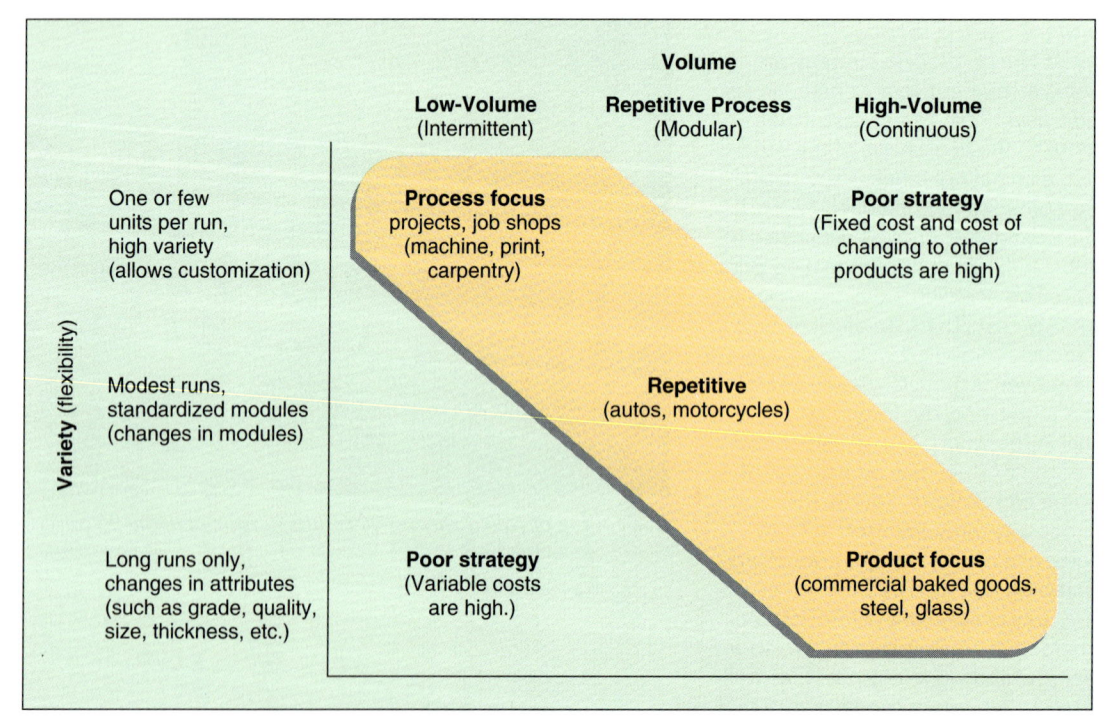

FIGURE 7.1 ■ Process Selected Must Fit with Volume and Variety

Process Focus

Seventy-five percent of all global production is devoted to making *low-volume, high-variety* products in places called "job shops." Such facilities are organized around performing processes. In a factory, these processes might be departments devoted to welding, grinding, and painting. In an office, the processes might be accounts payable, sales, and payroll. In a restaurant, they might be bar, grill, and bakery. Such facilities are **process focused** in terms of equipment, layout, and supervision. They provide a high degree of product flexibility as products move intermittently between processes. Each process is designed to perform a wide variety of activities and handle frequent changes. Consequently, they are also called *intermittent processes*.

These facilities have high variable costs with extremely low utilization of facilities, as low as 5%. This is the case for many restaurants, hospitals, and machine shops. However, some manufacturing facilities do a little better through the use of equipment with electronic controls. With the development of numerical-controlled equipment (machines controlled by computer software), it is possible to program machine tools and piece movement, tool changing, and even automate placement of the parts on the machine and the movement of materials between machines.

Example 1 shows how Standard Register, a billion-dollar printer and document processor headquartered in Dayton, Ohio, produces paper business forms.

Process focus A production facility organized around processes to facilitate low-volume, high-variety process.

EXAMPLE 1

Job Shop Process Focus at Standard Register

If you've had a pizza delivered to your home recently, there is a good chance that Standard Register printed the order and delivery tag on the box. You probably came in contact with one of Standard's forms this week without knowing it. Thousands of different products are made by the firm, a typical one being a multisheet (3- or 4-layer) business form. Forms used for student college applications, hospital patient admissions, bank drafts, store orders, and job applications are examples. The company has 11 U.S. plants in its Forms Division.

Figure 7.2 is a flow diagram of the entire production process, from order submission to shipment, at Standard's Kirkville, Missouri, plant. This job shop groups people and machines that perform specific activities, such as printing, cutting, or binding, into departments. Entire orders are processed in batches, moving from department to department, rather than in a continuous flow (as at Nucor Steel) or one at a time.

The process begins with a sales representative helping the customer design the business form. Once the form is established, the order is transmitted electronically to the Sales Support Department at the manufacturing plant. An order coordinator determines what materials will be needed in production (ink, paper, labels, etc.), computes the production time needed, and schedules the job on a particular machine.

The Prepress Department uses computer-aided design (CAD) to convert the product design into printing plates for the presses and then "burns" the image of the form onto an aluminum printing plate. Machine operators in the Printing Department install the plates and inks on their presses and print the forms. After leaving the presses, most products are collated on a machine that places up to 14 copies together, possibly with carbon paper between them. Some products undergo additional processing (for example, gluing, binding, stapling, or labeling). When the forms are completed, most are wrapped in polyethylene before being placed in cartons for shipping. The order is shipped, a "job ticket" is sent to Accounting, and an invoice goes to the customer.

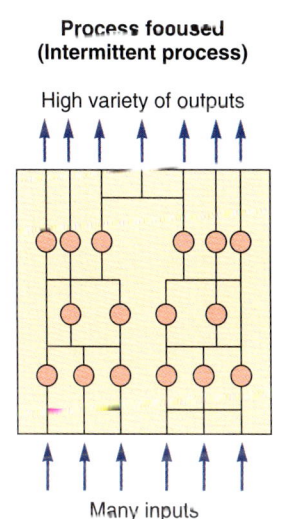

Process focused (Intermittent process)

High variety of outputs

Many inputs

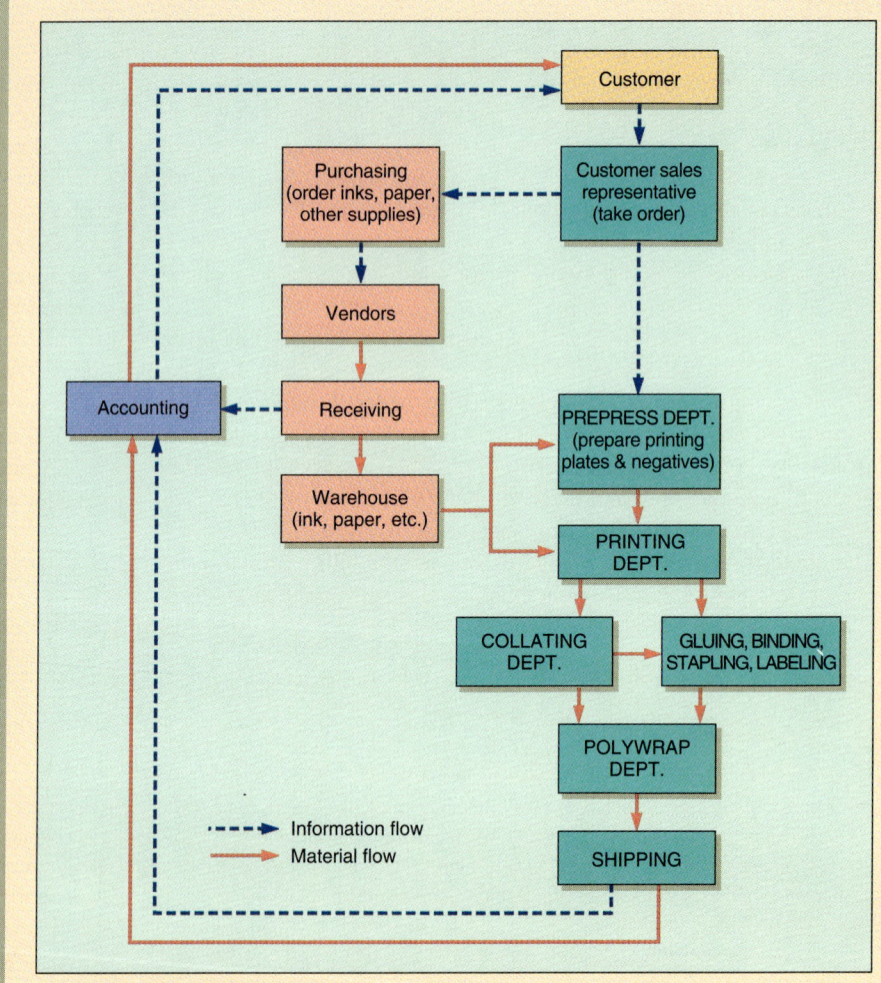

FIGURE 7.2 ■ **Flow Diagram of the Production Process at Standard Register's Plant in Kirksville, Missouri**
Source: Adapted from J. S. Martinich *Production and Operations Management* (New York: John Wiley, 1997), pp. 79–87.

Repetitive Focus

A repetitive process falls between the product and process focuses seen in Figure 7.1. Repetitive processes use modules. Modules are parts or components previously prepared, often in a continuous process.

The **repetitive process** line is the classic assembly line. Widely used in the assembly of virtually all automobiles and household appliances, it has more structure and consequently less flexibility than a process-focused facility.

Fast-food firms are an example of a repetitive process using **modules**. This type of production allows more customizing than a continuous process; so modules (for example, meat, cheese, sauce, tomatoes, onions) are assembled to get a quasi-custom product, a cheeseburger. In this manner, the firm obtains both the economic advantages of the continuous model (where many of the modules are prepared) and the custom advantage of the low-volume, high-variety model.

Repetitive process A product-oriented production process that uses modules.

Modules Parts or components of a product previously prepared, often in a continuous process.

Repetitive focus

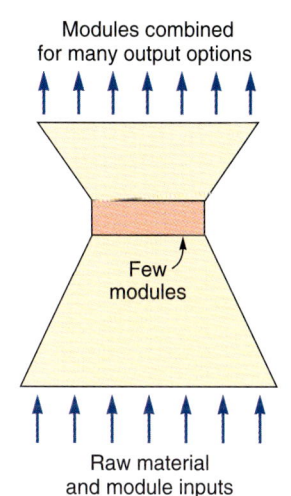

Modules combined for many output options

↑↑↑↑↑↑

Few modules

↑↑↑↑↑↑

Raw material and module inputs

Example 2 shows the Harley-Davidson assembly line. Harley is a repetitive manufacturer located toward the center of Figure 7.1.

EXAMPLE 2

Repetitive Manufacturing at Harley-Davidson

Harley-Davidson assembles modules. Most repetitive manufacturers produce on a form of assembly line where the end product can take a variety of shapes depending on the mix of modules. This is the case at Harley, where the modules are motorcycle components and options.

Harley engines are produced in Milwaukee and shipped on a just-in-time basis to the company's York, Pennsylvania, plant. At York, Harley groups parts that require similar processes together into families (see the flow diagram in Figure 7.3). The result is *work cells*. Work cells perform in one location all the operations necessary for the production of specific modules. These work cells feed the assembly line.

THE ASSEMBLY LINE

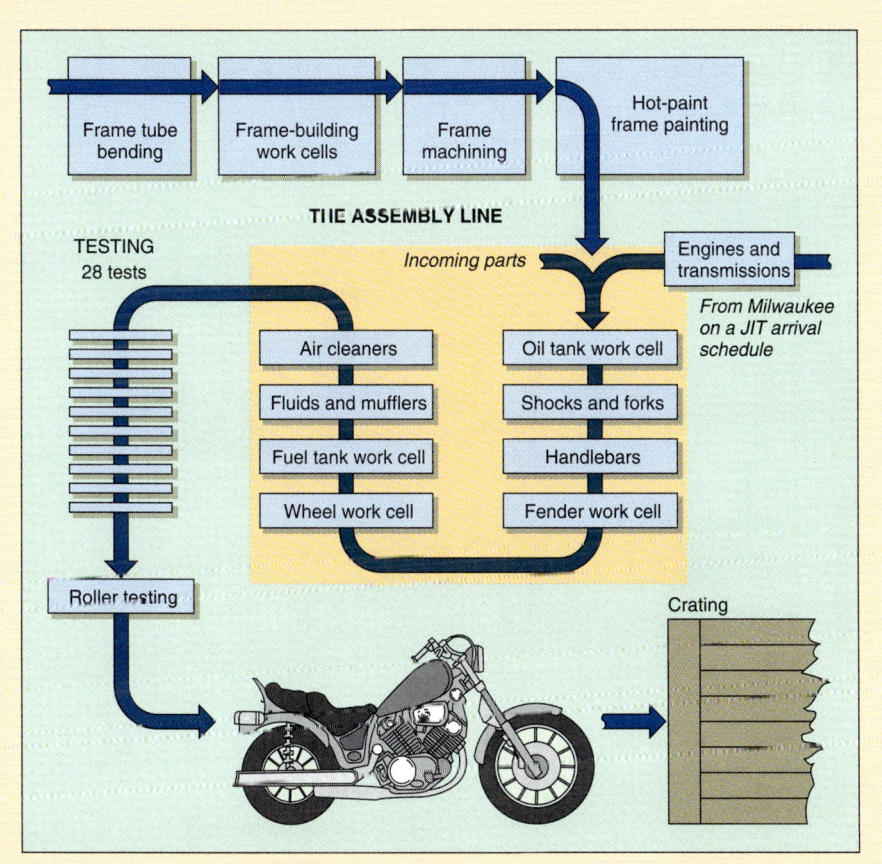

Frame tube bending → Frame-building work cells → Frame machining → Hot-paint frame painting

TESTING 28 tests

Incoming parts

Engines and transmissions — *From Milwaukee on a JIT arrival schedule*

Air cleaners | Oil tank work cell
Fluids and mufflers | Shocks and forks
Fuel tank work cell | Handlebars
Wheel work cell | Fender work cell

Roller testing

Crating

FIGURE 7.3 ■ Flow Diagram Showing the Production Process at Harley-Davidson's York, Pennsylvania, Assembly Plant

Harley-Davidson assembles 2 engine types in 3 displacement sizes for 20 street bike models, which are available in 13 colors and 2 wheel options adding up to 95 total combinations. Harley also produces 4 police, 2 Shriner, and many custom paint options. This strategy requires that no fewer than 20,000 different pieces be assembled into modules and then into motorcycles.

232 CHAPTER 7 PROCESS STRATEGY AND CAPACITY PLANNING

Product Focus

Product focus A facility organized around products; a product-oriented, high-volume, low-variety process.

High-volume, low-variety processes are **product focused**. The facilities are organized around *products*. They are also called *continuous processes*, because they have very long, continuous production runs. Products such as glass, paper, tin sheets, lightbulbs, beer, and bolts are made via a continuous process. Some products, such as lightbulbs, are discrete; others, such as rolls of paper, are nondiscrete. Still others, such as repaired hernias at Shouldice Hospital, are services. It is only with the standardization and effective quality control that firms have established product-focused facilities. An organization producing the same lightbulb or hot dog bun day after day can organize around a product. Such an organization has an inherent ability to set standards and maintain a given quality, as opposed to an organization that is producing unique products every day, such as a print shop or general-purpose hospital.

A product-focused facility produces high volume and low variety. The specialized nature of the facility requires high fixed cost, but low variable costs reward high facility utilization. The Nucor example follows.

EXAMPLE 3
Product-Focused Production at Nucor Steel

As we saw in the Nucor Global Company Profile, steel is manufactured in a product-oriented facility. Figure 7.4 illustrates Nucor's product-focused flow.

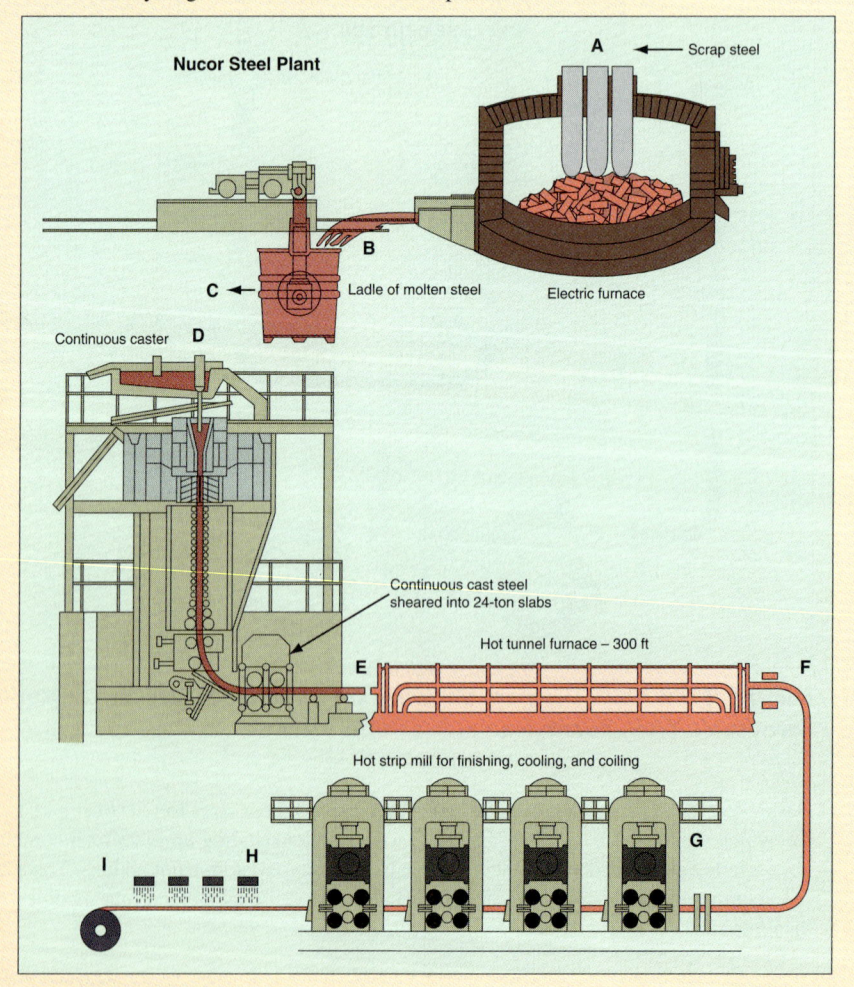

Product focused (Continuous process)

Output variations in size, shape, and packaging

Few inputs

FIGURE 7.4 ■ A Flow Diagram Showing the Steelmaking Process at Nucor's Crawfordsville, Indiana, Plant

In this process flow diagram, cold scrap steel is first lowered into a furnace that uses an electric arc to melt it in 20 seconds (A). Then molten steel pours from the furnace into a preheated ladle (B). The ladle moves on an overhead-track crane to the continuous caster (C). The ladle then opens and steel exits into the caster (D). Shaped steel exits the caster mold as a 2″ × 52″ slab (E). The slab exits the tunnel furnace (F) at a specific temperature needed for rolling. A higher-quality sheet can be produced if the slab temperature is uniform. The steel then enters the rolling mill (G). Water cools the hot-rolled steel before it is coiled (H). The rolled sheet of steel is coiled into rolls of about 25 tons each (I). Finally, a variety of finishing operations can modify the characteristics of the sheet steel to meet customer needs.

Nucor operates 24 hours a day, 6 days a week, with the seventh day reserved for scheduled maintenance.

Comparison of Process Choices

The characteristics of the three processes are shown in Table 7.1 and Figure 7.5. Advantages exist across the continuum of processes, and firms may find strategic advantage in any process. Each of the processes, when properly matched to volume and variety, can

TABLE 7.1 ■ Comparison of the Characteristics of Three Types of Processes

Process Focus (Low-Volume, High-Variety) (e.g., Standard Register)	Repetitive Focus (Modular) (e.g., Harley-Davidson)	Product Focus (High-Volume, Low-Variety) (e.g., Nucor Steel)
1. Small quantity and large variety of products are produced.	1. Long runs, usually a standardized product with options, are produced from modules.	1. Large quantity and small variety of products are produced.
2. Equipment used is general-purpose.	2. Special equipment aids in use of an assembly line.	2. Equipment used is special-purpose.
3. Operators are broadly skilled.	3. Employees are modestly trained.	3. Operators are less broadly skilled.
4. There are many job instructions because each job changes.	4. Repetitive operations reduce training and changes in job instructions.	4. Work orders and job instructions are few, because they are standardized.
5. Raw material inventories are high relative to the value of the product.	5. Just-in-time procurement techniques are used.	5. Raw materials inventories are low relative to the value of the product.
6. Work-in-process is high compared to output.	6. Just-in-time inventory techniques are used.	6. Inventory of work-in-process is low compared to output.
7. Units move slowly through the plant.	7. Movement is measured in hours and days.	7. Swift movement of units through the facility is typical.
8. Finished goods are usually made to order and not stored.	8. Finished goods are made to frequent forecasts.	8. Finished goods are usually made to a forecast and stored.
9. Scheduling to orders is complex and concerned with the trade-off between inventory availability, capacity, and customer service.	9. Scheduling is based on building various models from a variety of modules to forecasts.	9. Scheduling is relatively simple and concerned with establishing a rate of output sufficient to meet sales forecasts.
10. Fixed costs tend to be low and variable costs high.	10. Fixed costs are dependent on flexibility of the facility.	10. Fixed costs tend to be high and variable costs low.
11. Costing, often done by the job, is estimated prior to doing the job, but known only after the job.	11. Costs are usually known, because of extensive prior experience.	11. Because fixed costs are high, costs are highly dependent on utilization of capacity.

234 CHAPTER 7 PROCESS STRATEGY AND CAPACITY PLANNING

```
             Repetitive
Process focused    focus        Product focused
(intermittent process) (assembly line) (continuous process)

              ← Continuum →

High variety, low volume   Modular      Low variety, high volume
Low utilization (5% to 25%) Flexible equipment High utilization (70% to 90%)
General-purpose equipment             Specialized equipment
```

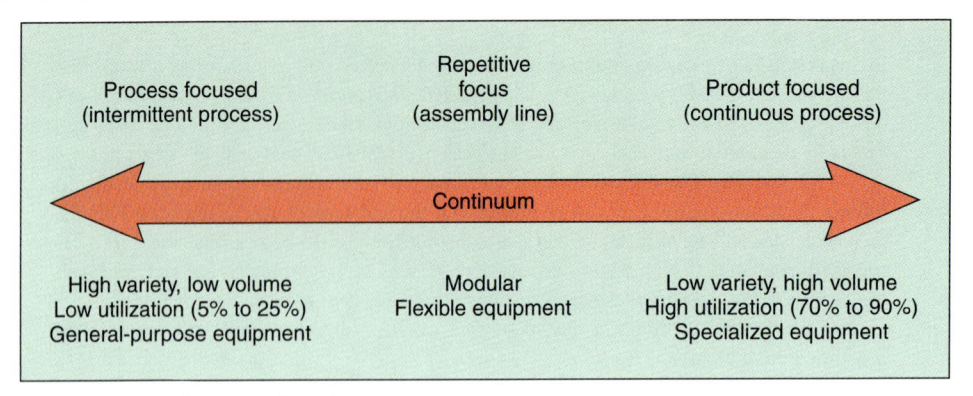

FIGURE 7.5 ■ **Process Continuum**

Manufactured housing is now 32% of all new homes sold in the U.S. This industry has increased sales as it reduced costs. It did so as it moved production from a process focus to repetitive.

produce a low-cost advantage. For instance, unit costs will be less in the continuous process case if high volume (and high utilization) exists. However, we do not always use the continuous process (that is, specialized equipment and facilities) because it is too expensive when volumes are low or flexibility is required. A low-volume, unique, highly differentiated good or service is more economical when produced under process focus; this is the way fine dining restaurants and hospitals are organized. Just as all three processes, when appropriately selected and well managed, can yield low cost, so too can all three be responsive and produce differentiated products.

Figure 7.5 indicates that equipment utilization in a process-focused facility is often in the range of 5% to 25%. When utilization goes above 15%, moving to the right on the process strategy continuum may be advantageous. A cost advantage usually exists by moving to the right as far as possible to reduce costs, provided the ability to do the necessary product customization is maintained. McDonald's started an entirely new industry by moving from the left toward the right of the continuum.

Flexibility The ability to respond with little penalty in time, cost, or customer value.

Modern technology is allowing innovative operations managers to enlarge the scope (as measured on the horizontal axis of Figure 7.5) of their process. Processes should be built with as much flexibility as possible. **Flexibility** is the ability to respond with little penalty in time, cost, or customer value. This may mean modular, movable, even cheap equipment. Flexibility may also mean the development of sophisticated electronic equipment. For instance, electronic-controlled equipment in repetitive plants (such as automobile assembly) and product-focused plants (such as weaving and knitting), have expanded the scope of their offerings. Using electronic controls, car makers build a larger variety of automobiles on the same assembly line. For instance, in Fairfax, Kansas, GM is now producing six different styles on one assembly line. GM's robot welders and other equipment are adjusted electronically as different models come down the assembly line. Similarly, electronic controls allow designers in the textile industry to rapidly revamp their lines and respond to seasonal changes.

Mass customization Rapid, low-cost production that caters to constantly changing unique customer desires.

Mass customization—rapidly mass-producing products that cater to sundry unique customer desires—is another benefit of efficient use of computers and electronic controls. National Bicycle (see photo), for example, produces custom bicycles in 3 hours. The idea is to use imagination and technology aggressively to make production processes so agile that mass customization can take place. Under mass customization, our three process models become flexible and the distinctions among them blurred, making variety and volume issues less significant. In the supplement to this chapter, we will look at ways technology aids operations managers in their move toward mass customization.

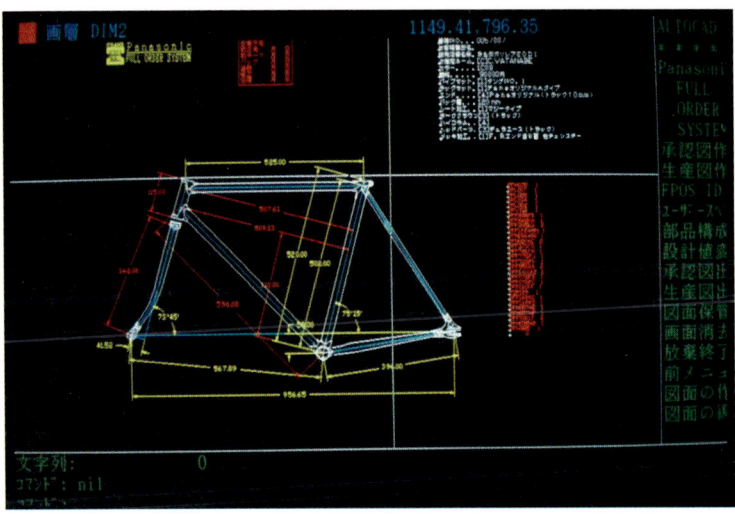

Flexible manufacturing can improve customer service and provide a competitive advantage. National Bicycle's customized Panasonic bicycle production process begins by defining individual customer needs. The customer mounts the special frame in a Panasonic bicycle store from which measurements are taken. These custom measurements are then sent to the factory, where CAD software produces a blueprint in about 3 minutes. At the same time, a bar-code label is prepared that will identify bicycle components as they move through production. Time—from beginning to end—is only 3 hours.

Changing the production system from one process model to another is still difficult and expensive. In some cases, the change may mean starting over. Consider what would be required of a rather simple change—McDonald's adding the flexibility necessary to serve you a charbroiled hamburger. What appears to be rather straightforward will require changes in many of our 10 OM decisions. For instance, changes may be necessary in (1) purchasing (a different quality of meat, perhaps with more fat content, and supplies such as charcoal); (2) quality standards (how long and at what temperature the patty will cook); (3) equipment (the charbroiler), (4) layout (space for the new process and for new exhaust vents), and (5) training. Like most firms, McDonald's will find changing the process difficult and expensive. Consequently, choosing where to operate on the process strategy continuum may determine the transformation strategy for an extended period. This critical decision must be done right the first time.

Agile organizations are quick and flexible in their response to ever-changing customer requirements.

PROCESS ANALYSIS AND DESIGN

When analyzing and designing processes to transform resources into goods and services, we ask questions such as:

- Is the process designed to achieve competitive advantage in terms of differentiation, response, or low cost?
- Does the process eliminate steps that do not add value?
- Does the process maximize customer value as perceived by the customer?
- Will the process win orders?

Each step of your process must add value.

A number of tools help us understand the complexities of process design and redesign. They are simply ways of making sense of what happens or must happen in a process. Let's look at four of these tools.

Flow Diagrams

Flow diagram A drawing used to analyze movement of people or material.

The first tool is the **flow diagram**, which is a schematic or drawing of the movement of material, product, or people. For instance, Figures 7.2, 7.3, and 7.4 showed the processes for Standard Register, Harley-Davidson and Nucor Steel, respectively. Such diagrams can help understanding, analysis, and communication of a process.

Process Charts

Process charts Charts using symbols to analyze the movement of people or material.

The second tool is the *process chart*. **Process charts** use symbols and sometimes time and distance to provide an objective and structured way to analyze and record the activities that make up a process.[1] They allow us to focus on value-added activities. For instance, the process chart shown in Figure 7.6, which includes the present method of hamburger assembly at a fast-food restaurant, includes a value-added line to help us distinguish between value-added activities and waste. Identifying all operational activities as value-added (as opposed to inspection, storage, delay, and transportation, which add no value) allows us to determine the percent of value added to total activities. We can see from the computation at the bottom of Figure 7.6 that the value added in this case is 85.7%. The operations manager's job is to reduce waste and increase the percent of value added. The nonvalue-added items are a waste; they are resources lost to the firm and to society forever.

PROCESS CHART

Present Method [X]   Proposed Method [ ]

SUBJECT CHARTED: Hamburger Assembly Process
DATE: 1/1/98
CHART BY: KH
CHART NO.: 1
DEPARTMENT: _____
SHEET NO. 1 OF 1

DIST. IN FEET	TIME IN MINS.	CHART SYMBOLS	PROCESS DESCRIPTION
—	—	▽	Meat Patty in Storage
1.5	.05	⇨	Transfer to Broiler
	2.50	○	Broiler
	.05	□	Visual Inspection
1.0	.05	⇨	Transfer to Rack
	.15	▽	Temporary Storage
.5	.10	⇨	Obtain Buns, Lettuce, etc.
	.20	○	Assemble Order
.5	.05	⇨	Place in Finish Rack
3.5	3.15	2 4 1 — 2	TOTALS

Value-added time = Operation time/Total time = (2.50+.20)/3.15 = 85.7%

○ = operation; ⇨ = transportation; □ = inspection; D = delay; ▽ = storage.

FIGURE 7.6 ■ Process Chart Showing a Hamburger Assembly Process at a Fast-Food Restaurant

---

[1] Additional examples of process charts are shown in chapter 4, "Managing Quality," and chapter 10, "Human Resources and Job Design."

PROCESS ANALYSIS AND DESIGN   237

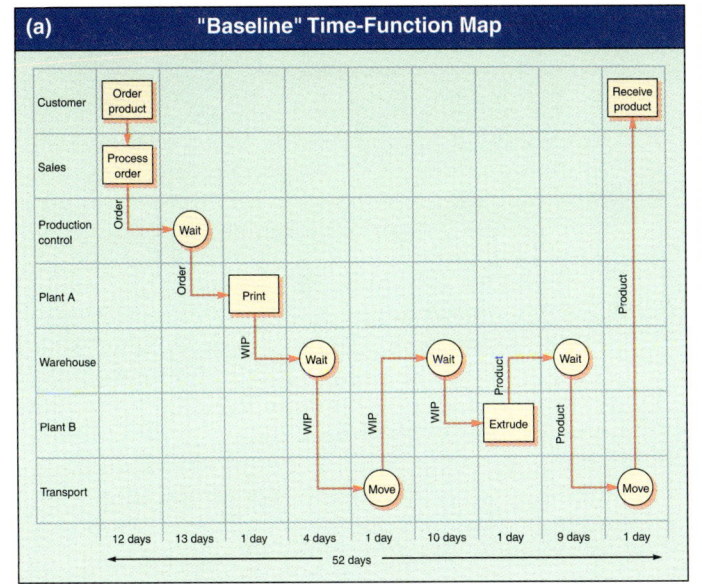

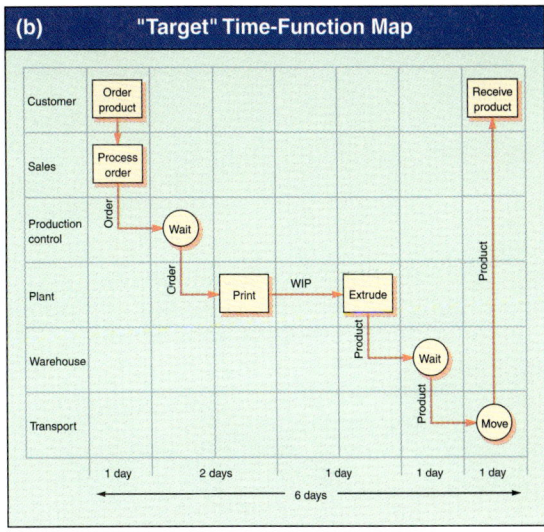

FIGURE 7.7 ■ Time-Function Mapping (Process Mapping) for a Product Requiring Printing and Extruding Operations at American National Can Company

This technique clearly shows that waiting and order processing contributed substantially to the 46 days that can be eliminated in this operation.

Source: Elaine J. Labach, "Faster, Better, and Cheaper," *Target* 7, no. 5 (winter 1991): 43. Excerpted from *Target* with permission of the Association for Manufacturing Excellence, 380 W. Palatine Road, Wheeling, IL 60090-5863, (847) 520-3282.

Time-Function Mapping

A third tool for process analysis and design is a traditional flow process chart, but with time added on the horizontal axis. Such charts are sometimes called **time-function mapping** or **process mapping**. With time-function mapping, nodes indicate the activities and the arrows indicate the flow direction, with time on the horizontal axis. As is the case with process charts, this type of analysis allows users to identify and eliminate waste such as extra steps, duplication, and delay. Figure 7.7(a, b) shows the use of process mapping before and after process improvement at American National Can Company. In this example, substantial reduction in waiting time and process improvement in order processing contributed to a savings of 46 days.

Time-function mapping (or process mapping) A flow process chart but with time added on the horizontal axis.

Work-Flow Analysis

A fourth technique, known as *work-flow analysis*, mimics the way people communicate. The idea is that everyone in an organization is a customer or a performer depending on the precise transaction. **Work-flow analysis** documents a network of transactions between customers and performers. The objective of each transaction is to achieve customer satisfaction. Work-flow analysis involves four phases:

1. *Request* from a customer or an offer to provide services by a performer.
2. *Negotiation*, allowing the customer and the performer to agree on how the work should be done and what will constitute customer satisfaction.
3. *Performance* of the assignment and completion.
4. *Acceptance*, closing the transaction provided the customer expresses satisfaction and agrees that the conditions were met.

Work-flow analysis A technique to document a network of transactions between cutomers and performance.

OM IN ACTION

REENGINEERING A SUCCESS AT WESTINGHOUSE

To Westinghouse, the problems were clear: Worldwide competition was increasing; the company was pressed to lower prices even though the cost of materials, employees, and overhead kept increasing; and higher customer expectations demanded shorter cycle times, superior quality, and greater customer satisfaction.

Reengineering was the answer. The phrase embraces such techniques as work teams—training employees in multiple skills so that they can do more than one job—and "empowerment," which means pushing decision-making authority as far down in the organization as possible. It also entails reorganizing processes, in both assembly lines and offices, to simplify and speed the flow of work.

The company developed WESTIP (Westinghouse Technology to Improve Process), a method to radically reengineer or improve business processes. Cross-functional employee teams used WESTIP to perform process analysis, redesign, and implementation quickly and simply.

The result was a Baldrige National Quality Award and these benefits: $22 million in savings in 1 year, two-thirds reduction in material costs, reduced drawing time from 90 to 10 days, 30% lower manufacturing costs through improved cellular layout, a drop in the time it takes to handle purchase orders from 14 days to 6 hours, and reduced order cost from $86 to $12. Finally, a factory that used to take 100,000 square feet to build Westinghouse components now needs only 40,000 square feet.

Sources: Industrial Engineering (March, 1995): 20, and *The Wall Street Journal* (March 16, 1993): A1.

Transactions can be very complex in a large organization, with a multitude of loops between customers and performers. Therefore this type of analysis is often done with computer programs that help chart various work flows. (See photo of work-flow software by Sterling Software, Inc.)

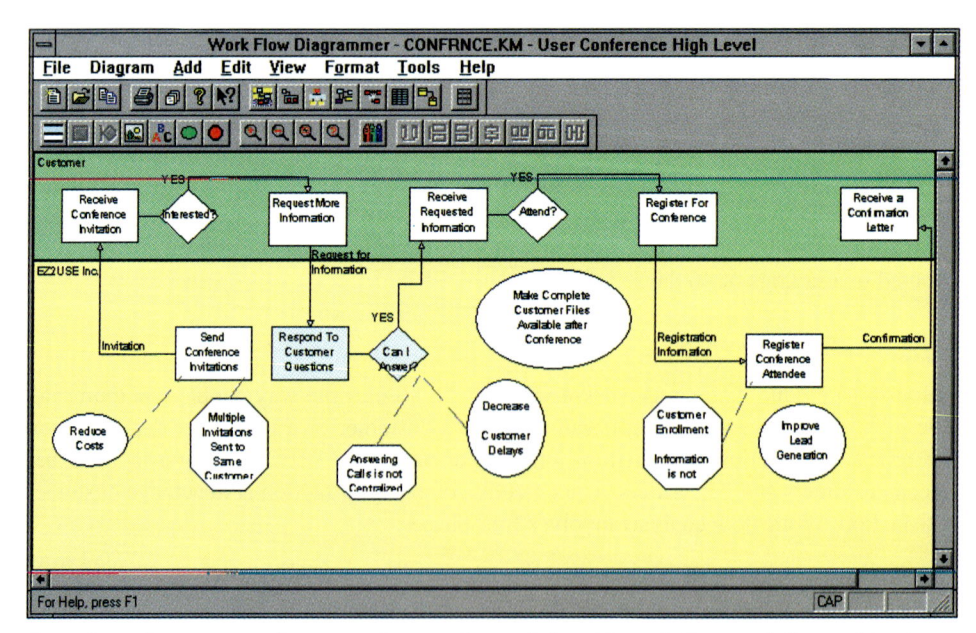

A number of computer software packages exists to help with work-flow modeling and business process reengineering. One such package is Key for Workgroup from Sterling Software, Inc., Atlanta.

PROCESS REENGINEERING

Because the world is so dynamic, with changes in customer desires, product, product mix, and technology, processes change. The competitive marketplace demands it. Consequently, processes are redesigned or, as it is sometimes called, *reengineered*. **Process reengineering** is the fundamental rethinking and radical redesign of business processes to bring about dramatic improvements in performance.[2]

Effective process reengineering relies on reevaluating the purpose of the process and questioning both purposes and underlying assumptions. It works only if the basic process and its objectives are reexamined. Often a firm finds that the initial assumptions of its process are no longer valid. (See the Westinghouse *OM in Action* box.)

Process reengineering focuses on those activities that cross functional lines. Because managers are often in charge of specific "functions" or specialized areas of responsibility, those activities (processes) that cross from one function or specialty to another may be neglected. Therefore, process reengineering often finds a fertile ground in these areas. Reengineering casts aside all notions of how the process is currently being done and focuses on dramatic improvements in cost, time, and customer value. Any process is a candidate for radical redesign. The process can be a factory layout, a purchasing procedure, or a new way of processing credit applications at IBM, as described in Example 4.

Process reengineering
The fundamental rethinking and radical design of business processes to bring about dramatic improvements in performance.

EXAMPLE 4

The traditional IBM credit application process took many steps. The first step consisted of 14 people answering phones and logging calls from field sales personnel requesting credit for customers. After receiving calls, phone personnel made paper notations that they sent upstairs to credit personnel for credit checks. Then the paper went down the hall to the business practice group where the data were entered into a computer for determination of terms and interest rates. From there, the packet of data went to a clerical group. A week or two after the request, the results of the request were available.

IBM tried to fix the process by keeping a log of each step of every request. Although logging allowed credit personnel to know where in the process the application was, it added a day to the turnaround. Finally, two managers tried a radical approach. They walked a loan request through each step from office to office and found that it took only 90 minutes of actual work. The additional week was spent shuttling the paperwork among departments. This meant that the work along the way was not the problem. Instead, the *process* was at fault. Reengineering resulted in IBM replacing all of its specialists with generalists, called caseworkers, who process applications from start to finish. The firm also developed software that uses the expertise of specialists to support caseworkers. The reengineered process reduced the number of employees and achieved better results. The week-plus turnaround time for a credit request is down to 4 hours. The company now handles 100 times the number of loan requests that it did under the old system.

Source: Adapted from Michael Hammer and James Campy, *Reengineering the Corporation: A Manifesto for Business Revolution* (New York: HarperCollins, 1993).

Moving toward Lean Production

The mission of **lean producers** is to achieve perfection through continuous learning, creativity, and teamwork.[3] Although this effort requires the full commitment and involvement

Lean producers
Repetitive producers who are world-class because they continuously drive out non-value–added activities.

---

[2] Michael Hammer and Steven Stanton, *The Reengineering Revolution* (New York: HarperCollins, 1995), p. 3.

[3] John Krafcik is given credit for coining the term *lean production*. Also see James P. Womack and Daniel T. Jones, *Lean Thinking* (New York: Simon & Schuster, 1996).

> ## OM IN ACTION
>
> ### UNIFORM PIGS CONTRIBUTE TO EFFICIENCY
>
> In the secluded hills of Princeton, Missouri, the life of a hog is brief, loveless, and focused on gaining weight. Meet the multibillion-dollar business called "techno-pork."
>
> Inside barn No. 5 of Premium Standard Farms Inc.'s sprawling complex, 1,100 hogs are being bred to a lean uniformity. Pellets rattle down plastic tubes when feed gets low. A computer closes curtains as the night grows chilly, and heaters whir into action. (Because bigger pigs like it cooler, a computer lowers the temperature a half degree per day as they age.) Just when the odor seems a bit ripe, a whoosh of water flushes away manure.
>
> A door cracks open and suddenly the pigs grunt and turn in unison to face two men in spotless blue jumpsuits—the hog-farmer outfit of the twenty-first century. VP Dan Skadburg gently pokes the ribs of a 235-pounder. Five days to slaughter, he figures.
>
> Factorylike operations such as this, which bring together technology and finance, are changing the face of the pork industry. Long a messy sideline for family farmers, pork population is characterized by an increasing number of mega farms that can produce a healthy, lean hog for 10% less than their smaller counterparts.
>
> And because Premium Standard's hogs are so uniform, its $50-million slaughterhouse is mechanized as never before. Loins are pulled off by robots and disassembling heads, a job once requiring a dozen knife-wielding workers, is automated. It all adds up to higher-quality, lower-priced pork at the market. It is a lesson learned long ago in manufacturing: Standardized products can boost efficient processes.
>
> Sources: *The Wall Street Journal* (May 4, 1995): A1–A6; *Fortune* (Oct. 14, 1996): 7; and *Economic Perspectives* (January-February, 1997): 2.

of all employees and the company's suppliers, the rewards reaped by lean producers are spectacular.

Lean producers share these attributes:

- They focus on *inventory reduction* to remove waste. They use just-in-time techniques to eliminate virtually all inventory. The removal of inventory removes the safety nets that allow a poor product to make its way through the production process.
- They *build systems that help employees* produce a perfect part every time.
- They *reduce space requirements*. The technique minimizes the distance a part travels and frees space for alternative uses.
- They *develop close relationships with suppliers* helping them to understand their needs and their customers' needs.
- They *educate suppliers* to accept responsibility for helping meet customer needs.
- They strive for continually declining costs by *eliminating all but value-added activities*. Material handling, inspection, inventory, and rework jobs are among the likely targets because these do not add value to the product.
- They *develop the workforce*. They constantly improve job design, training, employee participation and commitment, and work teams.
- They *make jobs more challenging*, pushing responsibility to the lowest level possible. They reduce the number of job classes and build workers flexibility.

Lean producers set their sights on perfection: no bad parts and no inventory. Lean production requires a commitment to continuously remove those activities that do not add value to the product. Meanwhile, customary production techniques have *limited* goals. Traditionally, for instance, managers have accepted the production of some defective parts and some safety stock inventory.

SERVICE PROCESS STRATEGY

Our process continuum, shown earlier in Figure 7.5, applies to services as well as to goods. Much of the service industry is producing in very small lots. This is true for legal services, medical services, dental services, and restaurants. They are often producing in lot sizes as small as one. Such organizations would be to the left of Figure 7.5.

Service-Sector Considerations

As Figure 7.5 indicates, equipment utilization is low in process-focused facilities—perhaps as low as 5%. This is true not only for manufacturing but also for services. An X-ray machine in a dentist's office and much of the equipment in a fine dining restaurant have low utilization. Hospitals, too, can be expected to be in that range, which would suggest why their costs are considered high. Why such low utilization? In part because excess capacity for peak loads is desirable. Hospital administrators, as well as managers of other service facilities and their patients and customers, expect equipment to be available as needed. Another reason is poor scheduling (although substantial efforts have been made to forecast demand in the service industry) and the resulting imbalance in the use of facilities.

The service industry moves to the right of Figure 7.5 by establishing fast-food restaurants, legal clinics, auto lubrication shops, auto tune up shops, and so on. As the variety of services is reduced, we would expect per-unit cost to drop. This is typically what happens.

Restaurants like Darden's Red Lobster are part of the service industry, but they are also the end of a long production line. At the beginning of the line, raw material goes in—at Red Lobster that means 60 million pounds of seafood a year. The seafood is purchased from all over the world. The shrimp arrives in frozen boxes from Ecuador and Thailand at a Red Lobster processing plant in St. Petersburg, Florida. There the shrimp is loaded onto a conveyor belt to be peeled, deveined, cooked, quick-frozen (left), sorted (right), and repacked for ultimate delivery to individual restaurants.

Customer Interaction and Process Strategy

Customer interaction is an important variable in process decisions. In a process that directly interfaces with the customer, one expects the customer to affect efficiency adversely. Activities in the service sector are a good example. In a restaurant, a medical facility, a law office, or a retail store, too much interaction between the customer and the process keeps the process from operating as smoothly as it otherwise might. Individual attention and customizing of the product or service for the customer can play havoc with a process. The more the process can be insulated from the customer's unique requirements, the lower will be the cost.

While services can be thought of as falling on the process continuum shown in Figure 7.5, the four quadrants in Figure 7.8 provide additional insight into service processes. The 10 operations management decisions we introduced in Chapter 2 are used with a different emphasis in each of these quadrants. For instance:

- In the upper sections (quadrants) of *mass service* and *professional service*, where *labor intensity is high*, we expect the manager to focus extensively on human resources. This is particularly true in the quadrant with *high interaction and customization*. These quadrants require that managers find ways of addressing unique issues that satisfy customers and win orders. This is often done with very personalized service, some of which requires high labor intensity and therefore significant selection and training issues in the human resources area.
- The quadrants with *low interaction and low customization* may be able (1) to standardize or restrict some offerings of the service, as do fast-food restaurants, (2) to automate, as have some airlines that have ticket-vending machines, or (3) to remove some services, such as seat assignments, as has Southwest Airlines. Off-loading some aspect of the service through automation may require innovations in process design as well as capital investment. Such was the case with airline ticket vending and bank ATMs. This move to standardization and automation may require added capital expenditure, as well as putting operations managers under pressure to develop new skills for the purchase and maintenance of such equipment. A reduction in a customization capability will require added strength in other areas.

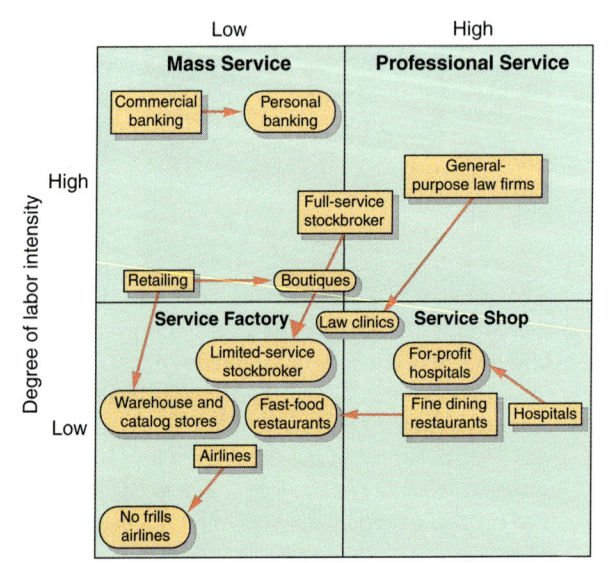

FIGURE 7.8 ■ Operation Changes within the Service Process Matrix

Source: Adapted from work by Roger Schmenner, "How Can Service Business Survive and Prosper?" *Sloan Management Review,* spring 1986, pp. 21–32. Reprinted by permission.

- Because customer feedback is lower in the quadrants with low interaction, tight control may be required to maintain quality standards.
- Operations with *low labor intensity* may lend themselves particularly well to innovations in process, technology, and scheduling capability.

These service process strategies can be summarized as (1) identifying and separating unique customer requirements so the high-cost personal service can be reduced, (2) automation, (3) excellent scheduling, and (4) outstanding training. Examples of some of these ideas are shown in Table 7.2.

More Opportunities to Improve Service Processes

Layout Layout design is an integral part of any service process, particularly in retailing, dining, and banking. In retailing, layout can provide not only product exposure but also customer education and product enhancement. In restaurants, layout can enhance the dining experience as well as provide an effective flow in both the kitchen and dining area. In banks, layout provides security as well as work flow and personal comfort. Because layout is such an integral part of many services, it provides continuing opportunity for winning orders.

TABLE 7.2 ■ Techniques for Improving Operations Productivity in Services

Strategy	Technique	Example
Separation	*Restricting* the offerings	Limited-menu restaurant
	Customizing at delivery	Customizing vans at delivery rather than at production
	Structuring service so customers must go where the service is offered	Banks where customers go to a manager to open a new account, to loan officers for loans, and to tellers for deposits
	Self-service so customers examine, compare, and evaluate at their own pace	Supermarkets and department stores
	Modular selection of service	Investment and insurance selection
	Product-focus production with some modules of the service	Prepackaged foods in restaurants
Automation	*Separating services* that may lend themselves to some type of automation	Automatic teller machines
Scheduling	Precise personnel *scheduling*	Scheduling ticket counter personnel at 15 minute intervals at airlines
Training	*Clarifying the service* options	Investment counselor, funeral directors
	Explaining problems	After sale maintenance personnel

Human Resources Because so many services involve direct interaction with the customer (as the upper quadrants of Figure 7.8 suggest), the human resource issues of recruiting and training can be particularly important ingredients in service processes. Additionally, a committed workforce that exhibits flexibility when schedules are made and is cross trained to fill in when the process requires less than a full-time person, can have a tremendous impact on overall process performance.

Technology Technology can also help improve services. Andersen Windows of Bayport, Minnesota, the world's largest maker of wooden windows and patio doors, is improving the service part of its manufacturing business through automation. Much in the way automatic teller machines improve customer banking services, Andersen has developed computer software that enables customers to design their own window specifications. The customer, with user-friendly software, calls up a product information guide, promotion material, a gallery of designs, and a sketch pad to create the designs desired. The software also allows the customer to determine likely energy savings and see a graphic view of their home fitted with the new window. It even determines the product numbers and creates a price and order list that initiates the order entry process. Similarly, computers and electronic communications in retail stores download prices quickly to reflect changing costs or market conditions. For instance, when devaluation struck Mexico, the drugstore chain Farmacias Benavides used computer systems to immediately stop the reorders of higher-priced items and to stock up instead on lower-cost generic product lines.

We will now deal with five additional topics that help managers choose the correct process. Those issues are selection of equipment, environmental issues, capacity, break-even analysis, and the investment itself.

SELECTION OF EQUIPMENT AND TECHNOLOGY

Ultimately, the decisions about a particular process require decisions about equipment and technology. Those decisions can be complex because alternative methods of production are present in virtually all operations functions, be they hospitals, restaurants, or manufacturing facilities. Picking the best equipment means understanding the specific industry and its established processes and technology. That choice of equipment, be it an X-ray machine for a hospital, a computer-controlled lathe for a factory, or a new computer for an office, requires considering cost, quality, capacity, and flexibility. To make this decision, operations personnel develop documentation that indicates the capacity, size, and tolerances of each option, as well as its maintenance requirements. Any one of these attributes may be the deciding factor regarding the use of a process.

The selection of equipment for a particular type of process can also provide competitive advantage. Many firms, for instance, develop unique machines or techniques within established processes that provide an advantage. This advantage may result in added flexibility in meeting customer requirements, lower cost, or higher quality. Innovations and equipment modification might also allow for a more stable production process that takes less adjustment, maintenance, and operator training. In any case, specialized equipment often provides a way to win orders.

The study of specific industries and their technology is outside the scope of this book. However, the technological advances that influence OM process strategy are substantial and are discussed in the supplement to this chapter.

ENVIRONMENTAL ISSUES

The past two decades have seen increasing pressure on firms to be more environmentally sensitive in the processes they use. Some companies have responded to environmental regulation with foot-dragging. Others recognize environmentally sound behavior as a socially responsible and profitable opportunity.

With a focus on such issues as waste by-products, emission controls, and material recycling, many firms have concentrated on changing production processes to reduce pollution and increase recycling. There are several ways companies can show their sensitivity to environmental issues in product and process design.[4]

1. *Make products recyclable.* Germany, a leader in the "green movement," passed a packaging ordinance in 1991 requiring beer brewers to use refillable bottles. BMW also uses a large number of metal and plastic parts that are designed to be recycled.
2. *Use recycled materials.* Standard Register, described in Example 1 in this chapter, produces considerable paper scrap—almost 20 tons of punch holes alone per month. The company developed ways to recycle paper scrap as well as aluminum and silver from the plate-making process shown in the flow diagram in Figure 7.2. And Scotch-Brite soap pads at 3M are made of recycled plastics, as are the park benches and other products at Plastic Recycling Corporation (see photo).
3. *Use less harmful ingredients.* Standard Register, like most of the printing industry, has replaced environmentally dangerous inks with soybean-based inks that reduce air and water pollution.

Technology can result in new processes. Shown here is an environmentally friendly process developed by Floyd Hammer (right) that converts plastic into weather-resistant park benches, parking lot curbs, and landscaping timbers. Hammer's company, Plastic Recycling Corp., based in Iowa Falls, expects to grow from only 2 plants to more than 16 as this new process provides what is becoming known as "green manufacturing."

---

[4] T. Saunders *The Bottom Line of Green Is Black* (San Francisco: HarperCollins, 1993), pp. 23–27; *The Economist,* June 3, 1995, p. 57; J. S. Martinich, *Production and Operations Management* (New York: John Wiley, 1997), pp. 86, 241, 348; and *The Wall Street Journal,* February 7, 1997, pp. B1, B8.

4. *Use lighter components.* The auto industry continues to expand the use of aluminum and plastic components to reduce weight. This change in material, while expensive, makes autos more environmentally friendly by improving mileage.
5. *Use less energy.* Ben and Jerry's Ice Cream saves $250,000 per year just by using energy-efficient florescent lighting. Anheuser-Busch saves $30 million per year in energy and waste-treatment costs by using treated plant wastewater to generate the gas that powers its St. Louis brewery. DuPont is so good at energy efficiency that it has turned its expertise into a consulting business.
6. *Use less material.* Most companies waste material—in the plant and in the packaging. An employee team at a Sony semiconductor plant achieved a 50% reduction in the amount of chemicals used in the silicon wafer etching process. This and similar successes reduce both production costs and environmental concerns. To conserve packaging, Boston's Park Plaza Hotel eliminated bars of soap and bottles of shampoo by installing pump dispensers in its bathrooms. This saved the need for 1 million plastic containers a year.

Green manufacturing Sensitivity to a wide variety of environmental issues in production processes.

The concept of **green manufacturing**—that is, making environmentally sound products through efficient processes—can be good business. The public appreciates it, and it can save money, material, and the environment we live in. These are the kind of win-win situations that operations managers seek.

CAPACITY

After considering the process options, managers still face a number of issues. Because determining the size of a facility is critical to a firm's success, we now investigate the concepts and techniques of capacity planning.

Defining Capacity

Capacity The maximum output of a system in a given period.

Capacity is the maximum output of a system in a given period. It is normally expressed as a rate, such as the number of tons of steel that can be produced per week, per month, or per year. For many companies, measuring capacity can be straightforward. It is the maximum number of units that can be produced in a specific time. However, for some organizations, determining capacity can be more difficult. Capacity can be measured in terms of beds (a hospital), active members (a church), or the number of counselors (a drug-abuse program). Other organizations use total work time available as a measure of overall capacity.

Most organizations operate their facilities at a rate less than the capacity. They do so because they have found that they can operate more efficiently when their resources are not stretched to the limit. Instead, they expect to operate at perhaps 92% of capacity. This concept is called effective capacity.

Effective capacity The maximum capacity a firm can expect to achieve given its product mix, methods of scheduling, maintenance, and standards of quality. Effective capacity is sometimes referred to as utilization.

Effective capacity is simply the percent of design capacity actually expected. It can be computed from the following formula:

$$\text{Effective capacity} = \frac{\text{Expected capacity}}{\text{Capacity}} \qquad (7.1)$$

Effective capacity is the capacity a firm can *expect* to achieve given its product mix, methods of scheduling, maintenance, and standards of quality.

Another consideration is efficiency. Depending on how facilities are used and managed, it may be difficult or impossible to reach 100% efficiency. Typically, efficiency is expressed as a percentage of effective capacity. **Efficiency** is a measure of actual output over effective capacity:

$$\text{Efficiency} = \frac{\text{Actual output}}{\text{Effective capacity}} \quad (7.2)$$

Efficiency A measure of actual output over effective capacity.

Rated capacity is a measure of the maximum usable capacity of a particular facility. Rated capacity will always be less than or equal to capacity. The equation used to compute rated capacity is:

$$\text{Rated capacity} = (\text{Capacity})(\text{Effective capacity})(\text{Efficiency}) \quad (7.3)$$

Rated capacity A measure of the maximum usable capacity of a particular facility.

We determine rated capacity in the following example.

EXAMPLE 5

The Sara James Bakery has a plant for processing breakfast rolls. The facility has an efficiency of 90%, and the effective capacity is 80%. Three process lines are used to produce the rolls. The lines operate 7 days a week and three 8-hour shifts per day. Each line was designed to process 120 standard (that is, plain) rolls per hour. What is the rated capacity?

Solution

In order to compute the rated capacity, we multiply the design capacity (which is equal to the number of lines times the number of hours times the number of rolls per hour) times the effective capacity times the efficiency. Each facility is used 7 days a week, 3 shifts a day. Therefore, each process line is utilized for 168 hours per week (168 = 7 days × 3 shifts per day × 8 hours per shift). With this information, the rated capacity can be determined. This is done below.

$$\begin{aligned}\text{Rated capacity} &= (\text{Capacity})(\text{Effective capacity})(\text{Efficiency}) \\ &= [(3)(168)(120)](.8)(.9) = 43{,}546 \text{ rolls per week}\end{aligned}$$

Forecasting Capacity Requirements

Determining future capacity requirements can be a complicated procedure, one based in large part on future demand. When demand for goods and services can be forecast with a reasonable degree of precision, determining capacity requirements can be straightforward. It normally requires two phases. During the first phase, future demand is forecast with traditional methods. During the second phase, this forecast is used to determine capacity requirements.

Once the rated capacity has been forecast, the next step is to determine the incremental size of each addition to capacity. At this point, the assumption is made that management knows the technology and the *type* of facilities to be employed to satisfy future demand requirements.

Figure 7.9 reveals how new capacity can be planned for future demand growth. As seen in Figure 7.9(a), new capacity is acquired at the beginning of year 1. This capacity will handle increased demand until the beginning of year 2. At the beginning of year 2, new capacity is again acquired, which will allow the organization to stay ahead of demand until the beginning of year 3. This process can be continued indefinitely into the future.

The capacity plan shown in Figure 7.9(a) is only one of an almost limitless number of plans to satisfy future demand. In this figure, new capacity was acquired *incrementally*—

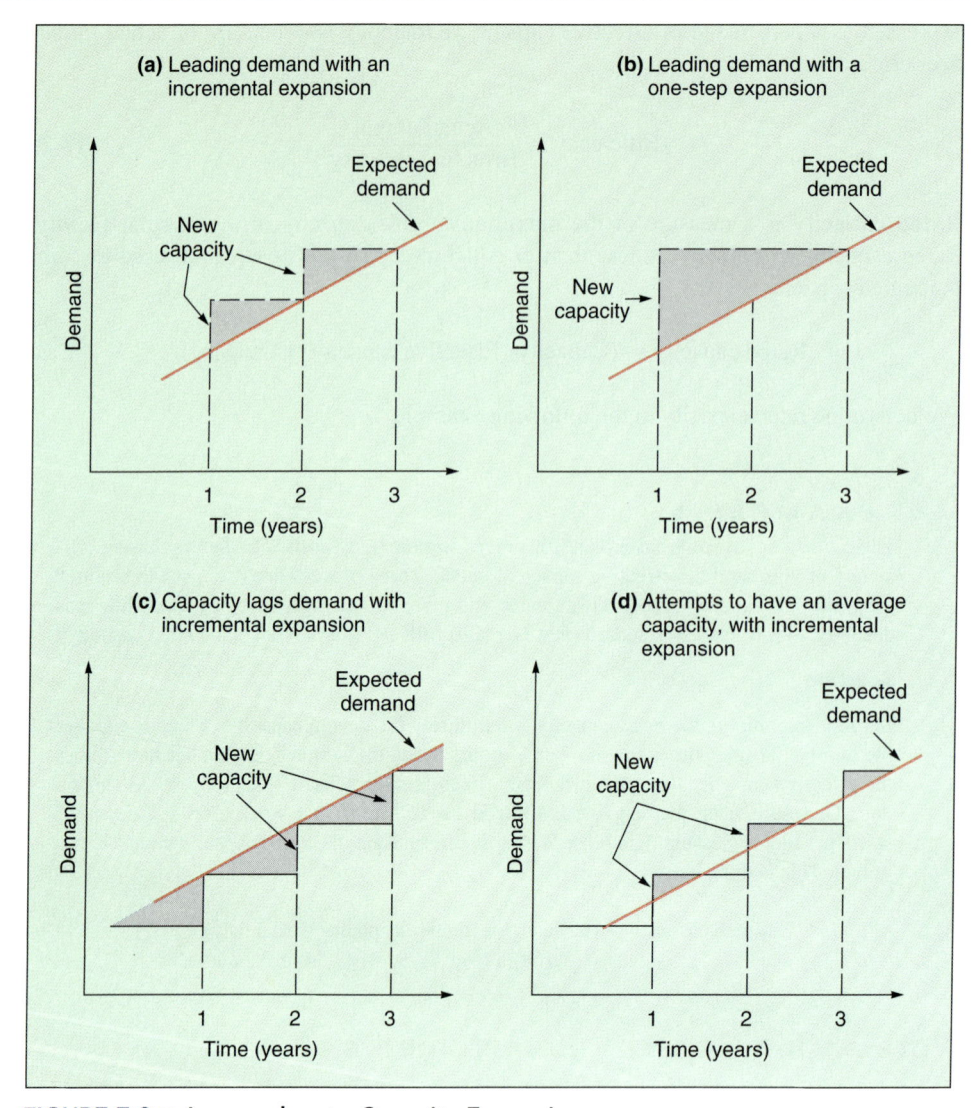

FIGURE 7.9 ■ **Approaches to Capacity Expansion**

(a) leads demand with an incremental expansion, (b) leads demand with a one-step expansion, (c) lags demand with incremental expansion, and (d) attempts to have an "average" capacity with incremental expansion.

at the beginning of year 1 *and* at the beginning of year 2. In Figure 7.9(b), a large increase in capacity is acquired at the beginning of year 1 in order to satisfy expected demand until the beginning of year 3.

Both of these alternatives *lead* capacity—that is, acquire capacity to stay ahead of demand—but Figure 7.9(c) shows an option that *lags* capacity, perhaps using overtime or subcontracting to accommodate excess demand. Figure 7.9(d) attempts to build capacity that is "average," sometimes lagging demand and sometimes leading it.

In some cases, deciding between alternatives can be relatively easy. The total cost of each alternative can be computed and the alternative with the least total cost selected. In other cases, determining the capacity and how to achieve it can be much more complicated. In most cases, numerous subjective factors are difficult to quantify and measure.

CAPACITY

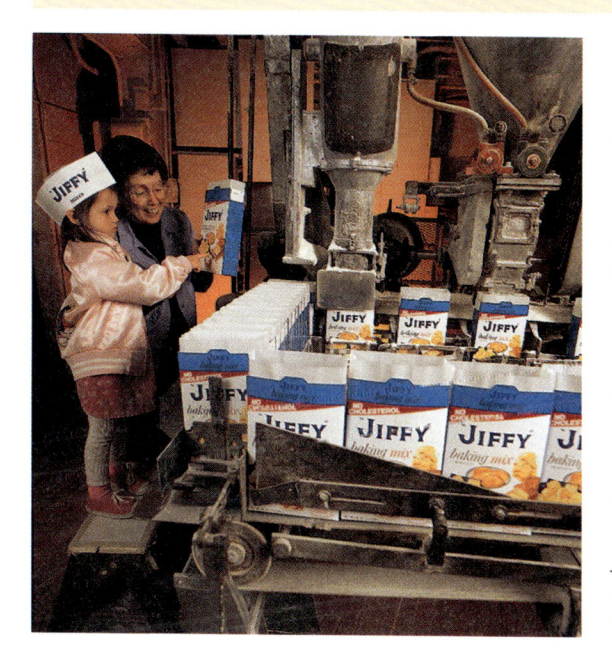

The capital expenditures for a capacity change can be tremendous. Many companies address this problem by making incremental changes when possible. Others adjust by modifying old equipment or using older equipment even though it may not be as efficient. For instance, managers at family-owned Chelsea Milling Company, makers of Jiffy brand mixes, decided that their company's OM strategy did not support additional capital investment in new equipment. Consequently, when making repairs, modifying equipment, or adjusting for peak loads, they draw on spare, often old, equipment.

These factors include technological options; competitor strategies; building restrictions; cost of capital; human resource options; and local, state, and federal laws and regulations.

When capacity requirements are subject to significant unknowns, "probabilistic" models may be appropriate. One technique for making successful capacity planning decisions with an uncertain demand is decision theory, including the use of decision trees.

Applying Decision Trees to Capacity Decisions

Decision trees require specifying alternatives and various states of nature. For capacity planning situations, the state of nature usually is future demand or market favorability. By assigning probability values to the various states of nature, we can make decisions that maximize the expected value of the alternatives. Example 6 shows how to apply decision trees to a capacity decision.

EXAMPLE 6

Southern Hospital Supplies, a company that makes hospital gowns, is considering capacity expansion. Its major alternatives are to do nothing, build a small plant, build a medium plant, or build a large plant. The new facility would produce a new type of gown, and currently the potential or marketability for this product is unknown. If a large plant is built and a favorable market exists, a profit of $100,000 could be realized. An unfavorable market would yield a $90,000 loss. However, a medium plant would earn a $60,000 profit with a favorable market. A $10,000 loss would result from an unfavorable market. A small plant, on the other hand, would return $40,000 with favorable market conditions and lose only $5,000 in an unfavorable market. Of course, there is always the option of doing nothing.

Recent market research indicates that there is a .4 probability of a favorable market, which means that there is also a .6 probability of an unfavorable market. With this information, the alternative that will result in the highest expected monetary value (EMV) can be selected:

EMV (large plant) = (.4)($100,000) + (.6)(−$90,000) = −$14,000

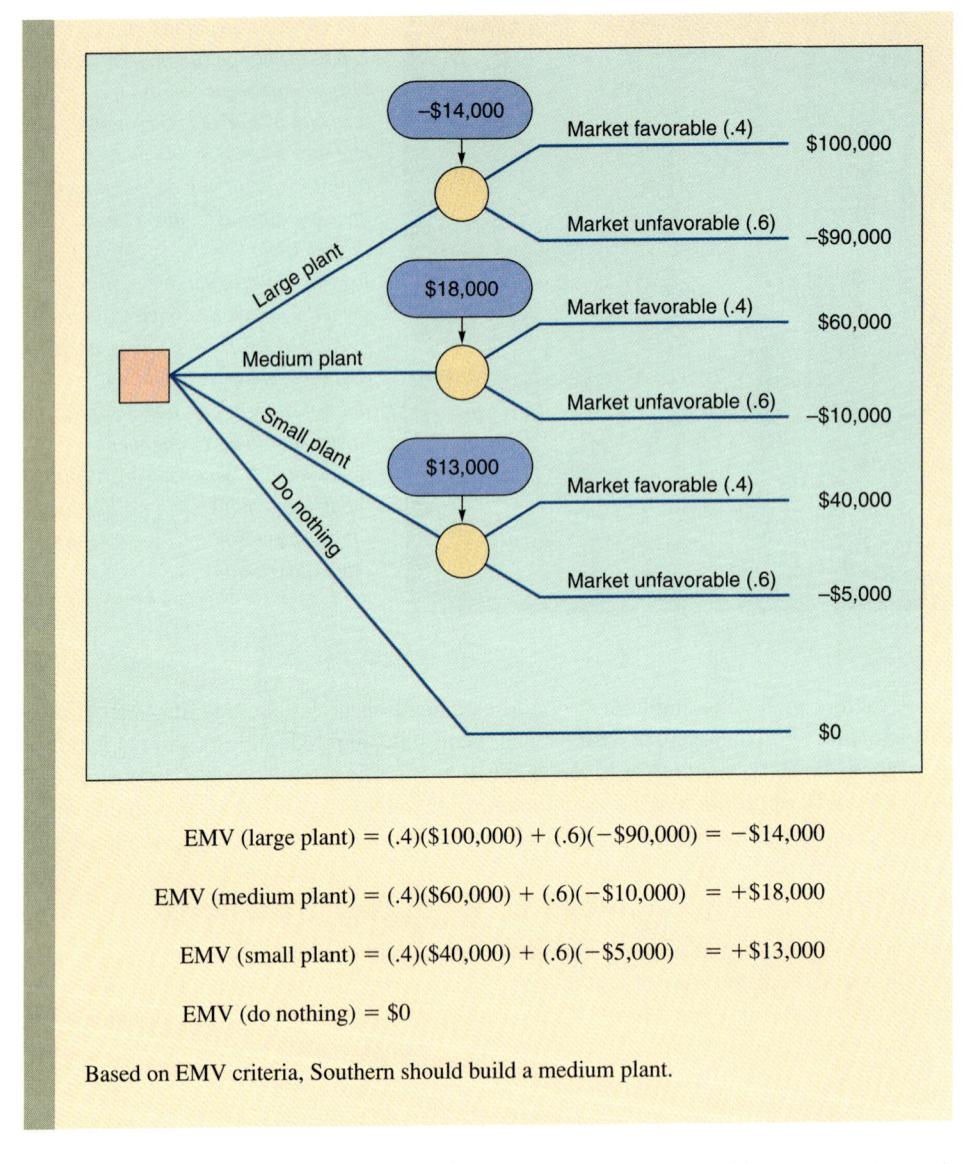

EMV (medium plant) = (.4)($60,000) + (.6)(−$10,000) = +$18,000

EMV (small plant) = (.4)($40,000) + (.6)(−$5,000) = +$13,000

EMV (do nothing) = $0

Based on EMV criteria, Southern should build a medium plant.

Rather than strategically manage capacity, managers may tactically manage demand. Here are some techniques for managing demand.

Managing Demand

Even with good forecasting and facilities built into that forecast, there may be a poor match between the actual demand that occurs and available capacity. A poor match may mean demand exceeds capacity or capacity exceeds demand. However, in both cases firms have options.

Demand Exceeds Capacity When *demand exceeds capacity*, the firm may be able to curtail demand simply by raising prices, scheduling long lead times (which may be inevitable), and discouraging marginally profitable business. Because inadequate facilities reduce revenue below what is possible, the long-term solution is usually to increase capacity.

Capacity Exceeds Demand When *capacity exceeds demand*, the firm may want to stimulate demand through price reductions or aggressive marketing, or it may accommodate the market through product changes.

Adjusting to Seasonal Demands A seasonal or cyclical pattern of demand is another capacity challenge. In such cases, management may find it helpful to offer products with complementing demand patterns—that is, products for which the demand is high for one when low for the other. For example, in Figure 7.10 the firm is adding a line of snowmobile engines to its line of jet ski engines to smooth demand. With appropriate complementing of products, perhaps the utilization of facility, equipment, and personnel can be smoothed.

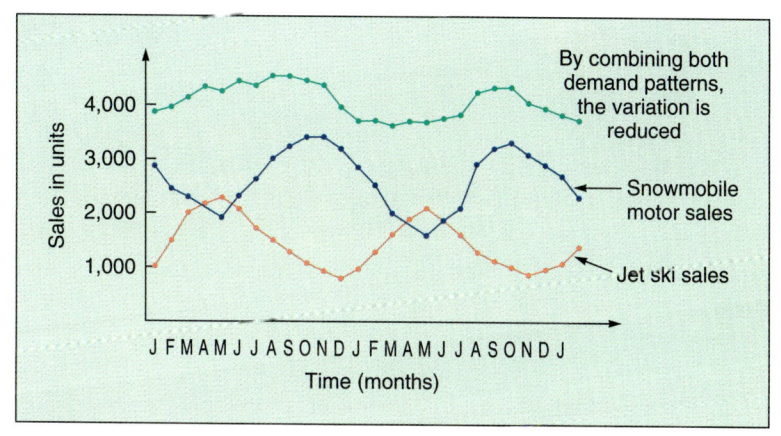

FIGURE 7.10 ■ By Combining Products That Have Complementary Seasonal Patterns, Capacity Can Be Better Utilized
A smoother sales demand contributes to improved scheduling and better human resource strategies.

Tactics for Matching Capacity to Demand Various tactics for matching capacity to demand exist. Internal changes include adjusting the process to a given volume through:

1. Making staffing changes;
2. Adjusting equipment and processes, which might include purchasing additional machinery or selling or leasing existing equipment;
3. Improving methods to increase throughput; and/or
4. Redesigning the product to facilitate more throughput.

The foregoing tactics can be used to adjust demand to existing facilities. The strategic issue is, of course, how to have a facility of the correct size. Break-even analysis helps with that decision.

BREAK-EVEN ANALYSIS

The objective of **break-even analysis** is to find the point, in dollars and units, at which costs equal revenues. This point is the break-even point. As shown in Figure 7.11, break-even analysis requires an estimation of fixed costs, variable costs, and revenue.

Fixed costs are costs that continue even if no units are produced. Examples include depreciation, taxes, debt, and mortgage payments. **Variable costs** are those that vary with

Break-even analysis
A means of finding the point, in dollars and units, at which costs equal revenues.

Fixed costs Costs that continue even if no units are produced.

Variable costs Costs that vary with the volume of units produced; also known as direct costs.

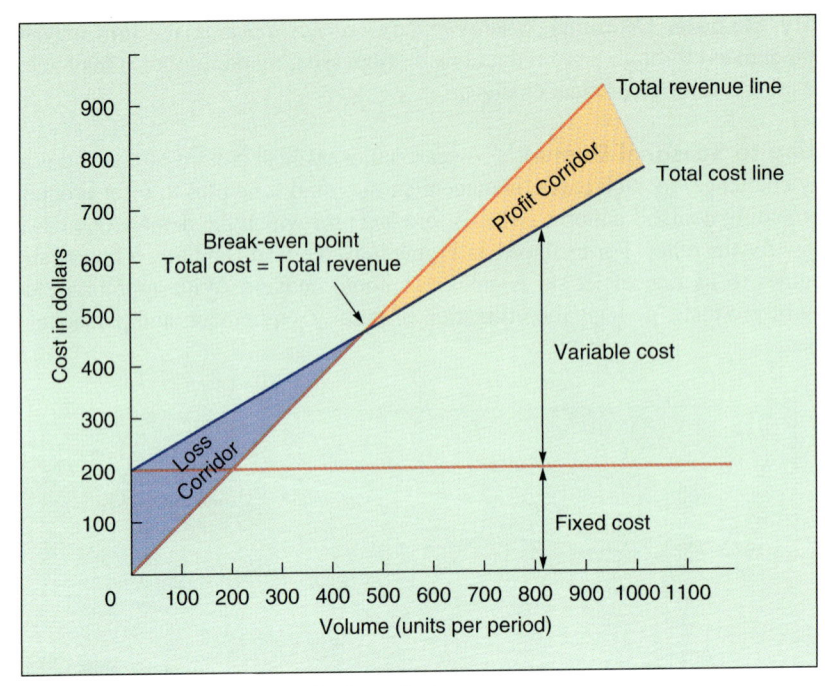

252 CHAPTER 7 PROCESS STRATEGY AND CAPACITY PLANNING

FIGURE 7.11 ■ **Basic Break-Even Point**

the volume of units produced. The major components of variable costs are labor and materials. However, other costs, such as the portion of the utilities that varies with volume, are also variable costs.

Another element in break-even analysis is the **revenue function**. In Figure 7.11, revenue begins at the origin and proceeds upward to the right, increasing by the selling price of each unit. Where the revenue function crosses the total cost line (the sum of fixed and variable costs), is the break-even point, with a profit corridor to the right and a loss corridor to the left.

Revenue function The function in break-even analysis that increases by the selling price of each unit.

Assumptions A number of assumptions underlie this basic break-even model. Notably, costs and revenue are shown as straight lines. They are shown to increase linearly—that is, in direct proportion to the volume of units being produced. However, neither fixed costs nor variable costs (nor, for that matter, the revenue function) need be a straight line. For example, fixed costs change as more capital equipment or warehouse space is used; labor costs change with overtime or as marginally skilled workers are employed; the revenue function may change with such factors as volume discounts.

Graphic Approach The first step in the graphic approach to break-even analysis is to define those costs that are fixed and sum them. The variable costs are then estimated by an analysis of labor, materials, and other costs connected with the production of each unit. The fixed costs are drawn as a horizontal line beginning at that dollar amount on the vertical axis. The variable costs are then shown as an incrementally increasing cost, originating at the intersection of the fixed cost on the vertical axis and increasing with each change in volume as we move to the right on the volume (or horizontal) axis. Both fixed- and variable-cost information is usually available from a firm's cost accounting department, although an industrial engineering department may also maintain cost information.

Fixed costs do not remain constant over all volume; new warehouses and new overhead charges result in step functions in fixed cost.

Virtually *no* variable costs are linear, but we make that assumption here.

Algebraic Approach The respective formulas for the break-even point in units and dollars are shown below. Let:

$BEP(x)$ = Break-even point in units

$BEP(\$)$ = Break-even point in dollars

P = Price per unit (dollars received per unit after all discounts)

x = Number of units produced

TR = Total revenue = Px

F = Fixed costs

V = Variable costs per unit

TC = Total costs = $F + Vx$

Setting total revenue equal to total costs, we get

$$TR = TC$$

or

$$Px = F + Vx$$

Solving for x, we get

$$BEP(x) = \frac{F}{P - V}$$

and

$$BEP(\$) = BEP(x)P$$

$$= \frac{F}{P - V}P = \frac{F}{(P - V)/P}$$

$$= \frac{F}{1 - V/P}$$

$$\text{Profit} = TR - TC$$

$$= Px - (F + Vx)$$

$$= Px - F - Vx$$

$$= (P - V)x - F$$

Using these equations, we can solve directly for break-even point and profitability. The two formulas that are of particular interest are:

These paper machines, recently upgraded at a cost of $500 million by International Paper in Texarkana, Texas, produce bleached board, which is used in cigarette cartons, signs, pharmaceutical boxes, and so on. This huge capital expenditure will result in a high fixed cost, but will allow production of these products at a very low variable cost. The production manager's job is to maintain utilization above the break-even point to achieve profitability.

$$\text{Break-even in units} = \frac{\text{Total fixed cost}}{\text{Price} - \text{Variable cost}} \qquad (7.4)$$

$$\text{Break-even in dollars} = \frac{\text{Total fixed cost}}{1 - \dfrac{\text{Variable cost}}{\text{Selling price}}} \qquad (7.5)$$

Crossover Charts Break-even analysis can aid process selection by identifying the processes with the lowest total cost for the volume expected. Such analysis will, of course, also indicate the largest profit corridor. We are, therefore, able to address two issues: the low-cost process and the absolute amount of profit. Only by directly addressing both issues can the process decision be successful. Figure 7.12 shows three alternative processes compared on a single chart. Such a chart is sometimes called a **crossover chart.** Process A has the lowest cost for volumes below V_1, process B has the lowest cost between V_1 and V_2, and process C has the lowest cost at volumes above V_2.

Crossover chart A chart of costs at the possible volumes for more than one process.

Single-Product Case

In Example 7, we determine the break-even point in dollars and units for one product.

EXAMPLE 7

Jimmy Stephens, Inc., has fixed costs of $10,000 this period. Direct labor is $1.50 per unit, and material is $.75 per unit. The selling price is $4.00 per unit.

The break-even point in dollars is computed as follows:

$$BEP(\$) = \frac{F}{1 - (V/P)} = \frac{\$10,000}{1 - [(1.50 + .75)/(4.00)]} = \frac{\$10,000}{.4375} = \$22,857.14$$

The break-even point in units is

$$BEP(x) = \frac{F}{P - V} = \frac{\$10,000}{4.00 - (1.50 + .75)} = 5,714$$

Note that in this example, we must use the total variable costs (that is, both labor and material).

Algebraic Approach The respective formulas for the break-even point in units and dollars are shown below. Let:

$BEP(x)$ = Break-even point in units

$BEP(\$)$ = Break-even point in dollars

P = Price per unit (dollars received per unit after all discounts)

x = Number of units produced

TR = Total revenue = Px

F = Fixed costs

V = Variable costs per unit

TC = Total costs = $F + Vx$

Setting total revenue equal to total costs, we get

$$TR = TC$$

or

$$Px = F + Vx$$

Solving for x, we get

$$BEP(x) = \frac{F}{P - V}$$

and

$$BEP(\$) = BEP(x)P$$

$$= \frac{F}{P - V} P = \frac{F}{(P - V)/P}$$

$$= \frac{F}{1 - V/P}$$

$$\text{Profit} = татTR - TC$$

$$= Px - (F + Vx)$$

$$= Px - F - Vx$$

$$= (P - V)x - F$$

Using these equations, we can solve directly for break-even point and profitability. The two formulas that are of particular interest are:

254 CHAPTER 7 PROCESS STRATEGY AND CAPACITY PLANNING

These paper machines, recently upgraded at a cost of $500 million by International Paper in Texarkana, Texas, produce bleached board, which is used in cigarette cartons, signs, pharmaceutical boxes, and so on. This huge capital expenditure will result in a high fixed cost, but will allow production of these products at a very low variable cost. The production manager's job is to maintain utilization above the break-even point to achieve profitability.

$$\text{Break-even in units} = \frac{\text{Total fixed cost}}{\text{Price} - \text{Variable cost}} \quad (7.4)$$

$$\text{Break-even in dollars} = \frac{\text{Total fixed cost}}{1 - \dfrac{\text{Variable cost}}{\text{Selling price}}} \quad (7.5)$$

Crossover Charts Break-even analysis can aid process selection by identifying the processes with the lowest total cost for the volume expected. Such analysis will, of course, also indicate the largest profit corridor. We are, therefore, able to address two issues: the low-cost process and the absolute amount of profit. Only by directly addressing both issues can the process decision be successful. Figure 7.12 shows three alternative processes compared on a single chart. Such a chart is sometimes called a **crossover chart**. Process A has the lowest cost for volumes below V_1, process B has the lowest cost between V_1 and V_2, and process C has the lowest cost at volumes above V_2.

Crossover chart A chart of costs at the possible volumes for more than one process.

Single-Product Case

In Example 7, we determine the break-even point in dollars and units for one product.

EXAMPLE 7

Jimmy Stephens, Inc., has fixed costs of $10,000 this period. Direct labor is $1.50 per unit, and material is $.75 per unit. The selling price is $4.00 per unit.

The break-even point in dollars is computed as follows:

$$BEP(\$) = \frac{F}{1 - (V/P)} = \frac{\$10,000}{1 - [(1.50 + .75)/(4.00)]} = \frac{\$10,000}{.4375} = \$22,857.14$$

The break-even point in units is

$$BEP(x) = \frac{F}{P - V} = \frac{\$10,000}{4.00 - (1.50 + .75)} = 5,714$$

Note that in this example, we must use the total variable costs (that is, both labor and material).

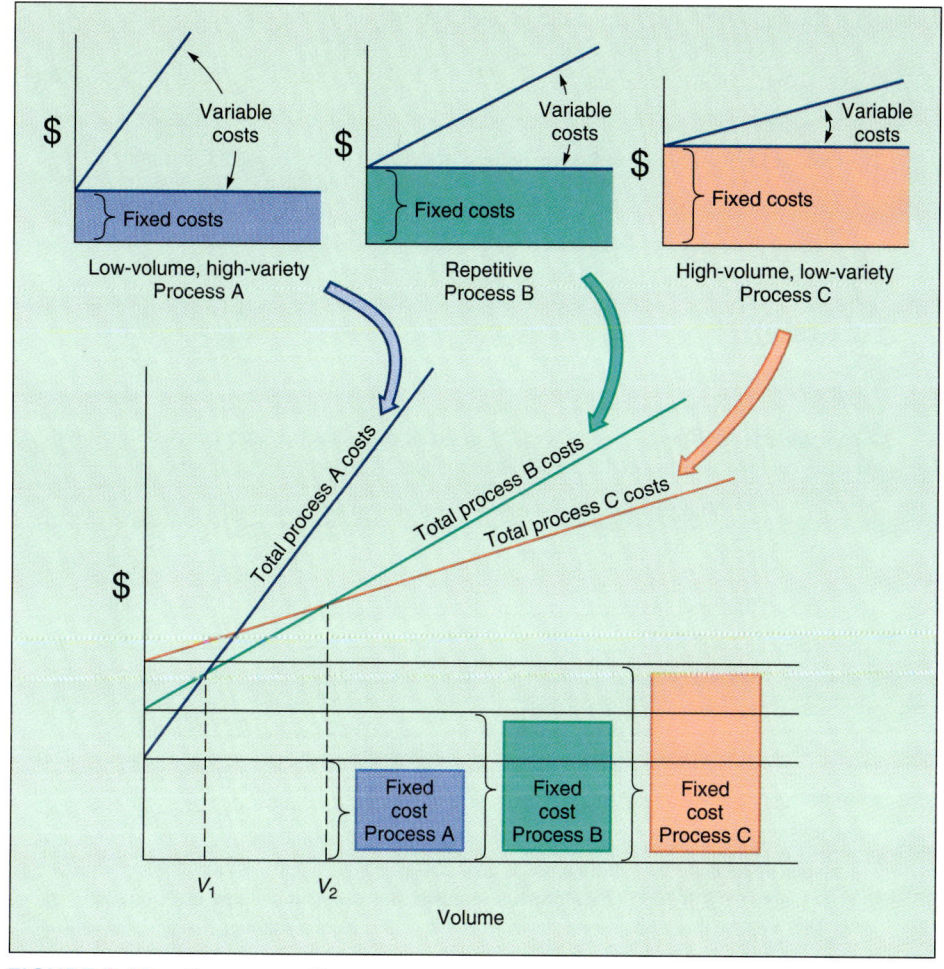

FIGURE 7.12 ■ **Crossover Charts**

Three different processes can be expected to have three different costs. However, at any given volume, only one will have the lowest cost.

Multiproduct Case

Most firms, from manufacturers to restaurants (even fast-food restaurants), have a variety of offerings. Each offering may have a different selling price and variable cost. Utilizing break-even analysis, we modify Equation (7.5) to reflect the proportion of sales for each product. We do this by "weighting" each product's contribution by its proportion of sales. The formula is then

$$BEP(\$) = \frac{F}{\sum\left[\left(1 - \frac{V_i}{P_i}\right) \times (W_i)\right]} \quad (7.6)$$

where V = variable cost per unit
P = price per unit
F = fixed cost
W = percent each product is of total dollar sales
i = each product

EXAMPLE 8

The costs at Le Bistro, a French-style deli, follow. Fixed costs are $3,500 per month.

Item	Price	Cost	Forecasted Sales Units
Sandwich	$2.95	$1.25	7,000
Soft drink	.80	.30	7,000
Baked potato	1.55	.47	5,000
Tea	.75	.25	5,000
Salad bar	2.85	1.00	3,000

With a variety of offerings, we proceed with break-even analysis just as in a single-product case, except that we weight each of the products by its proportion of total sales.

Multiproduct Break-Even–Determining Contribution

1	2	3	4	5	6	7	8
ITEM (i)	SELLING PRICE (P)	VARIABLE COST (V)	(V/P)	1 − (V/P)	FORECASTED SALES $	% OF SALES	WEIGHTED CONTRIBUTION (COL. 5 × COL. 7)
Sandwich	$2.95	$1.25	.42	.58	$20,650	.446	.259
Soft drink	.80	.30	.38	.62	5,600	.121	.075
Baked potato	1.55	.47	.30	.70	7,750	.167	.117
Tea	.75	.25	.33	.67	3,750	.081	.054
Salad bar	2.85	1.00	.35	.65	8,550	.185	.120
					$46,300	1.000	.625

For instance, revenue for sandwiches is $20,650 (2.95 × 7,000), which is 44.6% of the total revenue of $46,300. Therefore, the contribution for sandwiches is "weighted" by .446. The weighted contribution is .446 × .58 = .259. In this manner, its *relative* contribution is properly reflected.

Using this approach for each product, we find that the total weighted contribution is .625 for each dollar sales, and the break-even point in dollars is $67,200:

$$BEP(\$) = \frac{F}{\Sigma\left[\left(1 - \frac{V_i}{P_i}\right) \times (W_i)\right]}$$

$$= \frac{\$3,500 \times 12}{.625} = \frac{\$42,000}{.625}$$

$$= \$67,200$$

The information given in this example implies total daily sales (52 weeks at 6 days each) of

$$\frac{\$67,200}{312 \text{ days}} = \$215.38$$

Break-even figures by product provide the manager with added insight as to the realism of his or her sales forecast. They indicate exactly what must be sold each day, as we have done in Example 9.

EXAMPLE 9

Using the data in Example 8, we take the forecast sandwich sales of 44.6% times the daily break-even of $215.38 divided by the selling price of each sandwich ($2.95). Then sandwich sales must be

$$\frac{.446 \times \$215.38}{\$2.95} = \text{number of sandwiches} = 32.5 \approx 33 \text{ sandwiches each day}$$

Once break-even analysis has been prepared, analyzed, and judged to be reasonable, decisions can be made about the types of equipment needed. Indeed, a better judgment of the likelihood of success of the enterprise can now be made.

STRATEGY-DRIVEN INVESTMENTS

Let us now address the integration of strategy and investment with our process decision. Increasingly, managers realize that sustained profits come from building competitive advantage, not from a good financial return on a specific process.[5] We recommend that the traditional approach to investment analysis (just looking at financial returns) be enhanced by strategic considerations. Specifically, the strategic considerations we suggest are:

1. Select investments as *part of a coordinated strategic plan*. Where are these investments taking the organization? Investments should not be made as isolated expenditures, but as part of a coordinated strategic plan that will place the firm in an advantageous position. The questions to be asked are, "Will these investments eventually win customers?" and "What competitive advantage do we obtain?"
2. Choose investments *yielding a competitive advantage* (process flexibility, speed of delivery, improved quality, and so on).
3. *Consider product life cycles*.
4. Include a *variety of operating factors in the financial return analysis* (for instance, reductions in scrap, rework, floor space, and inventory increase returns).
5. Test investments *in light of several revenue projections* to ensure that upside potential and downside risk are considered.

Once the strategy implications of potential investments have been considered, traditional investment analysis is appropriate. We introduce the investment aspects of process selection next.

The operations manger may be the one held responsible for return-on-investment.

Investment, Variable Cost, and Cash Flow

Because process alternatives exist, so do options regarding capital investment and variable cost. Managers must choose from among different financial options as well as process alternatives. The number of initial alternatives may be large, but analysis of six major factors—cost, volume, human resource constraints, technology, quality, and reliability—typically reduces the number of alternatives to a few. Analysis should show the capital investment, variable cost, and cash flows as well as net present value for each alternative.

Capital investment requires cash flow as well as an evaluation of return on investments.

---

[5] For an excellent discussion on investments that support competitive advantage, see Terry Hill, *Manufacturing Strategy: Text and Cases* (Homewood, IL: Richard D. Irwin, 1989). Also see "Selling Rockwell on Automation," *Business Week*, June 6, 1988, p. 104.

Net Present Value

Net present value A means of determining the discounted value of a series of future cash receipts.

Determining the discount value of a series of future cash receipts is known as the **net present value** technique. By way of introduction, let us consider the time value of money. Say you invest $100.00 in a bank at 5% for 1 year. Your investment will be worth $100.00 + ($100.00)(.05) = $105.00. If you invest the $105.00 for a second year, it will be worth $105.00 + ($105.00)(.05) = $110.25 at the end of the second year. Of course, we could calculate the future value of $100.00 at 5% for as many years as we wanted by simply extending this analysis. However, there is an easier way to express this relationship mathematically. For the first year:

$$\$105 = \$100(1 + .05)$$

For the second year:

$$\$110.25 = \$105(1 + .05) = \$100(1 + .05)^2$$

In general,

$$F = P(1 + i)^N \qquad (7.7)$$

where F = future value (such as $110.25 or $105)
P = present value (such as $100.00)
i = interest rate (such as .05)
N = number of years (such as 1 year or 2 years)

In most investment decisions, however, we are interested in calculating the present value of a series of future cash receipts. Solving for P, we get

$$P = \frac{F}{(1 + i)^N} \qquad (7.8)$$

When the number of years is not too large, the preceding equation is effective. However, when the number of years, N, is large, the formula is cumbersome. For 20 years, you would have to compute $(1 + i)^{20}$. Without a sophisticated calculator, this computation would be difficult. Interest-rate tables, such as Table 7.3, alleviate this situation. First, let us rearrange the present value equation:

TABLE 7.3 ■ Present Value of $1

Year	5%	6%	7%	8%	9%	10%	12%	14%
1	.952	.943	.935	.926	.917	.909	.893	.877
2	.907	.890	.873	.857	.842	.826	.797	.769
3	.864	.840	.816	.794	.772	.751	.712	.675
4	.823	.792	.763	.735	.708	.683	.636	.592
5	.784	.747	.713	.681	.650	.621	.567	.519
6	.746	.705	.666	.630	.596	.564	.507	.456
7	.711	.665	.623	.583	.547	.513	.452	.400
8	.677	.627	.582	.540	.502	.467	.404	.351
9	.645	.592	.544	.500	.460	.424	.361	.308
10	.614	.558	.508	.463	.422	.386	.322	.270
15	.481	.417	.362	.315	.275	.239	.183	.140
20	.377	.312	.258	.215	.178	.149	.104	.073

Strategy-Driven Investments

$$P = \frac{F}{(1+i)^N} = FX \qquad (7.9)$$

where

$$X = \text{a factor defined as} = 1/(1+i)^N \qquad (7.10)$$

and

$$F = \text{future value}$$

Thus, all we have to do is find the factor X and multiply it by F to calculate the present value P. The factors, of course, are a function of the interest rate, i, and the number of years, N. Table 7.3 lists some of these factors.

Equations (7.7), (7.8), and (7.9) are used to determine the present value of one future cash amount, but there are situations in which an investment generates a series of uniform and equal cash amounts. This type of investment is called an *annuity*. For example, an investment might yield $300 per year for 3 years. Of course, you could use Equation (7.7) three times, for 1, 2, and 3 years, but there is a shorter method. Although there is a formula that can be used to solve for the present value of an annual series of uniform and equal cash flows (an annuity), an easy-to-use table has been developed for this purpose. Like the customary present value computations, this calculation involves a factor. The factors for annuities are in Table 7.4. The basic relationship is:

$$S = RX$$

where X = factor from Table 7.4
S = present value of a series of uniform annual receipts
R = receipts that are received every year for the life of the investment (the annuity)

The present value of a uniform annual series of amounts is an extension of the present value of a single amount, and thus Table 7.4 can be directly developed from Table 7.3. The factors for any given interest rate in Table 7.4 are nothing more than the cumulative sum of the values in Table 7.3. In Table 7.3, for example, .952, .907, and .864 are the factors for years 1, 2, and 3 when the interest rate is 5%. The cumulative sum of these factors is 2.723 = .952 + .907 + .864. Now look at the point in Table 7.4 where the interest rate is 5% and the number of years is 3. The factor for the present value of an annuity is 2.723, as you would expect. Table 7.4 can be very helpful in reducing the computations necessary to make financial decisions.

TABLE 7.4 ■ **Present Value of an Annuity of $1**

Year	5%	6%	7%	8%	9%	10%	12%	14%
1	.952	.943	.935	.926	.917	.90	.893	.877
2	1.859	1.833	1.808	1.783	1.759	1.73	1.690	1.647
3	2.723	2.673	2.624	2.577	2.531	2.48	2.402	2.322
4	3.546	3.465	3.387	3.312	3.240	3.17	3.037	2.914
5	4.329	4.212	4.100	3.993	3.890	3.79	3.605	3.433
6	5.076	4.917	4.766	4.623	4.486	4.35	4.111	3.889
7	5.786	5.582	5.389	5.206	5.033	4.86	4.564	4.288
8	6.463	6.210	5.971	5.747	5.535	5.33	4.968	4.639
9	7.108	6.802	6.515	6.247	5.985	5.75	5.328	4.946
10	7.722	7.360	7.024	6.710	6.418	6.14	5.650	5.216
15	10.380	9.712	9.108	8.559	8.060	7.60	6.811	6.142
20	12.462	11.470	10.594	9.818	9.128	8.51	7.469	6.623

Example 10 shows how to determine the present value of an annuity.

EXAMPLE 10

River Road Medical Clinic is thinking of investing in a sophisticated new piece of medical equipment. It will generate $7,000 per year in receipts for 5 years. What is the present value of this cash flow? Assume an interest rate of 6%.

$$S = RX = \$7,000(4.212) = \$29,484$$

The factor from Table 7.4 (4.212) was obtained by finding that value when the interest rate is 6% and the number of years is 5. There is another way of looking at this example. If you went to a bank and took a loan for $29,484 today, your payments would be $7,000 per year for 5 years if the bank used an interest rate of 6% compounded yearly. Thus, $29,484 is the present value.

The net present value method is one of the best methods of ranking investment alternatives. The procedure is straightforward: You simply compute the present value of all cash flows for each investment alternative. When deciding among investment alternatives, you pick the investment with the highest net present value. Similarly, when making several investments, those with higher net present values are preferable to investments with lower net present values.

Example 11 shows how to use the net present value to choose between investment alternatives.

EXAMPLE 11

Quality Plastics, Inc., is considering two different investment alternatives. Investment A has an initial cost of $25,000, and investment B has an initial cost of $26,000. Both investments have a useful life of 4 years. The cash flows for these investments follow. The cost of capital or the interest rate (i) is 8%.

Investment A's Cash Flow	Investment B's Cash Flow	Year	Present Value Factor at 8%
$10,000	$9,000	1	.926
9,000	9,000	2	.857
8,000	9,000	3	.794
7,000	9,000	4	.735

To find the present value of the cash flows for each investment, we multiply the present value factor by the cash flow for each investment for each year. The sum of these present value calculations minus the initial investment is the net present value of each investment. The computations appear in the following table.

Year	Investment A's Present Values	Investment B's Present Values
1	$ 9,260 = (.926)($10,000)	$ 8,334 = (.926)($9,000)
2	7,713 = (.857)($9,000)	7,713 = (.857)($9,000)
3	6,352 = (.794)($8,000)	7,146 = (.794)($9,000)
4	5,145 = (.735)($7,000)	6,615 = (.735)($9,000)
Totals:	$28,470	$29,808
Minus initial investment	−25,000	−26,000
Net present value	$ 3,470	$ 3,808

The net present value criterion shows investment B to be more attractive than investment A because it has a higher present value.

In Example 11, it was not necessary to make all of those present value computations for investment B. Because the cash flows are uniform, Table 7.4, the annuity table, gives the present value factor. Of course, we would expect to get the same answer. As you recall, Table 7.4 gives factors for the present value of an annuity. In this example, for payments of $9,000, cost of capital is 8% and the number of years is 4. Looking at Table 7.4 under 8% and 4 years, we find a factor of 3.312. Thus, the present value of this annuity is (3.312)($9,000) = $29,808, the same value as in Example 11.

Although net present value is one of the best approaches to evaluating investment alternatives, it does have its faults. Limitations of the net present value approach include the following:

1. Investments with the same present value may have significantly different projected lives and different salvage values.
2. Investments with the same net present value may have different cash flows. Different cash flows may make substantial differences in the company's ability to pay its bills.
3. The assumption is that we know future interest rates, which we do not.
4. Payments are always made at the end of the period (week, month, or year), which is not always the case.

SUMMARY

Effective operations managers understand how to use process strategy as a competitive weapon. They select a production process with the necessary quality, flexibility, and cost structure to meet product and volume requirements. They also seek creative ways to combine the low unit cost of high-volume, low-variety manufacturing with the customization available through low-volume, high-variety facilities. Managers use the techniques of lean production and employee participation to encourage the development of efficient proprietary equipment and processes. They design their equipment and processes to have capabilities beyond the tolerance required by their customers, while ensuring the flexibility needed for adjustments in technology, features, and volumes.

Good forecasting, break-even analysis, crossover charts, decision trees, cash flow, and net present value (NPV) techniques are particularly useful to operations managers when making the process decision.

Process investments are made effective by ensuring that the investments support a long-term strategy. The criteria for investment decisions are contribution to the overall strategic plan and winning profitable orders, not just return on investment. Efficient firms select the correct process and the correct capacity that contributes to their long-term strategy.

KEY TERMS

Process strategy *(p. 228)*
Process focus *(p. 229)*
Repetitive process *(p. 230)*
Modules *(p. 230)*
Product focus *(p. 232)*
Flexibility *(p. 234)*
Mass customization *(p. 234)*
Flow diagram *(p. 236)*
Process charts *(p. 236)*
Time function mapping (or process mapping) *(p. 237)*
Work-flow analysis *(p. 237)*
Process reengineering *(p. 239)*

Lean producers *(p. 239)*
Green manufacturing *(p. 246)*
Capacity *(p. 246)*
Effective capacity *(p. 246)*
Efficiency *(p. 247)*
Rated capacity *(p. 247)*
Break-even analysis *(p. 251)*
Fixed costs *(p. 251)*
Variable costs *(p. 251)*
Revenue function *(p. 252)*
Crossover chart *(p. 254)*
Net present value *(p. 258)*

USING EXCEL OM FOR BREAK-EVEN ANALYSIS

Excel OM's Break-Even Analysis module is illustrated in Programs 7.1 and 7.2. Using Jimmy Stephens Inc. data from Example 7, Program 7.1 shows input data and the Excel formulas used to compute the break-even points and optional volume analysis. Program 7.2 provides the solution and graphical output.

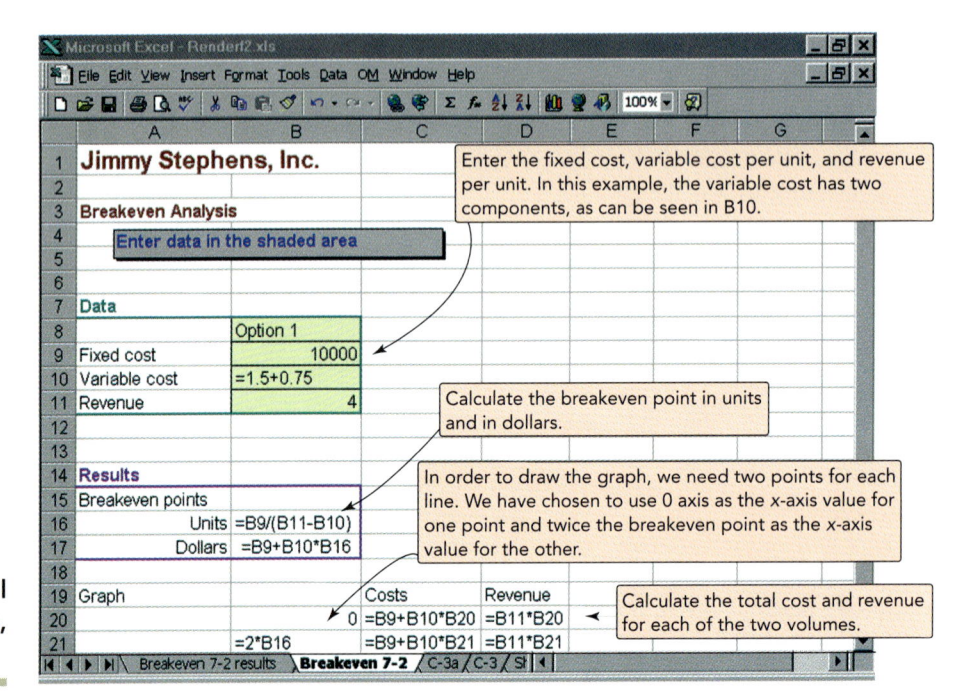

PROGRAM 7.1 ■ Excel OM's Break-Even Analysis, Using Example 7 Data

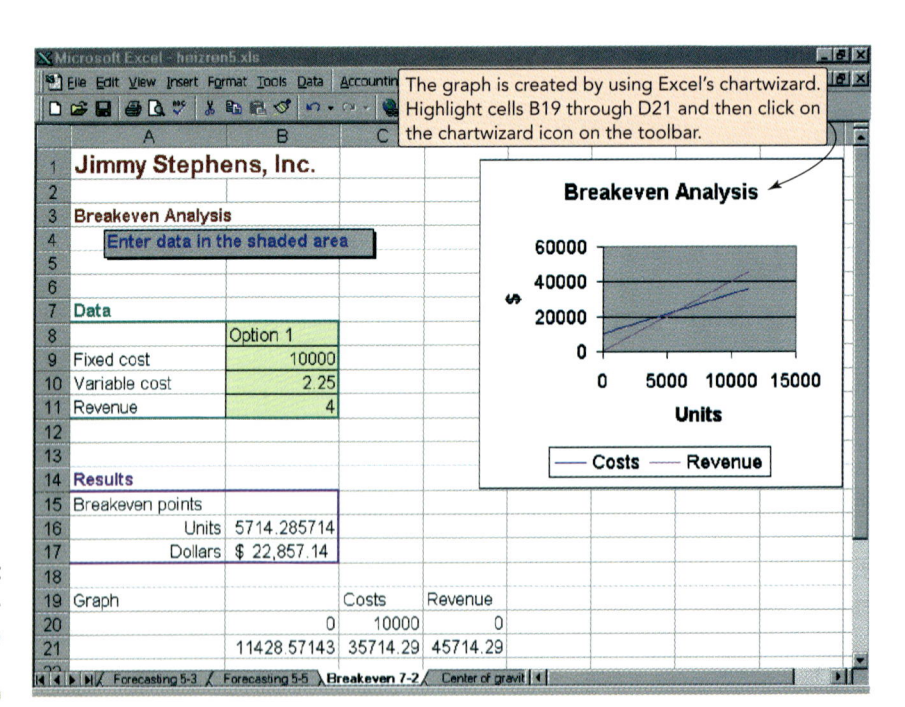

PROGRAM 7.2 ■ Output From Program 7.1, Including Optional Cost-Volume Graph

SOLVED PROBLEMS

Solved Problem 7.1

Sara James Bakery, described earlier in Example 5, has decided to increase its facilities by adding one additional process line. The firm will have 4 process lines, each working 7 days a week, 3 shifts per day, 8 hours per shift. Effective capacity is 90%. This addition, however, will reduce overall system efficiency to 85%. Compute the new rated capacity with this change in facilities.

Solution

$$\text{Rated capacity} = (\text{Capacity})(\text{Effective capacity})(\text{Efficiency})$$

$$= [(120)(4 \times 7 \times 3 \times 8)](.9)(.85)$$

$$= (80{,}640)(.9)(.85)$$

$$= 61{,}689.6 \text{ per week}$$

or

$$= (120)(4)(.9)(.85)$$

$$= 367.2 \text{ per hour}$$

Solved Problem 7.2

Marty McDonald works part-time packaging software in Wisconsin. His annual fixed cost is $10,000, direct labor is $3.50 per package, and material is $4.50 per package. The selling price will be $12.50 per package. What is the break-even point in dollars? What is break-even in units?

Solution

$$BEP(\$) = \frac{F}{1 - (V/P)} = \frac{\$10{,}000}{1 - (\$8.00/\$12.50)} = \frac{\$10{,}000}{.36} = \$27{,}777$$

$$BEP(x) = \frac{F}{P - V} = \frac{\$10{,}000}{\$12.50 - \$8.00} = \frac{\$10{,}000}{\$4.50} = 2{,}222 \text{ units}$$

DISCUSSION QUESTIONS

1. What are the advantages of standardization? How do we obtain variety while maintaining standardization?
2. What type of process is used for each of the following?
   a) beer
   b) business cards
   c) automobiles
   d) telephone
   e) "Big Macs"
   f) custom homes
3. In an affluent society, how do we produce a wide number of options for products at low cost?
4. What products would you expect to have made by a repetitive process?

5. Where does the manager obtain data for break-even analysis?
6. What keeps plotted variable and fixed-cost data from falling on a straight line?
7. What keeps plotted revenue data from falling on a straight line?
8. What are the assumptions of break-even analysis?
9. How might we isolate the production/operations process from the customer?
10. What are assumptions of the net present value technique?
11. Identify two services located at the process-focused side of the process strategy continuum (Figure 7.5).
12. Identify two services located at the product-focused side of the process strategy continuum (Figure 7.5).
13. Identify two services that are organized as repetitive.
14. Identify a service firm at each position on our process strategy continuum (process focused, repetitive, and product focused; Figure 7.5) and show how it competes (low cost, differentiation, or rapid response).
15. Identify a manufacturing firm at each position on our process strategy continuum (process focused, repetitive, and product focused; Figure 7.5) and show how it competes (low cost, differentiation, or response).
16. Distinguish between designed capacity, effective capacity, and efficiency.

CRITICAL THINKING EXERCISE

Premium Standard Farms, the firm described in the *OM in Action* box "Uniform Pigs Contribute to Efficiency," has turned pig production into a commodity—like toasters. Impregnated female sows wait for 40 days in metal stalls so small that they cannot turn around. After an ultrasound test, they wait 67 days in a similar stall until they give birth. Two weeks after delivering 10 or 11 piglets, the sows are moved back to breeding rooms for another cycle. After 3 years, the sow is slaughtered. Animal-welfare advocates say such confinement drives pigs crazy. Premium Standard replies that its hogs are in fact comfortable, arguing that only 1% die before Premium Standard wants them to. Discuss the productivity and ethical implications of this industry and these two divergent opinions.

PROBLEMS

7.1 River Road Medical Clinic, which runs an optometrist lab, experienced substantial growth over the last decade. It purchased additional increments of lens-grinding equipment in relatively small units. Prior analysis of its data (since its growth has been steady and constant) suggests that regression analysis (as described in chapter 5) is adequate to determine its capacity demands. Data for the past decade follow:

Year	1989	1990	1991	1992	1993	1994	1995	1996	1997	1998
Units Produced (in thousands)	15.0	15.5	16.25	16.75	16.9	17.24	17.5	17.3	17.75	18.1

   a) Determine the firm's capacity needs in units for 1999, 2001, and 2005.
   b) If each machine is capable of producing 2,500 lenses, how many machines should it expect to have in 2001?

7.2 Assume that in 1999, River Road Medical Clinic (Problem 7.1) has 8 machines, each capable of producing 2,500 lenses per year. However, the new and best machine then on the market has the capability of producing 5,000 per year.
   a) What is the status of capacity at the firm in the year 2005 if it buys the new and best machine in 1999?
   b) What is the status of capacity at the firm in the year 2005 if it buys the standard machine with a capacity of 2,500?

- **7.3** A work center operates 2 shifts per day 5 days per week (8 hours per shift) and has 4 machines of equal capability. If the machines are utilized 80% of the time at a system efficiency of 95%, what is the rated output in standard hours per week?
- **7.4** The minutes available for the next quarter of 1999 at MMU Mfg. in Waco, Texas, for each of three departments is shown. Recent data on effective capacity and efficiency are also shown.

Department	Minutes Available	Effective Capacity	Recent Efficiency
Design	93,600	.92	.95
Fabrication	156,000	.95	1.03
Finishing	62,400	.96	1.05

  Compute the expected capacity for next quarter for each department.
- **7.5** Butch Porter Manufacturing intends to increase capacity by overcoming a bottleneck operation through the addition of new equipment. Two vendors have presented proposals. The fixed costs for proposal A are $50,000 and $70,000 for proposal B. The variable cost for A is $12.00 and $10.00 for B. The revenue generated by each unit is $20.00.
  - a) What is the break-even point in units for proposal A?
  - b) What is the break-even point in units for proposal B?
- **7.6** You are given the data in Problem 7.5:
  - a) What is the break-even point in dollars for proposal A?
  - b) What is the break-even point in dollars for proposal B?
- **7.7** Given the data in Problem 7.5, at what volume (units) of output would the two alternatives yield the same profit?
- **7.8** Use the same data in Problem 7.5:
  - a) If the expected volume is 8,500 units, which alternative should be chosen?
  - b) If the expected volume is 15,000 units, which alternative should be chosen?
- **7.9** What is the net present value of an investment that costs $123,545, and has a salvage value of $44,560? The annual profit from the investment is $14,667 each year for 5 years. The cost of capital at this risk level is 12%.
- **7.10** The initial cost of an investment is $65,000 and the cost of capital is 10%. The return is $16,000 per year for 8 years. What is the net present value?
- **7.11** An investment will produce $1,000 2 years from now. What is the amount worth today? That is, what is the present value if the interest rate is 9%?
- **7.12** What is the present value of $5,600 when the interest rate is 8% and the return of $5,600 will not be received for 15 years?
- **7.13** Mr. Kulonda, VP of Operations at McClain Manufacturing, has to make a decision between two investment alternatives. Investment A has an initial cost of $61,000, and investment B has an initial cost of $74,000. The useful life of investment A is 6 years; the useful life of investment B is 7 years. Given a cost of capital of 9% and the following cash flows for each alternative, determine the most desirable investment alternative according to the net present value criterion.

Investment A's Cash Flow	Investment B's Cash Flow	Year
$19,000	$19,000	1
19,000	20,000	2
19,000	21,000	3
19,000	22,000	4
19,000	21,000	5
19,000	20,000	6
19,000	11,000	7

: 7.14 An electronics firm is currently manufacturing an item that has a variable cost of $.50 per unit and a selling price of $1.00 per unit. Fixed costs are $14,000. Current volume is 30,000 units. The firm can substantially improve the product quality by adding a new piece of equipment at an additional fixed cost of $6,000. Variable cost would increase to $.60, but volume should jump to 50,000 units due to a higher-quality product. Should the company buy the new equipment?

: 7.15 The electronics firm in Problem 7.14 is now considering the new equipment and increasing the selling price to $1.10 per unit. With the higher-quality product, the new volume is expected to be 45,000 units. Under these circumstances, should the company purchase the new equipment and increase the selling price?

· 7.16 Given the following data, calculate $BEP(x)$, $BEP(\$)$, and the profit at 100,000 units:

$$P = \$8/\text{unit} \qquad V = \$4/\text{unit} \qquad F = \$50,000$$

: 7.17 Kathleen Bentley has been asked to evaluate two machines. After some investigation, she determines that they have the following costs. She is told to assume that
a) the life of each machine is 3 years.
b) the company thinks it knows how to make 12% on investments no more risky than this one.

	Machine A	Machine B
Original cost	$10,000	$20,000
Labor per year	2,000	4,000
Maintenance per year	4,000	1,000
Salvage value	2,000	7,000

Determine, via the present value method, which machine Kathleen should recommend.

: 7.18 Your boss has told you to evaluate two ovens for Tink-the-Tinkers, a gourmet sandwich shop. After some questioning of vendors and receipt of specifications, you are assured that the ovens have the attributes and costs shown in the table below. The following two assumptions are appropriate:
1. The life of each machine is 5 years.
2. The company thinks it knows how to make 14% on investments no more risky than this one.

	Three Small Ovens at $1,250 Each	Two Large High-Quality Ovens at $2,500 Each
Original cost	$3,750	$5,000
Labor per year in excess of larger models	$ 750 (total)	
Cleaning/maintenance	$ 750 ($250 each)	$ 400 ($200 each)
Salvage value	$ 750 ($250 each)	$1,000 ($500 each)

a) Determine via the present value method which machine to tell your boss to purchase.
b) What assumption are you making about the ovens?
c) What assumptions are you making in your methodology?

: 7.19 Tom Miller and Jeff Vollmann have opened a copy service on Commonwealth Avenue. They estimate their fixed cost at $12,000 and their variable cost of each copy sold at $.01. They expect their selling price to average $.05.
a) What is their break-even point in dollars?
b) What is their break-even point in units?

7.20 Dr. Aleda Roth, a prolific author, is considering starting her own publishing company. She will call it DSI Publishing, Inc. DSI's estimated costs are

Fixed	$250,000.00
Variable cost per book	$20.00
Selling price per book	$30.00

How many books must DSI sell to break even?

7.21 In addition to the costs in Problem 7.20, Dr. Roth wants to pay herself a salary of $50,000 per year.
a) Now what is her break-even point in units?
b) What is her break-even point in dollars?

7.22 As a prospective owner of a club known as the Red Rose, you are interested in determining the volume of sales dollars necessary for the coming year to reach the break-even point. You have decided to break down the sales for the club into four categories, the first category being liquor and beer. Your estimate of the beer sales is that 30,000 drinks will be served. The selling price for each unit will average $1.50; the cost is $.75. The second major category is meals, which you expect to be 10,000 units with an average price of $10.00 and a cost of $5.00. The third major category is desserts and wine, of which you also expect to sell 10,000 units, but with an average price of $2.50 per unit sold and a cost of $1.00 per unit. The final category is lunches and inexpensive sandwiches, which you expect to total 20,000 units at an average price of $6.25 with a food cost of $3.25. Your fixed cost (that is, rent, utilities, and so on) is $1,800 per month plus $2,000 per month for entertainment.
a) What is your break-even point in dollars per month?
b) What is the expected number of meals each day if you are open 360 days a year?

7.23 Using the data in Problem 7.22, make the problem more realistic by adding labor cost at one-third the total cost of meals and sandwiches. Also add variable expenses (kitchen supplies, tablecloths, napkins, and so on) at 10% of cost for all categories.
a) What is your break-even point?
b) If you expect to make a profit of $35,000 (before taxes) for your 12-hour days, what must your total sales be?

7.24 As operations manager of Baby Furniture, Inc., you must make a decision about expanding your line of nursery furniture (that is, cribs, toy chests, dressers, and so on). In discussing the possibilities with your sales manager, Betsy Waugh-McCollum, you decide that there will definitely be a market and that your firm should enter that market. However, because nursery furniture is often painted rather than stained, you decide you need another process line. There is no doubt in your mind about the decision, and you are sure that you should have a second process. But you do question how large to make it. A large process line is going to cost $300,000; a small process line will cost $200,000. The question, therefore, is the demand for nursery furniture. After extensive discussion with Mrs. Waugh-McCollum and Mr. Utecht of Utecht Market Research, Inc., you determine that the best estimate you can make is that there is a two-out-of-three chance of profit from sales as large as $600,000 and a one-out-of-three chance as low as $300,000.

With a large process line, you could handle the high figure of $600,000. However, with a small process line you could not and would be forced to expand (at a cost of $150,000), after which time your profit from sales would be $500,000 rather than the $600,000 because of the lost time in expanding the process. If you do not expand the small process, your profit from sales would be held to $400,000. If you build a small process and the demand is low, you can handle all of the demand.

Should you open a large or small process line?

7.25 You are the new manager of the university basketball concession booths. You have been told in no uncertain terms that concession sales will support themselves. The following table provides the information you have been able to put together thus far:

Item	Selling Price	Variable Cost	% of Revenue
Soft drink			
Large	$1.10	$ .65	10
Medium	.75	.45	10
Small	.60	.40	20
Hot dog	.75	.45	10
Coffee	.50	.25	20
Miscellaneous snacks	.40	.30	30

Last year's manager, La Tonya Thompson, has advised you to be sure to add 10% of variable cost as a waste allowance for all categories.

You estimate labor cost to be $250.00 (5 booths with 3 people each). Even if nothing is sold, your cost will be $250.00, so you decide to consider this a fixed cost. Booth rental, which is a contractual cost at $50.00 *each* per game, is also a fixed cost.

a) What is break-even volume for all booths per game?
b) How many hot dogs would you expect to sell at the break-even point?

7.26 Rank the following investments according to net present value. Each alternative requires an initial investment of $20,000. Assume a 10% cost of capital.

Year	Cash Flow from Investment 1	Cash Flow from Investment 2	Cash Flow from Investment 3
1	$ 1,000	$ 7,000	$10,000
2	1,000	6,000	5,000
3	3,000	5,000	3,000
4	15,000	4,000	2,000
5	3,000	4,000	1,000
6	1,000	4,000	1,000
7	—	4,000	1,000
8	1,000	2,000	—
9	—	—	1,000

Case Study

Matthew Yachts, Inc.

Matthew Yachts, located in Montauk, Long Island, manufactured sailing yachts of all descriptions. The company began by building custom-designed yachts for a largely New York–based clientele. Custom-designed yachts still accounted for three fifths of Matthew's unit sales and four fifths of its dollar sales and earnings. Over the years, as Matthew Yachts' reputation for quality design and workmanship spread, sales broadened to cover all of the eastern seaboard.

To capitalize on this increased recognition and to secure a piece of the fastest growing market in sailing, Matthew Yachts began manufacturing a new standard, fixed-design craft. Matthew attacked only the high end of this market, as the boat measured 37 feet long. Nevertheless, even this end of the market was more price-sensitive and less conscious of performance than Matthew Yachts' custom-design customers were.

All of the company's yachts were manufactured at the Montauk plant and shared the same equipment and skilled labor force. Custom designs were given priority in scheduling, and the new boat was rotated into the schedule only when custom design demand slackened. As sales of the fixed-design boat increased, however, scheduling the new boat on a regular basis became necessary.

Matthew Yachts were built from the bottom up. Fabricating hulls was the first step. Increasingly, fiberglass hulls were demanded for their speed and easy maintenance. Afterward came the below-decks woodworking, followed by the fiberglass and woodworking on the deck itself. The masts were turned and drilled separately. Masts and hull were then joined and the finish work completed.

Over the past year, the fixed-design craft continued its steady increase in sales. However, costs were increasing and deliveries began to slide precipitously, especially on the fixed-design yachts. During this period, when push came to shove, construction of the fixed-design craft always yielded time and resources to the higher-profit-margin custom designs. As a result, many fixed-design yachts were strewn around the yard in various stages of construction. Moreover, space in the existing shipyard was becoming scarce, and a plant expansion of one sort or another appeared inevitable.

Discussion Questions

1. Should Matthew Yachts, Inc., stay in the business of building standard, fixed-design yachts?
2. If Matthew does so, how should it continue?

Source: Roger W. Schmenner, *Production/Operations Management*, 5th ed. (New York: Macmillan, 1993), p. 517.

Video Case 4

Process Strategy at Wheeled Coach

Wheeled Coach, based in Winter Park, Florida, is the world's largest manufacturer of ambulances. Working four 10-hour days, 350 employees make only custom-made ambulances: virtually every vehicle is different. Wheeled Coach accommodates the marketplace by providing a wide variety of options and an engineering staff accustomed to innovation and custom design. Continuing growth, which now requires that more than 20 ambulances roll off the assembly line each week, makes process design a continuing challenge. Wheeled Coach's response has been to build a focused factory: Wheeled Coach builds nothing but ambulances. Within the focused factory, Wheeled Coach established work cells for every major module feeding an assembly line, including aluminum bodies, electrical wiring harnesses, interior cabinets, windows, painting, and upholstery.

Labor standards drive the schedule so that every work cell feeds the assembly line on schedule, just-in-time for installations. The chassis, usually that of a Ford truck, moves to a station at which the aluminum body is mounted. Then the vehicle is moved to painting. Following a custom paint job, it moves to the assembly line, where it will spend seven days. During each of these 7 work days, each work cell delivers its respective module to the appropriate position on the assembly line. During the first day, electrical wiring is installed; on the second day, the unit moves forward to the station at which cabinetry is delivered and installed, then to a window and lighting station, on to upholstery, to fit and finish, to further customizing and finally to inspection and road testing. The *Global Company Profile* featuring Wheeled Coach (which opens chapter 14) provides further details about this process.

Discussion Questions

1. Why do you think major auto manufacturers do not build ambulances?
2. What is an alternative process strategy to the assembly line that Wheeled Coach currently uses?
3. Why is it more efficient for the work cells to prepare "modules" and deliver them to the assembly line than it would be to produce the component (e.g., interior upholstery) on the line?
4. How does Wheeled Coach determine what tasks are to be performed at each work station?

BIBLIOGRAPHY

Berry, Leonard L. *Great Service.* New York: The Free Press, 1995.

Berry, W. L., C. C. Bozarth, T. J. Hill, and J. E. Klompmaker. "Factory Focus: Segmenting Markets from an Operations Perspective." *Journal of Operations Management* 10, no. 3 (August 1991): 363.

Burbidge, J. L. "Production Flow Analysis for Planning Group Technology." *Journal of Operations Management* 10, no. 1 (January 1991): 5–27.

Bylinsky, G. "Manufacturing for Reuse." *Fortune,* February 6, 1995, pp. 102–112.

Cattanach, R. E., et al. *The Handbook of Environmentally Conscious Manufacturing.* Homewood, IL: Irwin Professional Publishing, 1995.

Ettlie, J. E. "What Makes a Manufacturing Firm Innovative." *The Executive,* November 1990, p. 10.

Ettlie, J. E., and E. M. Reza. "Organizational Integration and Process Innovation." *The Academy of Management Journal,* October 1992, p. 795.

Hall, Robert W., "Next Generation Manufacturing," *Target* 13, no. 1 (1997): 18–21.

Heizer, J. H. "Manufacturing Productivity: Japanese Techniques Not Enough." *Industrial Management,* September–October 1986, pp. 21–23.

Hounshell, D. A. *From the American System to Mass Production, 1800–1932.* Baltimore: Johns Hopkins University Press, 1984.

Mansfield, E. "The Diffusion of Flexible Manufacturing Systems in Japan, Europe, and the United States." *Management Science* 39, no. 2 (February 1993): 149–159.

McCutcheon, D. M., A. S. Raturi, and J. R. Meredith. "The Customization-Responsiveness Squeeze." *Sloan Management Review* 35, no. 2 (winter 1994): 89–100.

Morris, J. S., and R. J. Tersine. "A Simulation Analysis of Factors Influencing the Attractiveness of Group Technology Cellular Layout." *Management Science* 36 (December 1990): 1567–1578.

Parsaei, H. R., and A. Mital. *Economic Aspects of Advanced Production and Manufacturing Systems.* New York: Van Nostrand Reinhold, 1991.

Pine, B. J., II. *Mass Customization: The New Frontier in Business Competition.* Boston: Harvard Business School Press, 1993.

Primrose, P. *Investment in Manufacturing Technology.* New York: Van Nostrand Reinhold, 1991.

Russell, R. S., P. Y. Huang, and Y. Leu. "A Study of Labor Allocation Strategies in Cellular Manufacturing." *Decision Sciences* 22 (July–August 1991): 594.

Schonberger, Richard. *Building a Chain of Customers.* New York: The Free Press, 1995.

INTERNET RESOURCES

Agility Forum:
http://www.agilityforum.org

American Consulting Engineers Council:
http://www.acec.org

Association for Manufacturing Excellence:
http://www.ame.org

Business Process Reengineering Study Group:
http://www.bprsg.org.uk

Business Process Reengineering on-line
learning center tutorial: http://www.prosci.com/index.htm

Process Innovation (Department of Defense):
http://www.dtic.dla.mil/c3i/bpred/

SUPPLEMENT 7

STATE-OF-THE-ART TECHNOLOGY IN OPERATIONS

SUPPLEMENT OUTLINE

DESIGN TECHNOLOGY
  Computer-Aided Design (CAD)
  Standard for the Exchange of Product Data (STEP)
  Computer-Aided Manufacturing (CAM)
  Virtual Reality Technology
PRODUCTION TECHNOLOGY
  Numerical Control
  Process Control
  Vision Systems
  Robots
  Automated Storage and Retrieval System (ASRS)
  Automated Guided Vehicle (AGV)
  Flexible Manufacturing System (FMS)
  Computer-Integrated Manufacturing (CIM)

TECHNOLOGY IN SERVICES
INFORMATION SCIENCES IN OPERATIONS
  Transaction Processing
  Management Information System (MIS)
  The Internet
  Artificial Intelligence
MANAGING TECHNOLOGY IN A GLOBAL ENVIRONMENT
SUMMARY
KEY TERMS
DISCUSSION QUESTIONS
PROBLEMS
CASE STUDY: ROCHESTER MANUFACTURING CORPORATION
BIBLIOGRAPHY
INTERNET RESOURCES

LEARNING OBJECTIVES

When you complete this supplement you should be able to:

Identify or Define:
  Computer-aided design (CAD)
  Computer-aided manufacturing (CAM)
  Numerical control
  Process control
  Fuzzy logic
  Neural networks

Describe or Explain:
  Virtual reality in operations
  Flexible manufacturing systems (FMS)
  Computer-integrated manufacturing (CIM)
  Manufacturing uses of MIS
  Uses of the Internet in operations
  Expert systems

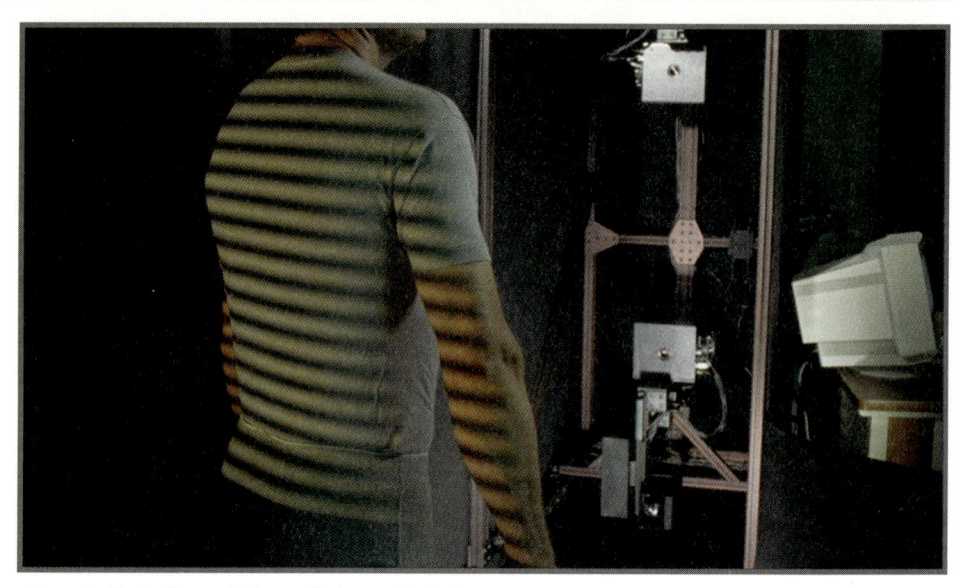

About half of all people buy off-the-rack clothing that does not fit well. With alterations posing such an expensive option, Textile/Clothing Technology Corp. (TC²) thinks it has the solution with **mass customization.** *Here is how TC²'s technology works. A person who has been outfitted in tight-fitting clothes enters a booth loaded with sensors and video cameras. The result, in 2 seconds, is 1.4 million data points in 3-D. The data points are then refined and a standard garment pattern is modified to the customer's dimensions. The digital data for the pattern are then sent to an agile factory where an automated pattern-adjustment system drives a laser, which cuts the cloth that is sewn into the final garment. Using this combination of lasers, electronic communication, automated equipment, and flexible sewing processes, TC² is able to deliver custom clothes in a few days.*
Sources: New York Times (February 19, 1996): C3 and (March 20, 1996): C1, C6.

Tremendous advances are being made in technology. That technology comes in many varieties, from custom clothing designs sent across continents, to innovative forms of production equipment such as lasers and robots. Technology is a significant ingredient in virtually all operations decisions, and opportunities for its innovative use exist throughout OM. Firms that know how to use technology find it an excellent vehicle for obtaining competitive advantage.[1] In this supplement, we look primarily at the electronic flow of information and how it improves operations management. The impact of this technology is pervasive.

DESIGN TECHNOLOGY

> Although technology is not a cure-all, managing technology is certainly a major ingredient in building firms with a future.

Among the tools provided by the information sciences that contribute to better, cheaper, and more rapidly designed products are (1) computer-aided design (CAD), (2) an exchange of information standard known as STEP, (3) computer-aided manufacturing (CAM), and (4) virtual reality technology.

---

[1] For instance, see discussions on the strategic uses of technology in product innovation in E. B. Roberts, "The Success of High-Technology Firms: Early Technological and Marketing Influences," *Interfaces* 22, no. 4 (July–August 1992): 3; Marco Iansiti and Jonathon West, "Technology Integration: Turning Great Research into Great Products," *Harvard Business Review* (May–June 1997): 69–82; and Joseph Morone, "Strategic Use of Technology," *California Management Review,* summer 1989, pp. 81–110.

Computer-Aided Design (CAD)

Computer-aided design (CAD) is the use of computers to interactively design products and prepare engineering documentation. Although the use and variety of CAD software is extensive, most of it is still used for drafting and three-dimensional drawings. However, its use is rapidly expanding. For instance, specialized CAD software exists for design and testing applications from electronic circuits to printed-circuit-board design. Still other CAD software is used for mechanical applications, including analysis of heat or stress.

CAD software allows designers to save time and money by shortening development cycles for virtually all products. The speed and ease with which sophisticated designs can be manipulated, analyzed, and modified with CAD makes review of numerous options possible before final commitments are made. Faster development, better products, accurate flow of information to other departments—all contribute to a tremendous payoff for CAD. The payoff is particularly significant because most product costs are determined at the design stage.[2]

Two extensions of CAD technology are Design for Manufacture and Assembly (DFMA) and 3-D object modeling. Both contribute to improved designs and faster product development.

DFMA DFMA software focuses on the effect of design upon assembly. It allows designers to examine the integration of product designs before the product is manufactured. For instance, DFMA allows automobile designers to examine how a transmission will be placed in a car on the production line, even while both the transmission and the car are still in the design stage. Changes are made rapidly and inexpensively at this stage. Ford Motor Co. believes that DFMA has reduced some of its manufacturing costs by 30%.

3-D Object Modeling 3-D object modeling allows the building of small models. This technology is particularly useful for small prototype development (as shown in the photo on page 274). 3-D object modeling rapidly builds up a model in very thin layers of synthetic materials for evaluation. This technology speeds development by avoiding a more lengthy and formal manufacturing process.

Standard for the Exchange of Product Data (STEP)

CAD technologies are based on electronic product-design information in digital form. This digital information has proven so important that a standard for its exchange has been developed known as **Standard for the Exchange of Product Data (STEP)**. STEP permits manufacturers to express 3-D product information in a standard format so it can be exchanged internationally, allowing geographically dispersed manufacturers to integrate design, manufacture, and support processes.[3]

Using STEP, Ford engineers are putting together designs on three continents. Engineers in England now electronically transmit detailed 3-D drawings to designers in Dearborn, Michigan, and subsequently to a design shop in Turin, Italy, where a computerized milling machine can turn out a model in a matter of hours.[4] STEP enhances collaboration, using talent wherever it is in the world, and at the same time reducing design lead time and development cost.

Computer-aided design (CAD) Interactive use of a computer to develop and document a design.

CAD implies computer-aided mechanical drafting. CAID implies computer-aided industrial design. MCAE implies mechanical computer-aided engineering. CAE implies computer-aided electronics engineering.

Computer-aided design (CAD) techniques are now used in mechanical engineering, electrical engineering, and even modeling large complex molecules.

STEP (Standard for the Exchange of Product Data) Provides a format allowing the electronic transmittal of three-dimensional data. It is defined in the European Community's ISO 10303.

---

[2] See Mohan V. Tatikunda, "Design for Assembly: A Critical Methodology for Product Reengineering and New Product Development," *Production and Inventory Management Journal*, first quarter 1994, pp. 31–38.

[3] The STEP format is documented in the European Community's standard called ISO 10303.

[4] *New York Times*, August 29, 1993; and *Forbes*, March 15, 1993, p. 54.

This 3-D object printer at Ford Motor Company reduces the time it takes to create a prototype part from weeks to just hours, and slashes prototype cost from $20,000 to less than $20 each.

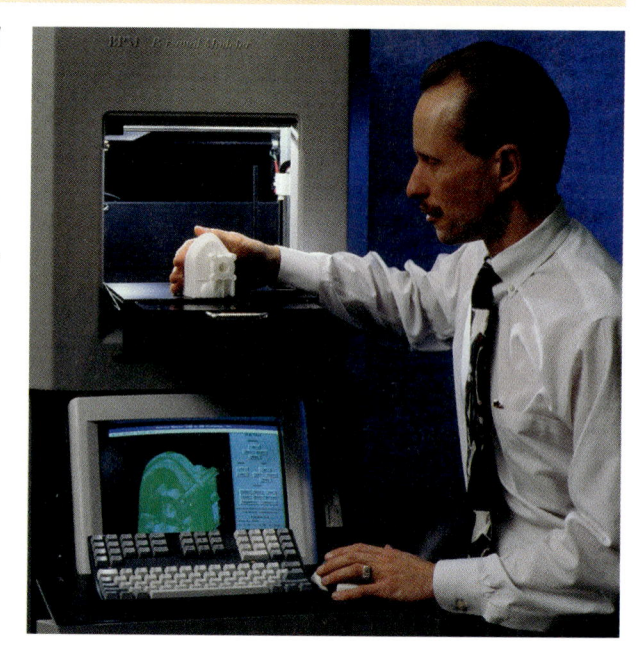

Computer-Aided Manufacturing (CAM)

Computer-aided manufacturing (CAM) refers to the use of specialized computer programs to direct and control manufacturing equipment. When computer-aided design (CAD) information is translated into instructions for computer-aided manufacturing (CAM), the result of these two technologies is CAD/CAM.

The benefits of CAD and CAM include:

1. *Product quality.* CAD permits the designer to investigate more alternatives, potential problems, and dangers.
2. *Shorter design time.* A shorter design phase lowers cost and allows a more rapid response to the market.
3. *Production cost reductions.* Reduced inventory, more efficient use of personnel through improved scheduling, and faster implementation of design changes lower costs.
4. *Database availability.* Consolidating accurate product data so everyone is operating from the same information results in dramatic cost reductions.
5. *New range of capabilities.* For instance, the ability to rotate and depict objects in three-dimensional form, to check clearances, to relate parts and attachments, to improve the use of numerically controlled machine tools—all provide new capability for manufacturing. CAD/CAM removes substantial detail work, allowing designers to concentrate on the conceptual and imaginative aspects of their task.

Virtual Reality Technology

Virtual reality is a visual form of communication in which images substitute for the real thing, but still allow the user to respond interactively. The roots of virtual reality technology in operations are in computer-aided design. As the foregoing discussion suggests, there is more to CAD than just a drawing board. Once design information is in a CAD system, it is also in electronic digital form for other uses. For instance, using a French software system called CATIA, Boeing assembled a virtual 777 to make sure the several

---

Computer-aided manufacturing (CAM) The use of information technology to control machinery.

Virtual reality A visual form of communication where images substitute for reality and typically allow the user to respond interactively.

hundred thousand parts fit. Similarly, General Motors creates its version of a "virtual car" using ceiling-mounted video projectors to project stereoscopic images on the floor of a small stark room. After donning a special pair of glasses, both designers and customers see a three-dimensional model of what the inside of a new design looks like. Virtual reality is also being used to develop 3-D layouts of everything from restaurants to amusement parks. Changes to the car, restaurant, or ride are made much less expensively at this design stage than they can be later.

Like Boeing and GM, many firms throughout the world are now using these design technologies to speed up product development, drive down costs, and improve products.

PRODUCTION TECHNOLOGY

In addition to exciting changes in design technology, a number of advances are also being made in technology to enhance *production*. We will review eight of these: (1) numerical control, (2) process control, (3) vision systems, (4) robots, (5) automated storage and retrieval systems (ASRS), (6) automated guided vehicles (AGVs), (7) flexible manufacturing systems (FMSs), and (8) Computer-integrated manufacturing (CIM).

Numerical Control

Much of the world's machinery that performs operations such as drilling, boring, and milling is now designed for electronic control. Electronic controls increase speed by reducing changeover time, reducing waste (because of fewer mistakes), and enhancing flexibility. Machinery that can be controlled electronically is called **numerical control (NC)** machinery. When machines have their own microcomputers *and* memories to store computer programs, they are called *computer numerical control (CNC)* machinery. Electronic control is accomplished by writing computer programs that are stored on magnetic media in the case of NC machines and in computer memory in the case of CNC machines. Computer languages used include APT (Automatically Programmed Tool) and Compact II. *Direct numeric control (DNC)* machines are wired to a central computer that can download the necessary code to the DNC machine memory.

Numerical control (NC) The controlling of machines by computer programs.

Process Control

Process control is the use of information technology to monitor and control a physical process. For instance, process control is used to measure the moisture content and thickness of paper as it travels over a paper machine at thousands of feet per minute. Process control is also used to determine and control temperatures, pressures, and quantities in petroleum refineries, petrochemical processes, cement plants, steel mills, nuclear reactors, and other product-focused facilities.

Process control systems operate in a number of ways, but the following is typical:

- Sensors—often analog devices—collect data.
- Analog devices read data on some periodic basis, perhaps once a minute or once every second.
- Measurements are translated into digital signals, which are transmitted to a digital computer.
- Computer programs read the file (the digital data) and analyze the data.
- The resulting output may take numerous forms. These include messages on computer consoles or printers, signals to motors to change valve settings, warning lights or horns, statistical process control charts, or schematics as shown in the photo on page 276.

Process control The use of information technology to control a physical process.

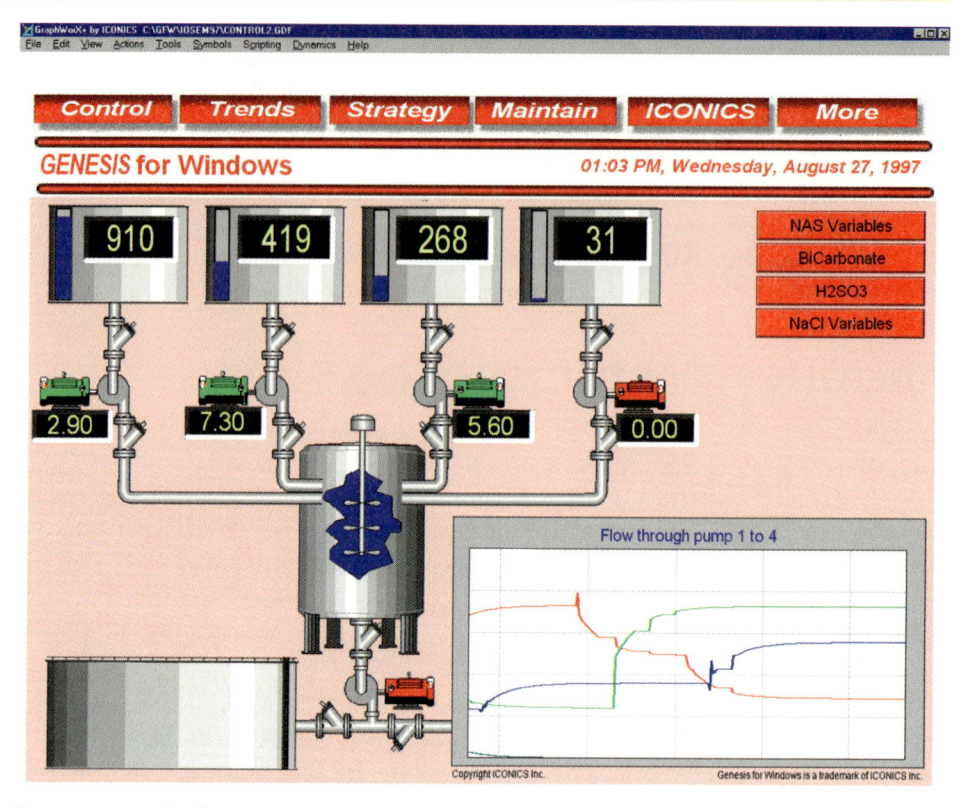

Process control software, such as "Genesis for Windows" shown here, controls the flow of materials for laundry detergents into a mixer. The trend window in the lower-right corner shows a graphical representation of the flow for the last 15 minutes.

Vision Systems

Vision systems Using video cameras and computer technology in inspection roles.

Vision systems combine video cameras and computer technology and are often used in inspection roles. Visual inspection is an important task in most food-processing and manufacturing organizations. Moreover, in many applications, visual inspection performed by humans is tedious, mind-numbing, and error-prone. Thus vision systems are widely used when the items being inspected are very similar. For instance, vision systems are used to inspect french fries so that imperfections can be identified as the fries proceed down the production line. Vision systems are used to ensure that sealant is present and in the proper amount on Whirlpool's washing-machine transmissions, and to inspect switch assemblies at the Foster Plant in Des Plaines, Illinois. Vision systems are consistently accurate, do not become bored, and are of modest cost. Consequently, these systems are vastly superior to individuals trying to perform these tasks.

Robots

Robot A flexible machine with the ability to hold, move, or grab items. It functions through electronic impulses that activate motors and switches.

When a machine is flexible and has the ability to hold, move, and perhaps "grab" items, we tend to use the word *robot*. **Robots** are mechanical devices that may have a few electronic impulses stored on semiconductor chips that will activate motors and switches. Robots may be used effectively to perform tasks that are especially monotonous or dangerous or those that can be improved by the substitution of mechanical for human effort.

Robots are used not only for labor savings but also more importantly, for those jobs that are dangerous or monotonous or require consistency, as in the even spraying of paint on an automobile (which robots do much more effectively than humans).

Such is the case when consistency, accuracy, speed, strength, or power can be enhanced by the substitution of machines for people. Ford, for example, uses robots to do 98% of the welding on its Taurus models.

Robots are now cost-competitive for a wide range of applications from small-batch production through long, continuous production. Less flexible and, consequently, less expensive robots may substitute for specialized equipment, even in continuous processes. Instructions to robots provide complete task control by providing position, orientation, velocity, and acceleration. Communication between the operator and the robot is typically provided by a computer, although robots can also be instructed via a "lead-through" method. (Lead through means that a "programmer" establishes the movements by physically moving the robot through each position.) Once instructions are entered, they are stored in computer memory and modified or edited as changes are made in the product or processing.

Computers can provide real-time changes in the position of a robot so that the work can be synchronized with other robots or moving parts.

Automated Storage and Retrieval System (ASRS)

Because of the tremendous labor involved in error-prone warehousing, computer-controlled warehouses have been developed. These systems, known as **automated storage and retrieval systems (ASRSs)**, provide for the automatic placement and withdrawal of parts and products into and from designated places in a warehouse. Such systems are commonly used in distribution facilities of retailers such as Wal-Mart, Tupperware, and Benetton. These systems are also found in inventory and test areas of manufacturing firms.

Automated storage and retrieval system (ASRS)
Computer controlled warehouses that provide for the automatic placement of parts into and from designated places within the warehouse.

Automated Guided Vehicle (AGV)

Automated material handling can take the form of monorails, conveyors, robots, or automated guided vehicles. **Automated guided vehicles (AGVs)** are electronically guided and controlled carts used in manufacturing to move parts and equipment. They are also used in offices to move mail and in hospitals and in jails to deliver meals.

Flexible Manufacturing System (FMS)

When a central computer provides instructions to each workstation *and* to the material-handling equipment (which moves material to that station), the system is known as an automated work cell or, more commonly, a **flexible manufacturing system (FMS)**. An FMS is flexible because both the material-handling devices and the machines themselves are controlled by easily changed electronic signals (computer programs). Operators simply load new programs, as necessary, to produce different products. The result is a system that can economically produce low volume but high variety. For example, the Lockheed-Martin facility, near Dallas, efficiently builds one-of-a-kind spare parts for military aircraft. The costs associated with changeover and low utilization have been reduced substantially. Consequently, FMSs bridge the gap between product-focused and process-focused facilities.

Automated guided vehicle (AGV) Electronically guided and controlled cart used to move materials.

Flexible manufacturing system (FMS) A system using an automated work cell controlled by electronic signals from a common centralized computer facility.

Computer Integrated Manufacturing (CIM)

- **Top management** decides to make a product based on market opportunities, the company's strength and weakness, and its strategic plan based on competitive advantage.
- **OM** runs the production process, coordinating supplies, requesting components and materials, planning and scheduling operations, overseeing cost accounting, and arranging outgoing shipments.
- **Computer-aided design (CAD)** designs the product, then analyzes it to assure quality and to extract data needed to plan the manufacturing process, design the molds and tools, and program the production machinery.

Management Information System

Flexible Manufacturing System (FMS)

- **Computer-aided manufacturing (CAM)** fabricates raw materials into components to be transferred to the assembly area.
- **Automated storage and retrieval system (ASRS) and automated guided vehicles (AGVs)** move incoming materials and parts, work-in-progress, and final product.
- **Robots** put the product together, test them with automated equipment, and box the finished product for shipment.

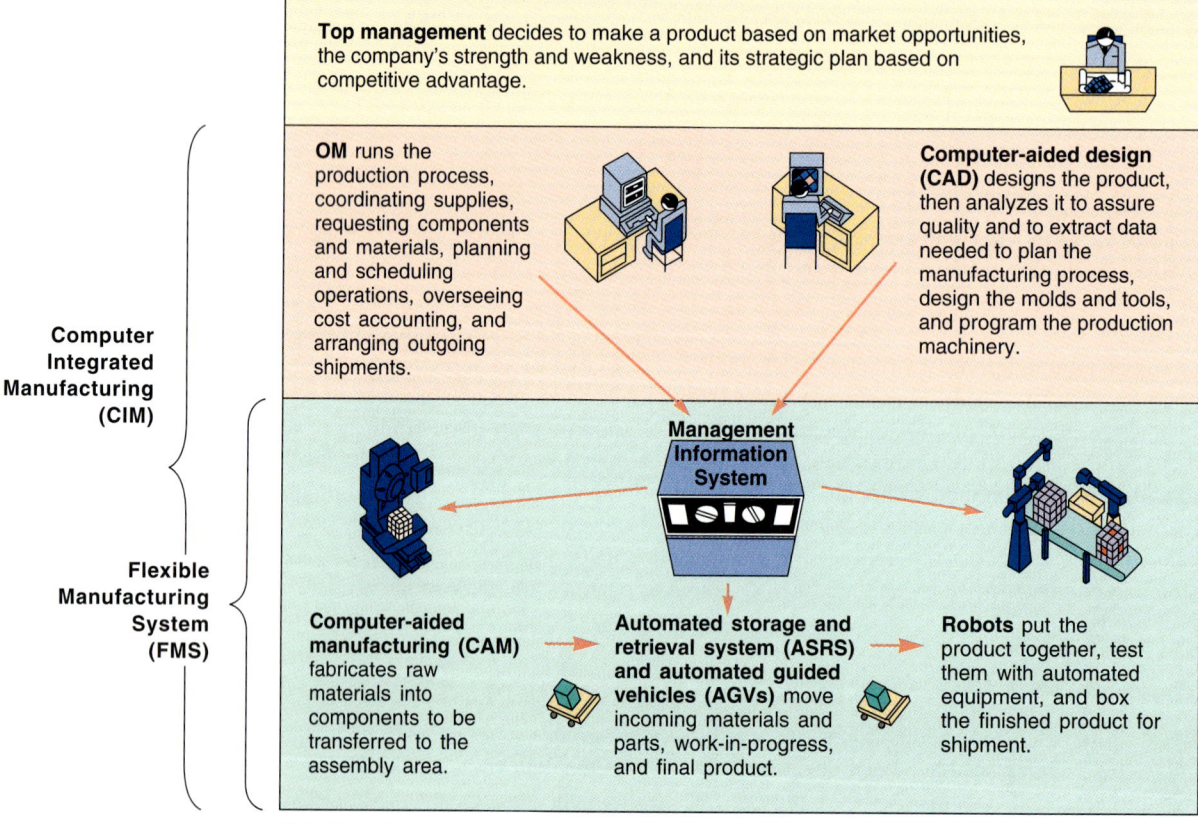

FIGURE S7.1 ■ *Computer-Integrated Manufacturing (CIM) includes computer-aided design (CAD), computer-aided manufacturing (CAM), flexible manufacturing systems (FMS), automated storage and retrieval systems (ASRS), and automated guided vehicles (AGV) to provide an integrated and flexible manufacturing process.*

FMSs are not a panacea, however, because the individual components (machines and material handling devices) have their own physical constraints. For instance, IBM's laptop manufacturing facility in Austin, Texas, can *only* assemble electronic products that fit in the FMS's 2-foot-×-2-foot-×-14-inch space. An FMS also has stringent communication requirements between unique components within it. However, reduced changeover time and more accurate scheduling result in faster throughput and improved utilization. Because there are fewer mistakes, reduced waste also contributes to lowering costs. These features are what operations managers are looking for: flexibility to provide customized products, improved utilization to reduce costs, and improved throughput to improve response. Consequently, FMSs are increasingly popular.

> Advantages of FMS include improved capital utilization, lower direct labor cost, reduced inventory, and consistent quality. Disadvantages of FMS include limited ability to adapt to product changes, substantial preplanning and capital, and tooling and fixture requirements.

Computer-Integrated Manufacturing (CIM)

Flexible manufacturing systems can be extended backward electronically into the engineering (CAD) and inventory control departments and forward to the warehousing and shipping departments. In this way, computer-aided drafting generates the necessary electronic instructions to run a direct numerically controlled (DNC) machine. In a computer-integrated manufacturing environment, a design change initiated at a CAD terminal can result in that change being made in the part produced on the shop floor in a matter of minutes. When this capability is integrated with inventory control, warehousing, and shipping as a part of a flexible manufacturing system, the entire system is called **computer-integrated manufacturing (CIM)** (Figure S7.1).

Flexible manufacturing systems and computer-integrated manufacturing are reducing the distinction between low-volume/high-variety and high-volume/low-variety production. Information technology is allowing FMS and CIM to handle increasing variety while expanding to include a growing range of volumes. Table S7.1 provides a synopsis of some of the major advances in production technology.

> **Computer-integrated manufacturing (CIM)** A manufacturing system in which CAD, FMS, inventory control, warehousing, and shipping are integrated.

> Because of capital and technological problems related to network communication, fully operational computer-integrated manufacturing (CIM) systems are still rare.

TABLE S7.1 ■ A Summary of the Elements of Production Technology

Numerical control (NC)	Instructions read from electronic media to control a machine.
Computer numerical control (CNC)	Computer memory resident at machine.
Direct numerical control (DNC)	Computer memory resident at machine and machine wired to a central computer.
Process control	Translates analog data into digital data to control a physical process.
Vision systems	Combines video cameras and computer technology.
Robots	Electronically controlled mechanical devices used to do monotonous, dangerous tasks or to substitute for human effort.
Automated storage and retrieval system (ASRS)	Computerized system that identifies, stores, and retrieves material; extensively used in warehouses and distribution centers.
Automated guided vehicle (AGV)	Electronically guided vehicles, typically following wires imbedded in the floor.
Flexible manufacturing system (FMS)	Electronic control of several DNC machines and the equipment (such as robots and AGVs) necessary to move material between them.
Computer-integrated manufacturing (CIM)	An FMS expanded to include design (CAD), inventory control, warehousing, and shipping.

OM IN ACTION

TECHNOLOGY IMPROVES PRODUCTIVITY IN THE HOSPITALITY INDUSTRY

Technology is making a difference in the hotel industry. Hotel owners can now precisely track a maid's time through the use of a security system. When a maid enters a room, a card is inserted that notifies the front desk computer as to the maid's location. "We can show her a printout of how long she takes to do a room," says the owner of one Maryland hotel chain.

The security system also enables guests to use their own credit cards as keys to unlock their door. There are also other uses for the system. The computer can bar a guest's access to the room after checkout time and automatically control the air conditioning or heat, turning it on at check-in and off at checkout.

Recently, one 92-room hotel with a new computer system opened with the equivalent of only 11 full-time employees—a general manager, 4.5 desk clerks, 5 housekeepers, and a part-time maintenance person. France's Formule 1 hotel chain even eliminated the night clerk completely. Guests check in via an automated teller machine.

Sources: The Wall Street Journal, July 23, 1997, p. A14; and *Cornell Hotel and Restaurant Administration Quarterly* (April, 1995): 16.

TECHNOLOGY IN SERVICES

Technology also has a wide range of applications in services. These include everything from diagnostic equipment at auto repair shops, to blood- and urine-testing equipment in hospitals, to improved materials for a knee replacement. The hospitality industry also provides a good example of the many ways technology can be used in services (see the *OM in Action* box, "Technology Improves Productivity in the Hospitality Industry"). As you

TABLE S7.2 ■ Examples of Technology's Impact on Services

Service Industry	Example
Financial services	Debit cards, electronic funds transfer, automatic teller machines.
Education	Multimedia presentations, electronic bulletin boards, library cataloging systems, Internet.
Utilities and government	Automated one-man garbage trucks, optical mail scanners, airborne warning and control systems.
Restaurant and foods	Optical checkout scanners, wireless orders from waiters to the kitchen, robot butchering.
Communications	Electronic publishing, interactive TV, voice mail, "notepad" computers, cellular phones.
Hotels	Electronic check-in and checkout systems, electronic key/lock systems.
Wholesale/retail trade	Point-of-sale electronic terminals, electronic communication between store and supplier, bar-coded data, automated security systems.
Transportation	Automatic toll booths, satellite-directed navigation systems.
Health care	MRI scanners, sonograms, patient-monitoring systems, on-line medical information systems.
Airlines	Ticketless travel, computer scheduling.

may have experienced, you can now authorize payment of your bill from your hotel room via a channel on the room's television set. The resulting labor savings at the registration desk and enhanced service for the customer are currently demonstrated at most major hotels.

Table S7.2 provides a glimpse of the impact of technology on services. Operations managers in services, as in manufacturing, must be able to evaluate the impact of technology on their firm. This ability requires particular skill when evaluating reliability, investment analysis, human resource requirements, and maintenance/service.

INFORMATION SCIENCES IN OPERATIONS

The information sciences are making a major impact in additional areas that have applications in operations. These areas are transaction processing, management information systems, the Internet, and artificial intelligence.

Transaction Processing

A **transaction processing system** addresses the many transactions that occur within and between firms. These transactions have traditionally been paper transactions and include payroll, order entry, invoicing, receipt of checks, inventory, personnel records, and so on. When these transactions are moved from paper to computerized processing and storage, we have a computer-based transaction system. To the extent that such systems can be automated beyond those of competitors, a competitive advantage in speed, accuracy, or cost reduction may be obtained. If General Motors conducts one billion paper transactions a year and can reduce the cost of each transaction by $5, the savings is tremendous.

Many transaction processing systems rely on electronic signals, which are a great vehicle for transmitting information, but they have a major limitation—most OM data do not start out in bits and bytes. Therefore, we must get the data into an electronic form. **Automatic identification systems (AIS)** are the technologies that provide the translation of data into electronic bits and bytes. Bar codes, radio frequencies, and those optical charac-

Transaction processing system A system that processes the transactions that occur within and between firms.

Automatic identification system (AIS) A system for transforming data into electronic form, for example, bar codes

State Farm Insurance is testing "notepad" computers, which have an electric pen that claims adjusters use to fill out forms and mark damage on a schematic of a car. The computer then uses stored parts and price lists to calculate damage. The information is transferred to a central computer at the end of the day. State Farm hopes that the system will improve accuracy and reduce time and costs associated with auto insurance claims.

Three critical success factors in the trucking industry are being addressed by information technology. They are (1) getting shipments to customers promptly (rapid response); (2) keeping trucks busy (capacity utilization); and (3) buying inexpensive fuel (driving down costs). Many firms have now developed devices like the one shown here to track location of trucks and facilitate communication between drivers and dispatchers. This system speeds shipment response, maximizes utilization of the truck, and ensures purchase of fuel at the most economical location.

ters on bank checks are automatic identification systems that help us move data to electronic media. Bar codes are used by Litton Industries for checking inventory and by nurses in hospitals to match bar codes on medication to ID bracelets on patients.

Management Information System (MIS)

Management information system (MIS) A system dedicated to obtaining, formatting, manipulating, and presenting data as information to managers when needed.

Management information systems (MIS) are dedicated to obtaining, formatting, manipulating, and presenting data in the form of information to managers when needed. Much of the control information for a firm is provided by the MIS. Information systems make their presence known in OM in a variety of ways, from scheduling to material requirements planning (MRP) (see Figure S7.2).

The Internet

Internet An international computer network connecting millions of people and companies around the world—it is the "information superhighway."

The **Internet** and the World Wide Web have become a great source of technical data for companies, suppliers, and customers. Internet information is enhancing communication, collaboration, and productivity. Lufthansa Airlines has put maintenance information on

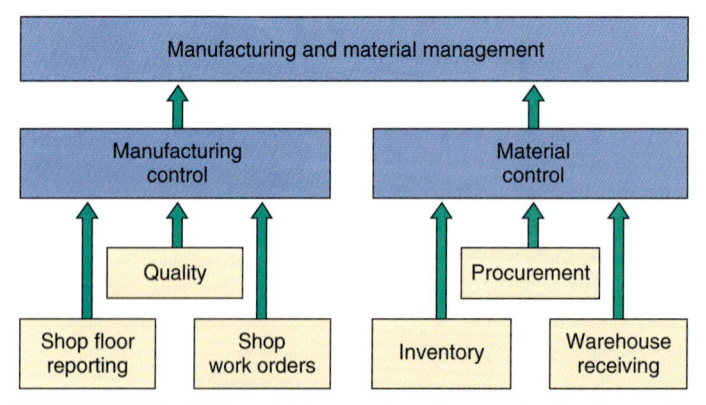

Management information systems (MIS) provide plans and performance measures and reports that provide feedback.

Transaction processing systems provide information reporting, data collection, and send information.

FIGURE S7.2 ■ MIS and Transaction Processing in Operations Management the web for use by its worldwide service personnel.[5] Ronal Tool Co. of York, Pennsylvania, builds stamping dies and injection molds from specifications that customers send via the Net.[6] Firms also place technical data for customers and suppliers in CAD and spreadsheet formats on Web pages. This practice allows customers not only to review the technical aspects of products, but also in some cases, to do more sophisticated analysis—say, simulations of stress or flow through a valve.[7]

Similarly, Hallmark Cards uses an in-house Internet, known as an *Intranet,* to view images of previous popular cards, share artwork, and even route new cards to production. Hallmark is joining those business processes together so that there is never a handoff until design goes to manufacturing, where a plate is created for the printing press.[8] In-house use, technical collaboration, and transfer of information to and from the customer are making both the Internet and the Intranet powerful new operations tools.

Artificial Intelligence

Constructing and programming computers to imitate human thought processes is a discipline known as **artificial intelligence.** Three tools, *expert systems, fuzzy logic,* and *neural networks,* are fundamental to the discipline.

Expert systems (ES) are computer programs that mimic human logic and "solve" problems much as a human expert would. The idea behind an expert system is to capture in a computer program the knowledge and skills of a person who is an expert in a given field. Indeed, five advantages of ESs are that they:

1. Make decisions faster than the expert;
2. Derive the benefits of having an expert at their disposal without having the expert present;
3. Equal and surpass, at least in terms of consistency, the human expert;
4. Free the human expert for other work;
5. Can be disseminated to numerous nonexperts for education and training.

Although the idea is quite simple, the mechanics of making an expert system work are difficult. To make the system function, there must be a knowledge base that is supplied by an expert. Every step of the process must be programmed meticulously, including any and all options to decisions made throughout the process. This computerized knowledge base is designed to be updated periodically to include new rules and facts. An electronic representation of the expert's thought process called the "inference engine" fuels the knowledge base.

Many decisions, however, are not sufficiently clear-cut for the use of expert systems. A yes or no may not be adequate. Consequently, another tool, *fuzzy logic,* has been developed for the operations manager's tool kit. **Fuzzy logic** can deal with *approximate* values, influences, and *incomplete* or *ambiguous* data to make decisions. For example, when making concrete or steel, the expertise of years of training is often the critical ingredient for a good batch. Knowing when to add material, heat, or a minor ingredient may be critical. Adding fuzzy rules—such as "If too hot, cut back on fuel" or "If mix is not consistent or if mix is too moist, mix longer"—deals with such ambiguities. Fuzzy logic is now written into computer programs to make both concrete and steel. It is also being used to add new features to consumer products ranging from washing machines to cameras.

Artificial intelligence computer-based systems that attempt to duplicate the functions of the human brain.

Expert system (ES) A computer program that mimics human logic and "solves" problems much as a human expert would.

Expert systems are used for medical diagnosis and to analyze data about petrochemicals such as viscosity or specific gravity.

Fuzzy logic A concept that deals with ambiguous and approximate information to make decisions.

---

[5] Lufthansa Internet location is http://www.lhsystems.com/.

[6] Thomas Petzinger, Jr., "The Front Lines," *The Wall Street Journal,* May 9, 1997, p. B1.

[7] The potential of the Internet/manufacturing interface is examined on the following Internet locations. http://www.isr.umd.edu/labs/CIM/cim.html and http://nii.nist.gov/manuf.html.

[8] Gene Koprowski, "Internets Unleashed," *Software,* August 1997, p. 78.

Paper moves through a modern paper machine at about 3000 feet per minute. Tiny holes in the web of paper can create costly problems. Mead Corporation, a paper maker, designed a computer-based artificial intelligence system that uses 1,200 sensing devices and computer systems to control some 750 process variables.

Neural networks Computer programs modeled on the brain's meshlike network of interconnected cells and programmed to recognize patterns and to solve related problems.

Modeled on the brain's meshlike network of interconnected cells, **neural networks** recognize patterns and program themselves to solve related problems. The advantage to the operations manager is that they are programmed to learn. They can, for instance, recognize unnatural patterns, such as cycles and trends in control charts. Because of this unique ability to learn and recognize patterns, they can provide valuable information for real-time process control.[9]

These three tools, and indeed the discipline of artificial intelligence, have developed to the point where they are now making a major impact on operations management.

MANAGING TECHNOLOGY IN A GLOBAL ENVIRONMENT

Agility and learning have emerged as important operations priorities in the global environment. The ability to switch products quickly and cheaply, and to tighten coordination with an international supply chain requires an agile organization. **Agile organizations** are quick and flexible in their response to changing customer requirements. They are learning organizations that manage change by combining a vision, a participative management environment, and *the application of technology*. Because technology and the global economy are changing so rapidly, it may be that only agile learning organizations will survive.

Agile organization An organization quick and flexible in its response to changing customer requirements.

Agile firms operating internationally need effective information systems so managers in any part of the world can communicate and share information. International banks do this very well, as do international shipping companies. They have no choice if they wish to survive; the global nature of their business requires it. In the apparel industry, as we note in the *OM in Action* box, Benetton is proving itself an agile organization, from design to distribution.

Another company that has moved toward global technological integration is Tiris, a subsidiary of Texas Instruments. Headquartered in the United Kingdom, Tiris has product development units in Germany and the Netherlands and manufacturing plants in Japan and Malaysia. Managers and engineers at each facility communicate with each other as if they were across the hall rather than thousands of miles apart. For example, a manager in

---

[9] H. Brian Hwarng and Norma Faris Habele, "X Control Chart Pattern Identification Through Efficient Off-Line Neural Network Training," *IIE Transactions* 25, no. 3 (May 1993): 27–40.

OM IN ACTION

BENETTON: THE WORLD'S FASTEST CLOTHING MANUFACTURER

Benetton, the Italian sportswear company, can probably claim to have the world's fastest factory *and* the most efficient distributor in the garment industry. Located in Ponzano, Italy, Benetton makes and ships 50 million pieces of clothing each year. That is 30,000 boxes every day—boxes that must be filled with exactly the items ordered going to the correct store of the 5,000 Benetton outlets in 60 countries. This highly automated distribution center uses only 19 people. Without automation, 400 people would be needed.

Here is how Benetton does it: Let's say a salesperson in a Boston shop finds that she is running out of a best-selling blue sweater. She calls a Benetton sales agent, who enters the order in a PC, which electronically forwards the order to the mainframe computer in Italy. Because the blue sweater was originally created by computer-aided design (CAD), the mainframe retains all the proper specifications, which it passes on to a knitting machine. The machine makes the sweaters, which are boxed with a bar code addressed to the Boston store, and the box goes to the Italian warehouse.

Once the blue sweaters are snugly sitting in one of the 300,000 slots in the warehouse, a robot flies by, reading bar codes. It picks out the right box and any other boxes ready for the Boston store and loads them for shipment.

Including manufacturing time, Benetton gets the order to Boston in 4 weeks if none is in stock, 1 week if a supply is already in the warehouse. In the notoriously slow garment industry, agile Benetton responds to the customer by using electronic communication, CAD/CAM, robots, and bar codes.

Sources: Fortune (February 20, 1995): 102–107; and *The Wall Street Journal*, July 23, 1997, p. A14.

England can respond to a customer order with an electronic request to a designer in the Netherlands to modify a part for that customer. The designer then electronically sends the new design specifications along with the order to Japan for production. At any time, manager or designer can monitor the order's progress electronically. This ability to compete globally provides competitive advantage through lower costs, speed, and flexibility in meeting the different needs of customers in different countries.

Understanding technology and how it influences your industry is a demanding task, as is implementing and managing it. Firms that achieve competitive advantage through technology are successful because they:[10]

- Have strategic vision (something Dilbert's boss, in the cartoon strip on page 286, seems to be missing);
- Plan for a more distant time horizon;
- Have a focused-product line and know their products and customers exceedingly well;
- Tie strong internal technical capabilities to their strategy;
- Build learning organizations that can effectively implement the changes necessary for the constructive use of technology.

Effectively managing technology can give operations managers the ability to hit all three strategic targets—low cost, differentiation, and rapid response.

---

[10] See, for example, S. C. Fleming, "Using Technology for Competitive Advantage," *Research Technology Management* 11, no. 5 (September–October 1994): 34–41; P. H. Biranbaum-Moore, A. R. Weiss, and R. W. Wright, "How Do Rivals Compete: Strategy, Technology, and Tactics," *Research Policy* 23, no. 3 (May 1994): 249–265; Andrew Bartmess and Keith Cerny, "Building Competitive Advantage Through a Global Network of Capabilities," *California Management Review* 35, no. 2 (winter 1993): 78–103; and M. E. Porter, "The Technological Dimension of Competitive Strategy," in *Research on Technology Innovation, Management and Policy*, ed., R. S. Rosenbloom, (Greenwich, CT: JAI Press), p. 3.

DILBERT
By Scott Adams

I've been asked to give a presentation at the trade show.

I'd like you to put that together for me, Alice.

What's your topic?

Technology. They didn't say if I'm for it or against it. I'll leave some wiggle room.

SUMMARY

Firms distinguish themselves not only by using the latest technology but also by the way they *strategically* use technology. The objective is not just to grab hold of the latest technological gimmick, but to use technology to achieve the firm's long-term strategic objectives. Return on investment, which is discussed in chapter 7, is only one criterion for technological investment. Companies must ask, "Does the technology win orders?" Successful firms ensure that they have the financial and human resources to make the technology work.

International competition is brutal. Markets are increasingly global, volatile, and customer driven. Labor costs in advanced economies are high and going higher. Environmental requirements are growing, and customers are more demanding. Firms in this new global marketplace must produce products faster, better (or more clearly differentiated), and cheaper. With proper management, technology helps them do so.

KEY TERMS

Computer-aided design (CAD) *(p. 273)*
STEP (Standard for the Exchange of Product Data) *(p. 273)*
Computer-aided manufacturing (CAM) *(p. 274)*
Virtual reality *(p. 274)*
Numerical control (NC) *(p. 275)*
Process control *(p. 275)*
Vision systems *(p. 276)*
Robot *(p. 276)*
Automated storage and retrieval system (ASRS) *(p. 277)*
Automated guided vehicle (AGV) *(p. 278)*
Flexible manufacturing system (FMS) *(p. 278)*
Computer-integrated manufacturing (CIM) *(p. 279)*
Transaction processing system *(p. 281)*
Automatic identification system (AIS) *(p. 281)*
Management information system (MIS) *(p. 282)*
Internet *(p. 282)*
Artificial intelligence *(p. 283)*
Expert system (ES) *(p. 283)*
Fuzzy logic *(p. 283)*
Neural networks *(p. 284)*
Agile organization *(p. 284)*

DISCUSSION QUESTIONS

1. What are some possible applications of an expert system?
2. What is an FMS?
3. What is the difference between a management information system (MIS) and transaction processing?
4. Give some recent examples of information technol-

ogy successfully applied to new products and new processes in (a) manufacturing and (b) services.
5. Distinguish between flexible manufacturing systems (FMS) and computer-integrated manufacturing (CIM).
6. What kinds of enhancements are being made to computer-aided design (CAD) systems?
7. Distinguish between expert systems, fuzzy logic, and neural networks.
8. How do "vision systems" work and where might they be used?
9. What are the advantages of a system like STEP (Standard for the Exchange of Product Data)?
10. What are the pressures on FMS and CIM to expand?
11. Explain the difference between NC, CNC, and DNC machines.
12. What are the different types of computer-aided design systems?

PROBLEMS

- **S7.1** Heyl Machine Shop, Inc., has a 1-year contract for the production of 200,000 gear housings for a new off-road vehicle. Owner Jeff Heyl hopes the contract will be extended and the volume increased next year. Heyl has developed costs for three alternatives. They are general-purpose equipment (GPE), flexible manufacturing system (FMS), and dedicated automation (DA). The cost data follow:

	General-Purpose Equipment (GPE)	Flexible Manufacturing System (FMS)	Dedicated Automation (DA)
Annual contracted units	200,000	200,000	200,000
Annual fixed cost	$100,000	$200,000	$500,000
Per unit variable cost	15.00	14.00	13.00

  Which process is best for this contract?
- **S7.2** Using the data in Problem S7.1, determine the economical volume for each process.
- **S7.3** Using the data in Problem S7.1, determine the best process for each of the following volumes: (1) 50,000, (2) 250,000, and (3) 350,000.
- **S7.4** Refer to Problem S7.1. If a contract for the second and third years is pending, what are the implications for process selection?
- **S7.5** Find two Internet locations that demonstrate the use of the Internet as a vehicle for communication of technical information.

Case Study

Rochester Manufacturing Corporation

Rochester Manufacturing Corporation (RMC) was considering moving some of its production from traditional numerically controlled machines to a flexible machining system (FMS). Its traditional numerical control machines have been operating in a high-variety/low-volume, intermittent manner. Machine utilization, as near as RMC can determine, is hovering around 10%. The machine tool salespeople and a consulting firm want to put the machines together in an FMS. They believe that a $3 million expenditure on machinery and the transfer machines will handle about 30% of RMC's work. The firm has not yet entered all of its parts into a comprehensive group technology system but believes that 30% is a good estimate. This 30% fits very nicely into a "family." Because of higher utilization, a reduction should take place in the number of pieces of machinery. The firm should be able to go from 15 to about 4 machines, and personnel should drop from 15 to perhaps 3. Similarly, required floorspace will be reduced from 20,000 feet to about 6,000. Throughput of orders should also improve with this family of parts being processed in 1 to 2 days rather than 7 to 10. Inventory reduction is estimated to yield a one-time $750,000 savings, and annual labor savings should be in the neighborhood of $300,000.

Although the projections all look very positive, an analysis of the project's return on investment showed it to be between 10% and 15% per year. The company has traditionally had an expectation that projects should yield well over 15% and have payback periods of substantially less than 5 years.

DISCUSSION QUESTIONS

1. As a production manager for RMC, what do you recommend? Why?
2. Prepare a case by a conservative plant manager for maintaining the status quo until the returns are more obvious.
3. Prepare the case for an optimistic sales manager that you should move ahead with the FMS now.

BIBLIOGRAPHY

Beatty, C. A. "Implementing Advanced Manufacturing Technologies: Rules of the Road." *Sloan Management Review* 33, no. 4 (summer 1992): 49.

Byrd, T. A. "Expert Systems in Production and Operations Management: Results of a Survey." *Interfaces* 23, no. 2 (March–April 1993): 118–129.

Davenport, T. H. *Process Innovation,* Cambridge, MA: Harvard Business School Press, 1993.

Grant, R. M., R. Krishnan, A. B. Shani, and R. Baer. "Appropriate Manufacturing Technology: A Strategic Approach." *Sloan Management Review* 33 (fall 1991): 43.

Iansiti, Marco, and Alan MacCormack. "Developing Products on Internet Time," *Harvard Business Review* (September–October 1997): 108–117.

Iansiti, Marco, and Jonathon West. "Technology Integration: Turning Great Research into Great Products," *Harvard Business Review* (May–June 1997): pp. 69–82.

Roberts, E. B. "The Success of High-Technology Firms: Early Technological and Marketing Influences." *Interfaces* 22, no. 4 (July–August 1992): 3.

Rodriquiz, A. A., and O. R. Mitchell. "A Vision System for Manufacturing Applications Under Moderately Unconstrained Conditions." *Industrial Engineering Research & Development* 25, no. 4 (July 1993): 15–25.

Roth, A. V., C. Gaimon, and L. Krajewski. "Optimal Acquisition of FMS Technology Subject to Technological Progress." *Decision Sciences,* 22 (spring 1991): 308.

Schonberger, Richard J. *World Class Manufacturing: The Next Decade.* New York: The Free Press, 1996.

Stefik, M., J. Aikins, R. Balzer, J. Benoit, L. Birnbaum, F. Hayes-Roth, and E. Sacerdoti. "The Organization of Expert Systems: A Tutorial." *Artificial Intelligence* 13 (March 1986): 135–173.

Sviokla, John J., "Knowledge Workers and Radically New Technology," *Sloan Management Review,* summer 1996.

Van Weelderen, J. A., and H. G. Sol. "MEDESS: A Methodology for Designing Expert Support Systems." *Interfaces* 23, no. 3 (May–June 1993): 51–61.

Wu, B. *Fundamentals of Manufacturing Systems Design and Analysis.* New York: Van Nostrand Reinhold, 1991.

INTERNET RESOURCES

Artificial Intelligence Applications Institute:
http://www.aiai.ed.ac.uk/

Business Research in Information and Technology:
http://www.brint.com

Electronic College of Innovation, Department of Defense:
http://www.dtic.dla.mil/

Oak Ridge Centers for Manufacturing Technology:
http://www.ornl.gov/orcmt/orcmt.html

The Robert C. Byrd Institute for Advanced Flexible Manufacturing Systems maintains an FMS newsletter at
http://199.217.7.39

TECHNOLOGY

As much as we have updated the text itself, we are even more excited with the wide array of resources that we are providing on a free student CD-ROM and on the text's Web site.

FREE STUDENT CD-ROM!

This disk, packaged with every copy of the book, includes free software and other valuable resources that will help students get more out of this course.

- **PowerPoint slides** - provide reinforcement of the main points of each chapter and allow students to review the material.
- **Chapter Quizzes and Practice Problems** - allow students to quiz their understanding of each chapter and practice solving homework problems and test questions.
- **NEW Excel OM** - these easy-to-use Excel add-ins will help students to easily solve many of the quantitative problems found in the book.
- **NEW EXTEND** simulation program - a student version of the Extend simulation package, developed by Imagine That, Inc.

WEB SITE SUPPORT!

Use the Internet to bring real business practices into your Operations Management course. Prentice Hall's "PHLIP" Web site contains an assortment of rich resources for both students and instructors.
The Web site, located at **http://www.prenhall.com/heizer** contains the following:

For the Student:
On-line quizzes, Lecture Notes and PowerPoints, links to *New York Times* articles, over 30 additional case studies, 15 virtual company tours with exercises, over 30 Internet exercises, Internet resources, and more.

For the Instructor:
- **PowerPoint slides** - includes hundreds of PowerPoint slides for lecture material.
- **Instructor's Resource Manual** - contains course outlines and syllabi, lecture notes, Internet assignments, student projects, video suggestions, chapter quizzes, simulation exercises, and more.
- **Instructor's Solutions Manual** - detailed solutions for all end-of-chapter exercises and cases. These solutions are provided electronically on the text's Web site, allowing instructors to electronically post individual solutions on their own course Web site.
- **Test Questions** - in Microsoft Word.
- **Excel OM** - these easy-to-use Excel add-ins can be distributed to students or placed on your computer network at your discretion.

LOCATION STRATEGIES

8

CHAPTER OUTLINE

GLOBAL COMPANY PROFILE: FEDERAL EXPRESS
THE STRATEGIC IMPORTANCE OF LOCATION
FACTORS THAT AFFECT LOCATION DECISIONS
    Labor Productivity
    Exchange Rates
    Costs
    Attitudes
    Proximity to Markets
    Proximity to Suppliers
METHODS OF EVALUATING LOCATION ALTERNATIVES
    The Factor-Rating Method
    Locational Break-Even Analysis
    Center-of-Gravity Method
    Transportation Model
SERVICE LOCATION STRATEGY
    How Hotel Chains Select Sites

The Telemarketing and Internet Industries
Geographic Information Systems
SUMMARY
KEY TERMS
USING POM FOR WINDOWS
USING EXCEL OM TO SOLVE LOCATION PROBLEMS
SOLVED PROBLEMS
DISCUSSION QUESTIONS
CRITICAL THINKING EXERCISE
PROBLEMS
DATA BASE APPLICATION
CASE STUDY: SOUTHERN RECREATIONAL VEHICLE COMPANY
INTERNET CASE STUDY
BIBLIOGRAPHY
INTERNET RESOURCES

LEARNING OBJECTIVES

When you complete this chapter you should be able to:

Identify or Define:

    Objective of location strategy

    International location issues

Describe or Explain:

    Three methods of solving the location problem:
- Factor-rating method
- Locational break-even analysis
- Center-of-gravity method

⊕ GLOBAL COMPANY PROFILE:

Location Provides Competitive Advantage for Federal Express

At the Federal Express hub in Memphis, Tennessee, approximately 100 Federal Express aircraft converge each night around midnight with more than 700,000 documents and packages.

At the preliminary sorting area, packages and documents are sorted and sent to a secondary sorting area. The Memphis facility covers 1,500,000 square feet; it is big enough to hold 33 football fields. Packages are sorted and exchanged until 4 A.M.

Overnight-delivery powerhouse Federal Express has believed in the hub concept for its 30-year existence. Even though Fred Smith, founder and CEO, got a C on his college paper proposing a hub for small package delivery, the idea has proven extremely successful. Starting with a hub in Memphis, Tennessee, the $10-billion firm has added a European hub in Paris and an Asian one in Subic Bay, Philippines. In 1998, a second Asian hub in Taipei, Taiwan, was added as a backup for Subic Bay, should political troubles or weather ever close that facility. Federal Express's fleet of over 600 planes flies into 325 airports worldwide, then delivers to the door with more than 38,000 vans.

Why was Memphis picked as Federal Express's central location? For one thing, it is located in the middle

290

FEDERAL EXPRESS

At the outbound slide/load area, packages and documents that have already gone through the primary and secondary sorts are checked by city, state, and zip code. They are then placed in containers that will be loaded onto aircraft for delivery to their final destinations in 211 countries.

of the U.S. For another, it has very few hours of bad weather closures, perhaps contributing to the firm's excellent flight-safety record.

Each night, except Sunday, Federal Express brings to Memphis packages from throughout the world that are going to cities for which Federal Express does not have direct flights. The central hub permits service to a far greater number of points with fewer aircraft than the traditional City-A-to-City-B system. It also allows Federal Express to match aircraft flights with package loads each night and to reroute flights when load volume requires it, a major cost savings. Moreover, Federal Express also believes that the central hub system helps reduce mishandling and delay in transit because there is total control over the packages from pickup point through delivery.

Federal Express jet departing the Subic Bay Asian hub. Subic Bay's 3,100 employees sort 6,000 boxes and 10,000 documents per hour in the 90,000-square-foot facility located on what used to be a U.S. military base in the Philippines.

291

THE STRATEGIC IMPORTANCE OF LOCATION

> **TEN DECISIONS OF OM**
> Managing Quality
> Design of Goods & Services
> Process Strategy
> **Location Strategies**
> Layout Strategies
> Human Resources
> Supply-Chain Management
> Inventory Management
> Scheduling
> Maintenance

When Federal Express opened its Asian hub in Taiwan in 1998 and doubled its flights to China, it set the stage for its new "round-the-world" flights linking its Paris and Memphis package hubs to Asia. When Mercedes-Benz announced its plans to build its first major overseas plant in Vance, Alabama, it completed a year of competition among 170 sites in 30 states and two countries. When McDonald's opened in Pushkin Square in Moscow, it ended six years of advance preparation of a Russian "food town" to supply its desired quality of ingredients.

One of the most important strategic decisions made by companies like Federal Express, Mercedes-Benz, and McDonald's is where to locate their operations. The international aspect of these decisions is an indication of the global nature of location decisions. With the opening of the Soviet and Chinese blocs, a great transformation is taking place. World markets have doubled and the global nature of business is accelerating.

Firms throughout the world are using the concepts and techniques of this chapter to address the location decision, because location greatly affects both fixed and variable costs. It has a major impact on the overall profit of the company. For instance, depending on the product and type of production or service taking place, transportation costs alone can total as much as 25% of the product's selling price. That is, one fourth of a firm's total revenue may be needed just to cover freight expenses of the raw materials coming in and finished products going out. Other costs that may be influenced by location include taxes, wages, raw material costs, and rents.

Because location is such a significant cost driver, the consulting firm McKinsey believes "location ultimately has the power to make (or break) a company's business strategy."[1] Key multinationals in every major industry, from automobiles to cellular phones now have or are planning a presence in each of their major markets. Motorola, however, has often rejected countries even when costs are lower if infrastructure and education levels cannot support specific production technologies. A low-cost strategy requires that the location decision be made only after careful consideration.

Once management is committed to a specific location, many costs are firmly in place and difficult to reduce. For instance, if a new factory location is in a region with high energy costs, even good management with an outstanding energy strategy is starting at a disadvantage. Management is in a similar bind with its human resource strategy if labor in the selected location is expensive, ill-trained, or has a poor work ethic. Consequently, hard work to determine an optimal facility location is a good investment.

The location decision often depends on the type of business. For industrial location decisions, the strategy is usually minimizing costs, whereas for retail and professional service organizations, the strategy focuses on maximizing revenue. Warehouse location strategy, however, may be driven by a combination of cost and speed of delivery. In general, the *objective of location strategy* is to maximize the benefit of location to the firm.

Companies make location decisions relatively infrequently, usually because demand has outgrown the current plant's capacity or because of changes in labor productivity, exchange rates, costs, or local attitudes. Companies may also relocate their manufacturing or service facilities because of shifts in demographics and customer demand.

Location options include (1) expanding an existing facility instead of moving, (2) maintaining current sites while adding another facility elsewhere, or (3) closing the existing facility and moving to another location.

List the factors most important to you in selecting a city in which to live.

---

[1] See Andrew D. Bartness, "The Plant Location Puzzle," *Harvard Business Review* (March–April 1994): 32.

FACTORS THAT AFFECT LOCATION DECISIONS

Selecting a facility location is becoming much more complex with the globalization of the workplace. As we saw in chapter 3, globalization has taken place because of the development of (1) market economics; (2) better international communications; (3) more rapid, reliable travel and shipping; (4) ease of capital flow between countries; and (5) high differences in labor costs. Many firms now consider opening new offices, factories, retail stores, or banks outside their home country. Location decisions transcend national borders. In fact, as Figure 8.1 shows, the sequence of location decisions often begins with choosing a country in which to operate. Before Germany's Mercedes-Benz chose Alabama, it first considered Mexico. In the end, the fear of marketing a $50,000 Mercedes that was "Made in Mexico" drove the firm back to the United States.

Once a firm decides which country is best for its location, it focuses on a region of the chosen country and a community. The final step in the location decision process is choosing a specific site within a community. The company must pick the one location that is best suited for shipping and receiving, zoning, utilities, size, and cost. Again, Figure 8.1 summarizes this series of decisions and the factors that affect them.

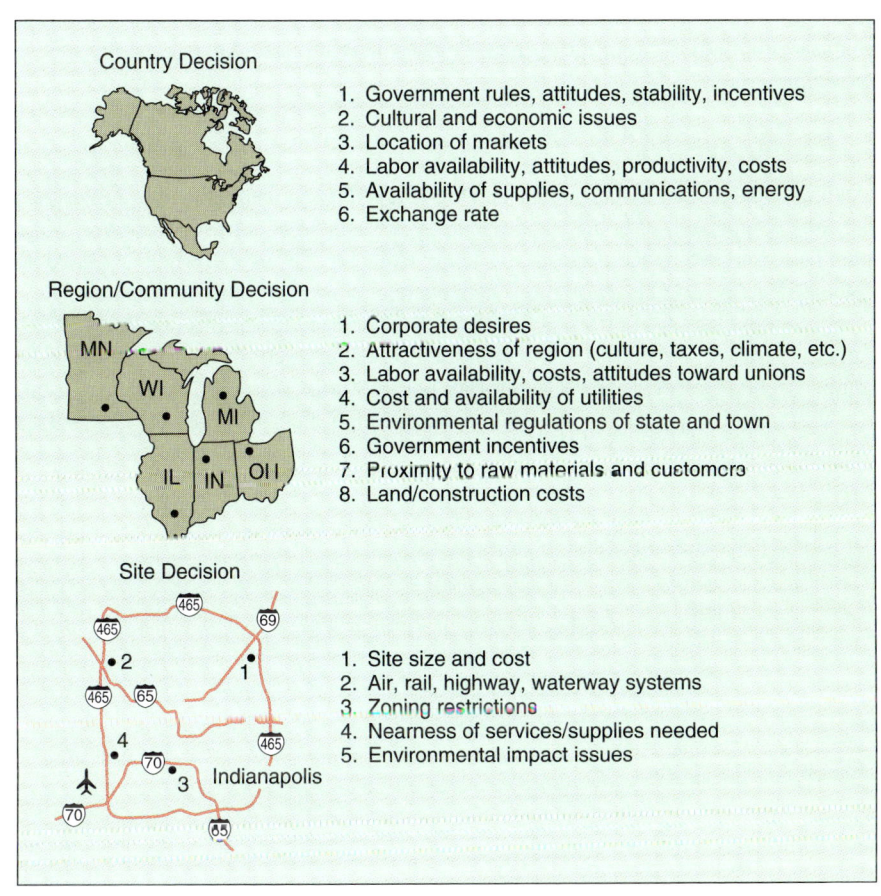

Country Decision
1. Government rules, attitudes, stability, incentives
2. Cultural and economic issues
3. Location of markets
4. Labor availability, attitudes, productivity, costs
5. Availability of supplies, communications, energy
6. Exchange rate

Region/Community Decision
1. Corporate desires
2. Attractiveness of region (culture, taxes, climate, etc.)
3. Labor availability, costs, attitudes toward unions
4. Cost and availability of utilities
5. Environmental regulations of state and town
6. Government incentives
7. Proximity to raw materials and customers
8. Land/construction costs

Site Decision
1. Site size and cost
2. Air, rail, highway, waterway systems
3. Zoning restrictions
4. Nearness of services/supplies needed
5. Environmental impact issues

FIGURE 8.1 ■ Some Considerations and Factors That Affect Location Decisions

OM IN ACTION

QUALITY COILS PULLS THE PLUG ON MEXICO

Keith Gibson, President of Quality Coils Inc., saw the savings of low Mexican wages and headed South. He shut down a factory in Connecticut and opened one in Juarez, where he could pay Mexicans one-third the wage rates he was paying Americans. "All the figures pointed out we should make a killing," says Gibson.

Instead, his company was nearly destroyed. The electromagnetic coil maker regularly lost money during 4 years in Mexico. High absenteeism, low productivity, and problems of long-distance management wore Gibson down until he finally pulled the plug on Juarez.

Moving back to the United States and rehiring some of his original workers, Gibson learned, "I can hire one person in Connecticut for what three were doing in Juarez."

When American unions complain that they cannot compete against the low wages in other countries and when the teamster rallies chant "$4 a day/No way!," they overlook several factors. First, productivity in low-wage countries often erases a wage advantage that is not nearly as great as people believe. Second, a host of problems, from poor roads to corrupt governments, run up operating costs. And most importantly, the cost of labor for most U.S. manufacturers is less important than such factors as the skill of the workforce, the quality of transportation, and access to technology.

Sources: The Wall Street Journal, September 15, 1993, p. A1; *CFO* (March 1994): 63–65; and *International Business* (September 1993): 72–74.

In most cases, it is cheaper to make clothes in Korea, Taiwan, or Hong Kong and ship them to the United States than it is to produce them in the United States. However, final cost is the critical factor and low productivity can negate low cost.

Labor costs in many underdeveloped countries are now one third of those in developed nations. However, when labor costs are only 15% of manufacturing costs, the difference may not overcome many other disadvantages of low-labor-cost countries.

Besides globalization, a number of other factors affect the location decision. Among these are labor productivity, foreign exchange, and changing attitudes toward the industry, unions, employment, zoning, pollution, and taxes.

Labor Productivity

When deciding on a location, management may be tempted by an area's low wage rates (see Figure 8.2 for a comparison of hourly manufacturing costs in 15 countries). However, wage rates cannot be considered by themselves, as Quality Coils Inc. discovered when it opened its plant in Mexico (see the *OM in Action* box). Management must also consider productivity.

As discussed in chapter 1, differences exist in productivity in various countries. What management is really interested in is the combination of productivity and the wage rate. For example, if Quality Coils pays $70 per day with 60 units produced per day in Connecticut, it will spend less on labor than at a Mexican plant that pays $25 per day with a productivity of 20 units per day:

$$\frac{\text{Labor cost per day}}{\text{Productivity (that is, units per day)}} = \text{cost per unit}$$

Case 1: Connecticut plant

$$\frac{\$70 \text{ Wages per day}}{60 \text{ Units produced per day}} = \frac{\$70}{60} = \$1.17 \text{ per unit}$$

Case 2: Juarez, Mexico, plant

$$\frac{\$25 \text{ Wages per day}}{20 \text{ Units produced per day}} = \frac{\$25}{20} = \$1.25 \text{ per unit}$$

Employees with poor training, poor education, or poor work habits may not be a good buy even at low wages. By the same token, employees who cannot or will not always reach

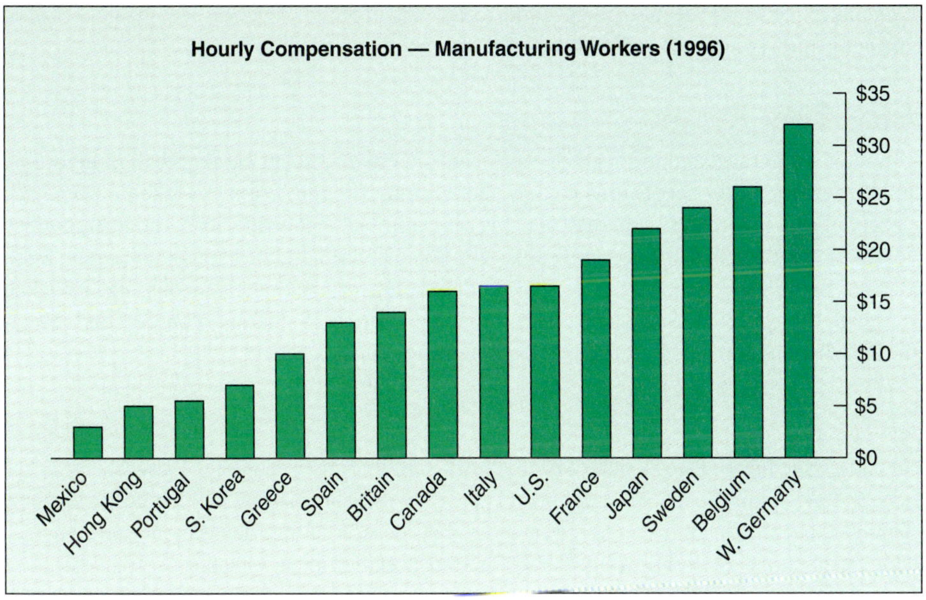
Hourly Compensation — Manufacturing Workers (1996)
$35
$30
$25
$20
$15
$10
$5
$0
Mexico
Hong Kong
Portugal
S. Korea
Greece
Spain
Britain
Canada
Italy
U.S.
France
Japan
Sweden
Belgium
W. Germany

FIGURE 8.2 ■ Labor Costs around the World

Sources: The Economist, May 24, 1997, p. 104; Swedish Employers' Confederation; and projections of the authors.

RCA
Componentes, S.A.deC.V
Entrada
Principal
RCA

Assembly plants operating along the Mexican side of the border, from Texas to California, are called maquiladoras. Some 2,000 firms and industrial giants, such as General Motors, Zenith, Hitachi, and GE, operate these plants, which were designed to help both sides of the impoverished border region. It is believed that by the year 2005, as many as 3 million workers will be employed in these cross-border plants. Mexican wages are low, and at current exchange rates, companies don't look to the Far East as they once did.

their places of work are not much good to the organization, even at low wages. (Labor cost per unit is sometimes called the *labor content* of the product.)

Exchange Rates

Although wage rates and productivity may make a country seem economical, unfavorable exchange rates might negate any savings. Sometimes, though, firms can take advantage of a particularly favorable exchange rate by relocating or exporting to a foreign country. However, the values of foreign currencies continually rise and fall in most countries. Such changes could well make what was a good location in 1998 a disastrous one in 2003. Many of the *maquiladora* plants, U.S.-owned factories in Juarez, Tijuana, and Matamoros, Mexico, expanded after the Mexican peso was devalued.

Costs

Tangible costs Readily identifiable costs that can be measured with some precision.

We can divide location costs into two categories, tangible and intangible. **Tangible costs** are those costs that are readily identifiable and precisely measured. They include utilities, labor, material, taxes, depreciation, and other costs that the accounting department and management can identify. In addition, such costs as transportation of raw materials, transportation of finished goods, and site construction are all factored into the overall cost of a location.

Intangible costs A category of location costs that cannot be easily quantified, such as quality of life and government.

Intangible costs are less easily quantified. They include quality of education, public transportation facilities, community attitudes toward the industry and the company, and quality and attitude of prospective employees. They also include quality-of-life variables, such as climate and sports teams, that may influence personnel recruiting.

Attitudes

Attitudes of national, state, and local governments toward private property, zoning, pollution, and employment stability may be in flux. Governmental attitudes at the time a location decision is made may not be lasting ones (see the *OM in Action* box, "O Governor, Won't You Buy Me a Mercedes Plant?"). Moreover, management may find that these attitudes can be influenced by their own leadership.

Table 8.1 ranks the top 20 countries in terms of their business environments. It is interesting to note that Hong Kong had held the number-one position over the period 1992–1996 but then dropped to number 14 with its takeover by mainland China.

"May I have my allowance in Deutsche Marks, Dad?"

TABLE 8.1 ■ Ranking of the Business Environment in 20 Countries, 1997–2001

Ranking calculation uses indicators such as market potential, tax and labor policies, infrastructure, skills, and political environment.

Rank	Country	Rank	Country
1	Netherlands	11	Finland
2	Britain	12	Belgium
3	Canada	13	New Zealand
4	Singapore	14	Hong Kong
5	U.S.	15	Austria
6	Denmark	16	Australia
7	Germany	17	Norway
8	France	18	Ireland
9	Switzerland	19	Italy
10	Sweden	20	Chile

Source: The Economist, May 17, 1997, p. 116, from the Economist Intelligence Unit.

> # OM IN ACTION
>
> ## OH GOVERNOR, WON'T YOU BUY ME A MERCEDES PLANT?
>
> When Mercedes-Benz (now DaimlerChrysler) announced plans in 1993 to build its first overseas plant in Vance, Alabama, the state hailed the German automaker as an industrial savior. Alabama's euphoria came after a year of competition among 170 sites in 30 states. Losers included finalists North Carolina and South Carolina and semifinalists Tennessee, Georgia, and Nebraska. Alabama Governor Jim Folsom warmly welcomed the $300-million complex and 1,500 high-paying new jobs as a symbol of prosperity. The city of Birmingham even spent $75,000 to erect a huge Mercedes hood ornament at the Legion Field football stadium just in time for the Alabama-Tennessee football game.
>
> However, as the details of the state's economic incentives to Mercedes have become public, not everyone has remained happy. Besides tax breaks and subsidies pushing $290 million (or $200,000 per job), the state agreed to buy 2,500 Mercedes vehicles for use by everyone from highway construction supervisors to agricultural agents. To clear land that the taxpayers bought for Mercedes, Governor Folsom even called out the National Guard for a "training mission," in effect using federal money to pay for one of Alabama's promised incentives.
>
> The trade-off, say local politicians, will be newfound prestige of making 60,000 Mercedes sports-utility vehicles a year and an extra 15,000 auto-related jobs. When Alabama missed a $43-million payment to Mercedes in 1994 and had to borrow from the state's pension fund, though, Governor Folsom was voted out of office. Critics said tax breaks were 18 times what Tennessee paid to get a Nissan plant and 4 times larger than what Kentucky paid for a Toyota plant. Says University of Alabama analyst William Gunther, "We're suffering from winner's curse." As for the $75,000 Mercedes emblem from Legion Field, it is lying these days in weeds in a storage yard.
>
> Sources: *New York Times* (January 1, 1996): 4–1, 4–10; and *Economist* (January 8, 1994): 32.

Worker attitudes may also differ from country to country, region to region, and small town to city. Worker views regarding turnover, unions, and absenteeism are all relevant factors. In turn, these attitudes can affect a company's decision whether to make offers to current workers if the firm relocates to a new location. The case study at the end of this chapter, Southern Recreational Vehicle Company, describes a St. Louis firm that actively chose *not to relocate* any of its workers when it moved to Mississippi.

Proximity to Markets

For many firms it is extremely important to locate near customers. Particularly, service organizations, like drugstores, restaurants, post offices, or barbers, find proximity to market is *the* primary location factor. Manufacturing firms find it useful to be close to customers when transporting finished goods is expensive or difficult (perhaps because they are bulky, heavy, or fragile). In addition, with the trend toward just-in-time production, suppliers want to locate near users to speed deliveries. For a firm like Coca-Cola, whose product's primary ingredient is water, it makes sense to have a bottling plant in many cities rather than shipping heavy (and sometimes fragile glass) containers cross country.

Proximity to Suppliers

Firms locate near their raw materials and suppliers because of (1) perishability, (2) transportation costs, or (3) bulk. Bakeries, dairy plants, and frozen seafood processors deal with *perishable* raw materials, so they often locate close to suppliers. Companies dependent on inputs of heavy or bulky raw materials (such as steel producers using coal and iron ore) face expensive inbound *transportation costs*, so transportation costs become a major factor. And goods for which there is a *reduction in bulk* during production (such as lumber mills locating in the Northwest near timber resources) typically need to be near the raw material.

The Texas city of Amarillo recently sent checks for $8 million apiece to 1,350 businesses as a "bribe." To cash the check, the business would have to set up shop in Amarillo and employ 800 workers. Only three takers so far. Why?

Masaki Kaneho, plant manager of Motorola's integrated semiconductor plant in Aizu, Japan, with author Jay Heizer. As a world-class manufacturer, Motorola has located facilities throughout the world. Where labor costs are a significant part of product cost, Southeast Asia may be appropriate. For other countries, such as Japan, exchange rates or a local presence may be critical. While a Southeast Asian worker can wire 120 integrated circuits to metal frames each hour, an automated machine can do 640. One worker can monitor 8 machines for a total hourly production of 5,120. Clearly, in integrated-circuit production, direct labor costs have become less critical and other considerations relatively more important.

METHODS OF EVALUATING LOCATION ALTERNATIVES

Four major methods are used for solving location problems: the factor-rating method, locational break-even analysis, the center-of-gravity method, and the transportation model. This section describes these approaches.

The Factor-Rating Method

There are many factors, both qualitative and quantitative, to consider in choosing a location. Some of these factors are more important than others, so managers can use weightings to make the decision process more objective. The **factor-rating method** is popular because a wide variety of factors, from education to recreation to labor skills, can be objectively included. Table 8.2 lists a few of the many factors that affect location decisions.

The factor-rating method has six steps:

1. Develop a list of relevant factors (such as those in Table 8.2).
2. Assign a weight to each factor to reflect its relative importance in the company's objectives.
3. Develop a scale for each factor (for example, 1 to 10 or 1 to 100 points).
4. Have management score each location for each factor, using the scale in step 3.
5. Multiply the score by the weights for each factor and total the score for each location.
6. Make a recommendation based on the maximum point score, considering the results of quantitative approaches as well.

Factor-rating method
A location method that instills objectivity into the process of identifying hard-to-evaluate costs.

The numbers used in factor weighting can be subjective and the model's results are not "exact" even though this is a quantitative approach.

TABLE 8.2 ■ Factors Affecting Location Selection

Labor costs (including wages, unionization, productivity)

Labor availability (including attitudes, age, distribution, skills)

Proximity to raw materials and suppliers

Proximity to markets

State and local government fiscal policies (including incentives, taxes, unemployment compensation)

Environmental regulations

Utilities (including gas, electric, water, and their costs)

Site costs (including land, expansion, parking, drainage)

Transportation availability (including rail, air, water, interstate roads)

Quality-of-life issues in the community (including all levels of education, cost of living, health care, sports, cultural activities, transportation, housing, entertainment, religious facilities)

Foreign exchange (including rates, stability)

Quality of government (including stability, honesty, attitudes toward new business—whether overseas or local)

A Grant Thornton study of U.S. locations showed North Dakota, Nebraska, and South Dakota to be the best places to locate and Montana, Ohio, and Michigan as the worst.

EXAMPLE 1

Five Flags over Florida, a U.S. chain of 10 family-oriented theme parks, has decided to expand overseas by opening its first park in Europe. The rating sheet in Table 8.3 provides a list of qualitative factors that management has decided are important; their weightings and their rating for two possible sites—Dijon, France, and Copenhagen, Denmark—are shown.

TABLE 8.3 Weights, Scores, and Solution

		SCORES (out of 100)		WEIGHTED SCORES	
FACTOR	WEIGHT	France	Denmark	France	Denmark
Labor availability and attitude	.25	70	60	(.25)(70) = 17.5	(.25)(60) = 15.0
People-to-car ratio	.05	50	60	(.05)(50) = 2.5	(.05)(60) = 3.0
Per capita income	.10	85	80	(.10)(85) = 8.5	(.10)(80) = 8.0
Tax structure	.39	75	70	(.39)(75) = 29.3	(.39)(70) = 27.3
Education and health	.21	60	70	(.21)(60) = 12.6	(.21)(70) = 14.7
Totals	1.00			70.4	68.0

Table 8.3 also indicates use of weights to evaluate alternative site locations. Given the option of 100 points assigned to each factor, the French location is preferable. By changing the points or weights slightly for those factors about which there is some doubt, we can analyze the sensitivity of the decision. For instance, we can see that changing the scores for "labor availability and attitude" by 10 points can change the decision.

When a decision is sensitive to minor changes, further analysis of either the weighting or the points assigned may be appropriate. Alternatively, management may conclude that these intangible factors are not the proper criteria on which to base a location decision. Managers therefore place primary weight on the more quantitative aspects of the decision.

Locational Break-Even Analysis

Locational break-even analysis A cost-volume analysis to make an economic comparison of location alternatives.

Locational break-even analysis is the use of cost-volume analysis to make an economic comparison of location alternatives. By identifying fixed and variable costs and graphing them for each location, we can determine which one provides the lowest cost. Locational break-even analysis can be done mathematically or graphically. The graphic approach has the advantage of providing the range of volume over which each location is preferable.

The three steps to locational break-even analysis are:

1. Determine the fixed and variable cost for each location.
2. Plot the costs for each location, with costs on the vertical axis of the graph and annual volume on the horizontal axis.
3. Select the location that has the lowest total cost for the expected production volume.

EXAMPLE 2

A manufacturer of automobile carburetors is considering three locations—Akron, Bowling Green, and Chicago—for a new plant. Cost studies indicate that fixed costs per year at the sites are $30,000, $60,000, and $110,000, respectively; and variable costs are $75 per unit, $45 per unit, and $25 per unit, respectively. The expected selling price of the carburetors produced is $120. The company wishes to find the most economical location for an expected volume of 2,000 units per year.

For each of the three, we can plot the fixed costs (those at a volume of zero units) and the total cost (fixed costs + variable costs) at the expected volume of output. These lines have been plotted in Figure 8.3.

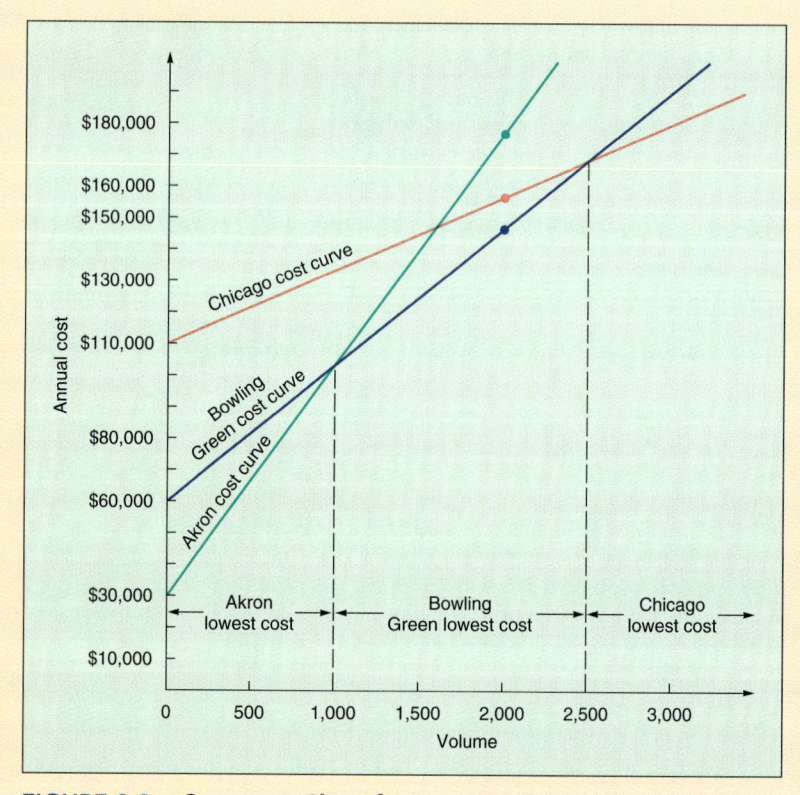

FIGURE 8.3 ■ **Crossover Chart for Locational Break-Even Analysis**

For Akron,

$$\text{Total cost} = \$30{,}000 + \$75(2{,}000) = \$180{,}000$$

For Bowling Green,

$$\text{Total cost} = \$60{,}000 + \$45(2{,}000) = \$150{,}000$$

For Chicago,

$$\text{Total cost} = \$110{,}000 + \$25(2{,}000) = \$160{,}000$$

With an expected volume of 2,000 units per year, Bowling Green provides the lowest cost location. The expected profit is:

$$\text{Total revenue} - \text{Total cost} = \$120(2{,}000) - \$150{,}000 = \$90{,}000 \text{ per year}$$

The chart also tells us that for a volume of less than 1,000, Akron would be preferred, and for a volume greater than 2,500, Chicago would yield the greatest profit. The crossover points are 1,000 and 2,500.

Center-of-Gravity Method

The **center-of-gravity method** is a mathematical technique used for finding the location of a distribution center that will minimize distribution costs. The method takes into account the location of markets, the volume of goods shipped to those markets, and shipping costs in finding the best location for a distribution center.

The first step in the center-of-gravity method is to place the locations on a coordinate system. This will be illustrated in Example 3. The origin of the coordinate system and the scale used are arbitrary, just as long as the relative distances are correctly represented. This can be done easily by placing a grid over an ordinary map. The center of gravity is determined by Equations (8.1) and (8.2):

Center-of-gravity method A mathematical technique used for finding the best location for a single distribution point that services several stores or areas.

$$C_x = \frac{\sum_i d_{ix} W_i}{\sum_i W_i} \qquad (8.1)$$

$$C_y = \frac{\sum_i d_{iy} W_i}{\sum_i W_i} \qquad (8.2)$$

where C_x = x-coordinate of the center of gravity
C_y = y-coordinate of the center of gravity
d_{ix} = x-coordinate of location i
d_{iy} = y-coordinate of location i
W_i = Volume of goods moved to or from location i

Note that Equations (8.1) and (8.2) include the term W_i, the volume of supplies transferred to or from location i.

Since the number of containers shipped each month affects cost, distance alone should not be the principal criterion. The center-of-gravity method assumes that cost is directly proportional to both distance and volume shipped. The ideal location is that which minimizes the weighted distance between the warehouse and its retail outlets, where the distance is weighted by the number of containers shipped.

EXAMPLE 3

Consider the case of Quain's Discount Department Stores, a chain of four large Kmart-type outlets. The firm's store locations are in Chicago, Pittsburgh, New York, and Atlanta; they are currently being supplied out of an old and inadequate warehouse in Pittsburgh, the site of the chain's first store. Data on demand rates at each outlet are shown in Table 8.4.

TABLE 8.4 ■ Demand for Quain's Discount Department Stores

Store Location	Number of Containers Shipped per Month
Chicago	2,000
Pittsburgh	1,000
New York	1,000
Atlanta	2,000

The firm has decided to find some "central" location in which to build a new warehouse. Its current store locations are shown in Figure 8.4. For example, location 1 is Chicago, and from Table 8.4 and Figure 8.4, we have:

$$d_{1x} = 30$$

$$d_{1y} = 120$$

$$W_1 = 2,000$$

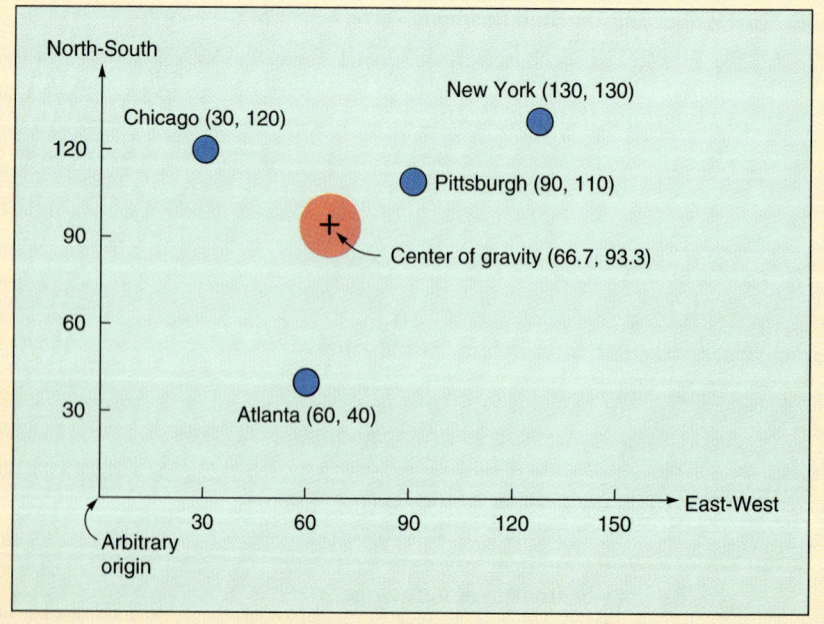

FIGURE 8.4 ■ Coordinate Locations of Four Quain's Department Stores and Center of Gravity

Using the data in Table 8.4 and Figure 8.4 for each of the other cities, in Equations (8.1) and (8.2) we find:

$$C_x = \frac{(30)(2000) + (90)(1000) + (130)(1000) + (60)(2000)}{2000 + 1000 + 1000 + 2000} = \frac{400,000}{6,000}$$

$$= 66.7$$

$$C_y = \frac{(120)(2000) + (110)(1000) + (130)(1000) + (40)(2000)}{2000 + 1000 + 1000 + 2000} = \frac{560,000}{6,000}$$

$$= 93.3$$

This location (66.7, 93.3) is shown by the crosshair in Figure 8.4. By overlaying a U.S. map on this exhibit, we find that this location is near central Ohio. The firm may well wish to consider Columbus, Ohio, or a nearby city as an appropriate location.

Transportation Model

The objective of the **transportation model** is to determine the best pattern of shipments from several points of supply (sources) to several points of demand (destinations) so as to minimize total production and transportation costs. Every firm with a network of supply-and-demand points faces such a problem. The complex Volkswagen supply network (shown in Figure 8.5) provides one such illustration. We note in Figure 8.5, for example, that VW de Mexico ships vehicles for assembly and parts to VW of Nigeria, sends assemblies to VW do Brazil, while it receives parts and assemblies from headquarters in Germany.

Although the linear programming (LP) technique can be used to solve this type of problem, more efficient, special-purpose algorithms have been developed for the trans-

Transportation model
A technique for solving a class of linear programming problems.

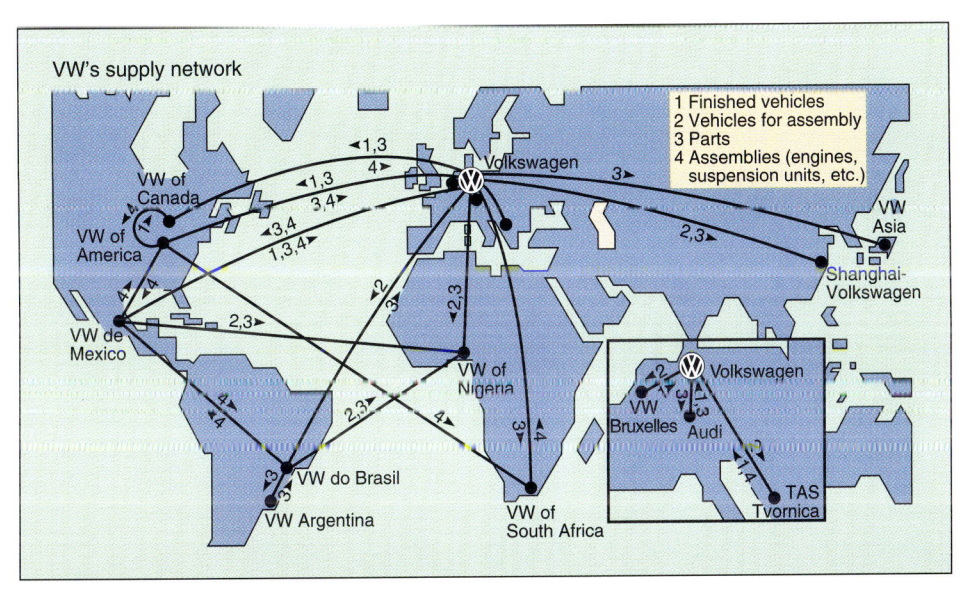

FIGURE 8.5 ■ Worldwide Distribution of Volkswagens and Parts
Source: The Economist, Ltd. Distributed by the *New York Times*/Special Features.

portation application. The transportation model finds an initial feasible solution and then makes step-by-step improvement until an optimal solution is reached.

SERVICE LOCATION STRATEGY

It is often desirable to locate near competition; large department stores often attract more shoppers when competitors are close by. The same applies to shoe stores, fast-food restaurants, and others.

While the focus in industrial-sector location analysis is on minimizing cost, the focus in the service sector is on maximizing revenue. This is because manufacturing firms find costs tend to vary substantially between locations, while service firms find location often has more impact on revenue than cost. Therefore, for the service firm, a specific location often influences revenue more than it does cost. This means that the location focus for service firms should be on determining the volume of business and revenue. There are eight major components of volume and revenue for the service firm. These are:

1. Purchasing power of the customer-drawing area.
2. Service and image compatibility with demographics of the customer-drawing area.
3. Competition in the area.
4. Quality of the competition.
5. Uniqueness of the firm's and competitors' locations.
6. Physical qualities of facilities and neighboring businesses.
7. Operating policies of the firm.
8. Quality of management.

TABLE 8.5 ■ Location Strategies—Service vs. Goods-Producing Organizations

Service/Retail/Professional Location	Goods-Producing Location
REVENUE FOCUS	**COST FOCUS**
Volume/revenue	**Tangible costs**
Drawing area; purchasing power	Transportation cost of raw material
Competition; advertising/pricing	Shipment cost of finished goods
Physical quality	Energy and utility cost; labor; raw material; taxes, and so on
Parking/access; security/lighting; appearance/image	**Intangible and future costs**
Cost determinants	Attitude toward union
Rent	Quality of life
Management caliber	Education expenditures by state
Operation policies (hours, wage rates)	Quality of state and local government
TECHNIQUES	**TECHNIQUES**
Regression models to determine importance of various factors	Transportation method
Factor-rating method	Factor-rating method
Traffic counts	Locational break-even analysis
Demographic analysis of drawing area	Crossover charts
Purchasing power analysis of area	
Center-of-gravity method	
Geographic information systems	
ASSUMPTIONS	**ASSUMPTIONS**
Location is a major determinant of revenue	Location is a major determinant of cost
High customer-contact issues are critical	Most major costs can be identified explicitly for each site
Costs are relatively constant for a given area; therefore, the revenue function is critical	Low customer contact allows focus on the identifiable costs
	Intangible costs can be evaluated

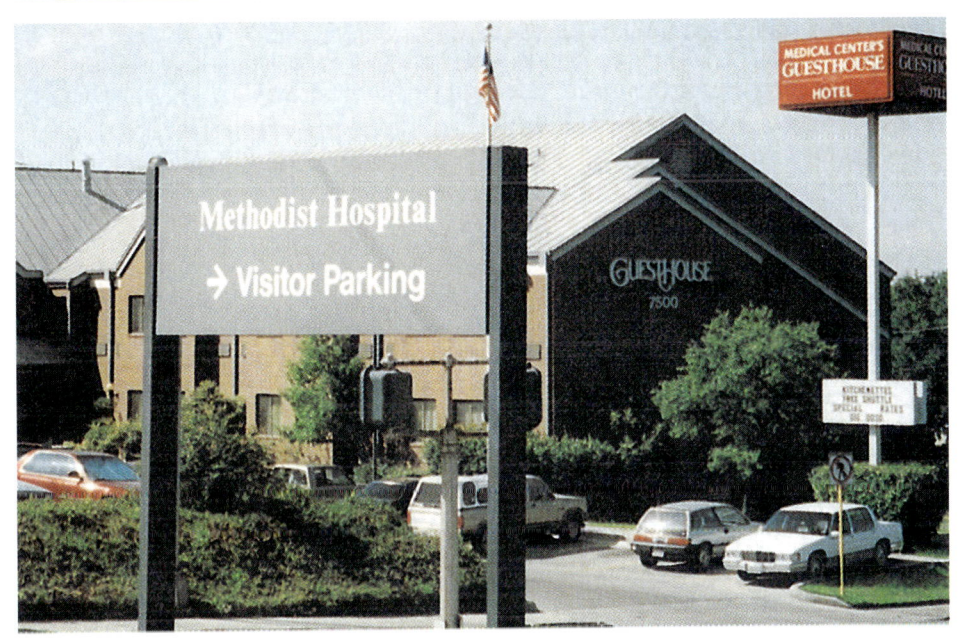

Even with reduced tax benefits and a saturated hotel market, opportunities still exist when hotel/motel locations are right. Good sites include those near hospitals and medical centers. As medical complexes in metropolitan areas continue to increase, so does the need for hotels to house patients' families. Additionally, medical services such as outpatient care, shorter hospital stays, and more diagnostic tests increase the need for hotels near hospitals.

Realistic analysis of these factors can provide a reasonable picture of the revenue expected. The techniques used in the service sector include correlation analysis, traffic counts, demographic analysis, purchasing power analysis, the factor-rating method, the center-of-gravity method, and geographic information systems. Table 8.5 provides a summary of location strategies for both service and goods-producing organizations.

How Hotel Chains Select Sites

One of the most important decisions in the hospitality industry is location. Hotel chains that pick good sites more accurately and quickly than competitors have a distinct strategic advantage. La Quinta Motor Inns, headquartered in San Antonio, Texas, is a moderately priced chain of 150 inns oriented toward frequent business travelers. To model motel-selection behavior and predict success of a site, La Quinta turned to statistical regression analysis.[2]

The hotel started by testing 35 independent variables, trying to find which of them would have the highest correlation with predicted profitability, the dependent variable. "Competitive" independent variables included the number of hotel rooms in the vicinity and average room rates. "Demand generator" variables were such local attractions as office buildings and hospitals that drew potential customers to a 4-mile-radius trade area. "Demographic" variables, such as local population and unemployment rate, can also affect the success of a hotel. "Market awareness" factors, such as the number of inns in a region, were a fourth category. Finally, "physical characteristics" of the site, such as ease of access or sign visibility, provided the last group of the 35 independent variables.

[2] Sheryl Kimes and James Fitzsimmons, "Selecting Profitable Hotel Sites at La Quinta Motor Inns," *Interfaces*, March–April 1990, pp. 12–20. Also see *The Wall Street Journal*, July 19, 1995, pp. B1, B5, for a discussion of how Amerihost Inns makes its location decisions.

> ## OM IN ACTION
>
> ### RETAILERS PAY BIG FOR PRIME INTERNET LOCATIONS
>
> One of the biggest cost savings for Internet retailers—no location, no location, no location—has turned out to be a location problem of a different sort. With hundreds of thousands of addresses on the World Wide Web, on-line retailers are discovering that customers are having a hard time finding them.
>
> Like bookstores, flower shops, and clothing stores in your town, on-line merchants need high-traffic sites to be successful. However, unlike the approaches described in this chapter, the key is prominent placement on the home pages of on-line service providers (like America Online, AOL) and search engines (like Excite or Yahoo).
>
> Two examples of premiere location deals are those made by Amazon.com (the discount bookstore) and 1-800-Flowers (the huge on-line florist). Entering into long-term relations with AOL and Excite, Amazon.com is paying top dollar ($19 million just to AOL) for promotional space on these heavily traveled sites. 1-800-Flowers inked a similar $25-million, 4-year deal with AOL. "Distribution is king," says George Bell, CEO of Excite, Inc. "If you have a terrific service but no eyeballs, it's likely the service will fail."
>
> *Sources: The Wall Street Journal* (July 8, 1997): B1, B8 and (August 5, 1997): B7 and; *Forbes* (June 2, 1997): 180.

In the end, the regression model chosen, with a coefficient of determination (r^2) of 51%, included just four predictive variables. They are the *price of the inn, median income levels, the state population per inn,* and the *location of nearby colleges* (which serves as a proxy for other demand generators). La Quinta then used the regression model to predict profitability and developed a cutoff that gave the best results for predicting success or failure of a site. A spreadsheet is now used to implement the model, which applies the decision rule and suggests "build" or "don't build."

The Telemarketing and Internet Industries

Where to locate telemarketers? Sixteen states now permit private companies to hire prisoners to pitch products, conduct surveys, or answer hotel/airline reservation systems.

Those industries and office activities that require neither face-to-face contact with the customer nor movement of material broaden location options substantially. A case in point is the telemarketing industry and those selling over the Internet, in which our traditional variables (as noted earlier) are no longer relevant. Where the electronic movement of information is good, the cost and availability of labor may drive the location decision. For instance, Fidelity Investments recently relocated many of its employees from Boston to Covington, Kentucky. Now employees in the low-cost Covington region connect, by inexpensive fiber-optic phone lines, to their colleagues in the Boston office at a cost of less than a penny per minute. That is less than Fidelity spends on local connections.

The changes in location criteria may also affect a number of other businesses. For instance, states with smaller tax burdens and owners of property in fringe suburbs and scenic rural areas should come out ahead. So should e-mail providers (like MCI), telecommuting software makers (like IBM/Lotus), videoconferencing firms (like PictureTel), makers of office electronic equipment (like Dell and Hewlett-Packard), and delivery firms (like UPS and Federal Express).

A whole separate category applies to service firms locating on the World Wide Web. Many of these "virtual" firms find their major location decision is *where to be on the Web.* As the *OM in Action* box, "Retailers Pay Big for Prime Internet Locations," indicates, virtual locations are becoming as important as physical ones.

Geographic Information Systems

Geographic information systems (GISs) are the latest tool to help firms make successful, analytical decisions with regard to location. Retailers, banks, food chains, and print shop

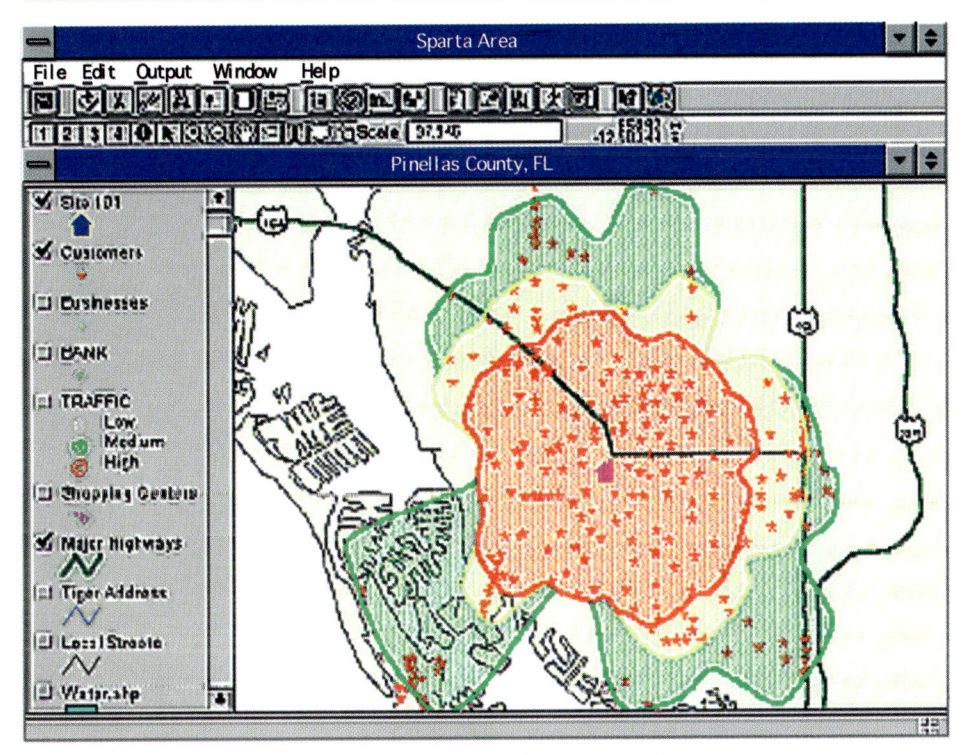

Geographic information systems, such as this one from National Decision Systems, can incorporate street-based data from the U.S. Census Bureau with traffic flow, local businesses, and income levels. Source: National Decision Systems, San Diego, CA.

franchises can all use geographically coded files from a GIS to conduct demographic analyses. By combining population, age, income, traffic flow, and density figures with geography, a retailer can pinpoint the best location for a new store or restaurant.

For example, Pep Boys, an auto parts retailer headquartered in Philadelphia, has developed models of how GIS technology can be used to identify where the company should locate new stores. It also uses its GIS to decide how many stores are needed to provide proper coverage in a certain geographic area.[3] Pep Boys uses a GIS software product called Atlas GIS (from Strategic Mapping Inc.). Other similar packages are Hemisphere Solutions (by Unisys Corp.), Map Info (from MapInfo Corp.), Arc/Info (by ESRI), SAS/GIS (by SAS Institute Inc.), and Market Base (by National Decision Systems, Inc.).

SUMMARY

Location may determine up to 10% of the total cost of an industrial firm. Location is also a critical element in determining revenue for the service, retail, or professional firm. Industrial firms need to consider both tangible and intangible costs. We typically address industrial location problems via a factor-rating method, locational break even analysis, the center-of-gravity method, and the transportation method of linear programming.

For service, retail, and professional organizations, analysis is typically made of a variety of variables including purchasing power of a drawing area, competition, advertising and promotion, physical qualities of the location, and operating policies of the organization.

---

[3] C. Frye, "Business Use Pushes GIS into Uncharted Territory," *Software Magazine,* November 1994, pp. 81–85.

308   CHAPTER 8   LOCATION STRATEGIES

KEY TERMS

Tangible costs *(p. 296)*
Intangible costs *(p. 296)*
Factor-rating method *(p. 298)*
Locational break-even analysis *(p. 300)*
Center-of-gravity method *(p. 301)*
Transportation model *(p. 303)*

USING POM FOR WINDOWS

POM for Windows includes two different facility location models. The first, the factor-rating method, was already illustrated in chapter 3 (see Program 3.1). The second, the center-of-gravity model, is illustrated in Program 8.1 using Example 3's data.

Quain's Department Store Solution

	Weight/# trips	x-coord	y-coord	X multiplied	Y multiplied
Chicago	2,000.	30.	120.	60,000.	240,000.
Pittsburgh	1,000.	90.	110.	90,000.	110,000.
New York	1,000.	130.	130.	130,000.	130,000.
Atlanta	2,000.	60.	40.	120,000.	80,000.
Total	6,000.	310.	400.	400,000.	560,000.
Average		77.5	100.		
Weighted Average				66.6667	93.3333
Median	3,000.			60.	110.

PROGRAM 8.1 ■ POM for Windows Center-of-Gravity Method, Applied to Example 3 Data (Quain's Discount Department Store)

USING EXCEL OM TO SOLVE LOCATION PROBLEMS

Excel is an excellent tool for solving both factor-rating and center-of-gravity problems. Earlier, in chapter 3 (see Programs 3.2 and 3.3), we illustrated the factor-rating model. Excel OM's center-of-gravity formulas are illustrated in Program 8.2, using the data from Example 3, Quain's Discount Department Store. The output that corresponds appears in Program 8.3.

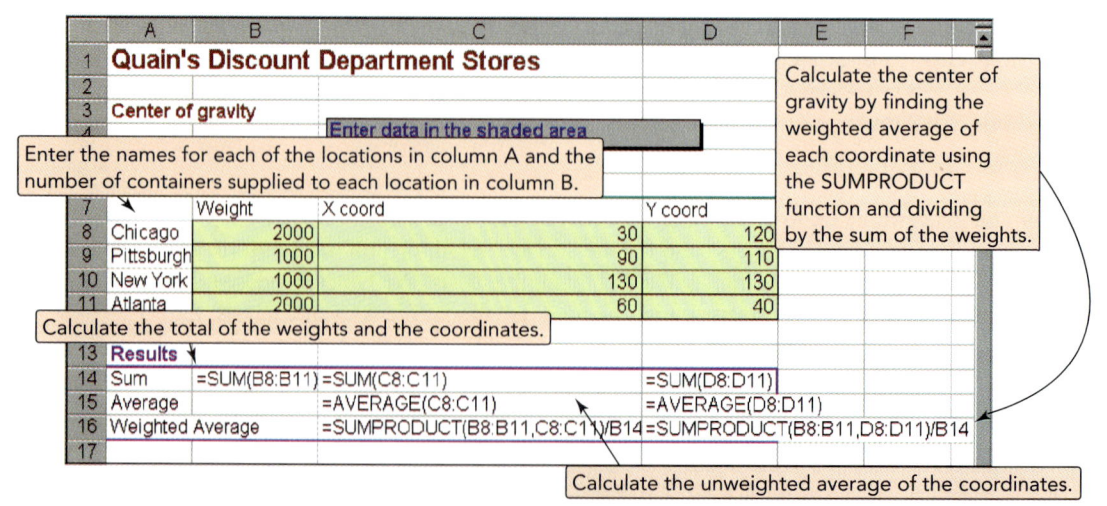

	A	B	C	D
1	Quain's Discount Department Stores			
2				
3	Center of gravity			
4		Enter data in the shaded area		
7		Weight	X coord	Y coord
8	Chicago	2000	30	120
9	Pittsburgh	1000	90	110
10	New York	1000	130	130
11	Atlanta	2000	60	40
13	Results			
14	Sum	=SUM(B8:B11)	=SUM(C8:C11)	=SUM(D8:D11)
15	Average		=AVERAGE(C8:C11)	=AVERAGE(D8:D11)
16	Weighted Average		=SUMPRODUCT(B8:B11,C8:C11)/B14	=SUMPRODUCT(B8:B11,D8:D11)/B14

Enter the names for each of the locations in column A and the number of containers supplied to each location in column B.

Calculate the center of gravity by finding the weighted average of each coordinate using the SUMPRODUCT function and dividing by the sum of the weights.

Calculate the total of the weights and the coordinates.

Calculate the unweighted average of the coordinates.

PROGRAM 8.2 ■ Excel OM's Center-of-Gravity Input Screen and Data from Example 3

Quain's Discount Department Stores

Center of gravity

Enter data in the shaded area

The graph is created by using Excel's chartwizard. Highlight cells C8 through D11 and then click on the chartwizard icon on the toolbar.

Data

	Weight	X coord	Y coord
Chicago	2000	30	120
Pittsburgh	1000	90	110
New York	1000	130	130
Atlanta	2000	60	40

Results

Sum	6000	310	400
Average		77.5	100
Weighted Average		66.66667	93.33333333

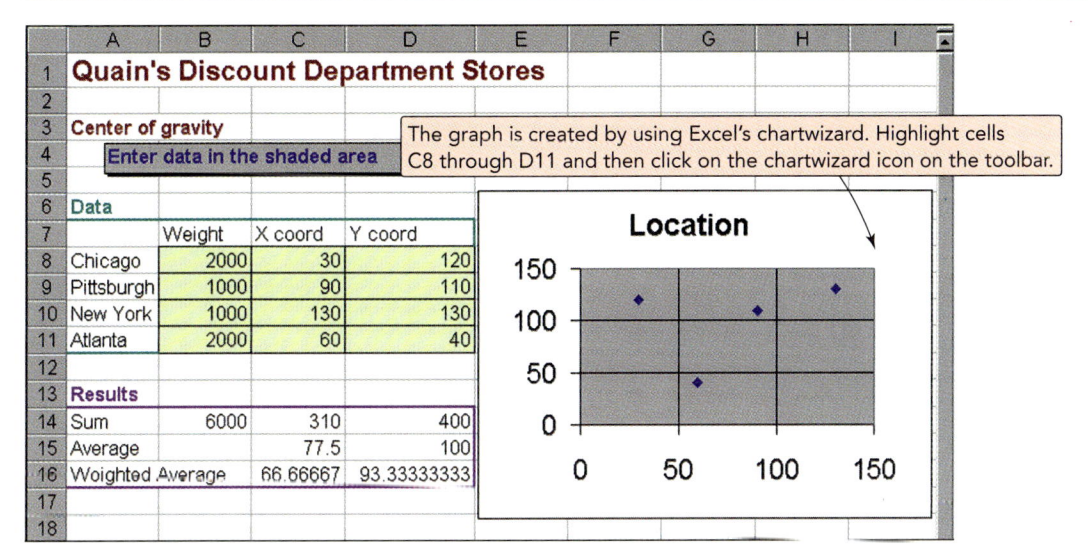

Location (graph showing points plotted between 0–150 on both axes)

PROGRAM 8.3 ■ Output from Program 8.2, Using Excel OM to Solve the Quain's Center-of-Gravity Problem

SOLVED PROBLEMS

Solved Problem 8.1

Just as cities and communities can be compared for location selection by the weighted approach model, as we saw earlier in this chapter, so can actual site decisions within those cities. Table 8.6 on page 310 illustrates four factors of importance to Washington, DC, and the health officials charged with opening that city's first public drug treatment clinic. Of primary concern (and given a weight of 5) was location of the clinic so it would be as accessible as possible to the largest number of patients. Due to a tight budget, the annual lease cost was also of some concern. A suite in the new City Hall, at 14th and U Streets, was highly rated because its rent would be free. An old office building near the downtown bus station received a much lower rating because of its cost. Equally important as lease cost was the need for confidentiality of patients and, therefore, for a relatively inconspicuous clinic. Finally, because so many of the staff at the clinic would be donating their time, the safety, parking, and accessibility of each site were of concern as well.

Using the factor-rating method, which site is preferred?

Solution

From the three rightmost columns in Table 8.6, the weighted scores are summed. The bus terminal area has a low score and can be excluded from further consideration. The other two sites are virtually identical in total score. The city may now want to consider other factors, including political ones, in selecting between the two remaining sites.

Source: R. Murdick, B. Render, and R. Russell, *Service Operations Management.* Copyright ©1990 by Allyn & Bacon. Reprinted by permission.

TABLE 8.6 ■ Potential Clinic Sites in Washington, DC

		Potential Locations*			Weighted Scores		
FACTOR	IMPORTANCE WEIGHT	HOMELESS SHELTER (2ND AND D, SE)	CITY HALL (14TH AND U, NW)	BUS TERMINAL AREA (7TH AND H, NW)	HOMELESS SHELTER	CITY HALL	BUS TERMINAL AREA
Accessibility for addicts	5	9	7	7	45	35	35
Annual lease cost	3	6	10	3	18	30	9
Inconspicuous	3	5	2	7	15	6	21
Accessibility for health staff	2	3	6	2	6	12	4
				Total scores:	84	83	69

*All sites are rated on a 1 to 10 basis, with 10 as the highest score and 1 as the lowest.

Solved Problem 8.2

Chuck Bimmerle is considering opening a new foundry in Denton, Texas; Edwardsville, Illinois; or Fayetteville, Arkansas, to produce high-quality rifle sights. He has assembled the following fixed cost and variable cost data:

		Per Unit Costs		
LOCATION	FIXED COST PER YEAR	MATERIAL	LABOR	VARIABLE OVERHEAD
Denton	$200,000	$ .20	$ .40	$ .40
Edwardsville	$180,000	$ .25	$ .75	$ .75
Fayetteville	$170,000	$1.00	$1.00	$1.00

a) Graph the total cost lines.
b) Over what range of annual volume is each facility going to have a competitive advantage?
c) What is the volume at the intersection of the Edwardsville and Fayetteville cost lines?

Solution

a) A graph of the total cost lines is shown in Figure 8.6.
b) Below 8,000 units, the Fayetteville facility will have a competitive advantage (lowest cost); between 8,000 units and 26,666 units, Edwardsville has an advantage; and above 26,666, Denton has the advantage. (We have made the assumption in this problem that other costs—that is, delivery and intangible factors—are constant regardless of the decision.)
c) From Figure 8.6, we see that the cost line for Fayetteville and the cost line for Edwardsville cross at about 8,000. We can also determine this point with a little algebra:

$$\$180{,}000 + 1.75Q = \$170{,}000 + 3.00Q$$

$$\$10{,}000 = 1.25Q$$

$$8{,}000 = Q$$

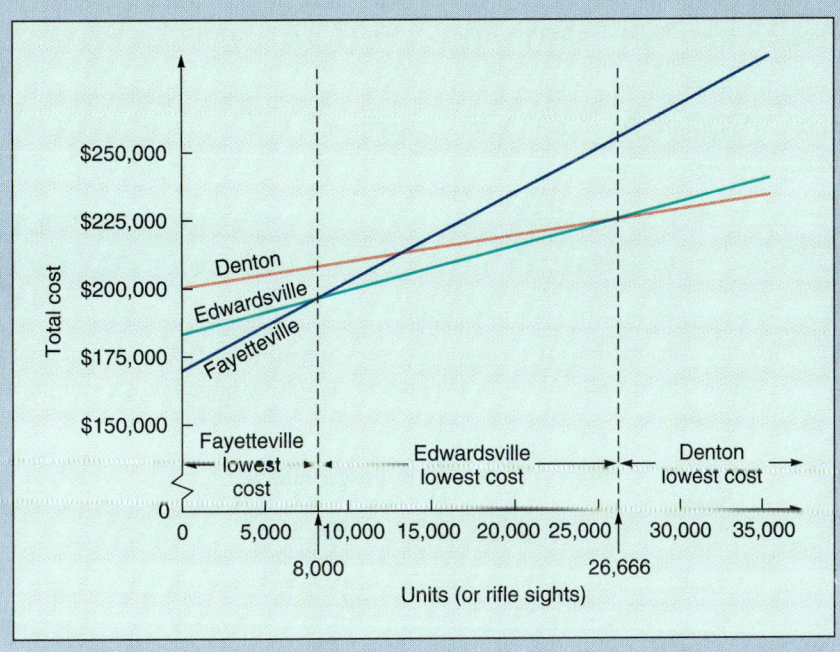

FIGURE 8.6 ■ Graph of Total Cost Lines for Chuck Bimmerle

DISCUSSION QUESTIONS

1. In terms of the strategic objective, how do goods-producing and service location decisions differ?
2. In recent years, the federal government has increased the latitude that railroads have in setting rates and has deregulated much of the rate-setting structure of trucks and airlines. What will be the long-range impact of this deregulation on location strategies?
3. Responding to a group of manufacturers who were complaining about the impact of increased taxes, Krishna Dir, city manager of a large eastern city, argued that taxes levied by a city were not an important consideration to a new business contemplating moving to that city. If you were president of the local chamber of commerce, how would you respond? If you are a person who is concerned about the unemployment rate in the inner city, how would you respond?
4. Explain the assumptions behind the center-of-gravity method. How can the model be used in a service facility location?
5. How do service facility location decisions differ from industrial location decisions in terms of the techniques used to analyze them?
6. What is the objective of location strategy?
7. What are the three steps to locational break-even analysis?
8. What are the major factors firms consider when choosing a country in which to locate?
9. What factors affect region/community location decisions?
10. Name several factors that affect site location.
11. How can quantitative and qualitative factors both be considered in a location decision?

CRITICAL THINKING EXERCISE

In this chapter, we have discussed a number of location decisions, including Mercedes-Benz's selection of Vance, Alabama, for its first U.S. plant. Similarly, United Airlines announced its competition to select a town for a new billion-dollar aircraft-repair base. The bidding for the prize of 7,000 jobs was fast and furious, with Orlando offering $154 million in incentives and Denver more than twice that amount. Kentucky's governor angrily rescinded Louisville's offer of $300 million, likening the bidding to "squeezing every drop of blood out of a turnip." What are the ethical, legal, and economic implications of such location bidding wars? Who pays for such giveaways? Are local citizens allowed to vote on offers made by their cities, counties, or states? Should there be limits on these incentives?

PROBLEMS

8.1 Consolidated Refineries, headquartered in Houston, must decide among three sites for the construction of a new oil-processing center. The firm has selected the six factors listed below as a basis for evaluation and has assigned rating weights from 1 to 5 on each factor:

Factor	Factor Name	Rating Weight
1	Proximity to port facilities	5
2	Power-source availability and cost	3
3	Workforce attitude and cost	4
4	Distance from Houston	2
5	Community desirability	2
6	Equipment suppliers in area	3

Management has rated each location for each factor on a 1 to 100 point basis.

Factor	Location A	Location B	Location C
1	100	80	80
2	80	70	100
3	30	60	70
4	10	80	60
5	90	60	80
6	50	60	90

Which site will be recommended?

8.2 The fixed and variable costs for four potential plant sites for a ski equipment manufacturer are shown below:

Site	Fixed Cost Per Year	Variable Cost Per Unit
Atlanta	$125,000	$ 6
Burlington	75,000	5
Cleveland	100,000	4
Denver	50,000	12

a) Graph the total-cost lines for the four potential sites.
b) Over what range of annual volume is each location the preferable one (that with lowest expected cost)?
c) If expected volume of the ski equipment is 5,000 units, which location would you recommend?

8.3 A Detroit seafood restaurant is considering opening a second facility in the suburb of West Bloomfield. The table below shows its ratings of five factors at each of four potential sites. Which site should be selected?

		Site			
Factor	Weight	1	2	3	4
Affluence of local population	10	70	60	85	90
Construction and land cost	10	85	90	80	60
Traffic flow	25	70	60	85	90
Parking availability	20	80	90	90	80
Growth potential	15	90	80	90	75

: **8.4** When placing a new medical clinic, county health offices wish to consider three sites. The pertinent data are given in the table below. Which is the best site?

		Scores		
Location Factor	Weight	Downtown	Suburb A	Suburb B
Facility utilization	9	9	7	6
Average time per emergency trip	8	6	6	8
Employee preferences	5	2	5	6
Accessibility to major roadways	5	8	4	5
Land costs	4	2	9	6

: **8.5** The main post office in Tampa, Florida, is due to be replaced with a much larger, more modern facility that can handle the tremendous flow of mail that has followed the city's growth since 1970. Since all mail, incoming or outgoing, travels from the seven regional post offices in Tampa through the main post office, its site selection can mean a big difference in overall delivery and movement efficiency. Using the data in the following table, calculate the center of gravity location for the proposed new facility.

Regional Post Office	Map Coordinates (x, y)	Truck Round Trips Per Day
Ybor City	(10, 5)	3
Davis Island	(3, 8)	3
Dale-Mabry	(4, 7)	2
Palma Ceia	(15, 10)	6
Bayshore	(13, 3)	5
Temple Terrace	(1, 12)	3
Hyde Park	(5, 5)	10

: **8.6** Katie Reynolds owns two exclusive women's clothing stores in Miami. In her plan to expand to a third location, she has narrowed her decision to three sites—one in a downtown office building, one in a shopping mall, and one in an old Victorian house in the suburban area of Coral Gables. She feels that rent is absolutely the most important factor to be considered, although walk-in traffic is 90% as important as rent. Further, the more distant the new store is from her two existing stores, the better. She weights this factor to be 80% as important as walk-in traffic. Katie developed the table below, in which she graded each site on the same system used in her MBA program in college. Which site is preferable?

	Downtown	Shopping Mall	Coral Gables House
Rent	D	C	A
Walk-in traffic	B	A	D
Distance from existing stores	B	A	C

8.7 The following table gives the map coordinates and the shipping loads for a set of cities that we wish to connect through a central "hub." Near which map coordinates should the hub be located?

City	Map Coordinate (x, y)	Shipping Load
A	(5, 10)	5
B	(6, 8)	10
C	(4, 9)	15
D	(9, 5)	5
E	(7, 9)	15
F	(3, 2)	10
G	(2, 6)	5

8.8 Beth Spenser Retailers is attempting to decide upon a location for a new retail outlet. At the moment, the firm has three alternatives—stay where it is but enlarge the facility; locate along the main street in nearby Newbury; or locate in a new shopping mall in Hyde Park. The company has selected the four factors listed in the following table as the basis for evaluation and has assigned weights as shown:

Factor	Factor Description	Weight
1	Average community income	.30
2	Community growth potential	.15
3	Availability of public transportation	.20
4	Labor availability, attitude, and cost	.35

Spenser has rated each location for each factor, on a 100-point basis. These ratings are given below:

	Location		
Factor	Present Location	Newbury	Hyde Park
1	40	60	50
2	20	20	80
3	30	60	50
4	80	50	50

Which site should be recommended?

8.9 The fixed and variable costs for three potential manufacturing plant sites for a rattan chair weaver are shown below:

Site	Fixed Cost Per Year	Variable Cost Per Unit
1	$ 500	$11
2	1,000	7
3	1,700	4

a) Over what range of production is each location optimal?
b) For a production of 200 units, which site is best?

8.10 Karen Fowler owns the Rocky Mountain Coolers, a semiprofessional basketball team in Northern Colorado. She wishes to move the Coolers east to either Atlanta or Charlotte.

The table below gives the factors that Karen thinks are important, their weights, and the scores for Atlanta and Charlotte. Which site should she select?

Factor	Weight	Atlanta	Charlotte
Incentive	.4	80	60
Player satisfaction	.3	20	50
Sports interest	.2	40	90
Size of city	.1	70	30

8.11 A British hospital chain wishes to make its first entry into the U.S. market by building a medical facility in the Midwest, a region with which its director, Marc Massoud, is comfortable because he got his medical degree at Northwestern University. After a preliminary analysis, four cities are chosen for further consideration. They are rated according to the factors shown below.

		City			
Factor	Weight	Chicago	Milwaukee	Madison	Detroit
Costs	2.0	8	5	6	7
Need for a facility	1.5	4	9	8	4
Staff availability	1.0	7	6	4	7
Local incentives	0.5	8	6	5	9

a) Which city should Massoud select?
b) Assume a cutoff of 5 is now used for all factors. Which city should be chosen?

8.12 Ramon Haynes owns an ambulance company that serves four hospitals in Claremont, California. Northwest Hospital has map coordinates of 20 West, 50 North. Northeast Hospital is located at 15 East, 30 North. Southwest Hospital is at 10 West, 40 South. Southeast Hospital is located on grid 25 East, 10 South. The average number of runs Haynes's service makes to each hospital is: Northwest (60), Northeast (40), Southwest (50) and Southeast (100). Using the map grid system, determine where Haynes should place his offices in order to make them most centrally located.

8.13 The fixed and variable costs (in U.S. dollars) for the new recycling plant that Eldon Yi is opening in Australia are computed as follows:

Cost	Victoria	Perth
Fixed	$1,000,000	$800,000
Variable	$73/unit	$112/unit

a) Over what range is each city preferable?
b) For a recycling of 5,000 units, which site is best?

DATA BASE APPLICATION

8.14. The unification of Europe has brought about changes in airline regulation that dramatically affect major European carriers such as British International Air, SAS, KLM, Air France, Alitalia, and Sabena. With ambitious expansion plans, British International Air (BIA) has decided it needs a second service hub on the continent, to complement its large

316   CHAPTER 8   LOCATION STRATEGIES

Heathrow (London) repair facility. The location selection is critical, and with the potential for 4,000 new skilled blue-collar jobs on the line, virtually every city in Western Europe is actively bidding for BIA's business.

After initial investigations by Holmes Miller, head of the Operations Department, BIA has narrowed the list to 16 cities. Each is then rated on 12 factors, with the following table resulting.

a) Help Miller rank the top three cities that BIA should consider as its new site for servicing aircraft.
b) After further investigation, Miller decides that an existing set of hangar facilities for repairs is not nearly as important as earlier thought. If he lowers the weight of that factor to 30, does the ranking change?
c) After Miller makes the change in part (b), Germany announces it has reconsidered its offer of financial incentives, with an additional 200 million deutsche mark package to entice BIA. Accordingly, BIA has raised Germany's rating to 10 on that factor. Is there any change in top rankings in part (b)?

Table for Data Base Application 8.14

		Italy			France			Germany		
Factor	Importance Weight	Milan	Rome	Genoa	Paris	Lyon	Nice	Munich	Bonn	Berlin
Financial incentives	85	8	8	8	7	7	7	7	7	7
Skilled labor pool	80	4	6	5	9	9	7	10	8	9
Existing facility	70	5	3	2	9	6	5	9	9	2
Wage rates	70	9	8	9	4	6	6	4	5	5
Competition for jobs	70	7	3	8	2	8	7	4	8	9
Ease of air traffic access	65	5	4	6	2	8	8	4	8	9
Real estate cost	40	6	4	7	4	6	6	3	4	5
Communication links	25	6	7	6	9	9	9	10	9	8
Attractiveness to relocating executives	15	4	8	3	9	6	6	2	3	3
Political considerations	10	6	6	6	8	8	8	8	8	8
Expansion possibilities	10	10	2	8	1	5	4	4	5	6
Union strength	10	1	1	1	5	5	5	6	6	6

		Spain	Switzerland		Holland		Denmark	Portugal
Factor	Importance Weight	Madrid	Bern	Zurich	Amsterdam	The Hague	Copenhagen	Lisbon
Financial incentives	85	9	8	8	9	9	8	10
Skilled labor pool	80	4	9	10	9	8	7	3
Existing facility	70	5	7	8	8	2	8	6
Wage rates	70	10	3	3	5	9	5	10
Competition for jobs	70	6	5	4	3	7	6	6
Ease of air traffic access	65	5	5	5	3	9	4	6
Real estate cost	40	8	2	1	3	5	4	7
Communication links	25	2	8	8	8	6	9	2
Attractiveness to relocating executives	15	4	9	8	9	6	7	3
Political considerations	10	5	9	9	8	8	8	2
Expansion possibilities	10	5	3	2	3	8	4	6
Union strength	10	9	8	8	7	7	5	9

Case Study

Southern Recreational Vehicle Company

In October 1997, top management of Southern Recreational Vehicle Company of St. Louis, Missouri, announced its plans to relocate its manufacturing and assembly operations by constructing a new plant in Ridgecrest, Mississippi. The firm, a major producer of pickup campers and camper trailers, had experienced five consecutive years of declining profits as a result of spiraling production costs. The costs of labor and raw materials had increased alarmingly, utility costs had gone up sharply, and taxes and transportation expenses had steadily climbed upward. In spite of increased sales, the company suffered its first net loss since operations were begun in 1977.

When management initially considered relocation, it closely scrutinized several geographic areas. Of primary importance to the relocation decision were the availability of adequate transportation facilities, state and municipal tax structures, an adequate labor supply, positive community attitudes, reasonable site costs, and financial inducements. Although several communities offered essentially the same incentives, the management of Southern Recreational Vehicle Company was favorably impressed by the efforts of the Mississippi Power and Light Company to attract "clean, labor-intensified" industry and the enthusiasm exhibited by state and local officials who actively sought to bolster the state's economy by enticing manufacturing firms to locate within its boundaries.

Two weeks prior to the announcement, management of Southern Recreational Vehicle Company finalized its relocation plans. An existing building in Ridgecrest's industrial park was selected (the physical facility had previously housed a mobile home manufacturer that had gone bankrupt due to inadequate financing and poor management); initial recruiting was begun through the state employment office; and efforts to lease or sell the St. Louis property were initiated. Among the inducements offered Southern Recreational Vehicle Company to locate in Ridgecrest were:

1. Exemption from county and municipal taxes for 5 years.
2. Free water and sewage services.
3. Construction of a second loading dock—free of cost—at the industrial site.
4. An agreement to issue $500,000 in industrial bonds for future expansion.
5. Public-financed training of workers in a local industrial trade school.

In addition to these inducements, other factors weighed heavily in the decision to locate in the small Mississippi town. Labor costs would be significantly less than those incurred in St. Louis; organized labor was not expected to be as powerful (Mississippi is a right-to-work state); and utility costs and taxes would be moderate. All in all, management of Southern Recreational Vehicle Company felt that its decision was sound.

On October 15, the following announcement was attached to each employee's paycheck:

> To: Employees of Southern Recreational Vehicle Company
> From: Gerald O'Brian, President
>
> The Management of Southern Recreational Vehicle Company regretfully announces its plans to cease all manufacturing operations in St. Louis on December 31. Because of increased operating costs and the unreasonable demands forced upon the company by the union, it has become impossible to operate profitably. I sincerely appreciate the fine service that each of you has rendered to the company during the past years. If I can be of assistance in helping you find suitable employment with another firm, please let me know. Thank you again for your cooperation and past service.

Discussion Questions

1. Evaluate the inducements offered Southern Recreational Vehicle Company by community leaders in Ridgecrest, Mississippi.
2. What problems would a company experience in relocating its executives from a heavily populated industrialized area to a small rural town?
3. Evaluate the reasons cited by O'Brian for relocation. Are they justifiable?
4. What responsibilities does a firm have to its employees when a decision to cease operations is made?

Source: Professor Jerry Kinard (Western Carolina University).

■ *Internet Case Study* ■

See our Internet home page at http://www.prenhall.com/heizer for this additional case study: Consolidated Bottling (A).

BIBLIOGRAPHY

Craig, C. S., et al. "Models of the Retail Location Process." *Journal of Retailing* 60 (April 1984): 5–36.

DeForest, M. E. "Thinking of a Plant in Mexico?" *The Academy of Management Executive* 8, no. 1 (February 1994): 33–40.

Domich, P. D., K. L. Hoffman, R. H. F. Jackson, and M. A. McClain. "Locating Tax Facilities: A Graphics-Based Microcomputer Optimization Model." *Management Science* 37 (August 1991): 960.

Drezner, Z. *Facility Location: A Survey of Applications and Methods.* Secaucus, NJ: Springer-Verlag, 1995.

Fitzsimmons, J. A. "A Warehouse Location Model Helps Texas Comptroller Select Out-of-State Audit Officers." *Interfaces* 13 (October 1983): 40–45.

Murdick, R., B. Render, and R. Russell. *Service Operations Management.* Boston: Allyn & Bacon, 1990.

Price, W. L., and M. Turcotte. "Locating a Blood Bank." *Interfaces* 16 (September–October 1986): 17–26.

Reed, R. *Plant Location, Layout, and Maintenance.* Homewood, IL: Richard D. Irwin, 1967.

Render, B., and R. M. Stair. *Quantitative Analysis for Management*, 6th ed. Upper Saddle River, NJ: Prentice Hall, 1997.

Schmenner, R. W. "Look Beyond the Obvious in Plant Location." *Harvard Business Review* 57 (January–February 1979): 126–132.

Vargas, G. A., and T. W. Johnson. "An Analysis of Operational Experience in the U.S./Mexico Production Sharing (Maquiladora) Program." *Journal of Operations Management* 11, no. 1 (March 1993): 17–34.

INTERNET RESOURCES

National Association of Manufacturers:
   http://www.nam.org/
Site Selection Magazine:
   http://www.conway.com/wcbss.htm
Economic Development Service (consulting service):
   http://www.sitelocationassistance.com/

LAYOUT STRATEGY

9

CHAPTER OUTLINE

GLOBAL COMPANY PROFILE: PITTSBURGH INTERNATIONAL AIRPORT
THE STRATEGIC IMPORTANCE OF LAYOUT DECISIONS
TYPES OF LAYOUT
FIXED-POSITION LAYOUT
PROCESS ORIENTED LAYOUT
  Expert Systems in Layout
  Work Cells
  The Focused Work Center and the Focused Factory
OFFICE LAYOUT
RETAIL LAYOUT
WAREHOUSING AND STORAGE LAYOUTS
  Cross-Docking
  Random Stocking
  Customizing
REPETITIVE AND PRODUCT-ORIENTED LAYOUT
  Assembly-Line Balancing

SUMMARY
KEY TERMS
USING POM FOR WINDOWS FOR LAYOUT DESIGN
SOLVED PROBLEMS
DISCUSSION QUESTIONS
CRITICAL THINKING EXERCISE
PROBLEMS
DATA BASE APPLICATION
CASE STUDIES: DES MOINES NATIONAL BANK; STATE AUTOMOBILE LICENSE RENEWALS
VIDEO CASE 5: FACILITY LAYOUT AT WHEELED COACH
INTERNET CASE STUDIES
BIBLIOGRAPHY
INTERNET RESOURCES

LEARNING OBJECTIVES

When you complete this chapter you should be able to:

Identify or Define:
  Fixed-position layout
  Process-oriented layout
  Work cells
  Focused work center
  Office layout
  Retail layout
  Warehouse layout
  Product-oriented layout
  Assembly-line factory

Describe or Explain:
  How to achieve a good layout for the process facility
  How to balance production flow in a repetitive or product oriented facility

GLOBAL COMPANY PROFILE:

Layout Provides a Competitive Advantage for Airlines at Pittsburgh International Airport

Just as operations techniques can assist in layouts for factories, stores, and hospitals, they can also aid in airport layout. Important layout criteria include reducing congestion, distance, and delays. These criteria have been successfully applied at Pittsburgh International Airport. The airport layout also had to accommodate passenger convenience, cost, and expandability as well as the traditional OM criterion of operational efficiency.

To address passenger convenience, designers created a revolutionary X-shaped airport. The facility includes a central shopping mall, a variety of people movers, and a $34-million baggage-handling system. The X shape positively influences the movement of passengers and aircraft. Combinations of escalators, moving sidewalks, and shuttle trains move passengers to any of the 75 gates in about 11 minutes. The X-shaped terminal has also proven to be an excellent vehicle for operational efficiency. Early in the design stage, elaborate simulations were done to evaluate flight activity and its impact on runways, taxiways, and gates.

The layout also provides dual apron taxi lanes around the jet gates

Pittsburgh International's X-shaped terminal reduces aircraft taxi time and improves gate access, thereby reducing airline fuel cost substantially. These dual taxiways contribute not only to reduced taxiing time but to faster takeoffs.

PITTSBURGH INTERNATIONAL AIRPORT

A variety of people movers—from shuttle trains to escalators to these moving walkways—improves passenger convenience.

to allow efficient aircraft access in and out of all positions. These are coupled with complementary dual taxiways running in opposite directions to and from existing runways. The combination contributes to reduced delays and allows faster takeoffs. The resultant efficiencies mean that airlines using the Pittsburgh airport can save as much as $15 million per year in operating expenses.

Pittsburgh International Airport, with the help of a new layout, is setting new standards for efficiency.

This $34 million dollar automated baggage-handling system uses a 10-digit tag to sort bags. The system uses computer-directed laser scanners to route bags along 6 miles of conveyor belts.

> **TEN DECISIONS OF OM**
>
> Managing Quality
> Design of Goods & Services
> Process Strategy
> Location Strategies
> **Layout Strategies**
> Human Resources
> Supply-Chain Management
> Inventory Management
> Scheduling
> Maintenance

THE STRATEGIC IMPORTANCE OF LAYOUT DECISIONS

Layout is one of the key decisions that determines the long-run efficiency of operations. Layout has numerous strategic implications because it establishes an organization's competitive priorities in regard to capacity, processes, flexibility, and cost, as well as quality of work life, customer contact, and image. An effective layout can help an organization achieve a strategic advantage that supports differentiation, low cost, or response. Benetton, for example, supports a *differentiation* strategy by heavy investment in warehouse layouts that contribute to fast, accurate sorting and shipping to its 5,000 outlets. Wal-Mart store layouts support a strategy of *low cost,* as do its warehouse techniques and layouts. Hallmark's office layouts, where many professionals operate in work cells, support *rapid development* of greeting cards. The objective of layout strategy is to develop an economic layout that will meet the firm's competitive requirements. These firms have done so.

In all cases, layout design must consider how to achieve the following:

1. Higher utilization of space, equipment, and people.
2. Improved flow of information, materials, or people.
3. Improved employee morale and safer working conditions.
4. Improved customer/client interaction.
5. Flexibility (whatever the layout is now, it will need to change).

Increasingly, layout designs need to be viewed as dynamic. This means considering small, movable, and flexible equipment. Store displays need to be movable, office desks and partitions modular, and warehouse racks prefabricated. In order to make quick and easy changes in product models and in production rates, operations managers must design flexibility into layouts. To obtain flexibility in layout, managers cross train their workers, maintain equipment, keep investments low, place workstations close together, and use small, movable, flexible equipment. In some cases, equipment on wheels is appropriate, in anticipation of the next change in product, process, or volume.

TYPES OF LAYOUT

Layout decisions include the best placement of machines (in production settings), offices and desks (in office settings), or service centers (in settings such as hospitals or department stores). An effective layout facilitates the flow of materials, people, and information within and between areas. To achieve these objectives, a variety of approaches have been developed. We will discuss six of them in this chapter:

1. *Fixed-position layout*—addresses the layout requirements of large, bulky projects such as ships and buildings.
2. *Process-oriented layout*—deals with low-volume, high-variety production (also called "job shop" or intermittent production).
3. *Office layout*—positions workers, their equipment, and spaces/offices to provide for movement of information.
4. *Retail layout*—allocates shelf space and responds to customer behavior.
5. *Warehouse layout*—addresses trade-offs between space and material handling.
6. *Product-oriented layout*—seeks the best personnel and machine utilization in repetitive or continuous production.

Examples for each of these classes of layout problems are noted in Table 9.1.

FIXED-POSITION LAYOUT

TABLE 9.1 ■ Layout Strategies

PROJECT (fixed-position)	JOB SHOP (process-oriented)	OFFICE	RETAIL	WAREHOUSE (storage)	REPETITIVE/ CONTINUOUS (product-oriented)
Examples:					
Ingall Ship Building Corp.	Shouldice Hospital	Allstate Insurance	Kroger's Supermarket	Federal-Mogul's warehouse	Sony's TV assembly line
Trump Plaza	Olive Garden Restaurants	Microsoft Corp.	Walgreens	The Gap's distribution center	Dodge Caravan minivans
Pittsburgh Airport			Bloomingdales		
Problem:					
Move material to the limited storage areas around the site	Manage varied material flow for each product	Locate workers requiring frequent contact close to one another	Expose customer to high-margin items	Balance low-cost storage with low-cost material handling	Equalize the task time at each workstation

Because only a few of these six classes can be modeled mathematically, layout and design of physical facilities are still something of an art. However, we do know that a good layout requires determining:

1. *Material handling equipment.* Managers must decide about equipment to be used, including conveyors, cranes, automated storage and retrieval systems, and automatic carts to deliver and store material.
2. *Capacity and space requirements.* Only when personnel, machines, and equipment requirements are known, can we proceed with layout and provide space for each component. In the case of office work, operations managers must make judgments about the space requirements for each employee. It may be a 6-×-6-foot cubicle plus allowance for hallways, aisles, rest rooms, cafeterias, stairwells, elevators, and so forth, or it may be spacious executive offices and conference rooms. Management must also consider allowances for safety requirements that address noise, dust, fumes, temperature, and space around equipment and machines.
3. *Environment and aesthetics.* Layout concerns often require decisions about windows, planters, and height of partitions to facilitate air flow, to reduce noise, to provide privacy, and so forth.
4. *Flows of information.* Communication is important to any company and must be facilitated by the layout. This issue may require decisions about proximity as well as decisions about open spaces versus half-height dividers versus private offices.
5. *Cost of moving between various work areas.* There may be unique considerations related to moving materials or the importance of certain areas being next to each other. For example, the movement of molten steel is more difficult than the movement of cold steel.

FIXED-POSITION LAYOUT

In a **fixed-position layout,** the project remains in one place and workers and equipment come to that one work area. Examples of this type of project are a ship, a highway, a bridge, a house, and an oil well.

Fixed-position layout
Addresses the layout requirements of stationary projects or large bulky projects (such as ships or buildings).

324   CHAPTER 9   LAYOUT STRATEGY

A house built via traditional fixed-position layout would be constructed on-site, with equipment, materials, and workers brought to the site. However, imaginative OM solutions allow the home pictured here to be built at a much lower cost. The house is built in two movable modules (shown joined here) in a factory, where equipment and material handling are expedited. Prepositioned scaffolding and hoists make the job easier, quicker, and cheaper. The indoor work environment also aids labor productivity, means no weather delays, and eliminates overnight thefts.

The techniques for addressing the fixed-position layout are not well developed and are complicated by three factors. First, there is limited space at virtually all sites. Second, at different stages in the construction process, different materials are needed; therefore, different items become critical as the project develops. Third, the volume of materials needed is dynamic. For example, the rate of use of steel panels for the hull of a ship changes as the project progresses.

Different industries handle these problems in different ways. The construction industry usually has a "meeting of the trades" to assign space for various time periods. As suspected, this often yields less than an optimum solution, as the discussion may be more political than analytical. Shipyards, however, have loading areas called "platens" adjacent to the ship, which are loaded by a scheduling department.

Because problems with fixed-position layouts are so difficult to solve well on-site, an alternative strategy is to complete as much of the project as possible off-site. This approach is used in the shipbuilding industry when standard units—say, pipe-holding brackets—are assembled on a nearby assembly line (a product-oriented facility). In an attempt to add efficiency to shipbuilding, Ingall Ship Building Corporation has moved toward product-oriented production when sections of a ship (modules) are similar or when it has a contract to build the same section of several similar ships.[1] Similarly, other shipbuilding

---

[1] "Ingall's 130 Million Dollar Ship Factory," *Shipbuilding and Shipping Record* 115, 22 (London: Transport and Technical Publications Ltd.): 25–26.

firms are experimenting with group technology (see chapter 6) to group components.[2] As the photo shows, many home builders are moving from a fixed-position layout strategy to one that is more product-oriented. About one third of all new homes in the U.S. are built this way.

PROCESS-ORIENTED LAYOUT

The **process-oriented layout** can simultaneously handle a wide variety of products or services. This is the traditional way to support a product differentiation strategy. It is most efficient when making products with different requirements or when handling customers, patients, or clients with different needs. A process-oriented layout is typically the low-volume, high-variety strategy discussed in chapter 7. In this job-shop environment, each product or each small group of products undergoes a different sequence of operations. A product or small order is produced by moving it from one department to another in the sequence required for that product. A good example of the process-oriented layout is a hospital or clinic. Figure 9.1 illustrates the process for two patients, A and B, at an emergency clinic in Chicago. An inflow of patients, each with his or her own needs, requires routing through admissions, laboratories, operating rooms, radiology, pharmacies, nursing beds, and so on. Equipment, skills, and supervision are organized around these processes.

A big advantage of process-oriented layout is its flexibility in equipment and labor assignments. The breakdown of one machine, for example, need not halt an entire process; work can be transferred to other machines in the department. Process-oriented layout is also especially good for handling the manufacture of parts in small batches, or **job lots,** and for the production of a wide variety of parts in different sizes or forms.

Process-oriented layout A layout that deals with low-volume, high-variety production; like machines and equipment are grouped together.

Job lots Groups or batches of parts processed together.

Process layouts are common not only in manufacturing, but in colleges, banks, auto-repair shops, airlines, and libraries.

FIGURE 9.1 ■ An Emergency Room Process Layout Showing the Routing of Two Patients *Patient A (broken leg) proceeds (blue arrow) to E.R. triage, to radiology, to surgery, to a bed, to pharmacy, to billing. Patient B (pacemaker problem) moves (red arrow) to E.R. triage, to surgery, to pharmacy, to lab, to a bed, to billing.*

---

[2] N. Yamamoto, K. Terai, and T. Kurioka, "The Continuous Flow Production System Which Has Applied to Hull Works in Shipbuilding Industry," *Selected Journal of the Society of Naval Architects of Japan*, No. 35, Society of Naval Architects of Japan, Shiba-Kotohiracho, Minato-Ku, Tokyo, Japan 5, 70: 153–174.

The disadvantages of process-oriented layout come from the general-purpose use of the equipment. Orders take more time to move through the system because of difficult scheduling, changing setups, and unique material handling. In addition, general-purpose equipment requires high labor skills, and work-in-process inventories are higher because of imbalances in the production process. High labor-skill needs also increase the required level of training and experience, and high work-in-process levels increase capital investment.

When designing a process layout, the most common tactic is to arrange departments or work centers so as to minimize the costs of material handling. In other words, departments with large flows of parts or people between them should be placed next to one another. Material handling costs in this approach depend on (1) the number of loads (or people) to be moved between two departments (*i* or *j*) during some period of time and (2) the distance-related costs of moving loads (or people) between departments. Cost is assumed to be a function of distance between departments. The objective can be expressed as follows:

$$\text{Minimize cost} = \sum_{i=1}^{n} \sum_{j=1}^{n} X_{ij} C_{ij} \qquad (9.1)$$

where n = total number of work centers or departments
  i, j = individual departments
  X_{ij} = number of loads moved from department i to department j
  C_{ij} = cost to move a load between department i and department j

Process-oriented facilities (and fixed-position layouts as well) try to minimize loads or trips times distance-related costs. The term C_{ij} combines distance and other costs into one factor. We thereby assume not only that the difficulty of movement is equal but also that the pickup and setdown costs are constant. Although they are not always constant, for simplicity's sake we summarize these data (that is, distance, difficulty, and pickup and setdown costs) in this one variable, cost. The best way to understand the steps involved in designing a process layout is to look at an example.

EXAMPLE 1

Walters Company management wants to arrange the six departments of its factory in a way that will minimize interdepartmental material handling costs. They make an initial assumption (to simplify the problem) that each department is 20 feet × 20 feet and that the building is 60 feet long and 40 feet wide. The process layout procedure that they follow involves six steps.

Step 1. *Construct a "from-to matrix"* showing the flow of parts or materials from department to department (Figure 9.2).

Step 2. *Determine the space requirements* for each department. (Figure 9.3 shows available plant space.)

Step 3. *Develop an initial schematic diagram* showing the sequence of departments through which parts must move. Try to place departments with a heavy flow of materials or parts next to one another. (See Figure 9.4 on page 328.)

Step 4. *Determine the cost* of this layout by using the material handling cost equation:

$$\text{Cost} = \sum_{i=1}^{n} \sum_{j=1}^{n} X_{ij} C_{ij}$$

Process-Oriented Layout 327

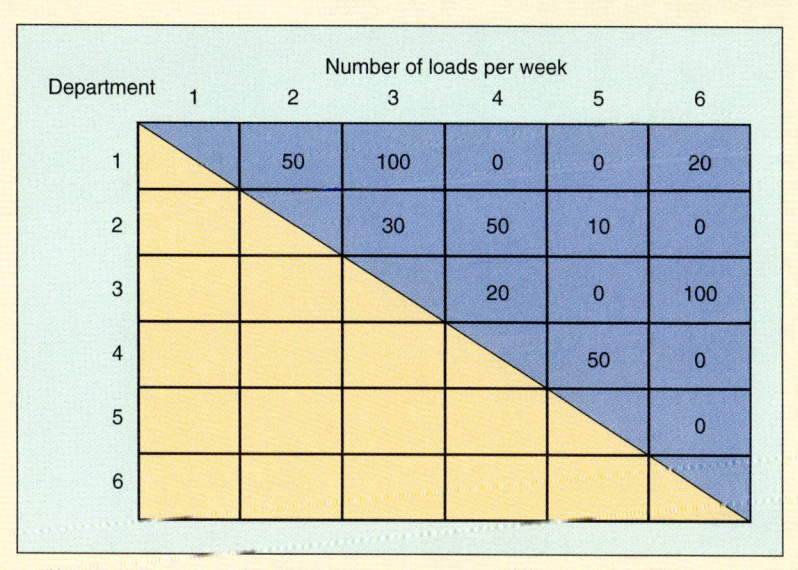

Department	1	2	3	4	5	6
1		50	100	0	0	20
2			30	50	10	0
3				20	0	100
4					50	0
5						0
6						

Number of loads per week

FIGURE 9.2 ■ **Interdepartmental Flow of Parts** *The high flows between 1 and 3, and 3 and 6 are immediately apparent. Departments 1, 3, and 6, therefore, should be close together.*

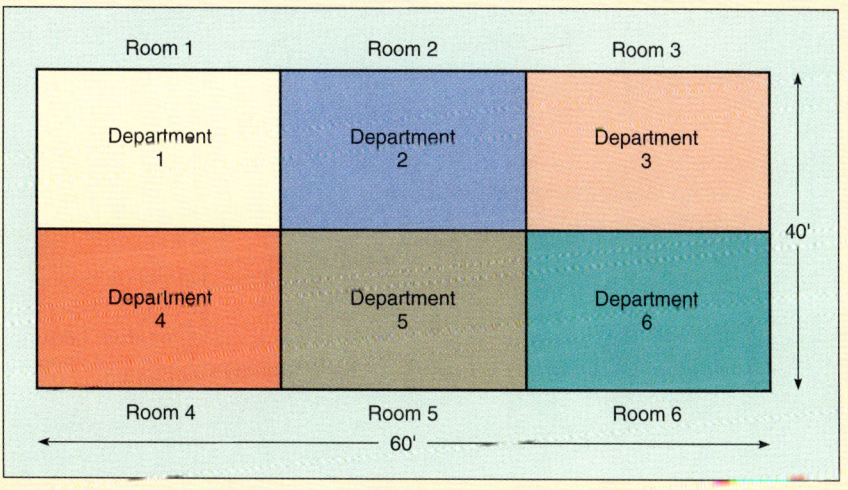

Room 1	Room 2	Room 3
Department 1	Department 2	Department 3
Department 4	Department 5	Department 6
Room 4	Room 5	Room 6

← 60' →   40'

FIGURE 9.3 ■ **Building Dimensions and a Possible Department Layout**

For this problem, Walters Company assumes that a forklift carries all interdepartmental loads. The cost of moving one load between adjacent departments is estimated to be $1. Moving a load between nonadjacent departments costs $2. Looking at Figure 9.2, we thus see that the handling cost between departments 1 and 2 is $50 ($1 × 50 loads), $200 between departments 1 and 3 ($2 × 100 loads), $40 between departments 1 and 6 ($2 × 20 loads), and so on. The total cost for the layout shown in Figure 9.4 is thus

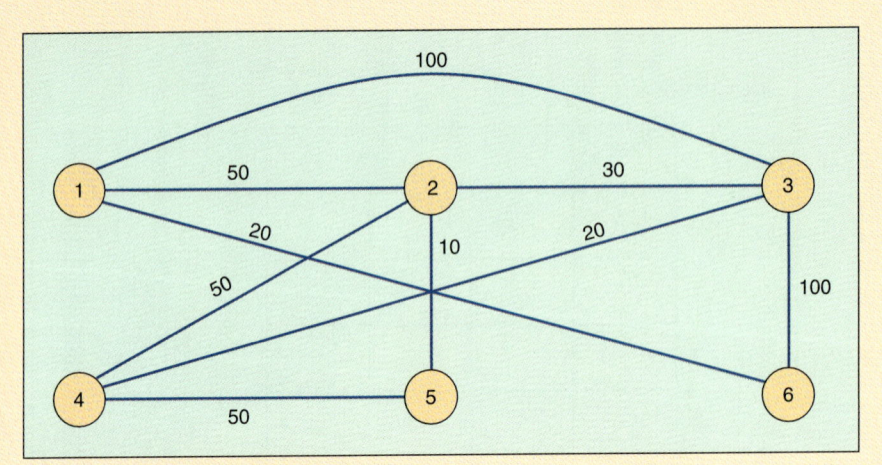

FIGURE 9.4 ■ Interdepartmental Flow Graph Showing Number of Weekly Loads

$$\text{Cost} = \underset{(1 \text{ and } 2)}{\$50} + \underset{(1 \text{ and } 3)}{\$200} + \underset{(1 \text{ and } 6)}{\$40} + \underset{(2 \text{ and } 3)}{\$30} + \underset{(2 \text{ and } 4)}{\$50}$$

$$+ \underset{(2 \text{ and } 5)}{\$10} + \underset{(3 \text{ and } 4)}{\$40} + \underset{(3 \text{ and } 6)}{\$100} + \underset{(4 \text{ and } 5)}{\$50}$$

$$= \$570$$

Step 5. By trial and error (or by a more sophisticated computer program approach that we discuss shortly), *try to improve the layout* pictured in Figure 9.3 to establish a reasonably good arrangement of departments.

By looking at both the flow graph (Figure 9.4) and the cost calculations, we see that placing departments 1 and 3 closer together appears desirable. They currently are nonadjacent, and the high volume of flow between them causes a large handling expense. Looking the situation over, we need to check the effect of shifting departments and possibly raising, instead of lowering, overall costs.

One possibility is to switch departments 1 and 2. This exchange produces a second departmental flow graph (Figure 9.5), which shows a reduction in cost to $480, a savings in material handling of $90.

$$\text{Cost} = \underset{(1 \text{ and } 2)}{\$50} + \underset{(1 \text{ and } 3)}{\$100} + \underset{(1 \text{ and } 6)}{\$20} + \underset{(2 \text{ and } 3)}{\$60} + \underset{(2 \text{ and } 4)}{\$50}$$

$$+ \underset{(2 \text{ and } 5)}{\$10} + \underset{(3 \text{ and } 4)}{\$40} + \underset{(3 \text{ and } 6)}{\$100} + \underset{(4 \text{ and } 5)}{\$50}$$

$$= \$480$$

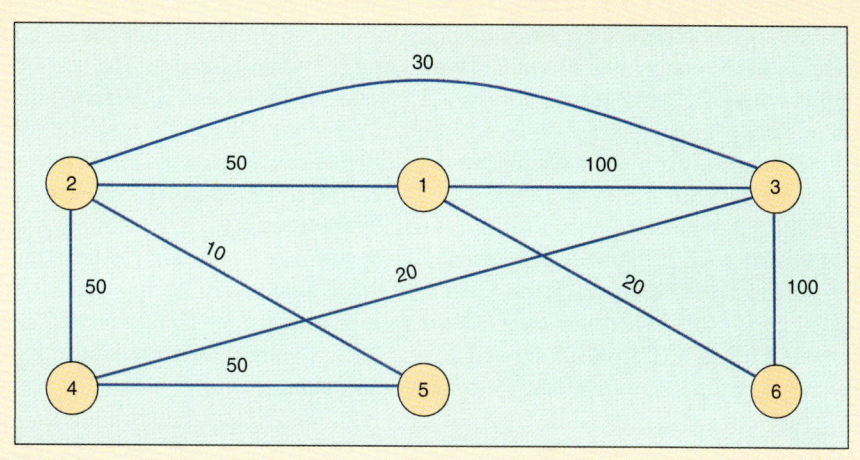

FIGURE 9.5 ■ Second Interdepartmental Flow Graph

This switch, of course, is only one of a large number of possible changes. For a six-department problem, there are actually 720 (or $6! = 6 \times 5 \times 4 \times 3 \times 2 \times 1$) potential arrangements! In layout problems, we seldom find the optimal solution and may have to be satisfied with a "reasonable" one reached after a few trials. Suppose Walters Company is satisfied with the cost figure of $480 and the flow graph of Figure 9.5. The problem may not be solved yet. Often a sixth step is necessary:

Step 6. *Prepare a detailed plan* arranging the departments to fit the shape of the building and its nonmovable areas (such as the loading dock, washrooms, and stairways). Often this step involves ensuring that the final plan can be accommodated by the electrical system, floor loads, aesthetics, and other factors.

In the case of Walters Company, space requirements are a simple matter (see Figure 9.6).

FIGURE 9.6 ■ A Feasible Layout for Walters Company

CRAFT A computer program that systematically examines alternative departmental rearrangements to reduce total material handling cost.

The graphic approach in Example 1 is fine for small problems.[3] It does not, however, suffice for larger problems. When 20 departments are involved in a layout problem, more than 600 *trillion* different department configurations are possible. Fortunately, computer programs have been written to handle layouts of up to 40 departments. The best-known of these is **CRAFT** (Computerized Relative Allocation of Facilities Technique),[4] a program that produces "good" but not always "optimal" solutions. CRAFT is a search technique that systematically examines alternative departmental rearrangements to reduce total material handling cost (see Figure 9.7). CRAFT has the added advantage of examining not only load and distance but also a third factor, a difficulty rating.

Computerized techniques have been developed for both two-dimensional and three-dimensional cases—the two-dimensional case being a one-story facility successfully addressed by CRAFT. The three-dimensional case is a multistory facility and is addressed by SPACECRAFT, CRAFT 3-D, and MULTIPLE.[5] Manual techniques also exist, but they are more difficult to use than are computer techniques.

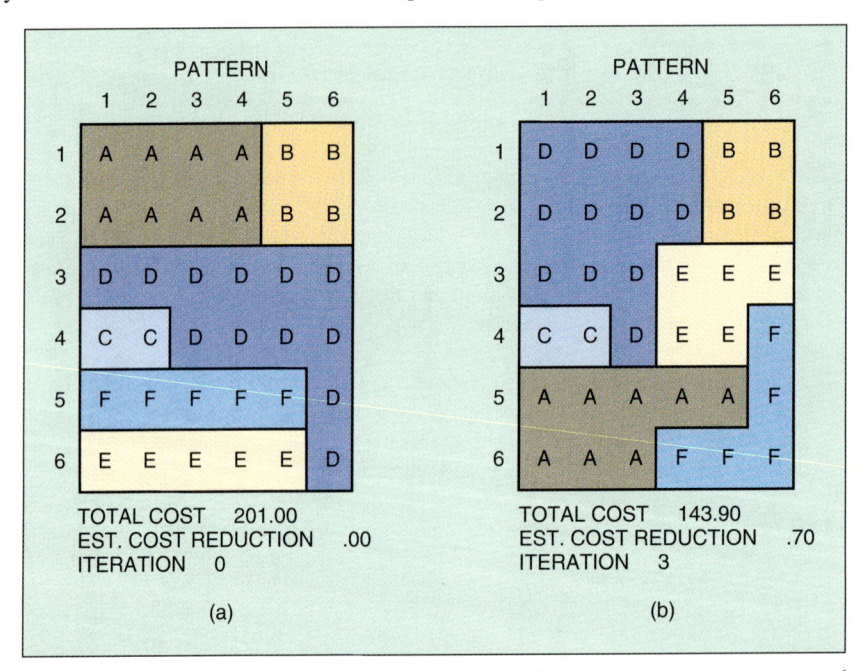

FIGURE 9.7 ■ **In This Six-Department Example, CRAFT Has Rearranged the Initial Layout** *(a), with a Cost of $201.00, into the New Layout with a Lower Cost of $143.90 (b). CRAFT does this by systematically testing pairs of departments to see if moving them closer to one another lowers total cost.*

---

[3] See also Richard Muther, *Systematic Layout Planning,* 2nd ed. (Boston: Cahners, 1976), for a similar approach to what the author calls simplified layout planning.

[4] E. S. Buffa, G. S. Armor, and T. E. Vollmann, "Allocating Facilities with CRAFT," *Harvard Business Review* 42, 2 (March–April 1964): 136–159.

[5] R. V. Johnson, "SPACECRAFT for Multi-Floor Layout Planning," *Management Science* 28, 4 (1982): 407–417. A discussion of CRAFT, COFAD, PLANET, CORELAP, and AIDED is available in James M. Moore and James A. Tompkins, *Computer Aided Layout: A User's Guide,* Publication Number 1 in the monograph series, *Facilities Planning and Design Division* (Norcross, GA: American Institute of Industrial Engineers), p. 77-1. For a discussion of CRAFT 3-D, see U. Cinar. "Facilities Planning: A Systems Analysis and Space Allocation Approach," in *Spatial Synthesis in Computer-Aided Building Design,* ed. C. M. Eastman (New York: John Wiley, 1975). For a discussion of MULTIPLE see Y. A. Bozer, R. D. Meller, and S. J. Erlebacher, "An Improvement-Type Layout Algorithm for Single and Multiple Floor Facilities," *Management Science* 40, 7 (1994):918–932.

Expert Systems in Layout

CRAFT, SPACECRAFT, CRAFT 3-D, and MULTIPLE are just a few of the computerized techniques available to aid in the design and layout of facilities. However, these and other popular programs, such as CORELAP, ALDEP, and COFAD, do not consider expert knowledge in ranking alternative plans. They do not have built-in rules to consider the creative aspects that a human designer would.

FADES (Facilities Design Expert System) is an *expert system*—a program that combines judgmental rules developed by human experts with the mathematical approach we introduced earlier in this section.[6] It develops good facility designs for unstructured situations. FADES reflects the new breed of artificial intelligence decision-making aids described in the supplement to chapter 7.

Work Cells

Cellular work arrangements are used when volume warrants a special arrangement of machinery and equipment. In a manufacturing environment, group technology identifies products that have similar characteristics and allows not just a particular batch (for example, several units of the same product) but also a family of batches, to be processed in a particular work cell.[7] *Work cells* can be thought of as a special case of process-oriented layout. Although the idea of work cells was first presented by R. E. Flanders in 1925,[8] only with the increasing use of group technology (see chapter 6) has the technique reasserted itself.

The **work cell** idea is to reorganize people and machines that would ordinarily be dispersed in various process departments and temporarily arrange them in a small group so that they can focus on making a single product or a group of related products (Figure 9.8 on page 332). The work cell therefore, is built around the product. Motorola, for instance, forms work cells to build and test engine control systems for John Deere tractors. These work cells are reconfigured as product design or volume changes. The advantages of work cells are:[9]

> **Work cell** A temporary product-oriented arrangement of machines and personnel in what is ordinarily a process-oriented facility.

1. *Reduced work-in-process inventory* because the work cell is set up to provide a balanced flow from machine to machine.
2. *Less floor space required* because less space is needed between machines to accommodate work-in-process inventory.
3. *Reduced raw material and finished goods inventories* because less work-in-process allows more rapid movement of materials through the work cell.
4. *Reduced direct labor cost* because of improved communication between employees, better material flow, and improved scheduling.
5. *Heightened sense of employee participation* in the organization and the product because employees accept the added responsibility of product quality being directly associated with them and their work cell.
6. *Increased use of equipment and machinery* because of better scheduling and faster material flow.

---

[6] See E. L. Fisher, "An AI Based Methodology for Factory Design," *AI Magazine* 3, 4 (fall 1986): 72–85; and E. L. Fisher and S. F. Nof, "FADES," *Proceedings of the Annual IIE Meeting* (1984): 74–82.

[7] Small batches in a process-oriented facility (e.g., a job shop) are called *job lots*.

[8] R. E. Flanders, "Design Manufacture and Production Control of a Standard Machine," *Transactions of ASME* 46 (1925).

[9] Burton I. Zisk, "Flexibility Is Key to Automated Material Transport System for Manufacturing Cells," *Industrial Engineering*, November 1983, pp. 58–64; and Williams J. Dumoliem and William P. Santen, "Cellular Manufacturing Becomes Philosophy of Management at Components Facility," *Industrial Engineering*, November 1983, pp. 72–76.

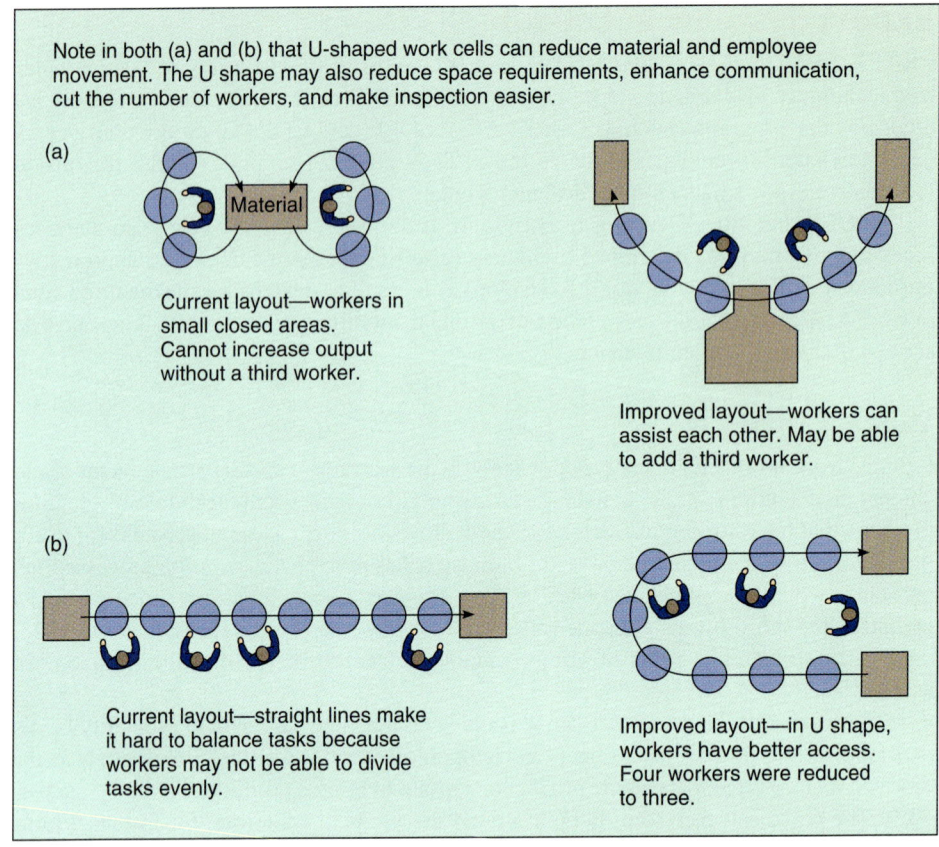

Note in both (a) and (b) that U-shaped work cells can reduce material and employee movement. The U shape may also reduce space requirements, enhance communication, cut the number of workers, and make inspection easier.

(a) Current layout—workers in small closed areas. Cannot increase output without a third worker.

Improved layout—workers can assist each other. May be able to add a third worker.

(b) Current layout—straight lines make it hard to balance tasks because workers may not be able to divide tasks evenly.

Improved layout—in U shape, workers have better access. Four workers were reduced to three.

FIGURE 9.8 ■ Improving Layouts by Moving to the Work Cell Concept

7. *Reduced investment in machinery and equipment* because good facility utilization reduces the number of machines and the amount of equipment and tooling.[10]

The requirements of cellular production include:

1. Identification of families of products, often through the use of group technology codes or equivalents.
2. A high level of training and flexibility on the part of employees.
3. Either staff support or flexible, imaginative employees to establish work cells initially.

Work cells and assembly lines are sometimes organized in a U shape. U-shaped facilities, as shown in Figure 9.8, have at least five advantages over straight ones: (1) because tasks can be grouped, inspection is often immediate; (2) fewer workers are needed; (3) workers can reach more of the work area; (4) the work area can be more efficiently balanced; and (5) communication is enhanced.

---

[10] Disputing advantages 6 and 7, two researchers have reported an increase in capital investment and lower machine use when work cells are utilized. Perhaps different firms achieve different utilization depending on their ability to switch cell configurations and move personnel, as well as on the initial cost of their particular machinery and equipment. See Timothy J. Greene and Randall P. Sadowski, "A Review of Cellular Manufacturing Assumptions, Advantages and Design Techniques," *Journal of Operations Management* 4, 2 (February 1984): 85–97.

OM IN ACTION

WORK CELLS AT ROWE FURNITURE

Many customers hate buying the standard product. This is particularly true of furniture customers, who usually want a much wider selection than most furniture showrooms can display. Customers really want customization, but they are unhappy waiting months for special orders. So Rowe Furniture Corp. of Salem, Virginia, created a computer network on which customers could order customized combinations of fabrics and styles. This strategy provided the customization, but the real trick was: How could operations people build ordered furniture rapidly and with no increase in cost?

First, Rowe annihilated the old assembly line. Then it formed work cells, each containing teams of workers with the necessary skills—gluers, sewers, staplers, and stuffers. Instead of being scattered along an assembly line, about 3 dozen team members found themselves in work cells. The work cells supported improved communication—perhaps even forced some communication between team members. Cross training followed; gluers began to understand what staplers needed, and stuffers began to understand sewing requirements. Soon, team members realized that they could successfully deal with daily problems and began to develop improved methods. Moreover, both team members and management began to work together to solve problems.

Today the Rowe plant operates at record productivity. "Everybody's a lot happier," says shop worker Sally Huffman.

Sources: The Wall Street Journal, September 13, 1996,: p. B1; and *Furniture Today*, January 13, 1997, as presented on www.rowefurniture.com.

Some 40% of U.S. plants with fewer than 100 employees use some sort of cellular system, whereas 74% of the larger plants surveyed have adopted cellular production methods.[11] Bayside Controls in Queens, N.Y., for example, has in the past decade increased sales from $300,000 per year to $11 million.[12] Much of the gain was attributed to its move to cellular manufacturing. As noted in the *OM in Action* box, Rowe Furniture, has had similar success with work cells.

The Focused Work Center and the Focused Factory

When a firm has *identified a large family of similar products that have a large and stable demand*, it may organize a focused work center. A **focused work center** moves production from a general-purpose, process-oriented facility to a large work cell that remains part of the present plant. If the focused work center is in a separate facility, it is often called a **focused factory**. A fast-food restaurant is a focused factory—most are easily reconfigured for adjustments to product mix and volume. Burger King, for example, changes the number of personnel and task assignments rather than moving machines and equipment. In this manner, the company balances the assembly line to meet changing production demands. In effect, the "layout" changes numerous times each day.

The term *focused factories* may also refer to facilities that are focused in ways other than by product line or layout. For instance, facilities may be focused in regard to meeting quality, new product introduction, or flexibility requirements.[13]

Focused facilities in manufacturing and in services appear to be better able to stay in tune with their customers, to produce quality products, and to operate at higher margins. This is true whether they are steel mills like SMI, Nucor, or Chaparral, restaurants like McDonald's and Burger King, or a hospital like Shouldice.

Focused work center A permanent or semipermanent product-oriented arrangement of machines and personnel.

Focused factory A facility designed to produce similar products or components.

---

[11] National Association of Manufacturers, Washington, DC, 1994.
[12] Stephanie N. Mehta, "Cell Manufacturing Gains Acceptance at Smaller Plants," *The Wall Street Journal*, September 15, 1996, p. B2.
[13] See for example, Wickham Skinner, "The Focused Factory," *Harvard Business Review* 52, 3 (May–June 1974): 113–121.

Table 9.2 summarizes our discussion of work cells, focused work centers, and focused factories.

TABLE 9.2 ■ Work Cells, Focused Work Centers, and the Focused Factory

Work Cell	Focused Work Center	Focused Factory
A work cell is a temporary product-oriented arrangement of machines and personnel in what is ordinarily a process-oriented facility.	A focused work center is a permanent product-oriented arrangement of machines and personnel in what is ordinarily a process-oriented facility.	A focused factory is a permanent facility to produce a product or component in a product-oriented facility. Many of the focused factories currently being built were originally part of a process-oriented facility.
Example: A job shop with machinery and personnel rearranged to produce 300 unique control panels.	*Example:* Pipe bracket manufacturing at a shipyard.	*Example:* A plant to produce window mechanisms for automobiles.

OFFICE LAYOUT

Office layout The grouping of workers, their equipment, and spaces/offices to provide for comfort, safety, and movement of information.

The main difference between **office** and factory **layouts** is the importance placed on information. However, in some office environments, just as in manufacturing, production relies on the flow of material. This is the case at Kansas City's Hallmark, which has over half the U.S. greeting card market and produces some 40,000 different cards. In the past, its 700 creative professionals would take up to 2 years to develop a new card. Hallmark's decision to create work cells of artists, writers, lithographers, merchandisers, and accountants, all located in the same area, has resulted in cards prepared in a fraction of the time that the old layout required.

Hallmark's example suggests that maintaining layout flexibility extends to offices as well as factories and remains an important principle of layout design. Just as operations managers build movable, modular equipment to maximize flexibility in the production process, so too should operations managers in office environments. The technological change sweeping manufacturing is also altering the way offices function, making office flexibility a necessity. Consequently, many varieties of modular office equipment that support changing layouts are now available.

Even though the movement of information is increasingly electronic, analysis of office layouts still requires a task-based approach. Managers must, therefore, examine both electronic and conventional communication patterns, separation needs, and other conditions affecting employee effectiveness.[14] A useful tool for such an analysis is the *relationship chart* shown in Figure 9.9. This chart, prepared for an office of software engineers, indicates that the chief technology officer must be (1) near the engineers' area, (2) less near the secretary and central files, and (3) not at all near the photocopy or storage room.

General office-area guidelines allot an average of about 100 square feet per person (including corridors). A major executive is allotted about 400 square feet, and a conference room area is based on 25 square feet per person, up to 30 people. In contrast, restaurants provide from 16 square feet to 50 square feet per customer (total kitchen and dining area divided by capacity). By making effective use of the vertical dimension in a work-

---

[14] Jacqueline C. Vischer, "Strategic Work-Space Planning," *Sloan Management Review,* fall 1995, p. 37.

Once the material and information flows of any layout provide a general arrangement, layout details must be added. This task has traditionally been done on a drafting board, cardboard cutouts, or 3-dimensional models. However, a new program from AutoDesk of Sausalito, California, Office Layout, has many of the features of a CAD (computer-aided design) program that allows dimensions, walls, dividers, and furniture, as well as people and even plants to be included and then printed.

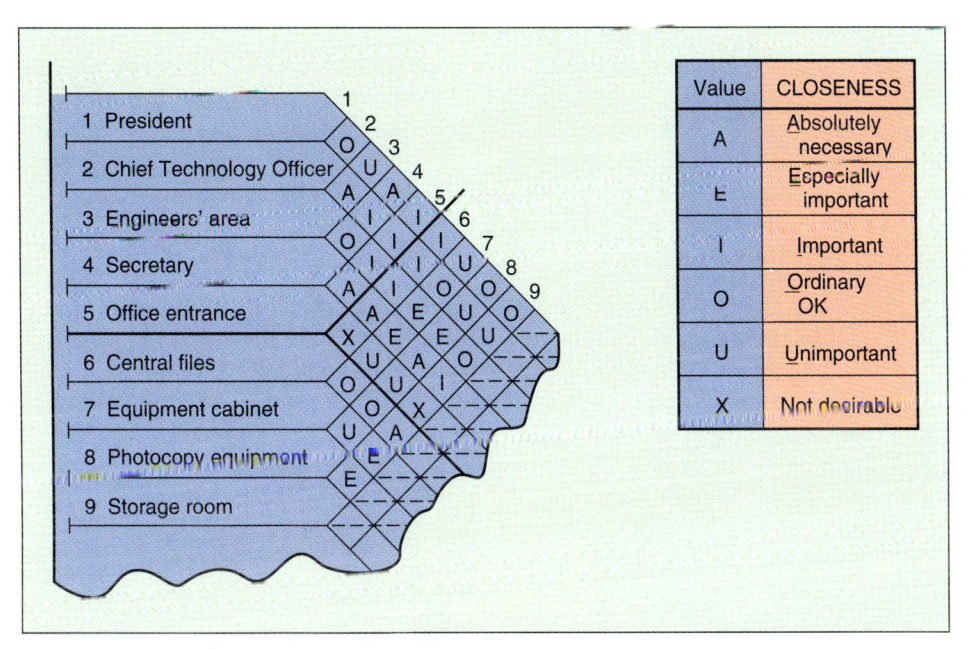

FIGURE 9.9 ■ Office Relationship Chart

Source: Adapted from Richard Muther, *Systematic Layout Planning*, 2nd ed., (Boston: Cahners Publishing Company, 1973). Used by permission of the publisher.

station, some office designers expand upward instead of outward. This approach keeps each workstation unit (what designers call the "footprint") as small as possible.

These American concepts of space are not universal, however. In the Tokyo office of Toyota, for example, about 110 people work in one large room. As is typical of Japanese offices, they work out in the open, with desks crammed together in clusters called "islands." Islands are arranged in long rows; managers sit at the ends of the rows with subordinates in full view. (When important visitors arrive for meetings, they are ushered into special rooms and do not see these cramped offices.)

On the other hand, some layout considerations are universal (many of which apply to factories as well as to offices). They have to do with working conditions, teamwork, authority, and status. Should all or only part of the work area be air-conditioned? Should all employees use the same entrance, rest rooms, lockers, and cafeteria? As mentioned earlier, layout decisions are part art and part science. Only the science part—which deals with the flow of materials and information—can be analyzed in the same manner as the flow of parts in a process layout.

As a final comment on office layout, we should note two major trends. First, *technology,* such as cellular phones, beepers, faxes, the Internet, home offices, laptop computers, and personal digital assistants (PDAs), allows increasing layout flexibility by moving information electronically. Second, *virtual companies* (discussed in chapter 11) create dynamic needs for space and services. These two changes tend to require fewer office employees on-site. For example, when accounting firm Ernst & Young's Chicago office found that 30% to 40% of desks were empty at any given time, the firm developed its new "hoteling programs." Five hundred junior consultants lost their permanent offices; anyone who plans to be in the office (rather than out with clients) for more than half a day books an office through a "concierge," who hangs that consultant's name on the door for the day.

RETAIL LAYOUT

Retail layout An approach that addresses flow, allocates space, and responds to customer behavior.

Retail layouts are based on the idea that sales and profitability vary directly with customer exposure to products. Thus, most retail operations managers try to expose customers to as many products as possible. Studies do show that the greater the rate of exposure, the greater the sales and the higher the return on investment. The operations manager can alter *both* with the overall arrangement of the store and the allocation of space to various products within that arrangement.

Five ideas are helpful for determining the overall arrangement of many stores:

1. Locate the high-draw items around the periphery of the store. Thus, we tend to find dairy products on one side of a supermarket and bread and bakery products on another. An example of this tactic is shown in Figure 9.10.
2. Use prominent locations for high-impulse and high-margin items such as housewares, beauty aids, and shampoos.
3. Distribute what are known in the trade as "power items"—items that may dominate a purchasing trip—to both sides of an aisle, and disperse them to increase the viewing of other items.
4. Use end-aisle locations because they have a very high exposure rate.
5. Convey the mission of the store by careful selection in the positioning of the lead-off department. For instance, if prepared foods are part of the mission, position the bakery and deli up front to appeal to convenience-oriented customers.

Once the overall layout of a retail store has been decided, products need to be arranged for sale. Many considerations go into this arrangement. However, the main *ob-*

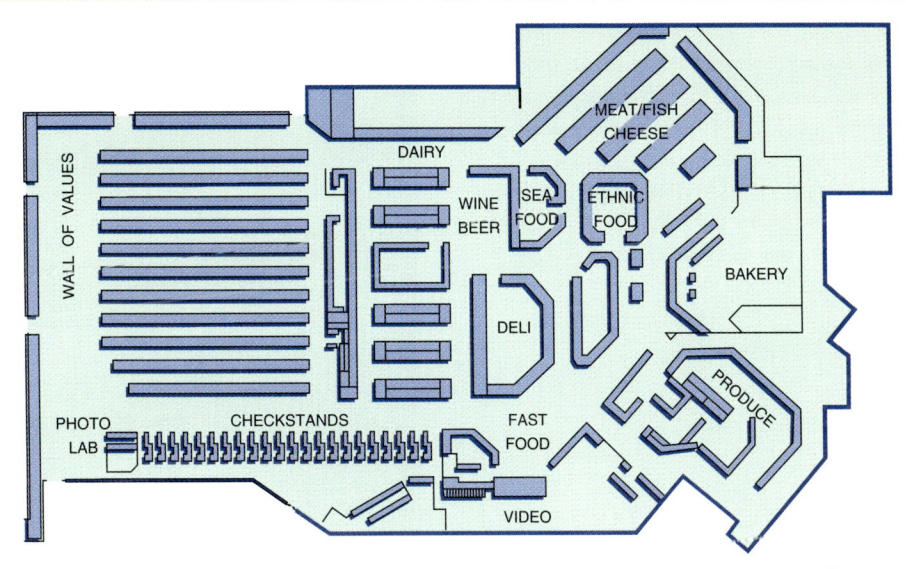

FIGURE 9.10 ■ Store Layout with Dairy and Bread, High-Draw Items, in Different Corners of the Store

jective of retail layout is to maximize profitability per square foot of floor space (or, in some stores, on linear foot of shelf space). Big-ticket, or expensive, items may yield greater dollar sales, but the profit per square foot may be lower. A number of computerized programs can assist managers in evaluating the profitability of various merchandise. One, SLIM (Store Labor and Inventory Management), can help store managers determine when shelf space is adequate to accommodate another full case. Another software package is COSMOS (Computerized Optimization and Simulation Modeling for Operating Supermarkets), which matches shelf space with delivery schedules, allocating sufficient space to minimize out-of-stock between receipts of orders.

WAREHOUSING AND STORAGE LAYOUTS

The objective of **warehouse layout** is to find the optimum trade-off between handling cost and warehouse space. Consequently, management's task is to maximize the utilization of the total "cube" of the warehouse—that is, utilize its full volume while maintaining low material handling costs. We define material handling costs as all the costs related to the incoming transport, storage, and outgoing transport of the materials to be warehoused. These costs include equipment, people, material, supervision, insurance, and depreciation. Effective warehouse layouts do, of course, also minimize the damage and spoilage of material within the warehouse.

Management minimizes the sum of the resources spent on finding and moving material plus the deterioration and damage to the material itself. The variety of items stored and the number of items "picked" has direct bearing on the optimum layout. A warehouse storing a few items lends itself to higher density than a warehouse storing a variety of items. Modern warehouse management is, in many instances, an automated procedure using automated storage and retrieval systems (ASRS).

An important component of warehouse layout is the relationship between the receiving/unloading area and the shipping/loading area. Facility design depends on the type of supplies unloaded, what they are unloaded from (trucks, rail cars, barges, and so on), and where they are unloaded. In some companies, the receiving and shipping facilities, or

Warehouse layout A design that attempts to minimize total cost by addressing trade-offs between space and material handling.

Automated storage and retrieval systems are reported to improve productivity by an estimated 500% over manual methods.

The Gap strives for both high quality and low costs. It does so by (1) designing its own clothes, (2) ensuring quality control among its vendors, and (3) maintaining downward pressure on distribution costs. A new automatic distribution center near Baltimore allows The Gap to stock East Coast stores daily rather than only three times a week.

"docks," as they are called, are even the same area; sometimes they are receiving docks in the morning and shipping docks in the afternoon.

Cross-Docking

Cross-docking Avoiding the placing of materials or supplies in storage by processing them as they are received for shipment.

Cross-docking means to avoid placing materials or supplies in storage by processing them as they are received. In a manufacturing facility, product is received directly to the assembly line. In a distribution center, labeled and presorted loads arrive at the shipping dock for immediate rerouting, thereby avoiding formal receiving, stocking/storing, and order-selection activities. Because these activities add no value to the product, their elimination is 100% cost savings. Wal-Mart, an early advocate of cross-docking, uses the technique as a major component of its continuing low-cost strategy. With cross-docking, Wal-Mart reduces distribution costs and speeds restocking of stores, thereby improving customer service. Although cross-docking reduces product handling, inventory, and facility costs, it requires both tight scheduling and that shipments received include accurate product identification, usually with bar codes.

Random Stocking

Random stocking Used in warehousing to locate stock wherever there is an open location. This technique means that space does not need to be allocated to particular items and the facility can be more fully utilized.

Automatic identification systems (AIS), usually in the form of bar codes, allow accurate and rapid item identification. When automatic identification systems are combined with effective management information systems, operations managers know the quantity and location of every unit. This information can be used with human operators or with automatic storage and retrieval systems to load units anywhere in the warehouse—randomly. Accurate inventory quantities and locations mean the potential utilization of the whole facility because space does not need to be reserved for certain stock-keeping units (SKUs) or part families. Computerized **random stocking** systems often include the following tasks:

1. Maintaining a list of "open" locations.
2. Maintaining accurate records of existing inventory and its locations.
3. Sequencing items on orders to minimize the travel time required to "pick" orders.
4. Combining orders to reduce picking time.
5. Assigning certain items or classes of items, such as high-usage items, to particular warehouse areas so that the total distance traveled within the warehouse is minimized.

In addition to accurate records, random stocking systems can increase facility utilization and decrease labor cost.

Customizing

Although we expect warehouses to store as little product as possible and hold it for as short a time as possible, we are now asking warehouses to customize products. The latest strategic planning for warehouses involves making them a place where value is added through **customizing** services. Warehouse customization is a particularly useful way to generate competitive advantage in markets with rapidly changing products. For instance, a warehouse is now a place where computer components are put together, software loaded, and repairs made. Many warehouses also provide customized labeling and packaging for retailers so items arrive ready for display.

Customizing Using warehousing to add value to the product through component modification, repair, labeling, and packaging.

Increasingly, this type of work goes on adjacent to major airports, in facilities such as the Federal Express terminal in Memphis. Adding value at warehouses adjacent to major airports facilitates overnight delivery. For instance, if your computer terminal has failed, the replacement may be sent to you from such a warehouse for delivery the next morning. When your old terminal arrives back at the warehouse, it is repaired and sent to someone else. These value-added activities at "quasi-warehouses" contribute to strategies of customization, low cost, and rapid response.

REPETITIVE AND PRODUCT-ORIENTED LAYOUT

Product-oriented layouts are organized around products or families of similar high-volume, low-variety products. Repetitive production and continuous production, which are discussed in chapter 7, use product layouts. The assumptions are:

1. Volume is adequate for high equipment utilization.
2. Product demand is stable enough to justify high investment in specialized equipment.
3. Product is standardized or approaching a phase of its life cycle that justifies investment in specialized equipment.
4. Supplies of raw materials and components are adequate and of uniform quality (adequately standardized) to ensure that they will work with the specialized equipment.

Two types of a product-oriented layout are fabrication and assembly lines. The **fabrication line** builds components, such as automobile tires or metal parts for a refrigerator, on a series of machines. An **assembly line** puts the fabricated parts together at a series of workstations. Both are repetitive processes, and in both cases, the line must be "balanced": That is, the time spent to perform work on one machine must equal or "balance" the time spent to perform work on the next machine in the fabrication line, just as the time spent at one workstation by one assembly-line employee must "balance" the time spent done at the next workstation by the next employee. The same issues arise when designing the "disassembly lines" of slaughterhouses and automobile makers (see the *OM in Action* box, "Automobile Disassembly Lines: Ecologically Correct").

Fabrication line A machine-paced, product-oriented facility for building components.

Assembly line An approach that puts fabricated parts together at a series of workstations; used in repetitive processes.

Fabrication lines tend to be machine-paced and require mechanical and engineering changes to facilitate balancing. Assembly lines, on the other hand, tend to be paced by work tasks assigned to individuals or to workstations. Assembly lines, therefore, can be balanced by moving tasks from one individual to another. In this manner, the amount of time required by each individual or station is equalized.

OM IN ACTION

AUTOMOBILE DISASSEMBLY LINES: ECOLOGICALLY CORRECT

Visionaries like Walter Chrysler and Louis Chevrolet could not have imagined the sprawling graveyards of rusting cars and trucks that bear testimony to the automotive culture they helped invent. These days, however, the graveyards are shrinking slightly. "Soon," says Ford's manager of vehicle recycling, "we think people will be buying cars based on how 'green' they are." At BMW, Horst Wolf agrees: "In the long term, all new vehicles will have to be designed in such a way that their materials can be easily reused in the next generation of cars."

In 1990, BMW, sensitive to the political power of Germany's Green Movement, built a pilot "auto disassembly" plant. In the U.S., the company offers $500 toward the purchase of a new-model BMW to anyone bringing a junked BMW to its salvage centers in New York, Los Angeles, or Orlando.

The disassembly line involves removing most of a car's plastic parts and sorting them for recycling. But this is not easy. Disassembly alone might take five people an hour. BMW also had to invent tools to safely puncture and drain fuel tanks with gas in them. Because various plastics are recycled differently, each must be labeled or color-coded. Some types of plastics can be remelted and turned into new parts, such as intake manifolds. Nissan Motor, with disassembly plants in Germany and Japan, now turns 2,000 bumpers a month into air ducts, foot rests, bumper parts, and shipping pallets.

The scrap-metal part of the disassembly line is easier. With shredders and magnets, baseball-sized chunks of metal are sorted after the engines, transmissions, radios, batteries, and exhausts have been removed. Steelmakers have helped over the past 20 years by building minimills that use scrap metal.

The ironic twist for an industry pushed to improve the crashworthiness of its vehicles is that automakers now also need to design cars and trucks that will come apart more easily.

Sources: California Management Review, winter 1995, pp. 114–137; Across the Board, June 1996, pp. 34–36; and Ward's Auto World, July 1995, p. 21.

The central problem in product-oriented layout planning is to balance the output at each workstation on the production line so that it is nearly the same, while obtaining the desired amount of output. Management's goal is to create a smooth, continuous flow along the assembly line with a minimum of idle time at each workstation. A well-balanced assembly line has the advantage of high personnel and facility utilization and equity between employees' work loads. Some union contracts require that work loads be nearly equal among those on the same assembly line. The term most often used to describe this process is **assembly line balancing.** Indeed, the *objective of the product-oriented layout is to minimize imbalance in the fabrication or assembly line.*

Assembly line balancing
Obtaining output at each workstation on the production line so delay is minimized.

The main advantages of product-oriented layout are:

1. The low variable cost per unit usually associated with high-volume, standardized products
2. Low material handling costs
3. Reduced work-in-process inventories
4. Easier training and supervision

The disadvantages of product layout are:

1. High volume is required because of the large investment needed to establish the process.
2. Work stoppage at any one point ties up the whole operation.
3. There is a lack of flexibility when handling a variety of products or production rates.

Because the problems of fabrication lines and assembly lines are similar, we focus our discussion on assembly lines. On an assembly line, the product typically moves via automated means, such as a conveyor, through a series of workstations until completed (Fig-

Repetitive and Product-Oriented Layout

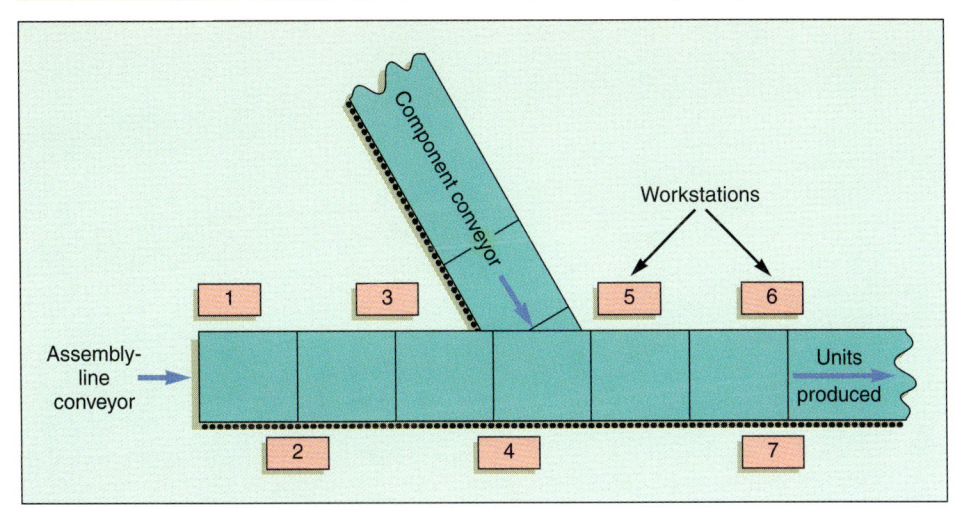

FIGURE 9.11 ■ An Assembly-Line Layout

ure 9.11). This is the way automobiles are assembled, television sets and ovens are produced, and fast-food hamburgers are made. Product-oriented layouts use more automated and specially designed equipment than do process layouts.

Assembly Line Balancing

Line balancing is usually undertaken to minimize imbalance between machines or personnel while meeting a required output from the line. In order to produce at a specified rate, management must know the tools, equipment, and work methods used. Then the time requirements for each assembly task (such as drilling a hole, tightening a nut, or spray-painting a part) must be determined. Management also needs to know the *precedence relationship* among the activities—that is, the sequence in which various tasks must be performed. Example 2 shows how to turn these task data into a precedence diagram.

Product layout can handle only a few products and process designs.

EXAMPLE 2

We want to develop a precedence diagram for an electrostatic copier that requires a total assembly time of 66 minutes. Table 9.3 (shown below) and Figure 9.12 on page 342 give the tasks, assembly times, and sequence requirements for the copier.

TABLE 9.3 ■ Precedence Data

TASK	PERFORMANCE TIME (minutes)	TASK MUST FOLLOW TASK LISTED BELOW	
A	10	—	
B	11	A	This means that
C	5	B	tasks B and E
D	4	B	cannot be done
E	12	A	until task A has been completed.
F	3	C, D	
G	7	F	
H	11	E	
I	3	G, H	
Total time	66		

FIGURE 9.12 ■ Precedence Diagram

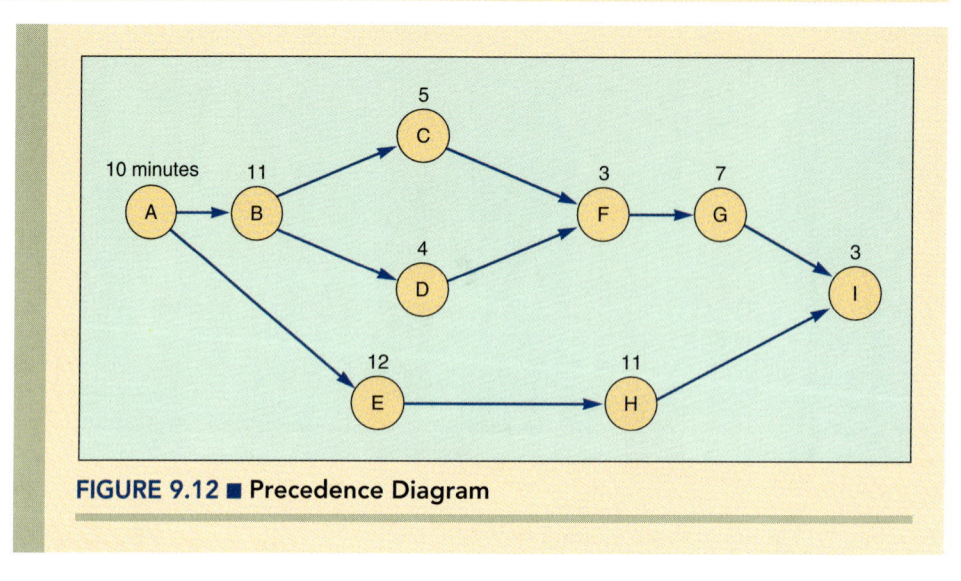

Once we have constructed a precedence chart summarizing the sequences and performance times, we turn to the job of grouping tasks into job stations so that we can meet the specified production rate. This process involves three steps:

1. Take the demand (or production rate) per day and divide it into the productive time available per day (in minutes or seconds). This operation gives us what is called the **cycle time**—namely, the maximum time that the product is available at each workstation if the production rate is to be achieved:

$$\text{Cycle time} = \frac{\text{Production time available per day}}{\text{Demand per day or production rate per day}} \quad (9.2)$$

2. Calculate the theoretical minimum number of workstations. This is the total task-duration time (the time it takes to make the product) divided by the cycle time. Fractions are rounded to the next higher whole number:

$$\text{Minimum number of workstations} = \frac{\sum_{i=1}^{n} \text{Time for task } i}{\text{Cycle time}} \quad (9.3)$$

where n is the number of assembly tasks.

3. Balance the line by assigning specific assembly tasks to each workstation. An efficient balance is one that will complete the required assembly, follow the specified sequence, and keep the idle time at each workstation to a minimum. A formal procedure for doing this is:
   a. Identify a master list of tasks.
   b. Eliminate those tasks that have been assigned.
   c. Eliminate those tasks whose precedence relationship has not been satisfied.
   d. Eliminate those tasks for which inadequate time is available at the workstation.
   e. Use one of the line-balancing "heuristics" described in Table 9.4. The five choices are: (1) longest task time, (2) most following tasks, (3) ranked positional weight, (4) shortest task time, and (5) least number of following tasks. You may wish to test several of these **heuristics** to see which generates the

---

Cycle time The maximum time that the product is available at each workstation.

The two issues in line balancing are the production rate and efficiency.

Some tasks simply cannot be grouped together in one workstation. There may be a variety of physical reasons for this.

Heuristic Problem solving using procedures and rules rather than by mathematical optimization.

TABLE 9.4 ■ **Layout Heuristics that may be Used to Assign Tasks to Work in Assembly Line Balancing**

1. Longest task (operation) time	From the available tasks, choose the task with the largest (longest) time.
2. Most following tasks	From the available tasks, choose the task with the largest number of following tasks.
3. Ranked positional weight	From the available tasks, choose the task where the sum of the times for each following task is longest. (In Example 3 we will see that the ranked positional weight of task C = 5(C) + 3(F) + 7(G) + 3(I) = 18, whereas the ranked positional weight of task D = 4(D) + 3(F) + 7(G) + 3(I) = 17; therefore, C would be chosen first.)
4. Shortest task (operations) time	From the available tasks, choose the task with the shortest task time.
5. Least number of following tasks	From the available tasks, choose the task with the least number of subsequent tasks.

"best" solution—that is, the smallest number of workstations and highest efficiency. Remember, however, that although heuristics provide solutions, they do not guarantee an optimal solution.

Example 3 illustrates a simple line-balancing procedure.

EXAMPLE 3

On the basis of the precedence diagram and activity times given in Example 2, the firm determines that there are 480 productive minutes of work available per day. Furthermore, the production schedule requires that 40 units be completed as output from the assembly line each day. Thus,

$$\text{Cycle time (in minutes)} = \frac{480 \text{ minutes}}{40 \text{ units}}$$

$$= 12 \text{ minutes/unit}$$

$$\text{Minimum number of workstations} = \frac{\text{total task time}}{\text{cycle time}} = \frac{66}{12}$$

$$= 5.5 \text{ or } 6 \text{ stations}$$

Use the *Most Following Tasks* heuristic to assign jobs to workstations.

Figure 9.13 on page 344 shows one solution that does not violate the sequence requirements and that groups tasks into six stations. To obtain this solution, activities with the most following tasks were moved into workstations to use as much of the available cycle time of 12 minutes as possible. The first workstation consumes 10 minutes and has an idle time of 2 minutes.

The second workstation uses 11 minutes, and the third consumes the full 12 minutes. The fourth workstation groups 3 small tasks and balances perfectly at 12 minutes. The fifth has 1 minute of idle time, and the sixth (consisting of tasks G and I) has 2 minutes of idle time per cycle. Total idle time for this solution is 6 minutes per cycle.

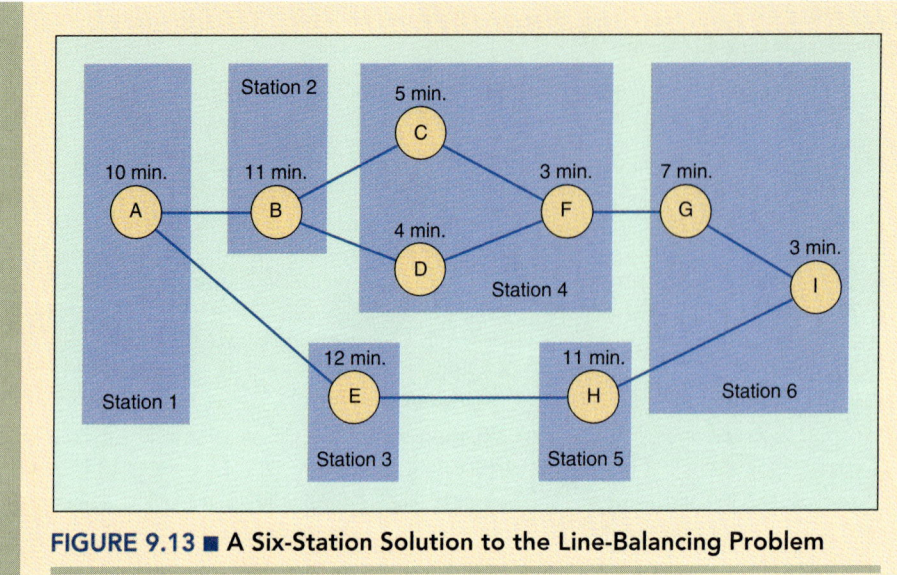

FIGURE 9.13 ■ A Six-Station Solution to the Line-Balancing Problem

We can compute the efficiency of a line balance by dividing the total task time by the product of the number of workstations required times the assigned cycle time:

$$\text{Efficiency} = \frac{\sum \text{task times}}{(\text{actual number of workstations}) \times (\text{assigned cycle time})} \quad (9.4)$$

Operations managers compare different levels of efficiency for various numbers of workstations. In this way, the firm can determine the sensitivity of the line to changes in the production rate and workstation assignments.

EXAMPLE 4

We can calculate the balance efficiency for Example 3 as follows:

$$\text{Efficiency} = \frac{66 \text{ minutes}}{(6 \text{ stations}) \times (12 \text{ minutes})} = \frac{66}{72} = 91.7\%$$

Note that opening a seventh workstation, for whatever reason, would decrease the efficiency of the balance to 78.6%:

$$\text{Efficiency} = \frac{66 \text{ minutes}}{(7 \text{ stations}) \times (12 \text{ minutes})} = 78.6\%$$

Large-scale line-balancing problems, like large process-layout problems, are often solved by computers. Several computer programs are available to handle the assignment of workstations on assembly lines with 100 (or more) individual work activities. Two computer routines COMSOAL (Computer Method for Sequencing Operations for Assembly Lines)[15] and ASYBL (General Electric's Assembly Line Configuration program), are

---

[15] A. L. Arcus, "COMSOAL: A Computer Method of Sequencing Operations for Assembly Line," *International Journal of Production Research* 4, 4 (1966).

SUMMARY

In the case of slaughtering operations, the assembly line is actually a disassembly *line. The line-balancing procedures described in this chapter are the same as for an assembly line. The chicken-processing plant shown here must balance the work of several hundred employees. Division of labor produces efficiency. Because one's skills develop with repetition, there is less time lost in changing tools, and specialized tools are developed. The total labor content in each of the chickens processed is a few minutes. How long would it take you to process a chicken by yourself?*

widely used in larger problems to evaluate the thousands, or even millions, of possible workstation combinations much more efficiently than could ever be done by hand.

The POM for Windows microcomputer software described at the end of this chapter also handles a variety of smaller problems and illustrates the problem described in Examples 2, 3, and 4. It offers five different heuristics for balancing the line.

Layouts make a substantial difference in operating efficiency. The six classic layout situations are (1) fixed-position, (2) process-oriented, (3) office, (4) retail, (5) warehouse, and (6) product-oriented. A variety of techniques have been developed in attempts to solve these layout problems. Industrial firms focus on reducing material movement and assembly line balancing. Retail firms focus on product exposure. Storage layouts focus on the optimum trade-off between storage costs and material handling costs.

Often the variables in the layout problem are so wide-ranging and numerous as to preclude finding an optimal solution. For this reason, layout decisions, although having received substantial research effort, remain something of an art.

KEY TERMS

Fixed-position layout *(p. 323)*
Process-oriented layout *(p. 325)*
Job lots *(p. 325)*
CRAFT *(p. 330)*
Work cell *(p. 331)*
Focused work center *(p. 333)*
Focused factory *(p. 333)*
Office layout *(p. 334)*
Retail layout *(p. 336)*

Warehouse layout *(p. 337)*
Cross-docking *(p. 338)*
Random stocking *(p. 338)*
Customizing *(p. 339)*
Fabrication line *(p. 339)*
Assembly line *(p. 339)*
Assembly line balancing *(p. 340)*
Cycle time *(p. 342)*
Heuristic *(p. 342)*

USING POM FOR WINDOWS FOR LAYOUT DESIGN

Solving Example 1 Using POM for Windows' Operations Layout Module

POM for Windows' facility layout module can be used to place up to 10 departments in ten rooms in order to minimize the total distance traveled as a function of the distances between the rooms and the flow between departments. The program performs pair-wise comparisons, exchanging departments until no exchange will reduce the total amount of movement.

The data screen in Program 9.1 consists of two tables of numbers—one for flows and one for distances. Output appears in Program 9.2.

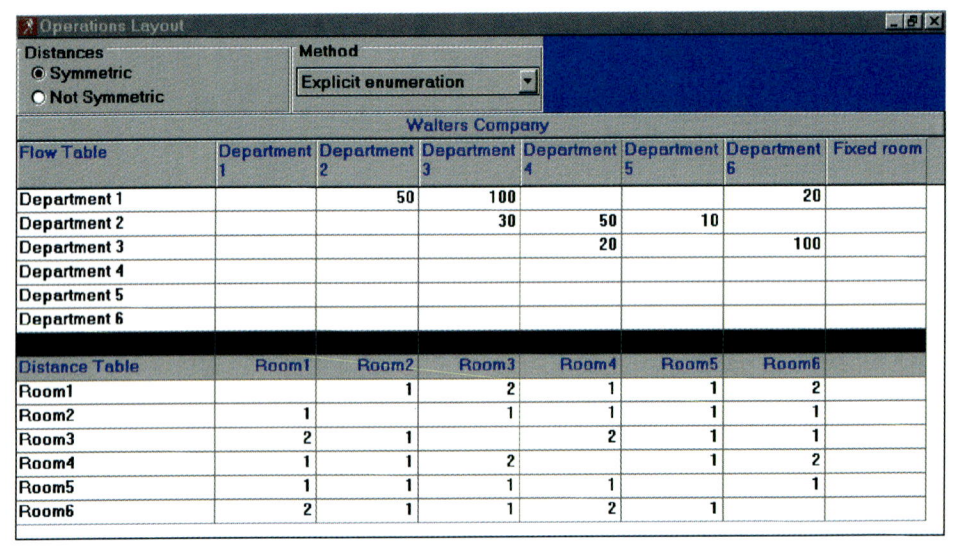

Flow Table

	Department 1	Department 2	Department 3	Department 4	Department 5	Department 6	Fixed room
Department 1		50	100			20	
Department 2			30	50	10		
Department 3				20		100	
Department 4							
Department 5							
Department 6							

Distance Table

	Room1	Room2	Room3	Room4	Room5	Room6
Room1		1	2	1	1	2
Room2	1		1	1	1	1
Room3	2	1		2	1	1
Room4	1	1	2		1	2
Room5	1	1	1	1		1
Room6	2	1	1	2	1	

Distances: Symmetric / Not Symmetric
Method: Explicit enumeration
Walters Company

PROGRAM 9.1 ■ POM for Windows' Operations Layout Program Applied to Walters Company Data in Example 1 *Departments may be named in their columns. Typically, the distance matrix will be symmetric. If not, all entries must be made. The solution appears in Program 9.2.*

Operations Layout Results — Room assignments

Department	Room
Total Movement	380
Department 1	Room1
Department 2	Room2
Department 3	Room5
Department 4	Room3
Department 5	Room6
Department 6	Room4

PROGRAM 9.2 ■ Solution to Program 9.1 POM for Windows' Input Screen for Walters Company Data

Solving Examples 2, 3, and 4 Using POM for Windows' Assembly Line-Balancing Module

POM for Windows' module for line balancing can handle a line with up to 99 tasks, each with up to 6 immediate predecessors. Programs 9.3 and 9.4 illustrate the input and output computer screens for this module as applied to Examples 2, 3, and 4.

TASK	Minutes	Predecessor 1	Predecessor 2	Predecessor 3	Predecessor 4	Predecessor 5
A	10					
B	11	a				
C	5	b				
D	4	b				
E	12	a				
F	3	c	d			
G	7	f				
H	11	e				
I	3	g	h			

Method: Longest operation time
Cycle time computation: Computed, 40 units per 8 hours
Task time unit: minutes

PROGRAM 9.3 ■ **POM for Windows' Assembly Line-Balancing Program Data Entry Screen** *Cycle time can be entered in two ways: (1) either given, if known or (2) demand rate can be entered with time available as shown. Five "heuristic rules" may be used: (1) longest operation (task) time, (2) most following tasks, (3) ranked positional weight, (4) shortest operation (task) time, and (5) least number of following tasks. No one rule can guarantee an optimal solution. The default rule is the longest operation time.*

Example Solution

Station	Task	Time (minutes)	Time left (minutes)	Ready tasks
				A
1	A	10.	2.	B,E
2	E	12.	0.	B,H
3	B	11.	1.	H,C,D
4	H	11.	1.	C,D
5	C	5.	7.	D
	D	4.	3.	F
	F	3	0.	G
6	G	7.	5.	I
	I	3.	2.	

Summary Statistics

Cycle time	12	minutes
Time allocated (cyc*sta)	72	minutes/cycle
Time needed (sum task)	66	minutes/unit
Idle time (allocated-needed)	6	minutes/cycle
Efficiency (needed/allocated)	91.66666%	
Balance Delay (1-efficiency)	8.333333%	
Min (theoretical) # of stations	6	

PROGRAM 9.4 ■ **POM for Windows' Assembly Line-Balancing Output for Examples 2 through 4 and Program 9.3** *Note that longest operation-time heuristic provides a different solution than the one that we found in Figure 9.13.*

SOLVED PROBLEMS

Solved Problem 9.1

The Snow-Bird Hospital is a small emergency-oriented facility located in a popular ski resort area in northern Michigan. Its new administrator, Mary Lord, decides to reorganize the hospital, using the process-layout method she studied in business school. The current layout of Snow-Bird's eight emergency departments is shown in Figure 9.14.

Snow-Bird Hospital Layout

Entrance/initial processing	Exam room 1	Exam room 2	X-ray
Laboratory tests/EKG	Operating room	Recovery room	Cast-setting room

(Each row is 10' tall; total width 40')

FIGURE 9.14 ■ Snow-Bird Hospital Layout

The only physical restriction perceived by Lord is the need to keep the combination entrance/initial processing room in its current location. All other departments or rooms (each 10-feet square) can be moved if layout analysis indicates a move would be beneficial.

First, Lord analyzes records in order to determine the number of trips made by patients between departments in an average month. The data are shown in Figure 9.15. Her objective, Lord decides, is to lay out the rooms so as to minimize the total distance walked by patients who enter for treatment. She writes her objective as:

$$\text{Minimize patient movement} = \sum_{i=1}^{8} \sum_{j=1}^{8} X_{ij} C_{ij}$$

where X_{ij} = number of patients per month (loads or trips) moving from department i to department j

C_{ij} = distance in feet between departments i and j (which, in this case, is the equivalent of cost per load to move between departments)

Note that this is only a slight modification of the cost-objective equation shown earlier in the chapter.

Lord assumes that adjacent departments, such as the entrance and examination room 1, have a walking distance of 10 feet. Diagonal departments are also con-

FIGURE 9.15 ■ Number of Patients Moving between Departments in One Month

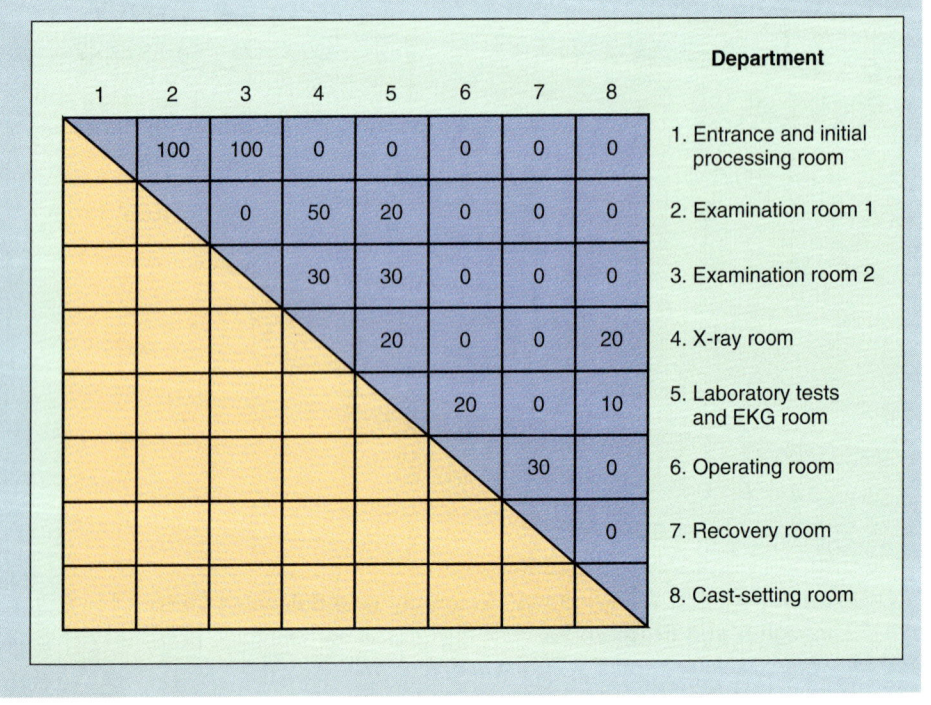

Department	2	3	4	5	6	7	8	
1	100	100	0	0	0	0	0	Entrance and initial processing room
2		0	50	20	0	0	0	Examination room 1
3			30	30	0	0	0	Examination room 2
4				20	0	0	20	X-ray room
5					20	0	10	Laboratory tests and EKG room
6						30	0	Operating room
7							0	Recovery room
8								Cast-setting room

sidered adjacent and assigned a distance of 10 feet. Nonadjacent departments, such as the entrance and examination room 2 or the entrance and recovery room, are 20 feet apart, and nonadjacent rooms, such as entrance and X-ray, are 30 feet apart. (Hence, 10 feet is considered 10 units of cost, 20 feet is 20 units of cost, and 30 feet is 30 units of cost.)

Given the above information, redo the layout of Snow-Bird Hospital to improve its efficiency in terms of patient flow.

Solution

First, establish Snow-Bird's current layout, as shown in Figure 9.16. By analyzing Snow-Bird's current layout, patient movement may be computed.

Total movement = $(100 \times 10') + (100 \times 20') + (50 \times 20') + (20 \times 10')$

          1 to 2   1 to 3   2 to 4   2 to 5

$+ (30 \times 10') + (30 \times 20') + (20 \times 30') + (20 \times 10')$

          3 to 4   3 to 5   4 to 5   4 to 8

$+ (20 \times 10') + (10 \times 30') + (30 \times 10')$

          5 to 6   5 to 8   6 to 7

$= 1{,}000 + 2{,}000 + 1{,}000 + 200 + 300 + 600 + 600 + 200 + 200 + 300 + 300$

$= 6{,}700$ feet

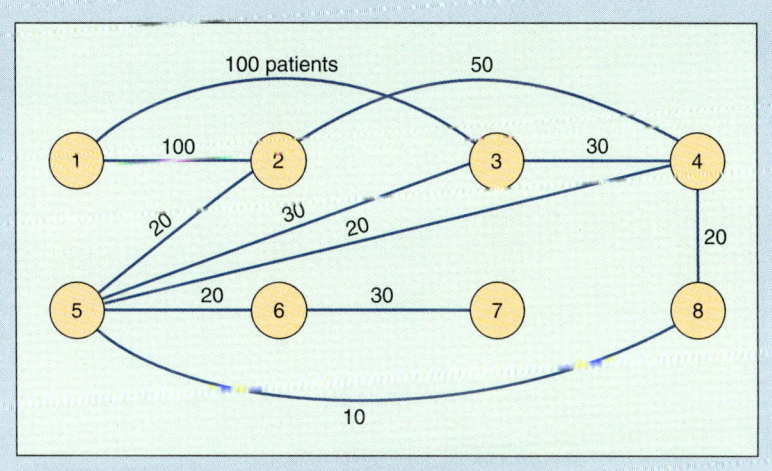

FIGURE 9.16 ■ **Current Snow-Bird Patient Flow**

Although it is not possible to prove a mathematically "optimal" solution, you should be able to propose a new layout that will reduce the current figure of 6,700 feet. Two useful changes, for example, are to switch rooms 3 and 5 and to interchange rooms 4 and 6. This change would result in the schematic shown in Figure 9.17.

Total movement = (100 × 10′) + (100 × 10′) + (50 × 10′) + (20 × 10′)

      1 to 2   1 to 3   2 to 4   2 to 5

   + (30 × 10′) + (30 × 20′) + (20 × 10′) + (20 × 20′)

      3 to 4   3 to 5   4 to 5   4 to 8

   + (20 × 10′) + (10 × 10′) + (30 × 10′)

      5 to 6   5 to 8   6 to 7

= 1,000 + 1,000 + 500 + 200 + 300 + 600 + 200
+ 400 + 200 + 100 + 300

= 4,800 feet

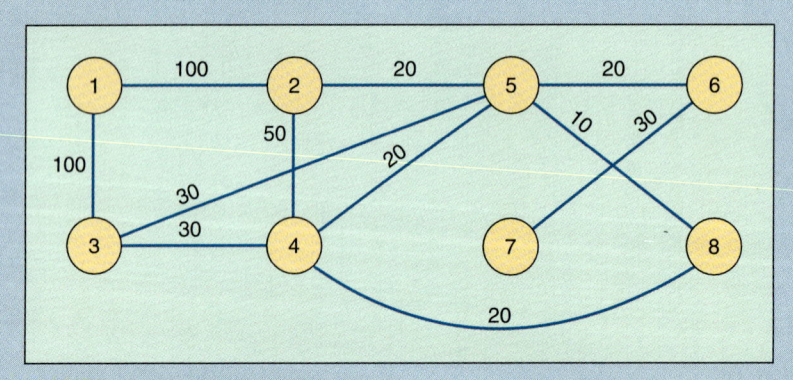

FIGURE 9.17 ■ **Improved Layout**

Do you see any room for further improvement? (See Homework Problem 9.2.)

Solved Problem 9.2

The assembly line whose activities are shown in Figure 9.18 has an 8-minute cycle time. Draw the precedence graph and find the minimum possible number of workstations. Then arrange the work activities into workstations so as to balance the line. What is the efficiency of your line balance?

Task	Performance Time (minutes)	Task Must Follow This Task
A	5	—
B	3	A
C	4	B
D	3	B
E	6	C
F	1	C
G	4	D, E, F
H	2	G
	28	

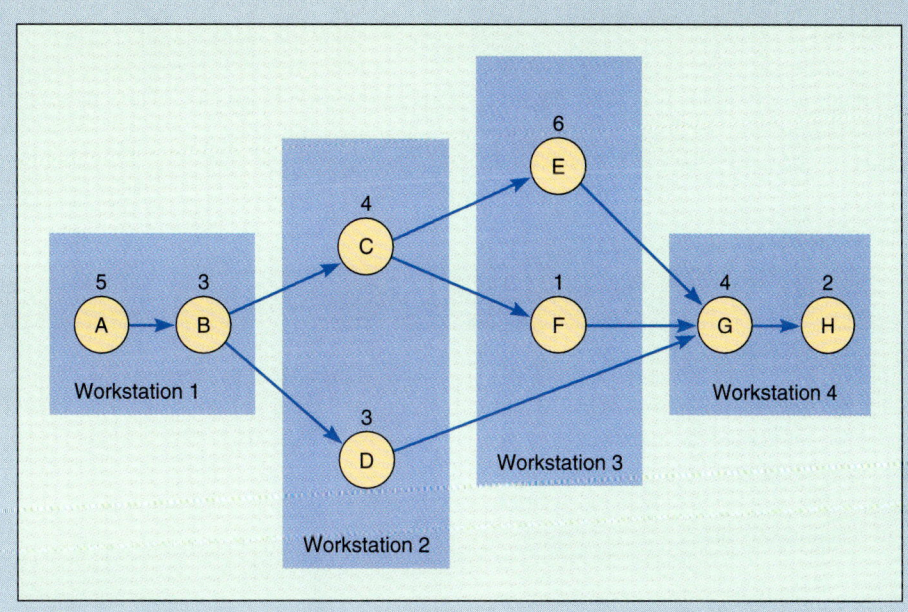

FIGURE 9.18 ■ **A Four-Station Solution to the Line-Balancing Problem**

Solution

The theoretical minimum number of workstations is

$$\frac{\sum t_i}{\text{Cycle time}} = \frac{28 \text{ minutes}}{8 \text{ minutes}} = 3.5 \text{ or 4 stations}$$

The precedence graph and one good layout are shown in Figure 9.18.

$$\text{Efficiency} = \frac{\text{total task time}}{(\text{number of workstations}) \times (\text{cycle time})} = \frac{28}{(4)(8)} = 87.5\%$$

DISCUSSION QUESTIONS

1. What is the layout strategy of your local print shop?
2. How would you go about collecting data to help a small business, like a print shop, improve its layout?
3. What are the six layout strategies presented in this chapter?
4. What are the advantages and disadvantages of product layout?
5. What are the advantages and disadvantages of process layout?
6. What are the advantages and disadvantages of work cells?
7. What layout innovations have you noticed recently in retail establishments?
8. What techniques can be used to overcome the inherent problems of fixed-position layout?
9. What layout variables would you consider particularly important in an office layout where computer programs are written?
10. What is required for a focused work center or focused factory to be appropriate?
11. Which of the layout types described in this chapter assume that demand is stable?

352 CHAPTER 9 LAYOUT STRATEGY

12. What are the variables that a manager can manipulate in a retail layout?
13. Visit a local supermarket and sketch its layout. What are your major observations regarding departments and their locations?
14. What information is necessary for random stocking to work?
15. What is cross-docking and how is it used?
16. Explain the concept of "customizing" at a warehouse.
17. What is a heuristic? Name several that can be used in assembly line balancing.

CRITICAL THINKING EXERCISE

Our discussion of office layout includes a note about the difference between U.S. and Japanese firms. Offices are more cramped and less automated in Japan; it is also common for two workers to share a telephone. No one at Tokyo's Toyota office has his or her own PC; rather, there is an alcove of machines to share.

Discuss your perceptions of the importance of the U.S. and Japanese styles of office layout. Which yields greater productivity?

PROBLEMS

9.1 Given the following flow and distance matrices in Roy Martin's job shop, what is the appropriate layout?

Flow Matrix

	Dept. A	Dept. B	Dept. C	Dept. D	Dept. E	Dept. F
Dept. A	0	100	50	0	0	50
Dept. B	25	0	0	50	0	0
Dept. C	25	0	0	0	50	0
Dept. D	0	25	0	0	20	0
Dept. E	50	0	100	0	0	0
Dept. F	10	0	20	0	0	0

Distance Matrix

	Dept. A	Dept. B	Dept. C	Dept. D	Dept. E	Dept. F
Dept. A	0	1	2	3	4	5
Dept. B	1	0	5	4	3	2
Dept. C	2	5	0	6	7	6
Dept. D	3	4	6	0	4	3
Dept. E	4	3	7	4	0	5
Dept. F	5	2	6	3	5	0

9.2 In Solved Problem 9.1 we improved Snow-Bird's layout to 4,800 feet of movement. Is further improvement possible? If so, what is it?

9.3 Registration period at Southeastern University has always been a time of emotion, commotion, and lines. Students must move among four stations to complete the trying semi-annual process. Last semester's registration, held in the fieldhouse, is described in Figure 9.19. You can see, for example, that 450 students moved from the paperwork station (A) to advising (B), and 550 went directly from A to picking up their class cards (C). Graduate students, who for the most part had preregistered, proceeded directly from A to the station where registration is verified and payment collected (D). The layout used last semester is also shown in Figure 9.19. The registrar is preparing to set up this semester's stations and is anticipating similar numbers.

a) What is the "load × distance," or cost, of the layout shown?
b) Provide an improved layout and compute its cost.

Interstation Activity Mix

	Pickup paperwork and forms (A)	Advising station (B)	Pickup class cards (C)	Verification of status and payment (D)
Paperwork/forms (A)	---	450	550	50
Advising (B)	250	---	200	0
Class cards (C)	0	0	---	750
Verification/payment (D)	0	0	0	---

Existing Layout

A — B — C — D (each segment 30')

FIGURE 9.19 ■ Registration Flow of Students

9.4 You have just been hired as the director of operations for Reid Chocolates, a purveyor of exceptionally fine candies. Reid Chocolates has two kitchen layouts under consideration for its recipe-making and -testing department. The strategy is to provide the best kitchen layout possible so that food scientists can devote their time and energy to product improvement, not wasted effort in the kitchen. You have been asked to evaluate these two kitchen layouts and to prepare a recommendation for your boss, Mr. Reid, so that he can proceed to place the contract for building the kitchens. (See Figure 9.20.)

Number of trips between work centers:

From \ To:	Refrigerator 1	Counter 2	Sink 3	Storage 4	Stove 5
Refrig. 1	0	8	13	0	0
Counter 2	5	0	3	3	8
Sink 3	3	12	0	4	0
Storage 4	3	0	0	0	5
Stove 5	0	8	4	10	0

Kitchen layout #1

Refrig.(1) — Counter(2) — Sink(3) — Storage(4) — Stove(5)
(distances 4, 4, 4, 4)

Kitchen layout #2

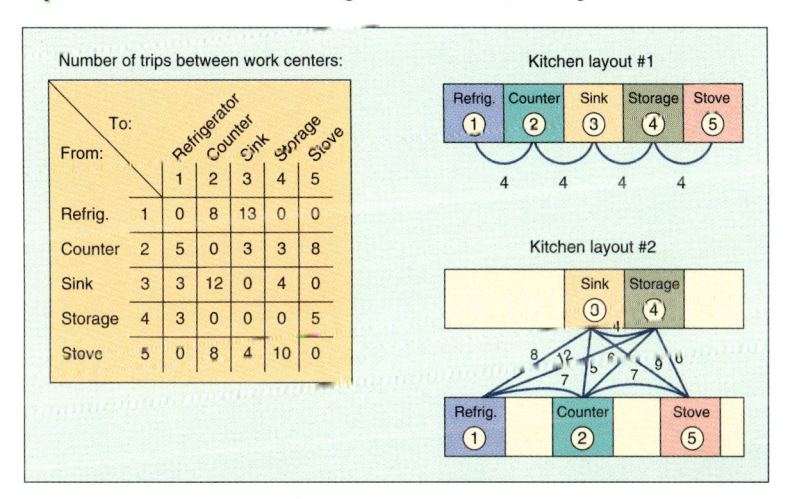

Sink(3), Storage(4)
Refrig.(1), Counter(2), Stove(5)

FIGURE 9.20 ■ Layout Options

9.5 Reid Chocolates (see problem 9.4) is considering a third layout, as shown below. Evaluate its effectiveness in trip-distance feet.

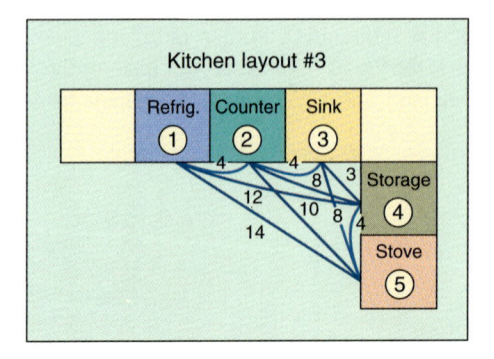

Kitchen layout #3

9.6 Reid Chocolates (see problems 9.4 and 9.5) has yet two more layouts to consider.
a) Layout #4 is shown below. What is the total trip distance?
b) Layout #5, also below, has what total trip distance?

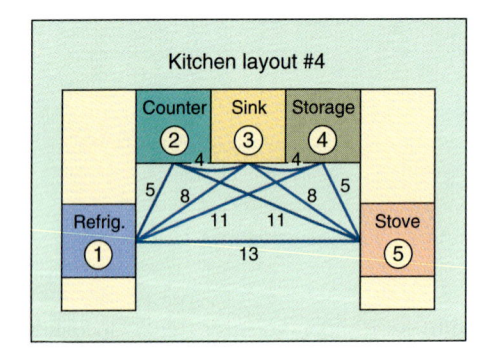

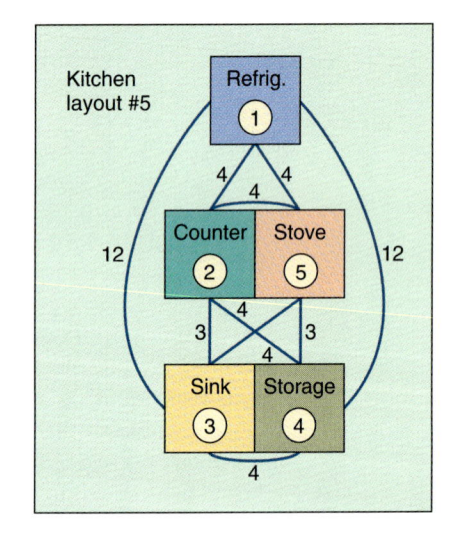

Kitchen layout #4

Kitchen layout #5

9.7 Given the following task, times, and sequence, develop a balanced line capable of operating with a 10-minute cycle time at Dave Visser's company. What is the efficiency of that line?

Task Element	Time (minutes)	Element Predecessor
A	3	—
B	5	A
C	7	B
D	5	—
E	3	C
F	3	B, D
G	5	D
H	6	G

9.8 The preinduction physical examination given by the U.S. Army involves the following seven activities:

Activity	Average Time (minutes)
Medical history	10
Blood tests	8
Eye examination	5
Measurements (i.e., weight, height, blood pressure)	7
Medical examination	16
Psychological interview	12
Exit medical evaluation	10

These activities can be performed in any order, with two exceptions: Medical history must be taken first, and exit medical evaluation is last. At present, there are three paramedics and two physicians on duty during each shift. Only physicians can perform exit evaluations and conduct psychological interviews. Other activities can be carried out by either physicians or paramedics.

a) Develop a layout and balance the line. How many people can be processed per hour?
b) Which activity accounts for the current bottleneck?
c) If one more physician and one more paramedic can be placed on duty, how would you redraw the layout? What is the new throughput?

: 9.9 A final assembly plant for Dictatape, a popular dictation company, produces the DT, a hand-held dictation unit. There are 400 minutes available in the final assembly plant for the DT, and the average demand is 80 units per day. Final assembly requires 6 separate tasks. Information concerning these tasks is given in the following table. What tasks should be assigned to various workstations, and what is the overall efficiency of the assembly line?

Task	Performance Time (minutes)	Task Must Follow Task Listed Below
1	1	—
2	1	1
3	4	1, 2
4	1	2, 3
5	2	4
6	4	5

: 9.10 South Carolina Furniture, Inc., produces all types of office furniture. The Executive Secretary is a chair that has been designed using ergonomics to provide comfort during long work hours. The chair sells for $130. There are 480 minutes available during the day, and the average daily demand has been 50 chairs. There are 8 tasks. Given the information below, solve this assembly line-balancing problem.

Task	Performance Time (minutes)	Task Must Follow Task Listed Below
1	4	—
2	7	1
3	6	1, 2
4	5	2, 3
5	6	4
6	7	5
7	8	5
8	6	6, 7

9.11 Tailwind, Inc., produces high-quality but expensive training shoes for runners. The Tailwind shoe, which sells for $110, contains both gas- and liquid-filled compartments to provide more stability and better protection against knee, foot, and back injuries. Manufacturing the shoes requires 10 separate tasks. How should these tasks be grouped into workstations? There are 400 minutes available for manufacturing the shoes in the plant each day. Daily demand is 60. The information for the tasks is as follows:

Task	Performance Time (minutes)	Task Must Follow Task Listed Below
1	1	—
2	3	1
3	2	2
4	4	2
5	1	3, 4
6	3	1
7	2	6
8	5	7
9	1	5, 8
10	3	9

9.12 Mach 10 is a one-person sailboat designed to be used in the ocean. Manufactured by Creative Leisure, Mach 10 can handle 40-mph winds and seas over 10 feet. The final assembly plant is in Cupertino, California. At this time, 200 minutes are available each day to manufacture Mach 10. The daily demand is 60 boats. Given the following information, how many workstations would you recommend?

Task	Performance Time (minutes)	Task Must Follow Task Listed Below
1	1	—
2	1	1
3	2	1
4	1	3
5	3	3
6	1	3
7	1	4, 5, 6
8	2	2
9	1	7, 8

9.13 Because of the expected high demand for Mach 10, Creative Leisure has decided to increase manufacturing time available to produce the Mach 10 (see problem 9.12). What impact would 300 available minutes per day have on the assembly line? What impact would 400 minutes have?

9.14 Nearbeer Products, Inc., manufactures drinks that taste the same as a good draft beer but contain no alcohol. With changes in drinking laws and demographics, there has been an increased interest in Nearbeer Lite. It has fewer calories than regular beer, is less filling, and tastes great. The final packing operation requires 13 tasks. Nearbeer bottles Nearbeer Lite 5 hours a day, 5 days a week. Each week, there is a demand for 3,000 bottles of Nearbeer Lite. Given the following information, solve this assembly line-balancing problem.

Data for Problems 9.14 and 9.15

Task	Performance Time (minutes)	Task Must Follow Task Listed Below
1	0.1	—
2	0.1	1
3	0.1	2
4	0.2	2
5	0.1	2
6	0.2	3, 4, 5
7	0.1	1
8	0.1	7
9	0.2	7, 8
10	0.1	9
11	0.2	6
12	0.2	10, 11
13	0.1	12

- **: 9.15** Nearbeer president Reed Doke believes that weekly demand for Nearbeer Lite could explode (see problem 9.14). What would happen if demand doubled?

- **: 9.16** Suppose production requirements in Solved Problem 9.2 increase and require a reduction in cycle time from 8 minutes to 7 minutes. Balance the line once again using the new cycle time. Note that it is not possible to combine task times so as to group tasks into the minimum number of workstations. This condition occurs in actual balancing problems fairly often.

- **: 9.17** Marilyn Hart, operations manager at Nesa Electronics, prides herself on excellent assembly line balancing. She has been told that the firm needs to complete 1,400 electronic relays per day. There are 420 minutes of productive time in each working day (which is equivalent to 25,200 seconds). Group the assembly-line activities below into appropriate workstations and calculate the efficiency of the balance.

Task	Time (seconds)	Must Follow Task	Task	Time (seconds)	Must Follow Task
A	13	—	G	5	E
B	4	A	H	6	F, G
C	10	B	I	7	H
D	10	—	J	5	H
E	6	D	K	4	I, J
F	12	E	L	15	C, K

- **: 9.18** Given the following data describing a line-balancing problem at Mayur Mehta's company, develop a solution allowing a cycle time of 3 minutes. What is the efficiency of that line?

Task Element	Time (minutes)	Element Predecessor
A	1	—
B	1	A
C	2	B
D	1	B
E	3	C, D
F	1	A
G	1	F
H	2	G
I	1	E, H

DATA BASE APPLICATION

9.19 As the Williams Bicycle Co. of Omaha completes plans for its new assembly line, it identifies 25 different tasks in the production process. VP of Operations Don Williams now faces the job of balancing the line. He lists precedences and provides time estimates for each step based on work-sampling techniques. His goal is to produce 1,000 bicycles per standard 40-hour workweek.

Task	Time (seconds)	Precedessor Tasks	Task	Time (seconds)	Precedessor Tasks
K3	60	—	E3	109	F3
K4	24	K3	D6	53	F4
K9	27	K3	D7	72	F9, E2, E3
J1	66	K3	D8	78	E3, D6
J2	22	K3	D9	37	D6
J3	3	—	C1	78	F7
G4	79	K4, K9	B3	72	D7, D8, D9, C1
G5	29	K9, J1	B5	108	C1
F3	32	J2	B7	18	B3
F4	92	J2	A1	52	B5
F7	21	J3	A2	72	B5
F9	126	G4	A3	114	B7, A1, A2
E2	18	G5, F3			

a) Balance this operation, using various heuristics. Which is best?
b) What happens if the firm can change to a 41-hour workweek?

■ *Case Study* ■

Des Moines National Bank

Des Moines National Bank (DNB) recently finished construction of a new building in the downtown business district. Moving into a new building provides an opportunity to arrange the various departments to optimize the efficiency and effectiveness of operations.

One primary operation of DNB is check processing. The check-processing division acts as a clearinghouse for commercial and personal checks. Checks are received from the tellers downstairs as well as from other, smaller financial institutions with which DNB has contracted. Using the magnetic-ink characters located at the bottom of each check, checks are sorted to be sent to the bank from which they are drawn. The reconcilement area ensures that incoming and outgoing totals balance, and the crediting area makes the entries to complete the transaction. Finally, sorted checks are bundled and shipped from the distribution area.

Personnel in this division are also responsible for processing government checks and for handling any returned checks coming back through the system. Because these checks require very different processing operations, they are placed in departments separate from the commercial check operations but are located on the same floor.

Because the service elevator travels only from the basement to the second floor, it has been decided that the check-processing division will be located on the second floor of the new building. The second floor is divided into 8 equal-sized rooms, as shown in Figure 9.21. (We call them rooms even though they are not separated by walls.) Each room is 75 feet square. Fortunately, this figure will not be a concern to bank management because each of the 8 departments to be located on this floor require roughly 5,000 square feet; these rooms will allow for some additional storage space and for future expansion.

The physical flow of materials—such as the checks being processed and computer printouts for the reconcilement and crediting areas—will be on aisles that run between the centers of the rooms, as shown in Figure 9.21. Because checks will arrive and be distributed from the service elevator, it is necessary to put the distribution department in the room with the elevator. There are no other physical restrictions that require any department to be placed in a given room.

For the first step in this analysis, it was necessary to determine the amount of work flow that travels between departments. Data collected for several weeks determined average daily traffic—measured in the number of trips between departments. Although there is some fluctuation in the number of checks processed on different days of the week, these average figures provide a good estimate of the relative work flow between each pair of departments.

A review of the work-flow data revealed that several important relationships were not being considered. For example, although no material flows directly between the commercial check-sorting area and the government check area, both areas use the same type of equipment. Because this equipment requires a "soundproof" wall to control the noise, it is necessary to keep them together to minimize the construction cost. Also, due to this noise, it is desirable to keep these departments removed from areas that require concentration, such as the reconcilement area and the offices. To account for these types of concerns, closeness ratings were identified for each pair of departments using the following rating scheme:

A—Absolutely necessary
E—Especially important
I—Important
O—Ordinary closeness OK
U—Unimportant
X—*Not* desirable

Table 9.5 on page 360 provides the average daily work flow between departments in the upper-right portion and the closeness ratings in the lower-left portion. For example, the work flow between check-sorting and reconcilement departments is 50 units per day, and there is a closeness rating of "X."

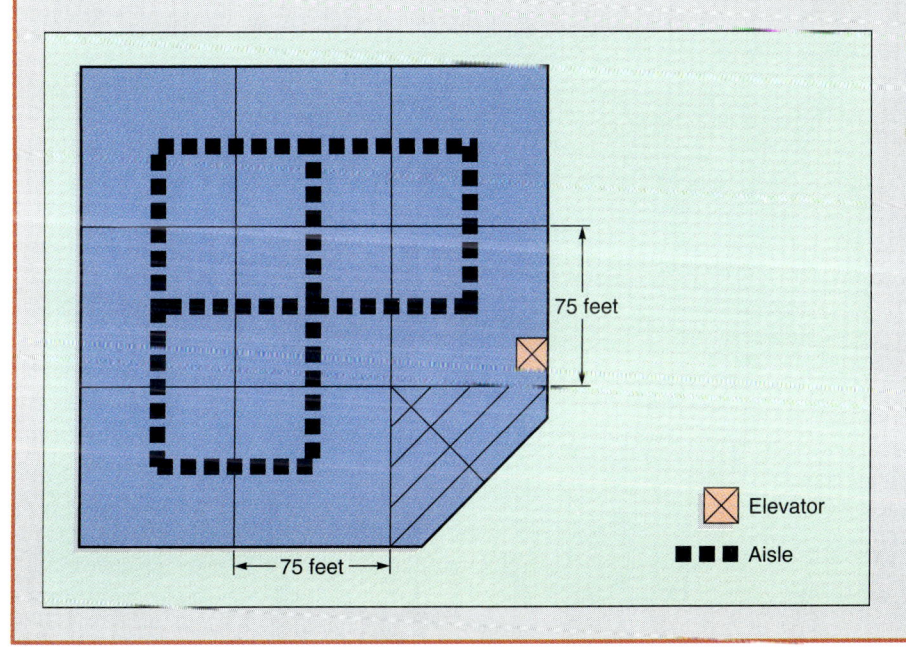

FIGURE 9.21 ■ Floor Plan of the Second Floor of the DNB Building

TABLE 9.5 ■ Work-flow and Closeness Relationships between Departments

Department	1	2	3	4	5	6	7	8
1. Check sorting	—	50	0	250	0	0	0	0
2. Check reconcilement	X	—	50	0	0	0	0	0
3. Check crediting	X	A	—	0	0	0	0	10
4. Check distribution	U	U	U	—	40	60	0	0
5. Government checks	A	U	U	E	—	0	0	0
6. Returned checks	U	U	U	E	U	—	12	0
7. Credit adjustment	X	A	A	U	U	E	—	10
8. Offices	X	I	I	U	O	O	I	—

Discussion Questions

1. Develop a layout that minimizes the total work flow.
2. Develop a layout using the relationships defined by the closeness ratings.
3. Develop a layout that considers both the work-flow and closeness relationships between departments.
4. Comment on the various layouts developed.
5. Discuss any other factors that should be considered when developing a layout of the check-processing division.

Source: Professor Timothy L. Urban, The University of Tulsa.

■ Case Study ■

State Automobile License Renewals

Henry Coupe, the manager of a metropolitan branch office of the state Department of Motor Vehicles, attempted to analyze the driver's license-renewal operations. He had to perform several steps. After examining the license-renewal process, he identified those steps and associated times required to perform each step, as shown in the following table:

State Automobile License Renewals Process Times

Step	Average Time To Perform (seconds)
1. Review renewal application for correctness	15
2. Process and record payment	30
3. Check file for violations and restrictions	60
4. Conduct eye test	40
5. Photograph applicant	20
6. Issue temporary license	30

Coupe found that each step was assigned to a different person. Each application was a separate process in the sequence shown above. He determined that his office should be prepared to accommodate a maximum demand of processing 120 renewal applicants per hour.

He observed that work was unevenly divided among clerks and that the clerk responsible for checking violations tended to shortcut her task to keep up with the others. Long lines built up during the maximum-demand periods.

Coupe also found that steps 1 to 4 were handled by general clerks who were each paid $6 per hour. Step 5 was performed by a photographer paid $8 per hour. (Branch offices were charged $5 per hour for each camera to perform photography.) Step 6, issuing temporary licenses, was required by state policy to be handled by uniformed motor vehicle officers. Officers were paid $9 per hour but could be assigned to any job except photography.

A review of the jobs indicated that step 1, reviewing applications for correctness, had to be performed before any other step could be taken. Similarly, step 6, issuing temporary licenses, could not be performed until all the other steps were completed.

Henry Coupe was under severe pressure to increase productivity and reduce costs, but he was also told by the regional director that he must accommodate the demand for renewals. Otherwise, "heads would roll."

Discussion Questions

1. What is the maximum number of applications per hour that can be handled by the present configuration of the process?
2. How many applications can be processed per hour if a second clerk is added to check for violations?
3. Assuming the addition of one more clerk, what is the maximum number of applications the process can handle?
4. How would you suggest modifying the process in order to accommodate 120 applications per hour?

Source: W. Earl Sasser, Paul R. Olson, and D. Daryl Wyckoff, *Management of Services Operations: Text, Cases, and Readings* (Boston: Allyn & Bacon, 1978).

Video Case 5

Facility Layout at Wheeled Coach

When President Bob Collins began his career at Wheeled Coach, the world's largest manufacturer of ambulances, there were only a handful of employees. Now the firm's Florida plant has a work force of 350. The physical plant has also expanded, with offices, R&D, final assembly, and wiring, cabinetry, and upholstery work cells in one large building. Growth has forced the painting work cell into a separate building, aluminum fabrication and body installation into another, inspection and shipping into a fourth, and warehousing into yet another.

Like many growing companies, Wheeled Coach was not able to design its facility from scratch. And while management realizes that material handling costs are a little higher than an ideal layout would provide, Collins is pleased with the way the facility has evolved and employees have adapted. The aluminum cutting work cell lies adjacent to body fabrication, which, in turn, is located next to the body-installation work cell. And while the vehicle must be driven across a street to one building for painting and then to another for final assembly, at least the ambulance is on wheels. Collins is also satisfied with the flexibility shown in design of the work cells. Cell construction is quite modular and can accommodate changes in product mix and volume. Additionally, work cells are typically small and movable, with many work benches and staging racks borne on wheels so that they can be easily rearranged and products transported to the assembly line.

Assembly line balancing is one key problem facing Wheeled Coach and every other repetitive manufacturer. Produced on a schedule calling for four 10-hour work days per week, once an ambulance is on one of the six final assembly lines, it *must* move forward each day to the next work station. Balancing just enough workers and tasks at each of the seven work stations is a never-ending challenge. Too many workers end up running into each other; too few can't finish an ambulance in 7 days. Constant shifting of design and mix and improved analysis has led to frequent changes. The *Global Company Profile* featuring Wheeled Coach (which opens chapter 14) provides further details about Wheeled Coach's facility layout.

Discussion Questions

1. What analytical techniques are available to help a company like Wheeled Coach deal with layout problems?
2. What suggestions would you make to Bob Collins about his layout?
3. How would you measure the "efficiency" of this layout?

▪ Internet Case Study ▪

See our Internet home page at http://www.prenhall.com/heizer for these additional case studies: Palm Beach Institute of Sports Medicine; W&G Beer Distributorship; and Microfix, Inc.

BIBLIOGRAPHY

Balakrishnan, J. "Notes: The Dynamics of Plant Layout." *Management Science* 39, 5 (May 1993): 654–655.

Ding, F., and L. Cheng. "An Effective Mixed-Model Assembly Line Sequencing Heuristic for Just-In-Time Production Systems." *Journal of Operations Management* 11, 1 (March 1993): 45–50.

Faaland, B. H., T. D. Klastorin, T. G. Schmitt, and A. Shtub. "Assembly Line Balancing with Resource Dependent Task Times." *Decision Sciences* 23, 2 (March–April 1992): 343.

Francis, R. L., L. F. McGinnis, and J. A. White. *Facility Layout and Location,* 2nd ed. Englewood Cliffs, NJ: Prentice Hall, 1992.

Heragu, Sunderesh, *Facilities Design.* Boston, MA: PWS Publishing Company, 1997.

Huang, P. Y., and B. L. W. Houck. "Cellular Manufacturing: An Overview and Bibliography." *Production and Inventory Management* 26 (fourth quarter 1985): 83–92.

Joshi, S., and M. Sudit. "Procedures for Solving Single-Pass Strip Layout Problems." *IIE Transactions* 26, 1 (January 1994): 27–37.

Leung, J. "A New Graph-Theoretic Heuristic for Facility Layout." *Management Science* 38, 4 (April 1992): 594.

Makens, P. K., D. F. Rossin, and M. C. Springer. "A Multivariate Approach for Assessing Facility Layout Complexity." *Journal of Operations Management* 9, 2 (April 1990): 185.

Montreuil, B., U. Venkatadri, and H. D. Ratliff. "Generating a Layout from a Design Skeleton." *Industrial Engineering Research & Development* 25, 1 (January 1993): 3–15.

Morris, J. S., and R. J. Tersine. "A Comparison of Cell Loading Practices in Group Technology." *Journal of Manufacturing and Operations Management* 2, 4 (winter 1989): 299.

Vakharia, A. J., and B. K. Kaku. "Redesigning a Cellular Manufacturing System to Handle Long-Term Demand Changes: A Methodology and Investigation." *Decision Sciences* 24, 5 (September–October 1993): 909.

INTERNET RESOURCES

Discussion of solutions to assembly-line problems that require parallel workstations:
http://darkwing.uoregon.edu/~gfrazier/abstract.htm

Discussion of branch and bound procedure to solve a variety of assembly line-balancing problems:
http://www.bwl.th-darmstadt.de/BWL3/forsch/projekte/alb/index.htm

Commercial layout software from Cimtechnologies:
http://www.cimtech.com

Various facility designs plans:
http://www.manufacturing.net/magazine/mmh/

HUMAN RESOURCES AND JOB DESIGN

10

CHAPTER OUTLINE

GLOBAL COMPANY PROFILE: LUCENT TECHNOLOGIES
HUMAN RESOURCE STRATEGY FOR COMPETITIVE ADVANTAGE
   Constraints on Human Resource Strategy
LABOR PLANNING
   Employment-Stability Policies
   Work Schedules
   Job Classifications and Work Rules
JOB DESIGN
   Labor Specialization
   Job Expansion
   Psychological Components of Job Design
   Self-Directed Teams

Motivation and Incentive Systems
Ergonomics and Work Methods
The Visual Workplace
LABOR STANDARDS
SUMMARY
KEY TERMS
SOLVED PROBLEM
DISCUSSION QUESTIONS
CRITICAL THINKING EXERCISE
PROBLEMS
CASE STUDIES: THE FLEET THAT WANDERS; LINCOLN ELECTRIC'S INCENTIVE PAY SYSTEM
BIBLIOGRAPHY
INTERNET RESOURCES

LEARNING OBJECTIVES

When you complete this chapter you should be able to:

Identify or Define:

   Job design

   Job specialization

   Job expansion

   Tools of methods analysis

   Ergonomics

   Labor standards

   Andon

Explain or Describe:

   Requirements of good job design

   The visual workplace

🌐 GLOBAL COMPANY PROFILE:

Lucent Technologies, a winner of the Shingo quality prize for manufacturing, is truly a global producer of computer chips. With fabrication plants in Pennsylvania, Florida, and Spain and manufacturing facilities in England, Mexico, Thailand, and Singapore, Lucent is one of the world's largest producers of chips for disk drives, cellular phones, and network switches.

Touring a fabrication plant is like entering a vacuum-sealed bag. It is not a place made for people, who are by nature "dirty" with flaking skin that creates showers of dust. Today's chips can be contaminated by a single particle of dust just 1/100 the width of a human hair.

What goes on in a fabrication or "fab" plant? Blank silicon wafers, valued at perhaps $200, are the starting product. The output is a wafer with complicated patterns—actually thousands of electronic components—transferred on it, now valued at $20,000 or more.

The real center of a fab is the photolithography bay. Here a photo-sensitive gel is sprayed onto the wafers; they then go into a machine that projects the circuit elements onto the wafer. The projector is called a "stepper" because it projects the same image about 100 times onto each wafer, moving the wafer in steps to receive each successive image.

The fab room's cleanliness is specified in terms of the number of particles larger than one half of 1 micron found in a cubic foot of air. A

A magnified view of Lucent's new technique to make internal measurements of integrated circuits.

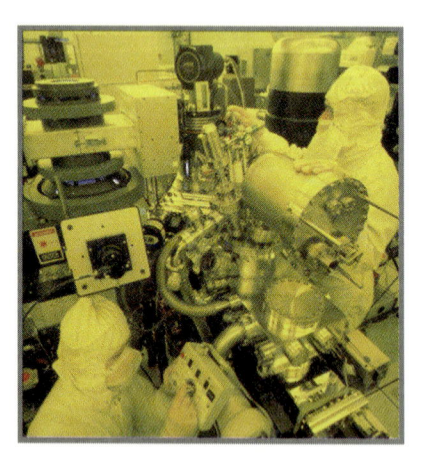

Workers in "bunny suits" complete one step in the photolithographic process of developing a wafer full of chips. The process of producing thousands of chips onto a silicon wafer is like printing a silk-screen reproduction with 20 different colors of ink. At each step, a fresh layer of silicon dioxide is baked on, parts of the new layer are etched away, and chemical elements are added to the exposed areas.

364

LUCENT TECHNOLOGIES

These three researchers are examining a wafer in a "clean room." Their clean-room "suits" consist of coats, gloves, and hoods, which are donned after the workers themselves are brushed and vacuumed. In some clean-room environments, only nonsmokers are permitted, as even a particulate of smoke residual in a man's mustache may contaminate the chip process.

typical college classroom might have a few hundred thousand particles per cubic foot. A surgical operating room brings the level down to about 20,000. In the wafer-handling areas of a Lucent fab, the level is brought down to 1! Cleanliness like this is expensive.

With the cost of the next generation of chip-fabrication plants approaching $2 billion, capital-intensive companies like Lucent are interested in maximizing the use of their investment. Therefore, Lucent operates its plants 24 hours a day, 7 days a week. Workers pull 12-hour shifts, working 3 days one week and 4 the next. Under this schedule, 4 crews alternate, with each crew working the day shift half the month and nights the other half. Although this schedule allows only 1 weekend day off each week and 2 fewer holidays each year, all days off total half a year. Still, some employees at Lucent remain on the standard 8-hour, 5-day workweek to facilitate working with suppliers, shippers, and customers who think 8-hour days are normal.

Various work shifts such as those at Lucent are repeated every day all over the world. One recent sample indicated that about one third of U.S. companies with over 1,000 employees use some kind of compressed workweek. Why do such jobs exist and is it good human resource strategy to have such jobs? In this chapter, we will examine these and related questions because an organization does not function without people. Moreover, it does not function well without competent, motivated people. Therefore, the operations manager's human resource strategy determines the talents and skills available to operations. Just to complicate matters, people are expensive, and most of them work for the operations manager.

However, as many organizations from Disney to Lincoln Electric to Lucent have demonstrated, competitive advantage can be built through human resource strategy. Good human resource strategies are expensive, difficult to achieve, and hard to sustain. However, the payoff potential is substantial, because they can be hard to copy! So a competitive advantage in this area is particularly beneficial. For these reasons, we now look at the operations manager's human resource options.

> **TEN DECISIONS OF OM**
> Managing Quality
> Design of Goods & Services
> Process Strategy
> Location Strategies
> Layout Strategies
> **Human Resources**
> Supply-Chain Management
> Inventory Management
> Scheduling
> Maintenance

HUMAN RESOURCE STRATEGY FOR COMPETITIVE ADVANTAGE

The *objective of a human resource strategy* is to manage labor and design jobs so people are *effectively* and *efficiently utilized*. As we focus on a human resource strategy, we want to ensure that people:

1. Are efficiently utilized within the constraints of other operations management decisions.
2. Have a reasonable quality of work life in an atmosphere of mutual commitment and trust.

By reasonable *quality of work life* we mean a job that is not only reasonably safe and for which the pay is equitable, but which also achieves an appropriate level of both physical and psychological requirements. *Mutual commitment* means that both management and employee strive to meet common objectives. *Mutual trust* is reflected in reasonable, documented employment policies that are honestly and equitably implemented to the satisfaction of both management and employee.[1] When management has a genuine respect for its employees and their contributions to the firm, establishing a reasonable quality of work life and mutual trust is not particularly difficult.

This chapter is devoted to showing how operations managers can achieve an effective human resource strategy.

Constraints on Human Resource Strategy

As Figure 10.1 suggests, many decisions made about people are constrained by other decisions. First, the product mix may determine seasonality and stability of employment. Second, technology, equipment, and processes may have implications for safety and job content. Third, the location decision may have an impact on the ambient environment in which the employees work. Finally, layout decisions, such as assembly line versus work cell, influence job content.

Technology decisions impose substantial constraints. For instance, some of the jobs in steel mills are dirty, noisy, and dangerous; slaughterhouse jobs may be stressful and

---

[1] With increasing frequency we find companies calling their employees *associates, individual contributors,* or members of a particular team.

LUCENT TECHNOLOGIES

These three researchers are examining a wafer in a "clean room." Their clean-room "suits" consist of coats, gloves, and hoods, which are donned after the workers themselves are brushed and vacuumed. In some clean-room environments, only nonsmokers are permitted, as even a particulate of smoke residual in a man's mustache may contaminate the chip process.

typical college classroom might have a few hundred thousand particles per cubic foot. A surgical operating room brings the level down to about 20,000. In the wafer-handling areas of a Lucent fab, the level is brought down to 1! Cleanliness like this is expensive.

With the cost of the next generation of chip-fabrication plants approaching $2 billion, capital-intensive companies like Lucent are interested in maximizing the use of their investment. Therefore, Lucent operates its plants 24 hours a day, 7 days a week. Workers pull 12-hour shifts, working 3 days one week and 4 the next. Under this schedule, 4 crews alternate, with each crew working the day shift half the month and nights the other half. Although this schedule allows only 1 weekend day off each week and 2 fewer holidays each year, all days off total half a year. Still, some employees at Lucent remain on the standard 8-hour, 5-day workweek to facilitate working with suppliers, shippers, and customers who think 8-hour days are normal.

365

Various work shifts such as those at Lucent are repeated every day all over the world. One recent sample indicated that about one third of U.S. companies with over 1,000 employees use some kind of compressed workweek. Why do such jobs exist and is it good human resource strategy to have such jobs? In this chapter, we will examine these and related questions because an organization does not function without people. Moreover, it does not function well without competent, motivated people. Therefore, the operations manager's human resource strategy determines the talents and skills available to operations. Just to complicate matters, people are expensive, and most of them work for the operations manager.

However, as many organizations from Disney to Lincoln Electric to Lucent have demonstrated, competitive advantage can be built through human resource strategy. Good human resource strategies are expensive, difficult to achieve, and hard to sustain. However, the payoff potential is substantial, because they can be hard to copy! So a competitive advantage in this area is particularly beneficial. For these reasons, we now look at the operations manager's human resource options.

TEN DECISIONS OF OM

Managing Quality
Design of Goods & Services
Process Strategy
Location Strategies
Layout Strategies
Human Resources
Supply-Chain Management
Inventory Management
Scheduling
Maintenance

HUMAN RESOURCE STRATEGY FOR COMPETITIVE ADVANTAGE

The *objective of a human resource strategy* is to manage labor and design jobs so people are *effectively* and *efficiently utilized*. As we focus on a human resource strategy, we want to ensure that people:

1. Are efficiently utilized within the constraints of other operations management decisions.
2. Have a reasonable quality of work life in an atmosphere of mutual commitment and trust.

By reasonable *quality of work life* we mean a job that is not only reasonably safe and for which the pay is equitable, but which also achieves an appropriate level of both physical and psychological requirements. *Mutual commitment* means that both management and employee strive to meet common objectives. *Mutual trust* is reflected in reasonable, documented employment policies that are honestly and equitably implemented to the satisfaction of both management and employee.[1] When management has a genuine respect for its employees and their contributions to the firm, establishing a reasonable quality of work life and mutual trust is not particularly difficult.

This chapter is devoted to showing how operations managers can achieve an effective human resource strategy.

Constraints on Human Resource Strategy

As Figure 10.1 suggests, many decisions made about people are constrained by other decisions. First, the product mix may determine seasonality and stability of employment. Second, technology, equipment, and processes may have implications for safety and job content. Third, the location decision may have an impact on the ambient environment in which the employees work. Finally, layout decisions, such as assembly line versus work cell, influence job content.

Technology decisions impose substantial constraints. For instance, some of the jobs in steel mills are dirty, noisy, and dangerous; slaughterhouse jobs may be stressful and

---

[1] With increasing frequency we find companies calling their employees *associates, individual contributors,* or members of a particular team.

Part III — Managing Operations

Supply-Chain Management

11

CHAPTER OUTLINE

GLOBAL COMPANY PROFILE: VOLKSWAGEN
THE STRATEGIC IMPORTANCE OF THE SUPPLY CHAIN
  Global Supply-Chain Issues
PURCHASING
  Manufacturing Environments
  Service Environments
  Make-or-Buy Decisions
SUPPLY-CHAIN STRATEGIES
  Many Suppliers
  Few Suppliers
  Vertical Integration
  Keiretsu Networks
  Virtual Companies
VENDOR SELECTION
  Vendor Evaluation
  Vendor Development
  Negotiations
MANAGING THE SUPPLY CHAIN
MATERIALS MANAGEMENT
  Distribution Systems
BENCHMARKING SUPPLY-CHAIN MANAGEMENT
SUMMARY
KEY TERMS
DISCUSSION QUESTIONS
CRITICAL THINKING EXERCISE
PROBLEMS
CASE STUDIES: FACTORY ENTERPRISES, INC.; THOMAS MANUFACTURING COMPANY
VIDEO CASE 6: SUPPLY CHAIN MANAGEMENT AT REGAL MARINE
INTERNET CASE STUDIES
BIBLIOGRAPHY
INTERNET RESOURCES

LEARNING OBJECTIVES

When you complete this chapter you should be able to:

Identify or Define:
  Supply-chain management
  Purchasing
  Materials management
  Keiretsu
  Virtual companies

Describe or Explain:
  Purchasing strategies
  Approaches to negotiations

413

GLOBAL COMPANY PROFILE:

Volkswagen's Radical Experiment in Supply-Chain Management

In its new Brazilian plant 100 miles northwest of Rio de Janeiro, Volkswagen is radically altering its supply chain. With this experimental truck factory, Volkswagen is betting that it has found a system that will reduce the number of defective parts, cut labor costs, and improve efficiency. Because VW's potential market is small, this is a relatively small plant, with scheduled production of only 100 trucks per day and only 1,000 workers. However, only 200 of the 1,000 work for Volkswagen. The VW employees are responsible for overall quality, marketing, research, and design. The other 800, who work for suppliers such as Rockwell International, Cummins Engines, Delga Automotiva, Remon, and VDO, do the assembly work. Volkswagen's innovative supply chain will, it hopes, improve quality and drive down costs, as each subcontractor accepts responsibility for its units and worker compensation. With this strategy, Volkswagen subcontractors accept more of the direct costs and risks.

As the schematic shows, at the first stop in the assembly process, workers from Iochpe-Maxion mount the gas tank, transmission lines, and steering blocks. As the chassis moves down the line, employees from Rockwell mount axles and brakes. Then workers from Remon put on wheels and adjust tire pressure. The MWM/Cummins team installs the engine and transmission. Truck cabs, produced by the Brazilian firm Delga Automotiva, are painted by Eisenmann, and then finished and upholstered by VDO, both of Germany. Volkswagen employees do an evaluation of the final truck.

Because technology and economic efficiency demand specialization, many firms, like Volkswagen, are increasing their commitment to out-

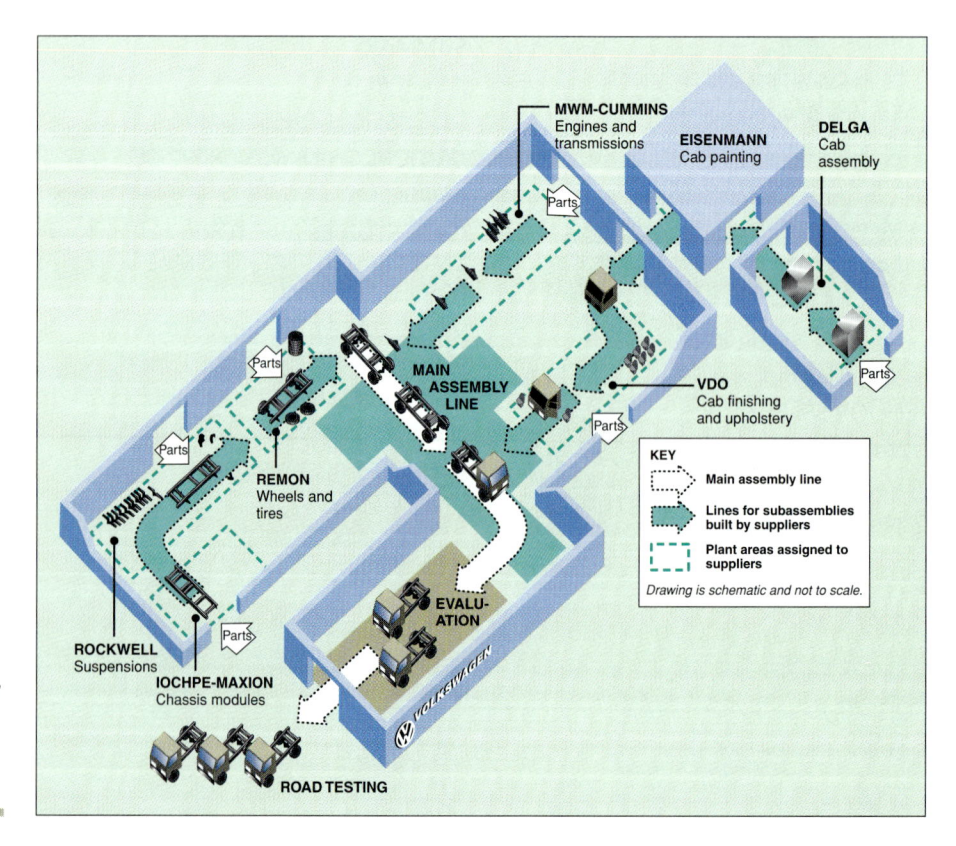

Volkswagen's major suppliers are assigned space in the VW plant, but supply their own components, supplies, and workers. Workers from various suppliers build the truck as it moves down the assembly line. Volkswagen personnel inspect.

414

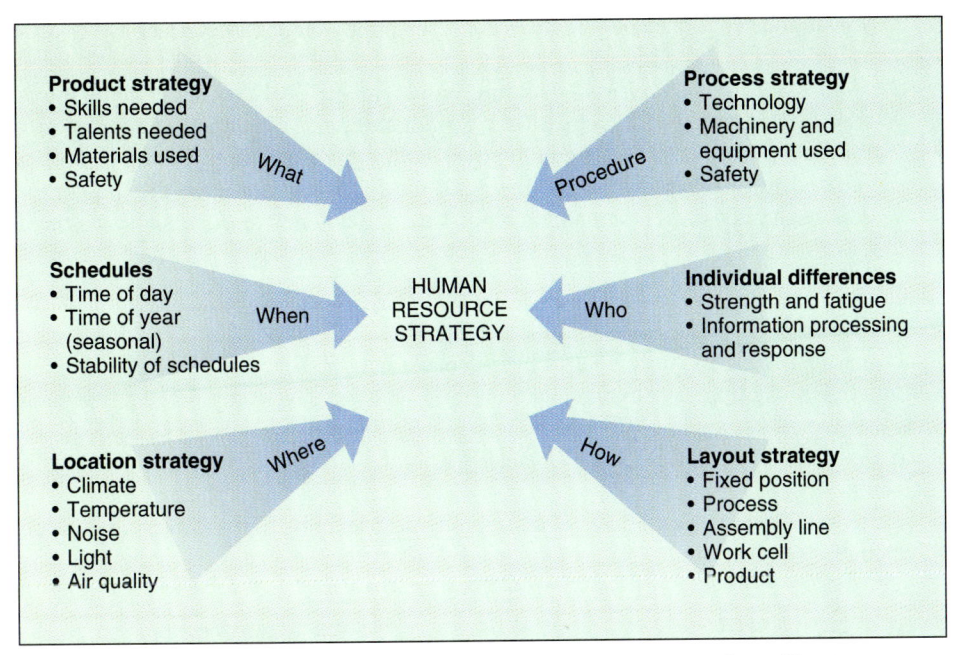

FIGURE 10.1 ■ Constraints on Human Resource Strategy. The effective operations manager understands how decisions blend together to constrain the human resource strategy.

subject workers to stomach-crunching stench; assembly-line jobs are often boring and mind-numbing; and high capital expenditures such as Lucent's fab plants may require 24-hour, 7-day-a-week operation in restrictive clothing.

We are not going to change these jobs without making changes in our other strategic decisions. So, the trade-offs necessary to reach a tolerable quality of work life are difficult. Effective managers consider such decisions simultaneously. The result: an effective, efficient system in which both individual and team performance are enhanced through optimum job design.

Acknowledging the constraints imposed on human resource strategy, we now look at three distinct decision areas of human resource strategy: labor planning, job design, and labor standards. The supplement to this chapter expands on the discussion of labor standards and introduces work measurement.

LABOR PLANNING

Labor planning is determining staffing policies that deal with (1) employment stability and (2) work schedules.

Employment-Stability Policies

Employment stability deals with the number of employees maintained by an organization at any given time. There are two very basic policies for dealing with stability:

1. *Follow demand exactly.* Following demand exactly keeps direct labor costs tied to production, but incurs other costs. These other costs include (a) hiring and termination costs, (b) unemployment insurance, and (c) premium wages to entice per-

Labor planning
A means of determining staffing policies dealing with employment stability and work schedules.

sonnel to accept unstable employment. This policy tends to treat labor as a variable cost.

2. *Hold employment constant.* Holding employment levels constant maintains a trained workforce and keeps hiring, termination, and unemployment costs to a minimum. However, with employment held constant, employees may not be utilized fully when demand is low, and the firm may not have the human resources it needs when demand is high. This policy tends to treat labor as a fixed cost.

Maintaining a stable workforce may allow a firm to pay lower wages than a firm that follows demand. This savings may provide a competitive advantage. However, firms with highly seasonal work and little control over demand may be best served by a fluctuating workforce. For example, a salmon canner on the Columbia River only processes salmon when the salmon are running. However, the firm may find complementary labor demands in other products or operations, such as making cans and labels or repairing and maintaining facilities.

Firms must determine policies about employment stability. The above policies are only two of many that can be efficient *and* provide a reasonable quality of work life.

Work Schedules

Standard work schedule
Five 8-hour days in the United States.

Although the **standard work schedule** in the United States is still five 8-hour days, variations do exist. A currently popular variation is a work schedule called flextime. **Flextime** allows employees, within limits, to determine their own schedules. A flextime policy might allow an employee (with proper notification) to be at work at 8 A.M. plus or minus 2 hours. This policy allows more autonomy and independence on the part of the employee. Some firms have found flextime a low-cost fringe benefit that enhances job satisfaction. The problem from the OM perspective is that much production work requires full staffing for efficient operations. A machine that requires 3 people cannot run at all if only 2 show up. Having a waiter show up to serve lunch at 1:30 P.M. rather than 11:30 A.M. is not much help either.

Flextime A system that allows employees, within limits, to determine their own work schedules.

Similarly, some industries find that their process strategies severely constrain their human resource scheduling options. For instance, paper manufacturing, petroleum refining, and power stations must be staffed around the clock except for maintenance and repair shutdown.

Flexible workweek
A work schedule that deviates from the normal or standard five 8-hour days (such as, four 10-hour days).

Another option is the **flexible workweek.** This plan often calls for fewer but longer days, such as four 10-hour days or, as in the case of Lucent Technologies, 12-hour shifts. Twelve-hour shifts usually mean working 3 days one week and 4 the next. Such shifts are sometimes called *compressed workweeks*. These schedules are viable for many operations functions—as long as suppliers and customers can be accommodated. Firms that have high process start-up times (say, to get a boiler up to operating temperature) find longer workday options particularly appealing. Compressed workweeks have long been common in fire and utility departments, where physical exertion is modest but 24-hour coverage desirable. A recent Gallup survey showed that two thirds of working adults would prefer toiling four 10-hour days to the standard 5-day schedule. Duke Power Co., Los Angeles county, AT&T, and General Motors are just a few organizations to offer the 4-day week.

Part-time status When an employee works less than a normal week; less than 32 hours per week often classifies an employee as "part-time."

Another option is shorter days rather than longer days. This plan often moves employees to **part-time status.** Such an option is particularly attractive in service industries, where staffing for peak loads is necessary. Banks and restaurants often hire part-time workers. Also, many firms reduce labor costs by reducing fringe benefits for part-time employees.

Job Classifications and Work Rules

Many organizations have strict job classifications and work rules that specify who can do what, when they can do it, and under what conditions they can do it, often as a result of union pressure. These job classifications and work rules restrict employee flexibility on the job, which in turn reduces the flexibility of the operations function. But, part of an operations manager's task is to manage the unexpected. Therefore, the more flexibility a firm has when staffing and establishing work schedules, the more efficient and responsive it *can* be. This is particularly true in service organizations, where extra capacity often resides in extra or flexible staff. Building morale and meeting staffing requirements that result in an efficient, responsive operation are easier if managers have fewer job classifications and work-rule constraints. If the strategy is to achieve a competitive advantage by responding rapidly to the customer, a flexible workforce may be a prerequisite.[2]

JOB DESIGN

Job design specifies the tasks that constitute a job for an individual or a group. We examine seven components of job design: (1) job specialization, (2) job expansion, (3) psychological components, (4) self-directed teams, (5) motivation and incentive systems, (6) ergonomics and work methods, and (7) visual workplace.

Job design
An approach that specifies the tasks that constitute a job for an individual or a group.

Labor Specialization

The importance of job design as a management variable is credited to the eighteenth-century economist Adam Smith.[3] Smith suggested that a division of labor, also known as **labor specialization** (or **job specialization**), would assist in reducing labor costs of multiskilled artisans. This is accomplished in several ways:

1. *Development of dexterity* and faster learning by the employee because of repetition,
2. *Less loss of time* because the employee would not be changing jobs or tools,
3. *Development of specialized tools* and the reduction of investment because each employee has only a few tools needed for a particular task.

Labor specialization (or job specialization) The division of labor into unique ("special") tasks.

The nineteenth-century British mathematician Charles Babbage determined that a fourth consideration was also important for labor efficiency.[4] Because pay tends to follow skill with a rather high correlation, Babbage suggested *paying exactly the wage needed for the particular skill required*. If the entire job consists of only one skill, then we would pay for only that skill. Otherwise, we would tend to pay for the highest skill contributed by the employee. These four advantages of labor specialization are still valid today.

A classic example of labor specialization is the assembly line. Such a system is often very efficient, although it may require employees to do repetitive, mind-numbing jobs. The wage rate for many of these jobs, however, is very good. Given the relatively high wage rate for the modest skills required in many of these jobs, there is often a large pool of employees from which to choose. This is not an incidental consideration for the manager with responsibility for staffing the operations function. It is estimated that 2% to 3% of the workforce in industrialized nations perform highly specialized, repetitive assembly-

---

[2] David M. Upton, "What Really Makes a Factory Flexible?" *Harvard Business Review* (July–August 1995): 74–84.

[3] Adam Smith, *On the Creation of the Wealth of Nations* (London, 1776).

[4] Charles Babbage, *On the Economy of Machinery and Manufacturers* (London: C. Knight, 1835), Chapter 18.

line jobs. The traditional way of developing and maintaining worker commitment under labor specialization has been good selection (matching people to the job), good wages, and incentive systems.

From the manager's point of view, a major limitation of specialized jobs is their failure to bring the whole person to the job. Job specialization tends to bring only the employee's manual skills to work. In an increasingly sophisticated knowledge-based society, managers may want employees to bring their mind to work as well.

Job Expansion

In recent years, there has been an effort to improve the quality of work life by moving from labor specialization toward more varied job design. Driving this effort is the theory that variety makes the job "better" and that the employee therefore enjoys a higher quality of work life. This flexibility thus benefits the employee and the organization.

We modify jobs in a variety of ways. The first approach is **job enlargement,** which occurs when we add tasks requiring similar skill to an existing job. **Job rotation** is a version of job enlargement that occurs when the employee is allowed to move from one specialized job to another. Variety has been added to the employee's perspective of the job. Another approach is **job enrichment,** which adds planning and control to the job. An example is to have department store salespeople responsible for ordering, as well as selling, their goods. Job enrichment can be thought of as *vertical expansion,* as opposed to job enlargement, which is *horizontal.* These ideas are shown in Figure 10.2.

A popular extension of job enrichment, **employee empowerment** is the practice of enriching jobs so employees accept responsibility for a variety of decisions normally associated with staff specialists.[5] Empowering employees helps them take "ownership" of their jobs so they have a personal interest in improving performance. (See the *OM in Action* box, "Empowerment at the Ritz-Carlton.")

> An enlarged job may give employees only a number of boring things to do.
>
> **Job enlargement** The grouping of a variety of tasks about the same skill level; horizontal enlargement.
>
> **Job rotation** A system in which an employee is moved from one specialized job to another.
>
> **Job enrichment** A method of giving an employee more responsibility that includes some of the planning and control necessary for job accomplishment; vertical enlargement.
>
> **Employee empowerment** Enlarging employee jobs so that the added responsibility and authority is moved to the lowest level possible in the organization. Empowerment allows the employee to assume both managerial and staff responsibilities.

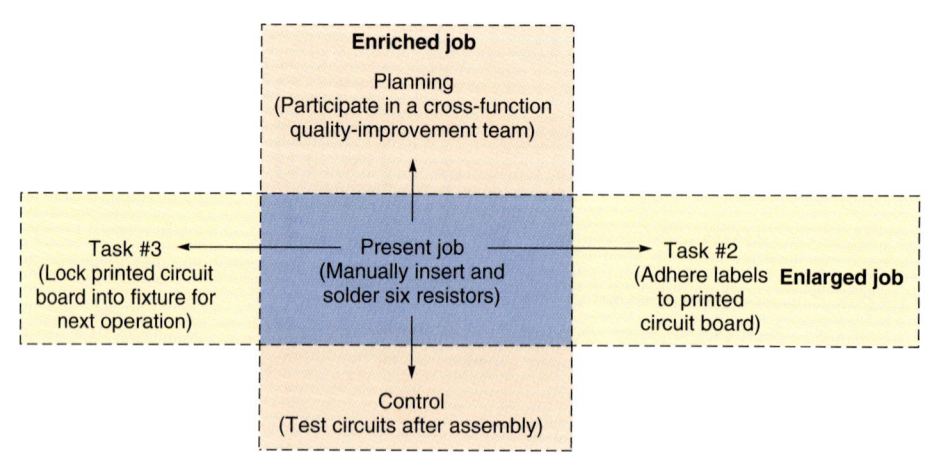

FIGURE 10.2 ■ **An Example of Job Enlargement (*horizontal* job expansion) and Job Enrichment (*vertical* job expansion)** *The job can be enlarged horizontally by job rotation to tasks 2 and 3 or these tasks can be made a part of the present job. Job enrichment, expanding the job vertically, can occur by adding other types of tasks, such as participation in a quality team (planning) and testing tasks (control).*

---

[5] See W. C. Byham, *Zapp! The Lightning of Empowerment* (New York: Ballantine, 1992).

OM IN ACTION

EMPOWERMENT AT THE RITZ-CARLTON

When the president of the Ritz-Carlton hotel chain introduces himself to employees, he begins with these lines: "My name is Horst Schulze. I'm president of this company; I'm very important. [Pause] But so are you. Absolutely. Equally important." This attitude may be the cause of a turnover rate that is less than half the industry average, and may be why the Ritz recently received a Malcolm Baldrige National Quality Award.

Schulze describes customer service in his organization as "Ladies and gentlemen serving ladies and gentlemen." He stresses that *both* groups be treated with dignity and respect.

To empower employees, Ritz front-desk clerks and sales managers can spend up to $2,000 and $5,000 of company money, respectively—to ensure that guests leave satisfied. For example, when the New York Ritz was overbooked once, 20 guests were sent to another hotel in 3 limousines packed with champagne and caviar. The cost: $5,000. "The idea was to please guests," says the Ritz manager.

Empowerment also includes taking suggestions of all employees seriously. When a room service waiter proposed the company spend $50,000 to implement a recycling plan, Schulze took a deep breath and then agreed. The idea paid off: Weekly garbage pickups have been reduced and the hotel now sells its paper products rather than paying others to haul it off. The changes have saved $80,000 a year and typify the hotel's reliance on employee suggestions for quality improvement.

Sources: Sloan Management Review, summer 1995, pp. 73–85; *The Wall Street Journal*, April 22, 1994: p. B1; and *Nation's Restaurant News*, July 8, 1996, p. 24.

Psychological Components of Job Design

An effective human resources strategy also requires consideration of the psychological components of job design. These components focus on how to design jobs that meet some minimum psychological requirements.

Hawthorne Studies The Hawthorne studies introduced psychology to the workplace. They were conducted in the late 1920s at Western Electric's Hawthorne plant near Chicago. Publication of the findings in 1939[6] showed conclusively that there is a dynamic social system in the workplace. Ironically, these studies were initiated to determine the impact of lighting on productivity. Instead they found the social system and distinct roles played by employees to be more important than the intensity of the lighting. They also found that individual differences may be dominant in what an employee expects from the job and what the employee thinks her or his contribution to the job should be.

"We hired workers and human beings came instead."
Max Frisch

Core Job Characteristics In the seven decades since the Hawthorne studies, substantial research regarding the psychological components of job design has taken place.[7] Hackman and Oldham have incorporated much of that work into five desirable characteristics of job design.[8] Their summary suggests that jobs should include the following characteristics:

---

[6] F. J. Roethlisberger and William J. Dickinson, *Management and the Workers* (New York: John Wiley, 1964, copyright 1939, by the President & Fellows of Harvard College).

[7] See, for instance, the work of Abraham H. Maslow, "A Theory of Human Motivation," *Psychological Review* 50 (1943): 370–396; and Frederick Herzberg, B. Mausner, and B. B. Snyderman, *The Motivation to Work* (New York: John Wiley, 1965).

[8] See "Motivation Through the Design of Work," in *Work Redesign*, eds. Jay Richard Hackman and Greg R. Oldham (Reading, MA: Addison-Wesley, 1980).

1. *Skill variety,* requiring the worker to use a variety of skills and talents.
2. *Job identity,* allowing the worker to perceive the job as a whole and recognize a start and a finish.
3. *Job significance,* providing a sense that the job has impact on the organization and society.
4. *Autonomy,* offering freedom, independence, and discretion.
5. *Feedback,* providing clear, timely information about performance.

> Empowerment can take many forms—planning, scheduling, quality, purchasing and even hiring authority.

Including these five ingredients in job design is consistent with job enlargement, job enrichment, and employee empowerment. We now want to look at some of the ways in which teams can be used to expand jobs and achieve these five job characteristics.

Self-Directed Teams

Many world-class organizations have adopted teams to foster mutual trust and commitment, and provide the core job characteristics. This practice is illustrated in the *OM in Action* box dealing with Mazda's worker selection. One team concept of particular note is the **self-directed team:** a group of empowered individuals working together to reach a common goal. These teams may be organized for long-term or short-term objectives. Teams are effective primarily because they can easily provide employee empowerment, ensure core job characteristics, and satisfy many of the psychological needs of individual team members.[9] A job design continuum is shown in Figure 10.3.

> **Self-directed team**
> A group of empowered individuals working together to reach a common goal.

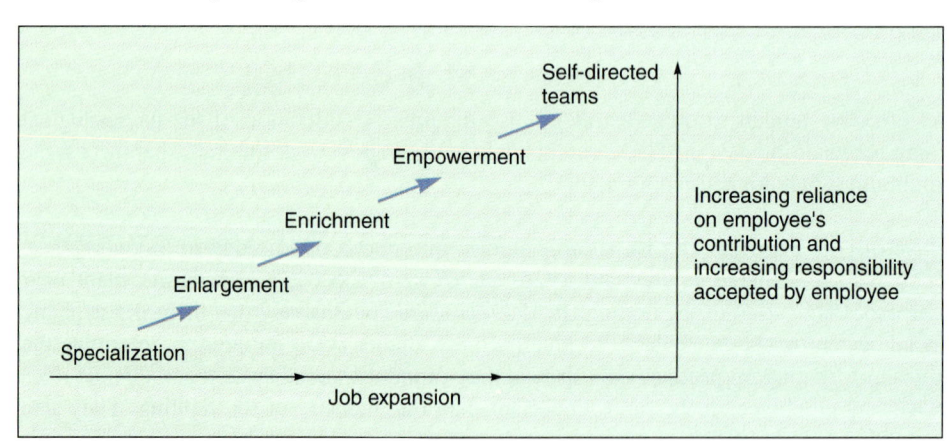

FIGURE 10.3 ■ Job Design Continuum

Of course, many good job designs *can* provide these psychological needs. Therefore, to maximize team effectiveness, managers do more than just form "teams." For instance, they (1) ensure that those who have a legitimate contribution are on the team, (2) provide management support, (3) ensure the necessary training, and (4) endorse clear objectives and goals. Successful teams should also receive financial and nonfinancial rewards. Finally, managers must recognize that teams have a life cycle and that achieving an objective may suggest disbanding the team. However, teams may be renewed with a change in members or new assignments.

Teams and other approaches to job expansion should not only improve the quality of work life and job satisfaction but also motivate employees to achieve strategic objectives.

---

[9] Per H. Engelstad, "Sociotechnical Approach to Problems of Process Control," in *Design of Jobs,* eds. Louis E. Davis and James C. Taylor (Santa Monica: Goodyear Publishing, 1979), pp. 184–205.

OM IN ACTION

HOW DOES MAZDA PICK WORKERS FOR ITS U.S. PLANTS? VERY CAREFULLY.

It was not long ago that the auto industry did not want educated people in its factories. As former United Auto Worker's President Douglas Fraser said, "You don't need to be a rocket scientist to assemble a car." But a new breed of auto worker is emerging. Over a quarter of the workers just hired for a new shift at a Chrysler plant in Ontario, Canada, have college degrees.

Mazda Motors' assembly plant in Flat Rock, Michigan, is even pickier, hiring only 3,500 of nearly 96,500 applicants who passed its five-step screening process. It spent about $40 million—over $11,000 per employee—to staff the plant. The Japanese firm believes that the key to success is picking the best employees and training them well.

A clear goal emerges. Interpersonal skills and team participation are mandatory. The basic philosophy: Reward flows not so much from your personal performance as from your impact on team and company.

In Mazda training rooms, employees learn to chart quality by building paper airplanes and checking their flight performance. "If a part doesn't meet specifications," they are told, "you reject it. That's your job." Mazda devotes 3 training days just to the philosophy of *Kaizen*, or continual improvement. After 3 weeks of this "basic training," each new hire spends 5 to 7 weeks on specific technical training and then 3 to 4 weeks being supervised on the assembly line.

Overkill? Maybe, but Mazda is not taking any chances. The company believes that teams are the key to its success and is building its plant around that concept from scratch.

Sources: Monthly Review, January 1996, pp. 48–55; *The Wall Street Journal,* March 11, 1994, p. A1; and *Industrial and Labor Review,* October 1995, pp. 88–105.

Both managers *and* employees need to be committed to achieving strategic objectives. However, employee contribution is fostered in a variety of ways, including organizational climate, supervisory action, *and* job design.

Expanded job designs allow employees to accept more responsibility. For employees who accept this responsibility, we may well expect some enhancement in productivity and product quality. Among the other positive aspects of job expansion are reduced turnover, tardiness, and absenteeism. Managers who expand jobs and build communication systems that elicit suggestions from employees have an added potential for efficiency and flexibility to meet market demands. However, these job designs have a number of limitations.

Limitations of Job Expansion If job designs that enlarge, enrich, empower, and use teams are so good, why are they not universally used? Let us identify some limitations of expanded job designs:

1. *Higher capital cost.* Job expansion may require facilities that cost more than those with a conventional layout. This extra expenditure must be generated through savings (greater efficiency) or higher prices.

2. *Individual differences.* Some studies indicate that many employees opt for the less complex jobs.[10] In a discussion about improving the quality of work life, we cannot forget the importance of individual differences. Differences in individuals provide latitude for the resourceful operations manager when designing jobs.

---

[10] Mitchell Fein, "Job Enrichment Does Not Work," *Atlanta Economic Review,* November–December 1975, pp 50–54. Also see interesting anecdotal evidence in Timothy Aeppel, "Not All Workers Find Idea of Empowerment as Neat as It Sounds," *The Wall Street Journal,* September 8, 1997, pp. A1–A13.

3. *Higher wage rates.* People often receive wages for their highest skills, not their lowest.[11] Thus expanded jobs may well require a higher average wage than jobs that are not.
4. *Smaller labor pool.* Because expanded jobs require more skill and acceptance of more responsibility, job requirements have increased. Depending upon the availability of labor, this may be a constraint.
5. *Increased accident rates.* Expanded jobs may contribute to a higher accident rate.[12] This indirectly increases wages, insurance costs, and worker's compensation. The alternative may be expanding training and safety budgets.
6. *Current technology may not lend itself to job expansion.* The disassembly jobs at a slaughterhouse and assembly jobs at automobile plants are that way because alternative technologies (if any) are thought to be unacceptable.

These six points provide the constraints on job expansion.

In short, job expansion often increases costs. Therefore, for the firm to have a competitive advantage, its savings must be greater than its costs. It is not always obvious that such is the case. The strategic decision may not be an easy one.

Despite the limitations of job expansion, firms are finding ways to make it work. Often the major limitations are not those listed above, but training budgets and the organization's culture. Training budgets must increase, and supervisors must release some control and learn to accept different job responsibilities. Self-directed teams may mean no supervisors on the factory floor. Removing supervisors from the factory floor, as has Harris-Farinon, a world leader in microwave equipment, is often a major culture change. However, Harris-Farinon is setting new performance standards with exactly this type of cultural change.

Service organizations have also reaped substantial advantage from successful human resources strategies. These success stories include Southwest Airlines, Ritz-Carlton, Nordstrom, Taco Bell, and Disney. Each has recognized that the creation of value for customers and shareholders begins with the creation of value for employees.[13]

Motivation and Incentive Systems

Our discussion of the psychological components of job design provides insight into the factors that contribute to job satisfaction and motivation. In addition to these psychological factors, there are monetary factors. Money often serves as a psychological as well as financial motivator. Monetary rewards take the form of bonuses, profit and gain sharing, and incentive systems.

Bonuses, typically in cash or stock options, are often used at executive levels to reward management. **Profit-sharing** systems provide some part of the profit for distribution to employees. A variation of profit sharing is **gain sharing,** which rewards employees for improvements made in an organization's performance. The most popular of these is the Scanlon plan, where any reduction in the cost of labor is shared between management and labor.[14]

Bonus A monetary reward, usually in cash or stock options, given to management or executives in an organization.

Profit sharing A system providing some portion of any profit for distribution to the employees.

Gain sharing A system of financial rewards to employees for improvements made in an organization's performance.

---

[11] Charles Babbage, *On the Economy of Machinery and Manufacturers* (London, 1832), chapter 18.

[12] J. Tsaari and J. Lahtella, "Job Enrichment: Cause of Increased Accidents?" *Industrial Engineering,* October 1978, pp. 41–45.

[13] Roger Hallowell, "Southwest Airlines: A Case Study Linking Employees' Needs, Satisfaction, and Organizational Capabilities to Competitive Advantage," *Human Resource Management,* winter, 1996, p. 530.

[14] Fred G. Lesieur and Elbridge S. Puckett, "The Scanlon Plan Has Proved Itself," *Harvard Business Review* 47, no. 5 (September–October 1969): 109–118.

The gain-sharing approach used by Panhandle Eastern Corp. of Houston, Texas, allows for employees to receive a bonus of 2% of their salary at year's end if the company earns at least $2.00 per share. When Panhandle earns $2.10 per share, the bonus climbs to 3%. Employees have become much more sensitive about costs since the plan began.

Incentive systems based on individual or group productivity are used in nearly half of the manufacturing firms in America. These systems often require employees or crews to achieve production above a predetermined standard. The standard can be based on a standard time per task or number of pieces made. Standard time systems are sometimes called *measured daywork*, where employees are paid based on the amount of standard time accomplished. A *piece-rate* system assigns a standard time for the production of each piece, and the employee is paid based on the number of pieces made. Both measured daywork and piece-rate systems typically guarantee the employee at least a base rate.

With the increasing use of teams, various forms of team-based pay are also being developed. Many are based on traditional pay systems supplemented with some form of bonus or incentive system. However, because many team environments require cross training of enlarged jobs, *knowledge-based* pay systems have also been developed. Under **knowledge-based** (or skill-based) **pay systems,** a portion of the employee's pay depends on demonstrated knowledge or skills possessed. Knowledge-based pay systems are designed to reward employees for the enlarged scope of their jobs. Some of these pay systems have three dimensions: *horizontal skills* that reflect the variety of tasks the employee can perform; *vertical skills* that reflect the planning and control aspects of the job; and *depth of skills* that reflect quality and productivity. At Wisconsin's Johnsonville Sausage Co., employees receive pay raises *only* by mastering new skills such as scheduling, budgeting, and quality control.

Incentive system An employee award system based on individual or group productivity.

Roger Penske, president of Detroit Diesel, which he purchased from GM, has used good relations with employees and a profit-sharing system to turn his firm around.

Knowledge-based pay systems A portion of the employee's pay depends on demonstrated knowledge or skills of the employee.

Ergonomics and Work Methods

As mentioned in chapter 1, Frederick W. Taylor began the era of scientific management in the late 1800s.[15] He and his contemporaries began to examine personnel selection, work methods, labor standards, and motivation.

With the foundation provided by Taylor, we have developed a body of knowledge about people's capabilities and limitations. This knowledge is necessary because humans are hand/eye animals possessing exceptional capabilities and some limitations. Because managers must design jobs that can be done, we now introduce a few of the issues related to people's capabilities and limitations.

Ergonomics The operations manager is interested in building a good interface between human and machine. Studies of this interface are known as **ergonomics.** Ergonomics means "the study of work." (*Ergon* is the Greek word for *work*.) In the United States, the term *human factors* is often substituted for the word *ergonomics.* Understanding ergonomics issues helps to improve human performance.

Male and female adults come in limited configurations.[16] Therefore, design of tools and the workplace depends on the study of people to determine what they can and cannot do. Substantial data have been collected that provide basic strength and measurement data needed to design tools and the workplace. The design of the workplace can make the job easier or impossible. Additionally, we now have the ability, through the use of computer modeling, to analyze human motions and efforts.

Ergonomics The study of work; often called *human factors.*

Many bicycle riders have seats set too low. The correct height is 103% of crotch to foot distance.

---

[15] Frederick W. Taylor, *Scientific Management* (New York: Harper & Row, 1911), p. 204.

[16] Henry Dreyfuss, *The Measure of Man* (New York: Whitney Library of Design, 1960).

Ergonomics issues occur in the office as well as in the factory. Here an ergonomics consultant is measuring the angle of a terminal operator's neck. Posture, which is related to desk height, chair height and position, keyboard placement, and computer screen, is an important factor in reducing back and neck pain that can be caused by extended hours at a computer.

Let's look briefly at one instance of human measurements: determining the proper height for a writing desk. The desk has an optimum height depending on the size of the individual and the task to be performed. The common height for a writing desk is 29 inches. For typing or data entry at a computer, the surface should be lower. The preferred chair and desk height should result in a very slight angle between the body and arm when the individual is viewed from the front and when the back is straight.[17] This is the critical measurement; it can be achieved via adjustment in either table or chair height.

Operator Input to Machines Operator response to machines, be they hand tools, pedals, levers, or buttons, needs to be evaluated. Operations managers need to be sure that operators have the strength, reflexes, perception, and mental capacity to provide necessary control. Such problems as *carpal tunnel syndrome* result when a tool as simple as a keyboard is poorly designed. The photos in Figure 10.4 indicate recent innovations designed to improve this common tool.

Feedback to Operators Feedback to operators is provided by sight, sound, and feel; it should not be left to chance. The mishap at the Three Mile Island nuclear facility, America's worst nuclear experience, was in large part the result of poor feedback to the operators about reactor performance. Nonfunctional groups of large, unclear instruments and inaccessible controls, combined with hundreds of confusing warning lights, contributed to that nuclear failure. Such relatively simple issues make a difference in operator response and, therefore, performance.

---

[17] Edwin R. Tichauer, "Biomechanics Sustains Occupational Safety and Health," *Industrial Engineering*, February 1976, pp. 46–55.

Apple Computers' adjustable keyboard is divided into two hinged sections that can be customized. (Apple Computers, Cupertino, California)

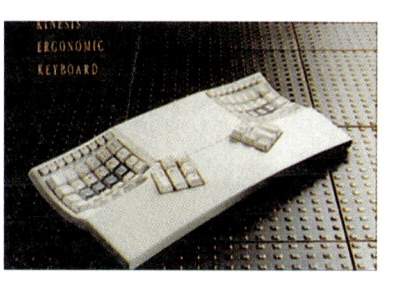

Tests indicate that this keyboard, which more closely fits the natural shape of the hand, is less physically demanding and more comfortable to use than a traditional computer keyboard. (Kinesis Corp., Bellevue, WA)

The "Data-Hand" keyboard allows each hand to rest on its own ergonomically shaped and padded palm support. Five keys surround each finger tip and thumb. (Industrial Innovations, Inc., Scottsdale, AZ)

FIGURE 10.4 ■ Job Design and the Keyboard

The Work Environment The physical environment in which employees work affects their performance, safety, and quality of work life. Illumination, noise and vibration, temperature, humidity, and air quality are work-environment factors under the control of the organization and the operations manager. The manager must approach them as controllable.

Illumination is necessary, but the proper level depends upon the work being performed. Table 10.1 on page 378 provides some guidelines. However, other lighting factors are important. These include reflective ability, contrast of the work surface with surroundings, glare, and shadows.

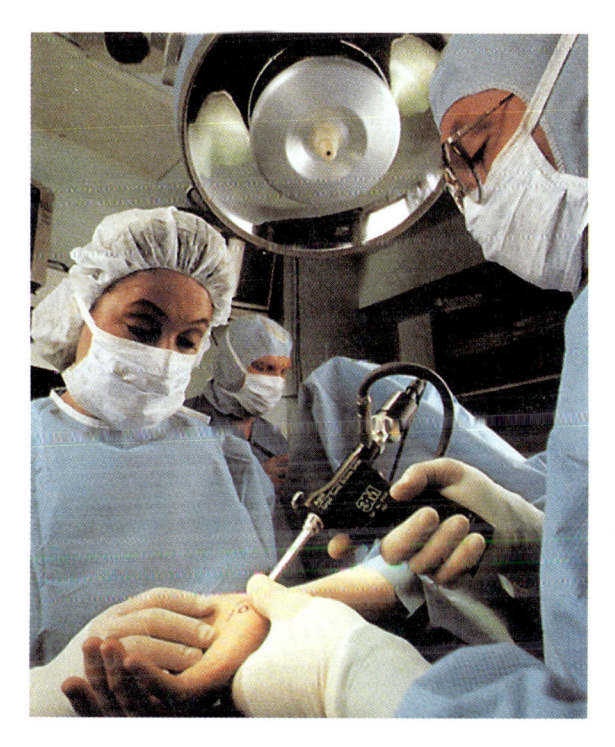

Carpal tunnel syndrome is a wrist disorder that afflicts 23,000 workers annually and costs employers and insurers an average of $30,000 per affected worker. Many of the tools, handles, and computer keyboards now in use put the wrists in an unnatural position. An unnatural position, combined with extended repetition, can cause carpal tunnel syndrome. One of the medical procedures to correct carpal tunnel syndrome is the operation shown here, which reduces the symptoms. The cure, however, lies in the ergonomics of workplace and tool design.

TABLE 10.1 ■ Levels of Illumination Recommended for Various Task Conditions

Task Condition	Type of Task or Area	Illumination Level (FT-C)*	Type of Illumination
Small detail, extreme accuracy	Sewing, inspecting dark materials	100	Overhead ceiling lights and desk lamp
Normal detail, prolonged periods	Reading, parts assembly, general office work	20–50	Overhead ceiling lights
Good contrast, fairly large objects	Recreational facilities	5–10	Overhead ceiling lights
Large objects	Restaurants, stairways, warehouses	2–5	Overhead ceiling lights

*FT-C (the footcandle) is a measure of illumination.
Source: C. T. Morgan, J. S. Cook III, A. Chapanis, and M. W. Lund, eds., *Human Engineering Guide to Equipment Design* (New York: McGraw-Hill, 1963).

TABLE 10.2 ■ Decibel (dB) Levels for Various Sounds. Decibel levels are A-weighted sound levels measured with a sound-level meter

Environment Noises	Common Noise Sources	Decibels	
	Jet takeoff (200 ft)	120	
Casting shakeout area	Riveting machine*	110	
Electric furnace area	Pneumatic peen hammer*	100	Very annoying
	Textile weaving plant*		
Printing press plant	Subway train (20 ft)	90	
			Ear protection required if exposed for 8 or more hours
	Pneumatic drill (50 ft)	80	
Inside sports car (50 mph)	Freight train (100 ft)		
	Vacuum cleaner (10 ft)	70	
Near freeway (auto traffic)	Speech (1 ft)		Intrusive
Large store		60	
Private business office			
Light traffic (100 ft)	Large transformer (200 ft)	50	Quiet
Minimum levels, residential areas in Chicago at night		40	
	Soft whisper (5 ft)		
Studio (speech)		30	Very quiet
		20	
		10	Threshold of hearing

*At operator's position
Source: Adapted from A. P. G. Peterson and E. E. Gross Jr., *Handbook of Noise Measurement*, 7th ed. (New Concord, MA: General Radio Co.).

Noise of some form is usually present in the work area, but most employees seem to adjust well. However, high levels of sound will damage hearing. Table 10.2 provides indications of the sound generated by various activities. Extended periods of exposure to decibel levels above 85 dB are permanently damaging. The Occupational Safety and Health Administration (OSHA) requires ear protection above this level if exposure equals or exceeds 8 hours. Even at low levels, noise and vibration can be distracting. Therefore, most managers make substantial effort to reduce noise and vibration through good machine design, enclosures, or segregation of sources of noise and vibration.

Temperature and humidity parameters have been well established. Managers with activities operating outside of the established comfort zone should expect adverse effect on performance.

Methods Analysis Methods analysis focuses on *how* a task is accomplished. Whether controlling a machine or making or assembling components, how a task is done makes a difference in performance, safety, and quality. Using knowledge from ergonomics and methods analysis, methods engineers are charged with ensuring that quality and quantity standards are achieved efficiently and safely. Methods analysis and related techniques are useful in office environments as well as the factory. Methods techniques are used to analyze:

1. Movement of individuals or material. The analysis is performed using *flow diagrams* and *process charts* with varying amounts of detail.
2. Activity of human and machine and crew activity. This analysis is performed using *activity charts* (also known as man-machine charts and crew charts).
3. Body movement (primarily arms and hands). This analysis is performed using *micro-motion charts*.

Methods analysis
Developing work procedures that are safe and produce quality products efficiently.

Performance during a pit stop makes a difference between winning and losing a race. Activity charts are used to orchestrate the movement of members of a pit crew, an operating room staff, or machine operators in a factory. Solved Problem 10.1 on page 384 shows an activity chart applied to a pit crew.

380　CHAPTER 10　HUMAN RESOURCES AND JOB DESIGN

Flow diagrams
Drawings used to analyze movement of people or material.

Process charts
A graphic representation that depicts a sequence of steps for a process.

Activity charts A way of improving utilization of an operator and a machine or some combination of operators (a crew) and machines.

Operations chart
A chart depicting right- and left-hand motions.

Flow diagrams are schematics (drawings) used to investigate movement of people or material. As shown for Britain's Paddy Hopkirk Factory in Figure 10.5, the flow diagram provides a systematic procedure for looking at long-cycle repetitive tasks. The old method is shown in Figure 10.5(a) and a new method, with improved work flow and requiring less storage and space, is shown in Figure 10.5(b). **Process charts** use symbols, as in Figure 10.5(c), to help us understand the movement of people or material. In this way, movement and delays can be reduced and operations made more efficient. Figure 10.5(c) is a process chart used to supplement the flow diagram shown in Figure 10.5(b).

Activity charts are used to study and improve the utilization of an operator and a machine or some combination of operators (a "crew") and machines. The typical approach is for the analyst to record the present method through direct observation and then propose the improvement on a second chart. Figure 10.6 is an activity chart to show a proposed improvement for a two-person crew at Quick Car Lube.

Body movement is analyzed by an **operations chart.** It is designed to show economy of motion by pointing out wasted motion and idle time (delay). The operations chart (also known as *right-hand/left-hand chart*) is shown in Figure 10.7.

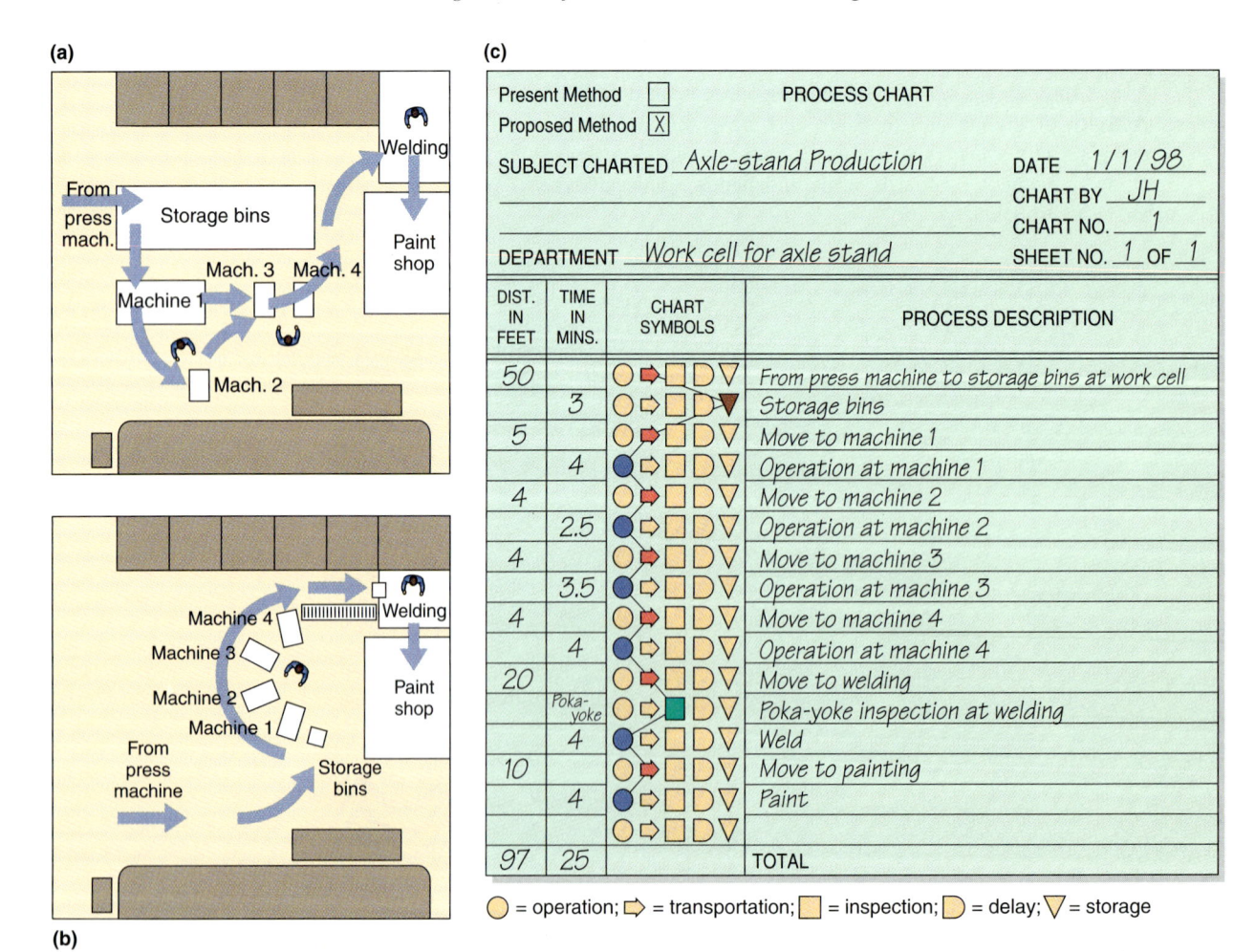

FIGURE 10.5 ■ Flow Diagram of Axle-Stand Production Line at Paddy Hopkirk Factory *(a) Old Method; (b) New Method; (c) Process chart of axle-stand production using Paddy Hopkirk's new method (shown in b).*

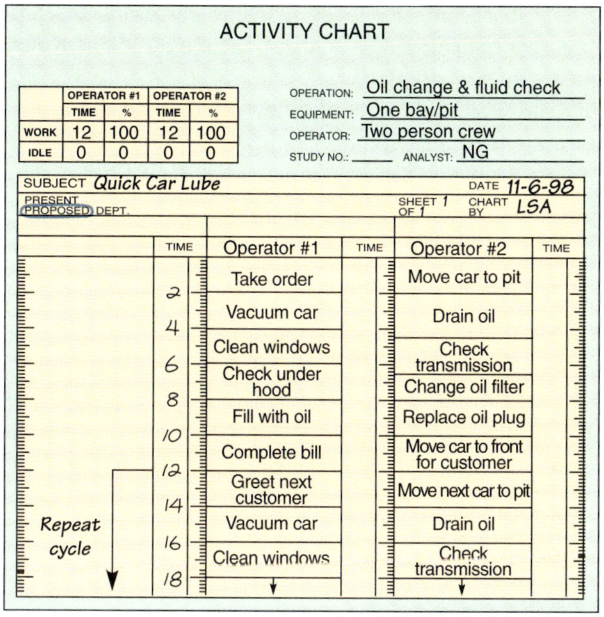

FIGURE 10.6 ■ Activity Chart for Two-person Crew Doing an Oil Change in 12 Minutes at Quick Car Lube

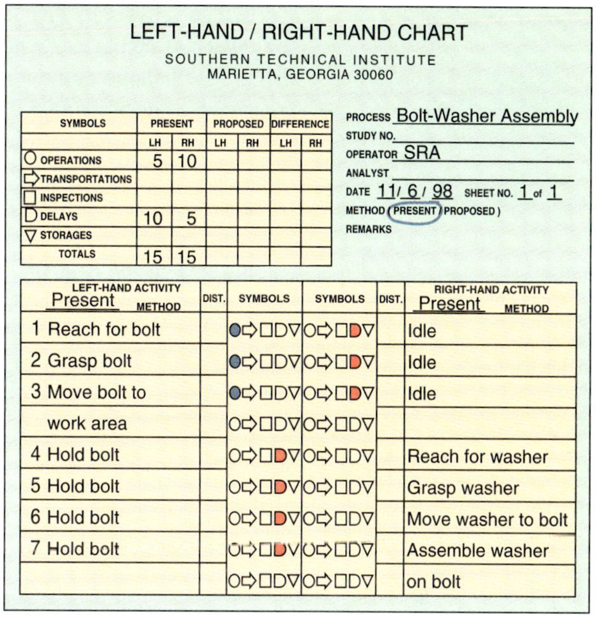

FIGURE 10.7 ■ Operation Chart (Right-Hand/Left-Hand Chart) for Bolt-Washer Assembly

Source: Adapted from L. S. Aft, *Productivity Measurement and Improvement* (Upper Saddle River, NJ: Prentice-Hall, 1992), p. 5. Reprinted by permission of Prentice-Hall, Inc.

THE VISUAL WORKPLACE

The **visual workplace** uses low-cost visual devices to share information quickly and accurately. Well-designed displays and graphs root out confusion and replace difficult-to-understand printouts and paperwork. Because workplace data change quickly and often, operations managers need to share accurate and up-to-date information. Workplace dynamics, with changing customer requirements, specifications, schedules, and other details on which an enterprise depends, must be rapidly communicated.

Visual systems can include statistical process control (SPC) charts, details of quality, accidents, service levels, delivery performance, costs, cycle time, and such traditional variables as attendance and tardiness. All visual systems should focus on improvement because progress almost always has motivational benefits. An assortment of visual signals and charts is an excellent tool for communication not only among people doing the work, but also among support people, management, visitors, and suppliers. All these stakeholders deserve feedback on the organization. Management reports, if held only in the hands of management, are often useless and perhaps counterproductive. Managers need to think in terms of visual management.

The visual workplace can take many forms. Kanbans are a type of visual signal indicating the need for more production. The three-minute clocks found in Burger Kings are a type of visual standard indicating the acceptable wait for service. Painted symbols indicating the place for tools are another visual standard to aid housekeeping. Some organizations have found it helpful to have performance standards indicated by hourly quota numbers for all to see. Andon lights are another visual signal. An **andon** is a signal that there is a problem. Andons can be manually initiated by employees when they notice a problem

Visual workplace Uses a variety of visual communication techniques to rapidly communicate information to stakeholders.

Andon Call light that signals problems.

or defect. They can also be triggered automatically when machine performance drops below a certain pace or when the number of cycles indicate that it is time for maintenance. Figure 10.8 shows some visual signals in the workplace.

Visual systems also communicate the larger picture, helping employees to understand the link between their day-to-day activities and the organization's overall performance. At Baldor Electric Co. in Fort Smith, Arkansas, the prior day's closing price of Baldor's stock is posted for all to see. The stock price is to remind employees that a portion of their pay is based on profit sharing and stock options, and to encourage them to keep looking for ways to increase productivity. Similarly, Missouri's Springfield Re Manufacturing Corp. has developed a concept called "open book management," where every employee is trained to understand the importance of financial measures (such as return on equity) and is provided with these measures regularly. When a huge copper mining company from Zambia asked its managers to benchmark the Springfield Re visual workplace, the mine company managers returned to spread

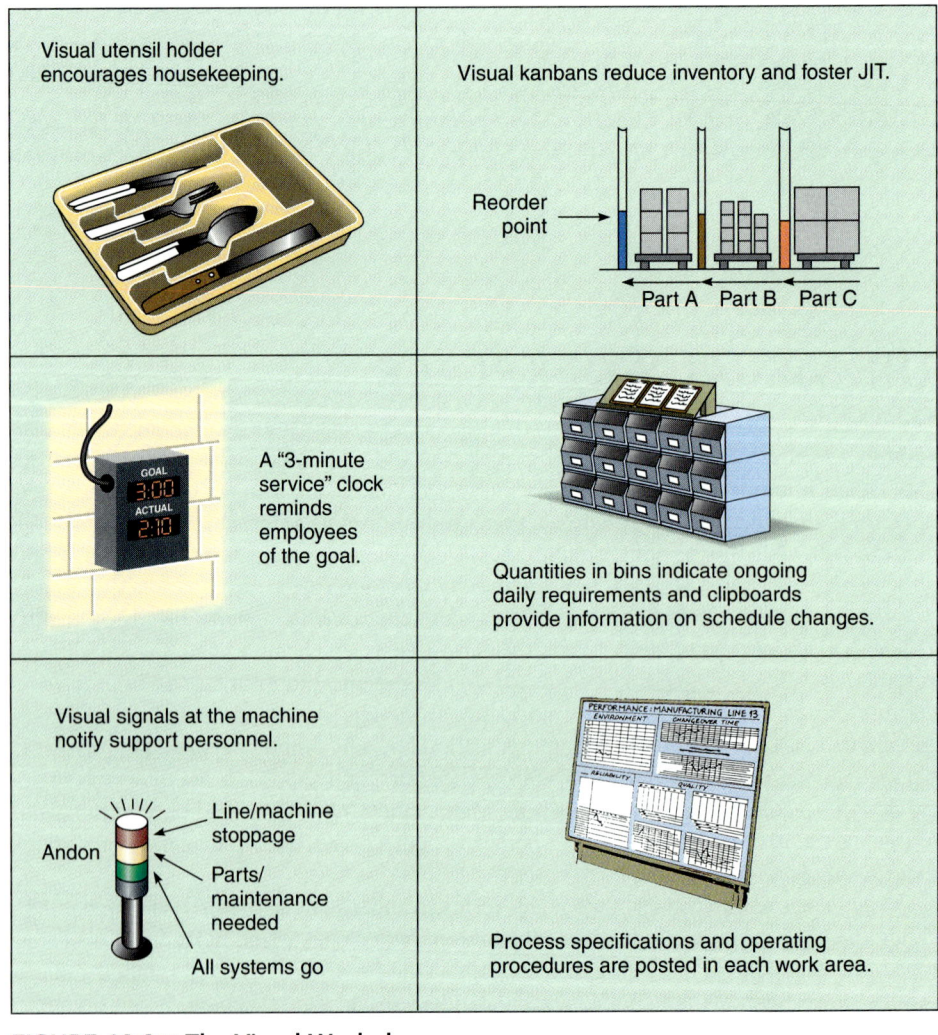

FIGURE 10.8 ■ The Visual Workplace

this philosophy to their 55,000 employees. Now as workers go in the front entrance of the mine, they cannot help but spot a 50-foot-high scoreboard that lists monthly and year-to-date financials.

The purpose of the visual workplace is to eliminate non-value-added activities and other forms of waste by making problems, abnormalities, and standards visual. This concept enhances communication and feedback by providing immediate information. The visual workplace needs less supervision because employees understand the standard, see the results, and know what to do.

LABOR STANDARDS

So far in this chapter, we have discussed labor planning and job design. The third requirement of an effective human resource strategy is the establishment of labor standards. Effective manpower planning is dependent upon a knowledge of the labor required.

Labor standards are the amount of time required to perform a job or part of a job. Every firm has labor standards, although they may vary from those established via informal methods to those established by professionals. Only when accurate labor standards exist can management know what its labor requirements are, what its costs should be, and what constitutes a fair day's work. Techniques for setting labor standards are presented in the supplement to this chapter.

Labor standards The amount of time required to perform a job or part of a job.

SUMMARY

Outstanding firms know the importance of an effective and efficient human resource strategy. Often a large percentage of employees and a large part of labor costs are under the direction of OM. Consequently, the operations manager usually has a large role to play in achieving human resource objectives. A prerequisite is to build an environment with mutual respect and commitment and a reasonable quality of work life. Outstanding organizations have designed jobs that use both the mental and physical capabilities of their employees. Regardless of the strategy chosen, the skill with which a firm manages its human resources ultimately determines its success.

KEY TERMS

Labor planning *(p. 367)*
Standard work schedule *(p. 368)*
Flextime *(p. 368)*
Flexible workweek *(p. 368)*
Part-time status *(p. 368)*
Job design *(p. 369)*
Labor specialization (or job specialization) *(p. 369)*
Job enlargement *(p. 370)*
Job rotation *(p. 370)*
Job enrichment *(p. 370)*
Employee empowerment *(p. 370)*
Self-directed team *(p. 372)*
Bonus *(p. 374)*
Profit sharing *(p. 374)*
Gain sharing *(p. 374)*
Incentive system *(p. 375)*
Knowledge-based pay systems *(p. 375)*
Ergonomics *(p. 375)*
Methods analysis *(p. 379)*
Flow diagrams *(p. 380)*
Process charts *(p. 380)*
Activity charts *(p. 380)*
Operations chart *(p. 380)*
Visual workplace *(p. 381)*
Andon *(p. 381)*
Labor standards *(p. 383)*

SOLVED PROBLEMS

Solved Problem 10.1

As pit crew manager for Prototype Sports Car, you have just been given the pit-stop rules for next season. You will be allowed only six people over the pit wall at any one time, and one of these must be a designated *fire extinguisher/safety* crewman. This crewman must carry a fire extinguisher and may not service the car. However, the fire extinguisher/safety crewman may also signal the driver where to stop the car in the pit lane and when to leave the pit.

You expect to have air jacks on this year's car. These built-in jacks require only an air hose to make them work. Fuel will also be supplied via a hose, with a second hose used for venting air from the fuel cells. The rate of flow for the fuel hose will be 1 gallon per second. The tank will hold 25 gallons. You expect to have to change all 4 tires on most pit stops. The length of the races will vary this year, but you expect that the longer races will also require the changing of drivers. Recent stopwatch studies have verified the following times for your experienced crew:

Activity	Time in Minutes
Install air hose	.075
Remove tire	.125
Mount new tire	.125
Move to air jack hose	.050
Move to rear of car	.050
Help driver	.175
Wipe windshield	.175
Load fuel (per gallon)	.016

Your job is to develop the initial plan for the best way to utilize your six-person pit crew. The six crewmen are identified with letters, as shown in Figure 10.9. You decide to use an activity chart similar to the one shown in Figure 10.6 (page 381) to aid you.

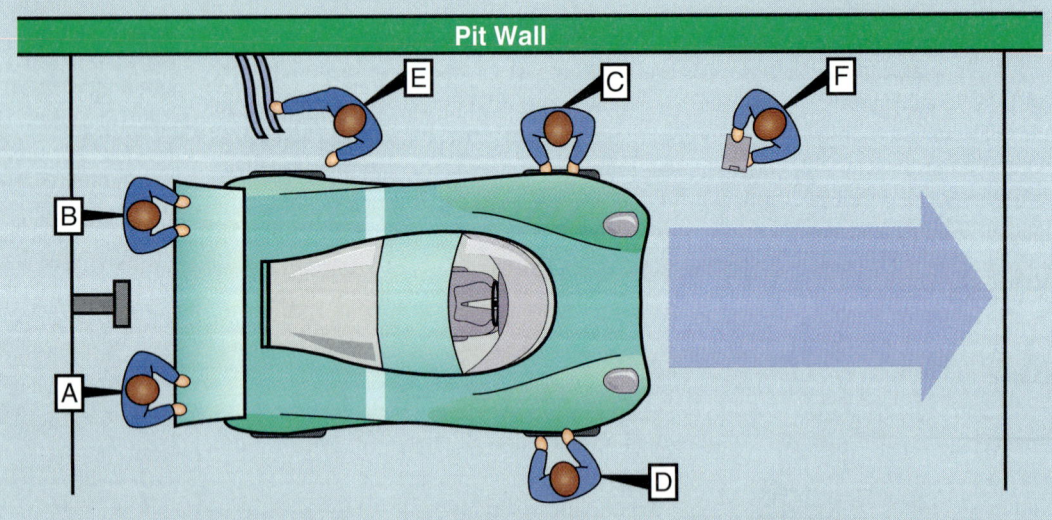

FIGURE 10.9 ■ Position of Car and Six Crewmen (see chart on next page)

Solution

Your activity chart shows each member of the crew what he or she is to do during each second of the pit stop.

Solved Problems

MULTIPLE ACTIVITY CHART

Chart No.:	Sheet No.:	Of:		S U M M A R Y		
PRODUCT:				PRESENT	PROPOSED	SAVING
			CYCLE TIME (min.)			
			Man			
PROCESS:	Pit stop for GTO cars		Machine			
			WORKING			
			Man			
			Machine			
MACHINE(S):			IDLE			
			Man			
			Machine			
OPERATIVE:		CLOCK NO.:	UTILIZATION			
CHARTED BY:		DATE:	Man			
			Machine			

TIME (min.)	CREW — A, B, C, D, E, F		NOTES	TIME (min.)

TIME (min.)	A	B	C	D	E	F	NOTES	TIME (min.)
0.025					Move to car/hoses	↓ 0.025	Fire Extinguisher/ Safety crewman F, goes over the pit wall to signal the driver where to stop the car.	0.025
0.050		Install air hose			Gas flows	S 0.050	Crewmen A, C, D, move to the car with tires.	0.050
0.075	Remove tire	↓	Remove tire	Remove tire		A 0.075	D places the air jack hose in the connection at the rear of the car.	0.075
0.100		Remove tire				F 0.100	B then returns to pit wall for the fourth tire. E moves to the car with two hoses (one for fuel & one to remove air).	0.100
0.125		↓	↓	↓		E 0.125		0.125
0.150						T 0.150	F is ready with the fire extinguisher. If the driver is to change, the first driver is out in the first 5 seconds.	0.150
0.175	Mount new tire		Mount new tire	Mount new tire		Y 0.175		0.175
0.200						0.200	If there is a driver change, the new driver enters the car.	0.200
0.225						C 0.225		0.225
0.250						R 0.250	A, C, D, have their tires mounted. D wipes the windshield with towels from belt.	0.250
0.275	Move to air jack hose	Mount new tire	Help driver	Wipe windshield		E 0.275	C helps the driver as necessary with seat belt & ice to cool suit.	0.275
0.300		↓				W 0.300	A removes the air jack hose.	0.300
0.325						M 0.325	B has tire mounted. B moves to the rear of the car.	0.325
0.350		Move to rear			24.5 gal of gas	A 0.350	A removes the air jack hose when B, C, and D signal their tires are mounted.	0.350
0.375						N 0.375	A and B prepare to push car. E (fuel man) disconnects fuel lines. F signals completion of fuel loading.	0.375
0.400	Idle	Idle			24.5 seconds	0.400	F moves to front of car on the pit side and prepares to signal driver when to leave.	0.400
0.425			↓	↓		↓ 0.425	A, B, C, and D, signal F when they are ready.	0.425
0.450			Idle	Idle	↓	0.450	F signals driver when all is ready. A and B push car out of pits.	0.450
0.475	Push	Push			Idle	Idle 0.475		0.475

FIGURE 10.9 ■ *(Continued)*

DISCUSSION QUESTIONS

1. What are some of the worst jobs you know about? Why are they bad jobs? Why do people want these jobs?
2. What factor would you add to, or delete from, the psychological factors given in the chapter?
3. If you were redesigning the job described in Question 1, what changes would you make? Are your changes realistic? Would they improve productivity (not just *production,* but *productivity*)?
4. How would you define a good quality of work life?
5. What are the differences among job enrichment, job enlargement, job rotation, job specialization, and employee empowerment?
6. Can you think of any jobs that push the man-machine interface to the limits of human capabilities?
7. Why prepare flow diagrams and process charts for tasks that are poorly done?
8. What are the six core characteristics of a good job design?
9. What is meant by the *visual workplace*? Provide two examples.
10. What is an andon? Give an example.
11. Whereas U.S. firms have invested substantially in training, that investment is much less than Japanese firms'. What may be the reason for that?

CRITICAL THINKING EXERCISE

The situation at the Lordstown, Ohio, airbag manufacturer was getting sticky. A skilled technician and member of the safety committee, Gregory White, suggested that the line be shut down because of horrible fumes created as employees inserted a chemical sensor into each airbag. A new bonding agent for sealing the sensors, though safe after drying, was highly toxic as a liquid. Additionally, the union steward was questioning safety standards, suggesting that the bonding agent remained toxic while drying. A recently installed ventilation system made little difference in the odor, but all tests had shown the chemical parts per million to be below the OSHA standard of 100. Plant manager Steve Goodman had discussed the issue with health and safety manager Nancy Kirschberg, who advised that although the OSHA standard is 100 ppm, the American Conference of Governmental Industrial Hygienists' (ACGIH) standard is only 50. Goodman was also well aware that although the new employee-empowerment program was important, the automobile assembly plant 15 miles away needed the airbags now. The automaker had no airbags in stock and depended on JIT delivery from the Lordstown plant. Therefore, shutting down airbag assembly would also shut down the assembly plant. Lordstown's reputation and the jobs of its people depended upon timely airbag delivery.

First, if you were Steve Goodman, what decision would you make? Justify your position as well as those of the union and Gregory White. Finally, propose a solution to deal with the very immediate problem.

PROBLEMS

- **10.1** Make a process chart for going from the living room to the kitchen for a glass, to the refrigerator for milk, and to a kitchen cabinet for cookies. Use a layout of your choosing. How can you make the task more efficient (that is, require less time or fewer steps)?
- **10.2** Draw an activity chart for a machine operator with the following operation. The relevant times are as follows:

Prepare mill for loading (cleaning, oiling, and so on)	.50 min.
Load mill	1.75 min.
Mill operating (cutting material)	2.25 min.
Unload mill	.75 min.

CASE STUDY

10.3 Draw an activity chart (a crew chart similar to figure 10.6) for a concert (for example, Billy Joel, Sheryl Crow, Jewel, Bruce Springsteen) and determine how to put the concert together so the star has reasonable breaks. For instance, at what point is there an instrumental number, a visual effect, a duet, a dance moment, that allows the star to pause and rest physically or at least rest his or her voice? Do other members of the show have moments of pause or rest?

10.4 Make an operations chart of one of the following:
  a) Putting a new eraser in (or on) a pencil.
  b) Putting a paper clip on two pieces of paper.
  c) Putting paper in a printer.

10.5 Having made the operations chart in Problem 10.4 and now being told that you were going to do the task 10,000 times, how would you improve the procedure? Prepare an operations chart of the improved task. What motion, time, and effort have you saved over the life of the task by redesigning it?

10.6 For a job you have had, rate each of Hackman and Oldham's core job characteristics (see pages 371–372) on a scale from 1 to 10. What is your total score? What about the job could have been changed to make you give it a higher score?

10.7 Using the data provided in Solved Problem 10.1, prepare an activity chart (a crew chart) similar to the one in the solved problem but based on a total of only five crew members.

10.8 Using the data provided in Solved Problem 10.1, prepare an activity chart similar to the one in the solved problem. However, consider the fact that fuel will now be delivered at the rate of 1 1/2 gallons per second.

10.9 Prepare an activity chart for a multi-operator
  a) car wash
  b) fast-food restaurant

▪ Case Study ▪

The Fleet That Wanders

Bill Southard, owner of Southard Truck Lines, recently purchased 10 new tractors for his operation from ARC Trucks. His relations with his drivers have been excellent, but they do not like the new tractors. They complain that the new tractors are hard to control on the highway; they "wander." When the drivers have a choice, they choose the older tractors. After numerous discussions with the drivers, Southard concludes that the new tractors do indeed have a problem. On the plus side, however, they get much better gas mileage, should have lower maintenance costs, and have the latest antilocking brakes.

Because each tractor costs over $50,000, Southard's investment exceeds $500,000 in the new fleet. He is trying to improve his fleet performance by reducing maintenance and fuel costs. However, these improvements have not happened. Additionally, he wants to keep his drivers happy. This has not happened either. Consequently, he has a serious talk with the manufacturer of the trucks.

The manufacturer, ARC Trucks of Canyon, Texas, redesigned the front suspension for this model of tractor. The firm tells him the new front end is great. Southard finds out, however, that since he purchased his trucks, there have been further (though minor) changes in some front-suspension parts.

ARC Trucks refuses to make any changes in the tractors Southard purchased. No one has suggested there is a safety problem, but the drivers are adamant that they have to work harder to keep the new tractors on the road. Southard has new tractors that spend much of their time sitting in the yard while drivers use the old tractors. His costs, therefore, are higher than they should be. He is considering court action, but legal counsel suggests that he document his case.

Discussion Questions

1. What suggestions do you have for Mr. Southard?
2. Having been exposed to introductory material about ergonomics, can you imagine an analytical approach to documenting the problems reported by the drivers?

Case Study

Lincoln Electric's Incentive Pay System

Cleveland's Lincoln Electric was founded by John C. Lincoln in 1895 to make an electric motor he had developed. When his brother James joined the organization in 1907, they began emphasizing employee motivation. Since that time, the company has endorsed the message that the business must prosper if employees are to benefit. Today, Lincoln is a $440-million firm with 2,400 employees. About 90% of its sales come from manufacturing arc-welding equipment and supplies.

The company has encouraged workers to own a stake in their employer by allowing them to buy stock at book value. (The employees are required to sell the stock at book value when they leave.) Approximately 70% of the employees own stock, and together they hold nearly 50% of the outstanding shares. Most of the remaining stock is held by members of the Lincoln family who are not involved in company operations.

Factory workers at Lincoln receive piece-rate wages with no guaranteed minimum hourly pay. After working for the firm for 2 years, employees begin to participate in the year-end bonus plan. Determined by a formula that considers the company's gross profits and both an employees' base piece rate and merit rating, it might be the most lucrative bonus system for factory workers in the United States. The *average* size of the bonus over the past 56 years has been 95.5% of base wages. Some Lincoln factory workers make more than $100,000 a year. In recent good years, average employees have earned about $85,000 a year, well above the average for U.S. manufacturing workers as a whole. However, in a bad year, Lincoln employees' average might fall as much as 40%.

The company has a guaranteed-employment policy in place since 1958. Since that time, it has not laid off a single worker. In return for job security, however, employees agree to several things. During slow times, they will accept reduced work periods. They also agree to accept work transfers, even to lower-paid jobs, if that is necessary to maintain a minimum of 30 hours of work per week.

The company calls the low cost of high wages its incentive-pay system. Each employee inspects his or her own parts and must correct any imperfect work on personal time. Each is responsible for the quality of his or her own work. Records are maintained to show who worked on each piece of equipment. Should inferior work slip by and be discovered by Lincoln's quality control people or customers, the worker's merit rating, bonus, and pay are lowered.

Some employees feel the system can cause some unfriendly competition. Because a certain number of merit points is allotted to each department, an exceptionally high rating for one person may mean a lower rating for another. These pressures have led Lincoln to occasionally consider modifications to the system.

Overall, however, the pressure has been good for productivity. One company executive estimates that Lincoln's overall productivity is about double that of its domestic competitors. The company has earned a profit every year since the depths of the 1930s' Depression and has never missed a quarterly dividend. Lincoln has one of the lowest employee turnover rates in U.S. industry. Recently, *Fortune* magazine cited Lincoln's two U.S. plants as among the 10 best managed in the country.

Discussion Questions

1. How are labor standards used to establish an incentive system such as this?
2. How and why does Lincoln's approach to motivating people work?
3. What problems might this system create for management?
4. What types of employee would be happy working at Lincoln?

BIBLIOGRAPHY

Alexander, D. C. *Industrial Ergonomics: A Practitioner's Guide*. Norcross, GA: IE & MP Publishers, 1985.

Barnes, R. M. *Motion and Time Study, Design and Measurement of Work*. New York: John Wiley, 1968.

Berggren, C. *Alternatives to Lean Production: Work Organization in the Swedish Auto Industry*. Ithaca, NY: ILR Press, 1993.

Carson, R. "Ergonomically Designed Tools: Selecting the Right Tool for the Job." *Industrial Engineering* 25, no. 7 (July 1993): 27–29.

Chapman, A. *Man-Machine Engineering*. Belmont, CA: Wadsworth, 1965.

Corlett, N., J. Wilson, and F. Manencia, eds. *Ergonomics of Working Posture*. New York: Taylor and Francis, 1986.

Dreyfuss, H. *The Measure of Man*. New York: Whitney Library of Design, 1970.

Franke, R. H. "The Ultimate Advantage: Creating the High-Involvement Organization." *The Executive* 7, no. 1 (February 1993): 105–106.

Galsworth, Gwendolyn D. *Visual Systems: Harnessing the Power of a Visual Workplace*. New York: AMACOM, 1997.

Greif, Michel. *The Visual Factory: Building Participation Through Shared Information*. Cambridge, Mass.: Productivity Press, 1991.

Hallowell, Roger. "Southwest Airlines: A Case Study Linking Employee Needs, Satisfaction, and Organizational Capabilities to Competitive Advantage." *Human Resource Management*, winter 1996, pp. 513–534.

Konz, S. *Work Design*. Columbia, OH: Grid, 1979.

McCormick, E. J. *Human Factors in Engineering and Design*, 4th ed. New York: McGraw-Hill, 1976.

Meyer, C. "How the Right Measures Help Teams Excel." *Harvard Business Review* (May–June 1994): 95.

Staughton, R., et al. "Modelling the Manufacturing Strategy Process." *OM Review* 9, no. 2 (April 1992): 48–68.

Zammuto, R. F., and E. J. O'Connor. "Gaining Advanced Manufacturing Technologies' Benefits." *The Academy of Management Review* 17, no. 4 (October 1992): 701.

INTERNET RESOURCES

American Compensation Association:
http://www.ahrm.org/aca/aca.htm

Bibliography on interpersonal relationships and teams:
http://mercury.hq.nasa.gov/office/hqlibrary/ppm/ppm29.htm

Bibliography on teams and teamwork:
http://mercury.hq.nasa.gov/office/hqlibrary/ppm/ppm5.htm

Ergonomics at University of Toronto:
http://vered.rose.toronto.edu/

Human Modeling by Transom Technologies:
http://www.transom.com/

IBM Report on Teams and Teamwork:
http://www.oise.on-ca/~bwillard/ideateam.htm

Occupational Safety and Health Administration:
http://www.osha.gov/

SUPPLEMENT 10

WORK MEASUREMENT

SUPPLEMENT OUTLINE

LABOR STANDARDS AND WORK MEASUREMENT
HISTORICAL EXPERIENCE
TIME STUDIES
PREDETERMINED TIME STANDARDS
WORK SAMPLING
SUMMARY
KEY TERMS
SOLVED PROBLEMS
DISCUSSION QUESTIONS
PROBLEMS
CASE STUDY: TELEPHONE OPERATOR STANDARDS AT AT&T
BIBLIOGRAPHY
INTERNET RESOURCES

LEARNING OBJECTIVES

When you complete this supplement you should be able to:

Identify or Define:

- Four ways of establishing labor standards

Describe or Explain

- Requirements for good labor standards
- Time study
- Predetermined time standards
- Work sampling

It was 2:36 P.M. and the 132 workers on the American Plastics Inc. factory floor were busy staffing their noisy machines. When Marc Schniederjans, a newly hired engineer, entered this production area through an office door, he was dressed in a white shirt and tie and carried a clipboard. He strode purposely to his destination, the lathe area, where he was to time three workers whose labor standards had not been updated in a decade. One pair of eyes after another followed his movement, almost like a wave building as it approaches the shore. Before Schniederjans was within 50 feet of his target, a loud whistle blew. The shop's union steward, Janet Wagner, had just called a work stoppage. A "suit" was on the floor to time workers without union authorization. American Plastics was silent.

LABOR STANDARDS AND WORK MEASUREMENT

Effective management of people requires knowledge of labor standards. Even though some employees and unions may be opposed to jobs being observed and timed, as in the preceding situation, labor standards are necessary. They help a firm determine the

1. Labor content of items produced (the labor cost);
2. Staffing needs (how many people it will take to meet required production);
3. Cost and time estimates prior to production (to assist in a variety of decisions, from cost estimates to make-or-buy decisions);
4. Crew size and work balance (who does what in a group activity or on an assembly line);
5. Expected production (so that both manager and worker know what constitutes a fair day's work);
6. Basis of wage-incentive plans (what provides a reasonable incentive);
7. Efficiency of employees and supervision (a standard is necessary against which to determine efficiency).

> Labor standards exist for telephone operators, auto mechanics, and UPS drivers, as well as factory workers.

Properly set labor standards represent the amount of time that it should take an average employee to perform specific job activities under normal working conditions. Labor standards are set in four ways:

1. Historical experience;
2. Time studies;
3. Predetermined time standards;
4. Work sampling.

This supplement covers each of these techniques.

HISTORICAL EXPERIENCE

Labor standards can be estimated based on *historical experience*—that is, how many labor-hours were required to do a task the last time it was performed. Historical standards have the advantage of being relatively easy and inexpensive to obtain. They are usually available from employee time cards or production records. However, they are not objective, and we do not know their accuracy, whether they represent a reasonable or a poor work pace, and whether unusual occurrences are included. Because these variables are unknown, their use is not recommended. Instead, time studies, predetermined time standards, and work sampling are preferred to set production standards.

TIME STUDIES

The classical stopwatch study, or time study, originally proposed by Frederick W. Taylor in 1881, is still the most widely used time-study method.[1] A **time-study** procedure involves timing a sample of a worker's performance and using it to set a standard. A trained and experienced person can establish a standard by following these eight steps:

1. Define the task to be studied (after methods analysis has been conducted).
2. Divide the task into precise elements (parts of a task that often take no more than a few seconds).
3. Decide how many times to measure the task (the number of cycles or samples needed).
4. Time and record elemental times and ratings of performance.
5. Compute the average actual cycle time. The **average actual cycle time** is the arithmetic mean of the times for *each* element measured, adjusted for unusual influence for each element:

$$\text{Average actual cycle time} = \frac{\begin{pmatrix}\text{sum of the times recorded}\\ \text{to perform each element}\end{pmatrix}}{\text{number of cycles observed}} \quad \text{(S10.1)}$$

6. Compute the **normal time** for each element. This measure is a "performance rating" for the particular worker pace observed:

$$\text{Normal time} = (\text{average actual cycle time}) \times (\text{rating factor}) \quad \text{(S10.2)}$$

The performance rating adjusts the observed time to what a normal worker could expect to accomplish. For example, a normal worker should be able to walk 3 miles per hour. He or she should also be able to deal a deck of 52 cards into 4 equal piles in 30 seconds. Numerous videos specify work pace on which professionals agree, and benchmarks have been established by the Society for the Advancement of Management. Performance rating, however, is still something of an art.

7. Add the normal times for each element to develop a total normal time for the task.
8. Compute the **standard time.** This adjustment to the total normal time provides for allowances such as *personal* needs, unavoidable work *delays*, and worker *fatigue*:

$$\text{Standard time} = \frac{\text{total normal time}}{1 - \text{allowance factor}} \quad \text{(S10.3)}$$

Time study The timing of a sample of a worker's performance and using it to set a standard.

Average actual cycle time The arithmetic mean of the times for each element measured, adjusted for unusual influence for each element.

Normal time The time, adjusted for pace, to complete a task observed during a time study.

Standard time A time-study adjustment to the total normal time; the adjustment provides allowances for personal needs, unavoidable work delays, and worker fatigue.

---

[1] For an illuminating look at the life and influence of Taylor, see Robert Kanigel, *The One Best Way: Frederick Winslow Taylor and the Enigma of Efficiency* (New York: Viking Press, 1997).

FIGURE S10.1 ■ Rest Allowances (in percentage) for Various Classes of Work

1. Constant allowances:
    (A) Personal allowance 5
    (B) Basic fatigue allowance 4
2. Variable allowances:
    (A) Standing allowance 2
    (B) Abnormal position allowance:
        (i) Awkward (bending) 2
        (ii) Very awkward (lying, stretching) 7
    (C) Use of force or muscular energy in
        lifting, pulling, pushing
        Weight lifted (pounds):
        20 3
        40 9
        60 17
    (D) Bad light:
        (i) Well below recommended 2
        (ii) Quite inadequate 5
    (E) Atmospheric conditions (heat and humidity):
        Variable 0–10
    (F) Close attention:
        (i) Fine or exacting 2
        (ii) Very fine or very exacting 5
    (G) Noise level:
        (i) Intermittent—loud 2
        (ii) Intermittent—very loud or high-pitched 5
    (H) Mental strain:
        (i) Complex or wide span of attention 4
        (ii) Very complex 8
    (I) Tediousness:
        (i) Tedious 2
        (ii) Very tedious 5

Source: Excerpted from B. W. Niebel, *Motion and Time Study,* 7th ed. (Homewood, IL: Richard D. Irwin, 1982) p. 393. Copyright © 1982 by Richard D. Irwin, Inc.

It is important to let a worker who is going to be observed know about the study in advance in order to avoid misunderstanding or suspicion.

In service jobs such as cleaning a Sheraton hotel bathtub, renting a Hertz car, or wrapping a Taco Bell burrito, time and motion studies are effective management tools.

Personal time allowances are often established in the range of 4% to 7% of total time, depending upon nearness to rest rooms, water fountains, and other facilities. *Delay allowances* are often set as a result of the actual studies of the delay that occurs. *Fatigue allowances* are based on our growing knowledge of human energy expenditure under various physical and environmental conditions. A sample set of personal and fatigue allowances is shown in Figure S10.1. Example S1 illustrates the computation of standard time.

EXAMPLE S1

The time study of a work operation yielded an average actual cycle time of 4.0 minutes. The analyst rated the observed worker at 85%. This means the worker performed at 85% of normal when the study was made. The firm uses a 13% allowance factor. We want to compute the standard time.

Solution

Average actual time = 4.0 min.

$$\text{Normal time} = (\text{average actual cycle time}) \times (\text{rating factor})$$

$$= (4.0)(.85)$$

$$= 3.4 \text{ min.}$$

$$\text{Standard time} = \frac{\text{normal time}}{1 - \text{allowance factor}} = \frac{3.4}{1 - .13} = \frac{3.4}{.87}$$

$$= 3.9 \text{ min.}$$

Example S2 works from a series of actual stopwatch times for each element.

EXAMPLE S2

Management Science Associates promotes its management development seminars by mailing thousands of individually typed letters to various firms. A time study has been conducted on the task of preparing letters for mailing. On the basis of the observations below, Management Science Associates wants to develop a time standard for this task. The firm's personal, delay, and fatigue allowance factor is 15%.

| | Cycle Observed (in minutes) | | | | | Performance |
Job Element	1	2	3	4	5	Rating
(A) Type letter	8	10	9	21*	11	120%
(B) Type envelope address	2	3	2	1	3	105%
(C) Stuff, stamp, seal, and sort envelopes	2	1	5*	2	1	110%

Solution

Once the data have been collected, the procedure is as follows:

1. Delete all unusual or nonrecurring observations such as those marked with an asterisk (*). (These might be due to unscheduled business interruptions, conferences with the boss, or mistakes of an unusual nature; they are not part of the job.)
2. Compute the average cycle time for each job element:

$$\text{Average time for A} = \frac{8 + 10 + 9 + 11}{4}$$

$$= 9.5 \text{ min.}$$

$$\text{Average time for B} = \frac{2 + 3 + 2 + 1 + 3}{5}$$

$$= 2.2 \text{ min.}$$

$$\text{Average time for C} = \frac{2 + 1 + 2 + 1}{4}$$

$$= 1.5 \text{ min.}$$

3. Compute the normal time for each job element:

$$\text{Normal time for A} = (\text{average actual time}) \times (\text{rating})$$

$$= (9.5)(1.2)$$

$$= 11.4 \text{ min.}$$

$$\text{Normal time for B} = (2.2)(1.05)$$

$$= 2.31 \text{ min.}$$

$$\text{Normal time for C} = (1.5)(1.10)$$

$$= 1.65 \text{ min.}$$

Note: Normal times are computed for each element because the rating factor may vary for each element, as it did in this case.

4. Add the normal times for each element to find the total normal time (the normal time for the whole job):

$$\text{Total normal time} = 11.40 + 2.31 + 1.65$$

$$= 15.36 \text{ min.}$$

5. Compute the standard time for the job:

$$\text{Standard time} = \frac{\text{total normal time}}{1 - \text{allowance factor}} = \frac{15.36}{1 - .15}$$

$$= 18.07 \text{ min.}$$

Thus, 18.07 minutes is the time standard for this job.

Time study is a sampling process, and the question of sampling error in the average actual cycle time naturally arises. In statistics, error varies inversely with sample size. So in order to determine just how many cycles we should time, we must consider the variability of each element in the study.

To determine an adequate sample size, three items must be considered:

1. How accurate we want to be (for example, is ±5% of actual cycle time close enough?).
2. The desired level of confidence (for example, the z value; is 95% adequate or is 99% required?).
3. How much variation exists within the job elements (for example, if the variation is large, a larger sample will be required).

The formula for finding the appropriate sample size given these three variables is

$$n = \left(\frac{zs}{h\bar{x}}\right)^2 \tag{S10.4}$$

Sleep Inn is showing the world that big gains in productivity can be made not only by manufacturers, but in the service industry as well. Designed with labor efficiency in mind, Sleep Inn is staffed with 13% fewer employees than similar budget hotels. Its features include a laundry room that is almost completely automated, round shower stalls that eliminate dirty corners, and closets that have no doors for maids to open and shut.

TIME STUDIES

where h = accuracy level desired in percent of the job element, expressed as a decimal (5% = .05)

z = number of standard deviations required for desired level of confidence (90% confidence = 1.65; see Table S10.1 or Appendix I for the more common z values)

s = standard deviation of the initial sample

$\bar{x}$ = mean of the initial sample

TABLE S10.1 ■ Common Z Values

Desired Confidence (%)	z Value (Standard Deviation Required for Desired Level of Confidence)
90.0	1.65
95.0	1.96
95.4	2.00
99.0	2.58
99.7	3.00

We demonstrate with Example S3.

EXAMPLE S3

Thomas W. Jones Manufacturing Co. has asked you to check a labor standard prepared by a recently terminated analyst. Your first task is to determine the correct sample size. Your accuracy is to be within 5% and your confidence level 95%. The standard deviation of the sample is 1.0 and the mean 3.00.

Solution

$$h = .05 \quad \bar{x} = 3.00 \quad s = 1.0$$

$$z = 1.96 \text{ (from Table S10.1 or Appendix I)}$$

$$n = \left(\frac{zs}{h\bar{x}}\right)^2$$

$$n = \left(\frac{(1.96 \times 1.0)}{(.05 \times 3)}\right)^2 = 170.74 \approx 171$$

Therefore, you recommend a sample size of 171.

Now let's look at two variations of Example S3.

First, if h, the desired accuracy, is expressed as an absolute amount of error (say, 1 minute of error is acceptable), then substitute e for $h\bar{x}$, and the appropriate formula is

$$n = \left(\frac{zs}{e}\right)^2 \tag{S10.5}$$

where e is the absolute amount of acceptable error.

Second, for those cases when s, the standard deviation of the sample, is not provided (which is typically the case outside the classroom), it must be computed. The formula for doing so is given in Equation (S10.6).

OM IN ACTION

UPS: THE TIGHTEST SHIP IN THE SHIPPING BUSINESS

United Parcel Service (UPS) employs 150,000 people and delivers an average of 9 million packages a day to locations throughout the United States and 180 other countries. To achieve its claim of "running the tightest ship in the shipping business," UPS methodically trains its delivery drivers in how to do their jobs as efficiently as possible.

Industrial engineers at UPS have time-studied each driver's route and set standards for each delivery, stop, and pickup. These engineers have recorded every second taken up by stoplights, traffic volume, detours, doorbells, walkways, stairways, and coffee breaks. Even bathroom stops are factored into the standards. All of this information is then fed into company computers to provide detailed time standards for every driver, every day.

To meet their objective of 200 deliveries and pickups each day (versus only 80 at Federal Express), UPS drivers must follow engineers' procedures exactly. As they approach a delivery stop, drivers unbuckle their seat belts, honk their horns, and cut their engines. In one seamless motion, they are required to yank up their emergency brakes and push their gearshifts into first. Then they slide to the ground with their clipboards under their right arms and their packages in their left hands. Ignition keys, teeth up, are in their right hands. They walk to the customer's door at the prescribed 3 feet per second and knock first to avoid lost seconds searching for the doorbell. After making the delivery, they do the paperwork on the way back to the truck.

Productivity experts describe UPS as one of the most efficient companies anywhere in applying the principles of scientific management.

Sources: The Wall Street Journal (May 24, 1995): B1, B4; and Gary A. Ferguson, *IEE Solutions* (May 1995): 28–33.

$$s = \sqrt{\frac{\sum(x_i - \bar{x})^2}{n - 1}} = \sqrt{\frac{\sum(\text{each sample observation} - \bar{x})^2}{\text{number in sample} - 1}} \quad \text{(S10.6)}$$

where x_i = value of each observation
$\bar{x}$ = mean of the observations
n = number of observations

An example of this computation is provided in Solved Problem S10.3 on page 404.

Although time studies provide accuracy in setting labor standards (see the *OM in Action* box on UPS), they have two disadvantages. First, they require a trained staff of analysts. Second, labor standards cannot be set before tasks are actually performed. This leads us to two alternative work-measurement techniques that we discuss next.

PREDETERMINED TIME STANDARDS

Predetermined time standards An approach that divides manual work into small basic elements that have established and widely accepted times.

In addition to historical experience and time studies, we can set production standards by using predetermined time standards. **Predetermined time standards** divide manual work into small basic elements that already have established times (based on very large samples of workers). To estimate the time for a particular task, the time factors for each basic element of that task are added together. Developing a comprehensive system of predetermined time standards would be prohibitively expensive for any given firm. Consequently, a number of systems are commercially available. The most common predetermined time standard is *methods time measurement* (MTM), which is a product of the MTM Association.[2]

---

[2] MTM is really a family of products available from the Methods Time Measurement Association. For example, MTM-HC deals with the health-care industry, MTM-C handles clerical activities, MTM-M involves microscope activities, MTM-V deals with machine shop tasks, and so on.

Predetermined Time Standards

GET AND PLACE			DISTANCE RANGE IN IN.	<8	>8 <20	>20 <32
WEIGHT	CONDITIONS OF GET	PLACE ACCURACY	CODE	1	2	3
<2 LBS	EASY	APPROXIMATE	AA	20	35	50
		LOOSE	AB	30	45	60
		TIGHT	AC	40	55	70
	DIFFICULT	APPROXIMATE	AD	20	45	60
		LOOSE	AE	30	55	70
		TIGHT	AF	40	65	80
	HANDFUL	APPROXIMATE	AG	40	65	80
>2 LBS <18 LBS		APPROXIMATE	AH	25	45	55
		LOOSE	AJ	40	65	75
		TIGHT	AK	50	75	85
>18 LBS <45 LBS		APPROXIMATE	AL	90	106	115
		LOOSE	AM	95	120	130
		TIGHT	AN	120	145	160

FIGURE S10.2 ■ **Sample MTM Table for GET and Place Motion** *Time values are in TMUs. Source:* Copyrighted by the MTM Association for Standards and Research. No reprint permission without consent from the MTM Association, 16-01 Broadway, Fair Lawn, NJ 07410.

Predetermined time standards are an outgrowth of basic motions called therbligs. The term *therblig* was coined by Frank Gilbreth (*Gilbreth* spelled backwards with the *t* and *h* reversed). **Therbligs** include such activities as select, grasp, position, assemble, reach, hold, rest, and inspect. These activities are stated in terms of **time measurement units (TMUs),** which are each equal to only .00001 hour, or .0006 minute. MTM values for various therbligs are specified in very detailed tables. Figure S10.2, for example, provides the set of time standards for the motion GET and PLACE. To use GET and PLACE (the most complex motion in the MTM system), one must know what is "gotten," its approximate weight, and where and how far it is supposed to be placed.

Example S4 shows a use of predetermined time standards in setting service labor standards.

Therbligs Basic physical elements of motion.

Time measurement units (TMU) Units for very basic micromotions where one TMU = .0006 minutes or 100,000 TMUs = 1 hour.

EXAMPLE S4

Pouring a tube specimen in a hospital lab is a repetitive task for which the MTM data in Figure S10.2 may be used to develop standard times. The sample tube is in a rack and the centrifuge tubes in a nearby box. A technician removes the sample tube from the rack, uncaps it, gets the centrifuge tube, pours, and places both tubes in the rack.

The first work element involves getting the tube from the rack. Suppose the conditions for GETTING the tube and PLACING it in front of the technician are

- weight (less than 2 pounds)
- conditions of GET (easy)
- place accuracy (approximate)
- distance range (8 to 20 inches)

Then the MTM element for this activity is AA2 (as seen from Figure S10.2). The rest of Table S10.2 on page 400 is developed from similar MTM tables. Most MTM calculations, by the way, are computerized, so the user need only key in the appropriate MTM codes, such as AA2 in Example S4.

TABLE S10.2 ■ MTM-HC Analysis: Pouring Tube Specimen

Element Description	Element	Time
Get tube from rack	AA2	35
Get stopper, place on counter	AA2	35
Get centrifuge tube, place at sample tube	AD2	45
Pour (3 sec.)	PT	83
Place tubes in rack (simo)	PC2	40
	Total TMU	238

.0006 × 238 = Total standard minutes = .14

Source: A. S. Helms, B. W. Shaw, and C. A. Lindner, "The Development of Laboratory Workload Standards through Computer-Based Work Measurement Technique, Part I," *Journal of Methods-Time Measurement,* 12, p. 43. Used with permission of MTM Association for Standards and Research.

Predetermined time standards have several advantages over direct time studies. First, they may be established in a laboratory environment, where the procedure will not upset actual production activities (which time studies tend to do). Second, because the standard can be set *before* a task is actually performed, it can be used for planning. Third, no performance ratings are necessary. Fourth, unions tend to accept this method as a fair means of setting standards. Finally, predetermined time standards are particularly effective in firms that do substantial numbers of studies of similar tasks. To ensure accurate labor standards, some firms use both time studies and predetermined time standards.

> Many firms use a combination of stopwatch studies and predetermined time standards when they are particularly interested in verifying results.

WORK SAMPLING

The fourth method of developing labor or production standards, work sampling, was developed in England by L. Tippet in the 1930s. **Work sampling** estimates the percent of the time that a worker spends on various tasks. It involves random observations to record the activity that a worker is performing.

> **Work sampling** An estimate, via sampling, of the percent of the time that a worker spends on various tasks.

Typically, work sampling is used in the following circumstances:

1. *Ratio delay studies.* These estimate the percentage of time that employees spend in unavoidable delays. The results are used to investigate work methods, to estimate activity costs, and to set allowances in labor standards.
2. *Setting labor standards.* For setting standard task times, the observer must be experienced enough to rate the worker's performance.
3. *Measuring worker performance.* Sampling can develop a performance index for periodic evaluations of workers.

The work-sampling procedure can be summarized in seven steps:

1. Take a preliminary sample to obtain an estimate of the parameter value (such as percent of time a worker is busy).
2. Compute the sample size required.
3. Prepare a schedule for observing the worker at appropriate times. The concept of random numbers is used to provide for random observation. For example, let's say we draw the following 5 random numbers from a table: 07, 12, 22, 25, and 49. These can then be used to create an observation schedule of 9:07 A.M., 9:12, 9:22, 9:25, 9:49.
4. Observe and record worker activities; rate the worker's performance.

WORK SAMPLING

5. Record the number of units or parts produced during the applicable portion of the study.
6. Compute the normal time per unit or part.
7. Compute the standard time per unit or part.

To determine the number of observations required, management must decide upon the desired confidence level and accuracy. First, however, the analyst must select a preliminary value for the parameter under study (step 1 above). The choice is usually based on a small sample of perhaps 50 observations. The following formula then gives the sample size for a desired confidence and accuracy:

$$n = \frac{z^2 p(1-p)}{h^2} \qquad (S10.7)$$

where n = required sample size
z = standard normal deviate for the desired confidence level
(z = 1 for 68% confidence, z = 2 for 95.45% confidence, and z = 3 for 99.7% confidence—these values are obtained from Table S10.1 or the normal table in Appendix I)
p = estimated value of sample proportion (of time worker is observed busy or idle)
h = accuracy level desired, in percent

Example S5 shows how to apply this formula.

> The cataloguer Land's End expects its sales reps to be busy 85% of the time and idle 15%. When the busy ratio hits 90%, the firm believes it is not reaching its goal of high-quality service.

EXAMPLE S5

The manager of one western state's welfare office estimates that assistants are idle 25% of the time. Her supervisor would like to take a work sample that is accurate within 3% and wants to have 95.45% confidence in the results.

Solution

In order to determine how many observations should be taken, the manager applies the equation:

$$n = \frac{z^2 p(1-p)}{h^2}$$

where n = sample size required
z = 2 for 95.45% confidence level
p = estimate of idle proportion = 25% = .25
h = accuracy desired of 3% = .03

She finds that

$$n = \frac{(2)^2(.25)(.75)}{(.03)^2} = 833 \text{ observations}$$

Thus, 833 observations should be taken. If the percent of idle time observed is not close to 25% as the study progresses, then the number of observations may have to be recalculated and increased or decreased as appropriate.

Work sampling is used to set labor standards in a fashion similar to that used in time studies. The analyst, however, simply records whether a worker is busy or idle during the observation. After all observations have been recorded, the worker rated, and the produced units counted (steps 4 and 5), we can determine the normal time by the following formula:

$$\text{Normal time} = \frac{\left(\begin{array}{c}\text{total study}\\\text{time}\end{array}\right) \times \left(\begin{array}{c}\text{percent of time employee}\\\text{observed working}\end{array}\right) \times \left(\begin{array}{c}\text{performance}\\\text{rating factor}\end{array}\right)}{\text{number of pieces produced}}$$

The standard time is the normal time adjusted by the allowance factor, computed as

$$\text{Standard time} = \frac{\text{normal time}}{1 - \text{allowance factor}}$$

Example S6 demonstrates the calculation of normal and standard times.

EXAMPLE S6

A work-sample study conducted over the 80 hours (or 4,800 minutes) of a 2-week period yielded the following data:

- The number of parts produced was 225 by an operator who was performance rated at 100%;
- The operator's idle time was 20%;
- The total allowance given by the company for this task is 25%.

The formulas for calculating normal and standard times are:

$$\text{Normal time} = \frac{\left(\begin{array}{c}\text{total}\\\text{time}\end{array}\right) \times \left(\begin{array}{c}\text{percent of time}\\\text{working}\end{array}\right) \times \left(\begin{array}{c}\text{rating}\\\text{factor}\end{array}\right)}{\text{number of units completed}}$$

$$= \frac{(4{,}800 \text{ min.})(.80)(1.00)}{225} = 17.07 \text{ min./part}$$

$$\text{Standard time} = \frac{\text{normal time}}{1 - \text{allowance factor}}$$

$$= \frac{17.07}{1 - .25} = 22.76 \text{ min./part}$$

Work sampling offers several advantages over time-study methods. First, because a single observer can observe several workers simultaneously, it is less expensive. Second, observers usually do not require much training, and no timing devices are needed. Third, the study can be temporarily delayed at any time with little impact on the results. And fourth, because work sampling uses instantaneous observations over a long period, the worker has little chance of affecting the study's outcome.

The disadvantages of work sampling are: (1) it does not divide work elements as completely as time studies, (2) it can yield biased or incorrect results if the observer does not follow random routes of travel and observation, and (3) it is less effective than time studies when cycle times are short.

To reduce the cost of work sampling, Kinemark, a Parsippany, New Jersey, firm, developed this small computer with options for 48 everyday office tasks. As each task is completed, the operator presses the appropriate key. After a week of such reporting, a rather complete picture of what is going on is available.

SUMMARY

Labor standards are required for an efficient operations system. They are needed for production planning, labor planning, costing, and evaluating performance. They can also be used as a basis for incentive systems. They are used in both the factory and the office. Standards may be established via historical data, time studies, predetermined time standards, and work sampling.

KEY TERMS

Time study *(p. 393)*
Average actual cycle time *(p. 393)*
Normal time *(p. 393)*
Standard time *(p. 393)*
Predetermined time standards *(p. 398)*
Therbligs *(p. 399)*
Time measurement units (TMU) *(p. 399)*
Work sampling *(p. 400)*

SOLVED PROBLEMS

Solved Problem S10.1

A work operation consisting of three elements has been subjected to a stopwatch time study. The recorded observations are shown in the following table. By union contract, the allowance time for the operation is personal time 5%, delay 5%, and fatigue 10%. Determine the standard time for the work operation.

| | Cycle Observations (in minutes) | | | | | | |
Job Element	1	2	3	4	5	6	Performance Rating (%)
A	.1	.3	.2	.9	.2	.1	90
B	.8	.6	.8	.5	3.2	.7	110
C	.5	.5	.4	.5	.6	.5	80

Solution

First, delete the two observations that appear to be very unusual (.9 minute for job element A and 3.2 minutes for job element B). Then,

$$\text{A's average cycle time} = \frac{.1 + .3 + .2 + .2 + .1}{5} = .18 \text{ min.}$$

$$\text{B's average cycle time} = \frac{.8 + .6 + .8 + .5 + .7}{5} = .68 \text{ min.}$$

$$\text{C's average cycle time} = \frac{.5 + .5 + .4 + .5 + .6 + .5}{6} = .50 \text{ min.}$$

A's normal time = (.18)(.90) = .16 min

B's normal time = (.68)(1.10) = .75 min

C's normal time = (.50)(.80) = .40 min

Normal time for job = .16 + .75 + .40 = 1.31 min.

Standard time = $\frac{1.31}{1 - .20}$ = 1.64 min.

Solved Problem S10.2

The preliminary work sample of an operation indicates the following:

Number of times operator working	60
Number of times operator idle	40
Total number of preliminary observations	100

What is the required sample size for a 99.7% confidence level with ±4% precision?

Solution

$$n = \frac{z^2 p(1-p)}{h^2} = \frac{(3)^2(.6)(.4)}{(.04)^2} = 1{,}350 \text{ sample size}$$

Solved Problem S10.3

Amor Manufacturing Co. of Geneva, Switzerland, has just studied a job in its laboratory in anticipation of releasing the job to the factory for production. It wants rather good accuracy for costing and labor forecasting. Specifically, it wants you to provide a 99% confidence level and a cycle time that is within 3% of the true

Solved Problems

value. How many observations should it make? The data collected so far are as follows:

Observation	Cycle Time
1	1.7
2	1.6
3	1.4
4	1.4
5	1.4

Solution

First, solve for the mean, $\bar{x}$, and the sample standard deviation, s.

$$s = \sqrt{\frac{\sum(\text{each sample observation} - \bar{x})^2}{\text{number in sample} - 1}}$$

Observation	x_i	$\bar{x}$	$x_i - \bar{x}$	$(x_i - \bar{x})^2$
1	1.7	1.5	.2	0.04
2	1.6	1.5	.1	0.01
3	1.4	1.5	−.1	0.01
4	1.4	1.5	−.1	0.01
5	1.4	1.5	.1	0.01
	$\bar{x} = 1.5$	7.5		$0.08 = \Sigma(x_i - \bar{x})^2$

$$s = \sqrt{\frac{.08}{n-1}} = \sqrt{\frac{.08}{4}} = .141$$

Then, solve for $n = \left(\frac{zs}{h\bar{x}}\right)^2 = \left[\frac{(2.58)(.141)}{(.03)(1.5)}\right]^2 = 65.3$

where $\bar{x} = 1.5$
$s = .141$
$z = 2.58$
$h = .03$

Therefore, you recommend 65 observations.

Solved Problem S10.4

At Maggard Micro Manufacturing, Inc., workers press semiconductors into predrilled slots on printed-circuit boards. The elemental motions for normal time used by the company are as follows:

Reach 6 inches for semiconductors	10.5 TMU
Grasp the semiconductor	8.0 TMU
Move semiconductor to printed-circuit board	9.5 TMU
Position semiconductor	20.1 TMU
Press semiconductor into slots	20.3 TMU
Move board aside	15.8 TMU

(Each time measurement unit is equal to .0006 min.) Determine the normal time for this operation in minutes and in seconds.

Solution

Add the time measurement units:

$10.5 + 8.0 + 9.5 + 20.1 + 20.3 + 15.8 = 84.2$

Time in minutes $= (84.2)(.0006 \text{ min.}) = .05052 \text{ min.}$

Time in seconds $= (.05052)(60 \text{ sec.}) = 3.0312 \text{ sec.}$

Solved Problem S10.5

To obtain the random sample needed for work sampling, a manager divides a typical workday into 480 minutes. Using a random-number table to decide what time to go to an area to sample work occurrences, the manager records observations on a tally sheet like the following:

Status	Tally	Frequency
Productively working	̶H̶H̶ ̶H̶H̶ ̶H̶H̶ I	16
Idle	IIII	4

Solution

In this case, the supervisor made 20 observations and found that employees were working 80% of the time. So, out of 480 minutes in an office workday, 20%, or 96 minutes, was idle time, and 384 minutes was productive. Note that this procedure describes what a worker *is* doing, not necessarily what he or she *should* be doing.

DISCUSSION QUESTIONS

1. Why do operations managers require labor standards?
2. How do we establish a fair day's work?
3. Is a "normal" pace the same thing as a 100% pace?
4. What is the difference between "normal" and "standard" times?
5. What kind of work pace would you expect from an employee during a time study? Why?
6. As a new time-study engineer in your plant, you are engaged in studying an employee operating a drill press. Somewhat to your surprise, one of the first things you notice is that the operator is performing a lot of operations besides just drilling holes. Your problem is what to include in your time study. From the following examples, indicate how, as the individual responsible for labor standards in your plant, you would handle them.
    a) Every so often, perhaps every 50 units or so, the drill press operator takes an extra-long look at the piece, which apparently is misshaped, and then typically throws it in the scrap barrel.
    b) Approximately 1 out of 100 units has a rough edge and will not fit in the jig properly; therefore, the drill press operator picks up the piece, hits the lower right-hand edge with a file a few times, puts the file down, and returns to normal operation.
    c) About every hour or so, the drill press operator stops to change the drill in the machine, even if he is in the middle of a job. (We can assume that the drill has become dull.)
    d) Between every job and sometimes in the middle of jobs, the drill press operator turns off the machine and goes for stock.
    e) The drill press operator is idle for a few minutes at the beginning of every job waiting for the setup man to complete the setup. Some of the setup time is used in going for stock, but the operator typically returns with stock before the setup man is finished with the setup.
    f) The operator stops to talk to you.
    g) The operator lights up a cigarette.
    h) The operator opens his lunch pail (it is not lunch time), removes an apple, and takes an occasional bite.
    i) The operator drops a part, which you pick up and hand to him. Does this make any difference in the time study? If so, how?
7. Describe Gilbreth's approach to setting work standards.

PROBLEMS

- **S10.1** After being observed many times, Sybil Gerand, a hospital lab analyst, had an average cycle time for blood tests of 6.525 minutes. Sybil's performance rating is a 95%. The hospital has a personal time allowance of 8%.
    a) Find the normal time for this process.
    b) Find the standard time for this blood test.

- **S10.2** A Northeast Airline gate agent, David Gillespie, gives out seat assignments to ticketed passengers. He takes an average of 50 seconds per passenger and is rated 110% in performance. How long should a *typical* agent be expected to take in making seat assignments?
- **S10.3** The cycle time for performing a certain task has been clocked at 10 minutes. The performance rating of the worker timed was estimated at 110%. Common practice in this department is to allow 5 minutes of personal time and 3 minutes of fatigue time per hour. In addition, it is estimated that there should be an extra allowance of 2 minutes per hour.
    a) Find the normal time for the operation.
    b) Compute the allowance factor and the standard time.
- **S10.4** A time study has revealed an average cycle time of 5 minutes, with a standard deviation of 1.25 minutes. These figures are based on a sample of 75 cycles. Is this sample large enough for an analyst to be 99% confident that the standard time is within 5% of the true value?
- **S10.5** The data in the following table represent time-study observations for an assembly process. On the basis of these observations, find the standard time for the process. Assume a 10% allowance factor.

	Performance	\multicolumn{5}{c}{Observation (minutes per cycle)}
Element	Rating (%)	1	2	3	4	5
1	100	1.5	1.6	1.4	1.5	1.5
2	90	2.3	2.5	2.1	2.2	2.4
3	120	1.7	1.9	1.9	1.4	1.6
4	100	3.5	3.6	3.6	3.6	3.2

- **S10.6** The following data represent observations for the cycle time of an assembly process. How many observations would be necessary for the observer to be 99% confident that the average cycle time is within 5% of the true value?

\multicolumn{5}{c}{Observation (in minutes)}
1	2	3	4	5
1.5	1.6	1.4	1.5	1.5

(*Hint:* Compute the sample standard deviation as shown in Solved Problem S10.3.)

- **S10.7** A work sample taken over a 100-hour work month produced the following results:

Units produced	200
Idle time (not part of task)	25%
Performance rating	110%
Allowance time	15%

What is the standard time for the job?

- **S10.8** Rebecca Page clocked the cycle time for welding a part onto truck doors at 5.3 minutes. The performance rating of the worker timed was estimated at 105%. Find the normal time for this operation.
    Note: According to the local union contract, each welder is allowed 3 minutes of personal time per hour and 2 minutes of fatigue time per hour. Further, it is estimated that there should be an average delay allowance of 1 minute per hour. Compute the allowance factor and then find the standard time for the welding activity.
- **S10.9** A time study of a factory worker has revealed an average cycle time of 3.20 minutes, with a standard deviation of 1.28 minutes. These figures were based on a sample of 45 cycles observed.

Is this sample adequate in size for the firm to be 99% confident that the standard time is within 5% of the true value? If not, what should be the proper number of observations?

: S10.10 The data in the following table represent time-study observations for a metalworking process. On the basis of these observations, find the standard time for the process, assuming a 25% allowance factor.

Element	Performance Rating (%)	1	2	3	4	5	6	7
1	90	1.80	1.70	1.66	1.91	1.85	1.77	1.60
2	100	6.9	7.3	6.8	7.1	15.3*	7.0	6.4
3	115	3.0	9.0*	9.5*	3.8	2.9	3.1	3.2
4	90	10.1	11.1	12.3	9.9	12.0	11.9	12.0

Observations (minutes per cycle)

*Disregard—unusual observation.

: S10.11 Based on a careful work study in the Julie Froelich Company, the results shown in the following table have been observed:

Element	1	2	3	4	5	Performance Rating (%)
Prepare daily reports	35	40	33	42	39	120
Photocopy results	12	10	36*	15	13	110
Label and package reports	3	3	5	5	4	90
Distribute reports	15	18	21	17	45†	85

Cycle Time (in minutes)

*Photocopying machine broken.
†Power outage.

a) Compute the normal time for each work element.
b) If the allowance for this type of work is 15%, what is the standard time?
c) How many observations are needed for a 95% confidence level within 5% accuracy? (*Hint:* Calculate the sample size of each element.)

: S10.12 The Division of Continuing Education at Virginia College promotes a wide variety of executive-training courses for firms in the Arlington, Virginia, region. Division director Christine Adams believes that individually typed letters add a personal touch to marketing. To prepare letters for mailing, she conducts a time study of her secretaries. On the basis of the observations shown in the following table, she wishes to develop a time standard for the whole job.

The college has an allowance factor of 12%. Adams decides to delete all unusual observations from the time study.

Element	1	2	3	4	5	6	Performance Rating (%)
Typing letter	2.5	3.5	2.8	2.1	2.6	3.3	85
Typing envelope	.8	.8	.6	.8	3.1	.7	100
Stuffing envelope	.4	.5	1.9	.3	.6	.5	95
Sealing, sorting	1.0	2.9	.9	1.0	4.4	.9	125

Cycle Time Observed (in minutes)

: S10.13 A time study at the phone company has observed a job containing three elements. The times and ratings for 10 cycles are shown in the following table.

	Performance	\multicolumn{10}{c}{Observation Time (minutes per cycle)}
Element	Rating (%)	1	2	3	4	5	6	7	8	9	10
1	85	.40	.45	.39	.48	.41	.50	.45	.39	.50	.40
2	88	1.5	1.7	1.9	1.7	1.8	1.6	1.8	1.8	2.0	2.1
3	90	3.8	3.4	3.0	4.8	4.0	4.2	3.5	3.6	3.7	4.3

a) Find the average cycle time for each element.
b) Find the normal time for each element.
c) Assuming an allowance factor for 20% of job time, determine the standard time for this job.

: S10.14 The Dubuque Cement Company packs 80-pound bags of concrete mix. Time-study data for the filling activity are shown in the following table.

The company's policy is a 20% allowance for workers. Compute the standard time for the bag-packing task. How many cycles are necessary for 99% confidence, within 5% accuracy?

	\multicolumn{5}{c}{Cycle Time (seconds per cycle)}	Performance
Element	1	2	3	4	5	Rating (%)
Grasp and place bag	8	9	8	11	7	110
Fill bag	36	41	39	35	112*	85
Seal bag	15	17	13	20	18	105
Place bag on conveyor	8	6	9	30†	35†	90

*Bag breaks open.
†Conveyor jams.

: S10.15 An office worker has been clocked performing three work elements, with the results shown in the following table. The allowance for tasks such as this is 15%.

	\multicolumn{6}{c}{Minutes per Cycle}	Performance
Element	1	2	3	4	5	6	Rating (%)
1	13	11	14	16	51	15	100
2	68	21	25	73	26	23	110
3	3.0	3.3	3.1	2.9	3.4	2.8	100

a) Find the normal time.
b) Find the standard time.

: S10.16 Installing mufflers at the McElroy Garage in Sacramento involves five work elements. Judy McElroy has timed workers performing these tasks seven times, with the results shown in the following table.

	Cycle Time Observations (minutes)							Performance Rating (%)
Job Element	1	2	3	4	5	6	7	
1. Select correct mufflers	4	5	4	6	4	15	4	110
2. Remove old muffler	6	8	7	6	7	6	7	90
3. Weld/install new muffler	15	14	14	12	15	16	13	105
4. Check/inspect work	3	4	24	5	4	3	18	100
5. Complete paperwork	5	6	8	—	7	6	7	130

By agreement with her workers, McElroy allows a 10% fatigue factor and a 10% personal-time factor. To compute standard time for the work operation, McElroy excludes all observations that appear to be unusual or nonrecurring. She does not want an error of more than 5%.

a) What is the standard time for the task?
b) How many cycles are needed to assure a 95% confidence level?

: **S10.17** Sample observations of an assembly-line worker made over a 40-hour workweek have revealed that the worker produced a total of 320 completed parts. The performance rating was 125%. The sample also showed that the worker was busy assembling the parts 80% of the time. Allowances for work on the assembly line total 10%. Find the normal time and standard time for this task.

• **S10.18** Bank manager Carrie Mattanini wants to determine the percent of time that tellers are working and idle. She decides to use work sampling, and her initial estimate is that the tellers are idle 30% of the time. How many observations should Mattanini take in order to be 95.45% confident that the results will not be more than 5% away from the true result?

: **S10.19** A work sample taken over a 160-hour work month has produced the following results. What is the standard time for the job?

Units manufactured	220
Idle time	20%
Performance rating	90%
Allowance time	10%

• **S10.20** Sharpening your pencil is an operation that may be divided into eight small elemental motions. In MTM terms, each element may be assigned a certain number of TMUs:

Reach 4 inches for the pencil	6 TMU
Grasp the pencil	2 TMU
Move the pencil 6 inches	10 TMU
Position the pencil	20 TMU
Insert the pencil into the sharpener	4 TMU
Sharpen the pencil	120 TMU
Disengage the pencil	10 TMU
Move the pencil 6 inches	10 TMU

What is the total normal time for sharpening one pencil? Convert your answer into minutes and seconds.

Case Study

Telephone Operator Standards at AT&T*

For well over a decade, many firms around the globe have employed sophisticated software to monitor the productivity of their clerical employees. Programs allow managers to measure keystrokes per hour, records entered, calls answered, and time on break.

For example, reservations agents at Delta Airlines may leave their workstations for personal break times only when approved by the software that controls staffing needs. Checkout clerks at Giant Food are monitored by dollars of sales scanned at their registers. If they fall behind the average, the manager can take corrective action. Data-entry clerks at Northwest Airlines are expected to type between 9,000 and 16,000 keystrokes per hour when feeding payroll and ticketing information into computers. The system at Northwest keeps track of speed; whereas slower typists can be penalized by losing pay, fast workers are rewarded with scheduling flexibility. A speed at least 75% as fast as the three fastest workers is expected. Not surprisingly, computer monitoring has been opposed by labor unions.

Beth Shader's Dismissal

Beth Shader, age 40, had been a telephone operator at AT&T Communications, in Richmond, Virginia, for 14 years. Beth viewed herself as a loyal employee and took pride in her job. A divorced mother of a 15-year-old son with only a high school education, Beth earned $22,000 per year as an experienced operator.

Like other firms, AT&T uses a computer to check each telephone operator's "average work time," or AWT. AWT is the time consumed on each call and has been set at AT&T as 30 seconds. In other words, from the moment an operator like Beth answered a 411 or 0 (operator) call at her station, she was expected to complete the call and move on the next one in an average time of a half minute.

In the period April to June 1997, Beth Shader consistently averaged 32 seconds. On July 1, she was dismissed. Beth approached her union steward at the Communication Workers of America (CWA), and on July 15, she filed a grievance against AT&T. Beth claimed that coworkers were under such pressure that they routinely risked disciplinary action by cutting off callers in order to maintain daily AWTs. She further stated that she felt it was her job to help people who needed help, especially the elderly who would often need the name and number of a nearby pharmacy or some other time-consuming information.

On March 6, 1998, the case of Beth Shader vs. AT&T came before James Gilbert, National Labor Relations Board chief arbitor for the Southeast Region in Norfolk, Virginia. Beth was represented by a CWA attorney, while AT&T had in-house counsel present.

DISCUSSION QUESTIONS

1. Make the case for Beth Shader and the CWA attorney and justify why the system should change.
2. Make the case for AT&T and justify why such labor standards are needed.

* Names of individuals, dates, and cities in this case study have been changed.

BIBLIOGRAPHY

Barnes, R. M. *Motion and Time Study*. New York: John Wiley, 1980.

Flynn, B. B., C. Blair, and M. Walters. "Flexible Compensation for World Class Manufacturers: Creating a Labor Skill Inventory Using Skill-Based Pay." *OM Review* 9, no. 3 (1992): 22–36.

Jacobs, L. W., and S. E. Bechtold. "Labor Utilization Effects of Labor Scheduling Flexibility Alternatives in a Tour Scheduling Environment." *Decision Sciences* 24, no. 1 (January–February 1993): 148–166.

Karger, D. W. *Advanced Work Measurement*. New York: Industrial Press, 1982.

Konz, S. *Work Design*. Columbus, OH: Grid, 1975.

Niebel, B. W. *Motion and Time Study,* 7th ed. Homewood, IL: Richard D. Irwin, 1982.

INTERNET RESOURCES

Institute of Industrial Engineers:
    http://www.iienet.org/
Methods Time Measurement Association:
    http://www.mtm.org/

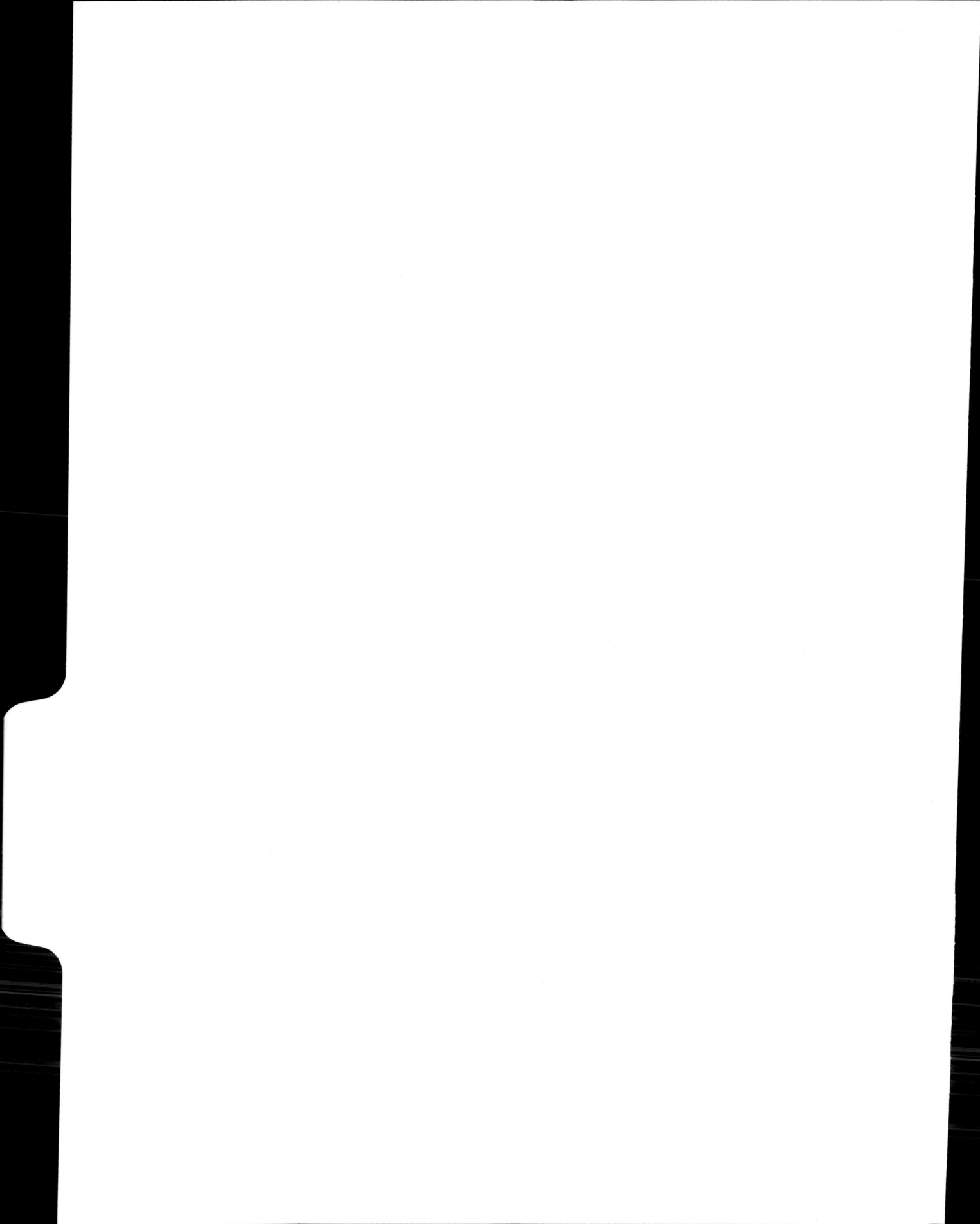

SOFTWARE

Two of the best student Operations Management software packages are available with our texts: **POM for Windows** and **Excel OM**. *POM for Windows* is a user friendly software package which helps students solve quantitative problems. This package contains numerous models relating to Operations Management and can be used to solve or approach problems as well as check answers that have been derived by hand. *It can be packaged as an option with this text, at a reasonable price.*

The *Excel OM* package is distributed **free** with this textbook on the **CD-ROM** in the back of the book. This is a program that is easy to install and very easy to use. Featuring a pull-down menu and Excel dialog boxes, the package will create a spreadsheet. Users need only to fill in the data and Excel will display and graph (where appropriate) the results. Because Excel illustrates the actual formulas used to make calculations, this exercise becomes an "Open" or "Symbolic" approach in which students can observe and even modify formulas.

For an example of our software, please see chapter 12 (Inventory Management).

VOLKSWAGEN

sourcing and supply-chain integration. At this Volkswagen plant, however, VW is buying not only the materials but also labor and the related services. Suppliers are integrated tightly into VW's own network, right down to the assembly work in the plant.

Because purchase costs in the auto industry exceed 60% of the sales dollar, even modest reductions in these costs could make Volkswagen's payoff substantial. The results are not in yet, but VW is already trying a similar approach in plants in Buenos Aires, Argentina, and Skoda, in the Czech Republic. Volkswagen's new level of integration in supply-chain management may be the wave of the future.

Sources: New York Times, November 19, 1996, pp. C1–C5; The Wall Street Journal, February 15, 1996, A11; and Business Week, October 7, 1996, pp. 55–56.

Remon workers attach the wheels as other parts of the truck are assembled simultaneously.

Nearly finished trucks move down the assembly line. The plant is expected to produce 100 trucks a day.

Most firms, like VW, spend over 50% of their sales dollars on purchases. Because such a high percentage of an organization's costs are determined by purchasing, relationships with suppliers are increasingly integrated and long-term. Joint efforts that improve innovation, speed design, and reduce costs are common. Such efforts can dramatically improve both partners' competitiveness. Consequently, a discipline known as *supply-chain management* has developed.

THE STRATEGIC IMPORTANCE OF THE SUPPLY CHAIN

Supply-chain management is the integration of the activities that procure materials, transform them into intermediate goods and final products, and deliver them to customers. These activities include the traditional purchasing function, plus many other activities that are important to the relationship with suppliers and distributors. As Figure 11.1 suggests, supply-chain management includes determining: (1) transportation vendors, (2) credit and cash transfers, (3) suppliers, (4) distributors and banks, (5) accounts payable and receivable, (6) warehousing and inventory levels, (7) order fulfillment, and (8) sharing customer, forecasting, and production information. The idea is to build a chain of suppliers that focus on both reducing waste and maximizing value to the ultimate customer. Activities of supply-chain managers cut across accounting, finance, marketing, and the operations discipline.

Supply-chain management
Management of activities that procure raw materials, transform those materials into intermediate goods and final products, and deliver the products through a distribution system.

The supplier must be treated as an extension of the company.

As firms strive to increase their competitiveness via product customization, high quality, cost reductions, and speed-to-market, they place added emphasis on the supply chain. The key to effective supply-chain management is to make the suppliers "partners" in the firm's strategy to satisfy an ever-changing marketplace.

To ensure that the supply chain supports the firm's strategy, we need to consider the supply-chain issues shown in Table 11.1. Just as the OM function supports the firm's overall strategy, the supply chain is designed to support the OM strategy. Strategies of low cost or rapid response demand different things from a supply chain than a strategy of differentiation. For instance, a low-cost strategy, as Table 11.1 indicates, requires that we

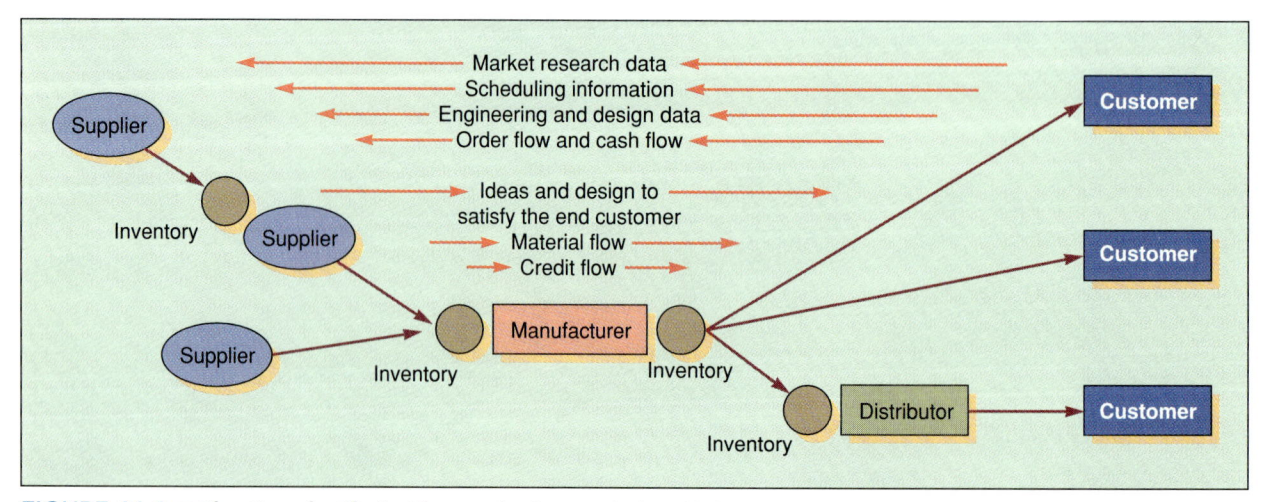

FIGURE 11.1 ■ The Supply Chain *The supply chain includes all the interactions between suppliers, manufacturers, distributors, and customers. The chain includes transportation, scheduling information, cash and credit transfers, as well as ideas, designs, and material transfers.*

TABLE 11.1 ■ How the Supply Chain Can Support the Overall Strategy

	Low-Cost Strategy	Response Strategy	Differentiation Strategy
Supplier's Goal	Supply demand at lowest possible cost (e.g., Emerson Electric, Taco Bell)	Respond quickly to changing requirements and demand to minimize stockouts (e.g., Dell Computers)	Share market research; jointly develop products and options (e.g., Benetton)
Primary Selection Criteria	Select primarily for cost	Select primarily for capacity, speed, and flexibility	Select primarily for product development skills
Process Characteristics	Maintain high average utilization	Invest in excess capacity and flexible processes	Modular processes that lend themselves to mass customization
Inventory Characteristics	Minimize inventory throughout the chain to hold down costs	Develop responsive system, with buffer stocks positioned to ensure supply	Minimize inventory in the chain to avoid obsolescence
Lead-Time Characteristics	Shorten lead time as long as it does not increase costs	Invest aggressively to reduce production lead time	Invest aggressively to reduce development lead time
Product-Design Characteristics	Maximize performance and minimize cost	Use product designs that lead to low setup time and rapid production ramp-up	Use modular design to postpone product differentiation for as long as possible

See related table and discussion in Marshall L. Fisher, "What Is the Right Supply Chain for Your Product?" *Harvard Business Review* (March–April 1997): 105.

select suppliers based primarily on cost. Such suppliers should have the ability to design low-cost products that meet the functional requirements, minimize inventory, and drive down lead times. To be effective and efficient, the firm must achieve integration of its selected strategy up and down the supply chain.

Global Supply-Chain Issues

When companies enter growing global markets such as eastern Europe, China, South America, or even Mexico, expanding their supply chains becomes a strategic challenge. Distribution systems in those areas may produce products of lower quality and be less reliable, suggesting higher inventory levels than would be needed in one's home country. Additionally, tariffs and quotas may block nonlocal companies from doing business. Moreover, market instabilities, such as major devaluations of the Thai bhat and Malaysian ringget in 1997, are common in newly emerging industrial economies.

So the development of a successful strategic plan for supply-chain management requires innovative planning and careful research. Supply chains in a global environment must be:

1. Flexible enough to react to sudden changes in parts availability, distribution or shipping channels, import duties, and currency rates.
2. Able to use the latest computer and transmission technologies to manage the shipment of parts in and finished products out.
3. Staffed with local specialists to handle duties, trade, freight, customs, and political issues.

TEN DECISIONS OF OM

Managing Quality

Design of Goods & Services

Process Strategy

Location Strategies

Layout Strategies

Human Resources

Supply-Chain Management

Inventory Management

Scheduling

Maintenance

McDonald's planned for this global supply-chain challenge 6 years in advance of its opening in Russia. Creating a $60-million *food town*, it developed independently owned supply plants in Moscow to keep its transportation costs and handling times low and its quality and customer-service levels high. Every component in this food chain—meat plant, chicken plant, bakery, fish plant, and lettuce plant—is closely monitored to make sure that all the system's links are strong.[1]

Firms like Ford and Boeing also face global procurement decisions. Ford's Mercury Mystique has only 227 suppliers worldwide, a small number compared to the 700 involved in previous models. Ford has set a trend to develop a global network of *fewer* suppliers who provide the lowest cost and highest quality regardless of home country.[2] So global is the production of the Boeing 777 that officials proclaim that "The Chinese now make so many Boeing parts, that when Boeing planes fly to China, they are going home."[3]

PURCHASING

TABLE 11.2 ■ Purchasing Costs as a Percent of Sales

Industry	% Purchased
All industry	52
Automobile	67
Food	60
Lumber	61
Paper	55
Petroleum	79
Transportation	62

The supply chain receives such attention because purchasing is the most costly activity in most firms. For both goods and services, the cost of purchases as a percent of sales is often substantial (see Table 11.2). Because such a huge portion of revenue is devoted to purchasing, an effective purchasing strategy is vital. Purchasing provides a major opportunity to reduce costs and increase contribution margins.

Table 11.3 illustrates the amount of leverage available to the operations manager through purchasing. Firms spending 50% of their sales dollar on purchases and having a net profit of 6% would require $3.57 worth of sales in order to equal the savings that accrues to the company from a $1 savings in procurement. These numbers indicate the strong role that procurement can play in profitability.

TABLE 11.3 ■ Dollars of Additional Sales Needed to Equal $1 Saved through Purchasing*

Percent Net Profit of Firm	30%	40%	50%	60%	70%	80%	90%
2	$2.78	$3.23	$3.85	$4.76	$6.25	$9.09	$16.67
4	$2.70	$3.13	$3.70	$4.55	$5.88	$8.33	$14.29
6	$2.63	$3.03	$3.57	$4.35	$5.56	$7.69	$12.50
8	$2.56	$2.94	$3.45	$4.17	$5.26	$7.14	$11.11
10	$2.50	$2.86	$3.33	$4.00	$5.00	$6.67	$10.00

Percent of Sales Spent for Purchases

*The required increase in sales assumes that 50% of the costs other than purchases are variable and that 1/2 of the remaining (less profit) are fixed. Therefore, at sales of $100 (50% purchases and 2% margin), $50 are purchases, $24 are other variable costs, $24 are fixed costs, and $2 profit. Increasing sales by $3.85 yields the following:

Purchases at 50%	$51.93
Other Variable Costs	24.92
Fixed Cost	24.00
Profit	3.00
	$103.85

Through $3.85 of additional sales, we have increased profit by $1, from $2 to $3. The same increase in margin could have been obtained by reducing purchasing costs by $1.

[1] P. Ritchie "McDonald's: A Winner Through Logistics," *International Journal of Physical Distribution and Logistics Management* 20, no. 3 (1990): 21–24.

[2] Alex Taylor, "The Auto Industry Meets The New Economy," *Fortune*, September 5, 1994, pp. 52–60.

[3] *New York Times*, October 21, 1997, p. A21.

> **EXAMPLE 1**
>
> The Goodwin Company spends 50% of its sales dollar on purchased goods. The firm has a net profit of 4%. Of the remaining 46%, 23% is fixed and the remaining 23% is variable. From Table 11.3, we see that the dollar value of sales needed to generate the same profit that results from $1 of purchase savings would be $3.70.

For most companies the percent of revenue spent on labor is going down, but the percent spent on purchases is going up.

Because the cost and quality of goods and services sold is directly related to the cost and quality of goods and services purchased, organizations must examine a number of strategies for effective purchasing. The need for a purchasing strategy and its accomplishment leads to the creation of a purchasing function. **Purchasing** is the acquisition of goods and services. The *objective of the purchasing* activity is:

1. To help identify the products and services that can be obtained externally.
2. To develop, evaluate, and determine the best supplier, price, and delivery for those products and services.

Purchasing takes place in both manufacturing and service environments.

Purchasing The acquisition of goods and services.

Manufacturing Environments

In the *manufacturing* environment, the purchasing function is usually managed by a **purchasing agent** who has legal authority to execute contracts on behalf of the firm. In a large firm, the purchasing agent may also have a staff that includes buyers and expediters. *Buyers* represent the company, performing all the activities of the purchasing department except the signing of contracts. *Expediters* assist buyers in following up on purchases to ensure timely delivery. The purchasing function is supported by product engineering drawings and specifications, quality-control documents, and testing activities that evaluate the purchased items.

Purchasing agent A person with legal authority to execute purchasing contracts on behalf of the firm.

Service Environments

In many *service* environments, purchasing's role is diminished because the primary product is an intellectual one. In legal and medical organizations, for example, the main items to be procured are office facilities, furniture and equipment, autos, and supplies. However, in other services such as transportation and restaurants, the purchasing function is critical. An airline that purchases planes that are inefficient for its route structure or a steak house that does not know how to buy steak is in trouble. In these and similar firms, resources must be expended and training provided to ensure that purchasing is competently addressed.

In the wholesale and retail segment of services, purchasing is performed by a **buyer** who has responsibility for the sale of and profit margins on purchased merchandise that will be resold. Buyers in this nonmanufacturing environment may have little support for standards and quality control other than historical customer behavior and standard grades. For instance, a USDA grade (such as *AA* eggs or *U.S. choice* meat), a textile standard or blend, or standard sizes may take the place of engineering drawings and quality-control documents found in manufacturing environments.

Buyer In wholesale and retail services, the purchaser who is responsible for the sale of and profit margins on merchandise that will be resold.

Make-or-Buy Decisions

A wholesaler or retailer buys everything that it sells; a manufacturing operation hardly ever does. Manufacturers, restaurants, and assemblers of products buy components and subassemblies that go into final products. As we saw in chapter 6, choosing products and

Make-or-buy decision
Choosing between producing a component or a service or purchasing it from an outside source.

services that can be advantageously obtained *externally* as opposed to produced *internally* is known as the **make-or-buy decision.** The purchasing department's role is to evaluate alternative suppliers and provide current, accurate, complete data relevant to the buy alternative. Table 11.4 lists a variety of considerations in the make-or-buy decision.

TABLE 11.4 ■ Considerations for the Make-or-Buy Decision

Reasons for Making	Reasons for Buying
1. Lower production cost	1. Lower acquisition cost
2. Unsuitable suppliers	2. Preserve supplier commitment
3. Assure adequate supply (quantity or delivery)	3. Obtain technical or management ability
4. Utilize surplus labor or facilities and make a marginal contribution	4. Inadequate capacity
	5. Reduce inventory costs
5. Obtain desired quality	6. Ensure alternative sources
6. Remove supplier collusion	7. Inadequate managerial or technical resources
7. Obtain unique item that would entail a prohibitive commitment for a supplier	8. Reciprocity
	9. Item is protected by a patent or trade secret
8. Maintain organizational talents and protect personnel from a layoff	10. Frees management to deal with its primary business
9. Protect proprietary design or quality	
10. Increase or maintain size of the company (management preference)	

Regardless of the decision, it should be reviewed periodically. Vendor competence and costs change, as do a firm's own production capabilities and costs.

SUPPLY-CHAIN STRATEGIES

Centralized purchasing almost always saves a firm money.

For those items to be purchased, companies must decide upon a supply-chain strategy. One such strategy is the traditional American approach of *negotiating with many suppliers* and playing one supplier against another. A second strategy is to develop *long-term, "partnering"* relationships with a few suppliers who will work with the purchaser to satisfy the end customer. A third strategy is *vertical integration,* where firms may decide to use vertical backward integration by actually buying the supplier. A fourth variation is a combination of few suppliers and vertical integration, known as a "keiretsu." In a keiretsu, *suppliers become part of a company coalition.* Finally, a fifth strategy is to develop virtual companies *that use suppliers on an as-needed basis.* We will now discuss each of these strategies.

Many Suppliers

With the many-supplier strategy, the supplier responds to the demands and specifications of a "request for quotation," with the order usually going to the low bidder. This strategy plays one supplier against another and places the burden of meeting the buyer's demands on the supplier. Suppliers aggressively compete with one another. Although many approaches to negotiations can be used with this strategy, long-term "partnering" relationships are not the goal. This approach holds the supplier responsible for maintaining the necessary technology, expertise, and forecasting abilities, as well as cost, quality, and delivery competencies.

Few Suppliers

A strategy of few suppliers implies that rather than looking for short-term attributes, such as low cost, a buyer is better off forming a long-term relationship with a few dedicated suppliers. Long-term suppliers are more likely to understand the broad objectives of the procuring firm and the end customer. Using few suppliers can create value by allowing suppliers to have economies of scale and a learning curve that yields both lower transaction costs and lower production costs.

Few suppliers, each with a large commitment to the buyer, may also be more willing to participate in JIT systems, as well as provide innovations and technological expertise. However, the most important factor may be the trust that comes with compatible organization cultures. A champion within one of the firms often promotes a positive relationship between purchase and supplier organizations by committing resources toward advancing the relationship. Such a commitment can foster both formal and informal contact, that may contribute to the alignment of organization cultures of the two firms, further strengthening the partnership.

Chrysler Corporation used this approach for the Dodge Stratus. Operations managers chose suppliers even before the parts were designed. Chrysler evaluated suppliers on many rigorous criteria but virtually eliminated traditional supplier bidding. As a part of this new process, Chrysler adopted contracts that run for at least the life of the model. By working with Chrysler as "partners," suppliers are expected to become more efficient, reducing prices as they move down the learning curve. This approach yields only a few suppliers, but Chrysler expects to develop long-term relationships with them. The success of this strategy on the Dodge Stratus and other models is evident in Table 11.5.

> Integrating suppliers, production, and distribution requires that operations be as agile as possible.

> Nearly 90 years ago, Henry Ford surrounded himself with reliable suppliers, many on his own property, making his assembly operation close to self-sufficient.

TABLE 11.5 ■ Chrysler's Supplier Cost Reduction Effort (Score) Produced $161 Million in Savings in Two Years

Supplier	Suggestion	Model	Annual Savings
Rockwell	Use passenger car door locks on Dodge trucks	Dodge trucks	$ 280,000
Rockwell	Simplify design and substitute materials on manual window-regulator systems	Various	300,000
3M	Change tooling for wood-grain panels to allow three parts to be made in one die instead of two	Caravan, Voyager	1,500,000
Trico	Change wiper-blade formulations to eliminate the disposable plastic shield used during assembly and shipping	Various	140,000
Leslie Metal Arts	Exterior lighting suggestions	Various	1,500,000

Source: James Welch, Laddie Cook, and Joseph Blackburn, "The Bridge to Competitiveness, Building Supplier-Customer Linkages," *Target,* November–December 1992, pp. 17–29. Reprinted from *Target* with permission of the Association for Manufacturing Excellence, Wheeling, IL.

Service companies like Marks and Spencer, a British retailer, have also demonstrated that cooperation with suppliers can yield cost savings for customers and suppliers alike. This strategy has resulted in suppliers that develop new products, winning customers for Marks and Spencer and the supplier.

Vertical integration
Developing the ability to produce goods or services previously purchased or actually buying a supplier or a distributor.

Like all strategies, a downside exists. With few suppliers, the cost of changing partners is huge, so both buyer and supplier run the risk of becoming captives of the other. Poor supplier performance is only one risk the purchaser faces. The purchaser must also be concerned about trade secrets and suppliers who make other alliances or venture out on their own. This happened when the U.S. Schwinn Bicycle Co., needing additional capacity, taught Taiwan's Giant Manufacturing Company to make and sell bicycles.[4] Giant Manufacturing is now the largest bicycle manufacturer in the world and Schwinn is trying to recover from bankruptcy.

Vertical Integration

Purchasing can be extended to take the form of vertical integration. By **vertical integration**, we mean developing the ability to produce goods or services previously purchased or actually buying a supplier or a distributor. As shown in Figure 11.2, vertical integration can take the form of *forward* or *backward integration*.

Backward integration suggests a firm purchase its suppliers, as in the case of Ford Motor Company deciding to manufacture its own car radios. Forward integration, on the other hand, suggests that a manufacturer of components make the finished product. An example is Texas Instruments, a manufacturer of integrated circuits that also makes calculators and computers containing integrated circuits.

Vertical integration can offer a strategic opportunity for the operations manager. For firms with the necessary capital, managerial talent, and required demand, vertical integration may provide substantial opportunities for cost reduction. Other advantages in inventory reduction and scheduling can accrue to the company that effectively manages vertical integration or close, mutually beneficial relationships with suppliers.

Because purchased items represent such a large part of the costs of sales, it is obvious why so many organizations find interest in vertical integration. Vertical integration can yield cost reduction, quality adherence, and timely delivery. Vertical integration appears to work best when the organization has large market share or the management talent to operate an acquired vendor successfully.[5] However, backward integration may be particu-

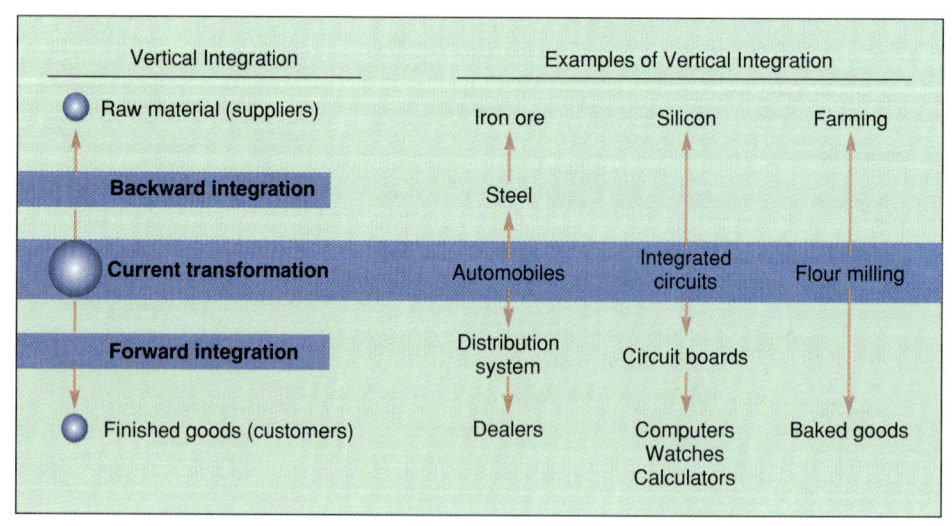

Vertical Integration	Examples of Vertical Integration		
Raw material (suppliers)	Iron ore	Silicon	Farming
Backward integration	Steel		
Current transformation	Automobiles	Integrated circuits	Flour milling
Forward integration	Distribution system	Circuit boards	
Finished goods (customers)	Dealers	Computers Watches Calculators	Baked goods

FIGURE 11.2 ■ Vertical Integration Can Be Forward or Backward

---

[4] Andrew Tanzer, "Bury Thy Teacher," *Forbes*, December 21, 1992, pp. 90–95.

[5] Robert D. Buzzell, "Is Vertical Integration Profitable?" *Harvard Business Review* 61 (January–February 1983): 92–102.

Sanford Corporation is one of America's largest producers of highlighters and markers. Sanford is vertically integrated, making its own inks—a strategy that gives it a research, development, quality, and product-flexibility advantage.

larly dangerous for firms in industries undergoing technological change if management cannot keep abreast of those changes or invest the financial resources necessary for the next wave of technology.

Keiretsu Networks

Many large Japanese manufacturers have found a middle ground between purchasing from few suppliers and vertical integration. These manufacturers are often financial supporters of suppliers through ownership or loans. The supplier then becomes part of a company coalition known as a **keiretsu.** Members of the keiretsu are assured long-term relationships and are therefore expected to function as partners, providing technical expertise and stable quality production to the manufacturer. Members of the keiretsu can also operate as suppliers further down the chain, making second- and even third-tier suppliers part of the coalition.

Keiretsu A Japanese term to describe suppliers who become part of a company coalition

Virtual Companies

As noted before, the limitations to vertical integration are severe. Our technological society continually demands more specialization that further complicates vertical integration. Similarly, a firm that has a department or division of its own for everything may be too bureaucratic to be world-class. On the other hand, rather than letting vertical integration

Virtual companies
Companies that rely on a variety of supplier relationships to provide services on demand. Also known as hollow corporations or network companies.

lock an organization into businesses that it may not understand or be able to manage, another approach is to find good flexible suppliers. **Virtual companies** rely on a variety of supplier relationships to provide services on demand. Virtual companies have fluid, moving organizational boundaries that allow them to create a unique enterprise to meet changing market demands. These relationships may provide a variety of vendor services that include doing the payroll, hiring personnel, designing products, providing consulting services, manufacturing components, conducting tests, or distributing products. The relationships may be short-term or long-term and may include true partners, collaborators, or simply able suppliers and subcontractors. Whatever the formal relationship, the result can be exceptionally lean performance. The advantages of virtual companies include specialized management expertise, low capital investment, flexibility, and speed. The result is efficiency.

The apparel business provides a *traditional* example of virtual organizations. The designers of clothes seldom manufacture their designs; rather, they license the manufacture. The manufacturer may then rent a loft, lease sewing machines, and contract for labor. The result is an organization that has low overhead, remains flexible, and can respond rapidly to the market.

A *contemporary* example is the semiconductor industry, exemplified by two California companies, S3 Inc. in Santa Clara and Visioneer in Palo Alto. Both firms subcontract almost everything. At Visioneer, software is written by several partners, hardware is manufactured by a subcontractor in Silicon Valley, printed circuit boards are made in Singapore, and plastic cases are made in Boston, where units are also tested and packed for shipment. In the virtual company, the purchasing function is demanding and dynamic.

Each company makes its own judgment about the appropriate degree of vertical integration. Jaguar has changed its approach to vertical integration. In the past, Jaguar made virtually every part it could, even when the strategy made little sense. It even manufactured some simple items such as washers. However, Jaguar now focuses on those items that make a car unique: the body, engine, and suspension. Outside suppliers with their own capabilities, expertise, and efficiencies provide most other components.

VENDOR SELECTION

A firm that decides to buy material rather than make it must select vendors. **Vendor selection** considers numerous factors, such as inventory and transportation costs, availability of supply, delivery performance, and quality of suppliers. A firm may have some competence in all areas and exceptional competence in only a few, but an outstanding operations function requires excellent vendors. We will now examine vendor selection as a three-stage process. Those three stages are: (1) vendor evaluation, (2) vendor development, and (3) negotiations.

Vendor selection A decision regarding who to buy materials from.

Vendor Evaluation

The first stage, *vendor evaluation,* involves finding potential vendors and determining the likelihood of their becoming good suppliers. This phase requires the development of evaluation criteria such as those in Figure 11.3. Both the criteria and the weights are dependent upon the needs of the organization. The selection of competent suppliers is critical. If good

VENDOR RATING REPORT — J.M. HUBER CORPORATION
COMPANY — TOTAL RATING

Company	Excellent (4)	Good (3)	Fair (2)	Poor (1)
Size and/or Capacity	4			
Financial Strength		3		
Operational Profit		3		
Manufacturing Range	4			
Research Facilities			2	
Technical Service		3		
Geographical Locations	4			
Management		3		
Labor Relations		3		
Trade Relations		3		
Total 32	12	18	2	
.63 × Total = 20.16				

Service	Excellent	Good	Fair	Poor
Deliveries on Time	4			
Condition on Arrival		3		
Follow Instructions		3		
Number of Rejections	4			
Handling of Complaints		3		
Technical Assistance			2	
Emergency Aid		3		
Supply Up-to-Date Catalogues, Etc.				1
Supply Price Changes Promptly	4			
Total 27	12	12	2	1
.69 × Total = 18.63				

Products	Excellent (4)	Good (3)	Fair (2)	Poor (1)
Quality	4			
Price		3		
Packaging	4			
Uniformity		3		
Warranty	4			
Total 18	12	6		
1.25 × Total = 22.50				

Sales Personnel				
1. Knowledge				
His Company		3		
His Products	4			
Our Industry		3		
Our Company		3		
2. Sales Calls				
Properly Spaced	4			
By Appointment		3		
Planned and Prepared		3		
Mutually Productive	4			
3. Sales Service				
Obtain Information		3		
Furnish Quotations Promptly	4			
Follow Orders		3		
Expedite Delivery		3		
Handle Complaints		3		
Total 43	16	27		
.48 × Total = 20.64				

FIGURE 11.3 ■ **Vendor Rating Form Used by J. M. Huber Corporation** *Evaluation categories are weighted according to importance (for example, product category is weighted 1.25; "service" is next at 0.69). Individual factors (for example, quality, delivery, and so on) have descending values, from 4 points for excellent to 1 point for poor. Total of points in each category is multiplied by the weight for that category.*
Source: Stuart F. Heinritz, Paul V. Farrell, Larry Giunipero, and Michael Kolchin, *Purchasing: Principles and Applications*, 8th ed. (Englewood Cliffs, NJ: Prentice Hall, 1992), p. 180.

suppliers are not selected, then all other purchasing efforts are wasted. As firms move toward fewer longer-term suppliers, the issues of financial strength, quality, management, research, technical ability, and potential for a close long-term relationship play an increasingly important role.[6] These attributes should be noted in the evaluation process.

Vendor Development

The second stage is *vendor development*. Assuming a firm wants to proceed with a particular vendor, how does it integrate this supplier into its system? Purchasing makes sure the vendor has an appreciation of quality requirements, engineering changes, schedules and delivery, the purchaser's payment system, and procurement policies. *Vendor development* may include everything from training, to engineering and production help, to formats for electronic information transfer. Purchasing policies might address issues such as percent of business done with any one supplier or with minority businesses.

Negotiations

Negotiation strategies
Approaches taken by purchasing personnel to develop contractual relationships with suppliers.

The third stage is *negotiations*. **Negotiation strategies** are of three classic types: the *cost-based price model*, the *market-based price model*, and *competitive bidding*.[7]

Cost-Based Price Model The *cost-based price model* requires that the supplier open its books to the purchaser. The contract price is then based on time and materials or on a fixed cost with an escalation clause to accommodate changes in the vendor's labor and materials cost.

Market-Based Price Model In the *market-based price model,* price is based on a published price or index. Paperboard prices, for instance, are published weekly in the "yellow sheet,"[8] and nonferrous metal prices in *Metals Week*.[9]

As a world-class telecommunications company, AT&T has an aggressive supplier evaluation and quality-improvement program. Part of this program requires that vendors provide company profile and capability information. Providing this information is often done in formal presentations, as Hitachi Cable Ltd. is doing here. Once vendors are approved and orders placed, AT&T tracks key supplier variables, such as order cycle time and quality yield, to determine effectiveness of the program.

---

[6] See Thomas Y. Choi and Janet L. Hartley, "An Exploration of Supplier Selection Practices across the Supply Chain," *Journal of Operations Management* 14, no. 4 (November 1996): 333–343.

[7] Gary J. Zenz, *Purchasing and the Management of Materials,* 7th ed. (New York: John Wiley, 1994).

[8] The "yellow sheet" is the commonly used name of the *Official Board Markets*, published by Magazines for Industry, Chicago. It contains announced paperboard prices for containerboard and boxboard.

[9] *Metals Week,* A. Patrick Ryan, editor and publisher, New York.

Competitive Bidding When suppliers are not willing to discuss costs or where near-perfect markets do not exist, *competitive bidding* is often appropriate. Competitive bidding is the typical policy in many firms for the majority of their purchases. The policy usually requires that the purchasing agent have several potential suppliers of the product (or its equivalent) and quotations from each. The major disadvantage of this method, as mentioned earlier, is that the development of long-term relations between buyer and seller are hindered. Competitive bidding may effectively determine cost. However, it may also make difficult the communication and performance that are vital for engineering changes, quality, and delivery.

Yet a fourth approach is *to combine one or more* of the preceding negotiation techniques. The supplier and purchaser may agree on review of certain cost data, accept some form of market data for raw material costs, or agree that the supplier will "remain competitive." In any case, a good supplier relationship is one in which both partners have established a degree of mutual trust and a belief in the competence of each other.

> Purchasing negotiations should not be viewed as a win/lose game; it can be a win/win game.

MANAGING THE SUPPLY CHAIN

Because supply-chain management deals with the complete cycle of materials as they flow from suppliers to production to warehousing to distribution to the customer, there are many opportunities to enhance value. We will now examine some of these opportunities.

Postponement Postponement withholds any modification or customization to the product (keeping it generic) as long as possible.[10] For instance, after analyzing the supply chain for its printers, Hewlett-Packard (H-P) determined that if the printer's power supply was moved out of the printer itself and into a power cord, H-P could ship the basic printer anywhere in the world. H-P modified the printer, its power cord, its packaging, and its documentation so that only the power cord and documentation needed to be added at the final distribution point. This modification allowed the firm to manufacture and hold centralized inventories of the generic printer for shipment as demand changed. Only the unique power system and documentation had to be held in each country. This understanding of the entire supply chain reduced both risk and investment in inventory.[11]

> **Postponement**
> Delaying any modifications or customization to the product as long as possible in the production process.

Channel Assembly Channel assembly is a variation of postponement. **Channel assembly** sends individual components and modules, rather than finished products, to the distributor. The distributor then assembles, tests, and ships. Channel assembly treats distributors more as manufacturing partners than as distributors. This technique has proven successful in industries where products are undergoing rapid change, such as personal computers. With this strategy, finished goods inventory is reduced because units are built to a shorter, more accurate forecast. Consequently, market response is better, with lower investment—a nice combination. Dell has successfully demonstrated the low-cost and rapid-response advantages of channel assembly, and IBM, H-P, and Compaq have all followed (see the *OM in Action* box on page 428 entitled, "IBM, H-P, and Compaq Move to Channel Assembly").

> **Channel assembly**
> Postpones final assembly of a product so the distribution channel can assemble it.

---

[10] Hau L. Lee and Corey Billington, "The Evolution of Supply-Chain-Management Models and Practice at Hewlett-Packard," *Interfaces* 25, no. 5 (September–October 1995): 42–63.

[11] M. Eric Johnson and Tom Davis, "Gaining an Edge with Supply Chain Management," *APICS: The Performance Advantage* 5, no. 12 (December 1995): 26–31.

> ## OM IN ACTION
>
> ### IBM, H-P, AND COMPAQ MOVE TO CHANNEL ASSEMBLY
>
> After some disastrous forecasting mistakes that either left the wrong personal computers (PCs) on dealer shelves or left dealers without the currently popular model, IBM, H-P, and Compaq have all moved to *channel assembly*. Because of rapid changes taking place in PCs—everything from monitors and processors to CD-ROMs and software—the PC industry is searching for ways to provide efficient mass customization.
>
> Bill Fairfield, CEO of Inacom Corp., an IBM distributor in Omaha, Nebraska, estimates that he can slash inventory by 50% and production time by 30% just by being able to build systems from scratch. In the past, he was often stuck with taking apart machines that IBM sent him and reconfiguring them to customer specifications. With 2,200 combinations of an IBM PC, as much as 80% of the units sent to distributors like Inacom had to be reconfigured before shipping to resellers. Channel assembly may be the answer. IBM built 50% of its units this way in 1998.
>
> The Inacom-IBM partnership should (1) increase flexibility by bringing new technology to market quickly, (2) make the right volume available when needed, and (3) reduce warranty claims and cost. Compaq believes in this approach so much that it recently cut prices 22% across the board. H-P's supply chain manager, Jeanne Wiseman, says, "The whole purpose is to work with our supply partners to reduce redundancies in the supply chain when these redundancies don't bring any value to our customer."
>
> The pace of change in the supply chain is increasing. The next step is to bypass a stop at the manufacturer for many of the components that the manufacturer traditionally purchases for its PCs so the components flow directly to the distributor. There is no point in double-shipping components.
>
> *Sources: VARBusiness* (September 15, 1997): pp. 80–100; and *Forbes* (March 24, 1997): p. 84.

Drop shipping Shipping directly from the supplier to the end consumer, rather than from the seller, saving both time and reshipping costs.

Drop Shipping and Special Packaging **Drop shipping** means the supplier will ship directly to the end consumer, rather than to the seller, saving both time and reshipping costs. Other cost-saving measures include the use of special packaging, labels, and optimal placement of labels and bar codes on containers. The final location down to the department and number of units in each shipping container can also be indicated. Substantial savings can be obtained through management techniques such as these. Some of these techniques can be of particular benefit to wholesalers and retailers by reducing shrinkage (lost, damaged, or stolen merchandise) and handling cost.

Blanket order A long-term purchase commitment to a supplier for items that are to be delivered against short-term releases to ship.

Blanket Orders Blanket orders are unfilled orders with a vendor.[12] A **blanket order** is a contract to purchase certain items from the vendor. It is not an authorization to ship anything. Shipment is made only upon receipt of an agreed-upon document, perhaps a shipping requisition or shipment release.

Invoiceless purchasing Units are paid for by the purchasing organization, without formal request by the supplier.

Invoiceless Purchasing **Invoiceless purchasing** is an extension of good purchaser-supplier relations. In an invoiceless purchasing environment, there is typically one supplier for all units of a particular product. If the supplier provides all four wheels for each lawn mower produced, then management knows how many wheels it purchased. It just multiplies the quantity of lawn mowers produced times four and issues a check to the supplier for that amount.

Electronic Ordering and Funds Transfer Electronic ordering and funds transfer reduce paper transactions. Paper transactions consist of a purchase order, a purchase release, a receiving document, authorization to pay an invoice (which is matched with the approved receiving report), and finally the issuance of a check. Purchasing departments

---

[12] Unfilled orders are also referred to as "open" orders or "incomplete" orders.

can reduce this barrage of paperwork by electronic ordering, acceptance of all parts as 100% good, and electronic funds transfer to pay for units received. Not only can electronic ordering reduce paperwork, but it also speeds up the traditionally long procurement cycle. General Motors has saved billions of dollars over the past few years through exactly this kind of electronic transfer.[13] See also the *OM in Action* box entitled "Streamlining the Supply Chain Moves Pampers Faster and Cuts Costs."

Transactions between firms are increasingly done via electronic data interchange. **Electronic data interchange (EDI)** is a standardized data-transmittal format for computerized communications between organizations. EDI provides data transfer for virtually any business application, including purchasing. Under EDI, for instance, data for a purchase order, such as order date, due date, quantity, part number, purchase order number, address, and so forth, are fitted into the standard EDI format.

A variation of EDI is **Advanced Shipping Notice (ASN),** which is a shipping notice delivered directly from vendor to purchaser. When the vendor is ready to ship, shipping labels are printed and the advanced shipping notice is created and transmitted to the purchaser. Both manufacturing and retail establishments are now using this technique.

Stockless Purchasing **Stockless purchasing** means that the supplier maintains inventory that is delivered directly to the purchaser's using department rather than to a stockroom. If the supplier can maintain the stock of inventory for a variety of customers who use the same product or whose differences are very minor (say, at the packaging stage), then there may be a net savings. Postponement and consignment inventories are related options.

Standardization The purchasing department should make special efforts to increase levels of **standardization:** That is, rather than obtaining a variety of similar components with labeling, coloring, packaging, or perhaps even slightly different engineering specifications, the purchasing agent should try to have those components standardized.

Other Techniques Under the umbrella of supply-chain management are a variety of other techniques. These include (1) establishing lines of credit for suppliers, (2) reducing bank "float" (the time money is in transit), (3) coordinating production and shipping schedules with suppliers and distributors, (4) sharing market research, and (5) making optimal use of warehouse space.

Electronic data interchange (EDI)
A standardized data-transmittal format for computerized communications between organizations.

Advanced Shipping Notice (ASN)
A shipping notice delivered directly from vendor to purchaser.

Stockless purchasing
Supplier delivers material directly to the purchaser's using department rather than to a central stockroom.

Standardization
Reducing the number of variations in materials and components as an aid to cost reduction.

MATERIALS MANAGEMENT

Purchasing may be combined with various warehousing and inventory activities to form a materials management system. The purpose of **materials management** is to obtain efficiency of operations through the integration of all material acquisition, movement, and storage activities. When transportation and inventory costs are substantial on both the input and output sides of the production process, an emphasis on materials management may be appropriate. The potential for competitive advantage is found via both reduced costs and improved customer service. Many manufacturing companies have moved to some form of materials management structure.

Firms recognize that the distribution of goods to and from their facilities can represent as much as 25% of the cost of products. In addition, the total distribution cost in the United States is over 10% of the gross national product (GNP).[14] Because of this high

Materials management
An approach that seeks efficiency of operations through the integration of all material acquisition, movement, and storage activities.

---

[13] See J. Carbonne, "G.M. After Lopez," *Electronic Business Buyer,* October 1993, pp. 56–60.

[14] Robert Millen, "JIT Logistics, Putting JIT on Wheels," *Target* 7, no. 2 (summer 1991). 4.

> **OM IN ACTION**
>
> ## STREAMLINING THE SUPPLY CHAIN MOVES PAMPERS FASTER AND CUTS COSTS
>
> Experts cite Procter & Gamble as a foremost example of how packaged goods and food manufacturers can work closely and form partnerships with major retailers to prune costs in the pipeline that connects manufacturers to consumers.
>
> Cutting inventories for both parties, smoothing out production schedules, and quickly identifying quality and service problems are the aims of these supply-chain partnerships. The identical benefits that automakers and other industrial companies have been reaping in recent years from just-in-time delivery arrangements with suppliers are exactly what they are looking for.
>
> Teams that mix data-processing experts, who automate order and record-keeping systems, with sales and purchasing representatives are assigned by companies like Procter & Gamble and Kmart to deal with each other.
>
> To help Procter & Gamble avoid sudden spikes and dips in orders for, say, Pampers, and coordinate delivery schedules with Kmart's warehouses, the companies' logistics managers share information. To coordinate Procter & Gamble's new product introductions with Kmart's promotional campaigns, marketing and finance managers share both up-to-date sales data on the latest promotions and long-range plans.
>
> "When we started looking at this," says Lawrence D. Milligan, P&G's senior vice president in charge of sales, "we saw a potential savings of $1 billion annually in the U.S. for Procter & Gamble and just as much, if not more, for our customers."
>
> Sources: *Fortune* (March 7, 1994): 74–80; and *Interfaces* (January–February 1997): 128–143.

cost, firms constantly evaluate their means of distribution. Five major means of distribution are trucking, railroads, airfreight, waterways, and pipelines.

Distribution Systems

Trucking The vast majority of manufactured goods moves by truck. The flexibility of shipping by truck is only one of its many advantages. Companies that have adopted JIT programs in recent years have put increased pressure on truckers to pick up and deliver on time, with no damage, with paperwork in order, and at low cost. Carriers such as Roadway Express and Skyway Freight Systems are now viewed as part of the chain of quality from supplier to processor to end customer. Trucking firms are increasingly using computers to monitor weather, find the most effective route, reduce fuel cost, and analyze the most efficient way to unload.[15]

Railroads Railroads in the United States employ 250,000 people and ship 60% of all coal, 67% of autos, 68% of paper products, and about one half of all food, lumber, and chemicals. Containerization has made intermodal shipping of truck trailers on railroad flat cars, often piggybacked as double-decks, a popular means of distribution. Over 4 million trailer loads are moved in the United States each year by rail. Norfolk and Southern uses piggybacked cars extensively to meet JIT demands of Detroit automakers. With the growth of JIT, however, rail transport has been the biggest loser because small-batch manufacture requires frequent, smaller shipments that are likely to move via truck or air.

Airfreight Airfreight represents only about 1% of tonnage shipped in the United States. However, the recent proliferation of airfreight carriers such as Federal Express, UPS, and Purolator makes it the fastest-growing mode of shipping. Clearly, for national and international movement of lightweight items such as medical and emergency supplies, flowers, fruits, and electronic components, airfreight offers speed and reliability.

---

[15] "New Gadgets Trace Truckers' Every Move," *The Wall Street Journal*, July 14, 1997, p. B1.

Waterways Waterways are one of the nation's oldest means of freight transportation, dating back to construction of the Erie Canal in 1817. Included in U.S. waterways are the nation's rivers, canals, the Great Lakes, coastlines, and oceans connecting to other countries. The usual cargo on waterways is bulky, low-value cargo such as iron ore, grains, cement, coal, chemicals, limestone, and petroleum products. This distribution system is important when shipping cost is more important than speed.

Pipelines Pipelines are an important form of transporting crude oil, natural gas, and other petroleum and chemical products. An amazing 90% of the state of Alaska's budget is derived from the 1.5 million barrels of oil pumped daily through the pipeline at Prudhoe Bay.

BENCHMARKING SUPPLY-CHAIN MANAGEMENT

As Table 11.6 shows, well-managed supply-chain relationships result in firms setting world-class benchmarks. Benchmark firms have driven down costs, lead times, late deliveries, and shortages, all while improving quality. Effective supply-chain management provides a competitive advantage by aiding firms in their response to a demanding global marketplace. Wal-Mart, for example, has developed a competitive edge by using supply-chain management. With its own fleet of 2,000 trucks, 19 distribution centers, and a satellite communication system, Wal-Mart (with the help of its suppliers) replenishes store shelves an average of twice per week. Competitors resupply every other week. Economical and speedy resupply means high levels of product availability and reductions in inventory investment.

TABLE 11.6 ■ Supply-Chain Performance Compared

	Typical Firms	Benchmark Firms
Number of suppliers per purchasing agent	34	5
Purchasing costs as percent of purchases	3.3%	.8%
Lead time (weeks)	15	8
Time spent placing an order	42 minutes	15 minutes
Percentage of late deliveries	33%	2%
Percentage of rejected material	1.5%	.0001%
Number of shortages per year	400	4

Source: Adapted from a McKinsey & Company report.

SUMMARY

A substantial portion of the cost and quality of the products of many firms, including most manufacturing, restaurant, wholesale, and retail firms, is determined by how efficiently they manage the supply chain. Consequently, supply-chain management provides a great opportunity for such firms to develop a competitive advantage. Supply-chain management is an approach to working with suppliers that includes not only purchasing but also a comprehensive approach to developing maximum value for the supply chain. Five purchasing strategies have been identified. They are (1) many suppliers, (2) few suppliers, (3) vertical integration, (4) keiretsu networks, and (5) virtual companies. Leading companies determine the right purchasing strategy and often develop a materials management organization to ensure effective warehousing and distribution.

KEY TERMS

Supply-chain management *(p. 416)*
Purchasing *(p. 419)*
Purchasing agent *(p. 419)*
Buyer *(p. 419)*
Make-or-buy decision *(p. 420)*
Vertical integration *(p. 422)*
Keiretsu *(p. 423)*
Virtual companies *(p. 424)*
Vendor selection *(p. 425)*
Negotiation strategies *(p. 426)*
Postponement *(p. 427)*
Channel assembly *(p. 427)*
Drop shipping *(p. 428)*
Blanket order *(p. 428)*
Invoiceless purchasing *(p. 428)*
Electronic data interchange (EDI) *(p. 429)*
Advanced Shipping Notice (ASN) *(p. 429)*
Stockless purchasing *(p. 429)*
Standardization *(p. 429)*
Materials management *(p. 429)*

DISCUSSION QUESTIONS

1. Under what conditions might a firm decide to organize its purchasing function as a materials management function?
2. What is a keiretsu?
3. What information does purchasing receive from other functional areas of the firm?
4. How does a traditional adversarial relationship with suppliers change when a firm makes a decision to move to a few suppliers?
5. What are the three basic approaches to negotiations?
6. What can purchasing do to implement just-in-time deliveries?
7. How does a traditional adversarial relationship with suppliers change when a firm decides to move to just-in-time deliveries?
8. How do we distinguish between supplier management, supply-chain management, purchasing, and materials management?
9. Both Brazil and Argentina have a strong labor union presence. What is the impact on unions in the VW approach to production described in the opening Global Company Profile?
10. What is the difference between postponement and channel assembly?
11. How does Wal-Mart use drop shipping?
12. What is vertical integration? Give examples of backward and forward integration.
13. What are blanket orders? How do they differ from invoiceless purchasing?

CRITICAL THINKING EXERCISE

What are the cultural impediments to establishing keiretsu networks in countries other than Japan? What would the antitrust division of the U.S. Department of Justice think of such arrangements? What would the European Community's position be on such arrangements? Find an example of a firm that has a keiretsu network and describe its effectiveness.

PROBLEMS

: 11.1 As a library or Internet assignment, identify organizations that are
   a) engaged in vertical integration
   b) engaged in reducing vertical integration
   c) moving toward "virtual" companies

: 11.2 As purchasing agent for Woolsey Enterprises in Golden, Colorado, you ask your buyer to provide you with a ranking of "excellent," "good," "fair," or "poor" for a variety of characteristics for two potential vendors. You suggest that the rankings be consistent with the vendor rating form shown in Figure 11.3 (p. 425). The buyer has returned the ranking shown below.

VENDOR RATING: DONNA INC. = D, KAY CORP. = K

Company	Excellent (4)	Good (3)	Fair (2)	Poor (1)
Size and/or Capacity		K	D	
Financial Strength			K	D
Operational Profit			K	D
Manufacturing Range			KD	
Research Facilities	K		D	
Technical Service		K	D	
Geographical Locations		K	D	
Management		K	D	
Labor Relations			K	D
Trade Relations			KD	

Service	Excellent (4)	Good (3)	Fair (2)	Poor (1)
Deliveries on Time		KD		
Condition on Arrival		KD		
Follow Instructions			D	K
Number of Rejections				KD
Handling of Complaints		KD		
Technical Assistance			K	D
Emergency Aid				KD
Supply Up-to-Date Catalogues, Etc.				KD
Supply Price Changes Promptly				KD

Products	Excellent (4)	Good (3)	Fair (2)	Poor (1)
Quality	KD			
Price			KD	
Packaging			KD	
Uniformity			KD	
Warranty			KD	

Sales Personnel	Excellent (4)	Good (3)	Fair (2)	Poor (1)
1. Knowledge				
His Company			D	K
His Products			K	D
Our Industry			KD	
Our Company			K	D
2. Sales Calls				
Properly Spaced			D	K
By Appointment				KD
Planned and Prepared			K	D
Mutually Productive			K	D
3. Sales Service				
Obtain Information			D	K
Furnish Quotations Promptly		K		D
Follow Orders			D	K
Expedite Delivery			K	D
Handle Complaints		KD		

Which of the two vendors would you select? (*Hint:* Figure 11.3 provides an excellent approach.)

- **11.3** Using the data in Problem 11.2, assume that both Donna Inc. and Kay Corp. are able to move all of their poor ratings from poor to fair. How would you then rank the two firms?
- **11.4** Determine the sales necessary to equal a dollar of savings on purchases for a company that has:
  - a) a net profit of 6% and spends 60% of its revenue on purchases.
  - b) a net profit of 8% and spends 80% of its revenue on purchases.

■ Case Study ■

Factory Enterprises, Inc.

Factory Enterprises, Inc., makes automobile air conditioners for car dealer installation. The firm owns the patents and makes the product at a sizable markup. As a result, the 20-year-old company pays its private owners very well.

The enterprise shows growth in overseas sales at the very time that domestic market demand is exploding. This exhausting situation calls for total effort by all company personnel: 8 managers and supervisors, 30 factory workers, and 6 office employees.

In addition to their regular duties, various people purchase materials and component parts. The production manager buys finned radiators and copper tubing. The shipping supervisor buys mounting assemblies, to which workers attach all of the component parts in the final process. The sales manager buys shipping cartons.

You have just joined the company as the purchasing manager.

Discussion Questions

1. Describe for the president the materials management concept. What would it do *for* the company and what would it do *to* the company?
2. What action steps would you follow to install the materials management concept if the president decides to adopt it?
3. Explain how sales and purchasing can help each other by establishing a good relationship.
4. European customers insist on ISO 9000 compliance. How should the company respond?

Source: Adapted from Gary J. Zenz, *Purchasing and the Management of Materials,* 7th ed. (New York: John Wiley, 1994), pp. 623–624.

■ Case Study ■

Thomas Manufacturing Company

Mr. Thomas, president of Thomas Manufacturing Company, and Mr. McDonnell, the vice president, were discussing how future economic conditions would affect their product, home air purifiers. They were particularly concerned about cost increases. They increased selling prices last year and thought another price increase would have an adverse affect on sales. They wondered if there was some way to reduce costs in order to maintain the existing price structure.

McDonnell had attended a purchasing association meeting the previous night and heard a presentation by the president of a tool company on how his firm was approaching cost reduction. The tool company had just hired a purchasing agent with a business degree who was reducing costs by 15%. McDonnell thought some of the ideas might be applicable to Thomas Manufacturing. The present purchasing agent, Mr. Older, had been with Thomas Manufacturing for 25 years, and management had no complaints. Production never stopped for lack of material. Yet a 15% cost reduction was something that could not be ignored. Thomas suggested that McDonnell look into this area and come up with a recommendation.

McDonnell contacted several business schools in the area. He said he would be interested in hiring a new graduate. One of the requirements for applicants was a paper on how to improve the company's purchasing function. Several applicants visited the plant and analyzed the purchasing department before they wrote their papers. The most dynamic paper was submitted by Tim Younger. He recommended:

1. Lower stock-reorder levels (from 60 days to 45 days) for many items, thus reducing inventory.
2. Analyze specifications on many parts.
3. Standardize many of the parts to reduce the variety of items.
4. Analyze items to see whether more products can be purchased by blanket purchase orders, with the ultimate goal of reducing the purchasing staff.
5. Look for new and lower-cost sources of supply.
6. Increase the number of requests for bids, to get still lower prices.
7. Be more aggressive in negotiations. Make fewer concessions.
8. Make sure that all trade, quantity, and cash discounts are taken.
9. Buy from the lowest-price source, disregarding local public relations.
10. Stop showing favoritism to customers who also buy from the company. Reciprocity comes second to price.
11. Purchase to current requirements rather than to market conditions; too much money is tied up in inventory.

After reading all the papers, McDonnell was debating with himself what he should recommend to Thomas. Just the previous week at the department meeting, Older was recommending many of the opposite actions. In particular, he recommended an increase in inventory levels in anticipation of future rising prices. Older also stressed the good relations that the company had with all its suppliers, who could be relied upon for good service and possible extensions of credit. Most of Thomas' suppliers bought their home air purifiers from Thomas Manufacturing. Yet Younger said that the practice of favoring them was wrong and should be eliminated. McDonnell was hesitant about what action he should recommend. Mr. Thomas wanted a decision in the morning.

Discussion Questions

1. What recommendation would you make if you were McDonnell? Why?
2. Analyze each of Younger's recommendations. Do you agree or disagree with them? Why?

Source: Professor Richard J. Tersine, University of Oklahoma.

Video Case 6

Supply Chain Management at Regal Marine

Like most manufacturers, Regal Marine finds that it must spend a huge portion of its revenue on purchases. Regal has also found that the better its suppliers understand its end users, the better both supplier's product and Regal's final product. As one of the ten largest U.S. power boat manufacturers, Regal is trying to differentiate its products from the vast number of boats supplied by 300 other companies. Thus, the Orlando firm works closely with suppliers to ensure innovation, quality, and timely delivery.

Regal has done a number of things to drive down costs while driving up quality, responsiveness, and innovation. First, working on partnering relationships with suppliers ranging from providers of windshields to providers of instrument panel controls, Regal has brought timely innovation at reasonable cost to its product. Key vendors are so tightly linked with the company that they meet with designers to discuss material changes to be incorporated into new product designs.

Second, the company has joined about 15 other boat manufacturers in a purchasing group, known as American Boat Builders Association, to work with suppliers on reducing the costs of large purchases. Third, Regal is working with a number of local vendors to supply hardware and fasteners directly to the assembly line on a just-in-time basis. In some of these cases, Regal has worked out an arrangement with the vendor so that title does not transfer until parts are used by Regal. In other cases, title transfers when items are delivered to the property. This practice drives down total inventory and the costs associated with large-lot delivery.

Finally, Regal works with an Orlando personnel agency to outsource part of the recruiting and screening process for employees. In all these cases, Regal is demonstrating innovative approaches to supply chain management that help the firm and, ultimately, the end user. The *Global Company Profile* featuring Regal Marine (which opens chapter 6) provides further background on Regal's operations.

Discussion Questions

1. What other techniques might be used by Regal to improve supply chain management?
2. What kind of response might members of the supply chain expect from Regal in response to their "partnering" in the supply chain?
3. Why is supply chain management important to Regal?

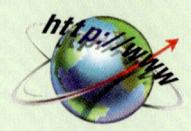

■ *Internet Case Studies* ■

See our Internet home page at http://www.prenhall.com/heizer for these additional case studies: AT&T Buys a Printer, and Blue and Gray, Inc.

BIBLIOGRAPHY

Akinc, U. "Selecting a Set of Vendors in a Manufacturing Environment." *Journal of Operations Management* 11, no. 2 (June 1993): 107–122.

Arnold, J. R. T. *Introduction to Material Management,* 2nd ed. Upper Saddle River, NJ: Prentice-Hall, 1996.

Bhote, K. *Supply Management: How to Make U.S. Suppliers Competitive*. New York: American Management Association, 1987.

Blumenfeld, D. E., L. D. Burns, C. F. Daganzo, M. C. Frick, and R. W. Hall. "Reducing Logistics Costs at General Motors." *Interfaces* 17 (January–February 1987): 26–47.

Bridleman, Dan, and Jeff Herrmann. "Supply Chain Management in a Make-to-Order World." *APICS* 7, no. 3 (March 1997): 32–38.

Burns, Kay. "Supplier Managed Inventory Sweeps Through Shell Chemical." *APICS* 7, no. 10 (October 1997): 34–39.

Burt, D. N., and W. R. Soukup. "Purchasing's Role in New Product Development." *Harvard Business Review* 63 (September–October 1985): 90–97.

Casey, Jeff T. "Predicting Buyer-Seller Pricing Disparities." *Management Science* 41, no. 6 (June 1995): 979–999.

Chesbrough, Henry W., and David J. Teece. "When Is Virtual Virtuous? Organizing for Innovation." *Harvard Business Review* (January–February 1996): 65–73.

Cleaves, Gerard W., and Vladimir A. Masch. "Strengthening Weak Links." *OR/MS Today* 23, no. 2 (April 1996): 32–37.

Copacino, William C. *Supply Chain Management*. St. Lucie Press, 1997.

Geoffrion, Arthur M., and Richard C. Grimes. "Twenty Years of Strategic Distribution System Design: An Evolutionary Perspective." *Interfaces* 25, no. 5 (1995).

Gumaer, Robert. "Synchronizing the Supply Chain." *APICS* 7, no. 1 (January 1997): 46–49.

Lee, Hau L., V. Padmanabhan, and Seungjin Whang. "Information Distortion in a Supply Chain: The Bullwhip Effect." *Management Science* 43, no. 4 (April 1997): 546–558.

Levy, David L. "Lean Production in an International Supply Chain." *Sloan Management Review*. 38, no. 2 (winter 1997): 94–101.

Lewis, Jordan D. *The Connected Corporation: How Leading Companies Win Through Customer-Supplier Alliances.* New York: The Free Press, 1996.

Magad, B. L., and J. M. Ames. *Total Material Management,* 2nd ed. New York: Chapman and Hall, 1995.

Metters, Richard. "Quantifying the Bullwhip Effect in Supply Chains." *Journal of Operations Management* 15, no. 2 (1997): 89–100.

Min, Hokey, and Dooyoung Shin. "A Group Technology Classification and Coding System for Value-Added Purchasing." *Production and Inventory Management Journal* 35, no. 1 (first quarter 1994).

Ross, David S. "Meeting the Challenge of Supply Chain Management." *APICS* 6, no. 9 (September 1996): 38–43.

Stein, Tom. "Orders from Chaos." *Information Week,* June 23, 1997, pp. 44–53.

INTERNET RESOURCES

Logistics Information on the Web:
  http://www.dsii.com/link1.html
Northwestern University Logistics Page:
  http://www.kellogg.nwu.edu/faculty/anupind:/ftp/omd55/logistics/download.html

Purchasing Magazine Web Site:
  http://www.manufacturing.net/magazine/purchasing/
American Supplier Institute:
  http://www.amsup.com

Inventory Management 12

CHAPTER OUTLINE

GLOBAL COMPANY PROFILE: HARLEY-DAVIDSON

FUNCTIONS OF INVENTORY
   Types of Inventory

INVENTORY MANAGEMENT
   ABC Analysis
   Record Accuracy
   Cycle Counting
   Control of Services Inventory

INVENTORY MODELS
   Independent versus Dependent Demand
   Holding, Ordering, and Setup Costs

INVENTORY MODELS FOR INDEPENDENT DEMAND
   The Basic Economic Order Quantity (EOQ) Model
   Minimizing Costs
   Reorder Points
   Production Order Quantity Model
   Quantity Discount Models

PROBABILISTIC MODELS WITH CONSTANT LEAD TIME

FIXED-PERIOD SYSTEMS

SUMMARY

KEY TERMS

USING POM FOR WINDOWS TO SOLVE INVENTORY PROBLEMS

USING EXCEL OM FOR INVENTORY

SOLVED PROBLEMS

DISCUSSION QUESTIONS

CRITICAL THINKING EXERCISE

PROBLEMS

CASE STUDIES: STURDIVANT SOUND SYSTEMS; LAPLACE POWER AND LIGHT

VIDEO CASE 7: INVENTORY CONTROL AT WHEELED COACH

INTERNET CASE STUDIES

BIBLIOGRAPHY

INTERNET RESOURCES

LEARNING OBJECTIVES

When you complete this chapter you should be able to:

Identify or Define:
   ABC analysis
   Record accuracy
   Cycle counting
   Independent and dependent demand
   Holding, ordering, and setup costs

Describe or Explain:
   The functions of inventory and basic inventory models

🌐 GLOBAL COMPANY PROFILE:

Inventory Control Brings a Competitive Advantage to Harley-Davidson

Harley-Davidson was founded in Milwaukee in 1903. Since that time, it has competed with hundreds of manufacturers, foreign and domestic. The competition has been tough, especially with the Japanese. Indeed, after nine decades, Harley is one of the few motorcycle companies still producing in the United States.

The Japanese motorcycle invasion of the 1970s caught Harley in the cross fire between Honda and Yamaha. The competition was so intense that Honda introduced 81 new models and Yamaha 34 in only 18 months. To meet the challenge, Harley-Davidson management emphasized quality improvement.

An emphasis on quality is a marvelous tonic for any management: It requires tighter inventory control, just-in-time techniques, product and process improvements, and a host of other modern manufacturing methods. However, mostly it means a total quality-control program driven by inventory-control policies.

By using JIT, Harley eliminated large parts inventories, along with their inherent problems and high costs. Now, management insists on delivery of small quantities of parts—with no defects—to the assembly line. The concept applies to suppliers as well as employees within Harley-Davidson itself. Indeed, Harley is so good at supplier development that it now does consulting in this area for other firms.

Most containers at Harley are specially made for individual parts, and many feature padding to protect the finish. Containers serve an important role in inventory reduction: Because they are the only place inventory is stored on the assembly line, they serve as a signal to supply new parts to the line. After all the pieces have been removed, the container is returned to its originating cell, signaling the worker there to build more.

438

HARLEY-DAVIDSON

Completed Harleys coming from the assembly line in preparation for a series of 28 tests and inspections.

Here a quick change fixture is used to hold fenders for laser-trimming. Harley workers have standardized die and fixture setups and located them near the machine where they will be used. An operator simply rolls up the next fixture or die and sets up for the next job in an average of 12 minutes, saving an average of 30 minutes over Harley's earlier processes. With more than 500 operations requiring such setups, the savings is substantial enough to give Harley a competitive edge.

440   CHAPTER 12   INVENTORY MANAGEMENT

Inventory investment: your company's largest asset.

As Harley-Davidson well knows, inventory is one of the most expensive assets of many companies, representing as much as 40% of total invested capital. Operations managers around the globe have long recognized that good inventory management is crucial. On the one hand, a firm can reduce costs by reducing on-hand inventory levels. On the other hand, production may stop and customers become dissatisfied when an item is out of stock. Thus, companies must strike a balance between inventory investment and customer service. You can never achieve a low-cost strategy without good inventory management.

All organizations have some type of inventory planning and control system. A bank has methods to control its inventory of cash. A hospital has methods to control blood supplies and pharmaceuticals. Government agencies, schools, and, of course, virtually every manufacturing and production organization are concerned with inventory planning and control.

In cases of physical products, the organization must determine whether to produce goods or to purchase them. Once this decision has been made, the next step is to forecast demand, as discussed in chapter 5. Then operations managers determine the inventory necessary to service that demand. In this chapter, we discuss the functions, types, and management of inventory. We then address two basic inventory issues: how much to order and when to order.

FUNCTIONS OF INVENTORY

TEN DECISIONS OF OM
Managing Quality
Design of Goods & Services
Process Strategy
Location Strategies
Layout Strategies
Human Resources
Supply-Chain Management
Inventory Management
  Independent Demand
  Dependent Demand
Scheduling
Maintenance

Inventory can serve several functions that add flexibility to a firm's operations. The six functions of inventory are:

1. To provide a stock of goods to *meet anticipated customer demand* and provide a "selection" of goods.
2. To *decouple suppliers from production and production from distribution.* For example, if a firm's supplies fluctuate, extra raw materials of inventory may be needed to "decouple" production processes from suppliers. Similarly, if product demand is high only during the summer, a firm may build up stock during the winter and thus avoid the costs of shortages and stockouts in the summer. Such a procedure "decouples" production from distribution.
3. To take advantage of *quantity discounts,* because purchases in larger quantities may reduce the cost of goods or delivery.
4. To *hedge against inflation* and upward price changes.
5. To *protect against delivery variation* due to weather, supplier shortages, quality problems, or improper deliveries. "Safety stocks"—namely, extra goods on hand—reduce the risk of shortages.
6. To *permit operations to continue smoothly* with the use of "work-in-process" inventory (goods that have been moved partway through production). These inventories exist because there may be disruptions in various stages of the production process.

Types of Inventory

To accomodate the functions of inventory, firms maintain four types of inventories. The types are: (1) raw material inventory, (2) work-in-process inventory, (3) maintenance/repair/operating supply (MRO) inventory, and (4) finished goods inventory.

Raw material inventory
Materials that are usually purchased but have yet to enter the manufacturing process.

Raw material inventory has been purchased but not processed. These items can be used to decouple (i.e., separate) suppliers from the production process. However, the preferred approach is to eliminate supplier variability in quality, quantity, or delivery time so

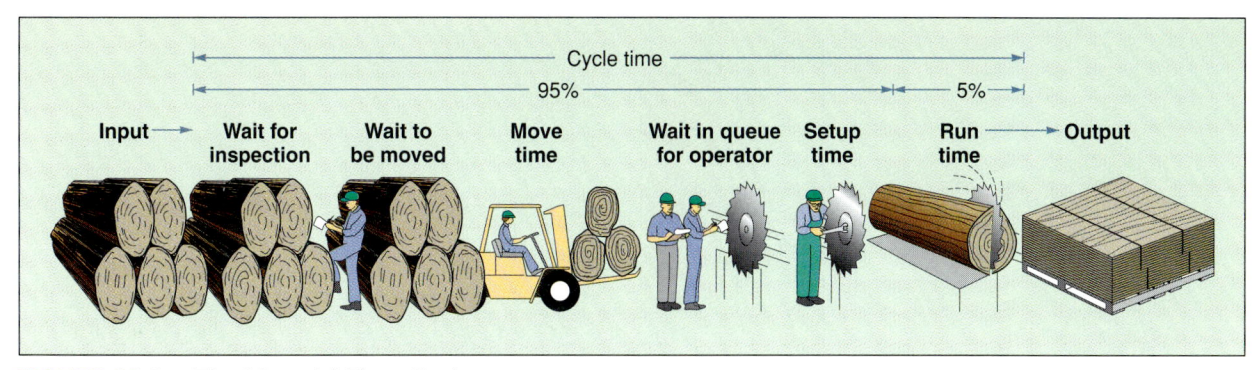

FIGURE 12.1 ■ **The Material Flow Cycle** *Most of the time that work is in-process (95% of the cycle time) is not productive time.*

that separation is not needed. **Work-in-process (WIP) inventory** are components or raw material that has undergone some change but is not completed. WIP exists because of the time it takes for a product to be made (called *cycle time*). Reducing cycle time reduces inventory. Often this task is not difficult: During most of the time a product is "being made," it is in fact sitting idle. As Figure 12.1 shows, actual work time or "run" time is a small portion of the material flow time, perhaps as low as 5%.

MROs are inventories devoted to **maintenance/repair/operating** supplies necessary to keep machinery and processes productive. They exist because the need and timing for maintenance and repair of some equipment are unknown. Although the demand for MRO inventories is often a function of maintenance schedules, other unscheduled MRO demands must be anticipated. However, **finished goods inventory** is completed product awaiting shipment. Finished goods may be inventoried because future customer demands are unknown.

Work-in-process inventory Incomplete products or components of products that are no longer considered raw material but have yet to become finished products.

MRO Maintenance, repair, and operating materials.

Finished goods inventory An end item ready to be sold, but still an asset on the company's books.

INVENTORY MANAGEMENT

Operations managers establish systems for managing inventory. In this section, we briefly examine two ingredients of such systems. (1) how inventory items can be classified (called *ABC analysis*) and (2) how accurate inventory records can be maintained. We will then look at inventory control in the service sector.

ABC Analysis

ABC analysis divides on-hand inventory into three classifications on the basis of annual dollar volume.[1] ABC analysis is an inventory application of what is known as the Pareto principle. The Pareto principle states that there are a "critical few and trivial many."[2] The idea is to establish inventory policies that focus resources on the *few critical* inventory parts and not the many trivial ones. It is not realistic to monitor inexpensive items with the same intensity as very expensive items.

To determine annual dollar volume for ABC analysis, we measure the *annual demand* of each inventory item times the *cost per unit*. *Class A* items are those on which the annual dollar volume is high. Although such items may represent only about 15% of the total inventory items, they represent 70% to 80% of the total dollar usage. *Class B* items are those inventory items of medium annual dollar volume. These items may represent

ABC analysis A method for dividing on-hand inventory into three classifications based on annual dollar volume.

---
[1] H. Ford Dickie, *Modern Manufacturing* (formerly *Factory Management and Maintenance*), July 1951.
[2] After Vilfredo Pareto, nineteenth-century Italian economist.

442 CHAPTER 12 INVENTORY MANAGEMENT

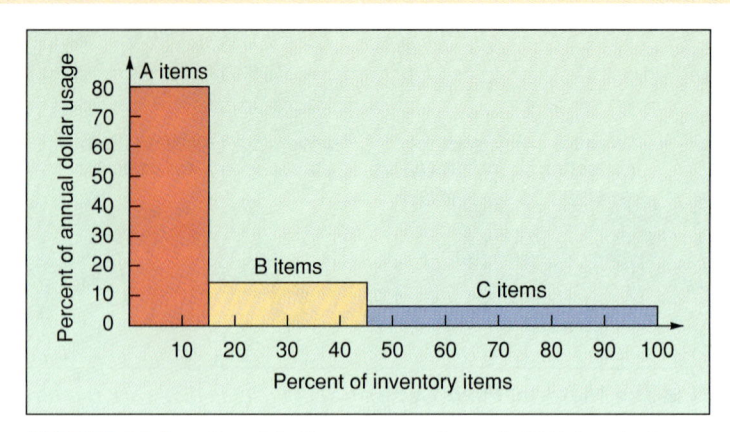

FIGURE 12.2 ■ Graphic Representation of ABC Analysis

Most automated inventory management systems include ABC analysis.

about 30% of inventory items and 15% to 25% of the total value. Those with low annual dollar volume are *Class C*, which may represent only 5% of the annual dollar volume but about 55% of the total inventory items.

Graphically, the inventory of many organizations would appear as presented in Figure 12.2. An example of the use of ABC analysis is shown in Example 1.

EXAMPLE 1

Silicon Chips, Inc., maker of super-fast DRAM chips, has organized its 10 inventory items on an annual dollar-volume basis. Shown below are the items (identified by stock number), their annual demand, unit cost, annual dollar volume, and the percentage of the total represented by each item. In the table below, we show these items grouped into ABC classifications:

ABC Calculation

Item Stock Number	Percent of Number of Items Stocked	Annual Volume (units)	× Unit Cost	= Annual Dollar Volume	Percent of Annual Dollar Volume		Class
#10286	} 20%	1,000	$ 90.00	$ 90,000	38.8% }	72%	A
#11526		500	154.00	77,000	33.2%		A
#12760	} 30%	1,550	17.00	26,350	11.3% }	23%	B
#10867		350	42.86	15,001	6.4%		B
#10500		1,000	12.50	12,500	5.4%		B
#12572	} 50%	600	$ 14.17	8,502	3.7% }	5%	C
#14075		2,000	.60	1,200	.5%		C
#01036		100	8.50	850	.4%		C
#01307		1,200	.42	504	.2%		C
#10572		250	.60	150	.1%		C
		8,550		$232,057	100.0%		

Criteria other than annual dollar volume can determine item classification. For instance, anticipated engineering changes, delivery problems, quality problems, or high unit cost may dictate upgrading items to a higher classification. The advantage of dividing inventory items into classes allows policies and controls to be established for each class.

OM IN ACTION

KMART'S REMOTE CONTROL INVENTORY CONTROL

Bar codes are old hat in retailing. But top American stores, like Kmart, are learning to apply their bar-code data in ways that radically change inventory control.

Employees at Kmart scurry around the aisles with hand-held lasers to zap bar-coded labels on products still sitting on the shelf. A display window on the laser, which is called a "remote maintenance unit," provides an instant scorecard. It shows how many units of the product ought to be on the shelf, how many are still in the stockroom, and the minimum number that the store should have on hand. It also reports whether an order has already been placed, what the price is, and whether that price is a sale or nonsale price.

Take, for example, Kmart's store at Auburn Hills, near Detroit. Bar codes scanned at checkout counters are recorded in the store's point-of-sales computer. They are *also* sent by satellite to Kmart's head office in Troy, Michigan. Troy logs the information for research purposes and then retransmits it to an inventory-distribution center, where more computers decide reorder points and what restocking is needed at Auburn Hills. Fresh stock arrives within 48 hours.

About 90% of everything Kmart sells is now subject to this centralized merchandising system. Staff at the stores is left managing the other 10%, usually fast-changing items like greeting cards.

Systems like this one are transforming retailing by keeping track of shoppers' preferences daily, enabling headquarters staff to predict selling trends more accurately than an individual store manager could do. For example, data showed that Kmart would do much better promoting a special line of soft toys by selling them next to infant's clothes instead of in the toy section.

Sources: Computerworld (December 16, 1996): 8; *The Economist* (May 29, 1993): 90–91; and *Chain Store Age* (January, 1994): 21–25.

Policies that may be based on ABC analysis include the following:

1. Purchasing resources expended on supplier development should be much higher for individual A items than for C items.
2. A items, as opposed to B and C items, should have tighter physical inventory control; perhaps they belong in a more secure area, and perhaps the accuracy of inventory records for A items should be verified more frequently.
3. Forecasting A items may warrant more care than forecasting other items.

Better forecasting, physical control, supplier reliability, and an ultimate reduction in safety stock can all result from appropriate inventory management policies. ABC analysis guides the development of those policies.

Record Accuracy

Good inventory policies are meaningless if management does not know what inventory is on hand. Accuracy of records is a critical ingredient in production and inventory systems. Record accuracy allows organizations to focus on those items that are needed, rather than settling for being sure that "some of everything" is in inventory. Only when an organization can determine accurately what it has on hand can it make precise decisions about ordering, scheduling, and shipping.

To ensure accuracy, incoming and outgoing record keeping must be good, as must be stockroom security. A well-organized stockroom will have limited access, good housekeeping, and storage areas that hold fixed amounts of inventory. Bins, shelf space, and parts will be labeled accurately. Kmart's approach to improved inventory record accuracy is discussed in the *OM in Action* box entitled "Kmart's Remote Control Inventory Control."

Cycle Counting

Cycle counting
A continuing reconciliation of inventory with inventory records.

Even though an organization may have made substantial efforts to record inventory accurately, these records must be verified through a continuing audit. Such audits are known as **cycle counting.** Historically, many firms performed annual physical inventories. This practice often meant shutting down the facility and having inexperienced people count parts and material. Inventory records should instead be verified via cycle counting. Cycle counting uses inventory classifications developed through ABC analysis. With cycle counting procedures, items are counted, records are verified, and inaccuracies are periodically documented. The cause of inaccuracies is then traced and appropriate remedial action taken to ensure integrity of the inventory system. A items will be counted frequently, perhaps once a month; B items will be counted less frequently, perhaps once a quarter; and C items will be counted perhaps once every 6 months. Example 2 illustrates how to compute the number of items of each classification to be counted each day.

EXAMPLE 2

Cole's Trucks, Inc., a builder of high-quality refuse trucks, has about 5,000 items in its inventory. After hiring Matt Clark, a bright young OM student, for the summer, the firm determined that it has 500 A items, 1,750 B items, and 2,750 C items. Company policy is to count all A items every month (every 20 working days), all B items every quarter (every 60 working days), and all C items every 6 months (every 120 working days). How many items should be counted each day?

Item Class	Quantity	Cycle Counting Policy	Number of Items Counted per Day
A	500	Each month (20 working days)	500/20 = 25/day
B	1,750	Each quarter (60 working days)	1,750/60 = 29/day
C	2,750	Every 6 months (120 working days)	2,750/120 = 23/day
			77/day

Seventy-seven items are counted each day.

In Example 2, the particular items to be cycle-counted can be sequentially or randomly selected each day. Another option is to cycle-count items when they are reordered.

Cycle counting also has the following advantages:

1. Eliminating the shutdown and interruption of production necessary for annual physical inventories;
2. Eliminating annual inventory adjustments;
3. Providing trained personnel to audit the accuracy of inventory;
4. Allowing the cause of the errors to be identified and remedial action to be taken;
5. Maintaining accurate inventory records.

Control of Service Inventories

Management of service inventories deserves some special consideration. Although we may think of services as not having inventory, that is not the case. For instance, extensive inventory is held in wholesale and retail businesses, making inventory management crucial. In the food-service business, for example, control of inventory can make the difference between success and failure. Moreover, inventory that is in transit or idle in a warehouse is lost value. Similarly, inventory damaged or stolen prior to sale is a loss. In

INVENTORY MANAGEMENT

> ## OM IN ACTION
>
> ### A TURN OF THE LISTERINE SKU
>
> Inventory identification and accurate records are revolutionizing inventory control at Wal-Mart and almost every other retailer. Wal-Mart Stores, the world's largest retailer, has invested one-half billion dollars annually over the past 3 years to automate inventory management. The objective is to have the right material in the right place at the right time. Through stock keeping units (SKUs), items are identified as they arrive at the store and as they are sold. With a single scan at the point of purchase, a continuous stream of information is provided to both Wal-Mart and Listerine manufacturer Warner-Lambert.
>
> When the universal product code (represented by a series of vertical bars) is scanned, the following information is written to the Wal-Mart database: SKU number, name of product, size of product, selling price, and cost.
>
> Locator Program: If the store anticipates a shortage (a stockout), store clerks or managers can, with a handheld computer, use Wal-Mart's *Item Locator Program* to find inventory elsewhere. Then a phone call is made to request the SKU.
>
> Data Transmission: Data are transmitted to and from Wal-Mart's home office several times a day. When some special event—say national news about a product—occurs, store managers and company executives can order changes in displays, pricing, or shipments.
>
> Retail Link: The data base is connected with 2,500 of Wal-Mart's 10,000 suppliers, including Warner-Lambert. To help both Wal-Mart and suppliers adjust to shifting demand, 65 weeks of sales data for each item are maintained.
>
> Forecasting: To further improve coordination between Wal-Mart and its suppliers, forecasting is being refined to address seasonal trends. In some instances, inventory has been cut in half.
>
> Sources: *Datamation* (November, 1996) 48; and *The New York Times Magazine* (April 6, 1997): S6.

retailing, inventory that is unaccounted for between receipt and time of sale is known as **shrinkage**. Shrinkage occurs from damage and theft as well as sloppy paperwork. In the retail business, theft is also known as **pilferage**. Retail inventory losses of 1% of sales is considered good, with losses in many stores exceeding 3%. Because the impact on profitability is substantial, inventory accuracy and control are critical. Applicable techniques include the following:

1. Good personnel selection, training, and discipline. These are never easy, but very necessary in food service, wholesale, and retail operations, where employees have access to directly consumable merchandise.
2. Tight control of incoming shipments. This task is being addressed by many firms through the use of bar-code systems that read every incoming shipment and automatically check tallies against purchase orders. When properly designed, these systems are very hard to defeat. Each item has its own stock keeping unit (SKU), pronounced "skew."
3. Effective control of all goods leaving the facility. This job is done with bar codes on items being shipped, magnetic strips on merchandise, or via direct observation. Direct observation can be personnel stationed at exits and in potentially high-loss areas or can take the form of one-way mirrors and video surveillance.

The *OM in Action* box "A Turn of the Listerine SKU" provides a look at how accurate product coding can aid record keeping and reduce inventory and shrinkage, while improving product availability.

Shrinkage Retail inventory that is unaccounted for between receipt and sale.

Pilferage A small amount of theft.

INVENTORY MODELS

We now examine a variety of inventory models and the costs associated with them.

Independent versus Dependent Demand

Inventory control models assume that demand for an item is either independent of or dependent on the demand for other items. For example, the demand for refrigerators is *independent* of the demand for toaster ovens. However, the demand for toaster oven components is *dependent* on the requirements of toaster ovens.

This chapter focuses on managing inventory where demand is *independent*. Chapter 14 presents *dependent* demand management.

Holding, Ordering, and Setup Costs

Holding costs are the costs associated with holding or "carrying" inventory over time. Therefore, holding costs also include obsolescence and costs related to storage, such as insurance, extra staffing, and interest payments. Table 12.1 shows the kinds of costs that need to be evaluated to determine holding costs. Many firms fail to include all of the inventory holding costs. Consequently, inventory holding costs are often understated.[3]

Ordering cost includes costs of supplies, forms, order processing, clerical support, and so forth. When orders are being manufactured, ordering costs also exist, but they are a part of what is called setup costs. **Setup cost** is the cost to prepare a machine or process for manufacturing an order. This includes time and labor to clean and change tools or holders. Operations managers can lower ordering costs by reducing setup costs and by using such efficient procedures as electronic ordering and payment.

> **Holding cost** The cost to keep or carry inventory in stock.

> **Ordering cost** The cost of the ordering process.

> **Setup cost** The cost to prepare a machine or process for production.

TABLE 12.1 ■ Determining Inventory Holding Costs

Category	Cost as a Percent of Inventory Value
Housing costs, such as building rent, depreciation, operating cost, taxes, insurance	6% (3–10%)
Material handling costs, including equipment, lease or depreciation, power, operating cost	3% (1–3.5%)
Labor cost from extra handling	3% (3–5%)
Investment costs, such as borrowing costs, taxes, and insurance on inventory	11% (6–24%)
Pilferage, scrap, and obsolescence	3% (2–5%)
Overall carrying cost	26%

Note: All numbers are approximate, as they vary substantially depending on the nature of the business, location, and current interest rates. Any inventory holding cost of less than 15% is suspect, but annual inventory holding costs often approach 40% of the value of inventory.

> **Setup time** The time required to prepare a machine or process for production.

In many environments, setup cost is highly correlated with **setup time.** Setups usually require a substantial amount of work prior to setup actually being performed at the work center. With proper planning much of the preparation required by a setup can be done prior to shutting down the machine or process. Setup times can thus be reduced substan-

---

[3] Jack G. Wacker, "Can Holding Costs Be Overstated for 'Just-in-Time' Manufacturing System?" *Production and Inventory Management* 27 (third quarter 1986): 11–14.

OM IN ACTION

A TURN OF THE LISTERINE SKU

Inventory identification and accurate records are revolutionizing inventory control at Wal-Mart and almost every other retailer. Wal-Mart Stores, the world's largest retailer, has invested one-half billion dollars annually over the past 3 years to automate inventory management. The objective is to have the right material in the right place at the right time. Through stock keeping units (SKUs), items are identified as they arrive at the store and as they are sold. With a single scan at the point of purchase, a continuous stream of information is provided to both Wal-Mart and Listerine manufacturer Warner-Lambert.

When the universal product code (represented by a series of vertical bars) is scanned, the following information is written to the Wal-Mart database: SKU number, name of product, size of product, selling price, and cost.

Locator Program. If the store anticipates a shortage (a stockout), store clerks or managers can, with a handheld computer, use Wal-Mart's *Item Locator Program* to find inventory elsewhere. Then a phone call is made to request the SKU.

Data Transmission: Data are transmitted to and from Wal-Mart's home office several times a day. When some special event—say national news about a product—occurs, store managers and company executives can order changes in displays, pricing, or shipments.

Retail Link: The data base is connected with 2,500 of Wal-Mart's 10,000 suppliers, including Warner-Lambert. To help both Wal-Mart and suppliers adjust to shifting demand, 65 weeks of sales data for each item are maintained.

Forecasting: To further improve coordination between Wal-Mart and its suppliers, forecasting is being refined to address seasonal trends. In some instances, inventory has been cut in half.

Sources: Datamation (November, 1996) 48; and *The New York Times Magazine* (April 6, 1997): S6.

---

retailing, inventory that is unaccounted for between receipt and time of sale is known as **shrinkage**. Shrinkage occurs from damage and theft as well as sloppy paperwork. In the retail business, theft is also known as **pilferage**. Retail inventory losses of 1% of sales is considered good, with losses in many stores exceeding 3%. Because the impact on profitability is substantial, inventory accuracy and control are critical. Applicable techniques include the following:

1. Good personnel selection, training, and discipline. These are never easy, but very necessary in food service, wholesale, and retail operations, where employees have access to directly consumable merchandise.
2. Tight control of incoming shipments. This task is being addressed by many firms through the use of bar-code systems that read every incoming shipment and automatically check tallies against purchase orders. When properly designed, these systems are very hard to defeat. Each item has its own stock keeping unit (SKU), pronounced "skew."
3. Effective control of all goods leaving the facility. This job is done with bar codes on items being shipped, magnetic strips on merchandise, or via direct observation. Direct observation can be personnel stationed at exits and in potentially high-loss areas or can take the form of one-way mirrors and video surveillance.

The *OM in Action* box "A Turn of the Listerine SKU" provides a look at how accurate product coding can aid record keeping and reduce inventory and shrinkage, while improving product availability.

Shrinkage Retail inventory that is unaccounted for between receipt and sale.

Pilferage A small amount of theft.

INVENTORY MODELS

We now examine a variety of inventory models and the costs associated with them.

Independent versus Dependent Demand

Inventory control models assume that demand for an item is either independent of or dependent on the demand for other items. For example, the demand for refrigerators is *independent* of the demand for toaster ovens. However, the demand for toaster oven components is *dependent* on the requirements of toaster ovens.

This chapter focuses on managing inventory where demand is *independent*. Chapter 14 presents *dependent* demand management.

Holding, Ordering, and Setup Costs

Holding costs are the costs associated with holding or "carrying" inventory over time. Therefore, holding costs also include obsolescence and costs related to storage, such as insurance, extra staffing, and interest payments. Table 12.1 shows the kinds of costs that need to be evaluated to determine holding costs. Many firms fail to include all of the inventory holding costs. Consequently, inventory holding costs are often understated.[3]

Ordering cost includes costs of supplies, forms, order processing, clerical support, and so forth. When orders are being manufactured, ordering costs also exist, but they are a part of what is called setup costs. **Setup cost** is the cost to prepare a machine or process for manufacturing an order. This includes time and labor to clean and change tools or holders. Operations managers can lower ordering costs by reducing setup costs and by using such efficient procedures as electronic ordering and payment.

> **Holding cost** The cost to keep or carry inventory in stock.
>
> **Ordering cost** The cost of the ordering process.
>
> **Setup cost** The cost to prepare a machine or process for production.

TABLE 12.1 ■ Determining Inventory Holding Costs

Category	Cost as a Percent of Inventory Value
Housing costs, such as building rent, depreciation, operating cost, taxes, insurance	6% (3–10%)
Material handling costs, including equipment, lease or depreciation, power, operating cost	3% (1–3.5%)
Labor cost from extra handling	3% (3–5%)
Investment costs, such as borrowing costs, taxes, and insurance on inventory	11% (6–24%)
Pilferage, scrap, and obsolescence	3% (2–5%)
Overall carrying cost	26%

Note: All numbers are approximate, as they vary substantially depending on the nature of the business, location, and current interest rates. Any inventory holding cost of less than 15% is suspect, but annual inventory holding costs often approach 40% of the value of inventory.

> **Setup time** The time required to prepare a machine or process for production.

In many environments, setup cost is highly correlated with **setup time.** Setups usually require a substantial amount of work prior to setup actually being performed at the work center. With proper planning much of the preparation required by a setup can be done prior to shutting down the machine or process. Setup times can thus be reduced substan-

---

[3] Jack G. Wacker, "Can Holding Costs Be Overstated for 'Just-in-Time' Manufacturing System?" *Production and Inventory Management* 27 (third quarter 1986): 11–14.

tially. Machines and processes that traditionally have taken hours to set up are now being set up in less than a minute by the more imaginative world-class manufacturers. As we shall see later in this chapter, reducing setup times is an excellent way to reduce inventory investment and to improve productivity.

INVENTORY MODELS FOR INDEPENDENT DEMAND

In this section, we introduce three inventory models that address two important questions: *when to order* and *how much to order*. These *independent* demand models are:

1. Basic economic order quantity (EOQ) model.
2. Production order quantity model.
3. Quantity discount model.

The Basic Economic Order Quantity (EOQ) Model

The **economic order quantity (EOQ) model** is one of the oldest and most commonly known inventory-control techniques.[4] This technique is relatively easy to use but is based on several assumptions:

1. Demand is known, constant, and independent.
2. *Lead time*—that is, the time between placement and receipt of the order—is known and constant.
3. Receipt of inventory is instantaneous and complete. In other words, the inventory from an order arrives in one batch at one time.
4. Quantity discounts are not possible.
5. The only variable costs are the cost of setting up or placing an order (setup cost) and the cost of holding or storing inventory over time (holding or carrying cost). These costs were discussed in the previous section.
6. Stockouts (shortages) can be completely avoided if orders are placed at the right time.

With these assumptions, the graph of inventory usage over time has a sawtooth shape, as in Figure 12.3 on page 448. In Figure 12.3, Q represents the amount that is ordered. If this amount is 500 dresses, all 500 dresses arrive at one time (when an order is received). Thus, the inventory level jumps from 0 to 500 dresses. In general, an inventory level increases from 0 to Q units when an order arrives.

Because demand is constant over time, inventory drops at a uniform rate over time. (Refer to the sloped lines in Figure 12.3.) When the inventory level reaches 0 each time, the new order is placed and received, and the inventory level again jumps to Q units (represented by the vertical lines). This process continues indefinitely over time.

Minimizing Costs

The objective of most inventory models is to minimize total costs. With the assumptions just given, significant costs are setup (or ordering) cost and holding (or carrying) cost. All other costs, such as the cost of the inventory itself, are constant. Thus, if we minimize the sum of setup and holding costs, we will also be minimizing total costs. To help you visu-

---

[4] The research on EOQ dates back to 1915; see Ford W. Harris, *Operations and Cost* (Chicago: A. W. Shaw, 1915).

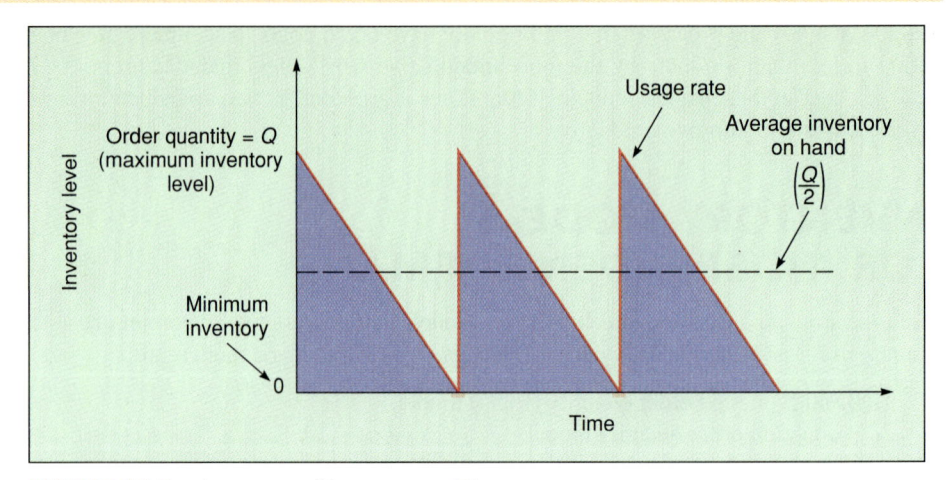

FIGURE 12.3 ■ Inventory Usage over Time

alize this, in Figure 12.4 we graph total costs as a function of the order quantity, Q. The optimal order size, Q^*, will be the quantity that minimizes the total costs. As the quantity ordered increases, the total number of orders placed per year will decrease. Thus, as the quantity ordered increases, the annual setup or ordering cost will decrease. But as the order quantity increases, the holding cost will increase due to the larger average inventories that are maintained.

As we can see in Figure 12.4, a reduction in either holding or setup cost will reduce the total cost curve. A reduction in the total cost curve also reduces the optimal order quantity (lot size). In addition, smaller lot sizes have a positive impact on quality[5] and production flexibility. The *OM in Action* box "Small Lot Sizes Contribute to Toshiba's Flexibility" discusses the competitive advantage found through smaller lot sizes.

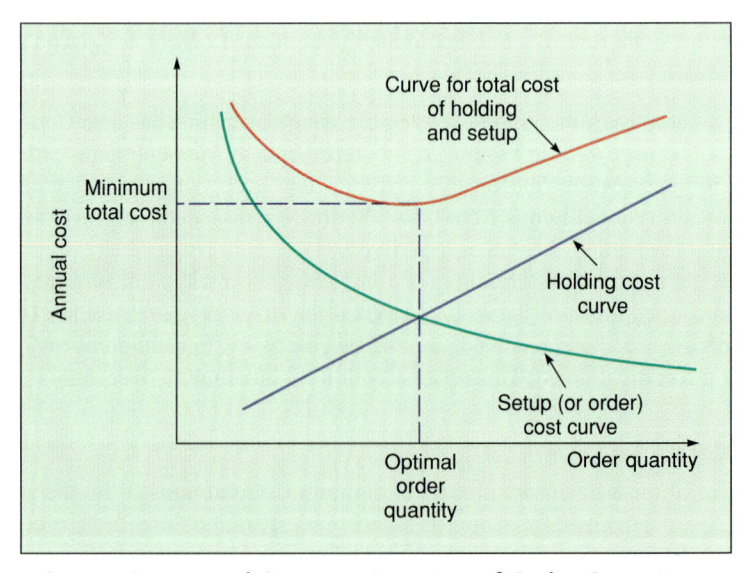

FIGURE 12.4 ■ Total Cost as a Function of Order Quantity

---

[5] R. Anthony Inman, "The Impact of Lot-Size Reduction on Quality," *Production and Inventory Management Journal* 35, 1 (first quarter 1994): 5–8.

OM IN ACTION

SMALL LOT SIZES CONTRIBUTE TO TOSHIBA'S FLEXIBILITY

A new challenge, called *flexibility*, faces global competitors today. Flexibility's watchwords are change, keep costs low, and respond quickly—all of which are supported by production in small lot sizes.

Flexibility is an explicit goal at Toshiba, Japan's $40-billion giant with products as diverse as computers, lightbulbs, and power plants. The idea, explains company president Fumio Sato, is to push Toshiba's two dozen factories to adapt faster to markets. "Customers wanted choices. They wanted a washing machine or a TV set that was precisely right for their needs. We needed variety, not mass production," says Sato.

The key to variety is finding ways to make money from ever-shorter production runs. Sato urges managers to reduce setup times, shrink lead times, and learn to make more products with the same equipment and people. "Smaller lot!" he yells at each plant he visits.

Toshiba's computer factory 30 miles outside of Tokyo got the message. Workers assemble 9 different word processors on the same line and, on an adjacent one, 20 varieties of laptop computers. Usually, they make a batch of 20 before changing models, but Toshiba can afford lot sizes as small as 10.

Because product life cycles for personal computers are now measured in months, not years, flexible lines allow the company to guard against running short of a hot model or overproducing one whose sales have slowed. The results are less inventory, less space devoted to inventory, less obsolete inventory, lower holding costs, and a focus on products currently in demand.

Sources: Information Week (November 21, 1994): 54–59; *Fortune* (September 21, 1992): 62–72; and *International Journal of Production Economics* (August 1, 1996): 37–46.

You should note that in Figure 12.4, the optimal order quantity occurs at the point where the ordering-cost curve and the carrying-cost curve intersect. This was not by chance. With the EOQ model, the optimal order quantity will occur at a point where the total setup cost is equal to the total holding cost.[6] We use this fact to develop equations that solve directly for Q^*. The necessary steps are:

1. Develop an expression for setup or ordering cost.
2. Develop an expression for holding cost.
3. Set setup cost equal to holding cost.
4. Solve the equation for the optimal order quantity.

Using the following variables, we can determine setup and holding costs and solve for Q^*:

Q = Number of pieces per order

Q^* = Optimum number of pieces per order (EOQ)

D = Annual demand in units for the inventory item

S = Setup or ordering cost for each order

H = Holding or carrying cost per unit per year

---

[6] This is the case where holding costs are linear and begin at the origin—that is, when inventory costs do not decline (or increase) as inventory volume increases and all holding costs are in small increments. Additionally, there is probably some learning each time a setup (or order) is executed—a fact that lowers subsequent setup costs. Consequently, the EOQ model is probably a special case. However, we abide by the conventional wisdom that this model is a reasonable approximation.

1. Annual setup cost = (Number of orders placed per year) × (Setup or order cost per order)

$$= \left(\frac{\text{Annual demand}}{\text{Number of units in each order}}\right)(\text{Setup or order cost per order})$$

$$= \left(\frac{D}{Q}\right)(S)$$

$$= \frac{D}{Q}S$$

2. Annual holding cost = (Average inventory level) × (Holding cost per unit per year)

$$= \left(\frac{\text{Order quantity}}{2}\right)(\text{Holding cost per unit per year})$$

$$= \left(\frac{Q}{2}\right)(H)$$

$$= \frac{Q}{2}H$$

3. Optimal order quantity is found when annual setup cost equals annual holding cost, namely,

$$\frac{D}{Q}S = \frac{Q}{2}H$$

4. To solve for Q^*, simply cross-multiply terms and isolate Q on the left of the equal sign.

$$2DS = Q^2H$$

$$Q^2 = \frac{2DS}{H}$$

$$Q^* = \sqrt{\frac{2DS}{H}} \quad (12.1)$$

Now that we have derived equations for the optimal order quantity, Q^*, it is possible to solve inventory problems directly, as in Example 3.

EXAMPLE 3

Sharp, Inc., a company that markets painless hypodermic needles to hospitals, would like to reduce its inventory cost by determining the optimal number of hypodermic needles to obtain per order. The annual demand is 1,000 units; the setup or ordering cost is $10 per order; and the holding cost per unit per year is $.50. Using these figures, we can calculate the optimal number of units per order:

$$Q^* = \sqrt{\frac{2DS}{H}}$$

$$Q^* = \sqrt{\frac{2(1,000)(10)}{0.50}} = \sqrt{40,000} = 200 \text{ units}$$

INVENTORY MODELS FOR INDEPENDENT DEMAND

We can also determine the expected number of orders placed during the year (N) and the expected time between orders (T) as follows:

$$\text{Expected number of orders} = N = \frac{\text{Demand}}{\text{Order quantity}} = \frac{D}{Q^*} \quad (12.2)$$

$$\text{Expected time between orders} = T = \frac{\text{Number of working days per year}}{N} \quad (12.3)$$

Example 4 illustrates this concept.

EXAMPLE 4

Using the data from Sharp, Inc., in Example 3, and assuming a 250-day working year, we find the number of orders (N) and the expected time between orders (T) as:

$$N = \frac{\text{Demand}}{\text{Order quantity}}$$

$$= \frac{1{,}000}{200} = 5 \text{ orders per year}$$

$$T = \frac{\text{Number of working days per year}}{\text{Expected number of orders}}$$

$$= \frac{250 \text{ working days per year}}{5 \text{ orders}} = 50 \text{ days between orders}$$

As mentioned earlier in this section, the total annual variable inventory cost is the sum of setup and holding costs:

$$\text{Total annual cost} = \text{Setup cost} + \text{Holding cost} \quad (12.4)$$

In terms of the variables in the model, we can express the total cost TC as:

$$TC = \frac{D}{Q}S + \frac{Q}{2}H \quad (12.5)$$

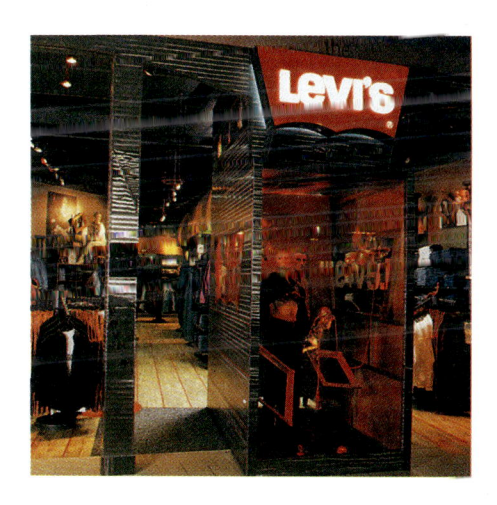

This store takes 4 weeks to get an order for Levis 501 jeans filled by the manufacturer. If the store sells 10 pairs of size 30–32 Levis a week, the store manager could set up 2 containers, keep 40 pairs of jeans in the second container, and place an order whenever the first container is empty. This would be a fixed-point reordering system. It is also called a "two-bin" system and is an example of a very elementary, but effective approach to inventory management.

452 CHAPTER 12 INVENTORY MANAGEMENT

Example 5 shows how to use this formula.

> **EXAMPLE 5**
> Again using the Sharp, Inc., data from Examples 3 and 4, we determine that the total annual inventory costs are:
>
> $$TC = \frac{D}{Q}S + \frac{Q}{2}H$$
>
> $$= \frac{1,000}{200}(\$10) + \frac{200}{2}(\$.50)$$
>
> $$= (5)(\$10) + (100)(\$.50)$$
>
> $$= \$50 + \$50 = \$100$$

The total inventory cost expression may also be written to include the actual cost of the material purchased. If we assume that the annual demand and the price per hypodermic needle are known values (for example, 1,000 hypodermics per year at $P = \$10$) and total annual cost should include purchase cost, then equation (12.5) becomes:

$$TC = \frac{D}{Q}S + \frac{Q}{2}H + PD$$

Because material cost does not depend on the particular order policy, we still incur an annual material cost of $D \times P = (1,000)(\$10) = \$10,000$. (Later in this chapter we will discuss the case in which this may not be true—namely, when a quantity discount is available.)

Robust A model that gives satisfactory answers even with substantial variation in its parameters.

Robust Model A benefit of the EOQ model is that it is robust. By **robust** we mean that it gives satisfactory answers even with substantial variation in its parameters. As we have observed, determining accurate ordering costs and holding costs for inventory is often difficult. Consequently, a robust model is advantageous. Total cost of the EOQ changes little in the neighborhood of the minimum. The curve is very shallow. This means that variations in setup costs, holding costs, demand, or even EOQ make relatively modest differences in total cost. Example 6 shows the robustness of EOQ.

> **EXAMPLE 6**
> If management in the Sharp, Inc., examples underestimated total annual demand by 50% (say demand is actually 1,500 needles rather than 1,000 needles) while using the same Q, the annual inventory cost increases only $25 ($100 versus $125), or 25%. Here is why.
> If demand in Example 5 is actually 1,500 needles rather than 1,000, but management uses an EOQ of $Q = 200$ (when it should be $Q = 244.9$ based on $D = 1,500$), the sum of holding and ordering cost increases 25%:
>
> $$\text{Annual cost} = \frac{D}{Q}S + \frac{Q}{2}H$$
>
> $$= \frac{1,500}{200}(\$10) + \frac{200}{2}(\$.50)$$
>
> $$= \$75 + \$50 = \$125$$

Inventory Models for Independent Demand

However, had we known that the demand was for 1,500 with an EOQ of 244.9 units, we would have spent $122.48, as shown below:

$$\text{Annual cost} = \frac{1{,}500}{244.9}(\$10) + \frac{244.9}{2}(\$.50)$$

$$= 6.125\,(\$10) + 122.45\,(\$.50)$$

$$= \$61.24 + \$61.24 = \$122.48$$

Note that the expenditure of $125.00, made with an estimate of demand that was substantially wrong, is only 2% ($2.52/$122.48) higher than we would have paid had we known the actual demand and ordered accordingly.

We may conclude that the EOQ is indeed robust and that significant errors do not cost us very much. This attribute of the EOQ model is most convenient because our ability to accurately forecast demand, holding cost, and ordering cost is limited.

Reorder Points

Now that we have decided *how much* to order, we will look at the second inventory question, *when* to order. Simple inventory models assume that receipt of an order is instantaneous. In other words, they assume (1) that a firm will place an order when the inventory level for that particular item reaches zero, and (2) that it will receive the ordered items immediately. However, the time between placement and receipt of an order, called **lead time** or delivery time, can be as short as a few hours or as long as months. Thus, the when-to-order decision is usually expressed in terms of a **reorder point (ROP)**— the inventory level at which an order should be placed (see Figure 12.5).

Lead time In purchasing systems, the time between placing an order and receiving it; in production systems, it is the wait, move, queue, setup, and run times for each component produced.

Reorder point (ROP) The inventory level (point) at which action is taken to replenish the stocked item.

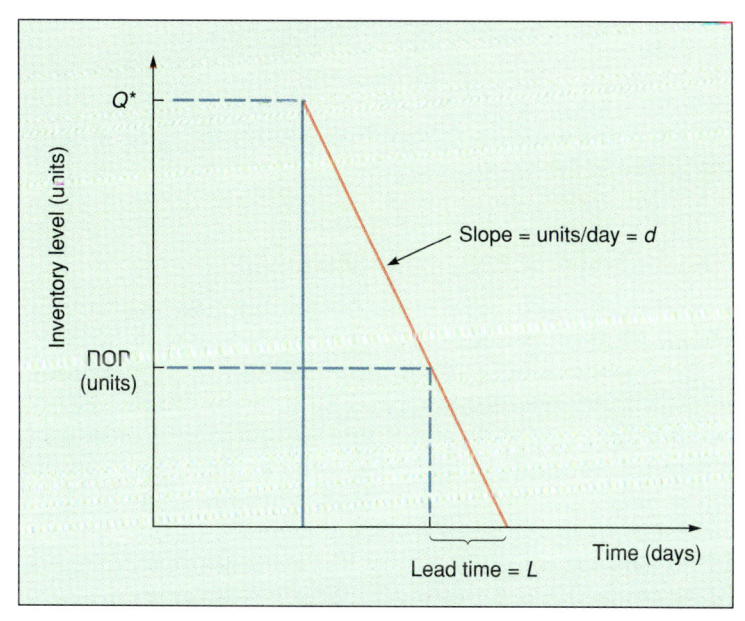

FIGURE 12.5 ■ **The Reorder Point (ROP) Curve** *Q* is the optimum order quantity, and lead time represents the time between placing and receiving an order.*

454　CHAPTER 12　INVENTORY MANAGEMENT

The reorder point (ROP) is given as:

$$\text{ROP} = (\text{Demand per day})(\text{Lead time for a new order in days})$$

$$= d \times L \tag{12.6}$$

Safety stock Extra stock to allow for uneven demand; a buffer.

This equation for ROP *assumes that demand during lead time and lead time itself are constant*. When this is not the case, extra stock, often called **safety stock,** should be added.

The demand per day, d, is found by dividing the annual demand, D, by the number of working days in a year:

$$d = \frac{D}{\text{Number of working days in a year}}$$

Computing the reorder point is demonstrated in Example 7.

EXAMPLE 7

Electronic Assembler, Inc., has a demand for 8,000 VCRs per year. The firm operates a 250-day working year. On average, delivery of an order takes 3 working days. We calculate the reorder point as

$$d = \frac{D}{\text{Number of working days in a year}} = \frac{8{,}000}{250}$$

$$= 32 \text{ units}$$

$$\text{ROP} = \text{Reorder point} = d \times L = 32 \text{ units per day} \times 3 \text{ days}$$

$$= 96 \text{ units}$$

Thus, when inventory stock drops to 96, an order should be placed. The order will arrive 3 days later, just as the firm's stock is depleted.

Production Order Quantity Model

In the previous inventory model, we assumed that the entire inventory order was received at one time. There are times, however, when the firm may receive its inventory over a period of time. Such cases require a different model, one that does not require the instantaneous-receipt assumption. This model is applicable under two situations: (1) when inventory continuously flows or builds up over a period of time after an order has been placed or (2) when units are produced and sold simultaneously. Under these circumstances, we take into account daily production (or inventory-flow) rate and daily demand rate. Figure 12.6 shows inventory levels as a function of time.

Production order quantity model An economic order quantity technique applied to production orders.

Because this model is especially suitable for the production environment, it is commonly called the **production order quantity model.** It is useful when inventory continuously builds up over time and traditional economic order quantity assumptions are valid. We derive this model by setting ordering or setup costs equal to holding costs and solving for optimal order size, Q^*. Using the following symbols, we can determine the expression for annual inventory holding cost for the production order quantity model:

Inventory Models for Independent Demand

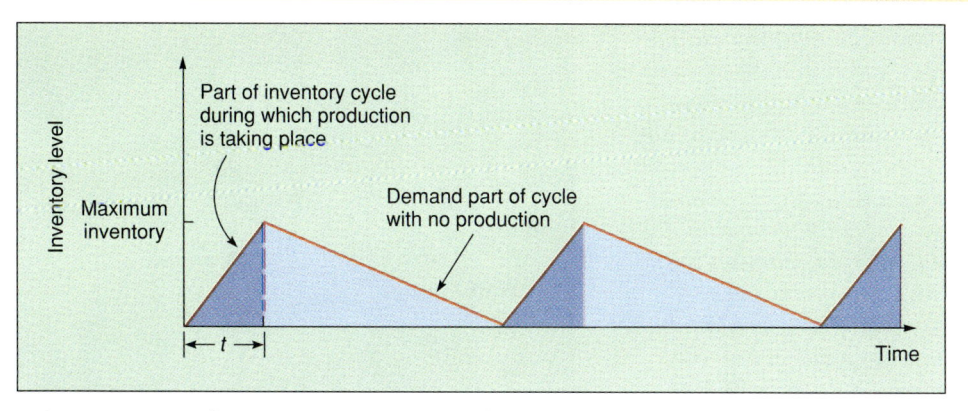

FIGURE 12.6 ■ Change in Inventory Levels over Time for the Production Model

Q = Number of pieces per order

H = Holding cost per unit per year

p = Daily production rate

d = Daily demand rate, or usage rate

t = Length of the production run in days

1. $\begin{pmatrix} \text{Annual inventory} \\ \text{holding cost} \end{pmatrix}$ = (Average inventory level) × $\begin{pmatrix} \text{Holding cost} \\ \text{per unit per year} \end{pmatrix}$

   = (Average inventory level) × H

2. $\begin{pmatrix} \text{Average inventory} \\ \text{level} \end{pmatrix}$ = (Maximum inventory level)/2

3. $\begin{pmatrix} \text{Maximum} \\ \text{inventory level} \end{pmatrix}$ = $\begin{pmatrix} \text{Total produced during} \\ \text{the production run} \end{pmatrix}$ − $\begin{pmatrix} \text{Total used during} \\ \text{the production run} \end{pmatrix}$

   = $pt - dt$

   However, Q = total produced = pt, and thus $t = Q/p$. Therefore,

   $$\text{Maximum inventory level} = p\left(\frac{Q}{p}\right) - d\left(\frac{Q}{p}\right)$$

   $$= Q - \frac{d}{p}Q$$

   $$= Q\left(1 - \frac{d}{p}\right)$$

4. Annual inventory holding cost (or simply holding cost) =
   $\dfrac{\text{Maximum inventory level}}{2}(H) = \dfrac{Q}{2}\left[1 - \left(\dfrac{d}{p}\right)\right]H$

Intermec Technologies uses bar-code readers to automate inventory control at its production and distribution facilities. Bar coding makes the data-collection process more accurate as well as faster and cheaper. With rapidly obtained data, shipments can be checked against production records and sales invoices to verify inventory accuracy and reduce losses. The scanning device shown is linked to the central computer by wireless data transmission.

A major difference between this model and the basic EOQ model is the annual holding cost, which is reduced in the production order quantity model.

Using the expression for holding cost above and the expression for setup cost developed in the basic EOQ model, we solve for the optimal number of pieces per order by equating setup cost and holding cost:

$$\text{Setup cost} = (D/Q)S$$

$$\text{Holding cost} = \tfrac{1}{2} HQ\,[1 - (d/p)]$$

Set ordering cost equal to holding cost to obtain Q^*_p:

$$\frac{D}{Q}S = \tfrac{1}{2} HQ\,[1 - (d/p)]$$

$$Q^2 = \frac{2DS}{H[1 - (d/p)]}$$

$$Q^*_p = \sqrt{\frac{2DS}{H[1 - (d/p)]}} \qquad (12.7)$$

In Example 8, we use the above equation, Q^*_p, to solve for the optimum order or production quantity when inventory is consumed as it is produced.

EXAMPLE 8

Nathan Manufacturing, Inc., makes and sells specialty hubcaps for the retail automobile aftermarket. Nathan's forecast for its wire-wheel hubcap is 1,000 units next year, with an average daily demand of 4 units. However, the production process is most efficient at 8 units per day. So the company produces 8 per day but uses only 4 per day. Given the following values, solve for the optimum number of units per order. (*Note:* This plant schedules production of this hubcap only as needed, about 250 days per year.)

$$\text{Annual demand} = D = 1{,}000 \text{ units}$$

$$\text{Setup cost} = S = \$10$$

$$\text{Holding cost} = H = \$0.50 \text{ per unit per year}$$

Inventory Models for Independent Demand

$$\text{Daily production rate} = p = 8 \text{ units daily}$$

$$\text{Daily demand rate} = d = 4 \text{ units daily}$$

$$Q^*_p = \sqrt{\frac{2DS}{H[1-(d/p)]}}$$

$$Q^*_p = \sqrt{\frac{2(1,000)(10)}{0.50[1-(4/8)]}}$$

$$= \sqrt{\frac{20,000}{0.50(1/2)}} = \sqrt{80,000}$$

$$= 282.8 \text{ hubcaps or 283 hubcaps}$$

You may want to compare this solution with the answer in Example 3. Eliminating the instantaneous-receipt assumption, where $p = 8$ and $d = 4$, has resulted in an increase in Q^* from 200 in Example 3 to 283. This increase in Q^* occurred because holding cost dropped from \$.50 to (\$.50 × $\frac{1}{2}$), making a larger Q^* optimal. Also note that:

$$d = 4 = \frac{D}{\text{Number of days the plant is in operation}} = \frac{1,000}{250}$$

We can also calculate Q^*_p when *annual* data are available. When annual data are used, we can express Q^*_p as:

$$Q^*_p = \sqrt{\frac{2DS}{H[1-(D/P)]}} \tag{12.8}$$

where D = Annual demand rate
        P = Annual production rate

Quantity Discount Models

To increase sales, many companies offer quantity discounts to their customers. A **quantity discount** is simply a reduced price (P) for an item when it is purchased in larger quantities. It is not uncommon to have a discount schedule with several discounts for large orders. A typical quantity discount schedule appears in Table 12.2.

Quantity discount A reduced price for items purchased in large quantities.

TABLE 12.2 ■ A Quantity Discount Schedule

Discount Number	Discount Quantity	Discount (%)	Discount Price (P)
1	0 to 999	no discount	\$5.00
2	1,000 to 1,999	4	\$4.80
3	2,000 and over	5	\$4.75

As can be seen in the table, the normal price of the item is \$5. When 1,000 to 1,999 units are ordered at one time, the price per unit drops to \$4.80; when the quantity ordered at one time is 2,000 units or more, the price is \$4.75 per unit. As always, management must decide when and how much to order. However, with an opportunity to save money on quantity discounts, how does the operations manager make these decisions?

As with other inventory models discussed so far, the overall objective is to minimize total cost. Because the unit cost for the third discount in Table 12.2 is the lowest, you might be tempted to order 2,000 units or more merely to take advantage of the lower product cost. Placing an order for that quantity, however, even with the greatest discount price, might not minimize total inventory cost. Granted, as discount quantity goes up, the product cost goes down. However, holding cost increases because orders are large. Thus the major trade-off when considering quantity discounts is between *reduced product cost* and *increased holding cost*. When we include the cost of the product, the equation for the total annual inventory cost can be calculated as follows:

$$\text{Total cost} = \text{Setup cost} + \text{Holding cost} + \text{Product cost}$$

or

$$T_c = \frac{D}{Q}S + \frac{QH}{2} + PD \tag{12.9}$$

where Q = Quantity ordered
D = Annual demand in units
S = Ordering or setup cost per order or per setup
P = Price per unit
H = Holding cost per unit per year

Now, we have to determine the quantity that will minimize the total annual inventory cost. Because there are several discounts, this process involves four steps:

Step 1: For each discount, calculate a value for optimal order size Q^*, using the following equation:

$$Q^* = \sqrt{\frac{2DS}{IP}} \tag{12.10}$$

Note that the holding cost is IP instead of H. Because the price of the item is a factor in annual holding cost, we cannot assume that the holding cost is a constant when the price per unit changes for each quantity discount. Thus, it is common to express the holding cost (I) as a percentage of unit price (P) instead of as a constant cost per unit per year, H.

Step 2: For any discount, if the order quantity is too low to qualify for the discount, adjust the order quantity upward to the lowest quantity that will qualify for the discount. For example, if Q^* for discount 2 in Table 12.2 were 500 units, you would adjust this value up to 1,000 units. Look at the second discount in Table 12.2. Order quantities between 1,000 and 1,999 will qualify for the 4% discount. Thus, if Q^* is below 1,000 units, we will adjust the order quantity up to 1,000 units.

Don't forget to adjust order quantity upward if the quantity is too low to qualify for the discount.

The reasoning for step 2 may not be obvious. If the order quantity, Q^*, is below the range that will qualify for a discount, a quantity within this range may still result in the lowest total cost.

As shown in Figure 12.7, the total cost curve is broken into three different total cost curves. There is a total cost curve for the first ($0 \leq Q \leq 999$), second ($1{,}000 \leq Q \leq 1{,}999$), and third ($2{,}000 \leq Q$) discount. Look at the

INVENTORY MODELS FOR INDEPENDENT DEMAND 459

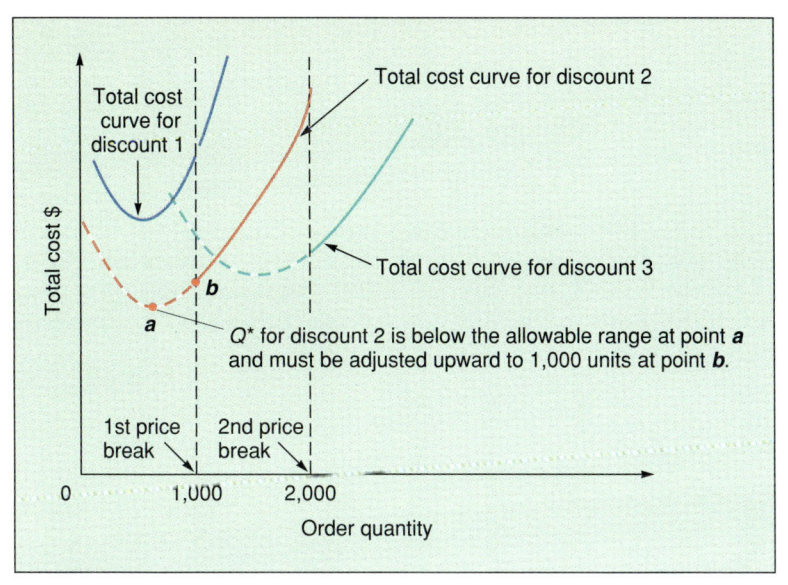

FIGURE 12.7 ■ Total Cost Curve for the Quantity Discount Model

total cost (T_c) curve for discount 2. Q^* for discount 2 is less than the allowable discount range, which is from 1,000 to 1,999 units. As the figure shows, the lowest allowable quantity in this range, which is 1,000 units, is the quantity that minimizes total cost. Thus, the second step is needed to ensure that we do not discard an order quantity that may indeed produce the minimum cost. Note that an order quantity computed in step 1 that is *greater* than the range that would qualify it for a discount may be discarded.

Step 3: Using the total cost equation above, compute a total cost for every Q^* determined in steps 1 and 2. If you had to adjust Q^* upward because it was below the allowable quantity range, be sure to use the adjusted value for Q^*.

Step 4: Select the Q^* that has the lowest total cost, as computed in step 3. It will be the quantity that will minimize the total inventory cost.

Let us see how this procedure can be applied with an example.

EXAMPLE 9

Wohl's Discount Store stocks toy race cars. Recently, the store has been given a quantity discount schedule for these cars. This quantity schedule was shown in Table 12.2. Thus, the normal cost for the toy race cars is $5.00. For orders between 1,000 and 1,999 units, the unit cost drops to $4.80; for orders of 2,000 or more units, the unit cost is only $4.75. Furthermore, ordering cost is $49.00 per order, annual demand is 5,000 race cars, and inventory carrying charge, as a percentage of cost, I, is 20% or .2. What order quantity will minimize the total inventory cost?

The first step is to compute Q^* for every discount in Table 12.2. This is done as follows:

$$Q_1^* = \sqrt{\frac{2(5{,}000)(49)}{(.2)(5.00)}} = 700 \text{ cars order}$$

$$Q_2^* = \sqrt{\frac{2(5,000)(49)}{(.2)(4.80)}} = 714 \text{ cars order}$$

$$Q_3^* = \sqrt{\frac{2(5,000)(49)}{(.2)(4.75)}} = 718 \text{ cars order}$$

The second step is to adjust upward those values of Q^* that are below the allowable discount range. Since Q_1^* is between 0 and 999, it need not be adjusted. Because Q_2^* is below the allowable range of 1,000 to 1,999, it must be adjusted to 1,000 units. The same is true for Q_3^*: It must be adjusted to 2,000 units. After this step, the following order quantities must be tested in the total cost equation:

$$Q_1^* = 700$$

$$Q_2^* = 1,000\text{—adjusted}$$

$$Q_3^* = 2,000\text{—adjusted}$$

The third step is to use the total cost equation and compute a total cost for each order quantity. This step is taken with the aid of Table 12.3, which presents the computations for each level of discount introduced in Table 12.2.

TABLE 12.3 ■ Total Cost Computations for Wohl's Discount Store

Discount Number	Unit Price	Order Quantity	Annual Product Cost	Annual Ordering Cost	Annual Holding Cost	Total
1	$5.00	700	$25,000	$350	$350	$25,700
2	$4.80	1,000	$24,000	$245	$480	$24,725
3	$4.75	2,000	$23,750	$122.50	$950	$24,822.50

The fourth step is to select that order quantity with the lowest total cost. Looking at Table 12.3, you can see that an order quantity of 1,000 toy race cars will minimize the total cost. You should see, however, that the total cost for ordering 2,000 cars is only slightly greater than the total cost for ordering 1,000 cars. Thus, if the third discount cost is lowered to $4.65, for example, then this quantity might be the one that minimizes total inventory cost.

PROBABILISTIC MODELS WITH CONSTANT LEAD TIME

Probabilistic model A statistical model applicable when product demand or any other variable is not known, but can be specified by means of a probability distribution.

All of the inventory models we have discussed so far make the assumption that demand for a product is constant and certain. We now relax this assumption. The following inventory models apply when product demand is not known but can be specified by means of a probability distribution. These types of models are called **probabilistic models.**

An important concern of management is maintaining an adequate service level in the face of uncertain demand. The **service level** is the complement of the probability of a stockout. For instance, if the probability of a stockout is 0.05, then the service level is .95. Uncertain demand raises the possibility of a stockout. One method of reducing stockouts is to hold extra units in inventory. As we noted, such inventory is usually referred to as safety stock. It involves adding a number of units as a buffer to the reorder point. As you recall from our previous discussion:

Service level The complement of the probability of a stockout.

PROBABILISTIC MODELS WITH CONSTANT LEAD TIME

$$\text{Reorder point} = \text{ROP} = d \times L$$

where d = Daily demand
  L = Order lead time, or number of working days it takes to deliver an order

The inclusion of safety stock (ss) changes the expression to:

$$\text{ROP} = d \times L + ss \qquad (12.11)$$

The amount of safety stock maintained depends on the cost of incurring a stockout and the cost of holding the extra inventory. Annual stockout cost is computed by:

$$\text{Annual stockout costs} = \text{the sum of the units short} \times \text{the probability} \\ \times \text{ the stockout cost/unit} \times \text{the number of orders per year} \qquad (12.12)$$

Example 10 illustrates this concept.

EXAMPLE 10

David Rivera Optical has determined that its reorder point for eyeglass frames is 50 ($d \times L$) units. Its carrying cost per frame per year is $5, and stockout (or lost sale) cost is $40 per frame. The store has experienced the following probability distribution for inventory demand during the reorder period. The optimum number of orders per year is six.

	Number of Units	Probability
	30	.2
	40	.2
ROP →	50	.3
	60	.2
	70	.1
		1.0

How much safety stock should David Rivera keep on hand?

Solution

The objective is to find the amount of safety stock that minimizes the sum of the additional inventory holding costs and stockout costs. The annual holding cost is simply the holding cost per unit multiplied by the units added to the ROP. For example, a safety stock of 20 frames, which implies that the new ROP, with safety stock, is 70 (= 50 + 20), raises the annual carrying cost by $5(20) = $100.

However, computing annual stockout cost is more interesting. For any level of safety stock, stockout cost is the expected cost of stocking out. We can compute it, as in equation (12.12), by multiplying the number of frames short by the probability of demand at that level, by the stockout cost, by the number of times per year the stockout can occur (which in our case is the number of orders per year). Then we add stockout costs for each possible stockout level for a given ROP. For zero safety stock, for example, a shortage of 10 frames will occur if demand is 60, and a shortage of 20 frames will occur if the demand is 70. Thus the stockout costs for zero safety stock are

(10 frames short) (.2) ($40 per stockout) (6 possible stockouts per year)
+ (20 frames short) (.1) ($40) (6) = $960

> The following table summarizes the total costs for each alternative:
>
> | Safety Stock | Additional Holding Cost | Stockout Cost | Total Cost |
> |---|---|---|---|
> | 20 | (20) ($5) = $100 | $0 | $100 |
> | 10 | (10) ($5) = $ 50 | (10) (.1) ($40) (6) = $240 | $290 |
> | 0 | $0 | (10) (.2) ($40) (6) + (20) (.1) ($40) (6) = $960 | $960 |
>
> The safety stock with the lowest total cost is 20 frames. Therefore, this safety stock changes the reorder point to 50 + 20 = 70 frames.

When it is difficult or impossible to determine the cost of being out of stock, a manager may decide to follow a policy of keeping enough safety stock on hand to meet a prescribed customer service level. For instance, Figure 12.8 shows the use of safety stock when demand (for hospital resuscitation kits) is probabilistic. We see that the safety stock in Figure 12.8 is 16.5 units, and the reorder point is also increased by 16.5.

The cost of the inventory policy increases dramatically with an increase in service levels. Indeed, inventory costs increase exponentially as service level increases.

The manager may want to define the service level as meeting 95% of the demand (or, conversely, having stockouts only 5% of the time). Assuming that demand during lead time (the reorder period) follows a normal curve, only the mean and standard deviation are needed to define the inventory requirements for any given service level. Sales data are usually adequate for computing the mean and standard deviation. In the following example we use a normal curve with a known mean (μ) and standard deviation (σ) to deter-

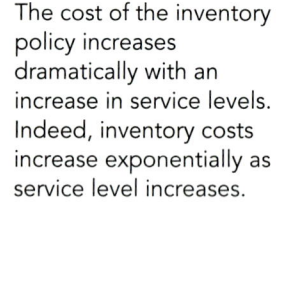

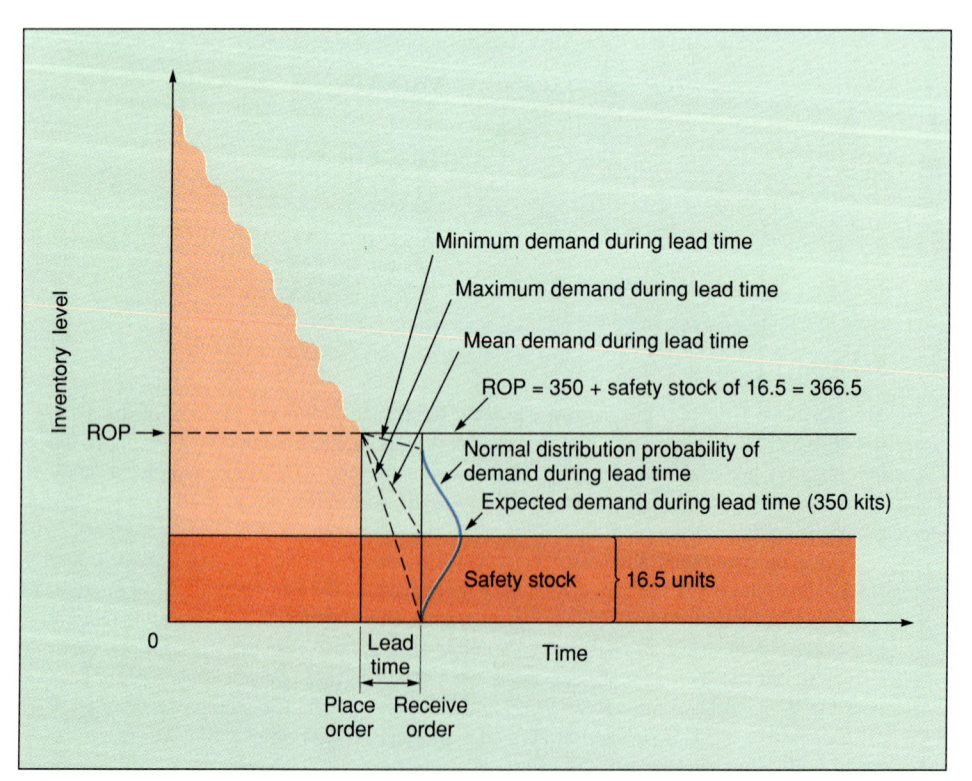

FIGURE 12.8 ■ **Probabilistic Demand for a Hospital Item** *Expected number of kits needed during lead time is 350, but for a 95% service level, the reorder point should be raised to 366.5.*

mine the reorder point and safety stock necessary for a 95% service level. We use the formula:

$$\text{ROP} = \text{expected demand during lead time} + Z\sigma \qquad (12.13)$$

where Z = number of standard deviations
          σ = standard deviation of lead time demand

EXAMPLE 11

Memphis Regional Hospital stocks a "code blue" resuscitation kit that has a normally distributed demand during the reorder period. The mean (average) demand during the reorder period is 350 kits, and the standard deviation is 10 kits. The hospital administrator wants to follow a policy that results in stockouts occurring only 5% of the time.

(a) What is the appropriate value of Z? (b) How much safety stock should the hospital maintain? (c) What reorder point should be used? The following figure may help you visualize the example:

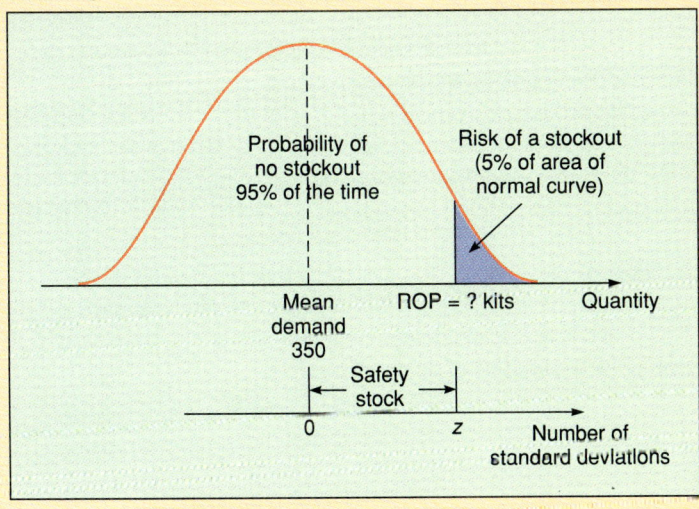

μ = Mean demand = 350 kits

σ = Standard deviation = 10 kits

Z = Number of standard normal deviates

Solution

a) We use the properties of a standardized normal curve to get a Z value for an area under the normal curve of .95 (or $1 - .05$). Using a normal table (see Appendix I), we find a Z value of 1.65 standard deviations from the mean.

b)
$$\text{Safety stock} = x - \mu$$
Because
$$Z = \frac{x - \mu}{\sigma}$$
Then   Safety stock = $Z\sigma$ \qquad (12.14)

Solving for safety stock, as in equation (12.14), gives

$$\text{Safety stock} = 1.65(10) = 16.5 \text{ kits}$$

> This is the situation illustrated in Figure 12.8.
>
> c) The reorder point is:
>
> $$\text{ROP} = \text{expected demand during lead time} + \text{safety stock}$$
> $$= 350 \text{ kits} + 16.5 \text{ kits of safety stock} = 366.5, \text{ or } 367 \text{ kits}$$

Equations (12.13) and (12.14) assume that both an estimate of expected demand during lead times and its standard deviation are available. When data on lead time demand are *not* at hand, these formulas cannot be applied and we need to determine if: (a) demand is variable and lead time is constant; or (b) only lead time is variable; or (c) both demand and lead time are variable. For each of these situations, a different formula is needed to compute ROP.[7]

FIXED-PERIOD SYSTEMS

The inventory models that we have considered so far are *fixed-quantity systems*. That is to say, the same fixed amount is added to inventory every time an order for an item is placed. We saw that orders are event-triggered, with the event triggering a reorder.

In a **fixed-period system,** however, inventory is ordered at the end of a given period. Then, and only then, is on-hand inventory counted. Only the amount necessary to bring total inventory up to a prespecified target level is ordered. Figure 12.9 illustrates this concept.

The advantage of the fixed-period system is that there is no physical count of inventory items after an item is withdrawn—this occurs only when the time for the next review comes up. This procedure is also convenient administratively, especially if inventory control is only one of several duties of an employee.

Fixed-period system
A sytem that triggers inventory ordering on a uniform time frequency.

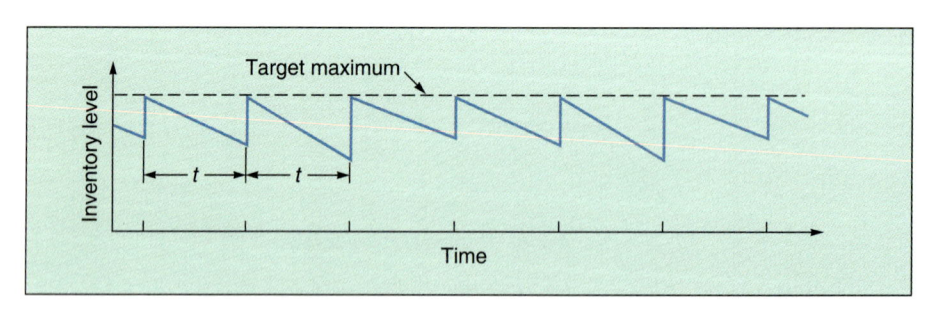

FIGURE 12.9 ■ **Inventory Level in a Fixed-Period System** *Various amounts are ordered based on the quantity necessary to bring inventory up to the target maximum.*

---

[7] (a) If *only* the *demand (d)* is variable, then
ROP = *average* daily demand × lead time in days + $Z\sigma_{dLT}$
where σ_{dLT} = standard deviation of demand per day
$= \sqrt{\text{lead time}} \times \sigma_d$
(b) If *only lead time* is variable, then
ROP = daily demand × *average* lead time in days + $Z \times d \times \sigma_{LT}$
(c) If *both* are variable, then
ROP = average daily demand × average lead time +
$Z\sqrt{\text{average lead time} \times \sigma_d^2 + \bar{d}^2 \sigma_{LT}^2}$

A fixed-period system is appropriate when vendors make routine (that is, at fixed-time interval) visits to customers to take fresh orders or when purchasers want to combine orders to save ordering and transportation costs (therefore, they will have the same review period for similar inventory items).

The disadvantage of this system is that because there is no tally of inventory during the review period, there is the possibility of a stockout during this time. This scenario is possible if a large order draws the inventory level down to zero right after an order is placed. Therefore, a higher level of safety stock (as compared to a fixed-quantity system) needs to be maintained to provide protection against stockout during both the time between reviews and the lead time.

SUMMARY

Inventory represents a major investment for many firms. This investment is often larger than it should be because firms find it easier to have "just-in-case" inventory rather than "just-in-time" inventory. Inventories are of four types:

1. Raw material and purchased components.
2. Work-in-process.
3. Maintenance, repair, and operating (MRO).
4. Finished goods.

In this chapter, we discussed independent inventory, ABC analysis, record accuracy, and inventory models used to control independent demands. The EOQ model, production order quantity model, and quantity discount model can all be solved using POM for Windows software or with Excel spreadsheets. A summary of the inventory models presented in this chapter is shown in Table 12.4.

TABLE 12.4 ■ Statistical Models for Independent Demand Summarized

Q = Number of pieces per order
EOQ = Optimum order quantity (Q^*)
D = Annual demand in units
S = Setup or ordering cost for each order
H = Holding or carrying cost per unit per year in dollars
p = Daily production rate
d = Daily demand rate

P = Price
I = Annual inventory carrying cost as a percentage of price
μ = Mean demand
σ = Standard deviation
x = Mean demand + Safety stock
Z = Standardized value under the normal curve

EOQ

$$Q^* = \sqrt{\frac{2DS}{H}} \quad (12.1)$$

Quantity discount EOQ model

$$Q^* = \sqrt{\frac{2DS}{IP}} \quad (12.10)$$

EOQ production order quantity model

$$Q_p^* = \sqrt{\frac{2DS}{H[1 - (d/p)]}} \quad (12.7)$$

Probability model

Safety stock = $Z\sigma = x - \mu$ (12.14)

Total cost for the EOQ and quantity discount EOQ models

T_c = Total cost
    = Setup cost + Holding cost + Product cost
    $= \dfrac{D}{Q}S + \dfrac{QH}{2} + PD \quad (12.9)$

466   CHAPTER 12   INVENTORY MANAGEMENT

KEY TERMS

Raw material inventory *(p. 440)*
Work-in-process inventory *(p. 441)*
MRO *(p. 441)*
Finished goods inventory *(p. 441)*
ABC analysis *(p. 441)*
Cycle counting *(p. 444)*
Shrinkage *(p. 445)*
Pilferage *(p. 445)*
Holding cost *(p. 446)*
Ordering cost *(p. 446)*
Setup cost *(p. 446)*

Setup time *(p. 446)*
Robust *(p. 452)*
Lead time *(p. 453)*
Reorder point (ROP) *(p. 453)*
Safety stock *(p. 454)*
Production order quantity model *(p. 454)*
Quantity discount *(p. 457)*
Probabilistic models *(p. 460)*
Service level *(p. 460)*
Fixed-period system *(p. 464)*

USING POM FOR WINDOWS TO SOLVE INVENTORY PROBLEMS

The POM for Windows inventory module can solve all of the EOQ family of problems, as well as ABC inventory management. Program 12.1 illustrates the application of this software to Example 9, using the Wohl quantity discount data. Input data are shown on the left side of the screen and output data on the right.

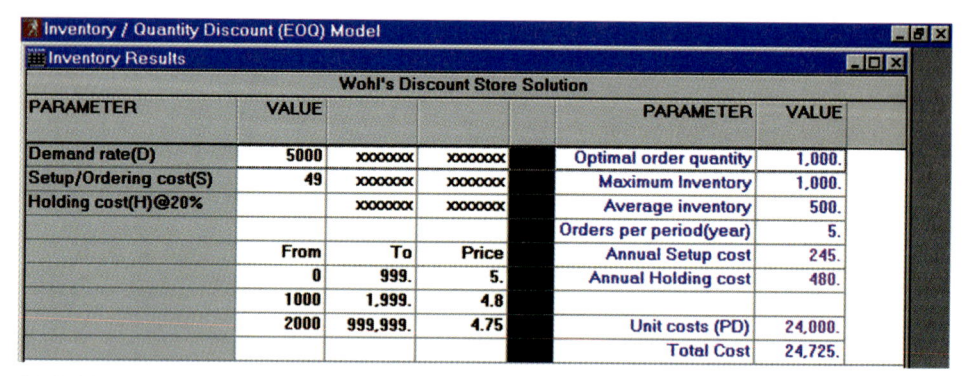

Inventory / Quantity Discount (EOQ) Model

Inventory Results — Wohl's Discount Store Solution

PARAMETER	VALUE				PARAMETER	VALUE
Demand rate(D)	5000	xxxxxxx	xxxxxxx		Optimal order quantity	1,000.
Setup/Ordering cost(S)	49	xxxxxxx	xxxxxxx		Maximum Inventory	1,000.
Holding cost(H)@20%		xxxxxxx	xxxxxxx		Average inventory	500.
					Orders per period(year)	5.
		From	To	Price	Annual Setup cost	245.
		0	999.	5.	Annual Holding cost	480.
		1000	1,999.	4.8		
		2000	999,999.	4.75	Unit costs (PD)	24,000.
					Total Cost	24,725.

PROGRAM 12.1 ■ Using POM for Windows to Solve the Quantity Discount Problem in Example 9

USING EXCEL OM FOR INVENTORY

Excel OM allows us to easily model inventory problems ranging from ABC analysis to the basic EOQ model to the production model to quantity discount situations. Two of these models are illustrated in this section.

Using Excel OM for Inventory

Silicon Chips, Inc.
Inventory ABC Analysis

Enter the item name or number, its sales volume, and the unit cost in columns A, B, and C.

Enter data in the shaded area, select items in columns a through e then DATA,

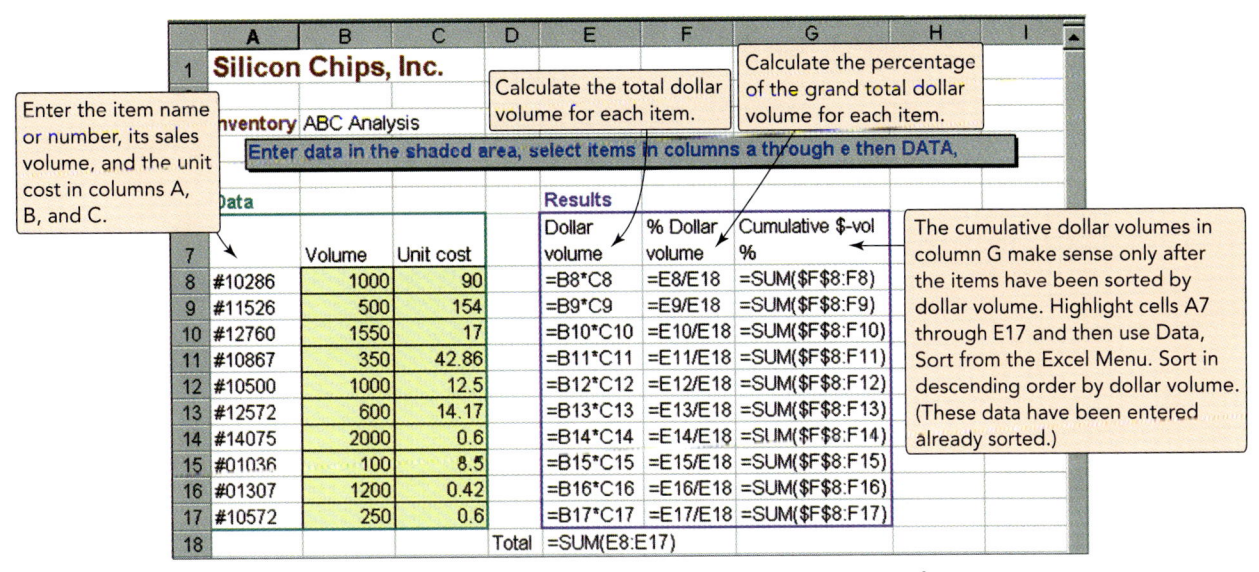

Calculate the total dollar volume for each item.

Calculate the percentage of the grand total dollar volume for each item.

The cumulative dollar volumes in column G make sense only after the items have been sorted by dollar volume. Highlight cells A7 through E17 and then use Data, Sort from the Excel Menu. Sort in descending order by dollar volume. (These data have been entered already sorted.)

	Volume	Unit cost	Dollar volume	% Dollar volume	Cumulative $-vol %
#10286	1000	90	=B8*C8	=E8/E18	=SUM($F$8:F8)
#11526	500	154	=B9*C9	=E9/E18	=SUM($F$8:F9)
#12760	1550	17	=B10*C10	=E10/E18	=SUM($F$8:F10)
#10867	350	42.86	=B11*C11	=E11/E18	=SUM($F$8:F11)
#10500	1000	12.5	=B12*C12	=E12/E18	=SUM($F$8:F12)
#12572	600	14.17	=B13*C13	=E13/E18	=SUM($F$8:F13)
#14075	2000	0.6	=B14*C14	=E14/E18	=SUM($F$8:F14)
#01036	100	8.5	=B15*C15	=E15/E18	=SUM($F$8:F15)
#01307	1200	0.42	=B16*C16	=E16/E18	=SUM($F$8:F16)
#10572	250	0.6	=B17*C17	=E17/E18	=SUM($F$8:F17)
		Total	=SUM(E8:E17)		

PROGRAM 12.2 ■ Using Excel OM for an ABC Analysis, with Data from Example 1

Program 12.2 shows the input data and formulas for an ABC analysis, using data from Example 1. After the data are entered, we use the *Data* and *Sort* Excel commands to rank the items from largest to smallest dollar volumes. The results appear in Program 12.3.

Silicon Chips, Inc.
Inventory ABC Analysis

Enter data in the shaded area, select items in columns a through e then DATA, SORT

	Volume	Unit cost	Dollar volume	% Dollar volume	Cumulative $-vol %
#10286	1000	90	90000	38.78%	38.78%
#11526	500	154	77000	33.18%	71.97%
#12760	1550	17	26350	11.35%	83.32%
#10867	350	42.86	15001	6.46%	89.78%
#10500	1000	12.5	12500	5.39%	95.17%
#12572	600	14.17	8502	3.66%	98.83%
#14075	2000	0.6	1200	0.52%	99.35%
#01036	100	8.5	850	0.37%	99.72%
#01307	1200	0.42	504	0.22%	99.94%
#10572	250	0.6	150	0.06%	100.00%
		Total	232057		

PROGRAM 12.3 ■ Output Screen from Excel OM ABC Analysis, Using Program 12.2 as Input

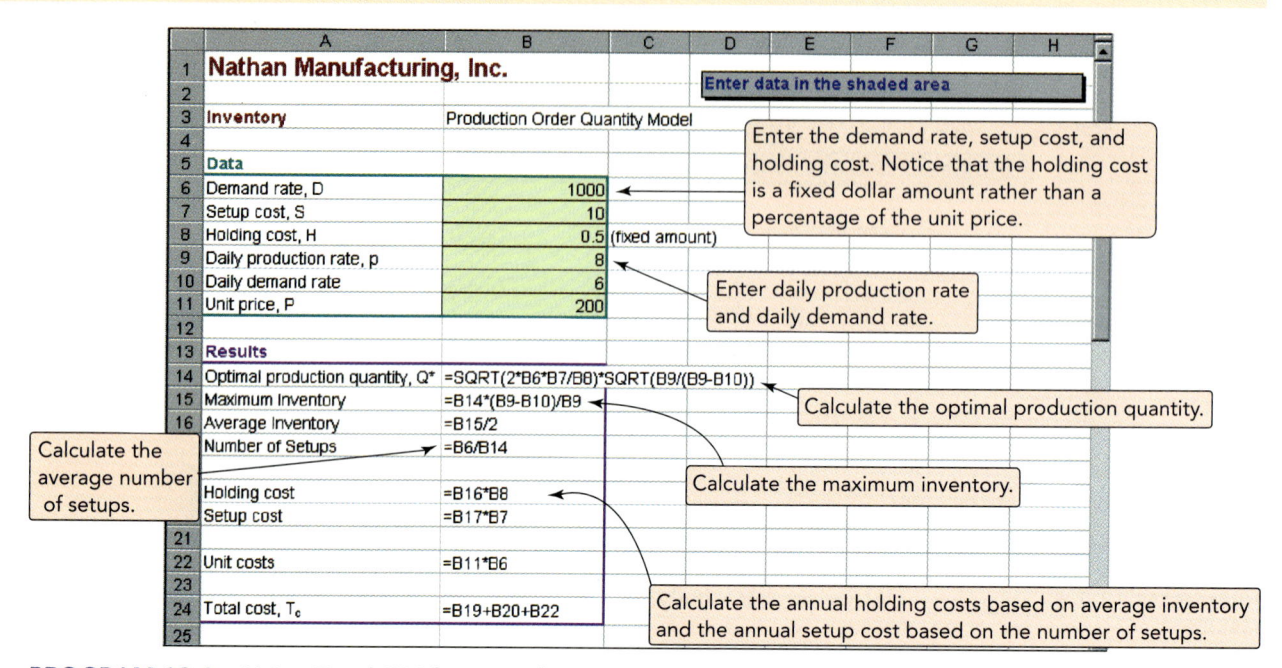

468 CHAPTER 12 INVENTORY MANAGEMENT

	A	B	C	D	E	F	G	H
1	Nathan Manufacturing, Inc.							
2					Enter data in the shaded area			
3	Inventory	Production Order Quantity Model						
4								
5	Data							
6	Demand rate, D	1000						
7	Setup cost, S	10						
8	Holding cost, H	0.5	(fixed amount)					
9	Daily production rate, p	8						
10	Daily demand rate	6						
11	Unit price, P	200						
12								
13	Results							
14	Optimal production quantity, Q*	=SQRT(2*B6*B7/B8)*SQRT(B9/(B9-B10))						
15	Maximum Inventory	=B14*(B9-B10)/B9						
16	Average Inventory	=B15/2						
17	Number of Setups	=B6/B14						
18								
19	Holding cost	=B16*B8						
20	Setup cost	=B17*B7						
21								
22	Unit costs	=B11*B6						
23								
24	Total cost, T_c	=B19+B20+B22						
25								

- Enter the demand rate, setup cost, and holding cost. Notice that the holding cost is a fixed dollar amount rather than a percentage of the unit price.
- Enter daily production rate and daily demand rate.
- Calculate the optimal production quantity.
- Calculate the maximum inventory.
- Calculate the average number of setups.
- Calculate the annual holding costs based on average inventory and the annual setup cost based on the number of setups.

PROGRAM 12.4 ■ Using Excel OM for a Production Model, with Data from Example 8

We illustrate the production inventory model in Programs 12.4 and 12.5 using the data from Example 8. Input data and Excel formulas appear in Program 12.4. Output, including an optional graph of order quantity versus cost, appears in Program 12.5.

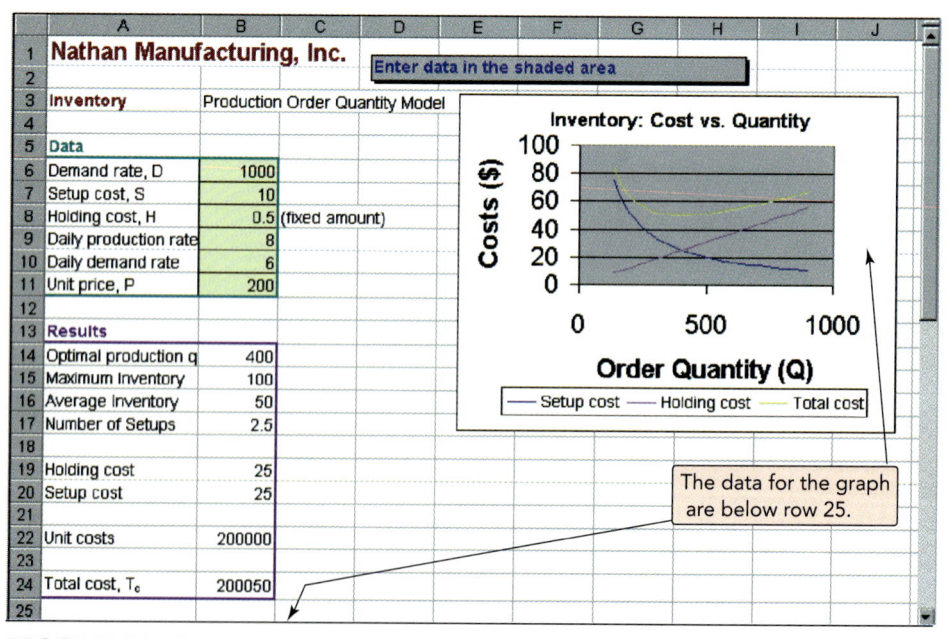

	A	B	C
1	Nathan Manufacturing, Inc.		
2			
3	Inventory	Production Order Quantity Model	
4			
5	Data		
6	Demand rate, D	1000	
7	Setup cost, S	10	
8	Holding cost, H	0.5	(fixed amount)
9	Daily production rate	8	
10	Daily demand rate	6	
11	Unit price, P	200	
12			
13	Results		
14	Optimal production q	400	
15	Maximum Inventory	100	
16	Average Inventory	50	
17	Number of Setups	2.5	
18			
19	Holding cost	25	
20	Setup cost	25	
21			
22	Unit costs	200000	
23			
24	Total cost, T_c	200050	
25			

Inventory: Cost vs. Quantity graph shows Setup cost, Holding cost, and Total cost versus Order Quantity (Q) from 0 to 1000, with Costs ($) on y-axis from 0 to 100.

The data for the graph are below row 25.

PROGRAM 12.5 ■ Output Screen from Excel OM Production Model, Using Program 12.4 as Input

SOLVED PROBLEMS

Solved Problem 12.1

The J. Spivey Computer Corporation purchases 8,000 transistors each year as components in minicomputers. The unit cost of each transistor is $10, and the cost of carrying one transistor in inventory for a year is $3. Ordering cost is $30 per order.

What are: (a) the optimal order quantity, (b) the expected number of orders placed each year, and (c) the expected time between orders? Assume that Spivey operates a 200-day working year.

Solution

a) $$Q^* = \sqrt{\frac{2DS}{H}} = \sqrt{\frac{2(8,000)(30)}{3}} = 400 \text{ units}$$

b) $$N = \frac{D}{Q^*} = \frac{8,000}{400} = 20 \text{ orders}$$

c) Time between orders = T

$$= \frac{\text{Number of working days}}{N} = \frac{200}{20}$$

$$= 10 \text{ working days}$$

Hence, an order for 400 transistors is placed every 10 days. Presumably, then, 20 orders are placed each year.

Solved Problem 12.2

Annual demand for notebook binders at Juenger's Stationery Shop is 10,000 units. Vanessa Juenger operates her business 300 days per year and finds that deliveries from her supplier generally take 5 working days. Calculate the reorder point for the notebook binders.

Solution

$$L = 5 \text{ days}$$

$$d = \frac{10,000}{300} = 33.3 \text{ units per day}$$

$$\text{ROP} = d \times L = (33.3 \text{ units per day})(5 \text{ days})$$

$$= 166.7 \text{ units}$$

Thus, Vanessa should reorder when her stock reaches 167 units.

Solved Problem 12.3

L. Alwayn, Inc., has an annual demand rate of 1,000 units but can produce at an average annual production rate of 2,000 units. Setup cost is $10; carrying cost $1. What is the optimal number of units to be produced each time?

Solution

$$Q^* = \sqrt{\frac{2DS}{H[1 - (D/P)]}}$$

$$= \sqrt{\frac{2(1,000)(10)}{1[1 - (1,000/2,000)]}} = \sqrt{\frac{20,000}{1/2}} = \sqrt{40,000}$$

$$= 200 \text{ units}$$

Solved Problem 12.4

What safety stock should James Gilbert Corporation maintain if mean sales are 80 during the reorder period, the standard deviation is 7, and Gilbert can tolerate stockouts 10% of the time?

Solution

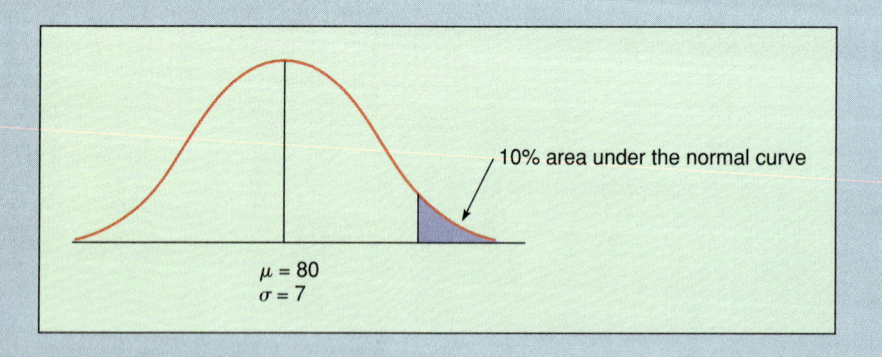

10% area under the normal curve

$\mu = 80$
$\sigma = 7$

From Appendix I, Z at an area of .9 (or $1 - .10$) = 1.28

$$Z = 1.28 = \frac{x - \mu}{\sigma} = \frac{ss}{\sigma}$$

$$ss = 1.28\sigma$$

$$= 1.28(7) = 8.96 \text{ units, or 9 units}$$

DISCUSSION QUESTIONS

1. With the advent of low-cost computing, do you see alternatives to the popular ABC classifications?
2. What is the difference between the standard EOQ model and the production inventory model?
3. What are the main reasons that an organization has inventory?
4. Describe the costs associated with ordering and maintaining inventory.
5. What are the assumptions of the EOQ model?
6. How sensitive is EOQ to variations in demand or costs?
7. Does the production model or the standard EOQ model yield a higher EOQ if setup costs and holding costs are the same? Why?
8. When is a good time for cycle-counting personnel to audit a particular item?
9. What impact does a decrease in setup time have on EOQ?
10. What is meant by *service level*?
11. How would a firm go about determining service level?
12. What happens to total inventory costs (and EOQ) if inventory holding costs per unit increase as inventory increases (that is, increase at an increasing rate)?
13. What happens to total inventory costs (and EOQ) if there is a fixed cost associated with inventory holding costs (for example, leasing the warehouse)?
14. Describe the difference between a fixed-quantity and a fixed-period inventory system.
15. Describe the four types of inventory.
16. What is meant by EOQ being suitable for independent demand?

CRITICAL THINKING EXERCISE

Wayne Hills Hospital in tiny Wayne, Nebraska, faces a problem common to large, urban hospitals as well as small, remote ones like itself. That problem is deciding how much of each type of whole blood to keep in stock. Because blood is expensive and has a limited shelf life (up to 5 weeks under 1–6°C refrigeration), Wayne Hills naturally wants to keep its stock as low as possible. Unfortunately, disasters such as a major tornado in 1986 and a train wreck in 1991 demonstrated that lives would be lost when not enough blood was available to handle massive needs. The hospital administrator wants to set an 85% service level based on demand over the past decade. Discuss the implications of this decision. What is the hospital's responsibility with regard to stocking lifesaving medicines with short shelf lives? How would you set the inventory level for a commodity such as blood?

PROBLEMS

12.1 Jacqueline Johnson's company has compiled the following data on a small set of products:

SKU	Annual Demand	Unit Cost
A	100	$250
B	75	100
C	50	50
D	200	150
E	150	75

Use her data to illustrate an ABC analysis.

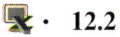

12.2 Stagg Enterprise has 10 items in inventory. Shane Stagg asks you, the recent OM graduate, to divide these items into ABC classifications. What do you report back?

Item	Annual Demand	Cost/Unit
A2	3,000	$ 50
B8	4,000	12
C7	1,500	45
D1	6,000	10
E9	1,000	20
F3	500	500
G2	300	1,500
H2	600	20
I5	1,750	10
J8	2,500	5

· **12.3** Judy Stamm opened a new beauty-products retail store. There are numerous items in inventory, and Judy knows that there are costs associated with inventory. However, because her time is limited she cannot carefully evaluate the inventory policy for all products. Judy wants to classify the items according to dollars invested in them. The following table provides information about the 10 items that she carries:

Item Number	Unit Cost	Demand (units)
E102	$4.00	800
D23	8.00	1,200
D27	3.00	700
R02	2.00	1,000
R19	8.00	200
S107	6.00	500
S123	1.00	1,200
U11	7.00	800
U23	1.00	1,500
V75	4.00	1,500

Use ABC analysis to classify these items into categories A, B, and C.

· **12.4** It takes approximately 2 weeks (14 days) for an order of steel bolts to arrive once the order has been placed.

The demand for bolts is fairly constant; on the average, the manager has observed that the hardware store sells 500 of these bolts each day. Because the demand is fairly constant, she believes that she can avoid stockouts completely if she orders the bolts at the correct time. What is the reorder point?

· **12.5** Lead time for one of your fastest-moving products is 21 days. Demand during this period averages 100 units per day. What would be an appropriate reorder point?

: **12.6** Teresa Cohan is attempting to perform an inventory analysis on one of her most popular products. Annual demand for this product is 5,000 units; unit cost is $200; carrying cost is considered to be approximately 25% of the unit price. Order costs for her company typically run nearly $30 per order and lead time averages 10 days. (Assume a 50-week year.)
  a) What is the economic order quantity?
  b) What is the reorder point?
  c) What is the total carrying + ordering cost?
  d) What is the optimal number of orders per year?
  e) What is the optimal number of days between orders (assume 250 working days per year)?

· **12.7** Betsy McCollum is the purchasing agent for Central Valve Company, which sells industrial valves and fluid-control devices. One of Central's most popular valves is the West-

ern, which has an annual demand of 4,000 units. The cost of each valve is $90, and the inventory carrying cost is estimated to be 10% of the cost of each valve. Betsy has made a study of the costs involved in placing an order for any of the valves that Central stocks, and she has concluded that the average ordering cost is $25 per order. Furthermore, it takes about 5 working days for an order to arrive from the supplier. During this time, the demand per week for valves is approximately 80.
   a) What is the economic order quantity?
   b) What is the reorder point?
   c) What is the total annual inventory cost (carrying cost + ordering cost)?
   d) What is the optimal number of orders per year?
   e) What is the optimal number of days between any two orders, assuming 250 working days per year?

: 12.8 Happy Pet, Inc., is a large pet store located in Long Beach Mall. Although the store specializes in dogs, it also sells fish, turtle, and bird supplies. The Everlast Leader, a leather lead for dogs, costs Happy Pet $7.00 each. There is an annual demand for 6,000 Everlast Leaders. The manager has determined that the ordering cost is $20 per order and the carrying cost, as a percentage of unit cost, is 15%. Happy Pet is now considering a new supplier of Everlast Leaders. Each lead would cost only $6.65; but in order to get this discount, Happy Pet would have to buy shipments of 3,000 at a time. Should Happy Pet use the new supplier and take this discount for quantity buying?

· 12.9 William Porter uses 1,500 per year of a certain subassembly that has an annual holding cost of $45 per unit. Each order placed costs Porter $150. He operates 300 days per year and has found that an order must be placed with his supplier 6 working days before he can expect to receive that order. For this subassembly, find:
   a) Economic order quantity.
   b) Annual holding cost.
   c) Annual ordering cost.
   d) Reorder point.

: 12.10 Francis Timoney, of Timoney Plumbing, uses 1,200 of a certain spare part that costs $25 for each order and $24 annual holding cost. Calculate the total cost for order sizes of 25, 40, 50, 60, and 100. Identify the economic order quantity and consider the implications for making an error in calculating economic order quantity.

· 12.11 Beth Rechsteiner's Dream Store sells water beds and assorted supplies. Her best-selling bed has an annual demand of 400 units. Ordering cost is $40; holding cost is $5 per unit per year. There are 250 working days per year, and lead time is 6 days.
   a) To minimize the total cost, how many units should be ordered each time an order is placed?
   b) If the holding cost per unit were $6 instead of $5, what would the optimal order quantity be?

: 12.12 James Walsh's Computer Store in Houston sells a printer for $200. Demand is constant during the year, and annual demand is forecasted to be 600 units. Holding cost is $20 per unit per year, whereas the cost of ordering is $60 per order. Currently, the company is ordering 12 times per year (50 units each time). There are 250 working days per year, and the lead time is 10 days.
   a) Given the current policy of ordering 50 units at a time, what is the total of the annual ordering cost and the annual holding cost?
   b) If the company used the absolute best inventory policy, what would be the total of ordering and holding costs?
   c) What is the reorder point?

: 12.13 Jan Kottas is the owner of a small company that produces electric knives used to cut fabric. The annual demand is for 8,000 knives, and Jan produces the knives in batches. On average,

Jan can produce 150 knives per day; during the production process, demand has been about 40 knives per day. The cost to set up the production process is $100.00, and it costs Jan $0.80 to carry a knife for one year. How many knives should Jan produce in each batch?

: 12.14 Jimmy Stephens, inventory control manager for Cal-Tex, receives wheel bearings from Wheel-Rite, a small producer of metal parts. Wheel-Rite can produce only 500 wheel bearings per day. Cal-Tex receives 10,000 wheel bearings from Wheel-Rite each year. Because Cal-Tex operates 200 working days each year, its average daily demand of wheel bearings is 50. Ordering cost for Cal-Tex is $40 per order, and carrying cost is $0.60 per wheel bearing per year. Wheel-Rite has agreed to ship the maximum number of wheel bearings that it produces each day to Cal-Tex once an order has been received. How many wheel bearings should Cal-Tex order at one time?

: 12.15 McLeavey Manufacturing has a demand for 1,000 pumps each year. The cost of a pump is $50. It costs McLeavey $40 to place an order, and carrying cost is 25% of unit cost. If pumps are ordered in quantities of 200, McLeavey can get a 3% discount. Should McLeavey order 200 pumps at a time and take the 3% discount?

: 12.16 Jack McCanna Products offers the following discount schedule for its 4-feet-by-8-feet sheets of quality plywood.

Order	Unit Cost
9 sheets or less	$18.00
10 to 50 sheets	$17.50
More than 50 sheets	$17.25

Home Sweet Home Company orders plywood from McCanna. Home Sweet Home has an ordering cost of $45. Carrying cost is 20%, and annual demand is 100 sheets. What do you recommend?

: 12.17 Given the following data on a hardware item stocked by Duncan McDougall Paint Store, should the quantity discount be taken?

$$D = 2,000 \text{ units}$$

$$S = \$10$$

$$H = \$1$$

$$P = \$1$$

$$\text{Discount price} = \$.75$$

$$\begin{pmatrix} \text{Quantity needed to} \\ \text{qualify for discount} \end{pmatrix} = 2,000 \text{ units}$$

: 12.18 The regular price of a tape deck component is $20.00. On orders of 75 units or more, the price is discounted to $18.50. On orders of 100 units or more, the discount price is $15.75. At present, Sound Business, Inc., a manufacturer of stereo components, has an inventory carrying cost of 5% per unit per year, and its ordering cost is $10.00. Annual demand is 45 components. What should Sound Business, Inc., do?

: 12.19 A product is ordered once each year, and the reorder point, without safety stock (dL), is 100 units. Inventory carrying cost is $10 per unit per year, and the cost of a stockout is $50 per unit per year. Given the following demand probabilities during the reorder period, how much safety stock should be carried?

Demand During Reorder Period	Probability
0	.1
50	.2
ROP → 100	.4
150	.2
200	.1
	1.0

: **12.20** Nancy Balaguer, Inc., which sells children's art sets, has an ordering cost of $40 for the BB-1 set. The carrying cost for BB-1 is $5 per set per year. In order to meet demand, Nancy orders large quantities of BB-1 seven times a year. The stockout cost is estimated to be $50 per set. Over the last several years, Nancy has observed the following demand for BB-1 during the lead time.

Demand During Lead Time	Probability
40	.1
50	.2
60	.2
70	.2
80	.2
90	.1
	1.0

The reorder point for BB-1 is 60 units. What level of safety stock should be maintained for BB-1?

: **12.21** Frederick Kohun's company produces a product for which annual demand is 10,000. Because it operates 200 days per year, demand is about 50 per day. Daily production is 200 units. Holding costs are $1.00 per unit per year; setup costs are $200.00. If you wish to produce this product in batches, what size batch should be used?

: **12.22** A product is delivered to Timothy Parson's company once a year. The reorder point, without safety stock, is 200 units. Carrying cost is $15 per unit per year, and the cost of a stockout is $70 per unit per year. Given the following demand probabilities during the reorder period, how much safety stock should be carried?

Demand During Reorder Period	Probability
0	0.1
100	0.1
200	0.2
300	0.2
400	0.2

: **12.23** Demand during lead time for one brand of TV is normally distributed with a mean of 36 TVs and a standard deviation of 15 TVs. What safety stock should be carried for a 90% service level? What is the appropriate reorder point?

: **12.24** Based on available information, lead time demand for CD-ROM drives averages 50 units (normally distributed), with a standard deviation of 5 drives. Management wants a 97% service level.
   a) What value of Z should be applied?
   b) How many drives should be carried as safety stock?
   c) What is the appropriate reorder point?

Case Study

Sturdivant Sound Systems

Sturdivant Sound Systems manufactures and sells sound systems for both home and auto. All parts of the sound systems, with the exception of CD players, are produced in the Rochester, New York, plant. CD players used in the assembly of Sturdivant systems are purchased from Morris Electronics of Concord, New Hampshire.

Sturdivant purchasing agent Mary Kim submits a purchase requisition for CD players once every 4 weeks. The company's annual requirements total 5,000 units (20 per working day), and the cost per unit is $60. (Sturdivant does not purchase in greater quantities because Morris Electronics does not offer quantity discounts.) Because Morris promises delivery within 1 week following receipt of a purchase requisition, rarely is there a shortage of CD players. (Total time between date of order and date of receipt is 10 days.)

Associated with the purchase of each shipment are procurement costs. These costs, which amount to $20 per order, include the costs of preparing the requisition, inspecting and storing the delivered goods, updating inventory records, and issuing a voucher and a check for payment. In addition to procurement costs, Sturdivant incurs inventory carrying costs that include insurance, storage, handling, taxes, and so forth. These costs equal $6 per unit per year.

Beginning in August of this year, Sturdivant management will embark on a companywide cost-control program in an attempt to improve its profits. One area to be closely scrutinized for possible cost savings is inventory procurement.

Discussion Questions

1. Compute the optimal order quantity of CD players.
2. Determine the appropriate reorder point (in units).
3. Compute the cost savings that the company will realize if it implements the optimal inventory procurement decision.
4. Should procurement costs be considered a linear function of the number of orders?

Source: Professor Jerry Kinard, Western Carolina University.

Case Study

LaPlace Power and Light

The southeastern Division of LaPlace Power and Light Company is responsible for providing dependable electric service to customers in and around the area of Metairie, Kenner, Destrehan, LaPlace, Lutcher, Hammond, Pontchatoula, Amite, and Bogalusa, Louisiana. One material used extensively to provide this service is the 1/0 AWG aluminum triplex cable, which delivers the electricity from the distribution pole to the meter loop on the house.

The Southeastern Division Storeroom purchases the cable that this division will use. For the coming year, this division will need 499,500 feet of this service cable. Because this cable is used only on routine service work, practically all of it is installed during the 5 normal workdays. The current cost of this cable is 41.4 cents per foot. Under the present arrangement with the supplier, the Southeastern Storeroom must take one twelfth of its annual need every month. This agreement was reached in order to reduce lead time by assuring LaPlace a regular spot on the supplier's production schedule. Without this agreement, the lead time would be about 12 weeks. No quantity discounts are offered on this cable; however, the supplier requires that a minimum of 15,000 feet be on an order. The Southeastern Storeroom has the space to store a maximum of 300,000 feet of 1/0 AWG aluminum service cable.

Associated with each shipment are ordering costs of $50, which include all the costs from making the purchase requisitions to issuing a check for payment. In addition, inventory carrying costs (including taxes) on all items are considered to be 10% of the purchase price per unit per year.

Because the company is a government-regulated, investor-owned utility, both the Louisiana Public Service Commission and its stockholders watch closely how effectively the company, including inventory management, is managed.

Discussion Questions

1. Evaluate the effectiveness of the current ordering system.
2. Can the current system be improved?

Video Case 7

Inventory Control at Wheeled Coach

Controlling inventory is one of Wheeled Coach's toughest problems. Operating according to a strategy of mass customization and responsiveness, management knows that success is dependent on tight inventory control. Anything else results in an inability to deliver promptly, chaos on the assembly line, and a huge inventory investment. Wheeled Coach finds that almost 50% of the $40,000–$100,000 cost of every vehicle is purchased materials. A large proportion of that 50% is in chassis (purchased from Ford), aluminum (from Reynolds Metal), and plywood used for flooring and cabinetry construction (from local suppliers). Wheeled Coach tracks these "A" inventory items quite carefully, maintaining tight security/control and ordering carefully so as to maximize quantity discounts while minimizing on-hand stock. Because of long lead times and scheduling needs at Reynolds, aluminum must actually be ordered as much as 8 months in advance.

In a crowded ambulance industry in which it is the only giant, its 45 competitors don't have the purchasing power to draw the same discounts as Wheeled Coach. But this competitive cost advantage cannot be taken lightly, according to President Bob Collins. "Cycle counting in our stock rooms is critical. No part can leave the locked stockrooms without appearing on a bill of materials."

Accurate bills of material (BOM) are a requirement if products are going to be built on time. Additionally, because of the custom nature of each vehicle, most orders are won only after a bidding process. Accurate BOMs are critical to cost estimation and the resulting bid. For these reasons, Collins was emphatic that Wheeled Coach maintain outstanding inventory control. The *Global Company Profile* featuring Wheeled Coach (which opens chapter 14) provides further details about the ambulance production process.

Discussion Questions

1. Explain how Wheeled Coach implements ABC analysis.
2. If you were to take over as inventory control manager at Wheeled Coach, what additional policies and techniques would you initiate to ensure accurate inventory records?
3. How would you go about implementing these suggestions?

■ Internet Case Studies ■

See our Internet home page at http://www.prenhall.com/heizer for these additional case studies: Martin-Pullin Bicycle Corp., Professional Video Management, Western Ranchman Outfitters, and Touro Infirmary.

BIBLIOGRAPHY

Bernard, Paul. "Are Your Customers Getting Better Service Than You Planned to Provide?" *APICS—The Performance Advantage,* July 1997, pp. 30–32.

Bowers, Melissa R., and Anurag Agarwal. "Lower In-Process Inventories and Better on Time Performance at Tanner Companies, Inc." *Interfaces* 25, no. 4 (July–August 1995): 30–43.

Brown, R. G. *Decision Rules for Inventory Management.* New York: Holt, Rinehart and Winston, 1967.

Denton, D. Keith. "Top Managements' Role in Inventory Control." *Industrial Engineering,* August 1994, pp. 26–27.

Freeland, J. R., J. P. Leschke, and E. N. Weiss. "Guidelines for Setup-Cost Reduction Programs to Achieve Zero Inventory." *Journal of Operations Management* 9 (January 1990): 85.

Groenevelt, H., L. Pintelon, and A. Seidmann. "Production Lot Sizing with Machine Breakdowns." *Management Science* 38, 1 (January 1992): 104.

Hall, R. *Zero Inventories.* Homewood, IL: Dow Jones-Irwin, 1983.

Jinchiro, N., and R. Hall. "Management Specs for Stockless Production." *Harvard Business Review* 63 (May–June 1983): 89–91.

Landvater, D. V. *World Class Production and Inventory Management.* Newburg, NH: Oliver Wight Publications, 1993.

Schniederjans, M. *Topics in Just-in-Time Management.* Boston: Allyn & Bacon, 1993.

Shingo, S. *A Revolution in Manufacturing: The SMED System.* Cambridge, MA: Productivity Press, 1986.

Vollmann, T. E., W. L. Berry, and D. C. Whybark. *Manufacturing Planning and Control Systems.* Homewood, IL: Irwin, 1988.

Wight, O. W. *Production and Inventory Management in the Computer Age.* Boston: Cahners, 1974.

INTERNET RESOURCES

APICS: The Educational Society for Resource Management:
http://www.apics.org

Center for Inventory Management:
http://www.inventorymanagement.com

Institute of Industrial Engineers:
http://www.iienet.org

Inventory Control Forum:
http://www.cris.com/~kthill/inventry.htm

List of inventory control related sites:
http://www.cris.com/~kthill/sites.htm

SUPPLEMENT 12

JUST-IN-TIME SYSTEMS

SUPPLEMENT OUTLINE

JUST-IN-TIME PHILOSOPHY
SUPPLIERS
   Goals of JIT Partnerships
   Concerns of Suppliers
JIT LAYOUT
   Distance Reduction
   Increased Flexibility
   Impact on Employees
   Reduced Space and Inventory
INVENTORY
   Reduce Variability
   Reduce Inventory
   Reduce Lot Sizes
   Reduce Setup Costs

SCHEDULING
   Level Material-Use Schedules
   Kanban
QUALITY
EMPLOYEE EMPOWERMENT
JIT IN SERVICES
SUMMARY
KEY TERMS
SOLVED PROBLEM
DISCUSSION QUESTIONS
PROBLEMS
CASE STUDY:
   ELECTRONIC SYSTEMS, INC.
BIBLIOGRAPHY
INTERNET RESOURCES

LEARNING OBJECTIVES

When you complete this supplement you should be able to:

Identify or Define:

Types of waste

Variability

Kanban

Describe or Explain:

Just-in-time philosophy

Pull systems

Push systems

The goals of JIT partnerships

The impact of JIT on layout

How JIT affects quality and employees

General Motors' plant in Lordstown, Ohio, is an example of the JIT drive for leanness. To eliminate the costly stockpiling of parts, supplies are kept so tight that sometimes helicopters have to fly in and out with deliveries. GM is using JIT, as are many other organizations, in its drive for continuous improvement.

General Motors' story is a common one in the auto industry. Toyota, the developer of JIT, also works aggressively with suppliers to reduce waste. Partnering with suppliers means Toyota shares complete information about operations, including schedules, costs, and quality levels. JIT extends to services as well. Restaurants, for instance, expect high-quality produce delivered without failure just when it is needed.

JUST-IN-TIME PHILOSOPHY

Just-in-time
A philosophy of continuous and forced problem solving that drives out waste.

Just-in-time (JIT) is a philosophy of continuous and forced problem solving. With JIT, supplies and components are "pulled" through a system to arrive *where* they are needed *when* they are needed. When good units do not arrive just as needed, a "problem" has been identified. This makes JIT an excellent tool to help operations managers add value by driving out waste and unwanted variability. Because there is no excess inventory or excess time in a JIT system, costs associated with unneeded inventory are eliminated and throughput improved. Consequently, the benefits of JIT are particularly helpful in supporting strategies of rapid response and low cost.

Because elimination of waste and variability and the concept of "pulling" materials are fundamental to JIT, we will briefly discuss these in this section. In the remainder of this supplement, we will introduce applications of JIT in dealing with suppliers, layout, inventory, scheduling, quality, and employee empowerment.

Waste Reduction When we talk about waste in the production of goods or services, we are describing *anything that does not add value*. Products being *stored, inspected,* or *de-*

layed, products waiting in queues, and *defective products* do not add value; they are 100% waste. Moreover, any activity that does not add value to a product *from the customer's perspective* is waste. JIT speeds up throughput, allowing faster delivery times and reducing work-in-process. Reducing work-in-process releases assets in inventory for other more productive purposes.

Variability Reduction To achieve just-in-time material movement, managers *reduce variability caused by both internal and external factors.* **Variability** is any deviation from the optimum process that delivers perfect product on time, every time. Inventory hides variability—a polite word for problems. The less variability in the system, the less waste in the system. Most variability is caused by tolerating waste or by poor management. Variability occurs because:

1. Employees, machines, and suppliers produce units that do not conform to standards, are late, or are not the proper quantity
2. Engineering drawings or specifications are inaccurate.
3. Production personnel try to produce before drawings or specifications are complete.
4. Customer demands are unknown.

Variability can often go unseen when inventory exists. This is why JIT is so effective. The JIT philosophy of continuous improvement removes variability. The removal of variability allows us to move good materials just-in-time for use. JIT reduces material throughout the supply chain. It helps us focus on adding value at each stage. Table S12.1 on page 482 outlines the contributions of JIT; we discuss each of these concepts in this supplement.

Pull versus Push The concept behind JIT is that of a **pull system:** a system that *pulls* a unit to where it is needed just as it is needed. A pull system uses signals to request production and delivery from stations upstream to the station that has production capacity available. The "pull" concept is used both within the immediate production process and with suppliers. By *pulling* material through the system in very small lots just as it is needed, the cushion of inventory that hides problems is removed, problems become evident, and continuous improvement is emphasized. Removing the cushion of inventory also reduces both investment in inventory and manufacturing cycle time.

Manufacturing cycle time is the time between the arrival of raw materials and the shipping of finished products. For example, at Northern Telecom, a phone switching-system manufacturer, materials are pulled directly from qualified suppliers to the assembly line. This effort reduced Northern's receiving segment of manufacturing cycle time from 3 weeks to just 4 hours, the incoming inspection staff from 47 to 24, and problems on the shop floor caused by defective materials by 97%.[1]

Many firms still move material through their facilities in a "push" fashion. A **push system** dumps orders on the next downstream workstation regardless of timeliness and resource availability. Push systems are the antithesis of JIT.

SUPPLIERS

Incoming material is often delayed at the shipper, in transit, at receiving departments, and at incoming inspection. Similarly, finished goods are often stored or held at warehouses prior to shipment to distributors or customers. Because holding inventory is wasteful, JIT partnerships are directed toward reducing such waste.

Variability Any deviation from the optimum process that delivers perfect product on time, every time.

Pull system A JIT concept that results in material being produced only when requested and moved to where it is needed just as it is needed.

Manufacturing cycle time The time between the arrival of raw materials and the shipping of finished products.

Push system A system that pushes materials into downstream workstations regardless of their timeliness or availability of resources to perform the work.

---

[1] Roy Merrils, "How Northern Telecom Competes on Time," *Harvard Business Review* 67 (July–August 1989): 108–114.

TABLE S12.1 ■ JIT Contributes to Competitive Advantage

JIT REQUIRES:

Suppliers:	Reduced number of vendors; Supportive supplier relationships; Quality deliveries on time
Layout:	Work-cell layouts with testing at each step of the process; Group technology; Movable, changeable, flexible machinery; High level of workplace organization and neatness; Reduced space for inventory; Delivery directly to work areas
Inventory:	Small lot sizes; Low setup time; Specialized bins for holding set number of parts
Scheduling:	Zero deviation from schedules; Level schedules; Suppliers informed of schedules; Kanban techniques
Preventive maintenance:	Scheduled; Daily routine; Operator involvement
Quality production:	Statistical process control; Quality suppliers; Quality within the firm
Employee empowerment:	Empowered and cross-trained employees; Training support; Few job classifications to ensure flexibility of employees
Commitment:	Support of management, employees, and suppliers

WHICH RESULTS IN:

Queue and delay reduction speeds throughput, frees assets, and wins orders

Quality improvement reduces waste and wins orders

Cost reduction increases margin or reduces selling price

Variability reduction in the workplace reduces wastes and wins orders

Rework reduction reduces wastes and wins orders

WHICH YIELDS:

Faster response to the customer at lower cost and higher quality—

A Competitive Advantage

JIT partnerships
Partnerships of suppliers and purchasers that remove waste and drive down costs for mutual benefits.

JIT partnerships exist when supplier and purchaser work together with a mutual goal of removing waste and driving down costs. Such relationships are critical for successful JIT. Every *moment* material is held, some process that adds value should be occurring. To ensure this is the case, Xerox, like other leading organizations, views the supplier as an extension of its own organization. Because of this view, the Xerox staff expects suppliers to be as fully committed to improvement as Xerox. This relationship requires a high degree of openness[2] by both supplier and purchaser. Table S12.2 shows the characteristics of JIT partnerships.

---

[2] J. Douglas Blocher, Charles W. Lackey, and Vincent A. Mabert, "From JIT Purchasing to Supplier Partnerships at Xerox," *Target* 9, no. 3 (May–June 1993): 12–18.

TABLE S12.2 ■ Characteristics of JIT Partnerships

Suppliers

Few suppliers
Nearby suppliers
Repeat business with same suppliers
Analysis to enable desirable suppliers to become or to stay price competitive
Competitive bidding mostly limited to new purchases
Buyer resists vertical integration and subsequent wipeout of supplier business
Suppliers encouraged to extend JIT buying to their suppliers

Quantities

Steady output rate
Frequent deliveries in small-lot quantities
Long-term contract agreements
Minimal paperwork to release orders
Delivery quantities fixed for whole contract term
Little or no permissible overage or underage
Suppliers package in exact quantities
Suppliers reduce their production lot sizes (or store unreleased material)

Quality

Minimal product specifications imposed on supplier
Help suppliers to meet quality requirements
Close relationships between buyers' and suppliers' quality assurance people
Suppliers use process control charts instead of lot-sampling inspection

Shipping

Scheduling of inbound freight
Gain control by use of company-owned or contract shipping and warehousing

Source: Adapted from Richard J. Schonberger and James P. Gilbert, "Just-in-Time Purchasing: A Challenge for U.S. Industry." Copyright © 1983 by The Regents of the University of California. Reprinted from the *California Management Review* 26, no. 1, by permission of The Regents.

Goals of JIT Partnerships

The Goals of JIT Partnerships:

1. *Elimination of unnecessary activities*. With good suppliers, for instance, receiving activity and incoming-inspection activity are unnecessary under JIT.
2. *Elimination of in-plant inventory*. JIT delivers materials where and when needed. Raw material inventory is necessary only if there is reason to believe that suppliers are undependable. Likewise, parts or components should be delivered in small lots directly to the using department as needed.
3. *Elimination of in-transit inventory*. General Motors once estimated that at any given time, over one half of its inventory is in transit. Modern purchasing departments are now addressing in-transit inventory reduction by encouraging suppliers and prospective suppliers to locate near manufacturing plants and provide frequent small shipments. The shorter the flow of material in the resource pipeline, the less inventory. Inventory can also be reduced by a technique known as *consignment*. Under a **consignment inventory** arrangement, the supplier maintains the title to the inventory until it is used. For instance, an assembly plant may find a hardware supplier that is willing to locate its warehouse where the user currently has its

To get JIT to work, the purchasing agent must communicate the company's goal to the supplier. This includes delivery, packaging, lot sizes, quality, and so on.

Consignment inventory
An arrangement where the supplier maintains title to the inventory until it is used.

stockroom. In this manner, when hardware is needed, it is no farther than the stockroom, and the supplier can ship to other, perhaps smaller, purchasers from the "stockroom."

4. *Elimination of poor suppliers.* When a firm reduces the number of suppliers, it increases long-term commitments. To obtain improved quality and reliability, vendors and purchasers have mutual understanding and trust. Achieving deliveries only when needed and in the exact quantities needed also requires *perfect quality*—or as it is also known, *zero defects.* Of course, *both* the supplier and the delivery system must be excellent.

Concerns of Suppliers

To establish JIT partnerships, several supplier concerns must be addressed.[3] The supplier concerns include:

1. *Desire for diversification.* Many suppliers do not want to tie themselves to long-term contracts with one customer. The suppliers' perception is that they reduce their risk if they have a variety of customers.
2. *Poor customer scheduling.* Many suppliers have little faith in the purchaser's ability to reduce orders to a smooth, coordinated schedule.
3. *Engineering changes.* Frequent engineering changes, with inadequate lead time for suppliers to carry out tooling and process changes, play havoc with JIT.
4. *Quality assurance.* Production with zero defects is not considered realistic by many suppliers.

Many services have adopted JIT techniques as a normal part of their business. Most restaurants, and certainly all fine-dining restaurants, expect and receive JIT deliveries. Both buyer and supplier expect fresh, high-quality produce delivered without fail just when it is needed. The system doesn't work any other way.

---

[3] This summary is based on a study by Tom Schmitt and Mary Connors, "A Survey of Suppliers' Attitudes Toward the Establishment of JIT," *Operations Management Review* 3, no. 4 (summer 1985): 36.

JIT LAYOUT 485

> ## OM IN ACTION
>
> ### JIT AIDS RAPID RESPONSE AT LIBRALTER PLASTICS
>
> Libralter Plastics, in Walled Lake, Michigan, makes wheel covers, grilles, and other plastic parts for the Big Three automakers. In only 3 years, the company went from chaos and waste to "the epitome of what every company is looking for in a supplier." Earning the *USA Today* Quality Cup Award for small organizations, Libralter employees developed new ways to respond to Big Three JIT demands. This meant being nimble enough to deliver parts on very short notice.
>
> First, workers developed a computer system that sharply reduced inventory. Before, supplies would sit on Libralter's factory floor an average of 23 days. Down to 14 days now, the changes helped slash inventory holding costs almost $250,000 a year.
>
> Libralter also responds to customers more quickly. Processing an order used to take 36 hours. Now, it takes less than 1 hour. Delivery trucks that used to sit idle until noon are loaded first thing in the morning.
>
> The team of 10 employees formed to fix the problem came from accounting, production, and information systems. However, most of the quality improvements at Libralter came after employees from the factory floor suggested them. As one Libralter manager says, "If you want to know the best way to do a job, ask the guy who's doing it."
>
> *Sources: Incentive* (June, 1994): 13 and *USA Today* (April 8, 1994): 2B.

5. *Small lot sizes.* Suppliers often have processes designed for large lot sizes and see frequent delivery to the customer in small lots as a way to transfer holding costs to the supplier.
6. *Proximity.* Depending upon the customer's location, frequent supplier delivery of small lots may be seen as economically prohibitive.

For those who remain skeptical of JIT partnerships, we would point out that virtually every restaurant in the world practices JIT, and with little staff support. Many restaurants order food for the next day in the middle of the night for delivery the next morning. They are ordering just *what* is needed, for delivery *when* it is needed, from reliable suppliers.

JIT LAYOUT

JIT layouts reduce another kind of waste—movement. The movement of material on a factory floor (or paper in an office) does not add value. Consequently, we want flexible layouts that reduce the movement of both people and material. JIT layouts move material directly to the location where needed. For instance, an assembly line should be designed with delivery points next to the line so material need not be delivered first to a receiving department elsewhere in the plant, then moved again. This is what VF Corporation's Wrangler Division in Greensboro, North Carolina, did. Now denim is delivered directly to the line. When a layout reduces distance, the firm also saves space and eliminates potential areas for unwanted inventory. Table S12.3 provides a list of layout tactics.

TABLE S12.3 ■ Layout Tactics
Build work cells for families of products
Minimize distance
Design little space for inventory
Improve employee communication
Use poka-yoke devices
Build flexible or movable equipment
Cross train workers to add flexibility

Distance Reduction

Reducing distance is a major contribution of work cells, work centers, and focused factories (see chapter 9). The days of long production lines and huge economic lots, with goods passing through monumental, single-operation machines, are gone. Now firms use work cells, often arranged in a U shape, containing several machines performing different operations. These work cells are often based on group technology codes (as discussed in chapter 6). Group technology codes help us identify components with similar characteristics so we can group them into families. Once families are identified, work cells are built for them. The result can be thought of as a small product-oriented facility where the "product" is actually a group of similar products—a family of products. The cells produce one good unit at a time, and ideally they produce the units *only* after a customer orders them.

Increased Flexibility

Modern work cells are designed so they can be easily rearranged to adapt to changes in volume, product improvements, or even new designs. Almost nothing in these new departments is bolted down. This same concept of layout flexibility applies to office environments. Not only are most office furniture and equipment movable, but so are office walls, computer connections, and telecommunications. Layout flexibility aids the changes that result from product *and* process improvements that are inevitable with a philosophy of continuous improvement.

Impact on Employees

> In a JIT system, each worker is inspecting the part as it comes to him or her. Each worker knows that the part must be good before it goes on to the next "customer."

Employees working together are cross-trained so they can bring flexibility and efficiency to the work cell. JIT layouts allow employees to work together so they can tell each other about problems and opportunities for improvement. When layouts provide for sequential operations, feedback can be immediate. Defects are waste. When workers produce units one at a time, they test each product or component at each subsequent production stage. Machines in work cells with self-testing "poka-yoke" functions detect defects and stop automatically when they occur. Before JIT, defective products were replaced from inventory. Because surplus inventory is not kept in JIT facilities, there are no such buffers. Getting it right the first time is critical.

Reduced Space and Inventory

Because JIT layouts reduce travel distance, they also reduce inventory by removing space for inventory. When there is little space, inventory must be moved in very small lots or even single units. Units are always moving because there is no storage. For instance, each month Security Pacific Corporation's focused facility sorts 7 million checks, processes 5 million statements, and mails 190,000 customer statements. With a JIT layout, mail processing time has been reduced by 33%, salary costs by $ tens of thousands per year, floor space by 50%, and in-process waiting lines by 75% to 90%.[4] Storage, including shelves and drawers, has been removed.

INVENTORY

> **Just-in-time inventory**
> The minimum inventory necessary to keep a perfect system running.

Inventories in production and distribution systems often exist "just in case" something goes wrong. That is, they are used just in case some variation from the production plan occurs. The "extra" inventory is then used to cover variations or problems. Effective inventory tactics require "just in time," not "just in case." **Just-in-time inventory** is the minimum inventory necessary to keep a perfect system running. With just-in-time inventory, the exact amount of goods arrives at the moment it is needed, not a minute before or a minute after. Some useful JIT inventory tactics are shown in Table S12.4 and discussed in more detail in the following sections.

---

[4] Paul Jackson, "White Collar JIT at Security Pacific," *Target* 7, no. 1 (spring 1991): 32–37.

OM IN ACTION

LET'S TRY ZERO INVENTORY

Just-in-time tactics are still being incorporated in manufacturing to improve quality, drive down inventory investment, and reduce other costs. However, JIT is also established practice in restaurants, where customers expect it, and a necessity in the produce business, where there is little choice. Pacific Pre-Cut Produce, a $14 million fruit and vegetable processing company in Tracy, California, holds inventory to zero. Buyers are in action in the wee hours of the morning. At 6 A.M., produce production crews show up. Orders for very specific cuts and mixtures of fruit and vegetable salads and stir-fry ingredients for supermarkets, restaurants, and institutional kitchens pour in from 8 A.M. until 4 P.M. Shipping begins at 10 P.M. and continues until the last order is filled and loaded at 5 A.M. the next morning. Inventories are once again zero, things are relatively quiet, and then the routine starts again. Pacific Pre-Cut Produce has accomplished a complete cycle of purchase, manufacture, and shipping in about 24 hours.

V.P. Bob Borzone calls the process the ultimate in mass-customization. "We buy everything as a bulk commodity, then slice and dice it to fit the exact requirements of the end user. There are 20 different stir-fry mixes. Some customers want the snow peas clipped on both ends, some just on one. Some want only red bell peppers in the mix, some only yellow. You tailor the product to the customer's requirements. You're trying to satisfy the need of a lot of end users, and each restaurant and retailer wants to look different."

Sources: Inbound Logistics, August, (1997): 26–32; and Restaurant Business (June 10, 1992): 16–20.

Reduce Variability

The idea behind JIT is to eliminate inventory that hides variability in the production system. This concept is illustrated in Figure S12.1, which shows a lake full of rocks. The water in the lake represents inventory flow, and the rocks represent problems such as late deliveries, machine breakdowns, and poor personnel performance. The water level in the lake hides variability and problems. Because inventory hides problems, they are hard to find.

Reduce Inventory

Operations managers move toward JIT by first removing inventory. Reducing inventory uncovers the "rocks" in Figure S12.1(a) that represent the variability and problems currently being tolerated. With reduced inventory, management chips away at the exposed

TABLE S12.4 ■
JIT Inventory Tactics

Use a pull system to move inventory
Reduce lot size
Develop just-in-time delivery systems with suppliers
Deliver directly to point of use
Perform to schedule
Reduce setup time
Use group technology

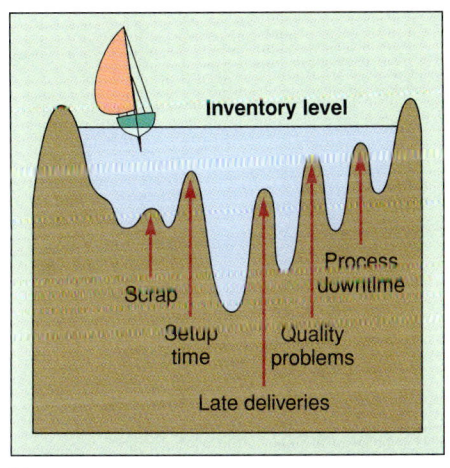

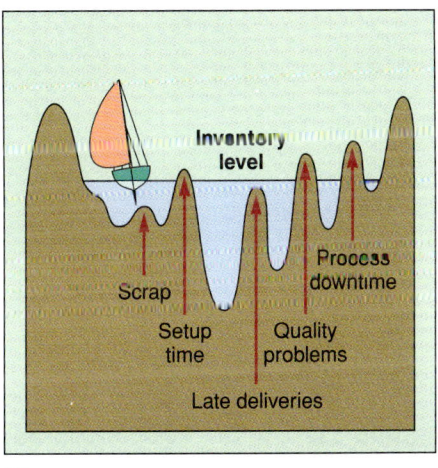

(a)   (b)

FIGURE S12.1 ■ Inventory Hides Problems, Just as Water in a Lake Hides the Rocks

"Inventory Is Evil."
Shigeo Shingo

problems until the lake is clear. After the lake is clear, managers make additional cuts in inventory and continue to chip away at the next level of exposed problems (see Figure S12.1(b)). Ultimately, there will be virtually no inventory and no problems (variability).

Shigeo Shingo, codeveloper of the Toyota JIT system, says, "Inventory is evil." He is not far from the truth. If inventory itself is not evil, it hides evil at great cost.

Reduce Lot Sizes

Just-in-time has also come to mean elimination of waste by reducing investment in inventory. The key to JIT is producing good product in small lot sizes. Reducing the size of batches can be a major help in reducing inventory and inventory costs. As we saw in chapter 12, when inventory usage is constant, the average inventory level is the sum of the maximum inventory plus the minimum inventory divided by two. Figure S12.2(a) shows

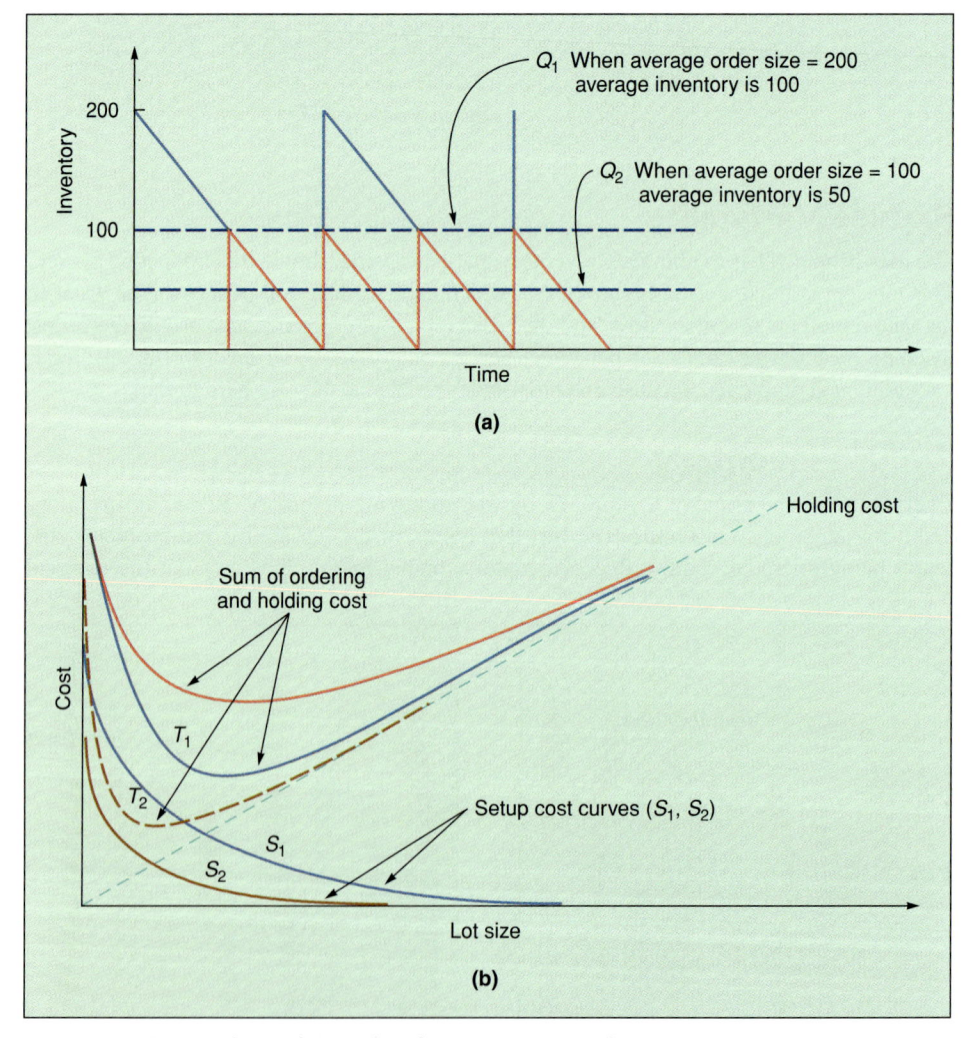

FIGURE S12.2 ■ **The Relationship between JIT and Setup** *(a) More frequent orders dramatically reduce average inventories, (b) but more frequent orders require reducing setup costs; otherwise, inventory costs will rise. As the setup costs are lowered (from S_1 to S_2), inventory costs also fall (from T_1 and T_2).*

that lowering the order size increases the number of orders but drops inventory levels dramatically.

Reduce Setup Costs

Both inventory and the cost of holding it go down as the inventory-reorder quantity and the maximum inventory level drops. However, because inventory requires incurring an ordering or setup cost that must be applied to the units produced, managers tend to purchase (or produce) large orders. With large orders, each unit purchased or ordered absorbs only a small part of the setup cost. Consequently, the way to drive down lot sizes *and* reduce average inventory is to reduce setup cost, which in turn lowers the optimum order size.

The effect of reduced setup costs on total cost and lot size is shown in Figure S12.2(b). Moreover, smaller lot sizes hide fewer problems. In many environments, setup cost is highly correlated with setup time. In a manufacturing facility, setups usually require a substantial amount of work prior to actually being accomplished at a work center. Much of the preparation required by a setup can be done prior to shutting down the machine or process. Setup times can be reduced substantially, as shown in Figure S12.3. Machines and processes that traditionally have taken hours to set up are now being set up in less than a minute by the more imaginative world-class manufacturers.

Just as setup costs can be reduced at a machine in a factory, setup time can also be reduced during the process of getting the order ready. It does little good to drive down factory setup time from hours to minutes if orders are going to take 2 weeks to process or "set up" in the office. This is exactly what happens in organizations that forget that JIT concepts have applications in offices as well as the factory. Reducing setup time (and cost) is an excellent way to reduce inventory investment and to improve productivity.

> Reduced lot sizes must be accompanied by reduced setup times; otherwise, the setup cost must be assigned to fewer units.

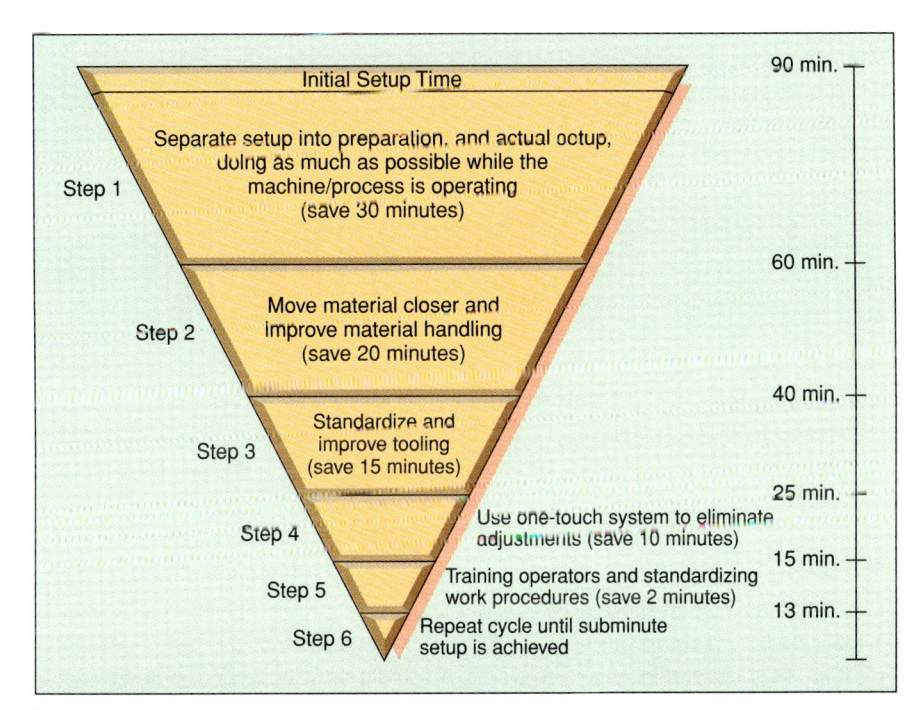

Step 1 — Separate setup into preparation, and actual setup, doing as much as possible while the machine/process is operating (save 30 minutes) — Initial Setup Time: 90 min.

Step 2 — Move material closer and improve material handling (save 20 minutes) — 60 min.

Step 3 — Standardize and improve tooling (save 15 minutes) — 40 min.

Step 4 — Use one-touch system to eliminate adjustments (save 10 minutes) — 25 min.

Step 5 — Training operators and standardizing work procedures (save 2 minutes) — 15 min.

Step 6 — Repeat cycle until subminute setup is achieved — 13 min.

FIGURE S12.3 ■ Steps to Reduce Setup Times *Reduced setup times are a major JIT component.*

TABLE S12.5 ■
JIT Scheduling Tactics
Communicate the schedule to suppliers
Make level schedules
Freeze part of the schedule
Perform to schedule
Seek one-piece-make and one-piece-move
Eliminate waste
Produce in small lots
Use kanbans
Make each operation produce a perfect part

SCHEDULING

Effective schedules, communicated both within the organization and to outside suppliers, support JIT. Better scheduling also improves the ability to meet customer orders, drives down inventory by allowing smaller lot sizes, and reduces work-in-process. For instance, Ford Motor Company now ties some suppliers to its final assembly schedule. Ford communicates its schedules to bumper manufacturer Polycon Industries from the Ford Oakville production control system. The scheduling system describes the style and color of the bumper needed for each vehicle moving down the final assembly line. The scheduling system transmits the information to portable terminals carried by Polycon warehouse personnel who load the bumpers onto conveyors leading to the loading dock. The bumpers are then trucked 50 miles to the Ford plant. Total time is 4 hours.[5] Table S12.5 suggests several items that can contribute to achieving these goals, but two techniques (in addition to communicating schedules) are paramount. They are *level material-use schedules* and *kanban*.

Level Material-Use Schedules

Level material-use schedules process frequent small batches rather than a few large batches. Because this technique schedules many small lots that are always changing, it has on occasion been called "jelly bean" scheduling. Figure S12.4 contrasts a traditional large-lot approach using large batches with a JIT level material-use schedule using many small batches. The operations manager's task is to make and move small lots so the level material-use schedule is economical. The scheduler may find that *freezing* the portion of the schedule closest to due dates allows the production system to function and the schedule to be met. Freezing means not allowing changes to be part of the schedule. Operations managers expect the schedule to be achieved with no deviations from the schedule.

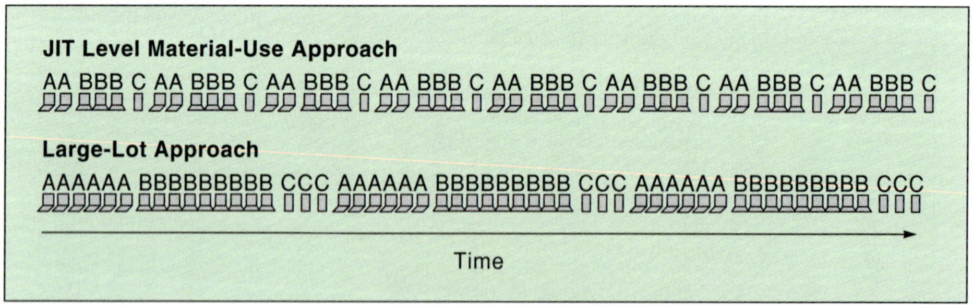

Level material-use schedules Scheduling products so that each day's production meets the demand for that day.

JIT Level Material-Use Approach
AA BBB C AA BBB C AA BBB C AA BBB C AA BBB C AA BBB C AA BBB C AA BBB C

Large-Lot Approach
AAAAAA BBBBBBBBB CCC AAAAAA BBBBBBBBB CCC AAAAAA BBBBBBBBB CCC

Time

FIGURE S12.4 ■ **Scheduling Small Lots of Parts A, B, and C Increases Flexibility to Meet Customer Demand and Reduces Inventory** *The JIT approach to scheduling produces just as many of each model per time period as the large-lot approach, provided setup times are lowered.*

Kanban

One way to achieve small lot sizes is to move inventory through the shop only as needed rather than *pushing* it on to the next workstation whether or not the personnel there are ready for it. As noted earlier, when inventory is moved only as needed, it is referred to as a *pull* system and the ideal lot size is one. The Japanese call this system *kanban*.

---

[5] Mike Ngo and Paul Szucs, "Four Hours," *APICS-The Performance Advantage* 6, no. 1 (January 1996): 30–32.

SCHEDULING 491

A kanban need not be as formal as signal lights or empty carts. In this photo, the cook in a fast-food restaurant knows that when six cars are in line, eight meat patties and six orders of french fries should be cooking.

Kanban is a Japanese word for *card*. In their effort to reduce inventory, the Japanese use systems that "pull" inventory through work centers. They often use a "card" to signal the need for another container of material—hence the name *kanban*. *The card is the authorization for the next container of material to be produced.* Typically, a kanban signal exists for each container of items to be obtained. An order for the container is then initiated by each kanban and "pulled" from the producing department or supplier. A sequence of kanbans "pulls" the material through the plant.

The system has been modified in many facilities so that, even though it is called a *kanban*, the card itself does not exist. In some cases, an empty position on the floor is sufficient indication that the next container is needed. In other cases, some sort of signal, such as a flag or rag (Figure S12.5) signifies that it is time for the next container.

Kanban The Japanese word for card that has come to mean "signal"; a kanban system moves parts through production via a "pull" from a signal.

Signal marker hanging on post for part C584 shows that production should start for that part. The post is located so that workers in normal locations can easily see it.

Signal marker on stack of boxes.

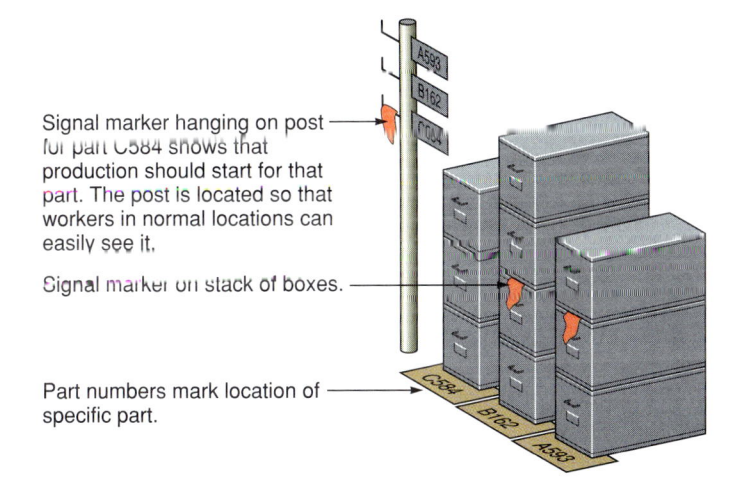

Part numbers mark location of specific part.

FIGURE S12.5 ■ **Diagram of Outbound Stockpoint with Warning-Signal Marker**
Source: Robert W. Hall, *Zero Inventories* (Homewood, IL: Dow Jones-Irwin, 1983), p. 51.

Determining the Number of Kanban Cards or Containers The number of kanban cards, or containers, in a JIT system sets the amount of authorized inventory. To determine the number of containers moving back and forth between the using area and the producing areas, management first sets the size of each container. This is done by computing the lot size, using a model such as the production order quantity model (discussed in chapter 12). Setting the number of containers involves knowing: (1) lead time needed to produce a container of parts and (2) the amount of safety stock needed to account for variability or uncertainty in the system. The number of kanban cards is computed as follows:

$$\text{Number of kanbans (containers)} = \frac{\text{Demand during lead time} + \text{Safety stock}}{\text{Size of container}}$$

Example S1 illustrates how to calculate the number of kanbans needed.

EXAMPLE S1

Hobbs Bakery produces short runs of cakes that are shipped to grocery stores. The owner, Ken Hobbs, wants to try to reduce inventory by changing to a kanban system. He has developed the following data and asked you to finish the project by telling him the number of kanbans (containers) needed.

Daily demand	500 cakes
Production lead time	2 days
Safety stock	1/2 day
Container size (determined on a production order size EOQ basis)	250 cakes

Solution

Demand during lead-time (= lead time × daily demand = 2 days × 500 cakes =)   1,000
Safety Stock   250
Number of kanbans (containers) needed =

$$\frac{\text{Demand during lead time} + \text{Safety stock}}{\text{Container size}} = \frac{1{,}000 + 250}{250} = 5$$

Advantages of Kanban Containers are typically very small, usually a matter of a few hours' worth of production. Such a system requires tight schedules. Small quantities must be produced several times a day. The process must run smoothly with little variability in quality of lead time because any shortage has an almost immediate impact on the entire system. Kanban places added emphasis on meeting schedules, reducing the time and cost required by setups, and economical material handling.

Whether it is called kanban or something else, the advantages of small inventory and *pulling* material through the plant only when needed are significant. For instance, small batches allow only a very limited amount of faulty or delayed material. Problems are immediately evident. Numerous aspects of inventory are bad; only one aspect—availability—is good. Among the bad aspects are poor quality, obsolescence, damage, occupied space, committed assets, increased insurance, increased material handling, and increased accidents. Kanban systems put downward pressure on all of these negative aspects of inventory.

In-plant kanban systems often use standardized, reusable containers that protect the specific quantities to be moved. Such containers are also desirable in the supply chain. Standardized containers reduce weight and disposal costs, generate less wasted space in trailers, and require less labor to pack, unpack, and prepare items.

Manufacturers' inventory/sales ratio was substantially lower in the last recession than in earlier recessions, thanks in large part to JIT inventories.

QUALITY

The relationship between JIT and quality is a strong one.[6] They are related in three ways. First, JIT cuts the cost of obtaining good quality. This saving occurs because scrap, rework, inventory investment, and damage costs are buried in inventory. JIT forces down inventory; therefore, fewer bad units are produced and fewer units must be reworked. In short, whereas inventory *hides* bad quality, JIT immediately *exposes* it.

Second, JIT improves quality. As JIT shrinks queues and lead time, it keeps evidence of errors fresh and limits the number of potential sources of error. In effect, JIT creates an early warning system for quality problems so that fewer bad units are produced and feedback is immediate. This advantage can accrue both within the firm and with goods received from outside vendors.

Finally, better quality means fewer buffers are needed and, therefore, a better, easier-to-employ JIT system can exist. Often the purpose of keeping inventory is to protect against poor production performance resulting from unreliable quality. If consistent quality exists, JIT allows firms to reduce all costs associated with inventory. Table S12.6 suggests some requirements for quality in a JIT environment.

TABLE S12.6 ■
JIT Quality Tactics
Use statistical process control
Empower employees
Build fail-safe methods (poka-yoke, checklists, and so on)
Provide immediate feedback

EMPLOYEE EMPOWERMENT

Whereas some JIT techniques require policy and strategy decisions, many are part of the purview of empowered employees. Empowered employees can bring their involvement to bear on most of the daily operations issues that are so much a part of a just-in-time philosophy. Since the dawn of the industrial revolution, much of management has been concerned with improving performance through the simplification of work. This policy made good sense in an age when many employees were illiterate and communication was complicated because of a variety of languages in the immigrant-filled workplaces of America. In much of the world, however, companies now have the opportunity to hire literate employees and use the techniques of the visual workplace. Consequently, communication problems are much less difficult than they were 100 or 200 years ago. This means that those tasks that have traditionally been assigned to staff can move to empowered employees. Aided by aggressive cross training and few job classifications, firms can engage the mental as well as physical capacities of employees in the challenging task of improving the workplace.

Employee empowerment follows the management adage that no one knows the job better than those who do it. Firms not only train and cross train, but need to take full advantage of that investment by enriching jobs.[7] For example, at a Thermofit plant in Britain, it once took machine operators 2 hours to change over machines for a new product—a costly waste of time when entire production runs last only 5 or 6 hours. Now with training and the aid of videotaped changeovers and analysis by the employees themselves, the changeover has been reduced to 45 minutes.[8]

JIT's philosophy of continuous improvement gives employees the opportunity to enrich their jobs and their lives. When empowerment is managed successfully, companies gain from mutual commitment and respect on the part of both employees and management.

---

[6] See related discussion in Barbara B. Flynn, Sadao Sakakibara, and Roger G. Schroeder. "Relationship Between JIT and TQM: Practices and Performance," *Academy of Management Journal* 38, no. 5 (1995): 1325–1360.

[7] Richard J. Schonberger, "Human Resource Management Lessons from a Decade of Total Quality Management and Reengineering," *California Management Review*, summer 1994, pp. 109–123.

[8] Seth Lubove, "A Long, Last Mile," *Forbes*, October 10, 1994, pp. 66–69.

JIT IN SERVICES

All of the JIT techniques for dealing with suppliers, layout, inventory, and scheduling are used in services.

Suppliers As we have noted, virtually every restaurant deals with its suppliers on a JIT basis. Those who do not are usually not successful. The waste is too evident—food spoils and customers complain.

Layouts JIT layouts work in restaurant kitchens, where cold food must be served cold and hot food hot. Layouts also make a difference in airline baggage claim, where customers expect their bags just-in-time.

Inventory Every stockbroker drives inventory down to nearly zero. Most sell and buy orders occur on a JIT basis because an unexecuted sell or buy order is not acceptable to most clients. A broker may be in serious trouble if left holding an unexecuted trade. Similarly, McDonald's maintains a finished goods inventory of only 10 minutes; after that, it is thrown away. Hospitals also endorse JIT inventory and low safety stocks, even for such critical supplies as pharmaceuticals, by developing community networks as backup systems. In this manner, if one pharmacy runs out of a needed drug, a member of the network can supply it until the next day's shipment arrives.[9]

Scheduling At airline ticket counters, the focus of a JIT system is customer demand, but rather than being satisfied by the inventory of a tangible product, that demand must be satisfied by personnel. Through elaborate scheduling, airline ticket-counter personnel show up just-in-time to satisfy customer demand, and they provide the service on a JIT basis. In other words, personnel are scheduled, rather than "things" inventoried. Personnel schedules are critical. At a beauty salon, the focus is only slightly different: The customer is scheduled to assure JIT service. Similarly, at McDonald's as at most fast-food restaurants, scheduling of personnel is down to 15-minute increments based on precise forecasting of

In a hospital with JIT, suppliers bring ready-to-use supplies directly to storage areas, nurses' stations, and operating rooms. Only a 24-hour reserve is maintained.

With good methods analysis and the proper tools, the setup time for french fries at McDonald's has been made very short. As a result, french fries are prepared frequently (almost for each order) to ensure that they are delivered hot, just as the customer requests them.

---

[9] Daniel Whitson, "Applying Just-in-Time Systems in Health Care," *Industrial Engineering Solutions,* August 1997, pp. 33–37.

demand. Additionally, production is done in small lots to ensure that fresh, hot hamburgers are delivered just-in-time. In short, both personnel and production are scheduled on a JIT basis to meet specific demand. Setup times are very low and lot sizes very small, approaching one. McDonald's comes very close to the JIT idea of one good product delivered when and where the customer wants it.

Notice that in all three of these examples—the airline ticket counter, the beauty salon, and McDonald's—scheduling is a key ingredient in effective JIT. Excellent forecasts drive those schedules. Those forecasts may be very elaborate, with seasonal, daily, and even hourly components in the case of the airline ticket counter (holiday sales, flight time, and so forth), seasonal and weekly components at the beauty salon (holidays and Fridays creating special problems), or down to a few minutes at McDonald's.

In order to deliver goods and services to customers under continuously changing demand, suppliers need to be good, inventories lean, cycle times short, and schedules nimble. These issues are currently being managed with great success in many firms regardless of their products. JIT techniques are widely used in both goods-producing and service-producing firms; they just look different.

SUMMARY

JIT is a philosophy of continuous improvement. It focuses on driving all waste out of the production process. Because waste is found in anything that does not add value, JIT facilities are adding value more efficiently than other facilities. Waste occurs when defects are produced within the production process or by outside suppliers. JIT attacks wasted space because of less-than-optimal layout; it attacks wasted time because of poor scheduling; it attacks waste in idle inventory; it attacks waste from poorly maintained machinery and equipment. JIT expects committed, empowered employees to work with committed management and suppliers to build systems that respond to customers with ever lower cost and ever higher quality.

KEY TERMS

Just-in-time (JIT) *(p. 480)*
Variability *(p. 481)*
Pull system *(p. 481)*
Manufacturing cycle time *(p. 481)*
Push system *(p. 481)*

JIT partnerships *(p. 482)*
Consignment inventory *(p. 483)*
Just-in-time inventory *(p. 486)*
Level material-use schedules *(p. 490)*
Kanban *(p. 491)*

SOLVED PROBLEM

Solved Problem S12.1

Krupp Refrigeration, Inc., is trying to reduce inventory and wants you to install a kanban system for compressors on one of its assembly lines. Determine the size of the kanban and the number of kanbans (containers) needed.

Setup cost = $10
Annual holding cost per compressor = $100
Daily production = 200 compressors
Annual usage = 25,000 (= 50 weeks × 5 days each
    × daily usage of 100 compressors)
Lead time = 3 days
Safety Stock = 1/2 day's production of compressors

Solution

First, we must determine kanban container size. To do this, we determine the production order quantity (see discussion in chapter 12), which determines our kanban size:

$$Q_p = \sqrt{\frac{2DS}{H\left(1 - \frac{d}{p}\right)}} = \sqrt{\frac{2(25,000)(10)}{H\left(1 - \frac{d}{p}\right)}} = \sqrt{\frac{500,000}{100\left(1 - \frac{100}{200}\right)}} = \sqrt{\frac{500,000}{50}}$$

$$= \sqrt{10,000} = 100 \text{ compressors}$$

Then we determine the number of kanbans:

Demand during lead time = 300 (= 3 days × daily usage of 100)

Safety stock = 100 (= 1/2 day's production × 200)

$$\text{Number of kanbans} = \frac{\text{Demand during lead time + Safety stock}}{\text{Size of container}}$$

$$= \frac{300 + 100}{100} = \frac{400}{100} = 4 \text{ containers}$$

DISCUSSION QUESTIONS

1. What is meant by "a JIT philosophy"?
2. What are the characteristics of JIT partnerships?
3. What are the types of waste JIT is designed to remove?
4. What is the difference between a "pull" system and a "push" system?
5. What are the types of variability that JIT is expected to help remove?
6. How does JIT help reduce distance, space, and inventory?
7. How do empowered employees aid the JIT effort?
8. What is the impact on JIT of reducing setup costs?
9. Identify the results from a JIT system that should lead to and yield a competitive advantage.
10. Identify some of the signals that kanban systems use.
11. What types of kanban signals might be used when dealing with outside suppliers?

PROBLEMS

- **S12.1** Ferdows Electronics, Inc. (FEI), produces short runs of custom microwave radios for railroads and other industrial clients. You have been asked to reduce inventory by introducing a kanban system. After several hours of analysis, you develop the following data for connectors used in one work cell. How many kanbans do you need for this connector?

Daily demand	1,500 radios
Production lead time	1 day
Safety stock	1/2 day
Kanban size	250 radios

PROBLEMS

• **S12.2** Fawcett Corp. wants to establish kanbans to feed a newly established work cell. The following data has been provided. How many kanbans are needed?

Daily demand	250 units
Production lead time	1/2 day
Safety stock	1/4 day
Kanban size	50 units

: **S12.3** Flores Manufacturing, Inc., is moving to kanbans to support its electronic board-assembly lines. Determine the size of the kanban for subassemblies and the number of kanbans needed.

Setup cost = $25.

Annual holding cost subassembly = $200 per subassembly

Daily production = 400 subassemblies

Annual usage = 50,000 (= 50 weeks × 5 days each × daily usage of 200 subassemblies)

Lead time = 6 days

Safety Stock = 1 day's production of subassemblies

: **S12.4** Heiko Motorcycle Corp. uses kanbans to support its transmission assembly line. Determine the size of the kanban for the mainshaft assembly and the number of kanbans needed.

Setup cost = $20

Annual holding cost of mainshaft assembly = $250 per unit

Daily production = 300 mainshafts

Annual usage = 20,000 (= 50 weeks × 5 days each × daily usage of 80 mainshafts)

Lead time = 3 days

Safety Stock = 1/2 day's production of mainshafts

• **S12.5** Discount-Mart, a major East Coast retailer, wants to determine the economic order quantity (see chapter 12 for EOQ formulas) for its halogen lamps. It currently buys all halogen lamps from Specialty Lighting Manufacturers, in Atlanta. Annual demand is 2,000 lamps, ordering cost per order is $30, carrying cost per lamp is $12.
  a) What is the EOQ?
  b) What are the total annual costs of holding and ordering?
  c) How many orders should Discount-Mart place with Specialty Lighting per year?

: **S12.6** Discount-Mart (see Problem S12.5), as part of its new JIT program, has signed a long-term contract with Specialty Lighting and will place orders electronically for its halogen

lamps. Ordering costs will drop to $.50 per order, but Discount-Mart also reassessed its carrying costs and raised them to $20 per lamp.
  a) What is the new economic order quantity?
  b) How many orders will now be placed?
  c) What is the total annual cost with this policy?

: **S12.7** How do your answers to Problems S12.5 and S12.6 provide insight into a JIT purchasing strategy?

Case Study

Electronic Systems, Inc.

Electronic System, Inc. (ESI), of Topeka, Kansas, is an electronic components manufacturer with a single production facility employing 2,000 assembly-line workers, 1,200 skilled workers, and 850 management and clerical personnel. Top management recently attended a JIT seminar offered by its major customer, the U.S. government. After some discussion, management sent down a dictum to first-line supervisors (plant foremen) that ESI was going to become a JIT operation.

ESI's components are used as replacement parts in military equipment and office equipment. The government purchases ESI's products in large lots and has no plans to change. The government's business represents about 80% of total sales for ESI.

Recently, government inspectors noticed that while ESI's JIT-oriented competitors were improving quality, ESI's quality was decreasing. ESI's past acceptance-sampling methods simply did not catch all defective products, while similar products from competitors were virtually defect-free. Also, a growing number of new customers had in recent months placed pressure on ESI to adopt JIT methods that would permit quicker response on orders. The new customers expressed a desire to receive smaller lot sizes instead of the large lot size the ESI system had been designed to provide. What's more, a foreign competitor recently entered the market and was providing a better-quality product, at less cost, and in a more timely manner than ESI.

The task of understanding JIT, devising an implementation plan, and implementing it was left entirely up to the first-line supervisors. ESI's management felt that the supervisors managing the workers who were going to be asked to perform JIT activities on the shop floor would be the best people to make the new system work. Management also realized that converting to a more responsive and quality-conscious system had to be accomplished as soon as possible. Therefore, the company established a deadline of 90 days for full implementation of JIT principles. Foremen and supervisors were given 30 days to develop a plan, 30 more to train and install it, and 30 to work out any bugs. As an added inducement, management informed employees that 100% of the savings from increased productivity would be given to them as a reward.

Supervisors felt that much of the JIT philosophy was based on identifying and reducing time-consuming, wasteful activities. At the same time, work activities that added value to the product should be identified and, where possible, given renewed effort or increased allocation of time. The supervisors' first act was to publish the list presented in Table S12.7. This list was designed to identify targeted areas of improvement or waste removal.

TABLE S12.7 ■ A List of Targeted Activities

Try to reduce the time it takes to perform these activities because they represent a waste of time and add little to the value of our products:
Counting component parts
Counting boxes
Cutting material used in the product
Maintaining equipment
Switching machine on
Overproducing stock
Handling materials

Try to do a better job, even if it takes more time, in performing the following activities since they add value to our products:
Making sure components fit in subassemblies
Checking other workers' jobs
Checking orders to see they are correct
Cleaning up work centers
Moving boxes
Setting up machines for a production run

Discussion Questions

1. Do you think ESI's assignment of first-line supervisors to implement its new JIT program was a correct move? Explain your answer.
2. What key JIT principles does the application in this case appear to violate? Which principles does it embrace?
3. Which of the items listed in Table S12.7 are waste and should be eliminated? Which add value to the product?
4. Do you think this JIT program will be successful? Give reasons why or why not.

Source: Adapted from Marc J. Schniederjans, *Topics in Just-in-Time Management* (Boston: Allyn & Bacon, 1993), pp. 21–23.

BIBLIOGRAPHY

Ansarl, A., and B. Modarress. "Just-in-Time Purchasing: Problems and Solutions." *Journal of Purchasing and Materials* 22 (summer 1986): 11–15.

Chapman, S. N., and P. L. Carter. "Supplier/Customer Inventory Relationships under JIT." *Decision Sciences,* winter 1990, pp. 35–51.

Chen, Shuyong, and Rongqiu Chen. "Manufacturer-Supplier Relationship in a JIT Environment," *Production and Inventory Management Journal* 38, no. 1 (first quarter 1997): 8–13.

Freeland, J. R. "A Survey of Just-in-Time Purchasing Practices in the United States." *Production and Inventory Management Journal* 32 (second quarter 1991): 43.

———, J. P. Leschke, and E. N. Weiss. "Guidelines for Setup-Cost Reduction Programs to Achieve Zero Inventory." *Journal of Operations Management* 9 (January 1990): 85.

Golhar, D. Y. "JIT Purchasing Practices in Manufacturing Firms." *Production and Inventory Management Journal* 34, no. 3 (third quarter 1993): 75–79.

Hall, R. *Zero Inventories.* Homewood, IL: Dow Jones-Irwin, 1983.

Handfield, R. "A Resource Dependence Perspective of Just-in-Time Purchasing." *Journal of Operations Management* 11 (1993): 289–311.

Hobbs, O. Kermit. "Managing JIT Toward Maturity." *Production and Inventory Management Journal* 38, no. 1 (first quarter 1997): 8–13.

Inman, R. A., and S. Mehra. "JIT Applications for Service Environments." *Production and Inventory Management Journal* 32, no. 3 (third quarter 1991): 16.

Jinchiro, N., and R. Hall. "Management Specs for Stockless Production." *Harvard Business Review* 63 (May–June 1983): 89–91.

Louis, R. S. *How to Implement Kanban for American Industry.* Cambridge, MA: Productivity Press, 1992.

Schniederjans, M. *Topics in Just-in-Time Management.* Boston: Allyn & Bacon, 1993.

Walleigh, R. C. "Getting Things Done. What's Your Excuse for Not Using JIT?" *Harvard Business Review* 64 (March–April 1986): 39–54.

Whitson, Daniel. "Applying Just-in-Time Systems in Health Care." *IIE Solutions* 29, no. 8 (August 1997): 33–37.

INTERNET RESOURCES

Business Open Learning Archive, United Kingdom:
http://wwwbs.wlihe.ac.uk/~jarvis/bola/jit/index.html

JIT Overview, Curtin University of Technology, Perth, Australia:
http://kcmow.curtin.edu.au/www/jit/jit.html

Kanban-An Integrated JIT System:
http://www.geocities.com/TimesSquare/1848/japan21.html

Aggregate Scheduling

13

CHAPTER OUTLINE

GLOBAL COMPANY PROFILE: ANHEUSER-BUSCH
THE PLANNING PROCESS
THE NATURE OF AGGREGATE SCHEDULING
AGGREGATE PLANNING STRATEGIES
   Capacity Options
   Demand Options
   Mixing Options to Develop a Plan
METHODS FOR AGGREGATE SCHEDULING
   Graphical and Charting Methods
   Mathematical Approaches to Planning
   Comparison of Aggregate Planning Methods
AGGREGATE SCHEDULING IN SERVICES
   Restaurants
   Miscellaneous Services
   National Chains of Small Service Firms
   Airline Industry
   Hospitals
SUMMARY
KEY TERMS
USING POM FOR WINDOWS FOR AGGREGATE PLANNING
USING EXCEL OM FOR AGGREGATE PLANNING
SOLVED PROBLEMS
DISCUSSION QUESTIONS
CRITICAL THINKING EXERCISE
PROBLEMS
CASE STUDY: SOUTHWESTERN STATE COLLEGE
INTERNET CASE STUDY
BIBLIOGRAPHY
INTERNET RESOURCES

LEARNING OBJECTIVES

When you complete this chapter you should be able to:

Identify or Define:

   Aggregate scheduling

   Tactical scheduling

   Graphic technique for aggregate planning

   Mathematical techniques for planning

Describe or Explain:

   How to do aggregate planning

   How service firms develop aggregate plans

🌐 GLOBAL COMPANY PROFILE:

Aggregate Scheduling Provides a Competitive Advantage at Anheuser-Busch

In the brewhouse control room, process control uses computers to monitor the starting-cellar process, where wort is in its final stage of preparation before being fermented into beer.

Anheuser-Busch produces close to 40% of the beer consumed in the United States. The company achieves efficiency at such volume by doing an excellent job of matching capacity to demand.

Matching capacity and demand in the intermediate term (3 to 18 months) is the heart of aggregate scheduling. Anheuser-Busch matches fluctuating demand by brand to specific plant, labor, and inventory capacity. Meticulous cleaning between batches, effective maintenance, and efficient employee and facility scheduling contribute to high facility utilization, a major factor in all high capital investment facilities.

Beer is made in a product-focused facility—one that produces high volume and low variety. Product-focused production

Shown are brew kettles in which wort, later to become beer, is boiled and hops are added for the flavor and bitter character they impart.

502

ANHEUSER-BUSCH

processes usually require high fixed cost but typically have the benefit of low variable costs. Maintaining high use of such facilities is critical because high capital costs require high use to be competitive. Performance above the break-even point requires high use, and downtime is disastrous.

Beer production can be divided into four stages. The first stage is the selection and assurance of raw material delivery and quality. The second stage is the actual brewing process from milling to aging. The third stage is packaging into the wide variety of containers desired by the market.

The fourth and final stage is distribution, which includes temperature-controlled delivery and storage. Each stage has its resource limitations. Developing the aggregate plan to make it all work is demanding. Effective aggregate scheduling is a major ingredient in competitive advantage at Anheuser-Busch.

The canning line imprints on each can: a code that identifies the day, year, and 15-minute period of production; the plant at which the product was brewed and packaged; and the production line used. This system allows any quality-control problems to be tracked and corrected.

503

Aggregate scheduling (or aggregate planning)
An approach to determine the quantity and timing of production for the intermediate future (usually 3 to 18 months ahead).

Manufacturers like Anheuser-Busch, GE, and Yamaha face tough decisions when trying to schedule products like beer, air conditioners, and jet skis, the demand for which is heavily dependent on seasonal variation. If the firms increase output and a summer is warmer than usual, they stand to increase sales and market share. However, if the summer is cool, they may be stuck with expensive unsold product. Developing plans that minimize costs connected with such forecasts is one of the main functions of an operations manager.

Aggregate scheduling (also known as **aggregate planning**) is concerned with determining the quantity and timing of production for the intermediate future, often from 3 to 18 months ahead. Operations managers try to determine the best way to meet forecasted demand by adjusting production rates, labor levels, inventory levels, overtime work, subcontracting rates, and other controllable variables. Usually, *the objective of aggregate planning is to minimize cost over the planning period.* However, other strategic issues may be more important than low cost. These strategies may be to smooth employment levels, to drive down inventory levels, or to meet a high level of service.

For manufacturers, the aggregate schedule ties the firm's strategic goals to production plans, but for service organizations, the aggregate schedule ties strategic goals to detailed workforce schedules.

Four things are needed for aggregate planning:

- A logical overall unit for measuring sales and output, such as air-conditioning units at GE or cases of beer at Anheuser-Busch.
- A forecast of demand for a reasonable intermediate planning period in these aggregate terms.
- A method for determining the costs that we discuss in this chapter.
- A model that combines forecasts and costs so that scheduling decisions can be made for the planning period.

In this chapter we describe the aggregate planning decision, show how the aggregate plan fits into the overall planning process, and describe several techniques that managers use when developing an aggregate plan. We stress both manufacturing and service-sector firms.

THE PLANNING PROCESS

In chapter 5, we saw that demand forecasting can address short-, medium-, and long-range problems. Long-range forecasts help managers deal with capacity and strategic issues and are the responsibility of top management (see Figure 13.1). Top management formulates policy-related questions, such as facility location and expansion, new product development, research funding, and investment over a period of several years.

Medium-range planning begins once long-term capacity decisions are made. This is the job of the operations manager. **Scheduling decisions** address the problem of matching productivity to fluctuating demands. All of these plans need to be consistent with top management's long-range strategy and work within the resources allocated by earlier strategic decisions. Medium- (or "intermediate-") range planning is accomplished by building an aggregate production plan.

Scheduling decisions
Making plans that match production to changes in demand.

Short-range planning may extend up to a year but is usually less than 3 months. This plan is also the responsibility of operations personnel, who work with supervisors and foremen to "disaggregate" the intermediate plan into weekly, daily, and hourly schedules. Tactics for dealing with short-term planning involve loading, sequencing, expediting, and dispatching which are discussed in chapter 15.

Figure 13.1 illustrates the time horizons and features for short-, intermediate-, and long-range planning.

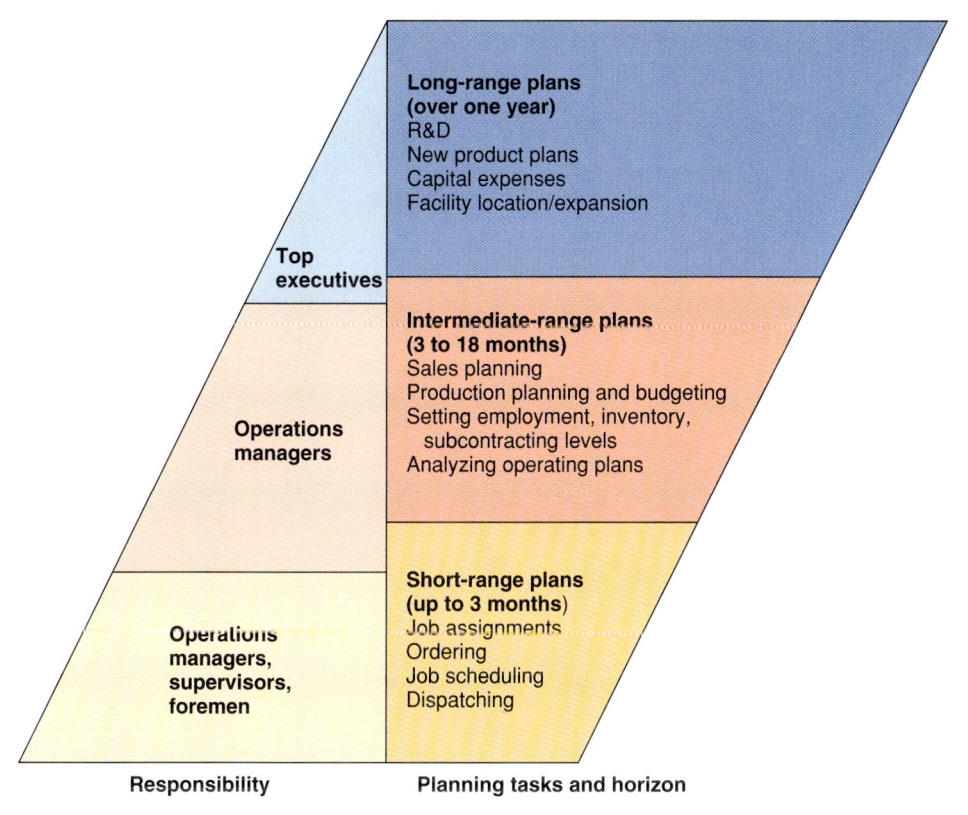

THE NATURE OF AGGREGATE SCHEDULING

FIGURE 13.1 ■ Planning Tasks and Responsibilities

Long-range plans (over one year)
- R&D
- New product plans
- Capital expenses
- Facility location/expansion

Top executives

Intermediate-range plans (3 to 18 months)
- Sales planning
- Production planning and budgeting
- Setting employment, inventory, subcontracting levels
- Analyzing operating plans

Operations managers

Short-range plans (up to 3 months)
- Job assignments
- Ordering
- Job scheduling
- Dispatching

Operations managers, supervisors, foremen

Responsibility | Planning tasks and horizon

If top management does a poor or inconsistent job of long-term planning, problems will develop that make the aggregate planner's job very tough.

THE NATURE OF AGGREGATE SCHEDULING

As the term *aggregate* implies, an aggregate plan means combining appropriate resources into general, or overall, terms. Given demand forecast, facility capacity, inventory levels, workforce size, and related inputs, the planner has to select the rate of output for a facility over the next 3 to 18 months. The plan can be for manufacturing firms such as Anheuser-Busch and Whirlpool, hospitals, colleges, or Prentice Hall, the company that published this textbook.

Take, for a manufacturing example, IBM or Compaq, each of which produces different models of microcomputers. They make (1) laptops, (2) desktops, (3) notebook computers, and (4) advanced technology machines with high-speed chips. For each month in the upcoming three quarters, the aggregate plan for IBM or Compaq might have the following output (in units of production) for this "family" of microcomputers:

QUARTER 1			QUARTER 2			QUARTER 3		
Jan.	Feb.	March	April	May	June	July	Aug.	Sept.
150,000	120,000	110,000	100,000	130,000	150,000	180,000	150,000	140,000

Note that the plan looks at production *in the aggregate*, not on a product-by-product breakdown. Likewise, an aggregate plan for GM tells the auto manufacturer how many cars to make, but not how many should be 2-door versus 4-door or red versus green. It

---

TEN DECISIONS OF OM

Managing Quality
Design of Goods & Services
Process Strategy
Location Strategies
Layout Strategies
Human Resources
Supply-Chain Management
Inventory Management
Scheduling
   Aggregate
   Short-Term
   Project
Maintenance

506 CHAPTER 13 AGGREGATE SCHEDULING

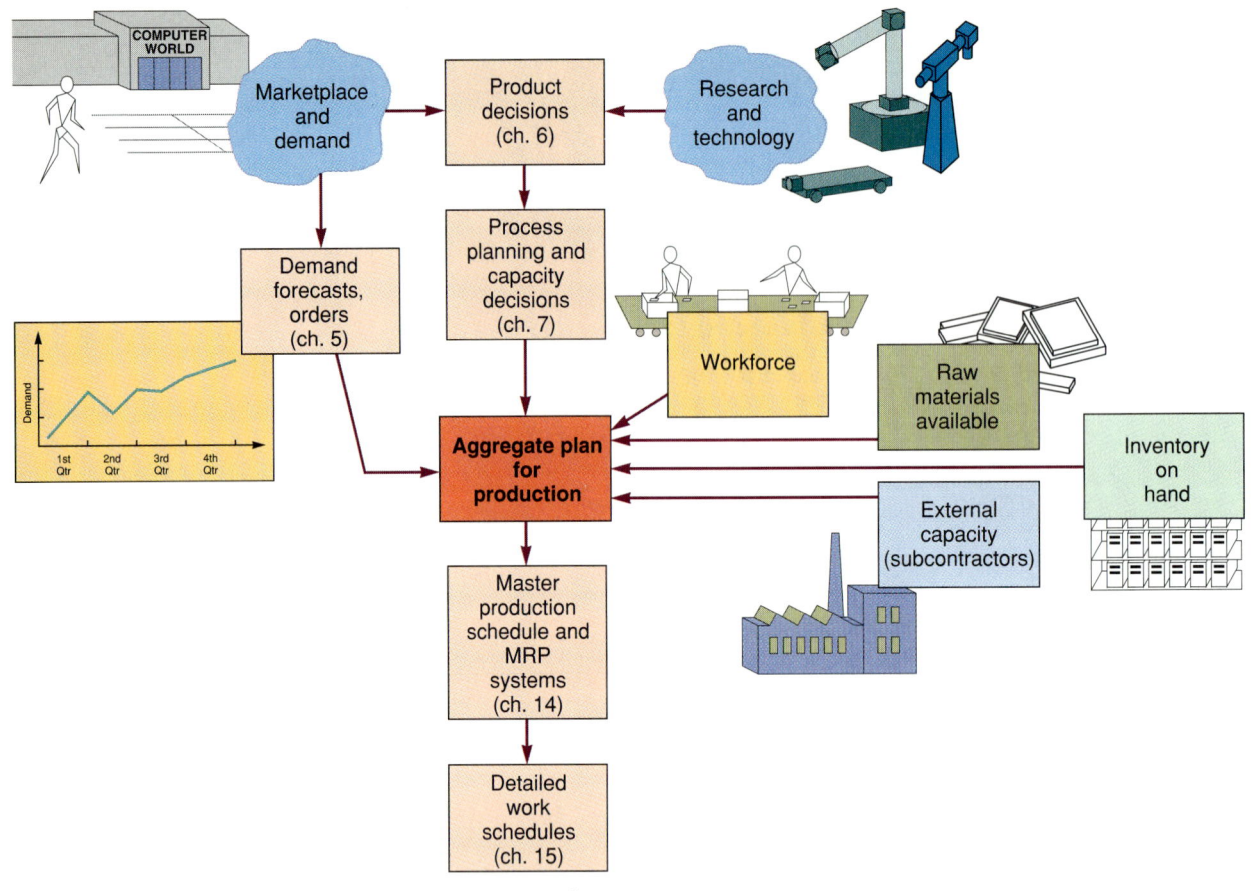

FIGURE 13.2 ■ Relationships of the Aggregate Plan

Disaggregation The process of breaking the aggregate plan into greater detail.

Master production schedule A timetable that specifies what is to be made and when.

tells Nucor Steel how many tons of steel to produce, but does not differentiate grades of steel.

In the service sector, consider Computrain, a company that provides microcomputer training for managers. The firm offers courses on spreadsheets, graphics, data bases, word processing, and the Internet, and employs several instructors to meet the demand for its services from business and government. Demand for training tends to be very low near holiday seasons and during summer, when many people take their vacations. To meet the fluctuating needs for courses, the company can hire and lay off instructors, advertise to increase demand in slow seasons, or subcontract its work to other training agencies during peak periods. Again, aggregate planning makes decisions about intermediate-range capacity, not specific courses or instructors.

Aggregate planning is part of a larger production planning system. Therefore, understanding the interfaces between the plan and several internal and external factors is useful. Figure 13.2 shows that not only does the operations manager receive input from the marketing department's demand forecast, but must also deal with financial data, personnel, capacity, and availability of raw materials. In a manufacturing environment, the process of breaking the aggregate plan down into greater detail is called **disaggregation.** Disaggregation results in a **master production schedule,** which provides input to material requirements planning (MRP) systems. The master production schedule addresses the purchasing or production of parts or components needed to make final products (see chapter

Federal Express's huge aircraft fleet is used to near capacity for nighttime delivery of packages but is 100% idle during the daytime. In an attempt to better utilize their capacity (and leverage its assets), Federal Express considered two services with opposite or countercyclical demand patterns to its nighttime service—commuter passenger service and passenger charter service. However, after a thorough analysis, the 12% to 13% return on investment was judged insufficient for the risks involved. Facing the same issues, though, UPS recently decided to begin a charter airline that operates on weekends.

14). Detailed work schedules for people and priority scheduling for products result as the final step of the production planning system (and are discussed in chapter 15).

AGGREGATE PLANNING STRATEGIES

When generating an aggregate plan, the operations manager must answer several questions:

1. Should inventories be used to absorb changes in demand during the planning period?
2. Should changes be accommodated by varying the size of the workforce?
3. Should part-timers be used, or should overtime and idle time absorb fluctuations?
4. Should subcontractors be used on fluctuating orders so a stable workforce can be maintained?
5. Should prices or other factors be changed to influence demand?

All of these are legitimate planning strategies. They involve the manipulation of inventory, production rates, labor levels, capacity, and other controllable variables. We will now examine eight options in more detail. The first five are called *capacity options* because they do not try to change demand but attempt to absorb the fluctuations in it. The last three are *demand options* through which firms try to smooth out changes in the demand pattern over the planning period.

Aggregate planning in the real world involves a lot of trial and error.

> # OM IN ACTION
>
> ## A TALE OF TWO DELIVERY SERVICES
>
> Federal Express and United Parcel Service are direct competitors in package delivery. Both firms are successful, but they approach aggregate planning quite differently.
>
> Managers at Federal Express use a large number of part-time employees in their huge package-sorting facility. This Memphis facility is designed and staffed to sort over a million envelopes and packages in a short 4-hour shift during the middle of the night. Federal Express found that college students provide a good source of labor. These high-energy part-timers help meet peak demands, and the firm believes that full-timers could not be effectively utilized for a full 8-hour shift.
>
> At UPS's package-sorting hub, managers are also faced with the decision whether to staff with mostly full-time or part-time employees. UPS chose the mostly full-time approach. The firm also researches job designs and work processes thoroughly, hoping to provide a high level of job satisfaction and a strong sense of teamwork. Hours at UPS are long, the work is hard, and UPS generates some complaints about its demanding levels of productivity. Yet when openings occur, UPS has never had a shortage of job applicants.
>
> *Sources: The Wall Street Journal* (May 24, 1995): B1, B4; *International Business* (September 1996): 14–17; and *U.S. News & World Report* (September 1, 1997): 44.

Capacity Options

A firm can choose from the following basic capacity (production) options:

1. *Changing inventory levels.* Managers can increase inventory during periods of low demand to meet high demand in future periods. If we select this strategy, costs associated with storage, insurance, handling, obsolescence, pilferage, and capital invested will increase. (These costs typically range from 15% to 40% of the value of an item annually.) On the other hand, when the firm enters a period of increasing demand, shortages can result in lost sales due to potentially longer lead times and poorer customer service.

2. *Varying workforce size by hiring or layoffs.* One way to meet demand is to hire or lay off production workers to match production rates. However, often new employees need to be trained, and the average productivity drops temporarily as they are absorbed into the firm. Layoffs or firings, of course, lower the morale of all workers and can lead to lower productivity.

3. *Varying production rates through overtime or idle time.* It is sometimes possible to keep a constant workforce while varying working hours, cutting back the number of hours worked when demand is low and increasing them when it rises. Yet when demand is on a large upswing, there is a limit on how much overtime is realistic. Overtime pay requires more money, and too much overtime can wear workers down to the point that overall productivity drops off. Overtime also implies the increased overhead needed to keep a facility open. On the other hand, when there is a period of decreased demand, the company must somehow absorb workers' idle time—usually a difficult process.

4. *Subcontracting.* A firm can acquire temporary capacity by subcontracting work during peak demand periods. Subcontracting, however, has several pitfalls. First, it may be costly; second, it risks opening your client's door to a competitor. Third, it is often hard to find the perfect subcontract supplier, one who always delivers the quality product on time.

5. *Using part-time workers.* Especially in the service sector, part-time workers can fill unskilled labor needs. This practice is common in fast-food restaurants, retail

stores, and supermarkets. The *OM in Action* box describing Federal Express and United Parcel Service provides two views of this strategy.

Demand Options

The basic demand options are the following:

1. *Influencing demand.* When demand is low, a company can try to increase demand through advertising, promotion, personal selling, and price cuts. Airlines and hotels have long offered weekend discounts and off-season rates; telephone companies charge less at night; some colleges give discounts to senior citizens; and air conditioners are least expensive in winter. However, even special advertising, promotions, selling, and pricing are not always able to balance demand with production capacity.

2. *Back ordering during high-demand periods.* Back orders are orders for goods or services that a firm accepts but is unable (either on purpose or by chance) to fill at the moment. If customers are willing to wait without loss of their goodwill or order, back ordering is a possible strategy. Many firms back order, but the approach often results in lost sales.

Negative inventory means we owe units to customers. We either lose sales or back order to make it up.

John Deere and Company, the "granddaddy" of farm equipment manufacturers, uses sales incentives to smooth demand. During the fall and winter off-seasons, sales are boosted with price cuts and other incentives. About 70% of Deere's big machines are ordered in advance of seasonal use—about double the industry rate. Incentives hurt margins, but Deere keeps its market share and controls costs by producing more steadily all year long. Similarly, in service businesses like L. L. Bean, some customers are offered free shipping on orders placed before the Christmas rush.

3. *Counterseasonal product and service mixing.* A widely used active smoothing technique among manufacturers is to develop a product mix of counterseasonal items. Examples include companies that make both furnaces and air conditioners or lawn mowers and snowblowers. However, companies who follow this approach may find themselves involved in products or services beyond their area of expertise or beyond their target market.

These eight options, along with their advantages and disadvantages, are summarized in Table 13.1.

TABLE 13.1 ■ Aggregate Planning Options: Advantages and Disadvantages

Option	Advantages	Disadvantages	Some Comments
Changing inventory levels.	Changes in human resources are gradual or none; no abrupt production changes.	Inventory holding costs. Shortages, resulting in lost sales, may occur if demand increases.	This applies mainly to production, not service, settings.
Varying workforce size by hiring or layoffs.	Avoids the costs of other alternatives.	Hiring, layoff, and training costs may be significant.	Used where many unskilled people seek extra income.
Varying production rates through overtime or idle time.	Matches seasonal fluctuations without hiring/training costs.	Overtime premiums; tired workers; may not meet demand.	Allows flexibility within the aggregate plan.
Subcontracting.	Permits flexibility and smoothing of the firm's output.	Loss of quality control; reduced profits; loss of future business.	Applies mainly in production settings.
Using part-time workers.	Is less costly and more flexible than full-time workers.	High turnover/training costs; quality suffers; scheduling difficult.	Good for unskilled jobs in areas with large temporary labor pools.
Influencing demand.	Tries to use excess capacity. Discounts draw new customers.	Uncertainty in demand. Hard to match demand to supply exactly.	Creates marketing ideas. Overbooking used in some businesses.
Back ordering during high-demand periods.	May avoid overtime. Keeps capacity constant.	Customer must be willing to wait, but goodwill is lost.	Many companies backorder.
Counterseasonal product and service mixing.	Fully utilizes resources; allows stable workforce.	May require skills or equipment outside firm's areas of expertise.	Risky finding products or services with opposite demand patterns.

Mixing Options to Develop a Plan

Although each of the five capacity options and three demand options might produce an effective aggregate schedule, some combination of capacity options and demand options may be better.

Many manufacturers assume that the use of the demand options has been fully explored by the marketing department and those reasonable options incorporated into the demand forecast. The operations manager then builds the aggregate plan based on that forecast. However, using the five capacity options at his command, the operations manager still has a multitude of possible plans. These plans can embody, at one extreme, a *chase strategy* and, at the other, a *level-scheduling strategy*. They may, of course, fall somewhere in between.

The most common options are regular time production, overtime production, and subcontracting.

Chase Strategy A **chase strategy** attempts to achieve output rates that match the demand forecast. This strategy can be accomplished in a variety of ways. For example, the operations manager can vary workforce levels by hiring or laying off or can vary production by means of overtime, idle time, part-time employees, or subcontracting. Many service organizations favor the chase strategy because the inventory option is difficult or impossible to adopt. Examples of diverse industries that have moved toward a chase strategy include education, hospitality, and construction.

> **Chase strategy** Sets production equal to forecasted demand.

Level Strategy A level strategy (or **level scheduling**) is an aggregate plan where daily production is uniform from period to period. Firms like Toyota and Nissan keep production at uniform levels and may: (1) let the finished goods inventory go up or down to buffer the difference between demand and production or (2) find alternative work for employees. Their philosophy is that a stable workforce leads to a better quality product, less turnover and absenteeism, and more employee commitment to corporate goals. Other hidden savings include employees that are more experienced, easier scheduling and supervision, and fewer dramatic startups and shutdowns. Level scheduling works well when demand is reasonably stable.

> **Level scheduling** Maintaining a constant output rate, production rate, or workforce level over the planning horizon.

METHODS FOR AGGREGATE SCHEDULING

For most firms, neither a chase strategy nor a level strategy is likely to prove ideal, so a combination of the eight options (called a **mixed strategy**) must be investigated to achieve minimum cost. However, because there are a huge number of possible mixed strategies, managers find that aggregate planning can be a challenging task. Finding the one "optimal" plan is not always possible. Indeed, some companies have no formal aggregate planning process: They use the same plan from year to year, making adjustments up or down just enough to fit the new annual demand. This method certainly does not provide much flexibility, and if the original plan was suboptimal, the entire production process will be locked into suboptimal performance.

In this section, we introduce several techniques that operations managers use to develop more useful and appropriate aggregate plans. They range from the widely used charting (or graphical) method to a series of more formal mathematical approaches, including the transportation method of linear programming.

> **Mixed strategy** A planning strategy that uses two or more controllable variables to set a feasible production plan.
>
> Mixed plans are more complex than single or "pure" ones but typically yield a better strategy.

Graphical and Charting Methods

Graphical and charting techniques are popular because they are easy to understand and use. Basically, these plans work with a few variables at a time to allow planners to compare projected demand with existing capacity. They are trial-and-error approaches that do not guarantee an optimal production plan, but they require only limited computations and can be performed by clerical staff. Following are the five steps in the graphical method:

1. Determine the demand in each period.
2. Determine capacity for regular time, overtime, and subcontracting each period.
3. Find labor costs, hiring and layoff costs, and inventory holding costs.
4. Consider company policy that may apply to the workers or to stock levels.
5. Develop alternative plans and examine their total costs.

> **Graphical and charting techniques** Aggregate planning techniques that work with a few variables at a time to allow planners to compare projected capacity with existing capacity.

512　CHAPTER 13　AGGREGATE SCHEDULING

These steps are illustrated in Examples 1 to 4.

EXAMPLE 1

A Charlotte, North Carolina, manufacturer of roofing supplies has developed monthly forecasts for an important product and presented the 6-month period January to June in Table 13.2:

TABLE 13.2

Month	Expected Demand	Production Days	Demand per Day (computed)
Jan.	900	22	41
Feb.	700	18	39
Mar.	800	21	38
Apr.	1,200	21	57
May	1,500	22	68
June	1,100	20	55
	6,200	124	

The demand per day is computed by simply dividing the expected demand by the number of production or working days each month.

To illustrate the nature of the aggregate planning problem, the firm also draws a graph (Figure 13.3) that charts daily demand each month. The dotted line across the chart represents the production rate required to meet average demand over the 6 month period. It is computed by:

$$\text{Average requirement} = \frac{\text{Total expected demand}}{\text{Number of production days}} = \frac{6{,}200}{124} = 50 \text{ units per day}$$

Note that in the first 3 months, expected demand is lower than average, while expected demand in April, May, and June is above average.

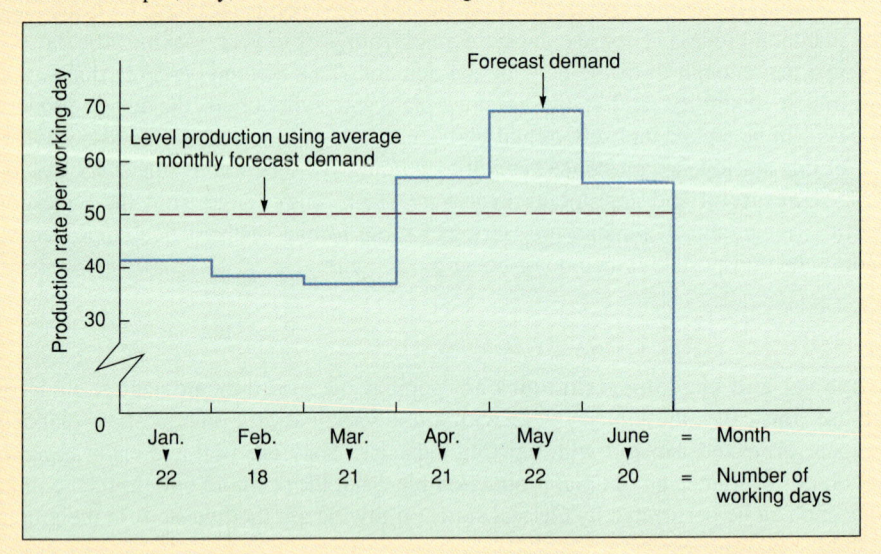

FIGURE 13.3 ■ Graph of Forecast and Average Forecast Demand

The graph in Figure 13.3 illustrates how the forecast differs from the average demand. Some strategies for meeting the forecast were listed earlier. The firm, for example, might staff in order to yield a production rate that meets *average* demand (as indicated by the dashed line). Or it might produce a steady rate of, say, 30 units and then subcontract ex-

METHODS FOR AGGREGATE SCHEDULING 513

cess demand to other roofing suppliers. A third plan might be to combine overtime work with some subcontracting to absorb demand. Examples 2 to 4 illustrate three possible strategies.

EXAMPLE 2

One possible strategy (call it plan 1) for the manufacturer described in Example 1 is to maintain a constant workforce throughout the 6-month period. A second (plan 2) is to maintain a constant workforce at a level necessary to meet the lowest demand month (March) and to meet all demand above this level by subcontracting. Both plan 1 and plan 2 have level production and are, therefore, called *level strategies*. Plan 3 is to hire and lay off workers as needed to produce exact monthly requirements—*a chase strategy*. Table 13.3 provides cost information necessary for analyzing these three alternatives:

TABLE 13.3 ■ Cost Information

Inventory carrying cost	$ 5 per unit per month
Subcontracting cost per unit	$10 per unit
Average pay rate	$ 5 per hour ($40 per day)
Overtime pay rate	$ 7 per hour (above 8 hours per day)
Labor-hours to produce a unit	1.6 hours per unit
Cost of increasing production rate (training and hiring)	$10 per unit
Cost of decreasing production rate (layoffs)	$15 per unit

Analysis of Plan 1. In analyzing this approach, which assumes that 50 units are produced per day, we have a constant workforce, no overtime or idle time, no safety stock, and no subcontractors. The firm accumulates inventory during the slack period of demand, January through March, and depletes it during the higher-demand warm season, April through June. We assume beginning inventory = 0 and planned ending inventory = 0:

Month	Production at 50 Units per Day	Demand Forecast	Monthly Inventory Change	Ending Inventory
Jan.	1,100	900	+200	200
Feb.	900	700	+200	400
Mar.	1,050	800	+250	650
Apr.	1,050	1,200	−150	500
May	1,100	1,500	−400	100
June	1,000	1,100	−100	0
				1,850

Total units of inventory carried over from one month to the next month = 1,850 units

Workforce required to produce 50 units per day = 10 workers

Because each unit requires 1.6 labor-hours to produce, each worker can make 5 units in an 8-hour day. Thus to produce 50 units, 10 workers are needed.

The costs of plan 1 are computed as follows:

Costs		Calculations
Inventory carrying	$ 9,250	(= 1,850 units carried × $5 per unit)
Regular-time labor	49,600	(= 10 workers × $40 per day × 124 days)
Other costs (overtime, hiring, layoffs, subcontracting)	0	
Total cost	$58,850	

514   CHAPTER 13   AGGREGATE SCHEDULING

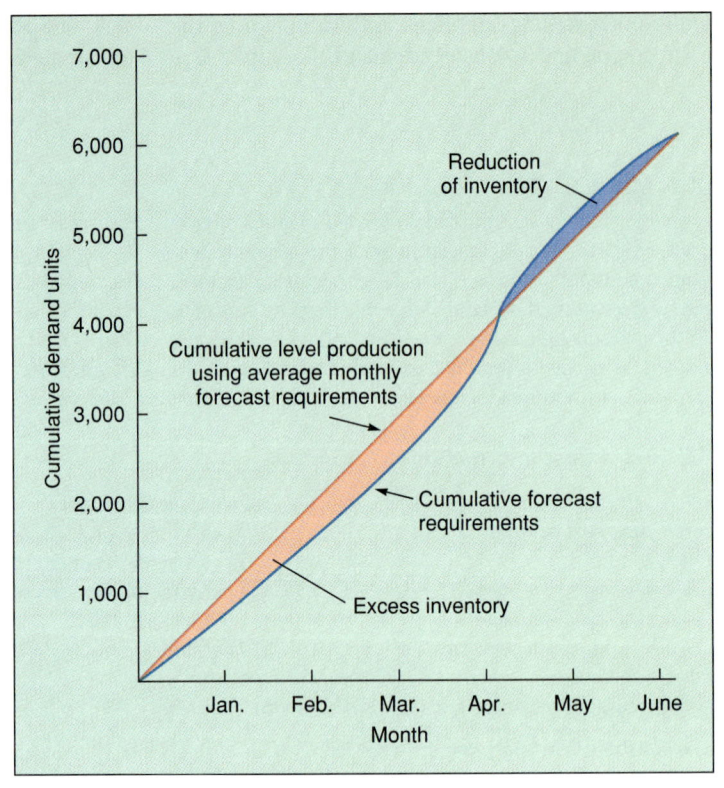

FIGURE 13.4 ■ Cumulative Graph for Plan 1

The graph for Example 2 was shown in Figure 13.3. Some planners prefer a *cumulative* graph to display visually how the forecast deviates from the average requirements. Note that both the level production line and the forecast line produce the same total production. Such a graph is provided in Figure 13.4.

EXAMPLE 3

Analysis of Plan 2. Although a constant workforce is also maintained in plan 2, it is set low enough to meet demand only in March, the lowest month. To produce 38 units per day in-house, 7.6 workers are needed. (You can think of this as 7 full-time workers and 1 part-timer.) *All* other demand is met by subcontracting. Subcontracting is thus required in every other month. No inventory holding costs are incurred in plan 2.

Because 6,200 units are required during the aggregate plan period, we must compute how many can be made by the firm and how many must be subcontracted:

In-house production = 38 units per day × 124 production days

= 4,712 units

Subcontract units = 6,200 − 4,712 = 1,488 units

The costs of plan 2 are computed as follows:

Costs		Calculations
Regular time labor	$37,696	(= 7.6 workers × $40 per day × 124 days)
Subcontracting	14,880	(= 1,488 units × $10 per unit)
Total cost	$52,576	

EXAMPLE 4

Analysis of Plan 3. The final strategy, plan 3, involves varying the workforce size by hiring and firing as necessary. The production rate will equal the demand. Table 13.4 shows the calculations and the total cost of plan 3. Recall that it costs $15 per unit produced to reduce production from the previous month's level and $10 per unit change to increase production through hirings:

TABLE 13.4 ■ Cost Computations for Plan 3

MONTH	FORECAST (units)	BASIC PRODUCTION COST (demand × 1.6 hrs per unit × $5 per hour)	EXTRA COST OF INCREASING PRODUCTION (hiring cost)	EXTRA COST OF DECREASING PRODUCTION (layoff cost)	TOTAL COST
Jan.	900	$ 7,200	—	—	$ 7,200
Feb.	700	5,600	—	$3,000 (= 200 × $15)	8,600
Mar.	800	6,400	$1,000 (= 100 × $10)	—	7,400
Apr.	1,200	9,600	$4,000 (= 400 × $10)	—	13,600
May	1,500	12,000	$3,000 (= 300 × $10)	—	15,000
June	1,100	8,800	—	$6,000 (= 400 × $15)	14,800
		$49,600	$8,000	$9,000	$66,600

So the total cost, including production, hiring, and layoff for plan 3 is $66,600.

The final step in the graphical method is to compare the costs of each proposed plan and to select the approach with the least total cost. A summary analysis is provided in Table 13.5. We see that because plan 2 has the lowest cost, it is the best of the three options.

TABLE 13.5 ■ Comparison of the Three Plans

COST	PLAN 1 (constant workforce of 10 workers)	PLAN 2 (workforce of 7.6 workers plus subcontract)	PLAN 3 (hiring and layoffs to meet demand)
Inventory carrying	$ 9,250	$ 0	$ 0
Regular labor	49,600	37,696	49,600
Overtime labor	0	0	0
Hiring	0	0	8,000
Layoffs	0	0	9,000
Subcontracting	0	14,880	0
Total cost	$58,850	$52,576	$66,600

Mathematical Approaches to Planning

This section briefly describes some of the mathematical approaches to aggregate planning that have been developed over the past 40 years.

The Transportation Method of Linear Programming When an aggregate planning problem is viewed as one of allocating operating capacity to meet forecasted demand, it can be formulated in a linear programming format. The **transportation method of linear programming** is not a trial-and-error approach like charting, but rather produces an optimal plan for minimizing costs. It is also flexible in that it can specify regular and overtime production in each time period, the number of units to be subcontracted, extra shifts, and the inventory carryover from period to period.

In Example 5, the supply consists of on-hand inventory and units produced by regular time, overtime, and subcontracting. Costs, in the upper right-hand corner of each cell of the matrix in Table 13.7, relate to units produced in a given period or units carried in inventory from an earlier period.

Transportation method of linear programming A way of solving for the optimal solution to an aggregate planning problem.

EXAMPLE 5

Farnsworth Tire Company developed data that relate to production, demand, capacity, and costs at its West Virginia plant. These data are shown in Table 13.6:

TABLE 13.6 ■ Farnsworth's Production, Demand, Capacity, and Cost Data

	Mar.	Apr.	May
Sales Period			
Demand	800	1,000	750
Capacity:			
Regular	700	700	700
Overtime	50	50	50
Subcontracting	150	150	130
Beginning inventory	100 tires		

Costs

Regular time	$40 per tire
Overtime	$50 per tire
Subcontract	$70 per tire
Carrying cost	$ 2 per tire per month

Table 13.7 illustrates the structure of the transportation table and an initial feasible solution.

In setting up and analyzing this table, you should note the following:

1. Carrying costs are $2/tire per month. Tires produced in 1 period and held for 1 month will have a $2 higher cost. Because holding cost is linear, 2 months' holdover costs $4. So when you move across a row from left to right, regular time, overtime, and

subcontracting costs are lowest when output is used the same period it is produced. If goods are made in one period and carried over to the next, holding costs are incurred.

2. Transportation problems require that supply equals demand; so, a dummy column called "unused capacity" has been added. Costs of not using capacity are zero.
3. Because back ordering is not a viable alternative in this model, no production is possible in those cells that represent production in a period to satisfy demand in a past period (i.e., those periods with an "X").
4. Quantities in each column of Table 13.7 designate the levels of inventory needed to meet demand requirements. Demand of 800 tires in March is met by using 100 tires from beginning inventory and 700 tires from regular time.
5. In general, to complete the table, allocate as much production as you can to a cell with the smallest cost without exceeding the unused capacity in that row or demand in that column. If there is still some demand left in that row, allocate as much as you can to the next-lowest-cost cell. You then repeat this process for periods 2 and 3 (and beyond, if necessary). When you are finished, the sum of all your entries in a row must equal the total row capacity, and the sum of all entries in a column must equal the demand for that period. (This step can be accomplished by the transportation method or by using POM for Windows or Excel OM software.)

TABLE 13.7 ■ Farnsworth's Transportation Table

SUPPLY FROM		Period 1 (Mar.)	Period 2 (Apr.)	Period 3 (May)	Unused Capacity (Dummy)	TOTAL CAPACITY AVAILABLE (supply)
	Beginning inventory	0 / 100	2	4	0	100
Period 1	Regular time	40 / 700	42	44	0	700
	Overtime	50	52 / 50	54	0	50
	Subcontract	70	72 / 150	74	0	150
Period 2	Regular time	X	40 / 700	42	0	700
	Overtime	X	50 / 50	52	0	50
	Subcontract	X	70 / 50	72	0 / 100	150
Period 3	Regular time	X	X	40 / 700	0	700
	Overtime	X	X	50 / 50	0	50
	Subcontract	X	X	70	0 / 130	130
TOTAL DEMAND		800	1,000	750	230	2,780

Management coefficients model A formal planning model built around a manager's experience and performance.

The transportation method of linear programming described above was originally formulated by E. H. Bowman in 1956.[1] Although it works well in analyzing the effects of holding inventories, using overtime, and subcontracting, it does not work when nonlinear or negative factors are introduced. So, when other factors such as hiring and layoffs are introduced, the more general method of linear programming must be used.

Management Coefficients Model Bowman's **management coefficients model**[2] builds a formal decision model around a manager's experience and performance. The assumption is that the manager's past performance is pretty good, so it can be used as a basis for future decisions. The technique uses a regression analysis of past production decisions made by managers. The regression line provides the relationship between variables (such as demand and labor) for future decisions. According to Bowman, managers' deficiencies are mostly inconsistencies in decision making.

Other Models Two additional aggregate planning models are the linear decision rule and simulation. The *linear decision rule (LDR)* attempts to specify an optimum production rate and workforce level over a specific period. It minimizes the total costs of payroll, hiring, layoffs, overtime, and inventory through a series of quadratic cost curves.[3]

A computer model called *scheduling by simulation* uses a search procedure to look for the minimum-cost combination of values for workforce size and production rate.[4]

Comparison of Aggregate Planning Methods

Although these mathematical models have been found by researchers to work well under certain conditions, and linear programming has found some acceptance in industry, the fact is that most sophisticated planning models are not widely used. Why? Perhaps it reflects the average manager's attitude about what he or she views as overly complex models. Like all of us, planners like to understand how and why the models on which they are basing important decisions work. Additionally, operations managers need to make decisions quickly based on the changing dynamics of the workplace. This may explain why the simpler charting and graphical approach is more generally accepted.

Table 13.8 highlights some of the main features of charting, transportation, and management coefficients planning models.

AGGREGATE SCHEDULING IN SERVICES

Some service organizations conduct aggregate scheduling in exactly the same way as we did in Examples 1 through 5 in this chapter, but with demand management taking a more active role. Because most services pursue *combinations* of the eight capacity and demand options discussed earlier, they usually formulate mixed aggregate planning strategies. In

---

[1] See E. H. Bowman, "Production Planning by the Transportation Method of Linear Programming," *Operations Research* 4, no. 1 (February 1956): 100–103.

[2] E. H. Bowman, "Consistency and Optimality in Managerial Decision Making," *Management Science* 9, no. 2 (January 1963): 310–321.

[3] Because LDR was developed by Charles C. Holt, Franco Modigliani, John F. Muth, and Nobel Prize–winner Herbert Simon, it is popularly known as the HMMS rule. For details, see C. C. Holt et al., *Production Planning, Inventories, and Work Force* (Englewood Cliffs, NJ: Prentice Hall, 1960).

[4] R. C. Vergin, "Production Scheduling under Seasonal Demand," *Journal of Industrial Engineering* 17, no. 5 (May 1966): 260–266.

AGGREGATE SCHEDULING IN SERVICES 519

TABLE 13.8 ■ Summary of Three Major Aggregate Planning Methods

Technique	Solution Approaches	Important Aspects
Graphical/charting methods	Trial and error	Simple to understand and easy to use. Many solutions; one chosen may not be optimal.
Transportation method of linear programmimg	Optimization	LP software available; permits sensitivity analysis and new constraints; linear functions may not be realistic.
Management coefficients model	Heuristic	Simple, easy to implement; tries to mimic manager's decision process; uses regression.

actuality, in such industries as banking, trucking, and fast foods, aggregate planning may be easier than in manufacturing.

Controlling the cost of labor in service firms is critical.[5] It involves:

1. Close control of labor-hours to assure quick response to customer demand.
2. Some form of on-call labor resource that can be added or deleted to meet unexpected demand.
3. Flexibility of individual worker skills that permits reallocation of available labor.
4. Individual worker flexibility in rate of output or hours of work to meet expanded demand.

These options may seem demanding, but they are not unusual in service industries where labor is the primary aggregate planning vehicle. For instance:

- Excess capacity is used to provide study and planning time by real estate and auto salespersons.
- Police and fire departments have provisions for calling in off-duty personnel for major emergencies. Where the emergency is extended, police or fire personnel may work longer hours and extra shifts.
- When business is unexpectedly light, restaurants and retail stores send personnel home early.
- Supermarket stock clerks work cash registers when checkout lines become too lengthy.
- Experienced waitresses increase their pace and efficiency of service as crowds of customers arrive.

Approaches to aggregate scheduling differ by the type of service provided. Here we discuss five service scenarios.[6]

Restaurants

Aggregate scheduling in a high-volume product output business such as a fast-food restaurant is directed toward (1) smoothing the production rate and (2) finding the size of the workforce to be employed. The general approach usually requires building very modest levels of inventory during slack periods and depleting inventory during peak periods, but using labor to accommodate most of the changes in demand.

---

[5] Glenn Bassett, *Operations Management for Service Industries* (Westport, CT: Quorum Books, 1992), p. 77

[6] The first four scenarios and their discussion are excerpted from R. Murdick, B. Render, and R. Russell, *Service Operations Management* (Boston: Allyn & Bacon, 1990), pp. 219–221.

> **OM IN ACTION**
>
> **YIELD MANAGEMENT AT HERTZ**
>
> For over 90 years, Hertz has been renting standard cars for a fixed amount per day. During the 2 past decades, however, a significant increase in demand has derived from airline travelers flying for business purposes. As the auto-rental market has changed and matured, Hertz has offered more options, including allowing customers to pick up and drop off in different locations. This option has resulted in excess capacity in some cities and shortages in others.
>
> These shortages and overages alerted Hertz to the need for a yield management system similar to those used at Delta and other airlines. The system is used to set prices, regulate the movement, and ultimately determine the availability of cars at each location. Through research Hertz found that different city locations peak on different days of the week. So cars are moved to peak-demand locations from locations where the demand is low. By altering both the price and quantity of cars at various locations, Hertz has been able to increase "yield" and boost revenue.
>
> The yield management system is primarily used by regional and local managers to better deal with changes in demand in the U.S. market. Hertz's plan to go global with the system, however, faces major challenges in foreign countries, where restrictions against moving empty cars across national borders are common.
>
> *Source:* William J. Carroll and Richard C. Grimes, "Evolutionary Change in Product Management," *Interfaces*, September–October 1995, pp. 84–104.

Because this situation is very similar to those found in manufacturing, traditional aggregate planning methods may be applied to high-volume services as well. One difference that should be noted is that the modest amounts of inventory may be perishable. In addition, the relevant units of time may be much smaller than in manufacturing. For example, in fast-food restaurants, peak and slack periods may be measured in hours and the "product" may be inventoried for only as long as 10 minutes.

Miscellaneous Services

Most "miscellaneous" services—financial, hospitality, transportation, and many communication and recreation services—provide high-volume but intangible output. Aggregate planning for these services deals mainly with planning for human resource requirements and managing demand. The twofold goal is to level demand peaks and to design methods for fully utilizing labor resources during forecasted low-demand periods.

National Chains of Small Service Firms

With the advent of national chains of small service businesses such as funeral homes, fast-food outlets, photocopy/printing centers, and computer centers, the question of aggregate planning versus independent planning at each business establishment becomes an issue. Both output and purchasing may be centrally planned when demand can be influenced through special promotions. This approach to aggregate scheduling is advantageous because it reduces purchasing and advertising costs and helps manage cash flow at independent sites.

Airline Industry

Airlines and auto-rental firms also have unique aggregate scheduling problems. Consider an airline that has its headquarters in New York, two hub sites in cities such as Atlanta and Dallas, and 150 offices in airports throughout the country. Aggregate planning consists of tables or schedules for: (1) number of flights in and out of each hub; (2) number of flights on all routes; (3) number of passengers to be serviced on all flights; and (4) number of air personnel and ground personnel required at each hub and airport.

Aggregate Scheduling in Services

This planning is considerably more complex than aggregate planning for a single site or even for a number of independent sites. Capacity decisions for airlines also include determining the percentage of seats to be allocated to various fare classes in order to maximize profit or yield. This type of capacity allocation problem is called **yield management**. The *OM in Action* box entitled "Yield Management at Hertz" shows that this practice has spread to the rental car industry as well.

Yield management
Capacity decisions that determine the allocation of classes of resources in order to maximize profit or yield.

Hospitals

Hospitals face aggregate planning problems in allocating money, staff, and supplies to meet the demands of patients. Michigan's Henry Ford Hospital, for example, plans for bed capacity and personnel needs in light of a patient-load forecast developed by moving averages. The necessary labor focus of its aggregate plan has led to the creation of a new floating staff pool serving each nursing pod.[7]

EXAMPLE 6

Aggregate Scheduling in a Law Firm

Klasson and Avalon, a medium-sized Tampa law firm of 32 legal professionals, has developed a 3-month forecast for 5 categories of legal business it anticipates (see Table 13.9). Assuming a 40-hour workweek and that 100% of each lawyer's hours are billed, about 500 billable hours are available from each lawyer this fiscal quarter. Hours of billable time are forecast and accumulated for the quarter by the 5 categories of skill (column 1), then divided by 500 to provide a count of lawyers needed to cover the estimated business. Between 30 and 39 lawyers will be needed to cover the variations in level of business between worst and best levels of demand. (For example, best-case scenario of 19,500 total hours, divided by 500 hours per lawyer, equals 39 lawyers needed.)

TABLE 13.9 ■ Labor Allocation at Klasson and Avalon, Attorneys-at-Law. Forecasts for Coming Quarter (1 Lawyer = 500 Hours of Labor)

	LABOR HOURS REQUIRED			CAPACITY CONSTRAINTS	
(1) Category of Legal Business	(2) Best Case (hours)	(3) Likely Case (hours)	(4) Worst Case (hours)	(5) Maximum Demand in People	(6) Number of Qualified Personnel
Trial work	1,800	1,500	1,200	3.6	4
Legal research	4,500	4,000	3,500	9.0	32
Corporate law	8,000	7,000	6,500	16.0	15
Real estate law	1,700	1,500	1,300	3.4	6
Criminal law	3,500	3,000	2,500	7.0	12
Total hours	19,500	17,000	15,000		
Lawyers needed	39	34	30		

Because all 32 lawyers at Klasson and Avalon are qualified to perform basic legal research, this skill area has maximum scheduling flexibility (column 6). The most highly skilled (and capacity-constrained) categories are trial work and corporate law. In these areas, the firm's best-case forecast just barely covers trial work with 3.6 lawyers needed (see column 5) and 4 qualified (column 6). Meanwhile, corporate law is short one full per-

---

[7] G. Buxey, "Production Planning for Seasonal Demand," *International Journal of Operations and Production Management* 13, no. 7 (1993): 4–21.

son. Overtime can be used to cover the excess this quarter, but as business expands, it might be necessary to hire or develop talent in both of these areas. Real estate and criminal practice are adequately covered by available staff, as long as other needs do not use their excess capacity.

With its current legal staff of 32, Klasson and Avalon's best-case forecast will increase the workload by 20% (assuming no new hires). This represents one extra day of work per lawyer per week. The worst-case scenario will result in about a 6% underutilization of talent. For both these scenarios, the firm has determined that available staff will provide adequate service.

Source: Adapted from Glenn Bassett, *Operations Management for Service Industries* (Westport, CT: Quorum Books, 1992), p. 110.

SUMMARY

Aggregate scheduling provides companies with a necessary weapon to help capture market shares in the global economy. The aggregate plan provides both manufacturing and service firms the ability to respond to changing customer demands while still producing at low-cost and high-quality levels.

The aggregate schedule sets levels of inventory, production, subcontracting, and employment over an intermediate time range, usually 3 to 18 months. This chapter describes several aggregate planning techniques, ranging from the popular charting approach to a variety of mathematical models such as linear programming.

The aggregate plan is an important responsibility of an operations manager and a key to efficient production. Output from the aggregate schedule leads to a more detailed master production schedule, which is the basis for disaggregation, job scheduling, and MRP systems.

Although the discussion in the early part of this chapter dealt mostly with the manufacturing environment, we also saw that aggregate plans for service systems are similar. Banks, restaurants, airlines, and auto-repair facilities are all service systems that employ aggregate plans. But regardless of the industry or planning method, the most important issue is the implementation of the plan. In this respect, managers appear to be more comfortable with faster, less complex, and less mathematical approaches to planning.

KEY TERMS

Aggregate scheduling (or aggregate planning) *(p. 504)*
Scheduling decisions *(p. 504)*
Disaggregation *(p. 506)*
Master production schedule *(p. 506)*
Chase strategy *(p. 511)*
Level scheduling *(p. 511)*
Mixed strategy *(p. 511)*
Graphical and charting techniques *(p. 511)*
Transportation method of linear programming *(p. 516)*
Management coefficients model *(p. 518)*
Yield management *(p. 521)*

USING POM FOR WINDOWS FOR AGGREGATE PLANNING

POM for Windows' Aggregate Planning module performs aggregate or production planning for up to 12 time periods. Given a set of demands for future periods, you can try various plans to determine the lowest-cost plan based on holding, shortage, production, and

USING EXCEL OM FOR AGGREGATE PLANNING

changeover costs. Four methods are available for planning. More help is available on each after you choose the method.

Programs 13.1 and 13.2 illustrate the use of POM for Windows for analyzing plan 1 (the first strategy) for Example 2. That "user-defined" plan maintained a constant workforce throughout the 6-month planning period.

Aggregate Planning

Shortage: ● Backordered ○ Lost sales
Method: User defined

Analysis of Plan 1 for Example 2

Period	Demand	Regular tm production	Overtime production	Subcontrac production	Unit costs	Value
January	900	1,100			Regular time	8.
February	700	900			Overtime	11.2
March	800	1,050			Subcontracting	10.
April	1,200	1,050			Holding cost	5.
May	1,500	1,100			Shortage cost	0.
June	1,100	1,000			Increase cost	0.
					Decrease cost	0.
					Initial Inventory	0.
					Units last period	0.

PROGRAM 13.1 ■ POM for Windows' Aggregate Planning Program with Data Entry Screen for Plan 1 of Example 2 *Note that the "user-defined" method was chosen for this analysis.*

Aggregate Planning Results

Analysis of Plan 1 for Example 2 Solution

	Demand	Regular tm production	Reg time Production	Inventory (end PD)	Units Increase	Units Decrease
Initial Inventory				0.		
January	900.	1,100.	1,100.	200.	0.	0.
February	700.	900.	900.	400.	0.	200.
March	800.	1,050.	1,050.	650.	150.	0.
April	1,200.	1,050.	1,050.	500.	0.	0.
May	1,500.	1,100.	1,100.	100.	50.	0.
June	1,100.	1,000.	1,000.	0.	0.	100.
Total(units)	6,200.	6,200.	6,200.	1,850.	200.	300.
			@$8 /unit	@$5 /unit	@$0 /unit	@$0 /unit
Subtotal Costs			49,600.	9,250.	0.	0.
Total Cost	58,850.					

PROGRAM 13.2 ■ POM for Windows Output for Aggregate Plan of Example 2

USING EXCEL OM FOR AGGREGATE PLANNING

Excel OM's Aggregate Planning module is illustrated in Programs 13.3 and 13.4 on page 524. Again using data from Example 2, Program 13.3 provides input and the formulas used to compute the costs of regular time, overtime, subcontracting, holding, shortage, and increase or decrease in production. The user must provide the production plan for Excel OM to analyze. The results of the analysis are shown in Program 13.4.

524 CHAPTER 13 AGGREGATE SCHEDULING

	A	B	C	F	G	H	I	J	K
1	Aggregate Planning								
2	Costs (per unit)						antities in area		
3	Reg time	=5*1.6							
4	Overtime	=7*1.6							
5	Subcontract		10						
6	Holding		5						
7	Shortage		0						
8	Increase		0						
9	Decrease		0						
10									
11	Starting Conditions								
12	Initial inventory								
13	Units last period		0	none given - therefore, do not calculate change in first period					
14									
15	Data				RESULTS				
16	Period	Demand	Reg Time Production		Inventory	Holding	Shortage		Change
17	Period 1	900	1100		=+B12+SUM(C17:E17)-B17	=IF(G17>=0,G17,0)	=IF(G17<=0,-G17,0)		
18	Period 2	700	900		=G17+SUM(C18:E18)-B18	=IF(G18>=0,G18,0)	=IF(G18<=0,-G18,0)	=C18-C17	=IF(J18>
19	Period 3	800	1050		=G18+SUM(C19:E19)-B19	=IF(G19>=0,G19,0)	=IF(G19<=0,-G19,0)	=C19-C18	=IF(J19>=
20	Period 4	1200	1050		=G19+SUM(C20:E20)-B20	=IF(G20>=0,G20,0)	=IF(G20<=0,-G20,0)	=C20-C19	=IF(J20>
21	Period 5	1500	1100		=G20+SUM(C21:E21)-B21	=IF(G21>=0,G21,0)	=IF(G21<=0,-G21,0)	=C21-C20	=IF(J21>=
22	Period 6	1100	1000		=G21+SUM(C22:E22)-B22	=IF(G22>=0,G22,0)	=IF(G22<=0,-G22,0)	=C22-C21	=IF(J22>
23	Total	=SUM(B17:B22)	=SUM(C17:C22)			=SUM(H17:H22)	=SUM(I17:I22)		=SUM(K1
24	Cost		=B3*C23			=B6*H23	=B7*I23		=B8*K23
25	Total Cost	=SUM(B24:L24)							

- Enter the costs. Regular time and overtime costs must be computed based on production hours and labor rates.
- Although the first period change depends on the production of the last period (B13), the others depend on the previous production in column J.
- The IF function is used to determine whether the inventory is positive (and therefore held) or negative (and therefore short).
- The IF function is used to determine whether the change is positive (and, therefore, an increase) or negative (and, therefore, a decrease). Columns K and L formulas are not shown.
- Enter the demands in column B and the number of units produced in each period in column C (and D and E, which are hidden on this particular spreadsheet because they are 0).
- Although the first period inventory relies on the initial inventory (B12), the others rely on the previous inventory in column G. Thus inventory in the first period is computed somewhat differently than the inventory in the other periods.

PROGRAM 13.3 ■ Excel OM Input and Formulas for Aggregate Planning, Using Example 2 Data

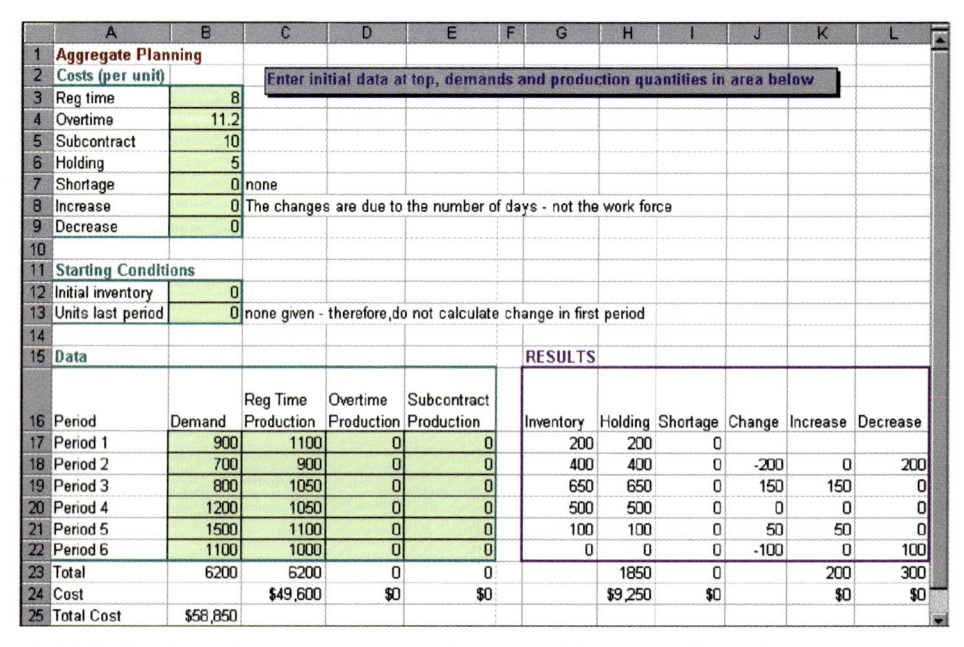

	A	B	C	D	E	G	H	I	J	K	L
1	Aggregate Planning										
2	Costs (per unit)		Enter initial data at top, demands and production quantities in area below								
3	Reg time	8									
4	Overtime	11.2									
5	Subcontract	10									
6	Holding	5									
7	Shortage	0	none								
8	Increase	0	The changes are due to the number of days - not the work force								
9	Decrease	0									
10											
11	Starting Conditions										
12	Initial inventory	0									
13	Units last period	0	none given - therefore, do not calculate change in first period								
14											
15	Data					RESULTS					
16	Period	Demand	Reg Time Production	Overtime Production	Subcontract Production	Inventory	Holding	Shortage	Change	Increase	Decrease
17	Period 1	900	1100	0	0	200	200	0			
18	Period 2	700	900	0	0	400	400	0	-200	0	200
19	Period 3	800	1050	0	0	650	650	0	150	150	0
20	Period 4	1200	1050	0	0	500	500	0	0	0	0
21	Period 5	1500	1100	0	0	100	100	0	50	50	0
22	Period 6	1100	1000	0	0	0	0	0	-100	0	100
23	Total	6200	6200	0	0		1850	0		200	300
24	Cost		$49,600	$0	$0		$9,250	$0		$0	$0
25	Total Cost	$58,850									

PROGRAM 13.4 ■ Output Results for Program 13.3 Using Excel OM

SOLVED PROBLEMS

Solved Problem 13.1

The roofing manufacturer described in Examples 1 to 4 of this chapter wishes to consider yet a fourth planning strategy (plan 4). This one maintains a constant workforce of eight people and uses overtime whenever necessary to meet demand. Use the cost information found in Table 13.3 on page 513. Again, assume beginning and ending inventories are equal to zero.

Solution

Employ eight workers and use overtime when necessary. Note that carrying costs will be encountered in this plan.

Month	Production at 40 Units per Day	Beginning-of-Month Inventory	Forecast Demand This Month	Overtime Production Needed	Ending Inventory
Jan.	880	—	900	20 units	0 units
Feb.	720	0	700	0 units	20 units
Mar.	840	20	800	0 units	60 units
Apr.	840	60	1,200	300 units	0 units
May	880	0	1,500	620 units	0 units
June	800	0	1,100	300 units	0 units
				1240 units	80 units

Carrying cost totals = 80 units × $5/unit/month = $400

Regular pay:

8 workers × $40/day × 124 days = $39,680

To produce 1,240 units at overtime rate (of $7/hour) requires 1,984 hours.

Overtime pay = $7/hour × 1,984 hours = $13,888

COSTS		PLAN 4 (workforce of 8 plus overtime)
Carrying cost	$ 400	(80 units carried × $5/unit)
Regular labor	39,680	(8 workers × $40/day × 124 days)
Overtime	13,888	(1,984 hours × $7/hour)
Hiring or firing	0	
Subcontracting	0	
Total costs	$53,968	

Solved Problem 13.2

A Dover, Delaware, plant has developed the accompanying supply, demand, cost, and inventory data. The firm has a constant workforce and meets all of its demand. Allocate production capacity to satisfy demand at a minimum cost. What is the cost of this plan?

526 CHAPTER 13 AGGREGATE SCHEDULING

Supply Capacity Available (in Units)

Period	Regular Time	Overtime	Subcontract
1	300	50	200
2	400	50	200
3	450	50	200

Demand Forecast

Period	Demand (units)
1	450
2	550
3	750

Other Data

Initial inventory	50 units
Regular-time cost per unit	$50
Overtime cost per unit	$65
Subcontract cost per unit	$80
Carrying cost per unit per period	$ 1

SUPPLY FROM		Period 1	Period 2	Period 3	Unused Capacity (Dummy)	TOTAL CAPACITY AVAILABLE (supply)
Beginning inventory		0 / 50	1	2	0	50
Period 1	Regular time	50 / 300	51	52	0	300
	Overtime	65 / 50	66	67	0	50
	Subcontract	80 / 50	81	82	0 / 150	200
Period 2	Regular time		50 / 400	51	0	400
	Overtime		65 / 50	66	0	50
	Subcontract		80 / 100	81 / 50	0 / 50	200
Period 3	Regular time			50 / 450	0	450
	Overtime			65 / 50	0	50
	Subcontract			80 / 200	0	200
TOTAL DEMAND		450	550	750	200	1,950

Solution

Cost of plan

Period 1: 50($0) + 300($50) + 50($65) + 50($80) = $22,250

Period 2: 400($50) + 50($65) + 100($80) = $31,250

Period 3: 50($81) + 450($50) + 50($65) + 200($80) = $45,800

Total cost $99,300

DISCUSSION QUESTIONS

1. What is the purpose of aggregate planning? Describe some demand and capacity options for implementing plans.
2. What is the difference between mixed production planning strategies and those eight demand and capacity options that are not mixed? Name four strategies that are not mixed.
3. Why are mathematical models not more widely used in aggregate planning?
4. What are the advantages and disadvantages of varying the size of the workforce to meet demand requirements each period?
5. Why do some firms have longer planning horizons than others?
6. What is the relationship between the aggregate plan and the master production schedule?
7. Briefly describe some mathematical approaches to aggregate planning.
9. Why are graphical aggregate planning methods useful?
10. What are major limitations of using the transportation method for aggregate planning?
11. What impact on quality do you think each of eight production planning strategies might have?
12. What are the disadvantages common to the following two strategies: (1) varying inventory levels and (2) back ordering during periods of high demand?
13. How does "yield management" impact the aggregate plan?

CRITICAL THINKING EXERCISE

Many companies deal with aggregate scheduling by forcing overtime on their employees to adjust for the peaks of seasonal demand. For example, a recent *Wall Street Journal* report on long and irregular hours in the United States highlights Angie Clark, a J.C. Penney supervisor in Springfield, Virginia. Clark works at least 44 hours a week, including evenings and frequent weekend shifts. Because of recent economic changes, staffers are busier than 5 years earlier, when Clark had 38 salespeople instead of the current 28. The result of this pressure is a 40% turnover. Because employee turnover is so large, training consists of the bare minimum—mostly how to operate the cash registers.

Discuss the implications of a strategy of heavy use of overtime in retailing, as well as in other fields, such as manufacturing, hospitals, and airlines. How does this U.S. approach compare to that in other countries?

PROBLEMS

: 13.1 Develop another plan for the roofing manufacturer described in Examples 1 to 4 (in the chapter) and Solved Problem 13.1 (at the end of the chapter). For this plan, plan 5, the firm wishes to maintain a constant workforce of six, paying overtime to meet demand. Is this plan preferable?

: 13.2 The same roofing manufacturer in Examples 1 to 4 (in this chapter) and Solved Problem 13.1 (at the end of the chapter) has yet a sixth plan. A constant workforce of seven is selected, with the remainder of demand filled by subcontracting. Is this a better plan?

: 13.3 The president of Daves Enterprises, Carla Daves, projects the firm's aggregate demand requirements over the next eight months as follows:

Jan.	1,400	May	2,200
Feb.	1,600	June	2,200
Mar.	1,800	July	1,800
Apr.	1,800	Aug.	1,400

Her operations manager is considering a new plan, which begins in January, with 200 units on hand. Stockout cost of lost sales is $100 per unit. Inventory holding cost is $20 per unit per month. Ignore any idle-time costs. The plan is called plan A.

Plan A. Vary the workforce level to execute a "chase" strategy by meeting demand requirements exactly. The December rate of production is 1,600 units per month. The cost of hiring additional workers is $5,000 per 100 units. The cost of laying off workers is $7,500 per 100 units. Evaluate this plan.

: 13.4 Refer to Problem 13.3. Daves is now looking at plan B. Beginning inventory, stockout costs, and holding costs are provided in Problem 13.3.

Plan B. Produce at a constant rate of 1,400 units per month, which will meet minimum demands. Then use subcontracting, with additional units at a premium price of $75 per unit. Evaluate this plan.

: 13.5 Daves is now considering plan C. (Refer to Problem 13.3.) Beginning inventory, stockout costs, and holding costs are provided in Problem 13.3.

Plan C. Keep a stable workforce by maintaining a constant production rate equal to the average requirements and allow varying inventory levels. Plot the demand with a graph that also shows average requirements.

: 13.6 Daves's operations manager (see Problems 13.3 through 13.5) is also considering two mixed strategies:

Plan D. Keep the current workforce stable at producing 1,600 units per month. Permit a maximum of 20% overtime at an additional cost of $50 per unit. A warehouse now constrains the maximum allowable inventory on hand to 400 units or less.

Plan E. Keep the current workforce, which is producing 1,600 units per month, and subcontract to meet the rest of the demand.

Evaluate plans D and E.

: 13.7 Dalen and Chiang is a VCR manufacturer in need of an aggregate plan for July through December. The company has gathered the following data:

Costs	
Holding cost	$8/VCR/month
Subcontracting	$80/VCR
Regular-time labor	$10/hour
Overtime labor	$16/hour for hours above 8 hours/worker/day
Hiring cost	$40/worker
Layoff cost	$80/worker

Demand	
July	400
Aug.	500
Sept.	550
Oct.	700
Nov.	800
Dec.	700

Other Data	
Current workforce	8 people
Labor hours/VCR	4 hours
Workdays/month	20 days
Beginning inventory	150 VCRs

What will each of the two following strategies cost?
a) Vary the workforce so that exact production meets forecast demand. Begin with eight workers on board at the end of June.
b) Vary overtime only and use a constant workforce of eight.

: 13.8 Develop your own aggregate plan for Dalen and Chiang (see Problem 13.7). Justify your approach.

: 13.9 Sue Badger, operations manager at Kimball Furniture, has received the following estimates of demand requirements.

Apr.	May	June	July	Aug.	Sept.
1,000	1,200	1,400	1,800	1,800	1,600

also available as a backup source to meet demand—but it insists on a firm contract and can provide only 500 bags total during the 6-month period. Develop a 6-month production plan for the feed mill.

Cost data are as follows:

Regular-time cost per bag (until April 30)	$12.00
Regular-time cost per bag (after May 1)	$11.00
Overtime cost per bag (during entire period)	$16.00
Cost of outside purchase per bag	$18.50
Carrying cost per bag per month	$ 1.00

: 13.17 The William Bistline Chemical Supply Company manufactures and packages expensive vials of mercury. Given the following demand, supply, cost, and inventory data, allocate production capacity to meet demand at minimum cost. A constant workforce is expected and no back orders are permitted.

	Supply Capacity (in units)			Demand
Period	Regular Time	Overtime	Subcontract	(in units)
1	25	5	6	32
2	28	4	6	32
3	30	8	6	40
4	29	6	7	40

Other Data

Initial inventory	4 units
Ending inventory desired	3 units
Regular-time cost per unit	$2,000
Overtime cost per unit	$2,475
Subcontract cost per unit	$3,200
Carrying cost per unit per period	$ 200

: 13.18 Given the following information, solve for the minimum-cost plan.

	Period				
	1	2	3	4	5
Demand	150	160	130	200	210
Capacity					
Regular	150	150	150	150	150
Overtime	20	20	10	10	10

Subcontracting: 100 units available over the 5-month period
Beginning inventory: 0 units
Ending inventory required: 20 units

Cost

Regular-time cost per unit	$100
Overtime cost per unit	$125
Subcontract cost per unit	$135
Inventory cost per unit per period	$ 3

Assume that back orders are not permitted.

CHAPTER 13 AGGREGATE SCHEDULING

DATA BASE APPLICATION

· 13.19 David Wood, owner of a dry-cleaning equipment manufacturer, develops an 8-month aggregate plan. Demand and capacity (in units) are forecast as follows:

Capacity Source	Jan.	Feb.	Mar.	Apr.	May	June	July	Aug.
Labor								
Regular time	235	255	290	300	300	290	300	290
Overtime	20	24	26	24	30	28	30	30
Subcontract	12	16	15	17	17	19	19	20
Demand	255	294	321	301	330	320	345	340

The cost of producing each unit is $1,000 on regular time, $1,300 on overtime, and $1,500 on a subcontract. Inventory carrying cost is $100 per unit per month. There is no beginning or ending inventory in stock and no back orders are permitted from period to period.

a) Set up a production plan that minimizes cost by producing exactly what the demand is each month and letting the workforce vary. What is this plan's cost?

b) Through better planning, regular-time production can be set at exactly the same value, 275, per month. Does this alter the solution?

c) If overtime costs rise from $1,300 to $1,400, will your answer to part (a) change? What if they fall to $1,200?

■ Case Study ■

Southwestern State College

The campus police chief at Southwestern State College wants to develop a 2-year plan that involves a request for additional resources.

The department currently has 26 sworn officers. The size of the force has not changed over the past 15 years, but the following changes have prompted the chief to seek more resources:

- The college has expanded geographically, with some new facilities now miles away from the main campus.
- Traffic and parking problems have increased.
- More portable, expensive computers with high theft potential are dispersed across the campus.
- Alcohol and drug problems have increased.
- The size of the athletic program has increased.
- The size of the surrounding community has doubled.
- The police need to spend more time on education and prevention programs.

The college is located in a small town. During the summer months, the student population is around 5,000. This number swells to 30,000 during fall and spring semesters. Thus demand for police and other services is significantly lower during the summer months. Demand for police services also varies by

- Time of day (peak time is between 10 P.M. and 2 A.M.).
- Day of the week (weekends are the busiest).
- Weekend of the year (on football weekends, 50,000 extra people come to campus).
- Special events (check-in, checkout, commencement).

Football weekends are especially difficult to staff. Extra police services are typically needed from 8:00 A.M. to 5:00 P.M. on 5 football Saturdays. All 26 officers are called in to work double shifts. Over 40 law enforcement officers from surrounding locations are paid to come in on their own time, and a dozen state police lend a hand free of charge (when available). Twenty-five students and local residents are paid to work traffic and parking. During the last academic year (a 9-month period), overtime payments to campus police officers totaled over $30,000.

Other relevant data include the following:

- The average starting salary for a police officer is $18,000.
- Work-study and part-time students and local residents who help with traffic and parking are paid $6.00 an hour.
- Overtime is paid to police officers who work over 40 hours a week at the rate of $13.00 an hour. Extra officers who are hired part-time from outside agencies also earn $13.00 an hour.
- There seems to be an unlimited supply of officers who will work for the college when needed for special events.
- With days off, vacations, and average sick leave considered, it takes 5 persons to cover one 24-hour, 7-day-a-week position.

The schedule of officers during fall and spring semesters is:

	Weekdays	Weekend
First shift (7 A.M.–3 P.M.)	5	4
Second shift (3 P.M.–11 P.M.)	5	6
Third shift (11 P.M.–7 A.M.)	6	8

Staffing for football weekends and special events is *in addition to* the preceding schedule. Summer staffing is, on average, half that shown.

The police chief thinks that his present staff is stretched to the limit. Fatigued officers are potential problems for the department and the community. In addition, neither time nor personnel has been set aside for crime prevention, safety, or health programs. Interactions of police officers with students, faculty, and staff are minimal and usually negative in nature. In light of these problems, the chief would like to request funding for four additional officers, two assigned to new programs and two to alleviate the overload on his current staff. He would also like to begin limiting overtime to 10 hours per week for each officer.

Discussion Questions

1. Which variations in demand for police services should be considered in an aggregate plan for resources? Which variations can be accomplished with short-term scheduling adjustments?
2. Evaluate the current staffing plan. What does it cost? Are 26 officers sufficient to handle the normal workload?
3. What would be the additional cost of the chief's proposal? How would you suggest that he justify his request?
4. How much does it currently cost the college to provide police services for football games? What would be the pros and cons of completely subcontracting this work to outside law enforcement agencies?
5. Propose other alternatives.

Source: From R. Murdick, Barry Render, and R. Russell, *Service Operations Management.* Copyright © 1990. Boston: Allyn & Bacon. Adapted by permission.

Internet Case Study

See our Internet home page at http://www.prenhall.com/heizer for this additional case study: Cornwell Glass.

BIBLIOGRAPHY

Armacost, R. L., R. J. Penlesky, and S. C. Ross. "Avoiding Problems Inherent in Spreadsheet-Based Simulation Models—An Aggregate Planning Application." *Production and Inventory Management* 31 (second quarter 1990): 62–68.

Bowers, M. R., and J. P. Jarvis. "A Hierarchical Production Planning and Scheduling Model." *Decision Sciences* 23 (January–February 1992):144–157.

Buxey, G. "Production Planning and Scheduling for Seasonal Demand." *International Journal of Operations and Production Management* 13, no. 7 (1993): 4–21.

DeMatta, R., and T. Miller. "A Note on the Growth of a Production Planning System." *Interfaces* 23 (April 1993): 27–31.

Fisher, M. L., J. H. Hammond, W. R. Obermeyer, and A. Raman. "Making Supply Meet Demand in an Uncertain World." *Harvard Business Review* 72, no. 3 (1994): 83–93.

Heskett, J., W. E. Sasser, and C. Hart. *Service Breakthroughs: Changing the Rules of the Game*. New York: The Free Press, 1990.

Leone, R. A., and J. R. Meyer. "Capacity Strategies for the 1980's." *Harvard Business Review* 58 (November–December 1980): 133.

Murdick, R., B. Render, and R. Russell. *Service Operations Management*. Boston: Allyn & Bacon, 1990.

Sasser, W. E. "Match Supply and Demand in Service Industries." *Harvard Business Review* 54 (November–December 1976): 133–140.

Schmenner, Roger W. *Service Operations Management*. Upper Saddle River, NJ: Prentice Hall, 1995.

Vollmann, T. E., W. L. Berry, and D. C. Whybark. *Manufacturing Planning and Control Systems,* 3rd ed. Homewood, IL: Irwin, 1992.

INTERNET RESOURCES

APICS courses:
   http://www.mgi.org/apics.html

Introductory discussion of aggregate scheduling:
   http://www.iaehv.nl/users/drshofm/kenc/TB/tech/aggreg.htm

Material Requirements Planning (MRP)

14

CHAPTER OUTLINE

GLOBAL COMPANY PROFILE: COLLINS INDUSTRIES

DEPENDENT INVENTORY MODEL REQUIREMENTS
- Master Production Schedule
- Bills of Material
- Accurate Inventory Records
- Purchase Orders Outstanding
- Lead Times for Each Component

MRP STRUCTURE

MRP MANAGEMENT
- MRP Dynamics
- MRP and JIT

LOT-SIZING TECHNIQUES

EXTENSIONS OF MRP
- Closed-Loop MRP
- Capacity Planning
- Material Requirements Planning II (MRP II)
- Enterprise Resource Planning (ERP)

MRP IN SERVICES

DISTRIBUTION RESOURCE PLANNING (DRP)
- DRP Structure
- Allocation

SUMMARY

KEY TERMS

USING POM FOR WINDOWS TO SOLVE MRP PROBLEMS

SOLVED PROBLEMS

DISCUSSION QUESTIONS

CRITICAL THINKING EXERCISE

PROBLEMS

DATA BASE APPLICATION

CASE STUDIES: SERVICE, INC.; RUCH MANUFACTURING

VIDEO CASE 8: MRP AT WHEELED COACH

BIBLIOGRAPHY

INTERNET RESOURCES

LEARNING OBJECTIVES

When you complete this chapter you should be able to:

Identify or Define:

   Planning bills and kits

   Phantom bills

   Low-level coding

   Lot sizing

Describe or Explain:

   Material requirements planning

   Distribution requirements planning

   Enterprise resource planning

🌐 GLOBAL COMPANY PROFILE:

MRP Provides a Competitive Advantage for Collins Industries

Collins Industries, headquartered in Hutchinson, Kansas, is the largest manufacturer of ambulances in the world. The $150-million firm is an international competitor that sells more than 20% of its vehicles to markets outside the United States. In its largest ambulance plant, located in Winter Park, Florida, vehicles are produced on assembly lines (i.e., a repetitive process). There are 12 major ambulance designs assembled at the Florida plant, and they use 18,000 different inventory items, including 6,000 manufactured parts and 12,000 purchased parts.

This variety of products and the nature of the process demand good material requirements planning. Effective use of an MRP system requires accurate bills of material and inventory records. The Collins system, which uses the MAPICS DB software on an IBM AS400 minicomputer, provides daily updates and has reduced inventory by over 30% in just 2 years.

Collins insists that four key tasks be performed properly. First, the material plan must meet both the requirements of the master schedule and the capabilities of the production facility. Second, the plan must be executed as designed. Third, effective "time-phased" material deliveries, consignment inventories, and a constant review of purchase methods reduce inventory investment. Finally, Collins maintains record integrity. Record accuracy is recognized as a fundamental ingredient of its successful MRP program. Collins's cycle counters are charged with material audits that not only correct errors, but also investigate and correct problems.

Collins Industries uses MRP as the catalyst for low inventory, high quality, tight schedules, and accurate records. Collins has found competitive advantage via MRP.

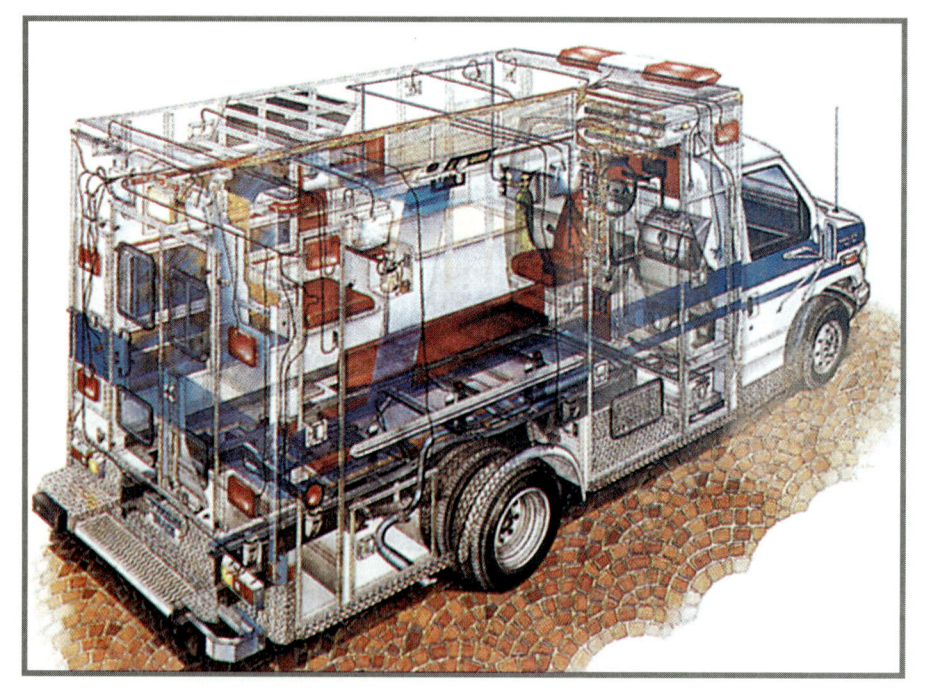

This cutaway of one ambulance interior indicates the complexity of the product, which for some rural locations may be the equivalent of a hospital emergency room in miniature. To complicate production, virtually every ambulance is custom-ordered, with 7,000 different options available. This customization necessitates precise orders and excellent bills of materials.

COLLINS INDUSTRIES

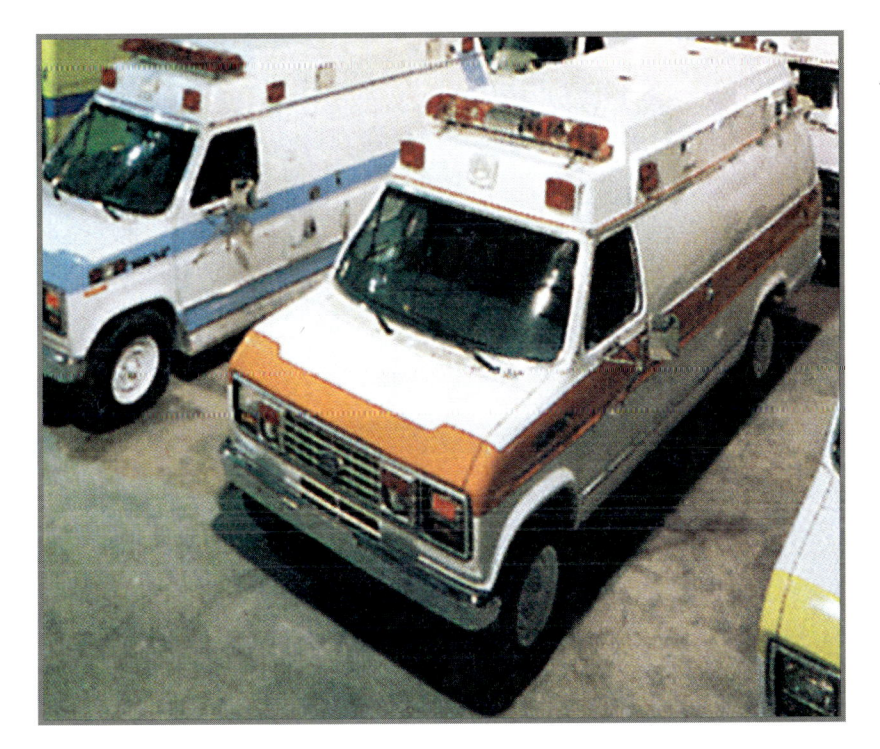

On six parallel lines, ambulances move forward each day to the next workstation. The MRP system makes certain that just the materials needed at each station arrive overnight for assembly the next day.

The company uses a job-shop environment to feed assembly-line needs. It maintains a complete carpentry shop (to provide interior cabinetry), a metal fabrication shop (to construct the shell of the ambulance), a paint shop (to prepare, paint, and detail each vehicle), an electrical shop (to provide for the complex electronics in a modern ambulance), and, as shown here, an upholstery shop (to make interior seats and benches).

537

538   CHAPTER 14   MATERIAL REQUIREMENTS PLANNING (MRP)

> **TEN DECISIONS OF OM**
> Managing Quality
> Design of Goods & Services
> Process Strategy
> Location Strategies
> Layout Strategies
> Human Resources
> Supply-Chain Management
> **Inventory Management**
>   **Independent Demand**
>   **Dependent Demand**
> Scheduling
> Maintenance

Material requirements planning (MRP) A dependent demand technique that uses bill-of-material, inventory, expected receipts, and a master production schedule to determine material requirements.

Collins Industries and many other firms have found important benefits in MRP. These benefits include: (1) better response to customer orders as the result of improved adherence to schedules, (2) faster response to market changes, (3) improved utilization of facilities and labor, and (4) reduced inventory levels. Better response to customer orders and to the market wins orders and market share. Better utilization of facilities and labor yields higher productivity and return on investment. Less inventory frees up capital and floor space for other uses. These benefits are the result of a strategic decision to use an inventory scheduling system that is dependent. Collins's demand for every component of an ambulance is dependent.

By *dependent demand,* we mean the demand for one item is related to the demand for another item. Consider the Ford Explorer. Ford's demand for auto tires and radiators depends on the production of Explorers. Four tires and one radiator go into each finished Explorer. Demand for items is *dependent* when the relationship between the items can be determined. Therefore, once management can make a forecast of the demand for the final product, quantities required for all components can be computed, because all components are dependent items. The Boeing Aircraft operations manager who schedules production of one plane per week, for example, knows the requirements down to the last rivet. For any product, all components of that product are dependent demand items. *More generally, for any item where a schedule can be established, dependent techniques should be used.*

When their requirements are met, dependent models are preferable to the EOQ models described in chapter 12.[1] Dependency exists for all component parts, subassemblies, and supplies once a master schedule is known. Dependent models are better not only for manufacturers and distributors but also for a wide variety of firms from restaurants[2] to hospitals.[3] The standard dependent techniques used in a production environment are variations of a technique called **material requirements planning (MRP).**

DEPENDENT INVENTORY MODEL REQUIREMENTS

Effective use of dependent inventory models requires that the operations manager know the:

1. Master production schedule (what is to be made and when);
2. Specifications or bill of material (materials and parts required to make the product);
3. Inventory availability (what is in stock);
4. Purchase orders outstanding (what is on order);
5. Lead times (how long it takes to get various components).

In this chapter, we discuss each of these requirements in the context of material requirements planning (MRP). We then introduce variations of MRP including distribution resource planning (DRP).

---

[1] The inventory models (EOQ) discussed in chapter 12 assumed that the demand for one item was independent of the demand for another item. For example, EOQ assumes the demand for refrigerators is *independent* of the demand for refrigerator parts and that the demand today may have little, if anything, to do with the demand tomorrow.

[2] John G. Wacker, "Effective Planning and Cost Control for Restaurants: Making Resource Requirements Planning Work," *Production and Inventory Management* 26 (first quarter 1985): 55–70.

[3] David W. Pentico, "Material Requirements Planning: A New Tool for Controlling Hospital Inventories," *Hospital Topics* 57 (May–June 1979): 40–43; and Aleda V. Roth and Roland van Dierdonck, "Hospital Resource Planning: Concepts, Feasibility, and Framework," *Production and Operations Management,* winter 1995, pp. 2–29.

Master Production Schedule

A **master production schedule (MPS)** specifies what is to be made (ie, the number of finished products or items) and when. The schedule must be in accordance with a production plan. The production plan sets the overall level of output in broad terms (for example, product families, standard hours, or dollar volume). The plan also includes a variety of inputs, including financial plans, customer demand, engineering capabilities, labor availability, inventory fluctuations, supplier performance, and other considerations. Each of these inputs contributes in its own way to the production plan, as shown in Figure 14.1.

Master production schedule (MPS) A timetable that specifies what is to be made and when.

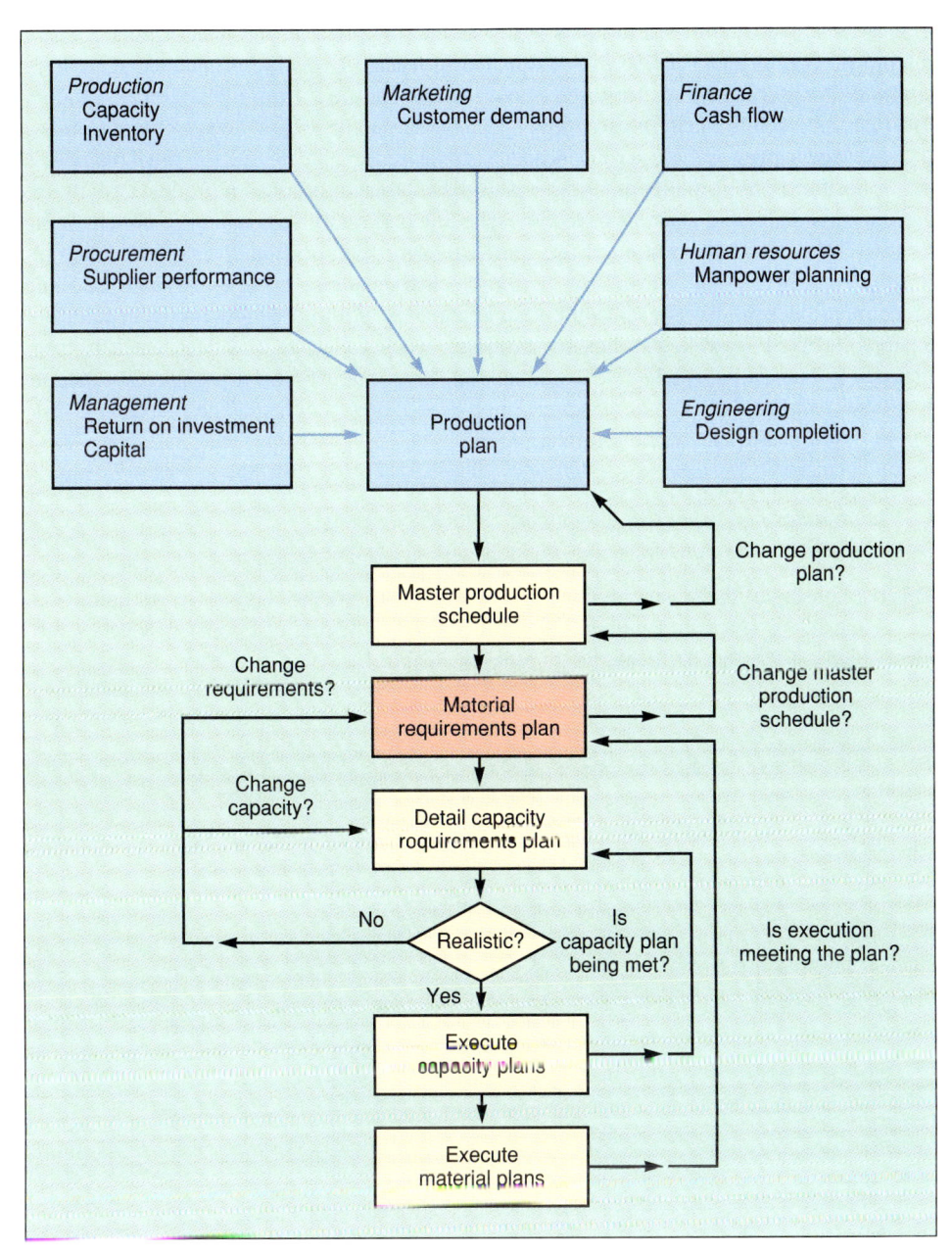

Regardless of the complexity of the planning process, the production plan and its derivative, the master production schedule, must be developed.

FIGURE 14.1 ■ **The Planning Process**

As the planning process moves from the production plan to execution, each of the lower-level plans must be feasible. When one is not, feedback to the next higher level is used to make the necessary adjustment. One of the major strengths of MRP is its ability to determine precisely the feasibility of a schedule within capacity constraints. This planning process can yield excellent results. The production plan sets the upper and lower bounds on the master production schedule. The result of this production planning process is the master production schedule.

The master production schedule tells us what is required to satisfy demand and meet the production plan. This schedule establishes what items to make and when: It *disaggregates* the aggregate production plan. While the *aggregate production plan* (as discussed in chapter 13) is established in gross terms such as families of products or tons of steel, the *master production schedule* is established in terms of specific products. Figure 14.2 shows the master schedules for three stereo models that flow from the aggregate production plan for a family of stereo amplifiers.

> The master production schedule is derived from the aggregate schedule.

Managers must adhere to the schedule for a reasonable length of time (usually a major portion of the production cycle—the time it takes to produce a product). Many organizations establish a master production schedule and establish a policy of not changing ("fixing") the near-term portion of the plan. This near-term portion of the plan is then referred to as the "fixed," "firm," or "frozen" schedule. Only changes beyond the fixed schedule are permitted. The schedule then becomes a "rolling" production schedule. For example, a fixed 7-week plan has an additional week added to it as each week is completed so a 7-week fixed schedule is maintained. Note that the master production schedule is a statement of *what is to be produced,* not a forecast of demand. The master schedule can be expressed in any of the following terms:

1. A *customer order in a job shop* (make-to-order) company;
2. *Modules in a repetitive* (assemble-to-stock) company;
3. An *end item in a continuous* (make-to-stock) company.

This relationship of the master production schedule to the processes is shown in Figure 14.3.

A master production schedule for two of Nancy's Specialty Foods' products, crabmeat quiche and spinach quiche, might look like Table 14.1.

Months	January				February			
Aggregate Production Plan (Shows the total quantity of amplifiers)	1,500				1,200			
Weeks	1	2	3	4	5	6	7	8
Master Production Schedule (Shows the specific type and quantity of amplifier to be produced)								
240 watt amplifier	100		100		100		100	
150 watt amplifier		500		500		450		450
75 watt amplifier			300				100	

FIGURE 14.2 ■ **The Aggregate Production Plan Provides the Basis for Development of the Detailed Master Production Schedule**

DEPENDENT INVENTORY MODEL REQUIREMENTS

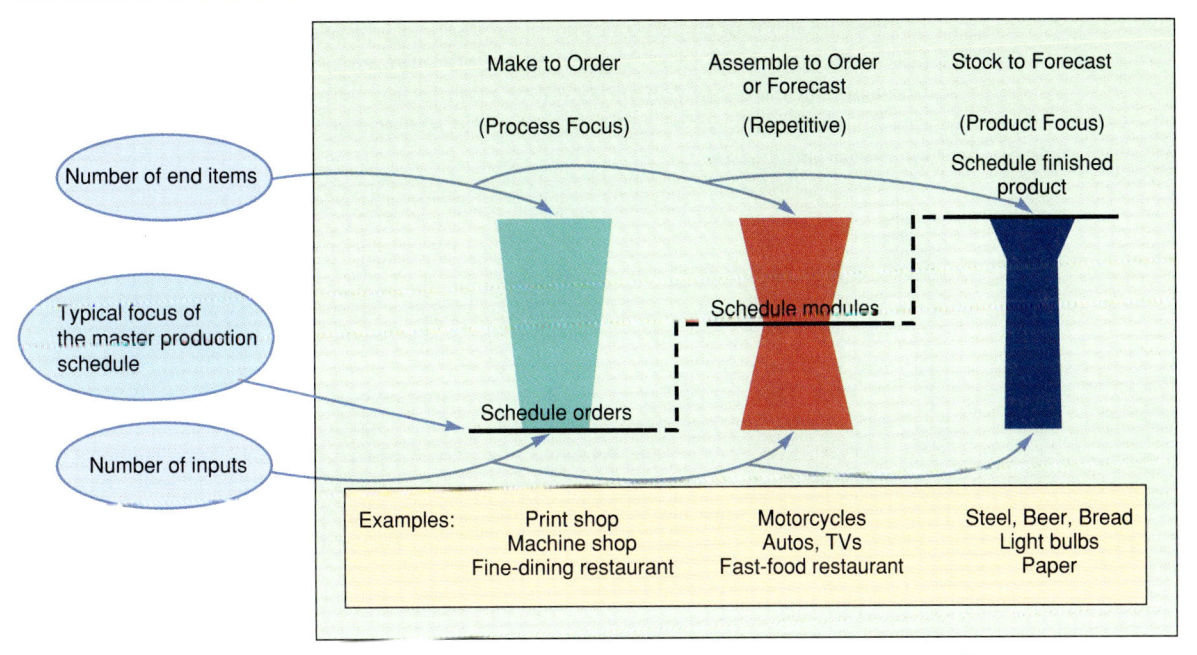

FIGURE 14.3 ■ Typical Focus of the Master Production Schedule in Three Process Strategies

TABLE 14.1 ■ Master Production Schedule for Products Crabmeat Quiche and Spinach Quiche

Gross Requirements for Product Crabmeat Quiche

Day	6	7	8	9	10	11	12	13	14	and so on
Amount	50		100	47	60		110	75		

Gross Requirements for Product Spinach Quiche

Day	7	8	9	10	11	12	13	14	15	16	and so on
Amount	100	200	150			60	75		100		

Bills of Material

Defining what goes into a product may seem simple, but it can be difficult in practice. As we noted in chapter 6, to aid this process, manufactured items are defined via a bill of material. A **bill of material (BOM)** is a list of quantities of components, ingredients, and materials required to make a product. Individual drawings describe not only physical dimensions but also any special processing as well as the raw material from which each part is made. Nancy's Specialty Foods' has a recipe for quiche, specifying ingredients and quantities, just as Collins Industries has a full set of drawings for an ambulance. Both are bills of material (although we call one a recipe and they do vary somewhat in scope).

Because there is often a rush to get a new product to market, however, drawings and bills of material may be incomplete or even nonexistent. Moreover, complete drawings and BOM (as well as other forms of specifications) often contain errors in dimensions, quantities, or countless other areas. When errors are identified, engineering change notices (ECNs) are created, further complicating the process. An *engineering change notice* is a change or correction to an engineering drawing or bill of material.

Bill of material (BOM)
A listing of the components, their description, and the quantity of each required to make one unit of a product.

542 CHAPTER 14 MATERIAL REQUIREMENTS PLANNING (MRP)

One way a bill of material defines a product is by providing a product structure. Example 1 shows how to develop the product structure and "explode" it to reveal the requirements for each component. A bill of material for item A in Example 1 consists of items B and C. Items above any level are called *parents;* items below any level are called *components* or *children.*

EXAMPLE 1

Speaker Kits, Inc., packages high-fidelity components for mail order. Components for the top-of-the-line speaker kit, "Awesome" (A), include 2 standard 12-inch speaker kits (B's) and 3 speaker kits with amp-boosters (C's).

Each B consists of 2 speakers (D's) and 2 shipping boxes each with an installation kit (E's). Each of the three 300-watt stereo kits (C's) has 2 speaker boosters (F's) and 2 installation kits (E's). Each speaker booster (F) includes 2 speakers (D's) and 1 amp-booster (G). The total for each Awesome is 4 standard 12-inch speakers and twelve 12-inch speakers with the amp-booster. (Most purchasers require hearing aids within 2 years, and at least one court case is pending because of structural damage to a men's dormitory.) As we can see, the demand for B, C, D, E, F, and G is completely dependent on the MPS for A—the Awesome speaker kits. Given this information, we can construct the following product structure:

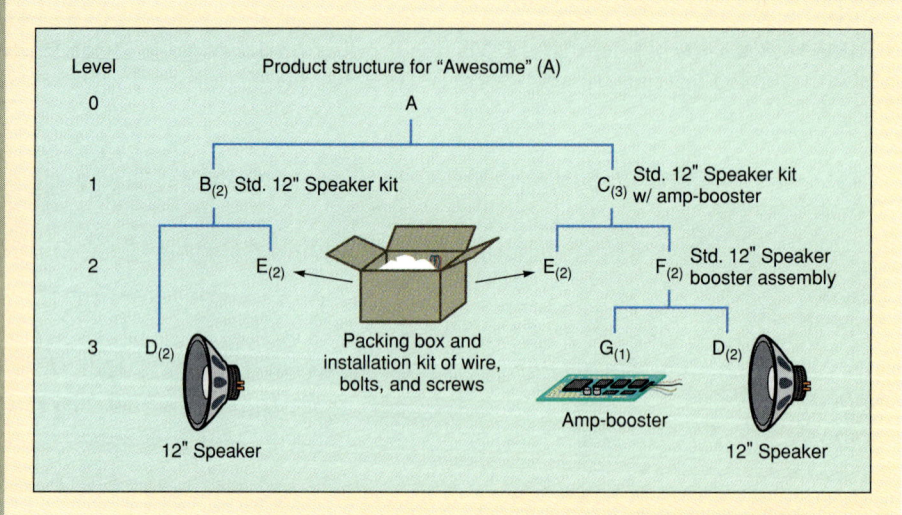

Level	Product structure for "Awesome" (A)
0	A
1	$B_{(2)}$ Std. 12" Speaker kit $C_{(3)}$ Std. 12" Speaker kit w/ amp-booster
2	$E_{(2)}$ ← Packing box and installation kit of wire, bolts, and screws → $E_{(2)}$ $F_{(2)}$ Std. 12" Speaker booster assembly
3	$D_{(2)}$ 12" Speaker $G_{(1)}$ Amp-booster $D_{(2)}$ 12" Speaker

This structure has four levels: 0, 1, 2, and 3. There are four parents: A, B, C, and F. Each parent item has at least one level below it. Items B, C, D, E, F, and G are components because each item has at least one level above it. In this structure, B, C, and F are both parents and components. The number in parentheses indicates how many units of that particular item are needed to make the item immediately above it. Thus, $B_{(2)}$ means that it takes 2 units of B for every unit of A, and $F_{(2)}$ means that it takes 2 units of F for every unit of C.

Once we have developed the product structure, we can determine the number of units of each item required to satisfy demand for a new order of 50 Awesome speaker kits. This information is displayed below:

Part B: 2 × number of A's =   (2)(50) =   100

Part C: 3 × number of A's =   (3)(50) =   150

Part D: 2 × number of B's + 2 × number of F's = (2)(100) + (2)(300) = 800

Part E:	2 × number of B's + 2 × number of C's =	(2)(100) + (2)(150) =	500
Part F:	2 × number of C's =	(2)(150) =	300
Part G:	1 × number of F's =	(1)(300) =	300

Thus, for 50 units of A, we will need 100 units of B, 150 units of C, 800 units of D, 500 units of E, 300 units of F, and 300 units of G.

Bills of material not only specify requirements but also are useful for costing, and they can serve as a list of items to be issued to production or assembly personnel. When bills of material are used in this way, they are usually called *pick lists*.

Modular Bills Bills of material may be organized around product modules (see chapter 6). *Modules* are not final products to be sold, but are components that can be produced and assembled into units. They are often major components of the final product or product options. Bills of material for modules are called **modular bills.** Bills of material are sometimes organized as modules (rather than as part of a final product) because production scheduling and production are often facilitated by organizing around relatively few modules rather than a multitude of final assemblies. For instance, a firm may make 138,000 different final products but have only 40 modules that are mixed and matched to produce those 138,000 final products. The firm builds an aggregate production plan and prepares its master production schedule for the 40 modules, not the 138,000 configurations of the final product. This approach allows the MPS to be prepared for a reasonable number of items (the narrow portion of the middle graphic in Figure 14.3) and to postpone assembly. The 40 modules can then be configured for specific orders at final assembly.

Modular bills Bills of material organized by major subassemblies or by product options.

Planning Bills and Phantom Bills Two other special kinds of bills of material are planning bills and phantom bills. **Planning bills** are created in order to assign an artificial parent to the bill of material. Such bills are used (1) when we want to group subassemblies so the number of items to be scheduled is reduced and (2) when we want to issue "kits" to the

Planning bills (or kits) A material grouping created in order to assign an artificial parent to the bill of material.

For manufacturers like Harley-Davidson, who produce a large number of end products from a relatively small number of options, modular bills of material provide an effective solution.

Phantom bills of material Bills of material for components, usually assemblies, that exist only temporarily; they are never inventoried.

production department. For instance, it may not be efficient to issue inexpensive items such as washers and cotter pins with each of numerous subassemblies, so we call this a *kit* and generate a planning bill. The planning bill specifies the *kit* to be issued. Consequently, a planning bill may also be known as **kitted material** or **kit. Phantom bills of material** are bills of material for components, usually subassemblies, that exist only temporarily. These components go directly into another assembly and are never inventoried. Therefore, components of phantom bills of material are coded to receive special treatment; lead times are zero, and they are handled as an integral part of their parent item.

Low-level coding Coding items at the lowest level at which they occur.

Low-level coding ensures that an item is always at the lowest level of usage.

Low-Level Coding Low-level coding of an item in a BOM is necessary when identical items exist at various levels in the BOM. **Low-level coding** means that the item is coded at the lowest level at which it occurs. For example, item D in Example 1 is coded at the lowest level at which it is used. Item D could be coded as part of B and occur at level 2. However, because D is also part of F, and F is level 2, item D becomes a level-3 item. Low-level coding is a convention to allow easy computing of the requirements of an item. When the BOM has thousands of items or when requirements are frequently recomputed, the ease and speed of computation become a major concern.

Accurate Inventory Records

As we saw in chapter 12, knowledge of what is in stock is the result of good inventory management. Good inventory management is an absolute necessity for an MRP system to work. If the firm has not yet achieved at least 99% record accuracy, then material requirements planning will not work.

Purchase Orders Outstanding

Knowledge of outstanding orders should exist as a by-product of well-managed purchasing and inventory-control departments. When purchase orders are executed, records of those orders and their scheduled delivery dates must be available to production personnel. Only with good purchasing data can managers prepare good production plans and effectively execute an MRP system.

Lead time In purchasing systems the time between placing an order and receiving it; in production systems, it is the wait, move, queue, setup, and run times for each component produced.

Lead Times for Each Component

Once managers determine when products are needed, they determine when to acquire them. The time required to acquire (that is, purchase, produce, or assemble) an item is known as **lead time.** Lead time for a manufactured item consists of *move, setup,* and *assembly* or *run times* for each component. For a purchased item, the lead time includes the time between when a part is ordered and when it is available for production.

When the bill of material for Awesome speaker kits (A's), in Example 1, is turned on its side and modified by adding lead times for each component (see Table 14.2), we then have a *time-phased product structure*. Time in this structure is shown on the horizontal axis of Figure 14.4 with item A due for completion in week 8. Each component is then offset to accommodate lead times.

TABLE 14.2 ■ Lead Times for Awesome Speaker Kits (A's)

Component	Lead Time
A	1 week
B	2 weeks
C	1 week
D	1 week
E	2 weeks
F	3 weeks
G	2 weeks

MRP STRUCTURE

Although most MRP systems are computerized, the MRP procedure is straightforward and can be done by hand. A master production schedule, a bill of material, inventory and purchase records, and lead times for each item are the ingredients of a material requirements planning system (see Figure 14.5).

MRP Structure

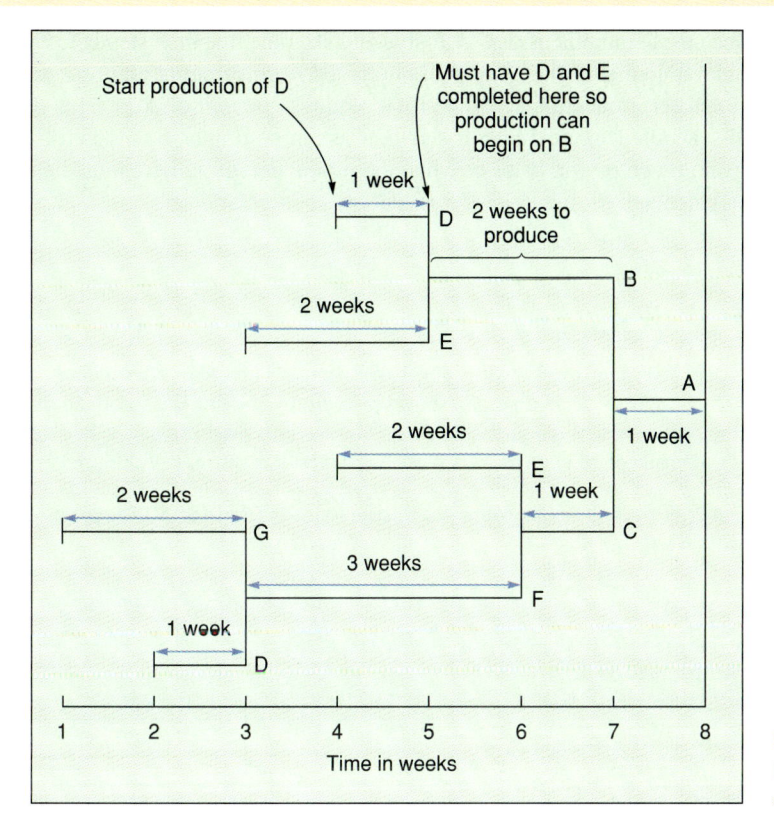

FIGURE 14.4 ■ Time-Phased Product Structure

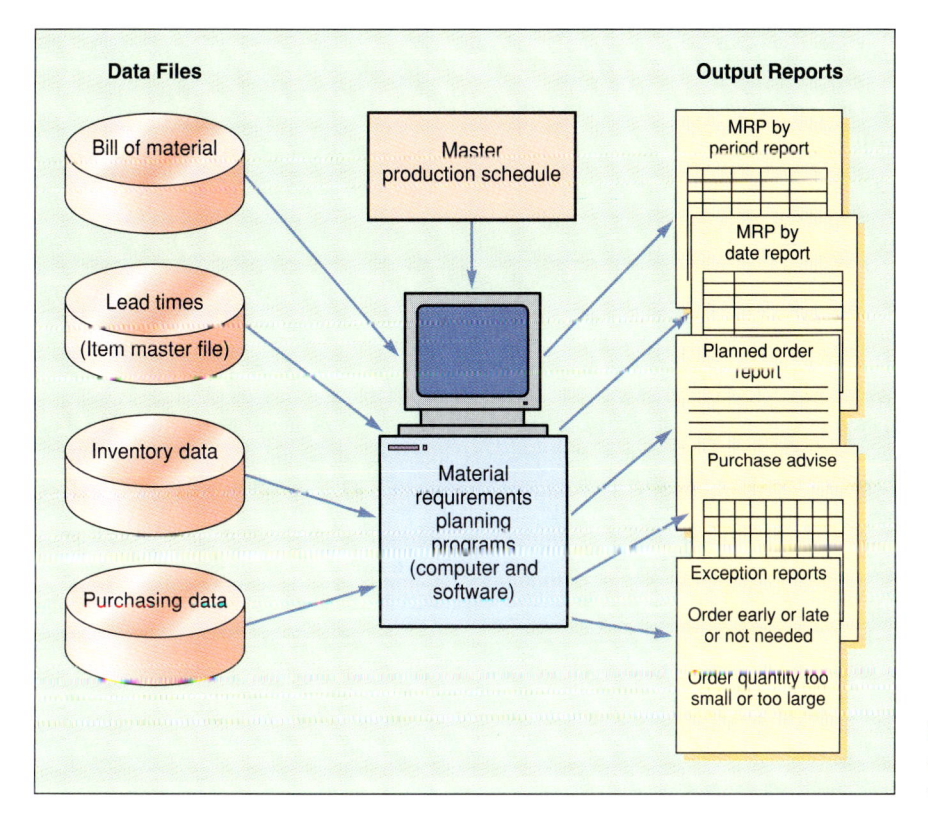

FIGURE 14.5 ■ Structure of the MRP System

MRP software programs are popular because many organizations face dependent demand situations.

Gross material requirements plan
A schedule that shows the total demand for an item (prior to subtraction of on-hand inventory and scheduled receipts) and when it must be ordered from suppliers, or production must be started in order to meet its demand by a particular date.

Once these ingredients are available and accurate, the next step is to construct a gross material requirements plan. The **gross material requirements plan** is a schedule. It combines a master production schedule (that requires one unit of A in week 8) and the time-phased schedule (Figure 14.4). It shows when an item must be ordered from suppliers if there is no inventory on hand or when the production of an item must be started in order to satisfy demand for the finished product by a particular date.

EXAMPLE 2

Each Awesome speaker kit (item A of Example 1) requires all the items in the product structure for A. Lead times are shown in Table 14.2. Using this information, we construct the gross material requirements plan and draw up a production schedule that will satisfy the demand of 50 units of A by week 8. The result is shown in Table 14.3.

TABLE 14.3 ■ Gross Material Requirements Plan for 50 Awesome Speaker Kits (A's)

	1	2	3	4	5	6	7	8	Lead Time
A. Required date								50	
Order release date							50		1 week
B. Required date							100		
Order release date					100				2 weeks
C. Required date							150		
Order release date						150			1 week
D. Required date						200			
Order release date					200				1 week
E. Required date						200	300		
Order release date				200	300				2 weeks
F. Required date						300			
Order release date			300						3 weeks
D. Required date				600					
Order release date			600						1 week
G. Required date				300					
Order release date	300								2 weeks

You can interpret the gross material requirements shown in Table 14.3 as follows: If you want 50 units of A at week 8, you must start assembling A in week 7. Thus, in week 7, you will need 100 units of B and 150 units of C. These two items take 2 weeks and 1 week, respectively, to produce. Production of B, therefore, should start in week 5, and production of C should start in week 6 (lead time subtracted from the required date for these items). Working backward, we can perform the same computations for all of the other items. The material requirements plan shows when production of each item should begin and end in order to have 50 units of A at week 8.

MRP Structure

So far, we have considered *gross material requirements,* which assumes that there is no inventory on hand. When there is inventory on hand, we prepare a *net requirements plan.* When considering on-hand inventory, we must realize that many items in inventory contain subassemblies or parts. If the gross requirement for Awesome speaker kits (A's) is 100 and there are 20 of those speakers on hand, the net requirement for Awesome speaker kits (A's) is 80 (that is, 100 − 20). However, each Awesome speaker kit on hand contains 2 B's. As a result, the requirement for B's drops by 40 B's (20 A kits on hand × 2 B's per A). Therefore, if inventory is on hand for a parent item, the requirements for the parent item and all its components decrease because each Awesome kit contains the components for lower-level items. Example 3 shows how to create a net requirements plan.

EXAMPLE 3

In Example 1, we developed a product structure from a bill of material, and in Example 2, we developed a gross requirements plan. Given the following on-hand inventory, we now construct a net requirements plan.

Item	On Hand	Item	On Hand
A	10	E	10
B	15	F	5
C	20	G	0
D	10		

A **net material requirements** plan includes gross requirements, on-hand inventory, net requirements, planned order receipt, and planned order release for each item. We begin with A and work backward through the components. Shown in the chart on page 548 is the net material requirements plan for product A.

Constructing a net requirements plan is similar to constructing the gross requirements plan. Starting with item A, we work backward to determine net requirements for all items. To do these computations, we refer to the product structure, on-hand inventory, and lead times. The gross requirement for A is 50 units in week 8. Ten items are on hand; therefore, the net requirements and the scheduled **planned order receipt** are both 40 items in week 8. Because of the 1-week lead time, the **planned order release** is 40 items in week 7 (see the arrow connecting the order receipt and order release). Referring to week 7 and the product structure in Example 1, we can see that 80 (2 × 40) items of B and 120 (3 × 40) items of C are required in week 7 in order to have a total for 50 items of A in week 8. The letter A to the right of the gross figure for items B and C was generated as a result of the demand for the parent, A. Performing the same type of analysis for B and C yields the net requirements for D, E, F, and G. Note the on-hand inventory in row E in week 6 is zero. It is zero because the on-hand inventory (10 units) was used to make B in week 5. By the same token, the inventory for D was used to make F.

Net material requirements The result of adjusting gross requirements for inventory on hand and scheduled receipts.

Planned order receipt The quantity planned to be received at a future date.

Planned order release The scheduled date for an order to be released.

Chapter 14 Material Requirements Planning (MRP)

Net Material Requirements Plan for Product A. Note that the superscript is the source of the demand.

Lot Size	Lead Time (weeks)	On Hand	Safety Stock	Allocated	Low-Level Code	Item Identification		Week 1	Week 2	Week 3	Week 4	Week 5	Week 6	Week 7	Week 8
Lot-for-Lot	1	10	—	—	0	A	Gross Requirements								50
							Scheduled Receipts								
							Projected on Hand 10	10	10	10	10	10	10	10	10
							Net Requirements								40
							Planned Order Receipts								40
							Planned Order Releases							40	
Lot-for-Lot	2	15	—	—	1	B	Gross Requirements							80^A	
							Scheduled Receipts								
							Projected on Hand 15	15	15	15	15	15	15	15	
							Net Requirements							65	
							Planned Order Receipts							65	
							Planned Order Releases						65		
Lot-for-Lot	1	20	—	—	1	C	Gross Requirements							120^A	
							Scheduled Receipts								
							Projected on Hand 20	20	20	20	20	20	20	20	
							Net Requirements							100	
							Planned Order Receipts							100	
							Planned Order Releases							100	
Lot-for-Lot	2	10	—	—	2	E	Gross Requirements						130^B	200^C	
							Scheduled Receipts								
							Projected on Hand 10	10	10	10	10	10	10		
							Net Requirements						120	200	
							Planned Order Receipts						120	200	
							Planned Order Releases				120	200			
Lot-for-Lot	3	5	—	—	2	F	Gross Requirements							200^C	
							Scheduled Receipts								
							Projected on Hand 5	5	5	5	5	5	5		
							Net Requirements							195	
							Planned Order Receipts							195	
							Planned Order Releases				195				
Lot-for-Lot	1	10	—	—	3	D	Gross Requirements					390^F		130^B	
							Scheduled Receipts								
							Projected on Hand 10	10	10	10					
							Net Requirements					380		130	
							Planned Order Receipts					380		130	
							Planned Order Releases				380		130		
Lot-for-Lot	2	0	—	—	3	G	Gross Requirements					195^F			
							Scheduled Receipts								
							Projected on Hand					0			
							Net Requirements					195			
							Planned Order Receipts					195			
							Planned Order Releases			195					

Examples 2 and 3 considered only product A, the Awesome speaker kit, and its completion only in week 8. Fifty units of A were required in week 8. Normally, however, there is a demand for many products over time. For each product, management must pre-

MRP Structure

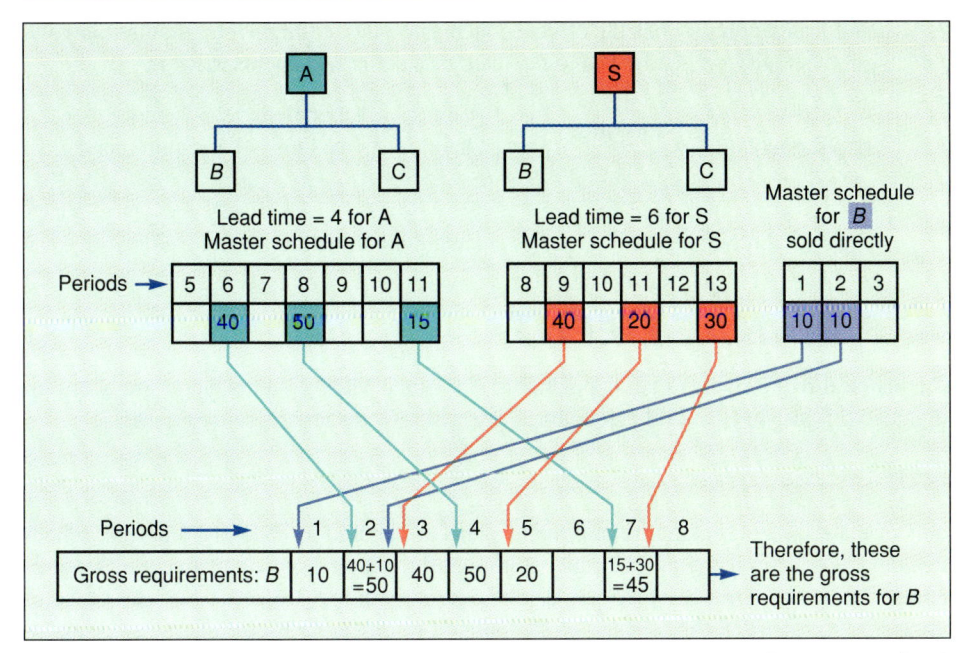

FIGURE 14.6 ■ Several Schedules Contributing to a Gross Requirements Schedule for B. One "B" is in each A and one "B" is in each S, and 10 B's sold directly are scheduled in week 1 and 10 more that are sold directly are scheduled in week 2.

pare a master production schedule (as we saw earlier in Table 14.1). Scheduled production of each product is added to the master schedule and ultimately to the net material requirements plan. Figure 14.6 shows how several product schedules, including requirements for components sold directly, can contribute to one gross material requirements plan.

Most inventory systems also note the number of units in inventory that have been assigned to specific future production but not yet used or issued from the stockroom. Such items are often referred to as *allocated* items. Allocated items increase requirements and may then be included in an MRP planning sheet, as shown in Figure 14.7.

Lot Size	Lead Time	On Hand	Safety Stock	Allocated	Low-Level Code	Item ID		Period							
								1	2	3	4	5	6	7	8
Lot For Lot	1	0	0	10	0	B	Gross Requirements							80	90
							Scheduled Receipts								0
							Projected On Hand 0	0	0	0	0	0	0	0	0
							Net Requirements								90
							Planned Order Receipts								90
							Planned Order Releases							90	

FIGURE 14.7 ■ Sample MRP Planning Sheet for Item A

The allocated quantity has the effect of increasing the requirements (or, alternatively, reducing the quantity on hand). The logic, then, of a net requirements MRP is:

$$\underbrace{\left[\begin{pmatrix}\text{gross}\\\text{requirements}\end{pmatrix} + \begin{pmatrix}\text{allocations}\end{pmatrix}\right]}_{\text{total requirements}} - \underbrace{\left[\begin{pmatrix}\text{on}\\\text{hand}\end{pmatrix} + \begin{pmatrix}\text{scheduled}\\\text{receipts}\end{pmatrix}\right]}_{\text{available inventory}} = \begin{matrix}\text{net}\\\text{requirements}\end{matrix}$$

MRP MANAGEMENT

The material requirements plan is not static. And since MRP systems increasingly are integrated with just-in-time (JIT) techniques, we will now discuss these two issues.

MRP Dynamics

Bills of material and material requirements plans are altered as changes in design, schedules, and production processes occur. Additionally, changes occur in material requirements whenever the master production schedule is modified. Regardless of the cause of any changes, the MRP model can be manipulated to reflect them. In this manner, an up-to-date requirements schedule is possible.

Due to the changes that occur in MRP data, it is not uncommon to recompute MRP requirements about once a week. Conveniently, a central strength of MRP is its timely and accurate *replanning* capability. However, many firms find they do not want to respond to minor scheduling or quantity changes even if they are aware of them. These frequent changes generate what is called **system nervousness** and can create havoc in purchasing and production departments if implemented. Consequently, OM personnel reduce such nervousness by evaluating the need and impact of changes prior to disseminating requests to other departments. Two tools are particularly helpful when trying to reduce MRP system nervousness.

The first is time fences. **Time fences** allow a segment of the master schedule to be designated as "not to be rescheduled." This segment of the master schedule is thus not changed during the periodic regeneration of schedules. The second tool is pegging. **Pegging** means tracing upward in the BOM from the component to the parent item. By pegging upward, the production planner can determine the cause for the requirement and make a judgment about the necessity for a change in the schedule.

With MRP, the operations manager *can* react to the dynamics of the real world. How frequently the manager wishes to impose those changes on the firm requires professional judgment. Moreover, if the nervousness is caused by legitimate changes, then the proper response of operations management may be to investigate the production environment—not adjust via MRP.[4]

MRP and JIT

MRP is a planning and scheduling technique with fixed lead times, while just-in-time (JIT) is a way to move material expeditiously. Fixed lead times can be a limitation. For instance, the lead time to produce 50 units may vary substantially from the lead time to produce 1 unit. This limitation complicates the marriage of JIT and MRP. In many respects, however, an MRP system combined with JIT provides the best of both worlds.

System nervousness Frequent changes in the MRP system.

Time fences A way of allowing a segment of the master schedule to be designated as "not to be rescheduled."

Pegging In material requirements planning systems, tracing upward in the bill of material (BOM) from the component to the parent item.

---

[4] Jay H. Heizer, "The Production Manager Can Be a Good Guy in the Factory with a Future," *APICS—The Performance Advantage*, July 1994, pp 30–34.

MRP provides a good master schedule and an accurate picture of requirements, and JIT reduces work-in-process inventory. Let's look at two approaches for integrating the two systems: small buckets and balanced flow.

Small Bucket Approach MRP is an excellent tool for resource and scheduling management in process-focused facilities that is, in job shops. Such facilities include machine shops, hospitals, and restaurants, where lead times are relatively stable and poor balance between work centers is expected. Schedules are often driven by work orders, and lot sizes are the exploded bill-of-material size. In these enterprises, MRP can be integrated with JIT through the following steps. First, reduce MRP "buckets" from weekly to daily to perhaps hourly. **Buckets** are time units in an MRP system. Although the examples in this chapter have used weekly *time buckets*, many firms now use daily or even fraction-of-a-day time buckets. Second, the planned receipts that are part of a firm's planned orders in an MRP system are communicated to the work areas for production purposes and used to sequence production. Third, inventory is moved through the plant on a JIT basis. Fourth, as products are completed, they are moved into inventory (typically finished goods inventory) in the normal way. Receipt of these products into inventory reduces the quantities required for subsequent planned orders in the MRP system. Finally, a system known as back flush is used to reduce inventory balances. **Back flushing** uses the bill of materials to reduce component inventory quantities as each product it is based upon is completed.

> **Buckets** Time units in a material requirements planning (MRP) system.

> **Back flush** A system to reduce inventory balances by deducting everything in the bill of material upon completion of the unit.

The focus in these facilities becomes one of maintaining schedules. Nissan achieves success with this approach by computer communication links to suppliers. These schedules are confirmed, updated, or changed every 15 to 20 minutes. Suppliers provide deliveries 4 to 16 times per day. Master schedule performance is 99% on time, as measured every hour. On-time delivery from suppliers is 99.9% and for manufactured piece parts, 99.5%.

Balanced Flow Approach MRP supports the planning and scheduling necessary for repetitive operations, such as the assembly lines at Harley-Davidson, Whirlpool, and a thousand other places. In these environments, the planning portion of MRP is combined with JIT execution. The JIT portion uses kanbans, visual signals, and reliable suppliers to pull the material through the facility. In these systems, execution is achieved by maintaining a carefully balanced flow of material to assembly areas with small lot sizes.[5]

LOT-SIZING TECHNIQUES

An MRP system is an excellent way to determine production schedules and net requirements. However, whenever we have a net requirement, a decision must be made about *how much* to order. This decision is called a **lot-sizing decision.** There are a variety of ways to determine lot sizes in an MRP system; commercial MRP software usually includes the choice of several lot-sizing techniques. We will now review a few of them.

> **Lot-sizing decisions** The process of, or techniques used in, determining lot size.

Lot-for-Lot In Example 3, we used a lot-sizing technique known as **lot-for-lot**, which produced exactly what was required. This decision is consistent with the objective of an MRP system, which is to meet the requirements of *dependent* demand. Thus, an MRP system should produce units only as needed, with no safety stock and no anticipation of further orders. When frequent orders are economical and just-in-time inventory tech-

> **Lot-for-lot** A lot-sizing technique producing exactly what was required to meet the plan.

---

[5] For a related discussion, see Sylvain Landry, Claude R. Duguay, Sylvain Chausse, and Jean-Luc Themens, "Integrating MRP, Kanban, and Bar-Coding Systems to Achieve JIT Procurement," *Production and Inventory Management Journal*, first quarter 1997, pp. 8–12.

niques implemented, lot-for-lot can be very efficient. However, when setup costs are significant or management has been unable to implement JIT, lot-for-lot can be expensive. Example 4 uses the lot-for-lot criteria and determines cost for 10 weeks of demand.

EXAMPLE 4

Speaker Kits, Inc., wants to compute its ordering and carrying cost of inventory on lot-for-lot criteria. Speaker Kits has determined that, for the 12-inch speaker/booster assembly, setup cost is $100 and holding cost is $1 per period. The production schedule, as reflected in net requirements for assemblies, is as follows:

MRP Lot-Sizing Problem: Lot-for-Lot Technique

		1	2	3	4	5	6	7	8	9	10
Gross Requirements		35	30	40	0	10	40	30	0	30	55
Scheduled Receipts											
Projected on Hand	35	35	0	0	0	0	0	0	0	0	0
Net Requirements		0	30	40	0	10	40	30	0	30	55
Planned Order Receipts			30	40		10	40	30		30	55
Planned Order Releases		30	40		10	40	30		30	55	

Holding costs = $1/unit/week; setup cost = $100; gross requirements average per week = 27; lead time = 1 week.

Shown above is the lot-sizing solution using the lot-for-lot technique and its cost. The holding cost is zero, but 7 separate setups (one associated with each order) yield a total cost of $700.

Economic Order Quantity As discussed in chapter 12, EOQ can be used as a lot-sizing technique. But as we indicated there, EOQ is preferable when *relatively constant* independent demand exists, not when we *know* the demand. EOQ is a statistical technique using averages, typically average demand for a year, whereas our MRP procedure assumes known (dependent) demand reflected in a master production schedule. Operations managers should take advantage of demand information when it is known, rather than assuming a constant demand. EOQ is examined in Example 5.

> MRP is preferable when demand is *dependent*. Statistical techniques such as EOQ are preferable when demand is *independent*.

This Nissan pickup truck assembly line in Smyrna, Tennessee, has little inventory because Nissan schedules to a razor's edge. At Nissan, MRP helps to reduce inventory to world-class standards. World-class automobile assembly requires that purchased parts have a turnover of slightly more than once a day and that overall turnover approaches 150 times per year.

EXAMPLE 5

With a setup cost of $100 and a holding cost per week of $1, Speaker Kits, Inc., examines its cost with lot sizes based on an EOQ criteria. Using the same requirements as in Example 4, the net requirements and lot sizes follow:

MRP Lot-Sizing Problem: EOQ Technique

		1	2	3	4	5	6	7	8	9	10
Gross Requirements		35	30	40	0	10	40	30	0	30	55
Scheduled Receipts											
Projected on Hand	35	35	0	43	3	3	66	26	69	69	39
Net Requirements		0	30	0	0	7	0	4	0	0	16
Planned Order Receipts			73			73		73			73
Planned Order Releases		73			73		73			73	

Holding costs = $1/unit/week; setup cost = $100; gross requirements average per week = 27; lead time = 1 week.

Ten-week usage equals gross requirement of 270 units; therefore, weekly usage equals 27, and 52 weeks (annual usage) equals 1,404 units. From chapter 12, the EOQ model is

$$Q^* = \sqrt{\frac{2DS}{H}}$$

where D = annual usage = 1,404
 S = setup cost = $100
 H = holding (carrying) cost, on an annual basis per unit
  = 1×52 weeks = $52

$$Q^* = 73 \text{ units}$$
Setups = 1,404/73 = 19 per year
Setup cost = 19 × $100 = $1,900
Holding cost = $\frac{73}{2} \times (\$1 \times 52 \text{ weeks}) = \$1,898$
Setup cost + holding cost = $1,900 + 1,898 = $3,798

The EOQ solution yields a computed 10-week cost of $730 [$3,798 × (10 weeks/52 weeks) = $730].

Notice that actual holding cost will vary from the computed $730, depending upon the rate of actual usage. From the preceding table, we can see that in our 10-week example, costs really are $400 for 4 setups, plus a holding cost of 353 units at $1 per week for a total of $753. Because usage was not constant, the actual computed cost was in fact more than the theoretical EOQ ($730) and more than the lot-for-lot rule ($700). If any stockouts had occurred, these costs too would need to be added to our actual EOQ of $753.

Part Period Balancing Part period balancing (PPB) is a more dynamic approach to balance setup and holding cost.[6] PPB uses additional information by changing the lot size to reflect requirements of the next lot size in the future. PPB attempts to balance setup and holding cost for known demands. Part period balancing develops an **economic part period (EPP)**, which is the ratio of setup cost to holding cost. For our Speaker Kits example, EPP = $100/$1 = 100 units. Therefore, holding 100 units for 1 period would cost

> **Part period balancing (PPB)** An inventory ordering technique that balances setup and holding costs by changing the lot size to reflect requirements of the next lot size in the future.
>
> **Economic part period (EPP)** That period of time when the ratio or setup cost to holding cost is equal.

---
[6] J. J. DeMatteis, "An Economic Lot-Sizing Technique: The Part-Period Algorithms," *IBM Systems Journal* 7 (1968): 30–38.

$100, exactly the cost of 1 setup. Similarly, holding 50 units for 2 periods also costs $100 (2 periods × $1 × 50 units). PPB merely adds requirements until the number of part periods approximates the EPP—in this case, 100. Example 6 shows the application of part period balancing.

> ### EXAMPLE 6
>
> Once again, Speaker Kits, Inc., computes the costs associated with a lot size by using a $100 setup cost and a $1 holding cost. This time, however, part period balancing is used. The data are shown in the following table:
>
> **PPB Calculations**
>
> | Periods Combined | Trial Lot Size (Cumulative Net Requirements) | Part Periods | Setup | Holding | Total |
> |---|---|---|---|---|---|
> | 2 | 30 | 0 | | | |
> | 2, 3 | 70 | 40 = 40 × 1 | | | |
> | 2, 3, 4 | 70 | 40 | | | |
> | 2, 3, 4, 5 | 80 | 70 = 40 × 1 + 10 × 3 | 100 | + 70 | = 170 |
> | 2, 3, 4, 5, 6 | 120 | 230 = 40 × 1 + 10 × 3 + 40 × 4 | | | |
>
> 40 units held for 1 period = $40
> 10 units held for 3 periods = $30
>
> (Therefore, combine periods 2 through 5; 70 is as close to our EPP of 100 as we are going to get.)
>
> | | | | | | |
> |---|---|---|---|---|---|
> | 6 | 40 | 0 | | | |
> | 6, 7 | 70 | 30 | | | |
> | 6, 7, 8 | 70 | 30 | | | |
> | 6, 7, 8, 9 | 100 | 120 = 30 × 1 + 30 × 3 | 100 | + 120 | = 220 |
>
> (Therefore, combine periods 6 through 9; 120 is as close to our EPP of 100 as we are going to get.)
>
> | | | | | | |
> |---|---|---|---|---|---|
> | 10 | 55 | 0 | 100 | + 0 | = 100 |
> | | | | 300 | + 190 | = 490 |
>
> **MRP Lot-Sizing Problem: PPB Technique**
>
> | | | 1 | 2 | 3 | 4 | 5 | 6 | 7 | 8 | 9 | 10 |
> |---|---|---|---|---|---|---|---|---|---|---|---|
> | Gross Requirements | | 35 | 30 | 40 | 0 | 10 | 40 | 30 | 0 | 30 | 55 |
> | Scheduled Receipts | | | | | | | | | | | |
> | Projected on Hand | 35 | 35 | 0 | 50 | 10 | 10 | 0 | 60 | 30 | 30 | 0 |
> | Net Requirements | | 0 | 30 | 0 | 0 | 0 | 40 | 0 | 0 | 0 | 55 |
> | Planned Order Receipts | | | 80 | | | | 100 | | | | 55 |
> | Planned Order Releases | | 80 | | | | 100 | | | 55 | | |
>
> Holding costs = $1/unit/week; setup cost = $100; gross requirements average per week = 27; lead time = 1 week.
>
> EPP is 100 (setup cost divided by holding cost = $100/$1). The first lot is to cover periods 1, 2, 3, 4, and 5 and is 80.
>
> The total costs are $490, with setup costs totaling $300 and holding costs totaling $190.

Wagner–Whitin procedure A programming model for lot-size computation that assumes a finite time horizon beyond which there are no additional net requirements.

Wagner–Whitin Algorithm The **Wagner-Whitin procedure** is a dynamic programming model that adds some complexity to the lot-size computation. It assumes a finite time horizon beyond which there are no additional net requirements. It does, however, provide good results.[7] The technique is seldom used in practice, but this may change with increasing understanding and software sophistication.

Lot-Sizing Summary In the three Speaker Kits lot-sizing examples, we found the following costs:

Lot-for-lot	$700
EOQ	$775
Part period balancing	$490

These examples should not, however, lead operations personnel to hasty conclusions about the preferred lot-sizing technique. In theory, new lot sizes should be computed whenever there is a schedule or lot-size change anywhere in the MRP hierarchy. However, in practice, such changes cause the instability and system nervousness referred to earlier in this chapter. Consequently, such frequent changes are not made. This means that all lot sizes are wrong because the production system can not respond to frequent changes.

In general, the lot-for-lot approach should be used wherever economical. Lot-for-lot is the goal. Lots can be modified as necessary for scrap allowances, process constraints (for example, a heat-treating process may require a lot of a given size), or raw material purchase lots (for example, a truckload of chemicals may be available in only one lot size). However, caution should be exercised prior to any modification of lot size because the modification can cause substantial distortion of actual requirements at lower levels in the MRP hierarchy. When setup costs are significant and demand is reasonably smooth, part period balancing (PPB), Wagner–Whitin, or even EOQ should provide satisfactory results. Too much concern with lot sizing yields false accuracy because of MRP dynamics. A correct lot size can be determined only after the fact, based on what actually happened in terms of requirements.[8]

EXTENSIONS OF MRP

Recent years have seen the development of a number of extensions of MRP. In this section, we review four of them.

Closed-Loop MRP

Closed-loop material requirements planning implies an MRP system that provides feedback to scheduling from the inventory control system. Specifically, a **closed-loop MRP system** provides feedback to the capacity plan, master production schedule, and ultimately to the production plan (as shown in Figure 14.8 on page 556). Virtually all commercial MRP systems are closed-loop.

Closed-loop MRP system A system that provides feedback to the capacity plan, master production schedule, and production plan

---

[7] See James M. Fordyce and Francis M. Webster, "The Wagner-Whitin Algorithm Made Simple," *Production and Inventory Management*, second quarter 1984, pp. 21–27. This article provides as straightforward an explanation of the Wagner–Whitin technique as the authors have found. The Wagner-Whitin Algorithm yields a cost of $455 for the data in Examples 4, 5, and 6.

[8] See discussions by Joseph Orlicky, *Material Requirements Planning* (New York: McGraw-Hill, 1975), pp. 136–137; and G. Nandakumar, "Lot-Sizing Techniques in a Multiproduct Multilevel Environment," *Production and Inventory Management* 26 (first quarter 1985): 46–54.

556 CHAPTER 14 MATERIAL REQUIREMENTS PLANNING (MRP)

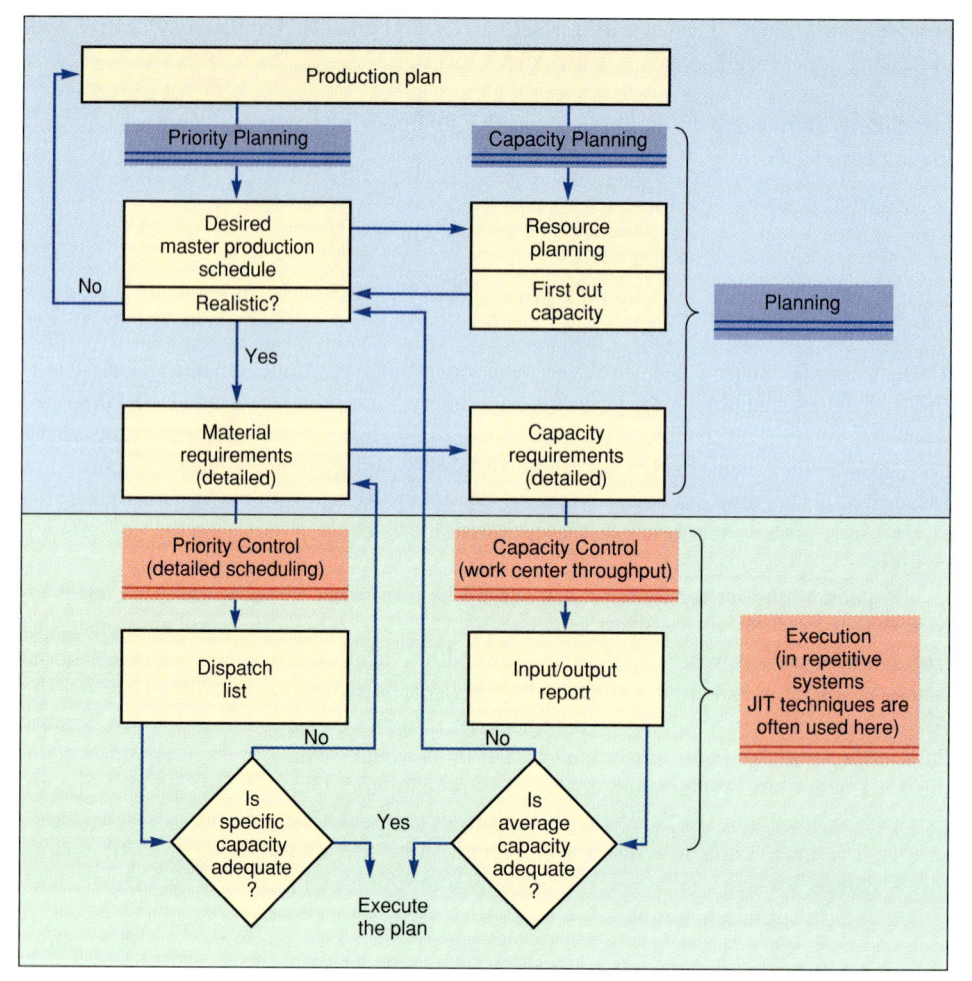

FIGURE 14.8 ■ **Closed-Loop Material Requirements Planning**
Source: Adapted from *Capacity Planning and Control Study Guide*. Falls Church, VA: American Production and Inventory Control Society.

Capacity Planning

Load report A report for showing the resource requirements in a work center for all work currently assigned there as well as all planned and expected orders.

In keeping with the definition of closed-loop MRP, feedback about workload is obtained from each work center. **Load reports** show the resource requirements in a work center for all work currently assigned to the work center, all work planned, and expected orders. Figure 14.9(a) shows that the initial load in the milling center exceeds capacity in weeks 4 and 6. Closed-loop MRP systems allow production planners to move the work between time periods in order to smooth the load or at least bring it within capacity. (This is the "Capacity Planning" side of Figure 14.8.) The closed-loop MRP system can then reschedule all items in the net requirements plan (see Figure 14.9[b]).

Tactics for smoothing the load and minimizing the impact of changed lead time include the following:

1. *Overlapping,* which reduces the lead time, sends pieces to the second operation before the entire lot is completed on the first operation.

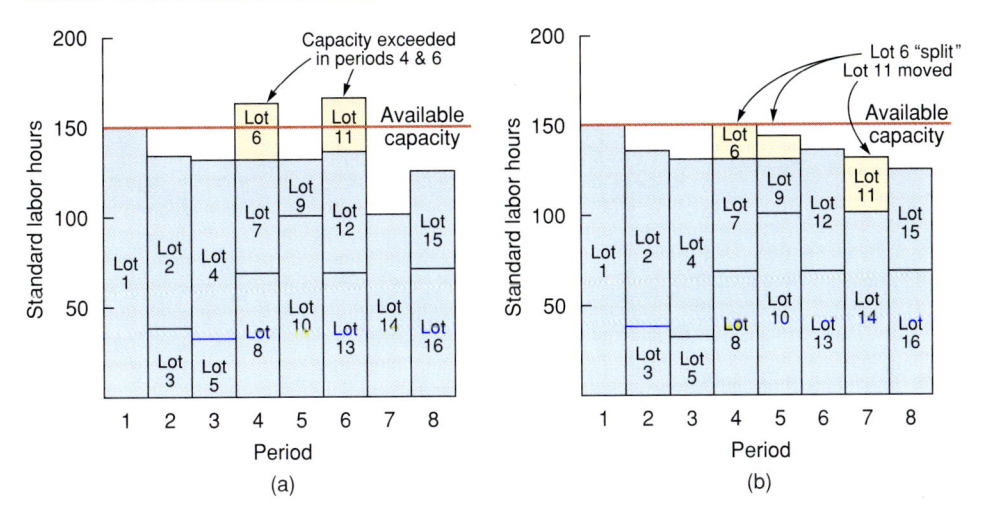

FIGURE 14.9 ■ (a) Initial Resource Requirements Profile for a Milling Center (b) Smoothed Resource Requirements Profile for a Milling Center

2. *Operations splitting* sends the lot to two different machines for the same operation. This involves an additional setup, but results in shorter throughput times, because only part of the lot is processed on each machine.
3. *Lot splitting* involves breaking up the order and running part of it ahead of schedule.

When the workload consistently exceeds work-center capacity, the tactics just discussed are not adequate. This may mean adding capacity. Options include adding capacity via personnel, machinery, overtime, or subcontracting.

Material Requirements Planning II (MRP II)

Material requirements planning II is an extremely powerful technique. Once a firm has MRP in place, inventory data can be augmented by labor-hours, by material cost (rather than material quantity), by capital cost, or by virtually any resource. When MRP is used this way, it is usually referred to as **MRP II,** and *resource* is usually substituted for *requirements*. MRP then stands for material *resource* planning.

For instance, so far in our discussion of MRP, we have scheduled units (quantities). However, each of these units requires resources in addition to its components. Those additional resources include labor-hours, machine-hours, and accounts payable (cash). Each of these resources can be used in an MRP format just as we used quantities. Table 14.4 on page 558 shows how to determine the labor-hours, machine-hours, and cash that a sample master production schedule will require in each period. These requirements are then compared with the respective capacity (that is, labor-hours, machine-hours, cash, and so forth), so operations managers can make schedules that will work. The potential of MRP II, combined with other information, is discussed further on page 558 in the *OM in Action* box entitled "MRP II Builds Profits at Compaq."

To aid the functioning of MRP II, most MRP II computer programs are tied into other computer files that provide data to the MRP system or receive data from the MRP system. Purchasing, production scheduling, capacity planning, and warehouse management are a few examples of this data integration.

Material requirements planning II (MRP II)
A system that allows, with MRP in place, inventory data to be augmented by other resource variables; in this case, MRP becomes *material resource planning*.

558 CHAPTER 14 MATERIAL REQUIREMENTS PLANNING (MRP)

TABLE 14.4 ■ Material Resource Planning (MRP II). By utilizing the logic of MRP, resources such as labor, machine-hours, and cost can be accurately determined and scheduled. Weekly demand for labor, machine-hours, and payables for 100 units are shown.

	Week 5	Week 6	Week 7	Week 8
A. Units (lead time 1 week)				100
Labor: 10 hours each				1,000
Machine: 2 hours each				200
Payable: $0 each				0
B. Units (lead time 2 weeks, 2 each required)			200	
Labor: 10 hours each			2,000	
Machine: 2 hours each			400	
Payable: Raw material at $5 each			1,000	
C. Units (lead time 4 weeks, 3 each required)	300			
Labor: 2 hours each	600			
Machine: 1 hour each	300			
Payable: Raw material at $10 each	3,000			

Enterprise Resource Planning (ERP)

Enterprise Resource Planning (ERP) An MRP II system that ties customers with suppliers.

MRP II has evolved to include order entry, purchasing, and direct interfaces with customers and suppliers such as electronic data interchange (EDI) and advanced shipping notice (ASN). These advanced MRP II systems that tie customers and suppliers to MRP II are now referred to as **Enterprise Resource Planning (ERP)** systems. For example, a company like Benetton may use a fully integrated ERP system to receive an order electronically from a customer in Brazil, issue the necessary purchase order to suppliers in Italy, change inventory levels, notify shippers on both ends of the transaction, update the MRP system, provide files for updating payables and receivables, and

---

OM IN ACTION

MRP II BUILDS PROFITS AT COMPAQ

Cal Monteith, Compaq Manager of Master Planning and Production Control in Houston, was in the process of phasing out one of Compaq's personal computer models when he was told that the company had underestimated demand. The new schedule suggested that he build 10,000 more PCs. Could he do it? Monteith faced the following questions: What parts were on hand and on order? What labor was available? Could the plant handle the capacity? Did vendors have the capacity? What product lines could be rescheduled? Traditionally, amassing such information required not only MRP reports but also a variety of additional reports. Even then a response was based on partial information.

New software that includes a combination of spreadsheets, inquiry languages, and report writers allowed Monteith to search huge data bases, isolate the relevant data (customer orders, forecasts, inventory, and capacity), and do some quick calculations. One such piece of software is available from FastMRP, which is based in Ottawa, Canada. Another is sold by Carp Systems International of Kanata, Ontario. The result: Compaq was able to make schedule adjustments that added millions of dollars to the bottom line.

Sources: Forbes (November 6, 1995): 124–125; *Computerworld* (April 10, 1995): 2; and *New York Times* (October 18, 1992): F9.

> ## OM IN ACTION
>
> ### MRP II, JIT, AND ERP GET MARRIED AT DETROIT DIESEL
>
> Detroit Diesel's five main production lines manufacture a wide variety of two- and four-cycle diesel engines. A major factor in the firm's success is its ability to deliver customized engines for highway, construction, mining, industrial, bus, marine, military, and power-generation markets worldwide. Engines are individually "configured" from options (modules) to meet these diverse needs as they are ordered. Detroit Diesel's success has pushed revenues to $40 million a week, with production running three shifts per day.
>
> The required engine customization puts a substantial burden on Detroit Diesel, as it would any organization. To respond, the firm has integrated MRP II, JIT, and ERP. As a result, Detroit Diesel issues work orders specifying individual treatment of every engine, component, routing, assembly instruction, and special procedure that may be necessary in the manufacturing process. The system monitors and measures all aspects of production as the order proceeds through the various steps of the production cycle. The work order provides a complete "audit trail."
>
> Key reports from the MRP/JIT/ERP system include inventory balances and receipts, assembly orders, customer orders, engineering orders and changes, purchase orders, payables, machine shop orders, and receivables. The JIT portion alone consists of a thousand reports, applications, and data-processing routines. With the new system installed, Detroit Diesel not only has more efficient purchasing and production strategies, but better cost tracking and communication with vendors. It also has a more flexible manufacturing process ready to accommodate continued growth. Detroit Diesel qualifies as an agile flexible manufacturer, responding rapidly and effectively to the diverse needs of its customers. Moreover, it now plans with MRP, drives down inventories with JIT, and uses ERP to incorporate suppliers into its competitive strategy.
>
> *Sources: APICS-Performance Advantage* (June 1996): 60–63; *IIE Solutions* (September 1996): 32–36; and *Industry Week* (February 3, 1997): 39–42.

do it all in the proper currency. This means performing exchange rate conversions so that the sale in the Brazilian *real* and the purchase of parts in the Italian *lira* are posted correctly.

Among the leading enterprise resource planning (ERP) systems are software packages sold by PeopleSoft, American Software, J. D. Edwards, BAAN, and SAP. SAP appears to be the current leader among these vendors with its R/3 software, a three-tier client/server configuration consisting of (1) high speed data base servers, (2) application servers, and (3) front end servers. ERP packages, because of the high level of integration, can be terribly expensive and complex to install. However, as firms seek competitive advantage by tying both suppliers and distributors more closely to their own organizations, more complex information systems seem inevitable.

When these systems work, they can be a major benefit, as noted in the *OM in Action* box describing Detroit Diesel's success with an ERP system.

Although the typical ERP system is an umbrella system, which ties together a variety of specialized systems, exactly what is tied together, and how, varies on a case-by-case basis. In some discussions, ERP may include not only MRP II, order entry, purchasing, and EDI, but also other major business processes, such as accounting, finance, and human resources, as well as supply-chain features. A schematic showing some of these relationships for a manufacturing firm appears in Figure 14.10 on page 560. Because ERP systems development is ongoing, the phrase is used to describe a variety of systems.[9]

For more information about SAP and its ERP systems, visit http://www.sap.com

---

[9] Ronald A. Hicks and Kathryn E. Stecke, "The ERP Maze," *IIE Solutions*, August 1995, pp. 12–16.

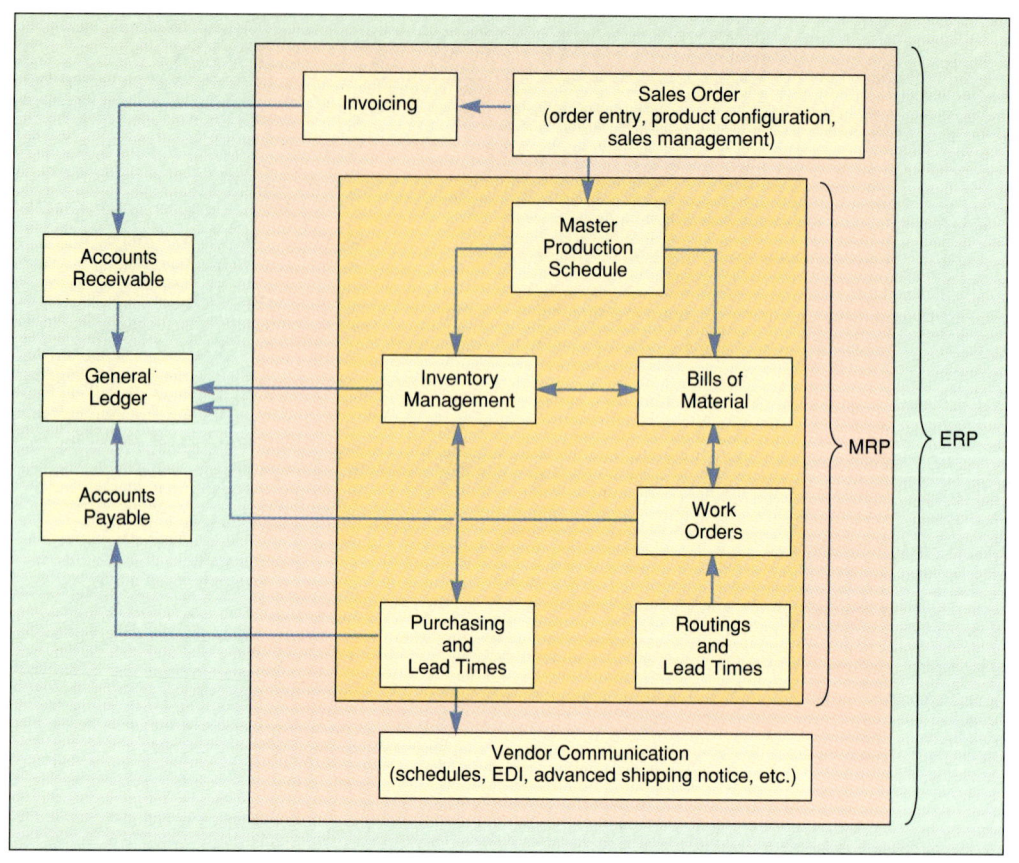

FIGURE 14.10 ■ MRP and ERP Information Flows Integrated with Other Information Systems. *Note:* Arrowheads indicate the flow of data.

MRP IN SERVICES

The demand for many services or service items is classified as dependent demand when it is directly related to or derived from the demand for other services. For example, in a restaurant where bread and vegetables are included in every meal ordered, the demand for bread and vegetables is dependent on the demand for meals. The meal is an end item and the bread and vegetables are component items.

Figure 14.11 shows a bill of material and accompanying product-structure tree for veal picante, a top-selling entrée in a New Orleans restaurant. Note that the various components of veal picante (that is, veal, sauce, and linguini) are prepared by different kitchen personnel (see part [a] of Figure 14.11). These preparations also require different amounts of time to complete. Figure 14.11(c) shows a bill of labor for the veal dish. It lists the operations to be performed, the order of operations, and the labor requirements for each operation (types of labor and labor-hours).

MRP is also applied in hospitals, especially when dealing with surgeries that require equipment, materials, and supplies. Houston's Park Plaza Hospital, for example, uses the technique to improve the management of expensive surgical inventory.[10]

---

[10] See E. Steinberg, B. Khumawala, and R. Scamell, "Requirements Planning in the Health Care Environment," *Journal of Operations Management* 2, no. 4 (August 1982): 251–259.

(a) PRODUCT STRUCTURE TREE

(b) BILL OF MATERIALS

Part Number	Description	Quantity	Unit of Measure	Unit Cost
10001	Veal picante	1	Serving	—
20002	Cooked linguini	1	Serving	—
20003	Prepared veal and sauce	1	Serving	—
20004	Spinach	0.1	Bag	0.94
30004	Uncooked linguini	0.5	Pound	—
30005	Veal	1	Serving	2.15
30006	Sauce	1	Serving	0.80

(c) BILL OF LABOR FOR VEAL PICANTE

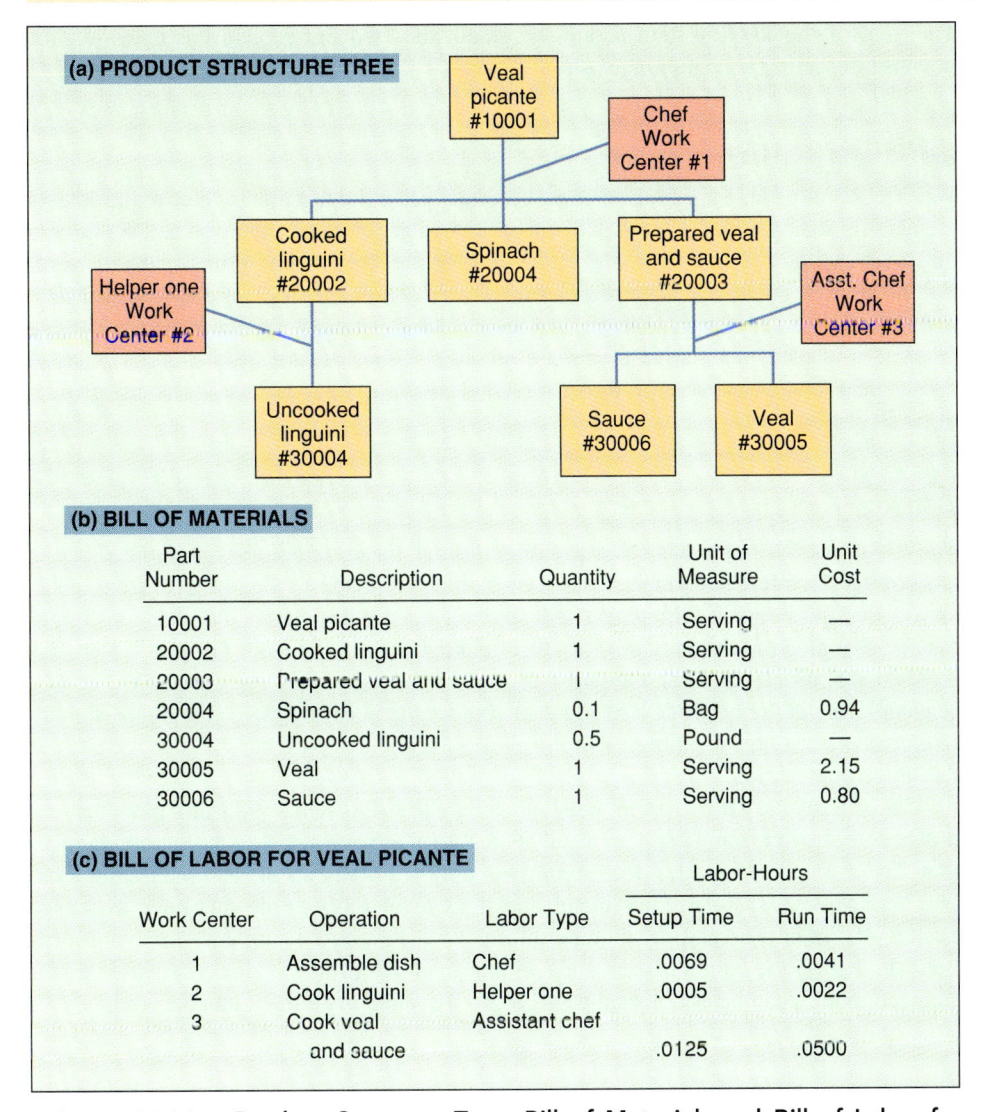

			Labor-Hours	
Work Center	Operation	Labor Type	Setup Time	Run Time
1	Assemble dish	Chef	.0069	.0041
2	Cook linguini	Helper one	.0005	.0022
3	Cook veal and sauce	Assistant chef	.0125	.0500

FIGURE 14.11 ■ Product Structure Tree, Bill of Material, and Bill of Labor for Veal Picante

Source: Adopted from John G. Wacker "Effective Planning and Cost Control for Restaurants," *Production and Inventory Management,* first quarter 1985, p. 60.

DISTRIBUTION RESOURCE PLANNING (DRP)

When dependent techniques are used in distribution environments, they are called distribution resource planning (DRP). **Distribution resource planning (DRP)** is a time-phased stock-replenishment plan for all levels of a distribution network. Its procedures and logic are analogous to MRP. DRP requires:

1. Gross requirements, which are the same as expected demand or sales forecasts;
2. Minimum levels of inventory to meet customer-service levels;
3. Accurate lead time;
4. Definition of the distribution structure.

Distribution resource planning (DRP) A time-phased stock-replenishment plan for all levels of a distribution network.

The goal of the DRP system should be small and frequent replenishment within the bounds of ordering and shipping costs.

DRP Structure

When DRP is used, expected demand becomes gross requirements. Net requirements are determined by allocating available inventory to gross requirements. The DRP procedure starts with the forecast at the retail level (or the most distant point of the distribution network being supplied). All other levels are computed. As is the case with MRP, inventory is then reviewed with an aim to satisfying demand. So that stock will arrive when it is needed, net requirements are offset by the necessary lead time. A planned order release quantity becomes the gross requirement at the next level down the distribution chain.

Allocation

The traditional DRP network *pulls* inventory through the system. Pulls are initiated by the top or retail level ordering more stock. Allocations are made to the top level from available stock after being modified to obtain shipping economies. These modifications might include changing the shipping quantity to a truckload or a pallet load. The pull system has three notable problems. First, the pulls (i.e., orders) are often distorted (increased) at subsequent levels in the network.[11] Second, each ordering location ignores the replenishment requirements at other locations. Third, ordering locations also ignore the stock status at the supplying location.

The alternative DRP system adds allocations to the system. With this modification, orders are received from upstream locations, but they are evaluated by the supplying location. The evaluation includes determining not only requirements at each requesting location but also total system requirements and stock availability at the supplying locations. Such a system is designed to combine information from both using and supplying locations. In theory, the combination yields an improved allocation of stock, because replenishment policies can be established based on both availability and system demand.

SUMMARY

Material requirements planning (MRP) is the preferred way to schedule production and inventory when demand is dependent. For MRP to work, management must have a master schedule, precise requirements for all components, accurate inventory and purchasing records, and accurate lead times. Distribution resource planning (DRP) is a time-phased stock-replacement technique for distribution networks based on MRP procedures and logic.

Production should often be lot-for-lot in an MRP system, and replenishment orders in a DRP system should be small and frequent, given the constraints of ordering and transportation costs.

---

[11] This is the same type of response recognized in Jay Forrester's *Industrial Dynamics*. Forrester noted that small changes in demand at the retail level stimulated wider variations at the wholesale level and even greater deviations at the factory level. J. Forrester, *Industrial Dynamics* (Cambridge, MA: MIT Press, 1964).

KEY TERMS

Material requirements planning (MRP) *(p. 538)*
Master production schedule (MPS) *(p. 539)*
Bill of material (BOM) *(p. 541)*
Modular bills *(p. 543)*
Planning bills (or kits *p. 543)*
Phantom bills of material *(p. 544)*
Low-level coding *(p. 544)*
Lead time *(p. 544)*
Gross material requirements plan *(p. 546)*
Net material requirements *(p. 547)*
Planned order receipt *(p. 547)*
Planned order release *(p. 547)*
System nervousness *(p. 550)*
Time fences *(p. 550)*
Pegging *(p. 550)*
Buckets *(p. 551)*
Back flush *(p. 551)*
Lot-sizing decision *(p. 551)*
Lot-for-lot *(p. 551)*
Part period balancing (PPB) *(p. 553)*
Economic part period (EPP) *(p. 553)*
Wagner-Whitin procedure *(p. 554)*
Closed-loop MRP system *(p. 555)*
Load report *(p. 556)*
Material requirements planning II (MRP II) *(p. 557)*
Enterprise Resource Planning (ERP) *(p. 558)*
Distribution resource planning (DRP) *(p. 561)*

Both MRP and DRP, when properly implemented, can contribute in a major way to reduction in inventory while improving customer-service levels. These techniques allow the operations manager to schedule and replenish stock on a "need-to-order" basis rather than simply a "time-to-order" basis.

USING POM FOR WINDOWS TO SOLVE MRP PROBLEMS

Programs 14.1 and 14.2 on page 564 show the detailed input and output, respectively, for solving Examples 1 to 3 using POM for Windows. Here are the inputs used in Program 14.1:

1. *Item names.* The item names are entered in the left column. The same item name will appear in more than one row if the item is used by two parent items. Each item must follow its parents, as shown in Program 14.1.
2. *Item level.* The level in the indented BOM must be given here. The item cannot be placed at a level more than one below the item immediately above.
3. *Lead time.* The lead time for an item is entered here. The default is 1 week.
4. *Number per parent.* The number of units of this subassembly needed for its parent is entered here. The default is one.
5. *On hand.* List current inventory on hand once, even if the subassembly is listed twice.
6. *Lot size.* The lot size can be specified here. A 0 or 1 will perform lot for lot ordering. If another number is placed here, then all orders for that item will be in integer multiples of that number.
7. *Demands.* The demands are entered in the end item row in the period in which the items are demanded.
8. *Scheduled receipts.* If units are scheduled to be received in the future, they should be listed in the appropriate time period (column) and item (row). (An entry here in level 1 is a demand; all other levels are receipts.)

564 CHAPTER 14 MATERIAL REQUIREMENTS PLANNING (MRP)

Item name	Level	Lead time	# per parent	Onhand	Lot size	pd1	pd2	pd3	pd4	pd5	pd6	pd7	pd8
a		1		10									50
b	1	2	2	15									
d	2	1	2	10									
e	2	2	3	10									
c	1	1	3	20									
e	2	2	1										
f	2	3	2		5								
g	3	2	1										
d	3	1	2										

PROGRAM 14.1 ■ **POM for Windows' MRP Module Applied to Examples 1, 2, and 3** *POM for Windows' material requirements planning (MRP) module can be used to perform an MRP analysis for up to 18 periods. The data screen shown is generated by indicating the number of lines in the bill of materials. In our sample problem, we created a BOM with 7 items but 9 lines.*

Example Solution

Item name (low level)	pd1	pd2	pd3	pd4	pd5	pd6	pd7	pd8
a (0)								
TOT.REQ.	0.	0.	0.	0.	0.	0.	0.	50.
ON HAND	10.	10.	10.	10.	10.	10.	10.	10.
SchdREC.	0.	0.	0.	0.	0.	0.	0.	0.
NET REQ	0.	0.	0.	0.	0.	0.	0.	40.
ORD REL	0.	0.	0.	0.	0.	0.	40.	0.
b (1)								
TOT.REQ.	0.	0.	0.	0.	0.	0.	80.	0.
ON HAND	15.	15.	15.	15.	15.	15.	15.	0.
SchdREC.	0.	0.	0.	0.	0.	0.	0.	0.
NET REQ	0.	0.	0.	0.	0.	0.	65.	0.
ORD REL	0.	0.	0.	0.	65.	0.	0.	0.
c (1)								
TOT.REQ.	0.	0.	0.	0.	0.	0.	120.	0.
ON HAND	20.	20.	20.	20.	20.	20.	20.	0.
SchdREC.	0.	0.	0.	0.	0.	0.	0.	0.
NET REQ	0.	0.	0.	0.	0.	0.	100.	0.
ORD REL	0.	0.	0.	0.	0.	100.	0.	0.
e (2)								
TOT.REQ.	0.	0.	0.	0.	195.	100.	0.	0.

PROGRAM 14.2 ■ **Solution to MRP Run on Examples 1, 2, and 3 Data** *The solution for items A, B, and D in Examples 1, 2, and 3 is shown in this output of Program 14.1. The meaning of each item on the left-hand column of the printed output is as follows:*

1. *Total required.* The total number of units required in each week is listed in the first row. For the end item, the first row contains the demand schedule that was input on the data screen (Program 14.1). Other requirements are computed.
2. *On hand.* The number on hand is listed here. The on-hand amount starts as given on the data screen and is reduced according to needs.
3. *Scheduled receipt.* The amount that was scheduled in the original data screen is shown here.
4. *Net required.* The net amount required is the amount needed after the on-hand inventory is used.
5. *Order release.* Order release is the net amount required, offset by the lead time.

SOLVED PROBLEMS

Solved Problem 14.1

Determine the low-level coding and the quantity of each component necessary to produce 10 units of an assembly we will call Alpha. The product structure and quantities of each component needed for each assembly are noted in parentheses.

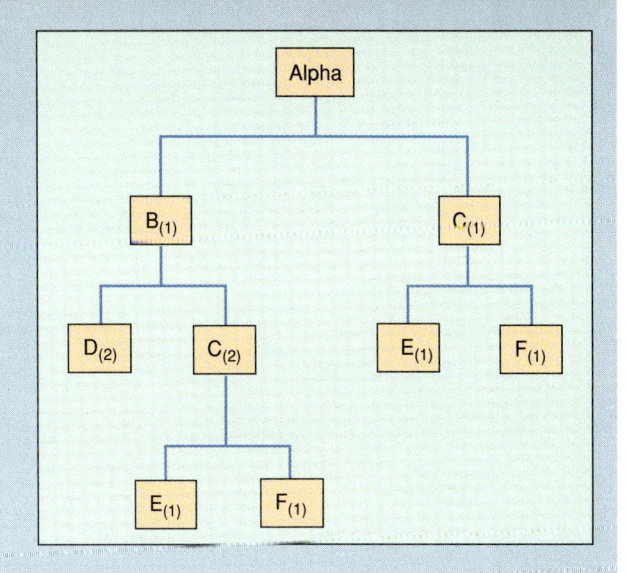

Solution

Redraw the product structure with low-level coding. Then multiply down the structure until the requirements of each branch are determined. Then add across the structure until the total for each is determined.

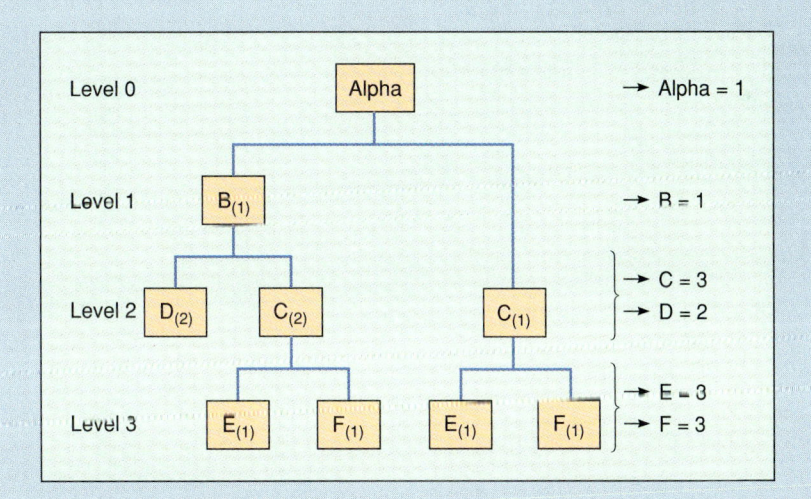

E's required for left branch:

$$(1_{alpha} \times 1_B \times 2_C \times 1_E) = 2$$

and E's required for right branch:

$$(1_{alpha} \times 1_C \times 1_E) = 1$$

3 E's required

Then "explode" the requirements by multiplying each by 10, as shown in the following table:

Level	Item	Quantity per Unit	Total Requirements for 10 Alpha
0	Alpha	1	10
1	B	1	10
2	C	3	30
2	D	2	20
3	E	3	30
3	F	3	30

Solved Problem 14.2

Using the product structure for Alpha in Solved Problem 14.1, and the lead times, quantity on hand, and master production schedule shown below, prepare a net MRP table for Alphas.

Item	Lead Time	Qty on Hand
Alpha	1	10
B	2	20
C	3	0
D	1	100
E	1	10
F	1	50

Master Production Schedule for Alpha

Period	6	7	8	9	10	11	12	13
Gross requirements			50			50		100

Solution

See the chart on the next page.

SOLVED PROBLEMS

Net Material Requirements Planning Sheet for Alpha. Note: The letter in parentheses (A) is the source of the demand.

Lot Size	Lead Time (# of Periods)	On Hand	Safety Stock	Allocated	Low-Level Code	Item ID		Period (week, day)													
								1	2	3	4	5	6	7	8	9	10	11	12	13
Lot-for-Lot	1	0	—	—	0	Alpha (A)	Gross Requirements								50			50		100
							Scheduled Receipts													
							Projected on Hand	10							10			—	—	—
							Net Requirements								40			50		100
							Planned Order Receipts								40			50		100
							Planned Order Releases							40			50		100	
Lot-for-Lot	2	20	—	—	1	B	Gross Requirements							40(A)			50(A)		100(A)	
							Scheduled Receipts													
							Projected on Hand	20						20			—	—	—	
							Net Requirements							20			50		100	
							Planned Order Receipts							20			50		100	
							Planned Order Releases					20				50	100			
Lot-for-Lot	3	0	—	—	2	C	Gross Requirements					40(B)		40(A)	100(E)	200(B) + 50(A)				
							Scheduled Receipts													
							Projected on Hand	0						—	—	—				
							Net Requirements					40		40	100	250				
							Planned Order Receipts					40		40	100	250				
							Planned Order Releases		40		40	100		250						
Lot-for-Lot	1	100	—	—	2	D	Gross Requirements					40(B)			100(B)		200(B)			
							Scheduled Receipts													
							Projected on Hand	100				100		60			—			
							Net Requirements					0		40	40		200			
							Planned Order Receipts					0		40	40		200			
							Planned Order Releases				0		250	40	200					
Lot-for-Lot	1	10	—	—	3	E	Gross Requirements		40(C)		40(C)	100(C)	250(C)		100(C)					
							Scheduled Receipts													
							Projected on Hand	10	10		—	—	—	—	—					
							Net Requirements		30		40	100	250		100					
							Planned Order Receipts		30		40	100	250		100					
							Planned Order Releases	30		40	100	250		100						
Lot-for-Lot	1	50	—	—	3	F	Gross Requirements		40(C)		40(C)	100(C)	250(C)		100(C)					
							Scheduled Receipts													
							Projected on Hand	50	50		10	—	—	—	—					
							Net Requirements		0		30	100	250		100					
							Planned Order Receipts		0		30	100	250		100					
							Planned Order Releases	—		30	100	250		100						

568　CHAPTER 14　MATERIAL REQUIREMENTS PLANNING (MRP)

DISCUSSION QUESTIONS

1. What is the difference between a *gross* requirements plan and a *net* requirements plan?
2. Once a material requirements plan (MRP) has been established, what other managerial applications might be found for the technique?
3. What are the similarities between MRP and DRP?
4. How does MRP II differ from MRP?
5. Which is the best lot-sizing policy for manufacturing organizations?
6. What impact does ignoring carrying cost in the allocation of stock in a DRP system have on lot sizes?
7. What do we mean by *closed-loop* MRP?
8. What are the options for the production planner who has (a) scheduled more than capacity in a work center next week, but (b) a consistent lack of capacity in that work center?
9. What types of resources might be scheduled via an MRP II?
10. What functions of the firm affect an MRP system? How?
11. What is the rationale for (a) a phantom bill of material, (b) a planning bill of material, and (c) a pseudo bill of material?
12. Identify five specific requirements of an effective MRP system.
13. What are some of the benefits of MRP?
14. What are the distinctions between MRP, ERP, and JIT?

CRITICAL THINKING EXERCISE

The very structure of MRP systems suggests fixed lead times. However, many firms are moving toward JIT and kanban techniques. What are the techniques, issues, and impact of adding JIT inventory and purchasing techniques to an organization that has MRP?

PROBLEMS

(Note: For several problems in this chapter, a copy of the form in Figure 14.12 may be helpful.)

• **14.1** The product structure for a product called Alpha is shown below. We need 10 units of Alpha in week 6. Three units of D and 2 units of F are required for each Alpha. The lead time for Alpha is 1 week. We have no units of Alpha, D, or F on hand. Lead time for D is 1 week and lead time for F is 2 weeks. Using the format in Figure 14.12, prepare a gross and net material requirements plan for Alpha.

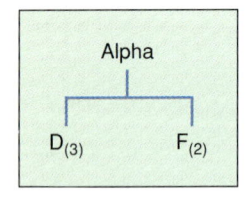

```
         Alpha
          |
    ┌─────┴─────┐
   D(3)       F(2)
```

: **14.2** The demand for subassembly S is 100 units in week 7. Each unit of S requires 1 unit of T and .5 unit of U. Each unit of T requires 1 unit of V, 2 units of W, and 1 unit of X. Finally, each unit of U requires .5 units of Y and 3 units of Z. One firm manufactures all items. It takes 2 weeks to make S, 1 week to make T, 2 weeks to make U, 2 weeks to make V, 3 weeks to make W, 1 week to make X, 2 weeks to make Y, and 1 week to make Z.
　　a) Construct a product structure and a gross material requirements plan for the dependent inventory items. Identify all levels, parents, and components.
　　b) Construct a net material requirements plan from the product structure and the following on-hand inventory.

Lot Size	Lead Time (# of periods)	On Hand	Safety Stock	Allo-cated	Low-Level Code	Item ID		Period (week, day)							
								1	2	3	4	5	6	7	8
							Gross Requirements								
							Scheduled Receipts								
							Projected on Hand								
							Net Requirements								
							Planned Order Receipts								
							Planned Order Releases								
							Gross Requirements								
							Scheduled Receipts								
							Projected on Hand								
							Net Requirements								
							Planned Order Receipts								
							Planned Order Releases								
							Gross Requirements								
							Scheduled Receipts								
							Projected on Hand								
							Net Requirements								
							Planned Order Receipts								
							Planned Order Releases								
							Gross Requirements								
							Scheduled Receipts								
							Projected on Hand								
							Net Requirements								
							Planned Order Receipts								
							Planned Order Releases								
							Gross Requirements								
							Scheduled Receipts								
							Projected on Hand								
							Net Requirements								
							Planned Order Receipts								
							Planned Order Releases								

FIGURE 14.12 ■ MRP Form for Homework Problems in Chapter 14

Item	On-Hand Inventory	Item	On-Hand Inventory
S	20	W	30
T	20	X	25
U	10	Y	15
V	30	Z	10

14.3 Look again at Problem 14.2. In addition to 100 units of S, there is also a demand for 20 units of U, which is a component of S. The 20 units of U are needed for maintenance purposes. These units are needed 1 week before S, in week 6. Modify the gross and net material requirements plan to reflect this change.

14.4 Given the following bill of material, master production schedule, and inventory status, develop: (a) a gross requirements plan for all items and (b) net materials requirements (planned order release) for all items.

CHAPTER 14 MATERIAL REQUIREMENTS PLANNING (MRP)

Master Production Schedule: X1

Period	7	8	9	10	11	12
Gross requirements		50		20		100

Item	Lead Time	On Hand	Item	Lead Time	On Hand
X1	1	50	C	3	10
B1	2	20	D	1	0
B2	2	20	E	1	0
A1	1	5			

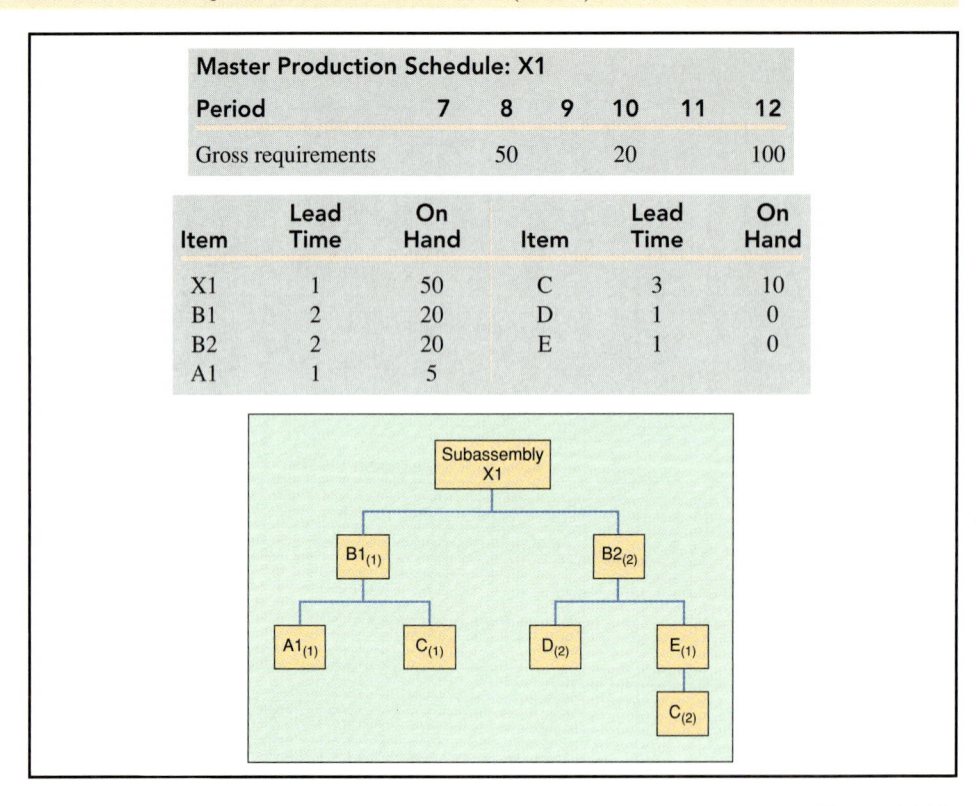

```
                Subassembly
                    X1
               /          \
            B1(1)         B2(2)
           /    \        /      \
        A1(1)  C(1)   D(2)    E(1)
                                |
                              C(2)
```

Problems 14.5 and 14.6 use the data shown in Tables 14.5 and 14.6 and Figure 14.13.

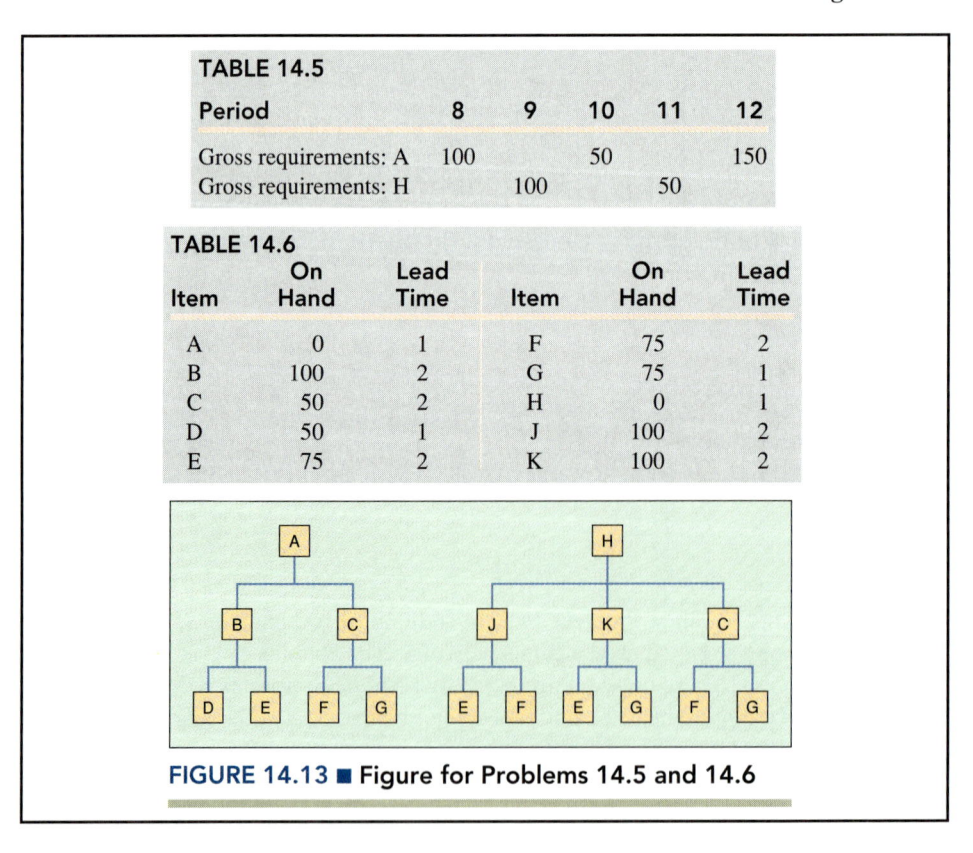

TABLE 14.5

Period	8	9	10	11	12
Gross requirements: A	100		50		150
Gross requirements: H		100		50	

TABLE 14.6

Item	On Hand	Lead Time	Item	On Hand	Lead Time
A	0	1	F	75	2
B	100	2	G	75	1
C	50	2	H	0	1
D	50	1	J	100	2
E	75	2	K	100	2

```
          A                         H
        /   \                    /  |  \
       B     C                  J   K   C
      /|\   /|\                /\  /\  /\
     D E F F G                E F E G F G
```

FIGURE 14.13 ■ Figure for Problems 14.5 and 14.6

14.5 Given the bill of material, master production schedule, and inventory status shown in Tables 14.5 and 14.6 and in Figure 14.13, develop (a) a gross requirements plan for C and (b) a planned order release for C.

14.6 Based on the preceding data (see Tables 14.5 and 14.6 and Figure 14.13), complete a net planned order release schedule for all items (10 schedules in all).

Problems 14.7 through 14.9 are based on an item that has the gross requirements shown in Table 14.7 and a beginning inventory of 40 units.

TABLE 14.7

Period	1	2	3	4	5	6	7	8	9	10	11	12
Gross requirements	30		40		30	70	20		10	80		50

Holding cost = $2.50/unit/week; setup cost = $150; lead time = 1 week.

14.7 Develop a lot-for-lot solution and calculate total relevant costs.

14.8 a) Develop an EOQ solution and calculate total relevant costs. Stockout costs equal $10 per unit.
b) Solve part (a) with lead time = 0.

14.9 a) Develop a PPB solution and calculate total relevant costs.
b) Solve part (a) with lead time = 0.

14.10 Keebock, a maker of outstanding running shoes, keeps the soles of its size-13 running shoes in inventory for one period at a cost of $.25 per unit. The setup costs are $50. Beginning inventory is zero and lead time is 1 week; stockout cost is $5 per unit. Shown in Table 14.8 are the net requirements per period.

TABLE 14.8

Period	0	1	2	3	4	5	6	7	8	9	10
Net requirements		35	30	45	0	10	40	30	0	30	55

Determine Keebock's cost based on:
a) EOQ.
b) Lot-for-lot.
c) Part period balancing (PPB).

Problems 14.11 through 14.14 are based on the data shown in Table 14.9. The parent item has a 1 week lead time, and the lot-for-lot rule is employed. Beginning inventory is 20 units. The parent item has a component whose lead time is also 1 week and whose starting inventory position is 30 units. At the component level, production occurs in lot sizes to cover 3 periods of net requirements.

TABLE 14.9

Period	1	2	3	4	5	6	7	8	9	10
Gross requirements	0	40	30	40	10	70	40	10	30	60

14.11 Develop the parent and component MRP tables to show the original planned positions.

14.12 At the parent level, gross requirements for period 2 are canceled. Develop the parent and component net MRP tables to show the net effect of this cancellation.

14.13 With the parent-level gross requirements canceled for period 2, what is the effect on inventory quantity, setup costs, and holding costs?

14.14 At the component level, there is enough capacity to produce 75 units in period 1. Gross requirements at the parent level increase from 40 to 50 units in period 2. What problem arises? What solution would you recommend?

14.15 A part structure, lead time (weeks), and on-hand quantities for product A are shown in Figure 14.14.

From the information shown, generate:
a) An indented bill of material for product A (see Figure 6.8 as an example of a BOM).
b) A bill of material showing the quantity of each part required to produce one A.
c) An exploded bill of material showing the quantity of each part required to produce ten A's.

PART	INVENTORY ON HAND
A	0
B	2
C	10
D	5
E	4
F	5
G	1
H	10

PART STRUCTURE TREE

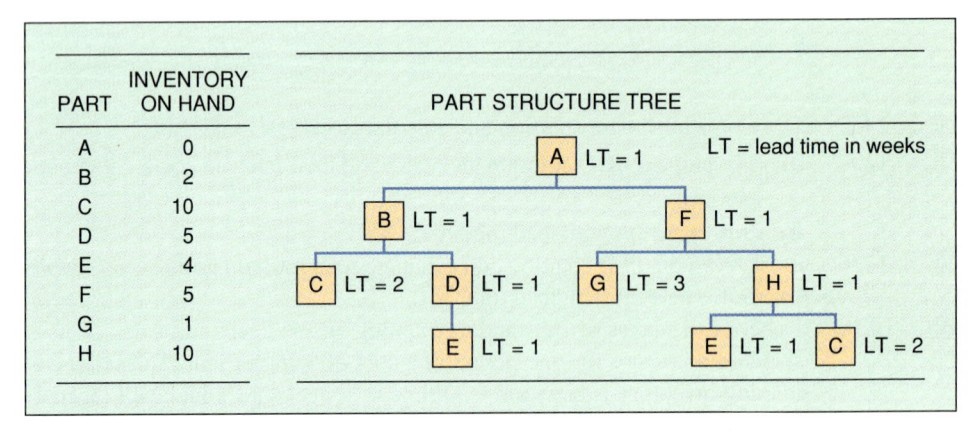

A (LT = 1)
├── B (LT = 1)
│   ├── C (LT = 2)
│   └── D (LT = 1)
│   └── E (LT = 1)
└── F (LT = 1)
    ├── G (LT = 3)
    └── H (LT = 1)
        ├── E (LT = 1)
        └── C (LT = 2)

LT = lead time in weeks

FIGURE 14.14 ■ Data for Problems 14.15, 14.16, 14.17, and the Data Base Application 14.19

d) Net requirements for each part to produce ten A's in week 8 using lot-for-lot.

(*Hint:* The POM for Windows software can help with parts [b] and [c], but cannot produce an output other than in MRP format.)

14.16 You are product planner for product A (in Problem 14.15). The field service manager, Al Trostel, has just called and told you that the requirements for B and F should each be increased by 10 units for his repair requirements in the field.
a) Prepare an exploded bill of material showing the quantity of each part required to produce the requirements for the service manager *and* the production request of 10.
b) What are the net requirements (i.e., exploded bill of materials less on-hand inventory)?
c) Prepare a net requirement plan by date for the new requirements (for both production and field service), assuming that the field service manager wants his 10 units in week 6 and the 10 production units are still due in week 8.

14.17 You have just been notified via fax that the lead time for component G of product A (Problem 14.16) has just been increased to 4 weeks.
a) Which items have changed and why?
b) What are the implications for the production plan?
c) As production planner, what can you do?

14.18 As director of operations, you have recently installed a distribution requirements planning (DRP) system. The company has East Coast and West Coast warehouses, as well as a main factory warehouse in Omaha, Nebraska. You have just received the orders for the next planning period from the managers at each of the three facilities. Their reports are shown below. The lead time to both the East and West Coast warehouses is 2 weeks, and there is a 1-week lead time to bring material to the factory warehouse. Shipments are in truckload quantities of 100 each. There is no initial inventory in the system. The factory is having trouble installing the level of material work schedule and still has a lot size in multiples of 100.

Data for East Coast Warehouse

Period	1	2	3	4	5	6	7	8	9	10	11	12
Forecast requirements			40	100	80	70	20	25	70	80	30	50

Lead time = 2 weeks

Data for West Coast Warehouse

Period	1	2	3	4	5	6	7	8	9	10
Forecast requirements	20	45	60	70	40	80	70	80	55	

Lead time = 2 weeks

Data for Factory Warehouse

Period	1	2	3	4	5	6	7	8	9	10
Forecast requirements			30	40	10	70	40	10	30	60

Lead time = 1 week

a) Show the plan for *receipt* of orders from the factory.
b) If the factory requires 2 weeks to produce the merchandise, when must the orders be *released* to the factory?

DATA BASE APPLICATION

14.19 Your stockroom manager, Yamil Bermudez, arrived at your desk just after you had completed the net requirements plan for product A (use data in Problem 14.15), exclaiming that the cycle counter should be fired. It seems that the cycle counter was wrong; there are three A's available now, not zero, as the original data showed; moreover, five E's are also available. About then, your boss, Sam Melnyk, who overheard the discussion, says, "You might as well extend the net requirements plan out to 16 weeks, because we just received an order for 10 more A's in week 12 and 5 more in week 15. Additionally, count on the field service department wanting 3 more B's in week 16, as well as those 10 units in week 8." You decide to use the lead times in Problem 14.15, but item G now has a lead time of 4 weeks.

Your assignment is to prepare a new net requirements plan, based on the actual inventory (as reported) and the new schedule.

Case Study

Service, Inc.

Service, Inc., is a distributor of automotive replacement parts. With no manufacturing capability, all the products it sells are purchased, assembled, and repackaged. Service, Inc. does have extensive inventory and final assembly facilities. Among its products are private-label carburetor and ignition kits. The company has been experiencing difficulties for the last 2 years. First, profits have fallen considerably. Second, customer-service levels have declined, with late deliveries now exceeding 25% of orders. Third, customer returns have been rising at a rate of 3% per month.

Phil Houghton, vice president of sales, claims that most of the problem lies with the assembly department. He says that although Service, Inc. has accurate BOM indicating what goes into each product, it is not producing the proper mix of the product. He also believes it has poor quality control, its productivity has fallen, and as a result, its costs are too high.

Treasurer Dick Houser, believes that problems are due to investment in the wrong inventories. He thinks that marketing has too many options and products. Dick also thinks that purchasing department buyers have been hedging their inventories and requirements with excess purchasing commitments.

Assembly manager John Burnham, says, "The symptom is that we have a lot of parts in inventory, but no place to assemble them in the production schedule. When we have the right part," he adds, "it is not very good, but we use it anyway to meet the schedule."

John Tolbert, manager of purchasing, has taken the stance that purchasing has not let Service, Inc. down. He has stuck by his old suppliers, used historical data to determine requirements, maintained what he views as excellent prices from suppliers, and evaluated new sources of supply with a view toward lowering cost. Where possible, John reacted to the increased pressure for profitability by emphasizing low cost and early delivery.

As president of Service, Inc. you must get the firm back on a course toward improved profitability.

Discussion Questions

1. Identify both the symptoms and problems at Service, Inc.
2. What specific changes would you implement?

Case Study

Ruch Manufacturing

Ruch Manufacturing is a truck manufacturer that recently relocated from Pennsylvania to North Carolina. Prior to the move, the company faced decreased demand, increasing labor costs, and deteriorating management-labor relations. Management offered positions in North Carolina to the entire workforce, and about half of the employees decided to make the move.

Prior to setting up the new operation, the new operations manager instructed each of his subordinates to examine various aspects of the production process. Although subordinates who had moved from Pennsylvania were already very familiar with the operations, new personnel needed to familiarize themselves with Ruch policies.

One of the assistant plant managers, a new graduate named Elton Clark, was assigned the task of examining ordering policies for supplies used in production. He found that Ruch was using an EOQ policy for ordering cases of lubricating oil. Elton called the finance department and was told that for purposes of analysis, the appropriate holding cost was 24% per year. Demand over the past 3 years was for 7,486 cases, or an average of 2,495 cases per year. At a cost of $6.32 per case, the cost of ordering the oil was estimated to be $83 per order. Clark used these numbers to find the EOQ:

$$EOQ = \sqrt{\frac{2DS}{H}} = \sqrt{\frac{(2)(7{,}486/3)(83)}{(.24)(\$6.32)}}$$

$$= \sqrt{\frac{414{,}225.32}{1.5168}} = \sqrt{273{,}091.58} \approx 523,$$

which basically agreed with Ruch's ordering size of 500. Clark then developed a table showing oil usage for the past 36 months.

Month	Year 1996	Year 1997	Year 1998
January	345	379	368
February	28	32	4
March	417	489	423
April	52	50	48
May	0	4	15
June	379	433	382
July	288	267	306
August	76	83	84
September	221	244	218
October	34	32	38
November	322	354	333
December	227	259	252
Total	2,389	2,626	2,471

Grand total = 7,486

Clark was somewhat dismayed. In business school, he had been led to believe that EOQ was appropriate only when the demand was somewhat constant. The numbers he saw here were far from constant. Furthermore, he had heard a great deal about just-in-time inventory and felt that perhaps the amount ordered each month should be the expected demand. Clark felt that a new policy should be implemented, but he wanted to test out his theory by experimenting with past data.

Discussion Questions

1. Would lot-for-lot ordering be better than the current EOQ policy?
2. Would lot-for-lot ordering be the best possible policy?
3. Is just-in-time a relevant notion for lot sizing?

Source: Professors Howard J. Weiss and Mark F. Gershon, Temple University.

Video Case 8

MRP at Wheeled Coach

Wheeled Coach, the world's largest manufacturer of ambulances, builds thousands of different and constantly changing configurations of its products. The custom nature of its business means lots of options and special designs—and a potential scheduling and inventory nightmare. Wheeled Coach addressed such problems, and succeeded in solving a lot of them, with an MRP system (described in the *Global Company Profile* that opens this chapter). As with most MRP installations, however, solving one set of problems uncovers a new set.

One of the new issues that had to be addressed by plant manager Lynn Whalen was newly discovered excess inventory. Managers discovered a substantial amount of inventory that was not called for in any finished products. Excess inventory was evident because of the new level of inventory accuracy required by the MRP system. The other reason was a new series of inventory reports generated by the IBM MAPICS MRP system purchased by Wheeled Coach. One of those reports indicates where items are used and is known as the "Where Used" report. Interestingly, many inventory items were not called out on bills-of-material (BOMs) for any current products. And in some cases, the reason some parts were in the stockroom remained a mystery.

The discovery of this excess inventory led to renewed efforts to ensure that the BOMs were accurate. With substantial work, BOM accuracy increased and the number of engineering change notices (ECNs) decreased. Similarly, purchase order accuracy, with regard to both part numbers and quantities ordered, was improved. Additionally, receiving department and stockroom accuracy went up, all helping to maintain schedule, costs, and, ultimately, shipping dates and quality.

Eventually, Lyn Whalen concluded that the residual amounts of excess inventory were the result, at least in part, of rapid changes in ambulance design and technology. Another source was customer changes made after specifications had been determined and materials ordered. This latter excess occurs because, even though Wheeled Coach's own throughput time is only 17 days, many of the items that it purchases require much longer lead times.

Discussion Questions

1. Why is accurate inventory such an important issue at Wheeled Coach?
2. What kind of a plan would you suggest for dealing with excess inventory at Wheeled Coach?
3. Be specific in your suggestions for reducing inventory and how to implement them.

BIBLIOGRAPHY

Bookbinder, J. H., and L. A. Koch. "Production Planning for Mixed Assembly/Arborescent Systems." *Journal of Operations Management* 9, no. 1 (1990): 7–23.

Brucker, H. D., G. A. Flowers, and R. D. Peck. "MRP Shop-Floor Control in a Job Shop: Definitely Works." *Production and Inventory Management Journal* 33, no. 2 (second quarter 1992): 43.

Campbell, G. M. "Master Production Scheduling under Rolling Planning Horizons with Fixed Order Intervals." *Decision Sciences* 23, no. 2 (March–April 1992): 312.

Ding, F., and M. Yuen. "A Modified MRP for a Production System with the Coexistence of MRP and Kanbans." *Journal of Operations Management* 10, no. 2 (April 1991): 267–277.

Dolinsky, L. R., T. E. Vollmann, and M. J. Maggard. "Adjusting Replenishment Orders to Reflect Learning in a Material Requirements Planning Environment." *Management Science* 36 (December 1990): 1,532–1,547.

Freeland, J. R., J. P. Leschke, and E. N. Weiss. "Guidelines for Setup Cost Reduction Programs to Achieve Zero Inventory." *Journal of Operations Management* 9 (January 1990): 85.

Gardiner, S. C., and J. H. Blackstone, Jr. "The Effects of Lot Sizing and Dispatching on Customer Service in an MRP Environment." *Journal of Operations Management* 11, no. 2 (June 1993): 143–160.

Haddock, J., and D. E. Hubicki. "Which Lot-Sizing Techniques Are Used in Material Requirements Planning?" *Production and Inventory Management* 30 (third quarter 1989): 53–56.

Hoy, P. "Client/Server MRP II Comes of Age." *APICS—The Performance Advantage,* June 1995, pp. 38–41.

Jacobs, F. R., and D. C. Whybark. "A Comparison of Reorder Point and Material Requirements Planning Inventory Control Logic." *Decision Sciences* 23, no. 2 (March–April 1992): 332.

Kumar, H., and R. Rachamadugu. "Is MRP II Dead?" *APICS—The Performance Advantage,* September 1995, pp. 24–27.

Ledbetter, M. E., C. A. Snyder, and S. C. Gardiner. "Work-in-Process Inventory Control for Repetitive Manufacturing in an MRP Environment: A Case Study." *Production and Inventory Management Journal* 34, no. 2 (second quarter 1993): 48–52.

Martin, A. J. *DRP: Distribution Resource Planning.* Englewood Cliffs, NJ: Prentice Hall, 1983.

Meckler, V. A. "Setup Cost Reduction in the Dynamic Lot-Size Model." *Journal of Operations Management* 11, no. 1 (March 1993): 35–44.

Proud, J. F. "Master Scheduling: More Art than Science." *Industrial Engineering Solutions,* September 1995, pp. 38–42.

St. Johns, R. "The Evils of Lot Sizing in MRP." *Production and Inventory Management* 25 (fourth quarter 1984): 75–85.

Sridharan, V., and R. Lawrence LaForge. "Freezing the Master Production Schedule: Implications for Customer Service." *Decision Sciences* 25, no. 3 (May–June 1994): 461–469.

Turbide, D. A. "MRP II: Still Number One!" *IIE Solutions,* July 1995, pp. 28–31.

Wagner, H. M., and T. M. Whitin. "Dynamic Version of the Economic Lot Size Model." *Management Science* 5, no. 1 (1958): 89–96.

Zhao, X., and T. S. Lee. "Freezing the Master Production Schedule for Material Requirements Planning Systems under Demand Uncertainty." *Journal of Operations Management* 11, no. 2 (June 1993): 185–206.

INTERNET RESOURCES

APICS Consulting Forum:
http://lionhrtpub.com/apics-6-96/consultant.html

APICS Study Material References provided by Business Systems Specialties, Inc.:
http://www.wp.com/BSSI/CPIMLST.htm

Armstrong Management Group Maintains a Web site with cases and articles related to ERP and MRP:
http://www.interlog.com/~arm

SAP America:
http://www.sap.com

Short-Term Scheduling

15

CHAPTER OUTLINE

GLOBAL COMPANY PROFILE: DELTA AIRLINES
THE STRATEGIC IMPORTANCE OF SHORT-TERM SCHEDULING
SCHEDULING ISSUES
  Forward and Backward Scheduling
  Scheduling Criteria
SCHEDULING PROCESS-FOCUSED WORK CENTERS
LOADING JOBS IN WORK CENTERS
  Input-Output Control
  Gantt Charts
  Assignment Method
SEQUENCING JOBS IN WORK CENTERS
PRIORITY RULES FOR DISPATCHING JOBS
CRITICAL RATIO
SEQUENCING N JOBS ON TWO MACHINES: JOHNSON'S RULE
LIMITATIONS OF RULE-BASED DISPATCHING SYSTEMS
FINITE SCHEDULING
THEORY OF CONSTRAINTS
  Bottleneck Work Centers
REPETITIVE MANUFACTURING
SCHEDULING FOR SERVICES
  Scheduling Nurses with Cyclical Scheduling
SUMMARY
KEY TERMS
USING POM FOR WINDOWS TO SOLVE SCHEDULING PROBLEMS
USING EXCEL OM FOR SHORT-TERM SCHEDULING
SOLVED PROBLEMS
DISCUSSION QUESTIONS
CRITICAL THINKING EXERCISE
PROBLEMS
DATA BASE APPLICATION
CASE STUDY: OLD OREGON WOOD STORE
BIBLIOGRAPHY
INTERNET RESOURCES

LEARNING OBJECTIVES

When you complete this chapter you should be able to:

Identify or Define:
  Gantt charts
  Assignment method
  Sequencing rules
  Johnson's rule
  Bottlenecks

Describe or Explain:
  Scheduling
  Sequencing
  Shop loading
  Theory of constraints

577

GLOBAL COMPANY PROFILE:

Scheduling Airplanes When Weather Is the Enemy

Throughout the ordeals of tornadoes, ice storms, and snowstorms, airlines across the globe struggle to cope with delays, cancellations, and furious passengers. Close to 10% of Delta Airlines' flights are disrupted in a typical year, half because of weather; the cost is $440 million in lost revenue, overtime pay, and food and lodging vouchers.

Now Delta is ready to take the sting out of the scheduling nightmares that come from weather-related problems. In 1997, it opened a $33-million high-tech nerve center adjacent to its major hub at the Atlanta Airport. From computers to telecommunications systems to de-icers, Delta's new Operations Control Center more quickly notifies customers of schedule changes, reroutes flights, and gets jets into the air.

With earlier access to information, the center's staff of 18 pores over streams of data transmitted by computers. Using mathematical scheduling models described in this chapter, Delta decides on schedule and route changes. Its software, called the Inconvenienced Passenger Rebooking System, notifies passengers of cancellations or delays and even books them onto rival airlines if necessary. With 100,000 passengers flying into and out of Atlanta every day, Delta figures its new scheduling efforts will save $35 million a year.

Sources: New York Times, January 21, 1997, pp. C1, C20; and P. R. Horner, OR/MS Today 22 (August 1995): 14–15.

To improve flight rescheduling efforts, Delta employees monitor giant screens that display meterological charts, weather patterns, and maps of Delta flights at its Operations Control Center in Atlanta.

4 A.M.	10 A.M.	1:30 P.M.	5 P.M.	10 P.M.
FORECAST: Rain with a chance of light snow for Atlanta.	**FORECAST:** Freezing rain after 5 P.M.	**FORECAST:** Rain changing to snow.	**FORECAST:** Less snow than expected.	**FORECAST:** Snow tapering off.
ACTION: Discuss status of planes and possible need for cancellations.	**ACTION:** Ready deicing trucks; develop plans to cancel 50 to 80% of flights after 6 P.M.	**ACTION:** Cancel half the flights from 6 P.M. to 10 A.M.; notify passengers and reroute planes.	**ACTION:** Continue calling passengers and arrange alternate flights.	**ACTION:** Find hotels for 1,600 passengers stranded by the storm.

Here is what Delta officials had to do one December day when a storm bore down on Atlanta.

Solved Problem 15.2

A defense contractor in Dallas has six jobs awaiting processing. Processing time and due dates are given in the table to the right. Assume that jobs arrive in the order shown. Set the processing sequence according to FCFS and evaluate.

Job	Job Processing Time (days)	Job Due Date (days)
A	6	22
B	12	14
C	14	30
D	2	18
E	10	25
F	4	34

Solution

FCFS has the sequence A-B-C-D-E-F.

Job Sequence	Job Processing Time	Flow Time	Due Date	Job Lateness
A	6	6	22	0
B	12	18	14	4
C	14	32	30	2
D	2	34	18	16
E	10	44	25	19
F	4	48	34	14
	48	182		55

1. Average completion time = 182/6 = 30.33 days
2. Average number of jobs in system = 182/48 = 3.79 jobs
3. Average job lateness = 55/6 = 9.16 days
4. Utilization = 48/182 = 26.4%

Solved Problem 15.3

The Dallas firm in Solved Problem 15.2 also wants to consider job sequencing by the SPT priority rule. Apply SPT to the same data and provide a recommendation.

Solution

SPT has the sequence D-F-A-E-B-C.

Job Sequence	Job Processing Time	Flow Time	Due Date	Job Lateness
D	2	2	18	0
F	4	6	34	0
A	6	12	22	0
E	10	22	25	0
B	12	34	14	20
C	14	48	30	18
	48	124		38

1. Average completion time = 124/6 = 20.67 days
2. Average number of jobs in system = 124/48 = 2.58 jobs
3. Average job lateness = 38/6 = 6.33 days
4. Utilization = 48/124 = 38.7%

SPT is superior to FCFS in this case on all four measures. If we were to also analyze EDD, we would, however, find its average job lateness to be lowest at 5.5 days. SPT is a good recommendation. SPT's major disadvantage is that it makes long jobs wait, sometimes for a long time.

Solved Problem 15.4

Use Johnson's rule to find the optimum sequence for processing the jobs shown on the right through two work centers. Times at each center are in hours.

Job	Work Center 1	Work Center 2
A	6	12
B	3	7
C	18	9
D	15	14
E	16	8
F	10	15

Solution

| B | A | F | D | C | E |

The sequential times are

Work center 1	3	6	10	15	18	16
Work center 2	7	12	15	14	9	8

Solved Problem 15.5

Illustrate the throughput time and idle time at the two work centers in Solved Problem 15.4 by constructing a time-phased chart.

Solution

| Work center 1 | B | A | F | D | C | E |
| Work center 2 | | B | A | F | D | C | E |

Work center 1: 0 3, 9, 19, 34, 52, 68
Work center 2: 0 3, 10, 22, 37, 51 52, 61, 68, 76

Completions: B at 10, A at 22, F at 37, D at 51, C at 61, E at 68

Idle time shown at start of Work center 2 and between jobs.

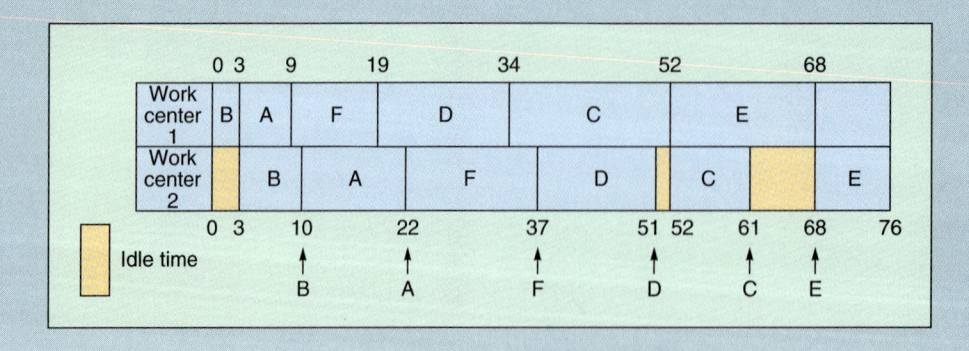

DISCUSSION QUESTIONS

1. Name five priority sequencing rules. Explain how each works to assign jobs.
2. When is Johnson's rule best applied in job-shop scheduling?
3. What is the difference between a Gantt load chart and a Gantt schedule chart?
4. What are the steps in the theory of constraints?
5. Why is the scheduling of services difficult?
6. What are the criteria by which we evaluate sequencing rules?
7. What are the advantages of level material flow?
8. Explain the difference between backward and forward scheduling.
9. What is input-output control?
10. What are the steps of the assignment method of linear programming?

CRITICAL THINKING EXERCISE

Scheduling people to work the late, or "graveyard," shift is a problem in almost every 24-hour company. An article in *The Wall Street Journal* titled "Scheduling Workers Who Fall Asleep on the Job Is Not Easy" describes night-shift dilemmas at an oil refinery and a police department. Scheduling is also difficult for airlines that fly long routes, such as El Al Airline's popular 11-hour nonstop Tel Aviv to New York flight.

Select five companies that require night shifts and discuss how each can deal with its staffing requirements. What are the major issues in each that affect morale, productivity, alertness, and safety?

PROBLEMS

15.1 Bob Swan's company has scheduled five jobs. Today, which is day 7, Swan is reviewing the Gantt chart depicting these schedules.

- Job A was scheduled to begin on day 3 and to take 6 days. As of now, it is 1 day ahead of schedule.
- Job B was scheduled to begin on day 1 and take 4 days. It is currently on time.
- Job C was scheduled to start on day 7 and take 3 days. It actually got started on day 6 and is progressing according to plan.
- Job D was scheduled to begin on day 5, but missing equipment delayed it until day 6. It is progressing as expected and should take 3 days.
- Job E was scheduled to begin on day 4 and take 5 days. It got started on time but has since fallen behind 2 days.

Draw the Gantt chart as it looks to Swan.

15.2 Mary Meyer's medical testing company wishes to assign a set of jobs to a set of machines. The following table provides data as to the productivity of each machine when performing the specific job.

| | Machine | | | |
Job	A	B	C	D
1	7	9	8	10
2	10	9	7	6
3	11	5	9	6
4	9	11	5	8

a) Determine the assignment of jobs to machines that will *maximize* total productivity.
b) What is the total productivity of your assignments?

· 15.3 Sharon Moore's company wishes to assign a set of jobs to a set of machines. The following table provides data as to the cost of each job when performed on a specific machine.
a) Determine the assignment of jobs to machines that will *minimize* Moore's total cost.
b) What is the total cost of your assignments?

| | Machine | | | |
Job	A	B	C	D
1	7	9	8	10
2	10	9	7	6
3	11	5	9	6
4	9	11	5	8

: 15.4 First Printing and Copy Center has 4 more jobs to be scheduled, in addition to those shown in Example 3 in the chapter. Production scheduling personnel are reviewing the Gantt chart at the end of day 4.

- Job D was scheduled to begin early on day 2 and to end on the middle of day 9. As of now (the review point after day 4), it is 2 days ahead of schedule.
- Job E should begin on day 1 and end on day 3. It was on time.
- Job F was to begin on day 3, but maintenance forced a delay of $1\frac{1}{2}$ days. The job should now take 5 full days. It is now on schedule.
- Job G is a day behind schedule. It started at the beginning of day 2 and should require 6 days to complete.

Develop a Gantt schedule chart for First Printing and Copy Center.

· 15.5 Paul Misselwitz, the managing partner at a large law firm in Memphis, must assign three clients to three attorneys. Cost data are presented below.

| | Attorney | | |
Client	1	2	3
Divorce case	$800	$1,100	$1,200
Felony case	$500	$1,600	$1,300
Discrimination case	$500	$1,000	$2,300

Use the assignment algorithm to solve this problem.

: 15.6 Coleen O'Dell, the scheduler at a small southwestern plant, has six jobs that can be processed on any of six machines, with respective times as shown (in hours) below. Determine the allocation of jobs to machines that will result in minimum time.

	Machine					
Job	1	2	3	4	5	6
A-52	60	22	34	42	30	60
A-53	22	52	16	32	18	48
A-56	29	16	58	28	22	55
A-59	42	32	28	46	15	30
A-60	30	18	25	15	45	42
A-61	50	48	57	30	44	60

· **15.7** Leslie Oliver, the hospital administrator at St. Charles General, must appoint head nurses to four newly established departments: urology, cardiology, orthopedics, and obstetrics. In anticipation of this staffing problem, she had hired four nurses; considered their backgrounds, personalities, and talents; and developed a cost scale ranging from 0 to 100 to be used in the assignment. A 0 for a nurse being assigned to the cardiology unit implies that she would be perfectly suited to that task. A value close to 100, on the other hand, would imply that she is not at all suited to head that unit. The accompanying table gives the complete set of cost figures that the hospital administrator feels represented all possible assignments. Which nurse should be assigned to which unit?

	Department			
Nurse	Urology	Cardiology	Orthopedics	Obstetrics
Hawkins	28	18	15	75
Condriac	32	48	23	38
Bardot	51	36	24	36
Hoolihan	25	38	55	12

· **15.8** The Gleaming Company has just developed a new dishwashing liquid and is preparing for a national television promotional campaign. The firm has decided to schedule a series of 1-minute commercials during the peak daytime audience viewing hours of 1:00 P.M. to 5:00 P.M. To reach the widest possible audience, Gleaming wants to schedule one commercial on each of 4 networks and have one commercial appear during each of the four 1-hour time blocks. The exposure ratings for each hour, representing the number of viewers per $1,000 spent, are presented in the accompanying table. Which network should be scheduled each hour in order to provide the maximum audience exposure?

	Networks			
Time	A	B	C	Independent
1:00–2:00 P.M.	27.1	18.1	11.3	9.5
2:00–3:00 P.M.	18.9	15.5	17.1	10.6
3:00–4:00 P.M.	19.2	18.5	9.9	7.7
4:00–5:00 P.M.	11.5	21.4	16.8	12.8

: **15.9** The Tim Parson's Manufacturing Company is putting out seven new electronic components. Each of Parson's eight plants has the capacity to add one more product to its current line of electronic parts. The unit manufacturing costs for producing the different parts at the eight plants are shown in the accompanying table. How should Parson assign the new products to the plants in order to minimize manufacturing costs?

| | Plants | | | | | | | |
Electronic Components	1	2	3	4	5	6	7	8
C53	$.10	$.12	$.13	$.11	$.10	$.06	$.16	$.12
C81	.05	.06	.04	.08	.04	.09	.06	.06
D5	.32	.40	.31	.30	.42	.35	.36	.49
D44	.17	.14	.19	.15	.10	.16	.19	.12
E2	.06	.07	.10	.05	.08	.10	.11	.05
E35	.08	.10	.12	.08	.09	.10	.09	.06
G99	.55	.62	.61	.70	.62	.63	.65	.59

: 15.10 The following jobs are waiting to be processed at the same machine center. Jobs are logged as they arrive:

Job	Due Date	Duration (days)
A	313	8
B	312	16
C	325	40
D	314	5
E	314	3

In what sequence would the jobs be ranked according to the following decision rules: (1) FCFS, (2) EDD, (3) SPT, (4) LPT? All dates are specified as manufacturing planning calendar days. Assume that all jobs arrive on day 275. Which decision is best and why?

· **15.11** Suppose that today is day 300 on the planning calendar and that we have not started any of the jobs given in Problem 15.10. Using the critical-ratio technique, in what sequence would you schedule these jobs?

: 15.12 An Alabama lumberyard has 4 jobs on order, as shown in the following table. Today is day 205 on the yard's schedule. Establish processing priorities.

Job	Due Date	Remaining Time in Days
A	212	6
B	209	3
C	208	3
D	210	8

: 15.13 The following jobs are waiting to be processed at a small machine center:

Job	Due Date	Duration (days)
010	260	30
020	258	16
030	260	8
040	270	20
050	275	10

In what sequence would the jobs be ranked according to the following decision rules: (1) FCFS, (2) EDD, (3) SPT, (4) LPT? All dates are specified as manufacturing planning calendar days. Assume that all jobs arrive on day 210. Which is the best decision rule?

Problems

: 15.14 The following jobs are waiting to be processed at Mike Perman's machine center:

Job	Date Order Received	Production Days Needed	Date Order Due
A	110	20	180
B	120	30	200
C	122	10	175
D	125	16	230
E	130	18	210

In what sequence would the jobs be ranked according to the following rules: (1) FCFS, (2) EDD, (3) SPT, (4) LPT? All dates are according to shop calendar days. Today on the planning calendar is day 130. Which rule is best?

· 15.15 Suppose that today is day 150 on the planning calendar and that we have not yet started any of the jobs in Problem 15.14. Using the critical-ratio technique, in what sequence would you schedule these jobs?

: 15.16 J. J. Ruppel Automation Company estimates the data entry and verifying times for four jobs as follows:

Job	Data Entry (hours)	Verify (hours)
A	2.5	1.7
B	3.8	2.6
C	1.9	1.0
D	1.8	3.0

In what order should the jobs be done if the company has one operator for each job? Illustrate the time-phased flow of this job sequence graphically.

: 15.17 Six jobs are to be processed through a two-step operation. The first operation involves sanding, and the second involves painting. Processing times are as follows:

Job	Operation 1 (hours)	Operation 2 (hours)
A	10	5
B	7	4
C	5	7
D	3	8
E	2	6
F	4	3

Determine a sequence that will minimize the total completion time for these jobs. Illustrate graphically.

: 15.18 Bill Penny has a repetitive manufacturing plant producing trailer hitches in Arlington, Texas. The plant has an average inventory turnover of only 12 times per year. He has, therefore, determined that he will reduce his component lot sizes. He has developed the following data for one component, the safety chain clip:

Annual demand = 31,200 units

Daily demand = 120 units

Daily production = 960 units

Desired lot size (1 hour of production) = 120 units

Holding cost per unit per year = $12

Setup labor cost per hour = $20

What setup time should he have his plant manager aim for regarding this component?

: **15.19** The following jobs are waiting to be processed at Scott Sambucci's machine center. Today is day 250.

Job	Date Job Received	Production Days Needed	Date Job Due
1	215	30	260
2	220	20	290
3	225	40	300
4	240	50	320
5	250	20	340

Using the critical-ratio scheduling rule, in what sequence would the jobs be processed?

: **15.20** Given the following information about a product, what is the appropriate setup time?

Annual demand = 39,000 units

Daily demand = 150 units

Daily production = 1,000 units

Desired lot size (1 hour of production) = 150 units

Holding cost per unit per year = $10

Setup labor cost per hour = $40

DATA BASE APPLICATION

: **15.21** NASA's astronaut crew currently includes 10 mission specialists who hold Ph.D.s in either astrophysics or astromedicine. One of these specialists will be assigned to each of the 10 flights scheduled for the upcoming 9 months. Mission specialists are responsible for carrying out scientific and medical experiments in space or for launching, retrieving, or repairing satellites. The chief of astronaut personnel, a former crew member with 3 missions under his belt, must decide who should be assigned and trained for each of the very different missions. Clearly, astronauts with medical educations are more suited to missions involving biological or medical experiments, whereas those with engineering- or physics-oriented degrees are best suited to other types of missions. The chief assigns each astronaut a rating on a scale of 1 to 10 for each possible mission, with a 10 being a perfect match for the task at hand and a 1 being a mismatch. Only one specialist is assigned to each flight, and none is reassigned until all others have flown at least once.

	Mission									
Astronaut	Jan. 12	Jan. 27	Feb. 5	Feb. 26	Mar. 26	Apr. 12	May 1	Jun. 9	Aug. 20	Sep. 19
Vincze	9	7	2	1	10	9	8	9	2	6
Veit	8	8	3	4	7	9	7	7	4	4
Anderson	2	1	10	10	1	4	7	6	6	7
Herbert	4	4	10	9	9	9	1	2	3	4
Schatz	10	10	9	9	8	9	1	1	1	1
Plane	1	3	5	7	9	7	10	10	9	2
Certo	9	9	8	8	9	1	1	2	2	9
Moses	3	2	7	6	4	3	9	7	7	9
Brandon	5	4	5	9	10	10	5	4	9	8
Drtina	10	10	9	7	6	7	5	4	8	8

a) Who should be assigned to which flight?

b) We have just been notified that Anderson is getting married in February and he has been granted a highly sought publicity tour in Europe that month. (He intends to take his wife and let the trip double as a honeymoon.) How does this change the final schedule?

c) Certo has complained that he was misrated on his January missions. Both ratings should be 10's, he claims to the chief, who agrees to recompute the schedule. Do any changes occur over the schedule set in part (b)?

d) What are the strengths and weaknesses of this approach to scheduling?

■ Case Study ■

Old Oregon Wood Store

In 1998, George Brown started the Old Oregon Wood Store to manufacture Old Oregon tables. Each table is carefully constructed by hand, using the highest-quality oak.

The manufacturing process consists of four steps: preparation, assembly, finishing, and packaging. Each step is performed by one person. In addition to overseeing the entire operation, George does all of the finishing. Tom Surowski performs the preparation step, which involves cutting and forming the basic components of the tables. Leon Davis is in charge of the assembly, and Cathy Stark performs the packaging.

Although each person is responsible for only one step in the manufacturing process, everyone can perform any one of the steps. It is George's policy that occasionally everyone should complete several tables on his or her own without any help or assistance. A small competition is used to see who can complete an entire table in the least amount of time. George maintains average total and intermediate completion times. The data are shown in Figure 15.6 on page 618.

It takes Cathy longer than the other employees to construct an Old Oregon table. In addition to being slower than the other employees, Cathy is also unhappy about her current responsibility of packaging, which leaves her idle most of the day. Her first preference is finishing, and her second preference is preparation.

In addition to quality, George is concerned with costs and efficiency. When one of the employees misses a day, it causes major scheduling problems. Overtime is expensive, and waiting for the employee to return to work causes delay and sometimes stops the entire manufacturing process.

To overcome some of these problems, Randy Lane was hired. Randy's major duties are to perform miscellaneous jobs and to help out if one of the employees is absent. George has given Randy training in all phases of the manufacturing process, and he is pleased with the speed at which Randy has been able to learn how to completely assemble Old Oregon tables. Total and in-

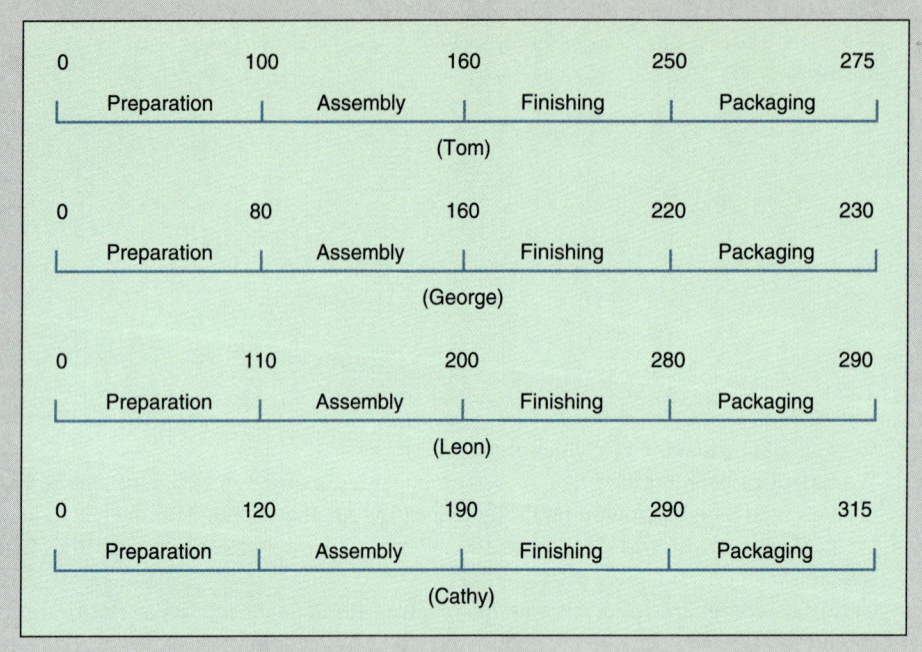

FIGURE 15.6 ■ Manufacturing Time in Minutes

```
0           100         160         250         275
|—Preparation—|—Assembly—|—Finishing—|—Packaging—|
                        (Tom)

0           80          160         220         230
|—Preparation—|—Assembly—|—Finishing—|—Packaging—|
                        (George)

0           110         200         280         290
|—Preparation—|—Assembly—|—Finishing—|—Packaging—|
                        (Leon)

0           120         190         290         315
|—Preparation—|—Assembly—|—Finishing—|—Packaging—|
                        (Cathy)
```

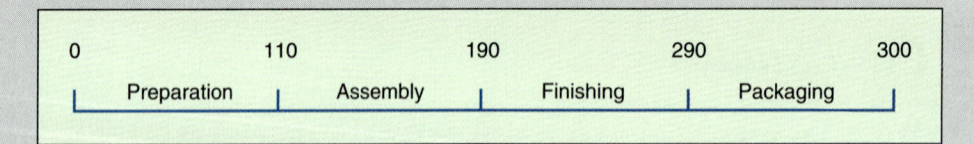

FIGURE 15.7 ■ Manufacturing Time in Minutes for Randy Lane

```
0           110         190         290         300
|—Preparation—|—Assembly—|—Finishing—|—Packaging—|
```

termediate completion times for Randy are given in Figure 15.7.

Discussion Questions

1. What is the fastest way to manufacture Old Oregon tables using the original crew? How many could be made per day?
2. Would production rates and quantities change significantly if George would allow Randy to perform one of the four functions and make one of the original crew the backup person?
3. What is the fastest time to manufacture a table with the original crew if Cathy is moved to either preparation or finishing?
4. Whoever performs the packaging function is severely underutilized. Can you find a better way of utilizing the four- or five-person crew than either giving each a single job or allowing each to manufacture an entire table? How many tables could be manufactured per day with this scheme?

Source: B. Render and R. M. Stair, *Quantitative Analysis for Management*, 6th ed. (Upper Saddle River, NJ: Prentice Hall, 1997).

BIBLIOGRAPHY

Akinc, U. "A Practical Approach to Lot and Setup Scheduling at a Textile Firm." *IIE Transactions* 25, no. 2 (March 1993): 54–64.

Anbil, R., E. Gelman, B. Patty, and R. Tanga. "Recent Advances in Crew-Pairing Optimization at American Airlines." *Interfaces* 21, no. 1 (January–February 1991): 62–74.

Bauer, A., J. Browne, R. Bowden, J. Duggan, and G. Lyons. *Shop Floor Control Systems*. New York: Van Nostrand Reinhold, 1991.

Ghosh, S., and C. Gaimon. "Production Scheduling in a Flexible Manufacturing System with Setups." *IIE Transactions* 25, no. 5 (September 1993): 21.

Gopalakrishnan, M., S. Gopalakrishnan, and D. M. Miller. "A Decision Support System for Scheduling Personnel in a Newspaper Publishing Environment." *Interfaces* 23, no. 4 (July–August 1993): 104–115.

Kim, Y., and C. A. Yano. "Heuristic Approaches for Loading Problems in Flexible Manufacturing Systems." *Industrial Engineering Research & Development* 25, no. 1 (January 1993): 26.

Morton, Thomas E., and David W. Pentico. *Heuristic Scheduling Systems*. New York: John Wiley, 1993.

Render, B., and R. M. Stair. *Quantitative Analysis for Management*, 6th ed. Upper Saddle River, NJ: Prentice Hall, 1997.

Schartner, A., and J. M. Pruett. "Interactive Job Shop Scheduling: An Experiment." *Decision Sciences* 22, no. 5 (November–December 1991).

Sivakumar, R. A., R. Batta, and K. Tehrani. "Scheduling Repairs at Texas Instruments." *Interfaces* 23, no. 4 (July–August 1993): 68–74.

Vollmann, T. E., W. L. Berry, and D. C. Whybark. *Manufacturing Planning and Control Systems*, 3rd ed. Homewood, IL: Irwin, 1992.

INTERNET RESOURCES

A Generic Approach to the Vehicle Dispatching Problem:
http://mjmi.engin.umich.edu/Conf/NO95/TALKS/TE14.2.html

Hierarchial Scheduling:
http://www.mech.kuleuven.ac.be/pma/project/complan/appsched.html

Scheduling Methods:
http://mjmi.engin.umich.edu/Conf/NO95/TALKS/TE03.html

Shop Floor Control:
http://www.business.sc.edu/business/CENTERS/TEMA25.HTM

Short-Term Scheduling in the Apparel Industry:
http://mjmi.engin.umich.edu/Conf/NO95/TALKS/TB08.3.html

Vehicle Routing & Dispatching for a Major US Blood Center:
http://www.informs.org/Conf/WA96/TALKS/TC18.3.html

Project Management 16

CHAPTER OUTLINE

GLOBAL COMPANY PROFILE: BECHTEL
THE STRATEGIC IMPORTANCE OF PROJECT MANAGEMENT
PROJECT PLANNING
   The Project Manager
   Work Breakdown Structure
PROJECT SCHEDULING
PROJECT CONTROLLING
PROJECT MANAGEMENT TECHNIQUES: PERT AND CPM
   The Framework of PERT and CPM
   Activities, Events, and Networks
   Dummy Activities and Events
   PERT and Activity Time Estimates
   Critical Path Analysis
   The Probability of Project Completion
   Case Study of PERT: Schware Foundry

COST-TIME TRADE-OFFS AND PROJECT CRASHING
APPLYING PROJECT SCHEDULING TO SERVICE FIRMS
A CRITIQUE OF PERT AND CPM
SUMMARY
KEY TERMS
USING POM FOR WINDOWS FOR PROJECT SCHEDULING
SOLVED PROBLEMS
DISCUSSION QUESTIONS
CRITICAL THINKING EXERCISE
PROBLEMS
DATA BASE APPLICATION
CASE STUDY: SHALE OIL COMPANY
INTERNET CASE STUDIES
BIBLIOGRAPHY
INTERNET RESOURCES

LEARNING OBJECTIVES

When you complete this chapter you should be able to:

Identify or Define:

   Work breakdown structure

   Critical path

   Event

   Activity

   Dummy activity

Describe or Explain:

   The role of the project manager

   Program evaluation and review technique (PERT)

   Critical path method (CPM)

   Crashing a project

GLOBAL COMPANY PROFILE:

Project Management Provides a Competitive Advantage for Bechtel

Fire-fighting crews relied on explosives and heavy machinery to remove the hardened petroleum residue that had formed around many wells. Even a day after a fire is out, the surface is still hot enough to boil water.

In the late fall of 1990, Iraq invaded Kuwait. In one final devastating act before Iraq's defeat in "Operation Desert Storm," Saddam Hussein torched the oil wells of Kuwait. To begin the rebuilding of its lands, the government of Kuwait called in one of the world's leading engineering and construction firms, Bechtel, which is headquartered in San Francisco. When the first three-member Bechtel advance team landed, within days of Desert Storm's end, the panorama of destruction was breathtaking.

Nearly 650 wells were ablaze, and others were gushing thousands of barrels of oil into dark lakes in the desert. Fire roared out of the ground from virtually every compass point.

Restoring the oil fields of Kuwait was a monumental project. There was no water, electricity, food, or facilities. Moreover, the country was littered with unexploded mines, bombs, grenades, and artillery shells. Finally, a good portion of the fires were inaccessible because lakes of oil-covered roads had spread to the ground surrounding many of the wells.

Even for Bechtel, whose competitive advantage is project management, this was a first-of-a-kind logistics problem. The number of specific project events that needed to be identified and accomplished was huge. Bechtel launched an on-site assessment effort, with a worldwide planning team to support the effort. A major global procurement program was needed. Bechtel equipment specialists in San Francisco, Houston, and London were called on to tap the company's computer network of buyers and suppliers worldwide.

About 550 miles to the southeast of Kuwait, at the port of Dubai, Bechtel established storage, docking, and

More than 200 lagoons filled with 1 million gallons of seawater were built. Pumps and hose lines to throw 6,000 gallons of water a minute were installed.

BECHTEL

The dense black clouds produced by burning oil wells turned day into night and added new meaning to "reading by firelight."

warehousing facilities. As a central transshipment point into Kuwait, the port received and processed hundreds of shipments from chartered seacraft and aircraft.

The Bechtel project management team procured, shipped, and deployed 125,000 tons of equipment and supplies, including some 4,000 pieces of operating equipment, ranging from bulldozers to ambulances. The team also managed a workforce that laid some 150 kilometers of pipeline, capable of delivering 20 million gallons of water a day to the fire site.

With the fires out, Kuwait again ships oil. And Bechtel has demonstrated its competitive advantage—project management.

Source: Adapted from *Bechtel Briefs* (San Francisco: Bechtel).

THE STRATEGIC IMPORTANCE OF PROJECT MANAGEMENT

- When the Bechtel project management team entered Kuwait, it quickly had to mobilize an international force of nearly 8,000 manual workers, 1,000 construction professionals, 100 medical personnel, and 2 helicopter evacuation teams. It also had to set up 6 full-service dining halls to provide 27,000 meals a day and build a 40-bed field hospital.
- When Microsoft Corporation set out to develop Windows 98—its biggest, most complex, and most important program to date—time was the critical thing for the project manager. With hundreds of programmers working on millions of lines of code in a program costing hundreds of millions to develop, immense stakes rode on the project being delivered on time.
- When Ford management decided to discontinue its fading former star, the Mustang, a group of Mustang loyalists at Ford persuaded the firm to let them take on the redesign. Promising a lower cost than the $1 billion that Ford had projected, the 450-member project team brought the new car on-line in 1994 for $700 million—25% faster and 30% cheaper than any comparable design project at Ford.

Bechtel, Microsoft, and Ford are just three examples of firms that face a modern phenomenon: growing project complexity and collapsing product/service life cycles. This change stems from awareness of the strategic value of time-based competition (noted in chapter 7) and a quality mandate for continuous improvement. Each new product/service introduction is a unique event—a project.

Moreover, every organization at one time or another will take on a large and complex project. The Hubbard Construction Company laying a highway in Orlando must complete thousands of costly activities. The U.S. State Department, installing and debugging an expensive computer system, spends months preparing the details for smooth conversion to new equipment. Avondale Shipyards in New Orleans requires tens of thousands of steps in constructing an oceangoing tugboat. A Shell Oil refinery about to shut down for a major maintenance project faces astronomical expenses if this difficult task is unduly delayed for any reason. Almost every industry worries about how to manage similar large-scale, complicated projects effectively.

Scheduling large, often one-time projects is a difficult challenge to operations managers and is one of the 10 OM decisions. The stakes in project management are high. Millions of dollars in cost overruns have been wasted due to poor planning on projects. Unnecessary delays have occurred due to poor scheduling. And companies have gone bankrupt due to poor controls.

Special projects that take months or years to complete are usually developed outside the normal production system. Project organizations within the firm are set up to handle such jobs and are often disbanded when the project is complete. The management of large projects involves three phases (see Figure 16.1):

1. *Planning.* This phase includes goal setting, defining the project, and team organization.
2. *Scheduling.* This phase relates people, money, and supplies to specific activities and relates activities to each other.
3. *Controlling.* Here the firm monitors resources, costs, quality, and budgets. It also revises or changes plans and shifts resources to meet time and cost demands.

We will begin this chapter with a brief overview of these functions. Three popular techniques to allow managers to plan, schedule, and control—Gantt charts, PERT, and CPM—are also described.

TEN DECISIONS OF OM

Managing Quality
Design of Goods & Services
Process Strategy
Location Strategies
Layout Strategies
Human Resources
Supply-Chain Management
Inventory Management
Scheduling
   Aggregate
   Short-Term
   Project
Maintenance

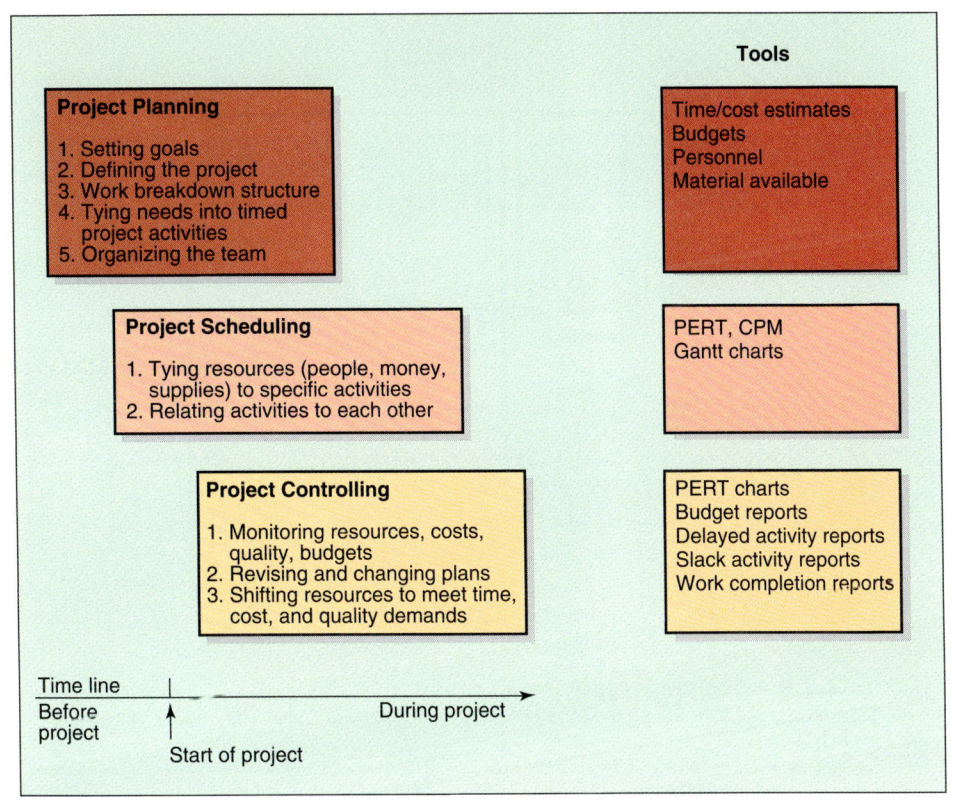

FIGURE 16.1 ■ Project Planning, Scheduling, and Controlling

PROJECT PLANNING

Projects can be defined as a series of related tasks directed toward a major output. A **project organization** is developed to make sure existing programs continue to run smoothly on a day-to-day basis while new projects are successfully completed.

A project organization is an effective way of pooling the people and physical resources needed for a limited time to complete a specific project. It is basically a temporary organization structure designed to achieve results by using specialists from throughout the firm. For many years, NASA successfully used the project approach to reach its goals. You may recall Project Gemini and Project Apollo. These terms were used to describe teams that NASA organized to reach space exploration objectives.

The project organization works best when

1. Work can be defined with a specific goal and deadline;
2. The job is unique or somewhat unfamiliar to the existing organization;
3. The work contains complex interrelated tasks requiring specialized skills;
4. The project is temporary but critical to the organization.

Project organization An organization formed to ensure that programs (projects) receive the proper management and attention.

The Project Manager

An example of a simplified project organization that is part of an ongoing firm is shown in Figure 16.2 on page 626. The project team members are temporarily assigned to the project and report to the project manager. The manager heading the project coordinates its ac-

When a project organization takes on a more permanent form, this is usually called a "matrix organization."

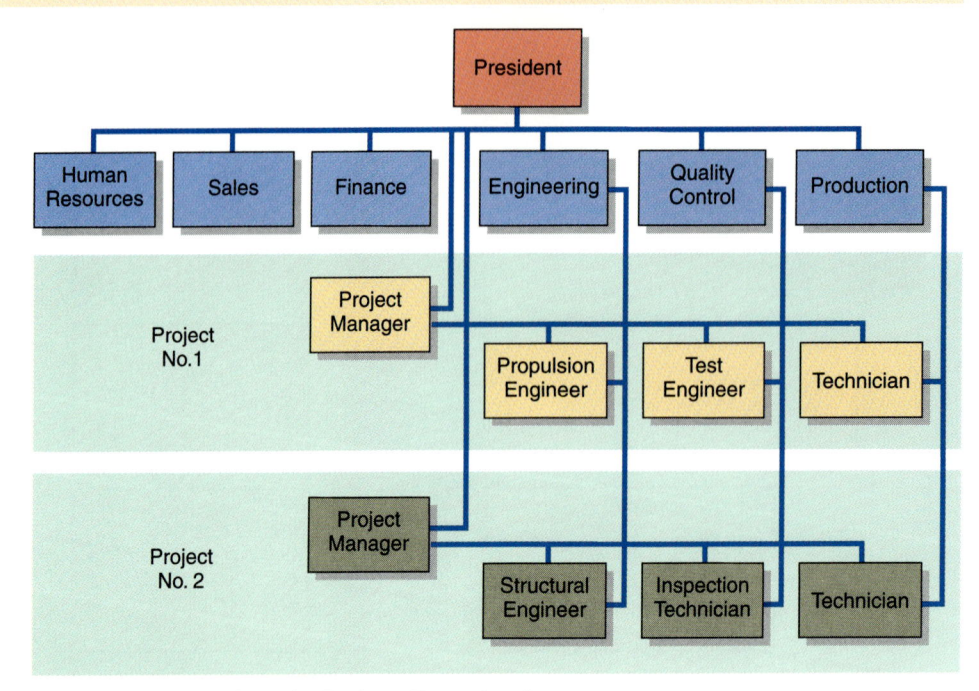

FIGURE 16.2 ■ A Sample Project Organization
Source: R.W. Mondy and S. R. Premeaux, *Management: Concepts, Practices and Skills,* 6th ed. (Boston: Allyn & Bacon, 1993), p. 247.

tivities with other departments and reports directly to top management, often the president, of the company. Project managers receive high visibility in a firm and are a key element in the planning and control of project activities.

Project managers are directly responsible for making sure that: (1) all necessary activities are finished in proper sequence and on time; (2) the project comes in within budget; (3) the project meets its quality goals; and (4) the people assigned to the project receive the motivation, direction, and information needed to do their jobs.

People are attracted to work on special projects because projects tend to be dynamic and exciting, providing team members with new challenges and new opportunities. Members get to meet workers from different areas of the firm, making new contacts. In addition, projects, such as developing and launching a new operating system at Microsoft, often inspire a special team spirit and boost in morale.

Work Breakdown Structure

The project management team begins its task well in advance of project execution so that a plan can be developed. One of its first steps is to carefully establish the project's objectives, then break the project down into manageable parts. This **work breakdown structure (WBS)** defines the project by dividing it into its major subcomponents (or tasks), which are then subdivided into more detailed components, and finally into a set of activities and their related costs. The division of the project into smaller and smaller tasks can be difficult, but is critical to managing the project and to scheduling success. Gross requirements for people, supplies, and equipment are also estimated in this planning phase.

Work breakdown structure (WBS)
Dividing a project into more and more detailed components.

The work breakdown structure typically decreases in size from top to bottom and is indented like this:

Level
1 Project
2   Major tasks in the project
3   Subtasks in major tasks
4   Activities (or "work packages") to be completed

This hierarchical framework can be illustrated with the development of Microsoft's operating system, Windows 98. As we see in Figure 16.3, the project, creating a new operating system, is labeled 1.0. The first step is to identify the major tasks in the project (level 2). Two examples would be development of graphic user interfaces or GUIs (1.1), and creating compatibility with previous versions of Windows (1.2). The major subtasks for 1.2 are creating a team to handle compatibility with Windows 3.1 (1.21), a compatibility team for Windows 95 (1.22), and compatibility with Windows NT (1.23). Then each major subtask is broken down into level-4 activities that need to be done, such as "importing files" created in Windows NT (1.231). There are usually many level-4 activities.

Level	Level ID Number	Activity
1	1.0	Develop/launch Windows 98 Operating System
2	1.1	Development of GUIs
2	1.2	Insure compatibility with earlier Windows versions
3	1.21	Compatibility with Windows 3.1
3	1.22	Compatibility with Windows 95
3	1.23	Compatibility with Windows NT
4	1.231	Ability to import files

FIGURE 16.3 ■ **Work Breakdown Structure**

PROJECT SCHEDULING

Project scheduling involves sequencing and allotting time to all project activities. At this stage, managers decide how long each activity will take and compute how many people and materials will be needed at each stage of production. Managers also chart separate schedules for personnel needs by type of skill (management, engineering, or pouring concrete, for example). Charts also can be developed for scheduling materials.

One popular project scheduling approach is the Gantt chart. **Gantt charts** are low-cost means of helping managers make sure that (1) all activities are planned for, (2) their order of performance is accounted for, (3) the activity time estimates are recorded, and (4) the overall project time is developed. As Figure 16.4 on page 628 shows, Gantt charts are easy to understand. Horizontal bars are drawn for each project activity along a time line. This illustration of a routine servicing of a Delta jetliner during a 60-minute layover shows that Gantt charts also can be used for scheduling repetitive operations. In this case, the chart helps point out potential delays. The *OM in Action* box on Delta (p. 628) provides additional insights. (An illustration of a Gantt chart is also provided in chapter 15, Figure 15.4.)

On simple projects, scheduling charts such as these can be used alone. They permit managers to observe the progress of each activity and to spot and tackle problem areas. Gantt charts, though, do not adequately illustrate the interrelationships between the activities and the resources.

Gantt charts Planning charts used to schedule resources and allocate time

OM IN ACTION

DELTA'S GROUND CREW ORCHESTRATES A SMOOTH TAKEOFF

Flight 199's 3 engines screech its arrival as the wide-bodied L-1011 jet lumbers down Orlando's taxiway with 200 passengers arriving from San Juan. In an hour, the plane is to be airborne again.

However, before this jet can depart, there is business to attend to: hundreds of passengers plus tons of luggage and cargo to unload and load; hundreds of meals, thousands of gallons of jet fuel, countless soft drinks and bottles of liquor to restock; cabin and restrooms to clean; toilet holding tanks to drain; and engines, wings, and landing gear to inspect.

The 12-person ground crew knows that a miscue anywhere—a broken cargo loader, lost baggage, misdirected passengers—can mean a late departure and trigger a chain reaction of headaches from Orlando to Dallas to every destination of a connecting flight.

Dennis Dettro, the operations manager for Delta's Orlando International Airport, likes to call the turnaround operation "a well-orchestrated symphony." Like a pit crew awaiting a race car, trained crews are in place for Flight 199 with baggage carts and tractors, hydraulic cargo loaders, a truck to load food and drinks, another to lift the cleanup crew, another to put fuel on, and a fourth to take water off. The "orchestra" usually performs so smoothly that most passengers never suspect the proportions of the effort. Gantt charts, such as the one in Figure 16.4, aid Delta and other airlines with the staffing and scheduling that are necessary for this symphony to perform.

Sources: New York Times (January 21, 1997): C1, C20; and *The Wall Street Journal* (August 4, 1994): B1.

PERT and CPM, the two widely used network techniques that we shall discuss shortly, *do* have the ability to consider precedence relationships and interdependency of activities. On complex projects, the scheduling of which is almost always computerized, PERT and CPM thus have an edge over the simpler Gantt charts. Even on huge projects, though, Gantt charts can be used as summaries of project status and may complement the other network approaches.

Gantt charts are an example of a widely used, nonmathematical technique that is very popular with managers because it is so simple and visual.

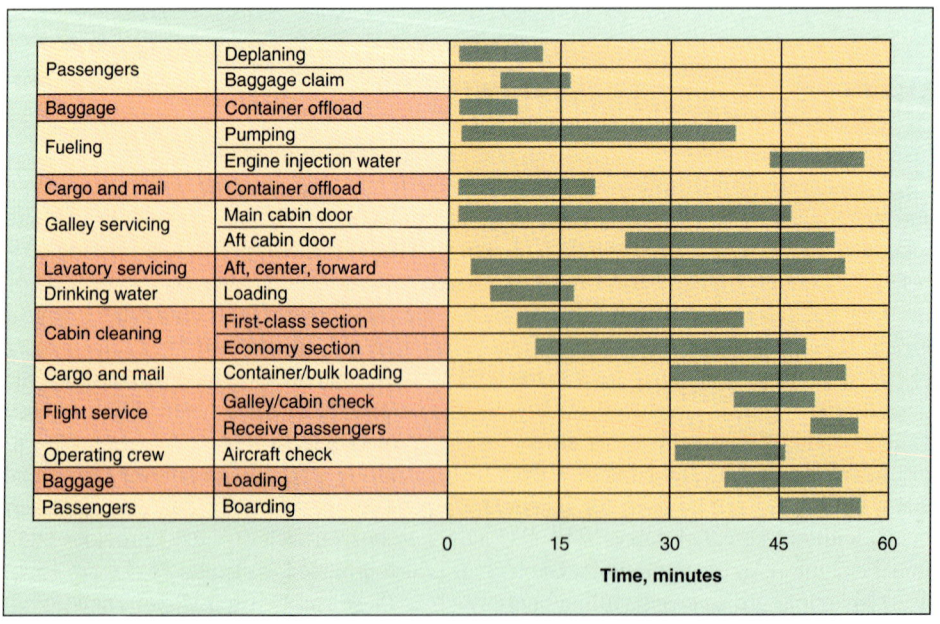

FIGURE 16.4 ■ Service Activities for a Commercial Jetliner during a 60-Minute Layover

To summarize, whatever the approach taken by a project manager, project scheduling serves several purposes:

1. It shows the relationship of each activity to others and to the whole project.
2. It identifies the precedence relationships among activities.
3. It encourages the setting of realistic time and cost estimates for each activity.
4. It helps make better use of people, money, and material resources by identifying critical bottlenecks in the project.

PROJECT CONTROLLING

The control of large projects, like the control of any management system, involves close monitoring of resources, costs, quality, and budgets. Control also means using a feedback loop to revise the project plan and having the ability to shift resources to where they are needed most. Computerized PERT/CPM reports and charts are widely available today on personal computers. Some of the more popular of these programs are Primavera (by Primavera Systems, Inc.), MS Project (by Microsoft Corp.), MacProject (by Apple Computer Corp.), Pertmaster (by Westminster Software, Inc.), VisiSchedule (by Paladin Software Corp.), and Time Line (by Symantec Corp.).

These programs produce a broad variety of reports including (1) detailed cost breakdowns for each task, (2) total program labor curves, (3) cost distribution tables, (4) functional cost and hour summaries, (5) raw material and expenditure forecasts, (6) variance reports, (7) time analysis reports, and (8) work status reports.

Due to the proliferation of microcomputer project management software, PERT/CPM have seen a resurgence of popularity in the 1990s.

PROJECT MANAGEMENT TECHNIQUES: PERT AND CPM

Program evaluation and review technique (PERT) and the **critical path method (CPM)** were both developed in the 1950s to help managers schedule, monitor, and control large and complex projects. CPM arrived first, in 1957, as a tool developed by J. E. Kelly of Remington Rand and M. R. Walker of duPont to assist in the building and maintenance of chemical plants at duPont. Independently, PERT was developed in 1958 by the Navy with Booz, Allen, and Hamilton.

The Framework of PERT and CPM

PERT and CPM both follow six basic steps:

1. Define the project and prepare the work breakdown structure.
2. Develop the relationships among the activities. Decide which activities must precede and which must follow others.
3. Draw the network connecting all of the activities.
4. Assign time and/or cost estimates to each activity.
5. Compute the longest time path through the network. This is called the **critical path**.
6. Use the network to help plan, schedule, monitor, and control the project.

Step 5, finding the critical path, is a major part of controlling a project. The activities on the critical path represent tasks that will delay the entire project unless they are completed on time. Managers can gain the flexibility needed to complete critical tasks by identifying noncritical activities and replanning, rescheduling, and reallocating resources such as labor and finances.

Program evaluation and review technique (PERT) A technique to enable managers to schedule, monitor, and control large and complex projects by employing three time estimates for each activity.

Critical path method (CPM) A network technique using only one time factor per activity that enables managers to schedule, monitor, and control large and complex projects.

Critical path The computed longest time path(s) through a network.

The Navy under the direction of Admiral Rickover successfully used PERT to build the first Polaris submarine ahead of schedule.

Although PERT and CPM differ to some extent in terminology and in the construction of the network, their objectives are the same. Furthermore, the analysis used in both techniques is very similar. The major difference is that PERT employs three time estimates for each activity. Each estimate has an associated probability of occurrence, which, in turn, is used in computing expected values and standard deviations for the activity times. CPM makes the assumption that activity times are known with certainty, and hence requires only one time factor for each activity.

For purposes of illustration, the rest of this chapter concentrates on a discussion of PERT. Most of the comments and procedures described, however, apply just as well to CPM.

PERT and CPM are important because they can help answer questions such as the following about projects with thousands of activities:

1. When will the entire project be completed?
2. What are the critical activities or tasks in the project—that is, the ones that will delay the entire project if they are late?
3. Which are the noncritical activities—the ones that can run late without delaying the whole project's completion?
4. What is the probability that the project will be completed by a specific date?
5. At any particular date, is the project on schedule, behind schedule, or ahead of schedule?
6. On any given date, is the money spent equal to, less than, or greater than the budgeted amount?
7. Are there enough resources available to finish the project on time?
8. If the project is to be finished in a shorter amount of time, what is the best way to accomplish this goal at the least cost?

Event An instant that marks the start or completion of a task or activity in a network.

Activity A task or a subproject in a CPM or PERT network that occurs between two events; a flow over time.

Activities, Events, and Networks

The first step in PERT is to divide the entire project into significant events and activities in accordance with the work breakdown structure. An **event** marks the start or completion of a particular task or activity. It is an instant in time. An **activity** is a task or a subproject that occurs between two events. Table 16.1 shows the symbols used to represent events and activities.

TABLE 16.1 ■ Events, Activities, and How They Relate

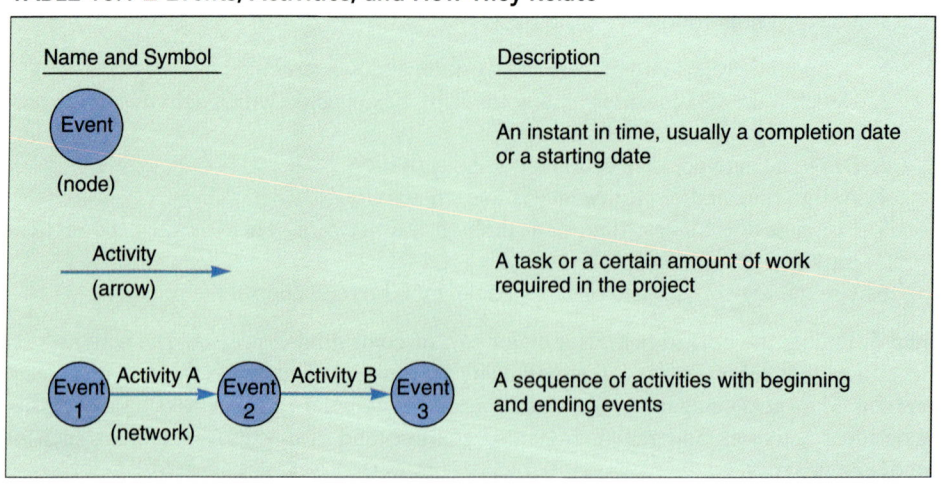

Name and Symbol	Description
Event (node)	An instant in time, usually a completion date or a starting date
Activity (arrow)	A task or a certain amount of work required in the project
Event 1 — Activity A → Event 2 — Activity B → Event 3 (network)	A sequence of activities with beginning and ending events

Project Management Techniques: PERT and CPM

This approach is the most common one in drawing networks and is also referred to as the **Activity-on-Arrow (AOA)** convention. A less popular convention, called **Activity-on-Node (AON)**, places activities on nodes. For simplicity, we will focus on AOA.

Any project that can be described by activities and events may be analyzed by a PERT **network**. A network, illustrated in Example 1, is a sequence of activities defined by starting and ending events.

Activity-on-Arrow (AOA) A network diagram in which arrows designate activities.

Activity-on-Node (AON) A network diagram in which nodes designate activities.

Network A sequence of activities defined by starting and ending events and the activites that occur between them.

EXAMPLE 1

Given the following information, develop an AOA network.

Activity	Immediate Predecessor(s)
A	—
B	—
C	A
D	B

In the AOA network below, we assign each event a number. It is also possible to identify each activity with a beginning and an ending event or node. For example, activity A is the activity that starts with event 1 and ends at node, or event, 2. Note that activity A immediately precedes activity C, which begins with event 2 and ends at event 4. In general, we number nodes from left to right. The beginning node, or event, of the entire project is number 1, and the last node, or event, in the entire project bears the largest number. The last node below shows the number 4.

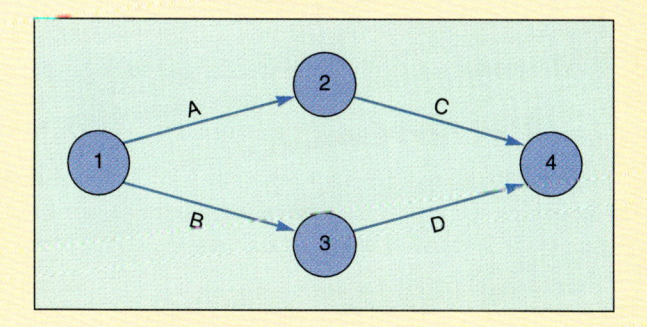

Alternatively, to provide a visual example of the activity-on-node (AON) approach, here is the network analogous to the one above.

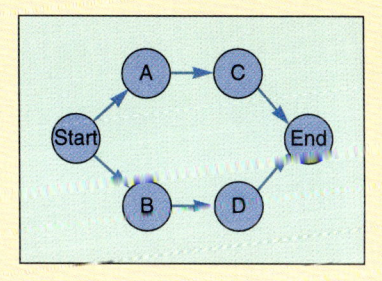

We can also specify networks by events and the activities that occur between events. Example 2 shows how to develop a network based on this type of specification scheme.

EXAMPLE 2

Given the following table, develop an AOA network.

Beginning Event	Ending Event	Activity
1	2	1–2
1	3	1–3
2	4	2–4
3	4	3–4
3	5	3–5
4	6	4–6
5	6	5–6

Instead of using a letter to signify activities and their predecessor activities, we can specify activities by their starting event and their ending event. Beginning with the activity that starts at event 1 and ends at event 2, we can construct the following network.

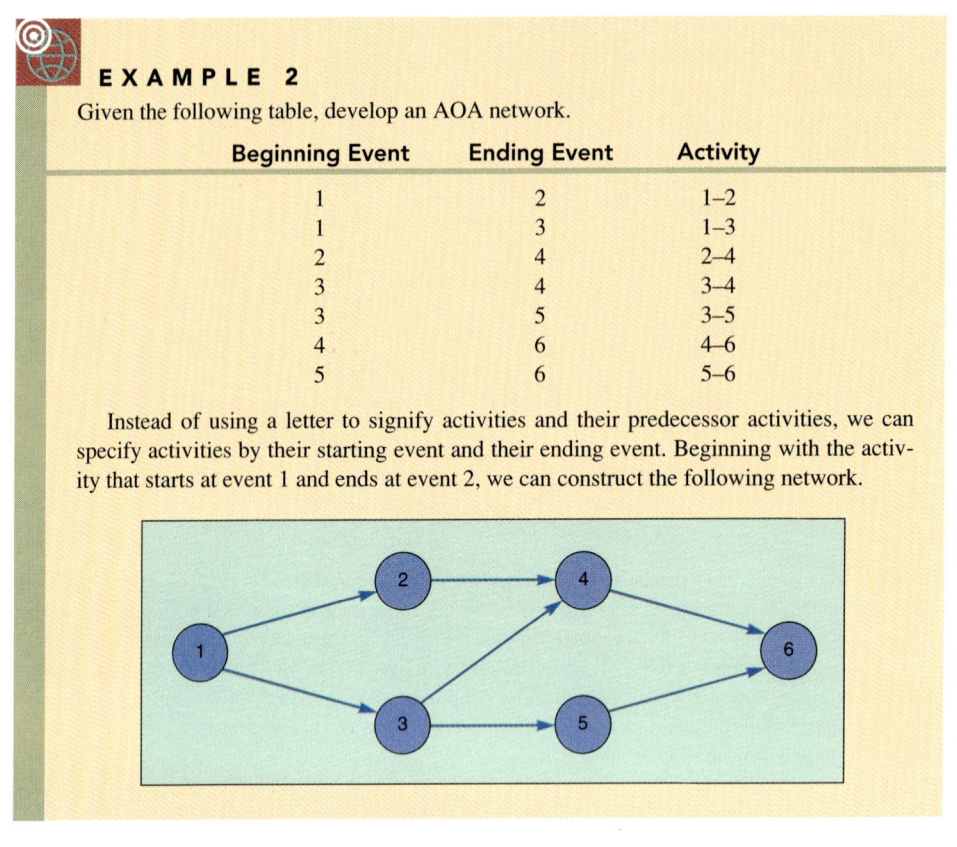

All that is required to construct a network is the starting and ending event for each activity.

Dummy Activities and Events

You may encounter a network that has two activities with identical starting and ending events. **Dummy activities** and events must be inserted into the network to deal with this problem (see Figure 16.5). The use of dummy activities and events is especially important

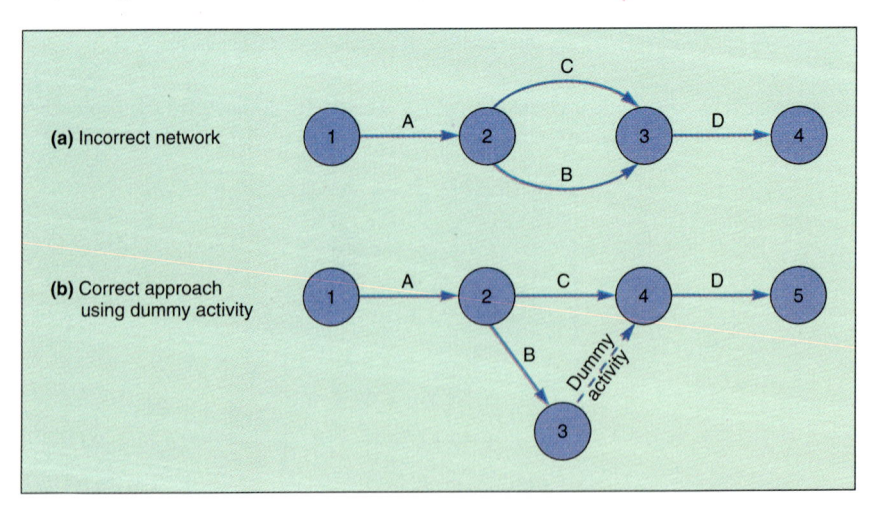

Dummy activities
Activities having no time, inserted into the network to maintain the logic of the network.

FIGURE 16.5 ■ **Incorrect and Correct Networks with Four Activities** *Activities B and C have identical starting and ending events.*

Project Management Techniques: PERT and CPM

when computer programs are to be employed in determining the critical path and project completion time. Dummy activities and events can also ensure that the network properly reflects the project under consideration. A dummy activity has a completion time, t, of zero. Example 3 illustrates the use of dummy activities.

EXAMPLE 3

Develop a network based on the following information:

Activity	Immediate Predecessor(s)	Activity	Immediate Predecessor(s)
A	—	E	C, D
B	—	F	D
C	A	G	E
D	B	H	F

Given these data, you might develop the following network.

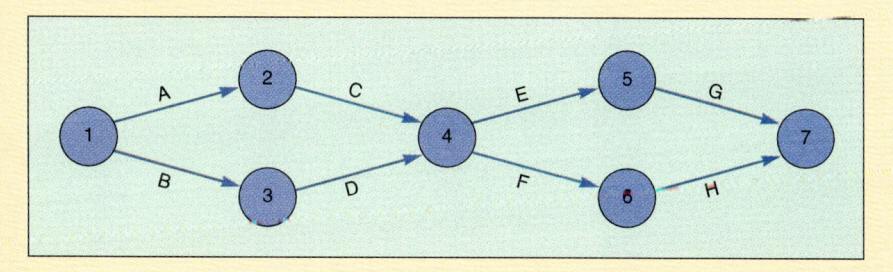

Look at activity F. According to the network, both activities C and D must be completed before we can start F, but in reality, only activity D must be completed (see the table). Thus, the network is not correct. The addition of a dummy activity and a dummy event can overcome this problem, as shown below.

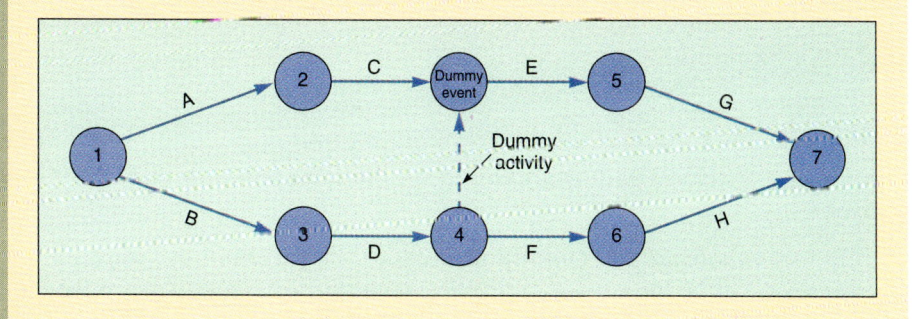

Now the network embodies all of the proper relationships and can be analyzed as usual.

PERT and Activity Time Estimates

As mentioned earlier, one distinguishing difference between PERT and CPM is the use of three **activity time estimates** for each activity in the PERT technique. Only one time factor is given for each activity in CPM.

For each activity in PERT, we must specify an **optimistic time**, a most **probable** (or most likely) **time**, and a **pessimistic time** estimate. We then use these three time estimates to calculate an expected completion time and variance for each activity. If we assume, as

Activity time estimates The time it takes to complete an activity in a network.

Optimistic time The "best" activity completion time that could be obtained in a PERT network.

Probable time The most likely time to complete an activity in a PERT network.

Pessimistic time The "worst" activity time that could be expected in a PERT network.

Beta probability distribution A mathematical distribution that may describe the activity time estimate distributions in a PERT network.

many researchers do, that activity times follow a **beta probability distribution**, we can use the formulas:[1]

$$t = \frac{a + 4m + b}{6} \quad \text{and} \quad v = \left(\frac{b - a}{6}\right)^2 \qquad (16.1)$$

where a = optimistic time for activity completion
b = pessimistic time for activity completion
m = most likely time for activity completion
t = expected time of activity completion
v = variance of activity completion time

In PERT, after we have developed the network, we compute expected times and variances for each activity. Example 4 shows these computations.

EXAMPLE 4

Compute expected times and variances of completion for each activity based on the following time estimates:

Activity	a	m	b
1–2	3	4	5
1–3	1	3	5
2–4	5	6	7
3–4	6	7	8

Activity	$a + 4m + b$	t	$\left(\dfrac{b-a}{6}\right)$	v
1–2	24	4	2/6	4/36
1–3	18	3	4/6	16/36
2–4	36	6	2/6	4/36
3–4	42	7	2/6	4/36

Critical Path Analysis

Critical path analysis A network model for finding the shortest possible schedule for a series of activities.

The objective of **critical path analysis** is to determine the following quantities for each activity:

- ES: Earliest activity start time. *All predecessor activities* must be completed before an activity can be started. The ending time of the predecessor activities is the earliest time an activity can be started.
- LS: Latest activity start time. *All following activities* must be completed without delaying the entire project. This is the latest time an activity can be started without delaying the entire project.
- EF: Earliest activity finish time.
- LF: Latest activity finish time.
- S: Activity **slack time**, which is equal to (LS − ES) or (LF − EF).

Slack time The amount of time an individual activity in a network can be delayed without delaying the entire project.

---

[1] Although the beta distribution has been widely used in PERT analysis for over 40 years, its applicability has been called into question. See M. W. Sasieni, "A Note on PERT Times," *Management Science* 32, no. 12 (December 1986): 1,662–1,663.

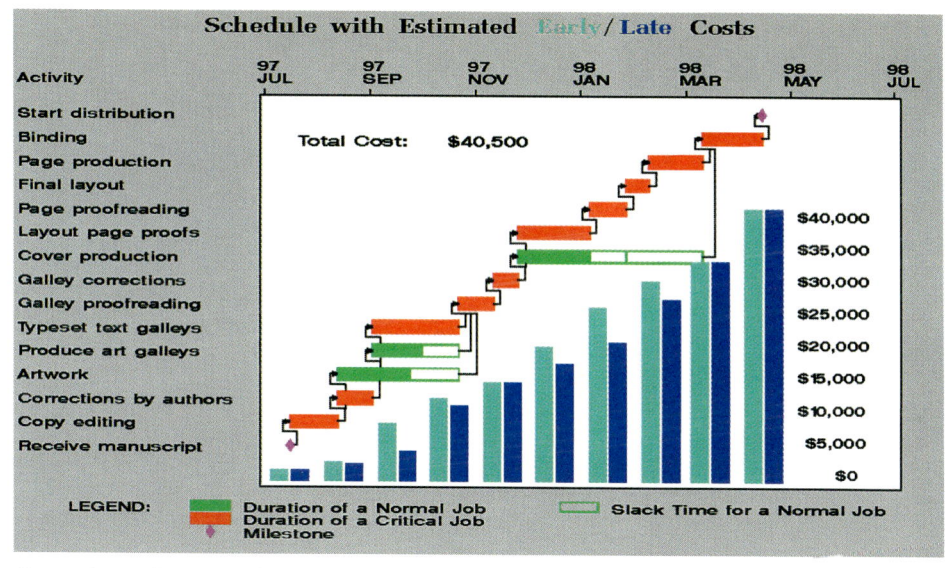

Gantt chart software, such as this one from the SAS Institute Inc. helps managers schedule projects easily. Time, resource, cost, and procedure constraints can be included to track project progress. Here, the SAS Gantt chart monitors the production of this textbook.

For any activity, if we can calculate ES and LS, we can find the other three quantities as follows:

$$EF = ES + t$$

$$LF = LS + t$$

$$S = LS - ES$$

or

$$S = LF - EF$$

Once we know these quantities for every activity, we can analyze the overall project. Typically, this analysis includes an examination of the following:

1. The critical path—the group of activities in the project that have a slack time of zero. This path is *critical* because a delay in any activity along it would delay the entire project.
2. *T*—the total project completion time, which is calculated by adding the expected time (*t*) values of those activities on the critical path.
3. *V*—variance of the critical path, which is computed by adding the variance (*v*) of those individual activities on the critical path.

Critical path analysis normally starts with the determination of ES and EF. Example 5 illustrates the procedure.

EXAMPLE 5

Given the following information, determine ES and EF for each activity.

Activity	t
1–2	2
1–3	7
2–3	4
2–4	3
3–4	2

In making a "forward pass," all activities must be completed before any activity can be started.

We find ES by moving from the starting activities of the project to the ending activities of the project. For the starting activities, ES is either zero or the actual starting date—say, August 1. For activities 1–2 and 1–3, ES is zero. (By convention, all projects start at time zero.)

There is one basic rule: Before an activity can be started, *all* of its predecessor activities must be completed. In other words, we search for the *longest* path leading to an activity in determining ES. For activity 2–3, ES is 2. Its only predecessor activity is 1–2, for which $t = 2$. By the same reasoning, ES for activity 2–4 also is 2. For activity 3–4, however, ES is 7. It has two predecessor paths: activity 1–3 with $t = 7$ and activities 1–2 and 2–3 with a total expected time of 6 (or $2 + 4$). Thus, ES for activity 3–4 is 7 because activity 1–3 must be completed before activity 3–4 can be started. We compute EF next by adding t to ES for each activity. See the following table.

Activity	ES	t	EF
1–2	0	2	2
1–3	0	7	7
2–3	2	4	6
2–4	2	3	5
3–4	7	2	9

In making a "backward pass," the latest time is computed by making sure the project would not be delayed for any activities.

The next step is to calculate LS, the latest starting time for each activity. We start with the last activities and work backward to the first activities to determine the latest possible starting time (LS) without making the earliest finishing time (EF) any later. This task seems more difficult than it really is. Example 6 shows how to calculate LS.

EXAMPLE 6

Determine LS, LF, and S (the slack) for each activity based on the following data:

Activity	t	ES	EF
1–2	2	0	2
1–3	7	0	7
2–3	4	2	6
2–4	3	2	5
3–4	2	7	9

The earliest time by which the entire project can be finished is 9 because activities 2–4 (EF = 5) and 3–4 (EF = 9) must *both* be completed. Using 9 as a basis, we now will work backward by subtracting the appropriate values of *t* from 9.

The latest time we can start activity 3–4 is at time 7 (or 9 − 2) in order to still complete the project by time period 9. Thus, LS for activity 3–4 is 7. By using the same reasoning, LS for activity 2–4 is 6 (or 9 − 3). If we start activity 2–4 at 6 and it takes 3 time units to complete the activity, we can still finish in 9 time units. The latest we can start activity 2–3 is 3 (or 9 − 2 − 4). If we start activity 2–3 at 3 and it takes 4 and 2 time units for activities 2–3 and 3–4, respectively, we can still finish on time. Thus, LS for activity 2–3 is 3. By using the same reasoning, LS for activity 1–3 is 0 (or 9 − 2 − 7).

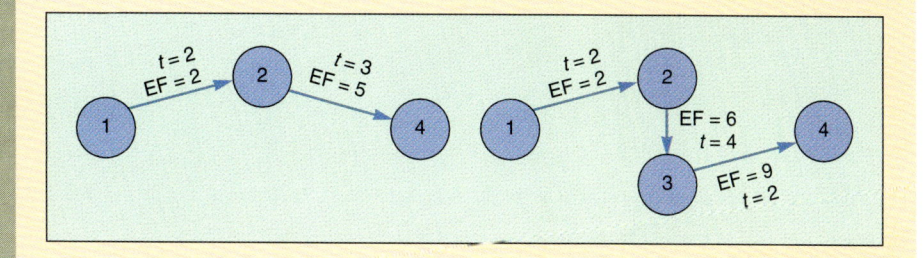

Analyzing activity 1–2 is more difficult because there are two paths. Both must be completed in 9 time units. Because both of the above paths must be completed, LS for activity 1–2 is computed from the most binding, or slowest, path. Thus, LS for activity 1–2 is 1 (or 9 − 2 − 4 − 2) and *not* 4 (or 9 − 3 − 2). Noting the following relationships, we can construct a table summarizing the results.

$$LF = LS + t$$

$$S = LF - EF$$

or

$$S = LS - ES$$

Activity	ES	EF	LS	LF	S
1–2	0	2	1	3	1
1–3	0	7	0	7	0
2–3	2	6	3	7	1
2–4	2	5	6	9	4
3–4	7	9	7	9	0

Once we have computed ES, EF, LS, LF, and S, we can finish analyzing the entire project. Analysis includes determining the critical path, project completion time, and project variance. Example 7 shows this procedure.

EXAMPLE 7

We have computed times, activity variances, and other information for the following network. What is the critical path, total completion time *T*, and project variance *V* of this network?

638 CHAPTER 16 PROJECT MANAGEMENT

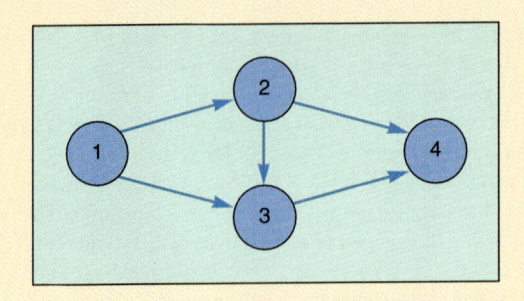

Activity	t	v	ES	EF	LS	LF	S
1–2	2	2/6	0	2	1	3	1
1–3	7	3/6	0	7	0	7	0
2–3	4	1/6	2	6	3	7	1
2–4	3	2/6	2	5	6	9	4
3–4	2	4/6	7	9	7	9	0

The critical path consists of those activities with zero slack. These are activities 1–3 and 3–4.

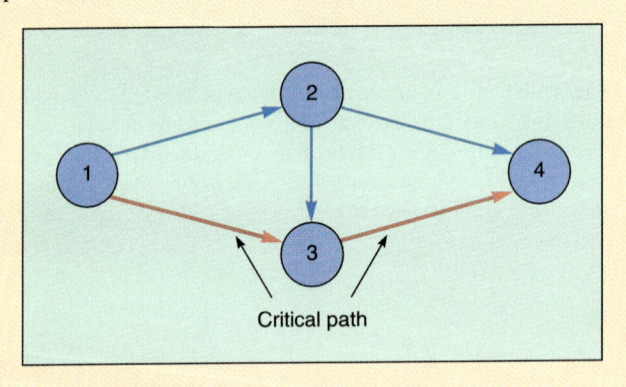

The total project completion time is 9 (or 7 + 2). The project variance is the sum of the *activity variances* along the *critical path*, which is 7/6 (or 3/6 + 4/6).

The Probability of Project Completion

Having computed the expected completion time T and completion variance V, we can determine the probability that the project will be completed at a specified date. If we make the assumption that the distribution of completion dates follows a normal curve, we can calculate the probability of completion as in Example 8.

EXAMPLE 8

If the expected project completion time T is 20 weeks and the project variance V is 100, what is the probability that the project will be finished on or before week 25?

$T = 20$

$V = 100$

σ = standard deviation = $\sqrt{\text{project variance}} = \sqrt{V} = \sqrt{100} = 10$

C = desired completion date = 25 weeks

The normal curve would appear as follows:

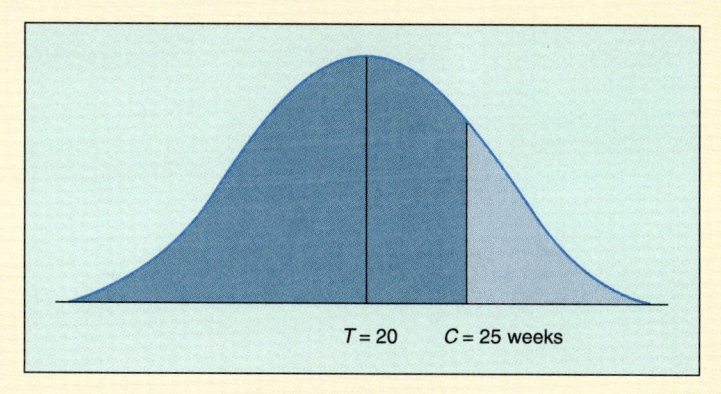

[Normal curve diagram with T = 20 and C = 25 weeks marked]

We solve for the probability by first computing Z:

$$Z = \frac{C - T}{\sigma} = \frac{25 - 20}{10} = .5$$

where Z equals the number of standard deviations from the mean. If we consult the normal curve table in Appendix I, we see that the area under the curve for Z = .5 is .6915. Thus, the probability of completing the project in 25 weeks is approximately .69, or 69%.

We must point out that probability analysis should be used with caution. For example, a noncritical path activity with a large variance could become a critical path activity. This occurrence would cause the analysis to be in error. Consider the network pictured in Figure 16.6. The critical path is 1–3 and 3–4 with $T = 12$ and $V = 4$. If the desired completion date is 14, the value of Z is 1 [or $(14 - 12)/\sqrt{4}$]. The chance of completion is 84%, from the normal distribution in Appendix I. But what would happen if activities 1–2 and 2–4 became the critical path? Because of the high variance, this event is not unlikely. With the same values for C and T, Z becomes 0.4 [or $(14 - 12)/\sqrt{25}$]. Looking at the normal distribution, we see that the chance of project completion is 66%. If activities 1–2 and 2–4 became the critical path, the chance of project completion would drop significantly due to the large total variance (25 = 16 + 9) of these activities. A simulation of the project could provide better data.

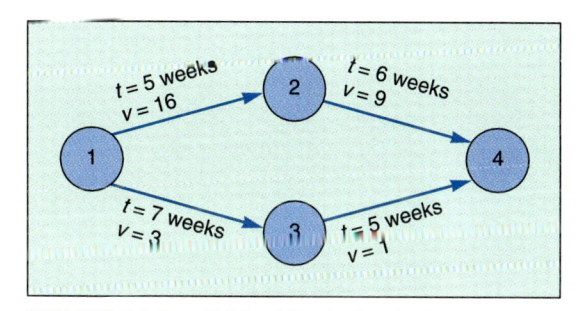

[Network diagram: Node 1 connects to Node 2 (t = 5 weeks, V = 16) and to Node 3 (t = 7 weeks, V = 3). Node 2 connects to Node 4 (t = 6 weeks, V = 9). Node 3 connects to Node 4 (t = 5 weeks, V = 1).]

FIGURE 16.6 ■ **Critical Path Analysis**

Case Study of PERT: Schware Foundry

Schware Foundry, Inc., a metalworks plant in Takoma Park, Maryland, has just decided to make a major investment in new air pollution control equipment. The plant, however, must be shut down during the installation process. Schware's board of directors estimates

640 CHAPTER 16 PROJECT MANAGEMENT

TABLE 16.2 ■ Activities and Immediate Predecessors for Schware Foundry, Inc.

Activity	Description	Immediate Predecessor(s)
A	Build internal components	—
B	Modify roof and floor	—
C	Construct collection stack	A
D	Pour concrete and install frame	B
E	Build high-temperature burner	C
F	Install control system	C
G	Install air pollution device	D, E
H	Inspection and testing	F, G

that the company can survive no more than 16 weeks without production in full swing. Alice Schware, the managing partner, wants to make sure that the installation progresses smoothly and on time.

All activities involved in the foundry project are shown in Table 16.2. We see in the table that before the collection stack can be constructed (activity C), the internal components must be built (activity A). Thus, activity A is the immediate predecessor to activity C. Likewise, both activities D and E must be performed just prior to installation of the air pollution device (activity G). The network for Schware Foundry is illustrated in Figure 16.7.

Table 16.3 shows Schware's optimistic, most probable, and pessimistic time estimates for each activity. It also reveals the expected time (t) and variance for each of the activities. Table 16.4 summarizes the critical path analysis for the activities and network. The total project completion time, 15 weeks, is seen as the largest number in the EF or LF columns of Table 16.4. Operations managers may refer to this as a *boundary time table*.

Probability of Project Completion The critical path analysis helped us determine that the foundry's expected project completion time is 15 weeks. Alice is aware, however, that there is significant variation in the time estimates for several activities. Variation in activities that are on the critical path can impact overall project completion, possibly delaying it. This is one occurrence that worries Alice considerably.

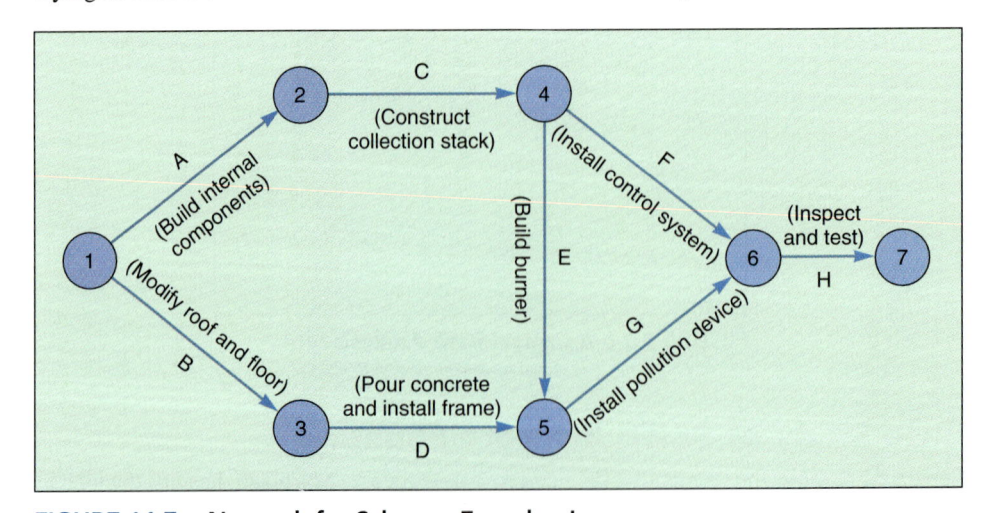

FIGURE 16.7 ■ Network for Schware Foundry, Inc.

TABLE 16.3 ■ Time Estimates (in weeks) for Schware Foundry, Inc.

Activity	Optimistic a	Most Probable m	Pessimistic b	Expected Time $t = (a + 4m + b)/6$	Variance $[(b - a)/6]^2$
A	1	2	3	2	$\left(\frac{3-1}{6}\right)^2 = \frac{4}{36}$
B	2	3	4	3	$\left(\frac{4-2}{6}\right)^2 = \frac{4}{36}$
C	1	2	3	2	$\left(\frac{3-1}{6}\right)^2 = \frac{4}{36}$
D	2	4	6	4	$\left(\frac{6-2}{6}\right)^2 = \frac{16}{36}$
E	1	4	7	4	$\left(\frac{7-1}{6}\right)^2 = \frac{36}{36}$
F	1	2	9	3	$\left(\frac{9-1}{6}\right)^2 = \frac{64}{36}$
G	3	4	11	5	$\left(\frac{11-3}{6}\right)^2 = \frac{64}{36}$
H	1	2	3	2	$\left(\frac{3-1}{6}\right)^2 = \frac{4}{36}$

TABLE 16.4 ■ Schware Foundry's Schedule and Slack Times

Activity	Earliest Start (ES)	Earliest Finish (EF)	Latest Start (LS)	Latest Finish (LF)	Slack (LS − ES)	On Critical Path?
A	0	2	0	2	0	Yes
B	0	3	1	4	1	No
C	2	4	2	4	0	Yes
D	3	7	4	8	1	No
E	4	8	4	8	0	Yes
F	4	7	10	13	6	No
G	8	13	8	13	0	Yes
H	13	15	13	15	0	Yes

PERT uses the variance of critical path activities to help determine the variance of the overall project. Project variance is computed by summing the variances of critical activities.

From Table 16.3 and equation (16.1), we know that

Critical Activity	Variance
A	4/36
C	4/36
E	36/36
G	64/36
H	4/36

Hence, the project variance = 4/36 + 4/36 + 36/36 + 64/36 + 4/36 = 3.111.

$$\text{Project standard deviation} = \sqrt{\text{project variance}}$$

$$= \sqrt{3.111} = 1.76 \text{ weeks}$$

In order for Alice to find the probability that her project will be finished on or before the 16-week deadline, she needs to determine the appropriate area under the normal curve in Figure 16.8. The standard normal equation can be applied as follows:

$$Z = \frac{\text{Due date } - \text{ Expected date of completion}}{\text{Standard deviation}} \quad (16.2)$$

$$= \frac{16 \text{ weeks } - 15 \text{ weeks}}{1.76 \text{ weeks}} = \frac{1}{1.76} = .57$$

where Z is the number of standard deviations the due date or target date lies from the mean or expected date.

Referring to the normal table in Appendix I, we find a probability of .71567. Thus, there is a 71.6% chance that the pollution-control equipment can be put in place in 16 weeks or less.

What PERT Was Able to Provide Schware Foundry PERT has thus far been able to provide Alice Schware with several valuable pieces of management information:

1. The project's expected completion date is 15 weeks.
2. There is a 71.6% chance the equipment will be in place within the 16-week deadline. Also, PERT can easily find the probability of finishing by any other date in which Alice is interested.
3. Five activities (A, C, E, G, H) are on the critical path. If any one of them is delayed for any reason, the whole project will be delayed.

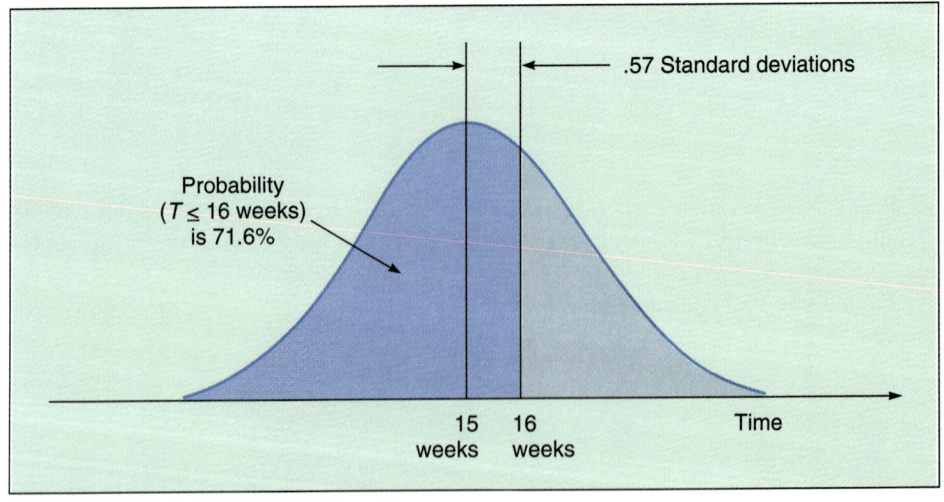

FIGURE 16.8 ■ **Probability of Schware Foundry's Meeting the 16-Week Deadline**

4. Three activities (B, D, F) are not critical but have some slack time built in. This means that Alice can borrow from their resources, and, if necessary, she may be able to speed up the whole project.
5. A detailed schedule of activity starting and ending dates has been made available (Table 16.4).

COST-TIME TRADE-OFFS AND PROJECT CRASHING

Until now, we have assumed that it is not possible to reduce activity times. This is usually not the case, however. Perhaps additional resources can reduce activity times for certain activities within the project. These resources might be additional labor, more equipment, and so on. Although shortening or "**crashing**" activity times can be expensive, doing so might be worthwhile. If a company faces costly penalties for being late with a project, using additional resources to complete the project on time might be economical. There may be fixed costs every day the project is in process. Thus, it might be profitable to use additional resources to shorten the project time and save some of the daily fixed costs. But what activities should be shortened? How much will this action cost? Will a reduction in the activity time in turn reduce the time needed to complete the entire project? Ideally, we would like to find the least expensive method of shortening the entire project.[2]

Crashing Shortening activity time in a network to reduce time on the critical path so total completion time is reduced.

Figure 16.9 shows cost-time curves for two activities. For activity 5–6, it costs $300 to complete the activity in 8 weeks, $400 for 7 weeks, and $600 for 6 weeks. Activity 2–4 requires $3,000 of additional resources for completion in 12 weeks and $1,000 for 14 weeks. Similar cost-time curves or relationships can usually be developed for all activities in the network.

The objective of crashing is to reduce the entire project completion time by a certain amount at the least cost. For each activity, there will exist a reduction in activity time and

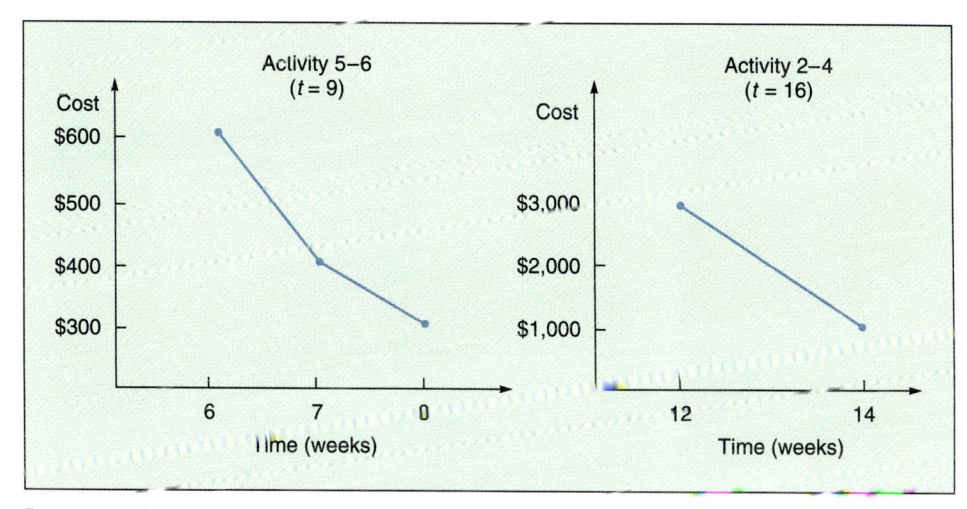

FIGURE 16.9 ■ Cost-Time Curves Used in Crashing Analysis

---

[2] The term *PERT/COST* is also used to describe cost-time trade-offs and crashing.

644 CHAPTER 16 PROJECT MANAGEMENT

Crashing is especially important when contracts for projects include bonuses or penalties for early or late finishes.

the cost incurred for that time reduction. For simplicity, we will assume that costs increase linearly as the activity time is reduced from its expected to its crash value. Let:

Normal time = expected time for an activity

Crash time = shortest possible time for that activity

Normal cost = cost of completing the activity in normal time

Crash cost = cost of completing the activity in the crash time

$$\text{Crash cost/time period} = \frac{\text{Crash cost} - \text{Normal time}}{\text{Normal time} - \text{Crash time}} \qquad (16.3)$$

With this information, it is possible to determine the least cost of reducing the project completion date. Example 9 illustrates the procedure.

EXAMPLE 9

Given the following information, determine the least cost of reducing the project completion time by 1 week.

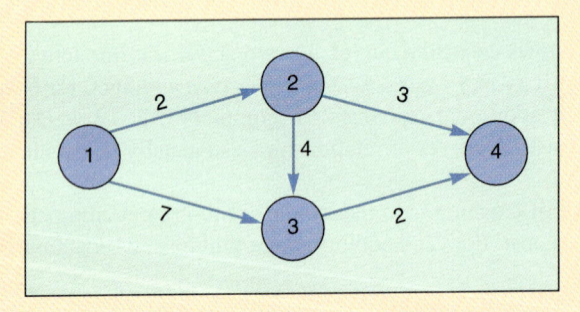

Activity	Normal or Expected time t (weeks)	Normal Cost	Crash Time (weeks)	Crash Cost	Activity	ES	EF	LS	LF	S
1–2	2	$ 100	1	$ 400	1–2	0	2	1	3	1
1–3	7	1,000	3	3,000	1–3	0	7	0	7	0
2–3	4	2,000	2	4,000	2–3	2	6	3	7	1
2–4	3	1,000	1	5,000	2–4	2	5	6	9	4
3–4	2	2,000	1	4,000	3–4	7	9	7	9	0

The first step is to compute the crash cost per week for each activity:

Activity	Normal Time − Crash Time	Crash Cost − Normal Cost	Crash Cost/week	Critical Path
1–2	1	$ 300	$ 300	No
1–3	4	2,000	500	Yes
2–3	2	2,000	1,000	No
2–4	2	4,000	2,000	No
3–4	1	2,000	2,000	Yes

APPLYING PROJECT SCHEDULING TO SERVICE FIRMS

The second step is to identify that activity on the critical path with the smallest crash cost per week. The critical path consists of activities 1–3 and 3–4. Because activity 1–3 has a lower crash cost per week, we can reduce the project completion time by 1 week, to 8 weeks, by incurring an additional cost of $500.

We must be very careful in using this procedure. Any further reduction in activity time along the critical path would cause activities on the path 1–2, 2–3, and 3–4 to also become critical. In other words, there would be *two* critical paths, and activities on both would need to be "crashed" to reduce project completion time.

> Remember that two or more critical paths may exist after performing project crashing.

APPLYING PROJECT SCHEDULING TO SERVICE FIRMS

PERT and CPM are certainly not tools that function only in manufacturing environments. Every firm needs to plan, schedule, and control large projects at one point or another. Here are two examples of how PERT and CPM are used in services.

Installing a New Computer System Figure 16.10 illustrates the steps involved in replacing one computer system with another at a large Denver consulting firm. The present computer is at capacity and no longer adequate. Additionally, the current software must be modified before it can be run on the new computer.

Relocating St. Vincent's Hospital When St. Vincent's Hospital moved from a 373-bed facility in Portland, Oregon, to a new 403-bed building in the suburbs approximately

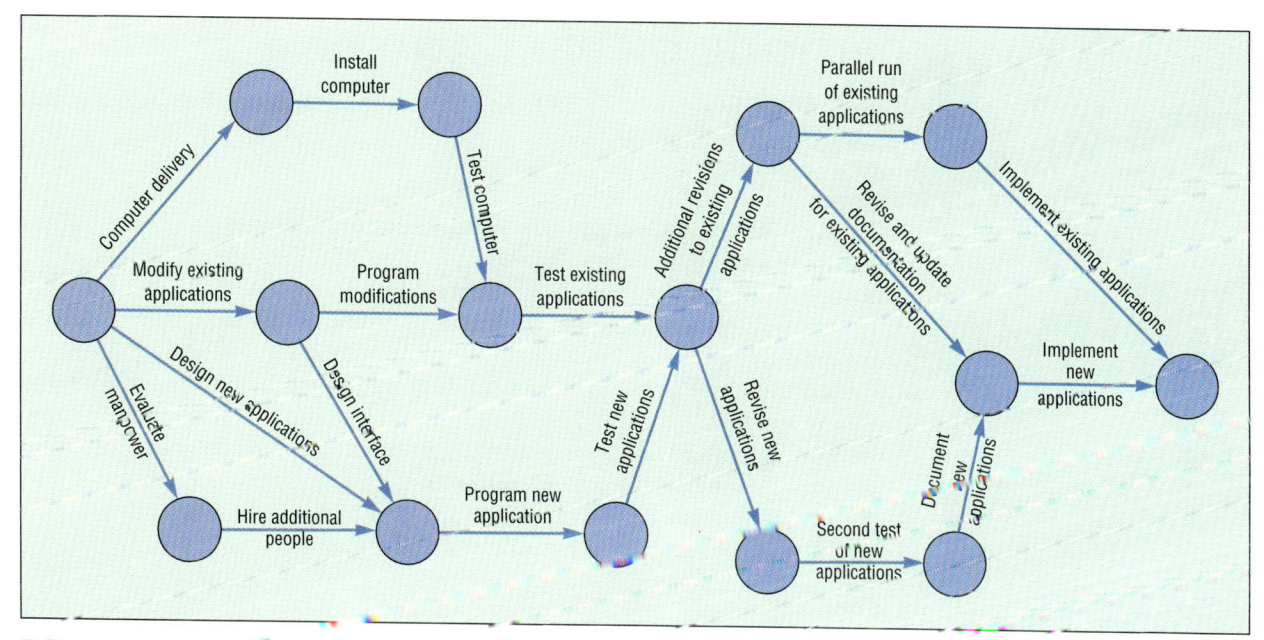

FIGURE 16.10 ■ **PERT Network Diagram for the Consulting Firm**

Source: S. A. Moscove and M. G. Simkin, *Accounting Information Systems*, 3rd ed. (New York: Wiley, 1987), p. 556. Copyright 1987 by John Wiley & Sons, Inc. Reprinted by permission of John Wiley & Sons, Inc.

OM IN ACTION

PROJECT MANAGEMENT AND SOFTWARE DEVELOPMENT

Although computers have revolutionized how companies conduct business and allowed some organizations to achieve a long-term competitive advantage in the marketplace, the software that controls these computers is often more expensive than intended and takes longer to develop than expected. In some cases, large software projects are never fully completed.

The London Stock Exchange, for example, had an ambitious software project called TAURUS that was intended to improve computer operations at the exchange. After numerous delays and cost overruns, however, the project, which cost hundreds of millions of dollars, was finally halted. The FLORIDA system, an ambitious software development project for the Department of Health and Rehabilitative Services (HRS) for the State of Florida, which was also delayed, cost $100 million more than expected, and didn't operate as everyone had hoped. While not all software development projects are delayed or over budget, it has been estimated that more than half of all software projects cost more than 189% of their original projections.

To control large software projects, many companies are now using project management techniques. Ryder Systems, Inc., American Express Financial Advisors, and United Airlines have all created project management departments for their software and information systems projects. These departments have the authority to monitor large software projects and make changes to deadlines, budgets, and resources used to complete software development efforts.

Sources: Computerworld (June 19, 1995): 25; Communications of the ACM (March 1995): 69–82; and D. H. Plummer, Productivity Management (Boston-Keane, Inc.) 1996.

In large networks there are too many activities to monitor closely, but we can concentrate on the critical activities.

5 miles away, a large variety of planning considerations had to be taken into account. Army vehicles and private ambulances had to be used to move patients; police escorts were needed; local stores would be affected by the move, among many other concerns. To coordinate all the activities, a project network was developed 8 months before the move. A *portion* of the large network is provided in Figure 16.11.

A CRITIQUE OF PERT AND CPM

As a critique of our discussions of PERT, here are some of its features about which operations managers need to be aware.

Advantages
1. Useful at several stages of project management, especially in the scheduling and control of large projects.
2. Straightforward in concept and not mathematically complex.
3. Graphical displays using networks help to perceive quickly relationships among project activities.
4. Critical path and slack time analyses help pinpoint activities that need to be closely watched.
5. Networks generated provide valuable project documentation and graphically point out who is responsible for various activities.
6. Applicable to a wide variety of projects and industries.
7. Useful in monitoring not only schedules, but costs as well.

Limitations
1. Project activities have to be clearly defined, independent, and stable in their relationships.
2. Precedence relationships must be specified and networked together.

SUMMARY

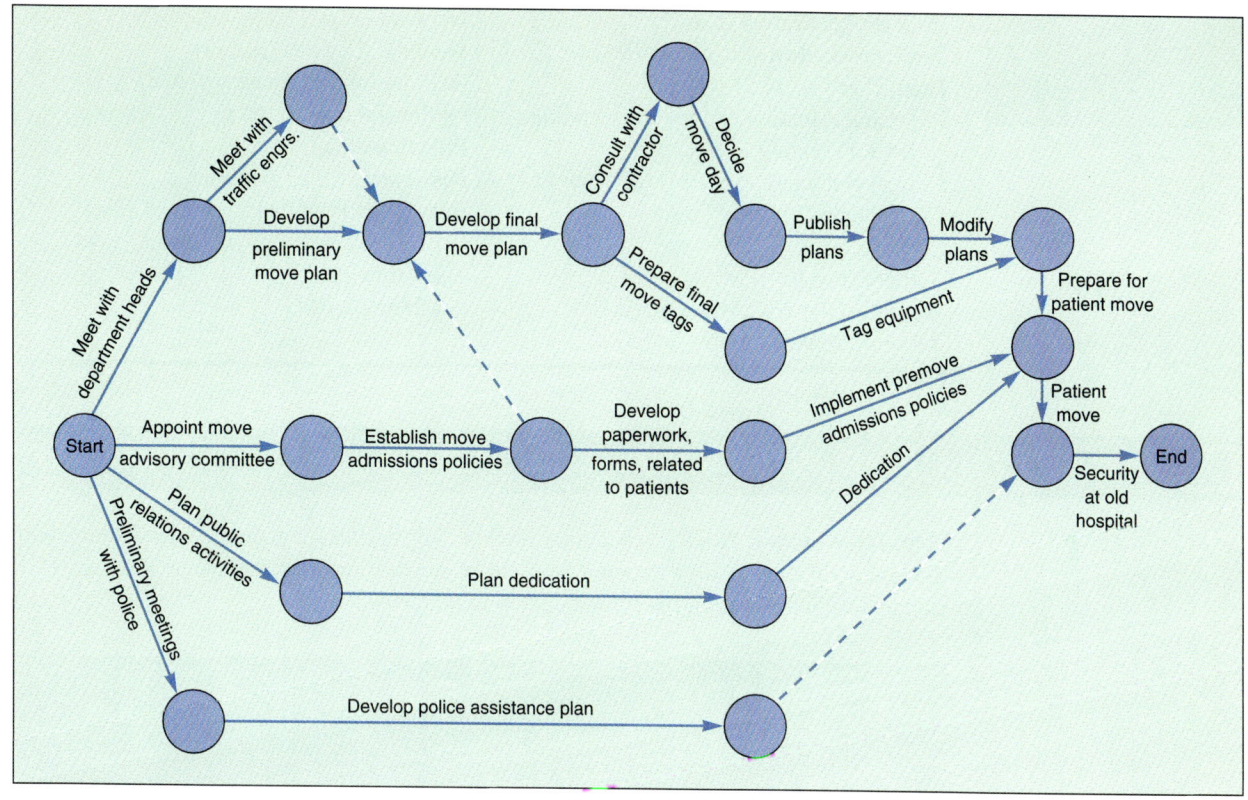

FIGURE 16.11 ■ **A Portion of St. Vincent's Hospital Project Network**
Source: Adapted from R. S. Hanson, "Moving the Hospital to a New Location," *Industrial Engineering*, November 1982. Copyright Institute of Industrial Engineers, 25 Technology Park/Atlanta, Norcross, GA 30092. Reprinted with permission.

3. Time estimates tend to be subjective and are subject to fudging by managers who fear the dangers of being overly optimistic or not pessimistic enough.
4. There is the inherent danger of too much emphasis being placed on the longest, or critical, path. Near-critical paths need to be monitored closely as well.

PERT, CPM, and other scheduling techniques have proven to be valuable tools in controlling large and complex projects. With these tools, managers understand the status of each activity and know which activities are critical and which have slack; in addition, they know where crashing makes the most sense. Projects are segmented into discrete activities, and specific resources are identified. This allows project managers to respond aggressively to global competition. Effective project management also allows firms to create products and services for global markets. A wide variety of software packages to help managers handle network modeling problems are available.

PERT and CPM do not, however, solve all the project scheduling and management problems of business and government. Good management practices, clear responsibilities for tasks, and straightforward and timely reporting systems are also needed. It is important to remember that the models we described in this chapter are only tools to help managers make better decisions.

CHAPTER 16 PROJECT MANAGEMENT

KEY TERMS

Project organization *(p. 625)*
Work breakdown structure (WBS) *(p. 626)*
Gantt charts *(p. 627)*
Program evaluation and review technique (PERT) *(p. 629)*
Critical path method (CPM) *(p. 629)*
Critical path *(p. 629)*
Event *(p. 630)*
Activity *(p. 630)*
Activity-on-arrow (AOA) *(p. 631)*
Activity-on-node (AON) *(p. 631)*
Network *(p. 631)*
Dummy activities *(p. 632)*
Activity time estimates *(p. 633)*
Optimistic time *(p. 633)*
Probable time *(p. 633)*
Pessimistic time *(p. 633)*
Beta probability distribution *(p. 634)*
Critical path analysis *(p. 634)*
Slack time *(p. 634)*
Crashing *(p. 643)*

USING POM FOR WINDOWS FOR PROJECT SCHEDULING

POM for Windows Project Scheduling module will find the expected project completion time for a CPM and PERT network with either one or three time estimates. Program 16.1 contains the input *and* output for the data in Example 6.

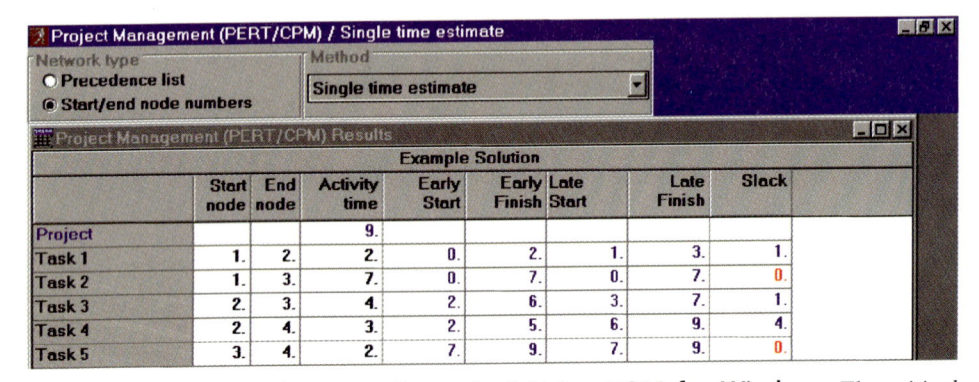

Example Solution

	Start node	End node	Activity time	Early Start	Early Finish	Late Start	Late Finish	Slack
Project			9.					
Task 1	1.	2.	2.	0.	2.	1.	3.	1.
Task 2	1.	3.	7.	0.	7.	0.	7.	0.
Task 3	2.	3.	4.	2.	6.	3.	7.	1.
Task 4	2.	4.	3.	2.	5.	6.	9.	4.
Task 5	3.	4.	2.	7.	9.	7.	9.	0.

PROGRAM 16.1 ■ **Solution to Example 6 Using POM for Windows** *The critical path consists of those activities that have zero slack, namely, Tasks 2 and 5 (i.e., Activities 1–3 and 3–4).*

SOLVED PROBLEMS

Solved Problem 16.1

Construct a network based on the following table.

Activity			
1–2	1–4	3–5	5–7
1–3	2–5	4–6	6–7

Solution

Solved Problem 16.2

Insert dummy activities and events to correct the following network:

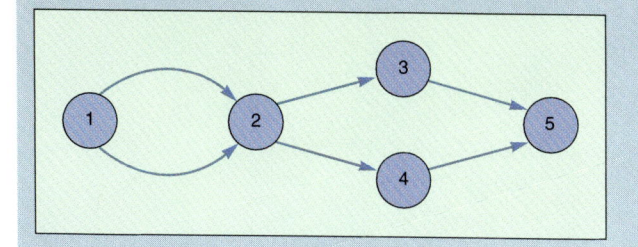

Solution

We can add the following dummy activity and dummy event to obtain the correct network:

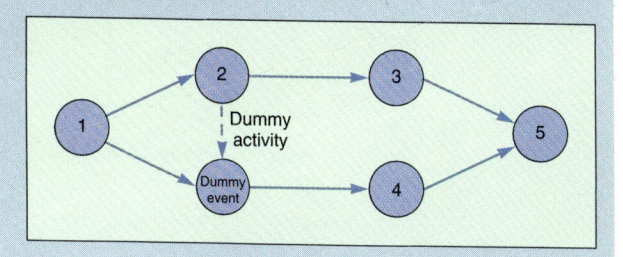

Solved Problem 16.3

Calculate the critical path, completion time T, and variance V based on the following information.

Activity	t	v	ES	EF	LS	LF	S
1–2	2	2/6	0	2	0	2	0
1–3	3	2/6	0	3	1	4	1
2–4	2	4/6	2	4	2	4	0
3–5	4	4/6	3	7	4	8	1
4–5	4	2/6	4	8	4	8	0
4–6	3	1/6	4	7	10	13	6
5–6	5	1/6	8	13	8	13	0

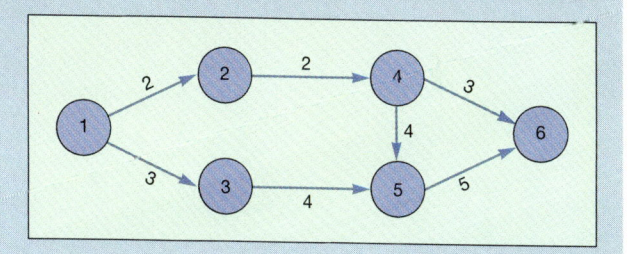

Solution

We conclude that the critical path is $1 \to 2 \to 4 \to 5 \to 6$.

$$T = 2 + 2 + 4 + 5 = 13$$

and

$$V = \frac{2}{6} + \frac{4}{6} + \frac{2}{6} + \frac{1}{6} = \frac{9}{6} = 1.5$$

Solved Problem 16.4

Given the following information, perform a critical path analysis.

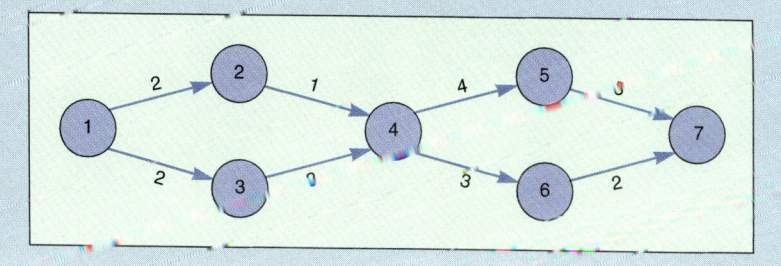

Activity	t	v	Activity	t	v
1–2	2	1/6	4–5	4	4/6
1–3	2	1/6	4–6	3	2/6
2–4	1	2/6	5–7	5	1/6
3–4	3	2/6	6–7	2	2/6

Solution

The solution begins with the determination of ES, EF, LS, LF, and S. We can find these values from the above information and then enter them into the following table:

Activity	t	v	ES	EF	LS	LF	S
1–2	2	1/6	0	2	2	4	2
1–3	2	1/6	0	2	0	2	0
2–4	1	2/6	2	3	4	5	2
3–4	3	2/6	2	5	2	5	0
4–5	4	4/6	5	9	5	9	0
4–6	3	2/6	5	8	9	12	4
5–7	5	1/6	9	14	9	14	0
6–7	2	2/6	8	10	12	14	4

Then we can find the critical path, T, and V. The critical path is 1-3, 3-4, 4-5, 5-7.

$$T = 2 + 3 + 4 + 5 = 14 \quad \text{and} \quad V = \frac{1}{6} + \frac{2}{6} + \frac{4}{6} + \frac{1}{6} = \frac{8}{6} = 1.33$$

Solved Problem 16.5

The following information has been computed from a project:

$T = 62$ weeks

$V = 81$

What is the probability that the project will be completed 18 weeks *before* its expected completion date?

Solution

The desired completion date is 18 weeks before the expected completion date, 62 weeks. The desired completion date is 44 (or 62 − 18) weeks.

$$Z = \frac{C - T}{\sigma} = \frac{44 - 62}{9} = \frac{-18}{9} = -2.0$$

The normal curve appears as follows:

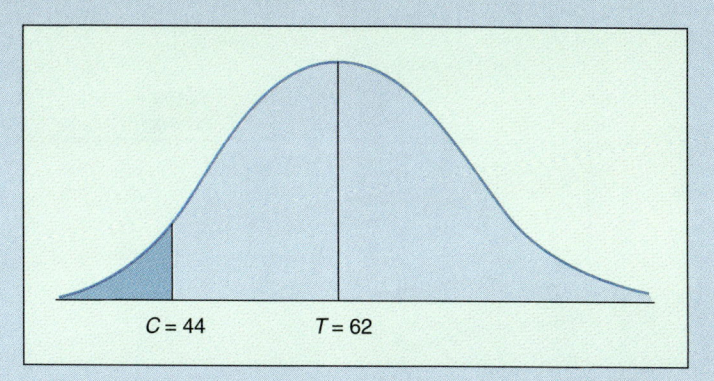

[Normal distribution curve with C = 44 on the left (shaded tail) and T = 62 at the center]

Because the normal curve is symmetrical and table values are calculated for positive values of Z, the area desired is equal to 1 − (table value). For Z = +2.0, the area from the table is .97725. Thus, the area corresponding to a Z value of −2.0 is .02275 (or 1 − 0.97725). Hence, the probability of completing the project 18 weeks before the expected completion date is approximately .02, or 2%.

Solved Problem 16.6

Determine the least cost of reducing the project completion date by 3 months based on the following information:

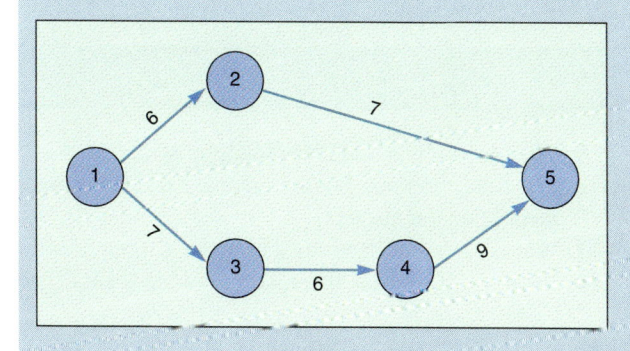

Activity	Normal Time (months)	Crash Time (months)	Normal Cost	Crash Cost
1–2	6	4	$2,000	$2,400
1–3	7	5	3,000	3,500
2–5	7	6	1,000	1,300
3–4	6	4	2,000	2,600
4–5	9	8	8,800	9,000

[Network diagram: Node 1 → Node 2 (6), Node 1 → Node 3 (7), Node 2 → Node 5 (7), Node 3 → Node 4 (6), Node 4 → Node 5 (9)]

Solution

The first step in this problem is to compute ES, EF, LS, LF, and S for each activity.

Activity	ES	EF	LS	LF	S
1–2	0	6	9	15	9
1–3	0	7	0	7	0
2–5	6	13	15	22	9
3–4	7	13	7	13	0
4–5	13	22	13	22	0

The critical path consists of activities 1–3, 3–4, and 4–5.
Next, crash cost/month must be computed for each activity.

Activity	Normal Time − Crash Time	Crash Cost − Normal Cost	Crash Cost/Month	Critical Path?
1–2	2	$400	$200/month	No
1–3	2	500	250/month	Yes
2–5	1	300	300/month	No
3–4	2	600	300/month	Yes
4–5	1	200	200/month	Yes

Finally, we will select that activity on the critical path with the smallest-crash cost/month. This is activity 4–5. Thus, we can reduce the total project completion date by 1 month for an additional cost of $200. We still need to reduce the project completion date by 2 more months. This reduction can be achieved at least cost along the critical path by reducing activity 1–3 by 2 months for an additional cost of $500. This solution is summarized in the following table:

Activity	Months Reduced	Cost
4–5	1	$200
1–3	2	500
	Total:	$700

DISCUSSION QUESTIONS

1. What are some of the questions that can be answered with PERT and CPM?
2. What is an activity? What is an event? What is an immediate predecessor?
3. Describe how expected activity times and variances can be computed in a PERT network.
4. Briefly discuss what is meant by critical path analysis. What are critical path activities and why are they important?
5. What are the earliest activity start time and latest activity start time, and how are they computed?
6. Describe the meaning of slack and discuss how it can be determined.
7. How can we determine the probability that a project will be completed by a certain date? What assumptions are made in this computation?
8. Briefly describe the concept of cost/time trade-off and how it is used.
9. What is crashing and how is it done by hand?
10. What are the three phases involved in the management of a large project?
11. What is a dummy activity and when is it required?
12. What is the basic difference between PERT and CPM?
13. How is the variance of the total project computed in PERT?
14. How is the expected completion time of a PERT project computed?
15. What is a project organization?
16. Describe the differences between a Gantt chart and a PERT/CPM network.
17. Name some of the widely used project management software programs.
18. What is the difference between an activity-on-arrow (AOA) network and an activity-on-node (AON) network? Which is primarily used in this chapter?

CRITICAL THINKING EXERCISE

The *OM in Action* box (p. 628) in this chapter that describes Delta Airlines' "well-orchestrated" ground turnaround procedures deals with a serious issue for all airlines. As a matter of fact, *The Wall Street Journal* article "New Airline Fad: Faster Airport Turnarounds" (August 4, 1994, pp. B1–B2) describes similar scheduling improvements at USAir, Continental, and Southwest. For years, Southwest has turned its planes around in 15 minutes.

Provide detailed suggestions as to how airlines can speed up turnaround times. What are Southwest's processes? What problems keep other airlines from emulating Southwest? Which is the preferable tool for turnaround analysis—Gantt charts or PERT/CPM, and why?

PROBLEMS

- **16.1** Draw the PERT network associated with the following activities for Bill Beville's next homework project.

Activity	Immediate Predecessor(s)	Activity	Immediate Predecessor(s)
A	—	E	B
B	A	F	C
C	A	G	D
D	B	H	E, F

- **16.2** Given the activities whose sequence is described by the following table, draw the appropriate PERT diagram.

Activity	Immediate Predecessor(s)	Activity	Immediate Predecessor(s)
A	—	F	C
B	A	G	E, F
C	A	H	D
D	B	I	G, H
E	B		

- **16.3** The following represent activities in Joan Blasco-Paul's Construction Company project. Draw the network to represent this situation.

Activity	Immediate Predecessor(s)	Activity	Immediate Predecessor(s)
A	—	E	B
B	—	F	C, E
C	A	G	D
D	B	H	F, G

- **16.4** Sally McPherson is the personnel director of Babson and Willcount, a company that specializes in consulting and research. One of the programs that Sally is considering for the middle-level managers is leadership training. Sally has listed a number of activities that must be completed before a training program of this nature could be conducted. The ac-

654 CHAPTER 16 PROJECT MANAGEMENT

tivities and immediate predecessors appear in the accompanying table. Develop a network for this problem.

Activity	Immediate Predecessor(s)	Activity	Immediate Predecessor(s)
A	—	E	A, D
B	—	F	C
C	—	G	E, F
D	B		

- 16.5 Sally McPherson was able to determine the activity times for the leadership training program. She would like to determine the total project completion time and the critical path. The activity times appear in the accompanying table. (See Problem 16.4).

Activity	Time (Days)
A	2
B	5
C	1
D	10
E	3
F	6
G	8
Total:	35 days

- 16.6 A large playground for the new town square in Celebration, Florida, is in the planning stages. Here are the six activities to be completed:

Activity	Hours needed	Immediate Predecessor(s)
Planning (A)	20	—
Buying supplies (B)	60	Planning (A)
Digging/grading (C)	100	Planning (A)
Sawing lumber (D)	30	Buying supplies (B)
Placing lumber (E)	20	Digging/grading (C) and Sawing (D)
Assembly/painting (F)	10	Placing lumber (E)

  a) Develop an activity-on-arrow (AOA) network for this project.
  b) What is the project completion time?

- 16.7 Refer to Problem 16.6. Develop an activity-on-node (AON) network for the project.
- 16.8 The activities needed to build an experimental weed-harvesting machine at Bill Bilderback Machinery Corp. are listed in the accompanying table. Construct a network for these activities.

Activity	Immediate Predecessor(s)	Activity	Immediate Predecessor(s)
A	—	E	B
B	—	F	B
C	A	G	C, E
D	A	H	D, F

- 16.9 Bill Bilderback (see Problem 16.8) was able to determine the activity times for constructing his weed-harvesting machine. Bilderback would like to determine ES, EF, LS, LF, and slack for each activity. The total project completion time and the critical path should also be determined. Here are the activity times:

Activity	Time (weeks)	Activity	Time (weeks)
A	6	E	4
B	5	F	6
C	3	G	10
D	2	H	7

- **16.10** Riddick Wiring and Electric installs wiring and electrical fixtures in residential construction. Anne Riddick has been very concerned with the amount of time it takes to complete wiring jobs. Some of her workers are very unreliable. A list of activities and their optimistic completion time, the most likely completion time and the pessimistic completion time (all in days) are given in the table below.
Determine the expected completion time and variance for each activity.

Activity	a	m	b	Immediate Predecessor(s)
A	3	6	8	—
B	2	4	4	—
C	1	2	3	—
D	6	7	8	C
E	2	4	6	B, D
F	6	10	14	A, E
G	1	2	4	A, E
H	3	6	9	F
I	10	11	12	G
J	14	16	20	C
K	2	8	10	H, I

- **16.11** Anne Riddick would like to determine the total project completion time and the critical path for installing electrical wiring and equipment in residential houses. See Problem 16.10 for details. In addition, determine ES, EF, LS, LF, and slack for each activity.
- **16.12** What is the probability that Riddick Wiring and Electric will finish the project described in Problems 16.10 and 16.11 in 40 days or less?
- **16.13** The activities described by the following table are given for the Bragg Corporation:

Activity	Immediate Predecessor(s)	Time
A	—	9
B	A	7
C	A	3
D	B	6
E	B	9
F	C	4
G	F, F	6
H	D	5
I	G, H	3

a) Draw the appropriate PERT diagram for John Bragg's management team.
b) Find the critical path.

: 16.14 A small software development project at Jack McGarrie's firm has five major activities. The times are estimated and provided in the table below. Find the expected time for completing McGarrie's project.

Activity	Immediate Predecessor	a	m	b
A	—	2	5	8
B	—	3	6	9
C	A	4	7	10
D	B	2	5	14
E	C	3	3	3

a) What is the expected completion time for this project?
b) What variance value would be used in finding probabilities of finishing by a certain time?

: 16.15 Given the activities described by the following table:

Activity	Expected Time	Standard Deviation of Time Estimate	Immediate Predecessor(s)
A	7	2	—
B	3	1	A
C	9	3	A
D	4	1	B, C
E	5	1	B, C
F	8	2	E
G	8	1	D, F
H	6	2	G

a) Draw the appropriate PERT diagram.
b) Find the critical path and project completion time.
c) Find the probability that the project will take more than 49 time periods to complete.

: 16.16 Development of a new deluxe version of a particular software product is being considered by Kathy Buhrow's software house. The activities necessary for the completion of this are listed in the table below.

Activity	Normal Time	Crash Time	Normal Cost	Crash Cost	Immediate Predecessor(s)
A	4	3	$2,000	$2,600	—
B	2	1	2,200	2,800	—
C	3	3	500	500	—
D	8	4	2,300	2,600	A
E	6	3	900	1,200	B
F	3	2	3,000	4,200	C
G	4	2	1,400	2,000	D, E

a) What is the project completion date?
b) What is the total cost required for completing this project on normal time?
c) If you wish to reduce the time required to complete this project by 1 week, which activity should be crashed, and how much will this increase the total cost?

: 16.17 A project in Julie Burgmeier's company has an expected completion time of 40 weeks and a standard deviation of 5 weeks. It is assumed that the project completion time is normally distributed.
a) What is the probability of finishing the project in 50 weeks or less?

b) What is the probability of finishing the project in 38 weeks or less?
c) The due date for the project is set so that there is a 90% chance that the project will be finished by this date. What is the due date?

: **16.18** B&R Manufacturing produces custom-built pollution-control devices for medium-sized steel mills. The most recent project undertaken by B&R requires 14 different activities. B&R's managers would like to determine the total project completion time and those activities that lie along the critical path. The appropriate data are shown in the table below.

Activity	Immediate Predecessor(s)	Optimistic Time	Most Likely Time	Pessimistic Time
A	—	4	6	7
B	—	1	2	3
C	A	6	6	6
D	A	5	8	11
E	B, C	1	9	18
F	D	2	3	6
G	D	1	7	8
H	E, F	4	4	6
I	G, H	1	6	8
J	I	2	5	7
K	I	8	9	11
L	J	2	4	6
M	K	1	2	3
N	L, M	6	8	10

: **16.19** Bill Trigiero, director of personnel of Trigiero Resources, Inc., is in the process of designing a program that his customers can use in the job-finding process. Some of the activities include preparing résumés, writing letters, making appointments to see prospective employers, researching companies and industries, and so on. Some of the information on the activities appears in the following table:

Activity	a	m	b	Immediate Predecessor(s)
A	8	10	12	—
B	6	7	9	—
C	3	3	4	—
D	10	20	30	A
E	6	7	8	C
F	9	10	11	B, D, E
G	6	7	10	B, D, E
H	14	15	16	F
I	10	11	13	F
J	6	7	8	G, H
K	4	7	8	I, J
L	1	2	4	G, H

a) Construct a network for this problem.
b) Determine the expected times and variances for each activity.
c) Determine ES, EF, LS, LF, and slack for each activity.
d) Determine the critical path and project completion time.
e) Determine the probability that the project will be finished in 70 days.

f) Determine the probability that the project will be finished in 80 days.
g) Determine the probability that the project will be finished in 90 days.

: 16.20 Using PERT, Brooke Cashion was able to determine that the expected project completion time for the construction of a pleasure yacht is 21 months and the project variance is 4.
a) What is the probability that the project will be completed in 17 months?
b) What is the probability that the project will be completed in 20 months?
c) What is the probability that the project will be completed in 23 months?
d) What is the probability that the project will be completed in 25 months?

: 16.21 Cole Builders manufactures steel storage sheds for commercial use. David Cole, president of Cole Builders, is contemplating producing sheds for home use. The activities necessary to build an experimental model and related data are given in the accompanying table.

Activity	Normal Time	Crash Time	Normal Cost ($)	Crash Cost ($)	Immediate Predecessor(s)
A	3	2	1,000	1,600	—
B	2	1	2,000	2,700	—
C	1	1	300	300	—
D	7	3	1,300	1,600	A
E	6	3	850	1,000	B
F	2	1	4,000	5,000	C
G	4	2	1,500	2,000	D, E

a) What is the project completion date?
b) Crash this project to 7 weeks (which is the maximum it can be crashed) at the least cost.

: 16.22 The Maser is a new custom-designed sports car. An analysis of the task of building the Maser reveals the following list of relevant activities, their immediate predecessors, and their duration.[3]

Job Letter	Description	Immediate Predecessor(s)	Normal Time (Days)
A	Start	—	0
B	Design	A	8
C	Order special accessories	B	0.1
D	Build frame	B	1
E	Build doors	B	1
F	Attach axles, wheels, gas tank	D	1
G	Build body shell	B	2
H	Build transmission and drivetrain	B	3
I	Fit doors to body shell	G, E	1
J	Build engine	B	4
K	Bench-test engine	J	2
L	Assemble chassis	F, H, K	1
M	Road-test chassis	L	0.5
N	Paint body	I	2
O	Install wiring	N	1
P	Install interior	N	1.5
Q	Accept delivery of special accessories	C	5

[3] Source: James A. F. Stoner and Charles Wankel, *Management*, 3rd ed. (Englewood Cliffs, NJ: Prentice Hall, 1986), p. 195.

Job Letter	Description	Immediate Predecessor(s)	Normal Time (Days)
R	Mount body and accessories on chassis	M, O, P, Q	1
S	Road-test car	R	0.5
T	Attach exterior trim	S	1
U	Finish	T	0

a) Draw a network diagram for the project.
b) Mark the critical path and state its length.
c) If the Maser had to be completed 2 days earlier, would it help to:
  i) Buy preassembled transmissions and drivetrains?
  ii) Install robots to halve engine-building time?
  iii) Speed delivery of special accessories by 3 days?
d) How might resources be borrowed from activities on the noncritical path to speed activities on the critical path?

16.23 Getting a degree from a college or university is a long and difficult task. Certain courses must be completed before other courses may be taken. Develop a network diagram in which every activity is a particular course that must be taken for a given degree program. The immediate predecessors will be course prerequisites. Do not forget to include all university, college, and departmental course requirements. Then try to group these courses into semesters or quarters for your particular school. Which courses, if not taken in the proper sequence, could delay your graduation?

DATA BASE APPLICATION

16.24 The Wood Construction Company is involved in constructing municipal buildings and other structures that are used primarily by city and state municipalities. This requires developing legal documents, drafting feasibility studies, obtaining bond ratings, and so forth. Recently, Elizabeth Wood was given a request to submit a proposal for the construction of a municipal building. The first step is to develop legal documents and to perform all necessary steps before the construction contract is signed. This requires approximately 20 separate activities that must be completed. These activities, their immediate predecessors, and time requirements are given in the table shown below. As you can see, optimistic (a), most likely (m), and pessimistic (b) time estimates have been given for all of the activities described in the table. Using these data, determine the total project completion time for this preliminary step, the critical path, and slack time for all activities involved.

Activity	a	m	b	Description	Immediate Predecessor(s)
1	1	4	5	Drafting legal documents	—
2	2	3	4	Preparation of financial statements	—
3	3	4	5	Draft of history	—
4	7	8	9	Draft demand portion of feasibility study	—
5	4	4	5	Review and approval of legal documents	1
6	1	2	4	Review and approval of history	3
7	4	5	6	Review feasibility study	4
8	1	2	4	Draft final financial portion of feasibility study	7

Activity	Time Required (Weeks) a	m	b	Description	Immediate Predecessor(s)
9	3	4	4	Draft facts relevant to the bond transaction	5
10	1	1	2	Review and approval of financial statements	2
11	18	20	26	Firm price received of project	—
12	1	2	3	Review and completion of financial portion of feasibility study	8
13	1	1	2	Draft statement completed	6, 9, 10, 11, 12
14	.10	.14	.16	All materials sent to bond rating services	13
15	.2	.3	.4	Statement printed and distributed to all interested parties	14
16	1	1	2	Presentation to bond rating services	14
17	1	2	3	Bond rating received	16
18	3	5	7	Marketing of bonds	15, 17
19	.1	.1	.2	Purchase contract executed	18
20	.1	.14	.16	Final statement authorized and completed	19
21	2	3	6	Purchase contract	19
22	.1	.1	.2	Bond proceeds available	20
23	.0	.2	.2	Sign construction contract	21, 22

Case Study

Shale Oil Company

Shale Oil Company contains several operating units that comprise its Aston, Ohio, manufacturing complex. These units process the crude oil that is pumped through and transform it into a multitude of hydrocarbon products. The units run 24 hours a day, 7 days a week, and must be shut down for maintenance on a predetermined schedule. One such unit is Distillation Unit No. 5, or DU5. Studies have shown that DU5 can operate only $3\frac{1}{2}$ years without major equipment breakdowns and excessive loss of efficiency. Therefore, DU5 is shut down every $3\frac{1}{2}$ years for cleaning, inspection, and repairs.

DU5 is the only distillation unit for crude oil in the Aston complex, and its shutdown severely affects all other operating units. Some of the production can be compensated for by Shale refineries in other locations, but the rest must be processed and stored before the shutdown. Without proper planning, a nationwide shortage of Shale gasoline could occur. The time of DU5's shutdown is critical, and the length of time the unit is down must be kept to a minimum to limit production loss. Shale uses PERT as a planning and controlling tool to minimize shutdown time.

The first phase of a shutdown is to open and clean the equipment. Inspectors can then enter the unit and examine the damage. Once damages are determined, the needed repairs can be carried out. Repair times can vary considerably, depending on what damage the inspection reveals. Based on previous inspection records, some repair work is known ahead of time. Thorough cleaning of the equipment is also necessary to improve the unit's operating efficiency. The table on page 661 lists the many maintenance activities and their estimated completion times.

Discussion Questions

1. Determine the expected shutdown time and the probability that the shutdown can be completed 1 week earlier.
2. What are the probabilities that Shale finishes the maintenance project 1, 2, 3, 4, 5, or 6 days earlier?
3. Shale Oil is considering increasing the budget to shorten the shutdown. How do you suggest the company proceed?

Preventive Maintenance of DU5

Activities		Time Estimates (in Days)		
		Optimistic	Most Likely	Pessimistic
1–2	Circulate wash water throughout unit	1	2	2.5
2–3	Install blinds	1.5	2	2.5
3–4	Open and clean vessels and columns	2	3	4
3–5	Open and clean heat exchangers; remove tube bundles	1	2	3
3–6	Open and clean furnaces	1	2	4
3–7	Open and clean mechanical equipment	2	2.5	3
3–8	Inspect instrumentation	2	4	5
4–9	Inspect vessels and columns	1	2	3
5–10	Inspect heat-exchanger shells	1	1.5	2
5–11	Inspect tube bundles	1	1.5	2
6–12	Inspect furnaces	2	2.5	3
6–17	Retube furnaces	15	20	30
7–13	Inspect mechanical equipment	1	1.5	2
7–18	Install new pump mechanical seals	3	5	8
8–19	Repair instrumentation	3	8	15
9–14	Repair vessels and columns	14	21	28
10–16	Repair heat-exchanger shells	1	5	10
11–15	Repair tube bundles; retube	2	5	10
12–17	Repair furnaces	5	10	20
13–18	Repair mechanical equipment	10	15	25
14–20	Test and close vessels and columns	4	5	8
15–16	Install tube bundles into heat-exchanger shells	1	2	3
16–20	Test and close heat exchangers	1	2	2.5
17–20	Test and close furnaces	1	2	3
18–20	Test and close mechanical equipment	1	2	3
19–20	Test instrumentation	2	4	6
20–21	Pull blinds	1.5	2	2.5
21–22	Purge all equipment with steam	1	3	5
22–23	Start up unit	3	5	10

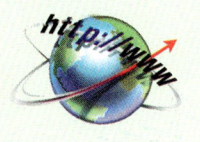

Internet Case Studies

See our Internet home page at http://www.prenhall.com/heizer for these additional case studies: Haywood Brothers Construction Company, The Family Planning Research Center of Nigeria, and Cranston Construction Company.

BIBLIOGRAPHY

Cleland, D. I., and W. R. King. *Project Management Handbook.* New York: Van Nostrand Reinhold, 1984.

Deans, B. V. "Getting the Job Done! Managing Project Teams and Task Forces for Success." *The Executive* 6, no. 4 (November 1992): 94.

Dusenberry, W. "CPM for New Product Introductions." *Harvard Business Review* (July–August 1967): pp. 124–139.

Hickman, Anita. "Refining the Process of Project Control." *Production and Inventory Management,* February 1992, pp. 26–27.

Keefer, D. L., and W. A. Verdini. "Better Estimation of PERT Activity Time Parameters." *Management Science* 39, no. 9 (September 1993): 1,086.

Kerzner, H., and H. Thamhain. *Project Management for Small and Medium Size Business.* New York: Van Nostrand Reinhold, 1984.

Kim, S., and R. C. Leachman. "Multi-Project Scheduling with Explicit Lateness Costs." *IIE Transactions* 25, no. 2 (March 1993): 34–44.

Pinto, M. B., J. K. Pinto, and J. E. Prescott. "Antecedents and Consequences of Project Team Cross-functional Cooperation." *Management Science* 39, no. 10 (October 1993): 1,281.

Render, B., and R. M. Stair. *Quantitative Analysis for Management,* 6th ed. Upper Saddle River: Prentice Hall, 1997.

INTERNET RESOURCES

Job Site Documentation Software for Windows™:
http://www.csiwin.com/project.html

PERT Chart EXPERT is an add-on product for Microsoft Project that adds extensive PERT charting:
http://www.jsaproj.com/prod02.htm

PERT Chart (and a Gantt Chart) for a Small Construction Project:
http://www.arch.uiuc.edu/courses/arch232/chart.html

PERT Chart and WBS Chart add-on products for Microsoft Project:
http://www.criticaltools.com/

Project Management uses traditional analytical tools to plan, schedule and track complex projects:
http://cher.eda.doc.gov/agencies/dac/projmgt.html

Maintenance and Reliability

17

CHAPTER OUTLINE

GLOBAL COMPANY PROFILE: NASA
THE STRATEGIC IMPORTANCE OF MAINTENANCE AND RELIABILITY
RELIABILITY
  Improving Individual Components
  Providing Redundancy
MAINTENANCE
  Implementing Preventive Maintenance
INCREASING REPAIR CAPABILITIES
  Total Productive Maintenance
TECHNIQUES FOR ESTABLISHING MAINTENANCE POLICIES

SUMMARY
KEY TERMS
USING POM FOR WINDOWS TO SOLVE RELIABILITY PROBLEMS
SOLVED PROBLEMS
DISCUSSION QUESTIONS
CRITICAL THINKING EXERCISE
PROBLEMS
CASE STUDY: WORLDWIDE CHEMICAL COMPANY
INTERNET CASE STUDIES
BIBLIOGRAPHY
INTERNET RESOURCES

LEARNING OBJECTIVES

When you complete this chapter you should be able to:

Identify or Define:

  Maintenance

  Mean time between failures

  Redundancy

  Preventive maintenance

  Breakdown maintenance

  Infant mortality

Describe or Explain:

  How to measure system reliability

  How to improve maintenance

  How to evaluate maintenance performance

GLOBAL COMPANY PROFILE:

Maintenance and Reliability Are the Critical Success Factors for NASA's Space Shuttles

Space Shuttle Columbia *is rolled from its hangar to the launch pad.*

Columbia's *main engine is installed in the Orbiter Processing facility.*

From miles away, a space shuttle looks gleaming white on the launch pad. Yet up close, in the hangars where the four NASA vehicles, *Columbia, Endeavor, Atlantis,* and *Discovery,* spend most of their lives, a shuttle can show her true colors: moldy green; burnt brown; grungy gray; sooty black.

In one Kennedy Space Center hangar, *Columbia* (officially, serial number 102) sits with her guts spread out. Her 3 engines (each the size of a Volkswagen) are detached and in another shop for maintenance. She has a gaping hole in her nose because her front jets are sitting on the floor. With 86 million miles on her odometer, *Columbia* is America's ultimate used car. However, NASA has no plans to retire this multibillion-dollar workhorse. *Columbia* is expected to make 77 more voyages as a global science lab, with her hold rented out to dozens of nations for scientific experiments and satellite launches.

Such a plan requires world-class reliability. It also requires maintenance. Indeed it means about 600 computer-generated maintenance jobs, each with hundreds of tasks, during the 3-month turnaround between flights. There are platforms to

664

NASA

A tunnel leading into the cargo bay space lab is inspected.

install, engine inspections, turbopump checks, tile reworks, lube-oil drainings, drag-chute removal and reinstallation. More than 100 men and women work behind the scenes to maintain *Columbia's* long-standing reputation of reliability. In the memory of each is the January 1986 *Challenger* explosion, a horrible commentary on reliability that almost caused NASA to shut its doors. How often do *Columbia* maintenance workers think about *Challenger*? "Every time it launches," admits senior engineer Jim Little.

THE STRATEGIC IMPORTANCE OF MAINTENANCE AND RELIABILITY

Managers at NASA must avoid the undesirable results of a shuttle that fails. The results of failure can be disruptive, inconvenient, wasteful, and expensive in dollars and in lives. Machine and product failures can have far-reaching effects on an organization's operation, reputation, and profitability. In complex, highly mechanized plants, an out-of-tolerance process or a machine breakdown may result in idle employees and facilities, loss of customers and goodwill, and profits turning into losses.[1] In an office, the failure of a generator, an air-conditioning system, or a computer may halt operations. A good maintenance and reliability strategy protects both a firm's performance and its investment.

The objective of maintenance and reliability is to maintain the capability of the system while controlling costs. A good maintenance system drives out system variability. Systems must be designed and maintained to reach expected performance and quality standards. **Maintenance** includes all activities involved in keeping a system's equipment in working order. **Reliability** is the probability that a machine part or product will function properly for a specified time under stated conditions.

Two firms that recognize the strategic importance of dedicated maintenance are Walt Disney Company and United Parcel Service. Disney World, in Florida, is intolerant of failures or breakdowns. Disney's reputation makes it not only one of the most popular vacation destinations in the world but also a mecca for benchmarking teams that want to study its maintenance and reliability practices.

Likewise, UPS's famed maintenance strategy keeps its delivery vehicles operating and looking as good as new for 20 years or more. The UPS program involves dedicated drivers who operate the same truck every day and dedicated mechanics who maintain the same group of vehicles. Drivers and mechanics are both responsible for the performance of a vehicle and stay closely in touch.

The interdependency of operator, machine, and mechanic is a hallmark of successful maintenance and reliability. As Figure 17.1 illustrates, it is not only good maintenance and reliability procedures that make Disney and UPS successful, but the involvement of their employees as well.

In this chapter, we examine four tactics for improving the reliability and maintenance not only of products and equipment but also of the systems that produce them. The four tactics are organized around reliability and maintenance.

The reliability tactics are:

1. Improving individual components;
2. Providing redundancy.

The maintenance tactics are:

1. Implementing or improving preventive maintenance;
2. Increasing repair capabilities or speed.

Maintenance All activities involved in keeping a system's equipment in working order.

Reliability The probability that a machine part or product will function properly for a specified time under stated conditions.

TEN DECISIONS OF OM
Managing Quality
Design of Goods & Services
Process Strategy
Location Strategies
Layout Strategies
Human Resources
Supply-Chain Management
Inventory Management
Scheduling
Maintenance

---

[1] Addressing the weaknesses in British productivity, a study in *The Economist* (March 9, 1985, pp. 62–63) compared British and German firms. It found that although the machinery in the British plants was no older than that in the German plants, it was poorly maintained. Breakdowns were more frequent and lasted longer. Operators were less able to do repairs themselves.

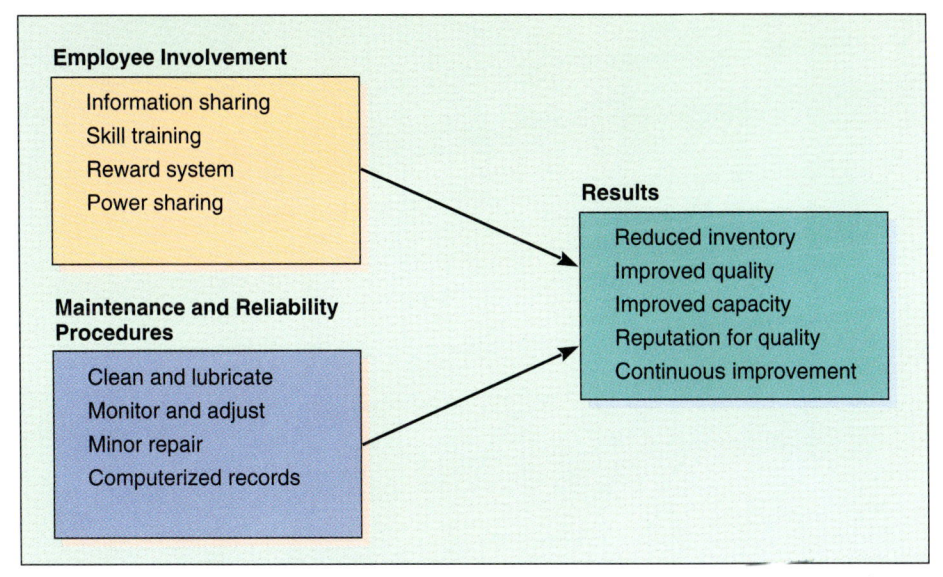

FIGURE 17.1 ■ **Good Maintenance and Reliability Strategy Requires Employee Involvement and Good Procedures**

RELIABILITY

Systems are composed of a series of individual interrelated components, each performing a specific job. If any *one* component fails to perform, for whatever reason, the overall system (for example, an airplane or machine) can fail.

Improving Individual Components

Because failures do occur in the real world, understanding their occurrence is an important reliability concept. We will now examine the impact of failure in a series. Figure 17.2 shows that as the number of components in a *series* increases, the reliability of the whole system declines very quickly. A system of $n = 50$ interacting parts, each of which has a 99.5% reliability, has an overall reliability of 78%. If the system or machine has 100 interacting parts, each with an individual reliability of 99.5%, the overall reliability will be only about 60%!

To measure reliability in a system in which each individual part or component may have its own unique rate of reliability, we cannot use the reliability curve in Figure 17.2. However, the method of computing system reliability (R_s) is simple. It consists of finding the product of individual reliabilities as follows:

$$R_s = R_1 \times R_2 \times R_3 \times \ldots \times R_n \qquad (17.1)$$

where R_1 = reliability of component 1
R_2 = reliability of component 2

and so on.

Equation (17.1) assumes that the reliability of an individual component does not depend on the reliability of other components (that is, each component is independent). Additionally, in this equation as in most reliability discussions, reliabilities are presented as

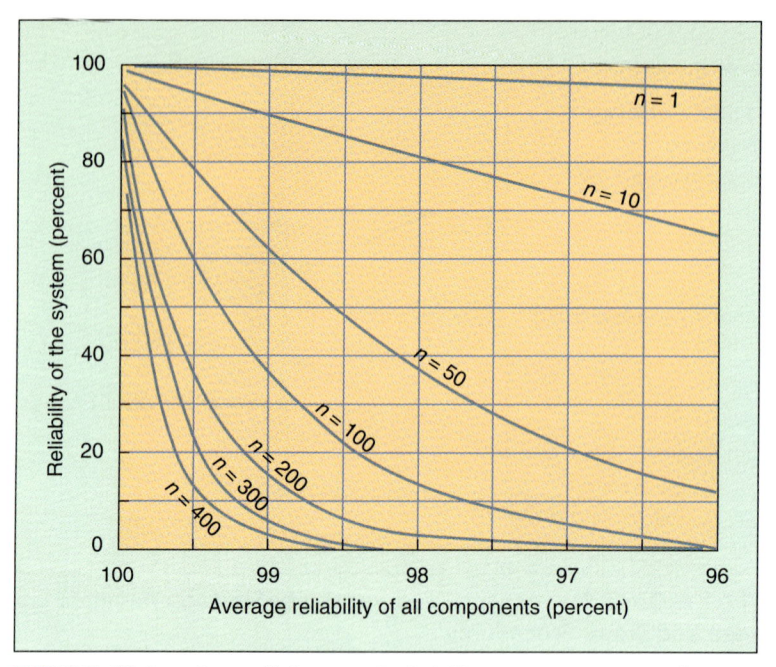

FIGURE 17.2 ■ Overall System Reliability as a Function of Number of Components and Component Reliability with Components in a Series

probabilities. Thus, a .90 reliability means that the unit will perform as intended 90% of the time. It also means that it will fail $1 - .90 = .10 = 10\%$ of the time. We can use this method to evaluate the reliability of a service or a product, such as the one we examine in Example 1.

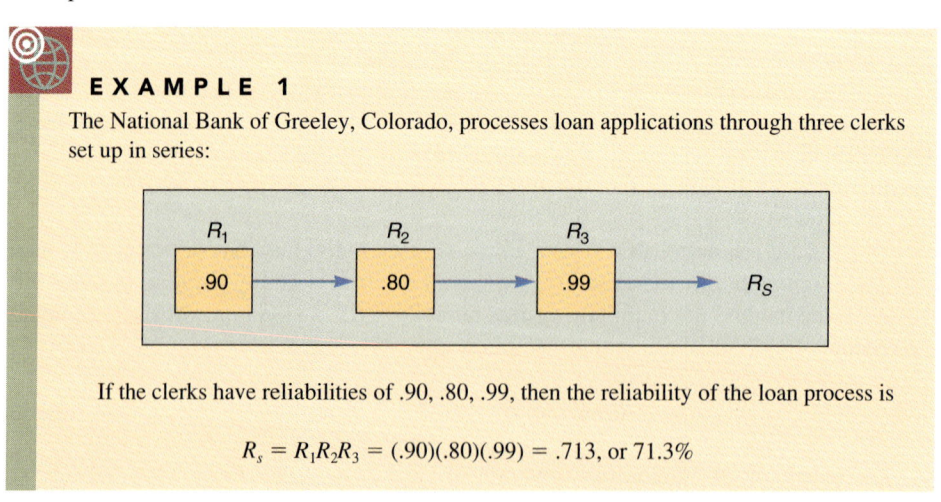

EXAMPLE 1

The National Bank of Greeley, Colorado, processes loan applications through three clerks set up in series:

R_1 .90 → R_2 .80 → R_3 .99 → R_S

If the clerks have reliabilities of .90, .80, .99, then the reliability of the loan process is

$$R_s = R_1 R_2 R_3 = (.90)(.80)(.99) = .713, \text{ or } 71.3\%$$

Component reliability is often a design or specification issue for which engineering design personnel may be responsible. However, purchasing personnel may be able to improve components of systems by staying abreast of suppliers' products and research efforts. Purchasing personnel can also contribute directly to the evaluation of supplier performance.

RELIABILITY

The basic unit of measure for reliability is the *product failure rate* (FR). Firms producing high-technology equipment often provide failure-rate data on their products. As shown in equations (17.2) and (17.3), the failure rate measures the percentage of failures among the total number of products tested, FR(%), or a number of failures during a period of time, FR(N):

$$FR(\%) = \frac{\text{Number of failures}}{\text{Number of units tested}} \times 100\% \quad (17.2)$$

$$FR(N) = \frac{\text{Number of failures}}{\text{Number of unit-hours of operating time}} \quad (17.3)$$

Perhaps the most common term in reliability analysis is the **mean time between failures (MTBF)**, which is the reciprocal of FR(N):

$$\text{MTBF} = \frac{1}{FR(N)} \quad (17.4)$$

In Example 2, we compute the percentage of failure FR(%), number of failures FR(N), and mean time between failures (MTBF).

Mean time between failures (MTBF) The expected time between a repair and the next failure of a component, machine, process, or product.

EXAMPLE 2

Twenty air-conditioning systems designed for use by astronauts in NASA space shuttles were operated for 1,000 hours at NASA's Huntsville, Alabama, test facility. Two of the systems failed during the test—one after 200 hours and the other after 600 hours. To compute the percentage of failures, we use the following equation:

$$FR(\%) = \frac{\text{Number of failures}}{\text{Number of tested}} = \frac{2}{20}(100\%) = 10\%$$

Next we compute the number of failures per operating hour:

$$FR(N) = \frac{\text{Number of failures}}{\text{Operating time}}$$

where

$$\text{Total time} = (1{,}000 \text{ hr})(20 \text{ units})$$

$$= 20{,}000 \text{ units-hr}$$

$$\text{Nonoperating time} = 800 \text{ hr for 1st failure} + 400 \text{ hr for 2nd failure}$$

$$= 1{,}200 \text{ unit-hr}$$

$$\text{Operating time} = \text{Total time} - \text{Nonoperating time}$$

$$FR(N) = \frac{2}{20{,}000 - 1{,}200} = \frac{2}{18{,}800}$$

$$= .000106 \text{ failure/unit-hr}$$

and because $\text{MTBF} = \frac{1}{FR(N)}$

$$\text{MTBF} = \frac{1}{.000106} = 9{,}434 \text{ hr}$$

670 CHAPTER 17 MAINTENANCE AND RELIABILITY

If the typical space shuttle trip lasts 60 days, NASA may be interested in the failure rate per trip:

$$\text{Failure rate} = (\text{failures/unit-hr})(24 \text{ hr/day})(60 \text{ days/trip})$$

$$= (.000106)(24)(60)$$

$$= .152 \text{ failure/trip}$$

Because the failure rate recorded in Example 2 is probably too high, NASA will have to either increase the reliability of individual components, and thus of the system, or else install several backup air-conditioning units on each space shuttle. Backup units provide redundancy.

Providing Redundancy

Redundancy The use of components in parallel to raise reliabilities.

To increase the reliability of systems, **redundancy** is added. The technique here is to "back up" components with additional components. This is known as putting units in parallel. Redundancy is provided to ensure that if one component fails the system has recourse to another. For instance, say that reliability of a component is .80 and we back it up with another component with reliability of .80. The resulting reliability is the probability of the first component working plus the probability of the backup (or parallel) component working multiplied by the probability of needing the backup component $(1 - .8 = .2)$. Therefore:

$$\begin{pmatrix}\text{Probability}\\\text{of first}\\\text{component}\\\text{working}\end{pmatrix} + \left[\begin{pmatrix}\text{Probability}\\\text{of second}\\\text{component}\\\text{working}\end{pmatrix} \times \begin{pmatrix}\text{Probability}\\\text{of needing}\\\text{second}\\\text{component}\end{pmatrix}\right] =$$

$$(.8) \quad + \quad [(.8) \quad \times \quad (1 - .8)] \quad = .8 + .16 = .96$$

Example 3 shows how redundancy can improve the reliability of the loan process presented in Example 1.

EXAMPLE 3

The National Bank is disturbed that its loan-application process has a reliability of only .713 (see Example 1). Therefore, the bank decides to provide redundancy for the 2 least reliable clerks. This procedure results in the system shown below:

$$\begin{array}{ccc}R_1 & R_2 & R_3\\ \boxed{0.90} & \boxed{0.8} & \\ \downarrow & \downarrow & \\ \boxed{0.90} \rightarrow \boxed{0.8} \rightarrow \boxed{0.99}\end{array} = [.9 + .9(1 - .9)] \times [.8 + .8(1 - .8)] \times .99$$

$$= [.9 + (.9)(.1)] \times [.8 + (.8)(.2)] \times .99$$

$$= .99 \times .96 \times .99 = .94$$

By providing redundancy for two clerks, National Bank has increased reliability of the loan process from .713 to .94.

MAINTENANCE

There are two types of maintenance: preventive maintenance and breakdown maintenance. **Preventive maintenance** involves performing routine inspections and servicing and keeping facilities in good repair. These activities are intended to build a system that will find potential failures and make changes or repairs that will prevent failure. Preventive maintenance is much more than just keeping machinery and equipment running. It also involves designing technical and human systems that will keep the productive process working within tolerance; it allows the system to perform. The emphasis of preventive maintenance is on understanding the process and allowing it to work without interruption. **Breakdown maintenance** occurs when equipment fails and must be repaired on an emergency or priority basis.

Implementing Preventive Maintenance

Preventive maintenance implies that we can determine when a system needs service or will need repair. Therefore, to perform preventive maintenance, we must know when a system requires service or when it is likely to fail. Failures occur at different rates during the life of a product. A high failure rate, known as **infant mortality**, may exist initially for many products. This is why many electronic firms "burn in" their products prior to shipment: That is to say, they execute a variety of tests (such as a full wash cycle at Maytag) to detect "start-up" problems prior to shipment. Firms may also provide 90-day warranties. We should note that many infant mortality failures are not product failures per se, but rather failure due to improper use. This fact points up the importance in many industries of operations management's building an after-sales service system that includes installing and training.

Preventive maintenance A plan that involves routine inspections, servicing, and keeping facilities in good repair to prevent failure.

Breakdown maintenance Remedial maintenance that occurs when equipment fails and must be repaired on an emergency or priority basis.

Infant mortality The failure rate early in the life of a product or process.

Preventive maintenance is critical to the Orlando Utilities Commission (OUC), a Central Florida electric utility company. Its coal-fired unit requires that maintenance personnel perform about 12,000 repair and preventive maintenance tasks a year. These are scheduled daily by a computerized maintenance program. An unexpected forced outage can cost OUC from $250,000 to $500,000 per day. The value of preventive maintenance was illustrated by the first overhaul of a new generator. A cracked rotor blade was discovered, which could have destroyed a $27 million piece of equipment.

Once the product, machine, or process "settles in," a study can be made of the MTBF (mean time between failure) distribution. When these distributions exhibit small standard deviations, then we know we have a candidate for preventive maintenance, even if the maintenance is expensive.[2]

Once our firm has a candidate for preventive maintenance, we want to determine *when* preventive maintenance is economical. Typically, the more expensive the maintenance, the narrower must be the MTBF distribution (that is, have a small standard deviation). Additionally, if the process is no more expensive to repair when it breaks down than the cost of preventive maintenance, perhaps we should let the process break down and then do the repair. However, the consequence of the breakdown must be fully considered. Even some relatively minor breakdowns have catastrophic consequences. At the other extreme, preventive maintenance costs may be so incidental that preventive maintenance is appropriate even if the MTBF distribution is rather flat (that is, it has a large standard deviation). In any event, all machine operators must be held responsible for preventive maintenance of their own equipment and tools.

With good reporting techniques, firms can maintain records of individual processes, machines, or equipment. Such records can provide a profile of both the kinds of maintenance required and the timing of maintenance needed. Maintaining equipment history is an important part of a preventive maintenance system, as is a record of the time and cost to make the repair. Such records can also contribute to similar information about the family of equipment as well as suppliers.

Record keeping is of such importance that most good maintenance systems are now computerized. Figure 17.3 shows the major components of such a system with files to be maintained on the left and reports generated on the right.

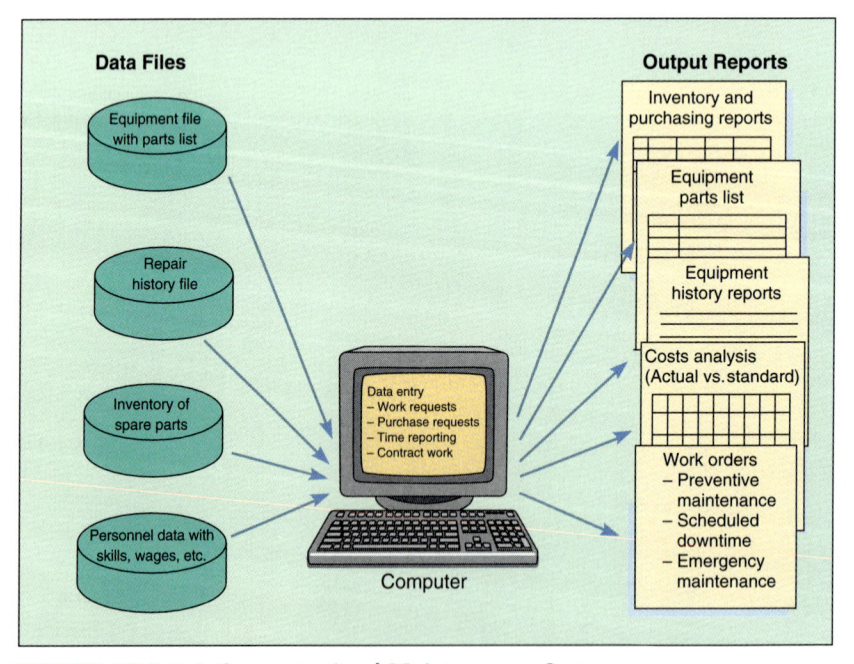

FIGURE 17.3 ■ A Computerized Maintenance System

---

[2] See, for example, the work of P. M. Morse, *Queues, Inventories, and Maintenance* (New York: John Wiley, 1958), pp. 161–168; and J. Michael Brock, John R. Michael, and David Morganstein, "Using Statistical Thinking to Solve Maintenance Problems," *Quality Progress*, May 1989, pp. 55–60.

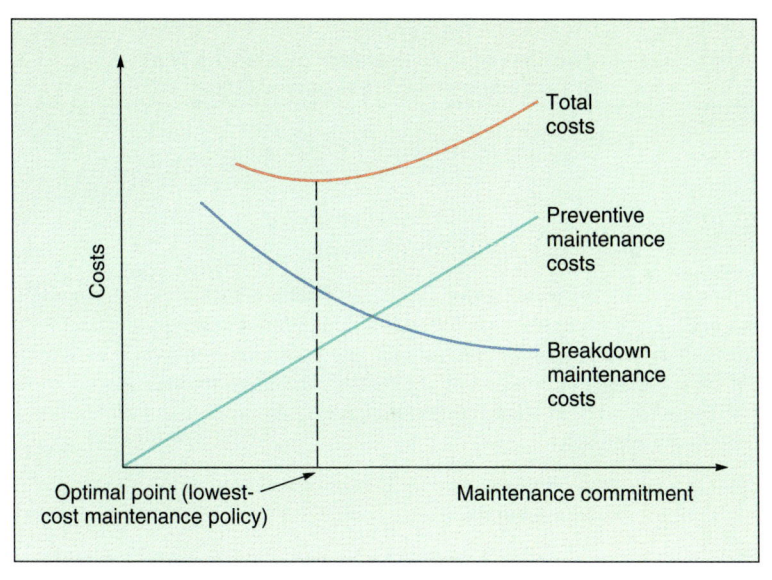

FIGURE 17.4 ■ Maintenance Costs

Figure 17.4 shows the relationship between preventive maintenance and breakdown maintenance. Operations managers must consider a *balance* between the two costs. On the one hand, allocating more money and crew to preventive maintenance will reduce the number of breakdowns. At some point, however, the decrease in breakdown maintenance costs will be less than the increase in preventive maintenance costs. At this point, the total cost curve will begin to rise. Beyond this optimal point, the firm will be better off waiting for breakdowns to occur and repairing them when they do.

Unfortunately, these cost curves seldom consider the *full costs of a breakdown*. Many costs are ignored because they are not *directly* related to the immediate breakdown. For instance, the cost of inventory maintained to compensate for downtime is not typically considered. Moreover, downtime can have a devastating effect on morale: Employees may begin to believe that performance to standard and maintaining equipment are not important. Finally, downtime can adversely affect delivery schedules, destroying customer relations and future sales.

Assuming that all potential costs associated with downtime have been identified, the operations staff can compute the optimal level of maintenance activity on a theoretical basis. Such analysis, of course, also requires accurate historical data on maintenance costs, breakdown probabilities, and repair times. Example 4 shows how to compare preventive and breakdown maintenance costs in order to select the least expensive maintenance policy.

EXAMPLE 4

Huntsman and Associates is a CPA firm specializing in payroll preparation. The firm has been successful in automating much of its work, using computers for processing and report preparation. The computerized approach, however, has problems. Over the past 20 months, the computer system has broken down at the rate indicated in the table that follows on page 674:

Number of Breakdowns	Number of Months That Breakdowns Occurred
0	4
1	8
2	6
3	2
Total:	20

Each time the computer breaks down, Huntsman estimates that it loses an average of $300 in time and service expenses. One alternative is to purchase a service contract for preventive maintenance. If Huntsman contracts for preventive maintenance, it expects an *average* of only 1 computer breakdown per month. The price for this service is $220 per month. To decide whether Huntsman should contract for preventive maintenance, we will follow a 4-step approach:

Step 1: Compute the *expected number* of breakdowns (based on past history) if the firm continues as is, without the service contract.

Step 2: Compute the expected breakdown cost per month with no preventive maintenance contract.

Step 3: Compute the cost of preventive maintenance.

Step 4: Compare the two options and select the one that will cost less.

1.

Number of Breakdowns	Frequency	Number of Breakdowns	Frequency
0	4/20 = .2	2	6/20 = 0.3
1	8/20 = .4	3	2/20 = 0.1

$$\begin{pmatrix}\text{Expected number}\\ \text{of breakdowns}\end{pmatrix} = \Sigma \left[\begin{pmatrix}\text{Number of}\\ \text{breakdowns}\end{pmatrix} \times \begin{pmatrix}\text{Corresponding}\\ \text{frequency}\end{pmatrix}\right]$$

$$= (0)(.2) + (1)(.4) + (2)(.3) + (3)(.1)$$

$$= 0 + .4 + .6 + .3$$

$$= 1.3 \text{ breakdowns/month}$$

2. Expected breakdown cost $= \begin{pmatrix}\text{Expected number}\\ \text{of breakdowns}\end{pmatrix} \times \begin{pmatrix}\text{Cost per}\\ \text{breakdown}\end{pmatrix}$

$$= (1.3)(\$300)$$

$$= \$390/\text{month}$$

3. $\begin{pmatrix}\text{Preventive}\\ \text{maintenance cost}\end{pmatrix} = \begin{pmatrix}\text{Cost of expected}\\ \text{breakdowns if service}\\ \text{contract signed}\end{pmatrix} + \begin{pmatrix}\text{Cost of}\\ \text{service contract}\end{pmatrix}$

$$= (1 \text{ breakdown/month})(\$300) + \$220/\text{month}$$

$$= \$520/\text{month}$$

4. Because it is less expensive to suffer the breakdowns *without* a maintenance service contract ($390) than with one ($520), the firm should continue its present policy.

Through variations of the technique shown in Example 4, operations managers can determine minimum-cost maintenance policies.

INCREASING REPAIR CAPABILITIES

Because reliability and preventive maintenance are seldom perfect, most firms opt for some level of repair capability. Enlarging or improving repair facilities can get the system back in operation faster. A good maintenance facility should have these six features:

1. Well-trained personnel;
2. Adequate resources;
3. Ability to establish a repair plan and priorities;[3]
4. Ability and authority to do material planning;
5. Ability to identify the cause of breakdowns;
6. Ability to design ways to extend MTBF.

However, not all repairs can be done in the firm's facility. Managers must, therefore, decide where repairs are to be performed. Figure 17.5 shows some of the options and how they rate in terms of speed, cost, and competence. Consistent with the advantages of employee empowerment, a strong case can be made for employees' maintaining their own equipment. This approach, however, may also be the weakest link in the repair chain because not every employee can be trained in all aspects of equipment repair. Moving to the right in Figure 17.5 may improve the competence of the repair work, but it also increases cost as it may entail expensive off-site repair with corresponding increases in replacement time and shipping.

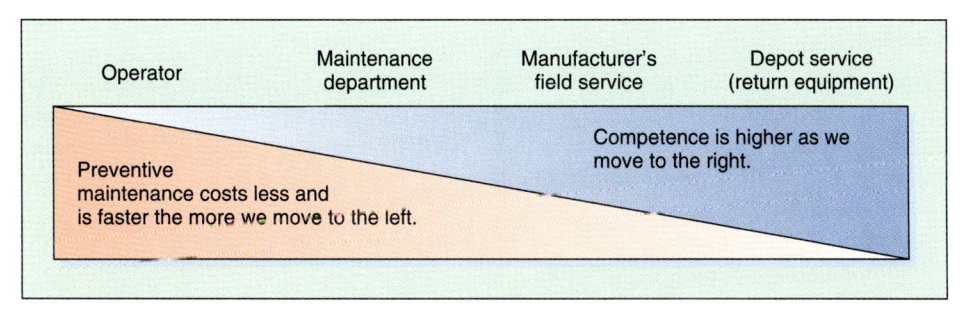

FIGURE 17.5 ■ **The Operations Manager Must Determine How Maintenance Will Be Performed**

However, preventive maintenance policies and techniques must include an emphasis on employees' accepting responsibility for the maintenance they are capable of doing. Employee maintenance may be only of the "clean, check, and observe" variety, but if each operator performs those activities within his or her capability, the manager has made a step toward both employee empowerment and maintaining system performance.

Total Productive Maintenance

Many firms have moved to bring total quality management concepts to the practice of preventive maintenance with an approach known as **Total Productive Maintenance (TPM)**.

Total productive maintenance (TPM)
Combines total quality management with a strategic view of maintenance from process equipment design to preventive maintenance.

---

[3] You may recall from our discussion of network planning in chapter 16 that DuPont developed the critical path method (CPM) to improve the scheduling of maintenance projects.

It involves the concept of reducing variability through employee involvement and excellent maintenance records. In addition, total productive maintenance includes:

- Designing machines that are reliable, easy to operate, and easy to maintain.
- Emphasizing total cost of ownership when purchasing machines, so that service and maintenance are included in the cost.
- Developing preventive maintenance plans that utilize the best practices of operators, maintenance departments, and depot service.
- Training workers to operate and maintain their own machines.

TECHNIQUES FOR ESTABLISHING MAINTENANCE POLICIES

Two other OM techniques have proven beneficial to establishing maintenance policies: simulation and expert systems.

Simulation Because of the complexity of some maintenance decisions, simulation is a good tool for evaluating the impact of various policies. For instance, operations personnel can decide whether to add more staff by determining the trade-offs between machine downtime costs and the costs of additional labor. Management can also simulate the replacement of parts that have not yet failed as a way of preventing future breakdowns. Simulation via physical models can also be useful. For example, a physical model can vibrate an airplane to simulate thousands of hours of flight time in order to evaluate maintenance needs.

Expert Systems OM managers use expert systems (that is, computer programs that mimic human logic) to assist staff in isolating and repairing various faults in machinery and equipment. For instance, General Electric's DELTA system asks a series of detailed questions that aid the user in identifying a problem. DuPont uses expert systems to monitor equipment and to train repair personnel.

SUMMARY

Reliable systems are a necessity. In spite of our best efforts to design reliable components, systems sometimes fail. Consequently, backup components are used. Reliability improvements also can be obtained through the use of preventive maintenance and excellent repair facilities.

Some firms use automated sensors and other controls to warn when production machinery is about to fail or is becoming damaged by heat, vibration, or fluid leaks. General Motors, for example, has developed a computer system to sense unusual vibrations in machines while they are running. The goal of such procedures is not only to avoid failures but also to perform preventive maintenance before machines are damaged.

Finally, many firms give employees a sense of "ownership" in their equipment. When workers repair or do preventive maintenance on their own machines, breakdowns are less common. Well-trained and empowered employees ensure reliable systems through preventive maintenance. In turn, reliable, well-maintained equipment not only provides higher utilization but also improves quality and performance to schedule. Top firms build and maintain systems so that customers can count on products and services that are produced to specifications and on time.

KEY TERMS

Maintenance *(p. 666)*
Reliability *(p. 666)*
Mean time between failures (MTBF) *(p. 669)*
Redundancy *(p. 670)*

Preventive maintenance *(p. 671)*
Breakdown maintenance *(p. 671)*
Infant mortality *(p. 671)*
Total productive maintenance (TPM) *(p. 675)*

USING POM FOR WINDOWS TO SOLVE RELIABILITY PROBLEMS

Program 17.1 illustrates POM for Windows Reliability module applied to the National Bank scenario in Example 3.

Reliability Results — National Bank

	Parallel system 1	Parallel system 2	Parallel system 3
Component 1	0.9	0.8	
Component 2	0.9	0.8	0.99
Prll System Rel	0.99	0.96	0.99
Overall Reliability	0.940896		

PROGRAM 17.1 ■ POM for Windows Reliability Module Example *The entries for reliability are: (1) number of systems (components) in the series (1 through 10); (2) number of backup or parallel components (1 through 12); (3) component reliability. Enter the reliability of each component in the body of the table. Series data are entered across the table, and backup or parallel data down the table. The program will disregard any zeros in the table.*

SOLVED PROBLEMS

Solved Problem 17.1

The semiconductor used in the Sullivan Wrist Calculator has 5 parts, each of which has its own reliability rate. Component 1 has a reliability of .90; component 2, .95; component 3, .98; component 4, .90; and component 5, .99. What is the reliability of one semiconductor?

Solution

$$\text{Semiconductor reliability}, R_s = R_1 R_2 R_3 R_4 R_5$$

$$= (.90)(.95)(.98)(.90)(.99)$$

$$= .7466$$

Solved Problem 17.2

A recent engineering change at Sullivan Wrist Calculator places a backup component in each of the two least reliable transistor circuits. The new circuit will look like the following:

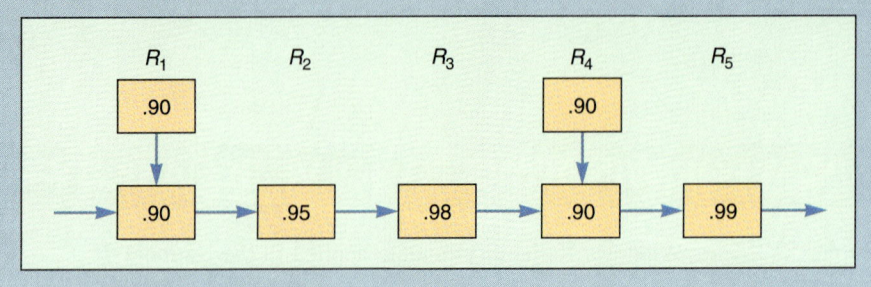

```
        R₁           R₂          R₃          R₄          R₅
       .90                                   .90
        ↓                                     ↓
       .90  →  .95  →  .98  →  .90  →  .99
```

What is the reliability of the new system?

Solution

Reliability = $[.9 + (1 - .9) \times .9] \times .95 \times .98 \times [.90 + (1 - .9) \times .9] \times .99$

$= [.9 + .09] \times .95 \times .98 \times [.90 + .09] \times .99$

$= .99 \times .95 \times .98 \times .99 \times .99$

$= .903$

DISCUSSION QUESTIONS

1. What variables contribute to infant mortality for new machinery?
2. What techniques can management use to improve system reliability?
3. Under what conditions is preventive maintenance likely to be appropriate?
4. Why is simulation often an appropriate technique for maintenance problems?
5. What is the trade-off between operator-performed maintenance versus supplier-performed maintenance?
6. How can a manager evaluate the effectiveness of the maintenance function?
7. What kind of records are helpful when developing a good maintenance system?
8. How do expert systems improve maintenance systems?
9. How can a firm improve or speed up its repair facilities?

CRITICAL THINKING EXERCISE

The 1989 crash of a McDonnell Douglas DC-10 over Iowa suggests the plane's hydraulic systems may not provide enough protection. The DC-10 has three separate hydraulic systems, all of which failed when an engine exploded. The engine threw off shreds of metal that severed two of the lines, and the third line required power from the demolished engine that was no longer available. The DC-10, unlike other commercial jets, has no shutoff valves that might have stemmed the flow of hydraulic fluid. Lockheed's similar L-1011 trijet has four hydraulic systems. A McDonnell Douglas VP said at the time, "You can always be extreme and not have a practical airplane. You can be perfectly safe and never get off the ground." Discuss the pros and cons of McDonnell's position. How might you design a reliability experiment? What has since happened to the McDonnell Douglas Corporation?

PROBLEMS

- **17.1** The credit card issuing process at Atlanta Bank's VISA program consists of 10 steps performed in series by different bank employees. The average reliability of each employee is 98%. Use Figure 17.2 (p. 668) to find the overall reliability of the credit card issuing process.
- **17.2** A testing process at Boeing Aircraft has 400 components in series. The average reliability of each component is 99.5%. What is the overall reliability of the whole testing process?
- **17.3** What are the *expected* number of yearly breakdowns for the power generator at Orlando Utilities that has exhibited the following data over the past 20 years?

Number of breakdowns	0	1	2	3	4	5	6
Number of years in which breakdown occurred	2	2	5	4	5	2	0

- **17.4** Each breakdown of a graphic plotter table at Airbus Industries costs $50. Find the expected daily breakdown cost given the following data:

Number of breakdowns	0	1	2	3	4
Daily breakdown probability	.1	.2	.4	.2	.1

- **17.5** The Beta II computer's electronic processing unit contains 50 components in series. The average reliability of each component is 99.0%. Using Figure 17.2, determine the overall reliability of the processing unit.
- **: 17.6** Greg Duncan Manufacturing, a medical equipment manufacturer, has subjected 100 heart pacemakers to 5,000 hours of testing. Halfway through the testing, 5 pacemakers failed. What was the failure rate in terms of the following:
    a) Percent of failures?
    b) Number of failures per unit-hour?
    c) Number of failures per unit-year?
    d) If 1,100 people receive pacemaker implants, how many units can we expect to fail during the following 1 year?
- **17.7** Given the probabilities that follow for a Wayne Froelich's print shop, find the expected breakdown cost.

Number of Breakdowns	0	1	2	3
Daily Frequency	.3	.2	.2	.3

The cost per breakdown is $10.

- **: 17.8** You have a system composed of 4 components in series. The reliability of each component is .95. What is the reliability of the system?
- **: 17.9** You have a system composed of a serial connection of four components with the following reliabilities:

Component	Reliability
1	.90
2	.95
3	.80
4	.85

What is the reliability of the system?

: 17.10 Jane Manning Hyatt has a system composed of three components in parallel. The components have the following reliabilities:

$$R_1 = 0.90, \quad R_2 = 0.95, \quad R_3 = 0.85$$

What is the reliability of the system? (*Hint:* See Example 3.)

· 17.11 A medical control system has three components in series with individual reliabilities ($R_1, R_2,$ and R_3) as shown.

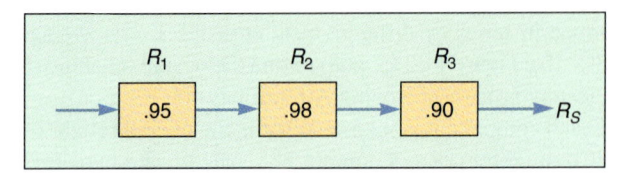

R_1 .95 → R_2 .98 → R_3 .90 → R_S

What is the reliability of the system?

: 17.12 What is the reliability of the system shown below?

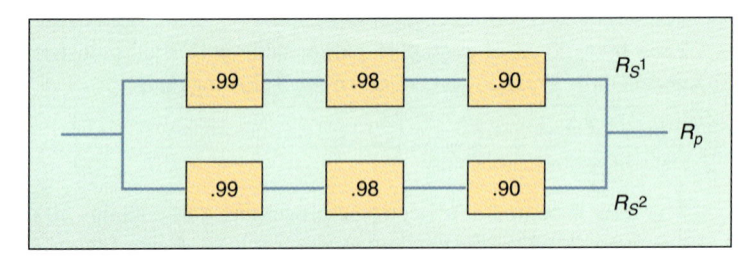

Top branch: .99 → .98 → .90 → R_{S^1}
Bottom branch: .99 → .98 → .90 → R_{S^2}
Combined: R_p

: 17.13 What is the impact on reliability if the medical control system shown in Problem 17.11 is changed to the parallel system shown in Problem 17.12?

: 17.14 Your design team has proposed the following system with component reliabilities as indicated.

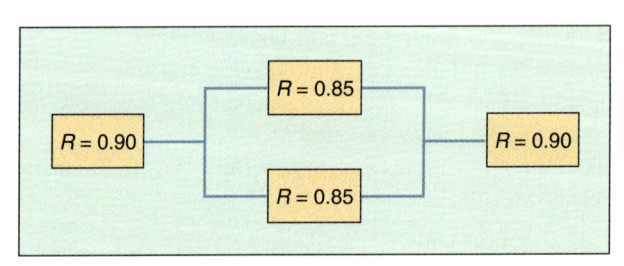

R = 0.90 → [R = 0.85 parallel with R = 0.85] → R = 0.90

What is the reliability of the system?

: 17.15 Paul Feyen Manufacturing has tested 200 units of a product. After 2,000 hours, 4 units have failed; the remainder functioned for the full 4,000 hours of the testing.
   a) What is the percent of failures?
   b) What is the number of failures per unit-hour?
   c) What is the number of failures per unit-year?
   d) If you sell 500 units, how many are likely to fail within a 1-year time period?

: 17.16 Wharton Manufacturing Company operates its 23 large and expensive grinding and lathe machines from 7 A.M. to 11 P.M., 7 days a week. For the past year, the firm has been under contract with Simkin and Sons for daily preventive maintenance (lubrication, cleaning, inspection, and so on). Simkin's crew works between 11 P.M. and 2 A.M. so as not to interfere with the daily manufacturing crew. Simkin charges $645 per week for this service. Since signing the maintenance contract, Wharton Manufacturing has noted an average of only 3 breakdowns per week. When a grinding or lathe machine *does* break down during a working shift, it costs Wharton about $250 in lost production and repair costs.

After reviewing past breakdown records (for the period before signing a preventive maintenance contract with Simkin and Sons), Wharton's production manager was able to summarize the following patterns:

Number of breakdowns per week	0	1	2	3	4	5	6	7	8
Number of weeks in which breakdowns occurred	1	1	3	5	9	11	7	8	5

Total weeks of historical data: 50

The production manager is not certain that the contract for preventive maintenance with Simkin is in Wharton's best financial interest. He recognizes that much of his breakdown data are old but is fairly certain that they are representative of the present picture.

What is your analysis of this situation and what recommendations do you think the production manager should make?

: 17.17 Bridgette Hunt, salesperson for Wave Soldering Systems, Inc. (WSSI), has provided you with a proposal for improving the temperature control on your present machine. The machine uses a hot-air knife to cleanly remove excess solder from printed circuit boards; this is a great concept, but the hot-air temperature control lacks reliability. According to Hunt, engineers at WSSI have improved the reliability of the critical temperature controls. The new system still has the 4 sensitive integrated circuits controlling the temperature, but the new machine has a backup for each. The 4 integrated circuits have reliabilities of .90, .92, .94, and .96. The 4 backup circuits all have a reliability of .90.

a) What is the reliability of the new temperature controller?
b) If you pay a premium, Hunt says she can improve all 4 of the backup units to .93. What is the reliability of this option?

▪ Case Study ▪

Worldwide Chemical Company

Jack Smith wiped the perspiration from his face. It was another scorching-hot summer day, and one of the four process refrigeration units was down. The units were critical to the operation of Worldwide Chemical Company's Fibers Plant, which produces synthetic fibers and polymer flake for a global market.

Before long, Al Henson, the day-shift production superintendent, was on the intercom, shouting his familiar proclamation that "heads would roll" if the unit was not back on-line within the hour. However, Jack Smith, the maintenance superintendent, had heard it all before—nothing ever happened as a result of Henson's temper tantrums. "Serves him right," he thought. "Henson is uncooperative when we want to perform scheduled maintenance, so it doesn't get done and equipment goes down."

At that moment, however, Henson was genuinely furious over the impact that the breakdown would have on his process yield figures. Meeting with plant manager Beth Conner, he was charging that all the maintenance department did was "sit around" and play cards like firemen waiting for an alarm to send them to a three-alarm blaze across town. The "fix-it" approach to maintenance was costing the plant throughput that was vital to meeting standard costs and avoiding serious variances. Foreign competitors were delivering high-quality fibers in less time and at lower prices. Conner had already been called on the carpet at corporate headquarters over output levels that were significantly below the budgeted numbers. The business cycle contained predictable seasonal variations. That meant building inventories that would be carried for months, tying up scarce capital, a characteristic of most continuous processes. Monthly shipments would look bad. Year-to-date shipments would look even worse because of machine breakdowns and lost output to date. Conner knew that something had to be done to develop machine reliability. Capacity on demand was needed to respond to growing foreign competition. Unreliable production equipment was jeopardizing the company's TQM effort by causing process variations that affected both first-quality product yields and on-time deliveries, but no one seemed to have the answer to the problem of machine breakdowns.

The maintenance department operated much like a fire department, rushing to a breakdown with a swarm of mechanics, some who disassembled the machine while others poured over wiring schematics and still others hunted for spare parts in the maintenance warehouse. Eventually, they would have the machine back up, though sometimes only after working through the night to get the production line going again. Maintenance had always been done this way. However, with new competitors, machine reliability had suddenly become a major barrier to competing successfully.

Rumors of a plant closing were beginning to circulate and morale was suffering, making good performance that much more difficult. Beth Conner knew she needed solutions if the plant had any chance of survival.

Discussion Questions

1. Can Smith and Hensen do anything to improve performance?
2. Is there an alternative to the current operations approach of the maintenance department?
3. How could production make up for lost output resulting from scheduled maintenance?
4. How could maintenance mechanics be better utilized?
5. Is there any way to know when a machine breakdown is probable?

Source: Patrick Owings, under the supervision of Professor Marilyn M. Helms, University of Tennessee at Chattanooga.

Internet Case Studies

See our Internet home page at http://www.prenhall.com/heizer for these additional case studies: Buffalo Alkali and Cartak's Department Store.

BIBLIOGRAPHY

Gray, D. "Airworthy—Decision Support for Aircraft Overhaul Maintenance Planning." *OR/MS Today* 19 (December 1992): 24–29.

Hayes, R. H., and K. B. Clark. "Why Some Factories Are More Productive than Others." *Harvard Business Review* 64, no. 5 (September–October 1986): 66–73.

Joshi, S., and R. Gupta. "Scheduling of Routine Maintenance Using Production Schedules and Equipment Failure History." *Computers and Industrial Engineering* 10, no. 1 (1986): 11–20.

Linder-Dutton, L., M. Jordan, and M. Karwan. "Beyond Mean Time to Failure." *OR/MS Today* 21, no. 2 (April 1994): 30–33.

Maggard, B. N., and D. M. Rhyne. "Total Productive Maintenance: A Timely Integration of Production and Maintenance." *Production and Inventory Management Journal* 33, no. 4 (fourth quarter 1992): 6–10.

Mann, L., Jr. *Maintenance Management.* Lexington, MA: Lexington Books, 1983.

Schneeweiss, C. A., and H. Schroder. "Planning and Scheduling the Repair Shops of the Deutsche Lufthansa AG: A Hierarchical Approach." *Production and Operations Management* 1, no. 1 (winter 1992): 22.

Sherwin, D. J. "Inspect or Monitor." *Engineering Costs and Production Economics* 18 (January 1990): 223–231.

Vaziri, H. K. "Using Competitive Benchmarking to Set Goals." *Quality Progress* 25, no. 10 (October 1992): 81.

INTERNET RESOURCES

National Information Center for Reliability Engineering:
http://enre.umd.edu//reinfo.htm

Penn State University reliability Home Page:
http://wisdom.arl.psu.edu/

Society for Maintenance and Reliability Professionals:
http://www.smrp.org/smrp.html

Society for Reliability:
http://www.sre.org/

Part IV Quantitative Modules

QUANTITATIVE MODULE A

Decision-Making Tools

MODULE OUTLINE

THE DECISION PROCESS IN OPERATIONS

FUNDAMENTALS OF DECISION MAKING

DECISION TABLES
- Decision Making under Risk
- Expected Value of Perfect Information (EVPI)

DECISION TREES
- A More Complex Decision Tree

SUMMARY

KEY TERMS

USING POM FOR WINDOWS TO SOLVE DECISION TABLE AND TREE PROBLEMS

USING EXCEL OM FOR DECISION MODELS

SOLVED PROBLEMS

DISCUSSION QUESTIONS

PROBLEMS

CASE STUDY: NIGEL SMYTHE'S HEART BYPASS OPERATION

INTERNET CASE STUDIES

BIBLIOGRAPHY

LEARNING OBJECTIVES

When you complete this module you should be able to:

Identify or Define:

Decision trees and decision tables

Highest monetary value

Expected value of perfect information

Sequential decisions

Describe or Explain:

Decision making under risk

The wildcatter's decision was a tough one. Which of his new Kentucky lease areas—Blair East or Blair West—should he drill for oil? A wrong decision in this type of wildcat oil drilling could mean the difference between success and bankruptcy for the company. Talk about decision making under uncertainty and pressure! But using a decision tree, Tomco Oil President Thomas E. Blair identified 74 different options, each with its own potential net profit. What had begun as an overwhelming number of geological, engineering, economic, and political factors now became much clearer. Says Blair, "Decision tree analysis provided us with a systematic way of planning these decisions and clearer insight into the numerous and varied financial outcomes that are possible."
Source: Adapted from J. Hosseini, "Decision Analysis and Its Application in the Choice between Two Wildcat Ventures," *Interfaces,* March–April 1986, pp. 75–85.

Operations managers are decision makers. To achieve the goals of their organizations, managers must understand how decisions are made and know which decision-making tools to use. To a great extent, the success or failure of both people and companies depends on the quality of their decisions. The manager who insisted on launching the space shuttle *Challenger* (which exploded in 1986), despite being advised against it, did not rise to power within NASA. However, Bill Gates, who developed DOS and Windows, operating systems for personal computers, became president of the most powerful software firm in the world (Microsoft) and a billionaire.

THE DECISION PROCESS IN OPERATIONS

What makes the difference between a good decision and a bad decision? A "good" decision—one that uses analytic decision making—is based on logic and considers all available data and possible alternatives. It also follows these six steps:

1. Clearly define the problem and the factors that influence it.
2. Develop specific and measurable objectives.

3. Develop a model—that is, a relationship between objectives and variables (which are measurable quantities).
4. Evaluate each alternative solution based on its merits and drawbacks.
5. Select the best alternative.
6. Implement the decision and set a timetable for completion.

Throughout this book, we introduce a broad range of mathematical models and tools to help operations managers make better decisions. The *types* of decisions that managers make include deciding: (1) what the firm's quality objectives are, (2) what its products and processes should be, (3) what its capacity should be, (4) where to locate its facilities, (5) how to layout its facilities, (6) what its job designs should include, (7) what the purchasing/supply chain should be, (8) how to manage inventory, (9) how to schedule over the short term (days or weeks) and intermediate term (months), (10) how to schedule projects, and (11) how to maintain systems and facilities.

All of these OM decisions tie to corporate strategy. In addition, none of them can be made independently of others. Effective operations depend on careful decision making. Fortunately, there are a whole variety of analytic tools to help make these decisions. This module introduces two of them—decision tables and decision trees. They are used in a wide number of OM situations, ranging from new product analysis (chapter 6), to equipment selection (chapter 7), to location planning (chapter 8), to scheduling (chapter 15), and to maintenance planning (chapter 17).

FUNDAMENTALS OF DECISION MAKING

Regardless of the complexity of a decision or the sophistication of the technique used to analyze it, all decision makers are faced with alternatives and "states of nature." The following notation will be used in this module:

1. Terms:
   a. *Alternative*—a course of action or strategy that may be chosen by a decision maker (for example, not carrying an umbrella tomorrow).
   b. *State of nature*—an occurrence or a situation over which the decision maker has little or no control (for example, tomorrow's weather).
2. Symbols used in a decision tree:
   a. □—a decision node from which one of several alternatives may be selected.
   b. ○—a state-of-nature node out of which one state of nature will occur.

To present a manager's decision alternatives, we can develop *decision trees* using the above symbols. When constructing a decision tree, we must be sure that all alternatives and states of nature are in their correct and logical places and that we include *all* possible alternatives and states of nature.

EXAMPLE A1

Getz Products Company is investigating the possibility of producing and marketing backyard storage sheds. Undertaking this project would require the construction of either a large or a small manufacturing plant. The market for the product produced—storage sheds—could be either favorable or unfavorable. Getz, of course, has the option of not developing the new product line at all. A decision tree for this situation is presented in Figure A.1.

FIGURE A.1 ■ Getz Products Decision Tree

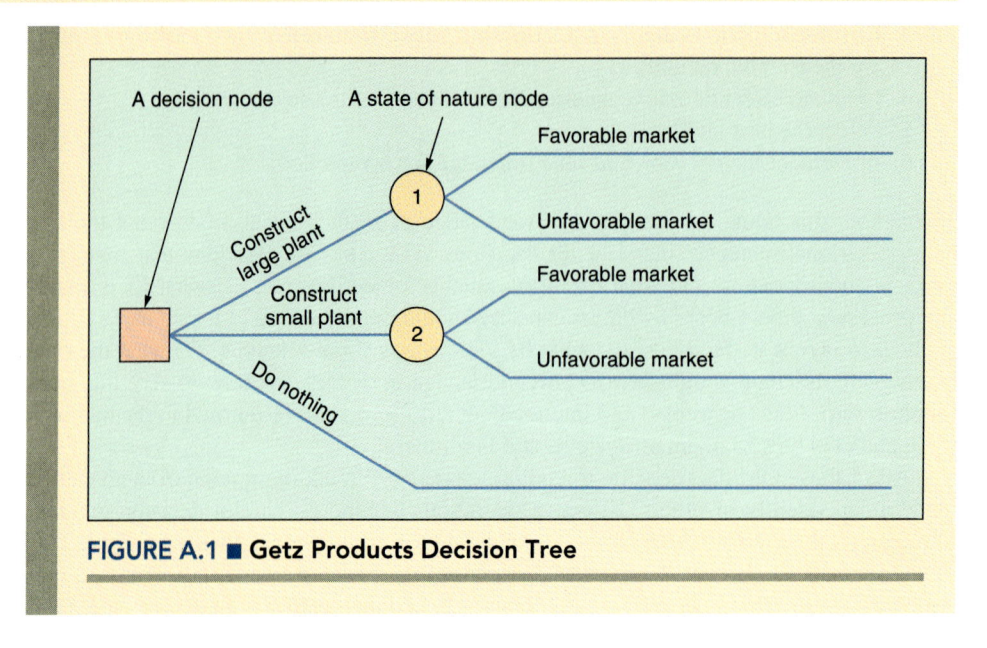

DECISION TABLES

We may also develop a decision or payoff table to help Getz Products define its alternatives. For any alternative and a particular state of nature, there is a *consequence* or *outcome*, which is usually expressed as a monetary value. This is called a *conditional value*. Note that all of the alternatives in Example A2 are listed down the left side of the table, that states of nature (outcomes) are listed across the top, and that conditional values (payoffs) are in the body of the **decision table.**

Decision table A tabular means of analyzing decision alternatives and states of nature.

EXAMPLE A2

We construct a decision table for Getz Products (see Table A.1), including conditional values based on the following information. With a favorable market, a large facility would give Getz Products a net profit of $200,000. If the market is unfavorable, a $180,000 net loss would occur. A small plant would result in a net profit of $100,000 in a favorable market, but a net loss of $20,000 would be encountered if the market is unfavorable.

TABLE A.1 ■ Decision Table with Conditional Values for Getz Products

| | States of Nature ||
Alternatives	Favorable Market	Unfavorable Market
Construct large plant	$200,000	–$180,000
Construct small plant	$100,000	–$ 20,000
Do nothing	$ 0	$ 0

The toughest part of decision tables is getting the data to analyze.

Decision Making under Risk

The situation facing Getz constitutes decision making "under risk." It is a *probabilistic* decision situation: That is, several possible states of nature occur, each with a given probability. Given a decision table with conditional values and probability assessments for all states of nature, we can determine the **expected monetary value (EMV)** for each alternative. This figure represents the expected value or *average* return for each alternative *if we could repeat the decision a large number of times.*

The EMV for an alternative is the sum of all possible payoffs from the alternative, each weighted by the probability of that payoff occurring.

EMV (Alternative *i*) = (Payoff of 1st state of nature)

× (Probability of 1st state of nature)

+ (Payoff of 2nd state of nature)

× (Probability of 2nd state of nature)

+ ⋯ + (Payoff of last state of nature)

× (Probability of last state of nature)

Expected monetary value (EMV) The expected payout or value of a variable that has different possible states of nature, each with an associated probability.

The following example illustrates the computational procedure used to determine the maximum EMV.

EXAMPLE A3

Getz Products operations manager believes that the probability of a favorable market is exactly the same as that of an unfavorable market; that is, each state of nature has a .50 chance of occurring. We can now determine the EMV for each alternative (see Table A.2):

1. EMV(A_1) = (.5)($200,000) + (.5)(−$180,000) = $10,000
2. EMV(A_2) = (.5)($100,000) + (.5)(−$20,000) = $40,000
3. EMV(A_3) = (.5)($0) + (.5)($0) = $0

The maximum EMV is seen in alternative A_2. Thus, according to the EMV decision criterion, we would build the small facility.

TABLE A.2 ■ Decision Table for Getz Products

	States of Nature	
Alternatives	Favorable Market	Unfavorable Market
Construct large plant (A_1)	$200,000	−$180,000
Construct small plant (A_2)	$100,000	−$ 20,000
Do nothing (A_3)	$0	$0
Probabilities	.50	.50

Now suppose that the Getz operations manager has been approached by a marketing research firm that proposes to help him make the decision about whether or not to build the plant to produce storage sheds. The marketing researchers claim that their technical analysis will tell Getz with certainty whether or not the market is favorable for the proposed product. In other words, it will change Getz's environment from one of decision making *under risk* to one of decision making *under certainty*. This information could prevent Getz from making a very expensive mistake. The marketing research firm would charge Getz $65,000 for the information. What would you recommend? Should the operations

EVPI places an upper limit on what you should pay for information.

manager hire the firm to make the study? Even if the information from the study is perfectly accurate, is it worth $65,000? What might it be worth? Although some of these questions are difficult to answer, determining the value of such *perfect information* can be very useful. It places an upper bound on what you would be willing to spend on information, such as that being sold by a marketing consultant. This is the concept of the expected value of perfect information, which we now introduce.

Expected Value of Perfect Information (EVPI)

Expected value of perfect information (EVPI) The difference between the payoff under certainty and the payoff under risk.

If a manager were able to determine which state of nature would occur, then he or she would know which decision to make. Once a manager knows which decision to make, the payoff increases because the payoff is now a certainty, not a probability. Because the payoff will increase with knowledge of which state of nature will occur, this knowledge has value. Therefore, we now look at how to determine the value of this information. We call this difference between the payoff under certainty and the payoff under risk the **expected value of perfect information (EVPI).**

$$\text{EVPI} = \text{Expected value under certainty} - \text{Maximum EMV}$$

Expected value under certainty The expected (average) return if perfect information is available.

To find the EVPI, we must first compute the **expected value under certainty,** which is the expected (average) return, if we have perfect information before a decision has to be made. In order to calculate this value, we choose the best alternative for each state of nature and multiply its payoff times the probability of occurrence of that state of nature.

Expected value under certainty = (Best outcome or consequence for 1st state of nature)

$\times$ (Probability of 1st state of nature)

+ (Best outcome for 2nd state of nature)

$\times$ (Probability of 2nd state of nature)

+ $\cdots$ + (Best outcome for last state of nature)

$\times$ (Probability of last state of nature)

We will use the data and decision table from Example A3 to examine the expected value of perfect information. We do so in Example A4.

EXAMPLE A4

By referring back to Table A.2, the Getz operations manager can calculate the maximum that he would pay for information—that is, the expected value of perfect information, or EVPI. He follows a two-stage process. First, the expected value under certainty is computed. Then, using this information, EVPI is calculated. The procedure is outlined as follows:

1. The best outcome for the state of nature "favorable market" is "build a large facility" with a payoff of $200,000. The best outcome for the state of nature "unfavorable market" is "do nothing" with a payoff of $0. Expected value under certainty = ($200,000)(0.50) + ($0)(0.50) = $100,000. Thus, if we had perfect information, we would expect (on the average) $100,000 if the decision could be repeated many times.

> **2.** The maximum EMV is $40,000, which is the expected outcome without perfect information. Thus:
>
> $$\text{EVPI} = \text{Expected value under certainty} - \text{Maximum EMV}$$
>
> $$= \$100,000 - \$40,000 = \$60,000$$
>
> In other words, the *most* Getz should be willing to pay for perfect information is $60,000. This conclusion, of course, is again based on the assumption that the probability of each state of nature is 0.50.

DECISION TREES

Decisions that lend themselves to display in a decision table also lend themselves to display in a decision tree. We will, therefore, analyze some decisions using decision trees. Although the use of a decision table is convenient in problems having one set of decisions and one set of states of nature, many problems include *sequential* decisions and states of nature. When there are two or more sequential decisions and later decisions are based on the outcome of prior ones, the decision tree approach becomes appropriate. A **decision tree** is a graphic display of the decision process that indicates decision alternatives, states of nature and their respective probabilities, and payoffs for each combination of decision alternative and state of nature.

Decision tree A graphical means of analyzing decision alternatives and states of nature.

Expected monetary value (EMV) is the most commonly used criterion for decision tree analysis. One of the first steps in such analysis is to graph the decision tree and to specify the monetary consequences of all outcomes for a particular problem.

Analyzing problems with *decision trees* involves five steps:

1. Define the problem.
2. Structure or draw the decision tree.
3. Assign probabilities to the states of nature.
4. Estimate payoffs for each possible combination of decision alternatives and states of nature.
5. Solve the problem by computing expected monetary values (EMV) for each state-of-nature node. This is done by working *backward*—that is, by starting at the right of the tree and working back to decision nodes on the left.

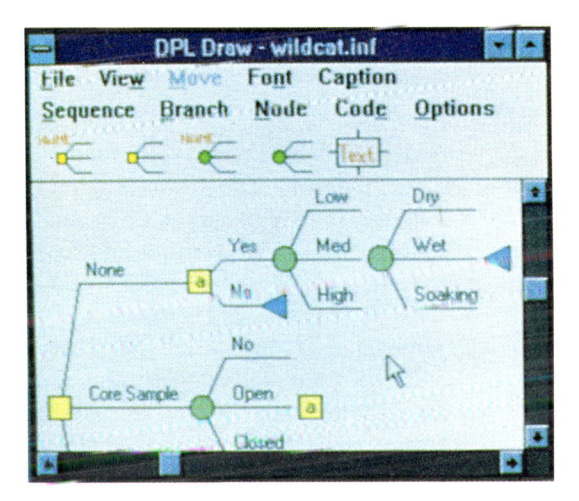

Decision tree software is a relatively new advance that permits users to solve decision-analysis problems with flexibility, power, and ease. Programs such as DPL, Tree Plan, and Supertree allow decision problems to be analyzed with less effort and in greater depth than ever before. Full-color presentations of the options open to managers always have impact. In this photo, wildcat drilling options are explored with DPL, a product of Applied Decision Analysis.

EXAMPLE A5

A completed and solved decision tree for Getz Products is presented in Figure A.2. Note that the payoffs are placed at the right-hand side of each of the tree's branches. The probabilities (first used by Getz in Example A3) are placed in parentheses next to each state of nature. The expected monetary values for each state-of-nature node are then calculated and placed by their respective nodes. The EMV of the first node is $10,000. This represents the branch from the decision node to "construct a large plant." The EMV for node 2, to "construct a small plant," is $40,000. The option of "doing nothing" has, of course, a payoff of $0. The branch leaving the decision node leading to the state of nature node with the highest EMV will be chosen. In Getz's case, a small plant should be built.

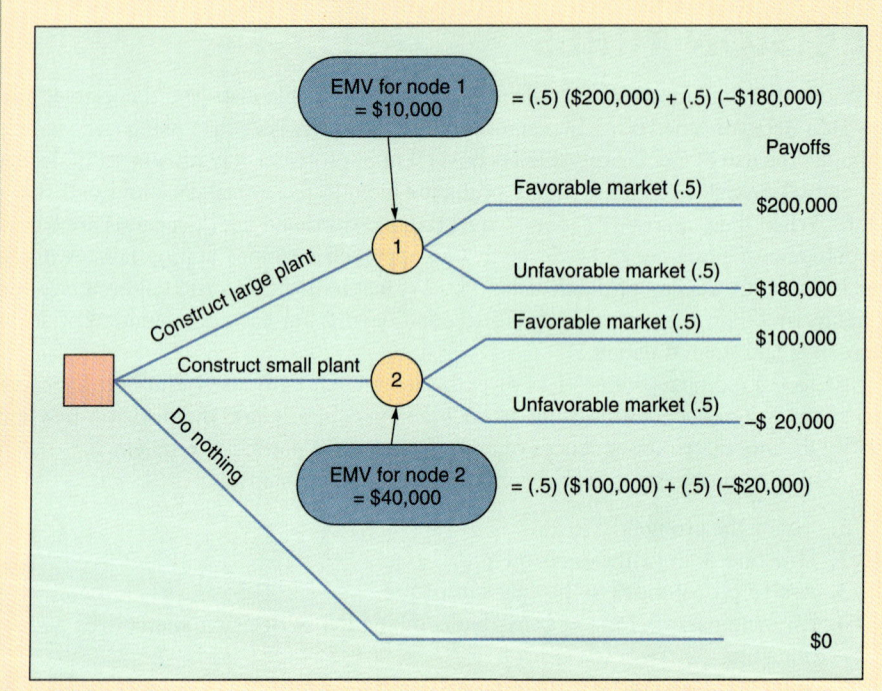

FIGURE A.2 ■ Completed and Solved Decision Tree for Getz Products

EMV for node 1 = $10,000 = (.5) ($200,000) + (.5) (−$180,000)

Payoffs
- Construct large plant → Node 1
  - Favorable market (.5) → $200,000
  - Unfavorable market (.5) → −$180,000
- Construct small plant → Node 2
  - Favorable market (.5) → $100,000
  - Unfavorable market (.5) → −$20,000
- Do nothing → $0

EMV for node 2 = $40,000 = (.5) ($100,000) + (.5) (−$20,000)

A More Complex Decision Tree

When a *sequence* of decisions must be made, decision trees are much more powerful tools than are decision tables. Let's say that Getz Products has two decisions to make, with the second decision dependent on the outcome of the first. Before deciding about building a new plant, Getz has the option of conducting its own marketing research survey, at a cost of $10,000. The information from this survey could help it decide whether to build a large plant, to build a small plant, or not to build at all. Getz recognizes that although such a survey will not provide it with *perfect* information, it may be extremely helpful.

Getz's new decision tree is represented in Figure A.3 of Example A6. Take a careful look at this more complex tree. Note that *all possible outcomes and alternatives* are included in their logical sequence. This procedure is one of the strengths of using decision trees. The manager is forced to examine all possible outcomes, including unfavorable ones. He or she is also forced to make decisions in a logical, sequential manner.

> You can reduce complexity by viewing and solving a number of smaller trees—start at the end branches of a large one. Take one decision at a time.

DECISION TREES

EXAMPLE A6

Examining the tree in Figure A.3, we see that Getz's first decision point is whether to conduct the $10,000 market survey. If it chooses not to do the study (the lower part of the tree), it can either build a large plant, a small plant, or no plant. This is Getz's second decision point. If the decision is to build, the market will be either favorable (.50 probability) or unfavorable (also .50 probability). The payoffs for each of the possible consequences are listed along the right-hand side. As a matter of fact, this lower portion of Getz's tree is *identical* to the simpler decision tree shown in Figure A.2.

There is a widespread use of decision trees beyond OM. Managers often appreciate a graphical display of a tough problem.

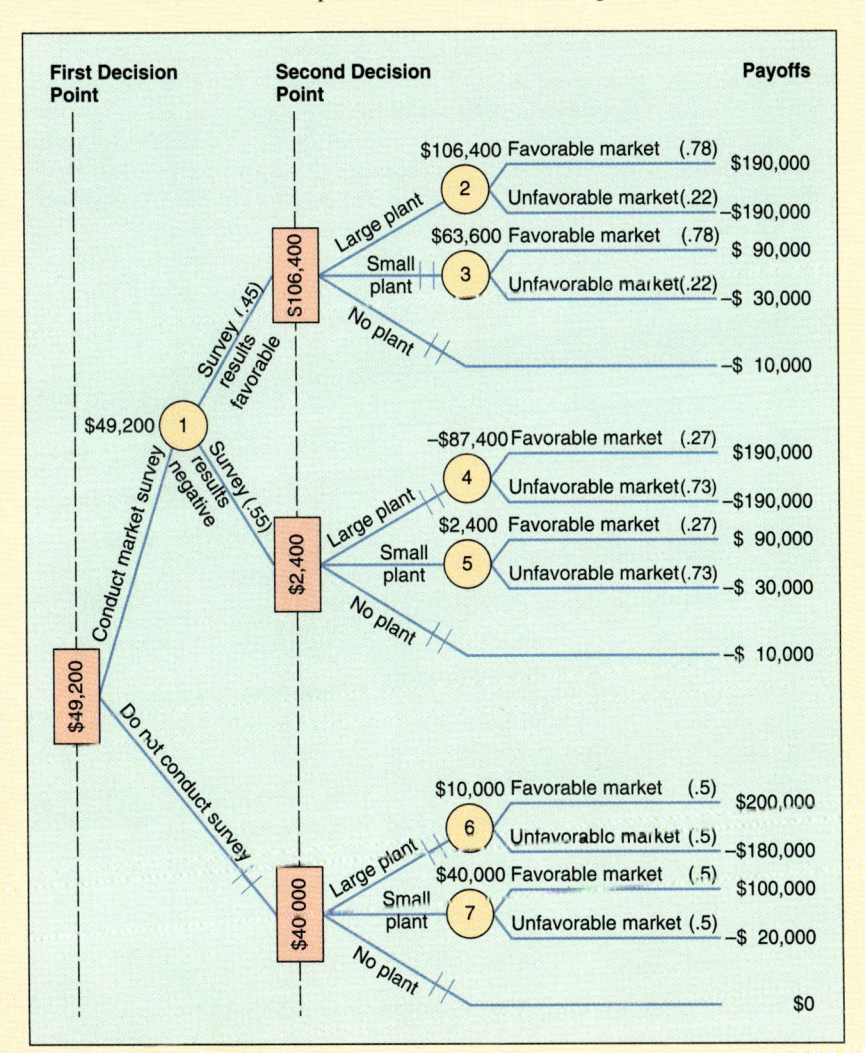

FIGURE A.3 ■ **Getz Products Decision Tree with Probabilities and EMVs Shown** *The short parallel lines mean "prune" that branch, as it is less favorable than another available option and may be dropped.*

The upper part of Figure A.3 reflects the decision to conduct the market survey. State-of-nature node number 1 has 2 branches coming out of it. Let us say there is a 45% chance that the survey results will indicate a favorable market for the storage sheds. We also note that the probability is .55 that the survey results will be negative.

The rest of the probabilities shown in parentheses in Figure A.3 are all *conditional* probabilities. For example, .78 is the probability of a favorable market for the sheds given a favorable result from the market survey. Of course, you would expect to find a high probability of a favorable market given that the research indicated that the market was good. Don't forget, though: There is a chance that Getz's $10,000 market survey did not result in perfect or even reliable information. Any market research study is subject to error. In this case, there remains a 22% chance that the market for sheds will be unfavorable given that the survey results are positive.

Likewise, we note that there is a 27% chance that the market for sheds will be favorable given that Getz's survey results are negative. The probability is much higher, .73, that the market will actually be unfavorable given that the survey was negative.

Finally, when we look to the payoff column in Figure A.3, we see that $10,000—the cost of the marketing study—must be subtracted from each of the top 10 tree branches. Thus, a large plant constructed in a favorable market would normally net a $200,000 profit. Yet because the market study was conducted, this figure is reduced by $10,000. In the unfavorable case, the loss of $180,000 would increase to $190,000. Similarly, conducting the survey and building *no plant* now results in a −$10,000 payoff.

With all probabilities and payoffs specified, we can start calculating the expected monetary value of each branch. We begin at the end or right-hand side of the decision tree and work back toward the origin. When we finish, the best decision will be known.

1. Given favorable survey results,

    EMV(node 2) = (.78)($190,000) + (.22)(−$190,000) = $106,400

    EMV(node 3) = (.78)($90,000) + (.22)(−$30,000) = $63,600

    The EMV of no plant in this case is −$10,000. Thus, if the survey results are favorable, a large plant should be built.

2. Given negative survey results,

    EMV(node 4) = (.27)($190,000) + (.73)(−$190,000) = −$87,400

    EMV(node 5) = (.27)($90,000) + (.73)(−$30,000) = $2,400

    The EMV of no plant is again −$10,000 for this branch. Thus, given a negative survey result, Getz should build a small plant with an expected value of $2,400.

3. Continuing on the upper part of the tree and moving backward, we compute the expected value of conducting the market survey.

    EMV(node 1) = (.45)($106,400) + (.55)($2,400) = $49,200

4. If the market survey is *not* conducted,

    EMV(node 6) = (.50)($200,000) + (.50)(−$180,000) = $10,000

    EMV(node 7) = (.50)($100,000) + (.50)(−$20,000) = $40,000

    The EMV of no plant is $0. Thus, building a small plant is the best choice, given the marketing research is not performed.

5. Because the expected monetary value of conducting the survey is $49,200—versus an EMV of $40,000 for not conducting the study—the best choice is to *seek marketing information*. If the survey results are favorable, Getz should build the large plant; if they are unfavorable, it should build the small plant.

SUMMARY

This module examines two of the most widely used decision techniques—decision tables and trees. Decision tables and trees are especially useful for making decisions under risk. Investments in research and development, plant and equipment, and even new buildings

KEY TERMS

and structures can be analyzed with these decision models. Problems in inventory control, aggregate planning, maintenance, scheduling, and production control are just a few other decision table and decision tree applications.

Decision table *(p. 686)*
Expected monetary value (EMV) *(p. 687)*
Expected value of perfect information (EVPI) *(p. 688)*
Expected value under certainty *(p. 688)*
Decision tree *(p. 689)*

USING POM FOR WINDOWS TO SOLVE DECISION TABLE AND TREE PROBLEMS

POM for Windows can be used to calculate all of the information described in the decision tables and trees in this module. Program A.1 illustrates the decision table input and output. Program A.2 shows how a decision tree can be analyzed with the software.

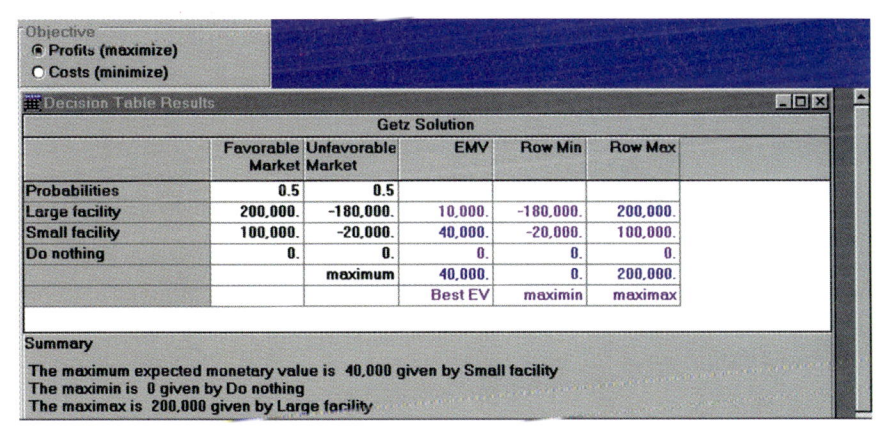

PROGRAM A.1 ■ **POM for Windows Decision Table Program for Getz Products (Examples A2 to A5)** *The user can request details by clicking on the icons that will appear at the bottom of the screen.*

PROGRAM A.2 ■ **Using POM for Windows to Analyze a Decision Tree Using Getz Data in Example A5 and Figure A.2** *Note that node numbering is different because the square decision box in Figure A.2 is node number 1.*

USING EXCEL OM FOR DECISION MODELS

Excel OM allows decision makers to evaluate decisions quickly and to perform sensitivity analysis on the results. Program A.3 again uses the Getz data to illustrate the formulas needed to compute the EMV and EVPI values. The results of these formulas are shown in Program A.4.

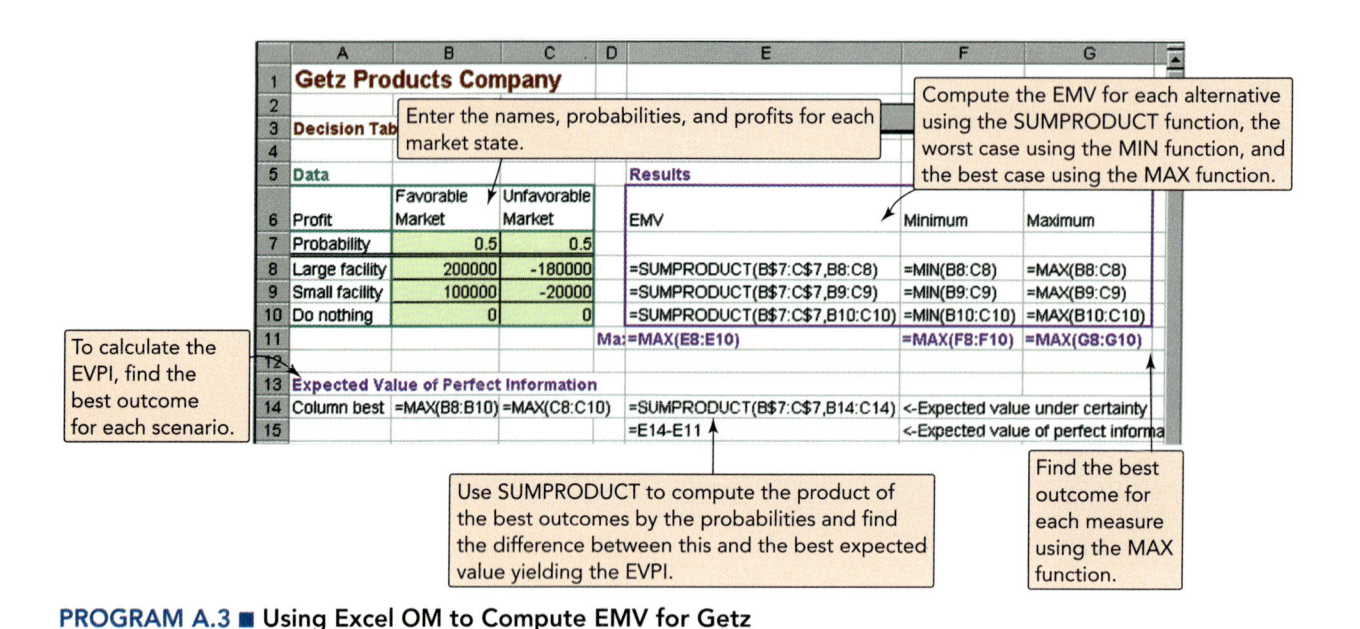

	A	B	C	D	E	F	G
1	Getz Products Company						
2							
3	Decision Tab						
4							
5	Data				Results		
6	Profit	Favorable Market	Unfavorable Market		EMV	Minimum	Maximum
7	Probability	0.5	0.5				
8	Large facility	200000	-180000		=SUMPRODUCT(B$7:C$7,B8:C8)	=MIN(B8:C8)	=MAX(B8:C8)
9	Small facility	100000	-20000		=SUMPRODUCT(B$7:C$7,B9:C9)	=MIN(B9:C9)	=MAX(B9:C9)
10	Do nothing	0	0		=SUMPRODUCT(B$7:C$7,B10:C10)	=MIN(B10:C10)	=MAX(B10:C10)
11					Ma:=MAX(E8:E10)	=MAX(F8:F10)	=MAX(G8:G10)
12							
13	Expected Value of Perfect Information						
14	Column best	=MAX(B8:B10)	=MAX(C8:C10)		=SUMPRODUCT(B$7:C$7,B14:C14)	<-Expected value under certainty	
15					=E14-E11	<-Expected value of perfect informa	

- Enter the names, probabilities, and profits for each market state.
- Compute the EMV for each alternative using the SUMPRODUCT function, the worst case using the MIN function, and the best case using the MAX function.
- To calculate the EVPI, find the best outcome for each scenario.
- Use SUMPRODUCT to compute the product of the best outcomes by the probabilities and find the difference between this and the best expected value yielding the EVPI.
- Find the best outcome for each measure using the MAX function.

PROGRAM A.3 ■ Using Excel OM to Compute EMV for Getz

	A	B	C	D	E	F	G	H
1	Getz Products Company							
2								
3	Decision Tables		Enter data in the shaded area					
4								
5	Data				Results			
6	Profit	Favorable Market	Unfavorable Market		EMV	Minimum	Maximum	
7	Probability	0.5	0.5					
8	Large facility	200000	-180000		10000	-180000	200000	
9	Small facility	100000	-20000		40000	-20000	100000	
10	Do nothing	0	0		0	0	0	
11					Maximum	40000	0	200000
12								
13	Expected Value of Perfect Information							
14	Column best	200000	0		100000	<-Expected value under certainty		
15					60000	<-Expected value of perfect information		

PROGRAM A.4 ■ Results of Excel OM Analysis in Program A.3

SOLVED PROBLEMS

Solved Problem A.1

Debbie Clair is considering the possibility of opening a small dress shop on Fairbanks Avenue, a few blocks from the university. She has located a good mall that attracts students. Her options are to open a small shop, a medium-sized shop, or no shop at all. The market for a dress shop can be good, average, or bad. The probabilities for these three possibilities are .2 for a good market, .5 for an average market, and .3 for a bad market. The net profit or loss for the medium-sized or small shops for the various market conditions are given in the following table. Building no shop at all yields no loss and no gain. What do you recommend?

Alternatives	Good Market ($)	Average Market ($)	Bad Market ($)
Small shop	75,000	25,000	−40,000
Medium-sized shop	100,000	35,000	−60,000
No shop	0	0	0
Probabilities	.20	.50	.30

Solution

The problem can be solved by computing the expected monetary value (EMV) for each alternative.

$$\text{EMV (Small shop)} = (.2)(\$75{,}000) + (.5)(\$25{,}000) + (.3)(-\$40{,}000) = \$15{,}500$$

$$\text{EMV (Medium-sized shop)} = (.2)(\$100{,}000) + (.5)(\$35{,}000) + (.3)(-\$60{,}000) = \$19{,}500$$

$$\text{EMV (No shop)} = (.2)(\$0) + (.5)(\$0) + (.3)(\$0) = \$0$$

As you can see, the best decision is to build the medium-sized shop. The EMV for this alternative is $19,500.

Solved Problem A.2

Daily demand for cases of Tidy Bowl cleaner at Ravinder Nath's Supermarket has always been 5, 6, or 7 cases. Develop a decision tree that illustrates her decision alternatives as to whether to stock 5, 6, or 7 cases.

Solution

The decision tree is shown in Figure A.4.

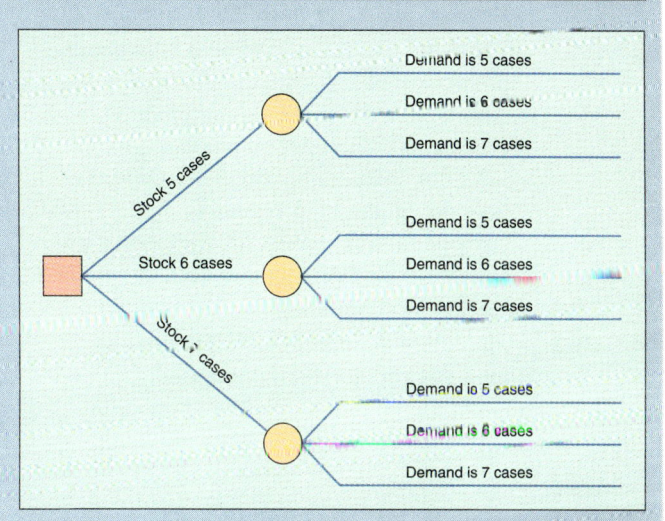

FIGURE A.4 ■ **Demand at Ravinder Nath's Supermarket**

DISCUSSION QUESTIONS

1. Give an example of a good decision you made that resulted in a bad outcome. Also give an example of a bad decision you made that had a good outcome. Why was each decision good or bad?
2. What is an alternative? What is a state of nature?
3. Jenine Duffey is trying to decide whether to invest in three different production processes. How well she does depends on whether the economy enters a period of recession or inflation. Develop a decision table (excluding the conditional values) to describe this situation.
4. Describe the meaning of EMV and EVPI. Provide an example in which EVPI can help a manager.
5. When are decision trees most useful?
6. Expected value is considered to be a reasonable, analytic criterion for decision making. What are its weaknesses? What are its assumptions?
7. Explain how decision trees might be used in several of the ten OM decisions.

PROBLEMS

A.1 A T-shirt salesperson at a David Bowie concert tour created a table of conditional values for the various alternatives (stocking decision) and states of nature (size of crowd):

Alternatives	States of Nature (demand)		
	BIG	AVERAGE	SMALL
Large Stock	$22,000	$12,000	−$2,000
Average Stock	$14,000	$10,000	$6,000
Small Stock	$ 9,000	$ 8,000	$4,000

If the probabilities associated with the states of nature are 0.3 for a big demand, 0.5 for an average demand, and 0.2 for a small demand, determine the alternative that provides the greatest expected monetary value (EMV).

A.2 For Problem A.1, compute the expected value of perfect information (EVPI).

A.3 The ABC Co. is considering a new consumer product. Managers believe that there is a probability of 0.4 that the XYZ Co. will come out with a competitive product. If ABC adds an assembly line for the product and XYZ Co. does not follow with a competitive product, ABC's expected profit is $40,000; if ABC adds an assembly line and XYZ follows suit, ABC still expects $10,000 profit. If ABC adds a new plant addition and XYZ does not produce a competitive product, ABC expects a profit of $600,000; if XYZ does compete for this market, ABC expects a loss of $100,000.
Determine the EMV of each decision.

A.4 For Problem A.3, compute the expected value of perfect information.

A.5 The following payoff table provides profits based on various possible decision alternatives and various levels of demand:

	Demand		
	LOW	MEDIUM	HIGH
Alternative 1	80	120	140
Alternative 2	90	90	90
Alternative 3	50	70	150

The probability of low demand is 0.4, whereas the probability of medium and high demand is each 0.3.
  a) What is the highest possible expected monetary value?
  b) Calculate the expected value of perfect information for this situation.

· A.6 Legal Services of Tampa is going to increase its capacity to provide free legal advice but must decide whether to do so by hiring another full-time lawyer or by using part-time lawyers. The table below shows the expected *costs* of the two options for three possible demand levels:

	States of Nature		
Alternatives	LOW DEMAND	MEDIUM DEMAND	HIGH DEMAND
Hire full-time	$300	$500	$ 700
Hire part-time	$ 0	$350	$1,000
Probabilities	.2	.5	.3

Using expected value, what should Legal Services do?

· A.7 Given the following conditional value table, determine the appropriate decision assuming that each state of nature has an equal likelihood of occurring:

	States of Nature		
Alternatives	VERY FAVORABLE MARKET	AVERAGE MARKET	UNFAVORABLE MARKET
Large plant	$275,000	$100,000	−$150,000
Small plant	$200,000	$ 60,000	−$ 10,000
Overtime	$100,000	$ 40,000	−$ 1,000
Do nothing	$ 0	$ 0	$ 0

· A.8 Jerry Bauman's company is considering expansion of its current facility to meet increasing demand. If demand is high in the future, a major expansion would result in an additional profit of $800,000, but if demand is low there would be a loss of $500,000. If demand is high, a minor expansion will result in an increase in profits of $200,000, but if demand is low, there is a loss of $100,000. The company has the option of not expanding. If there is a 50% chance demand will be high, what should the company do to maximize long-run average profits?

: A.9 Foto Color is a small supplier of chemicals and equipment used by some photographic stores to process 35 mm film. One product that Foto Color supplies is BC-6. Doug Niles, president of Foto Color, normally stocks 11, 12, or 13 cases of BC-6 each week. For each case that Doug sells, he receives a profit of $35. Because BC-6, like many photographic chemicals, has a very short shelf life, if a case is not sold by the end of the week Doug must discard it. Because each case costs Doug $56, he loses $56 for every case that is not sold by the end of the week. There is a probability of 0.45 of selling 11 cases, a probability of 0.35 of selling 12 cases, and a probability of 0.2 of selling 13 cases.
  a) What is your recommended course of action?
  b) If Doug is able to develop BC-6 with an ingredient that stabilizes BC-6 so it no longer has to be discarded, how would this change your recommended course of action?

: A.10 Smith Cheese Company is a small manufacturer of several different cheese products. One product is a cheese spread sold to retail outlets. Maureen Smith must decide how many cases of cheese spread to manufacture each month. The probability that demand will be 6 cases is .1, for 7 cases it is .3, for 8 cases it is .5, and for 9 cases it is .1. The cost of every case is $45, and the price Maureen gets for each case is $95. Unfortunately, any cases not sold by the end of the month are of no value as a result of spoilage. How many cases should Maureen manufacture each month?

: **A.11** Russell Slater, chief engineer at Atlantic Chemical, Inc., has to decide whether or not to build a new state-of-the-art processing facility. If the new facility works, the company could realize a profit of $200,000. If it fails, Atlantic could lose $150,000. At this time, Russell estimates a 60% chance that the new process will fail.

The other option is to build a pilot plant and then decide whether or not to build a complete facility. The pilot plant would cost $10,000 to build. Russell estimates a 50-50 chance that the pilot plant will work. If the pilot plant works, there is a 90% probability that the complete plant, if it is built, will also work. If the pilot plant does not work, there is only a 20% chance that the complete project (if it is constructed) will work. Russell faces a dilemma. Should he build the plant? Should he build the pilot project and then make a decision? Help Russell by analyzing this problem.

: **A.12** Penny Walk, president of PW Industries, is considering whether or not to build a manufacturing plant in the Ozarks. Her decision is summarized in the following table:

Alternatives	Favorable Market	Unfavorable Market
Build large plant	$400,000	−$300,000
Build small plant	$ 80,000	−$ 10,000
Don't build	$ 0	$ 0
Market probabilities	0.4	0.6

a) Construct a decision tree.
b) Determine the best strategy using expected monetary value (EMV).
c) What is the expected value of perfect information (EVPI)?

· **A.13** Varzandeh Mfg. Corp. buys on-off switches from two suppliers. The quality of the switches from the suppliers is indicated in the following table:

Percent Defective	Probability for Supplier A	Probability for Supplier B
1	.70	.30
3	.20	.40
5	.10	.30

For example, the probability of getting a batch of switches that are 1% defective from supplier A is .70. Since Varzandeh orders 10,000 switches per order, this would mean that there is a .7 probability of getting 100 defective switches out of the 10,000 switches if supplier A is used to fill the order. A defective switch can be repaired for $0.50. Although the quality of supplier B is lower, it will sell an order of 10,000 switches for $37 less than supplier A.

a) Develop a decision tree.
b) Which supplier should Varzandeh use?

: **A.14** Susan Williams, a concessionaire for the local ballpark, has developed a table of conditional values for the various alternatives (stocking decision) and states of nature (size of crowd).

	States of Nature (size of crowd)		
Alternatives	LARGE	AVERAGE	SMALL
Large inventory	$20,000	$10,000	−$2,000
Average inventory	$15,000	$12,000	$6,000
Small inventory	$ 9,000	$ 6,000	$5,000

If the probabilities associated with the states of nature are 0.3 for a large crowd, 0.5 for an average crowd, and 0.2 for a small crowd, determine:
a) The alternative that provides the greatest expected monetary value (EMV).
b) The expected value of perfect information (EVPI).

: **A.15** Even though independent gasoline stations have been having a difficult time, Kimberly Yeager has been thinking about opening one. Kimberly's problem is to decide how large her station should be. The annual returns will depend on both the size of her station and a number of marketing factors related to the oil industry and demand for gasoline. After a careful analysis, Kimberly developed the following table:

Size of First Station	Good Market	Fair Market	Poor Market
Small	$ 50,000	$20,000	−$ 10,000
Medium	$ 80,000	$30,000	−$ 20,000
Large	$100,000	$30,000	−$ 40,000
Very large	$300,000	$25,000	−$160,000

For example, if Yeager constructs a small station and the market is good, she will realize a profit of $50,000. Without further information on the market, Yeager assumes that each state of nature has an equal likelihood. Compute the expected value.

: **A.16** Using the data in Problem A.15, develop a decision tree and determine the best decision based on the highest expected monetary value. Assume that each outcome is equally likely.

: **A.17** Chris Suit is administrator for Lowell Hospital. She is trying to determine whether to build a large wing on the existing hospital, a small wing, or no wing at all. If the population of Lowell continues to grow, a large wing could return $150,000 to the hospital each year. If a small wing were built, it would return $60,000 to the hospital each year if the population continues to grow. If the population of Lowell remains the same, the hospital would encounter a loss of $85,000 with a large wing and a loss of $45,000 with a small wing. Unfortunately, Suit does not have any information about the future population of Lowell.
a) Construct a decision tree.
b) Construct a decision table.
c) Assuming that each state of nature has the same likelihood, determine the best alternative.
d) If the likelihood of growth is .6 and that of remaining the same is .4 and the decision criterion is expected monetary value, which decision should Suit make?

• **A.18** Paul Zipkin is considering opening a bicycle shop in Oshkosh. Zipkin enjoys biking, but this is to be a business endeavor from which he expects to make a living. He can open a small shop, a large shop, or no shop at all. Because there will be a 5-year lease on the building that Zipkin is thinking about using, he wants to make sure he makes the correct decision. Zipkin is also thinking about hiring his old marketing professor to conduct a marketing research study to see if there is a market for his services. The results of such a study could be either favorable or unfavorable. Develop a decision tree for Zipkin.

: **A.19** Paul Zipkin (of Problem A.10) has done some analysis of his bicycle shop decision. If he builds a large shop, he will earn $60,000 if the market is favorable; he will lose $40,000 if the market is unfavorable. A small shop will return a $30,000 profit with a favorable market and a $10,000 loss if the market is unfavorable. At the present time, he believes that there is a 50-50 chance of a favorable market. His former marketing professor, Jim Freeland, will charge him $5,000 for the market research. He has estimated that there is a .6 probability that the market survey will be favorable. Furthermore, there is a .9 probability that the market will be favorable given a favorable outcome of the study. However, Freeland has warned Zipkin that there is a probability of only .12 of a favorable market if the marketing research results are not favorable. Expand the decision tree of Problem A.18 to help Zipkin decide what to do.

- A.20 Dick Holliday is not sure what he should do. He can build either a large video rental section or a small one in his drugstore. He can also gather additional information or simply do nothing. If he gathers additional information, the results could suggest either a favorable or an unfavorable market, but it would cost him $3,000 to gather the information. Holliday believes that there is a 50–50 chance that the information will be favorable. If the rental market is favorable, Holliday will earn $15,000 with a large section or $5,000 with a small. With an unfavorable video-rental market, however, Holliday could lose $20,000 with a large section or $10,000 with a small section. Without gathering additional information, Holliday estimates that the probability of a favorable rental market is .7. A favorable report from the study would increase the probability of a favorable rental market to .9. Furthermore, an unfavorable report from the additional information would decrease the probability of a favorable rental market to .4. Of course, Holliday could forget all of these numbers and do nothing. What is your advice to Holliday?

- A.21 Bakery Products is considering the introduction of a new line of pastries. In order to produce the new line, the bakery is considering either a major or a minor renovation of its current plant. The following conditional values table has been developed by Bill Wicker, head of operations:

Alternatives	Favorable Market	Unfavorable Market
Major renovation	$100,000	−$90,000
Minor renovation	$ 40,000	−$20,000
Do nothing	$ 0	$ 0

Under the assumption that the probability of a favorable market is equal to the probability of an unfavorable market, determine:
a) The appropriate decision tree showing payoffs and probabilities.
b) The best alternative using expected monetary value (EMV).

■ Case Study ■

Nigel Smythe's Heart Bypass Operation

Nigel Smythe, a robust 50-year-old college administrator living in the northern suburbs of Dallas, has been diagnosed by a University of Texas cardiologist as having a defective heart valve. Although he is otherwise healthy, Smythe's heart problem could prove fatal if left untreated.

Firm research data are not yet available to predict the likelihood of survival for a man of Smythe's age and condition without surgery. However, based on her own experience and recent medical journal articles, the cardiologist tells him that if he elects to avoid surgical treatment of the valve problem, chances of survival would be approximately as follows: only a 50% chance of living 1 year, a 20% chance of surviving for 2 years, a 20% chance for 5 years, and a 10% chance of living to age 58. She places his probability of survival beyond age 58 without a heart bypass to be extremely low.

The bypass operation, however, is a serious surgical procedure. Five percent of patients die during the operation or its recovery stage, with an additional 45% dying during the first year. Twenty percent survive for 5 years, 13% survive for 10 years, and 8%, 5%, and 4% survive, respectively, for 15, 20, and 25 years.

Discussion Questions

1. Do you think that Smythe should select the bypass operation?
2. What other factors might be considered?

■ Internet Case Studies ■

See our Internet home page at http://www.prenhall.com/heizer for these additional case studies: Drink-at-Home, Inc., Arctic, Inc., and Toledo Leather Company.

BIBLIOGRAPHY

Brown, R. "Do Managers Find Decision Theory Useful?" *Harvard Business Review* 48 (May–June 1970): 78–89.

Hess, Sidney W. "Swinging on the Branch of a Tree." *Interfaces* 23 (November–December 1993): 5–12.

Pratt, J. W., H. Raiffa, and R. Schlaifer. *Introduction to Statistical Decision Theory.* New York: McGraw-Hill, 1965.

Raiffa, H. *Decision Analysis: Introductory Lectures on Choices Under Certainty.* Reading, MA: Addison-Wesley, 1968.

Render, B., and R. M. Stair Jr. *Quantitative Analysis for Management,* 6th ed. Upper Saddle River, NJ: Prentice Hall, 1997.

Schlaifer, R. *Analysis of Decisions Under Certainty.* New York: McGraw-Hill, 1969.

Ulvila, J. "Postal Automation Technology: A Decision Analysis." *Interfaces* 17 (March–April 1987): 1–12.

———, and R. Brown. "Decision Analysis Comes of Age." *Harvard Business Review* 60 (September–October 1982): 130.

QUANTITATIVE MODULE B

LINEAR PROGRAMMING

MODULE OUTLINE

REQUIREMENTS OF A LINEAR PROGRAMMING PROBLEM

FORMULATING LINEAR PROGRAMMING PROBLEMS
- Shader Electronics Example

GRAPHICAL SOLUTION TO A LINEAR PROGRAMMING PROBLEM
- Graphical Representation of Constraints
- Iso-Profit Line Solution Method
- Corner-Point Solution Method

SENSITIVITY ANALYSIS

SOLVING MINIMIZATION PROBLEMS

LINEAR PROGRAMMING APPLICATIONS
- Production-Mix Example
- Diet Problem Example
- Production Scheduling Example
- Labor Scheduling Example

THE SIMPLEX METHOD OF LP

SUMMARY

KEY TERMS

USING POM FOR WINDOWS TO SOLVE LP PROBLEMS

USING EXCEL SPREADSHEETS TO SOLVE LP PROBLEMS

SOLVED PROBLEMS

DISCUSSION QUESTIONS

PROBLEMS

DATA BASE APPLICATION

CASE STUDY: GOLDING LANDSCAPING AND PLANTS, INC.

INTERNET CASE STUDIES

BIBLIOGRAPHY

LEARNING OBJECTIVES

When you complete this module you should be able to:

Identify or Define:
- Objective function
- Constraints
- Feasible region
- Iso-profit/iso-cost methods
- Corner-point solution
- Shadow price

Describe or Explain:
- How to formulate linear models
- Graphical method of linear programming
- How to intrepret sensitivity analysis

The storm front closed in quickly on Chicago's O'Hare Airport, shutting it without warning. The heavy thunderstorms, lightning, and poor visibility sent American Airlines passengers and ground crew scurrying. Because American Airlines uses linear programming (LP) to schedule flights, hotels, crews, and refueling, LP has a direct impact on profitability. As Thomas Cook, president of AA's Decision Technology Group, says, "Finding fast solutions to LP problems is essential. If we get a major weather disruption at one of the hubs, such as Dallas or Chicago, then a lot of flights may get canceled, which means we have a lot of crews and airplanes in the wrong places. What we need is a way to put that whole operation back together again." LP is the tool that helps airlines such as American unsnarl and cope with this weather mess.

Linear programming (LP) A mathematical technique designed to help operations managers plan and make decisions relative to the trade-offs necessary to allocate resources.

Many operations management decisions involve trying to make the most effective use of an organization's resources. Resources typically include machinery (such as planes, in the case of an airline), labor (such as pilots), money, time, and raw materials (such as jet fuel). These resources may be used to produce products (such as machines, furniture, food, or clothing) or services (such as airline schedules, advertising policies, or investment decisions). **Linear programming (LP)** is a widely used mathematical technique designed to help operations managers plan and make the decisions necessary to allocate resources.

A few examples of problems in which LP has been successfully applied in operations management are:

1. Scheduling school buses to *minimize* the total distance traveled when carrying students.
2. Allocating police patrol units to high crime areas in order to *minimize* response time to 911 calls.
3. Scheduling tellers at banks so that needs are met during each hour of the day while *minimizing* the total cost of labor.
4. Selecting the product mix in a factory to make best use of machine- and labor-hours available while *maximizing* the firm's profit.

SUPPLEMENT PACKAGE

This edition has gone through extensive accuracy checking to ensure quality and consistency throughout the text and support package. Our integrated package includes for the Instructor:

- **Instructor's Resource Manual** - Fully detailed lectures, student projects, Internet assignments, and much, much, more.
- **PowerPoints**
- **Videos**
    - Competitiveness and Continuous Improvement at Xerox
    - Teams and Employee Involvement at Hewlett Packard
    - Statistical Process Control at Kurt Manufacturing
    - Process Strategy and Selection
    - Technology and Manufacturing: Flexible Manufacturing Systems
    - Overview of Operations Management and Strategy at Whirlpool
    - Product Design and Supplier Partnerships at Motorola
    - Service Quality and Service Design at Marriott
    - Winnebago Industries Plant Tour
    - Wheeled Coach-Custom Videos integrated with the text
    - Regal Marine-Custom Videos integrated with the text
- **Solutions Manual**
- **Test Item File**
- **Computerized Test Item File**
- **Instructor's CD-ROM also containing Presentation Manager**

Presentation Manager enables instructors to customize their own lecture or presentation by pulling resources such as photos, figures, and PowerPoints from a library of resources placed on the instructor's CD-ROM. This presentation program helps users create exciting multimedia lectures and also allows for the inclusion of their personal notes.

OM IN ACTION

USING LP TO SELECT TENANTS IN A SHOPPING MALL

Homart Development Company is one of the largest shopping-center developers in the United States. When starting a new center, Homart produces a tentative floor plan, or "footprint," for the mall. This plan outlines sizes, shapes, and spaces for large department stores. Leasing agreements are reached with the two or three major department stores that will become anchor stores in the mall. The anchor stores are able to negotiate highly favorable occupancy agreements. Homart's profits come primarily from the rent paid by the nonanchor tenants—the smaller stores that lease space along the aisles of the mall. The decision as to allocating space to potential tenants is, therefore, crucial to the success of the investment.

The tenant mix describes the desired stores in the mall by their size, general location, and type of merchandise or service provided. For example, the mix might specify two small jewelry stores in a central section of the mall and a medium-sized shoe store and a large restaurant in one of the side aisles. In the past, Homart developed a plan for tenant mix using "rules of thumb" developed over years of experience in mall development.

Now, to improve its bottom line in an increasingly competitive marketplace, Homart treats the tenant-mix problem as an LP model. First, the model assumes that tenants can be classified into categories according to the type of merchandise or service they provide. Second, the model assumes that for each store type, store sizes can be estimated by distinct category. For example, a small jewelry store is said to contain about 700 square feet and a large one about 2,200 square feet. The tenant-mix model is a powerful tool for enhancing Homart's mall planning and leasing activities.

Source: James Bean et al., "Selecting Tenants in a Shopping Mall," *Interfaces*, March–April 1988, pp 1–9.

---

5. Picking blends of raw materials in feed mills to produce finished feed combinations at *minimum* cost.
6. Determining the distribution system that will *minimize* total shipping cost from several warehouses to various market locations.
7. Developing a production schedule that will satisfy future demands for a firm's product and at the same time *minimize* total production and inventory costs.
8. Allocating space for a tenant mix in a new shopping mall so as to *maximize* revenues to the leasing company. (See the *OM in Action* box "Using LP to Select Tenants in a Shopping Mall.")

REQUIREMENTS OF A LINEAR PROGRAMMING PROBLEM

All LP problems have four properties in common:

1. LP problems seek to *maximize* or *minimize* some quantity (usually profit or cost). We refer to this property as the **objective function** of an LP problem. The major objective of a typical firm is to maximize dollar profits in the long run. In the case of a trucking or airline distribution system, the objective might be to minimize shipping costs.
2. The presence of restrictions, or **constraints,** limits the degree to which we can pursue our objective. For example, deciding how many units of each product in a firm's product line to manufacture is restricted by available labor and machinery. We want, therefore, to maximize or minimize a quantity (the objective function) subject to limited resources (the constraints).
3. There must be *alternative courses of action* to choose from. For example, if a company produces three different products, management may use LP to decide

Objective function A mathematical expression in linear programming that maximizes or minimizes some quantity (often profit or cost but any goal may be used.)

Constraints Restrictions that limit the degree to which a manager can pursue an objective.

how to allocate among them its limited production resources (of labor, machinery, and so on). If there were no alternatives to select from, we would not need LP.
4. The objective and constraints in linear programming problems must be expressed in terms of *linear equations* or inequalities.

FORMULATING LINEAR PROGRAMMING PROBLEMS

One of the most common linear programming applications is the *product-mix problem*. Two or more products are usually produced using limited resources. The company would like to determine how many units of each product it should produce in order to maximize overall profit given its limited resources. Let's look at an example.

Shader Electronics Example

The Shader Electronics Company produces two products: (1) the Shader Walkman, a portable AM/FM cassette player, and (2) the Shader Watch-TV, a wristwatch-sized black-and-white television. The production process for each product is similar in that both require a certain number of hours of electronic work and a certain number of labor-hours in the assembly department. Each Walkman takes 4 hours of electronic work and 2 hours in the assembly shop. Each Watch-TV requires 3 hours in electronics and 1 hour in assembly. During the current production period, 240 hours of electronic time are available and 100 hours of assembly department time are available. Each Walkman sold yields a profit of $7; each Watch-TV produced may be sold for a $5 profit.

Shader's problem is to determine the best possible combination of Walkmans and Watch-TVs to manufacture in order to reach the maximum profit. This product-mix situation can be formulated as a linear programming problem.

We begin by summarizing the information needed to formulate and solve this problem (see Table B.1). Further, let's introduce some simple notation for use in the objective function and constraints. Let

X_1 = number of Walkmans to be produced

X_2 = number of Watch-TVs to be produced

> We name the decision variables X_1 and X_2 here but point out that any notation (such as WM and WT) would be fine as well.

TABLE B.1 ■ **Shader Electronics Company Problem Data**

Hours Required to Produce 1 Unit

Department	WALKMANS (X_1)	WATCH-TVs (X_2)	Available Hours This Week
Electronic	4	3	240
Assembly	2	1	100
Profit per unit	$7	$5	

Now we can create the LP *objective function* in terms of X_1 and X_2:

$$\text{Maximize profit} = \$7X_1 + \$5X_2$$

Our next step is to develop mathematical relationships to describe the two constraints in this problem. One general relationship is that the amount of a resource used is to be less than or equal to ($\leq$) the amount of resource *available*.

First constraint: Electronic time used is ≤ Electronic time available.

$$4X_1 + 3X_2 \leq 240 \text{ (hours of electronic time)}$$

Second constraint: Assembly time used is ≤ Assembly time available.

$$2X_1 + 1X_2 \leq 100 \text{ (hours of assembly time)}$$

Both of these constraints represent production capacity restrictions and, of course, affect the total profit. For example, Shader Electronics cannot produce 70 Walkmans during the production period because if $X_1 = 70$, both constraints will be violated. It also cannot make $X_1 = 50$ Walkmans and $X_2 = 10$ Watch-TVs. This constraint brings out another important aspect of linear programming: That is, certain interactions will exist between variables. The more units of one product that a firm produces, the fewer it can make of other products.

GRAPHICAL SOLUTION TO A LINEAR PROGRAMMING PROBLEM

The easiest way to solve a small LP problem such as that of the Shader Electronics Company is the **graphical solution approach.** The graphical procedure can be used only when there are two **decision variables** (such as number of Walkmans to produce, X_1, and number of Watch-TVs to produce, X_2). When there are more than two variables, it is *not* possible to plot the solution on a two-dimensional graph; we then must turn to more complex approaches described later in this module.

Graphical solution approach A means of plotting a solution to a two-variable problem on a graph.

Graphical Representation of Constraints

In order to find the optimal solution to a linear programming problem, we must first identify a set, or region, of feasible solutions. The first step in doing so is to plot the problem's constraints on a graph.

Decision variables Choices available to a decision maker.

The variable X_1 (Walkmans, in our example) is usually plotted as the horizontal axis of the graph, and the variable X_2 (Watch-TVs) is plotted as the vertical axis. The complete problem may be restated as:

$$\text{Maximize profit} = \$7X_1 + \$5X_2$$

Subject to the constraints:

$$4X_1 + 3X_2 \leq 240 \text{ (electronics constraint)}$$

$$2X_1 + 1X_2 \leq 100 \text{ (assembly constraint)}$$

$$X_1 \geq 0 \text{ (number of Walkmans produced is greater than or equal to 0)}$$

$$X_2 \geq 0 \text{ (number of Watch-TVs produced is greater than or equal to 0)}$$

These two constraints are also called the nonnegativity constraints.

The first step in graphing the constraints of the problem is to convert the constraint inequalities into equalities (or equations).

Constraint A: $4X_1 + 3X_2 = 240$

Constraint B: $2X_1 + 1X_2 = 100$

The equation for constraint A is plotted in Figure B.1 and for constraint B in Figure B.2 at the top of the next page.

FIGURE B.1 ■ Constraint A

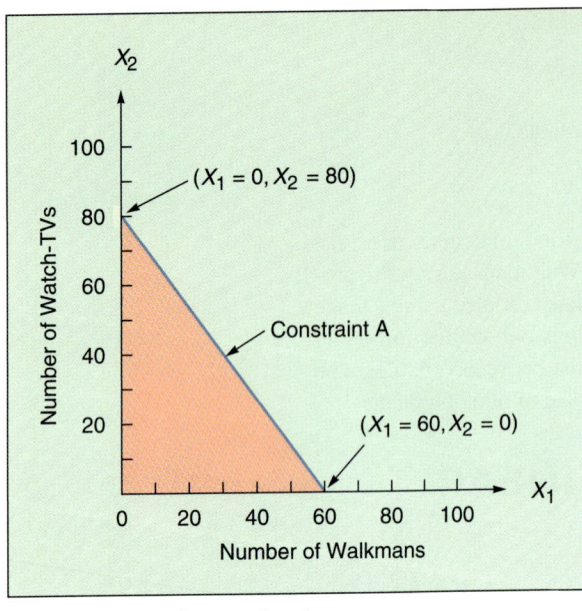

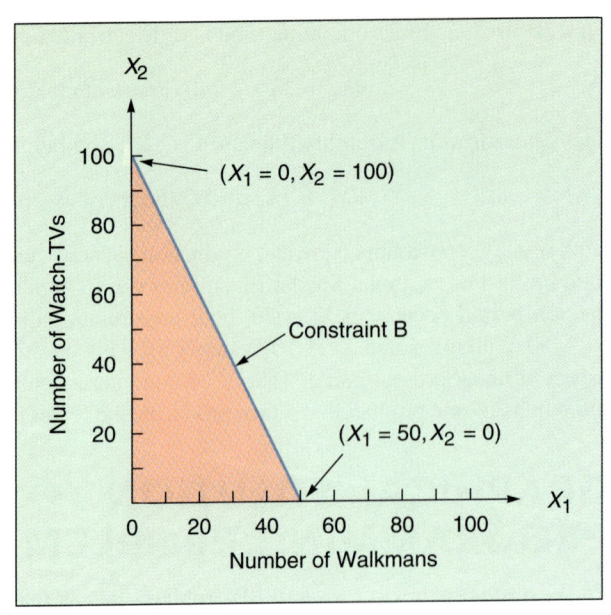

FIGURE B.2 ■ Constraint B

To plot the line in Figure B.1, all we need to do is to find the points at which the line $4X_1 + 3X_2 = 240$ intersects the X_1 and X_2 axes. When $X_1 = 0$ (the location where the line touches the X_2 axis), it implies that $3X_2 = 240$ and that $X_2 = 80$. Likewise, when $X_2 = 0$, we see that $4X_1 = 240$ and that $X_1 = 60$. Thus, constraint A is bounded by the line running from ($X_1 = 0$, $X_2 = 80$) to ($X_1 = 60$, $X_2 = 0$). The shaded area represents all points that satisfy the original *inequality*.

Constraint B is illustrated similarly in Figure B.2. When $X_1 = 0$, then $X_2 = 100$; and when $X_2 = 0$, then $X_1 = 50$. Constraint B, then, is bounded by the line between ($X_1 = 0$, $X_2 = 100$) and ($X_1 = 50$, $X_2 = 0$). The shaded area represents the original inequality.

Figure B.3 shows both constraints together. The shaded region is the part that satisfies both restrictions. The shaded region in Figure B.3 is called the *area of feasible solutions*, or simply the **feasible region.** This region must satisfy *all* conditions specified by the program's constraints and is thus the region where all constraints overlap. Any point in the region would be a *feasible solution* to the Shader Electronics Company problem. Any point outside the shaded area would represent an *infeasible solution*. Hence, it would be feasible to manufacture 30 Walkmans and 20 Watch-TVs ($X_1 = 30$, $X_2 = 20$), but it would violate the constraints to produce 70 Walkmans and 40 Watch-TVs. This can be seen by plotting these points on the graph of Figure B.3.

Feasible region The set of all feasible combinations of decision variables.

Iso-Profit Line Solution Method

Now that the feasible region has been graphed, we can proceed to find the *optimal* solution to the problem. The optimal solution is the point lying in the feasible region that produces the highest profit.

Once the feasible region has been established, several approaches can be taken in solving for the optimal solution. The speediest one to apply is called the **iso-profit line method**.[1]

Iso-profit line method An approach to solving a linear programming maximization problem graphically.

---

[1] *Iso* means "equal" or "similar." Thus, an iso-profit line represents a line with all profits the same, in this case $210.

GRAPHICAL SOLUTION TO A LINEAR PROGRAMMING PROBLEM

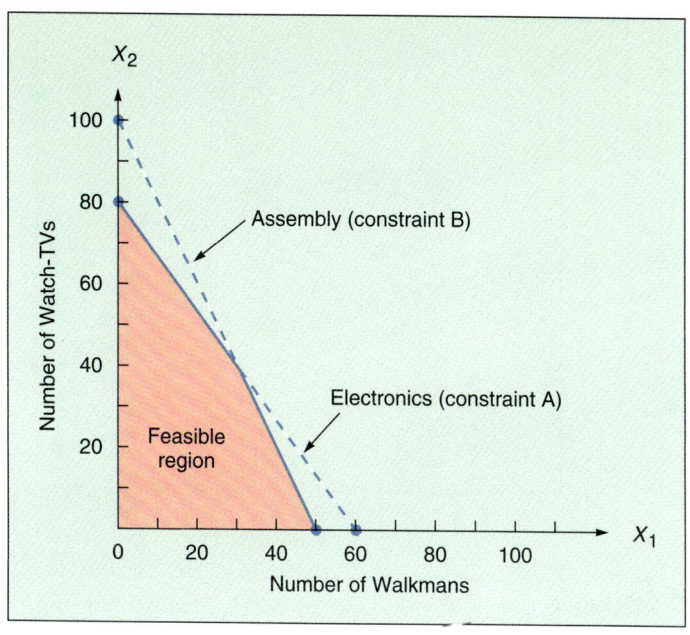

FIGURE B.3 ■ **Feasible Solution Region for the Shader Electronics Company Problem**

We start by letting profits equal some arbitrary but small dollar amount. For the Shader Electronics problem, we may choose a profit of $210. This is a profit level that can easily be obtained without violating either of the two constraints. The objective function can be written as $210 = 7X_1 + 5X_2$.

This expression is just the equation of a line; we call it an *iso-profit line*. It represents all combinations (of X_1, X_2) that would yield a total profit of $210. To plot the profit line, we proceed exactly as we did to plot a constraint line. First, let $X_1 = 0$ and solve for the point at which the line crosses the X_2 axis.

$$\$210 = \$7(0) + \$5X_2$$

$$X_2 = 42 \text{ Watch-TVs}$$

Then let $X_2 = 0$ and solve for X_1.

$$\$210 = \$7X_1 + \$5(0)$$

$$X_1 = 30 \text{ Walkmans}$$

We can now connect these two points with a straight line. This profit line is illustrated in Figure B.4 on page 710. All points on the line represent feasible solutions that produce a profit of $210.

We see, however, that the iso-profit line for $210 does not produce the highest possible profit to the firm. In Figure B.5 on page 710, we try graphing two more lines, each yielding a higher profit. The middle equation, $280 = \$7X_1 + \$5X_2$, was plotted in the same fashion as the lower line. When $X_1 = 0$,

$$\$280 = \$7(0) + \$5X_2$$

$$X_2 = 56 \text{ Watch-TVs}$$

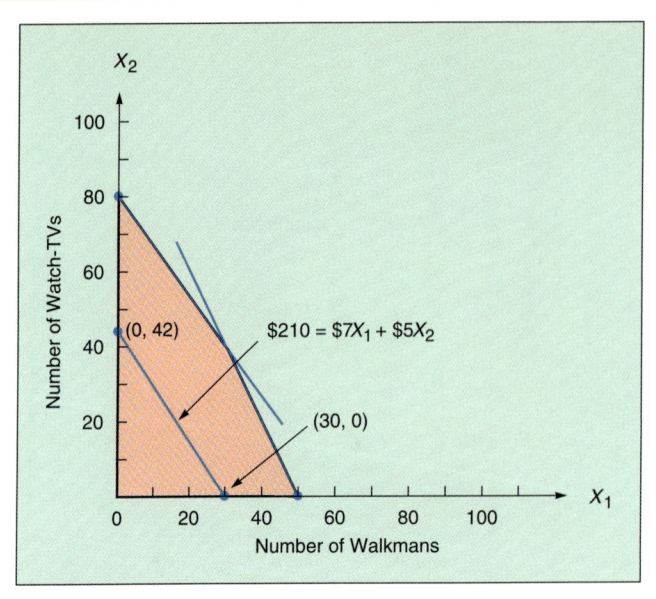

FIGURE B.4 ■ A Profit Line of $210 Plotted for the Shader Electronics Company

When $X_2 = 0$,

$$\$280 = \$7X_1 + \$5(0)$$

$$X_1 = 40 \text{ Walkmans}$$

Again, any combination of Walkmans (X_1) and Watch-TVs (X_2) on this iso-profit line will produce a total profit of $280.

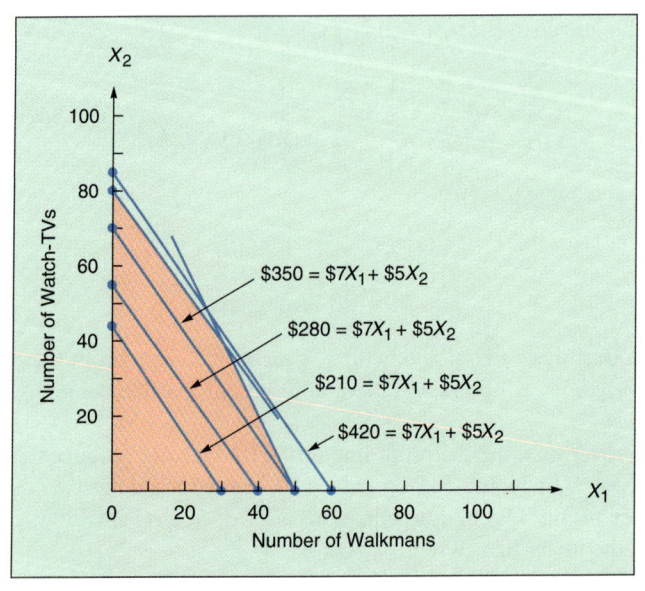

FIGURE B.5 ■ Four Iso-Profit Lines Plotted for the Shader Electronics Company

Graphical Solution to a Linear Programming Problem

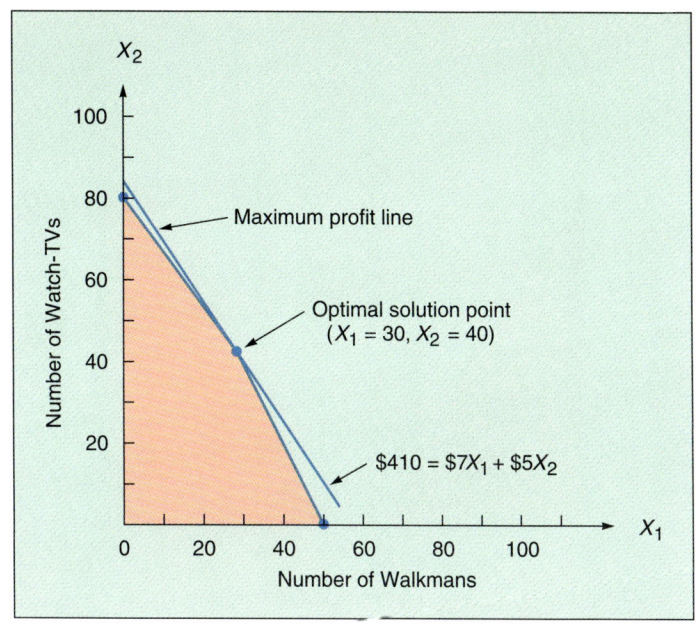

FIGURE B.6 ■ **Optimal Solution for the Shader Electronics Problem**

Note that the third line generates a profit of $350, even more of an improvement. The farther we move from the 0 origin, the higher our profit will be. Another important point to note is that these iso-profit lines are parallel. We now have two clues as to how to find the optimal solution to the original problem. We can draw a series of parallel profit lines (by carefully moving our ruler in a plane parallel to the first profit line). The highest profit line that still touches some point of the feasible region will pinpoint the optimal solution. Notice that the fourth line ($420) is too high to count because it does not touch the feasible region.

The highest possible iso-profit line is illustrated in Figure B.6. It touches the tip of the feasible region at the corner point ($X_1 = 30$, $X_2 = 40$) and yields a profit of $410.

Corner-Point Solution Method

A second approach to solving linear programming problems employs the **corner-point method**. This technique is simpler in concept than the iso-profit line approach, but it involves looking at the profit at every corner point of the feasible region.

The mathematical theory behind linear programming states that an optimal solution to any problem (that is, the values of X_1, X_2 that yield the maximum profit) will lie at a *corner point*, or *extreme point*, of the feasible region. Hence, it is necessary to find only the values of the variables at each corner; the maximum profit or optimal solution will lie at one (or more) of them.

Once again we can see (in Figure B.7 on page 712) that the feasible region for the Shader Electronics Company problem is a four-sided polygon with four corner, or extreme, points. These points are labeled ①, ②, ③, and ④ on the graph. To find the (X_1, X_2) values producing the maximum profit, we find out what the coordinates of each corner point are, then determine and compare their profit levels.

Corner-point method
A method for solving graphical linear programming problems.

Module B Linear Programming

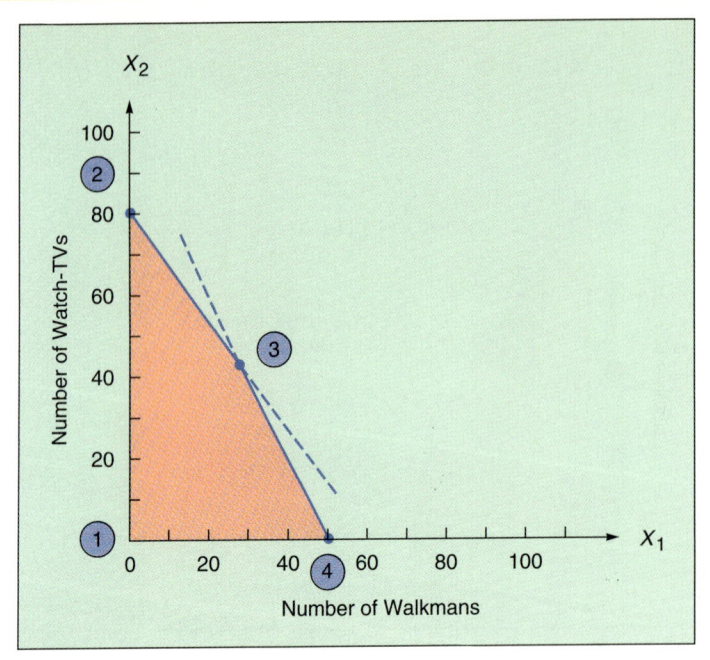

FIGURE B.7 ■ The Four Corner Points of the Feasible Region

Point ①: $(X_1 = 0, X_2 = 0)$ Profit $7(0) + $5(0) = $0

Point ②: $(X_1 = 0, X_2 = 80)$ Profit $7(0) + $5(80) = $400

Point ④: $(X_1 = 50, X_2 = 0)$ Profit $7(50) + $5(0) = $350

We skipped corner point ③ momentarily because in order to find its coordinates *accurately*, we will have to solve for the intersection of the two constraint lines. As you may recall from algebra, we can apply the method of *simultaneous equations* to the two constraint equations.

$$4X_1 + 3X_2 = 240 \quad (\textit{electronics time})$$

$$2X_1 + 1X_2 = 100 \quad (\textit{assembly time})$$

To solve these equations simultaneously, we multiply the second equation by -2:

$$-2(2X_1 + 1X_2 = 100) = -4X_1 - 2X_2 = -200$$

and then add it to the first equation:

$$+4X_1 + 3X_2 = 240$$
$$-4X_1 - 2X_2 = -200$$
$$\overline{\, + 1X_2 = 40}$$

or

$$X_2 = 40$$

Doing this has enabled us to eliminate one variable, X_1, and to solve for X_2. We can now substitute 40 for X_2 in either of the original equations and solve for X_1. Let us use the first equation. When $X_2 = 40$, then

$$4X_1 + 3(40) = 240$$

$$4X_1 + 120 = 240$$

or

$$4X_1 = 120$$

$$X_1 = 30$$

Thus, point ③ has the coordinates ($X_1 = 30$, $X_2 = 40$). We can compute its profit level to complete the analysis.

Point ③: ($X_1 = 30, X_2 = 40$) Profit = $7(30) + $5(40) = $410

Although the values for X_1 and X_2 are integers for Shader Electronics, this will not always be the case.

Because point ③ produces the highest profit of any corner point, the product mix of $X_1 = 30$ Walkmans and $X_2 = 40$ Watch-TVs is the optimal solution to the Shader Electronics problem. This solution will yield a profit of $410 per production period; it is the same solution we obtained using the iso-profit line method.

SENSITIVITY ANALYSIS

Operations managers are usually interested in more than the optimal solution to an LP problem. In addition to knowing the value of each decision variable (the X_i's) and the value of the objective function, they want to know how sensitive these answers are to input **parameter** changes. For example, what happens if the coefficients of the objective function are not exact, or if they change by 10% or 15%? What happens if right-hand-side values of the constraints change? Because solutions are based on the assumption that input parameters are constant, the subject of sensitivity analysis comes into play. **Sensitivity analysis**, or postoptimality analysis, is the study of how sensitive solutions are to parameter changes.

LP software like POM for Windows, Excel, or LINDO enables you to perform sensitivity analysis for situations such as these. Let us examine several scenarios relating to the Shader Electronics example.

We begin by introducing the concept of a **shadow price**, which is also called the **dual**. The dual is the value of 1 additional unit of a resource in the form of 1 more hour of machine time, labor time, or other scarce resource. It answers the question: Exactly how much should a firm be willing to pay to make additional resources available? Is it worthwhile to pay workers an overtime rate to stay 1 extra hour each night in order to increase production output?

We just saw that the optimal solution to the Shader problem is $X_1 = 30$ Walkmans, $X_2 = 40$ Watch-TVs, and profit = $410. Suppose Shader is considering adding an extra assembler at a salary of $5.00 per hour. Should the firm do so? The answer is *no*—the dual value of the assembly department resource is only $.50 (see Program B.1 on page 714). Thus, the firm will lose $4.50 for every hour the new assembler works.

Let us ask a second question relating to sensitivity analysis. What would happen, for example, if the manager at Shader Electronics had been off by 17% in setting the net

Parameter Numerical value that is given in a model.

Sensitivity analysis An analysis that projects how much a solution might change if there were changes in the variables or input data.

Shadow price (or **dual**) The value of 1 additional unit of a resource in the form of 1 more hour of machine time or labor time or other scarce resource in linear programming.

profit per Walkman at $7. Would that error drastically alter the decision to produce 30 Walkmans and 40 Watch-TVs? What would be the impact of 265 electronic hours being available instead of 240?

Program B.1 is part of the POM for Windows computer-generated output available to help a decision maker know whether or not a solution is relatively insensitive to reasonable changes in one or more of the parameters of the problem. (The complete computer run for these data, including input and full output, is illustrated in Program B.2 later in this module.)

Shader electronics Solution

Variable	Value	Reduced	Original Val	Lower Bound	Upper Bound
Walkmans	30.	0.	7.	6.6667	10.
Watch-TVs	40.	0.	5.	3.5	5.25
Constraint	Dual Value	Slack/Surplus	Original Val	Lower Bound	Upper Bound
Electronics	1.5	0.	240.	200.	300.
Assembly	0.5	0.	100.	80.	120.

PROGRAM B.1 ■ Sensitivity Analysis for Shader Electronics Using POM for Windows Software

First, let us consider changes to the right-hand side of a constraint. In Program B.1, we assume that changes are made in only one constraint at a time, while the other one remains fixed at its original values. *Right-hand side ranging* tells us over what range of right-hand side values the dual (shadow) prices for that constraint will remain valid. In the Shader example, the $1.50 dual value for the electronic constraint will apply even if the original value of 240 hours drops as low as 200 (lower bound) or increases as high as 300 (upper bound).

This concept that the right-hand side range limits the dual, or shadow price, is important in sensitivity analysis. Suppose Shader Electronics could obtain additional electronic hours at a cost less than the dual. The question of how much to obtain is answered by the upper bound in Program B.1—that is, secure 60 hours (300–240) more than the original 240 hours.

SOLVING MINIMIZATION PROBLEMS

Many linear programming problems involve *minimizing* an objective such as cost instead of maximizing a profit function. A restaurant, for example, may wish to develop a work schedule to meet staffing needs while minimizing the total number of employees. Also, a manufacturer may seek to distribute its products from several factories to its many regional warehouses in such a way as to minimize total shipping costs.

Minimization problems can be solved graphically by first setting up the feasible solution region and then using either the corner-point method or an **iso-cost** line approach (which is analogous to the iso-profit approach in maximization problems) to find the values of X_1 and X_2 that yield the minimum cost.

Example B1 shows how to solve a minimization problem.

Iso-cost An approach to solving a linear programming minimization problem graphically.

EXAMPLE B1

Cohen Chemicals, Inc., produces two types of photo-developing fluids. The first, a black-and-white picture chemical, costs Cohen $2,500 per ton to produce. The second, a color photo chemical, costs $3,000 per ton.

Solving Minimization Problems

Based on an analysis of current inventory levels and outstanding orders, Cohen's production manager has specified that at least 30 tons of the black-and-white chemical and at least 20 tons of the color chemical must be produced during the next month. In addition, the manager notes that an existing inventory of a highly perishable raw material needed in both chemicals must be used within 30 days. In order to avoid wasting the expensive raw material, Cohen must produce a total of at least 60 tons of the photo chemicals in the next month.

We may formulate this information as a minimization LP problem. Let

X_1 = number of tons of black-and-white picture chemical produced

X_2 = number of tons of color picture chemical produced

Subject to:

$X_1 \geq 30$ tons of black-and-white chemical

$X_2 \geq 20$ tons of color chemical

$X_1 + X_2 \geq 60$ tons total

$X_1, X_2 \geq 0$ nonnegativity requirements

To solve the Cohen Chemicals problem graphically, we construct the problem's feasible region, shown in Figure B.8.

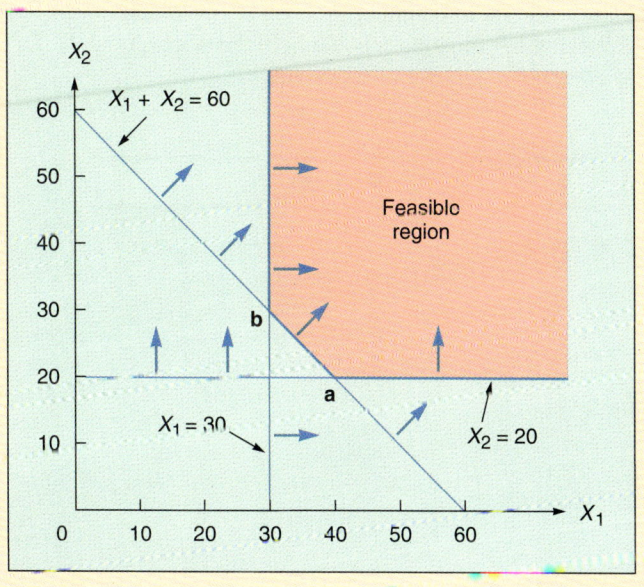

FIGURE B.8 ■ **Cohen Chemicals' Feasible Region**

The area is not unbounded to the right in a minimization problem as it is in a maximization problem.

Minimization problems are often unbounded outward (that is, on the right side and on the top), but this characteristic causes no problem in solving them. As long as they are bounded inward (on the left side and the bottom), we can establish corner points. The optimal solution will lie at one of the corners.

In this case, there are only two corner points, **a** and **b** in Figure B.8. It is easy to determine that at point **a**, $X_1 = 40$ and $X_2 = 20$, and that at point **b**, $X_1 = 30$ and $X_2 = 30$. The optimal solution is found at the point yielding the lowest total cost.

Thus

$$\text{Total cost at } \mathbf{a} = 2{,}500X_1 + 3{,}000X_2$$

$$= 2{,}500(40) + 3{,}000(20)$$

$$= \$160{,}000$$

$$\text{Total cost at } \mathbf{b} = 2{,}500X_1 + 3{,}000X_2$$

$$= 2{,}500(30) + 3{,}000(30)$$

$$= \$165{,}000$$

The lowest cost to Cohen Chemicals is at point **a**. Hence the operations manager should produce 40 tons of the black-and-white chemical and 20 tons of the color chemical.

LINEAR PROGRAMMING APPLICATIONS

The foregoing examples each contained just two variables (X_1 and X_2). Most real-world problems contain many more variables, however. Let's use the principles already developed to formulate a few more complex problems. The practice you will get by "paraphrasing" the following LP situations should help develop your skills for applying linear programming to other common operations situations.

OM IN ACTION

SCHEDULING PLANES AT DELTA AIRLINES WITH COLDSTART

It has been said that an airline seat is the most perishable commodity in the world. Each time an airliner takes off with an empty seat, a revenue opportunity is lost forever. For Delta Airlines, which flies over 2,500 domestic flight legs per day using about 450 aircraft of 10 different models, its schedule is the very heartbeat of the airline.

One flight leg for Delta might consist of a Boeing 757 jet assigned to fly at 6:21 A.M. from Atlanta to arrive in Boston at 8:45 A.M. Delta's problem, like that of every competitor, is to match airplanes such as 747s, 757s, or 767s to flight legs such as Atlanta–Boston and to fill seats with paying passengers. Recent advances in linear programming algorithms and computer hardware have made it possible to solve optimization problems of this scope for the first time. Delta calls its huge LP model Coldstart and runs the model every day. Delta is the first airline to solve a problem of this scope.

The typical size of a daily Coldstart model is about 40,000 constraints and 60,000 variables. The constraints include aircraft availability, balancing arrivals and departures at airports, aircraft maintenance needs, and so on. Coldstart's objective is to minimize a combination of operating costs and lost passenger revenue, called "spill costs."

The savings from the model so far have been phenomenal, estimated at $220,000 per day over Delta's earlier schedule planning tool, which was nicknamed "Warmstart." Delta expects to save $300 million over the next three years through this use of linear programming.

Sources: R. Subramanian et al., *Interfaces* 24, 1 (January–February 1994): 104–120; Peter R. Horner, *OR/MS Today* 22, 4 (August 1995): 14–15.

Production-Mix Example

Example B2 involves another *production-mix* decision. Limited resources must be allocated among various products that a firm produces. The firm's overall objective is to manufacture the selected products in such quantities as to maximize total profits.

EXAMPLE B2

Failsafe Electronics Corporation primarily manufactures four highly technical products, which it supplies to aerospace firms that hold NASA contracts. Each of the products must pass through the following departments before they are shipped: wiring, drilling, assembly, and inspection. The time requirements in each department (in hours) for each unit produced and its corresponding profit value are summarized in this table:

Product	Wiring	Drilling	Assembly	Inspection	Unit Profit
XJ201	.5	3	2	.5	$ 9
XM897	1.5	1	4	1.0	$12
TR29	1.5	2	1	.5	$15
BR788	1.0	3	2	.5	$11

The production time available in each department each month and the minimum monthly production requirement to fulfill contracts are as follows:

Department	Capacity (in hours)	Product	Minimum Production Level
Wiring	1,500	XJ201	150
Drilling	1,700	XM897	100
Assembly	2,600	TR29	300
Inspection	1,200	BR788	400

The production manager has the responsibility of specifying production levels for each product for the coming month. Let

$$X_1 = \text{number of units of XJ201 produced}$$
$$X_2 = \text{number of units of XM897 produced}$$
$$X_3 = \text{number of units of TR29 produced}$$
$$X_4 = \text{number of units of BR788 produced}$$

Maximize profit = $9X_1 + 12X_2 + 15X_3 + 11X_4$

subject to $.5X_1 + 1.5X_2 + 1.5X_3 + 1X_4 \leq 1,500$ hours of wiring available
$3X_1 + 1X_2 + 2X_3 + 3X_4 \leq 1,700$ hours of drilling available
$2X_1 + 4X_2 + 1X_3 + 2X_4 \leq 2,600$ hours of assembly available
$.5X_1 + 1X_2 + .5X_3 + .5X_4 \leq 1,200$ hours of inspection

$X_1 \geq 150$ units of XJ201
$X_2 \geq 100$ units of XM897
$X_3 \geq 300$ units of TR29
$X_4 \geq 400$ units of BR788

$X_1, X_2, X_3, X_4 \geq 0$

Diet Problem Example

Example B3 illustrates the *diet problem*, which was originally used by hospitals to determine the most economical diet for patients. Known in agricultural applications as the *feed-mix problem*, the diet problem involves specifying a food or feed ingredient combination that will satisfy stated nutritional requirements at a minimum cost level.

EXAMPLE B3

The Feed 'N Ship feedlot fattens cattle for local farmers and ships them to meat markets in Kansas City and Omaha. The owners of the feedlot seek to determine the amounts of cattle feed to buy in order to satisfy minimum nutritional standards and, at the same time, minimize total feed costs.

The feed mix may contain three grains in the following proportions *per pound of feed:*

	Feed		
Ingredient	Stock X	Stock Y	Stock Z
A	3 oz.	2 oz.	4 oz.
B	2 oz.	3 oz.	1 oz.
C	1 oz.	0 oz.	2 oz.
D	6 oz.	8 oz.	4 oz.

The cost per pound of grains X, Y, and Z is $.02, $.04, and $.025, respectively. The minimum requirement per cow per month is 64 ounces of ingredient A, 80 ounces of ingredient B, 16 ounces of ingredient C, and 128 ounces of ingredient D.

The feedlot faces one additional restriction—it can obtain only 500 pounds of stock Z per month from the feed supplier, regardless of its need. Because there are usually 100 cows at the Feed 'N Ship feedlot at any given time, this constraint limits the amount of stock Z for use in the feed of each cow to no more than 5 pounds, or 80 ounces, per month. Let

X_1 = number of pounds of stock X purchased per cow each month

X_2 = number of pounds of stock Y purchased per cow each month

X_3 = number of pounds of stock Z purchased per cow each month

Minimum cost = $.02X_1 + .04X_2 + .025X_3$ subject to

Ingredient A requirement: $3X_1 + 2X_2 + 4X_3 \geq 64$

Ingredient B requirement: $2X_1 + 3X_2 + 1X_3 \geq 80$

Ingredient C requirement: $1X_1 + 0X_2 + 2X_3 \geq 16$

Ingredient D requirement: $6X_1 + 8X_2 + 4X_3 \geq 128$

Stock Z limitation: $X_3 \leq 80$

$X_1, X_2, X_3 \geq 0$

Production Scheduling Example

One of the most important areas of linear programming application is *production scheduling*. Solving a production scheduling problem allows the production manager to set an efficient, low-cost production schedule for a product over several production periods. Basically, the problem resembles the common product-mix model for each period in the future. Production levels must allow the firm to meet demand for its product within manpower and inventory limitations. The objective is either to maximize profit or to minimize the total cost (of production plus inventory).

EXAMPLE B4

The T. E. Callarman Appliance Company is thinking of manufacturing and selling trash compactors on an experimental basis over the next 6 months. The manufacturing costs and selling prices of the compactors are projected to vary from month to month. Table B.2 gives these forecast costs and prices.

TABLE B.2 ■ Manufacturing Costs and Selling Prices

Month	Manufacturing Cost	Selling Price (during month)
July	$60	—
August	$60	$80
September	$50	$60
October	$60	$70
November	$70	$80
December	—	$90

All compactors manufactured during any month are shipped out in one large load at the end of that month. The firm can sell as many units as it produces, but its operation is limited by the size of its warehouse, which holds a maximum of 100 compactors.

Callarman's operations manager, Richard Deckro, needs to determine the number of compactors to manufacture and sell each month in order to maximize the firm's profit. Callarman has no compactors on hand at the beginning of July and wishes to have no compactors on hand at the end of the test period in December.

To formulate this LP problem, Deckro lets

$$X_1, X_2, X_3, X_4, X_5, X_6 = \text{number of units } \textit{manufactured} \text{ during July (first month), August (second month), etc.}$$

$$Y_1, Y_2, Y_3, Y_4, Y_5, Y_6 = \text{number of units } \textit{sold} \text{ during July, August, etc.}$$

He notes that because the company starts with no compactors (and because it takes 1 month to gear up and ship out the first batch), it cannot sell any units in July (that is, $Y_1 = 0$). Also, because it wants zero inventory at the end of the year, manufacture during the month of December must be zero (that is, $X_6 = 0$).

Profit for Callarman Appliances is sales minus manufacture cost. Hence, Deckro's objective function is

$$\text{Maximize profit} = 80Y_2 + 60Y_3 + 70Y_4 + 80Y_5 + 90Y_6 \\ - (60X_1 + 60X_2 + 50X_3 + 60X_4 + 70X_5)$$

The first part of this expression is the sales price times the units sold each month. The second part is the manufacture cost, namely, the costs from Table B.2 times the units manufactured.

To set up the constraints, Deckro needs to introduce a new set of variables: $I_1, I_2, I_3, I_4, I_5, I_6$. These represent the inventory at the end of a month (after all sales have been made and after the amount produced during the month has been stocked in the warehouse). Thus,

$$\text{Inventory at end of this month} = \text{Inventory at end of previous month} + \text{Current month's production} - \text{This month's sales}$$

For July, this is $I_1 = X_1$, because there is neither previous inventory nor sales. For August,

$$I_2 = I_1 + X_2 - Y_2$$

Constraints for the remaining months are as follows:

September: $I_3 = I_2 + X_3 - Y_3$

October: $I_4 = I_3 + X_4 - Y_4$

November: $I_5 = I_4 + X_5 - Y_5$

December: $I_6 = I_5 - Y_6$

Constraints for the storage capacity are:

$I_1 \leq 100$

$I_2 \leq 100$

$I_3 \leq 100$

$I_4 \leq 100$

$I_5 \leq 100$

$I_6 = 0$ (in order to end up with zero inventory at the end of December)

Labor Scheduling Example

Labor scheduling problems address staffing needs over a specific time period. They are especially useful when managers have some flexibility in assigning workers to jobs that require overlapping or interchangeable talents. Large banks and hospitals frequently use LP to tackle their labor scheduling. Example B5 describes how one bank uses LP to schedule tellers.

EXAMPLE B5

Arlington Bank of Commerce and Industry is a busy bank that has requirements for between 10 and 18 tellers depending on the time of day. Lunch time, from noon to 2 P.M., is usually heaviest. The table below indicates the workers needed at various hours that the bank is open.

Time Period	Number of Tellers Required	Time Period	Number of Tellers Required
9 A.M.–10 A.M.	10	1 P.M.–2 P.M.	18
10 A.M.–11 A.M.	12	2 P.M.–3 P.M.	17
11 A.M.–Noon	14	3 P.M.–4 P.M.	15
Noon–1 P.M.	16	4 P.M.–5 P.M.	10

Linear Programming Applications

The bank now employs 12 full-time tellers, but many people are on its roster of available part-time employees. A part-time employee must put in exactly 4 hours per day, but can start anytime between 9 A.M. and 1 P.M. Part-timers are a fairly inexpensive labor pool, because no retirement or lunch benefits are provided them. Full-timers, on the other hand, work from 9 A.M. to 5 P.M. but are allowed 1 hour for lunch. (Half the full-timers eat at 11 A.M., the other half at noon.) Full-timers thus provide 35 hours per week of productive labor time.

By corporate policy, the bank limits part-time hours to a maximum of 50% of the day's total requirement.

Part-timers earn $6 per hour (or $24 per day) on average, whereas full-timers earn $75 per day in salary and benefits on average. The bank would like to set a schedule that would minimize its total manpower costs. It will release 1 or more of its full-time tellers if it is profitable to do so.

We can let

F = Full-time tellers

P_1 = Part-timers starting at 9 A.M. (leaving at 1 P.M.)

P_2 = Part-timers starting at 10 A.M. (leaving at 2 P.M.)

P_3 = Part-timers starting at 11 A.M. (leaving at 3 P.M.)

P_4 = Part-timers starting at noon (leaving at 4 P.M.)

P_5 = Part-timers starting at 1 P.M. (leaving at 5 P.M.)

Objective function:

$$\text{Minimize total daily manpower cost} = \$75F + \$24(P_1 + P_2 + P_3 + P_4 + P_5)$$

Constraints: For each hour, the available labor-hours must be at least equal to the required labor-hours.

$F + P_1$	≥ 10	(9 A.M. to 10 A.M. needs)
$F + P_1 + P_2$	≥ 12	(10 A.M. to 11 A.M. needs)
$\frac{1}{2}F + P_1 + P_2 + P_3$	≥ 14	(11 A.M. to noon needs)
$\frac{1}{2}F + P_1 + P_2 + P_3 + P_4$	≥ 16	(noon to 1 P.M. needs)
$F + P_2 + P_3 + P_4 + P_5$	≥ 18	(1 P.M. to 2 P.M. needs)
$F + P_3 + P_4 + P_5$	≥ 17	(2 P.M. to 3 P.M. needs)
$F + P_4 + P_5$	≥ 15	(3 P.M. to 4 P.M. needs)
$F + P_5$	≥ 10	(4 P.M. to 5 P.M. needs)

Only 12 full-time tellers are available, so

$$F \leq 12$$

Part-time worker-hours cannot exceed 50% of total hours required each day, which is the sum of the tellers needed each hour.

$$4(P_1 + P_2 + P_3 + P_4 + P_5) \leq .50(10 + 12 + 14 + 16 + 18 + 17 + 15 + 10)$$

or

$$4P_1 + 4P_2 + 4P_3 + 4P_4 + 4P_5 \leq 0.50(112)$$
$$F, P_1, P_2, P_3, P_4, P_5 \geq 0$$

There are two alternative optimal schedules that Arlington Bank can follow. The first is to employ only 10 full-time tellers ($F = 10$) and to start 7 part-timers at 10 A.M. ($P_2 = 7$), 2 part-timers at 11 A.M. and noon ($P_3 = 2$ and $P_4 = 2$), and 3 part-timers at 1 P.M. ($P_5 = 3$). No part-timers would begin at 9 A.M.

The second solution also employs 10 full-time tellers, but starts 6 part-timers at 9 A.M. ($P_1 = 6$), 1 part-timer at 10 A.M. ($P_2 = 1$), 2 part-timers at 11 A.M. and noon ($P_3 = 2$ and $P_4 = 2$), and 3 part-timers at 1 P.M. ($P_5 = 3$). The cost of either of these two policies is $1,086 per day.

THE SIMPLEX METHOD OF LP

Simplex method An algorithm developed by Dantzig for solving linear programming problems of all sizes.

Most real-world linear programming problems have more than two variables and thus are too complex for graphical solution. A procedure called the **simplex method** may be used to find the optimal solution to such problems. The simplex method is actually an algorithm (or a set of instructions) with which we examine corner points in a methodical fashion until we arrive at the best solution—highest profit or lowest cost. Computer programs (such as POM for Windows) and Excel spreadsheets are both described later in this module and are available to solve linear programming problems via the simplex method.

If you are interested in the detailed algebraic steps of the simplex algorithm, refer to a management science textbook.[2]

SUMMARY

This module introduces a special kind of model, linear programming. LP has proven to be especially useful when trying to make the most effective use of an organization's resources.

The first step in dealing with LP models is problem formulation, which involves identifying and creating an objective function and constraints. The second step is to solve the problem. If there are only two decision variables, the problem can be solved graphically, using the corner-point method or the iso-profit/iso-cost line method. With either approach, we first identify the feasible region, then find the corner point yielding the greatest profit or least cost.

All LP problems can also be solved with the simplex method, using software such as POM for Windows or Excel. This approach produces valuable economic information such as the shadow price, or dual, and provides complete sensitivity analysis on other inputs to the problem. LP is used in a wide variety of business applications, as the examples and homework problems in this module reveal.

---

[2] See, for example, Barry Render and Ralph Stair, *Quantitative Analysis for Management*, 6th ed. (Upper Saddle River, NJ: Prentice Hall, 1997), chaps. 7–9.

KEY TERMS

Linear programming (LP) *(p. 704)*
Objective function *(p. 705)*
Constraints *(p. 705)*
Graphical solution approach *(p. 707)*
Decision variables *(p. 707)*
Feasible region *(p. 708)*
Iso-profit line method *(p. 708)*

Corner-point method *(p. 711)*
Parameter *(p. 713)*
Sensitivity analysis *(p. 713)*
Shadow price or dual *(p. 713)*
Iso-cost *(p. 714)*
Simplex method *(p. 722)*

USING POM FOR WINDOWS TO SOLVE LP PROBLEMS

POM for Windows can handle LP problems with up to 22 constraints and 99 variables. Data entry and output for the Shader Electronics example used in this module are provided in Program B.2. As output, the software provides optimal values for the variables, optimal profit or cost ($410 here), and sensitivity analysis (which we saw earlier in Program B.1). In addition, POM for Windows provides graphical output for problems with only two variables, as shown in Program B.3.

	Walkmans	Watch-TVs		RHS	Dual
Maximize	7.	5.			
Electronics	4.	3.	<=	240.	1.5
Assembly	2.	1.	<=	100.	0.5
Solution->	30.	40.		410.	

PROGRAM B.2 ■ POM for Windows Analysis of Shader Electronics LP Problem

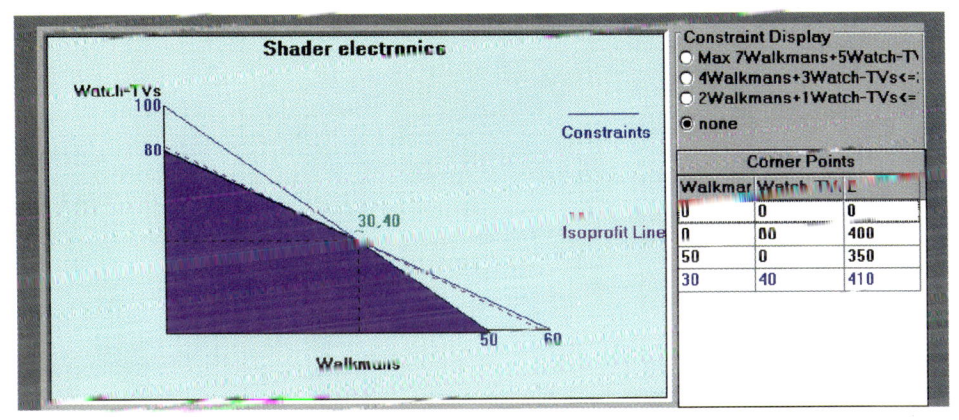

Corner Points:
Walkmans	Watch-TVs	E
0	0	0
0	80	400
50	0	350
30	40	410

PROGRAM B.3 ■ Shader Electronics Graphics Output Using POM for Windows

USING EXCEL SPREADSHEETS TO SOLVE LP PROBLEMS

Excel and other spreadsheets offer the ability to analyze linear programming problems using built-in problem-solving tools. Excel OM is not illustrated because Excel uses a *built-in* tool named Solver to find LP solutions. Solver is limited to 200 changing cells (variables), each with 2 boundary constraints and up to 100 additional constraints. These capabilities make Solver suitable for the solution of complex, real-world problems.

We use Excel to solve the Shader Electronics problem in Program B.4. The objective and constraints are repeated here:

Objective function: Maximize profit =

$$\$7(\text{No. of Walkmans}) + \$5(\text{No. of Watch-TVs})$$

Subject to: $4(\text{Walkmans}) + 3(\text{Watch-TVs}) \leq 240$

$2(\text{Walkmans}) + 1(\text{Watch-TVs}) \leq 100$

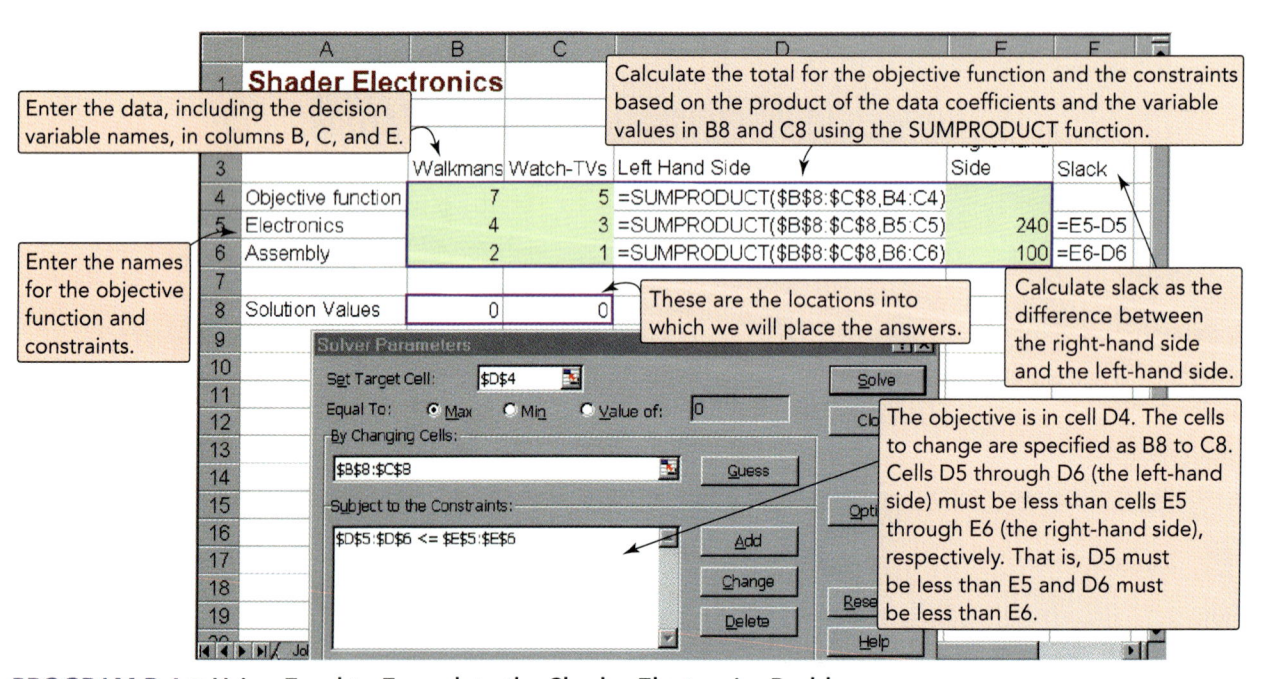

PROGRAM B.4 ■ **Using Excel to Formulate the Shader Electronics Problem**

The Excel screen in Program B.5 shows Solver's solution to the Shader Electronics Company problem. Note that the optimal solution is now shown in the *changing cells* (cells B8 and C8, which served as the variables). The Reports selection performs more extensive analysis of the solution and its environment.

SOLVED PROBLEMS

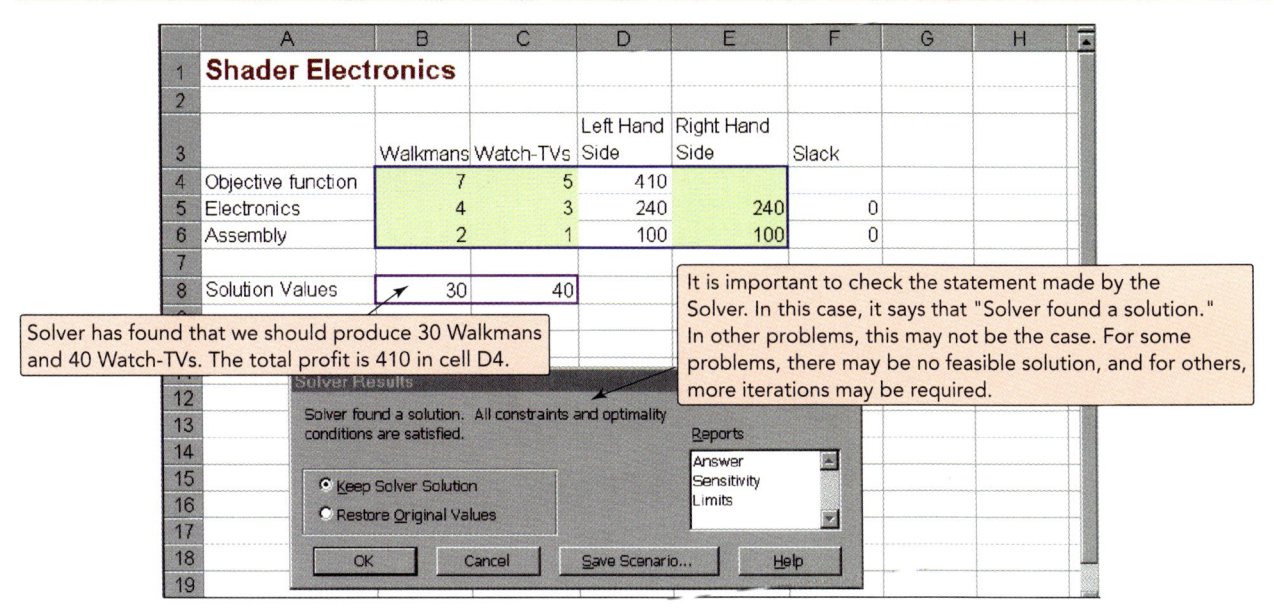

	A	B	C	D	E	F	G	H
1	**Shader Electronics**							
2								
3		Walkmans	Watch-TVs	Left Hand Side	Right Hand Side	Slack		
4	Objective function	7	5	410				
5	Electronics	4	3	240	240	0		
6	Assembly	2	1	100	100	0		
7								
8	Solution Values	30	40					

Solver has found that we should produce 30 Walkmans and 40 Watch-TVs. The total profit is 410 in cell D4.

It is important to check the statement made by the Solver. In this case, it says that "Solver found a solution." In other problems, this may not be the case. For some problems, there may be no feasible solution, and for others, more iterations may be required.

Solver Results

Solver found a solution. All constraints and optimality conditions are satisfied.

- ● Keep Solver Solution
- ○ Restore Original Values

Reports:
Answer
Sensitivity
Limits

[OK] [Cancel] [Save Scenario...] [Help]

PROGRAM B.5 ■ Excel Solution to Shader Electronics LP Problem

---

SOLVED PROBLEMS

Solved Problem B.1

Smitty's, a clothing manufacturer that produces men's shirts and pajamas, has two primary resources available: sewing-machine time (in the sewing department) and cutting-machine time (in the cutting department). Over the next month, Smitty can schedule up to 280 hours of work on sewing machines and up to 450 hours of work on cutting machines. Each shirt produced requires 1.00 hour of sewing time and 1.50 hours of cutting time. Producing each pair of pajamas requires .75 hour of sewing time and 2.00 hours of cutting time.

To express the LP constraints for this problem mathematically, we let

X_1 = number of shirts produced

X_2 = number of pajamas produced

Solution

First constraint: $1X_1 + .75X_2 \leq 280$ hours of sewing-machine time available—our first scarce resource

Second constraint: $1.5X_1 + 2X_2 \leq 450$ hours of cutting-machine time available—our second scarce resource

Note: This means that each pair of pajamas takes 2 hours of the cutting resource.

Smitty's accounting department analyzes cost and sales figures and states that each shirt produced will yield a $4 contribution to profit and that each pair of pajamas will yield a $3 contribution to profit.

This information can be used to create the LP *objective function* for this problem:

Objective function: maximize total contribution to profit = $4X_1 + $3X_2

Solved Problem B.2

We want to solve the following LP problem for Failsafe Computers using the corner-point method.

Maximize profit = $9X_1 + $7X_2$

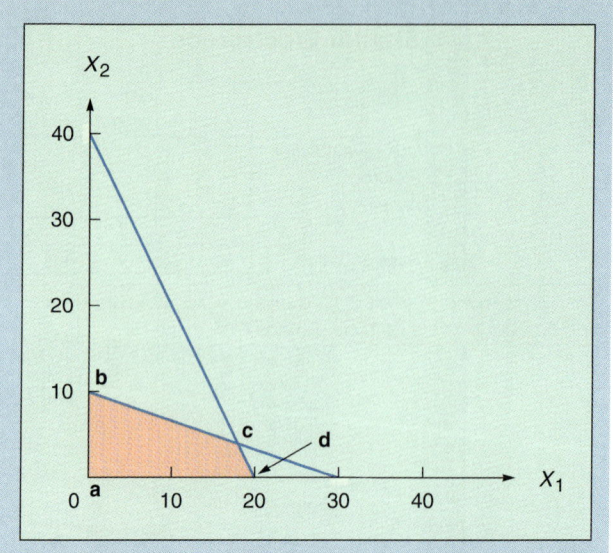

$$2X_1 + 1X_2 \leq 40$$

$$X_1 + 3X_2 \leq 30$$

FIGURE B.9 ■ **Failsafe Computers Feasible Region**

Solution

Figure B.9 illustrates these constraints:

Corner-point **a**: $(X_1 = 0, X_2 = 0)$ Profit = 0

Corner-point **b**: $(X_1 = 0, X_2 = 10)$ Profit = 9(0) + 7(10) = $ 70

Corner-point **d**: $(X_1 = 20, X_2 = 0)$ Profit = 9(20) + 7(0) = $180

Corner-point **c** is obtained by solving equations $2X_1 + 1X_2 = 40$ and $X_1 + 3X_2 = 30$ simultaneously. Multiply the second equation by -2 and add it to the first.

$$2X_1 + 1X_2 = 40$$
$$-2X_1 - 6X_2 = -60$$
$$\overline{ -5X_2 = -20}$$

Thus $X_2 = 4$.

$$X_1 + 3(X_2 = 4) = 30 \text{ or } X_1 + 12 = 30 \text{ or } X_1 = 18$$

Corner-point **c**: $(X_1 = 18, X_2 = 4)$ Profit = 9(18) + 7(4) = $190

Hence the optimal solution is

$$(x_1 = 18, x_2 = 4) \quad \text{Profit} = \$190$$

Solved Problem B.3

Holiday Meal Turkey Ranch is considering buying two different types of turkey feed. Each feed contains, in varying proportions, some or all of the three nutritional ingredients essential for fattening turkeys. Brand Y feed costs the ranch $.02 per pound. Brand Z costs $.03 per pound. The rancher would like to determine the lowest-cost diet that meets the minimum monthly intake requirement for each nutritional ingredient.

The following table contains relevant information about the composition of brand Y and brand Z feeds, as well as the minimum monthly requirement for each nutritional ingredient per turkey.

Composition of Each Pound of Feed

Ingredient	Brand Y Feed	Brand Z Feed	Minimum Monthly Requirement
A	5 oz.	10 oz.	90 oz.
B	4 oz.	3 oz.	48 oz.
C	.5 oz.	0	1.5 oz.
Cost/lb	$.02	$.03	

Solution

If we let

X_1 = number of pounds of brand Y feed purchased

X_2 = number of pounds of brand Z feed purchased

then we may proceed to formulate this linear programming problem as follows:

Minimize cost (in cents) = $2X_1 + 3X_2$

subject to these constraints:

$5X_1 + 10X_2 \geq 90$ ounces   (*ingredient A constraint*)

$4X_1 + 3X_2 \geq 48$ ounces   (*ingredient B constraint*)

$\frac{1}{2}X_1 \geq 1\frac{1}{2}$ ounces   (*ingredient C constraint*)

Figure B.10 illustrates these constraints.

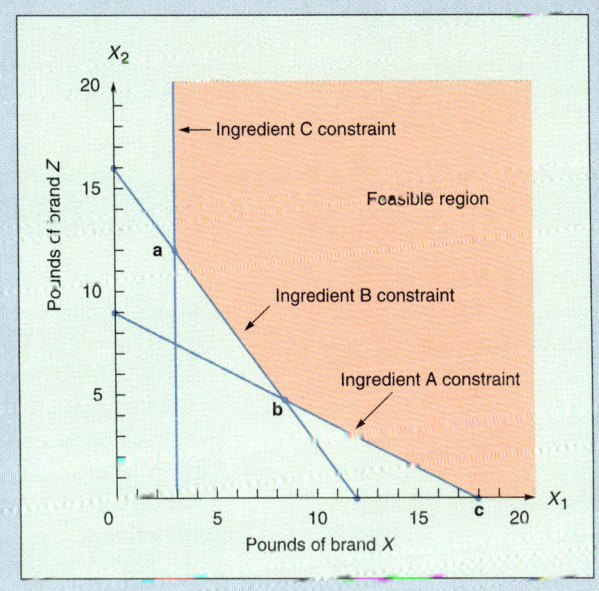

FIGURE B.10 ■ **Feasible Region for the Holiday Meal Turkey Ranch Problem**

The iso-cost line approach may be used to solve LP minimization problems such as that of the Holiday Meal Turkey Ranch. As with iso-profit lines, we need not compute the cost at each corner point, but instead draw a series of parallel cost lines. The lowest cost line (that is, the one closest in toward the origin) to touch the feasible region provides us with the optimal solution corner.

For example, we start in Figure B.11 by drawing a 54¢ cost line, namely, $54 = 2X_1 + 3X_2$. Obviously, there are many points in the feasible region that would yield a lower total cost. We proceed to move our iso-cost line toward the lower left, in a plane parallel to the 54¢ solution line. The last point we touch while still in contact with the feasible region is the same as corner point **b** of Figure B.10. It has the coordinates ($X_1 = 8.4$, $X_2 = 4.8$) and an associated cost of 31.2 cents.

FIGURE B.11 ■ Graphical Solution to the Holiday Meal Turkey Ranch Problem Using the Iso-Cost Line. Note that the last line parallel to the 54¢ iso-cost line that touches the feasible region indicates the optimal corner point.

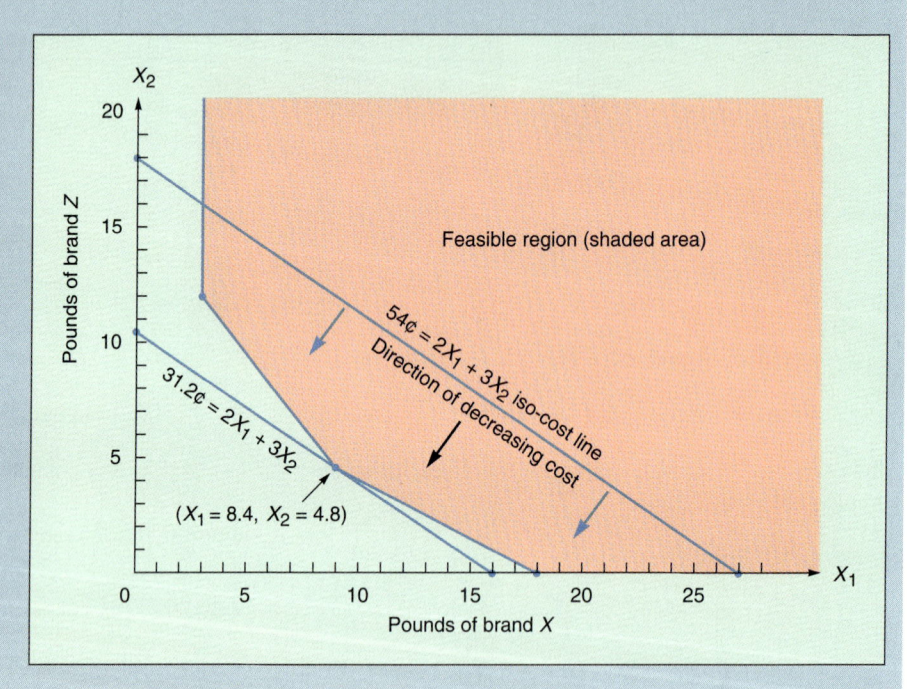

DISCUSSION QUESTIONS

1. Discuss the similarities and differences between minimization and maximization problems using the graphical solution approach of linear programming.
2. It has been said that each linear programming problem that has a feasible region has an infinite number of solutions. Explain.
3. The production manager of a large Cincinnati manufacturing firm once made this statement: "I should like to use linear programming, but it's a technique that operates under conditions of certainty. My plant doesn't have that certainty; it's a world of uncertainty. So LP can't be used here." Do you think this statement has any merit? Explain why the manager may have said it.
4. Should people who will be using the results of a new quantitative model such as linear programming become involved in the technical aspects of the problem-solving procedure?
5. Explain how to use the iso-profit line in a graphical maximization problem.
6. Explain how to use the iso-cost line in a graphical minimization problem.
7. Compare how the corner-point and iso-profit line methods work for solving graphical problems.
8. Define the feasible region of a graphical LP problem. What is a feasible solution?
9. What are the properties of all LP problems?

PROBLEMS

B.1 Andrew McCarroll is trying to determine how many units each of 2 cordless telephones to produce each day. One of these is the standard model; the other is the deluxe model. The profit per unit on the standard model is $40, on the deluxe model $60. Each unit requires 30 minutes of assembly time. The standard model requires 10 minutes of inspection time, the deluxe model 15 minutes. The company must fill an order for 6 standard phones. There are 450 minutes of assembly time and 180 minutes of inspection time available each day. How many units of each product should be manufactured to maximize profits?

B.2 Solve the following linear programming problem graphically.

$$\text{Maximize} \quad Z = X + 10Y$$

$$\text{Subject to:} \quad 4X + 3Y \le 36$$

$$2X + 4Y \le 40$$

$$Y \ge 3$$

$$X, Y \ge 0$$

B.3 Solve the following linear programming problem graphically.

$$\text{Maximize} \quad Z = 3X + 5Y$$

$$\text{Subject to:} \quad 4X + 4Y \le 48$$

$$1X + 2Y \le 20$$

$$Y \ge 2$$

$$X, Y \ge 0$$

B.4 Consider the following linear programming problem;

$$\text{Maximize} \quad Z = 30X_1 + 10X_2$$

$$\text{Subject to:} \quad 3X_1 + X_2 \le 300$$

$$X_1 + X_2 \le 200$$

$$X_1 \le 100$$

$$X_2 \ge 50$$

$$X_1 - X_2 \le 0$$

$$X_1, X_2 \ge 0$$

a) Solve the problem graphically.
b) Is there more than one optimal solution? Explain.

- **B.5** Suppose a linear programming (maximization) problem has been solved and that the optimal value of the objective function is $300. Suppose an additional constraint is added to this problem. Explain how this might affect each of the following:
  - a) The feasible region.
  - b) The optimal value of the objective function.

- **B.6** Tricia Liscio's Dog Food Company wishes to introduce a new brand of dog biscuits composed of chicken- and liver-flavored biscuits that meet certain nutritional requirements. The liver-flavored biscuits contain 1 unit of nutrient A and 2 units of nutrient B; the chicken-flavored biscuits contain 1 unit of nutrient A and 4 units of nutrient B. According to federal requirements, there must be at least 40 units of nutrient A and 60 units of nutrient B in a package of the new mix. In addition, the company has decided that there can be no more than 15 liver-flavored biscuits in a package. If it costs 1 cent to make 1 liver-flavored biscuit and 2 cents to make 1 chicken-flavored, what is the optimal product mix for a package of the biscuits in order to minimize the firm's cost?
  - a) Formulate this as a linear programming problem.
  - b) Solve this problem graphically, giving the optimal values of all variables.
  - c) What is the total cost of a package of dog biscuits using the optimal mix?

- **B.7** The Electrocomp Corporation manufactures 2 electrical products: air conditioners and large fans. The assembly process for each is similar in that both require a certain amount of wiring and drilling. Each air conditioner takes 3 hours of wiring and 2 hours of drilling. Each fan must go through 2 hours of wiring and 1 hour of drilling. During the next production period, 240 hours of wiring time are available and up to 140 hours of drilling time may be used. Each air conditioner sold yields a profit of $25. Each fan assembled may be sold for a $15 profit.

    Formulate and solve this LP production-mix situation, and find the best combination of air conditioners and fans that yields the highest profit.

- **B.8** The Shari Meffert Tub Company manufactures 2 lines of bathtubs, called model A and model B. Every tub requires blending a certain amount of steel and zinc; the company has available a total of 25,000 pounds of steel and 6,000 pounds of zinc. Each model A bathtub requires a mixture of 125 pounds of steel and 20 pounds of zinc, and each yields a profit of $90. Each model B tub requires 100 pounds of steel and 30 pounds of zinc and can be sold for a profit of $70.

    Find by graphical linear programming the best production mix of bathtubs.

- **B.9** The Outdoor Furniture Corporation manufactures 2 products, benches and picnic tables, for use in yards and parks. The firm has 2 main resources: its carpenters (labor force) and a supply of redwood for use in the furniture. During the next production cycle, 1,200 hours of labor are available under a union agreement. The firm also has a stock of 3,500 board feet of quality redwood. Each bench that Outdoor Furniture produces requires 4 labor-hours and 10 board feet of redwood; each picnic table takes 6 labor-hours and 35 board feet of redwood. Completed benches will yield a profit of $9 each, and tables will result in a profit of $20 each. How many benches and tables should Outdoor Furniture produce in order to obtain the largest possible profit? Use the graphical linear programming approach.

- **B.10** MSA Computer Corporation manufactures two models of minicomputers, the Alpha 4 and the Beta 5. The firm employs 5 technicians, working 160 hours each per month, on its assembly line. Management insists that full employment (that is, *all* 160 hours of time) be maintained for each worker during next month's operations. It requires 20 labor-hours to assemble each Alpha 4 computer and 25 labor-hours to assemble each Beta 5 model. MSA wants to see at least 10 Alpha 4s and at least 15 Beta 5s produced during the production period. Alpha 4s generate a $1,200 profit per unit, and Betas yield $1,800 each.

    Determine the most profitable number of each model of minicomputer to produce during the coming month.

Problems

B.11 Solve the following linear programming problem graphically:

Maximize $Z = 4X_1 + 4X_2$

Subject to: $3X_1 + 5X_2 \leq 150$

$X_1 - 2X_2 \leq 10$

$5X_1 + 3X_2 \leq 150$

$X_1, X_2 \geq 0$

B.12 Consider this linear programming formulation:

Minimize cost = $\$1X_1 + \$2X_2$

Subject to: $X_1 + 3X_2 \geq 90$

$8X_1 + 2X_2 \geq 160$

$3X_1 + 2X_2 \geq 120$

$X_2 \leq 70$

a) Graphically illustrate the feasible region and apply the iso-cost line procedure to indicate which corner point produces the optimal solution.
b) What is the cost of this solution?

B.13 The mathematical relationships that follow were formulated by an operations research analyst at the Kari Jabe Chemical Company. Which ones are invalid for use in a linear programming problem, and why?

Maximize = $4X_1 + 3X_1X_2 + 5X_3$

Subject to: $2X_1X_2 + 2X_3 \leq 50$

$8X_1 - 4X_2 \geq 6$

$1.5X_1 + 6X_2 + 3X_3 \geq 21$

$19X_2 - \frac{1}{3}X_3 = 17$

$5X_1 + 4X_2 + 3\sqrt{X_3} \leq 80$

$-X_1 - X_2 + X_3 = 5$

B.14 Kalyan Singhal Corp. makes three products, and it has three machines available as resources as given in the following LP problem.

Maximize contribution = $4X_1 + 4X_2 + 7X_3$

Subject to: $1X_1 + 7X_2 + 4X_3 \leq 100$ (hours on machine 1)

$2X_1 + 1X_2 + 7X_3 \leq 110$ (hours on machine 2)

$8X_1 + 4X_2 + 1X_3 \leq 100$ (hours on machine 3)

- **: B.15** Using the data from Kalyan Singhal Corp. in Problem B.14, determine:
  a) What would it be worth to the firm to make an additional hour of time available on the third machine?
  b) How much would the firm's profit increase if an extra 10 hours of time were made available on the second machine at no extra cost?

- **: B.16** The Burton Dean Mfg. Corp. has $250,000 available to invest for 12 months prior to its plant expansion. The money can be placed in Treasury notes yielding an 8% return or in municipal bonds at an average rate of 9%. Management requires that at least 50% of the investment be placed in Treasury notes. Because of defaults in municipal bonds, it is decided that no more than 40% of the investment be placed in such bonds.

  How much should be invested in each security to maximize return on investment?

- **: B.17** Gupta Furniture manufactures 2 different types of china cabinets, a French provincial model and a Danish modern model. Each cabinet produced must go through 3 departments: carpentry, painting, and finishing. The accompanying table contains all relevant information concerning production times per cabinet produced and production capacities for each operation per day, along with net revenue per unit produced. The firm has a contract with a Miami distributor to produce a minimum of 300 of each cabinet per week (or 60 cabinets per day). Owner Sushil Gupta would like to determine a product mix to maximize his daily revenue.

Cabinet Style	Carpentry (hours per cabinet)	Painting (hours per cabinet)	Finishing (hours per cabinet)	Net Revenue Per Cabinet
French provincial	3	$1\frac{1}{2}$	$\frac{3}{4}$	$28
Danish modern	2	1	$\frac{3}{4}$	$25
Department capacity (hours)	360	200	125	

Formulate this as a linear programming problem and solve.

- **: B.18** The famous Gary Eppen Restaurant is open 24 hours a day. Servers report for duty at 3 A.M., 7 A.M., 11 A.M., 3 P.M., 7 P.M., or 11 P.M., and each works an 8-hour shift. The following table shows the minimum number of workers needed during the 6 periods into which the day is divided.

Period	Time	Number of Servers Required
1	3 A.M.– 7 A.M.	3
2	7 A.M.–11 A.M.	12
3	11 A.M.– 3 P.M.	16
4	3 P.M.– 7 P.M.	9
5	7 P.M.–11 P.M.	11
6	11 P.M.– 3 A.M.	4

Eppen's scheduling problem is to determine how many servers should report for work at the start of each time period in order to minimize the total staff required for one day's op-

: **B.19** eration. (*Hint:* Let X_i equal the number of servers beginning work in time period i, where $i = 1, 2, 3, 4, 5, 6$.)

This is the slack time of year at JES, Inc. The firm would actually like to shut down the plant, but if it laid off its core employees, they would probably go to work for a competitor. JES could keep its core (full-time, year-round) employees busy by making 10,000 round tables per month, or by making 20,000 square tables per month (**or** some ratio thereof). JES, does, however, have a contract with a supplier to buy a minimum of 5,000 square tabletops per month. Handling and storage costs per round table will be $10; these costs would be $8 per square table.

Draw a graph, algebraically describe the constraint inequalities and the objective function, identify the points bounding the feasible solution area, and find the cost at each point and the optimum solution. Let X_1 equal the thousands of round tables per month and X_2 equal the thousands of square tables per month.

: **B.20** Each coffee table produced by Timothy Kent Designers nets the firm a profit of $9. Each bookcase yields a $12 profit. Kent's firm is small and its resources limited. During any given production period (of 1 week), 10 gallons of varnish and 12 lengths of high-quality redwood are available. Each coffee table requires approximately 1 gallon of varnish and 1 length of redwood. Each bookcase takes 1 gallon of varnish and 2 lengths of wood.

Formulate Kent's production-mix decision as a linear programming problem, and solve. How many tables and bookcases should be produced each week? What will the maximum profit be?

· **B.21** Solve the following linear programming problem graphically. Indicate the corner points on your graph.

Maximize profit = $3X_1 + \$5X_2$

Subject to: $X_2 \leq 6$

$3X_1 + \$2X_2 \leq 18$

$X_1, \quad X_2 \geq 0$

· **B.22** Solve the following linear programming problem graphically.

Minimize cost = $4X_1 + 5X_2$

Subject to: $X_1 + 2X_2 \geq 80$

$3X_1 + X_2 \geq 75$

$X_1, \quad X_2 \geq 0$

: **B.23** Gross Distributors packages and distributes industrial supplies. A standard shipment can be packaged in a class A container, a class K container, or a class T container. A single class A container yields a profit of $8; a class K container, a profit of $6; and a class T container, a profit of $14. Each shipment prepared requires a certain amount of packing material and a certain amount of time.

Resources Needed per Standard Shipment		
Class of Container	Packing Material (pounds)	Packing Time (hours)
A	2	2
K	1	6
T	3	4
Total amount of resource available each week	120 pounds	240 hours

Jim Gross, head of the firm, must decide the optimal number of each class of container to pack each week. He is bound by the previously mentioned resource restrictions but also decides that he must keep his 6 full-time packers employed all 240 hours (6 workers × 40 hours) each week.

Formulate and solve this problem using LP software.

- **B.24** Using the data from Problem B.7 and LP software, determine the range within which the unit profit contribution of an air conditioner must fall for the current solution to remain optimal.

- **B.25** Greg Middleton, the advertising director for Diversey Paint and Supply, a chain of four retail stores on Chicago's North Side, is considering two media possibilities. One plan is for a series of half-page ads in the Sunday *Chicago Tribune* newspaper, and the other is for advertising time on Chicago TV. The stores are expanding their line of do-it-yourself tools, and the advertising director is interested in an exposure level of at least 40% within the city's neighborhoods and 60% in northwest suburban areas.

  The TV viewing time under consideration has an exposure rating per spot of 5% in city homes and 3% in the northwest suburbs. The Sunday newspaper has corresponding exposure rates of 4% and 3% per ad. The cost of a half-page *Tribune* advertisement is $925; a television spot costs $2,000.

  Diversey Paint would like to select the least costly advertising strategy that would meet desired exposure levels. Formulate and solve this LP problem.

- **B.26** Gerry Johnson Manufacturing has three factories (1, 2, and 3) and three warehouses (A, B, and C). The following table shows the shipping costs between each factory and warehouse, the factory manufacturing capabilities (in 1,000's) and the warehouse capacities (in 1,000's).
  a) Write the objective function and the constraint inequations. Let X1A = 1,000s of units shipped from factory 1 to warehouse A, and so on.
  b) Solve by computer.

TO / FROM	A	B	C	PRODUCTION CAPABILITY
Factory 1	$ 6	$ 5	$ 3	6
Factory 2	$ 8	$10	$ 8	8
Factory 3	$11	$14	$18	10
Capacity	7	12	5	

- **B.27** Andy's Bicycle Company (ABC) has the hottest new product on the upscale toy market—boys' and girls' bikes in bright fashion colors, with oversized hubs and axles; shell design safety tires; strong padded frames; chrome-plated chains, brackets, and valves; and non-

slip handlebars. Due to the seller's market for high-quality toys for the newest baby boomers, ABC can sell all the bicycles it manufactures at the following prices: boys' bikes, $220; girls' bikes, $175. This is the price payable to ABC at its Orlando plant.

The firm's accountant, V. R. Dondeti, has determined that direct labor costs will be 45% of the price that ABC receives for the boys' model and 40% of the price received for the girls' model. Production costs, other than labor but excluding painting and packaging, are $44 per boys' bicycle and $30 per girls' bicycle. Painting and packaging are $20 per bike, regardless of model.

The Orlando plant's overall production capacity is 390 bicycles per day. Each boys' bike requires 2.5 labor-hours, each girls' model 2.4 hours. ABC currently employs 120 workers, each of whom puts in an 8-hour day. The firm has no desire to hire or fire to affect labor availability, for it believes its stable workforce is one of its biggest assets.

Using a graphic approach, determine the best product mix for ABC.

B.28 New Orleans's Mt. Sinai Hospital is a large, private, 600-bed facility complete with laboratories, operating rooms, and X-ray equipment. In seeking to increase revenues, Mt. Sinai's administration has decided to make a 90-bed addition on a portion of adjacent land currently used for staff parking. The administrators feel that the labs, operating rooms, and X-ray department are not being fully utilized at present and do not need to be expanded to handle additional patients. The addition of 90 beds, however, involves deciding how many beds should be allocated to the medical staff (for medical patients) and how many to the surgical staff (for surgical patients).

The hospital's accounting and medical records departments have provided the following pertinent information. The average hospital stay for a medical patient is 8 days, and the average medical patient generates $2,280 in revenues. The average surgical patient is in the hospital 5 days and generates $1,515 in revenues. The laboratory is capable of handling 15,000 tests per year more than it *was* handling. The average medical patient requires 3.1 lab tests, the average surgical patient 2.6 lab tests. Furthermore, the average medical patient uses 1 X-ray, the average surgical patient 2 X-rays. If the hospital were expanded by 90 beds, the X-ray department could handle up to 7,000 X-rays without significant additional cost. Finally, the administration estimates that up to 2,800 additional operations could be performed in existing operating-room facilities. Medical patients, of course, require no surgery, whereas each surgical patient generally has one surgery performed.

Formulate this problem so as to determine how many medical beds and how many surgical beds should be added in order to maximize revenues. Assume that the hospital is open 365 days per year.

DATA BASE APPLICATION

B.29 Mann Enterprises is a Houston manufacturer of tables and accessories for personal computers. The company is caught in a vicious cross fire between rapidly dropping market prices from competitors worldwide for its products and stable domestic costs for its materials. The 15 different products noted below must be scheduled to maximize profits or there will be no jobs and no firm in another 3 months. Your job as the new OM graduate is to address the issues raised this morning by Laura Mann, the president, in an emergency meeting in her office. Without being told so explicitly, you conclude that if you don't get the schedule done accurately and in a timely manner, you will be history. To your relief, the industrial engineers and accountants have provided the data shown on the following page. The issues, as recorded in your notes, are identified in (a) through (f).

Module B   Linear Programming

Product	Steel Alloy Required (Lb.)	Plastic Required (Sq. Ft.)	Wood Required (Bd. Ft.)	Aluminum Required (Lb.)	Formica Required (Bd. Ft.)	Labor Required (Hr.)	Minimum Monthly Demand (Units)	Contribution to Profit
A158	—	.4	.7	5.8	10.9	3.1	—	$18.79
B179	4	.5	1.8	10.3	2.0	1.0	20	6.31
C023	6	—	1.5	1.1	2.3	1.2	10	8.19
D045	10	.4	2.0	—	—	4.8	10	45.88
E388	12	1.2	1.2	8.1	4.9	5.5	—	63.00
F422	—	1.4	1.5	7.1	10.0	.8	20	4.10
G366	10	1.4	7.0	6.2	11.1	9.1	10	81.15
H600	5	1.0	5.0	7.3	12.4	4.8	20	50.06
I701	1	.4	—	10.0	5.2	1.9	50	12.79
J802	1	.3	—	11.0	6.1	1.4	20	15.88
K900	—	.2	—	12.5	7.7	1.0	20	17.91
L901	2	1.8	1.5	13.1	5.0	5.1	10	49.99
M050	—	2.7	5.0	—	2.1	3.1	20	24.00
N150	10	1.1	5.8	—	—	7.7	10	88.88
P259	10	—	6.2	15.0	1.0	6.6	10	77.01
Availability per month	980	400	600	2,500	1,800	1,000		

a) How many of each of the 15 products should be produced each month?
b) Clearly explain the meaning of each shadow price.
c) A number of workers interested in saving money for the holidays have offered to work overtime next month at a rate of $12.50 per hour. What should the response of management be?
d) Two tons of steel alloy are available from an overstocked supplier at a total cost of $8,000. Should the steel be purchased? All or part of the supply?
e) The accountants have just discovered that an error was made in the contribution to profit for product N150. The correct value is actually $8.88. What are the implications of this error?
f) Management is considering the abandonment of five product lines (those beginning with letters A through E). If no minimum monthly demand is established, what are the implications? Note that there already is no minimum for two of these products. Use the corrected value for N150.

■ Case Study ■

Golding Landscaping and Plants, Inc.

Kenneth and Patricia Golding spent a career as a husband-and-wife real estate investment partnership in Washington, DC. When they finally retired to a 25-acre farm in northern Virginia's Fairfax County, they became ardent amateur gardeners. Kenneth Golding planted shrubs and fruit trees, and Patricia spent her hours potting all sizes of plants. When the volume of shrubs and plants reached the point where the Goldings began to think of their hobby in a serious vein, they built a greenhouse adjacent to their home and installed heating and watering systems.

By 1994, the Goldings realized their retirement from real estate had really only led to a second career—in the plant and shrub business—and they filed for a Virginia business license. Within a matter of months, they asked their attorney to file incorporation documents and formed the firm Golding Landscaping and Plants, Inc.

Early in the new business's existence, Kenneth Golding recognized the need for a high-quality commercial fertilizer that he could blend himself, both for sale and for his own nursery. His goal was to keep his costs to a minimum while producing a top-notch product that was especially suited to the northern Virginia climate.

Working with chemists at Virginia Tech and George Mason Universities, Golding blended "Golding-Grow." It consists of four chemical compounds, C-30, C-92, D-21, and E-11. The cost per pound for each compound is indicated in the following table.

Chemical Compound	Cost per Pound
C-30	$.12
C-92	.09
D-21	.11
E-11	.04

The specifications for Golding-Grow are established as:

a) Chemical E-11 must comprise at least 15% of the blend.
b) C-92 and C-30 must together constitute at least 45% of the blend.
c) D-21 and C-92 can together constitute no more than 30% of the blend.
d) Golding-Grow is packaged and sold in 50-pound bags.

Discussion Questions

1. Formulate an LP problem to determine what blend of the 4 chemicals will allow Golding to minimize the cost of a 50-pound bag of the fertilizer.
2. Solve to find the best solution.

Source: Barry Render and Ralph Stair, *Quantitative Analysis for Management*, 6th ed. (Upper Saddle River: Prentice Hall, 1997).

Internet Case Studies

See our Internet home page at http://www.prenhall.com/heizer for these three additional case studies: Mexicana Wire Works, Coastal States Chemical, and Chase Manhatten Bank.

BIBLIOGRAPHY

Farley, A. A. "Planning the Cutting of Photographic Color Paper Rolls for Kodak (Australasia) Pty. Ltd." *Interfaces* 21, no. 1 (January–February 1991): 92–106.

Gass, S. I. *An Illustrated Guide to Linear Programming*. New York: Dover, 1990.

Greenberg, H. J. "How to Analyze the Results of Linear Programs—Part 1: Preliminaries." *Interfaces* 23, no. 4 (July–August 1993): 56–68.

Orden, A. "LP from the '40s to the '90s." *Interfaces* 23, no. 5 (September–October 1993): 2.

Quinn, P., B. Andrews, and H. Parsons. "Allocating Telecommunications Resources at L. L. Bean, Inc." *Interfaces* 21, no. 1 (January–February 1991): 75–91.

Render, B., and R. M. Stair. *Quantitative Analysis for Management*, 6th ed. Upper Saddle River, NJ: Prentice Hall, 1997.

Saltzman, M. J. "Survey: Mixed Integer Programming." *OR/MS Today* 21, no. 2 (April 1994): 42–51.

Schindler, S., and T. Semmel. "Station Staffing at Pan American World Airways." *Interfaces* 23, no. 3 (May–June 1993): 91.

Sexton, T. R., S. Sleeper, and R. E. Taggart, Jr. "Improving Pupil Transportation in North Carolina." *Interfaces* 24, no. 1 (January–February 1994): 87–104.

QUANTITATIVE MODULE C

Transportation Models

MODULE OUTLINE

TRANSPORTATION MODELING

DEVELOPING AN INITIAL SOLUTION:
THE NORTHWEST-CORNER RULE

THE STEPPING-STONE METHOD

SPECIAL ISSUES IN MODELING
  Demand Not Equal to Supply
  Degeneracy

SUMMARY

KEY TERMS

USING POM FOR WINDOWS TO SOLVE TRANSPORTATION PROBLEMS

USING EXCEL OM TO SOLVE TRANSPORTATION PROBLEMS

SOLVED PROBLEMS

DISCUSSION QUESTIONS

PROBLEMS

DATA BASE APPLICATION

CASE STUDY: ANDREW-CARTER, INC.

INTERNET CASE STUDIES

BIBLIOGRAPHY

LEARNING OBJECTIVES

When you complete this module you should be able to:

Identify or Define:

  Transportation modeling

  Facility location analysis

Explain or be able to use:

  Northwest-corner rule

  Stepping-stone method

The problem facing the Avis car rental company was cross-country travel. Lots of it. Cars rented in New York ended up in Chicago, cars from L.A. came to Philadelphia, and cars from Boston came to Miami. The scene was repeated in over 100 cities around the United States. As a result, there were too many cars in some cities and too few in others. Avis operations managers had to decide how many of these rentals should be trucked (by costly auto carriers) from each city with excess capacity to each city that needed more rentals. The process required quick action at the most economical routing, so Avis turned to transportation modeling.

Because location of a new factory, warehouse, or distribution center is a strategic issue with substantial cost implications, most companies consider and evaluate several alternative locations. With a wide variety of objective and subjective factors to be considered, rational decisions are aided by a number of techniques. One of those techniques is transportation modeling.

The transportation models described in this module prove useful when considering alternative facility locations *within the framework of an existing distribution system.* Each new potential plant, warehouse, or distribution center will require a different allocation of shipments, depending on its own production and shipping costs and the costs of each existing facility. The choice of a new location depends on which will yield the minimum cost *for the entire system.*

TRANSPORTATION MODELING

Transportation modeling finds the least-cost means of shipping supplies from several origins to several destinations. *Origin points* (or *sources*) can be factories, warehouses, car rental agencies like Avis, or any other points from which goods are shipped. *Destinations* are any points that receive goods. To use the transportation model, we need to know the following:

1. The origin points and the capacity or supply per period at each.
2. The destination points and the demand per period at each.
3. The cost of shipping one unit from each origin to each destination.

Transportation modeling An iterative procedure for solving problems that involve minimizing the cost of shipping products from a series of sources to a series of destinations.

The transportation model is actually a class of the linear programming models discussed in quantitative module B. As it is for linear programming, software is available to solve transportation problems. To fully use such programs, though, you need to understand the assumptions that underlie the model. To illustrate one transportation problem, in this module we will look at a company called Arizona Plumbing, which makes, among other products, a full line of bathtubs. In our example, the firm must decide which of its factories should supply which of its warehouses. Relevent data for Arizona Plumbing are presented in Table C.1 and Figure C.1. Table C.1 shows, for example, that it costs Arizona Plumbing $5 to ship one bathtub from its Des Moines factory to its Albuquerque warehouse, $4 to Boston, and $3 to Cleveland. Likewise, we see in Figure C.1 that the 300 units required by Arizona Plumbing's Albuquerque warehouse might be shipped in various combinations from its Des Moines, Evansville, and Fort Lauderdale factories.

The first step in the modeling process is to set up a *transportation matrix*. Its purpose is to summarize all relevant data and to keep track of algorithm computations. Using the information displayed in Figure C.1 and Table C.1, we can construct a transportation matrix as shown in Figure C.2 on page 742.

TABLE C.1 ■ Transportation Costs per Bathtub for Arizona Plumbing

FROM \ TO	ALBUQUERQUE	BOSTON	CLEVELAND
Des Moines	$5	$4	$3
Evansville	$8	$4	$3
Fort Lauderdale	$9	$7	$5

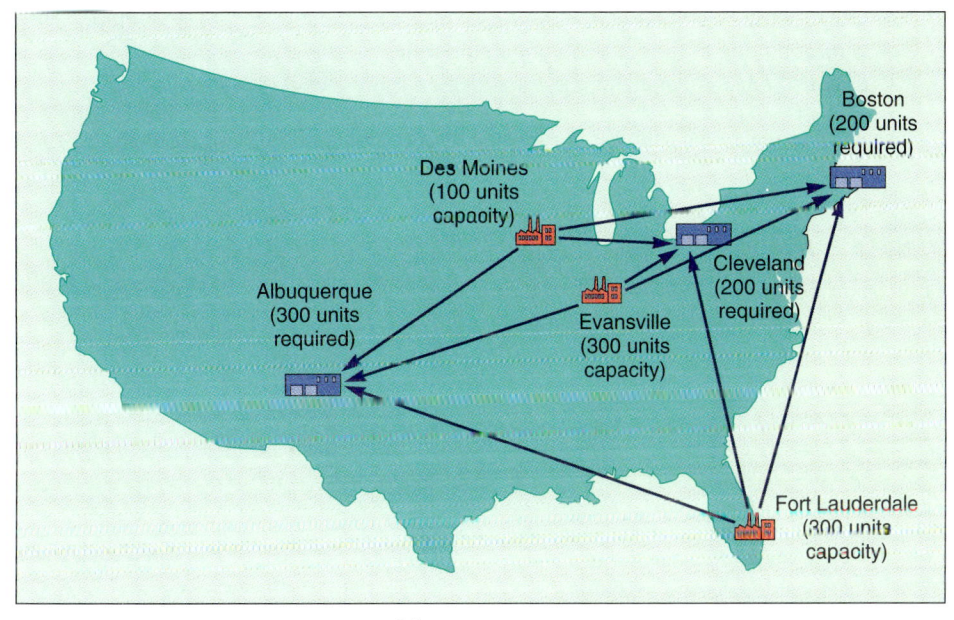

FIGURE C.1 ■ Transportation Problem

From \ To	Albuquerque	Boston	Cleveland	Factory capacity
Des Moines	$5	$4	$3	100
Evansville	$8	$4	$3	300
Fort Lauderdale	$9	$7	$5	300
Warehouse requirements	300	200	200	700

- Des Moines capacity constraint
- Cell representing a possible source-to-destination shipping assignment (Evansville to Cleveland)
- Cost of shipping 1 unit from Fort Lauderdale factory to Boston warehouse
- Cleveland warehouse demand
- Total demand and total supply

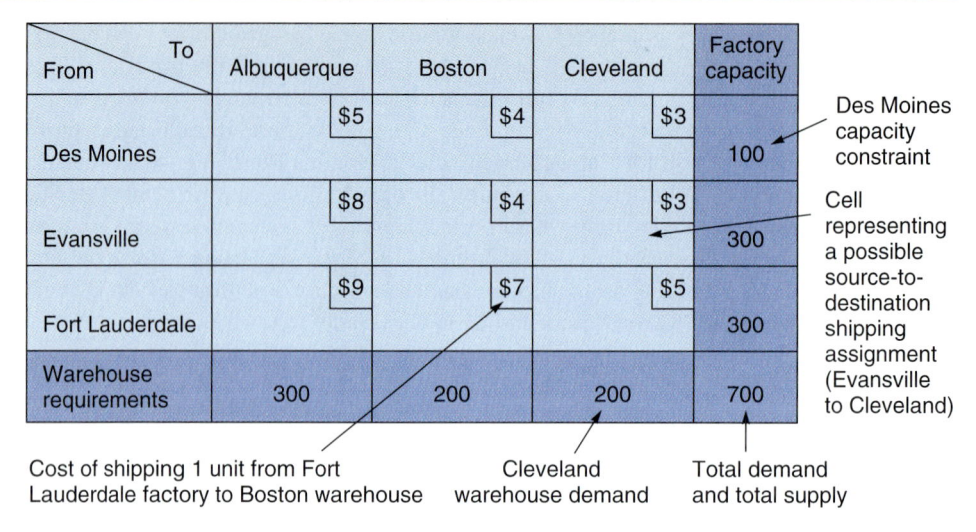

FIGURE C.2 ■ Transportation Matrix for Arizona Plumbing

DEVELOPING AN INITIAL SOLUTION: THE NORTHWEST-CORNER RULE

Northwest-corner rule
A procedure in the transportation model where one starts at the upper left-hand cell of a table (the northwest corner) and systematically allocates units to shipping routes.

Once the data are arranged in tabular form, we must establish an *initial feasible solution* to the problem. One systematic procedure, known as the **northwest-corner rule,** requires that we start in the upper left-hand cell (or northwest corner) of the table and allocate units to shipping routes as follows:

1. Exhaust the supply (factory capacity) of each row (e.g., Des Moines: 100) before moving down to the next row.
2. Exhaust the (warehouse) requirements of each column (e.g., Albuquerque: 300) before moving to the next column on the right.
3. Check to ensure that all supplies and demands are met.

Example C1 applies the northwest-corner rule to our Arizona Plumbing problem.

EXAMPLE C1

In Figure C.3 we use the northwest-corner rule to find an initial feasible solution to the Arizona Plumbing problem. To make our initial shipping assignments, we need five steps:

1. Assign 100 tubs from Des Moines to Albuquerque (exhausting Des Moines' supply).
2. Assign 200 tubs from Evansville to Albuquerque (exhausting Albuquerque's demand).
3. Assign 100 tubs from Evansville to Boston (exhausting Evansville's supply).
4. Assign 100 tubs from Fort Lauderdale to Boston (exhausting Boston's demand).
5. Assign 200 tubs from Fort Lauderdale to Cleveland (exhausting Cleveland's demand and Fort Lauderdale's supply).

The northwest-corner rule is easy to use, but totally ignores costs. Can you propose better approaches (i.e., new algorithms) to finding initial solutions?

From \ To	(A) Albuquerque	(B) Boston	(C) Cleveland	Factory capacity
(D) Des Moines	$5 100	$4	$3	100
(E) Evansville	$8 200	$4 100	$3	300
(F) Fort Lauderdale	$9	$7 (100)	$5 200	300
Warehouse requirements	300	200	200	700

Means that the firm is shipping 100 bathtubs from Fort Lauderdale to Boston

FIGURE C.3 ■ Northwest-Corner Solution to Arizona Plumbing Problem

The total cost of this shipping assignment is $4,200 (see Table C.2).

TABLE C.2 ■ Computed Shipping Cost

Route From	To	Tubs Shipped	Cost per Unit	Total Cost
D	A	100	$5	$ 500
E	A	200	8	1,600
E	B	100	4	400
F	B	100	7	700
F	C	200	5	1,000
			Total:	$4,200

The solution given is feasible because it satisfies all demand and supply constraints. However, we would be very lucky if this solution yielded the minimum transportation cost for the problem. Because the northwest-corner method is meant only to provide us with a starting point, we will have to employ an additional procedure to reach an *optimal* solution.

THE STEPPING-STONE METHOD

The **stepping-stone method** will help us move from an initial feasible solution to an optimal solution. It is used to evaluate the cost effectiveness of shipping goods via transportation routes not currently in the solution. When applying it, we test each unused cell, or square, in the transportation table by asking: "What would happen to total shipping costs if one unit of the product (for example, one bathtub) were tentatively shipped on an unused route?" We conduct the test as follows:

1. Select any unused square to evaluate.
2. Beginning at this square, trace a closed path back to the original square via squares that are currently being used (only horizontal and vertical moves are permissible). You may, however, step over either an empty or an occupied square.

Stepping-stone method
An iterative technique for moving from an initial feasible solution to an optimal solution in the transportation method.

3. Beginning with a plus (+) sign at the unused square, place alternate minus signs and plus signs on each corner square of the closed path just traced.
4. Calculate an improvement index by first adding the unit-cost figures found in each square containing a plus sign, and then by subtracting the unit costs in each square containing a minus sign.
5. Repeat steps 1 through 4 until you have calculated an improvement index for all unused squares. If all indices computed are *greater than or equal to zero,* you have reached an optimal solution. If not, it is possible to improve the current solution still further in order to decrease total shipping costs.

Example C2 illustrates how to use the stepping-stone method to move toward an optimal solution.

EXAMPLE C2

We can apply the stepping-stone method to the Arizona Plumbing data in Figure C.3 to evaluate unused shipping routes. As you can see, the four currently unassigned routes are: Des Moines to Boston, Des Moines to Cleveland, Evansville to Cleveland, and Fort Lauderdale to Albuquerque.

Steps 1 and 2. Beginning with the Des Moines-to-Boston route, first trace a closed path *using only currently occupied squares* (see Figure C.4). Place alternate plus signs and minus signs in the corners of this path. In the upper left square, for example, we place

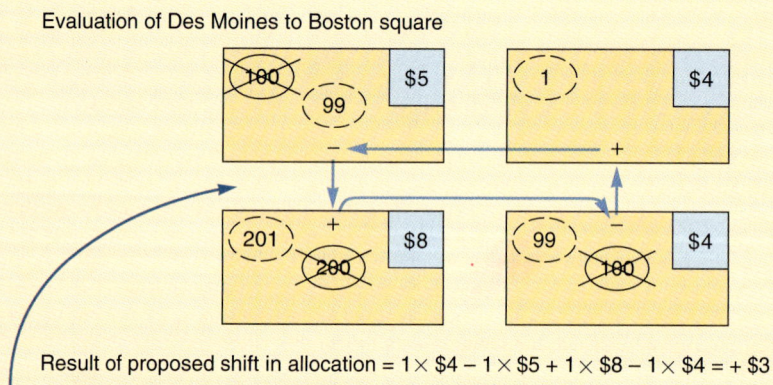

Evaluation of Des Moines to Boston square

Result of proposed shift in allocation = 1 × $4 − 1 × $5 + 1 × $8 − 1 × $4 = + $3

From \ To	(A) Albuquerque	(B) Boston	(C) Cleveland	Factory capacity
(D) Des Moines	$5 100	$4 Start	$3	100
(E) Evansville	$8 200	$4 100	$3	300
(F) Fort Lauderdale	$9	$7 100	$5 200	300
Warehouse requirements	300	200	200	700

FIGURE C.4 ■ Stepping-Stone Evaluation of Alternative Routes for Arizona Plumbing

The Stepping-Stone Method

a minus sign because we have *subtracted* 1 unit from the original 100. Note that we can use only squares currently used for shipping to turn the corners of the route we are tracing. Hence, the path Des Moines–Boston to Des Moines–Albuquerque to Fort Lauderdale–Albuquerque to Fort Lauderdale–Boston to Des Moines–Boston would not be acceptable, because the Fort Lauderdale–Albuquerque square is empty. It turns out that *only one closed route exists for each empty square*. Once this one closed path is identified, we can begin assigning plus and minus signs to these squares in the path.

Step 3. How do we decide which squares get plus signs and which squares get minus signs? The answer is simple. Because we are testing the cost effectiveness of the Des Moines–Boston shipping route, we try shipping 1 bathtub from Des Moines to Boston. This is 1 *more* unit than we *were* sending between the 2 cities, so place a plus sign in the box. However, if we ship 1 more unit than before from Des Moines to Boston, we end up sending 101 bathtubs out of the Des Moines factory. Because the Des Moines factory's capacity is only 100 units, we must ship 1 bathtub less from Des Moines to Albuquerque. This change prevents us from violating the capacity constraint.

To indicate that we have reduced the Des Moines–Albuquerque shipment, place a minus sign in its box. As you continue along the closed path, notice that we are no longer meeting our Albuquerque warehouse requirement for 300 units. In fact, if we reduce the Des Moines–Albuquerque shipment to 99 units, we must increase the Evansville–Albuquerque load by 1 unit, to 201 bathtubs. Therefore, place a plus sign in that box to indicate the increase. You may also observe that those squares in which we turn a corner (and only those squares) will have plus or minus signs.

Finally, note that if we assign 201 bathtubs to the Evansville–Albuquerque route, then we must reduce the Evansville–Boston route by 1 unit, to 99 bathtubs, in order to maintain the Evansville factory's capacity constraint of 300 units. To account for this reduction, we thus insert a minus sign in the Evansville–Boston box. By so doing we have balanced supply limitations among all 4 routes on the closed path.

Step 4. Compute an improvement index for the Des Moines–Boston route by adding unit costs in squares with plus signs and subtracting costs in squares with minus signs.

$$\text{Des Moines–Boston index} = \$4 - \$5 + \$8 - \$4 = +\$3$$

This means that for every bathtub shipped via the Des Moines–Boston route, total transportation costs will increase by $3 over their current level.

Let us now examine the unused Des Moines–Cleveland route, which is slightly more difficult to trace with a closed path (see Figure C.5). Again, notice that we turn each corner along the path only at squares on the existing route. Our path, for example, can go

> There is *only one* closed path that can be traced for each unused cell.

From \ To	(A) Albuquerque	(B) Boston	(C) Cleveland	Factory capacity
(D) Des Moines	$5 100 −	$4 +	$3 Start	100
(E) Evansville	$8 200	$4 100	$3	300
(F) Fort Lauderdale	$9	$7 + 100	$5 − 200	300
Warehouse requirements	300	200	200	700

FIGURE C.5 ■ **Testing Des Moines to Cleveland**

Because the cities in the tables are in random order, crossing an unoccupied cell is fine.

through the Evansville–Cleveland box but cannot turn a corner; thus we cannot place a plus or minus sign there. We may use occupied squares only as stepping-stones:

Des Moines–Cleveland index = $3 − $5 + $8 − $4 + $7 − $5 = +$4

Again, opening this route fails to lower our total shipping costs.

Two other routes can be evaluated in a similar fashion:

Evansville–Cleveland index = $3 − $4 + $7 − $5 = +$1

(Closed path = EC − EB + FB − FC)

Fort Lauderdale–Albuquerque index = $9 − $7 + $4 − $8 = −$2

(Closed path = FA − FB + EB − EA)

Because this last index is negative, we can realize cost savings by using the (currently unused) Fort Lauderdale–Albuquerque route.

In Example C2, we see that a better solution is indeed possible because we can calculate a negative improvement index on one of our unused routes. *Each negative index represents the amount by which total transportation costs could be decreased if one unit were shipped by the source-destination combination.* The next step, then, is to choose that route (unused square) with the *largest* negative improvement index. We can then ship the maximum allowable number of units on that route and reduce the total cost accordingly.

What is the maximum quantity that can be shipped on our new money-saving route? That quantity is found by referring to the closed path of plus signs and minus signs drawn for the route and then selecting the *smallest number found in the squares containing minus signs*. To obtain a new solution, we add this number to all squares on the closed path with plus signs and subtract it from all squares on the path to which we have assigned minus signs.

One iteration of the stepping-stone method is now complete. Again, of course, we must test to see if the solution is optimal or whether we can make any further improvements. We do this by evaluating each unused square, as previously described. Example C3 continues our effort to help Arizona Plumbing arrive at a final solution.

EXAMPLE C3

To improve our Arizona Plumbing solution, we can use the improvement indices calculated in Example C2. We found in Example C2 that the largest (and only) negative index is on the Fort Lauderdale–Albuquerque route (which is the route depicted in Figure C.6).

The maximum quantity that may be shipped on the newly opened route, Fort Lauderdale–Albuquerque (FA), is the smallest number found in squares containing minus signs—in this case, 100 units. Why 100 units? Because the total cost decreases by $2 per unit shipped, we know we would like to ship the maximum possible number of units. Previous stepping-stone calculations indicate that each unit shipped over the FA route results in an increase of 1 unit shipped from Evansville (E) to Boston (B) and a decrease of 1 unit in amounts shipped both from F to B (now 100 units) and from E to A (now 200 units). Hence, the maximum we can ship over the FA route is 100 units.

THE STEPPING-STONE METHOD

From \ To	(A) Albuquerque	(B) Boston	(C) Cleveland	Factory capacity
(D) Des Moines	$5 100	$4	$3	100
(E) Evansville	$8 200 −	$4 100 +	$3	300
(F) Fort Lauderdale	$9 +	$7 100 −	$5 200	300
Warehouse demands	300	200	200	700

FIGURE C.6 ■ **Transportation Table: Route FA**

This solution results in zero units being shipped from F to B. Now we take the following 4 steps:

1. Add 100 units (to the zero currently being shipped) on route FA;
2. Subtract 100 from route FB, leaving zero in that square (though still balancing the row total for F);
3. Add 100 to route EB, yielding 200; and,
4. Finally, subtract 100 from route EA, leaving 100 units shipped.

Note that the new numbers still produce the correct row and column totals as required. The new solution is shown in Figure C.7.

From \ To	(A) Albuquerque	(B) Boston	(C) Cleveland	Factory capacity
(D) Des Moines	$5 100	$4	$3	100
(E) Evansville	$8 100	$4 200	$3	300
(F) Fort Lauderdale	$9 100	$7	$5 200	300
Warehouse demands	300	200	200	700

FIGURE C.7 ■ **Solution at Next Iteration (Still Not Optimal)**

Total shipping cost has been reduced by (100 units) × ($2 saved per unit) = $200 and is now $4,000. This cost figure, of course, can also be derived by multiplying the cost of shipping each unit by the number of units transported on its respective route, namely: 100($5) + 100($8) + 200($4) + 100($9) + 200($5) = $4,000.

Looking carefully at Figure C.7, however, you can see that it, too, is not yet optimal. Route EC (Evansville–Cleveland) has a negative cost improvement index. See if you can find the final solution for this route on your own. (Programs C.1–C.4, at the end of this module, provide POM for Windows and Excel OM solutions.)

SPECIAL ISSUES IN MODELING

Demand Not Equal to Supply

A common situation in real-world problems is the case in which total demand is not equal to total supply. We can easily handle these so-called "unbalanced" problems with the solution procedures that we have just discussed by introducing **dummy sources** or **dummy destinations.** If total supply is greater than total demand, we make demand exactly equal the surplus by creating a dummy destination. Conversely, if total demand is greater than total supply, we introduce a dummy source (factory) with a supply equal to the excess of demand. Because these units will not in fact be shipped, we assign cost coefficients of zero to each square on the dummy location. In each case, then, the cost is zero. Example C4 demonstrates the use of a dummy destination.

Dummy sources Artificial shipping source points created in the transportation method when total demand is greater than total supply in order to affect a supply equal to the excess of demand over supply.

Dummy destinations Artificial destination points created in the transportation method when the total supply is greater than the total demand; they serve to equalize the total demand and supply.

EXAMPLE C4

Let's assume that Arizona Plumbing increases the production in its Des Moines factory to 250 bathtubs, thereby increasing supply over demand. To reformulate this unbalanced problem, we refer back to the data presented in Example C1 and present the new matrix in Figure C.8. First, we use the northwest-corner rule to find the initial feasible solution. Then, once the problem is balanced, we can proceed to the solution in the normal way.

From \ To	(A) Albuquerque	(B) Boston	(C) Cleveland	Dummy	Factory capacity
(D) Des Moines	$5 250	$4	$3	0	250
(E) Evansville	$8 50	$4 200	$3 50	0	300
(F) Fort Lauderdale	$9	$7	$5 150	0 150	300
Warehouse requirements	300	200	200	150	850

(Arrow points to 250 as "New Des Moines capacity")

FIGURE C.8 ■ **Northwest-Corner Rule with Dummy**

Total cost = 250($5) + 50($8) + 200($4) + 50($3) + 150($5) + 150(0) = $3,350

Degeneracy

To apply the stepping-stone method to a transportation problem, we must observe a rule about the number of shipping routes being used: *The number of occupied squares in any solution (initial or later) must be equal to the number of rows in the table plus the number of columns minus 1*. Solutions that do not satisfy this rule are called degenerate.

Degeneracy occurs when too few squares or shipping routes are being used. As a result, it becomes impossible to trace a closed path for 1 or more unused squares. The Ari-

Degeneracy An occurrence in transportation models when too few squares or shipping routes are being used so that tracing a closed path for each unused square becomes impossible.

SPECIAL ISSUES IN MODELING   749

When the navy in Thailand drafts a young man, he first reports to the induction center closest to his home. From one of 36 centers, he is transported by truck to one of 4 naval bases. The problem of deciding how many men should be assigned and transported from each center to each base is solved using the transportation model. Each base gets the number of recruits it needs, and costly extra trips are avoided.

zona Plumbing problem we just examined was not degenerate as it had 5 assigned routes (3 rows or factories + 3 columns or warehouses − 1).

To handle degenerate problems, we must artificially create an occupied cell: That is, we place a zero or a *very* small amount (representing a fake shipment) in one of the unused squares and *then treat that square as if it were occupied*. Remember that the chosen square must be in such a position as to allow all stepping-stone paths to be closed. We illustrate this procedure in Example C5.

> Check the unused squares to be sure that $m + n - 1$ equals the number of filled squares.

EXAMPLE C5

Martin Shipping Company has three warehouses from which it supplies its three major retail customers in San Jose. Martin's shipping costs, warehouse supplies, and customer demands are presented in the transportation table in Figure C.9 on page 750. To make the initial shipping assignments in that table, we apply the northwest-corner rule.

The initial solution is degenerate because it violates the rule that the number of used squares must equal the number of rows plus the number of columns minus 1. To correct the problem, we may place a zero in the unused square that permits evaluation of all empty cells. Some experimenting may be needed because not every cell will allow tracing a closed path for the remaining cells. Also, we want to avoid placing the 0 in a cell that has the negative sign in a closed path. No reallocation will be possible if we do this.

From \ To	Customer 1	Customer 2	Customer 3	Warehouse supply
Warehouse 1	$8 100	$2	$6	100
Warehouse 2	$10 0	$9 100	$9 20	120
Warehouse 3	$7	$10	$7 80	80
Customer demand	100	100	100	300

FIGURE C.9 ■ Martin's Northwest-Corner Rule

For this example, we try the empty square that represents the shipping route from Warehouse 2 to Customer 1. Now we can close all stepping-stone paths and compute improvement indices.

SUMMARY

The transportation model, a form of linear programming, is used to help find the least-cost solutions to systemwide shipping problems. The northwest-corner method, which begins in the upper-left corner of the transportation table, is used for finding an initial feasible solution. The stepping-stone algorithm is then used for finding optimal solutions. Unbalanced problems are those in which the total demand and total supply are not equal. Degeneracy refers to the case in which the number of rows + the number of columns − 1, is not equal to the number of occupied squares. The transportation model approach is one of the four location models described earlier in chapter 8.

KEY TERMS

Transportation modeling *(p. 740)*
Northwest-corner rule *(p. 742)*
Stepping-stone method *(p. 743)*
Dummy sources *(p. 748)*
Dummy destinations *(p. 748)*
Degeneracy *(p. 748)*

USING POM FOR WINDOWS TO SOLVE TRANSPORTATION PROBLEMS

In this transportation modeling example, we use the data from Arizona Plumbing. Program C.1 reflects the input of demand data, supply data, and unit shipping costs. Program C.2 displays the output. Several optional screens are also available.

PROGRAM C.1 ■ Input Screen of POM for Windows Transportation Module Applied to Arizona Plumbing Data

Objective: Minimize
Starting method: Any starting method

Arizona Plumbing

COSTS	Albuquerque	Boston	Cleveland	Total
Des Moines	5	4	3	100
Evansville	8	4	3	300
Ft. Lauderdale	9	7	5	300
Total	300	200	200	

USING EXCEL OM TO SOLVE TRANSPORTATION PROBLEMS

Transportation Shipments

Arizona Plumbing Solution

Optimal cost = $3,900	Albuquerque	Boston	Cleveland
Des Moines	100.		
Evansville		200.	100.
Ft. Lauderdale	200.		100.

PROGRAM C.2 ■ POM for Windows Output for Arizona Plumbing Transportation Problem

USING EXCEL OM TO SOLVE TRANSPORTATION PROBLEMS

Excel OM's Transportation module uses Excel's built-in Solver routine to find opimal solutions to transportation problems. Program C.3 illustrates the input data (from Arizona Plumbing) and total cost formulas. To reach an optimal solution, we must go to Excel's *Tools* bar, request *Solver*, then select *Solve*. The output appears in Program C.4 on page 752.

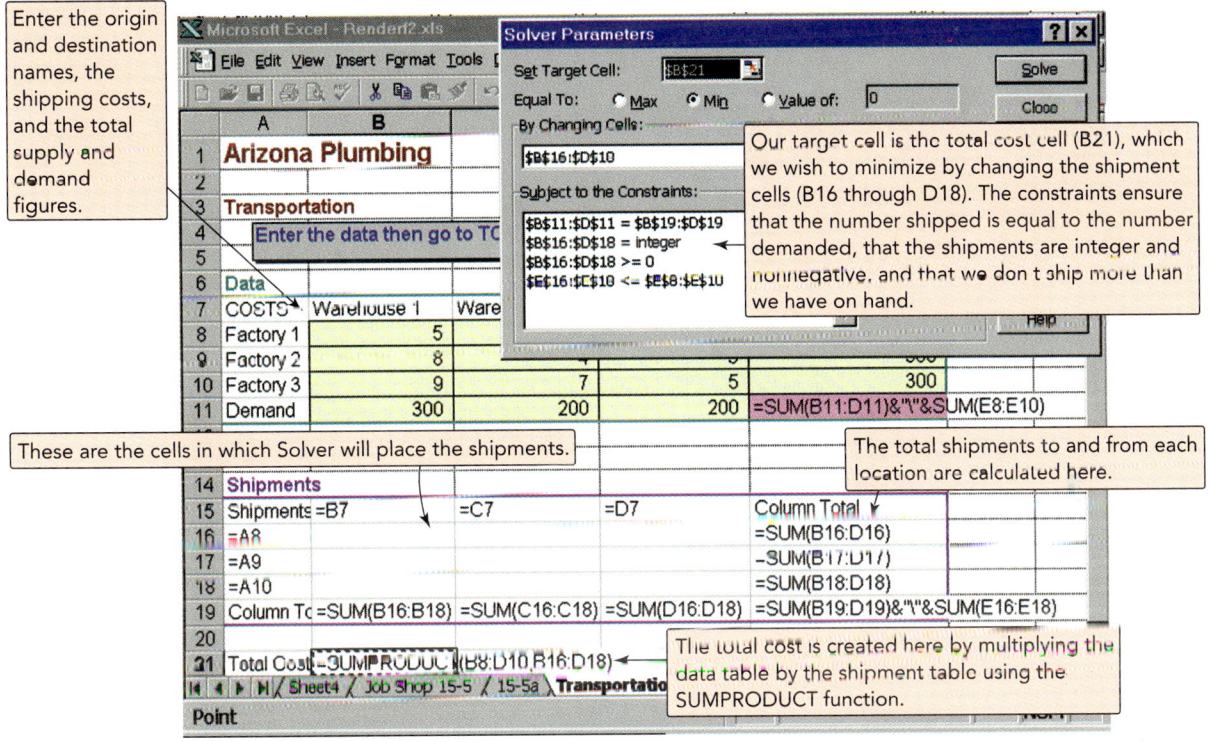

Enter the origin and destination names, the shipping costs, and the total supply and demand figures.

Our target cell is the total cost cell (B21), which we wish to minimize by changing the shipment cells (B16 through D18). The constraints ensure that the number shipped is equal to the number demanded, that the shipments are integer and nonnegative, and that we don't ship more than we have on hand.

These are the cells in which Solver will place the shipments.

The total shipments to and from each location are calculated here.

The total cost is created here by multiplying the data table by the shipment table using the SUMPRODUCT function.

PROGRAM C.3 ■ Excel OM Input Screen and Formulas, Using Arizona Plumbing Data

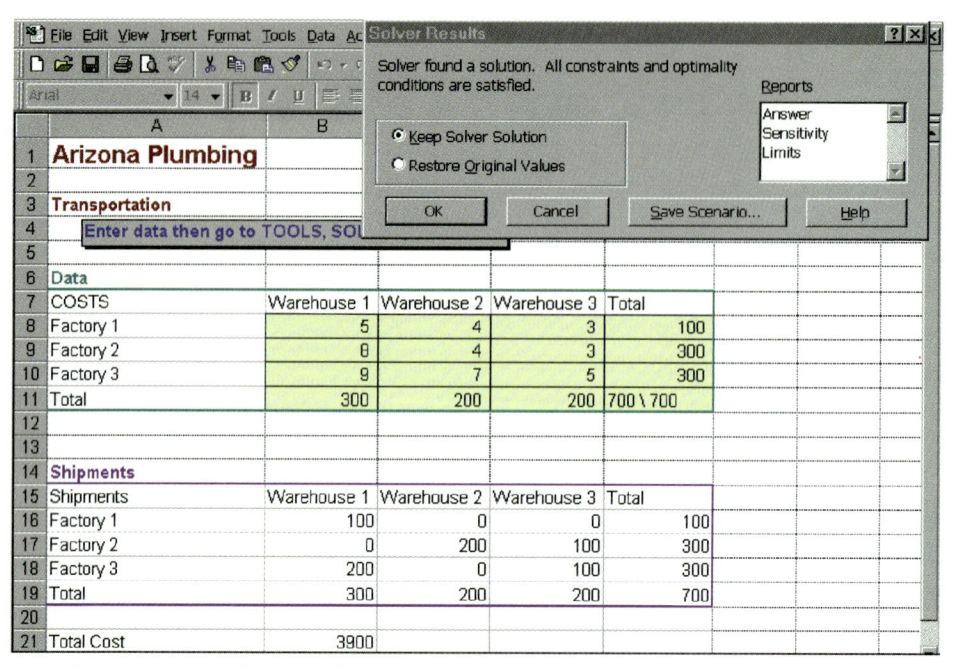

PROGRAM C.4 ■ Output from Excel OM with Optimal Solution to Arizona Plumbing Problem

Arizona Plumbing

Transportation

Enter data then go to TOOLS, SOL...

Data

COSTS	Warehouse 1	Warehouse 2	Warehouse 3	Total
Factory 1	5	4	3	100
Factory 2	8	4	3	300
Factory 3	9	7	5	300
Total	300	200	200	700 \ 700

Shipments

Shipments	Warehouse 1	Warehouse 2	Warehouse 3	Total
Factory 1	100	0	0	100
Factory 2	0	200	100	300
Factory 3	200	0	100	300
Total	300	200	200	700
Total Cost	3900			

Solver Results: Solver found a solution. All constraints and optimality conditions are satisfied.

SOLVED PROBLEMS

Solved Problem C.1

Williams Auto Top Carriers currently maintains plants in Atlanta and Tulsa to supply auto top carriers to distribution centers in Los Angeles and New York. Because of expanding demand, Williams has decided to open a third plant and has narrowed the choice to one of two cities—New Orleans and Houston. Table C.3 provides pertinent production and distribution costs as well as plant capacities and distribution demands.

Which of the new locations, in combination with the existing plants and distribution centers, yields a lower cost for the firm?

TABLE C.3 ■ Production Costs, Distribution Costs, Plant Capabilities, and Market Demands for Williams Auto Top Carriers

	To Distribution Centers		Normal Production	Unit Production Cost
From Plants	Los Angeles	New York		
Existing plants				
Atlanta	$8	$5	600	$6
Tulsa	$4	$7	900	$5
Proposed locations				
New Orleans	$5	$6	500	$4 (anticipated)
Houston	$4	$6[a]	500	$3 (anticipated)
Forecast demand	800	1,200	2,000	

[a] Indicates distribution cost (shipping, handling, storage) will be $6 per carrier between Houston and New York.

Solution

To answer this question, we must solve two transportation problems, one for each combination. We will recommend the location that yields a lower total cost of distribution and production in combination with the existing system.

We begin by setting up a transportation table that represents the opening of a third plant in New Orleans (see Figure C.10). Then we use the northwest-corner method to find an initial solution. The total cost of this first solution is $23,600. Note that the cost of each individual "plant-to-distribution-center" route is found by adding the distribution costs (in the body of Table C.3) to the respective unit production costs (in the right-hand column of Table C.3). Thus, the total production-plus-shipping cost of one auto top carrier from Atlanta to Los Angeles is $14 ($8 for shipping plus $6 for production).

From \ To	Los Angeles	New York	Production capacity
Atlanta	$14 — 600	$11	600
Tulsa	$9 — 200	$12 — 700	900
New Orleans	$9	$10 — 500	500
Demand	800	1,200	2,000

FIGURE C.10 ■ Williams Transportation Table for New Orleans

$$\text{Total cost} = (600 \text{ units} \times \$14) + (200 \text{ units} \times \$9)$$
$$+ (700 \text{ units} \times \$12) + (500 \text{ units} \times \$10)$$
$$= \$8,400 + \$1,800 + \$8,400 + \$5,000$$
$$= \$23,600$$

Is this initial solution optimal? We can use the stepping-stone method to test it and compute improvement indices for unused routes:

Improvement index for Atlanta–New York route

$$= +\$11 \text{ (Atlanta–New York)} - \$14 \text{ (Atlanta–L.A.)}$$
$$+ \$9 \text{ (Tulsa–L.A.)} - \$12 \text{ (Tulsa–New York)}$$
$$= -\$6$$

Improvement index for New Orleans–Los Angeles route

= + $9 (New Orleans–L.A.)

− $10 (New Orleans–New York)

+ $12 (Tulsa–New York)

− $9 (Tulsa–L.A.)

= $2

Because the firm can save $6 for every unit shipped from Atlanta to New York, it will want to improve the initial solution and send as many units as possible (600, in this case) on this currently unused route (see Figure C.11). You may also want to confirm that the total cost is now $20,000, a savings of $3,600 over the initial solution.

From \ To	Los Angeles	New York	Production capacity
Atlanta	$14	$11 / 600	600
Tulsa	$9 / 800	$12 / 100	900
New Orleans	$9	$10 / 500	500
Demand	800	1,200	2,000

FIGURE C.11 ■ **Improved Transportation Table for Williams**

Next, we must test the two unused routes to see if their improvement indices are also negative numbers:

Index for Atlanta–Los Angeles

= $14 − $11 + $12 − $9 = $6

Index for New Orleans–Los Angeles

= $9 − $10 + $12 − $9 = $2

Because both indices are greater than zero, we have already reached our optimal solution using the New Orleans plant. If Williams elects to open the New Orleans plant, the firm's total production and distribution cost will be $20,000.

This analysis, however, provides only half the answer to Williams's problem. The same procedure must still be followed to determine the minimum cost if the new plant is built in Houston. Determining this cost is left as a homework problem. You can help provide complete information and recommend a solution by solving Problem C.8.

Solved Problem C.2

In Solved Problem C.1, we examined the Williams Auto Top Carriers problem by using a transportation table. An alternative approach is to structure the same decision analysis using linear programming (LP), which we explained in detail in quantitative module B.

Solution

Using the data in Figure C.10 (p. 753), we write the objective function and constraints as follows:

Minimize total cost = $14X_{Atl,LA} + \$11X_{Atl,NY} + \$9X_{Tul,LA} + \$12X_{Tul,NY} + \$9X_{NO,LA} + 10X_{NO,NY}$

Subject to: $X_{Atl,LA} + X_{Atl,NY} \leq 600$ (production capacity at Atlanta)

$X_{Tul,LA} + X_{Tul,NY} \leq 900$ (production capacity at Tulsa)

$X_{NO,LA} + X_{NO,NY} \leq 500$ (production capacity at New Orleans)

$X_{Atl,LA} + X_{Tul,LA} + X_{NO,LA} \geq 800$ (Los Angeles demand constraint)

$X_{Atl,NY} + X_{Tul,NY} + X_{NO,NY} \geq 1200$ (New York demand constraint)

DISCUSSION QUESTIONS

1. What is a *balanced* transportation problem? Describe the approach you would use to solve an *unbalanced* problem.
2. Develop a *northeast*-corner rule and explain how it would work. Set up an initial solution for the Arizona Plumbing problem analyzed in Example C1.
3. In solving a transportation problem, when is a northwest-corner solution optimal?
4. How can the transportation method address production costs in addition to transportation costs?
5. What is the difference between a feasible solution and an optimal one?
6. What is the purpose of the stepping-stone method?
7. What is the purpose of introducing a *dummy source* or *dummy destination* into a transportation problem?
8. Identify the three "steps" in the northwest-corner rule.

PROBLEMS

C.1 Find an initial solution to the following transportation problem using the northwest-corner method. What is the total cost?

FROM \ TO	SAN DIEGO	TORONTO	MEXICO CITY	SUPPLY
Tijuana	$ 6	$18	$ 8	100
Boston	$17	$13	$19	60
Montreal	$20	$10	$24	40
Demand	50	80	70	

· C.2 Using the stepping-stone method, find the optimal solution to Problem C.1. Compute the total cost.

· C.3 Use the northwest-corner method to find an initial feasible solution to the following problem. What must you do before beginning the solution steps?

TO FROM	A	B	C	SUPPLY
X	10	18	12	100
Y	17	13	9	50
Z	20	18	14	75
Demand	50	80	70	

· C.4 Find the optimal solution to Problem C.3 using the stepping-stone method.

: C.5 The following table presents cost, capacity, and supply data for a transportation problem in Stephanie Robbin's furniture company. Set up the appropriate transportation table and find the initial solution using northwest-corner data. Note that a "dummy" source is needed to balance the problem.

To From	1	2	3	Capacity
A	$30	$10	$5	20
B	$10	$10	$10	30
C	$20	$10	$25	75
Supply	40	60	55	

: C.6 The following table is the result of one or more iterations:

To From	1	2	3	Capacity
A	30 40	10	5 10	50
B	10	10 30	10 10	30
C	20	10 30	25 45	75
Demands	40	60	55	155

a) Complete the next iteration using the stepping-stone method.
b) Calculate the "total cost" incurred if your results were to be accepted as the final solution.

- **C.7** Determine whether the new solution table presented in Example C3 in this module contains the optimal transportation allocation for Arizona Plumbing. If not, compute an improved solution and test it for optimality.

- **C.8** In Solved Problem C.1, at the end of this module, Williams Auto Top Carriers proposed opening a new plant in either New Orleans or Houston. Management found that the total system cost (of production plus distribution) would be $20,000 for the New Orleans site. What would be the total cost if Williams opened a plant in Houston? At which of the two proposed locations (New Orleans or Houston) should Williams open the new facility?

- **C.9** After one iteration of the stepping-stone method, G. W. Willis Paint Company produced the following transportation table. Complete the analysis, determining an optimal shipping solution.

G. W. Willis Paint Company

From \ To	Warehouse 1	Warehouse 2	Warehouse 3	Factory capacity
Factory A	$8 120	$5	$6	120
Factory B	$15	$10 80	$14	80
Factory C	$3 30	$9	$10 50	80
Warehouse requirements	150	80	50	280

Cost = $2,350

- **C.10** The Todd Corbin Clothing Group owns factories in three towns (W, Y, and Z), which distribute to three Corbin retail dress shops in three other cities (A, B, and C). The following table summarizes factory availabilities, projected store demands, and unit shipping costs.

Corbin Clothing Group

From \ To	Dress Shop A	Dress Shop B	Dress Shop C	Factory availability
Factory W	$4	$3	$3	35
Factory Y	$6	$7	$6	50
Factory Z	$8	$2	$5	50
Store demand	30	65	40	135

  a) Complete the analysis, determining the optimal solution for shipping at the Todd Corbin Clothing Group.

  b) How do you know if it is optimal or not?

- **C.11** Sound Track Stereos assembles its high-fidelity stereophonic systems at three plants and distributes them from three regional warehouses. The production capacities at each plant, demand at each warehouse, and unit shipping costs are presented in the following table:

Sound Track Stereos

From \ To	Warehouse A	Warehouse B	Warehouse C	Plant supply
Plant W	$6	$4	$9	200
Plant Y	$10	$5	$6	175
Plant Z	$12	$7	$8	75
Warehouse demand	250	100	150	450 / 500

a) Set up this transportation problem by adding a dummy plant. Then use the northwest-corner rule to find an initial basic feasible solution.

b) What is the optimal solution?

: C.12 Whybark Mill Works (WMW) ships French doors to three building-supply houses from mills in Mountpelier, Nixon, and Oak Ridge. Determine the best shipment schedule for WMW from the data provided by Tad Hixon, the traffic manager at WMW. Use the northwest-corner starting procedure and the stepping-stone method. Refer to the following table. (*Note:* you may face a degenerate solution in one of your iterations.)

Whybark Mill Works

From \ To	Supply House 1	Supply House 2	Supply House 3	Mill capacity (in tons)
Mountpelier	$3	$3	$2	25
Nixon	$4	$2	$3	40
Oak Ridge	$3	$2	$3	30
Supply house demand (in tons)	30	30	35	95

: C.13 Jim Lloyd, vice president for operations of HHN, Inc., a manufacturer of cabinets for telephone switches, is constrained from meeting his 5-year forecast by limited capacity at the company's 3 existing plants. These plants are Waterloo, Pusan, and Bogota. As his able assistant, you have been told that because of existing capacity constraints and the expanding world market for HHN cabinets, a new plant is to be added to the current 3 plants. The real estate department has advised Lloyd that two sites seem particularly good because of stable political situations and tolerable exchange rates. These two locations are Dublin, Ireland, and Fontainebleau, France. Lloyd suggests that from the data in the following table, which provide production and transportation costs, you should be able to determine where the fourth plant should be located. (*Note:* This problem is degenerate with the data for both locations.)

Problems

	Plant Location				
Market Area	Waterloo	Pusan	Bogota	Fontainebleau	Dublin
Canada: Demand 4,000					
Production cost	50	30	40	50	45
Transportation cost	10	25	20	25	25
South America: Demand 5,000					
Production cost	50	30	40	50	45
Transportation cost	20	25	10	30	30
Pacific Rim: Demand 10,000					
Production cost	50	30	40	50	45
Transportation cost	25	10	25	40	40
Europe: Demand 5,000					
Production cost	50	30	40	50	45
Transportation cost	25	40	30	10	20
Capacity	8,000	2,000	5,000	9,000	9,000

- : **C.14** Susan Helms Manufacturing Co. has hired you to evaluate its shipping costs. The table below shows present demand, capacity, and freight costs between each factory and each warehouse. Find the shipping pattern with the lowest cost.

Susan Helms Manufacturing Data

From \ To	Warehouse 1	Warehouse 2	Warehouse 3	Warehouse 4	Plant capacity
Factory 1	4	7	10	12	2,000
Factory 2	7	5	8	11	2,500
Factory 3	9	8	6	9	2,200
Warehouse demand	1,000	2,000	2,000	1,200	6,700 / 6,200

- : **C.15** Drew Rosen Corp. is considering adding a fourth plant to its three existing facilities in Decatur, Minneapolis, and Carbondale. Both St. Louis and East St. Louis are being considered. Evaluating only the transportation costs per unit as shown in the table below, decide which site is best.

	From Existing Plants			
To	Decatur	Minneapolis	Carbondale	Demand
Blue Earth	$20	$17	$21	250
Ciro	25	27	20	200
Des Moines	22	25	22	350
Capacity	300	200	150	

	From Proposed Plants	
To	East St. Louis	St. Louis
Blue Earth	$29	$27
Ciro	30	28
Des Moines	30	31
Capacity	150	150

: C.16 Using the data from Problem C.15 and the unit production costs in the following table, show which locations yield the lowest cost.

Location	Production Costs ($)
Decatur	$50
Minneapolis	60
Carbondale	70
East St. Louis	40
St. Louis	50

DATA BASE APPLICATION

: C.17 Culman Pharmaceuticals enjoys a dominant position in the southeast United States, with over 800 discount retail outlets. These stores are served by twice-weekly deliveries from Culman's 13 warehouses, which are in turn supplied daily by 7 factories that manufacture about 70% of all of the chain's products.

It is clear to Christine Culman, VP Operations, that an additional warehouse is desperately needed to handle growth and backlogs. Three cities, Mobile, Tampa, and Huntsville, are under final consideration. The following table illustrates the current and proposed factory/warehouse capacities/demands and shipping costs per average box of supplies.

a) Based on shipping costs only, which city should be selected for the new warehouse?
b) One study shows that Ocala's capacity can increase to 500 boxes per day. Would this affect your decision in part (a)?
c) Because of a new intrastate shipping agreement, rates for shipping from each factory in Florida to each warehouse in Florida drop by $1 per carton. How does this factor affect your answer to parts (a) and (b)?

Table for Data Base Application C.17

	Warehouse								
Factory	Atlanta, GA	New Orleans, LA	Jackson, MS	Birmingham, AL	Montgomery, AL	Raleigh, NC	Ashville, NC	Columbia, SC	Capacity (cartons per day)
Valdosta, GA	$3	$5	$4	$3	$4	$6	$8	$8	500
Ocala, FL	4	6	5	5	6	7	6	7	300
Augusta, GA	1	4	3	2	2	6	7	8	400
Stuart, FL	3	5	2	6	6	5	5	6	200
Biloxi, MS	4	1	4	3	3	8	9	10	600
Starkville, MS	3	3	1	2	2	6	5	6	400
Durham, NC	4	8	8	7	7	2	2	2	500
Requirements (cartons/day)	150	250	50	150	100	200	150	300	

Table for Data Base Application C.17 (Continued)

Factory	Orlando, FL	Miami, FL	Jacksonville, FL	Wilmington, NC	Charlotte, NC	Mobile, AL	Tampa, FL	Huntsville, AL	Capacity (cartons per day)
Valdosta, GA	$9	$10	$8	$8	$11	$4	$6	$3	500
Ocala, FL	2	3	2	6	7	5	2	5	300
Augusta, GA	7	9	6	8	9	3	5	2	400
Stuart, FL	2	2	3	5	5	6	3	5	200
Biloxi, MS	7	13	9	8	8	2	6	3	600
Starkville, MS	6	8	7	7	8	3	6	2	400
Durham, NC	6	8	5	1	2	8	7	8	500
Requirements (cartons/day)	250	300	300	100	150	300	300	300	

Case Study

Andrew-Carter, Inc.

Andrew-Carter, Inc. (A-C) is a major Canadian producer and distributor of outdoor lighting fixtures. Its products are distributed throughout South and North America and have been in high demand for several years. The company operates three plants to manufacture fixtures and distribute them to five distribution centers (warehouses).

During the present global slowdown, A-C has seen a major drop in demand for its products, largely because the housing market has declined. Based on the forecast of interest rates, the head of operations feels that demand for housing and thus for A-C's products will remain depressed for the foreseeable future. A-C is considering closing one of its plants, as it is now operating with a forecast excess capacity of 34,000 units per week. The forecast weekly demands for the coming year are as follows:

Warehouse 1	9,000 units
Warehouse 2	13,000
Warehouse 3	11,000
Warehouse 4	15,000
Warehouse 5	8,000

Plant capacities, in units per week, are:

Plant 1, regular time	27,000 units
Plant 1, on overtime	7,000
Plant 2, regular time	20,000
Plant 2, on overtime	5,000
Plant 3, regular time	25,000
Plant 3, on overtime	6,000

If A-C shuts down any plants, its weekly costs will change, because fixed costs will be lower for a nonoperating plant. Table 1 on page 762 shows production costs at each plant, both variable at regular time and overtime, and fixed when operating and shut down. Table 2 (p. 762) shows distribution costs from each plant to each distribution center.

Discussion Questions

1. Evaluate the various configurations of operating and closed plants that will meet weekly demand. Determine which configuration minimizes total costs.
2. Discuss the implications of closing a plant.

Source: Reprinted by permission of Professor Michael Ballot, University of the Pacific, Stockton, CA.

TABLE 1 ■ Andrew-Carter, Inc., Variable Costs and Fixed Production Costs per Week

Plant	Variable Cost (per unit)	Fixed Cost per Week Operating	Fixed Cost per Week Not Operating
1, regular time	$2.80	$14,000	$6,000
1, overtime	3.52		
2, regular time	2.78	12,000	5,000
2, overtime	3.48		
3, regular time	2.72	15,000	7,500
3, overtime	3.42		

TABLE 2 ■ Andrew-Carter, Inc., Distribution Costs per Unit

From Plants	W1	W2	W3	W4	W5
1	$.50	$.44	$.49	$.46	$.56
2	.40	.52	.50	.56	.57
3	.56	.53	.51	.54	.35

■ *Internet Case Studies* ■

See our Internet home page at http://www.prenhall.com/heizer for these additional case studies: Custom Vans, Inc.; Consolidated Bottling (B); and Northwest General Hospital.

BIBLIOGRAPHY

Drezner, Z. *Facility Location: A Survey of Applications and Methods*. Secaucus, NJ: Springer-Verlag, 1995.

Fitzsimmons, J. A. "A Warehouse Location Model Helps Texas Comptroller Select Out-of-State Audit Officers." *Interfaces* 13 (October 1983): 40–45.

Murdick, R., B. Render, and R. Russell. *Service Operations Management*. Boston: Allyn & Bacon, 1990.

Price, W. L., and M. Turcotte. "Locating a Blood Bank." *Interfaces* 16 (September–October 1986): 17–26.

Reed, R. *Plant Location, Layout, and Maintenance*. Homewood, IL: Richard D. Irwin, 1967.

Render, B., and R. M. Stair. *Quantitative Analysis for Management*, 6th ed. Upper Saddle River, NJ: Prentice Hall, 1997.

Schmenner, R. W. "Look Beyond the Obvious in Plant Location." *Harvard Business Review* 57 (January–February 1979): 126–132.

QUANTITATIVE MODULE D

Waiting-Line Models

MODULE OUTLINE

QUEUING COSTS

CHARACTERISTICS OF A WAITING-LINE SYSTEM
  Arrival Characteristics
  Waiting-Line Characteristics
  Service Facility Characteristics
  Measuring the Queue's Performance

THE VARIETY OF QUEUING MODELS
  Model A: Single-Channel Queuing Model with Poisson Arrivals and Exponential Service Times
  Model B: Multiple-Channel Queuing Model
  Model C: Constant Service Time Model
  Model D: Limited Population Model

OTHER QUEUING APPROACHES

SUMMARY

KEY TERMS

USING POM FOR WINDOWS FOR QUEUING

USING EXCEL OM FOR QUEUING

SOLVED PROBLEMS

DISCUSSION QUESTIONS

PROBLEMS

CASE STUDIES: NEW ENGLAND CASTINGS; THE WINTER PARK HOTEL

INTERNET CASE STUDY

BIBLIOGRAPHY

LEARNING OBJECTIVES

When you complete this module you should be able to:

Identify or Define:

  The assumptions of the four basic waiting-line models

Describe or Explain:

  How to apply waiting-line models

  How to conduct an economic analysis of queues

Paris's Euro Disney, Tokyo's Disney Japan, and the U.S.'s Disney World and Disneyland all have one feature in common—long lines and seemingly endless waits. However, Disney is one of the world's leading companies in the scientific analysis of queuing theory. It analyzes queuing behaviors and can predict which rides will draw what length crowds. To keep visitors happy, Disney makes lines appear to be constantly moving forward, entertains people while they wait, and posts signs telling visitors how many minutes until they reach each ride.

Queuing theory A body of knowledge about waiting lines.

Waiting line (Queue) items or people in a line awaiting service.

The body of knowledge about waiting lines, often called **queuing theory**, is an important part of operations and a valuable tool for the operations manager. **Waiting lines** are a common situation—they may, for example, take the form of cars waiting for repair at a Midas Muffler Shop, copying jobs waiting to be completed at a Kinko's print shop, or vacationers waiting to enter Mr. Frogg's Wild Ride at Disney. Table D.1 lists just a few OM uses of waiting-line models.

TABLE D.1 ■ Common Queuing Situations

Situation	Arrivals in Queue	Service Process
Supermarket	Grocery shoppers	Checkout clerks at cash register
Highway toll booth	Automobiles	Collection of tolls at booth
Doctor's office	Patients	Treatment by doctors and nurses
Computer system	Programs to be run	Computer processes jobs
Telephone company	Callers	Switching equipment to forward calls
Bank	Customers	Transactions handled by teller
Machine maintenance	Broken machines	Repair people fix machines
Harbor	Ships and barges	Dock workers load and unload

Two interesting quotes:
"The other line always moves faster."
   Etorre's Observation
"If you change lines, the one you just left will start to move faster than the one you are now in."
   O'Brien's Variation

Waiting-line models are useful in both manufacturing and service areas. Analysis of queues in terms of waiting-line length, average waiting time, and other factors helps us to understand service systems (such as bank teller stations), maintenance activities (that might repair broken machinery), and shop-floor control activities. As a matter of fact, patients waiting in a doctor's office and broken drill presses waiting in a repair facility have a lot in common from an OM perspective. Both use human and equipment resources to restore valuable production assets (people and machines) to good condition.

QUEUING COSTS

Operations managers recognize the trade-off that must take place between two costs: the cost of providing good service and the cost of customer or machine waiting time. Managers want queues that are short enough so that customers do not become unhappy and either leave without buying or buy but never return. However, managers are willing to allow some waiting if it is balanced by a significant savings in service costs.

One means of evaluating a service facility is to look at total expected cost. Total cost is the sum of expected service costs plus expected waiting costs.

As you can see in Figure D.1, service costs increase as a firm attempts to raise its level of service. Managers in *some* service centers can vary capacity by having standby personnel and machines that they can assign to specific service stations in order to prevent or shorten excessively long lines. In grocery stores, for example, managers and stock clerks can open extra checkout counters. In banks and airport check-in points, part-time workers may be called in to help. As the level of service improves (that is, speeds up), however, the cost of time spent waiting in lines decreases. (Refer again to Figure D.1.) Waiting cost may reflect lost productivity of workers while tools or machines await repairs or may simply be an estimate of the cost of customers lost because of poor service and long queues. In some service systems (for example, an emergency ambulance service), the cost of long waiting lines may be intolerably high.

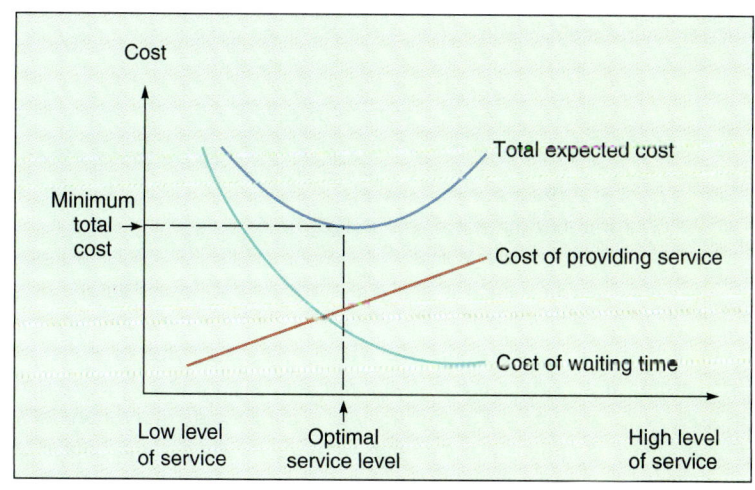

FIGURE D.1 ■ **The Trade-Off between Waiting Costs and Service Costs**

As we look at Figure D.1, it becomes clear that different organizations place different values on their customers' time (with many colleges and motor vehicle offices placing minimal cost on waiting time).

CHARACTERISTICS OF A WAITING-LINE SYSTEM

In this section, we take a look at the three parts of a waiting-line, or queuing, system:

1. Arrivals or inputs to the system;
2. Queue discipline, or the waiting line itself;
3. The service facility.

Arrival Characteristics

The input source that generates arrivals or customers for a service system has three major characteristics:

- The *size* of the arrival population,
- The *pattern* of arrivals at the queuing system, and
- The *behavior* of arrivals.

Size of the Source Population Population sizes are considered either unlimited (essentially infinite) or limited (finite). When the number of customers or arrivals on hand at any given moment is just a small portion of all potential arrivals, the arrival population is considered **unlimited**, or **infinite**. Examples of unlimited populations include cars arriving at a highway toll booth, shoppers arriving at a supermarket, and students arriving to register for classes at a large university. Most queuing models assume such an infinite arrival population. An example of a **limited**, or **finite**, population is found in a copying shop that has, say, eight copying machines. Each of the copiers is a potential "customer" that might break down and require service.

Unlimited, or infinite, population A queue in which a virtually unlimited number of people or items that could request the services, or the number of customers or arrivals on hand at any given moment is a very small portion of potential arrivals.

Limited, or finite, population A queue in which there are only a limited number of potential users of the service.

Poisson distribution A discrete probability distribution that often describes the arrival rate in queuing theory.

Pattern of Arrivals at the System Customers arrive at a service facility either according to some known schedule (for example, 1 patient every 15 minutes or 1 student every half hour) or else they arrive *randomly*. Arrivals are considered random when they are independent of one another and their occurrence cannot be predicted exactly. Frequently in queuing problems, the number of arrivals per unit of time can be estimated by a probability distribution known as the **Poisson distribution.** For any given arrival time (such as 2 customers per hour or 4 trucks per minute), a discrete Poisson distribution can be established by using the formula

$$P(x) = \frac{e^{-\lambda}\lambda^x}{x!} \quad \text{for } x = 0, 1, 2, 3, 4, \ldots \quad \text{(D.1)}$$

where $P(x)$ = probability of x arrivals
 x = number of arrivals per unit of time
 λ = average arrival rate
 e = 2.7183 (which is the base of the natural logarithms)

With the help of the table in Appendix III, which gives the value of $e^{-\lambda}$ for use in the Poisson distribution, these values are easy to compute. Figure D.2 illustrates the Poisson distribution for $\lambda = 2$ and $\lambda = 4$. This means that if the average arrival rate is $\lambda = 2$ customers per hour, the probability of 0 customers arriving in any random hour is about 13%, probability of 1 customer is about 27%, 2 customers about 27%, 3 customers about 18%, 4 customers about 9%, and so on. The chances that 9 or more will arrive are virtually nil. Arrivals, of course, are not always Poisson distributed (they may follow some other distribution). Patterns, therefore, should be examined to make certain that they are well-approximated by Poisson before that distribution is applied.

Behavior of Arrivals Most queuing models assume that an arriving customer is a patient customer. Patient customers are people or machines that wait in the queue until they are served and do not switch between lines. Unfortunately, life is complicated by the fact that people have been known to balk or to renege. Customers who *balk* refuse to join the waiting line because it is too long to suit their needs or interests. *Reneging* customers are those who enter the queue but then become impatient and leave without completing their

$$\text{Probability} = P(x) = \frac{e^{-\lambda}\lambda^x}{x!}$$

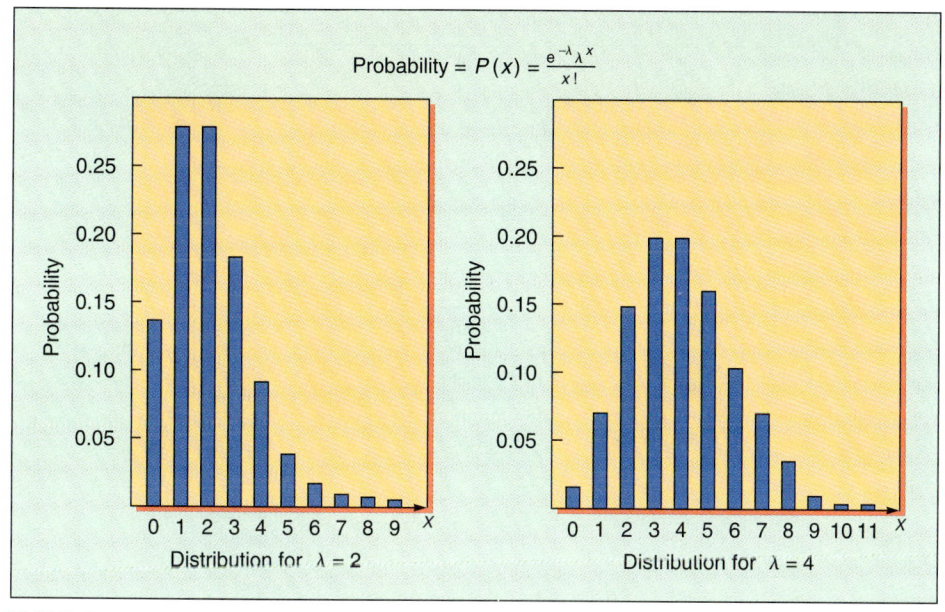

FIGURE D.2 ■ **Two Examples of the Poisson Distribution for Arrival Times**

transaction. Actually, both of these situations just serve to highlight the need for queuing theory and waiting-line analysis.

Waiting-Line Characteristics

The waiting line itself is the second component of a queuing system. The length of a line can be either limited or unlimited. A queue is *limited* when it cannot, either by law or because of physical restrictions, increase to an infinite length. A small barbershop, for example, will have only a limited number of waiting chairs. Queuing models are treated in this module under an assumption of *unlimited* queue length. A queue is *unlimited* when its size is unrestricted, as in the case of the toll booth serving arriving automobiles.

A second waiting-line characteristic deals with *queue discipline*. This refers to the rule by which customers in the line are to receive service. Most systems use a queue discipline known as the **first-in, first-out (FIFO) rule**. In a hospital emergency room or an express checkout line at a supermarket, however, various assigned priorities may preempt FIFO. Patients who are critically injured will move ahead in treatment priority over patients with broken fingers or noses. Shoppers with fewer than 10 items may be allowed to enter the express checkout queue (but are *then* treated as first-come, first-served). Computer-programming runs also operate under priority scheduling. In most large companies, when computer-produced paychecks are due on a specific date, the payroll program gets highest priority.[1]

First-in, first-out (FIFO) rule A queuing discipline where the first customers in line receive the first service.

Service Facility Characteristics

The third part of any queuing system is the service facility. Two basic properties are important: (1) the configuration of the service system and (2) the pattern of service times.

---

[1] The term *FIFS* (first-in, first-served) is often used in place of FIFO. Another discipline, LIFS (last-in, first-served) also called last-in, first-out (LIFO), is common when material is stacked or piled so that the items on top are used first.

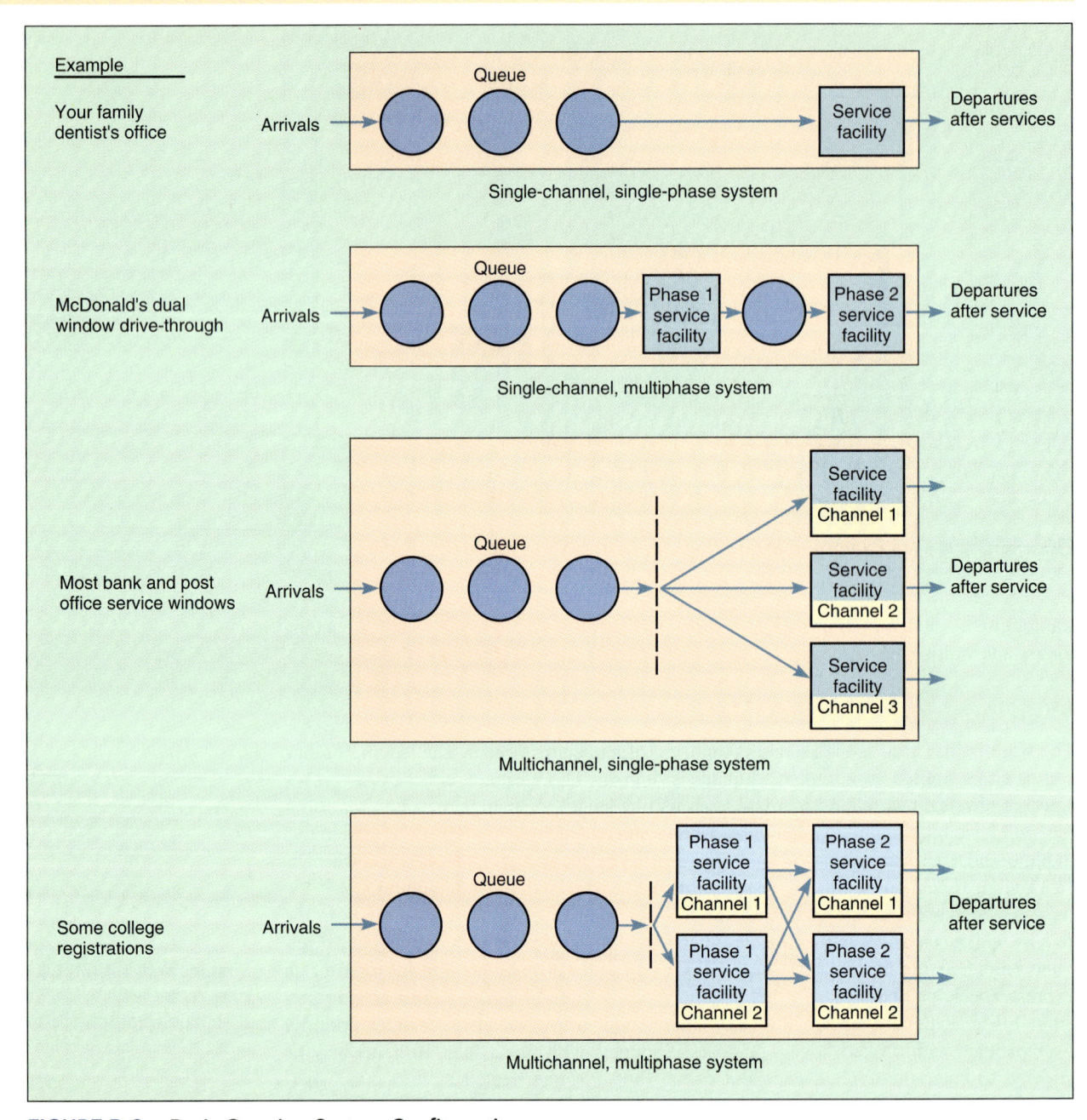

FIGURE D.3 ■ Basic Queuing System Configurations

Example	Configuration
Your family dentist's office	Single-channel, single-phase system
McDonald's dual window drive-through	Single-channel, multiphase system
Most bank and post office service windows	Multichannel, single-phase system
Some college registrations	Multichannel, multiphase system

Basic Queuing System Configurations Service systems are usually classified in terms of their number of channels (for example, number of servers) and number of phases (for example, number of service stops that must be made). A **single-channel queuing system**, with one server, is typified by the drive-in bank with only one open teller. If, on the other hand, the bank has several tellers on duty, with each customer waiting in one common line for the first available teller, then we would have a **multiple-channel queuing system**. Most banks today are multichannel service systems, as are most large barbershops, airline ticket counters, and post offices.

Single-channel queuing system A service system with one line and one server.

CHARACTERISTICS OF A WAITING-LINE SYSTEM

In a **single-phase system,** the customer receives service from only one station and then exits the system. A fast-food restaurant in which the person who takes your order also brings your food and takes your money is a single-phase system. So is a driver's license agency in which the person taking your application also grades your test and collects your license fee. However, say, the restaurant requires you to place your order at one station, pay at a second, and pick up your food at a third. In this case, it is a **multiphase system**. Likewise, if the driver's license agency is large or busy, you will probably have to wait in one line to complete your application (the first service stop), queue again to have your test graded and finally go to a third counter to pay your fee. To help you relate the concepts of channels and phases, Figure D.3 presents four possible channel configurations.

Service Time Distribution Service patterns are like arrival patterns in that they may be either constant or random. If service time is constant, it takes the same amount of time to take care of each customer. This is the case in a machine-performed service operation such as an automatic car wash. More often, service times are randomly distributed. In many cases, we can assume that random service times are described by the **negative exponential probability distribution**.

Figure D.4 shows that if *service times* follow a negative exponential distribution, the probability of any very long service time is low. For example, when an average service time is 20 minutes, seldom if ever will a customer require more than 90 minutes in the service facility. If the mean service time is 1 hour, the probability of spending more than 180 minutes in service is virtually zero.

> **Multiple-channel queuing system**
> A service system with one waiting line but with several servers.
>
> **Single-phase system**
> A system in which the customer receives service from only one station and then exits the system.
>
> **Multiphase system**
> A system in which the customer receives services from several stations before exiting the system.
>
> **Negative exponential probability distribution**
> A continuous probability distribution often used to describe the service time in a queuing system.

Probability (service takes longer than x minutes) = $e^{-\mu x}$ for $x \geq 0$

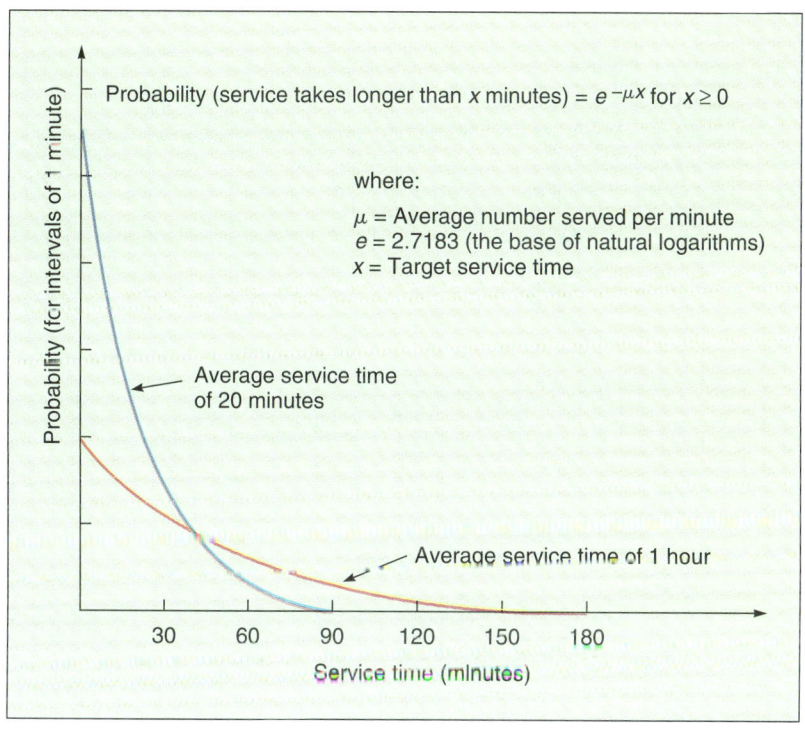

where:
μ = Average number served per minute
e = 2.7183 (the base of natural logarithms)
x = Target service time

FIGURE D.4 ■ Two Examples of the Negative Exponential Distribution for Service Times

> Although Poisson and exponential distributions are commonly used to describe arrival rates and service times, you should not take them for granted; Normal and Erlang or others may be more valid.

Measuring the Queue's Performance

Queuing models help managers make decisions that balance service costs with waiting-line costs. Queuing analysis can obtain many measures of a waiting-line system's performance, including the following:

1. Average time that each customer or object spends in the queue;
2. Average queue length;
3. Average time that each customer spends in the system (waiting time plus service time);
4. Average number of customers in the system;
5. Probability that the service facility will be idle;
6. Utilization factor for the system;
7. Probability of a specific number of customers in the system.

THE VARIETY OF QUEUING MODELS

Visit a bank or a drive-through restaurant and time arrivals to see what kind of distribution (Poisson or other) they might reflect.

A wide variety of queuing models may be applied in operations management. We will introduce you to four of the most widely used models. These are outlined in Table D.2, and examples of each follow in the next few sections. More complex models are described in queuing theory textbooks[2] or can be developed through the use of simulation (which is the topic of module F). Note that all four queuing models listed in Table D.2 have three characteristics in common. They all assume:

1. Poisson distribution arrivals;
2. FIFO discipline;
3. A single-service phase.

TABLE D.2 ■ Queuing Models Described in This Chapter

Model	Name (technical name in parentheses)	Example	Number of Channels	Number of Phases	Arrival Rate Pattern	Service Time Pattern	Population Size	Queue Discipline
A	Simple system (M/M/1)	Information counter at department store	Single	Single	Poisson	Exponential	Unlimited	FIFO
B	Multichannel (M/M/S)	Airline ticket counter	Multi-channel	Single	Poisson	Exponential	Unlimited	FIFO
C	Constant service (M/D/1)	Automated car wash	Single	Single	Poisson	Constant	Unlimited	FIFO
D	Limited population (finite population)	Shop with only a dozen machines that might break	Single	Single	Poisson	Exponential	Limited	FIFO

[2] See, for example, W. Griffin, *Queuing: Basic Theories and Applications* (Columbus: Grid Publishing, 1978); or R. B. Cooper, *Introduction to Queuing Theory,* 2nd ed. (New York: Elsevier-North Holland, 1980).

In addition, they all describe service systems that operate under steady, ongoing conditions. This means that arrival and service rates remain stable during the analysis.

Model A: Single-Channel Queuing Model with Poisson Arrivals and Exponential Service Times

The most common case of queuing problems involves the *single-channel*, or single-server, waiting line. In this situation, arrivals form a single line to be serviced by a single station (see Figure D.3 on p. 768). We assume that the following conditions exist in this type of system:

1. Arrivals are served on a first-in, first-out (FIFO) basis, and every arrival waits to be served, regardless of the length of the line or queue.
2. Arrivals are independent of preceding arrivals, but the average number of arrivals (*arrival rate*) does not change over time.
3. Arrivals are described by a Poisson probability distribution and come from an infinite (or very, very large) population.
4. Service times vary from one customer to the next and are independent of one another, but their average rate is known.
5. Service times occur according to the negative exponential probability distribution.
6. The service rate is faster than the arrival rate.

What would be the impact of equal service and arrival rates?

When these conditions are met, the series of equations shown in Table D.3 can be developed. Examples D1 and D2 illustrate how Model A (which in technical journals is known as the M/M/1 model) may be used.

Table D.3 ■ Queuing Formulas for Model A: Simple System, also called M/M/1

λ = mean number of arrivals per time period
μ = mean number of people or items served per time period
L_s = average number of units (customers) in the system
$$= \frac{\lambda}{\mu - \lambda}$$
W_s = Average time a unit spends in the system (waiting time plus service time)
$$= \frac{1}{\mu - \lambda}$$
L_q = Average number of units in the queue
$$= \frac{\lambda^2}{\mu(\mu - \lambda)}$$
W_q = Average time a unit spends waiting in the queue
$$= \frac{\lambda}{\mu(\mu - \lambda)}$$
ρ = Utilization factor for the system
$$= \frac{\lambda}{\mu}$$
P_0 = Probability of 0 units in the system (that is, the service unit is idle)
$$= 1 - \frac{\lambda}{\mu}$$
$P_{n>k}$ = Probability of more than k units in the system, where n is the number of units in the system
$$= \left(\frac{\lambda}{\mu}\right)^{k+1}$$

OM IN ACTION

L. L. BEAN TURNS TO QUEUING THEORY

L. L. Bean faced severe problems. It was the peak selling season, and the service level to incoming calls was simply unacceptable. Widely known as a high-quality outdoor goods retailer, about 65% of L. L. Bean's sales volume is generated through telephone orders via its toll-free service centers located in Maine.

Here is how bad the situation was: During certain periods, 80% of the calls received a busy signal, and those who did not often had to wait up to 10 minutes before speaking with a sales agent. L. L. Bean estimated it lost $10 million in profit because of the way it allocated telemarketing resources. Keeping customers waiting "in line" (on the phone) was costing $25,000 per day. On exceptionally busy days, the total orders lost because of queuing problems approached $500,000 in gross revenues.

Developing queuing models similar to those presented here, L. L. Bean was able to set the number of phone lines and the number of agents to have on duty for each half hour of every day of the season. Within a year, use of the model resulted in 24% more calls answered, 17% more orders taken, and 16% more revenues. The new system also meant 81% fewer abandoned callers and an 84% faster answering time. The percent of callers spending less than 20 seconds in the queue increased from 25% to 77%. Needless to say, queuing theory changed the way L. L. Bean thought about telecommunications.

Sources: P. Quinn, B. Andrews, and H. Parsons, *Interfaces* (January/February 1991): 75–91; and B. Render and R. Stair, *Quantitative Analysis for Management*, 6th ed. (Upper Saddle River, NJ: Prentice Hall, 1997), p. 658.

EXAMPLE D1

Jones, the mechanic at Golden Muffler Shop, is able to install new mufflers at an average rate of 3 per hour (or about 1 every 20 minutes), according to a negative exponential distribution. Customers seeking this service arrive at the shop on the average of 2 per hour, following a Poisson distribution. They are served on a first-in, first-out basis and come from a very large (almost infinite) population of possible buyers.

From this description, we are able to obtain the operating characteristics of Golden Muffler's queuing system:

$\lambda = 2$ cars arriving per hour

$\mu = 3$ cars serviced per hour

$$L_s = \frac{\lambda}{\mu - \lambda} = \frac{2}{3 - 2} = \frac{2}{1}$$

= 2 cars in the system, on average

$$W_s = \frac{1}{\mu - \lambda} = \frac{1}{3 - 2} = 1$$

= 1-hour average waiting time in the system

$$L_q = \frac{\lambda^2}{\mu(\mu - \lambda)} = \frac{2^2}{3(3 - 2)} = \frac{4}{3(1)} = \frac{4}{3}$$

= 1.33 cars waiting in line, on average

$$W_q = \frac{\lambda}{\mu(\mu - \lambda)} = \frac{2}{3(3 - 2)} = \frac{2}{3} \text{ hour}$$

= 40-minute average waiting time per car

$$\rho = \frac{\lambda}{\mu} = \frac{2}{3}$$

= 66.6% of time mechanic is busy

$$P_0 = 1 - \frac{\lambda}{\mu} = 1 - \frac{2}{3}$$

= .33 probability there are 0 cars in the system

Probability of More Than *k* Cars in the System

k	$P_{n>k} = (2/3)^{k+1}$
0	.667 ← Note that this is equal to $1 - P_0 = 1 - .33 = .667$.
1	.444
2	.296
3	.198 ← Implies that there is a 19.8% chance that more than 3 cars are in the system.
4	.132
5	.088
6	.058
7	.039

Once we have computed the operating characteristics of a queuing system, it is often important to do an economic analysis of their impact. Although the waiting-line model described above is valuable in predicting potential waiting times, queue lengths, idle times, and so on, it does not identify optimal decisions or consider cost factors. As we saw earlier, the solution to a queuing problem may require management to make a trade-off between the increased cost of providing better service and the decreased waiting costs derived from providing that service.

A $P_{n>3}$ of .0625 means that the chance of having more than 3 customers in an airport check-in line at a certain time of day is 1 in 16. If this British Airways office in Barbados can live with 4 or more passengers in line about 6% of the time, one service agent will suffice. If not, more check-in positions and staff will have to be added.

Example D2 examines the costs involved in Example D1.

> ### EXAMPLE D2
>
> The owner of the Golden Muffler Shop estimates that the cost of customer waiting time, in terms of customer dissatisfaction and lost goodwill, is $10 per hour of time spent *waiting* in line. Because the average car has a 2/3-hour wait (W_q) and because there are approximately 16 cars serviced per day (2 arrivals per hour times 8 working hours per day), the total number of hours that customers spend waiting each day for mufflers to be installed is
>
> $$\frac{2}{3}(16) = \frac{32}{3} = 10\frac{2}{3} \text{ hour}$$
>
> Hence, in this case,
>
> $$\text{Customer waiting-time cost} = \$10 \left(10\frac{2}{3}\right) = \$107 \text{ per day}$$
>
> The only other major cost that Golden's owner can identify in the queuing situation is the salary of Jones, the mechanic, who earns $7 per hour, or $56 per day. Thus,
>
> $$\text{Total expected costs} = \$107 + \$56$$
> $$= \$163 \text{ per day}$$
>
> This approach will be useful in Solved Problem D.2 on page 784.

Although many parameters are computed for a queuing study, L_q and W_q are the two most important when it comes to actual cost analysis.

Model B: Multiple-Channel Queuing Model

Now let's turn to a multiple-channel queuing system in which two or more servers or channels are available to handle arriving customers. We still assume that customers awaiting service form one single line and then proceed to the first available server. Multichannel, single-phase waiting lines are found in many banks today: a common line is formed, and the customer at the head of the line proceeds to the first free teller. (Refer to Figure D.3 on p. 768 for a typical multichannel configuration.)

The multiple-channel system presented in Example D3 again assumes that arrivals follow a Poisson probability distribution and that service times are exponentially distributed. Service is first-come, first-served, and all servers are assumed to perform at the same rate. Other assumptions listed earlier for the single-channel model also apply.

The queuing equations for Model B (which also has the technical name of M/M/S) are shown in Table D.4. These equations are obviously more complex than those used in

---

TABLE D.4 ■ Queuing Formulas for Model B: Multichannel System, also Called M/M/S

M = number of channels open
λ = average arrival rate
μ = average service rate at each channel

The probability that there are zero people or units in the system is

$$P_0 = \frac{1}{\left[\sum_{n=0}^{M-1} \frac{1}{n!}\left(\frac{\lambda}{\mu}\right)^n\right] + \frac{1}{M!}\left(\frac{\lambda}{\mu}\right)^M \frac{M\mu}{M\mu - \lambda}} \quad \text{for } M\mu > \lambda$$

TABLE D.4 ■ (continued)

The average number of people or units in the system is

$$L_s = \frac{\lambda\mu(\lambda/\mu)^M}{(M-1)!(M\mu-\lambda)^2} P_0 + \frac{\lambda}{\mu}$$

The average time a unit spends in the waiting line or being serviced (namely, in the system) is

$$W_s = \frac{\mu(\lambda/\mu)^M}{(M-1)!(M\mu-\lambda)^2} P_0 + \frac{1}{\mu} = \frac{L_s}{\lambda}$$

The average number of people or units in line waiting for service is

$$L_q = L_s - \frac{\lambda}{\mu}$$

The average time a person or unit spends in the queue waiting for service is

$$W_q = W_s - \frac{1}{\mu} = \frac{L_q}{\lambda}$$

the single-channel model; yet they are used in exactly the same fashion and provide the same type of information as the simpler model. (Note that the POM for Windows and Excel OM software described later in this chapter can prove very useful in solving multiple-channel, as well as other, queuing problems.)

EXAMPLE D3

The Golden Muffler Shop has decided to open a second garage bay and hire a second mechanic to handle installations. Customers, who arrive at the rate of about $\lambda = 2$ per hour, will wait in a single line until 1 of the 2 mechanics is free. Each mechanic installs mufflers at the rate of about $\mu = 3$ per hour.

To find out how this system compares to the old single-channel waiting-line system, we will compute several operating characteristics for the $M = 2$ channel system and compare the results with those found in Example D1:

$$P_0 = \frac{1}{\left[\sum_{n=0}^{1}\frac{1}{n!}\left(\frac{2}{3}\right)^n\right] + \frac{1}{2!}\left(\frac{2}{3}\right)^2 \frac{2(3)}{2(3)-2}}$$

$$= \frac{1}{1 + \frac{2}{3} + \frac{1}{2}\left(\frac{4}{9}\right)\left(\frac{6}{6-2}\right)} = \frac{1}{1 + \frac{2}{3} + \frac{1}{3}} = \frac{1}{2}$$

$= .5$ probability of zero cars in the system

Then,

$$L_s = \frac{(2)(3)(2/3)^2}{1![2(3)-2]^2}\left(\frac{1}{2}\right) + \frac{2}{3} = \frac{8/3}{16}\left(\frac{1}{2}\right) + \frac{2}{3} = \frac{3}{4}$$

$= .75$ average number of cars in the system

$$W_s = \frac{L_s}{\lambda} = \frac{3/4}{2} = \frac{3}{8} \text{ hour}$$

$= 22.5$ minutes average time a car spends in the system

$$L_q = L_s - \frac{\lambda}{\mu} = \frac{3}{4} - \frac{2}{3} = \frac{1}{12}$$

$$= .083 \text{ average number of cars in the queue}$$

$$W_q = \frac{L_q}{\lambda} = \frac{.083}{2} = .0415 \text{ hour}$$

$$= 2.5 \text{ minutes average time a car spends in the queue}$$

We can summarize these characteristics and compare them to those of the single-channel model as follows:

	Single Channel	Two Channels
P_0	.33	.5
L_s	2 cars	.75 car
W_s	60 minutes	22.5 minutes
L_q	1.33 cars	.083 car
W_q	40 minutes	2.5 minutes

The increased service has a dramatic effect on almost all characteristics. In particular, time spent waiting in line drops from 40 minutes to only 2.5 minutes.

Model C: Constant Service Time Model

Some service systems have constant, instead of exponentially distributed service times. When customers or equipment are processed according to a fixed cycle, as in the case of an automatic car wash or an amusement park ride, constant service times are appropriate.

Queues exist not only in every industry but also around the world. Here, the Moscow McDonald's on Puskin Square, 4 blocks from the Kremlin, boasts 700 indoor and 200 outdoor seats, employs 800 Russian citizens, and generates annual revenues of $80 million. In spite of its size and volume, it still has queues and has had to develop a strategy for dealing with them.

Because constant rates are certain, the values for L_q, W_q, L_s, and W_s are always less than they would be in Model A, which has variable service rates. As a matter of fact, both the average queue length and the average waiting time in the queue are halved with Model C. Constant service model formulas are given in Table D.5. Model C also has the technical name of M/D/1 in the literature of queuing theory. Example D4 gives a constant-service time analysis.

TABLE D.5 ■ Queuing Formulas for Model C: Constant Service, also Called M/D/1

Average length of queue: $L_q = \dfrac{\lambda^2}{2\mu(\mu - \lambda)}$

Average waiting time in queue: $W_q = \dfrac{\lambda}{2\mu(\mu - \lambda)}$

Average number of customers in system: $L_s = L_q + \dfrac{\lambda}{\mu}$

Average waiting time in system: $W_s = W_q + \dfrac{1}{\mu}$

EXAMPLE D4

Garcia-Golding Recycling, Inc., collects and compacts aluminum cans and glass bottles in New York City. Its truck drivers currently wait an average of 15 minutes before emptying their loads for recycling. The cost of driver and truck time while they are in queues is valued at $60 per hour. A new automated compactor can be purchased to process truckloads at a constant rate of 12 trucks per hour (that is, 5 minutes per truck). Trucks arrive according to a Poisson distribution at an average rate of 8 per hour. If the new compactor is put in use, the cost will be amortized at a rate of $3 per truck unloaded. The firm hires a summer college intern, who conducts the following analysis to evaluate the costs versus benefits of the purchase:

Current waiting cost/trip = (1/4 hr. waiting now) ($60/hr. cost) = $15/trip

New system: $\lambda = 8$ trucks/hr. arriving $\quad \mu = 12$ trucks/hr. served

Average waiting time in queue $= W_q = \dfrac{\lambda}{2\mu(\mu - \lambda)} = \dfrac{8}{2(12)(12 - 8)} = \dfrac{1}{12}$ hr.

Waiting cost/trip with new compactor = (1/12 hr. wait) ($60/hr. cost) = $ 5/trip

Savings with new equipment = $15 (current system) − $5 (new system) = $10/trip

Cost of new equipment amortized = $ 3/trip

Net savings $ 7/trip

Model D: Limited Population Model

When there is a limited population of potential customers for a service facility, we must consider a different queuing model. This model would be used, for example, if we were considering equipment repairs in a factory that has 5 machines, if we were in charge of maintenance for a fleet of 10 commuter airplanes, or if we ran a hospital ward that has 20 beds. The limited population model allows any number of repair people (servers) to be considered.

This model differs from the three earlier queuing models because there is now a *dependent* relationship between the length of the queue and the arrival rate. Let's illustrate the extreme situation: If your factory had five machines and all were broken and awaiting repair, the arrival rate would drop to zero. In general, then, as the *waiting line* becomes longer in the limited population model, the *arrival rate* of customers or machines drops.

Table D.6 displays the queuing formulas for the limited population model. Note that they employ a different notation than Models A, B, and C. To simplify what can become time-consuming calculations, finite queuing tables have been developed that determine D and F. D represents the probability a machine needing repair will have to wait in line. F is a waiting-time efficiency factor. D and F are needed to compute most of the other finite model formulas.

TABLE D.6 ■ Queuing Formulas and Notation for Model D: Limited Population Formulas

Service factor: $X = \dfrac{T}{T + U}$　　　　　　　　　　　Average number running: $J = NF(1 - X)$

Average number waiting: $L = N(1 - F)$　　　　　　Average number being serviced: $H = FNX$

Average waiting time: $W = \dfrac{L(T + U)}{N - L} = \dfrac{T(1 - F)}{XF}$　　Number of population: $N = J + L + H$

Notation

D = probability that a unit will have to wait in queue　　N = number of potential customers

F = efficiency factor　　　　　　　　　　　　　　　　　T = average service time

H = average number of units being served　　　　　　U = average time between unit service requirements

J = average number of units not in queue or in service bay　　W = average time a unit waits in line

L = average number of units waiting for service　　　　X = service factor

M = number of service channels

Source: L. G. Peck and R. N. Hazelwood, *Finite Queuing Tables* (New York: John Wiley, 1958).

A small part of the published finite queuing tables is illustrated in this section. Table D.7 provides for a population of $N = 5$.[3]

To use Table D.7, we follow four steps:

1. Compute X (the service factor, where $X = T/(T + U)$).
2. Find the value of X in the table and then find the line for M (where M is the number of service channels).
3. Note the corresponding values for D and F.
4. Compute L, W, J, H, or whichever are needed to measure the service system's performance.

---

[3] Limited, or finite, queuing tables are available to handle arrival populations of up to 250. Although there is no definite number that we can use as a dividing point between limited and unlimited populations, the general rule of thumb is this: If the number in the queue is a significant proportion of the arrival population, use a limited population queuing model. For a complete set of N values, see L. G. Peck and R. N. Hazelwood, *Finite Queuing Tables* (New York: John Wiley, 1958).

TABLE D.7 ■ Finite Queuing Tables for a Population of N = 5

X	M	D	F	X	M	D	F	X	M	D	F	X	M	D	F	X	M	D	F
.012	1	.048	.999		1	.404	.945		1	.689	.801	.330	4	.012	.999		3	.359	.927
.019	1	.076	.998	.110	2	.065	.996	.210	3	.032	.998		3	.112	.986	.520	2	.779	.728
.025	1	.100	.997		1	.421	.939		2	.211	.973		2	.442	.904		1	.988	.384
.030	1	.120	.996	.115	2	.071	.995		1	.713	.783		1	.902	.583	.540	4	.085	.989
.034	1	.135	.995		1	.439	.933	.220	3	.036	.997	.340	4	.013	.999		3	.392	.917
.036	1	.143	.994	.120	2	.076	.995		2	.229	.969		3	.121	.985		2	.806	.708
.040	1	.159	.993		1	.456	.927		1	.735	.765		2	.462	.896		1	.991	.370
.042	1	.167	.992	.125	2	.082	.994	.230	3	.041	.997		1	.911	.569	.560	4	.098	.986
.044	1	.175	.991		1	.473	.920		2	.247	.965	.360	4	.017	.998		3	.426	.906
.046	1	.183	.990	.130	2	.089	.933		1	.756	.747		3	.141	.981		2	.831	.689
.050	1	.198	.989		1	.489	.914	.240	3	.046	.996		2	.501	.880		1	.993	.357
.052	1	.206	.988	.135	2	.095	.993		2	.265	.960		1	.927	.542	.580	4	.113	.984
.054	1	.214	.987		1	.505	.907		1	.775	.730	.380	4	.021	.998		3	.461	.895
.056	2	.018	.999	.140	2	.102	.992	.250	3	.052	.995		3	.163	.976		2	.854	.670
	1	.222	.985		1	.521	.900		2	.284	.955		2	.540	.863		1	.994	.345
.058	2	.019	.999	.145	3	.011	.999		1	.794	.712		1	.941	.516	.600	4	.130	.981
	1	.229	.984		2	.109	.991	.260	3	.058	.944	.400	4	.026	.977		3	.497	.883
.060	2	.020	.999		1	.537	.892		2	.303	.950		3	.186	.972		2	.875	.652
	1	.237	.983	.150	3	.012	.999		1	.811	.695		2	.579	.845		1	.996	.333
.062	2	.022	.999		2	.115	.990	.270	3	.064	.994		1	.952	.493	.650	4	.179	.972
	1	.245	.982		1	.553	.885		2	.323	.944	.420	4	.031	.997		3	.588	.850
.064	2	.023	.999	.155	3	.013	.999		1	.827	.677		3	.211	.966		2	.918	.608
	1	.253	.981		2	.123	.989	.280	3	.071	.993		2	.616	.826		1	.998	.308
.066	2	.024	.999		1	.568	.877		2	.342	.938		1	.961	.471	.700	4	.240	.960
	1	.260	.979	.160	3	.015	.999		1	.842	.661	.440	4	.037	.996		3	.678	.815
.068	2	.026	.999		2	.130	.988	.290	4	.007	.999		3	.238	.960		2	.950	.568
	1	.268	.978		1	.582	.869		3	.079	.992		2	.652	.807		1	.999	.286
.070	2	.027	.999	.165	3	.016	.999		2	.362	.932		1	.969	.451	.750	4	.316	.944
	1	.275	.977		2	.137	.987		1	.856	.644	.460	4	.045	.995		3	.763	.777
.075	2	.031	.999		1	.597	.861	.300	4	.008	.999		3	.266	.953		2	.972	.532
	1	.294	.973	.170	3	.017	.999		3	.086	.990		2	.686	.787	.800	4	.410	.924
.080	2	.035	.998		2	.145	.985		2	.382	.926		1	.975	.432		3	.841	.739
	1	.313	.969		1	.611	.853		1	.869	.628	.480	4	.053	.994		2	.987	.500
.085	2	.040	.998	.180	3	.021	.999	.310	4	.009	.999		3	.296	.945	.850	4	.522	.900
	1	.332	.965		2	.161	.983		3	.094	.989		2	.719	.767		3	.907	.702
.090	2	.044	.998		1	.638	.836		2	.402	.919		1	.980	.415		2	.995	.470
	1	.350	.960	.190	3	.024	.998		1	.881	.613	.500	4	.063	.992	.900	4	.656	.871
.095	2	.049	.997		2	.117	.980	.320	4	.010	.999		3	.327	.936		3	.957	.666
	1	.368	.955		1	.665	.819		3	.103	.988		2	.750	.748		2	.998	.444
.100	2	.054	.997	.200	3	.028	.998		2	.422	.912		1	.985	.399	.950	4	.815	.838
.100	1	.386	.950	.200	2	.194	.976		1	.892	.597	.520	4	.073	.991		3	.989	.631
.105	2	.059	.997																

Source: From L. G. Peck and R. N. Hazelwood, *Finite Queuing Tables* (New York: John Wiley, 1958, p. 4) © 1985, John Wiley & Sons, Inc.

Example D5 illustrates these steps.

EXAMPLE D5

Past records indicate that each of the 5 laser computer printers at the U.S. Department of Energy, in Washington, DC, needs repair after about 20 hours of use. Breakdowns have been determined to be Poisson-distributed. The one technician on duty can service a printer in an average of 2 hours, following an exponential distribution. Printer downtime costs $120 per hour. Technicians are paid $25 per hour. Should the DOE hire a second technician?

Assuming the second technician can repair a printer in an average of 2 hours, we can use Table D.7 (because there are $N = 5$ machines in this limited population) to compare the costs of 1 versus 2 technicians.

1. First, we note that $T = 2$ hours and $U = 20$ hours.
2. Then, $X = \dfrac{T}{T + U} = \dfrac{2}{2 + 20} = \dfrac{2}{22} = .091$ (close to .090).
3. For $M = 1$ server, $D = .350$ and $F = .960$.
4. For $M = 2$ servers, $D = .044$ and $F = .998$.
5. The average number of printers *working* is $J = NF(1 - X)$.
   For $M = 1$, this is $J = (5)(.960)(1 - .091) = 4.36$.
   For $M = 2$, it is $J = (5)(.998)(1 - .091) = 4.54$.
6. The cost analysis follows:

Number of Technicians	Average Number Printers Down (N – J)	Average Cost/Hr. For Downtime (N – J)($120/Hr.)	Cost/Hr. For Technicians (at $25/Hr.)	Total Cost/Hr.
1	.64	$76.80	$25.00	$101.80
2	.46	$55.20	$50.00	$105.20

This analysis suggests that having only one technician on duty will save a few dollars per hour ($105.20 − $101.80 = $3.40).

OTHER QUEUING APPROACHES

Many practical waiting-line problems that occur in service systems have characteristics like those of the four mathematical models described above. Often, however, *variations* of these specific cases are present in an analysis. Service times in an automobile repair shop, for example, tend to follow the normal probability distribution instead of the exponential. A college registration system in which seniors have first choice of courses and hours over other students is an example of a first-come, first-served model with a preemptive priority queue discipline. A physical examination for military recruits is an example of a multiphase system, one that differs from the single-phase models discussed earlier in this module. A recruit first lines up to have blood drawn at one station, then waits for an eye exam at the next station, talks to a psychiatrist at the third, and is examined by a doctor for medical problems at the fourth. At each phase, the recruit must enter another queue and wait his or her turn. Many models, some very complex, have been developed to deal with situations such as these. One of these is described in the *OM in Action* box called "Shortening Arraignment Times in New York's Police Department."

OM IN ACTION

SHORTENING ARRAIGNMENT TIMES IN NEW YORK'S POLICE DEPARTMENT

On March 23, 1990, the *New York Times* ran a front-page story about a woman who spent 45 hours in pre-arraignment detention under the headline "Trapped in the Terror of New York's Holding Pens." Indeed, people arrested in New York City at that time averaged a 40-hour wait (some more than 70 hours) prior to arraignment. They were kept in crowded, noisy, stressful, unhealthy, and often dangerous holding facilities and, in effect, denied speedy court appearances. That same year, the New York Supreme Court ruled that the city must attempt to arraign within 24 hours or to release the prisoner.

The arrest-to-arraignment (ATA) process, which has the general characteristics of a large queuing system, involves these steps: arrest of suspected criminal, transport to a police precinct, search/fingerprinting, paperwork for arrest, transport to a central booking facility, additional paperwork, processing of fingerprints, a bail interview, transport to either the courthouse or an outlying precinct, checks for a criminal record, and finally, an assistant district attorney drawing up a complaint document.

To solve the complex problem of improving this system, the city hired Queues Enforth Development, Inc., a Massachusetts consulting firm. The firm's Monte Carlo simulation of the ATA process included single- and multiple-server queuing models. The modeling approach successfully reduced the average ATA time to 24 hours and resulted in an annual cost savings of $9.5 million for the city and state.

Source: R. C. Larson, M. F. Colan, and M. C. Shell, "Improving the New York Arrest-to-Arraignment System," *Interfaces* 23, 1 (January–February 1993): 76–96.

SUMMARY

Queues are an important part of the world of operations management. In this module, we describe several common queuing systems and present mathematical models for analyzing them.

The most widely used queuing models include Model A, the basic single-channel, single-phase system with Poisson arrivals and exponential service times; Model B, the multichannel equivalent of Model A; Model C, a constant service rate model; and Model D, a limited population system. All four models allow for Poisson arrivals, first-in, first-out service, and a single-service phase. Typical operating characteristics we examine include average time spent waiting in the queue and system, average number of customers in the queue and system, idle time, and utilization rate.

A variety of queuing models exists for which all of the assumptions of the traditional models need not be met. In these cases, we use more complex mathematical models or turn to a technique called simulation. The application of simulation to problems of queuing systems is addressed in quantitative module F.

KEY TERMS

Queuing theory *(p. 764)*
Waiting line *(p. 764)*
Unlimited, or infinite, population *(p. 766)*
Limited, or finite, population *(p. 766)*
Poisson distribution *(p. 766)*
First-in, first-out (FIFO) rule *(p. 767)*
Single-channel queuing system *(p. 768)*
Multiple-channel queuing system *(p. 769)*
Single-phase system *(p. 769)*
Multiphase system *(p. 769)*
Negative exponential probability distribution *(p. 769)*

USING POM FOR WINDOWS FOR QUEUING

There are several POM for Windows queuing models from which to select. The left-hand side of Program D.1 shows the input data for Example D3, in which the Golden Muffler Shop has added a second mechanic. The right-hand side illustrates the program's outputs. As an option, you may click an icon below the screen and display probabilities of various numbers of people/items in the system.

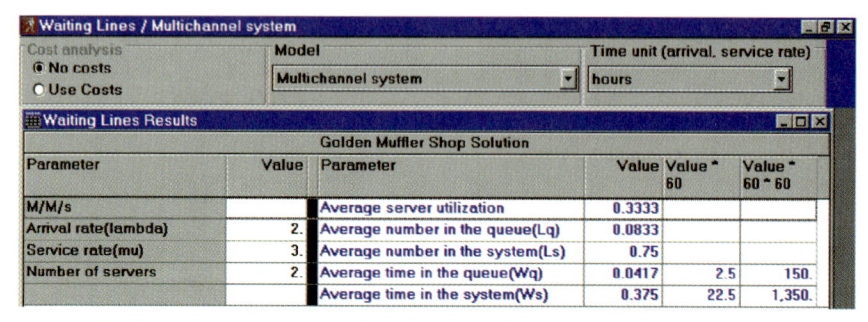

PROGRAM D.1 ■ POM for Windows Analysis of Golden Muffler Shop's (Example D3) Two-Server Queuing Problem

USING EXCEL OM FOR QUEUING

Excel OM's Waiting Line program handles all four of the models developed in this module. Programs D.2 and D.3 illustrate our first model, the M/M/1 system, using the data from Example D1. Formulas are shown in Program D.2 and the results in Program D.3.

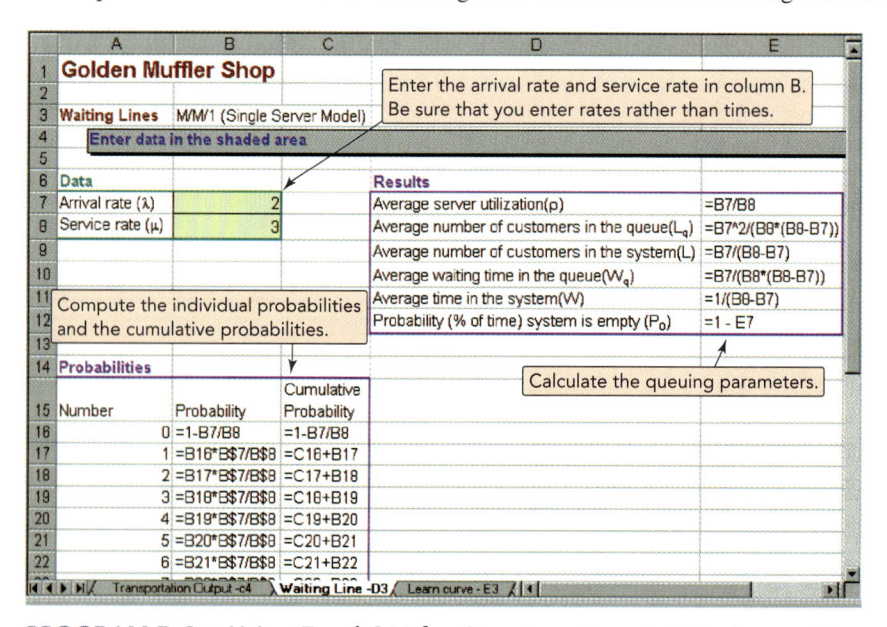

PROGRAM D.2 ■ Using Excel OM for Queuing. *Example D1's data are illustrated in the M/M/1 model.*

OM IN ACTION

SHORTENING ARRAIGNMENT TIMES IN NEW YORK'S POLICE DEPARTMENT

On March 23, 1990, the *New York Times* ran a front-page story about a woman who spent 45 hours in pre-arraignment detention under the headline "Trapped in the Terror of New York's Holding Pens." Indeed, people arrested in New York City at that time averaged a 40-hour wait (some more than 70 hours) prior to arraignment. They were kept in crowded, noisy, stressful, unhealthy, and often dangerous holding facilities and, in effect, denied speedy court appearances. That same year, the New York Supreme Court ruled that the city must attempt to arraign within 24 hours or to release the prisoner.

The arrest-to-arraignment (ATA) process, which has the general characteristics of a large queuing system, involves these steps: arrest of suspected criminal, transport to a police precinct, search/fingerprinting, paperwork for arrest, transport to a central booking facility, additional paperwork, processing of fingerprints, a bail interview, transport to either the courthouse or an outlying precinct, checks for a criminal record, and finally, an assistant district attorney drawing up a complaint document.

To solve the complex problem of improving this system, the city hired Queues Enforth Development, Inc., a Massachusetts consulting firm. The firm's Monte Carlo simulation of the ATA process included single- and multiple-server queuing models. The modeling approach successfully reduced the average ATA time to 24 hours and resulted in an annual cost savings of $9.5 million for the city and state.

Source: R. C. Larson, M. F. Colan, and M. C. Shell, "Improving the New York Arrest-to-Arraignment System," *Interfaces* 23, 1 (January–February 1993): 76–96.

SUMMARY

Queues are an important part of the world of operations management. In this module, we describe several common queuing systems and present mathematical models for analyzing them.

The most widely used queuing models include Model A, the basic single-channel, single-phase system with Poisson arrivals and exponential service times; Model B, the multichannel equivalent of Model A; Model C, a constant service rate model; and Model D, a limited population system. All four models allow for Poisson arrivals, first-in, first-out service, and a single-service phase. Typical operating characteristics we examine include average time spent waiting in the queue and system, average number of customers in the queue and system, idle time, and utilization rate.

A variety of queuing models exists for which all of the assumptions of the traditional models need not be met. In these cases, we use more complex mathematical models or turn to a technique called simulation. The application of simulation to problems of queuing systems is addressed in quantitative module F.

KEY TERMS

Queuing theory *(p. 764)*
Waiting line *(p. 764)*
Unlimited, or infinite, population *(p. 766)*
Limited, or finite, population *(p. 766)*
Poisson distribution *(p. 766)*
First-in, first-out (FIFO) rule *(p. 767)*
Single-channel queuing system *(p. 768)*
Multiple-channel queuing system *(p. 769)*
Single-phase system *(p. 769)*
Multiphase system *(p. 769)*
Negative exponential probability distribution *(p. 769)*

USING POM FOR WINDOWS FOR QUEUING

There are several POM for Windows queuing models from which to select. The left-hand side of Program D.1 shows the input data for Example D3, in which the Golden Muffler Shop has added a second mechanic. The right-hand side illustrates the program's outputs. As an option, you may click an icon below the screen and display probabilities of various numbers of people/items in the system.

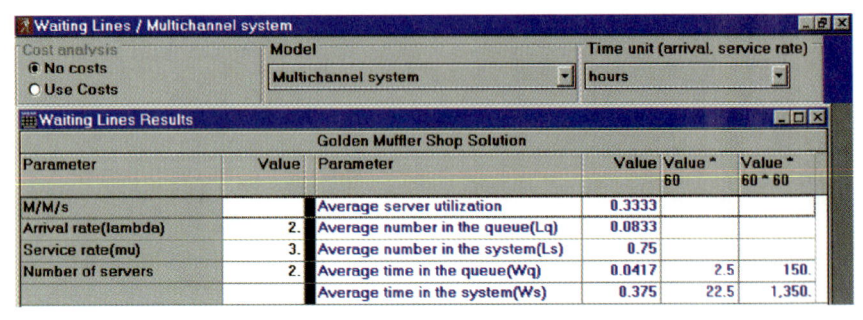

Parameter	Value	Parameter	Value	Value * 60	Value * 60 * 60
M/M/s		Average server utilization	0.3333		
Arrival rate(lambda)	2.	Average number in the queue(Lq)	0.0833		
Service rate(mu)	3.	Average number in the system(Ls)	0.75		
Number of servers	2.	Average time in the queue(Wq)	0.0417	2.5	150
		Average time in the system(Ws)	0.375	22.5	1,350

PROGRAM D.1 ■ POM for Windows Analysis of Golden Muffler Shop's (Example D3) Two-Server Queuing Problem

USING EXCEL OM FOR QUEUING

Excel OM's Waiting Line program handles all four of the models developed in this module. Programs D.2 and D.3 illustrate our first model, the M/M/1 system, using the data from Example D1. Formulas are shown in Program D.2 and the results in Program D.3.

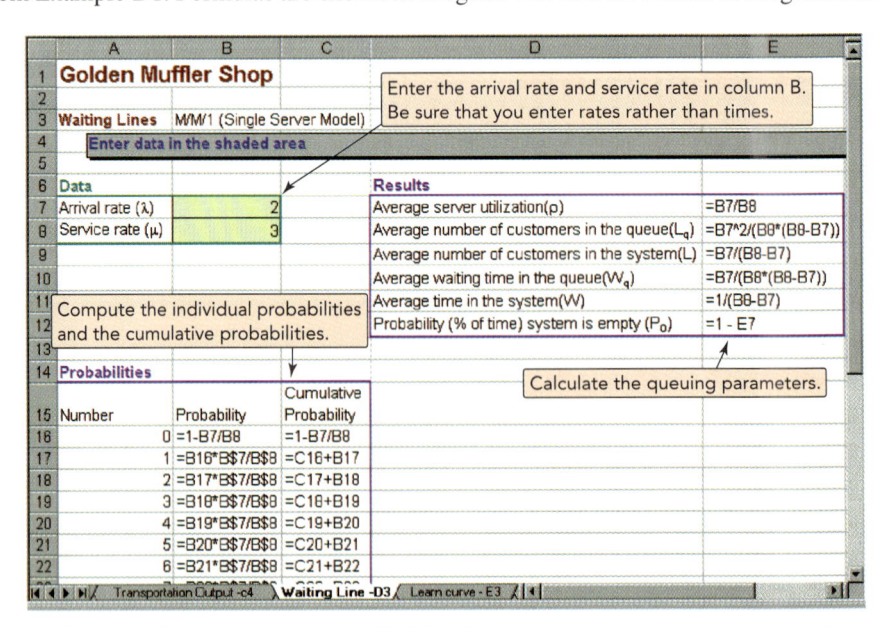

	A	B	C	D	E
1	Golden Muffler Shop				
3	Waiting Lines	M/M/1 (Single Server Model)			
4	Enter data in the shaded area				
6	Data			Results	
7	Arrival rate (λ)	2		Average server utilization(ρ)	=B7/B8
8	Service rate (μ)	3		Average number of customers in the queue(Lq)	=B7^2/(B8*(B8-B7))
9				Average number of customers in the system(L)	=B7/(B8-B7)
10				Average waiting time in the queue(Wq)	=B7/(B8*(B8-B7))
11				Average time in the system(W)	=1/(B8-B7)
12				Probability (% of time) system is empty (P₀)	=1 - E7
14	Probabilities				
15	Number	Probability	Cumulative Probability		
16	0	=1-B7/B8	=1-B7/B8		
17	1	=B16*B$7/B$8	=C16+B17		
18	2	=B17*B$7/B$8	=C17+B18		
19	3	=B18*B$7/B$8	=C18+B19		
20	4	=B19*B$7/B$8	=C19+B20		
21	5	=B20*B$7/B$8	=C20+B21		
22	6	=B21*B$7/B$8	=C21+B22		

Enter the arrival rate and service rate in column B. Be sure that you enter rates rather than times.

Compute the individual probabilities and the cumulative probabilities.

Calculate the queuing parameters.

PROGRAM D.2 ■ Using Excel OM for Queuing. *Example D1's data are illustrated in the M/M/1 model.*

SOLVED PROBLEMS

PROGRAM D.3 ■ Output from Excel OM Analysis in Program D.2

SOLVED PROBLEMS

Solved Problem D.1

Sid Das Brick Distributors currently employs 1 worker whose job is to load bricks on outgoing company trucks. An average of 24 trucks per day, or 3 per hour, arrive at the loading platform, according to a Poisson distribution. The worker loads them at a rate of 4 trucks per hour, following approximately the exponential distribution in his service times.

Das believes that adding a second brick loader will substantially improve the firm's productivity. He estimates that a two-person crew at the loading gate will double the loading rate from four trucks per hour to eight trucks per hour. Analyze the effect on the queue of such a change and compare the results to those achieved with one worker. What is the probability that there will be more than three trucks either being loaded or waiting?

Solution

	Number of Brick Loaders	
	1	2
Truck arrival rate (λ)	3/hr.	3/hr.
Loading rate (μ)	4/hr.	8/hr.
Average number in system (L_s)	3 trucks	.6 truck
Average time in system (W_s)	1 hr.	.2 hr.
Average number in queue (L_q)	2.25 trucks	.225 truck
Average time in queue (W_q)	.75 hr.	.075 hr.
Utilization rate (ρ)	.75	.375
Probability system empty (P_0)	.25	.625

Probability of More Than k Trucks in System

k	Probability N > k One Loader	Two Loaders
0	.75	.375
1	.56	.141
2	.42	.053
3	.32	.020

These results indicate that when only one loader is employed, the average truck must wait three quarters of an hour before it is loaded. Furthermore, there is an average of 2.25 trucks waiting in line to be loaded. This situation may be unacceptable to management. Note also the decline in queue size after the addition of a second loader.

Solved Problem D.2

Truck drivers working for Sid Das (see Solved Problem D.1) earn an average of $10 per hour. Brick loaders receive about $6 per hour. Truck drivers waiting *in the queue or at the loading platform* are drawing a salary but are productively idle and unable to generate revenue during that time. What would be the *hourly* cost savings to the firm if it employed 2 loaders instead of 1?

Referring to the data in Solved Problem D.1, we note that the average number of trucks *in the system* is 3 when there is only 1 loader and .6 when there are 2 loaders.

Solution

	Number of Loaders 1	2
Truck driver idle time costs [(average number of trucks) × (hourly rate)] = (3)($10) =	$30	$ 6 = (.6)($10)
Loading costs	6	12 = (2)($6)
Total expected cost per hour	$36	$18

The firm will save $18 per hour by adding a second loader.

Solved Problem D.3

Sid Das is considering building a second platform or gate to speed the process of loading trucks. This system, he thinks, will be even more efficient than simply hiring another loader to help out on the first platform (as in Solved Problem D.1).

Assume that workers at each platform will be able to load four trucks per hour each and that trucks will continue to arrive at the rate of three per hour. Then apply the appropriate equations to find the waiting line's new operating conditions. Is this new approach indeed speedier than the other two that Das has considered?

Solution

$$P_0 = \frac{1}{\left[\sum_{n=0}^{1} \frac{1}{n!}\left(\frac{3}{4}\right)^n\right] + \frac{1}{2!}\left(\frac{3}{4}\right)^2 \frac{2(4)}{2(4) - 3}}$$

$$= \cfrac{1}{1 + \cfrac{3}{4} + \cfrac{1}{2}\left(\cfrac{3}{4}\right)^2 \left(\cfrac{8}{8-3}\right)} = .454$$

$$L_s = \frac{3(4)(3/4)^2}{(1)!(8-3)^2}(.4545) + \frac{3}{4} = .873$$

$$W_s = \frac{.873}{3} = .291 \text{ hr.}$$

$$L_q = .873 - 3/4 = .123$$

$$W_q = \frac{.123}{3} = .041 \text{ hr.}$$

Looking back at Solved Problem D.1, we see that although length of the *queue* and average time in the queue are lowest when a second platform is open, the average number of trucks in the *system* and average time spent waiting in the system are smallest when two workers are employed at a *single* platform. Thus, we would probably recommend not building a second platform.

Solved Problem D.4

St. Elsewhere Hospital's Cardiac Care Unit (CCU) has 5 beds, which are virtually always occupied by patients who have just undergone major heart surgery. Two registered nurses are on duty in the CCU in each of the three 8-hour shifts. About every 2 hours (following a Poisson distribution), one of the patients requires a nurse's attention. The nurse will then spend an average of 30 minutes (exponentially distributed) assisting the patient and updating medical records regarding the problem and care provided.

Because immediate service is critical to the five patients, two important questions are: What is the average number of patients being attended by the nurses? What is the average time that a patient spends waiting for one of the nurses to arrive?

Solution

$$N = 5 \text{ patients}$$

$$M = 2 \text{ nurses}$$

$$T = 30 \text{ minutes}$$

$$U = 120 \text{ minutes}$$

$$X = \frac{T}{T + U} = \frac{30}{30 + 120} = .20$$

From Table D.7 (p. 779), with $X = .20$ and $M = 2$, we see that

$$F = .976$$

$$H = \text{average number being attended to} = FNX$$
$$= (.976)(5)(.20) = .98 \approx 1 \text{ patient at any given time}$$

$$W = \text{average waiting time for a nurse} = \frac{T(1 - F)}{XF}$$

$$= \frac{30(1 - .976)}{(.20)(.976)} = 3.69 \text{ minutes}$$

MODULE D WAITING-LINE MODELS

DISCUSSION QUESTIONS

1. What is the waiting-line problem? What are the components in a waiting-line system?
2. What are the assumptions underlying the queuing models described in this chapter?
3. Describe the important operating characteristics of a queuing system.
4. Why must the service rate be greater than the arrival rate in a single-channel queuing system?
5. Briefly describe three situations in which the first-in, first-out (FIFO) discipline rule is not applicable in queuing analysis.
6. Provide examples of four situations in which there is a limited, or finite, waiting line.
7. What are the components of the following queuing systems? Draw and explain the configuration of each:
   a) barbershop
   b) car wash
   c) laundromat
   d) small grocery store
8. Do doctors' offices generally have random arrival rates for patients? Are service times random? Under what circumstances might service times be constant?
9. Do you think the Poisson distribution, which assumes independent arrivals, is a good estimation of arrival rates in the following queuing systems? Defend your position in each case:
   a) school cafeteria
   b) barbershop
   c) hardware store
   d) dentist's office
   e) college class
   f) movie theater
10. What is the utilization factor for a system?
11. What happens if two single-channel systems have the same mean arrival and service rates, but the service time is constant in one and exponential in the other?
12. What dollar value do you place on yourself per hour that you spend waiting in lines? What value do your classmates place on themselves? Why do they differ?
13. Provide an example of a situation in which a manager actually wants a queue. Why might this be the case?
14. Most banks have changed from having a line in front of each teller to a system whereby one line feeds all tellers. Which system is better? Why?
15. Justify the queuing system used in most supermarkets today (i.e., a line for each register, with those customers having 10 or fewer items going to special registers).
16. What cost trade-offs must be considered in queuing analysis?

PROBLEMS

D.1 Customers arrive at a local 7–11 at the rate of $\lambda = 40$ per hour (and follow a Poisson process). The only employee in the store can check them out at a rate of $\mu = 60$ per hour (following an exponential distribution). Compute the following:
a) the percentage of time that the employee is busy with checkouts.
b) the average length of the queue.
c) the average number of customers in the system.
d) the average time spent waiting in the queue.
e) the average time in the system.

D.2 There is only 1 copying machine in the student lounge of the business school. Students arrive at the rate of $\lambda = 40$ per hour (according to a Poisson distribution). Copying takes an average of 40 seconds, or $\mu = 90$ per hour (according to an exponential distribution). Compute the following:
a) the percentage of time that the machine is used.
b) the average length of the queue.
c) the average number of students in the system.
d) the average time spent waiting in the queue.
e) the average time in the system.

PROBLEMS

D.3 Due to a recent increase in business, a law firm secretary must now word-process an average of 20 letters a day (assume a Poisson distribution). It takes him approximately 20 minutes to type each letter (assume an exponential distribution). Assuming the secretary works 8 hours a day:
a) What is the secretary's utilization rate?
b) What is the average waiting time before the secretary word-processes a letter?
c) What is the average number of letters waiting to be done?
d) What is the probability that the secretary has more than 5 letters to do?

D.4 Sam the Vet is running a rabies-vaccination clinic for dogs at the local grade school. Sam can "shoot" a dog every 3 minutes. It is estimated that the dogs will arrive independently and randomly throughout the day at a rate of 1 dog every 6 minutes according to a Poisson distribution. Also assume that Sam's shooting times are exponentially distributed. Compute the following:
a) the probability that Sam is idle.
b) the proportion of the time that Sam is busy.
c) the average number of dogs being vaccinated and waiting to be vaccinated.
d) the average number of dogs waiting to be vaccinated.
e) the average time a dog waits before getting vaccinated.
f) the average amount of time a dog spends waiting in line and being vaccinated.

D.5 Refer to Problem D.4. Contrary to estimates, dogs arrive at the rate of 1 dog every 4 minutes (*not* every 6 minutes). Recompute your answers to parts (a) through (f) in Problem D.4.

D.6 Calls arrive at John DeBruzzi's hotel switchboard at a rate of 2 per minute. The average time to handle each is 20 seconds. There is only 1 switchboard operator at the current time. The Poisson and exponential distributions appear to be relevant in this situation.
a) What is the probability that the operator is busy?
b) What is the average time that a caller must wait before reaching the operator?
c) What is the average number of calls waiting to be answered?

D.7 At the start of football season, the ticket office gets very busy the day before the first game. Customers arrive at the rate of 4 every 10 minutes, and the average time to transact business is 2 minutes.
a) What is the average number of people in line?
b) What is the average time that a person will spend at the ticket office?
c) What proportion of time is the server busy?

D.8 The Charles Leitle Electronics Corporation retains a service crew to repair machine breakdowns that occur on an average of $\lambda = 3$ per day (approximately Poisson in nature). The crew can service an average of $\mu = 8$ machines per day, with a repair time distribution that resembles the exponential distribution.
a) What is the utilization rate of this service system?
b) What is the average downtime for a broken machine?
c) How many machines are waiting to be serviced at any given time?
d) What is the probability that more than one machine is in the system? The probability that more than two are broken and waiting to be repaired or being serviced? More than three? More than four?

D.9 Bryce Dodson's Car Wash is open 6 days a week, but its busiest day is always Saturday. From historical data, Dan estimates that dirty cars arrive at the rate of 20 per hour all day Saturday. With a full crew working the hand-wash line, he figures that cars can be cleaned at the rate of one every 2 minutes. One car at a time is cleaned in this example of a single-channel waiting line.

Assuming Poisson arrivals and exponential service times, find the following:
a) The average number of cars in line.
b) The average time that a car waits before it is washed.

c) The average time that a car spends in the service system.
d) The utilization rate of the car wash.
e) The probability that no cars are in the system.
f) Bryce is thinking of switching to an all-automated car wash that uses no crew. The equipment under consideration washes one car every minute at a constant rate. How will your answers to parts (a) and (b) change with the new system?

: D.10 Gabrielle Dudnyk manages a large Montgomery, Alabama, movie theater complex called Cinema I, II, III, and IV. Each of the 4 auditoriums plays a different film; the schedule staggers starting times to avoid the large crowds that would occur if all 4 movies started at the same time. The theater has a single ticket booth and a cashier who can maintain an average service rate of 280 patrons per hour. Service times are assumed to follow an exponential distribution. Arrivals on a normally active day are Poisson-distributed and average 210 per hour.

In order to determine the efficiency of the current ticket operation, Gabrielle wishes to examine several queue-operating characteristics.
a) Find the average number of moviegoers waiting in line to purchase a ticket.
b) What percentage of the time is the cashier busy?
c) What is the average time that a customer spends in the system?
d) What is the average time spent waiting in line to get to the ticket window?
e) What is the probability that there are more than two people in the system? More than three people? More than four?

: D.11 The cafeteria line in the university student center is a self-serve facility in which students select the items they want and then form a single line to pay the cashier. Students arrive at a rate of about 4 per minute according to a Poisson distribution. The single cashier takes about 12 seconds per customer, following an exponential distribution.
a) What is the probability there are more than two students in the system? More than three students? More than four?
b) What is the probability that the system is empty?
c) How long will the average student have to wait before reaching the cashier?
d) What is the expected number of students in the queue?
e) What is the average number in the system?
f) If a second cashier is added and works at the same pace, how will the operating characteristics computed in parts (b), (c), (d), and (e) change? Assume customers wait in a single line and go to the first available cashier.

: D.12 The wheat harvesting season in the American Midwest is short, and farmers deliver their truckloads of wheat to a giant central storage bin within a 2-week span. Because of this, wheat-filled trucks waiting to unload and return to the fields have been known to back up for a block at the receiving bin. The central bin is owned cooperatively, and it is to every farmer's benefit to make the unloading/storage process as efficient as possible. The cost of grain deterioration caused by unloading delays and the cost of truck rental and idle driver time are significant concerns to the cooperative members. Although farmers have difficulty quantifying crop damage, it is easy to assign a waiting and unloading cost for truck and driver of $18 per hour. During the 2-week harvest season, the storage bin is open and operated 16 hours per day, 7 days per week, and can unload 35 trucks per hour according to an exponential distribution. Full trucks arrive all day long (during the hours the bin is open) at a rate of about 30 per hour, following a Poisson pattern.

To help the cooperative get a handle on the problem of lost time while trucks are waiting in line or unloading at the bin, find the following:
a) The average number of trucks in the unloading system.
b) The average time per truck in the system.
c) The utilization rate for the bin area.

d) The probability that there are more than three trucks in the system at any given time.
e) The total daily cost to the farmers of having their trucks tied up in the unloading process.
f) As mentioned, the cooperative uses the storage bin heavily only 2 weeks per year. Farmers estimate that enlarging the bin would cut unloading costs by 50% next year. It will cost $9,000 to do so during the off-season. Would it be worth the expense to enlarge the storage area?

D.13 Michael Hanna's Department Store in Clear Lake, Texas, maintains a successful catalog sales department in which a clerk takes orders by telephone. If the clerk is occupied on 1 line, incoming phone calls to the catalog department are answered automatically by a recording machine and asked to wait. As soon as the clerk is free, the party that has waited the longest is transferred and serviced first. Calls come in at a rate of about 12 per hour. The clerk can take an order in an average of 4 minutes. Calls tend to follow a Poisson distribution, and service times tend to be exponential.

The clerk is paid $5 per hour, but because of lost goodwill and sales, Hanna's loses about $25 per hour of customer time spent waiting for the clerk to take an order.

a) What is the average time that catalog customers must wait before their calls are transferred to the order clerk?
b) What is the average number of callers waiting to place an order?
c) Hanna's is considering adding a second clerk to take calls. The store would pay that person the same $5 per hour. Should it hire another clerk? Explain your decision.

D.14 Customers arrive at an automated coffee-vending machine at a rate of 4 per minute, following a Poisson distribution. The coffee machine dispenses cups of coffee at a constant time of 10 seconds.

a) What is the average number of people waiting in line?
b) What is the average number in the system?
c) How long does the average person wait in line before receiving service?

D.15 Robert Olney's Barbershop is a popular haircutting and styling salon near the campus of the University of New Haven. Four barbers work full-time and spend an average of 15 minutes on each customer. Customers arrive all day long at an average rate of 12 per hour. Arrivals tend to follow the Poisson distribution, and service times are exponentially distributed. The software described in this quantitative module may be used to answer the following questions:

a) What is the probability that the shop is empty?
b) What is the average number of customers in the barber shop?
c) What is the average time spent in the shop?
d) What is the average time that a customer waits to be called to the barber chair?
e) What is the average number waiting to be served?
f) Robert is thinking of adding a fifth barber. How will this affect the utilization rate of his shop?

D.16 The administrator at a large hospital emergency room faces the problem of providing treatment for patients who arrive at different rates during the day. There are 4 doctors available to treat patients when needed. If not needed, they can be assigned other responsibilities (such as doing lab tests, reports, X-ray diagnoses) or else rescheduled to work at other hours.

It is important to provide quick and responsive treatment, and the administrator feels that, on the average, patients should not have to sit in the waiting area for more than 5 minutes before being seen by a doctor. Patients are treated on a first-come, first-served basis and see the first available doctor after waiting in the queue. The arrival pattern for a typical day is as follows:

Time	Arrival Rate
9 A.M.–3 P.M.	6 patients/hour
3 P.M.–8 P.M.	4 patients/hour
8 P.M.–midnight	12 patients/hour

Arrivals follow a Poisson distribution, and treatment times, 12 minutes on the average, follow the exponential pattern.

How many doctors should be on duty during each period in order to maintain the level of patient care expected?

D.17 One mechanic services 5 drilling machines for a steel plate manufacturer. Machines break down on an average of once every 6 working days, and breakdowns tend to follow a Poisson distribution. The mechanic can handle an average of one repair job per day. Repairs follow an exponential distribution.
   a) On the average, how many machines are waiting for service?
   b) On the average, how many drills are in running order?
   c) How much would waiting time be reduced if a second mechanic were hired?

D.18 Two technicians, working as a team, monitor a group of 5 computers that run an automated manufacturing facility. It takes an average of 15 minutes (exponentially distributed) to adjust a computer that develops a problem. Computers run for an average of 85 minutes (Poisson-distributed) without requiring adjustments. Determine the following:
   a) The average number of computers waiting for adjustment.
   b) The average number being adjusted.
   c) The average number of computers not in working order.

D.19 There are approximately 300 customers shopping in Fackert Department Store between 9 A.M. and 5 P.M. on Saturdays. When deciding how many cash registers to keep open each Saturday, owner Susan Fackert considers 2 factors: customer waiting time (and the associated waiting cost) and the service costs of employing additional checkout clerks. Checkout clerks are paid an average of $4 per hour. When only 1 is on duty, the waiting time per customer is about 10 minutes (or 1/6 of an hour); when 2 clerks are on duty, average checkout time is 6 minutes per person; 4 minutes when 3 clerks are working; and 3 minutes with 4 clerks.

Ms. Fackert has conducted customer satisfaction surveys and has been able to estimate that the store suffers approximately $5 in lost sales and goodwill for every *hour* of customer time spent waiting in checkout lines. Using the information provided, determine the optimal number of clerks to have on duty each Saturday in order to minimize the store's total expected cost.

D.20 Kathleen Kelly's Kar Wash takes a constant time of 4.5 minutes in its automated car wash cycle. Autos arrive following a Poisson distribution at the rate of 10 per hour. Kathleen wants to know:
   a) the average waiting time in line.
   b) the average length of the line.

Case Study

New England Castings

For over 75 years, New England Castings, Inc. (NECI), has manufactured wood stoves for home use. In recent years, with increasing energy prices, president George Mathison, has seen sales triple. This dramatic increase has made it difficult for George to maintain quality in all of his wood stoves and related products.

Unlike other companies manufacturing wood stoves, NECI is *only* in the business of making stoves and stove-related products. Its major products are the Warmglo I, the Warmglo II, the Warmglo III, and the Warmglo IV. The Warmglo I is the smallest wood stove, with a heat output of 30,000 BTUs, and the Warmglo IV is the largest, with a heat output of 60,000 BTUs.

The Warmglo III outsold all other models by a wide margin. Its heat output and available accessories were ideal for the typical home. The Warmglo III also had a number of other outstanding features that made it one of the most attractive and heat-efficient stoves on the market. These features, along with the accessories, resulted in expanding sales and prompted George to build a new factory to manufacture the Warmglo III model. An overview diagram of the factory is shown in Figure D.5.

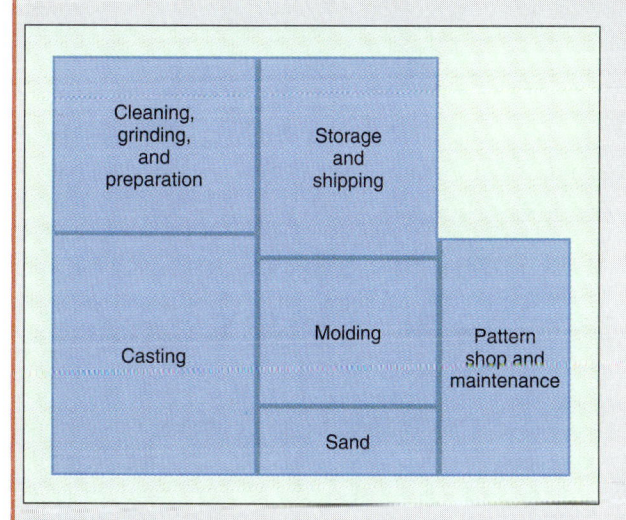

FIGURE D.5 ■ **Overview of Factory**

The new foundry used the latest equipment, including a new Disamatic that helped in manufacturing stove parts. Regardless of new equipment or procedures, casting operations have remained basically unchanged for hundreds of years. To begin with, a wooden pattern is made for every cast-iron piece in the stove. The wooden pattern is an exact duplicate of the cast-iron piece that is to be manufactured. All NECI patterns are made by Precision Patterns, Inc., and are stored in the pattern shop and maintenance room. Next, a specially formulated sand is molded around the wooden pattern. There can be two or more sand molds for each pattern. Mixing the sand and making the molds is done in the molding room. When the wooden pattern is removed, the resulting sand molds form a negative image of the desired casting. Next, molds are transported to the casting room, where molten iron is poured into them and allowed to cool. When the iron has solidified, molds are moved into the cleaning, grinding, and preparation room, where they are dumped into large vibrators that shake most of the sand from the casting. The rough castings are then subjected to both sandblasting to remove the rest of the sand and grinding to finish some of their surfaces. Castings are then painted with a special heat-resistant paint, assembled into workable stoves, and inspected for manufacturing defects that may have gone undetected. Finally, finished stoves are moved to storage and shipping, where they are packaged and transported to the appropriate locations.

At present, the pattern shop and the maintenance department are located in the same room. One large counter is used by both maintenance personnel, who store tools and parts, and sand molders, who need various patterns for the molding operation. Pete Nawler and Bob Dillman, who work behind the counter can service a total of 10 people per hour (about 5 per hour each). On the average, 4 people from maintenance and 3 from molding arrive at the counter each hour. People from molding and maintenance departments arrive randomly, and to be served, they form a single line.

Pete and Bob have always had a policy of first-come, first-served. Because of the location of the pattern shop and maintenance department, it takes about 3 minutes for an individual from the maintenance department to walk to the pattern and maintenance room, and it takes about 1 minute for an individual to walk from the molding department to the pattern and maintenance room.

After observing the operation of the pattern shop and maintenance room for several weeks, George decided to make some changes to the factory layout. An overview of these changes appears in Figure D.6 on page 792.

Separating the maintenance shop from the pattern shop had a number of advantages. It would take people from the maintenance department only 1 minute instead of 3 to get to the new maintenance room. Using motion and time studies, George was also able to determine that improving the layout of the maintenance room would allow Bob to serve 6 people from the maintenance department per hour; improving the layout of the pattern department would allow Pete to serve 7 people from the molding shop per hour.

Discussion Questions

1. How much time would the new layout save?
2. If maintenance personnel were paid $9.50 per hour and molding personnel were paid $11.75 per hour, how much could be saved per hour with the new factory layout?
3. Should George have made the change in layout?

Source: B. Render and R. M. Stair, Jr., *Quantitative Analysis for Management*, 6th ed. (Upper Saddle River, NJ: Prentice Hall, 1997)

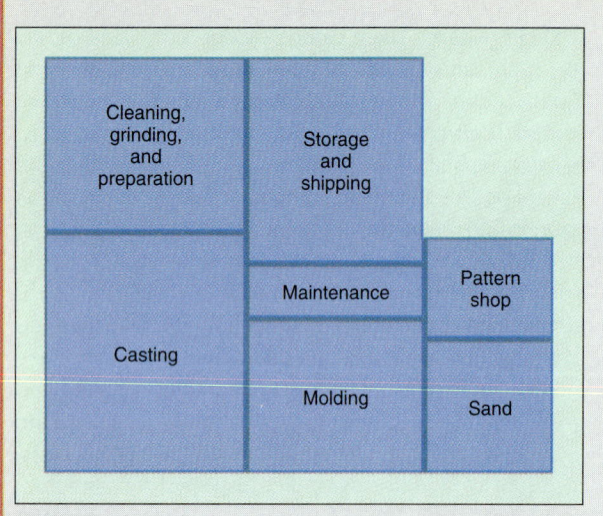

FIGURE D.6 ■ Overview of Factory after Changes

■ Case Study ■

The Winter Park Hotel

Donna Shader, manager of the Winter Park Hotel, is considering how to restructure the front desk to reach an optimum level of staff efficiency and guest service. At present, the hotel has 5 clerks on duty, each with a separate waiting line, during peak check-in time of 3:00 P.M. to 5:00 P.M. Observation of arrivals during this period shows that an average of 90 guests arrive each hour (although there is no upward limit on the number that could arrive at any given time). It takes an average of 3 minutes for the front-desk clerk to register each guest.

Ms. Shader is considering 3 plans for improving guest service by reducing the length of time that guests spend waiting in line. The first proposal would designate one employee as a quick-service clerk for guests registering under corporate accounts, a market segment that fills about 30% of all occupied rooms. Because corporate guests are preregistered, their registration takes just 2 minutes. With these guests separated from the rest of the clientele, the average time for registering a typical guest would climb to 3.4 minutes. Under this plan, noncorporate guests would choose any of the remaining 4 lines.

The second plan is to implement a single-line system. All guests could form a single waiting line to be served by whichever of 5 clerks became available. This option would require sufficient lobby space for what could be a substantial queue.

The use of an automatic teller machine (ATM) for check-ins is the basis of the third proposal. Because initial use of this technology might be minimal, Shader estimates that 20% of customers, primarily frequent guests, would be willing to use the machines. (This might be a conservative estimate if guests perceive direct benefits from using the ATM, as bank customers do. Citibank reports that some 80% of its Manhattan customers use its ATMs.) Ms. Shader would set up a single queue for customers who prefer human check-in clerks. This line would be served by the 5 clerks, although Shader is hopeful that the ATM machine will allow a reduction to 4.

Discussion Questions

1. Determine the average amount of time that a guest spends checking in. How would this change under each of the stated options?
2. Which option do you recommend?

Source: B. Render and R. M. Stair, Jr., *Quantitative Analysis for Management*, 6th ed. (Upper Saddle River, NJ: Prentice Hall, 1997)

▪ *Internet Case Study* ▪

See our Internet home page at http://www.prenhall.com/heizer for this additional case study: Pantry Shopper.

BIBLIOGRAPHY

Becker, L. C., and E. G. Landauer. "Reducing Waiting Time at Security Checkpoints." *Interfaces* 19, no. 5 (September–October 1989): 57–65.

Byrd, J. "The Value of Queuing Theory." *Interfaces* 8, no. 3 (May 1978): 22–26.

Cooper, R. B. *Introduction to Queuing Theory,* 2nd ed. New York: Elsevier-North Holland, 1980.

Foote, B. L. "Queuing Case Study of Drive-In Banking." *Interfaces* 6, no. 4 (August 1976): 31.

Grassmann, W. K. "Finding the Right Number of Servers in Real-World Queuing Systems." *Interfaces* 18, no. 2 (March–April 1988): 94–104.

Ho, C., and H. Lau. "Minimizing Total Cost in Scheduling Outpatient Appointments." *Management Science* 38, no. 12 (December 1992): 1750.

Katz, K., B. Larson, and R. Larson. "Prescription for the Waiting-in-Line Blues: Entertain, Enlighten, and Engage." *Sloan Management Review,* winter 1991, pp. 44–53.

Prabhu, N. U. *Foundations of Queuing Theory*. Klewer Academic Publishers, 1997.

Render, B., and R. M. Stair. *Introduction to Management Science*. Boston: Allyn & Bacon, 1992.

———. *Quantitative Analysis for Management,* 6th ed. Upper Saddle River, Prentice Hall, NJ: 1997.

Solomon, S. *Simulation of Waiting Lines*. Englewood Cliffs, NJ: Prentice Hall, 1983.

Sze, D. Y. "A Queuing Model for Telephone Operator Staffing." *Operations Research* 3, no. 2 (March–April 1984): 229–249.

Worthington, D. J. "Queuing Models for Hospital Waiting Lists." *Journal of the Operational Research Society* 38, no. 5 (May 1987): 413–422.

QUANTITATIVE MODULE E

LEARNING CURVES

MODULE OUTLINE

LEARNING CURVES IN SERVICES AND MANUFACTURING

APPLYING THE LEARNING CURVE
- Arithmetic Approach
- Logarithmic Approach
- Learning-Curve Coefficient Approach

STRATEGIC IMPLICATIONS OF LEARNING CURVES

SUMMARY

KEY TERM

USING POM FOR WINDOWS FOR LEARNING CURVES

USING EXCEL OM FOR LEARNING CURVES

SOLVED PROBLEMS

DISCUSSION QUESTIONS

PROBLEMS

CASE STUDY: SMT'S NEGOTIATION WITH IBM

BIBLIOGRAPHY

LEARNING OBJECTIVES

When you complete this module you should be able to:

Identify or Define:

- What a learning curve is
- Example of learning curves
- The doubling concept

Describe or Explain:

- How to compute learning curve effects
- Why learning curves are important
- The strategic implication of learning curves

When Korean electronics giant Samsung entered the microwave oven market over a decade ago, its production team began making 1 oven a day on a makeshift assembly line. As employees began to learn the assembly process, they went to 2 microwaves a day, then 5. With long hours spent redesigning the line at night, Samsung engineers worked out the bugs discovered by day. Production improved to 10 ovens a day, then 15, and soon to 50. Within 3 years, the learning process had allowed workers to produce 300 ovens a day, and within 4 years, that number had doubled again. By its fifth year in business, Samsung was making 2,500 microwaves a day and continuing to improve.[1]

Most organizations learn and improve over time. Learning takes place as firms and employees perform a task over and over; they learn how to perform more efficiently. This means that task times and costs decrease.

Learning curves are based on the premise that people and organizations become better at their tasks as the tasks are repeated. A learning curve graph (illustrated in Figure E.1) displays labor-hours per unit versus the number of units produced. From it we see that the time needed to produce a unit decreases, usually following a negative exponential curve, as the person or company produces more units. In other words, *it takes less time to complete each additional unit a firm produces.* However, we also see in Figure E.1 that the time *savings* in completing each subsequent unit *decreases.* These are the major attributes of the learning curve.

Learning curves The premise that people and organizations get better at their tasks as the tasks are repeated; sometimes called experience curves.

Learning curves were first applied to industry in a report by T. P. Wright of Curtis-Wright Corp. in 1936.[2] Wright described how direct labor costs of making a particular airplane decreased with learning, a theory since confirmed by other aircraft manufacturers. Regardless of the time needed to produce the first plane, learning curves are found to apply to various categories of air frames (e.g., jet fighters versus passenger planes versus bombers). Learning curves have since been applied not only to labor but also to a wide variety of other costs, including material and purchased components. The power of the learning curve is so significant that it plays a major role in many strategic decisions related to employment levels, costs, capacity, and pricing.

The learning curve is based on a *doubling* of productivity: That is, when production doubles, the decrease in time per unit affects the rate of the learning curve. So, if the learning curve is an 80% rate, the second unit takes 80% of the time of the first unit, the fourth unit takes 80% of the time of the second unit, the eighth unit takes 80% of the time of the fourth unit, and so forth. This principle is shown as

$$T \times L^n = \text{Time required for the } n\text{th unit} \tag{E.1}$$

---

[1] Ira C. Magaziner and Mark Patinkin, "Fast Heat: How Korea Won the Microwave War," *Harvard Business Review* 89, 10 (January–February 1989): 83–92.

[2] T. P. Wright, "Factors Affecting the Cost of Airplanes," *Journal of the Aeronautical Sciences,* February 1936.

LEARNING CURVES IN SERVICES AND MANUFACTURING

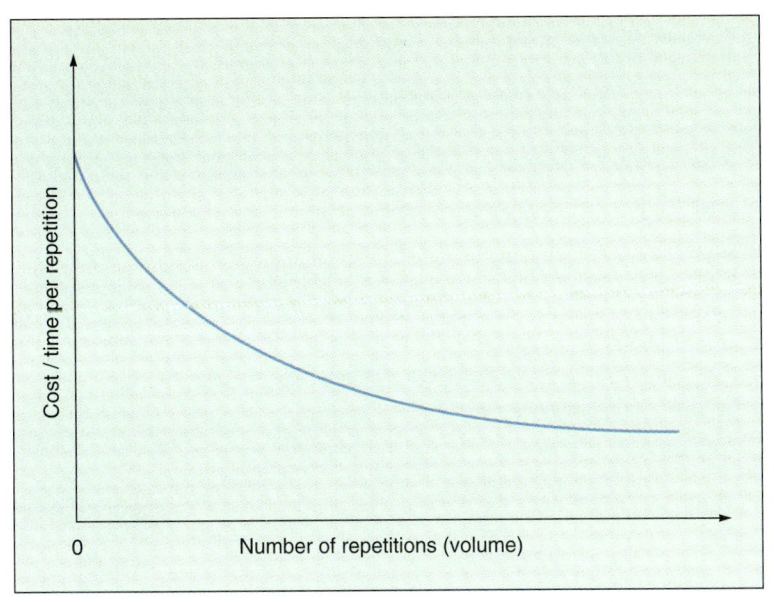

FIGURE E.1 ■ The Learning-Curve Effect States That Time per Repetition Decreases as the Number of Repetitions Increases

where T = unit cost or unit time of the first unit
        L = learning curve rate
        n = number of times T is doubled

If the first unit of a particular product took 10 labor-hours, and if a 70% learning curve is present, the hours the fourth unit will take require doubling twice—from 1 to 2 to 4. Therefore, the formula is

$$\text{Hours required for unit } 4 = 10 \times (.7)^2 = 4.9 \text{ hours}$$

LEARNING CURVES IN SERVICES AND MANUFACTURING

Different organizations—indeed, different products—have different learning curves. The rate of learning varies depending upon the quality of management and the potential of the process and product. *Any change in process, product, or personnel disrupts the learning curve.* Therefore, caution should be exercised in assuming that a learning curve is continuing and permanent.

As you can see in Table E.1 on page 798, industry learning curves vary widely. The lower the number, (say 70% compared to 90%), the steeper the slope and the faster the drop in costs. By tradition, learning curves are defined in terms of the *complements* of their improvement rates. For example, a 70% learning curve implies a 30% decrease in time each time the number of repetitions is doubled. A 90% curve means there is a corresponding 10% rate of improvement.

Stable, standardized products and processes tend to have costs that decline more steeply than others. Between 1920 and 1955, for instance, the steel industry was able to reduce labor-hours per unit to 79% each time cumulative production doubled.

Try testing the learning-curve effect on some activity you may be performing. For example, if you need to assemble four bookshelves, time your work on each and note the rate of improvement.

TABLE E.1 ■ Examples of Learning-Curve Effects

Example	Improving Parameter	Cumulative Parameter	Learning-Curve Slope (%)	Time Frame
1. Model-T Ford production	Price	Units produced	86	1910–1926
2. Aircraft assembly	Direct labor-hours per unit	Units produced	80	1925–1957
3. Equipment maintenance at GE	Average time to replace a group of parts	Number of replacements	76	Around 1957
4. Steel production	Production worker labor-hours per unit produced	Units produced	79	1920–1955
5. Integrated circuits	Average price per unit	Units produced	72[a]	1964–1972
6. Hand-held calculator	Average factory selling price	Units produced	74	1975–1978
7. Disk memory drives	Average price per bit	Number of bits	76	1975–1978
8. Heart transplants	One-year death rates	Transplants completed	79	1985–1988

[a]Constant dollars.

Sources: James A. Cunningham, "Using the Learning Curve as a Management Tool," *IEEE Spectrum,* June 1980, p. 45. © 1980 IEEE; and David B. Smith and Jan L. Larsson, "The Impact of Learning on Cost: The Case of Heart Transplantation," *Hospital and Health Services Administration,* spring 1989, pp. 85–97.

By coincidence, the learning curve for a very service-oriented task, performing heart transplants, was found to follow the same 79% slope by researchers at Temple University Hospital. The results of that hospital's 3-year study of 62 patients receiving transplants found that every 3 operations resulted in a halving of the 1-year death rate. As more hospitals face pressure from both insurance companies and the government to enter fixed-price negotiations for their services, their ability to learn from experience becomes increasingly critical.

Learning curves are useful for a variety of applications. These include:

1. Internal labor forecasting, scheduling, establishing costs and budgets.
2. External purchasing and subcontracting (see the SMT case study at the end of this module).
3. Strategic evaluation of company and industry performance.

> Failure to consider the effects of learning can lead to *overestimates* of labor needs and *underestimates* of material needs.

APPLYING THE LEARNING CURVE

A mathematical relationship enables us to express the time it takes to produce a certain unit. This relationship is a function of how many units have been produced before the unit in question and how long it took to produce them. Although this procedure determines how long it takes to produce a given unit, the consequences of this analysis are more far-reaching. Costs drop and efficiency goes up for individual firms and the industry. Therefore, severe problems in scheduling occur if operations are not adjusted for implications of the learning curve. For instance, if learning-curve improvement is not considered when scheduling, the result may be labor and productive facilities being idle a portion of the time. Furthermore, firms may refuse additional work because they do not consider the improvement in their own efficiency that results from learning. From a purchasing perspective, our interest is in negotiating what our suppliers' costs should be for further production of units based on the size of our order. The foregoing are only a few of the ramifications of the effect of learning curves.

With this in mind, let us look at three approaches to learning curves: arithmetic analysis, logarithmic analysis, and learning-curve coefficients.

> Although in many cases analysts can examine their company and fit a learning rate to it, trade journals also publish industrywide data on specific types of operations.

Arithmetic Approach

The arithmetic approach is the simplest approach to learning-curve problems. As we noted at the beginning of this module, each time that production doubles, labor per unit declines by a constant factor, known as the learning rate. So, if we know that the learning rate is 80% and that the first unit produced took 100 hours, the hours required to produce the second, fourth, eighth, and sixteenth units are as follows:

Nth Unit Produced	Hours for Nth Unit
1	100.0
2	80.0 = (.8 × 100)
4	64.0 = (.8 × 80)
8	51.2 = (.8 × 64)
16	41.0 = (.8 × 51.2)

As long as we wish to find the hours required to produce N units and N is one of the doubled values, then this approach works. Arithmetic analysis does not tell us how many hours will be needed to produce other units. For this flexibility, we must turn to the logarithmic approach.

Logarithmic Approach

The logarithmic approach allows us to determine labor for *any* unit, T_N, by the formula

$$T_N = T_1(N^b) \tag{E.2}$$

where T_1 = hours to produce the first unit
       b = slope of the learning curve
       = (log of the learning rate)/(log 2)

Some of the values for b are presented in Table E.2. Example E1 shows how this formula works.

TABLE E.2 ■ Learning Curve Values of b

Learning Rate (%)	b
70	−.515
75	−.415
80	−.322
85	−.234
90	−.152

EXAMPLE E1

The learning rate for a particular operation is 80%, and the first unit of production took 100 hours. The hours required to produce the third unit may be computed as follows:

$$T_N = T_1 (N^b)$$

$$T_3 = (100 \text{ hours}) (3^b)$$

$$= (100)(3^{\log .8/\log 2})$$

$$= (100)(3^{-.322}) = 70.2 \text{ labor-hours}$$

The logarithmic approach allows us to determine the hours required for *any* unit produced, but there *is* a simpler method.

Learning-Curve Coefficient Approach

The learning-curve coefficient technique is embodied in Table E.3 and the following equation:

$$T_N = T_1 C \qquad (E.3)$$

where T_N = number of labor-hours required to produce the Nth unit
T_1 = number of labor-hours required to produce the first unit
C = learning-curve coefficient found in Table E.3

The learning-curve coefficient, C, depends on both the learning rate (70%, 75%, 80%, and so on) and the unit of interest.

Example E2 uses the preceding equation and Table E.3 to calculate learning-curve effects.

EXAMPLE E2

It took a Korean shipyard 125,000 labor-hours to produce the first of several tugboats that you expect to purchase for your shipping company, Great Lakes, Inc. Boats 2 and 3 have been produced by the Koreans with a learning factor of 85%. At $40 per hour, what should you, as purchasing agent, expect to pay for the fourth unit?

First, search Table E.3 for the fourth unit and a learning factor of 85%. The learning-curve coefficient, C, is .723. To produce the fourth unit, then, takes

$$T_N = T_1 C$$

$$T_4 = (125,000 \text{ hours})(.723)$$

$$= 90,375 \text{ hours}$$

To find the cost, multiply by $40:

$$90,375 \text{ hours} \times \$40 \text{ per hour} = \$3,615,000$$

Applying the Learning Curve

TABLE E.3 ■ Learning-Curve Coefficients

Unit Number (N)	70% Unit Time	70% Total Time	75% Unit Time	75% Total Time	80% Unit Time	80% Total Time	85% Unit Time	85% Total Time	90% Unit Time	90% Total Time
1	1.000	1.000	1.000	1.000	1.000	1.000	1.000	1.000	1.000	1.000
2	.700	1.700	.750	1.750	.800	1.800	.850	1.850	.900	1.900
3	.568	2.268	.634	2.384	.702	2.502	.773	2.623	.846	2.746
4	.490	2.758	.562	2.946	.640	3.142	.723	3.345	.810	3.556
5	.437	3.195	.513	3.459	.596	3.738	.686	4.031	.783	4.339
6	.398	3.593	.475	3.934	.562	4.299	.657	4.688	.762	5.101
7	.367	3.960	.446	4.380	.534	4.834	.634	5.322	.744	5.845
8	.343	4.303	.422	4.802	.512	5.346	.614	5.936	.729	6.574
9	.323	4.626	.402	5.204	.493	5.839	.597	6.533	.716	7.290
10	.306	4.932	.385	5.589	.477	6.315	.583	7.116	.705	7.994
11	.291	5.223	.370	5.958	.462	6.777	.570	7.686	.695	8.689
12	.278	5.501	.357	6.315	.449	7.227	.558	8.244	.685	9.374
13	.267	5.769	.345	6.660	.438	7.665	.548	8.792	.677	10.052
14	.257	6.026	.334	6.994	.428	8.092	.539	9.331	.670	10.721
15	.248	6.274	.325	7.319	.418	8.511	.530	9.861	.663	11.384
16	.240	6.514	.316	7.635	.410	8.920	.522	10.383	.656	12.040
17	.233	6.747	.309	7.944	.402	9.322	.515	10.898	.650	12.690
18	.226	6.973	.301	8.245	.394	9.716	.508	11.405	.644	13.334
19	.220	7.192	.295	8.540	.388	10.104	.501	11.907	.639	13.974
20	.214	7.407	.288	8.828	.381	10.485	.495	12.402	.634	14.608
25	.191	8.404	.263	10.191	.355	12.309	.470	14.801	.613	17.713
30	.174	9.305	.244	11.446	.335	14.020	.450	17.091	.596	20.727
35	.160	10.133	.229	12.618	.318	15.643	.434	19.294	.583	23.666
40	.150	10.902	.216	13.723	.305	17.193	.421	21.425	.571	26.543
45	.141	11.625	.206	14.773	.294	18.684	.410	23.500	.561	29.366
50	.134	12.307	.197	15.776	.284	20.122	.400	25.513	.552	32.142

Table E.3 also shows *cumulative values*. These allow us to compute the total number of hours needed to complete a specified number of units. Again, the computation is straightforward. Just multiply the table value times the time required for the first unit. Example E3 illustrates this concept.

EXAMPLE E3

Example E2 computed the time to complete the fourth tugboat that Great Lakes plans to buy. How long will *all four* boats require?

Looking this time at the "total time" column in Table E.3, we find that the cumulative coefficient is 3.345. Thus, the time required is

$$T_N = T_1 C$$

$$T_4 = (125,000)(3.345) = 418,125 \text{ hours in total for all 4 boats}$$

For an illustration of how POM for Windows and Excel OM can be used to solve Examples E2 and E3, see Programs E.1–E.4 at the end of this module.

As later times become available, it can be useful to revise the basic unit; this is especially so when the first unit is estimated prior to production.

Using Table E.3 requires that we know how long it takes to complete the first unit. Yet, what happens if our most recent or most reliable information available pertains to some other unit? The answer is that we must use these data to find a revised estimate for the first unit and then apply the table to that number. Example E4 illustrates this concept.

EXAMPLE E4

Great Lakes, Inc., believes that unusual circumstances in producing the first boat (see Example E2) imply that the time estimate of 125,000 hours is not as valid a base as the time required to produce the third boat. Boat number 3 was completed in 100,000 hours.

To solve for the revised estimate for boat number 1, we return to Table E.3, with a unit value of $N = 3$ and a learning-curve coefficient of $C = .773$ in the 85% column. To find the revised estimate, we divide the actual time for boat number 3, 100,000 hours, by $C = .773$

$$\frac{100,000}{.773} = 129,366 \text{ hours}$$

STRATEGIC IMPLICATIONS OF LEARNING CURVES

So far, we have shown how operations managers can forecast labor-hour requirements for a product. We have also shown how purchasing agents can determine a supplier's cost, knowledge that can help in price negotiations. Another important application of learning curves concerns strategic planning.

An example of a company cost line and industry price line are so labeled in Figure E.2. These learning curves are straight because both scales are log scales. When the *rate* of change is constant, a log-log graph yields a straight line. If an organization believes its cost line to be the "company cost" line and the industry price is indicated by the dashed horizontal line, then the company must have costs at the points below the dotted line (for example, point *a* or *b*) or else operate at a loss (point *c*).

Applications of the learning curve:
1. Internal → determine labor standards and rates of material supply required.
2. External → determine purchase costs.
3. Strategic → determine volume-cost changes.

Lower costs are not automatic; they must be managed down. When a firm's strategy is to pursue a curve steeper than the industry average (the company cost line in Figure E.2), it does this by:

1. Following an aggressive pricing policy;
2. Focusing on continuing cost reduction and productivity improvement;
3. Building on shared experience;
4. Keeping capacity growing ahead of demand.

Costs may drop as a firm pursues the learning curve, but volume must increase for the learning curve to exist. In recent years, much of the computer industry, for instance, has operated at a 25% cost reduction per year, with steep learning curves. Texas Instruments (TI), however, discovered that developing a competitive strategy via the learning curve is not for everyone:[3] TI allowed other PC producers to lead in cost reductions and price-cutting. It paid the price for its mistake when sales of its PC line dropped.

Managers must understand competitors before embarking on a learning-curve strategy. Weak competitors are undercapitalized, stuck with high costs, or do not understand the logic of learning curves. However, strong and dangerous competitors control their

---

[3] Pankaj Ghemawat, "Building Strategy on the Experience Curve," *Harvard Business Review* 63 (March–April 1985): 148.

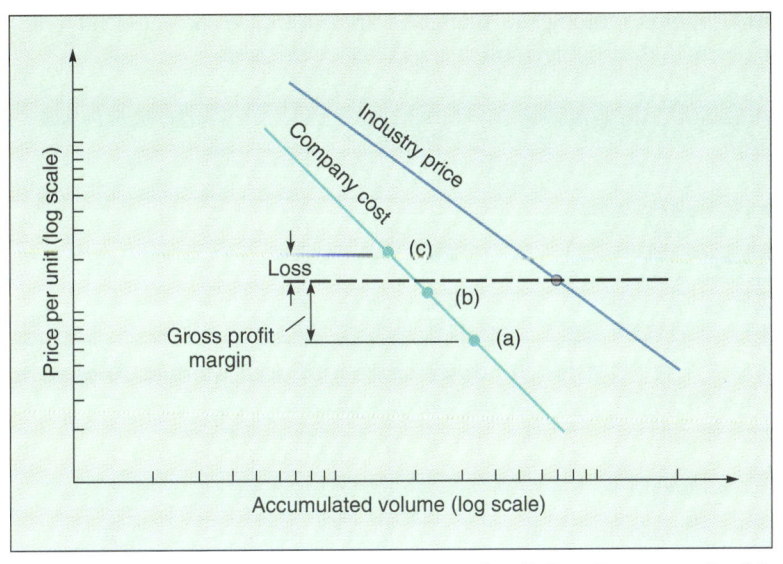

FIGURE E.2 ■ **Industry Learning Curve for Price Compared with Company Learning Curve for Cost** *Note: Both the vertical and horizontal axes of this figure are log scales. This is known as a log-log graph.*

costs, have solid financial positions for the large investments needed, and have a track record of using an aggressive learning-curve strategy. Taking on such a competitor in a price war may help only the consumer.

SUMMARY

The learning curve is a powerful tool for the operations manager. This tool can assist operations managers in determining future cost standards for items produced as well as purchased. In addition, the learning curve can provide understanding about company and industry performance. We saw three approaches to learning curves: arithmetic analysis, logarithmic analysis, and learning-curve coefficients found in tables. Software can also help analyze learning curves.

KEY TERM

Learning curves *(p. 796)*

USING POM FOR WINDOWS FOR LEARNING CURVES

POM for Windows' Learning Curve module computes the length of time that future units will take, given the time required for the base unit and the learning rate (expressed as a number between 0 and 1). As an option, if the times required for the first and *N*th units are already known, the learning *rate* can be computed. Programs E.1 and E.2 on page 804 illustrate the software applied to Examples E2 and E3. Program E.1 provides an input screen, plus the output time for the fourth unit. Program E.2 shows individual and cumulative times for units 1 through 4. Note that outputs from the software tend to be more accurate (in decimal places) than those using tabled coefficients.

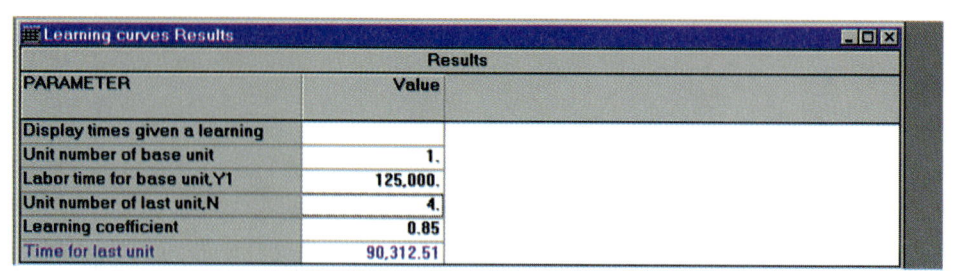

PARAMETER	Results Value
Display times given a learning	
Unit number of base unit	1.
Labor time for base unit, Y1	125,000.
Unit number of last unit, N	4.
Learning coefficient	0.85
Time for last unit	90,312.51

PROGRAM E.1 ■ POM for Windows Learning-Curve Module Applied to Examples E2 and E3 *The program also has graphic capability.*

Example Solution

Unit	Production Time	Cumulative Time
1	125,000.	125,000.
2	106,250.	231,250.
3	96,614.36	327,864.4
4	90,312.51	418,176.9

PROGRAM E.2 ■ POM for Windows Second Output Screen for Examples E2 and E3 *Unit and cumulative times are shown.*

USING EXCEL OM FOR LEARNING CURVES

Program E.3 and E.4 show how Excel OM develops a spreadsheet for learning-curve calculations. Program E.3 illustrates the input data, from Examples E2 and E3, and the formulas. Program E.4 is an output screen.

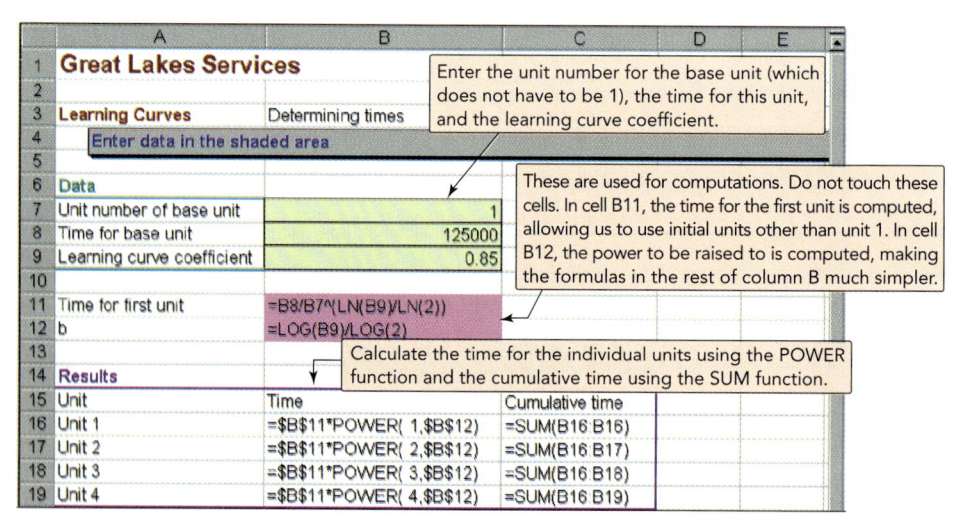

	A	B	C	D	E
1	**Great Lakes Services**				
2					
3	Learning Curves	Determining times			
4	Enter data in the shaded area				
5					
6	Data				
7	Unit number of base unit	1			
8	Time for base unit	125000			
9	Learning curve coefficient	0.85			
10					
11	Time for first unit	=B8/B7^(LN(B9)/LN(2))			
12	b	=LOG(B9)/LOG(2)			
13					
14	Results				
15	Unit	Time	Cumulative time		
16	Unit 1	=$B$11*POWER(1,$B$12)	=SUM(B16:B16)		
17	Unit 2	=$B$11*POWER(2,$B$12)	=SUM(B16:B17)		
18	Unit 3	=$B$11*POWER(3,$B$12)	=SUM(B16:B18)		
19	Unit 4	=$B$11*POWER(4,$B$12)	=SUM(B16:B19)		

Enter the unit number for the base unit (which does not have to be 1), the time for this unit, and the learning curve coefficient.

These are used for computations. Do not touch these cells. In cell B11, the time for the first unit is computed, allowing us to use initial units other than unit 1. In cell B12, the power to be raised to is computed, making the formulas in the rest of column B much simpler.

Calculate the time for the individual units using the POWER function and the cumulative time using the SUM function.

PROGRAM E.3 ■ Excel OM's Learning-Curve Module, Using Data from Examples E2 and E3

	A	B	C	D	E	F	G	H
1	**Great Lakes Services**							
2								
3	Learning Curves	Determining times						
4	Enter data in the shaded area							
5								
6	Data							
7	Unit number of base unit	1						
8	Time for base unit	125000						
9	Learning curve coefficient	0.85						
10								
11	Time for first unit	125000						
12	b	-0.23447						
13								
14	Results							
15	Unit	Time	Cumulative time					
16	Unit 1	125000	125000					
17	Unit 2	106250	231250					
18	Unit 3	96614.35	327864.355					
19	Unit 4	90312.5	418176.855					

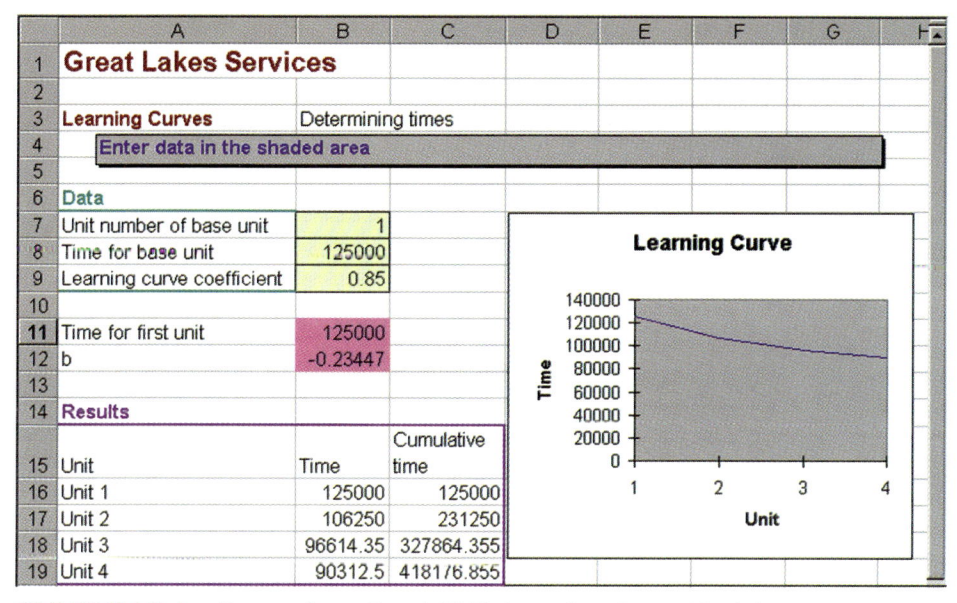

PROGRAM E.4 ■ Output from Excel OM's Learning-Curve Module

SOLVED PROBLEMS

Solved Problem E.1

Digicomp produces a new telephone system with built-in TV screens. Its learning rate is 80%.

a) If the first one took 56 hours, how long will it take Digicomp to make the eleventh system?

b) How long will the first 11 systems take in total?

c) As a purchasing agent, you expect to buy units 12 through 15 of the new phone system. What would be your expected cost for the units if Digicomp charges $30 for each labor-hour?

Solution

a) $T_N = T_1 C$ — from Table E.3—80% unit time
$T_{11} = (56 \text{ hours})(.462) = 25.9$ hours

b) Total time for the first 11 units = (56 hours)(6.777) = 379.5 hours

— from Table E.3—80% unit time —

c) To find the time for units 12 through 15, we take the total cumulative time for units 1 to 15 and subtract the total time for units 1 to 11, which was computed in part (b). Total time for the first 15 units = (56 hours) (8.511) = 476.6 hours. So, the time for units 12 through 15 is 476.6 − 379.5 = 97.1 hours. (This figure could also be confirmed by computing the times for units 12, 13, 14, and 15 separately using the unit-time column and then adding them.) Expected cost for units 12 through 15 = (97.1 hours) ($30 per hour) = $2,913.

Solved Problem E.2

If the first time you perform a job it takes 60 minutes, how long will the eighth job take if you are on an 80% learning curve?

Solution

Three doublings from 1 to 2 to 4 to 8 implies $.8^3$. Therefore, we have

$$60 \times (.8)^3 = 60 \times .512 = 30.72 \text{ minutes}$$

or, using Table E.3, we have $C = .512$. Therefore:

$$60 \times .512 = 30.72 \text{ minutes}$$

DISCUSSION QUESTIONS

1. What are some of the limitations to the use of learning curves?
2. What techniques can a firm use to move to a steeper learning curve?
3. What are the approaches to solving learning-curve problems?
4. Refer to Example E1: What are the implications for Great Lakes, Inc., if the engineering department wants to change the engine in the third and subsequent tugboats that the firm purchases?
5. Why isn't the learning-curve concept as applicable in a high-volume assembly line as it is in most other human activities?
6. What can cause a learning curve to vary from a smooth downward slope?
7. Explain the concept of the "doubling" effect in learning curves.

PROBLEMS

E.1 An IRS auditor took 45 minutes to process her first tax return. The IRS uses an 85% learning curve. How long will the:
  a) second return take?
  b) fourth return take?
  c) eighth return take?

E.2 Seton Hall Trucking Co. just hired a new person to verify daily invoices and accounts payable. It took her 9 hours and 23 minutes to complete her task on the first day. Prior employees in this job have tended to follow a 90% learning curve. How long will the task take at the end of:
  a) the second day?
  b) the fourth day?
  c) the eighth day?
  d) the sixteenth day?

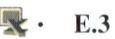

E.3 If it took 563 minutes to complete a hospital's first liver transplant, and the hospital uses a 90% learning rate, how long should:
  a) the third transplant take?
  b) the sixth transplant take?

Problems

      c)   the eighth transplant take?
      d)   the sixteenth transplant take?

E.4   Refer to Problem E.3: Compute the *cumulative* time to complete:
      a)   the first 3 transplants.
      b)   the first 6 transplants.
      c)   the first 8 transplants.
      d)   the first 16 transplants.

E.5   Beth Zion Hospital has received initial certification from the state of California to become a center for kidney transplants. The hospital, however, must complete its first 18 transplants under great scrutiny and at no cost to the patients. The very first transplant, just completed, required 30 hours. On the basis of research at the hospital, Beth Zion estimates that it will have an 80% learning curve. Estimate the time it will take to complete the following:
      a)   the fifth kidney transplant.
      b)   all of the first 5 transplants.
      c)   the eighteenth transplant.
      d)   all 18 transplants.

E.6   Refer to Problem E.5: Beth Zion Hospital has just been informed that only the first 10 transplants must be performed at the hospital's expense. The cost per hour of surgery is estimated to be $5,000. Again, the learning rate is 80% and the first surgery took 30 hours.
      a)   How long will the tenth surgery take?
      b)   How much will the tenth surgery cost?
      c)   How much will all 10 cost the hospital?

E.7   If the fourth oil change and lube job at Trendo-Lube took 18 minutes and the second took 20 minutes, estimate how long:
      a)   the first job took.
      b)   the third job took.
      c)   the eighth job will take.
      d)   the actual learning rate is.

E.8   A student at San Diego State University bought 6 bookcases for her dorm room. Each required unpacking of parts and assembly, which included some nailing and bolting. She completed the first bookcase in 5 hours and the second in 4 hours.
      a)   What is her learning rate?
      b)   Assuming the same rate continues, how long will the third bookcase take?
      c)   The fourth, fifth, and sixth cases?
      d)   All six cases?

E.9   Cleaning a toxic landfill took one EPA contractor 300 labor-days. If the contractor follows an 85% learning rate, how long will it take, in total, to clean the next 5 (that is, landfills 2 through 6)?

E.10   The first vending machine that Smith Inc. assembled took 80 labor-hours. Estimate how long the fourth machine will require for each of the following learning rates:
      a)   95%
      b)   87%
      c)   72%

E.11   Refer to Problem E.10, in which the time for the fourth unit was estimated. How long will the sixteenth vending machine take to assemble under the same three learning rates—namely:
      a)   95%
      b)   87%
      c)   72%

Module E Learning Curves

: E.12 As the purchasing agent for Northeast Airlines, you are interested in determining what you can expect to pay for airplane number 4 if the third plane took 20,000 hours to produce. What would you expect to pay for plane number 5? Number 6? Use an 85% learning curve and a $40-per-hour labor charge.

: E.13 Using the data from Problem E.12, how long will it take to complete the twelfth plane? The fifteenth plane? How long will it take to complete planes 12 through 15 inclusive? At $40 per hour, what can you, as purchasing agent, expect to pay for all 4 planes?

: E.14 Dynamic RAM Corp. produces semiconductors and has a learning curve of .7. The price per bit is 100 millicents when the volume is $.7 \times 10^{12}$ bits. What is the expected price at 1.4×10^{12} bits? What is the expected price at 89.6×10^{12} bits?

· E.15 It takes 80,000 hours to produce the first jet engine at T.R.'s aerospace division and the learning factor is 90%. How long does it take to produce the eighth engine?

: E.16 It takes 28,718 hours to produce the eighth locomotive at a large French manufacturing firm. If the learning factor is 80%, how long does it take to produce the tenth locomotive?

: E.17 If the first unit of a production run takes 1 hour and the firm is on an 80% learning curve, how long will unit 100 take? (*Hint:* Apply the coefficient in Table E.3 twice.)

: E.18 As the estimator for Umble Enterprises, your job is to prepare an estimate for a potential customer service contract. The contract is for the service of diesel locomotive cylinder heads. The shop has done some of these in the past on a sporadic basis. The time required to service each cylinder head has been exactly 4 hours, and similar work has been accomplished at an 85% learning curve. The customer wants you to quote in batches of 12 and 20.
a) Prepare the quote.
b) After preparing the quote, you find a labor ticket for this customer for 5 locomotive cylinder heads. From the sundry notations on the labor ticket, you conclude that the fifth unit took 2.5 hours. What do you conclude about the learning curve and your quote?

: E.19 Using the log-log graph below, answer the following questions.
a) What are the implications for management if it has forecast its cost on the optimum line?
b) What could be causing the fluctuations above the optimum line?
c) If management forecast the tenth unit on the optimum line, what was that forecast in hours?
d) If management built the tenth unit as indicated by the actual line, how many hours did it take?

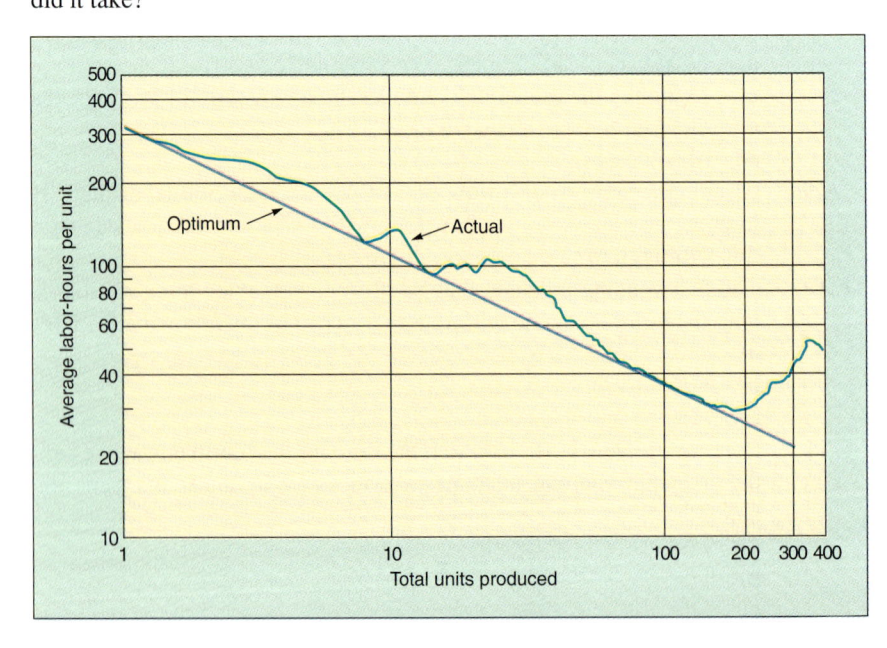

Case Study

SMT's Negotiation with IBM

SMT and one other, much larger company were asked by IBM to bid on 80 more units of a particular computer product. The RFQ (request for quote) asked that the overall bid be broken down to show the hourly rate, the parts and materials component in the price, and any charges for subcontracted services. SMT quoted $1.62 million and supplied the cost breakdown as requested. The second company submitted only one total figure, $5 million, with no cost breakdown. The decision was made to negotiate with SMT.

The IBM negotiating team included two purchasing managers and two cost engineers. One cost engineer had developed manufacturing cost estimates for every component, working from engineering drawings and cost-data books that he had built up from previous experience and that contained time factors, both setup and run times, for a large variety of operations. He estimated materials costs by working both from data supplied by the IBM corporate purchasing staff and from purchasing journals. He visited SMT facilities to see the tooling available so that he would know what processes were being used. He assumed that there would be perfect conditions and trained operators, and he developed cost estimates for the 158th unit (previous orders were for 25, 15, and 38 units). He added 5% for scrap-and-flow loss; 2% for the use of temporary tools, jigs, and fixtures; 5% for quality control; and 9% for purchasing burden. Then, using an 85% learning curve, he backed up his costs to get an estimate for the first unit. He next checked the data on hours and materials for the 25, 15, and 38 units already made and found that his estimate for the first unit was within 4% of actual cost. His check, however, had indicated a 90% learning curve effect on hours per unit.

In the negotiations, SMT was represented by one of the two owners of the business, two engineers, and one cost estimator. The sessions opened with a discussion of learning curves. The IBM cost estimator demonstrated that SMT had in fact been operating on a 90% learning curve. But, he argued, it should be possible to move to an 85% curve, given the longer runs, reduced setup time, and increased continuity of workers on the job that would be possible with an order for 80 units. The owner agreed with this analysis and was willing to reduce his price by 4%.

However, as each operation in the manufacturing process was discussed, it became clear that some IBM cost estimates were too low because certain crating and shipping expenses had been overlooked. These oversights were minor, however, and in the following discussions, the two parties arrived at a common understanding of specifications and reached agreements on the costs of each manufacturing operation.

At this point, SMT representatives expressed great concern about the possibility of inflation in materials costs. The IBM negotiators volunteered to include a form of price escalation in the contract, as previously agreed among themselves. IBM representatives suggested that if overall materials costs changed by more than 10%, the price could be adjusted accordingly. However, if one party took the initiative to have the price revised, the other could require an analysis of *all* parts and materials invoices in arriving at the new price.

Another concern of the SMT representatives was that a large amount of overtime and subcontracting would be required to meet IBM's specified delivery schedule. IBM negotiators thought that a relaxation in the delivery schedule might be possible if a price concession could be obtained. In response, the SMT team offered a 5% discount, and this was accepted. As a result of these negotiations, the SMT price was reduced almost 20% below its original bid price.

In a subsequent meeting called to negotiate the prices of certain pipes to be used in the system, it became apparent to an IBM cost estimator that SMT representatives had seriously underestimated their costs. He pointed out this apparent error because he could not understand why SMT had quoted such a low figure. He wanted to be sure that SMT was using the correct manufacturing process. In any case, if SMT estimators had made a mistake, it should be noted. It was IBM's policy to seek a fair price both for itself and for its suppliers. IBM procurement managers believed that if a vendor was losing money on a job, there would be a tendency to cut corners. In addition, the IBM negotiator felt that by pointing out the error, he generated some goodwill that would help in future sessions.

Discussion Questions

1. What are the advantages and disadvantages to IBM and SMT from this approach?
2. How does SMT's proposed learning rate compare with that of other companies?
3. What are the limitations of the learning curve in this case?

Source: Adapted from E. Raymond Corey, *Procurement Management: Strategy, Organization, and Decision Making* (New York: Van Nostrand Reinhold).

BIBLIOGRAPHY

Abernathy, W. J., and K. Wayne. "Limits of the Learning Curve." *Harvard Business Review* 52 (September–October 1974): 109–119.

Camm, J. "A Note on Learning Curve Parameters." *Decision Sciences*, summer 1985, pp. 325–327.

Hall, G., and S. Howell. "The Experience Curve from the Economist's Perspective." *Strategic Management Journal*, July–September 1985, pp. 197–210.

Hart, C. W., G. Spizizen, and D. D. Wyckoff. "Scale Economies and the Experience Curve." *The Cornell H.R.A. Quarterly* 25 (May 1984): 91–103.

Taylor, M. L. "The Learning Curve—A Basic Cost Projection Tool." *N.A.A. Bulletin,* February 1961, pp. 21–26.

QUANTITATIVE MODULE F

Simulation

MODULE OUTLINE

WHAT IS SIMULATION?
ADVANTAGES AND DISADVANTAGES OF SIMULATION
MONTE CARLO SIMULATION
SIMULATION OF A QUEUING PROBLEM
SIMULATION AND INVENTORY ANALYSIS
THE ROLE OF COMPUTERS IN SIMULATION
SUMMARY
KEY TERMS
USING POM FOR WINDOWS FOR SIMULATION
SIMULATION WITH EXCEL SPREADSHEETS
SOLVED PROBLEMS
DISCUSSION QUESTIONS
PROBLEMS
CASE STUDY: ALABAMA AIRLINES
INTERNET CASE STUDIES
BIBLIOGRAPHY

LEARNING OBJECTIVES

When you complete this module you should be able to:

Identify or Define:

Monte Carlo simulation
Random numbers
Random number interval
Simulation software

Describe or Explain:

The advantages and disadvantages of modeling with simulation

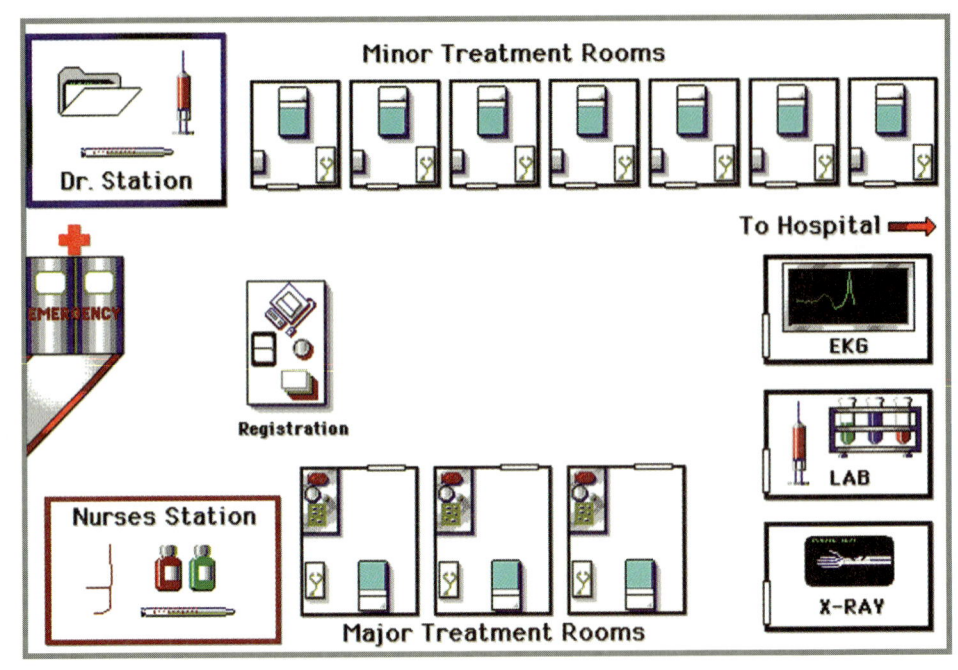

When Bay Medical Center faced severe overcrowding at its outpatient clinic, it turned to computer simulation to try to reduce bottlenecks and improve patient flow. A simulation language called Micro Saint analyzed current data relating to patient service times between clinic rooms. By simulating different numbers of doctors and staff, simulating the use of another clinic for overflow, and simulating a redesign of the existing clinic, Bay Medical Center was able to make decisions based on an understanding of both costs and benefits. This resulted in better patient service at lower cost.
Source: Micro Analysis and Design Simulation Software, Inc., Boulder, CO.

Simulation models abound in our world. The city of Atlanta, for example, uses them to control traffic. Europe's Airbus Industries uses them to test the aerodynamics of proposed jets. The U.S. Army simulates war games on computers. Business students use management gaming to simulate realistic business competition. And thousands of organizations like Bay Medical Center develop simulation models to help make operations decisions.

Most of the large companies in the world use simulation models. Table F.1 lists just a few areas in which simulation is now being applied.

TABLE F.1 ■ Some Applications of Simulation

Ambulance location and dispatching	Bus scheduling
Assembly line balancing	Design of library operations
Parking lot and harbor design	Taxi, truck, and railroad dispatching
Distribution system design	Production facility scheduling
Scheduling aircraft	Plant layout
Labor-hiring decisions	Capital investments
Personnel scheduling	Production scheduling
Traffic-light timing	Sales forecasting
Voting pattern prediction	Inventory planning and control

There are many kinds of simulations, and although this module stresses Monte Carlo simulations, you should be aware of "physical" simulations (such as a wind tunnel model) as well.

WHAT IS SIMULATION?

Simulation is the attempt to duplicate the features, appearance, and characteristics of a real system. In this module, we will show how to simulate part of an operations management system by building a mathematical model that comes as close as possible to representing the reality of the system. The model will then be used to estimate the effects of various actions. The idea behind simulation is threefold:

1. To imitate a real-world situation mathematically,
2. Then to study its properties and operating characteristics, and
3. Finally to draw conclusions and make action decisions based on the results of the simulation.

In this way, a real-life system need not be touched until the advantages and disadvantages of a major policy decision are first measured on the model.

To use simulation, an OM manager should:

1. Define the problem;
2. Introduce the important variables associated with the problem;
3. Construct a numerical model;
4. Set up possible courses of action for testing;
5. Run the experiment;
6. Consider the results (possibly modifying the model or changing data inputs);
7. Decide what course of action to take.

These steps are illustrated in Figure F.1.

The problems tackled by simulation may range from very simple to extremely complex, from bank teller lines to an analysis of the U.S. economy. Although small simulations can be conducted by hand, effective use of the technique requires a computer. Even large-scale models, simulating perhaps years of business decisions, are handled by computer.

In this module, we examine the basic principles of simulation and then tackle some problems in the areas of waiting-line analysis and inventory control. Why do we use simulation in these areas when mathematical models described in other chapters can solve similar problems? The answer is that simulation provides an alternative approach for problems that are very complex mathematically. It can handle, for example, inventory problems in which demand or lead time is not constant.

Simulation The attempt to duplicate the features, appearance, and characteristics of a real system, usually via a computerized model.

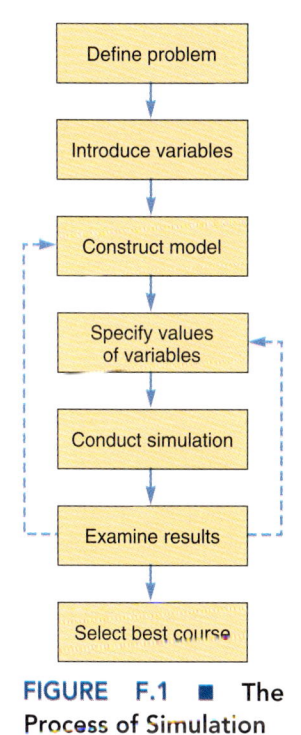

FIGURE F.1 ■ The Process of Simulation

ADVANTAGES AND DISADVANTAGES OF SIMULATION

Simulation is a tool that has become widely accepted by managers for several reasons. The main *advantages* of simulation are as follows:

1. Simulation is relatively straightforward and flexible.
2. It can be used to analyze large and complex real-world situations that cannot be solved by conventional operations management models.
3. Real-world complications can be included that most OM models cannot permit. For example, simulation can use *any* probability distribution the user defines; it does not require standard distributions.
4. "Time compression" is possible. The effects of OM policies over many months or years can be obtained by computer simulation in a short time.

814   MODULE F   SIMULATION

The cost of simulating a frontal car crash at Ford was $60,000 in 1985. Today's computers can simulate the event for $200, and by 2001 it will cost only $10. Using Ford's new supercomputer, the simulation takes just 15 minutes.

5. Simulation allows "what-if" types of questions. Managers like to know in advance what options will be most attractive. With a computerized model, a manager can try out several policy decisions within a matter of minutes.
6. Simulations do not interfere with real-world systems. It may be too disruptive, for example, to experiment physically with new policies or ideas in a hospital or manufacturing plant.
7. Simulation can study the interactive effects of individual components or variables in order to determine which ones are important.

The main *disadvantages* of simulation are as follows:

1. Good simulation models can be very expensive; they may take many months to develop.
2. It is a trial-and-error approach that may produce different solutions in repeated runs. It does not generate optimal solutions to problems (as does linear programming).
3. Managers must generate all of the conditions and constraints for solutions that they want to examine. The simulation model does not produce answers without adequate, realistic input.
4. Each simulation model is unique. Its solutions and inferences are not usually transferable to other problems.

Can you think of a real-world business application in which a math model would be much better than playing with the actual operation of the firm?

Computer simulation models have been developed to address a variety of productivity issues at Burger King. In one, the ideal distance between the drive-through order station and the pickup window was simulated. For example, because a longer distance reduced waiting time, 12 to 13 additional customers could be served per hour—a benefit of over $10,000 in extra sales per restaurant per year. In another simulation, a second drive-through window was considered. This model predicted a sales increase of 15%, $13,000 per year per restaurant.

WHAT IS SIMULATION?

Simulation is the attempt to duplicate the features, appearance, and characteristics of a real system. In this module, we will show how to simulate part of an operations management system by building a mathematical model that comes as close as possible to representing the reality of the system. The model will then be used to estimate the effects of various actions. The idea behind simulation is threefold:

1. To imitate a real-world situation mathematically,
2. Then to study its properties and operating characteristics, and
3. Finally to draw conclusions and make action decisions based on the results of the simulation.

In this way, a real-life system need not be touched until the advantages and disadvantages of a major policy decision are first measured on the model.

To use simulation, an OM manager should:

1. Define the problem;
2. Introduce the important variables associated with the problem;
3. Construct a numerical model;
4. Set up possible courses of action for testing;
5. Run the experiment;
6. Consider the results (possibly modifying the model or changing data inputs);
7. Decide what course of action to take.

These steps are illustrated in Figure F.1.

The problems tackled by simulation may range from very simple to extremely complex, from bank teller lines to an analysis of the U.S. economy. Although small simulations can be conducted by hand, effective use of the technique requires a computer. Even large-scale models, simulating perhaps years of business decisions, are handled by computer.

In this module, we examine the basic principles of simulation and then tackle some problems in the areas of waiting-line analysis and inventory control. Why do we use simulation in these areas when mathematical models described in other chapters can solve similar problems? The answer is that simulation provides an alternative approach for problems that are very complex mathematically. It can handle, for example, inventory problems in which demand or lead time is not constant.

Simulation The attempt to duplicate the features, appearance, and characteristics of a real system, usually via a computerized model.

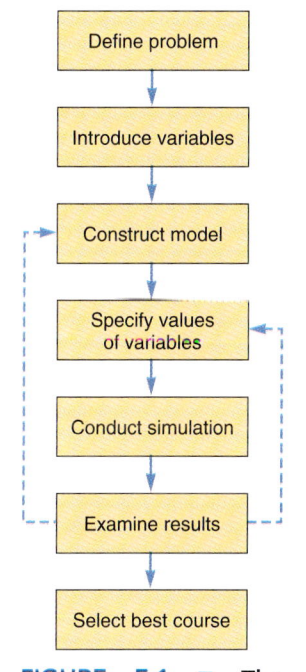

FIGURE F.1 ■ The Process of Simulation

ADVANTAGES AND DISADVANTAGES OF SIMULATION

Simulation is a tool that has become widely accepted by managers for several reasons. The main *advantages* of simulation are as follows:

1. Simulation is relatively straightforward and flexible.
2. It can be used to analyze large and complex real-world situations that cannot be solved by conventional operations management models.
3. Real-world complications can be included that most OM models cannot permit. For example, simulation can use *any* probability distribution the user defines; it does not require standard distributions.
4. "Time compression" is possible. The effects of OM policies over many months or years can be obtained by computer simulation in a short time.

> The cost of simulating a frontal car crash at Ford was $60,000 in 1985. Today's computers can simulate the event for $200, and by 2001 it will cost only $10. Using Ford's new supercomputer, the simulation takes just 15 minutes.

5. Simulation allows "what-if" types of questions. Managers like to know in advance what options will be most attractive. With a computerized model, a manager can try out several policy decisions within a matter of minutes.
6. Simulations do not interfere with real-world systems. It may be too disruptive, for example, to experiment physically with new policies or ideas in a hospital or manufacturing plant.
7. Simulation can study the interactive effects of individual components or variables in order to determine which ones are important.

The main *disadvantages* of simulation are as follows:

1. Good simulation models can be very expensive; they may take many months to develop.
2. It is a trial-and-error approach that may produce different solutions in repeated runs. It does not generate optimal solutions to problems (as does linear programming).
3. Managers must generate all of the conditions and constraints for solutions that they want to examine. The simulation model does not produce answers without adequate, realistic input.
4. Each simulation model is unique. Its solutions and inferences are not usually transferable to other problems.

> Can you think of a real-world business application in which a math model would be much better than playing with the actual operation of the firm?

Computer simulation models have been developed to address a variety of productivity issues at Burger King. In one, the ideal distance between the drive-through order station and the pickup window was simulated. For example, because a longer distance reduced waiting time, 12 to 13 additional customers could be served per hour—a benefit of over $10,000 in extra sales per restaurant per year. In another simulation, a second drive-through window was considered. This model predicted a sales increase of 15%, $13,000 per year per restaurant.

MONTE CARLO SIMULATION

When a system contains elements that exhibit *chance* in their behavior, the **Monte Carlo method** of simulation may be applied. The basis of Monte Carlo simulation is experimentation on chance (or *probabilistic*) elements by means of random sampling.

The technique breaks down into five simple steps:

1. Setting up a probability distribution for important variables.
2. Building a cumulative probability distribution for each variable.
3. Establishing an interval of random numbers for each variable.
4. Generating random numbers.
5. Actually simulating a series of trials.

> **Monte Carlo method** A simulation technique that uses random elements when chance exists in their behavior.

Let's examine these steps in turn.

Step 1. Establishing Probability Distributions. The basic idea in the Monte Carlo simulation is to generate values for the variables making up the model under study. In real-world systems, a lot of variables are probabilistic in nature. To name just a few: inventory demand; lead time for orders to arrive; times between machine breakdowns; times between customer arrivals at a service facility; service times; times required to complete project activities; and number of employees absent from work each day.

One common way to establish a *probability distribution* for a given variable is to examine historical outcomes. We can find the probability, or relative frequency, for each possible outcome of a variable by dividing the frequency of observation by the total number of observations. Here's an example.

The daily demand for radial tires at Barry's Auto Tire over the past 200 days is shown in columns 1 and 2 of Table F.2. Assuming that past arrival rates will hold in the future, we can convert this demand to a probability distribution by dividing each demand frequency by the total demand, 200. The results are shown in column 3.

> To establish a probability distribution for tires, we assume that historical demand is a good indicator of future outcomes.

TABLE F.2 ■ Demand for Barry's Auto Tire

(1) Demand for Tires	(2) Frequency	(3) Probability of Occurrence	(4) Cumulative Probability
0	10	10/200 = .05	.05
1	20	20/200 = .10	.15
2	40	40/200 = .20	.35
3	60	60/200 = .30	.65
4	40	40/200 = .20	.85
5	30	30/200 = .15	1.00
	200 days	200/200 = 1.00	

Step 2. Building a Cumulative Probability Distribution for Each Variable. The conversion from a regular probability distribution, such as in column 3 of Table F.2, to a **cumulative probability distribution** is an easy job. In column 4, we see that the cumulative probability for each level of demand is the sum of the number in the probability column (column 3) added to the previous cumulative probability.

Step 3. Setting Random-Number Intervals. Once we have established a cumulative probability distribution for each variable in the simulation, we must assign a set of numbers to represent each possible value or outcome. These are referred to as **random-number intervals.** Basically, a **random number** is a series of digits (say, two digits from 01, 02, ..., 98, 99, 00) that have been selected by a totally random process—a process where each random number has an equal chance of being selected.

> **Cumulative probability distribution** The accumulation of individual probabilities of a distribution.
>
> **Random-number intervals** A set of numbers to represent each possible value or outcome in a computer simulation.
>
> **Random number** A series of digits that have been selected by a totally random process; all digits have an equal chance of occurring.

You may start random number intervals at either 01 or 00, but the text starts at 01 so that the top of each range is the cumulative probability.

If, for example, there is a 5% chance that demand for Barry's radial tires will be 0 units per day, then we will want 5% of the random numbers available to correspond to a demand of 0 units. If a total of 100 two-digit numbers is used in the simulation, we could assign a demand of 0 units to the first 5 random numbers: 01, 02, 03, 04, and 05.[1] Then a simulated demand for 0 units would be created every time one of the numbers 01 to 05 was drawn. If there is also a 10% chance that demand for the same product will be 1 unit per day, we could let the next 10 random numbers (06, 07, 08, 09, 10, 11, 12, 13, 14, and 15) represent that demand—and so on for other demand levels.

Similarly, we can see in Table F.3 that the length of each interval on the right corresponds to the probability of 1 of each of the possible daily demands. Thus, in assigning

Table F.3 ■ The Assignment of Random-Number Intervals for Barry's Auto Tire

Daily Demand	Probability	Cumulative Probability	Interval of Random Numbers
0	.05	.05	01 through 05
1	.10	.15	06 through 15
2	.20	.35	16 through 35
3	.30	.65	36 through 65
4	.20	.85	66 through 85
5	.15	1.00	86 through 00

TABLE F.4 ■ Table of Random Numbers

52	06	50	88	53	30	10	47	99	37	66	91	35	32	00	84	57	07
37	63	28	02	74	35	24	03	29	60	74	85	90	73	59	55	17	60
82	57	68	28	05	94	03	11	27	79	90	87	92	41	09	25	36	77
69	02	36	49	71	99	32	10	75	21	95	90	94	38	97	71	72	49
98	94	90	36	06	78	23	67	89	85	29	21	25	73	69	34	85	76
96	52	62	87	49	56	59	23	78	71	72	90	57	01	98	57	31	95
33	69	27	21	11	60	95	89	68	48	17	89	34	09	93	50	44	51
50	33	50	95	13	44	34	62	64	39	55	29	30	64	49	44	30	16
88	32	18	50	62	57	34	56	62	31	15	40	90	34	51	95	26	14
90	30	36	24	69	82	51	74	30	35	36	85	01	55	92	64	09	85
50	48	61	18	85	23	08	54	17	12	80	69	24	84	92	16	49	59
27	88	21	62	69	64	48	31	12	73	02	68	00	16	16	46	13	85
45	14	46	32	13	49	66	62	74	41	86	98	92	98	84	54	33	40
81	02	01	78	82	74	97	37	45	31	94	99	42	49	27	64	89	42
66	83	14	74	27	76	03	33	11	97	59	81	72	00	64	61	13	52
74	05	81	82	93	09	96	33	52	78	13	06	28	30	94	23	37	39
30	34	87	01	74	11	46	82	59	94	25	34	32	23	17	01	58	73
59	55	72	33	62	13	74	68	22	44	42	09	32	46	71	79	45	89
67	09	80	98	99	25	77	50	03	32	36	63	65	75	94	19	95	88
60	77	46	63	71	69	44	22	03	85	14	48	69	13	30	50	33	24
60	08	19	29	36	72	30	27	50	64	85	72	75	29	87	05	75	01
80	45	86	99	02	34	87	08	86	84	49	76	24	08	01	86	29	11
53	84	49	63	26	65	72	84	85	63	26	02	75	26	92	62	40	67
69	84	12	94	51	36	17	02	15	29	16	52	56	43	26	22	08	62
37	77	13	10	02	18	31	19	32	85	31	94	81	43	31	58	33	51

Source: Reprinted from *A Million Random Digits with 100,000 Normal Deviates,* Rand (New York: The Free Press, 1995). Used by permission.

[1] Alternatively, we could have assigned the random numbers 00, 01, 02, 03, and 04 to represent a demand of 0 units. The two digits 00 can be thought of as either 0 or 100. As long as 5 numbers out of 100 are assigned to the 0 demand, it does not make any difference which 5 they are.

random numbers to the daily demand for 3 radial tires, the range of the random-number interval (36 through 65) corresponds *exactly* to the probability (or proportion) of that outcome. A daily demand for 3 radial tires occurs 30% of the time. All of the 30 random numbers greater than 35 up to and including 65 are assigned to that event.

Step 4. Generating Random Numbers. Random numbers may be generated for simulation problems in two ways. If the problem is large and the process under study involves many simulation trials, computer programs are available to generate the needed random numbers. If the simulation is being done by hand, the numbers may be selected from a table of random digits.

Step 5. Simulating the Experiment. We may simulate outcomes of an experiment by simply selecting random numbers from Table F.4. Beginning anywhere in the table, we note the interval in Table F.3 into which each number falls. For example, if the random number chosen is 81 and the interval 66 through 85 represents a daily demand for 4 tires, then we select a demand of 4 tires. Example F1 carries the simulation further.

EXAMPLE F1

Let's illustrate the concept of random numbers by simulating 10 days of demand for radial tires at Barry's Auto Tire (see Table F.3). We select the random numbers needed from Table F.4, starting in the upper left-hand corner and continuing down the first column:

Day Number	Random Number	Simulated Daily Demand
1	52	3
2	37	3
3	82	4
4	69	4
5	98	5
6	96	5
7	33	2
8	50	3
9	88	5
10	90	5
		39 Total 10-day demand

39/10 = 3.9 = Tires average daily demand

It is interesting to note that the average demand of 3.9 tires in this 10-day simulation differs significantly from the *expected* daily demand, which we may calculate from the data in Table F.3:

$$\text{Expected demand} = \sum_{i=1}^{5} (\text{probability of } i \text{ units}) \times (\text{demand of } i \text{ units})$$

$$= (.05)(0) + (.10)(1) + (.20)(2) + (.30)(3) + (.20)(4) + (.15)(5)$$

$$= 0 + .1 + .4 + .9 + .8 + .75$$

$$= 2.95 \text{ tires}$$

However, if this simulation were repeated hundreds or thousands of times, the average *simulated* demand would be nearly the same as the *expected* demand.

Naturally, it would be risky to draw any hard and fast conclusions about the operation of a firm from only a short simulation like this one. It is also unlikely that anyone would actually want to go to the effort of simulating such a simple model containing only one vari-

> ## OM IN ACTION
>
> ### USING SIMULATION AT MEXICO'S LARGEST TRUCK MANUFACTURER
>
> The manufacturing world has gone global. To remain competitive, many firms have made strategic and cultural alliances with international partners. Mexico is the United States' third-largest trading partner ($27 billion), after Canada and Japan. Trading breakthroughs, such as the North American Economic Community (NAEC), have fundamental implications for industries in the United States and Mexico, including the truck manufacturer Vilpac, which is headquartered in Mexicali, Mexico.
>
> Vilpac developed a comprehensive simulation model for the analysis and design of its manufacturing operation using SIMNET II (a network-based simulation language on an IBM 3090 supercomputer). The idea was to allow manufacturing engineers to experiment with alternative systems and strategies to seek the best overall factory performance.
>
> Ninety-five machines and 1,900 parts were included in the model, which performed a wide variety of experiments. SIMNET II was used to study the effects of policies on (1) the flexibility of the factory to adapt to change in demand and product mix, (2) the factory's responsiveness to customer orders, (3) product quality, and (4) total cost. Benefits of the simulation approach included a 260% increase in production, a 70% decrease in work-in-process, and an increase in market share.
>
> *Source:* J. P. Nuno et al., "Mexico's Vilpac Truck Company Uses a CIM Implementation to Become a World Class Manufacturer," *Interfaces* 23, 1 (January–February 1993): 59–75.

able. Simulating by hand does, however, demonstrate the important principles involved and may be useful in small-scale studies.

SIMULATION OF A QUEUING PROBLEM

Barge arrivals and unloading rates are both probabilistic variables. Unless they follow the queuing probability distributions of module D, we must turn to a simulation approach.

An important use of simulation is in the analysis of waiting-line problems. As we saw in module D, the assumptions required for solving queuing problems are quite restrictive. For most realistic queuing systems, simulation may be the only approach available.

Example F2 illustrates the use of simulation for a large unloading dock and its associated queue. Arrivals of barges at the dock are not Poisson-distributed, and unloading rates (service times) are not exponential or constant. As such, the mathematical waiting-line models of quantitative module D cannot be used.

EXAMPLE F2

Following long trips down the Mississippi River from industrial midwestern cities, fully loaded barges arrive at night in New Orleans. The number of barges docking on any given night ranges from 0 to 5. The probability of 0, 1, 2, 3, 4, and 5 arrivals is displayed in Table F.5. In the same table, we establish cumulative probabilities and corresponding random-number intervals for each possible value.

TABLE F.5 ■ Overnight Barge Arrival Rates and Random-Number Intervals

Number of Arrivals	Probability	Cumulative Probability	Random-Number Interval
0	.13	.13	01 through 13
1	.17	.30	14 through 30
2	.15	.45	31 through 45
3	.25	.70	46 through 70
4	.20	.90	71 through 90
5	.10	1.00	91 through 00
	1.00		

A study by the dock superintendent reveals that the number of barges unloaded also tends to vary from day to day. In Table F.6, the superintendent provides information from which we can create a probability distribution for the variable *daily unloading rate*. As we just did for the arrival variable, we can set up an interval of random numbers for the unloading rates.

TABLE F.6 ■ Unloading Rates and Random-Number Intervals

Daily Unloading Rates	Probability	Cumulative Probability	Random-Number Interval
1	.05	.05	01 through 05
2	.15	.20	06 through 20
3	.50	.70	21 through 70
4	.20	.90	71 through 90
5	.10	1.00	91 through 00
	1.00		

The relation between intervals and cumulative probability is that the top end of each interval is equal to the cumulative probability percentage.

Barges are unloaded on a first-in, first-out basis. Any barges not unloaded on the day of arrival must wait until the following day. However, tying up barges in dock is an expensive proposition, and the superintendent cannot ignore the angry phone calls from barge owners reminding him that "time is money!" He decides that, before going to the Port of New Orleans controller to request additional unloading crews, he should conduct a simulation study of arrivals, unloadings, and delays. A 100-day simulation would be ideal, but for purposes of illustration, the superintendent begins with a shorter 15-day analysis. Random numbers are drawn from the top row of Table F.4 to generate daily arrival rates. To create daily unloading rates, they are drawn from the second row of Table F.4. Table F.7 shows the day-to-day port simulation.

TABLE F.7 ■ Queuing Simulation of Port of New Orleans Barge Unloadings

(1) Day	(2) Number Delayed from Previous Day	(3) Random Number	(4) Number of Nightly Arrivals	(5) Total to Be Unloaded	(6) Random Number	(7) Number Unloaded
1	—[1]	52	3	3	37	3
2	0	06	0	0	63	0[2]
3	0	50	3	3	28	3
4	0	88	4	4	02	1
5	3	53	3	6	74	4
6	2	30	1	3	35	3
7	0	10	0	0	24	0[3]
8	0	47	3	3	03	1
9	2	99	5	7	29	3
10	4	37	2	6	60	3
11	3	66	3	6	74	4
12	2	91	5	7	85	4
13	3	35	2	5	90	4
14	1	32	2	3	73	3[4]
15	20	00	25	5	59	23
	20 Total delays		41 Total arrivals			39 Total unloadings

[1] We can begin with no delays from the previous day. In a long simulation, even if we started with five overnight delays, that initial condition would be averaged out.
[2] Three barges could have been unloaded on day 2. Yet because there were no arrivals and no backlog existed, zero unloadings took place.
[3] The same situation as noted in footnote 2 takes place.
[4] This time, 4 barges could have been unloaded, but because only 3 were in queue, the number unloaded is recorded as 3.

> The superintendent will likely be interested in at least three useful and important pieces of information:
>
> $$\begin{pmatrix} \text{Average number of barges} \\ \text{delayed to the next day} \end{pmatrix} = \frac{20 \text{ delays}}{15 \text{ days}}$$
>
> $$= 1.33 \text{ barges delayed per day}$$
>
> $$\text{Average number of nightly arrivals} = \frac{41 \text{ arrivals}}{15 \text{ days}}$$
>
> $$= 2.73 \text{ arrivals per night}$$
>
> $$\text{Average number of barges unloaded each day} = \frac{39 \text{ unloadings}}{15 \text{ days}}$$
>
> $$= 2.60 \text{ unloadings per day}$$

When the data from Example F2 are analyzed in terms of delay costs, idle labor costs, and the cost of hiring extra unloading crew, the dock superintendent and port controller can make a better staffing decision. They may even choose to resimulate the process assuming different unloading rates that would correspond to increased crew sizes. Although simulation cannot guarantee an optimal solution to problems such as this, it can be helpful in recreating a process and identifying good decision alternatives.

SIMULATION AND INVENTORY ANALYSIS

In chapter 12, we introduced inventory models. The commonly used EOQ models are based on the assumption that both product demand and reorder lead time are known, constant values. In most real-world inventory situations, though, demand and lead time are variables, so accurate analysis becomes extremely difficult to handle by any means other than simulation.

In this section, we present an inventory problem with two decision variables and two probabilistic components. The owner of the hardware store in Example F3 would like to establish *order quantity* and *reorder point* decisions for a particular product that has probabilistic (uncertain) daily demand and reorder lead time. He wants to make a series of simulation runs, trying out various order quantities and reorder points, in order to minimize his total inventory cost for the item. Inventory costs in this case will include ordering, holding, and stockout costs.

> ### EXAMPLE F3
>
> Simkin's Hardware sells the Ace model electric drill. Daily demand for the drill is relatively low but subject to some variability. Over the past 300 days, Simkin has observed the sales shown in column 2 of Table F.8. He converts this historical frequency into a probability distribution for the variable daily demand (column 3). A cumulative probability distribution is formed in column 4 of Table F.8. Finally, Simkin establishes an interval of random numbers to represent each possible daily demand (column 5).

TABLE F.8 ■ Probabilities and Random-Number Intervals for Daily Ace Drill Demand

(1) Demand for Ace Drill	(2) Frequency	(3) Probability	(4) Cumulative Probability	(5) Interval of Random Numbers
0	15	.05	.05	01 through 05
1	30	.10	.15	06 through 15
2	60	.20	.35	16 through 35
3	120	.40	.75	36 through 75
4	45	.15	.90	76 through 90
5	30	.10	1.00	91 through 00
	300 days	1.00		

When Simkin places an order to replenish his inventory of drills, there is a delivery lag of from 1 to 3 days. This means that lead time may also be considered a probabilistic variable. The number of days that it took to receive the past 50 orders is presented in Table F.9. In a fashion similar to the creation of the demand variable, Simkin establishes a probability distribution for the lead time variable (column 3 of Table F.9), computes the cumulative distribution (column 4), and assigns random-number intervals for each possible time (column 5).

TABLE F.9 ■ Probabilities and Random-Number Intervals for Reorder Lead Time

(1) Lead Time (days)	(2) Frequency	(3) Probability	(4) Cumulative Probability	(5) Random-Number Interval
1	10	.20	.20	01 through 20
2	25	.50	.70	21 through 70
3	15	.30	1.00	71 through 00
	50 orders	1.00		

The first inventory policy that Simkin wants to simulate is an order quantity of 10 with a reorder point of 5. That is, every time the on-hand inventory level at the end of the day is 5 or less, Simkin will call his supplier that evening and place an order for 10 more drills. Note that if the lead time is 1 day, the order will not arrive the next morning, but rather at the beginning of the following workday.

The entire process is simulated in Table F.10 on page 822 for a 10-day period. We assume that beginning inventory (column 3) is 10 units on day 1. We took the random numbers (column 4) from column 2 of Table F.4.

Table F.10 was filled in by proceeding 1 day (or line) at a time, working from left to right. It is a four-step process:

1. Begin each simulated day by checking to see whether any ordered inventory has just arrived. If it has, increase current inventory by the quantity ordered (10 units, in this case).
2. Generate a daily demand from the demand probability distribution by selecting a random number.
3. Compute ending inventory = beginning inventory minus demand. If on-hand inventory is insufficient to meet the day's demand, satisfy as much as possible and note the number of lost sales.
4. Determine whether the day's ending inventory has reached the reorder point (5 units). If it has, and if there are no outstanding orders, place an order. Lead time for a new order is simulated by choosing a random number and using the distribution in Table F.9.

Simkin's first inventory simulation yields some interesting results. The average daily ending inventory is:

$$\text{Average ending inventory} = \frac{41 \text{ total units}}{10 \text{ days}} = 4.1 \text{ units/day}$$

We also note the average lost sales and number of orders placed per day:

$$\text{Average lost sales} = \frac{2 \text{ sales lost}}{10 \text{ days}} = .2 \text{ unit/day}$$

$$\text{Average number of orders placed} = \frac{3 \text{ orders}}{10 \text{ days}} = .3 \text{ order/day}$$

TABLE F.10 ■ Simkin Hardware's First Inventory Simulation. Order quantity = 10 units; reorder point = 5 units

(1) Day	(2) Units Received	(3) Beginning Inventory	(4) Random Number	(5) Demand	(6) Ending Inventory	(7) Lost Sales	(8) Order?	(9) Random Number	(10) Lead Time
1		10	06	1	9	0	No		
2	0	9	63	3	6	0	No		
3	0	6	57	3	⑤[1]	0	Yes	⑫[2]	1
4	0	3	⑨④[3]	5	0	2	Ⓝⓞ[4]		
5	⑩[5]	10	52	3	7	0	No		
6	0	7	69	3	4	0	Yes	33	2
7	0	4	32	2	2	0	No		
8	0	2	30	2	0	0	No		
9	⑩[6]	10	48	3	7	0	No		
10	0	7	88	4	3	0	Yes	14	
				Totals:	41	2			

[1] This is the first time inventory dropped to the reorder point of 5 drills. Because no prior order was outstanding, an order is placed.

[2] The random number 02 is generated to represent the first lead time. It was drawn from column 2 of Table F.4 as the next number in the list being used. A separate column could have been used from which to draw lead-time random numbers if we had wanted to do so, but in this example, we did not do so.

[3] Again, notice that the random digits 02 were used for lead time (see footnote 2). So the next number in the column is 94.

[4] No order is placed on day 4 because there is an order outstanding from the previous day that has not yet arrived.

[5] The lead time for the first order placed is 1 day, but as noted in the text, an order does not arrive the next morning, but rather the beginning of the following day. Thus, the first order arrives at the start of day 5.

[6] This is the arrival of the order placed at the close of business on day 6. Fortunately for Simkin, no lost sales occurred during the 2-day lead time before the order arrived.

Example F4 shows how these data can be useful in studying the inventory costs of the policy being simulated.

EXAMPLE F4

Simkin estimates that the cost of placing each order for Ace drills is $10, the holding cost per drill held at the end of each day is $.50, and the cost of each lost sale is $8. This information enables us to compute the total daily inventory cost for the simulated policy in Example F3. Let's examine the 3 cost components:

> Daily order cost = (cost of placing one order)
> 　　　　　　　　× (number of orders placed per day)
> 　　　　　　　　= $10 per order × .3 order per day = $3
>
> Daily holding cost = (cost of holding one unit for 1 day)
> 　　　　　　　　× (average ending inventory)
> 　　　　　　　　= 50¢ per unit per day × 4.1 units per day = $2.05
>
> Daily stockout cost = (cost per lost sale)
> 　　　　　　　　× (average number of lost sales per day)
> 　　　　　　　　= $8 per lost sale × .2 lost sales per day = $1.60
>
> Total daily inventory cost = Daily order cost + Daily holding cost
> 　　　　　　　　+ Daily stockout cost = $6.65

Now that we have worked through Example F3, we want to emphasize something very important: This simulation should be extended many more days before we draw any conclusions as to the cost of the order policy being tested. If a hand simulation is being conducted, 100 days would provide a better representation. If a computer is doing the calculations, 1,000 days would be helpful in reaching accurate cost estimates. (Moreover, remember that even with a 1,000-day simulation, the generated distribution should be compared with the desired distribution to ensure valid results.)

Let us say that Simkin *does* complete a 1,000-day simulation of the policy from Example F3 (order quantity = 10 drills, reorder point = 5 drills). Does this complete his analysis? The answer is no—this is just the beginning! Simkin must now compare *this* potential strategy to other possibilities. For example, what about order quantity = 10, reorder point = 4? Or order quantity = 12, reorder point = 6? Or order quantity = 14, reorder point = 5? Perhaps every combination of values—of order quantity from 6 to 20 drills and reorder points from 3 to 10—should be simulated. After simulating all reasonable combinations of order quantities and reorder points, Simkin would likely select the pair yielding the lowest total inventory cost. Problem F.12 gives you a chance to help Simkin begin this series of comparisons.

THE ROLE OF COMPUTERS IN SIMULATION

Computers are critical in simulating complex tasks. They can generate random numbers, simulate thousands of time periods in a matter of seconds or minutes, and provide management with reports that make decision making easier. A computer approach is almost a necessity in order to draw valid conclusions from a simulation.

Computer programming languages can help the simulation process. *General-purpose languages*, such as BASIC, C++, or PASCAL, constitute one approach. *Special purpose simulation languages*, such as GPSS, SIMSCRIPT, and DYNAMO, have a few advantages: (1) they require less programming time for large simulations, (2) they are usually more efficient and easier to check for errors, and (3) random-number generators are already built in as subroutines.

Commercial, easy-to-use prewritten simulation programs are also available. Some are generalized to handle a wide variety of situations ranging from queuing to inventory.

The explosion of personal computers has created a wealth of computer simulation languages and broadened the use of simulation. Now, even spreadsheet software can be used to conduct fairly complex simulations.

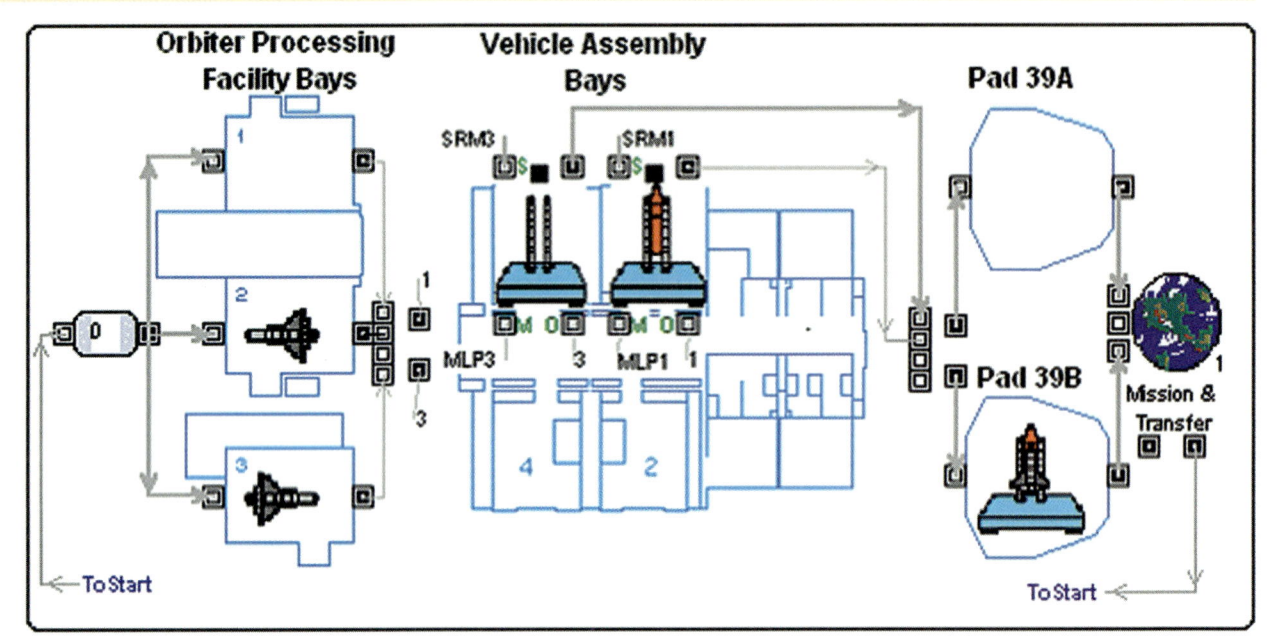

Simulation software is an excellent tool for examining both large and small processes in a wide variety of applications. Here, Extend+Manufacturing is used to simulate refurbishment, assembly, and launch of the Orbiters over ten years. A limited version of this software is supplied on the CD-ROM included with this text.

These include programs such as Extend, Witness, MAP/1, Slam II, Simfactory, Arena, Micro Saint, and Taylor II. A student version of Extend is included on the CD-ROM that accompanies this text.

Spreadsheet software such as Excel can also be used to develop simulations quickly and easily. Such packages have built-in random-number generators and develop outputs through "data-fill" table commands.

SUMMARY

Simulation involves building mathematical models that attempt to act like real operating systems. In this way, a real-world situation can be studied without imposing on the actual system. Although simulation models can be developed manually, simulation by computer is generally more desirable. The Monte Carlo approach uses random numbers to represent variables, such as inventory demand or people waiting in line, which are then simulated in a series of trials. Simulation is widely used as an operations tool because its advantages usually outweigh its disadvantages.

KEY TERMS

Simulation *(p. 813)*
Monte Carlo method *(p. 815)*
Cumulative probability distribution *(p. 815)*
Random-number intervals *(p. 815)*
Random number *(p. 815)*

USING POM FOR WINDOWS FOR SIMULATION

Program F.1 is a Monte Carlo simulation using our accompanying software, POM for Windows. It conducts the same analysis we saw in Example F1, Barry's Auto Tires. Program F.1 reveals that after 250 runs, the average daily demand is 2.824 tires. If even more repetitions occurred, we would come even closer to the expected value of 2.95 tires computed in Example F1.

Category name	Value	Frequency	Probability	Cumulative Probability	Value * Frequency	Occurrence	Percentage	Occurrence * Value
Category 1	0.	0.06	0.05	0.05	0.	18.	0.072	0.
Category 2	1.	0.1	0.1	0.15	0.1	20.	0.08	20.
Category 3	2.	0.2	0.2	0.35	0.4	62.	0.248	124.
Category 4	3.	0.3	0.3	0.65	0.9	72.	0.288	216.
Category 5	4.	0.2	0.2	0.85	0.8	44.	0.176	176.
Category 6	5.	0.15	0.15	1.	0.75	34.	0.136	170.
Total		1.	1.	Expected	2.95	250.	1.	706.
							Average	2.824

PROGRAM F.1 ■ **Pom for Windows Monte Carlo Computer Simulation of Barry's Auto Tire, Example F1**

SIMULATION WITH EXCEL SPREADSHEETS

The ability to generate random numbers and then "look up" these numbers in a table in order to associate them with a specific event makes spreadsheets excellent tools for conducting simulations. Excel OM does not have a simulation module, because we are able to model all simulation problems directly in Excel. Program F.2 on page 826 illustrates an Excel simulation for Example F1.

Notice that the cumulative probabilities are calculated in column D of Program F.2. This procedure reduces the chance of error and is useful in larger simulations involving more levels of demand.

The =VLOOKUP function in column I looks up the random number (generated in column H) in the leftmost column of the defined lookup table ($C$3:$E$8). It moves downward through this column until it finds a cell that is bigger than the random number. It then goes to the previous row and gets the value from column E of the table.

826 MODULE F SIMULATION

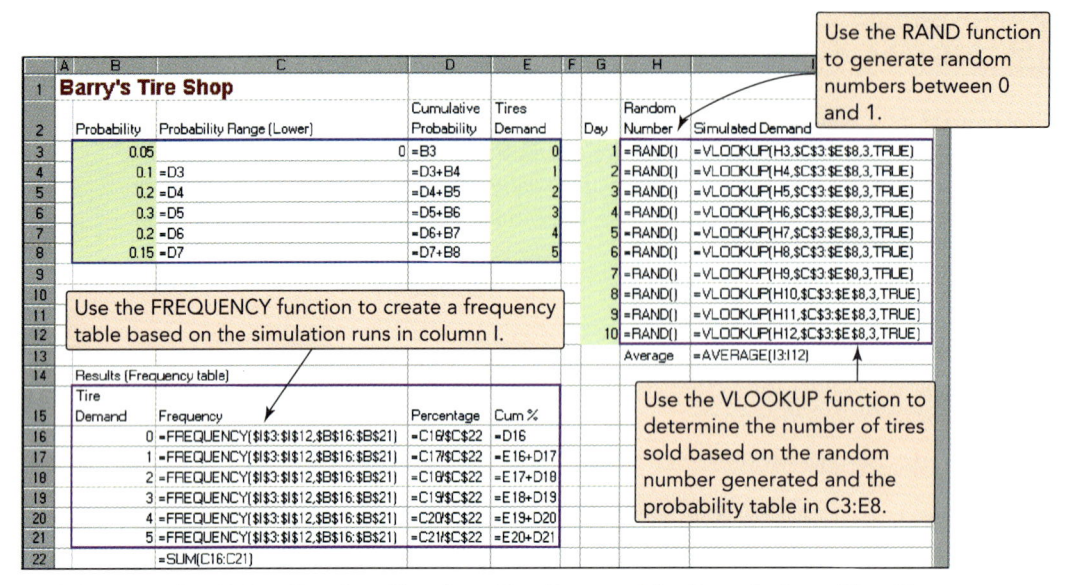

PROGRAM F.2 ■ **Using Excel to Simulate Tire Demand for Barry's Auto Tire Shop**

In the output screen of Program F.3, for example, the first random number shown is .300. Excel looked down the left-hand column of the lookup table ($C$3:$E$8) of Program F.2 until it found .35. From the previous row it retrieved the value in column E which is 2. Pressing the F9 function key recalculates the random numbers and the simulation.

PROGRAM F.3 ■ **Excel Simulation Results for Barry's Auto Tire Shop** *The spreadsheet output in Program F.3 shows a simulated average of 3.0 tires per day.*

SOLVED PROBLEMS

Solved Problem F.1

Higgins Plumbing and Heating maintains a stock of 30-gallon hot-water heaters that it sells to homeowners and installs for them. Owner Jerry Higgins likes the idea of having a large supply on hand to meet any customer demand. However, he also recognizes that it is expensive to do so. He examines hot-water heater sales over the past 50 weeks and notes the following:

Hot-Water Heater Sales per Week	Number of Weeks This Number Was Sold
4	6
5	5
6	9
7	12
8	8
9	7
10	3
	50 weeks total data

a) If Higgins maintains a constant supply of 8 hot-water heaters in any given week, how many times will he stock out during a 20-week simulation? We use random numbers from the seventh column of Table F.4, beginning with the random digit 10.

b) What is the average number of sales per week over the 20-week period?

c) Using an analytic nonsimulation technique, what is the expected number of sales per week? How does this compare to the answer in part (b)?

Solution

Heater Sales	Probability	Random-Number Intervals
4	.12	01 through 12
5	.10	13 through 22
6	.18	23 through 40
7	.24	41 through 64
8	.16	65 through 80
9	.14	81 through 94
10	.06	95 through 100
	1.00	

a)

Week	Random Number	Simulated Sales	Week	Random Number	Simulated Sales
1	10	4	11	08	4
2	24	6	12	48	7
3	03	4	13	66	8
4	32	6	14	97	10
5	23	6	15	03	4
6	59	7	16	96	10
7	95	10	17	46	7
8	34	6	18	74	8
9	34	6	19	77	8
10	51	7	20	44	7

With a supply of 8 heaters, Higgins will stock out 3 times during the 20-week period (in weeks 7, 14, and 16).

b) Average sales by simulation = total sales/20 weeks = 135/20
   = 6.75 per week

c) Using expected values,

$$E(\text{sales}) = .12(4 \text{ heaters}) + .10(5)$$

$$+ .18(6) + .24(7) + .16(8)$$

$$+ .14(9) + .06(10) = 6.88 \text{ heaters}$$

With a longer simulation, these two approaches will lead to even closer values.

Solved Problem F.2

Random numbers may be used to simulate continuous distributions. As a simple example, assume that fixed cost equals $300, profit contribution equals $10 per item sold, and you expect an equally likely chance of 0 to 99 units to be sold. That is, profit equals $-\$300 + \$10X$, where X is the number sold. The mean amount you expect to sell is 49.5 units.

a) Calculate the expected value.
b) Simulate the sale of 5 items, using the following double-digit random numbers:
   37 77 13 10 85
c) Calculate the expected value of part (b) and compare with the results of part (a).

Solution

a) Expected value = $-300 + 10(49.5) = \$195$
b) $-300 + \$10(37) = \$70$
   $-300 + \$10(77) = \$470$
   $-300 + \$10(13) = -\$170$
   $-300 + \$10(10) = -\$200$
   $-300 + \$10(85) = \$550$
c) The mean of these simulated sales is $144. If the sample size were larger, we would expect the two values to be closer.

DISCUSSION QUESTIONS

1. What are the advantages and limitations of simulation models?
2. Why might a manager be forced to use simulation instead of an analytical model in dealing with a problem of:
   a) inventory order policy?
   b) ships docking in a port to unload?
   c) bank teller service windows?
   d) the U.S. economy?
3. What types of management problems can be solved more easily by techniques other than simulation?
4. What are the major steps in the simulation process?
5. What is Monte Carlo simulation? What principles underlie its use, and what steps are followed in applying it?
6. In the simulation of an order policy for drills at Simkin's Hardware (Example F3), would the results (of Table F.10) change significantly if a longer pe-

PROBLEMS 829

riod were simulated? Why is the 10-day simulation valid or invalid?

7. Why is a computer necessary in conducting a real-world simulation?
8. Do you think the application of simulation will increase significantly in the next 10 years? Why?
9. Why would an analyst ever prefer a general-purpose language such as BASIC or PASCAL in a simulation when there are advantages to using a special-purpose language such as GPSS or SIM-SCRIPT?
10. What is the role of random numbers in a Monte Carlo simulation?
11. Why do the results of a simulation differ each time you make a run?
12. List six ways that simulation can be used in business.
13. Why is simulation such a widely used technique?

PROBLEMS

The problems that follow involve simulations that can be done by hand. However, to obtain accurate and meaningful results, long periods must be simulated. This task is usually handled by a computer. If you are able to program some of the problems in Excel or a computer language with which you are familiar, we suggest you try to do so. If not, the hand simulations will still help you understand the simulation process.

- **F.1** The daily demand for newspapers at a particular vending machine is either 20, 21, 22, or 23, with probabilities 0.4, 0.3, 0.2, or 0.1, respectively. Assume the following random numbers have been generated: 08, 54, 74, 66, 52, 58, 03, 22, 89, and 85. Using these numbers, generate daily newspaper sales for 10 days.

- **F.2** The number of machine breakdowns per day at Katie Park's factory is either 0, 1, or 2, with probabilities 0.5, 0.3, or 0.2, respectively. The following random numbers have been generated: 13, 14, 02, 18, 31, 19, 32, 85, 31, and 94. Use these numbers to generate the number of breakdowns for 10 consecutive days. What proportion of these days had at least 1 breakdown?

- **F.3** The number of cars arriving at Dave Cole's self-service gasoline station during the last 50 hours of operation are as follows:

Number of Cars Arriving	Frequency
6	10
7	12
8	20
9	8

The following random numbers have been generated: 44, 30, 26, 09, 49, 13, 33, 89, 13, and 37. Simulate 10 hours of arrivals. What is the average number of arrivals during this period?

- **F.4** Kate Moore sells papers at a newspaper stand for $.35. The papers cost her $.25, giving her a $.10 profit on each one she sells. From past experience Kate knows that
  - 20% of the time she sells 100 papers
  - 20% of the time she sells 150 papers
  - 30% of the time she sells 200 papers
  - 30% of the time she sells 250 papers

  Assuming that Kate believes the cost of a lost sale to be $.05 and any unsold papers cost her $.25, simulate her profit outlook over 5 days if she orders 200 papers for each of the 5 days. Use the following random numbers: 52, 06, 50, 88, and 53.

- **F.5** Refer to Problem F.4. Kate's new strategy is to order 175 papers for each of the 5 days. Use the same random numbers and simulate Kate's profits. What is the average daily profit?

: F.6 Marissa Feliberty's grocery store has noted the following figures with regard to the number of people who arrive at the store's three checkout stands and the time it takes to check them out:

Arrivals/min.	Frequency
0	.3
1	.5
2	.2

Service Time in Min.	Frequency
1	.1
2	.3
3	.4
4	.2

Simulate the utilization of the three checkout stands over 5 minutes, using the following random numbers: 07, 60, 77, 49, 76, 95, 51, and 16. Record the results at the end of the 5-minute period.

: F.7 Average daily sales of a product in Hector Fernandez's store are 8 units. The actual number of sales each day is either 7, 8, or 9, with probabilities 0.3, 0.4, or 0.3, respectively. The lead time for delivery averages 4 days, although the time may be 3, 4, or 5 days, with probabilities of .2, .6, and .2. Fernandez plans to place an order when the inventory level drops to 32 units (based on the average demand and average lead time). The following random numbers have been generated:

60, 87, 46, 63 (set 1)

52, 78, 13, 06, 99, 98, 80, 09, 67, 89, 45 (set 2)

Use set 1 to generate lead times and set 2 to simulate daily demand. Simulate 2 ordering periods and determine how often the company runs out of stock before an order arrives.

: F.8 The time between arrivals at the drive-through window of Mary Gallagher's fast-food restaurant follows the distribution given below. The service-time distribution is also given. Use the random numbers provided to simulate the activity of the first 5 arrivals. Assume that the window opens at 11:00 A.M. and that the first arrival occurs afterward, based on the first interarrival time generated.

Time between Arrivals	Probability	Service Time	Probability
1	.2	1	.3
2	.3	2	.5
3	.3	3	.2
4	.2		

Random numbers for arrivals: 14, 74, 27, 03
Random numbers for service times: 88, 32, 36, 24

At what time does the fourth customer leave the system?

: F.9 Ventra Property Management is responsible for the maintenance, rental, and day-to-day operation of a large apartment complex. Mark Ventra is especially concerned about the cost projections for replacing air conditioner compressors. He would like to simulate the number of compressor failures each year over the next 20 years. Using data from a similar apartment building that he also manages, Ventra establishes the following table of relative frequency of failures during a year:

Number of A.C. Compressor Failures	Probability (relative frequency)
0	.06
1	.13
2	.25
3	.28
4	.20
5	.07
6	.01

He decides to simulate the 20-year period by selecting 2-digit random numbers from column 3 of Table F.4 (starting with the random number 50). Conduct the simulation for Ventra. Is it common to have 3 or more consecutive years of operation with 2 or fewer compressor failures per year?

- **F.10** The number of cars arriving at Barry Harmon's Car Wash during the last 200 hours of operation is observed to be the following:

Number of Cars Arriving	Frequency
3 or less	0
4	20
5	30
6	50
7	60
8	40
9 or more	0
	200

  a) Set up a probability and cumulative-probability distribution for the variable of car arrivals.
  b) Establish random-number intervals for the variable.
  c) Simulate 15 hours of car arrivals and compute the average number of arrivals per hour. Select the random numbers needed from column 1, Table F.4, beginning with the digits 52.

- **F.11** Refer to Example F2 on page 818. An increase in the size of the barge-unloading crew at the Port of New Orleans has resulted in a new probability distribution for daily unloading rates. In particular, Table F.6 in that example may be revised as shown here:

Daily Unloading Rate	Probability
1	.03
2	.12
3	.40
4	.28
5	.12
6	.05

  a) Resimulate 15 days of barge unloading and compute the average number of barges delayed, average number of nightly arrivals, and average number of barges unloaded each day. Draw random numbers from the bottom row of Table F.4 to generate daily arrivals and from the second-from-the-bottom row to generate daily unloading rates.

b) How do these simulated results compare to those in the Example F2?

F.12 Simkin's Hardware simulated an inventory-ordering policy for Ace electric drills that involved an order quantity of 10 drills, with a reorder point of 5. This first attempt to develop a cost-effective ordering strategy was illustrated in Table F.10 of Example F3. The brief simulation resulted in a total daily inventory cost of $6.65.

Simkin would now like to compare this strategy to one in which he orders 12 drills, with a reorder point of 6. Conduct a 10-day simulation and discuss the cost implications.

F.13 Carol Pharo, a Ph.D. student at Northern Virginia University, has been having problems balancing her checkbook. Her monthly income is derived from a graduate research assistantship; in most months, however, she also makes extra money by tutoring undergraduates in a quantitative analysis course. In the following table, her chances of various income levels are shown on the left.

Pharo's expenditures also vary from month to month, and she estimates that they will follow the distribution on the right.

Monthly Income	Probability	Monthly Expenses	Probability
$350	.40	$300	.10
$400	.20	$400	.45
$450	.30	$500	.30
$500	.10	$600	.15

Assume that Pharo's income is received at the beginning of each month and that she begins her final year with $600 in her checking account. Simulate the entire year (12 months) and discuss Pharo's financial picture.

F.14 Refer to the data in Solved Problem F.1, on page 827, which deals with Higgins Plumbing and Heating. Higgins has now collected 100 weeks of data and finds the following distribution for sales:

Hot-Water Heater Sales per Week	Number of Weeks This Number Was Sold	Hot-Water Heater Sales per Week	Number of Weeks This Number Was Sold
3	2	8	12
4	9	9	12
5	10	10	10
6	15	11	5
7	25		100

a) Assuming Higgins maintains a constant supply of 8 heaters, resimulate the number of stockouts incurred over a 20-week period.

b) Conduct this 20-week simulation 2 more times and compare your answers with those in part (a). Did they change significantly? Why or why not?

c) What is the new expected number of sales per week?

F.15 Helms Aircraft Co. operates a large number of computerized plotting machines. The machines are highly reliable, with the exception of the 4 sophisticated built-in ink pens. The pens constantly clog and jam in a raised or lowered position. When this occurs, the plotter is unusable.

Currently, Helms replaces every pen as it fails. The service manager, however, has proposed replacing all 4 pens every time one fails. This practice, he contends, should cut down the frequency of plotter failures. At present, it takes 1 hour to replace 1 pen. All 4 pens could be replaced in 2 hours. The total cost of an unusable plotter is $50 per hour. Each pen costs $8.

If only one pen is replaced each time a clog or jam occurs, the following breakdown data are thought to be valid:

Hours between Plotter Failures if One Pen Is Replaced during a Repair	Probability
10	.05
20	.15
30	.15
40	.20
50	.20
60	.15
70	.10

Based on the service manager's estimates, if all 4 pens are replaced each time 1 pen fails, the probability distribution between failures is:

Hours between Plotter Failures if All Four Pens Are Replaced during a Repair	Probability
100	.15
110	.25
120	.35
130	.20
140	.05

a) Simulate Helms's problem and determine the best policy. Should the firm replace 1 pen or all 4 pens each time a failure occurs?

b) Develop a second approach to solving this problem (this time without simulation). Compare the results. How does it affect the policy decision that Helms reached using simulation?

F.16 Tia Thompson owns and operates one of the largest Mercedes-Benz auto dealerships in Washington, DC. In the past 36 months, her sales have ranged from a low of 6 new cars to a high of 12 new cars, as reflected in the following table:

Sales of New Cars/Month	Frequency
6	3
7	4
8	6
9	12
10	9
11	1
12	1
	36 months

Thompson believes that sales will continue during the next 24 months at about the same historical rates, and that delivery times will also continue to follow the following pace (stated in probability form):

Delivery Time (in months)	Probability
1	.44
2	.33
3	.16
4	.07
	1.00

Thompson's current policy is to order 14 cars at a time (2 full truckloads, with 7 autos on each truck), and to place a new order whenever the stock on hand reaches 12 autos. What are the results of this policy when simulated over the next 2 years?

- **F.17** Refer to Problem F.16. Tia Thompson establishes the following relevant costs: (1) carrying cost per Mercedes per month is $600; (2) cost of a lost sale averages $4,350; and (3) cost of placing an order is $570. What is the total inventory cost of the policy simulated in Problem F.16?

- **F.18** Refer to Problems F.16 and F.17. Thompson wishes to try a new simulated policy: ordering 21 cars per order, with a reorder point of 10 autos. Which policy is better, this one or the one formulated in Problems F.16 and F.17?

- **F.19** The Eichler Corp. is the nation's largest manufacturer of industrial-size washing machines. A main ingredient in the production process is 8-by-10-foot sheets of stainless steel. The steel is used for both interior washer drums and outer casings.

    Steel is purchased weekly on a contractual basis from the RTT Foundry, which, because of limited availability and lot sizing, can ship either 8,000 or 11,000 square feet of stainless steel each week. When Eichler's weekly order is placed, there is a 45% chance that 8,000 square feet will arrive and a 55% chance of receiving the larger-size order.

    Eichler uses the stainless steel on a stochastic (nonconstant) basis. The probabilities of demand each week are

Steel Needed per Week (sq. ft)	Probability
6,000	.05
7,000	.15
8,000	.20
9,000	.30
10,000	.20
11,000	.10

Eichler has a capacity to store no more than 25,000 square feet of steel at any time. Because of the contract, orders *must* be placed each week regardless of on-hand supply.

  a) Simulate stainless steel order arrivals and use for 20 weeks. (Begin the first week with a starting inventory of 0.) If an end-of-week inventory is ever negative, assume that "back orders" are permitted and fill the demand from the next arriving order.
  b) Should Eichler add more storage area? If so, how much? If not, comment on its present system.

- **F.20** General Hospital in Blacksburg, Virginia has an emergency room that is divided into six departments: (1) an initial exam station to treat minor problems or make diagnosis; (2) an X-ray department; (3) an operating room; (4) a cast-fitting room; (5) an observation room (for recovery and general observation before final diagnosis or release); and (6) an outprocessing department (where clerks check out patients and arrange for payment or insurance forms).

    The probabilities that a patient will go from one department to another are presented in the following table.

From	To	Probability
Initial exam at emergency room entrance	X-ray department	.45
	Operating room	.15
	Observation room	.10
	Outprocessing clerk	.30
X-ray department	Operating room	.10
	Cast-fitting room	.25
	Observation room	.35
	Outprocessing clerk	.30
Operating room	Cast-fitting room	.25
	Observation room	.70
	Outprocessing clerk	.05
Cast-fitting room	Observation room	.55
	X-ray department	.05
	Outprocessing clerk	.40
Observation room	Operating room	.15
	X-ray department	.15
	Outprocessing clerk	.70

a) Simulate the trail followed by 10 emergency room patients. Proceed, 1 patient at a time, from each one's entry at the initial exam station until he or she leaves through outprocessing. You should be aware that a patient can enter the same department more than once.

b) Using your simulation data, determine the chances that a patient enters the X-ray department twice.

F.21 Management of First Syracuse Bank is concerned over a loss of customers at its main office. One proposed solution calls for adding 1 or more drive-through teller stations so that customers can get quick service without parking. President Steve Shoff thinks the bank should risk only the cost of installing one drive-through. He is informed by his staff that the cost (amortized over a 20-year period) of building a drive-through is $12,000 per year. It also costs $16,000 per year in wages and benefits to staff each new teller window.

The director of Management Analysis, Jennifer Jaenicke, believes that the following 2 factors encourage the immediate construction of 2 drive-through stations. According to a recent article in *Banking Research* magazine, customers who wait in long lines for drive-through teller service will cost banks an average of $1 per minute in lost goodwill. Also, although adding a second drive-through will cost an additional $16,000 in staffing, amortized construction costs can be cut to a total of $20,000 per year if 2 drive-throughs are installed simultaneously, instead of 1 at a time. To complete her analysis, Jaenicke collected 1 month's worth of arrival and service rates at a competing bank. These data follow:

Interarrival Times for 1,000 Observations

Time between Arrivals (in minutes)	Number of Occurrences
1	200
2	250
3	300
4	150
5	100

| Customer Service Time for 1,000 Customers ||
Service Time (in minutes)	Number of Occurrences
1	100
2	150
3	350
4	150
5	150
6	100

a) Simulate a 1-hour time period, from 1 P.M. to 2 P.M., for a single-teller drive-through.
b) Simulate a 1-hour time period, from 1 P.M. to 2 P.M., for a 2-teller system.
c) Conduct a cost analysis of the 2 options. Assume that the bank is open 7 hours per day and 200 days per year.

■ Case Study ■

Alabama Airlines

Alabama Airlines opened it doors in June 1998 as a commuter service with its headquarters and only hub located in Birmingham. A product of airline deregulation, Alabama Air joined the growing number of successful short-haul, point-to-point airlines, including Lone Star, Comair, Atlantic Southeast, Skywest, and Business Express.

Alabama Air was started and managed by 2 former pilots, David Douglas (who had been with now defunct Eastern Airlines) and Michael Hanna (formerly with Pan Am). It acquired a fleet of 12 used prop-jet planes and the airport gates vacated by Delta Airlines' 1997 downsizing.

With business growing quickly, Douglas turned his attention to Alabama Air's "800" reservations system. Between midnight and 6:00 A.M., only 1 telephone reservations agent had been on duty. The time between incoming calls during this period is distributed as shown in Table 1. Carefully observing and timing the agent, Douglas estimated that the time required to process passenger inquiries is distributed as shown in Table 2.

All customers calling Alabama Air go "on hold" and are served in the order of the calls unless the reservations agent is available for immediate service. Douglas is deciding whether a second agent should be on duty to cope with customer demand. To maintain customer satisfaction, Alabama Air wants a customer to be "on hold" for no more than 3 to 4 minutes; it also wants to maintain a "high" operator utilization.

Furthermore, the airline is planning a new TV advertising campaign. As a result, it expects an increase in "800" line phone inquiries. Based on similar campaigns in the past, the incoming call distribution from

| TABLE 1 ■ Incoming Call Distribution ||
Time between Calls (in minutes)	Probability
1	.11
2	.21
3	.22
4	.20
5	.16
6	.10

| TABLE 2 ■ Service-Time Distribution ||
Time to Process Customer Enquiries (in minutes)	Probability
1	.20
2	.19
3	.18
4	.17
5	.13
6	.10
7	.03

midnight to 6 A.M. is expected to be as shown in Table 3. (The same service time distribution will apply).

TABLE 3 ■ Incoming Call Distribution

Time between Calls (in minutes)	Probability
1	.22
2	.25
3	.19
4	.15
5	.12
6	.07

Discussion Questions

1. Given the original call distribution, what would you advise Alabama Air to do for the current reservation system? Create a simulation model to investigate the scenario. Describe the model carefully and justify the duration of the simulation, assumptions, and measures of performance.
2. What are your recommendations regarding operator utilization and customer satisfaction if the airline proceeds with the advertising campaign?

Source: Professor Zbigniew H. Przasnyski, Loyola Marymount University. Reprinted by permission.

■ *Internet Case Study* ■

See our Internet home page at http://www.prenhall.com/heizer for these additional case studies: Abjar Transport and Bialis Waste Disposal.

BIBLIOGRAPHY

Abdou, G., and S. P. Dutta. "A Systematic Simulation Approach for the Design of JIT Manufacturing Systems." *Journal of Operations Management* 11, no. 3 (September 1993): 25–38.

Brennan, J. E., B. L. Golden, and H. K. Rappoport. "Go with the Flow: Improving Red Cross Bloodmobiles Using Simulation Analysis." *Interfaces* 22, no. 5 (September–October 1992): 1.

Evans, J. R. "A Little Knowledge Can Be Dangerous: Handle Simulation with Care." *Production and Inventory Management Journal* 33, no. 2 (second quarter 1992): 51.

Flowers, A. D., and J. R. Cole. "An Application of Computer Simulation to Quality Control in Manufacturing." *IIE Transactions* 17, no. 3 (September 1985): 277–283.

Hutchinson, J., G. K. Loong, and P. T. Ward. "Improving Delivery Performance in Gear Manufacturing at Jeffrey Division of Dresser Industries." *Interfaces* 23, no. 2 (March–April 1993): 69–79.

Lev, B. "Simulation of Manufacturing Systems." *Interfaces* 20, no. 3 (May–June 1990): 99.

Render, B., and R. M. Stair. *Introduction to Management Science*. Boston: Allyn & Bacon, 1992.

———. *Quantitative Analysis for Management*, 6th ed. Upper Saddle River NJ: Prentice Hall, 1997.

Russell, R. A., and R. Hickle. "Simulation of a CD Portfolio." *Interfaces* 16, no. 3 (May–June 1986): 49–54.

Solomon, S. L. *Simulation of Waiting Lines*. Englewood Cliffs, NJ: Prentice Hall, 1983.

Trunk, C. "Simulation for Success in the Automated Factory." *Material Handling Engineering*, May 1989, pp. 64–76.

Appendices

APPENDIX I
NORMAL CURVE AREAS AND HOW TO USE THE NORMAL DISTRIBUTION

APPENDIX II
POISSON DISTRIBUTION VALUES

APPENDIX III
VALUES OF $e^{-\lambda}$ FOR USE IN THE POISSON DISTRIBUTION

APPENDIX IV
TABLE OF RANDOM NUMBERS

APPENDIX V
USING POM FOR WINDOWS AND EXCEL OM

APPENDIX VI
SOLUTION TO EVEN-NUMBERED PROBLEMS

APPENDIX I: NORMAL CURVE AREAS AND HOW TO USE THE NORMAL DISTRIBUTION

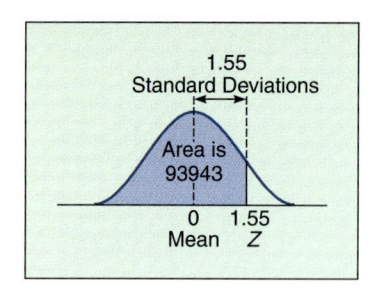

To find the area under the normal curve, you must know how many standard deviations that point is to the right of the mean. Then, the area under the normal curve can be read directly from the normal table. For example, the total area under the normal curve for a point that is 1.55 standard deviations to the right of the mean is .93943.

	.00	.01	.02	.03	.04	.05	.06	.07	.08	.09
.0	.50000	.50399	.50798	.51197	.51595	.51994	.52392	.52790	.53188	.53586
.1	.53983	.54380	.54776	.55172	.55567	.55962	.56356	.56749	.57142	.57535
.2	.57926	.58317	.58706	.59095	.59483	.59871	.60257	.60642	.61026	.61409
.3	.61791	.62172	.62552	.62930	.63307	.63683	.64058	.64431	.64803	.65173
.4	.65542	.65910	.66276	.66640	.67003	.67364	.67724	.68082	.68439	.68793
.5	.69146	.69497	.69847	.70194	.70540	.70884	.71226	.71566	.71904	.72240
.6	.72575	.72907	.73237	.73536	.73891	.74215	.74537	.74857	.75175	.75490
.7	.75804	.76115	.76424	.76730	.77035	.77337	.77637	.77935	.78230	.78524
.8	.78814	.79103	.79389	.79673	.79955	.80234	.80511	.80785	.81057	.81327
.9	.81594	.81859	.82121	.82381	.82639	.82894	.83147	.83398	.83646	.83891
1.0	.84134	.84375	.84614	.84849	.85083	.85314	.85543	.85769	.85993	.86214
1.1	.86433	.86650	.86864	.87076	.87286	.87493	.87698	.87900	.88100	.88298
1.2	.88493	.88686	.88877	.89065	.89251	.89435	.89617	.89796	.89973	.90147
1.3	.90320	.90490	.90658	.90824	.90988	.91149	.91309	.91466	.91621	.91774
1.4	.91924	.92073	.92220	.92364	.92507	.92647	.92785	.92922	.93056	.93189
1.5	.93319	.93448	.93574	.93699	.93822	.93943	.94062	.94179	.94295	.94408
1.6	.94520	.94630	.94738	.94845	.94950	.95053	.95154	.95254	.95352	.95449
1.7	.95543	.95637	.95728	.95818	.95907	.95994	.96080	.96164	.96246	.96327
1.8	.96407	.96485	.96562	.96638	.96712	.96784	.96856	.96926	.96995	.97062
1.9	.97128	.97193	.97257	.97320	.97381	.97441	.97500	.97558	.97615	.97670
2.0	.97725	.97784	.97831	.97882	.97932	.97982	.98030	.98077	.98124	.98169
2.1	.98214	.98257	.98300	.98341	.98382	.98422	.98461	.98500	.98537	.98574
2.2	.98610	.98645	.98679	.98713	.98745	.98778	.98809	.98840	.98870	.98899
2.3	.98928	.98956	.98983	.99010	.99036	.99061	.99086	.99111	.99134	.99158
2.4	.99180	.99202	.99224	.99245	.99266	.99286	.99305	.99324	.99343	.99361
2.5	.99379	.99396	.99413	.99430	.99446	.99461	.99477	.99492	.99506	.99520
2.6	.99534	.99547	.99560	.99573	.99585	.99598	.99609	.99621	.99632	.99643
2.7	.99653	.99664	.99674	.99683	.99693	.99702	.99711	.99720	.99728	.99736
2.8	.99744	.99752	.99760	.99767	.99774	.99781	.99788	.99795	.99801	.99807
2.9	.99813	.99819	.99825	.99831	.99836	.99841	.99846	.99851	.99856	.99861
3.0	.99865	.99869	.99874	.99878	.99882	.99886	.99899	.99893	.99896	.99900
3.1	.99903	.99906	.99910	.99913	.99916	.99918	.99921	.99924	.99926	.99929
3.2	.99931	.99934	.99936	.99938	.99940	.99942	.99944	.99946	.99948	.99950
3.3	.99952	.99953	.99955	.99957	.99958	.99960	.99961	.99962	.99964	.99965
3.4	.99966	.99968	.99969	.99970	.99971	.99972	.99973	.99974	.99975	.99976
3.5	.99977	.99978	.99978	.99979	.99980	.99981	.99981	.99982	.99983	.99983
3.6	.99984	.99985	.99985	.99986	.99986	.99987	.99987	.99988	.99988	.99989
3.7	.99989	.99990	.99990	.99990	.99991	.99991	.99992	.99992	.99992	.99992
3.8	.99993	.99993	.99993	.99994	.99994	.99994	.99994	.99995	.99995	.99995
3.9	.99995	.99995	.99996	.99996	.99996	.99996	.99996	.99996	.99997	.99997

Source: From Richard I. Levin and Charles A. Kirkpatrick, *Quantitative Approaches to Management*, 4th ed. Copyright © 1978, 1975, 1971, 1965 by McGraw-Hill, Inc. Used with permission of McGraw-Hill Book Company.

HOW TO USE NORMAL DISTRIBUTION

A popular and useful continuous probability distribution is the normal distribution, characterized by a bell-shaped curve. The normal distribution is completely specified when values for the mean, μ, and the standard deviation, σ, are known.

The Area under the Normal Curve

Because the normal distribution is symmetrical, its midpoint (and highest point) is at the mean. Values of the *x*-axis are then measured in terms of how many standard deviations they are from the mean.

The area under the curve (in a continuous distribution) describes the probability that a variable has a value in the specified interval. For example, Figure I.1 illustrates three commonly used relationships that have been derived from the accompanying standard normal table. The area from point *a* to point *b* in the first drawing represents the probability, 68%, that the variable will be within 1 standard deviation of the mean. In the middle graph, we see that about 95.4% (more precisely 95.45%) of the area lies within plus or minus 2 standard deviations of the mean. The third figure shows that 99.7% lies between $\pm 3\sigma$.

Translated into an application, Figure I.1 implies that if the expected lifetime of a computer chip is $\mu = 100$ days, and if the standard deviation is $\sigma = 15$ days, we can make the following statements:

1. 68% of the population of computer chips studied have lives between 85 and 115 days (namely, $\pm 1\sigma$).
2. 95.4% of the chips have lives between 70 and 130 days ($\pm 2\sigma$).
3. 99.7% of the computer chips have lives in the range from 55 to 145 days ($\pm 3\sigma$).
4. Only 16% of the chips have lives greater than 115 days (from first graph, the area to the right of $+1\sigma$).

Using the Standard Normal Table

To use a table to find normal probability values, we follow two steps.

Step 1 Convert the normal distribution to what we call a *standard normal distribution*. A standard normal distribution is one that has a mean of 0 and a standard deviation of 1. All normal tables are designed to handle variables with $\mu = 0$ and $\sigma = 1$. Without a standard normal distribution, a different table would be needed for each pair of μ and σ values. We call the new standard variable *z*. The value of *z* for any normal distribution is computed from the equation:

$$z = \frac{x - \mu}{\sigma}$$

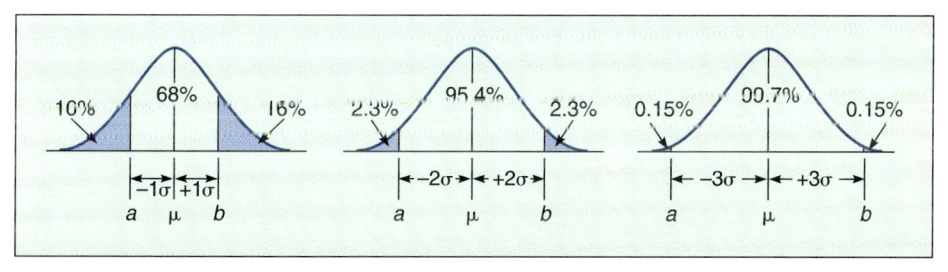

FIGURE I.1 ■ Three Common Areas under Normal Curves

where x = value of the variable we want to measure
μ = mean of the distribution
σ = standard deviation of the distribution
z = number of standard deviations from x to the mean, μ

For example, if $\mu = 100$, $\sigma = 15$, and we are interested in finding the probability that the variable x is less than 130, then we want $P(x < 130)$.

$$z = \frac{x - \mu}{\sigma} = \frac{130 - 100}{15} = \frac{30}{15} = 2 \text{ standard deviations}$$

This means that the point x is 2.0 standard deviations to the right of the mean. This is shown in Figure I.2.

Step 2 Look up the probability from the table of normal curve areas. It is set up to provide the area under the curve to the left of any specified value of z.

Let's see how the table in this appendix can be used. The column on the left lists values of z, with the second decimal place of z appearing in the top row. For example, for a value of $z = 2.00$ as just computed, find 2.0 in the left-hand column and .00 in the top row. In the body of the table, we find that the area sought is .97725, or 97.7%. Thus,

$$P(x < 130) = P(z < 2.00) = 97.7\%$$

This suggests that if the mean lifetime of a computer chip is 100 days with a standard deviation of 15 days, the probability that the life of a randomly selected chip is less than 130 is 97.7%. By referring back to Figure I.1, we see that this probability could also have been derived from the middle graph. (Note that $1.0 - .977 = .023 = 2.3\%$, which is the area in the right-hand tail of the curve.)

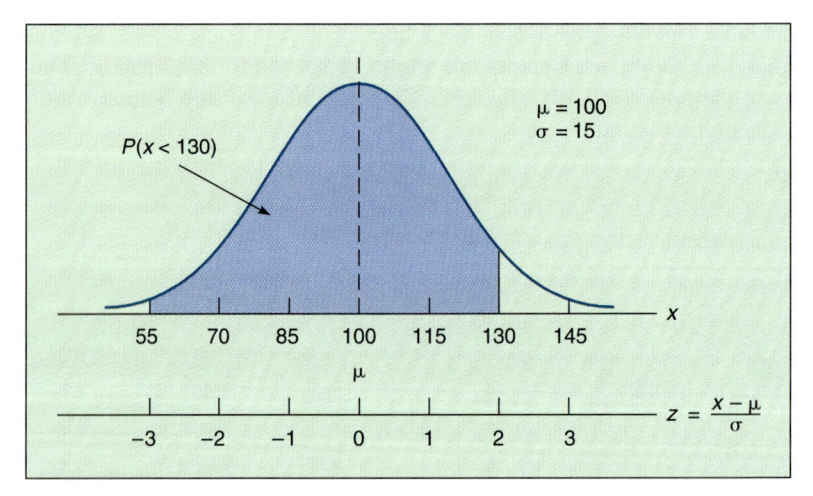

FIGURE I.2 ■ Normal Distribution Showing the Relationship between z Values and x Values

APPENDIX II POISSON DISTRIBUTION VALUES

$$P(X \leq c; \lambda) = \sum_{0}^{c} \frac{\lambda^x e^{-\lambda}}{x!}$$

The following table shows 1,000 times the probability of c or fewer occurrences of an event that has an average number of occurrences of λ.

Values of c

λ	0	1	2	3	4	5	6	7	8	9	10
.02	980	1000									
.04	961	999	1000								
.06	942	998	1000								
.08	923	997	1000								
.10	905	995	1000								
.15	861	990	999	1000							
.20	819	982	999	1000							
.25	779	974	998	1000							
.30	741	963	996	1000							
.35	705	951	994	1000							
.40	670	938	992	999	1000						
.45	638	925	989	999	1000						
.50	607	910	986	998	1000						
.55	577	894	982	998	1000						
.60	549	878	977	997	1000						
.65	522	861	972	996	999	1000					
.70	497	844	966	994	999	1000					
.75	472	827	959	993	999	1000					
.80	449	809	953	991	999	1000					
.85	427	791	945	989	998	1000					
.90	407	772	937	987	998	1000					
.95	387	754	929	984	997	1000					
1.00	368	736	920	981	996	999	1000				
1.1	333	699	900	974	995	999	1000				
1.2	301	663	879	966	992	998	1000				
1.3	273	627	857	957	989	998	1000				
1.4	247	592	833	946	986	997	999	1000			
1.5	223	558	809	934	981	996	999	1000			
1.6	202	525	783	921	976	994	999	1000			
1.7	183	493	757	907	970	992	998	1000			
1.8	165	463	731	891	964	990	997	999	1000		
1.9	150	434	704	875	956	987	997	999	1000		
2.0	135	406	677	857	947	983	995	999	1000		

Source: Adapted from E. L. Grant, *Statistical Quality Control*, McGraw-Hill Book Company, New York, 1964. Reproduced by permission of the publisher.

APPENDIX II POISSON DISTRIBUTION VALUES (CONTINUED)

Values of c

λ	0	1	2	3	4	5	6	7	8	9	10	11	12	13	14	15	16	17	18	19	20	21	22
2.2	111	359	623	819	928	975	993	998	1000														
2.4	091	308	570	779	904	964	988	997	999	1000													
2.6	074	267	518	736	877	951	983	995	999	1000													
2.8	061	231	469	692	848	935	976	992	998	999	1000												
3.0	050	199	423	647	815	916	966	988	996	999	1000												
3.2	041	171	380	603	781	895	955	983	994	998	1000												
3.4	033	147	340	558	744	871	942	977	992	997	999	1000											
3.6	027	126	303	515	706	844	927	969	988	996	999	1000											
3.8	022	107	269	473	668	816	909	960	984	994	998	999	1000										
4.0	018	092	238	433	629	785	889	949	979	992	997	999	1000										
4.2	015	078	210	395	590	753	867	936	972	989	996	999	1000										
4.4	012	066	185	359	551	720	844	921	964	985	994	998	999	1000									
4.6	010	056	163	326	513	686	818	905	955	980	992	997	999	1000									
4.8	008	048	143	294	476	651	791	887	944	975	990	996	999	1000									
5.0	007	040	125	265	440	616	762	867	932	968	986	995	998	999	1000								
5.2	006	034	109	238	406	581	732	845	918	960	982	993	997	999	1000								
5.4	005	029	095	213	373	546	702	822	903	951	977	990	996	999	1000								
5.6	004	024	082	191	342	512	670	797	886	941	972	988	995	998	999	1000							
5.8	003	021	072	170	313	478	638	771	867	929	965	984	993	997	999	1000							
6.0	002	017	062	151	285	446	606	744	847	916	957	980	991	996	999	999	1000						
6.2	002	015	054	134	259	414	574	716	826	902	949	975	989	995	998	999	1000						
6.4	002	012	046	119	235	384	542	687	803	886	939	969	986	994	997	999	1000						
6.6	001	010	040	105	213	355	511	658	780	869	927	963	982	992	997	999	999	1000					
6.8	001	009	034	093	192	327	480	628	755	850	915	955	978	990	996	998	999	1000					
7.0	001	007	030	082	173	301	450	599	729	830	901	947	973	987	994	998	999	1000					
7.2	001	006	025	072	156	276	420	569	703	810	887	937	967	984	993	997	999	999	1000				
7.4	001	005	022	063	140	253	392	539	676	788	871	926	961	980	991	996	998	999	1000				
7.6	001	004	019	055	125	231	365	510	648	765	854	915	954	976	989	995	998	999	1000				
7.8	000	004	016	048	112	210	338	481	620	741	835	902	945	971	986	993	997	999	1000				
8.0	000	003	014	042	100	191	313	453	593	717	816	888	936	966	983	992	996	998	999	1000			
8.5	000	002	009	030	074	150	256	386	523	653	763	849	909	949	973	986	993	997	999	999	1000		
9.0	000	001	006	021	055	116	207	324	456	587	706	803	876	926	959	978	989	995	998	999	1000		
9.5	000	001	004	015	040	089	165	269	392	522	645	752	836	898	940	967	982	991	996	998	999	1000	
10.0	000	000	003	010	029	067	130	220	333	458	583	697	792	864	917	951	973	986	993	997	998	999	1000

APPENDIX III VALUES OF $e^{-\lambda}$ FOR USE IN THE POISSON DISTRIBUTION

Values of $e^{-\lambda}$

λ	$e^{-\lambda}$	λ	$e^{-\lambda}$	λ	$e^{-\lambda}$	λ	$e^{-\lambda}$
.0	1.0000	1.6	.2019	3.1	.0450	4.6	.0101
.1	.9048	1.7	.1827	3.2	.0408	4.7	.0091
.2	.8187	1.8	.1653	3.3	.0369	4.8	.0082
.3	.7408	1.9	.1496	3.4	.0334	4.9	.0074
.4	.6703	2.0	.1353	3.5	.0302	5.0	.0067
.5	.6065	2.1	.1225	3.6	.0273	5.1	.0061
.6	.5488	2.2	.1108	3.7	.0247	5.2	.0055
.7	.4966	2.3	.1003	3.8	.0224	5.3	.0050
.8	.4493	2.4	.0907	3.9	.0202	5.4	.0045
.9	.4066	2.5	.0821	4.0	.0183	5.5	.0041
1.0	.3679	2.6	.0743	4.1	.0166	5.6	.0037
1.1	.3329	2.7	.0672	4.2	.0150	5.7	.0033
1.2	.3012	2.8	.0608	4.3	.0136	5.8	.0030
1.3	.2725	2.9	.0550	4.4	.0123	5.9	.0027
1.4	.2466	3.0	.0498	4.5	.0111	6.0	.0025
1.5	.2231						

APPENDIX IV TABLE OF RANDOM NUMBERS

52	06	50	88	53	30	10	47	99	37	66	91	35	32	00	84	57	07		
37	63	28	02	74	35	24	03	29	60	74	85	90	73	59	55	17	60		
82	57	68	28	05	94	03	11	27	79	90	87	92	41	09	25	36	77		
69	02	36	49	71	99	32	10	75	21	95	90	94	38	97	71	72	49		
98	94	90	36	06	78	23	67	89	85	29	21	25	73	69	34	85	76		
96	52	62	87	49	56	59	23	78	71	72	90	57	01	98	57	31	95		
33	69	27	21	11	60	95	89	68	48	17	89	34	09	93	30	44	51		
50	33	50	95	13	44	34	62	64	39	55	29	30	64	49	44	30	16		
88	32	18	50	62	57	34	56	62	31	15	40	90	34	51	95	26	14		
90	30	36	24	69	82	51	74	30	35	36	85	01	55	92	64	09	85		
50	48	61	18	85	23	08	54	17	12	80	69	24	84	92	16	49	59		
27	88	21	62	69	64	48	31	12	73	02	68	00	16	16	46	13	85		
45	14	46	32	13	49	66	62	74	41	86	98	92	98	84	54	33	40		
81	02	01	78	82	74	97	37	45	31	94	99	42	49	27	64	89	42		
66	83	14	74	27	76	03	33	11	97	59	81	72	00	64	61	13	52		
74	05	81	82	93	09	96	33	52	78	13	06	28	30	94	23	37	39		
30	34	87	01	74	11	46	82	59	94	25	34	32	23	17	01	58	73		
59	55	72	33	62	13	74	68	22	44	42	09	32	46	71	79	45	89		
67	09	80	98	99	25	77	50	03	32	36	63	65	75	94	19	95	88		
60	77	46	63	71	69	44	22	03	85	14	48	69	13	30	50	33	24		
60	08	19	29	36	72	30	27	30	64	85	72	75	29	87	05	75	01		
80	45	86	99	02	34	87	08	86	84	49	76	24	08	01	86	29	11		
53	84	49	63	26	65	72	84	85	63	26	02	75	26	92	62	40	67		
69	84	12	94	51	36	17	02	15	29	16	52	56	43	26	22	08	62		
37	77	13	10	02	18	31	19	32	85	31	94	81	43	31	58	33	51		

Source: Excerpted from *A Million Random Digits with 100,000 Normal Deviates,* The Free Press, 1955, p. 7, with permission of the Rand Corporation.

APPENDIX V USING POM FOR WINDOWS AND EXCEL OM

Two approaches to computer-aided decision making are available with this text: **POM** (Production and Operations Management) **for Windows** and **Excel OM.** These are the two most user-friendly software packages available to help you learn and understand operations management. Both programs can be used either to solve homework problems identified with a computer logo or to check answers you have developed by hand. Both software packages use the standard Windows interface and run on any IBM-PC compatible 386 or higher with at least 3-MB RAM and operating Windows 3.1 or better. There are essentially no differences when operating the software under Windows 3.1, or Windows 95, or on a Macintosh.

POM for Windows

POM for Windows is decision support software that may be ordered as an option with this textbook. Program V.1 shows a list of 20 OM programs on the disk you may install on your hard drive. Once you follow the standard setup instructions, a POM for Windows program icon will be added to your program group. The program may be accessed by double-clicking on the icon. Upgrades to POM for Windows are available on the Internet through the Prentice-Hall download library, found at http://www.prenhall.com/weiss.

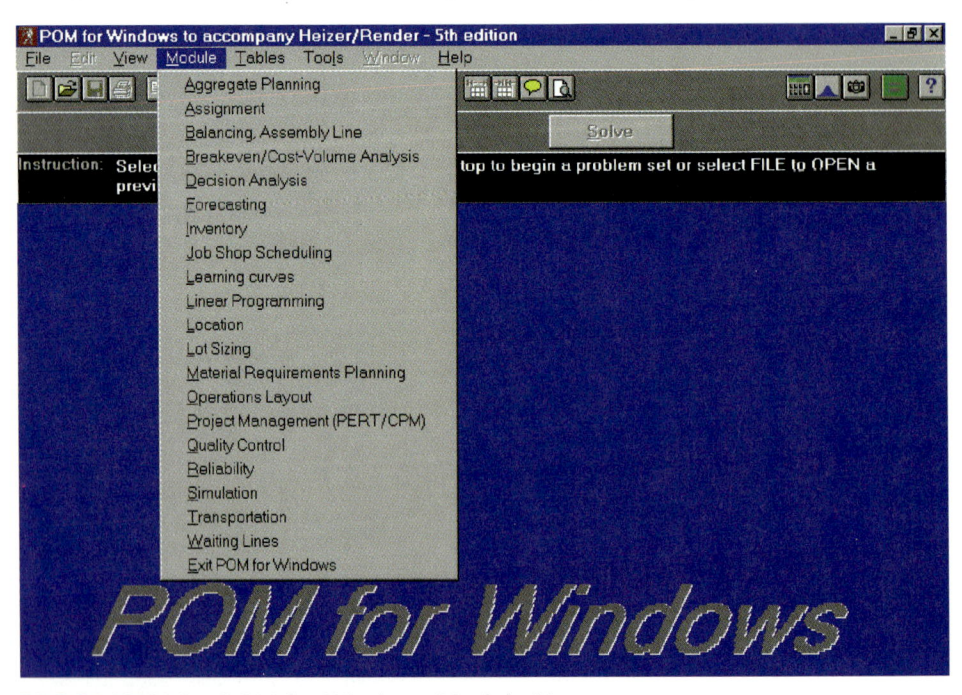

PROGRAM V.1 ■ POM for Windows Module List

Excel OM

Excel OM also has been designed to help you to better learn and understand both OM and Excel. Even though the software contains 14 modules and over 35 submodules, the screens for every module are consistent and easy to use. The modules are illustrated in

Program V.2. This software is provided by means of the CD-ROM that is included in the back of this text, or via the Internet at no cost to purchasers of this textbook. No floppy disk drive is required, but Excel version 5 or better must be on your PC.

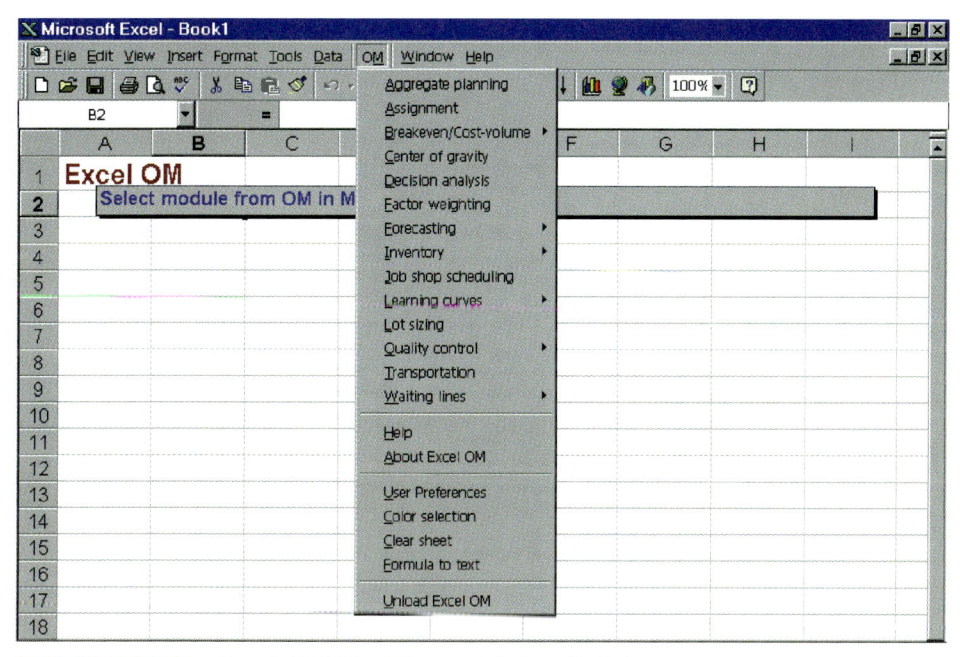

PROGRAM V.2 ■ **Excel OM Modules and Other Utilities**

To install Excel OM, exit and reenter Windows, then:

1. Insert the CD-ROM or download the file ExcelOM.exe from the Prentice-Hall Web site and store in any directory.
2. Run Excel OM. There are several ways to do this. For example, from the Windows Program Manager (Win 3.1), select FILE, RUN or in Win 95, use START, RUN. In the box, type the name of the directory in which you have stored the program and SETUP. For example, temp\setup.exe. Alternatively from File Manager (Win 3.1) or Explorer (Win 95), double-click on the file name ExcelOM.exe.
3. Follow the setup instructions on the screen.

Default values have been assigned in the setup program, but you may change them if you like. The default values in Windows 3.1 are that the program will be installed to a directory on the C: drive named C:\ExcelOM and that the program group will be named Excel OM. The default folder in Windows 95 is C:\Program Files\ExcelOM. Generally speaking, it is simply necessary to click NEXT each time the installation program asks a question.

The Program Group Under Windows 3.1, you will have a program group added to your program manager. The group will be called Excel OM, and after you open the group it will appear with five icons displayed. Under Windows 95, a program group with four options will be added to the Start menu. Prior to starting the program, check the README file by clicking on the *Readme* icon in the program group.

The Excel OM icon is the option used to begin the program. Help is available from within the program, but first use the Excel OM *Help* icon if you want to read some information about the program without starting it.

Under either Windows 3.1 or Windows 95, the program group contains an icon named *Prentice-Hall Web Site Gateway*. If you have an association for HTM files with a Web browser (e.g., Netscape or Internet Explorer), this document will point you to program upgrades.

Starting the Program If you do not already have Excel open, then to start Excel OM under Windows 3.1, double-click on the Excel OM program icon. For Windows 95, click on START, PROGRAMS and then the Excel OM icon in order to use the software. In addition, under Windows 95 the installation will create a shortcut and place it on your desktop. This can be used to start Excel OM. If you already have Excel open, then simply load the file Excel OM.xla, which is in the default directory (C:\ExcelOM or C:\Program Files\Excel OM) if you did not change this at the time of installation.

It is also possible to install Excel OM as an add-in. This will load Excel OM each time you start Excel. To do this, simply go to TOOLS, ADDINS, BROWSE and select ExcelOM.xla.

Excel OM serves two purposes in the learning process. First, it can simply help you solve homework problems. You enter the appropriate data, and the program provides numerical solutions. POM for Windows operates on the same principle. However, *Excel OM* allows for a second approach; that is, noting the Excel *formulas* used to develop solutions and modifying them to deal with a wider variety of problems. This "open" approach enables you to observe, understand, and even change the formulas underlying the Excel calculations, hopefully conveying Excel's power as an OM analysis tool.

APPENDIX VI SOLUTIONS TO EVEN-NUMBERED PROBLEMS

Chapter 1

1.2. (a) 20 ornaments/hour
(b) 26.7 ornaments/hour
(c) 33.5%
1.4. 6.0% or 6.4% depending on the approach taken.
1.6. 6.75% or 7.3% depending on the approach taken.
1.8. It is unlikely that U.S. productivity will exceed 2% per year.

Chapter 2

2.2. (a) For a producer with high energy costs, major oil prices change the cost structure, result in higher selling prices, and, if the company is energy-inefficient compared to other producers, result in a change in competitive position. Conversely, when oil prices dipped in 1997, it was a bonanza for the airline industry, heavy users of fuel.

2.4. The mission, for example, for Microsoft is:
At Microsoft, our long-held vision of a computer on every desk and in every home continues to be at the core of everything we do. We are committed to the belief that software is the tool that empowers people both at work and at home. Since our company was founded in 1975, our charter has been to deliver on this vision of the power of personal computing.

Chapter 3

3.2. Thailand, with a 3.1 weighted average
3.4. Italy
3.6. England has the highest rating of 3.55; Italy is second with 3.3.

Chapter 4

4.2. Individual answer. The student should build a house-of-quality similar to the one shown at the top of the next page, entering the *wants* on the left and entering the *hows* at the top.

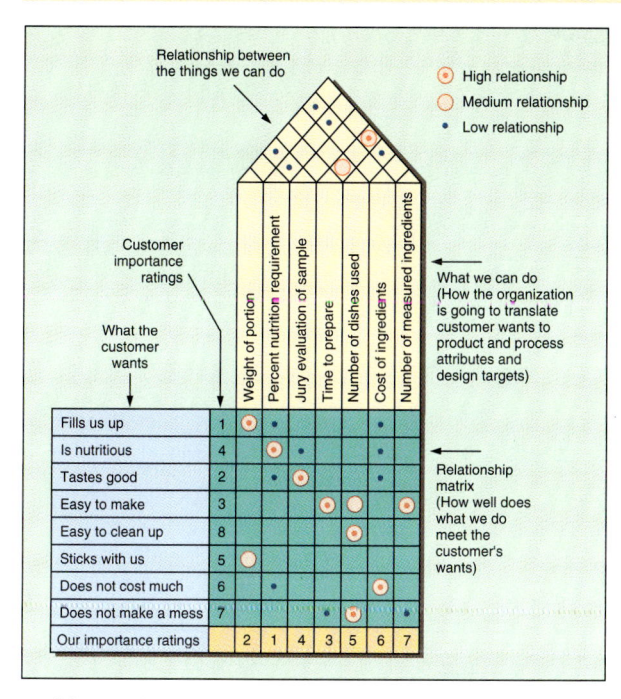

Chapter 4 Supplement

S4.2. $UCL_{\bar{x}} = 52.308$
$LCL_{\bar{x}} = 47.692$
$UCL_R = 8.456$
$LCL_R = 0.0$

S4.4. $UCL_{\bar{x}} = 46.966$
$LCL_{\bar{x}} = 45.034$
$UCL_R = 4.008$
$LCL_R = 0$

S4.6. $UCL_{\bar{x}} = 17.187$
$LCL_{\bar{x}} = 16.814$
$UCL_R = .932$
$LCL_R = .068$

S4.8. $UCL_{\bar{x}} = 3.728$
$LCL_{\bar{x}} = 2.236$
$UCL_R = 2.336$
$LCL_R = 0.0$
The process is in control

S4.10. $UCL_p = .0596$
$LCL_p = .0104$

S4.12. $UCL_p = .0311$ to $.1636$
$LCL_p = 0.0$ to $.0364$

S4.14. $UCL_{\bar{x}} = 64.6$
$LCL_{\bar{x}} = 62.4$
$UCL_R = 3.42$
$LCL_R = 0$

S4.16. $UCL_p = .0581$
$LCL_p = 0$

S4.18. $UCL_c = 33.4$
$LCL_c = 7$

S4.20. $C_{pk} = .166$

S4.22. $C_{pk} = 1.04$

Chapter 5

5.2. MAD = 30.33/7 = 4.33

5.4. MAD for 2-week moving average is lower:
MAD = 33.5/8 = 4.1875

5.6. (a) $y = 50 + 18x$
(b) $410. Each guest accounts for an additional $18 in bar sales.

5.8. Confirm that you match all the numbers in Table 5.1.

5.10. 18.67, 16.67, 14, 14.33, 15.33, 17, 18.33, 19.33, 20.33, 21.33

5.12. (a) 337; (b) 380; (c) 423

5.14. 2 year: 5, 5, 4.5, 7.5, 9.0, 7.5, 8.0, 10.5, 13.0
4 year: 4.75, 6.25, 6.75, 7.50, 8.50, 9.00, 10.50

5.16. Wtd. M.A. MAD = 2,312
Exp. Smooth MAD = 2,581

5.18. MAD ($\alpha = .3$) = 74.6
MAD ($\alpha = .6$) = 51.8
MAD ($\alpha = .9$) = 38.1 (best)

5.20. $y = 522 + 33.6x - 622$ if x's are coded as $-2, -1, 0, +1, +2$. Or $y = 421 + 33.6x$ if x's are coded as 1, 2, 3, 4, 5.

5.22. (a) 43.4, 47.4, 50.2, 53.7, 56.3 for $\alpha = .6$; 44.6, 49.5, 51.8, 55.6, 57.8 for $\alpha = .9$
(b) 49, 52.7, 55.3
(c) 45.8, 49.0, 52.2, 55.4, 58.6, 61.8
(d) Trend with MAD = .6

5.24. 5, 5.4, 6.12, 5.90, 6.52, 7.82

5.26. MAD = 3.99; $\beta = .8$ is better than $\beta = .2$

4.4. Individual answer, but in the style of problem 4.2.

4.6. (a) 8′ ↓ move to trunk
○ open trunk
○ loosen tire and jack
○ remove tire and jack
8′ ↓ move the tire and jack to wheel
○ position jack
☐ inspect
○ loosen wheel lugs
○ jack up car
○ remove wheel lugs
○ remove wheel
○ position good wheel
○ tighten lugs
○ lower car
○ finish tightening lugs
☐ inspect
8′ ↓ move tire and jack to trunk
○ position tire and jack
○ close trunk
8′ ↓ move to driver's seat

4.8.

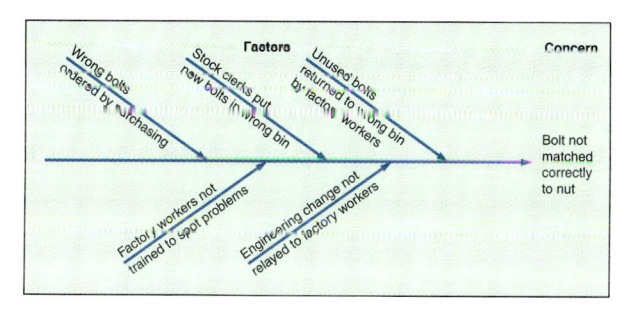

4.10. Individual answer, but in the style of problem 4.8 above.

- **5.28.** $y = 5.26 + 1.11x$
  Period 7 demand = 13.03
- **5.30.** (a) Moving average forecast for February is 13.6667.
  (b) Weighted moving average forecast for February is 13.17.
  (c) MAD for Avg is 2.2.
  MAD for Weighted Avg is 2.7.
  (d) seasonality, causal variables such as advertising budget
- **5.32.** (a) $\hat{y} = 1 + 1x$; $r = .45$
  (b) $S_{yx} = 3.65$
- **5.34.** $y = .972 + .0035x$ using a hand calculator, or $y = 1.03 + .0034x$ by computer; $r^2 = 0.479$; $x = 350$; $y = 2.197$; $x = 800$; $y = 3.77$
- **5.36.** $131.2 \rightarrow 72.7$ patients; $90.6 \rightarrow 50.6$ patients
- **5.38.** Fall = 270; Winter = 390; Spring = 189; Summer = 351
- **5.40.** (a) 1785
  (b) 1560
- **5.42.** (a) 17.00; 17.80; 18.04; 19.03; 18.83; 18.26; 18.61; 18.49; 19.19; 19.35; 18.48
  (b) 2.60
  (c) No, tracking signal exceeds 5 sigma at week 10.
- **5.44.** (a, b)

Week	$\alpha = .1$ Forecast	$\alpha = .6$ Forecast
25	46.9	57.6

  (c) On the basis of forecast and standard error of estimate, $\alpha = .6$ is better. Yet other α's should be tried.
- **5.46.** Each answer will differ, but note the presence of both seasonal and trend factors.
- **5.48.** 150,000; 126,000; 120,000; and 207,000 for the 4 respective quarters.

Chapter 6

- **6.2.** Assembly chart for a ballpoint pen

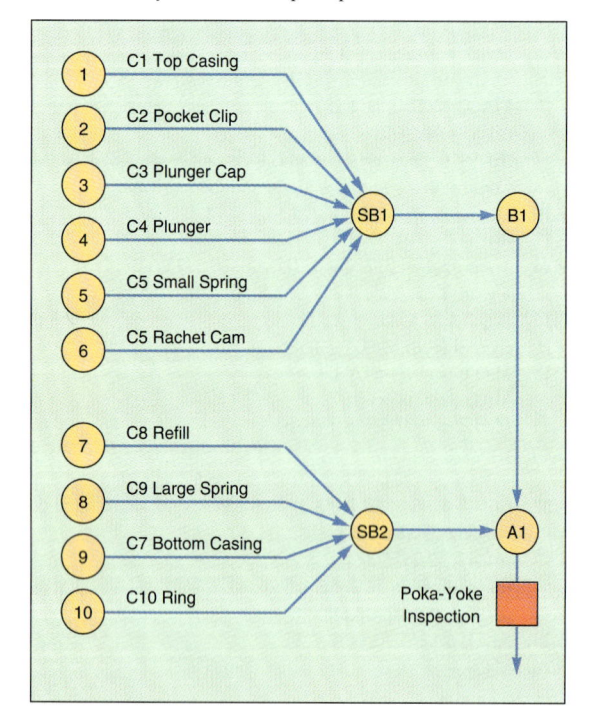

- **6.4.**

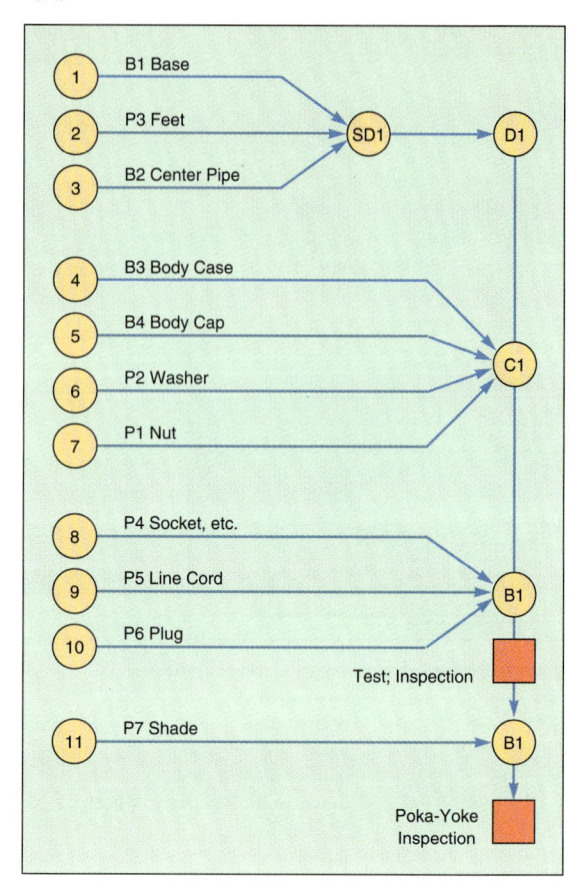

- **6.6.** *Possible strategies:*

Notebook computers (growth phase):
  Increase capacity and improve balance of production system. Attempt to make production facilities more efficient.

Palm held computer (introductory phase)
  Increase R&D to better define required product characteristics.
  Modify and improve production process.
  Develop supplier and distribution systems.

Hand calculator (decline phase):
  Concentrate on production and distribution cost reduction.

- **6.8.** EMV of Proceed = $49,500,000
  EMV of Do Value Analysis = $55,025,000
  Therefore, Do Value Analysis.
- **6.10.** EMV of Design A = $875,000
  EMV of Design B = $700,000

Chapter 7

- **7.2.** (a) 4,590 in excess capacity
  (b) 2,090 in excess capacity
- **7.4.** Design = 81,806
  Fabrication = 152,646
  Finishing = 62,899
- **7.6.** (a) $BEP_\$ = \$125,000$
  (b) $BEP_\$ = \$140,000$

APPENDIX VI SOLUTIONS TO EVEN-NUMBERED PROBLEMS A13

7.8. (a) Proposal A is best; $a = \$18,000$; $b = \$15,000$
(b) Proposal B is best; $a = \$70,000$; $b = \$80,000$
7.10. NPV = $20,280
7.12. NPV = $1,764
7.14. Present equipment = $1,000
New equipment = 0
7.16. (a) $100,000
(b) 12,500 units
(c) $350,000
7.18. (a) Purchase two large ovens
(b) Equal quality, equal capacity
(c) Payments are made at end of each time period. And future interest rates are known.
7.20. BEP(x) = 25,000
7.22. BEP($) = $7,584.83 per month
Daily meals = 9
7.24. Payoff from small line equals $133,000; payoff from large line equals $200,000; open large process line.
7.26. NPV for investment 1 = $17,127
NPV for investment 2 = $25,532
NPV for investment 3 = $18,962

Chapter 7 Supplement

S7.2. GPE is best below 100,000
FMS is best between 100,000 and 300,000
DA is best over 300,000
S7.4. Optimal process will change with each additional 100,000 units.

Chapter 8

8.2. (b) Denver, 0–3,570 units; Burlington, 3,571–24,999 units; Cleveland, more than 25,000 units
(c) Burlington
8.4. Suburb B, rating = 6.35 but all are close.
8.6. Shopping mall is best.
8.8. Hyde Park with 54.5 points
8.10. Atlanta = 53; Charlotte = 60; select Charlotte.
8.12. Weighted location is 5.6 East, 4.8 North.
8.14. (a) Lyon, 3,970; The Hague, 3,920; Bonn, 3,915
(b) The Hague, 3,840; Lyon, 3,730; Berlin, 3,585
(c) Berlin, 3,840; The Hague, 3,840; Bonn, 3,810

Chapter 9

9.2. Yes, with POM for Windows patient movement = 4,500 feet.
9.4. Layout #1, distance = 600
Layout #2, distance = 602
9.6. Layout #4, distance = 609
Layout #5, distance = 372
9.8. (a) Throughput of 3.75 people/hour possible
(b) Medical exam—16 minutes
(c) At least 5 per hour now
9.10. Cycle time = 9.6 minutes; 8 workstations with 63.8% efficiency is possible.
9.12. 5 workstations; Station #1, tasks 1, 3; #2, task 5; #3, tasks 2, 4; #4, tasks 6, 8; #5, tasks 7, 9. Efficiency = 78%
9.14. Cycle time = .5 minute/bottle. Possible assignments with 4 workstations yields efficiency = 90%.

9.16. Minimum (theoretical) = 4 stations. Efficiency = 80% with 5 stations. Several assignments with 5 are possible.
9.18. There are 3 alternatives each with an efficiency = 86.67%.

Chapter 10

10.2.

Time	Operator	Time	Machine	Time
1	Prepare Mill	1	Idle	1
2	Load Mill	2		2
3	Idle	3	Mill Operating (Cutting Material)	3
4		4		4
5	Unload Mill	5	Idle	5
6		6		6

10.4. The first 10 steps of 10.4(a) are shown below. The remaining 10 steps are similar.

OPERATIONS CHART			SUMMARY					
PROCESS: CHANGE ERASER			SYMBOL		PRESENT		DIFF.	
ANALYST:				LH	RH	LH	RH	LH	RH
DATE:			○ OPERATIONS	1	8				
SHEET: 1 of 2			⇨ TRANSPORTS	3	8				
METHOD: (PRESENT) PROPOSED			□ INSPECTIONS	1					
REMARKS:			D DELAYS	15	4				
			▽ STORAGE						
			TOTALS	20	20				
LEFT HAND	DIST.	SYMBOL	SYMBOL	DIST	RIGHT HAND			
1 Reach for pencil		⇨	D		Idle			
2 Grasp pencil		○	D		Idle			
3 Move to work area		⇨	⇨		Move to pencil top			
4 Hold pencil		D	○		Grasp pencil top			
5 Hold pencil		D	○		Remove pencil top			
6 Hold pencil		D	⇨		Set top aside			
7 Hold pencil		D	⇨		Reach for old eraser			
8 Hold pencil		D	○		Grasp old eraser			
9 Hold pencil		D	○		Remove old eraser			
10 Hold pencil		D	⇨		Set aside old eraser			

10.6. Individual solution.
10.8. The answer is similar to Solved Problem 10.1, but crew activities C and D become the limiting activities.

Chapter 10 Supplement

S10.2. Normal time = 55 sec.
S10.4. Sample size of 166 is required.
S10.6. Six observations are required.
S10.8. Normal time = 5.565 min.
Allowance = 10%
Std. time = 6.183
S10.10. 29.8 min.

APPENDIX VI

S10.12. 5.4 or 6.67 depending upon the observations deleted
S10.14. 82.35 seconds, 106 samples
S10.16. (a) 47.55 min.
(b) 60 observations are required for element 4.
S10.18. 336 observations.
S10.20. .1092 min., or 6.55 sec.

Chapter 11
11.2. Kay Corp. = 54.15
11.4. (a) $4.35
(b) $7.14

Chapter 12
12.2. A items are G2 and F3; B items are A2, C7, and D1; all others are C.
12.4. 7,000 units
12.6. (a) 78
(b) 200
(c) $3,873
(d) 64
(e) 3.91 days
12.8. Quantity discount: Cost = $41,436.25
12.10. $Q = 25$, $C = \$1,500$; $Q = 40$, $C = \$1,230$; $Q = 50$, $C = \$1,200$; $Q = 60$; $C = \$1,220$; $Q = 100$, $C = \$1,500$
12.12. (a) $1,220
(b) $1,200 with $Q = 60$
(c) 24 units
12.14. 1,217 units
12.16. 51 units; $1,901.22
12.18. $752.63 (Order 100 units each time at discount level of $15.75).
12.20. Safety stock = 30 units; ROP = 90 units
12.22. Safety stock = 100 units: ROP = 300 units
12.24. (a) $z = 1.88$
(b) 9.4 drives = safety stock
(c) ROP = 59.4 drives

Chapter 12 Supplement
S12.2. 3.75, or 4 kanbans
S12.4. Size of kanban = 66; number of kanbans = 5.9, or 6
S12.6. (a) EOQ = 10 lamps
(b) 200 orders/year
(c) $200

Chapter 13
13.2. Cost = $53,320
No, plan 2 is better.
13.4. Cost = $214,000 for plan B
13.6. Plan D; $122,000; Plan E is $129,000
13.8. Each answer you develop will differ.
13.10. Plan C, $92,000; Plan D, $82,300 assuming initial inventory = 0
13.12. $11,790
13.14. $1,186,810
13.16. $100,750
13.18. $88,150

Chapter 14
14.2. (a)

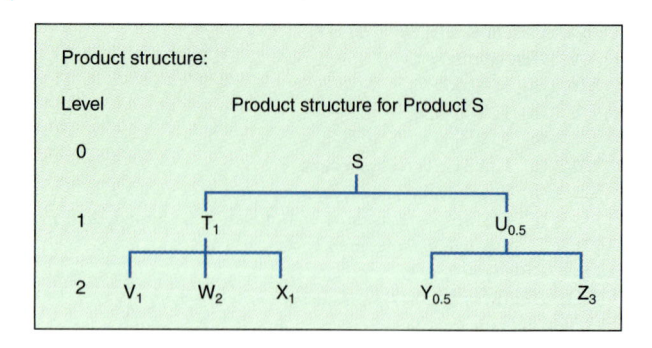

Product structure:

Product structure for Product S

Level 0: S
Level 1: T_1, $U_{0.5}$
Level 2: V_1, W_2, X_1, $Y_{0.5}$, Z_3

Gross material requirements plan:

Item		1	2	3	4	5	6	7	8	Lead Time (wks)
S	Gr. Required							100		
	Order release					100				2
T	Gr. Required					100				
	Order release				100					1
U	Gr. Required					50				
	Order release			50						2
V	Gr. Required				100					
	Order release		100							2
W	Gr. Required				200					
	Order release	200								3
X	Gr. Required				100					
	Order release			100						1
Y	Gr. Required			25						
	Order release	25								2
Z	Gr. Required		150							
	Order release	150								1

(b) Net material requirements plan (only items S and T are shown):

Item		1	2	3	4	5	6	7	8	Lead Time (wks)
S	Gross required							100		
	On hand							20		
	Net required							80		2
	Order receipt							80		
	Order release					80				
T	Gross required					80				
	On hand					20				
	Net required					60				1
	Order receipt					60				
	Order release				60					

APPENDIX VI SOLUTIONS TO EVEN-NUMBERED PROBLEMS

14.4. (a) Gross material requirements plan:

		\multicolumn{12}{c}{Week}
		1	2	3	4	5	6	7	8	9	10	11	12
X_1	Gr. Required								50		20		100
	Order release							50		20		100	
B_1	Gr. Required								50		20		100
	Order release					50		20		100			
B_2	Gr. Required							100		40		200	
	Order release				100		40			200			
A_1	Gr. Required					50		20		100			
	Order release			50		20		100					
D	Gr. Required				200		80		400				
	Order release			200		80		400					
E	Gr. Required				100		40		200				
	Order release			100		40		200					
C	Gr. Required				200	50	80	20	400	100			
	Order release	200	50	80	20	400	100						

(b) Net material requirements (planned order release) plan:

		\multicolumn{12}{c}{Week}
		1	2	3	4	5	6	7	8	9	10	11	12
X_1	Gr. Required										20		100
	Order release									20		100	
B_1	Gr. Required												100
	Order release									100			
B_2	Gr. Required									20		200	
	Order release							20		200			
A_1	Gr. Required									95			
	Order release							95					
D	Gr. Required							40		400			
	Order release						40		400				
E	Gr. Required							20		200			
	Order release					20		200					
C	Gr. Required						30		400	100			
	Order release			30		400	100						

14.6. Net material requirements plan (only items A and H are shown):

		\multicolumn{12}{c}{Week}
		1	2	3	4	5	6	7	8	9	10	11	12
A	Gross required							100		50		150	
	On hand							0		0		0	
	Net required							100		50		150	
	Order receipt							100		50		150	
	Order release						100		50		150		
H	Gross required								100		50		
	On hand								0		0		
	Net required								100		50		
	Order receipt								100		50		
	Order release							100		50			

14.8. (a) EOQ = 57.4 units
Theoretical total cost: $1,723.42
Actual total cost: $2,365.00

(b) EOQ = 57.4 units
Theoretical total cost: $1,723.42
Actual total cost: $1,810.00

14.10. (a) EOQ = $332.50
(b) Lot-for-lot = $400
(c) PPB cost = $220

14.12. New master production schedule:

		\multicolumn{11}{c}{Week}
		0	1	2	3	4	5	6	7	8	9	10
P	Gross required	0	0	30	40	10	70	40	10	30	60	

Gross material requirements plan:

		\multicolumn{11}{c}{Week}
		0	1	2	3	4	5	6	7	8	9	10
P	Gr. Required			30	40	10	70	40	10	30	60	
	Order release		30	40	10	70	40	10	30	60		
C	Gr. Required			30	40	10	70	40	10	30	60	
	Order release	80			120			90				

Net material requirements plan:

		\multicolumn{11}{c}{Week}
		0	1	2	3	4	5	6	7	8	9	10
P	Gross required	0	0	0	30	40	10	70	40	10	30	60
	On hand	20	20	20	20	0	0	0	0	0	0	0
	Net required				10	40	10	70	40	10	30	60
	Order receipt				10	40	10	70	40	10	30	60
	Order release			10	40	10	70	40	10	30	60	
C	Gross required			10	40	10	70	40	10	30	60	
	On hand	30	30	30	20	80	70	0	40	30	0	
	Net required	0	0	0	40	10	70	40	10	30	60	
	Order receipt			100			80				60	
	Order release	40		100			80			60		

14.14. The limit of 75 components per week constrains component production in weeks 4 and 7. Some production will need to be moved to weeks 2 and 5.

14.16. (a) Ten units are required for production, and 10 for field service repair.

(b)

Components	Quantity		Components	Quantity
A	10		A	10
B	20		B	18
C	40		C	13
D	20		D	13
E	40		E	14
F	20		F	15
G	20		G	14
H	20		H	5

(c) Not shown here

14.18. **(a)**

Requirements

	1	2	3	4	5	6	7	8	9	10	11	12
E.C.W.			40	100	80	70	20	25	70	80	30	50
W.C.W.		20	45	60	70	40	80	70	80	55		
F.W.			30	40	10	70	40	10	30	60		

Requirements Offset for Lead times

	0	1	2	3	4	5	6	7	8	9	10	11	12
E.C.W.		40	100	80	70	20	25	70	80	30	50		
W.C.W.	20	45	60	70	40	80	70	80	55				
F.W.			30	40	10	70	40	10	30	60			

Receipts from Factory at Factory Warehouse

	0	1	2	3	4	5	6	7	8	9	10	11	12
Gross required	20	85	190	190	120	170	135	160	165	90	50		
On hand		80	95	5	15	95	25	90	30	65	75	25	
Planned receipt from factory	100	100	100	200	200	100	200	100	200	100			

(b) Release all orders 2 weeks prior to the schedule above (the planned "Receipts from Factory" date).

If the schedule is late, as suggested above, then the initial order for receipt in week 3 should be for all requirements needed prior to that (i.e., weeks 0, 1, 2, and 3, for a total of 500 units). The release schedule would then be

	Week						
	1	2	3	4	5	6	7
Planned order release	500	200	100	200	100	200	100

Chapter 15

15.2. **(a)** 1-D, 2-A, 3-C, 4-B
(b) 40

15.4.

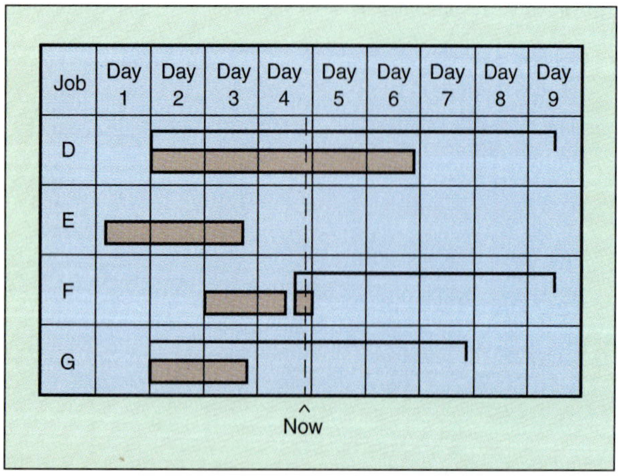

15.6. A-61 to 4; A-60 to 1; A-53 to 3; A-56 to 5; A-52 to 2; A-59 to 6; 150 hours

15.8. 1–2 P.M. on A; 2–3 P.M. on C; 3–4 P.M. on B; 4–5 P.M. on Independent; 75.5 rating

15.10. **(a)** A, B, C, D, E
(b) B, A, D, E, C
(c) E, D, A, B, C
(d) C, B, A, D, E
SPT is best

15.12. D, C, A, B sequence

15.14. **(a)** A, B, C, D, E
(b) C, A, B, E, D
(c) C, D, E, A, B
(d) B, A, E, D, C
EDD and FCFS are best on lateness, SPT on other two measures.

15.16. D, B, A, C

15.18. 7.26 minutes per setup

15.20. 3.67 minutes per setup

Chapter 16

16.2.

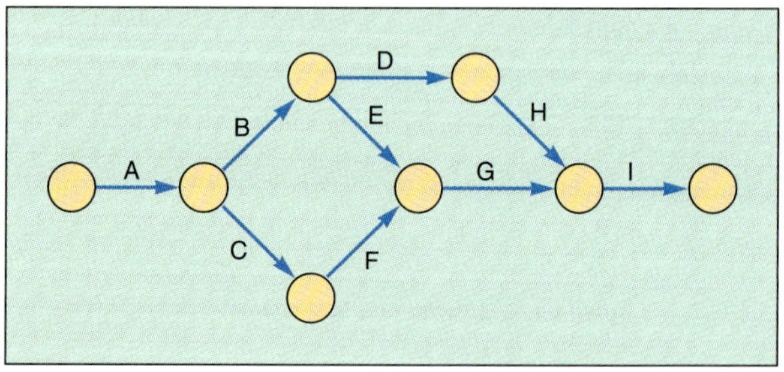

16.4.

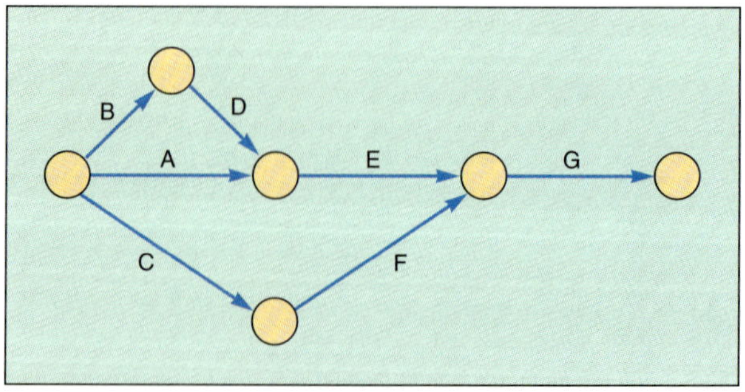

16.6. (a)

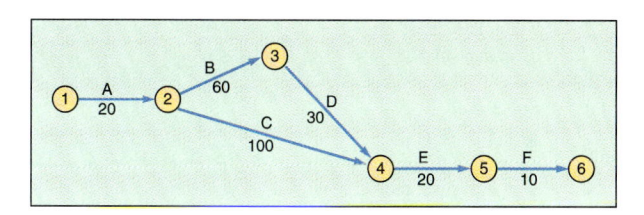

[Network diagram: Node 1 →A,20→ Node 2 →B,60→ Node 3; Node 2 →C,100→ Node 4; Node 3 →D,30→ Node 4; Node 4 →E,20→ Node 5 →F,10→ Node 6]

(b) project completion time = 150 hours

16.8.

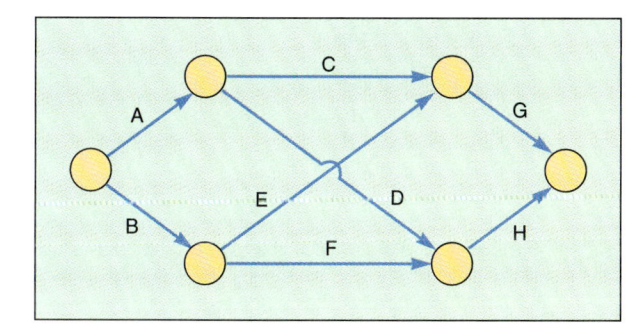

[Network diagram showing activities A, B, C, D, E, F, G, H connecting nodes]

16.10. A, 5.83, 0.69
B, 3.67, 0.11
C, 2.00, 0.11
D, 7.00, 0.11
E, 4.00, 0.44
F, 10.00, 1.78
G, 2.17, 0.25
H, 6.00, 1.00
I, 11.00, 0.11
J, 16.33, 1.00
K, 7.33, 1.78

16.12. .9463

16.14. (a) 15 (A, C, E)
(b) 2

16.16. (a) 16 (A, D, G)
(b) $12,300
(c) D, 1 week for $75

16.18. A, C, E, H, I, K, M, N; 50 weeks

16.20. (a) .0228
(b) .3085
(c) .8413
(d) .9772

16.22. (a, b) Critical path = A, B, J, K, L, M, R, S, T, U; time = 18
(c) Transmissions and drive trains are not on the critical path; halving engine time reduces the critical path by 2 days; speeding accessory delivery is not critical.
(d) Reallocating workers can reduce the critical path length.

16.24. Length = 34 weeks; critical path is composed of activities 11, 13, 14, 16, 17, 18, 19, 21, and 23.

Chapter 17

17.2. From Figure 17.2, about 13% overall reliability.
17.4. Expected daily breakdowns = 2.0.
Expected cost = $100 daily

17.6. (a) 5.0%
(b) .00001025 failures/unit-hr.
(c) .08979
(d) 98.77
17.8. $R_s = .8145$
17.10. $R_p = .99925$
17.12. $R_p = .984$
17.14. $R = .7918$
17.16. Cost without maintenance contract = $1,255/week
Cost with maintenance contract = $1,395/week

Quantitative Module A

A.2. EVPI = $13,800 − 12,200 = $1,600
where $13,800 = .3(22,000) + .5(12,000) + .2(6,000)
A.4. EVPI = $364,000 − $320,000 = $44,000
A.6. E(cost full-time) = $520
E(cost part-timers) = $475
A.8. Major expansion; EMV = $150,000
A.10. 8 cases
A.12. (a)

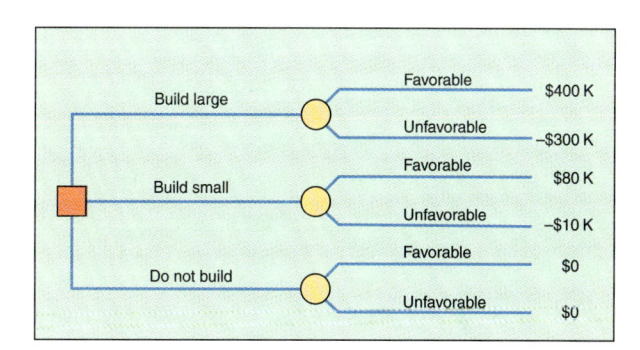

[Decision tree: Build large → Favorable $400K / Unfavorable −$300K; Build small → Favorable $80K / Unfavorable −$10K; Do not build → Favorable $0 / Unfavorable $0]

(b) Small plant with EMV = $26,000
(c) EVPI = $134,000
A.14. (a) Max EMV = $11,700
(b) EVPI = $13,200 − $11,700 = $1,500
A.16.

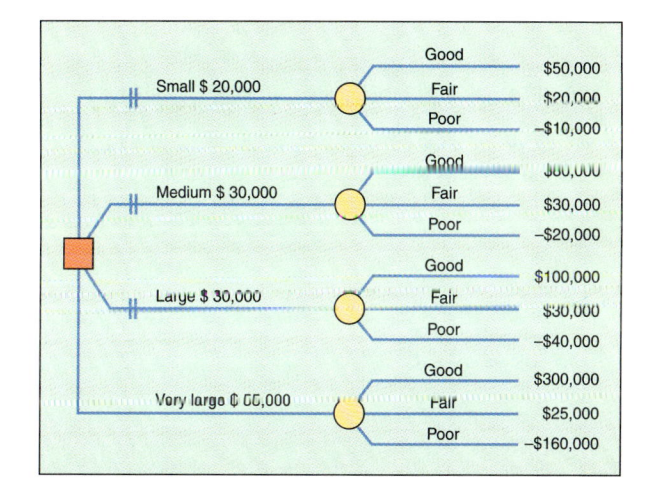

[Decision tree: Small $20,000 → Good $50,000 / Fair $20,000 / Poor −$10,000; Medium $30,000 → Good $80,000 / Fair $30,000 / Poor −$20,000; Large $30,000 → Good $100,000 / Fair $30,000 / Poor −$40,000; Very large $60,000 → Good $300,000 / Fair $25,000 / Poor −$160,000]

A.18.

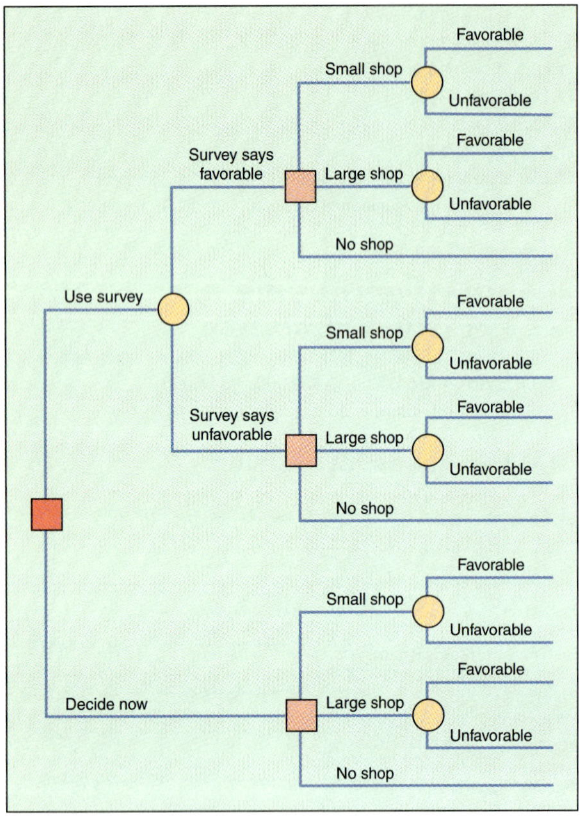

Use survey
Survey says favorable
Survey says unfavorable
Decide now
Small shop
Large shop
No shop
Favorable
Unfavorable

A.20. No information and build large; $4,500

Quantitative Module B

B.2. $P = 100$ at (0, 10)

B.4. **(a)** $P = \$3{,}000$ at (75, 75) and (50, 150)

B.6. **(a)** Min $X_1 + 2X_2$

$X_1 + X_2 \geq 40$

$2X_1 + 4X_2 \geq 60$

$x_1 \leq 15$

(b) Cost = $.65 at (15, 25)

(c) 65¢

B.8. $x_1 = 200, x_2 = 0$, profit = $18,000

B.10. 10 Alpha 4s, 24 Beta 5s, profit = $55,200

B.12. **(a)** $x_1 = 25.71, x_2 = 21.43$

(b) Cost = $68.57

B.14. **(a)** $x_1 = 7.9, x_2 = 5.9, x_3 = 12.6, P = \$143.40$

(b) No unused time

B.16. Treasury notes = $150,000; bonds = $100,000; ROI = $21,000

B.18. Hire 30 workers

16 begin at 7 A.M.

9 begin at 3 P.M.

2 begin at 7 P.M.

3 begin at 11 P.M.

An alternate optimum is:

3 begin at 3 A.M.

9 begin at 7 A.M.

7 begin at 11 A.M.

2 begin at 3 P.M.

9 begin at 7 P.M.

0 begin at 11 P.M.

B.20. Max $P = 9x_1 + 12x_2$

Subject to:

$x_1 + x_2 \leq 10$

$x_1 + 2x_2 \leq 12$

$x_1 = 8, x_2 = 2$; profit = $96

B.22. $x_1 = 14, x_2 = 33$, cost = 221

B.24. $22.50–$30.00

B.26. **(a)** Minimize = 6X1A + 5X1B + 3X1C + 8X2A + 10X2B + 8X2C + 11X3A + 14X3B + 18X3C

Subject to:

X1A + X2A + X3A = 7

X1B + X2B + X3B = 12

X1C + X2C + X3C = 5

X1A + X1B + X1C ≤ 6

X2A + X2B + X2C ≤ 8

X3A + X3B + X3C ≤ 10

(b) Minimum cost = $219,000

B.28. One approach results in 2,791 medical patients and 2,105 surgical patients, with a revenue of $9,551,668 per year (which can change slightly with rounding). This yields 61 medical beds and 29 surgical beds.

Quantitative Module C

C.2. Total cost = $2,000. Multiple optimal solutions exist. Cost after second iteration = $2,640; after third iteration = $2,160.

C.4. Optimal cost = $2,570

X-A = 50; X-C = 50; Y-B = 50; Z-B = 30; Z-C = 20; Z-Dummy = 25

C.6. **(a)** A-1, 10; B-1, 30; C-2, 60; A-3, 40; C-3, 15.

(b) $1,775

C.8. Houston, $19,500

C.10. Total cost = $505

C.12. Initial cost = $260

Improved solution = $255

Final solution = $230

C.14. F1-W1, 1,000; F1-W4, 500; F2-W2, 2,000; F2-W3, 500; F3-W3, 1,500; F3-W4, 700; cost = $39,300

C.16. $60,900 with East St. Louis; $62,250 with St. Louis.

Quantitative Module D

D.2. **(a)** 44%

(b) .36 people

(c) .8 people

(d) .53 minutes

(e) 1.2 minutes

D.4. **(a)** .5

(b) .5

(c) 1

(d) .5

(e) .05 hr.

(f) .1 hr.

D.6. **(a)** .667

(b) .667 min.

(c) 1.33

D.8. (a) .375
(b) 1.6 hr. (or .2 days)
(c) .225
(d) 0.141, 0.053, 0.020, 0.007

D.10. (a) 2.25
(b) .75
(c) .857 min. (.014 hours)
(d) .64 min. (.011 hours)
(e) 42%, 32%, 24%

D.12. (a) 6 trucks
(b) 12 min.
(c) .857
(d) 54%
(e) $1,728/day
(f) Yes, save $3,096 is the first year.

D.14. (a) .666
(b) 1.33
(c) 10 sec.

D.16. 3, 2, 4 MDs, respectively

D.18. (a) .05
(b) .743
(c) .795

D.20. (a) .113 hour = 6.8 min.
(b) 1.13 cars

Quantitative Module E

E.2. (a) 507 min.
(b) 456 min.
(c) 410 min.
(d) 369 min.

E.4. (a) 1,546 min.
(b) 2,872 min.
(c) 3,701 min.
(d) 6,779 min.

E.6. (a) 14.31 hr.
(b) $71,550
(c) $947,250

E.8. (a) 80%
(b) 3.51
(c) 3.2, 2.98, 2.81
(d) 21.5

E.10. (a) 72.2 hr.
(b) 60.55 hr.
(c) 41.47 hr.

E.12. $748,240 for fourth, $709,960 for fifth, and $679,942 for sixth

E.14. (a) 70 millicents/bit
(b) 8.2 millicents/bit

E.16. 26,755 lu.

E.18. (a) 32.98 hr, 49.61 hr.
(b) Initial quote is high.

Quantitative Module F

F.2. 0, 0, 0, 0, 0, 0, 0, 2, 0, 2
F.4. Profits = 20, −15, 20, 17.50, 20; average equals 12.50
F.6. At the end of 5 minutes, 2 checkouts are still busy and one is available.

F.8.

Arrivals	Arrival Time	Service Time	Departure Time
1	11:01	3	11:04
2	11:04	2	11:06
3	11:06	2	11:08
4	11:07	1	11:09

F.10. (a, b)

No. Cars	Prob.	Cum. Prob.	R.N. Interval
3 or less	0	0	—
4	.10	.10	01 through 10
5	.15	.25	11 through 25
6	.25	.50	26 through 50
7	.30	.80	51 through 80
8	.20	1.00	81 through 00
9 or more	0	—	—

(c) Average no. arrivals/hour = 105/15 = 7 cars

F.12. Each simulation will differ. Using random numbers from right-hand column of the random number table, reading top to bottom, in the order used, results in a $9.20 cost. This is greater than the $6.65 in Example F3.

F.14. (a) 5 times
(b) 6.95 times; yes
(c) 7.16 heaters

F.16. Average demand is about 8.75, average lead time is 1.86, average end inventory = 6.50, average lost sales = 4.04. Values will vary with different sets of random numbers.

F.18. Average end inventory = 8.90; average lost sales = 3.41; total cost = $488,568 or $20,357/month. This new policy seems preferable.

F.20. Here are the random-number intervals for the first two departments. Random number intervals correspond to probability of occurrence.

From	To	R.N. Interval
Initial exam	X-ray	01 through 45
	OR	46 through 60
	Observ.	61 through 70
	Out	71 through 00

From	To	R.N. Interval
X-ray	OR	01 through 10
	Cast	11 through 35
	Observ.	36 through 70
	Out	71 through 00

Each simulation will produce different results. Some will indeed show a person entering X-ray twice.

Name Index

Aaker, David, 43n
Abadow, G., 837n
Abernathy, William J., 810n
Aeppel, Timothy, 373n
Aft, L.S., 381n
Agarwal, Anurag, 478n
Aikins, J., 288n
Akao, Yoji, 87n, 106n, 224n
Akinc, U., 436n, 619n
Alexander, D.C., 388n
Ali, A., 224
Ames, J.M., 436n
Anard, Sam, 597n
Anbil, R.E., 619n
Anderson, John C., 82n
Andrews, B., 737n, 772n
Ansarl, A., 499n
Arcus, A.L., 344n
Armacost, R.L., 534n
Armor, G.S., 330n
Armstrong, J.S., 190n
Arnold, J.R.T., 436n
Atanasoff, John Vincent, 6
Atkinson, A. A., 199n

Babbage, Charles, 28n, 369, 369n, 374n
Baer, R., 288n
Balakrishnan, J., 362n
Baldwin, C.Y., 204n
Ballot, Michael, 761n
Balzer, R., 288n
Banker, R. D., 199n
Barney, Jay B., 51n
Barnes, R.M., 388n, 412n
Bartlett, Christopher, 58n
Bartmess, Andrew, 285n, 292n
Bassett, Glenn, 519n
Batta, R., 619n
Batterson, R., 74n
Bauer, A., 619n
Bayus, Barry L., 146n
Bean, James, 705n
Beaty, C A , 288n
Bechtold, S.E., 412n
Becker, L.C., 793n
Bell, George, 306
Bell, Glen, 23
Benoit, J., 288n
Berggren, C., 388n

Berle, G., 67n, 74n
Bernard, Paul, 478n
Berry, W.L., 270n, 478n, 534n, 619n
Berry, L., 23n, 97n, 98n, 106n, 221n, 270n
Besterfield, D.H., 137n
Bhote, K., 436n
Billington, C., 427n
Biranbaum-Moore, P.H., 285n
Birnbaum, L., 288n
Black, Simon A., 106n
Blackburn, J., 204n, 421
Blackstone, Jr., J.H., 576n
Blair, C., 412n
Blair, Thomas E., 684
Bleeke, J., 74n
Blocker, Douglas J., 482n
Blumenthal, D.E., 436n
Bookbinder, J.H., 576
Borzone, Bob, 487
Bowden, R., 619n
Bower, J.L., 224n
Bowers, M.R., 478n, 534n
Bowman, E.H., 518, 518n
Box, G.E.P., 190n
Boxley, Al, 601
Bozarth, C.C., 270n
Brennan, J.E., 837n
Bridleman, Dan, 436n
Brock, Michael, 672n
Brown, R., 701n
Brown, R.G., 190n, 203n, 478n
Browne, J., 619n
Brozer, Y.A., 330n
Brucker, H.D., 576n
Buffa, E.S., 330n
Burbidge, J.L., 224n, 270n
Burke, Sir Edmund, 147
Burns, Kay, 436n
Burns, L.D., 436n
Burt, D.N., 436n
Buxey, G., 521n, 534n
Buzzell, Robert D., 42n, 422
Byham, W.C., 370n
Bylinsky, G., 270n
Byrd, J., 793n
Byrd, T.A., 288n

Camm, Jeff, 810n
Camp, Robert, 86

Campbell, G.M., 576n
Campy, James, 239n
Capon, N.J., 224n
Carbonne, J., 429n
Carlzon, Jan, 213n
Carr, L.P., 106n
Carroll, S.J., 66n, 74n
Carson, R., 388n
Carter, P.L., 499n
Casey, Jeff T., 436n
Cattanach, R.E., 270n
Cerny, Keith, 285n
Chambers, J.C., 190n
Chapman, S.N., 499n
Chapman, A., 389n
Carroll, William J., 520n
Chausse, Sylvain, 551n
Chen, Rongqui, 499n
Chen, Shuyong, 499n
Cheng, L., 362n
Chesbrough, Henry W., 436n
Chevrolet, Louis, 340
Chew, Bruce W., 224n
Chilton, K., 74n
Choi, M., 224
Choi, Thomas Y., 426n
Chrysler, Walter, 340
Cinar, U., 330n
Clark, Kim B., 204n, 682n
Cleaves, Gerard, 436n
Cleland, D.I., 661n
Colan, M. F., 781n
Cole, J.R., 837n
Collopy, F., 190n
Connors, Mary, 484n
Cook, Laddie, 421n
Cook, Thomas, 704
Cooper, R. B., 224n, 770n, 793n
Copacino, William C., 436n
Corlett, N., 389n
Costin, H., 106n
Cox, Jeff, 598, 598n
Craig, C.S., 318n
Crosby, Philip B., 81, 81n, 84, 85, 106n
Cunningham, James A., 798n
Czerwinski, F. L., 224n

Daganzo, F., 436n
Dator, S. M., 105n

Name Index

D'Aveni, Richard, 39
Davenport, T.H., 288n
Davis, Louis E., 372n
Davis, T., 427n
Dean, B.V., 661n
Dean, J., 204n
Dean, James, 223n
Deere, John, 161
DeForest, M.E., 318n
DeMatta, R., 534n
DeMatteis, J.J., 553n
Deming, W. Edwards, 6, 82, 83n, 84, 106n, 109n
Denton, D.K., 106n, 478n
Dettro, Dennis, 628
Dickie, Ford H., 441n
Dickinson, William J., 371n
Ding, F., 362n, 576n
Dodge, H.F., 125n
Dolinsky, L.R., 576n
Domich, P.D., 318n
Draper, A.B., 224n
Dreyfuss, Henry, 375n, 389n
Drezner, Z., 318n
Drucker, P.F., 28n, 47n, 51n
Duggan, J., 619n
Duguary, Claude R., 551n
Dumoliem, Williams J., 331n
Dusenberry, W., 661n
Dutta, S.P., 837n
Dwinells, E.E., 116n

Ealey, Lance, 89n
Eastman, C.M., 330n
Eckert, J. Presper, 6
Edmonson, H.E., 51n
Engelstad, H., 372n
Epstein, Marc J., 199n
Erlebacher, S.J., 330n
Ernst, D., 74n
Ettlie, J.E., 270n
Evans, J., 204n
Evans, James R., 106n, 137n, 223n, 837n

Faaland, B.H., 362n
Fabricant, Solomon, 28n
Fairfield, Bill, 428
Farley, A.A., 737n
Farrell, Paul V., 425n
Feigenbaum, A.V., 106n
Fein, Mitchell, 373n
Ferdows, K., 59n, 60n, 74n
Fields, Debbie, 603
Fisher, Bradley, 83n
Fisher, E.L., 331n
Fisher, Marshall L., 417n, 534n
Fitzsimmons, James, 224n, 305n
Flanders, R.E., 331, 331n
Fleming, S.C., 285n
Flowers, A.D., 837n

Flowers, G.A., 576n
Flynn, B.B., 412n, 493n
Foote, B.L., 793n
Ford, Henry, 5, 421
Fordyce, James M., 555n
Forrester, Jay, 562n
Foss, Murray, 16n
Foster, G., 105n
Foster, Jr., S.T., 106n
Francis, R.L., 362n
Franke, R.H., 389n
Fraser, Douglas, 373
Freeland, J.R., 478n, 499n, 576n
Frick, M.D., 436n
Frye, C., 307n

Gagnon, Roger J., 102
Gaimon, C., 288n, 619n
Gale, B.T., 28n, 42n
Galsworth, Gwendolyn D., 389n
Galvin, Robert, 76
Gannon, M.J., 66n, 74n
Gantt, Henry L., 5
Gardiner, S.C., 576n
Gardner, E.S., 158n, 190n
Garvin, D.A., 78n, 79n
Garza, O., 224n
Gass, S.I., 737n
Gates, Bill, 684
Gelman, E., 619
Geoffrion, Arthur M., 436n
Georgoff, D.M., 190n
Gerwin, D., 51n
Ghemawat, Pankaj, 802n
Ghosh, S., 619n
Ghoshal, Sumantra, 58
Gibson, Keith, 294
Gibson, Richard, 198n
Gilbert, James P., 483n
Gilbreth, Frank, 5, 399
Gilbreth, Lillian, 5
Gilman, Andrew, 596n
Gips, J., 190n
Giunipero, Larry, 425n
Golden, B.L., 837n
Goldratt, Eliyahu M., 598, 598n
Golhar, D.Y., 499n
Gopalakrishnan, M., 619n
Gopalakrishnan, S., 619n
Grant, R.M., 288n
Grassman, W.K., 793n
Gray, D., 682n
Greenberg, H.J., 737n
Greene, Timothy J., 332n
Greenwald, Bruce, 23n, 29n
Greif, Michael, 389n
Griffin, W., 50n, 56n, 57n, 68n, 73n, 205n, 770n
Grimes, Richard C., 436n, 520n
Groenevelt, H., 478n
Gross, E.E., 378n

Grover, Varun, 52n
Gumaer, Robert, 436n
Gunther, William, 297
Gupta, Y.P., 137n, 682n

Habele, Norma Faris, 284n
Hackman, J.R., 371, 371n
Haddock, J., 576n
Hadlley, Leonard, 66
Hall, G., 810n
Hall, R.W., 270n, 436n, 478n, 491n
Hallowell, Roger, 374n, 389n
Hammer, Floyd, 245
Hammer, Michael, 239n
Hammond, J. H., 534n
Hanfield, R., 499n
Hansen, Bertrand L., 94n
Hanson, R.S., 647n
Harbison, Frederick, 28n
Harris, Ford W., 447n
Hart, C., 534n, 810n
Hart, M.K., 106n
Hartley, Janet L., 426n
Hastings, N.A., 224n
Hauser, J.R., 106n
Hayes, Robert H., 682n
Hayes-Roth, F., 288n
Hazelwood, R.N., 778n, 779n
Heinritz, Stuart F., 425n
Heizer, Jay, 270n, 298, 550n
Helms, Marilyn M., 28n, 682n
Henry, Patrick, 147
Herager, Sunderesh, 362n
Herrmann, Jeff, 436n
Hertzberg, Frederick, 371n
Heskett, J., 534n
Hess, S.W., 701n
Hickle, R., 837n
Hickman, Anita, 661n
Hicks, Ronald A., 559n
Hill, Charles W. L., 59n
Hill, T.J., 270n
Hill, Terry, 257n
Ho, C., 793n
Hobbs, Kermit O., 499n
Hoey, James, 601n
Hoffman, J.J., 74n
Hoffman, K.L., 318n
Hokey, Min, 436n
Holmes, Sherlock, 110
Holt, Charles, 518n
Horner, P. R., 578n, 716n
Horngren, C.T., 105n
Hosseini, J., 684n
Hotchkiss, C., 66n, 74n
Houck, B.L.W., 362n
Hounshell, D.A., 29n, 270n
Hout, T.M., 224n
Howell, S., 810n
Hoy P., 576n
Huang, P.Y., 270n, 362n

Name Index

Hubicki, D.E., 576n
Hulbert, J.M., 224n
Hutchinson, J., 837n
Hwarng, H.B., 284n

Iansiti, M., 224n, 272n, 288n
Inman, A.R., 448n, 499n
Irwin, Richard D., 257n
Israeli, Asher, 83n

Jackson, Paul, 486n
Jackson, R.H.F., 318n
Jacobs, F.R., 576n
Jacobs, L.W., 412n
Janaro, R.E., 224n
Jarvis, J.P., 534n
Jenkins, G., 190n
Jinchiro, N., 478n, 499n
Johnson, Eric, 427n
Johnson, R.V., 330n
Johnson, Ross, 79n
Johnson, S.M., 595n
Johnson, T.W., 318n
Jones, Daniel T., 52n, 204n, 239n
Jones, Marilyn, 105n
Jordan, M., 682n
Joshi, S., 362n, 682n
Juran, J.M., 84, 90, 106n

Kaku, B.K., 362n
Kalwani, M.V., 224n
Kanigel, Robert, 393n
Kanter, Rosabeth Moss, 198n
Kao, John, 198n
Kaplan, Robert S., 51n, 199n
Karger, D.W., 412n
Karwan, M., 682n
Katz, K., 793n
Keefer, D.L., 662n
Kelly, J.E., 629
Kerzner, H., 662n
Khumawala, B., 560n
Khurana, A., 224n
Kim, S., 662n
Kim, Y., 619n
Kimes, Sheryl, 305n
Kinard, Jerry, 135n, 137n, 317n, 476n
King, W.R., 661n
Kirshner, P., 67n, 74n
Klastorin, T.D., 362n
Klopmaker, J.E., 270n
Koch, L.A., 576n
Kolchin, Michael, 425n
Konz, S., 389n, 412n
Koprowski, Gene, 283n
Koslow, L.E., 60n, 67n, 74n
Kouvelis, P., 224n
Kovenock, D., 224n
Krafcik, John, 239n
Krajewski, L.J., 288n
Krishnan, R., 288n

Kuck, Paul, 192
Kumar, H., 576n
Kumar, S., 137n
Kurioka, Tatsumi, 325n

Labach, Elaine J., 237n
Lackey, Charles W., 482n
LaForge, Lawrence R., 576n
Lahtella, J., 374n
Landauer, E.G., 793n
Landry, Sylvain, 551n
Landvater, D.V., 478n
Larson, B., 793n
Larson, R., 793n
Larson, R.C., 781n
Larsson, Jan L., 798n
Lau, H., 793n
Leachman, R.C., 662n
Ledbetter, M.E., 576n
Lee, Hau L., 427n, 436n
Lee, T.S., 576n
Lehmann, D.R., 224n
Leone, R.A., 534n
Leong, Keong G., 142n, 837n
Leschke, J.P., 478n, 499n, 576n
Lesieur, Fred G., 374n
Leu, Y, 270n
Leung, J., 362n
Lev, B., 837n
Levy, David L., 436n
Lewis, Jordan D., 436n
Lincoln, John C., 388
Lincoln, James, 388
Linder-Dutton, L., 682n
Lindsay, W.M., 106n, 137n
Louis, R.S., 499n
Love, Robert, 601n
Low, James T., 598n
Lubove, Seth, 493n
Lyons, G., 619n

Mabert, Vincent A., 482n
Macelli, Carlos, 66
MacCormick, Alan, 288n
MacMillan, Ian C., 51n
Magad, B. L., 436n
Maggard, M.J., 576n
Maggard, B.N., 682n
Makens, P.K., 362n
Malhotra, Manoj K., 52n
Mallick, D.N., 224n
Manencia, F., 389n
Mann, Jr., L., 682n
Mansfield, E., 270n
Markides, Constantinos, 37, 52n
Markland, Robert K., 36n
Marquardt, M., 74n
Martin, A.J., 576n
Martinich, J.S., 230n, 245n
Masch, Vladimir A., 436n
Maslow, Abraham H., 371n

Mauchly, John, 6
Mausner, B., 371n
McClain, M.A., 318n
McCormick, E.J., 389n
McCutcheon, D.M., 270n
McGinnis, L.F., 362n
McGrath, Rita Gunther, 51n
Meckler, V.A., 576n
Mehra, S., 499n
Mehtra, Stephanie, 333n
Meller, R.D., 330n
Meredith, J.R., 270n
Merrils, Roy, 481n
Metters, Richard, 436n
Meyer, C., 389n
Meyers, C.A., 28n
Meyer, J.R., 534n
Michael, John R., 672n
Millen, Robert, 430n
Miller, D.M., 619n
Miller, Jeffrey G., 39n, 106n
Miller, T., 534n
Mulligan, Lawrence D., 429
Mital, A., 270n
Mitchell, O.R., 288n
Modarress, B., 499n
Modigliani, Franco, 518n
Mondy, R.W., 626n
Monteith, Cal, 558
Montgomery, D.C., 137n
Montreuil, B., 362n
More, James M., 330n
Morganstein, David, 672n
Morone, Joseph, 272n
Morris, J.S., 270n, 362n
Morse, P.M., 672n
Morton, Thomas E., 619n
Moscove, S.A., 645n
Mosier, C.T., 224n
Mullick, S.K., 190n
Murdick, Robert, 190n, 212n, 309n, 318, 519n, 533n, 534n, 602n
Muth, John F., 518n
Muther, Richard, 330n, 335n

Nandakumar, G., 555n
Neter, J., 166n
Ngo, Mile, 490n
Nicolin, M., 62n, 63n
Nicbel, D.W., 224n, 412n
Norton, David P., 51n

Obermeyer, W.R., 534n
O'Connor, E.J., 389n
Ohmae, K., 52n
Oldham, Greg R., 371, 371n
Olson, Ken, 170
Olson, Paul R., 14n, 361n
Orden, A., 736n
Orlicky, Joseph, 555n
Owings, Patrick, 682n

Name Index

Padmanabhan, V., 436n
Parasuraman, A., 97n, 98n, 106n
Pareto, Vilfredo, 90, 441n
Parsaei, H.R., 270n
Parsons, H., 737n, 772n
Pascale, Richard, 43
Paton, S.M., 106n
Patty, B., 619n
Peace, G.S., 106n
Pearson, Jim, 122n
Peck, R.D., 576n
Peck, L.G., 778n, 779n
Penlesky, R.J., 534n
Pentico, David W., 538n, 619n
Peterson, A.P.G., 378n
Petzinger, Thomas Jr., 283n
Pine, II, B.J., 270n
Pintelon, L., 478n
Pinto, M.B., 662n
Pinto, J.K., 662n
Plossl, George, 170n
Plummer, D.H., 646n
Porter, Leslie J., 106n
Porter, Michael E., 36n, 44n, 45n, 52n, 74n, 285n
Prabhu, N.U., 793n
Pratt, J.W., 701n
Premeaux, S.R., 626n
Prescott, J.E., 662n
Price, F., 106n
Price, W.L., 318n
Primrose, P., 270n
Proud, J.F., 576n
Pruett, J.M., 619n
Przasnyski, Zbigniew H., 837n
Puckett, Elbridge S., 374n
Pugliese, Phil, 28n
Pustay, M.W., 50n, 56n, 57n, 68n, 73n, 205n

Quinn, P., 737n

Rachamaduger, R., 576n
Raiffa, H., 701n
Raman, A., 534n
Rappoport, H.K., 837n
Ratliff, H.D., 362n
Raturi, A.S., 270n
Reed, R., 318n
Reich, R.B., 59n
Reinersten, D.G., 224n
Render Barry, 190n, 212n, 309n, 318n, 519n, 533n, 534n, 602n, 618n, 619n, 662n, 701n, 722n, 737n, 772n, 792n, 793n, 837n
Rengshida, Hefei, 66
Reynolds, A., 74n
Reza, E.M., 270n
Rhyne, D.M., 682n
Riggs, W.E., 224n
Ritchie, P., 418n
Roberts, E.B., 272n, 288n

Robertson, Thomas S., 204n
Robinson, Alan, 96n
Robinson, H.K., 62n, 63n
Rodrigues, C., 74n
Rodriquez, A.A., 288n
Roethlisberger, F.J., 371n
Romig, H.C., 125n
Roos, Daniel, 52n, 204n
Rosenbloom, R.S., 285n
Rosenthal, S.R., 224n
Ross, David S., 436n
Ross, S.C., 534n
Rossin, D.F., 362n
Roth, Adela, 39n, 538n
Roth, A.V., 288n
Runger, G.C., 137n
Rungtusanatham, Manus, 82n
Ruskin, John, 86
Russell, R.A., 190n, 837n
Russell, Roberta, 212n, 270n, 309n, 318n, 519n, 534n, 602
Ryan, Patrick, 426n

Sacerdoti, E., 288n
Sadowski, Randell P., 332n
Sakakibara, Sadao, 493n
Saltzman, M.J., 737n
Samoris, T.T., 224
Santen, William P., 331n
Sasieni, M.W., 634n
Sasser, W. Earl, 14n, 224n, 361n, 534n
Satinder, C., 190n
Sato, Fumio, 449
Saunders, T., 245n
Scamell, R., 560n
Schaaf, Dick, 214n
Schartner, A., 619n
Schindler, S., 737n
Schlaifer, R., 701n
Schmenner, Roger W., 269n, 318n, 534n
Schmitt, T.G., 362n
Schmitt, Tom, 484n
Schneeweis, C.A., 682n
Schniederjans, Marc J., 56, 59n, 74n, 478n, 499n
Schonberger, Richard J., 106n, 270n, 288n, 483n, 493n
Schroder, H., 682n
Schroeder, Roger G., 82n, 493n
Schulze, Horst, 371
Seidmann, A., 478n
Semmel, T., 737n
Sexton, T.R., 737n
Shani, A.B., 288n
Sheffer, J.P., 116n
Shell, M.C., 781n
Sherwin, D.J., 682n
Shewhart, Walter, 5, 108
Shin, Dooyoung, 436n
Shingo, Shingeo, 478n
Shostack, Lynn G., 14n

Shtub, A., 362n
Simkin, M.G., 645n
Simon, Herbert, 518n
Simmons, Bruce F. III, 189n
Sinai, Allen, 22n
Sivakumar, R., 619n
Skadburg, Dan, 240
Skinner, W., 52n
Skinner, Wickham, 333n
Sleeper, S., 737n
Smith, A., 29n
Smith, Adam, 369, 369n
Smith, Bernard, 172, 172n
Smith, David B., 798n
Smith, D.D., 189n, 190n
Smith, Fred, 290
Smith, P.G., 224n
Smunt, T.L., 224n
Snyder, C.A., 576n
Snyderman, B.B., 371n
Sofianou, Zaharo, 22n
Sol, H.G., 288n
Solomon, S., 793n
Solomon, S.L., 837n
Sorensen, Charles, 5, 6
Soukup, W.R., 436n
Southard, Bill, 387
Sower, Victor E., 102
Spendolini, Michael J., 84n
Spizizen, G., 810n
Springer, M.C., 362n
Sridharan, V., 576n
St. Johns, R., 576n
Stair, Jr., R.M., 190n, 318n, 618n, 619n, 662n, 701n, 722n, 737n, 772n, 792n, 793n, 837n
Stanton, Steven, 239n
Stalk Jr. George, 52n, 224n
Staughton, R.V.W., 389n
Stecke, Kathryn E., 558n
Steele, Daniel C., 27, 52n
Stefik, M., 288n
Stein, Herbert, 16n
Stein, Tom, 436n
Steinberg, E., 560n
Stone, Nan, 20
Stonebraker, Peter W., 142n
Stryker, Homer, 196
Subramanian, R., 716n
Sudit, M., 362n
Sullivan, B., 190n
Sviokla, John J., 288n
Sze, D.Y., 793n
Szucs, Paul, 490n

Taggart, Jr., R.E., 737n
Taguchi, Genichi, 89–90
Tanga, R., 619n
Tanzer, Andrew, 422n
Tatikunda, Mohan V., 273n
Taylor, Alex, 418n

Name Index

Taylor, Frederick W., 5, 6, 29n, 375, 375n, 393
Taylor, James C., 372n
Taylor, M.L., 810n
Tedone, Mark J., 169n
Teece, David J., 436n
Tehrani, K., 619n
Terai, Kiyohi, 325n
Tersine, Richard J., 270n, 362n, 435n
Thamhain, H., 662n
Themens, Jean-Luc, 551n
Thompson, Arthur A., 47n
Tichauer, Edwin R., 376n
Toffler, Alvin, 58, 58n
Tompkins, James A., 330n
Trunk, C., 837n
Tsaari, J., 374n
Turbide, D.A., 576n
Turcotte, M., 318n

Ulvila, J., 701n
Upton, David M., 369n
Urban, Timonty, 360n

Vakharia, A.J., 362n
Van Biema, Michael, 23n, 29n
Van Dierdonck, Roland, 538n
Van Weelderen, J.A., 288n
Vargas, G.A., 318n

Vaziri, H.K., 682n
Venkatadri, U., 362n
Verdini, W.A., 662n
Vergin, R.C., 518n
Vischer, Jacquelilne C., 334n
Vollmann, T.E., 330n, 478n, 534n, 576n, 619n

Wacker, John G., 446n, 538n, 561n
Wagner, H.M., 576n
Walker, M.R., 629
Walleigh, R.C., 499n
Walters, M., 412n
Ward, P.T., 837n
Wasserman, W., 166n
Watson, Thomas, 170
Wayne, K., 810n
Webster, Francis M., 555n
Weidenbaum, M., 74n
Weiss, A.R., 285n
Weiss, E.N., 478n, 499n, 576n
Weiss, Howard J., 575n
Welsh, James, 421n
West, Jonathan, 272n, 288n
Whang, Seungjin, 436n
Wheeler, Donald J., 137n
Wheelwright, Steven C., 51n, 224n
White, J.A., 362n
Whitin, T.M., 576n
Whitmore, S., 166n

Whitney, Eli, 5
Whitson, Daniel, 494n, 499n
Whybark, D.C., 478n, 534n, 576n, 619n
Wiersema, Fred, 198n
Wight, Oliver W., 170n, 478n
Williams, Robert, 99
Wilson, Joe, 102, 389n
Winchell, William O., 79n
Wolf, Horst, 340
Womack, James P., 52n, 204n, 239n
Worthington, D.J., 793n
Wrege, C.D., 29n
Wren, D.A., 29n
Wright, R.W., 285n
Wu, B., 288n
Wyckoff, Daryl D., 14n, 361n, 810n

Yamanato, Noboru, 325n
Yano, C.A., 619n
Yeh, C., 224n
Young, S.M., 199n
Yuen, M., 576n

Zammuto, R.F., 389n
Zeithaml, V., 97n, 98n, 106n
Zemke, Ron, 214n
Zenz, G.J., 426n, 434n
Zhao, X., 576n
Zisk, Burton, 331n

General Index

ABC analysis, 441–443
Acceptable quality level (AQL), 124
Acceptance sampling, 108, 123–125
    average outgoing quality and (AOQ), 125
    average outgoing quality limit (AOQL), 125
    operating characteristic curves and, 123–125
    producer's and consumer's risk and, 123–124
Accurate records, inventory and, 544
Activities,
    dummy, 632–633
    in PERT, 630–632
Activity charts, job design and, 380
Activity-on-Arrow (AOA), 631
Activity-on-Node (AON), 631
Activity time estimates, in PERT, 633–634
Adaptive forecasting, 172
Adaptive smoothing, 172
Advanced shipping notice (ASN), 429
Aggregate planning, *See* Aggregate scheduling
Aggregate scheduling, 501–534
    comparison of methods for, 518
    graphical and charting methods in, 511–516
    level material use schedule, 490, 599
    mathematical approach and, 516–518
    methods for, 511–518
    mixed strategies for, 511
    nature of, 505–507
    objective of, 504
    planning process and, 504
    scheduling, OM and, 8
    services and, 518–522
    strategies for, 507–511
Agile organization, 284
Airbus Industries, 54, 205, 812
Airfreight, materials management and, 430
Airline Industry
    aggregate scheduling and, 520–521
    global operations and, 68
    scheduling in, 601–602
Akron Zoological Park, 189
Alabama Airlines, 836–837
Alaska, Delphi method, 146
ALDEP, 331
Allocation, distribution resource planning and, 562

Amazon.com, 306
American Airlines, 81, 169, 704
American Electronics Association, 146
American Hardware Supply, 172
American League umpires, scheduling and, 590
American National Can Co., 237
American Plastics, Inc., 392
American Society of Mechanical Engineers (ASME), symbols of, 92
American Society for Quality (ASQ), 79, 82
American Software, 559
Andon, 381–382
Andrew Carter, Inc., 761
Anheuser-Busch, 246, 502–504, 505
APT, 275
Apple Computer, 377
Application of decision trees, product design and, 215–216
Applied Decision Analysis, 689
Applying learning curve, 798–802
Approaches to forecasting, 145–147
Area of feasible solutions, 708
ARENA, 824
Arithmetic approach, learning curves and, 799
Arrival characteristics, waiting line systems and, 766
Arrival population, 765–770
    characteristics of, 766
    pattern of arrivals and, 766
    size of, 766
Artificial intelligence, 283–284
Asea Brown Boveri, 58
ASRS (Automated Storage & Retreival Systems) 277
Assembly chart, 210
Assembly drawing, 210
Assembly line, product-oriented layout and, 339
Assembly line balancing, product-oriented layout and, 340–345
    objectives of, 340
Assignable causes, statistical process control and, 108
Assignable variations, statistical process control and, 108–110
Assignment method, loading and, 587–589
Assumptions, break-even analysis and, 252

ASYBL (Assembly Line Configuration), 344
AT&T, 82, 204, 368, 411, 426
Attitudes, location strategies and, 296
Attracting and retaining global talent, 61–62
Attracting new markets, global operations and, 61
Attribute(s), control charts for, 116–120
    p-charts and, 118
Attribute inspection, 96
Auto Desk, 335
Automated Storage and Retrieval Systems (ASRS), 277
Automatic guided vehicles (AGVs), 278
Automatic identification systems (AIS), 281, 338
Automatically Programmed Tool (APT), 275
Automation, service design and, 213
Average actual cycle time, 393
Average outgoing quality (AOQ), acceptance sampling and, 125
Average outgoing quality limit (AOQL), 125
Avis Car Rental, 740

BAAN, 559
Backflush, 551
Backward scheduling, 582
Balanced flow approach, MRP and, 551
Baldor Electric Co., 382
Balking customers, 766
BASIC, 823
Bay Medical Center, 812
Bayfield Mud Co., 135
Bayside Controls, 333
Bechtel, 622–624
Bell Laboratories, 108
Ben & Jerry's Ice Cream, 246
Benchmarking, 84–85
    supply-chain management and, 431
Benneton, 56, 277, 284, 285, 322
Bertelsmann, 58
Betamax, 196
Beta probability distribution, PERT and, 634
BetzDearborn, Inc., 108
B.F. Goodrich, 206
Bill-of-material (BOM), 208–209
    master production schedule (MPS) and, 541–544
Biological sciences, 6
BIOMED, 172

General Index

Blanket orders, 428
BMW, 200, 245, 340
Body Shop, 199
Boeing Aircraft, 54–56, 204, 205, 211, 274, 275, 418, 538
BOM, 208–209
Bonuses, 374
Booz, Allen & Hamilton, 629
Bose Corp., 78
Bottleneck work centers, 598–599
Brazil
    IBM, 62
    Volkswagen, 303, 414–416
    Whirlpool, 2
Breakdown maintenance, 671
Break-even analysis
    algebraic approach, 253
    assumptions and, 252
    crossover chart, 254, 255
    fixed costs, 251
    graphic approach, 252
    location strategies and, 300–301
    multiproduct case and, 255–257
    objective of, 251
    process strategy, capacity planning and, 251–257
    revenue function, 252
    single-product case and, 254
    variable costs, 251
Bristol-Myers Squib Company, 145, 199
British Airways, 773
Buckets, MRP and, 551
Burger King, 205, 333, 381, 814
Buyer, 419

C_{pk}, 121–123, 125–126
C++, 823
CAD, 205–206, 273, 335
CAD/CAM approach, 192, 273, 274
Cadillac, 81
CAE, 273
Canada, Whirlpool and, 2
Capacity, 246–251
    decision trees applied and, 249–250
    defined, 246–247
    demand management and, 250–251
    design, operations decisions and, 39–42
    effective, 246
    efficiency, 247
    forecasting and, 144
    forecasting requirements and, 247–249
    process strategy and, 225–270
    utilization, 246
Capacity options, aggregate strategies and, 507–509
Capacity planning, material requirements planning and, 556–557
Capital, as productivity variable, 19–22
Carpal tunnel syndrome, job design and, 376–377
Carrier Corp., 20

Case Studies
    Akron Zoological Park, chapter 5, 189
    Alabama Airlines, Quant. Mod. F, 836–837
    Andrew Carter, Inc., Quant. Mod. C, 761
    AT&T, supplement 10, 411
    Bayfield Mud Co., supplement 4, 135
    DeMar, chapter 6, 221
    Des Moines National Bank, chapter 9, 358
    Electronic Systems, Inc., supplement 12, 498
    Factory Enterprises, Inc., chapter 11, 433
    Ford, chapter 3, 73
    General Electric, chapter 6, 222–223
    Golding Landscaping & Plants, Inc., Quant. Mod. B, 736
    Heart bypass operation, Quant. Mod. A, 700
    LaPlace Power & Light, chapter 12, 476
    Lincoln Electric, chapter 10, 388
    Mathew Yachts, Inc., chapter 7, 268–269
    Mazda, chapter 3, 73
    Minit-Lube, Inc., chapter 2, 49
    Motorola, chapter 2, 50
    National Air Express, chapter 1, 28
    New England Castings, Quant. Mod. D, 790
    North-South Airline, chapter 5, 188
    Old Oregon Wood Store, chapter 15, 617–618
    Quality Cleaners, chapter 4, 104
    Rochester Manufacturing Corp., supplement 7, 287–288
    Ruch Manufacturing, chapter 14, 574–575
    Service, Inc., chapter 14, 574
    Shale Oil Co., chapter 16, 660
    Southard Truck Lines, chapter 10, 387
    Southern Recreational Vehicle Co., chapter 8, 317
    Southwestern State College, chapter 13, 532
    SMT's negotiation with IBM, Quant. Mod. D, 809
    SPC at the Gazette, supplement 4, 136–137
    Sturdivant Sound Systems, chapter 12, 476
    Thomas Manufacturing Co., chapter 11, 434
    Winter Park Hotel, Quant. Mod. D, 792
    Worldwide Chemical Company, chapter 17, 681–682
Cash flow, strategy driven investments and, 257
Caterpillar, 32–33
Causal methods, forecasting and, 146–147, 163–169
    correlation coefficients for regression lines, 167–168
    linear regression as method for, 146, 163–165
    multiple regression analysis, 168–169
    standard error of the estimate, 165–167
Causal models, 146–147
Cause and effect diagrams, 92, 95
c-charts, 120–121
Center of gravity method, location strategies and, 301–303
Central limit theorem, x-bar charts and, 111–112
Channel assembly, supply-chain mgt. and, 427–428
Chaparral, 333
Charting methods, for aggregate scheduling and, 511–516
Chase strategy, aggregate scheduling and, 510–511
Chelsea Milling Company, 249
China
    Boeing Aircraft, 418
    Federal Express, 292
    Global operations, 56, 67
    Johnson Electric Holdings, Ltd., 38
    Maytag, 66
    Whirlpool, 2
Chrysler Corporation, 85, 86
Circle K, 34
Citicorp, 58, 194
Closed-loop material requirements planning, 555–556
Coca-Cola, 63, 297
Coefficient of correlation, 167–168
Coefficient of determination, 168
COFAD, 331
Coleco, 56
Columbia, Bogata's Mobil Oil, 81
Collins Industries, 536–538
Colorado General Hospital, 603
Compact II, 275
Company reputation, quality and, 80
Compaq Computer Corp., 37–38, 46, 427–428, 505, 558
Competitive advantage, operations and, 36–39
    cost and, 37
    differentiation and, 36–37
    human resource strategy and, 366
    response and, 37–38
Competitive bidding, 426–427
Components, MRP, lead times and, 545
Compressed workweeks, 368
Computers, forecasting and, 172
Computer-aided design (CAD), 205–206, 273
Computer-aided manufacture (CAM), 274
Computer-integrated manufacturing (CIM), 279
Computer numerical control (CNC) machinery, 275
Computers in simulation, 823–824
Computrain, 506

General Index

COMSOAL (Computer Method for Sequencing Operations for Assemby Lines), 344, 344n
Concurrrent engineering, 202
Configuration management, 211
Consignment inventory, 483
Constant service time model, 776–777
Constraints
    graphical representation of, 707–708
    linear programming problem, 705
    on human resource strategy, 366–367
Consumer market survey, forecasting and, 146
Consumer's risk, 123–125
Continuous improvement, quality and, 83
Continuous processes, 232
Control charts, 108–121
    for attributes, 116–121
    c-charts, 120–121
    defined, 108
    p-charts, 118–119
    R-charts, 110, 115–116
    TQM and, 93
    for variables, 110
    x-bar, 110, 111–116
Control files, scheduling and, 584
Control of service inventory, 444–445
Controlling forecasts, 170–172
Coors, 147
Core job characteristics, 371–372
CORELAP, 331
Corner point method, 711
COSMOS (Computerized Optimization Modeling for Operating Supermarkets), 337
Cost(s)
    competitive advantage and, 37
    intangible, 296
    location strategies and, 296
    reduction OM and, 10
    tangible, 296
    variable, 251–252
Cost-based price model, 426
CPM see Critical path method
CRAFT (Computerized Relative Allocation of Facilities Techniques), 330, 330n, 331
CRAFT-3D, 330, 330n, 331
Crashing, project mgt. and, 643–645
Crime factor, global operations and, 64
Critical path, 629
Critical path analysis, 634–638
Critical path method (CPM):
    activities, events, and networks and, 630–632
    critique of, 646–647
    dummy activities & events in, 632–634
    framework of, 629–630
Critical ratio (CR), sequencing and, 594
Critical success factors, 45–47, 63–65

Cross-docking, 338
Cross-functional team, 202
Crossover chart, 254, 255
Culture and ethics, global operations and, 66
Cummins Engine, 414
Cumulative probability distribution, Monte Carlo simulation and, 815
Customer service, OM and, 10
Customization, service design and, 205, 213
Customizing, warehousing layout and, 339
Cycle counting, inventory management and, 444
Cycles, decomposition of a time series, 147
Cycle time
    assembly line balancing and, 342
    types of inventory and, 441
Cyclical scheduling, 602–603

Daimler Chrysler, 297
Darden, 241
Decision making, 683–700
    decision tables, 686–689
    decision trees, 685, 689–693
    fundamentals of, 685
    process in operations, 684–685
Decisions of OM, 8, 39, 78, *See also* Operations decisions
    efficiency and, 16n
Decision tables, 686–689
    expected value of perfect information and, 688–689
    risk and, 686–688
Decision trees, 689–698
    capacity decisions and, 249–250
    definition, 689
    more complex, 690–693
    product design and, 215–216
Decision variables, linear programing and, 707
Decline phase, product life cycle and, 199
Decomposition of a time series, 147–148
Degeneracy, transportation modeling and, 748–750
Delga Automatic, 414
Dell Computers, 36, 78, 194, 427
Delphi method, forecasting and, 146
Delta Airlines, 578–580, 628, 716
Demand
    dependent, MRP and, 538
    independent, inventory models and, 447–460
    management and capacity planning, 250–251
    unequal to supply, transportation models and, 748
Demand forecasts, 143
Demand options, aggregate strategies and, 509–510
De Mar, 221
Deming's 14 points for quality improvement, 83

Demographic change, new product opportunities and, 196
Dependent demand, MRP and, 538
Dependent inventory models, 538–545
    accurate records and, 544
    bills-of-material and, 541–544
    lead times for components and, 545
    master production schedule and, 539–540
    purchase orders outstanding and, 545
Dependent variable, 163
Design for Manufacture & Assembly (DFMA), 273
Design for manufacturability, 202
Design of goods and services, 191–224
    application of decision trees to product design, 215–216
    defining the product, 207–210
    documents for production, 210–211
    goods and services selection, 194–200
    issues for product development, 203–207
    product development, 200–203
    service design, 211–215
    transition to production, 217
Design technology
    computer-aided design (CAD), 273
    computer-aided manufacturing (CAM), 274
    standard for exchange of product data (STEP), 273
    virtual reality technology, 274–275
Detroit Diesel, 559
Detroit Edison, 583
Differentiation, competitive advantage and, 36–37
Direct numerically controlled (DNC) machines, 275
Disaggregation, aggregate scheduling and, 506
Disney, 366, 374, 666, 764
Disney, global operations and, 68
Distance reduction, JIT layout and, 485–486
Distribution resource planning (DRP), 561–563
    allocation and, 562
    structure for, 562
Distribution systems, supply-chain management, 430–431
Distributors, new product opportunities and, 196
Documents for services, 213–215
Dodge-Romig table, 125, 125n
Dow Chemical, 583
DPL, 689
Dresser Industries, 32–33
Drop shipping, 428
Dual, 713
Duke Power Company, 368
Dummy activities, 632–633
Dummy destinations, 748
Dummy sources, 748
DuPont, 116, 198, 246

Dynamics, operations strategy and, 43–44
DYNAMO, 823

Earliest due date (EDD), 590–593
EC, see European Community
Economic change, new product opportunities and, 195
Economic forecasts, 143
Economic order quantity (EOQ) model, 447
　lot sizing and, 552–553
　minimize costs, 447
　production order quantity model, 454–457
　quantity discount model, 457–460
　robust model, 452
Economic part period (EPP), lot sizing, and, 553–554
Effective capacity, 246
Efficiency, 16n, 247
Electronic data interchange (EDI), 429
Electronic ordering and funds transfer, 428–429
Electronic Systems, Inc., 498
Electrolux, 2
Employee empowerment, 12, 83, 370
　just-in-time and, 493
Employment stability policies, 367
Engineering change notice (ECN), 211
　material requirements planning and, 541
Engineering drawing, 207–209
England
　engineers using STEP, 273
　globalization of production, 59
　Hewlett-Packard, 63
　Lucent Technologies, 364
　Paddy Hopkick Factory, 380
　Tiris, 284
ENIAC, 6
Enterprise Resource Planning (ERP) 558–559
Environment 2000, 199
Environmental issues, process strategy and, 245–246
Environmental management standard, quality and, 82
Environmentally friendly products, 199–200
EOQ, See Economic order quantity models
Ergonomics, job design and, 375–380
Ernst & Young Accounting, 336
ESRI, 307
Ethics and culture, global operations and, 66
Euro-Disney, 68
European Community (EC)
　environmental mgt. standard and, 82
　ISO 9000, 81
　ISO 10303, 273n
　ISO 14000, 82
Events, PERT and, 630–632
Excel OM, 172
　aggregate scheduling, 523–524
　break-even analysis, 262
　decision models, 694
　forecasting, 174–176
　how to use, A8–A10
　inventory, 466–468
　learning curves, 804
　linear programing, 724
　location problems, 69–70, 308–309
　queuing, 782
　short term scheduling, 605–606
　simulation, 825
　statistical process control, 127
　transportation problems, 751–752
Exchange rates, location strategies and, 296
Excite, Inc., 306
Exogenous variables, 19n
Expected monetary value (EMV), 687
Expected value of perfect information (EVPI), 688–689
Expediters, 419
Expert systems (ES), 283
　in layout, 331
　in maintenance, 676
Exponential smoothing, quantitative forecasting and, 146–147, 151–155
　mean absolute deviation (MAD), 153–154
　mean square error (MSE), 154–155
　smoothing constants and, 151–153
　with trend adjustment, 155–161
Extensions of MRP, 555–559
　capacity planning, 556–557
　closed look, 555–556
　enterprise resource planning (ERP), 558–559
　material requirements planning, 11, 557–558
Extreme point, 711
Exxon, 583

Fabrication line, production-oriented layout and, 339
Facilities/space utilization, OM and, 10
Factor-rating method, location strategies and, 298–299
Factory Enterprises, Inc., 433
Factory, focused, 333–334
FADES (Facilities Design Expert System), 331
Failure, See also Maintenance
　mean time between failure distribution (MTBF) and, 669–670
Feasible region, 708
Feasible solution, 708
Federal Express, 82, 290–292, 339, 430, 507, 508
FIFS (first in, first served), 767n
Financial/accounting, OM and, 10
Finished goods inventory, 441
Finite population, 766
Finite scheduling, 596–597
First-come, first served (FCFS) system, 590–594

First-in, first-out (FIFO), 767
First-in, first-served (FIFS), 767n
First Printing & Copy Center, 586
Fish-bone chart, 92
Fixed costs, 251
Fixed-period inventory systems, 464–465
Fixed-position layout, 322, 323–325
Flexibility, JIT layout and, 486
Flexible manufacturing system (FMS), 278–279
Flexible response, 37–38, 234
Flexible work week, 368
Flex-time, 368
Flow diagrams, 236
　job design and, 380
Flow process charts, job design and, 380
Focus forecasting, 172
Focused factory, 333–334
Focused work center, 333–334
Ford Motor Company, 4, 59, 73, 273, 274, 277, 340, 418, 422, 490, 538, 624
Forecasting, 139–147, See Time-series forecasting, 147–163
　approaches to, 145–147
　capacity and, 144
　causal methods and, 163–169
　computer's role in, 172
　defined, 142
　monitoring and controlling forecasts and, 170–172
　product life cycle and, 143
　service sector and, 172–173
　steps in, 144–145
　strategic importance of, 143–144
　time horizons and, 142
　types of, 143
Forward scheduling, 582
France
　EuroDisney, 68
　Federal Express, 292
　globalization of production, 59, 61
　Software, CATIA, 274
　TRW, 95
Fundamentals of decision making, 685–686
Funds transfer, electronic ordering and, 428–429
Future time horizon, forcasting and, 142
Fuzzy logic, 283

Gain sharing, 374
Gantt charts
　load chart, 585
　loading and, 585–586
　project scheduling and, 586n, 627, 635
　schedule chart, 586
GATT, 60, 66
Gazette, 136–137
General agreement of tariffs and trade, 60, 66
General Electric Corporation, 2, 42, 63, 108, 199, 222–223, 295, 344

General Electric Hawthorne Plant, 371
General Mills, 197
General Motors Corporation, 59, 61, 142, 194–195, 234, 275, 281, 295, 368, 480, 483, 507
General purpose languages, 823
Genesis for Windows, 276
Geographic information systems (GISs), location strategies and, 306–307
Germany
  environmental issues and, 245
  globalization of production, 59
  Green Movement, 245, 340
  Hewlett-Packard, 63
  Nissan, 340
  productivity comparison with U.S. and Japan, 21
  Tiris, 284
  Volkswagen, 303
Giant Manufacturing Co., 422
Gillette, 4
Glidden Paints, 65
Global company, 57
Global Company Profile
  Anheuser-Busch, 502–504
  Bechtel, 622–624
  Boeing Aircraft, 54–56
  Collins Industries, 536–538
  Delta Airlines, 578–580
  Federal Express, 290–292
  Harley-Davidson, 438–440
  Komatsu, 32–34
  Lucent Technologies, 364–366
  Motorola, 76–78
  NASA, 664–666
  Nucor, 226–228
  Pittsburgh International Airport, 320–322
  Regal Marine, 192–194
  Tupperware Corp., 140–142
  Volkswagen, 414–416
  Whirlpool, 2–4
Global environment, managing technology and, 284–286
Global facility location analysis, 63–65
Global factory, 57
Global focus, OM and, 11
Global implications, quality and, 80
Global operations *See* Operations in a global environment, 53–74
Global process design and technology, 63
Global product, 57, 59
Global product design, 62–63
Global service operations, mgt. of, 68
Global supply-chain issues, 417–418
Global village, 57
Globalization of production, 59
Golding Landscaping & Plants, Inc., 736
Goods
  design of, services and, 191–224
  differences from services, 12–14

operations decisions and, 39–42
selection of, 194–200
GPSS (General Purpose System Simulator), 823
Grant Thornton, 299
Graphic approach, break-even analysis and, 252
Graphical and charting methods, for aggregate scheduling and, 511–516
Graphical representation of constraints, 707–708
Graphical solution approach, linear programing and, 707–713
Green manufacturing, 200, 245, 246
Green movement, 245, 340
Gross material requirements plan, MRP and, 546
Group technology, 209–210
Growth phase, product life cycle and, 199
GTE, 213
Guatemala, global operations and, 66

Hallmark Cards, 283, 322, 334
Harley-Davidson, 118, 213, 228, 231, 233, 438–440, 543, 551
Hawthorne studies, 371
Henry Ford Hospital, 521
Heuristics, assembly-line balancing and, 342–344
Hertz, 394, 520
Hewlett-Packard, 63, 427
Historical experience, work measurement and, 393
Hitachi, 295, 426
HMMS rule, 518n
Holding costs, 446
Holland, globalization of production, 59
Homart Development Company, 705
Honda, 194
Hospitals, aggregate scheduling and, 521
  short-term scheduling and, 601
Hotel site selection, location strategies and, 305–306
House of quality, 87
H-P, 427–428
Hugo Boss AG, 59
Human resources
  forecasting and, 144
  operations decisions and, 40–42
  service process strategy and, 244
Human resource strategy, 366–369
  competitive advantage for, 366–367
  constraints on, 366–367
  OM and, 8
  job design and, 8, 369–380
  labor planning and, 367–369
  labor standards and, 383
  objective of, 366
  visual work place, 381–383
Humidity, job design and, 377, 379
Hungary, global operations and, 63
Hunter Fan, 36

IBM, 60, 62, 67, 108, 152, 163, 172, 239, 279, 427–428, 505, 809–810, 818
Illumination, job design and, 377
IMPACT (Inventory Management Program and Control Technique), 172
Impact on employees, JIT layout and, 486
Improving chain-supply, global operation and, 60–61
Inacom Corp., 428
Incentive systems, job design and, 375
"Incomplete" orders, 428n
Independent demand, inventory models and, 447–460
  basic economic order quantity (EOQ) model, 447
  production order quantity model, 454–457
  quantity discount model, 457–460
Independent variable, 163
India, Whirlpool and, 2
Industrial engineering, 6
Industrial Innovations, Inc., 377
Industrial standards, Z8108–1981, 80
Infant mortality, 671
Infeasible solution, 708
Infinite population, 766
Information science, 6
Information sciences in operations, 281–284
  artificial intelligence, 283–284
  management information system and, 282
  transaction processing system and, 281–282
Ingall Ship Building Corp., 324, 324n
Initial feasable solution, 742
Input-output control, loading and, 584–586
Inspection,
  of attributes versus variables, 96
  quality management and, 93–97
  service industry in, 96
  when and where, 95–96
Intangible costs, location strategies and, 296
Intel, 194
Intermec Technologies, 456
Intermittent processes, 229, 583
International business, 57
International Paper, 254
International quality standards, 80–82
International service provider, 67
Internet, 282, 306
  location and, 306
Introductory phase, of product life cycle, 198
Inventory analysis, simulation and, 820–823
Inventory management, 437–478
  dependent inventory models and, *See* Dependent inventory models
  fixed period systems and, 464–465
  functions of, 440
  independent inventory models, *See* Independent demand
  independent versus dependent demand and, 446

General Index

Inventory management (cont.)
   just-in-time, 486–489
   Kanban, 490–492
   management and, 441–445
   models, 446–447
   operations decisions and, 40–42
   probabilistic models with constant lead time, 460–464
   types of, 440–441
Inventory models, 446–447, *See also* Independent demand
   holding costs, 446
   independent vs. dependent demand, 446
   ordering costs, 446
   set-up costs, 446
   set-up time, 446–447
Inventory records, accuracy and, 544
Inventory reduction, OM and, 11
Investment(s), strategy-driven, 257–261
Invoiceless purchasing, 428
Ireland, globalization of production, 59
Ishikawa diagrams, 29
"ISO", 708n
ISO 9000, 81
ISO 10303, 273n
ISO 14000, 82
Iso-cost line, 709, 714
Isometric drawing, 210
Iso-profit line method, 708
Italy
   Benetton, 56
   globalization in production, 59
Item master file, 584

J.C. Penney, 66
Jaguar, 424
J.M. Huber Corp., 425
J.R. Simplot, 209
Japan
   Boeing Aircraft, 54–56
   General Motors, 61
   globalization of production, 59
   Hewlett-Packard, 63
   Honda, 438
   IBM, 62
   Industrial Standard Z8101–1981, 80
   Kaizen, 83
   Kanban system in, 490–492
   Keiretsu, 423
   Komatsu, 32–34
   layout strategy, perspective and, 336
   Mazda, 73, 121
   Motorola, 298
   Nissan Motor Co., 340
   poka-yoke, 96
   productivity comparison with United States and Germany, 21
   Ricoh Corp., 99
   Tiris, 284
   Toshiba, 449

   Toyota, 336
   Yamaha, 438
Job classifications, 369
Job design, 369–380
   components of, 369
   ergonomics and work methods and, 375–380
   human resource strategy and, 8, 363–389
   job expansion, 370, 373–374
   labor specialization, 369–370
   labor standards, 383
   motivation and incentive systems and, 374–375
   operations decisions and, 40–42
   psychological components of, 371–372
   self-directed teams, 372–374
   visual workplace, 381–383
Job enlargement, human resource strategy and, 370
Job expansion, 370
   limitations of, 373–374
Job enrichment, 370
Job lots, 325, 331n
Job rotation, 370
Job shops, 229, 583
Job shop scheduling, 583n
Job specialization, 369–370
Jobs, OM and, 10–11
John Deere & Company, 32, 331, 509
Johnson Electric, 38
Johnson's rule, sequencing and, 594–596
Johnsonville Sausage Co., 375
Jury of executive opinion, 145
Just-in-time (JIT) inventory, 192, 486–489
   reduce inventory, 487–488
   reduce lot sizes, 488–489
   reduce setup costs, 489
   reduce variability, 487
Just-in-time partnerships, 482–485
   goals of, 484–484
Just-in-time performance, OM and, 12
Just-in-time:
   MRP and, 550–551
   quality mgt. and, 85–86
Just-in time systems, 479–498
   employee empowerment and, 493
   inventory and, 486–489
   layout and, 485–486
   philosphy and, 480–481
   quality and, 493
   scheduling and, 490–492
   services, 494–495
   suppliers, 481–485

Kaizen, 83, 373
Kanban system, 381, 490–492
   advantages of, 492
   number of cards or containers and, 492
Keiretsu, 420, 423
Kinemark, 403
Kinesis Corporation, 377

Kinko, 764
Kit, 544
Kitted material, MRP and, 544
Kmart, 429, 443
Knowledge-based pay systems, 375
Knowledge society, 21
Kodak, 204
Komatsu, 32–34, 44
Kuwait, Bechtel and, 622–624

Labor
   productivity of, location strategies and, 294–296
   as productivity variable, 19–22
Labor planning, human resource strategy, 367–369
   employment-stability policies, 367–368
   job classifications and work rules, 369
   work schedules, 368
Labor scheduling problems, linear programming and, 720–722
Labor specialization, 369–370
Labor standards
   human resource strategy, 383
   work measurement and, 392
Lands End, 401
LaPlace Power & Light, 476
LaQuinta Motor Inns, 305–306
Layout design, operations decisions and, 39–42
   service process strategy and, 243
Layout strategy, 319–362
   fixed-position layout and, 323–325
   importance of, 322
   Japanese perspective, 336
   just-in-time and, 485–486
   OM and, 8
   office layout and, 322, 334–336
   process-oriented layout and, 322, 325–334
   product-oriented layout and, 322, 339–345
   retail/layout and, 322, 336–337
   types of, 322–323
   warehouse layouts and, 322, 337–339
Lead time
   dependent inventory model and, 544
   reorder point and, 453
Lean producer, 239
Lean production, 239–240
Learning curve coefficient approach, 800–802
Learning curves, 795–810
   applying, 798–802
   services and manufacturing and, 797–798
   strategic implications of, 802–803
Learning to improve global operations, 61
Least squares method, trend projections and, 158–161
Legal change, new product opportunities and, 196
Level material use schedule, 490, 599

General Index

Level scheduling, 511
Level strategy, aggregate scheduling and, 511
Levis, 451
Libralter Plastics, 485
Life cycle, 61
    strategy and, 198–199
LIFO (Last in, first out), 767n
LIFS (Last in, first served), 767n
Limited population, 766, 777–780
Limited queue, 767
Lincoln Electric, 366, 388
Linear decision rule (LDR), aggregate scheduling and, 518
Linear programing (LP)
    applications and, 716–722
    constraints, 705
    corner point method, 711–713
    feed-mix problem, 718
    formulating, 706–707
    graphical solution to, 707–713
    iso-profit line method, 710–711
    labor scheduling, 720–722
    minimization problems, 714–716
    production mix problem, 717
    production scheduling, 718–720
    requirements of programing problems, 705–706
    sensitivity analysis, 713–714
    simplex method of, 722
Linear regression analysis, quantitative forecasting and, 146–147, 163–165
    standard error of estimate and, 165–167
Litton Industries, 282
L.L. Bean, 85, 86, 149, 509, 772
Load reports, 556
Loading jobs in work centers, short term scheduling and, 584–590
    assignment method, 587–589
    Gantt charts, 585–586
    input-output control, 584–586
Location decisions, factors affecting in, 293–294
Location strategies, 289–318
    attitudes and, 296–297
    break-even analysis and, 300–301
    center of gravity method and, 301–303
    costs and, 296
    exchange rates and, 296
    factors affecting location decisions, 293–294
    factor-rating method, 298–299
    geographic information systems, 306–307
    labor productivity and, 294–296
    methods of evaluating location alternatives, 298–304
    OM and, 8
    operations decisions and, 39–42
    proximity to markets, 297
    proximitiy to suppliers, 297
    service location, 304–306
    strategic importance of, 292
    transportation model and, 303–304
Locational break-even analysis, 300–301
Lockheed-Martin, 278, 580
Logarithmic approach, learning curves and, 799–800
Longest processing time (LPT), 590–593
Long-range forecast, 142–143
Lot sizing decision, 551
Lot sizing, MRP and, 551–555
    economic order quantity, as technique for, 552–553
    lot-for-lot technique for, 551–552
    part period balancing, (PPB), 553–554
    summary, 555
    Wagner-Whitin procedure for, 554–555
Lot tolerance percent defective (LTPD), 124–125
Low-cost leadership, 37
Low-level coding, 544
Lucent Technologies, 364–366
Lufthansa Airlines, 282–283, 283n

Maintenance, 663–682
    defined, 666
    expert systems applied to, 676
    increasing repair capabilities and, 675–676
    OM and, 8
    operations decisions and, 40–42
    preventive, 671–675
    strategic importance of, 666
    techniques for establishing policies and, 676
Maintenance/repair/operating (MROs), 441
Make-or-buy decisions, 209, 419–420
Malaysia
    global operations and, 56
    Motorola, 77
    Tiris, 284
Malcolm Baldrige National Quality Awards, 76, 82, 104
Management
    as productivity variable, 19–22
    process of OM and, 7–8
Management coefficients model, aggregate scheduling and, 518
Management information system (MIS), 282
Management science, 6
Managing quality, 75–106
    quality and strategy, 78
    role of inspection, 93–97
    Taguchi technique, 89–93
    tools of TQM, 86–88
    total quality mgt., 82–86
    total quality mgt. in services, 97–99
Manila, cartoon industry in, 60
MapInfo Corp., 307
Manufacturability, product development and, 202–203
Manufacturing-based category, quality and, 80

Manufacturing cycle time, 481
Manufacturing environments, supply-chain management and, 419
MAP/1, 824
Maquiladora assembly plant, 60, 295, 296
Market-based price model, 426
Marketing, OM and, 10
Marketing option, 7
Market practice, new product opportunities and, 196
Mass customization, OM and, 12
    process strategy and, 234–235
Master production schedule (MPS), 506, 539–540
Matching capacity to demand, 251
Materials management, 429–431
Material requirements planning (MRP), 535–576
    capacity planning and, 556–557
    closed-loop, 555–556
    dependent inventory model requirements and, 538–545. *See also* Dependent inventory models
    distribution resource planning (DRP) and, 561–563
    dynamics, 550
    extensions of, 555
    lot-sizing techniques and, 551–555
    management and, 550–551
    services and, 560
    structure for, 544–550
Material requirements planning II (MRP II), 557–558
Mathematical approach, aggregate scheduling and, 516–518
Maturity phase, product life cycle and, 199
Maytag, 2, 66, 203
Mazda, 73, 121, 372, 373
MCAE, 273
McDonald's Corp., 4, 96, 194, 205, 207, 209, 213, 234, 235, 292, 333, 418, 494, 601, 776
McDonnell Douglas, 56
M/D/1 model, 777
Mean absolute deviation (MAD), 153–154
Mean chart limits, setting of, 113–114
    using of, 115–116
Mean squared error (MSE), 154–155
Mean time between failure (MTBF) distribution, 669–670
Measured daywork, 375
Medium-range forecast, 142–143
Mercedes-Benz, 292, 293, 297
Merck, 34
Metals Week, 426, 426n
Methods analysis, job design and, 379–380
Methods for aggregate scheduling, 511–518
Methods Time Measurement Association, 398–399, 398n
Methods Time Measurement (MTM), 398–399

Mexico
- global operations and, 59–60, 64
- Lucent Technologies, 364
- Maquiladora assembly plants, 60, 295, 296
- Quality Coils, Inc., 294–296
- Vilpac, 818
- Vitromatic, 2
- Volkswagen, 303
- Whirlpool, 2

Microsoft Corporation, 4, 44, 46, 57, 147, 161, 194, 624, 627, 684
Midas Muffler, 764
Milliken and Company, 82
M/M/1 model, 771
M/M/S model, 774
Minimization problems, linear programing and, 714–716
Minimizing costs, independent demand inventory and, 447–453
Minitab, 172
Minit-Lube, Inc., 49
Miscellaneous services, aggregate scheduling and, 520
Mission, 34–35
Mixed strategy, 511
Mixing options, aggregate scheduling and, 510–511
MNC, 57
Mobil Oil, 81
Models, inventory and, 446–447
Modular bills, MRP and, 543
Modular design, product development and, 204–205, 213
Modules, repetitive focus and, 230–231
Moment-of-truth, service design and, 213
Monte Carlo simulation, 815–818
Monitoring forecasts, 170–172
Motivation systems, job design and, 374–375
Motorola, 38, 50, 76–78, 82, 108, 148, 194, 198, 204, 298, 331
Moving averages, forecasting and, 146–151
 weighted, 149–151
MRP, *See also* Material requirements planning
Mrs. Field's Cookies, 603
Multifactor productivity, 18
Multinational corporation, 57
Multiphase queuing system, 769
MULTIPLE, 330, 330n, 331
Multiple-channel queuing system, 768–769, 774–776
Multiple regression analysis, 168–169
Multiplicative seasonal model, forecasting and, 161
Mutual commitment, human resources strategy and, 366
Mutual trust, human resources strategy and, 366

Nabisco, 144
NAFTA, 60, 60n, 67

Naive approach, quantitative forecasting and, 146–148
NASA, 625, 664–666
National Air Express, 28
National chains, aggregate scheduling and, 520
National Decision Systems, Inc., 307
Natural causes, statistical process control and, 108–110
Natural variations, statistical process control and, 108–110
Nature of aggregate scheduling, 505–507
NCR Corporation, 63, 200
Negative exponential probability distribution, 769
Negotiation strategies, vendor selection and, 426–427
Nestle's, 58
Net material requirements plan, MRP and, 547
Net present value, strategy-driven investments and, 258–261
Net requirements plan, MRP and, 547
Netherlands
 N.V. Philips, 2
 Tiris, 284
Network(s), PERT, 631
Neural networks, 283–284
New England Castings, Inc. 790
New United Motor Manufacturing (NUMMI), 116
New York Police Department, 781
Nigeria, Volkswagen and, 303
Nike, 147
Nissan Motor Company, 340, 552
Noise, job design and, 377–399
Nordstrom, 374
Normal probability distribution, how to use it and table, A2–A4
Normal time, work measurement and, 393
North American Economic Community (NAEC), 818
North American Free Trade Agreement, 60, 60n, 67
North-South Airline, 188
Northwest corner rule, 742–743
Nucor, 36, 78, 226–228, 232–233, 333, 506
Numerical control (NC), 275

Objective function, linear programing problems and, 705
Office layout, layout strategy and, 334–336
Official Board Markets, 426n
Old Oregon Wood Store, 617–618
OM in Action
 automobile disassembly lines, chapter 9, 340
 Benetton, supplement 7, 285
 Boeing Aircraft, chapter 6, 205
 Carrier Corp., chapter 1, 20
 cartoon industry in Manila, chapter 3, 60

Compaq, chapter 2, 46: chapter 11, 428: chapter 14, 558
crime in foreign site selection, chapter 3, 64
Delta Airlines, chapter 16, 628: Quant. Module B, 716
Detroit Diesel, chapter 14, 559
Federal Express, chapter 13, 508
Forecasting: American Airlines, chapter 5, 169
HDTV sales, chapter 5, 146
H-P, chapter 11, 428
Hertz, chapter 13, 520
Homart Development Co., Quant. Module B, 705
IBM, chapter 11, 428
Internet locations, chapter 8, 306
Johnson Electric Holdings, Inc., chapter 2, 38
Kmart, chapter 12, 443
L.L. Bean, chapter 4, 86, Quant. Module D, 772
Libralter Plastics, supplement 12, 485
Listerine & Wal-Mart stores, chapter 12, 445
Maytag Corp., chapter 3, 66
Mazda, chapter 4S, 121: chapter 10, 373
McDonald's, chapter 15, 601
Mercedes-Benz, chapter 8, 297
Microsoft, chapter 2, 46
New York's Police Department, Quant. Module D, 781
operations management, chapter 1, 20–22
Pacific Pre-Cut Produce, chapter 12S, 487
Premium Standard Farms, Inc., chapter 7, 240
Proctor & Gamble, chapter 11, 430
project management & software development, chapter 16, 646
Quality Coils, Inc., chapter 8, 294
Ritz Carlton Hotel, chapter 10, 371
Rowe Furniture Corp. chapter 9, 333
Scheduling and falling asleep on the job, chapter 15, 583
SPC, Dupont and the environment, supplement 4, 116
Stryker Corp., chapter 6, 196
Taco Bell, chapter 1, 23
Technology in hospitality industry, supplement 7, 280
Toshiba, chapter 12, 449
TQM in service sector, chapter 4, 99
United Parcel Services (UPS), supplement, 10, 398: chapter 13, 508
U. S. Airways and scheduling, chapter 15, 602
Vilpac, simulation and, Quant. Mod. F, 818
Warner-Lambert, chapter 12, 445

Westinghouse, chapter 7, 238
Whirlpool, chapter 1, 17
1-800-FLOWERS, 306
"Open" orders, 428n
Operating characteristics (OC) curves, 123–125
Operations and productivity, 1–29
Operations chart, job design and, 380
Operations decisions, *See* Ten decisions of OM
Operations in a global environment, 53–74
    achieving, 62–66
    defining, 57–59
    importance of, 59–62
    service operations issues, 67–68
Operations layout strategy, *See* Layout strategy
Operations management
    definition, 4
    heritage of, 4–6
    introduction to, 1–29
    jobs in, 10–11
    manager responsibilities, 7–8
    new trends, 11–12
    organizing to produce goods & services, 8–10
    productivity challenge, 16–20
    reasons to study, 6–7
    service sector, 12–14
    significant events in, 5
Operations manager, challenges for, 11
    job of, 47
Operations strategy for competitive advantage, 31–52
    competitive advantage through operations, 36–39
    issues in, 42–44
    mission, 34–35
    strategy, 36
    strategy development and implementation, 44–47
    ten decisions of OM, 39–42
Opportunity cost, assignment method and, 587, 587n
Optimistic time in PERT, 633–634
Ordering cost, 446
Organization, building & staffing of, 47
Organizing, to produce goods and services, 8–10
Origin points, 740

Pacific Bell, 91
Pacific Pre-Cut Produce, 487
Paddy-Hopkirk Factory, 380
Pakistan, global operations and, 67
Pampers, 429
Panhandle Eastern Corp., 375
Parameter, sensitivity analysis and, 713
Pareto charts, 90–91, 95, 96
Pareto principle, 206
Park Plaza Hospital, 560

Park Plaza Hotel, 246
Part period balancing (PPB), lot sizing and, 553–554
Part-time status, 368
PASCAL, 823
p-charts, 118–121
Pegging, 550
Pennzoil, 583
People Soft, 559
People/team development, OM and, 10
Pep Boys, 307
Pepsi Co., 23
PERT, 629–643
PERT-Cost, 643n
PERT network, 631
Pessimistic time estimate, in PERT, 633–634
Phantom bills-of-material, MRP and, 543–544
Philippines
    cartoon industry and, 60
    Federal Express, 291
Philips, 2
Philosophy, JIT and, 480–481
Physical sciences, 6
Pick lists in MRP, 543
Piece rate, 375
Pilferage, 445
PIMS, 42
Pipelines, 431
Pittsburgh International Airport, 320–322
Planned order receipt, MRP and, 547
Planned order release, MRP and, 547
Planning bills, MRP and, 543
Planning files, scheduling and, 584
Plastic Recycling Corp., 245
Poisson distribution, 766
Poka-yoke, 96
Political change, new product opportunities and, 196
Polycon Industries, 490
POM for Windows, 172
    aggregate scheduling, 522–523
    assembly line-balancing, 347
    decision table and tree, 693
    forecasting, 174
    how to use, A8
    inventory problems, 466
    layout design, 346
    learning curves, 803–804
    linear programming, 723
    location analysis, 69
    location strategies, 308
    material requirements planning (MRP), 563–564
    project scheduling, 648
    queuing, 782
    reliability, 677
    scheduling, 604
    simulation, 825
    statistical process control, 126
    transportation problems, 750

Population of waiting line system,
    unlimited or infinite, 766
    limited or finite, 766
Portion-control standards, 208
Postponement, supply-chain mgt. and, 427
Precedence relationship, assembly line balancing and, 341–342
Preconditions, operations strategy and, 43
Predetermined time standards, 398–400
Premium Standard Farms Inc., 240
Prentice Hall, 505
Preventive maintenance, 671–675
Priority rules, for dispatching jobs, 590–594
Probabilistic inventory models with constant lead time, 460–464
Probability distributions, Monte Carlo simulation and, 815–818
Probable time estimate, in PERT, 633–634
Process analysis and design, 235–238
Process capability, SPC and, 121–123
Process charts,
    analysis design and, 236
    job design and, 380
    TQM and, 91–92, 95, 96
Process control, 275
Process design, operations decisions and, 39–42
Process-focused facilities, 583
Process focus, process strategies and, 229, 233
Process mapping, 237
Process-oriented layout, 322, 325–334
    expert systems in, 331
    focused work center and focused factory and, 333–334
    work cells and, 331–333
Process reengineering, 239–240
Process sheets, 211
Process strategies, OM and, 8
Process strategy and capacity planning, 225–270
    capacity and, 246–251
    comparison of, 233–235
    continuous processes, 232
    defined, 228
    environmental issues, 245–246
    equipment selection, 244
    high-volume, low-variety (continuous) processes and, 232–233
    lean producers, 239
    lean production, 239–240
    low-volume, high-variety (intermittent) processes and, 229
    modules, 230–231
    process focus, 229, 233
    product focus, 232–233
    repetitive focus and, 230–231, 233
    service process and, 241–244
Process strategy, customer interaction and, 242–243
Procter & Gamble, 205, 430

General Index

Producer's risk, 123–125
Product(s)
  defining, 207–210
  documenting, 210–211
Product based category, quality and, 80
Product-by-value analysis, 206–207
Product design, decision trees, OM and, 8, 194
Product development, 200–203
  issues for, 203–207
  manufacturability and value engineering teams and, 202–203
  organizing and, 201–202
  system and, 200–201
  teams and, 202
Product focus, 232–233
Product liability, quality and, 80
Product life cycle, 196–199
  forecasting and, 143
  strategy and, 198–199
Product mix problem, linear programming and, 706–707
Product-oriented layout, 322, 339–345
  assembly line balancing and, 339–345
Product strategy
  generation of new opportunities, 195–196
  options of, 194–195
Production defined, 4, 17
Production-mix, linear programing and, 717
Production order quantity model, 454–457
Production/operations, OM and,10
Production scheduling, linear programing and, 718–720
Production technology, 275–280
  automated guided vehicles (AGV), 278
  automated storage & retrieval system (ASRS), 277
  computer-integrated manufacturing (CIM), 279
  flexible manufacturing system (FMS), 278
  numerical control, 275
  process control, 275
  robots, 276–277
  vision systems, 276
Productivity
  challenge and OM, 16
  improvement, OM and, 11, 17
  measurement of, 17–19
  service sector and, 22–23
  variables, 19–21
Professional standards, new product opportunities and, 196
Profit sharing, 374
Program evaluation and review technique (PERT), 629
  activities, events, and networks and, 630–632
  activity time estimates and, 633–634
  critique of, 646–647
  dummy activities and events in, 632–634

framework of, 629–630
  probability of project completion, 638–639
Project controlling, 629
Project management, 621–622
  cost-time trade-offs, 643–645
  CPM in *See* Critical path method
  Critique of PERT & CPM, 646–647
  PERT/CPM in, 629–643
  PERT/COST, 643n
  PERT in *See* Program evaluation and review technique
  project controlling and, 629
  project crashing, 643–645
  project planning and, 625–627
  project scheduling and, 627–629
  service firms and, 645
  strategic importance of, 624
  techniques of, 629–643
Project manager, 625–626
Project organization, 625
Project planning, 625–627
Project scheduling, OM and, 8
Providing better good and services, global operations and, 61
Psychological components, job design and, 371–372
Pull system, 481, 562
Pull versus push system, 481
Purchase orders, outstanding, 544
Purchasing agent, 419
Pure service, 13
Purolator, 430
Push system, 481, 562

Qualitative forecasting methods, 145–146
  consumer marketing survey, 146
  Delphi method, 146
  jury of executive opinion, 145
  sales force composite, 145
Quality, *See also* Total Quality Management (TQM), 82–86
  defined, 79, 99
  just-in-time and, 493
  OM and, 10
  operations decisions and, 39–42
Quality circles, 84
Quality Cleaners, 104
Quality Coils, Inc., 294
Quality control (QC), *See* Tools of TQM & International Quality Standards
Quality Function Deployment (QFD), 86–87
Quality loss function (QLF), 89–90
Quality management, OM and, 8 see Managing Quality
Quality of work life, 366
Quality robust, 89
Quantitative forecasting methods, 145–147
  time series models and, 146–147
  causal models and, 146–147
Quantity discount, 457

Quantity discount models, inventory management and, 457–460
Queue(s), limited and unlimited, 767
QueuesEnforth Development, Inc., 781
Queue discipline, 767
Queuing models, variety of, 770–780, *See also* Waiting line models
  constant service time, 776–777
  limited population, 777–780
  multiple-channel, 774–776
  other approaches, 780–781
  single channel/Poisson arrivals/exponential service times, 771–774
Queuing problems, simulation of, 818–820
Queuing theory, 764
Quickness, response and, 38

Railroads, materials mgt. and, 430
Random arrivals, waiting line systems and, 766
Random number, 815–818
Random number intervals, Monte Carlo simulation and, 815–818
Random stocking, warehouse layout and, 338–339
Random variations, decomposition of a time series, 147
Range chart limits, setting of, 115
Rapid product development, OM and, 12
Rated capacity, 247
Raw material inventory, 440–441
R-chart, 110
  setting limits for, 115
  using, 115–116
Re Manufacturing Corp., 382
Record accuracy, inventory mgt. and, 443
Reduced customer interaction, service design and, 213
Reduced space and inventory, JIT layout and, 486
Reduction of costs, global operations and, 59–60
Reduction of risks, global operations and, 60
Redundancy, reliability and, 670
Regal Marine, 51, 192–194, 205, 223, 435
Regression analysis, forecasting and, 163–165
Relationship chart, 334–335
Reliability, 663–682, *See also* Maintenance
  defined, 666
  improving individual components and, 667–670
  redundancy and, 670
  response and, 37–38
  strategic importance of, 666
Remon, 414–415
Reneging customers, 766–767
Reorder point (ROP) inventory management and, 453–454
Repair capabilities, increasing, 675–676

Repetitive manufacturing, scheduling and, 599–600
Research, operations strategy and, 42–43
Response, competitive advantage and, 37–38
    flexibility of, 37
    reliability of, 37–38
    quickness of, 38
Restaurants, aggregate scheduling and, 519–520
Retail store layout, 322, 336–337
Reuters, 58
Revenue function, 252
Rice Aircraft, 81
Right-hand/left-hand chart, 380
Right-hand side ranging, 714
Ritz-Carlton Hotels, 82, 105, 371, 374
Roadway Express, 430
Robots, 276–277
Robust design, product development and, 203–204
Robust model, economic order quantity model and, 452
Rochester Manufacturing Corp., 287–288
ROI, 42, 42n
Role of inspection, managing quality and, 93–97
Ronal Tool Co., 283
Route sheet, 211
Routing file, 584
Rowe Furniture Corp., 333
Rubbermaid, 194, 198
Rule-based dispatching systems, limitations of, 596
Russia, McDonald's and, 292, 418

Saatchi & Saatchi, 67
Safeskin Corp., 36
Sales force composite, forecasting and, 145
SAE, 209
Samsung, 796
Sanford Corp., 423
SAP, 559
SAS, 172
SAS Institute, Inc., 307, 635
Savin Corporation, 99
Scanlon plan, 374
Scheduling,
    backward, 582
    criteria, 582
    decisions, 504
    finite scheduling, 596
    forward, 582
    just-in-time and, 490–492
    OM and, 8
    operations decisions and, 40–42
    services and, 601–603
    short-term issues and, 580–583
    simulation and, 518
    strategic importance of, 580
Schwinn Bicycle Co., 422
Scotland, global operations and, 63

SDRC, 206
Seasonal forecast, 161
Seasonality, decomposition of a time series, 147
Seasonal variations, time series, 161–163
Security Pacific Corp., 486
Self-directed teams, 372–374
Sensitivity analysis, linear programing and, 713–714
Sequencing, jobs in work centers, 590–595
    critical ratio and, 594
    Johnson's rule and, 594–596
    priority rules for dispatching jobs, 590–594
    scheduling and, 590–595
Service(s), *See also* Service Sector
    defined, 12
    design and, 211–215
    design of, goods and, 191–224
    differences from goods and, 12–14
    just-in-time and, 494
    OM and, 8
    operations decisions and, 39–42
    pure and, 13
    selection of, 194–200
    technology in, 280–281
Service environments, supply chain mgt. and, 419
Service facility characteristics, waiting line systems and, 767–769
Service, Inc., 574
Service level, probabilistic models and, 460
Service pay, OM and, 16
Service process strategy, 241–244
    customer interaction and, 242–243
    opportunities to improve and, 243–244
    service sector considerations and, 241
Service quality, determinants of, 98
Service sector
    aggregate scheduling and, 518–522
    defined, 15
    forecasting and, 172–173
    inspection in, 96
    learning curves and, 797–798
    location strategies and, 304–306
    material requirements planning (MRP) and, 560
    organizations in, 15
    productivity and, 22–23
    project scheduling and, 645
    scheduling personnel in, 601–603
    service process strategy and, 241–244
Setup cost, 446
Setup time, 446–447
Shader Electronics, 706–713
Shadow price, 713
Sheraton Hotels, 394
Shortest processing time (SPT), 590–593
Short-range forecast, 142–143
Short-term scheduling, 577–618
    finite scheduling, 596–597

limitations of rule-based dispatching systems, 596
loading jobs in work centers, 584–590
OM and, 8
process focused work centers and, 583–584
repetitive manufacturing and, 599–600
scheduling issues, 580–583
sequencing, jobs in work center, 590–595
services and, 601–603
strategic importance of, 580
theory of constraints (TOC), 597–599
Shouldice Hospital, 194–195, 333
Shrinkage, 445
Siemens Corp., 22
Simplex method of LP, 722
Simfactory, 824
SIMNET II, 818
SIMSCRIPT, 823
Simulation, 811–837
    advantages and disadvantages of, 813–814
    computers in, 823–824
    defined, 813
    inventory analysis and, 820–823
    for maintenance policy, 676
    Monte Carlo, 815–818
    of queuing problems, 818–820
Singapore
    globalization of production, 59
    Hewlett-Packard, 63
    Lucent Technologies, 364
    Visioneer, 424
Single-channel queuing system, 768
Single channel queuing/poisson arrivals/exponential service times, 771–774
Single factor productivity, 18
Single-phase queuing system, 769
Six sigma, 77, 83
Skill-based pay systems, 375
SKU, 144
Skyway Freight Systems, 430
Slack time, critical path analysis and, 634–638
Slam II, 824
Sleep Inn, 396
SLIM (Store Labor and Inventory Management), 337
SMI, 333
SMT, 809–810
Small bucket approach, MRP and, 551
Smoothing constant, 151–153
    selecting, 153
Society of Automotive Engineers (SAE), 209
Sociological change, new product opportunities and, 196
SONY, 56, 246
Source inspection, 96
South Korea, globalization of product and, 59
Southard Truck Lines, 387

Southern Recreational Vehicle Co., 297, 317
Southwest Airlines, 37, 213, 242, 374
Southwestern State College, 532
SPACECRAFT, 330, 330n, 331
Spain
    Euro-Disney, 68
    globalization of production, 59
    Lucent Technologies, 364
Special packaging, 428
Special purpose simulation languages, 823
SPSS, 172
Standard error of estimate, 165–167
Standard for the Exchange of Product Data, 273
Standard Register, 228–229, 233, 245
Standardization, supply chain mgt. and, 429
Standard time, work measurement and, 393–394
Standard work schedule, 368
State Farm Insurance, 281
State-of-the-Art Technology in Operations, 271–288
    design technology, 272–275
    information sciences in operations, 281–284
    management in global environment, 284–286
    production technology, 275–280
    services and, 280–281
State of nature, decision making and, 685
Statistical process control (SPC), 107–138
    acceptance sampling, 123–125
    assignable causes, 108
    assignable variations, 109–110
    c-charts, 120–121
    central limit theorem and, 111–112
    control charts for attributes and, 116–121
    control charts for variables and, 110
    definition, 92
    natural causes, 108
    natural variations, 108–109
    p-charts, 118–119
    process capability, 121–123
    R-chart limits and, 110, 115–116
    x-bar chart and, 110–116
Statistical control, 108
STEP, 273, 273n
Stepping-stone method, 743–747
Steps in forecasting, 144–145
Sterling Software, Inc., 238
Stockless purchasing, 429
Storage layout, 337–339
    cross docking, 338
    customizing, 339
    random stocking, 338–339
Strategic concepts, 36
Strategic importance of:
    forecasting, 143–144
    layout decisions, 332

    learning curves, 802–803
    location, 292
    maintenance and reliability, 6
    project management, 624
    short term scheduling, 580
    supply chain-mgt., 416–418
Strategic issues, OM and, 10
Strategic Mapping, Inc. 307
Strategy,
    aggregate scheduling, 507–511
    definition, 36
Strategy driven investments, 257–261
    investment, variable cost, and cash flow and, 257
    net present value and, 258–261
Structural Dynamics Research Corporation (SDRC), 206
Stryker Corp., 196
Sturdivant Sound Systems, 476
St. Vincent's Hospital, 646, 647
Sumitomo Bank, 67
Supertree, 689
Suppliers
    just-in-time systems and, 481–485
    new product opportunities and, 196
    supply chain-management and, 420–422
Supply-chain management, 413–436
    benchmarking and, 431
    forecasting and, 144
    importance of, 416–418
    managing the supply chain, 427–430
    materials management and, 430–431
    OM and, 8, 11
    operatons decisions and, 40–42
    purchasing and, 418–420
    supply chain strategies and, 420–424
    vendor selections and, 425–427
Supply chain partnering, OM and, 12
Supply, demand unequal to, transportation method and, 748
Sweden, global operations and, 58, 61
Switzerland, global operations and, 58
SWOT analysis, 44–45
Symbols, decision trees and, 685
SYSTAB, 172
System design, Taguchi technique, 89–90
System nervousness, 550

Taco Bell, 23, 194–195, 374, 394
Taguchi technique, 89–90
Taiwan
    Federal Express, 292
    Giant Manufacturing Co., 422
    globalization of production, 59
Tangible costs, location strategies and, 296
Target oriented quality, 89, 90
Taylor, II, 824
Technical change, new products opportunities and, 196
Technological forecasts, 143

Technology
    methods, OM and, 10
    process strategy and, 244
    services in, 280–281
Technology in operations, 271–288
    Automated Storage and Retrieval Systems (ASRS), 277
    Automatic Guided Vehicles (AGVs), 278
    CAD/CAM, 273, 274
    Computer-Integrated Manufacturing (CIM), 279
    computer numerical control, 275
    Flexible Manufacturing Systems (FMSs), 278–279
    hospitality industry and, 75
    management in global environment, 284–286
    numerical control, 275
    process control, 275
    robots, 276–277
    vision systems, 276
Telemarketing, locations strategies and, 306
Temperature, job design and, 377, 379
Ten decisions of OM, 39–42
    design of goods and services, 194
    human resources, 366
    inventory management, 440
    layout strategy, 322
    maintenance, 666
    material requirements planning (MRP), 538
    project management, 624
    scheduling, 194
Texas Instruments, 63, 82, 284
Textile/Clothing Technology Corp., 272
Thailand,
    global operations and, 56
    Lucent Technologies, 364
    transportation model and, 749
The Gap, Inc. 338
Theory of constraints (TOC), scheduling and, 597–599
    bottleneck work centers, 598–599
Therblig, 399
Thomas Manufacturing Co., 434
3-D object modeling, 273
3M, 245
Three Mile Island, 376
3S Inc., 424
Time-based competition, product development and, 203, 204
Time fences, 550
Time-function mapping, analysis, design and, 237
Time horizons, forecasting and, 142–143
Time Measurement Units (TMUs), 399
Time-phased product structure, MRP and, 544
Time series forecasting, 147–163, 172
    decomposition of time series and, 147–148

General Index

exponential smoothing and, 151–155
exponential smoothing with trend adjustment, 155–161
moving averages and, 146–151
naive approach to, 148
seasonal variations in data, 161–163
trend projections and, 158–161
weighted moving averages and, 149–151
Times series models, 146–147
Time studies, work measurement and, 393–398
Tomco Oil, 684
Tompkins Associates, Inc., 10n
Tools of TQM, 86–93
 cause & effect diagrams, 92
 Pareto charts, 90
 process charts, 91–92
 quality function deployment, 86–88
 statistical process control, 92–93
 Taguchi technique, 89–90
Toshiba, 449
Total factor productivity, 18
Total productive maintenance (TPM), 675–676
Total quality management (TQM), 82–86, 99
 continuous improvement, 83
 definition, 82
 employee empowerment, 83
 benchmarking, 84–85
 hospital measurement in, 99
 just-in-time, 85–86
 services and, 97
 TQM tools, 86–88
Toyota, 195, 336, 480
Tracking signal, 170
Transaction processing system, 281–282
Transformation strategy, 228
Transition to production, 217
Transitional company, 58
Transportation models, 739–762
 degeneracy and, 748–750
 demand not equal to supply, 748
 location strategies and, 303–304
 northwest corner rule and, 742–743
 stepping-stone method and, 743–747
 transportation modeling, 740–742
Transportation method of linear programming, 516–518
Tree Plan, 689
Trend, decomposition of a time series, 147
Trend adjustment, exponential smoothing with, 155–161
Trend projections, forecasting and, 146–147, 158–161
Trucking, materials management and, 430
TRW, 95, 144
Tupperware, 140–142, 144–145, 277
"two bin" systems, 451
Type I error, 125
Type II error, 125

Types of forecasts, 143
Types of inventory, 440–441

Unisys Corp., 307
United States
 Coleco, 56
 Hewlett Packard, 63
 IBM, 62
 MIL-STD, 105, 125, 125n
 productivity comparison with Japan & Germany, 21
 quality standards, 82
Unlimited queue, 766
UPS (United Parcel Service), 398, 430, 507, 508, 666
User-based category, quality and, 79
Utilization, capacity and, 246

Value analysis, 206–207
Value engineering,
 product development and, 202–203
 teams, 202
Variability, 481
Variability reduction, JIT and, 481
Variable(s)
 control charts for, 110
 exogenous, 19n
Variable costs, 251–252
 strategy driven investments and, 257
Variable inspection, 96
VDO, 414
Velcro Industries, 96
Vendor development, 426
Vendor evaluation, 425
Vendor selection, supply-chain mgt. and, 425–427
Vertical integration, supply-chain mgt. and, 420–422–423
VF Corp. 485
Video Case Studies
 Facility layout at Wheeled Coach, 361
 Inventory control at Wheeled Coach, 477
 Material requirements planning (MRP) at Wheeled Coach, 575–576
 Process strategy at Wheeled Coach, 269
 Product design at Regal Marine, 223
 Quality at Ritz-Carlton Hotel, 105
 Strategy at Regal Marine, 51
 Supply chain-management at Regal Marine, 435
Vietnam, global operations and, 67
Vilpac, 818
Virtual companies, 336, 423–424
Virtual reality technology, 274–275
Vision systems, design technology and manufacturing, 276
Visioneer, 424
Visual workplace, job design and, 381–383
Vitromatic, 2
Volkswagen, 196, 303, 414–416

Wagner-Whitin algorithm, lot sizing and, 554–555
Waiting line models, 763–793, See also Queuing models
 arrival characteristics of, 766–767
 characteristics of waiting line system and, 765–770
 measuring queue performance and, 770
 queuing costs, 765
 queuing models, varieties of, 770–780
 service facility characteristics and, 767–769
 waiting line characteristics and, 767
 waiting line queue, 764
Walmart, 277, 322, 431, 445
Warehouse layout, 322, 337–339
 crossdocking, 338
 customizing, 339
 random stocking, 338–339
Warner-Lambert, 445
Waste Management Corp., 120
Waste reduction, JIT philosophy and, 480–481
Waterways, materials management and, 431
Weighted moving averages, 149–151
Western Electric Hawthorne plant, 371
Westinghouse Electric Corporation, 238
Westover Electrical, Inc., 102
Wheeled Coach, 269, 361, 477, 575–576
Whirlpool, 2–3, 4, 17, 276, 505, 551
Winter Park Hotel, 792
Witness software, 824
Work breakdown structure (WBS), project mgt. and, 626–627
Work cells, layout and, 331–333
Work center master file, 584
Work-flow analysis, 237–238
Work-in-process (WIP) inventory, 441
Work measurement, 391–412
 historical experience and, 393
 labor standards and, 392
 predetermined time standards and, 398–400
 time studies and, 393–398
 work sampling and, 400–403
Work methods, job design and, 375–380
Work order, 211
Work rules, job design and, 369
Work sampling, 400–403
Work schedules, 368–369
World Wide Chemical Co., 681–682
World Wide Web, 282, 306

x-bar chart, 110
 central limit theorem and, 111–112
 setting limits for, 113–114
 using, 115–116
Xerox, 82, 85, 86

"Yellow sheet", 426, 426n
Yield management, 521

Zenith, 295
Zero defects, 83, 484

GENERAL INDEX

exponential smoothing and, 151–155
exponential smoothing with trend adjustment, 155–161
moving averages and, 146–151
naive approach to, 148
seasonal variations in data, 161–163
trend projections and, 158–161
weighted moving averages and, 149–151
Times series models, 146–147
Time studies, work measurement and, 393–398
Tomco Oil, 684
Tompkins Associates, Inc., 10n
Tools of TQM, 86–93
   cause & effect diagrams, 92
   Pareto charts, 90
   process charts, 91–92
   quality function deployment, 86–88
   statistical process control, 92–93
   Taguchi technique, 89–90
Toshiba, 449
Total factor productivity, 18
Total productive maintenance (TPM), 675–676
Total quality management (TQM), 82–86, 99
   continuous improvement, 83
   definition, 82
   employee empowerment, 83
   benchmarking, 84–85
   hospital measurement in, 99
   just-in-time, 85–86
   services and, 97
   TQM tools, 86–88
Toyota, 195, 336, 480
Tracking signal, 170
Transaction processing system, 281–282
Transformation strategy, 228
Transition to production, 217
Transitional company, 58
Transportation models, 739–762
   degeneracy and, 748–750
   demand not equal to supply, 748
   location strategies and, 303–304
   northwest corner rule and, 742–743
   stepping-stone method and, 743–747
   transportation modeling, 740–742
Transportation method of linear programming, 516–518
Tree Plan, 689
Trend, decomposition of a time series, 147
Trend adjustment, exponential smoothing with, 155–161
Trend projections, forecasting and, 146–147, 158–161
Trucking, materials management and, 430
TRW, 95, 144
Tupperware, 140–142, 144–145, 277
"two bin" systems, 451
Type I error, 125
Type II error, 125

Types of forecasts, 143
Types of inventory, 440–441

Unisys Corp., 307
United States
   Coleco, 56
   Hewlett Packard, 63
   IBM, 62
   MIL-STD, 105, 125, 125n
   productivity comparison with Japan & Germany, 21
   quality standards, 82
Unlimited queue, 766
UPS (United Parcel Service), 398, 430, 507, 508, 666
User-based category, quality and, 79
Utilization, capacity and, 246

Value analysis, 206–207
Value engineering,
   product development and, 202–203
   teams, 202
Variability, 481
Variability reduction, JIT and, 481
Variable(s)
   control charts for, 110
   exogenous, 19n
Variable costs, 251–252
   strategy driven investments and, 257
Variable inspection, 96
VDO, 414
Velcro Industries, 96
Vendor development, 426
Vendor evaluation, 425
Vendor selection, supply-chain mgt. and, 425–427
Vertical integration, supply-chain mgt. and, 420-422–423
VF Corp. 485
Video Case Studies
   Facility layout at Wheeled Coach, 361
   Inventory control at Wheeled Coach, 477
   Material requirements planning (MRP) at Wheeled Coach, 575–576
   Process strategy at Wheeled Coach, 269
   Product design at Regal Marine, 223
   Quality at Ritz-Carlton Hotel, 105
   Strategy at Regal Marine, 51
   Supply chain-management at Regal Marine, 435
Vietnam, global operations and, 67
Vilpac, 818
Virtual companies, 336, 423–424
Virtual reality technology, 274–275
Vision systems, design technology and manufacturing, 276
Visioneer, 424
Visual workplace, job design and, 381–383
Vitromatic, 2
Volkswagen, 196, 303, 414–416

Wagner-Whitin algorithm, lot sizing and, 554–555
Waiting line models, 763–793, *See also* Queuing models
   arrival characteristics of, 766–767
   characteristics of waiting line system and, 765–770
   measuring queue performance and, 770
   queuing costs, 765
   queuing models, varieties of, 770–780
   service facility characteristics and, 767–769
   waiting line characteristics and, 767
   waiting line queue, 764
Walmart, 277, 322, 431, 445
Warehouse layout, 322, 337–339
   crossdocking, 338
   customizing, 339
   random stocking, 338–339
Warner-Lambert, 445
Waste Management Corp., 120
Waste reduction, JIT philosophy and, 480–481
Waterways, materials management and, 431
Weighted moving averages, 149–151
Western Electric Hawthorne plant, 371
Westinghouse Electric Corporation, 238
Westover Electrical, Inc., 102
Wheeled Coach, 269, 361, 477, 575–576
Whirlpool, 2–3, 4, 17, 276, 505, 551
Winter Park Hotel, 792
Witness software, 824
Work breakdown structure (WBS), project mgt. and, 626–627
Work cells, layout and, 331–333
Work center master file, 584
Work-flow analysis, 237–238
Work-in-process (WIP) inventory, 441
Work measurement, 391–412
   historical experience and, 393
   labor standards and, 392
   predetermined time standards and, 398–400
   time studies and, 393–398
   work sampling and, 400–403
Work methods, job design and, 375–380
Work order, 211
Work rules, job design and, 369
Work sampling, 400–403
Work schedules, 368–369
World Wide Chemical Co., 681–682
World Wide Web, 282, 306

x-bar chart, 110
   central limit theorem and, 111–112
   setting limits for, 113–114
   using, 115–116
Xerox, 82, 85, 86

"Yellow sheet", 426, 426n
Yield management, 521

Zenith, 295
Zero defects, 83, 484

LICENSE AGREEMENT AND LIMITED WARRANTY
POM FOR WINDOWS AND/OR THE CD-ROM

READ THE FOLLOWING TERMS AND CONDITIONS CAREFULLY BEFORE OPENING EITHER THE **POM FOR WINDOWS** DISK PACKAGE OR THE **CD-ROM** DISK PACKAGE, EITHER OF WHICH MAY BE PACKAGED WITH THIS BOOK, AND COLLECTIVELY HEREINAFTER REFERRED TO AS THE "SOFTWARE". THIS LEGAL DOCUMENT IS AN AGREEMENT BETWEEN YOU AND PRENTICE HALL, INC. (THE COMPANY). BY OPENING EITHER SEALED DISK PACKAGE(S), YOU ARE AGREEING TO THE TERMS AND CONDITIONS OF THIS AGREEMENT. IF YOU DO NOT AGREE WITH THESE TERMS AND CONDITIONS, DO NOT OPEN THE DISK PACKAGE. PROMPTLY RETURN THE UNOPENED DISK PACKAGE AND ALL ACCOMPANYING ITEMS TO THE PLACE YOU OBTAINED THEM. [[FOR A FULL REFUND OF ANY SUMS YOU HAVE PAID.]]

1. GRANT OF LICENSE:
In consideration of your payment of the license fee, which is part of the price you paid for this product, and your agreement to abide by the terms and conditions of this Agreement, the Company grants you to a nonexclusive right to use and display the copy of the enclosed software (hereinafter the SOFTWARE). The Company reserves all rights not expressly granted to you under this Agreement.

2. OWNERSHIP OF SOFTWARE:
You own only the magnetic or physical media (the enclosed disks) on which the SOFTWARE is recorded or fixed, but the Company retains all the rights, title, and ownership to the SOFTWARE recorded on the original disk copy(ies) and all subsequent copies of the SOFTWARE, regardless of the form or media on which the original or other copies may exist. This license is not a sale of the original software, or any copy to you.

3A. RESTRICTIONS ON USE AND TRANSFER OF THE **CD-ROM** DISK PACKAGE:
This SOFTWARE and the accompanying printed materials and user manual (the Documentation), if any, are the subject of copyright and is licensed to you only. You may not sell or license copies of the SOFTWARE or the documentation to others and you may not transfer or distribute it, except to instructors and students in your school who are users of the Company textbook that accompanies this SOFTWARE. You have the right to place this SOFTWARE on the university network only for as long as you are a user of the company textbook that accompanies this SOFTWARE. You may not reverse engineer, disassemble, decompile, modify, adapt, translate or create derivative works based on the SOFTWARE or the Documentation without the prior written consent of the Company. You may be held legally responsible for any copying or copyright infringement which is caused or encouraged by your failure to abide by the terms of these restrictions.

3B. RESTRICTIONS ON USE AND TRANSFER OF THE **POM FOR WINDOWS** DISK PACKAGE:
This SOFTWARE and the accompanying printed materials and user manual (the Documentation) are the subject of copyright and is licensed to you only. You may not sell or license copies of the SOFTWARE or the documentation to others and you may not transfer or distribute it, except with the express written consent of the publisher. You may not reverse engineer, disassemble, decompile, modify, adapt, translate or create derivative works based on the SOFTWARE or the Documentation without the prior written consent of the Company. You may be held legally responsible for any copying or copyright infringement which is caused or encouraged by your failure to abide by the terms of these restrictions.

4. TERMINATION:
This license is effective until terminated. This license will terminate automatically without notice from the Company and become null and void if you fail to comply with any provisions or limitations of this license. Upon termination, you shall destroy the Documentation and all copies of the SOFTWARE. All provisions of this Agreement as to warranties, limitation of liability, remedies or damages, and our ownership rights shall survive termination.

5. MISCELLANEOUS:
THIS AGREEMENT SHALL BE CONSTRUED IN ACCORDANCE WITH THE LAWS OF THE UNITED STATES OF AMERICA AND THE STATE OF NEW YORK, APPLICABLE TO CONTRACTS MADE IN NEW YORK, AND SHALL BENEFIT THE COMPANY, ITS AFFILIATES AND ASSIGNEES.

6. LIMITED WARRANTY AND DISCLAIMER OF WARRANTY:
The Company warrants that the SOFTWARE, when properly used in accordance with the Documentation, will operate in substantial conformity with the description of the SOFTWARE set forth in the Documentation. The Company does not warrant that the SOFTWARE will meet your requirements or that the operation of the SOFTWARE will be uninterrupted or error-free. The Company warrants that the media on which the SOFTWARE is delivered shall be free from defects in materials and workmanship under normal use for a period of thirty (30) days from the date of your purchase. Your only remedy and the Company's only obligation under these limited warranties is, [[at the company's option,]] return of the warranted item for [[a refund of any amounts paid by you or]] replacement of the item. Any replacement of SOFTWARE or media under the warranties shall not extend the original warranty period. The limited warranty set forth above shall not apply to any SOFTWARE which the Company determines in good faith has been subject to misuse, neglect, improper installation, repair, alteration, or damage by you. EXCEPT FOR THE EXPRESSED WARRANTIES SET FORTH ABOVE, THE COMPANY DISCLAIMS ALL WARRANTIES, EXPRESSED OR IMPLIED, INCLUDING WITHOUT LIMITATION, THE IMPLIED WARRANTIES OF MERCHANTABILITY AND FITNESS FOR A PARTICULAR PURPOSE. EXCEPT FOR THE EXPRESSED WARRANTY SET FORTH ABOVE, THE COMPANY DOES NOT WARRANT, GUARANTEE, OR MAKE ANY REPRESENTATION REGARDING THE USE OR THE RESULTS OF THE USE OF THE SOFTWARE IN TERMS OF ITS CORRECTNESS, ACCURACY, RELIABILITY, CURRENTNESS, OR OTHERWISE. IN NO EVENT, SHALL THE COMPANY OR ITS EMPLOYEES, AGENTS, SUPPLIERS, OR CONTRACTORS BE LIABLE FOR ANY INCIDENTAL, INDIRECT, SPECIAL, OR CONSEQUENTIAL DAMAGES ARISING OUT OF OR IN CONNECTION WITH THE LICENSE GRANTED UNDER THIS AGREEMENT, OR FOR LOSS OF USE, LOSS OF DATA, LOSS OF INCOME OR PROFIT, OR OTHER LOSSES, SUSTAINED AS A RESULT OF INJURY TO ANY PERSON, OR LOSS OF DAMAGE TO PROPERTY, OR CLAIMS OF THIRD PARTIES, EVEN IF THE COMPANY OR AN AUTHORIZED REPRESENTATIVE OF THE COMPANY HAS BEEN ADVISED OF THE POSSIBILITY OF SUCH DAMAGES. [[IN NO EVENT SHALL LIABILITY OF THE COMPANY FOR DAMAGES WITH RESPECT TO THE SOFTWARE EXCEED THE AMOUNTS ACTUALLY PAID BY YOU, IF ANY, FOR THE SOFTWARE.]]

7. SOME JURISDICTIONS DO NOT ALLOW THE LIMITATION OF IMPLIED WARRANTIES OR LIABILITY FOR INCIDENTAL, INDIRECT, SPECIAL, OR CONSEQUENTIAL DAMAGES, SO THE ABOVE LIMITATIONS MAY NOT ALWAYS APPLY. THE WARRANTIES IN THIS AGREEMENT GIVE YOU SPECIFIC LEGAL RIGHTS AND YOU MAY ALSO HAVE OTHER RIGHTS WHICH VARY IN ACCORDANCE WITH LOCAL LAW.

8. ACKNOWLEDGMENT:
YOU ACKNOWLEDGE THAT YOU HAVE READ THIS AGREEMENT, UNDERSTAND IT, AND AGREE TO BE BOUND BY ITS TERMS AND CONDITIONS. YOU ALSO AGREE THAT THIS AGREEMENT IS THE COMPLETE AND EXCLUSIVE STATEMENT OF THE AGREEMENT BETWEEN YOU AND THE COMPANY AND SUPERSEDES ALL PROPOSALS OR PRIOR AGREEMENTS, ORAL, OR WRITTEN, AND ANY OTHER COMMUNICATIONS BETWEEN YOU AND THE COMPANY OR ANY OTHER REPRESENTATIVE OF THE COMPANY RELATING TO THE SUBJECT MATTER OF THIS AGREEMENT.

Should you have any questions concerning this agreement or if you wish to contact the Company for any reason, please contact Customer Service at (800) 922-0579.